MILESTONES—REAL LIFE, REAL DEVELOPMENT

With **Milestones of Child Development**, students track the early stages of physical, social, and emotional development. By watching one child over time, or by comparing various children, Milestones provides a unique, experiential learning environment that can only be achieved by watching real human development as it happens—all in pre-transitional and post-milestone segments.

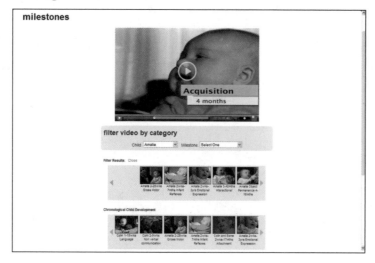

The **LEARNSMART** adaptive learning system helps students learn faster, study more efficiently, and retain more knowledge for greater success.

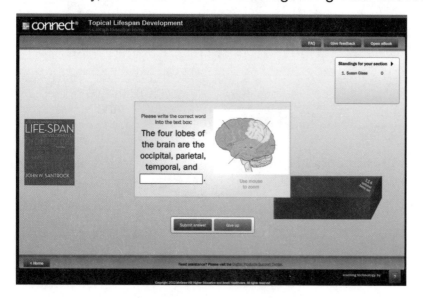

Students come to class with a range of preparedness. With a focus on course-critical concepts, **LearnSmart** is like a personal tutor guiding students to spend less time on what they already know and more time on what they don't.

A TOPICAL APPROACH TO
LIFE-SPAN
DEVELOPMENT

Sixth Edition

A TOPICAL APPROACH TO
LIFE-SPAN
DEVELOPMENT

Sixth Edition

JOHN W. SANTROCK

University of Texas at Dallas

Connect
Learn
Succeed™

Published by McGraw-Hill, an imprint of The McGraw-Hill Companies, Inc., 1221 Avenue of the Americas, New York, NY 10020. Copyright © 2012, 2010, 2008, 2007, 2005, 2002. All rights reserved. No part of this publication may be reproduced or distributed in any form or by any means, or stored in a database or retrieval system, without the prior written consent of The McGraw-Hill Companies, Inc., including, but not limited to, in any network or other electronic storage or transmission, or broadcast for distance learning.

This book is printed on acid-free paper.

3 4 5 6 7 8 9 0 RJE/RJE 1 0 9 8 7 6 5 4 3 2

ISBN: 978-0-07-803513-5
MHID: 0-07-803513-9

Sponsoring Editor: *Allison McNamara*
Marketing Manager: *Julia Larkin*
Development Editors: *Cara Labell and Elisa Adams*
Editorial Coordinator: *Sarah Kiefer*
Production Editor: *Brett Coker*
Production Service: *Melanie Field, Strawberry Field Publishing*
Manuscript Editor: *Janet Tilden*
Cover Designer: *Preston Thomas*
Interior Designers: *Pam Verros and Preston Thomas*
Art Editor: *Janet Robbins*
Illustrator: *Judy Waller*
Photo Researcher: *Jennifer Blankenship*
Buyer: *Carol Bielski*
Media Project Manager: *Adam Dweck*
Digital Product Manager: *Jay Gubernick*
Composition: *9.5/12 Meridien Roman by Aptara®, Inc.*
Printing: *45# New Era Thin Plus by R.R. Donnelley*

Vice President Editorial: *Michael Ryan*
Publisher: *Michael J. Sugarman*
Director of Development: *Dawn Groundwater*

Credits: The credits section for this book begins on page C-1 and is considered an extension of the copyright page.

Library of Congress Cataloging-in-Publication Data

Santrock, John W.
  A topical approach to lifespan development / John Santrock. — 6th ed.
      p. cm.
  Includes bibliographical references and index.
  ISBN-13: 978-0-07-803513-5 (hbk. : alk. paper)
  ISBN-10: 0-07-803513-9 (hbk. : alk. paper)
1. Developmental psychology. I. Title.
  BF713.S257 2012
  305.2—dc23

                                                          2011034203

The Internet addresses listed in the text were accurate at the time of publication. The inclusion of a website does not indicate an endorsement by the authors or McGraw-Hill, and McGraw-Hill does not guarantee the accuracy of the information presented at these sites.

Printed in the USA

www.mhhe.com

With special appreciation to my wife, Mary Jo

about the author

John W. Santrock

John Santrock received his Ph.D. from the University of Minnesota in 1973. He taught at the University of Charleston and the University of Georgia before joining the program in Psychology and Human Development at the University of Texas at Dallas, where he currently teaches a number of undergraduate courses.

John Santrock, teaching an undergraduate class

John has been a member of the editorial boards of *Child Development* and *Developmental Psychology*. His research on father custody is widely cited and used in expert witness testimony to promote flexibility and alternative considerations in custody disputes. John also has authored these exceptional McGraw-Hill texts: *Psychology* (7th edition), *Children* (11th edition), *Adolescence* (14th edition), *Life-Span Development* (13th edition), and *Educational Psychology* (5th edition).

For many years John was involved in tennis as a player, a teaching professional, and a coach of professional tennis players. As an undergraduate, he was a member of the University of Miami (FL) tennis team that still holds the record for consecutive wins (137) in any NCAA Division I sport. John has been married for more than 35 years to his wife, Mary Jo, who is a Realtor. He has two daughters—Tracy, who is also a Realtor, and Jennifer, who is a medical sales specialist. He has one granddaughter, Jordan, age 20, and two grandsons, Alex, age 7, and Luke, age 5. In the last decade, John also has spent time painting expressionist art.

brief contents

contents

SECTION 1   THE LIFE-SPAN PERSPECTIVE   2

SECTION 2   BIOLOGICAL PROCESSES, PHYSICAL DEVELOPMENT, AND HEALTH   46

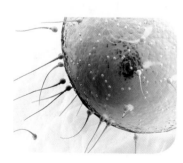

Contents **ix**

SECTION 4   SOCIOEMOTIONAL PROCESSES AND DEVELOPMENT   298

SECTION 6 ENDINGS 560

expert consultants

Life-span development has become an enormous, complex field, and no single author, or even several authors, could possibly keep up with all of the rapidly changing content in the many different areas in this field. To solve this problem, author John Santrock has sought the input of leading experts about content in a number of areas of life-span development across each of the six editions of this text. The experts provide detailed evaluations and recommendations in their area(s) of expertise.

The following individuals were among those who served as expert consultants for one or more of the first five editions of this text: James Birren, Denise Park, Charles Nelson, Rachel Keen, Robert J. Sternberg, Susanne Denham, Gilbert Gottlieb, Linda Mayes, William Hoyer, Carolyn Saarni, Doug Wahlsten, Elena Grigorenko, Ross Parke, James Marcia, Crystal Park, Daniel Mroczek, Janet Shibley Hyde, Ross Thompson, Linda George, James Garbarino, Jay Belsky, Scott Hofer, Allan Wigfield, Bert Hayslip, and Robert Kastenbaum.

The biographies and photographs of the expert consultants for the sixth edition of this text, who (like the expert consultants for the first five editions) literally represent a Who's Who *in the field of life-span development, follow:*

David Almeida

David Almeida is one of the world's leading experts on stress and coping in the field of life-span development. He obtained his Ph.D. from the University of Victoria and currently is Professor of Human Development at Pennsylvania State University. Dr. Almeida's research focuses on how daily experiences in families and other social contexts, such as work and leisure, influence health and well-being in adulthood and aging. His research has been funded by grants from the National Institute of Mental Health, the National Institute on Aging, the MacArthur Foundation, the Kellogg Foundation, and the Sloan Foundation. Dr. Almeida has published extensively in leading research journals in adult development and aging and recently contributed this chapter to the *Handbook of the Psychology of Aging:* "The Speedometer of Life: Stress, Health, and Aging" (Almeida, Piazza, Stawski, & Kline, 2011).

"I have been teaching Introduction to Human Development for 15 years and have always used one of John Santrock's textbooks. The students find the textbooks engaging, easy to understand, and applicable to their own lives. As an instructor, I've always been impressed with Professor Santrock's ability to organize and synthesize such a broad array of material while at the same time keeping up to date on the latest and most relevant research findings. Indeed, I always learn new developments in the field after teaching the course with a new textbook. The new edition of A Topical Approach to Life-Span Development *is no exception. The volume of new material is impressive! There are scores of citations from 2009 and 2010. There are even 2011 citations in this edition."*
—**Dr. David Almeida**

Karen Adolph

Karen Adolph is one of the world's leading experts on infant motor development. She obtained her Ph.D. in experimental/developmental psychology from Emory University. Dr. Adolph currently is a professor of psychology and neural science at New York University. She has received a James McKeen Cattell Sabbatical Award, the Robert L. Fantz Memorial Award from the American Psychological Foundation, the Boyd McCandless Award from the American Psychological Association, the Young Investigator Award from the International Society for Infant Studies, FIRST and MERIT awards from the National Institutes of Health, and is a Fellow of the American Psychological Association and the Association for Psychological Science. Her research is supported by grants from the National Institutes of Health. Dr. Adolph's work is inspired by a developmental systems approach, and her research interests include learning and development in the context of infant motor skill acquisition.

"It (Chapter 5, Motor, Sensory, and Perceptual Development) is a wonderful chapter! I learned a lot reading about declines during aging, and now I've got that to look forward to. The coverage is broad and deep. The illustrations are interesting. The tone is accessible and very readable." —**Karen Adolph**

Ross Thompson

Ross Thompson is one of the world's leading experts on children's socioemotional development. He currently is Professor of Psychology at the University of California–Davis, where he directs the Social and Emotional Development Lab. A developmental psychologist, Dr. Thompson studies early parent-child relationships, the development of emotion understanding and emotion regulation, early moral development, and the growth of self-understanding in young children. He also works on the applications of developmental research to public policy concerns, including school readiness and its development, early childhood investments, and early mental health. Dr. Thompson is a founding member of the National Scientific Council on the Developing Child. Dr. Thompson has twice been Associate Editor of *Child Development*. He received the Boyd McCandless Young Scientist Award for Early Distinguished Achievement from the American Psychological Association, the Scholarship in Teaching Award, and the Outstanding Research and Creative Activity Award from the University of Nebraska, where he was also a lifetime member of the Academy of Distinguished Teachers.

"Reading this chapter (10, Emotional Development) was a pleasure. The writing is animated and engaging, the coverage interesting, and the organization of the chapter makes it flow effortlessly. These qualities are even more remarkable because of the astonishing amount of coverage that is required of this chapter on emotional development, including the development of emotion, temperament, and attachment . . . The discussion of attachment is rich and thought-provoking . . . With the upsurge of biologically-oriented research and thinking in the field of socioemotional development, John Santrock has done a fine job of not only tackling issues of genetics and developmental neurobiology earlier in the text, but also of integrating these topics into the coverage of this chapter . . . I thought the "Connections" sidebars were a real strength of this chapter. On several occasions, these one-sentence references added an "aha!" moment of realization of the relevance to the discussion of a topic or idea that had been discussed elsewhere. The format of these is nicely done: enough to be provocative, not too much to be intrusive . . . Great chapter!" —**Ross Thompson**

Martha Ann Bell

Martha Bell is a leading expert in developmental cognitive neuroscience. She currently is a professor of psychology at Virginia Tech University. Dr. Bell obtained her Ph.D. in Human Development from the University of Maryland. Her research focuses on developmental changes in the brain's frontal lobe using both behavioral and electrophysiological methods. Dr. Bell's current work, funded by NIH/NICHD, centers on individual differences in the development of working memory and inhibitory control during infancy and early childhood. Dr. Bell is Editor of *Infancy* and her research has been published in journals such as *Developmental Psychobiology, Developmental Neuropsychology, Child Development*, and *Brain and Cognition*. Dr. Bell has contributed chapters to several edited books that highlight developmental neuroscience research, including most recently *The Developing Brain*.

". . . It is clear that Professor Santrock took great care in writing the revision of this Topical Life-Span Development textbook. The research discussed is the most current in the field and the references are excellent and very appropriate for this undergraduate text." —**Martha Ann Bell**

Kirby Deater-Deckard

Dr. Deater-Deckard is a leading expert on biological foundations of development, heredity-environment interaction, and parenting. He obtained his Ph.D. from the University of Virginia and currently is a professor and the director of graduate programs in psychology at Virginia Polytechnic Institute and State University. Dr. Deater-Deckard's research focuses on the development of individual differences in childhood and adolescence, with emphasis on gene-environment processes. He has written papers and book chapters in the areas of developmental psychology and psychopathology. His current research on parenting and children's development is funded by the NICHD. Dr. Deater-Deckard has been joint editor of the *Journal of Child Psychology and Psychiatry*, and currently is on the editorial boards of *Infant and Child Development, Journal of Family Psychology*, and *Parenting: Science and Practice*.

"The research base is timely and covers the most important major topics (Ch. 2, Biological Beginnings). The chapter is thorough and incredibly comprehensive with respect to evolutionary, behavioral genetic, molecular genetic, and prenatal/perinatal health perspectives. The overall presentation is fair and balanced, raising the major 'big ideas,' theories, empirical evidence, and commonly raised limitations. Inclusion of gene-environment interaction, gene-gene interaction, and epigenetic systems concepts further strengthens the chapter. . . The chapter was a real pleasure to read." —**Kirby Deater-Deckard**

Darcia Narváez

Darcia Narváez is one of the world's leading experts on moral development. She obtained her Ph.D. from the University of Minnesota and currently is a professor in the Department of Psychology at the University of Notre Dame. Dr. Narváez is director of the Collaborative for Ethical Education. She studies and teaches about moral development, moral discourse processing, and moral identity. Her Triune Ethics Theory (TET) (Narváez, 2008) is a comprehensive account of moral psychology rooted in neurobiology and early experience. Integrating cognitive science, expertise development, and classical notions of virtue cultivation, she developed the Integrative Ethical Education model (2006). Her work has appeared in more than 90 publications, including *Journal of Educational Psychology, Developmental Psychology,* and several books, including the award-winning *Postconventional Moral Thinking.*

"I enjoyed reading this chapter (13, Moral Development, Values, and Religion) very much. It is loaded with good information and easy to read." —**Darcia Narváez**

Ross Parke

Ross Parke is one of the world's leading experts on socioemotional development and family processes. Dr. Parke obtained his Ph.D. from the University of Waterloo, Ontario, Canada, and he is currently Professor Emeritus at the University of California–Riverside, where he formerly was Distinguished Professor of Psychology and director of the Center for Family Studies. His research has focused on early social relationships in infancy and childhood. Dr. Parke is well known for his early work on the effects of punishment, aggression, and child abuse, as well as his research on the father's role in infancy and early childhood. His current research focuses on links between family and peer social systems, and on the impact of parenting on youth in families of diverse ethnic backgrounds. He is a past president of Division 7, the Developmental Psychology Division, of the American Psychological Association, and has received the G. Stanley Hall Award from this APA division. Dr. Parke has served as president of SRCD and received the Distinguished Scientific Contribution to Child Development Award from this organization. He has been the editor of the *Journal of Family Psychology* and of *Developmental Psychology.* Dr. Parke has authored and edited a number of books, including most recently (2011) *Social Development* (with K. Alison Clarke-Stewart).

"As expected, John Santrock continues his tradition of providing up-to-date, but highly accessible coverage of this topic (Ch. 14, Families, Lifestyles, and Parenting)." —**Ross Parke**

JoNell Strough

JoNell Strough is a leading expert on gender development**.** She obtained her Ph.D. from the University of Utah and currently is Professor of Psychology at West Virginia University, where she also serves as the Coordinator of the Graduate Training Program in Life-Span Developmental Psychology. Dr. Strough conducts two lines of research: (1) gender development across the life span, with an emphasis on adolescence and early and later adulthood, and (2) everyday problem solving and decision making. Dr. Strough serves on the editorial boards of *Experimental Aging Research* and the *Journal of Gerontology: Psychological Sciences.* Her research has been funded by the National Institute on Aging. She has published extensively in a number of leading research journals.

"John Santrock is to be commended for integrating research on a variety of topics pertaining to gender and sexuality across the life span. . . The connections theme—especially those that link the content of the chapters to (a) careers, (b) the real world, and (c) across chapters—is a feature of this textbook that students likely find useful. The connections across chapters will help students integrate the information and may make the sheer amount of the material more manageable." —**JoNell Strough**

Elizabeth M. Zelinski

Elizabeth Zelinski is a leading expert on cognitive development and aging. She obtained her Ph.D. from the University of Southern California and was a postdoctoral fellow at Claremont University. Dr. Zelinski is currently Professor of Psychology and Gerontology at the University of Southern California, where she also holds the Rita and Edward Polunsky Chair in Education and Aging. Her research focuses on changes in memory, intelligence, and language in healthy adults from 30 to 97 years of age. Dr. Zelinski's recent projects include using video games to improve older adults' cognitive skills and using virtual reality to assess older adults' real-world problem-solving ability. Her current research is funded by multiple grants from the National Institute on Aging, and she is the author of more than 50 publications. Dr. Zelinski recently served as President of the Division of Adult Development and Aging in the American Psychological Association. She also has received teaching awards at the University of Southern California.

A Topical Approach

Examining life-span development topically allows developmental changes through the life span to be described in close proximity to one another so that students can make better connections between them. **Connections** play a key role in student learning and are a driving force behind *A Topical Approach to Life-Span Development*.

---

developmental connection

Brain Development. Might changes in the development of the adolescent brain be related to teens' mood swings and increased risk taking? Chapter 3, p. 104

Connecting Topical Processes Across the Life Span

✳ ***Developmental Connections*** highlight links across topics of development *and* connections between biological, cognitive, and socioemotional processes.

✳ ***Connect*** questions within chapters and end-of-chapter Review, Connect, and Reflect sections allow students to practice making connections among development topics.

Connecting Research to What We Know About Development

✳ ***Connecting with Research*** describes a study or program to illustrate how research in development is conducted and how it influences our understanding of the discipline.

✳ ***Leading experts*** in the field provided detailed input on the content and offered key insights on new research and findings in their fields of study (see pp. xv–xvii for their bios and photos).

✳ ***The most current coverage of research***—More than 1,000 citations from 2009, 2010, 2011, and 2012.

Connecting Development to the Real World

✳ ***Connecting Development to Life*** describes the influence of development in a real-world context of topics such as exercise, living a more creative life, and strategies for making friends.

✳ ***Connecting with Careers*** and the ***Careers Appendix*** profile careers that require education and training in various areas of human development to show students where knowledge of human development could lead them.

✳ ***Reflect: Your Own Personal Journey of Life*** questions at the end of each chapter ask students to reflect on some aspect of the discussion in the section they have just read and to connect it to their own life.

✳ The ***Milestones*** program enables students to track the early age periods that involve physical, social, and emotional development in real children. This video program captures a handful of children as they reach developmental milestones in a longitudinal view of real development.

Connect

PSYCHOLOGY

Connect Psychology is a groundbreaking digital learning solution that makes managing assignments easier for instructors—and makes learning and studying more motivational and efficient for students.

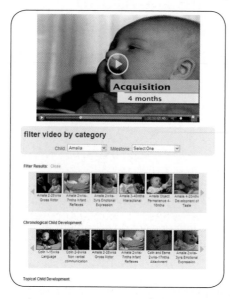

✳ ***Milestones of Development.*** The ***Milestones*** program enables students to track the early stages of physical, social, and emotional development. This video program tracks a handful of children as they reach developmental milestones in a longitudinal view of real development from infancy and beyond. Assignable and assessable, these segments allow students to demonstrate mastery of core course outcomes by applying concepts to real children as their development unfolds.

✳ **Adaptive.** The adaptive learning system helps students "know what they know"—while guiding them to focus on what they *don't* know. The adaptive diagnostic creates a unique path for each student as they work toward mastering key concepts for the course.

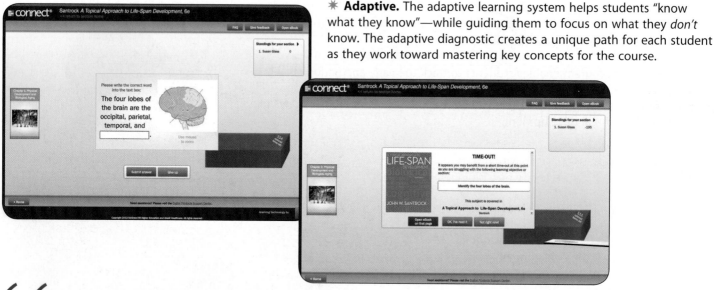

❝❝ Connect Psychology (especially the adaptive testing of LearnSmart) is a highly effective and innovative way to get students more engaged with the text and course material. Students ask more interesting questions in class because they seem to have already grasped the most basic principles before they arrive. ❞❞

Joy Berrenberg, University of Colorado—Denver

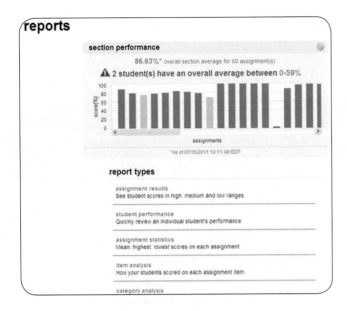

✳ **Real-Time Reports.** Printable, exportable reports show how well each student is performing. Instructors can use this feature to spot problem areas—for individual students or the class as a whole—*before* they crop up on an exam.

✳ **Learning Objectives.** Every assignment and all course resources can be sorted by learning objective, with point-and-click flexibility. Instructors can use this feature to customize the content and course materials to meet the particular needs of their course and the reporting needs of their department.

✳ **Assignable and Assessable Activities.** Instructors can deliver assignments and tests easily online, and students can practice skills and fulfill learning goals at their own pace and on their own schedule.

McGraw-Hill Higher Education and Blackboard have teamed up. What does this mean for you?

✳ **Your life, simplified.** Now you and your students can access McGraw-Hill's Connect™ and Create™ right from within your Blackboard course—all with one single sign-on. Say goodbye to the days of logging in to multiple applications.

✳ **Deep integration of content and tools.** Not only do you get single sign-on with Connect and Create, you also get deep integration of McGraw-Hill content and content engines right in Blackboard. Whether you're choosing a book for your course or building Connect assignments, all the tools you need are right where you want them—inside Blackboard.

✳ **Seamless gradebooks.** Are you tired of keeping multiple gradebooks and manually synchronizing grades into Blackboard? We thought so. When a student completes an integrated Connect assignment, the grade for that assignment automatically (and instantly) feeds your Blackboard grade center.

✳ **A solution for everyone.** Whether your institution is already using Blackboard or you just want to try Blackboard on your own, we have a solution for you. McGraw-Hill and Blackboard can now offer you easy access to industry-leading technology and content, whether your campus hosts it or we do. Be sure to ask your local McGraw-Hill representative for details.

A Topical Approach to Life-Span Development and APA Goals and Outcomes

1 KNOWLEDGE BASE OF PSYCHOLOGY
Demonstrate familiarity with the major concepts, theoretical perspectives, empirical findings, and historical trends in psychology.

1.1 Characterize the nature of psychology as a discipline.

1.2 Demonstrate knowledge and understanding representing appropriate breadth and depth in selected content areas of psychology.

1.3 Use the concepts, language, and major theories of the discipline to account for psychological phenomena.

1.4 Explain major perspectives of psychology (e.g., behavioral, biological, cognitive, evolutionary, humanistic, psychodynamic, and sociocultural).

- **Ch. 1:** Characteristics of the Life-Span Perspective, pp. 1–8; Nature of Development, pp. 12–18; Theories of Development, pp. 20–27
- **Ch. 2:** The Evolutionary Perspective, pp. 49–51; Genetic Foundations of Development, pp. 52–59; Heredity and Environment Interaction: The Nature-Nurture Debate, pp. 59–64; Prenatal Development, pp. 64–76; Birth and the Postpartum Period, pp. 76–85
- **Ch. 3:** Body Growth and Change, pp. 90–98; The Brain, pp. 99–108; Sleep, pp.109–113; Longevity, pp. 114–118
- **Ch. 4:** Health, Illness, and Disease, pp. 123–130; Nutrition and Eating Behavior, pp. 131–139; Exercise, pp. 140–144; Substance Use, pp. 145–150
- **Ch. 5:** Motor Development, pp. 153–161; Sensory and Perceptual Development, pp. 162–175; Perceptual-Motor Coupling, pp. 176–177
- **Ch. 6:** Piaget's Theory of Cognitive Development, pp. 183–196; Applying and Evaluating Piaget's Theory, pp. 197–198; Vygotsky's Theory of Cognitive Development, pp.199–203; Cognitive Changes in Adulthood, pp. 204–207
- **Ch. 7:** The Information-Processing Approach, pp. 211–212; Attention, pp. 213–217; Memory, pp. 218–225; Thinking, pp. 226–237; Metacognition, pp. 238–243
- **Ch. 8:** The Concept of Intelligence, pp. 247–252; Controversies and Group Comparisons, pp. 253–257; The Development of Intelligence, pp. 258–262; The Extremes of Intelligence and Creativity, pp. 263–271
- **Ch. 9:** What is Language?, pp. 275–277; How Language Develops, pp. 278–289; Biological and Environmental Influences, pp. 290–295
- **Ch. 10:** Exploring Emotion, pp. 301–303; Development of Emotion, pp. 304–311; Temperament, pp. 312–316; Attachment and Love, pp. 317–335
- **Ch. 11:** The Self, pp. 339–351; Identity, pp. 352–357; Personality, pp. 358–367
- **Ch. 12:** Biological, Social, and Cognitive Influences on Gender, pp. 371–376; Gender Stereotypes, Similarities, and Differences, pp. 377–380; Gender Development Through the Life Span, pp. 381–385; Exploring Sexuality, pp. 386 –392; Sexuality Through the Life Span, pp. 392–403
- **Ch. 13:** Domains of Moral Development, pp. 408–417; Contexts of Moral Development, pp. 418–422; Prosocial and Antisocial Behavior, pp. 423–429; Values, Religion, Spirituality, and Meaning in Life, pp. 430–438
- **Ch. 14:** Family Processes, pp. 445–447; The Diversity of Adult Lifestyles, pp. 448–457; Parenting, pp. 458–476; Other Family Relationships, pp. 477–482
- **Ch. 15:** Peer Relations in Childhood and Adolescence, pp. 487–494; Friendship, pp. 495–499; Play and Leisure, pp. 500–503; Aging and the Social World, pp. 504–506; Sociocultural Influences, pp. 507–520
- **Ch. 16:** Schools, pp. 525–539; Achievement, pp. 540–546; Careers, Work, and Retirement, pp. 547–556
- **Ch. 17:** The Death System and Cultural Contexts, pp. 563–564; Defining Death and Life/Death Issues, pp. 565–568; A Developmental Perspective on Death, pp. 568–572; Facing One's Own Death, pp. 573–575; Coping with the Death of Someone Else, pp. 576–583

2 RESEARCH METHODS IN PSYCHOLOGY
Understand and apply basic research methods in psychology, including research design, data analysis, and interpretation.

2.1 Describe the basic characteristics of the science of psychology.

2.2 Explain different research methods used by psychologists.

2.3 Evaluate the appropriateness of conclusions derived from psychological research.

2.4 Design and conduct basic studies to address psychological questions using appropriate research methods.

2.5 Follow the APA Codes of Ethics in the treatment of human and nonhuman participants in the design, data collection, interpretation, and reporting of psychological research.

2.6 Generate research conclusions appropriately based on the parameters of particular research methods.

- **Ch. 1:** Connecting Development to Life, p.11; Connecting with Research, p. 16; Theories of Development—Scientific Method, p. 20; Psychoanalytic Theory, p. 20; Ethological Method, p. 26; Research in Life-Span Development, p. 28–29; Methods for Collecting Data, pp. 29–30; Research Designs, pp. 31–32; Time-Span Research, pp. 33–34; Conducting Ethical Research, pp. 34–35; Minimizing Bias, pp. 35–36
- **Ch. 2:** Connecting with Research, p. 83
- **Ch. 3:** Connecting with Research, p. 108
- **Ch. 4:** Connecting with Research, p. 129; Treatment for Older Adults, p. 130; Nutrition, Infancy, Outcomes of Breast-Feeding, p. 132
- **Ch. 5:** Connecting with Research, pp. 164–165
- **Ch. 6:** Connecting with Research, pp. 188
- **Ch. 7:** Connecting with Research, p. 225; Scientific Thinking, pp. 229–230; Education, Work, and Health, p. 234
- **Ch. 8:** Connecting with Research, p. 256; Fluid and Crystallized Intelligence/Seattle Longitudinal Study, p. 260
- **Ch. 9:** Connecting with Research, p. 283; How Language Develops—Middle and Late Childhood (Bilingualism and Second Language Learning), p. 288
- **Ch. 10:** Attachment and Love—Infancy and Childhood, p. 318; Connecting with Research, p. 334
- **Ch. 11:** Connecting with Research, p. 364; Stability and Change (Berkeley Longitudinal Studies), pp. 364–365; Stability and Change (Vaillant's Studies), p. 365
- **Ch. 12:** Biological, Social, and Cognitive Influences on Gender, pp. 371–376; Connecting with Research, p. 376; Gender Stereotypes, Similarities, and Differences, pp. 377–381
- **Ch. 13:** Moral Thought—Kohlberg's Critics, p. 413; Moral Feeling, p. 415; Antisocial Behavior, p. 428; Connecting with Research, p. 429
- **Ch. 14:** Married Adults, p. 452; Connecting with Research, p. 464; Adoptive Parents and Adopted Children, p. 476
- **Ch. 15:** Connecting with Research, p. 493; Socioeconomic Status and Poverty, p. 516
- **Ch. 16:** Educating Children with Disabilities (Autism Spectrum Disorders), p. 536; Achievement—Mastery Motivation and Mindset, p. 543; Achievement—Expectations, pp. 544–545; Connecting with Research, p. 546
- **Ch. 17:** Connecting with Research, p. 580

3 CRITICAL THINKING SKILLS IN PSYCHOLOGY
Respect and use critical and creative thinking, skeptical inquiry, and, when possible, the scientific approach to solving problems related to behavior and mental processes.

3.1 Use critical thinking effectively.

3.2 Engage in creative thinking.

3.3 Use reasoning to recognize, develop, defend, and criticize arguments and other persuasive appeals.

3.4 Approach problems effectively.

- **Ch. 1:** Connecting Development to Life, p. 11; Developmental Connection, p. 13; Developmental Connection, p. 18; Evaluating Psychoanalytic Theories, p. 22; Evaluating Cognitive Theories, p. 24; Evaluating Behavioral and Social Cognitive Theories, p. 24; Review, Connect, Reflect sections
- **Ch. 2:** Evaluating Evolutionary Psychology, p. 51; Connecting Development to Life, p. 75; Connecting with Research, p. 83; Review, Connect, Reflect sections
- **Ch. 3:** Connecting Development to Life, p. 105; Connecting with Research, p. 108; Review, Connect, Reflect sections
- **Ch. 4:** Connecting with Research, p. 129; Controversy over Vitamins, p. 140; Connecting Development to Life, p. 143; Connecting with Research, p. 129; Review, Connect, Reflect sections

3 | CRITICAL THINKING SKILLS IN PSYCHOLOGY *continued*

Respect and use critical and creative thinking, skeptical inquiry, and, when possible, the scientific approach to solving problems related to behavior and mental processes.

- **Ch. 5:** Connecting Development to Life, p. 159; Connecting with Research, p. 165; Review, Connect, Reflect sections
- **Ch. 6:** Connecting with Research, p. 188; Perceptual Development and Expectations, p. 189; Concrete and Formal Operations, pp. 194–195; Applying and Evaluating Piaget's Theory, p. 197; Connecting Development to Life, p. 202; Evaluating Vygotsky's Theory, p. 203; Piaget's View, p. 204; Review, Connect, Reflect sections
- **Ch. 7:** Connecting Development to Life, p. 237; Connecting with Research, p. 225; Review, Connect, Reflect sections
- **Ch. 8:** Ethnic Comparisons, p. 257; Connecting Development to Life, p. 270; Connecting with Research, p. 256; Review, Connect, Reflect sections
- **Ch. 9:** Connecting with Research, p. 283; Connecting Development to Life, p. 294; Review, Connect, Reflect sections
- **Ch. 10:** What Are Emotions?, p. 302; Connecting Development to Life, p. 316; Connecting with Research, p. 334; Review, Connect, Reflect sections
- **Ch. 11:** Connecting Development to Life, p. 351; Connecting with Research, p. 364; Review, Connect, Reflect sections
- **Ch. 12:** Connecting Development to Life, p. 399; Connecting with Research, p. 376; Review, Connect, Reflect sections
- **Ch. 13:** Connecting Development to Life, p. 436; Connecting with Research, p. 429; Review, Connect, Reflect sections
- **Ch. 14:** Connecting Development to Life, p. 473; Connecting with Research, p. 464; Review, Connect, Reflect sections
- **Ch. 15:** Connecting with Research, p. 493; Connecting Development to Life, p. 496; Review, Connect, Reflect sections
- **Ch. 16:** Connecting with Research, p. 546; Connecting Development to Life, p. 550; Review, Connect, Reflect sections
- **Ch. 17:** Connecting Development to Life, p. 202; Connecting with Research, p. 580; Review, Connect, Reflect sections

4 | APPLICATION OF PSYCHOLOGY

Understand and apply psychological principles to personal, social, and organizational issues.

4.1 Describe major applied areas (e.g., clinical, counseling, industrial/organizational, school, etc.) and emerging (e.g., health, forensics, media, military, etc.) applied areas of psychology.

4.2 Identify appropriate applications of psychology in solving problems.

4.3 Articulate how psychological principles can be used to explain social issues and inform public policy.

4.4 Apply psychological concepts, theories, and research findings as these relate to everyday life.

4.5 Recognize that ethically complex situations can develop in the application of psychological principles.

- **Ch. 1:** Life-Span Perspective, p. 5; Some Contemporary Concerns, p. 8; Parenting and Education, p. 8; Social Policy, pp. 9–12; Connecting Development to Life, p. 11; Connecting Biological . . . Processes, p. 13; Nature and Nurture, p. 18; Ethological Theory, pp. 25–26; fMRI, p. 30; Connecting with Careers, p. 36; Connecting with Research, p. 16
- **Appendix:** Careers in Life-Span Development, pp. 41–45
- **Ch. 2:** Evolution and Life-Span Development, p. 51; Genetic Principles, pp. 55–56; Sickle-Cell Anemia, p. 58; Behavior Genetics, p. 60; Shared/Nonshared Environmental Issues, pp. 61–62; Prenatal Diagnostic Tests, pp. 67–68; Hazards to Prenatal Development, pp. 68–74; Connecting Development to Life, p. 75; Connecting with Research, p. 83.; Connecting with Careers, p. 81
- **Ch. 3:** Psychological Accompaniments, p. 95; Connecting Development to Life, p.105; Connecting with Research, p. 108; SIDS, p. 111; Developmental Connection, p. 117; Connecting with Careers, p. 98
- **Ch. 4:** Alzheimer's Disease, p. 127; Treatment for Older Adults, p. 130; Nutrition, Infancy, Breast vs. Bottle Feeding, pp. 131–132; Substance Abuse, p. 147; Connecting with Research, p. 129; Connecting with Careers, p. 129; Connecting Development to Life, p. 143

4 APPLICATION OF PSYCHOLOGY *continued*
Understand and apply psychological principles to personal, social, and organizational issues.

- **Ch. 5:** Connecting Development to Life, p.159; Connecting with Research, p. 164
- **Ch. 6:** Piaget's Theory of Cognitive Development, pp. 183–194; Applying and Evaluating Piaget's Theory, p. 197; Vygotsky's Theory of Cognitive Development, pp. 199–203; Evaluating Vygotsky's Theory, p. 203; Connecting Development to Life, p. 202; Connecting with Research, p. 188
- **Ch. 7:** Memory/Teaching Strategies, p. 223; Executive Function, p. 229; Adolescent Decision-Making, p. 232; Education, Work, and Health, pp. 234–235; Cognitive Neuroscience, pp. 235–236; Connecting Development to Life, p. 237; Theory of Mind and Autism, p. 241; Connecting with Research, p. 225; Connecting with Careers, p. 229
- **Ch. 8:** Use/Misuse of Intelligence Tests, p. 250; Theories of Multiple Intelligences, pp. 250–252; Controversies and Group Comparisons, pp. 253–255; Connecting with Research, p. 256; Tests of Infant Intelligence, p. 259; Education of Children Who Are Gifted, p. 266; Creativity in Schools, pp. 268–269; Connecting Development to Life, p. 270; Connecting with Careers, p. 258
- **Ch. 9:** How Language Develops—Early Literacy, pp. 283–284; Writing, p. 286; Bilingualism and Second Language Learning, p. 287–288; Environmental Influences, pp. 292–293; Connecting Development to Life, p. 294. Connecting with Careers, p. 288.; Connecting with Research, p. 283
- **Ch. 10:** Emotional Competence, p. 303; Development of Emotion—Coping with Stress, pp. 308–309; Temperament, p. 313; Connecting Development to Life, p. 316; Goodness of Fit and Parenting, p. 316; Attachment and Love, pp. 317–334; Connecting with Research, p. 334. Connecting with Careers, p. 326
- **Ch. 11:** Self-Understanding, pp. 342–345; Self-Esteem and Self-Concept (Strategies for Increasing Self-Esteem), p. 348; Self-Regulation, p. 348; Connecting Development to Life, p. 351; Connecting with Careers, p. 358; Connecting with Research, p. 364
- **Ch. 12:** Biological, Social, and Cognitive Influences on Gender, pp. 371–376; Gender Stereotypes, Similarities, and Differences, pp. 377–380; Exploring Sexuality, pp. 386–391; Sexuality Through the Life Span, pp. 392–402; Connecting Development to Life, p. 399; Connecting with Careers, pp. 384, p. 398; Connecting with Research, p. 376
- **Ch. 13:** Domains of Moral Development, pp. 408–417; Contexts of Moral Development, pp. 418–422; Prosocial and Antisocial Behavior, pp. 423–427; Values, Religion, Spirituality, and Meaning in Life, pp. 430–436; Connecting Development to Life, p. 436; Connecting with Careers, p. 428
- **Ch. 14:** Family Processes, pp. 445–448; The Diversity of Adult Lifestyles, pp. 448–457; Parenting, p. 458; Connecting Development to Life, p. 473; Other Family Relationships, pp. 477–481; Connecting with Careers, p. 460, p. 465; Connecting with Research, p. 464
- **Ch. 15:** Connecting Development to Life, p. 496; Sociocultural Influences, pp. 507–518; Connecting with Research, p. 493; Connecting with Careers, p. 519
- **Ch. 16:** Schools, pp. 525–539; Achievement, pp. 540–546; Careers, Work, and Retirement, pp. 547–555; Connecting Development to Life, p. 550; Connecting with Careers, p. 529, p. 539; Connecting with Research, p. 546
- **Ch. 17:** The Death System and Cultural Contexts, pp. 563–565; Defining Death and Life/Death Issues, pp. 565–568; Kubler-Ross's Stages of Dying, p. 574; Connecting Development to Life, p. 577; Dimensions of Grief, p. 578; Making Sense of the World, p. 579; Connecting with Research, p. 580; Connecting with Careers, p. 568

5 VALUES IN PSYCHOLOGY

Value empirical evidence, tolerate ambiguity, act ethically, and reflect other values that are the underpinnings of psychology as a science.

5.1 Recognize the necessity for ethical behavior in all aspects of the science and practice of psychology.

5.2 Demonstrate reasonable skepticism and intellectual curiosity by asking questions about causes of behavior.

5.3 Seek and evaluate scientific evidence for psychological claims.

5.4 Tolerate ambiguity and realize that psychological explanations are often complex and tentative.

5.5 Recognize and respect human diversity.

5.6 Assess and justify their engagement with respect to civic, social, and global responsibilities.

5.7 Understand the limitations of their psychological knowledge and skills.

- **Ch. 1:** Evaluating Psychoanalytic Theories, p. 22; Evaluating Cognitive Theories, p. 24; Air-Crib Question, p. 24; Evaluating Behavioral and Social Cognitive Theories, p. 24; Evaluating Ethological Theory, p. 26; Criticism of Methods for Collecting Data, pp. 29–30; Criticism of Types of Research Designs, pp. 31–32; Criticisms of Time-Span Research, pp. 33–34; Conducting Ethical Research, pp. 34–35; Minimizing Bias, pp. 35–36; Connecting with Research, p. 16

- **Ch. 2:** Evolutionary Perspective, p. 50; Evaluating Evolutionary Psychology, p. 51; The Nature-Nurture Debate, pp. 59–63; Connecting with Research, p. 83

- **Ch. 4:** Health and Aging—Alzheimer's Disease, p. 126; Connecting with Research, p. 129; Nutrition, Infancy, Outcomes of Breast-Feeding, p. 132; Controversy over Vitamins, p. 140; Childhood, p. 141; Connecting with Research, p. 129

- **Ch. 5:** Depth Perception, p. 168; Ecological Viewpoint, p. 175

- **Ch. 6:** Conservation Discrepancies, p. 193; Criticisms of Piaget, p. 199

- **Ch. 7:** Memory, p. 224; Prospective Memory, p. 225; Executive Function, p. 229; Scientific Thinking, pp. 230–231; Education, Work, and Health, p. 234

- **Ch. 8:** Genetic Influences, p. 254; Cultural Bias in Testing, pp. 256–257; Bias/Ethnic Comparisons in Testing, pp. 256–257; Fluid and Crystallized Intelligence, p. 260

- **Ch. 9:** Connecting with Research, p. 283; How Language Develops—Reading, p. 285; Bilingualism and Second Language Learning, pp. 287–288; Biological Influences, p. 292; An Interactionist View of Language, p. 295

- **Ch. 10:** Development of Emotion—Infancy (Early Emotions), pp. 304–307; What are Emotions?, p. 302; Adult/Aging, p. 310; Attachment and Love—Infancy and Childhood (Evaluating the Strange Situation), p. 322; Interpreting Differences in Attachment, p. 322; Adolescence (Dating and Adjustment), p. 329; Attachment, p. 330; Adulthood (Romantic Love), p. 332

- **Ch. 11:** Self-Understanding (Understanding Others), p. 341; Self-Esteem and Self-Concept, p. 347; Ethnic Identity, pp. 357–358; Views on Adult Personality Development, p. 361

- **Ch. 13:** Moral Thought—Kohlberg's Critics (Culture and Moral Reasoning), p. 412; Moral Thought—Kohlberg's Critics (Gender and Care Perspective), p. 412

- **Ch. 14:** Divorced Adults (Coping with Divorce), p. 455; Divorced Adults (Main Causes for Men), p. 455; Step-Families, p. 474; Gay and Lesbian Parents, p. 474; Adoptive Parents and Adopted Children (Developmental Outcomes), p. 476; Sibling Relationships and Birth Order, pp. 478–479; Intergenerational Relationships, p. 481

- **Ch. 15:** Bullying, pp. 492–493; Friendship During Childhood, p. 497; Culture (Individualism and Collectivism), p. 508

- **Ch. 16:** Approaches to Student Learning and Assessment, pp. 525–527

- **Ch. 17:** Death System and Its Cultural Variation, pp. 563–564; Changing Historical Circumstances, pp. 565–566; Decisions Regarding Life, Death, and Health Care, pp. 566–567; Attitudes Toward Death at Different Points in the Life Span, p. 570

6 INFORMATION AND TECHNOLOGICAL LITERACY
Demonstrate information competence and the ability to use computers and other technology for many purposes.

6.1 Demonstrate information competence at each stage in the following process:
   a. Formulate a researchable topic that can be supported by database search strategies
   b. Locate and choose relevant sources from appropriate media, which may include data and perspectives outside traditional psychology and Western boundaries
   c. Use selected sources after evaluating their suitability based on
      (1) Appropriateness, accuracy, quality, and value of the source
      (2) Potential bias of the source
      (3) The relative value of primary versus secondary sources, empirical versus nonempirical sources, and peer-reviewed versus non-peer-reviewed sources
   d. Read and accurately summarize the general scientific literature of psychology
6.2 Use appropriate software to produce understandable reports of the psychological literature, methods, and statistical and qualitative analyses in APA or other appropriate style, including graphic representations of data.
6.3 Use information and technology ethically and responsibly.
6.4 Demonstrate these computer skills:
   a. Use basic word processing, database, e-mail, spreadsheet, and data analysis program
   b. Search the Web for high-quality information
   c. Use proper etiquette and security safeguards when communicating through e-mail

- **Ch. 1:** Connecting Development to Life (graph), p. 11
- **Ch. 2:** Figures 2.17 and 2.18, p. 84
- **Ch. 3:** Figure 3.12, p. 103
- **Ch. 4:** Emerging and Young Adults' Health, p. 124; Figure 4.2, p. 125; Connecting with Research, p. 129; Treatment for Older Adults, Figure 4.8, p. 130; Figure 4.12, p. 138; Figure 4.16, p. 142
- **Ch. 7:** Attention, p. 216
- **Ch. 8:** Intelligence, Figure 8.1, p. 249

7 COMMUNICATION SKILLS
Communicate effectively in a variety of formats.

7.1 Demonstrate effective writing skills in various formats (e.g., essays, correspondence, technical papers, note taking) and for various purposes (e.g., informing, defending, explaining, persuading, arguing, teaching).
7.2 Demonstrate effective oral communication skills in various formats (e.g., group discussion, debate, lecture) and for various purposes (e.g., informing, defending, explaining, persuading, arguing, teaching).
7.3 Exhibit quantitative literacy.
7.4 Demonstrate interpersonal communication skills.
7.5 Exhibit the ability to collaborate effectively.

- **Ch. 1:** Connecting Development to Life (graph), p. 11; Review, Connect, Reflect sections
- **Ch. 2:** Evolutionary Perspective, Figure 2.1, p. 50; Figures 2.17 and 2.18 (graph), p. 84; Review, Connect, Reflect sections
- **Ch. 3:** Connecting with Research, p. 108; Review, Connect, Reflect sections
- **Ch. 4:** Review, Connect, Reflect sections
- **Ch. 5:** Review, Connect, Reflect sections
- **Ch. 6:** Figures 6.1 and 6.2, p. 185; Concrete Operations, Figure 6.9, p. 194; Figure 6.12, p. 203; Review, Connect, Reflect sections
- **Ch. 7:** Figure 7.1, p. 211; Review, Connect, Reflect sections
- **Ch. 8:** Figure 8.5, p. 254; Figures 8.11 and 8.12, p. 264; Review, Connect, Reflect sections
- **Ch. 9:** Review, Connect, Reflect sections
- **Ch. 10:** Review, Connect, Reflect sections
- **Ch. 11:** Review, Connect, Reflect sections
- **Ch. 12:** Review, Connect, Reflect sections
- **Ch. 13:** Review, Connect, Reflect sections
- **Ch. 14:** Review, Connect, Reflect sections
- **Ch. 15:** Review, Connect, Reflect sections
- **Ch. 16:** Review, Connect, Reflect sections
- **Ch. 17:** Review, Connect, Reflect sections

8 SOCIOCULTURAL AND INTERNATIONAL AWARENESS

Recognize, understand, and respect the complexity of sociocultural and international diversity.

8.1 Interact effectively and sensitively with people from diverse backgrounds and cultural perspectives.

8.2 Examine the sociocultural and international contexts that influence individual differences.

8.3 Explain how individual differences influence beliefs, values, and interactions with others and vice versa.

8.4 Understand how privilege, power, and oppression may affect prejudice, discrimination, and inequity.

8.5 Recognize prejudicial attitudes and discriminatory behaviors that might exist in themselves and others.

8.6 Predict how interaction among diverse people can challenge conventional understanding of psychological processes and behavior.

- **Ch. 1:** Development Is Contextual, p. 7; Development Is Co-construction . . . Individual, p. 8; Sociocultural . . . Diversity, pp. 8–10; Reflect Question, p. 12; Connecting Biological . . . Processes, p. 13; Age and Happiness, p. 15; Connecting with Research—Experiment, Figure 1.7, p. 16; Conceptions of Age, p. 17; Vygotsky's Theory, p. 23; Skinner's Operant Conditioning, p. 24; Social Cognitive Theories, p. 25; Ecological Theory, p. 27; Cohort Effects, p. 33; Minimizing Bias, pp. 35–36
- **Ch. 2:** Sickle-Cell Anemia, p. 58; Childbirth Settings, p. 77; Methods of Childbirth, pp. 78–79; Low Birth Weight, p. 81
- **Ch. 3:** Puberty—Timing and Variations, p. 94; Middle Adulthood—Physical Appearance, p. 96; Sexuality, p. 97; Connecting Development to Life, p. 105; Connecting with Research, p. 108; Shared Sleeping, p. 110; SIDS, p. 111; Life Expectancy, p. 115
- **Ch. 4:** Nutrition, Adolescence—Obesity, p. 136; Adolescence, p. 142
- **Ch. 5:** The First Year: Motor Development, p. 156; Cultural Variations in Infant Motor Development, pp. 157–158
- **Ch. 6:** Formal Operations, p. 195; Applying and Evaluating Piaget's Theory, p. 197; Evaluating Piaget's Theory, p. 199; Review, Connect, Reflect, p. 199
- **Ch. 7:** Attention, p. 216
- **Ch. 8:** Cultural Factors in Intelligence, pp. 256–257; Bias/Ethnic Comparisons in Testing, pp. 256–257; Creativity in Schools, p. 268
- **Ch. 9:** Language's Rule Systems (Phonology), p. 276; Syntax, p. 276; Pragmatics, p. 277; How Language Develops—Infancy (Gestures), p. 278; Early Literacy, pp. 283–284; Bilingualism and Second Language Learning, pp. 287–288
- **Ch. 10:** Attachment and Love—Infancy and Childhood (Evaluating the Strange Situation), p. 322; Interpreting Differences in Attachment, p. 323; Mothers and Fathers as Caregivers, p. 324; Child Care—Parental Leave, p. 325; Sociocultural Contexts and Dating, pp. 329–330
- **Ch. 11:** Self-Esteem and Self-Concept (Developmental Changes), pp. 346–347; Ethnic Identity, p. 357
- **Ch. 12:** Social Influences, pp. 373–374; Gender Stereotyping, p. 377; Sexual Orientation, p. 387; Forcible Sexual Behavior and Sexual Harassment, p. 391
- **Ch. 13:** Moral Thought—Kohlberg's Critics (Culture and Moral Reasoning), p. 412; Gender and Care Perspective, p. 412; Review, Connect, Reflect, p. 418; Religion and Spirituality, pp. 432–435
- **Ch. 14:** Family Processes (Sociocultural and Historical Influences), p. 447; Cohabiting Adults, pp. 449–450; Married Adults (Social Contexts), pp. 451–452; Parenting Styles and Discipline (Parenting Styles in Context), p. 462; Punishment, pp. 463–464; Child Maltreatment—Context of Abuse, p. 466; Parent-Adolescent Relationships—Autonomy and Attachment, pp. 467–468; Children in Divorced Families, p. 471; Role of SES, p. 472; Gay and Lesbian Parents, p. 474; Adoptive Parents and Adopted Children (Increased Diversity), p. 475; Sibling Relationships and Birth Order, p. 478; Grandparenting and Great-Grandparenting, p. 479
- **Ch. 15:** Exploring Peer Relations, pp. 488–490; Adolescent Peer Relations, p. 494; Culture, p. 507; Individualism and Collectivism, p. 508; Technology, Media, and Culture, pp. 510–511; Aging and Culture, pp. 512–513; Socioeconomic Status and Poverty, p. 513; Socioeconomic Variations, pp. 513–514; Poverty, p. 514; Psychological Ramifications of Poverty, p. 515; Ethnicity (Immigration), p. 517; Ethnicity and Aging, p. 519
- **Ch. 16:** Schools and Developmental Status (High School), pp. 531–532; Socioeconomic Status and Ethnicity in Schools (Education of Students from Low-Income Backgrounds), p. 537; Ethnicity, pp. 538–539; Achievement—Ethnicity and Culture, pp. 545–547; Careers, Work, and Retirement (Monitoring the Occupational Outlook), p. 548; Work in Adolescence, p. 549; Work and Retirement around the World, p. 554
- **Ch. 17:** Death System and Its Cultural Variation, pp. 563–564; Decisions Regarding Life, Death, and Health Care (Euthanasia), p. 567; Suicide, pp. 571–572; Communicating with a Dying Person, p. 579; Forms of Mourning, pp. 581–582; Review, Connect, Reflect, p. 576

9 PERSONAL DEVELOPMENT

Develop insight into their own and others' behavior and mental processes and apply effective strategies for self-management and self-improvement.

9.1 Reflect on their experiences and find meaning in them.

9.2 Apply psychological principles to promote personal development.

9.3 Enact self-management strategies that maximize health outcomes.

9.4 Display high standards of personal integrity with others.

9.5 Seek input from and experiences with diverse people to enhance the quality of solutions.

- **Ch. 1:** Importance of Studying, p. 5; Development Is Multidirectional, p. 6; Development = Growth . . . Loss, p. 8; Social Policy, p. 12; Happiness, bottom of p. 16 and Figure 1.8, p. 17; Conceptions of Age, p. 17; Piaget's Theory/Formal Operations, p. 23; Skinner's Operant Conditioning, p. 24; Social Cognitive Theories, p. 25; Review, Connect, Reflect sections
- **Ch. 2:** Review, Connect, Reflect sections
- **Ch. 3:** Review, Connect, Reflect sections; REM sleep, p. 110; Chart for Life Expectancy, p. 116
- **Ch. 4:** Review, Connect, Reflect sections; Connecting Development to Life, p. 143
- **Ch. 6:** Review, Connect, Reflect sections; Piaget's Theory of Cognitive Development, pp. 186–187; Piaget's Processes of Development, pp. 183–184; Preoperational Stage, pp. 191–192; Concrete and Formal Operations, pp. 194–195; Adolescent Egocentrism, p. 196; Cognitive Changes in Adulthood, p. 205; Figure 6.13, p. 206
- **Ch. 7:** Review, Connect, Reflect sections
- **Ch. 8:** Review, Connect, Reflect sections; Connecting Development to Life, p. 270
- **Ch. 9:** Review, Connect, Reflect sections
- **Ch. 10:** Review, Connect, Reflect sections; Attachment and Love—Adulthood, p. 331
- **Ch. 11:** Review, Connect, Reflect sections
- **Ch. 12:** Review, Connect, Reflect sections
- **Ch. 13:** Review, Connect, Reflect sections; Values, Religion, Spirituality, and Meaning in Life, p. 430
- **Ch. 14:** Review, Connect, Reflect sections; Family Processes (Developmental Connection), p. 447
- **Ch. 15:** Review, Connect, Reflect sections
- **Ch. 16:** Review, Connect, Reflect sections
- **Ch. 17:** Review, Connect, Reflect sections

10 CAREER PLANNING AND DEVELOPMENT

Pursue realistic ideas about how to implement their psychological knowledge, skills, and values in occupational pursuits in a variety of settings that meet personal goals and societal needs.

10.1 Apply knowledge of psychology (e.g., decision strategies, life-span processes, psychological assessment, types of psychological careers) when formulating career choices.

10.2 Identify the types of academic experience and performance in psychology and the liberal arts that will facilitate entry into the workforce, post-baccalaureate education, or both.

10.3 Describe preferred career paths based on accurate self-assessment of abilities, achievement, motivation, and work habits.

10.4 Identify and develop skills and experiences relevant to achieving selected career goals.

10.5 Articulate how changing societal needs can influence career opportunities and foster flexibility about managing changing conditions.

10.6 Demonstrate an understanding of the importance of lifelong learning and personal flexibility to sustain personal and professional development as the nature of work evolves.

- **Ch. 1:** Connecting with Careers, p. 36
- **Appendix:** Careers in Life-Span Development, pp. 41–47
- **Ch. 2:** Connecting with Careers, p. 59; Connecting with Careers, p. 81
- **Ch. 3:** Connecting with Careers, p. 98
- **Ch. 4:** Connecting with Careers, p. 133
- **Ch. 7:** Connecting with Careers, p. 229; Connecting Development to Life, p. 237
- **Ch. 8:** Connecting with Careers, p. 258
- **Ch. 9:** Connecting with Careers, p. 281; Connecting with Careers, p. 288
- **Ch. 10:** Connecting with Careers, p. 326
- **Ch. 11:** Connecting with Careers, p. 358
- **Ch. 12:** Connecting with Careers, p. 384; Connecting with Careers, p. 398
- **Ch. 13:** Connecting with Careers, p. 428; Connecting with Careers, p. 435
- **Ch. 14:** Connecting with Careers, p. 460; Connecting with Research, p. 465
- **Ch. 15:** Connecting with Careers, p. 519
- **Ch. 16:** Connecting with Careers, p. 529; Connecting with Careers, p. 539; Connecting with Careers, p. 548
- **Ch. 17:** Connecting with Careers, p. 568

Making Connections . . . From My Classroom to *A Topical Approach to Life-Span Development* to You

Having taught life-span development every semester for 25 years now, I'm always looking for ways to improve my course and texts. Just as McGraw-Hill looks to those who teach the life-span development course for input, each year I ask the almost 200 students in my life-span development course to tell me what they like about the course and the text, and what they think could be improved. What have my students told me lately about my course and text? Students said that highlighting connections among the different aspects of life-span development would help them to better understand the concepts. As I thought about this, it became clear that a *connections* theme would provide a systematic, integrative approach to the course material. I used this theme to shape my current goals for my life-span development course, which, in turn, I've now incorporated into the main goals of this text:

1. **Connecting research to what we know about development.** To provide students with the best and most recent *theory and research* in the world today about each of the periods of the human life span.

2. **Connecting topical processes in development.** To guide students in making *topical connections* across different aspects of development through the life span.

3. **Connecting development to the real world.** To help students understand ways to *apply* content about the human life span to the real world and improve people's lives; and to motivate them to think deeply about *their own personal journey through life* and better understand who they were, are, and will be.

Connecting with Today's Students

I recognize that today's students are as different in some ways from the learners of the last generation as today's discipline of life-span development is different from the field 30 years ago. Students are now learning in multiple modalities; rather than sitting down and reading traditional printed chapters in linear fashion from beginning to end, their work preferences tend to be more visual and more interactive. Their reading and study often occur in short bursts. For many students, a traditionally formatted printed textbook is no longer enough when they have instant, 24/7 access to news and information from around the globe. **Connect Psychology,** our **adaptive learning system** and integrated **learning goals system** provide the kind of access and flexibility today's students demand.

Chapter-by-Chapter Changes

Numerous content changes were made in each of the 17 chapters in *A Topical Approach to Life-Span Development*, Sixth Edition. The major ones are described below.

Chapter 1: Introduction

- Substantial updating of research and citations
- Extensive editing for improved student understanding
- Expanded discussion of poverty and children, including updated statistics on the percentage of U.S. children under 18 years of age living in poverty (Childstats.gov, 2010)
- Description of a recent study of more than 300,000 U.S. adults that revealed an increase in psychological well-being after 50 years of age (Stone & others, 2010)
- New Figure 1.8, "How Satisfied Am I with My Life?" that gives students an opportunity to evaluate their life satisfaction on the most widely used measure in research on life satisfaction (Diener, 2011; Diener & others, 1985)
- Expanded coverage of Bronfenbrenner's contributions (Gauvain & Parke, 2010; Parke & Clarke-Stewart, 2011)

Chapter 2: Biological Beginnings

- Expanded discussion of criticisms of evolutionary psychology to include it being on a time scale that does not allow its empirical study
- New introductory material connecting the discussion of evolution and genetics
- Description of a recent study that found exposure to radiation changes the rate of DNA synthesis (Lee & others, 2011)
- Updated coverage of susceptibility (Paquette & others, 2010) and longevity genes (Bauer & others, 2010)
- Updated material on the concept of gene-gene interaction (Bapal & others, 2010; Chen & others, 2010)
- Updated coverage of the concept of $G \times E$, which involves the interaction of a specific measured variation in the DNA sequence and a specific measured aspect of the environment (Goldman & others, 2010; Keers & others, 2011)
- Expanded and updated commentary about the transport of drugs across the placenta (Eshkoli & others, 2011)
- Description of a recent study that found cigarette smoking weakened and increased oxidative stress in the fetal membranes from which the placenta develops (Menon & others, 2011)
- New coverage of a link between maternal diabetes and obesity and the development of neural tube defects (Yazdy & others, 2010)
- Updated coverage of the offspring of diabetic mothers (Huda & others, 2010)
- Description of a recent research study linking failure to take folic acid supplements in the first trimester of pregnancy with toddlers' behavioral problems (Roza & others, 2010)

- Coverage of a recent experimental study of the effects of a CenteringPregnancy Plus program on high-stress pregnant women (Ickovics & others, 2011)
- Inclusion of information from a recent research review indicating that high amounts of caffeine consumption by pregnant women do not increase the risk of miscarriage (Brent, Christian, & Diener, 2011)
- Discussion of a recent meta-analysis linking maternal smoking in pregnancy to a modest increase in non-Hodgkin lymphoma in children (Antonopoulos & others, 2011)
- Description of recent research on the negative effects of cocaine exposure and elevated blood pressure at 9 years of age (Shankaran & others, 2011)
- Discussion of prenatal methamphetamine exposure and decreased brain activation, especially in the frontal lobes, in 7- to 15-year-olds (Roussotte, 2011)
- Coverage of recent research on more than 30,000 offspring and the time during prenatal development when stress was most likely to increase the risk of preterm birth (Class & others, 2011)
- Coverage of two recent research reviews that linked maternal depression to preterm birth and low birth weight (Dunkel Schetter, 2011; Field, 2011)
- Discussion of a recent study that found waterbirth was related to having a shorter second stage of labor (Cortes, Basra, & Kelleher, 2011)
- Update on the dramatic increase in cesarean deliveries in the United States (Solheim & others, 2011)
- Description of a recent study indicating that low Apgar scores were linked to developing ADHD in childhood (Li & others, 2011)
- New material on ethnic variations in preterm births in the United States (National Center for Health Statistics, 2009)
- Updated statistics on the percentage of preterm and low birth weight infants in the United States (Hamilton & others, 2009)
- Significant updating of research on the role of progestin in preventing preterm births, indicating the conditions under which progestin is most successful (da Fonseca & others, 2009; Norman & others, 2009)
- New section on the postpartum period
- Discussion of a recent study on the percentage of women with postpartum depression who seek help for their depression (McGarry & others, 2009)
- Updated coverage of fathers' adjustment during the postpartum period (Dietz & others, 2009; Smith & Howard, 2008)

- Coverage of a recent research review of the interaction difficulties of depressed mothers and their infants (Field, 2010)

Chapter 3: Physical Development and Biological Aging

- Updated commentary on the recent interest in molecular genetic studies that seek to identify genes that are linked to the onset of puberty (He & others, 2010)
- Description of a recent study on the role of weight in girls' pubertal development (Christensen & others, 2010)
- Inclusion of recent information on a longitudinal study of the sequence of pubertal events in boys and girls (Susman & others, 2010)
- Discussion of a recent study of gender differences in the aesthetic aspects of adolescents' body image (Abbott & Barber, 2010)
- Coverage of a recent longitudinal study of early- and late-maturing girls from adolescence through emerging adulthood (Copeland & others, 2010)
- Discussion of a recent study on early maturing girls' higher level of depression and its link to a heightened sensitivity to interpersonal stress (Natsuaki & others, 2010)
- Description of recent research linking maternal harshness in early childhood with early maturation and sexual risk taking in adolescence (Belsky & others, 2010)
- Coverage of a recent study that found a link between early maturation and substance abuse as well as early sexual intercourse (Gaudineau & others, 2010)
- Discussion of a recent study linking a low level of HDL cholesterol with a higher probability of still being alive at 85 years of age (Rahilly-Tierney & others, 2011)
- Inclusion of recent research on physical activity, metabolic syndrome, and cardiovascular disease (Broekhuizen & others, 2011)
- Addition of John Richards and his colleagues (2010; Richards, Reynolds, & Courage, 2010) as conducting important research on the development of the brain in infancy
- Updated coverage of the role of myelination in providing energy for neurons (Campbell & Mahad, 2011)
- New description of how the information about changes in the adolescent brain reflects the rapidly emerging field of developmental social neuroscience (Casey & others, 2010)
- Inclusion of Laurence Steinberg and his colleagues' (Albert & Steinberg, 2011a, b; Caufman & others, 2010; Steinberg & others, 2008, 2009) recent research and theory on changes during adolescence in preference for immediate rewards, benefits versus costs in risk taking, and impulse control
- New discussion of the potential positive outcomes of some aspects of risk taking in adolescence (Allen & Allen, 2009)
- Updated information about neuronal loss not being substantial in healthy older adults (Richard, Taylor, & Greer, 2010)
- Updated coverage of neurogenesis and aging, including a recent study in which coping with stress stimulated hippocampal neurogenesis in adult monkeys (Lyons & others, 2010)
- Discussion of recent research on variation in the link between cognitive processing and asymmetry in the prefrontal cortex in older adults (Manenti, Cotelli, & Miniussi, 2010)
- New material on the most common sleep problem in infancy (Hospital for Sick Children & others, 2010)
- Coverage of a recent study linking maternal emotional availability to infants with fewer sleep problems (Teti & others, 2010)
- Discussion of a recent study indicating that paternal involvement in infant care was related to fewer infant sleep problems (Tikotzky, Sadeh, & Glickman-Gavrieli, 2010)
- Description of recent research on early life risk factors that are linked to infant sleep duration (Nevarez & others, 2010)
- Updated information about infant-parent bed sharing and an increasing trend of recommending that this not occur until the infant is at least 6 months old (McIntosh, Tonkin, & Gunn, 2010)
- Coverage of a recent study indicating that infant-parent bed sharing was linked with more infant sleep problems, such as disordered breathing (Kelmanson, 2010)
- Updated and expanded coverage of SIDS, including the role of brain stem functioning and the neurotransmitter serotonin (Duncan & others, 2010)
- Description of a recent study linking sleep problems in early childhood with subsequent attention problems that in some cases persist into early adolescence (O'Callaghan & others, 2010)
- Coverage of a recent study indicating that having trouble sleeping in childhood was related to alcohol use problems in adolescence and early adulthood (Wong & others, 2010)
- Discussion of a recent study of emotional security in parent-child and marital relationships in the third grade and their link to fewer sleep problems in the fifth grade (Keller & El-Sheikh, 2010)
- Coverage of a recent analysis indicating that chronic child sleep disorders that deprive children of adequate sleep may lead to impaired brain development (Jan & others, 2010)
- Description of a recent study on delaying school start time for ninth- to twelfth-grade students and their improved sleep, alertness, mood, and health (Owens, Belon, & Moss, 2010)
- New content on sleep in emerging adulthood (Galambos, Howard, & Maggs, 2011)

- Discussion of recent research indicating that first-year college students have bedtimes and risetimes that are later than those of high school seniors but that bedtimes and risetimes decline by the third and fourth year of college (Lund & others, 2010)

- Description of a recent study that found first-year college students' sleep was of poorer quality in the months in which they were experiencing the most stress (Galambos, Howard, & Maggs, 2011)

- Updated coverage of the percentage of older adults who have difficulty in sleeping (Neikrug & Ancoli-Israel, 2010)

- Discussion of recent research on sleep and memory in older adults (Aly & Moscovitch, 2010)

- New discussion of the evolutionary theory of aging in the section on biological theories of aging (Austad, 2009; Kittas, 2010)

- Updated and expanded material on telomeres and telomerase, including the increasing interest in the role they likely play in stem cell regeneration (Flores & Blasco, 2010)

- New material on the allostatic load view of stress in the coverage of the hormonal stress theory of aging (Almeida & others, 2011)

Chapter 4: Health

- Updated and expanded information about the increase in health problems in emerging adulthood compared to adolescence (Fatusi & Hindin, 2010)

- New coverage of why it is important to focus on biological and environmental risk factors, preventive strategies, and maintenance of cognitive reserves in middle adulthood in research on Alzheimer disease

- New discussion of the role that oxidative stress might play in Alzheimer disease (Bonda & others, 2010)

- New coverage of a research review indicating that fMRI measurement of neuron loss in the medial temporal lobe predicts memory loss and eventually dementia (Vellas & Aisen, 2010)

- Expanded discussion of drug treatment of Alzheimer disease including recent indications of how effective the drugs are

- Inclusion of estimates of the percentage of individuals 65 years of age and older who have mild cognitive impairment (MCI) (Alzheimer's Association, 2010)

- Inclusion of information that the Federal Drug Administration has yet to approve any drugs for the treatment of MCI

- Description of recent research indicating that the presence of amyloid protein in the spinal fluid of individuals with mild cognitive impairment predicted whether they would develop Alzheimer disease within the next five years (De Meyer & others, 2010)

- Updated coverage of new treatments for Parkinson disease, including stem cell research (Fricker-Gates & Gates, 2010)

- Description of research indicating that preschool children who were overweight had a significant risk of being overweight/obese at 11 years of age (Shankaran & others, 2011)

- Updated discussion of research indicating that certain types of dance, such as the tango, can improve the motor skills of individuals with Parkinson disease (Hackney & Earhart, 2010a, b)

- New coverage of a recent study of child health and nutrition programs in Haiti that helped to reduce the impact of economic hardship on stunting of children's growth (Donegan & others, 2010)

- Coverage of a recent meta-analysis linking obesity with depression in women but not men (de Wit & others, 2010)

- Discussion of a recent study on parents' roles in limiting children's sedentary activity (Edwardson & Gorely, 2010)

- Coverage of a recent study on the effectiveness of a school-based program for increasing children's physical activity (Kriemler & others, 2010)

- Discussion of a recent study linking low levels of exercise to depressive symptoms in young adolescents (Sund, Larsson, & Wichstrom, 2010)

- Description of a recent study that found a relation between vigorous physical activity and lower drug use in adolescents (Delisle & others, 2010)

- Discussion of a recent study of overweight and obesity from 14 to 24 years of age (Patton & others, 2011)

- Inclusion of recent research indicating that the main reason overweight adolescents were depressed was their body dissatisfaction (Mond & others, 2011)

- New section on binge eating disorder (BED), including recent research on factors that differentiate BED from other eating disorders (White & Grillo, 2011; Zeeck & others, 2011)

- Updated statistics on the increase in overweight/obesity in adulthood (Flegal & others, 2010)

- New coverage of the highest and lowest percentage of obese adults in 33 developed countries, including a new Figure 4.12 (OECD, 2010a)

- Description of recent research showing links between aerobic exercise and a number of children's and adolescents' cognitive skills (Best, 2011; Davis & others, 2011)

- New discussion of links between screen-based activity and physical exercise in adolescents (Sisson & others 2010)

- Expanded and updated research on telomere length, exercise, and aging (La Rocca, Seals, & Pierce, 2010)

- Updated description of improved brain functioning related to exercise (McGregor & others, 2011)

- Updated coverage of the Monitoring the Future study's assessment of drug use by secondary school students (Johnston & others, 2011)

- Coverage of recent research that found parental monitoring was linked to lower substance abuse in adolescence (Tobler & Komro, 2010)
- Description of a recent research review that indicated adolescents who more frequently ate dinner with their family were less likely to have substance abuse problems (Sen, 2010)
- Discussion of recent research on positive and negative aspects of adolescents' interaction and relationships with parents and adolescent drinking and smoking (Gutman & others, 2011)
- Updated material on college students' drinking habits, including new data on extreme binge drinking (Johnston & others, 2010a)
- New coverage of pregaming and gaming as becoming increasingly common rituals on college campuses, including recent research (DeJong, DeRicco, & Schneider, 2010; Read, Merrill, & Bytschkow, 2010)

Chapter 5: Motor, Sensory, and Perceptual Development

- A number of changes made in the discussion of motor development based on leading expert Karen Adolph's feedback
- Numerous updates and changes in the chapter based on Scott Johnson's feedback
- Updated discussion of infant reflexes arguing that reflexes are not exclusively inborn, genetic mechanisms but rather that infants can deliberately control such movements (Adolph & Robinson, 2011)
- New coverage of recent research indicating that alternating leg movements occur during the fetal period and at birth (Adolph & Robinson, 2011)
- Revised information about the percentage of infants who do not crawl in some cultures with information that about one-fourth of infants in Jamaica don't crawl (Hopkins, 1991)
- Revised and updated information about cultural variations in promoting or restricting motor development and outcomes of these practices (Adolph, Karasik, & Tamis-LeMonda, 2010)
- Added commentary about the traditional practice in many sub-Saharan villages of engaging babies in exercise (Super & Harkness, 2011)
- Coverage of a recent study linking sports participation to a lower incidence of being overweight or obese (Antonogeorgos & others, 2011)
- Inclusion of recent research indicating that training infants to use sticky mittens resulted in advances in their reaching behavior (Libertus & Needham, 2010) New Figure 5.4 showing age-related slowing of movement that occurs across a range of mobility
- Coverage of recent research on obesity and mobility restrictions in older adults (Jensen & Hsiao, 2010; Vincent, Vincent, & Lamb, 2010)

- Inclusion of recent research indicating that a combined program of physical activity and weight loss was linked to preserving mobility in older, obese adults in poor cardiovascular health (Rejeski & others, 2011)
- Discussion of recent research indicating that less frequent social activity in older adults was linked to more rapid loss of motor function (Buchman & others, 2009)
- New description of falls in older adults and the role that exercise can play in reducing risk of falling (Yokoya, Demura, & Sato, 2009)
- Discussion of recent research linking a lower education level to higher mobility disability in older adults (Gregory & others, 2011)
- Inclusion of recent information about the development of sophisticated eye-tracking equipment to study infant perception, including a new figure of an infant in a study using eye-tracking equipment (Franchak & others, 2010)
- Deletion of figure on eye tracking because it was done almost 30 years ago with rudimentary equipment and does not accurately portray newborns' eye movements
- Coverage of a recent study indicating that young infants looked longest at reddish hues and shortest at greenish hues (Franklin & others, 2010)
- New figure illustrating the study by Bennett Bertenthal and his colleagues (2007) of infants' predictive tracking of briefly occluded moving objects
- New commentary about critics of the visual cliff concluding that it likely is a better test of social referencing and fear of heights than depth perception
- Inclusion of recent research linking visual decline in older adults with a lower level of cognitive functioning (Clay & others, 2009)
- New commentary that diabetes is a risk factor in the development of cataracts (De Fine & others, 2011; Grausland, 2011)
- Description of a study linking macular degeneration to an increased risk of falls in older adults (Wood & others, 2011)
- Coverage of a recent national survey of the percentage of adults 70 years and older with hearing loss (Lin & others, 2011)
- Added commentary that most perception is intermodal (Bahrick, 2010)

Chapter 6: Cognitive Developmental Approaches

- New discussion of Baillargeon's view of innate bias as expressed in the principle of persistence (Baillargeon & others, 2009)
- Inclusion of criticism of Spelke's core knowledge approach by Mark Johnson (2008)
- Description of a recent research study indicating that adolescents envision that they are vulnerable

to experiencing a premature death (Fischhoff & others, 2010)

- Expanded and updated coverage of the importance of perspective taking and ego development in explaining the imaginary audience and personal fable (Lapsley & Hill, 2010)
- New section, "Cognition and Emotion," in the discussion of cognitive changes in emerging and early adulthood
- New discussion of the views of Labouvie-Vief and her colleagues (2010) on the role of developmental changes in the integration and complexity of cognition and emotion, as well as the presence of increasing internal reflection and less context-dependent thinking in middle-aged adults as compared with young adults
- Revision of the definition of postformal thought to include the view of Labouvie-Vief and her colleagues (2010) on the role of emotion in cognitive changes
- Inclusion of recent information about the assessment of postformal thinking, including a new Figure 6.13 that gives students an opportunity to evaluate their postformal thinking (Cartwright & others, 2009)
- Discussion of a recent study indicating that college students with a higher number of cross-category friends have a higher level of postformal thinking than their counterparts with fewer cross-category friends (Galupo, Cartwright, & Savage, 2010)

Chapter 7: Information Processing

- Inclusion of recent research on speed of processing training with older drivers who have difficulties with speed of processing (Edwards, Delahunt, & Mahncke, 2009; Edwards & others, 2010)
- Discussion of a recent study indicating that joint attention enhanced the long-term memory of 9-month-old infants (Kopp & Lindenberger, 2011)
- Description of a recent study linking early joint attention with a specific area in the prefrontal cortex (Grossmann & Johnson, 2010)
- New material on using computer exercises to improve children's attention (Jaeggi, Berman, & Jonides, 2009; Tang & Posner, 2009)
- Coverage of a recent research study linking television watching and video game playing to children's attention problems (Swing & others, 2010)
- Discussion of a recent study showing a decline in executive attention in older adults (Mahoney & others, 2010)
- Description of a recent study of sustained attention from early adulthood through late adulthood (Carriere & others, 2010)
- New coverage of three recent studies of working memory that illustrate the importance of working memory capacity for children's cognitive development and achievement (Andersson, 2010; Aslan, Zellner, & Bauml, 2010; Welsh & others, 2010)

- New section on improving children's memory
- Expanded coverage of strategies for improving children's memory skills, including memory development expert Patricia Bauer's (2009) emphasis on the importance of consolidation and reconsolidation in memory by varying an instructional theme and linking often
- New material on Peter Ornstein and his colleagues' view (2010) that it is important for instructors to embed memory-relevant language in their teaching
- Description of a recent study of the reminiscence bump and its link to certain types of memories (Demiray, Gulgoz, & Bluck, 2009)
- Added commentary by infant researcher Alison Gopnik (2010) on the importance of putting things into the right categories
- New coverage of the increasing interest in children's executive functioning, including its importance in the preschool years (Zelazo & Muller, 2011)
- Inclusion of recent research by Stephanie Carlson (2010, 2011) on developmental changes in young children's executive functioning, including a description and photograph of the research setting used in her research
- Updated and revised description of the *Connecting with Careers* box on Helen Hadani and her new work
- Expanded and updated content on executive functioning in adolescence
- New section on the importance of controlling attention and interfering thoughts in adolescence
- Inclusion of information about a recent study of the important role of metacognition in adolescents' ability to effectively generate hypotheses (Kim & Pedersen, 2010)
- Description of a recent study with college students indicating that metacognition is a key factor in the ability to engage effectively in critical thinking (Magno, 2010)
- Description of a recent study that linked a reduction in decision-making quality in risky situations by older adults to declines in memory and processing speed (Henninger, Madden, & Huettel, 2010)
- Coverage of a recent study linking education and cognitive abilities in older adults, and describing how engaging in cognitive activities can improve cognitive functioning in older adults with less education (Lachman & others, 2010)
- Discussion of a recent study on differences in connectivity between brain regions in younger and older adults (Leshikar & others, 2010)
- Description of recent research indicating that when older adults engage in cognitively stimulating activities, the onset of rapid memory decline is delayed (Hall & others, 2009)
- Coverage of a recent study of older adults who engaged in a memory training program and how it affected their source memory and brain (Engvig & others, 2010)

- Expanded, updated, and revised content in the *Connecting with Research* box on interventions in cognitive aging to include the views of a consensus of leading experts at the Stanford University Center for Longevity (2011)
- Discussion of a recent research review of dietary supplements and cognitive aging (Gorby, Brownell, & Falk, 2010)

Chapter 8: Intelligence

- Substantial updating of research with addition of a number of 2010 and 2011 research citations
- Description of a recent study of predicting academic performance with measures of general mental abilities and emotional intelligence (Song & others, 2010)
- Coverage of a recent analysis indicating that the Flynn effect may be due to improvements in prenatal and early postnatal nutrition (Lynn, 2009)
- Discussion of a recent study that revealed an accelerated Flynn effect for children whose mothers have more education and for children from higher-income families (Ang, Rodgers, & Wanstrom, 2010)
- Description of a recent study linking children's scores on the WISC performance scale IQ and gray and white temporal lobe matter, as well as frontal lobe white matter (Lange & others, 2010)
- Discussion of a study linking selective attention to novelty at 6 to 12 months of age with intelligence at 21 years of age (Fagan, Holland, & Wheeler, 2007)
- Coverage of a recent longitudinal study on the stability of intelligence from 12 months to 4 years of age (Blaga & others, 2009)
- Expanded and updated coverage of predicting children's intelligence from assessment of habituation in early infancy (Domsch, Lohaus, & Thomas, 2009)
- Coverage of a recent study that compared the wisdom of college students and older adults on three dimensions: cognitive, reflective, and affective (Ardelt, 2010)
- Added examples of different aspects of wisdom to provide students with an indication of the types of items that are assessed in studies of wisdom (Ardelt, 2010)
- Expanded discussion of children's creative thinking, including recent research indicating a decline in creative thinking by U.S. schoolchildren and increased interest in teaching creative thinking in Chinese schools (Kim, 2010; Plucker, 2010)

Chapter 9: Language Development

- Modifications and updates of the discussion of language development based on comments by leading expert Catherine McBride-Chang
- New material on strategies for using books with preschoolers (Galinsky, 2010)
- Expanded coverage of reading, including the importance of fluency and metacognitive strategies in becoming a good reader (Snowling & Gobel, 2011)

- Inclusion of information about a recent study indicating that a computer-based program that emphasizes phonics improved first-grade students' reading skills (Savage & others, 2009)
- Discussion of a recent study of U.S. high school teachers' writing assignments that caused concern about the nature and frequency of the writing assignments students are required to do (Kiuhara, Graham, & Hawken, 2009)
- Discussion of recent research on differences in early gesture as explanations for SES disparities in child vocabulary at school entry (Rowe & Goldin-Meadow, 2009)
- Coverage of a recent research review indicating that bilingual children have lower formal language proficiency than monolingual children (Bialystok & Craik, 2010a)
- Description of recent research indicating that bilingual children have a smaller vocabulary in each language than monolingual children (Bialystok, 2011)
- New discussion of variations in early literacy across countries, including comparisons of children learning English and Chinese (McBride-Chang & others, 2008)
- Coverage of a recent study of 4-year-olds that revealed peers' expressive language abilities were positively linked to the 4-year-olds' receptive and expressive language development (Mashburn & others, 2009)
- New commentary suggesting that if infants don't hear language or develop an emotional bond with an adult, the neural connections that are linked to language may be weakened (Berko Gleason, 2009)
- Expanded and updated material on how parents can facilitate their infants' and toddlers' language development based on recommendations by Ellen Galinsky (2010)

Chapter 10: Emotional Development

- Added commentary about the importance of the communication aspect of emotion, especially in infancy (Witherington & others, 2011)
- Expanded coverage of the onset of emotions in infancy, including Jerome Kagan's (2010) recent conclusion that emotions such as guilt, pride, despair, shame, and jealousy, which require thought, cannot be experienced in the first year because of the structural immaturity of the infant's brain
- New material on the importance of smiling in infancy as a means of developing a new social skill and providing a key social signal (Campos, 2009)
- Revised definition of temperament to include individual differences in emotions, based on the view of leading expert Joseph Campos (2009)
- Discussion of a recent study linking young children's emotional understanding with their prosocial behavior (Ensor, Spencer, & Hughes, 2010)
- New descriptions of recent studies on how various aspects of disasters and traumatic events affect children (Catani & others, 2010; Chemtob & others, 2010; Peek & Stough, 2010)

- New material on dose/response effects in the study of how disasters and traumatic events affect children's adjustment and adaptation (Masten & Osofsky, 2010; Obradovic, Shaffer, & Master, 2011)
- Coverage of research by Laura Carstensen and her colleagues (2011) on links between aging and emotional well-being, emotional stability, and longevity
- Discussion of a recent study of younger and older adults' information-focus and emotion-focus in health-care decision making (Mikels & others, 2010)
- Updated information about temperament based on feedback from leading expert John Bates
- Coverage of a recent study linking behavioral inhibition at 3 years of age with shyness four years later (Volbrecht & Goldsmith, 2010)
- Added commentary about the importance of locomotion for the development of independence in the infant and toddler years (Campos, 2009)
- Description of a recent study linking security of attachment at 24 and 36 months to the child's social problem-solving skills at 54 months (Raikes & Thompson, 2009)
- Discussion of a recent study of maternal sensitive parenting and infant attachment security (Finger & others, 2009)
- Coverage of a recent meta-analysis linking Type D insecure attachment to externalizing problems (Fearon & others, 2010)
- Added information about the link of maternal sensitivity to secure infant attachment not being especially strong (Campos, 2009)
- Expanded discussion of fathers and mothers as caregivers
- New coverage of the Aka pygmy culture, where fathers are as involved in infant caregiving as much as mothers are (Hewlett, 2000; Hewlett & McFarlan, 2010)
- Description of a recent study of multiple child-care arrangements and young children's behavioral outcomes (Morrissey, 2009)
- New *Connecting with Careers* box on Wanda Mitchell, Child-Care Director
- Coverage of recent research linking early higher quality of child care with higher cognitive-academic achievement and lower externalizing behavior at 15 years of age (Vandell & others, 2010)
- Inclusion of the following important point about the NICHD SECC research: findings consistently show that family factors are considerably stronger and more consistent predictors of a wide variety of child outcomes than are child care experiences (quality, quantity, type)
- Description of a recent study using NICHD SECC data indicating that the worst socioeconomic outcomes for children occurred when both home and child care settings conferred risk (Watamura & others, 2011)
- Discussion of Joseph Allen and his colleagues' (2009) recent research linking secure attachment at age 14 with positive outcomes at age 21

- Description of a recent analysis that concluded the most consistent outcomes of secure attachment in adolescence involve positive peer relations and the development of emotion regulation capacities (Allen & Miga, 2010)
- Coverage of recent research on the negative outcomes of adolescent girls having an older romantic partner (Haydon & Halpern, 2010)
- Inclusion of recent research on 18- to 25-year-olds' linking attachment security with the quality of romantic relationships (Holland & Roisman, 2010)
- Discussion of recent research on links between anxious and avoidant attachment styles and various health problems (McWilliams & Bailey, 2010)
- Coverage of a recent analysis that revealed a link between insecure attachment in adults and depression (Bakermans-Kranenburg & van IJzendoorn, 2009)
- Discussion of a recent study that revealed attachment-anxious individuals show strong ambivalence toward a romantic partner (Mikulincer & others, 2010)
- Description of a recent study linking recent secure attachment to parents with ease in forming friendships in college (Parade, Leerkes, & Blankson, 2010)

Chapter 11: The Self, Identity, and Personality

- Inclusion of recent research on the early appearance of infants' conscious awareness of their bodies, which doesn't emerge until the second year (Brownell & others, 2009)
- Description of recent research on young children's understanding of joint commitments (Grafenhain & others, 2009)
- New coverage of leading expert Ross Thompson's (2009a) commentary about how current research on theory of mind and young children's social understanding is so dissonant with Piaget's egocentrism concept
- New material on perspective taking in understanding others, including the role of executive functioning in perspective taking (Galinsky, 2010)
- Discussion of a recent study that focused on the positive aspects of perspective-taking skills in children who are emotionally reactive (Bengtsson & Arvidsson, 2011)
- Inclusion of recent research on institutionalized older adults that revealed reminiscence therapy increased their life satisfaction and reduced their depression (Chiang & others, 2010)
- Discussion of a recent study that found a life-review course, "Looking for Meaning," reduced middle-aged and older adults' depressive symptoms (Pot & others, 2010)
- Coverage of a recent study on the developmental increase in self-control in middle and late childhood and its link to lower levels of deviant behavior and to warmth and positive affect in parenting (Vazsonyi & Huang, 2010)
- Inclusion of a recent study of self-regulation in children from low-income families (Buckner, Mezzacappa, & Beardslee, 2009)

- Description of a recent study on the consistency of identity over the course of adolescence and the percentage of adolescents who have identity conflicts throughout adolescence (Meeus & others, 2010)
- Coverage of a recent meta-analysis of 127 studies focused on developmental changes in Marcia's identity statuses (Kroger, Martinussen, & Marcia, 2010)
- Coverage of a recent study indicating the importance of exploration in ethnic identity development (Whitehead & others, 2009)
- Description of a recent study of older adult women's daily stressors and negative affect (Charles & others, 2010)
- New discussion of the manner in which different stressors—chronic and daily—affect health events (Piazza & others, 2010)
- New discussion of a recent study linking generativity with positive social engagement in such contexts as family life and community involvement (Cox & others, 2010)

Chapter 12: Gender and Sexuality

- New discussion of greater social acceptance of masculine girls who are described as tomboys than feminine boys described as sissies (Pasterski, Golombok, & Hines, 2011)
- New commentary about friendships mainly being same-sex in adolescence through late adulthood (Mehta & Strough, 2009, 2010)
- Inclusion of information about a recent meta-analysis that revealed no gender differences in math for adolescents (Lindberg & others, 2010)
- Revised and updated discussion of gender differences in relationships, including information from recent research reviews that concluded girls are more people-oriented, while boys are more object-oriented (Galambos & others, 2009; Perry & Pauletti, 2011)
- Discussion of a recent study indicating that relational aggression increases in middle and late childhood (Dishion & Piehler, 2009)
- Inclusion of information from a recent research review that girls engage in more relational aggression than boys in adolescence but not in childhood (Smith, Rose, & Schwartz-Mette, 2010)
- Discussion of recent research on developmental changes and cohort effects in masculinity, femininity, and androgyny from adolescence through late adulthood (Strough & others, 2007)
- Coverage of a recent study of adolescents' sexual experience and having multiple sexual partners from 1991 to 2007 (Santelli & others, 2009)
- Revised and updated data (Figure 12.6) on the percentage of adolescents who reported having had sexual intercourse, including a reversal for twelfth-graders with a higher percentage of twelfth-grade girls reporting having had sex than twelfth-grade boys (Eaton & others, 2010)
- Updated data on the percentage of U.S. adolescents who report that they are currently sexually active (Eaton & others, 2010)
- Description of the American Academy of Pediatrics policy statement regarding sexuality, contraception, and the media
- Discussion of a recent study that linked alcohol use, early menarche, and poor parent-child communication to early sexually intimate behavior in girls (Hipwell & others, 2011)
- Coverage of a recent study of early initiation of sexual intercourse in five countries (Madkour & others, 2010)
- Reorganized, updated, and expanded material on risk factors in adolescent pregnancy
- Description of recent research linking deviant peer relations in early adolescence with an increase in multiple sexual partners at age 16 (Lansford & others, 2010)
- Updated data on trends in the percentage of sexually active adolescents who used a condom the last time they had sexual intercourse (Eaton & others, 2010)
- Coverage of the reversal in increase of births to adolescents with a decline in 2007 and 2008, and a new Figure 12.7 (Hamilton, Martin, & Ventura, 2010)
- Discussion of the high fertility rate of Latina adolescents and comparison of their recent adolescent pregnancy and birth rates with those of other ethnic groups (Santelli, Abraido-Lanza, & Melnikas, 2009)
- New coverage of information comparing ethnic groups on the likelihood of having a second child in adolescence (Rosengard, 2009)
- Inclusion of a recent meta-analysis of studies on gender differences in sexuality (Peterson & Hyde, 2010)
- New discussion of the positive role of sexuality in well-being, including recent research (Brody & Costa, 2009)
- Expanded coverage of causes of homosexual behavior, including a recent large-scale study in Sweden (King, 2011; Langstrom & others, 2010)
- Updated description of HIV and AIDS in the United States (National Center for Health Statistics, 2010b)
- Discussion of recent research on a link between men's sexual narcissism and their sexual aggression (Wildman & McNulty, 2010)
- Updated data on the percentage of ninth- to twelfth-grade U.S. students who have been physically forced to have sex (Eaton & others, 2010)
- Coverage of a recent study that indicated sexual assault was more likely to occur if the offender was using substances, regardless of whether or not the victim was doing so (Brecklin & Ullman, 2010)
- New description of the red zone on college and university campuses and the time in their college years when

women are most likely to have unwanted sexual experiences (Kimble & others, 2008)

- Discussion of a recent research review indicating that there is no clear evidence that depressive disorders occur more frequently during menopause than at other times in a woman's reproductive life (Judd, Hickey, & Bryant, 2011)

- New description of later menopause being linked to increased risk of breast cancer (Mishra & others, 2009)

- Description of recent analyses confirming a link between combined estrogen/progestin hormone therapy and increased risk of cardiovascular disease (Toh & others, 2010)

- Coverage of recent research studies in a number of countries indicating that coinciding with the decrease in HRT in recent years has been a related decline in breast cancer (Baber, 2011; Chlebowski & others, 2010; Howell & Evans, 2011)

- Update on the percentage of aging men who experience erectile dysfunction (Berookhim & Bar-Chama, 2011)

Chapter 13: Moral Development, Values, and Religion

- Description of a recent study of children's unwillingness to donate any money after watching a UNICEF film on children suffering from poverty until an adult gently probed their intentions, which supports the situational nature of moral behavior (van IJzendoorn & others, 2010)

- Coverage of a recent study that revealed links between a higher level of multicultural experience and a lower level of closed-mindedness, a growth mindset, and higher moral judgment (Narváez & Hill, 2010)

- Description of a recent study of young children's internalization of parents' rules and children's competent behavior (Kochanska & others, 2010)

- Expanded discussion of moral identity with an emphasis on Darcia Narváez's (2010a) recent view that moral metacognition, especially through self-monitoring and self-reflection, is linked to moral maturity

- Discussion of two recent studies that revealed an important role of early secure attachment in children's future successful socialization and behavioral outcomes (Kochanska, Barry, & others, 2010; Kochanska, Woodard, & others, 2010)

- Description of a recent study that linked authoritative parenting to an increase in adolescents' moral identity (Hardy & others, 2010)

- Inclusion of research indicating that adolescents' moral motivation was related to the quality of their relationship with their parents (Malti & Buchmann, 2010)

- Discussion of recent research by Gustavo Carlo and his colleagues (2010) that illustrated the importance of considering the multidimensional aspects of prosocial behavior

- Inclusion of recent research on factors linked to forgiveness in older adults (Hantman & Cohen, 2010)

- Description of a recent longitudinal study of older adults with functional limitations that explored whether volunteering decreased their risk of dying over a six-year period (Okun & others, 2010)

- Discussion of recent research on the role of parental monitoring and support during adolescence in reducing criminal behavior in emerging adulthood (Johnson & others, 2011)

- Inclusion of recent research on the role of engaged parenting and mothers' social network support in reducing delinquency in low-income families (Ghazarian & Roche, 2010)

- Description of a recent study that found repeated poverty was a high risk factor for delinquency (Najman & others, 2010)

- Updated coverage of outcomes for the Fast Track delinquency intervention study through age 19 that found the program was successful in reducing juvenile arrest rates (Conduct Problems Prevention Research Group, 2010a)

- Updated coverage of the percentage of college freshmen who view being well-off financially versus pursuing a meaningful philosophy of life as a very important or essential goal (Pryor & others, 2010)

- Updated material on the percentage of college freshmen who estimate that there is a very good chance they will participate in volunteer or community work (Pryor & others, 2009)

- New coverage of the distinctions between religion, religiousness, and spirituality based on a recent analysis by Pamela King and her colleagues (2011)

- Description of a recent study of religious activity across the first three semesters of college (Stoppa & Lefkowitz, 2010)

- Discussion of recent research on church engagement and a lower level of depression in adolescents (Kang & Romo, 2010)

- Update of college freshmen's religious activities and preference (Pryor & others, 2009)

- Description of the increasing evidence that religion has a positive link to health (McCullough & Willoughby, 2009)

- Coverage of a recent study that indicated personal religiosity reduced the negative effects of a spouse's death on the psychological well-being of widowed individuals (Momtaz & others, 2010)

- Inclusion of recent research that found a higher level of spirituality was linked to resilience in older women (Vahia & others, 2011a)

- Discussion of the religious interest of older African American adults (Williams, Keigher, & Williams, 2010)

- New material on the factors that shape an individual's exploration of meaning in life and whether developing a sense of meaning in life is linked to positive developmental outcomes (Krause, 2008, 2009)

Chapter 14: Families, Lifestyles, and Parenting

- Inclusion of new information about the concept of transactions reflecting reciprocal socialization (Sameroff, 2009)

- Discussion of a recent study linking maternal scaffolding and young children's reasoning skills (Stright, Herr, & Neitzel, 2009)

- New coverage of Andrew Cherlin's analysis of how Americans move in and out of relationship styles more often than people do in other countries

- Updated data on single adults in the United States—for the first time, in 2009 the number of U.S. single adults from 25 to 34 years of age surpassed the number of married adults (U.S. Census Bureau, 2010c)

- New coverage of Bella DePaulo's (2006, 2011) conclusion that there is widespread bias against unmarried adults

- Discussion of a recent large-scale study of U.S. singles that found women are now more likely than men to want their independence in relationships (Match.com, 2011)

- Description of a recent meta-analysis of links between cohabitation and marital quality/stability (Jose, O'Leary, & Moyer, 2010)

- Discussion of recent research that found a link between cohabitation prior to becoming engaged and negative marital outcomes for first marriages but not second marriages (Stanley & others, 2010)

- Updated coverage of the continuing decline in the rate of marriage in the United States from 2007 to 2009 (National Center for Health Statistics, 2010)

- Further clarification of factors involved in whether cohabiting results in negative marital outcomes (Cherlin, 2009)

- Revised and updated analysis of marriage trends, including recent research on the percentage of U.S. adults under 30 who think marriage is headed for extinction and the percentage of those young adults who still plan to get married (Pew Research Center, 2010a)

- Discussion of a recent study of premarital education in first and second marriages (Doss & others, 2009)

- Expanded and updated discussion on the benefits of a good marriage, including a recent study on a lower proportion of time spent in marriage being linked to a likelihood of earlier death (Henretta, 2010)

- Updated statistics on the percentage of older adults who are married (U.S. Census Bureau, 2010c)

- Updated information on the percentage of older adult women and men who are divorced or separated (U.S. Census Bureau, 2010c)

- Description of research on marital satisfaction in octogenarians and its ability to protect their happiness from the effects of daily fluctuations in perceived health (Waldinger & others, 2011)

- Updated coverage on the resumption of a decline in the rate of divorce in the United States from 2007 to 2009 following an increase from 2005 to 2007 (National Center for Health Statistics, 2010)

- New material on the characteristics and timing of adults who get remarried (Sweeney, 2009, 2010)

- Discussion of recent research on parent-adolescent relationships of Asian American parents and adolescents (Russell, Crockett, & Chao, 2010)

- Coverage of a recent study of mothers' use of physical punishment in six countries and its link to their children's aggression (Gershoff & others, 2010)

- Expanded discussion of the effects of punishment on children, including the current conclusion of some experts that adequate research evidence has not yet been obtained about the effects of abusive physical punishment and mild physical punishment

- Conclusions regarding punishment research that if physical punishment is used it needs to be mild, infrequent, age-appropriate, and used in the context of a positive parent-child relationship (Grusec, 2011)

- Coverage of a recent study linking fathers' play with young children to an increase in supportive coparenting (Jia & Schoppe-Sullivan, 2011)

- Inclusion of recent research on factors linked to new mothers' low marital satisfaction (Dew & Wilcox, 2011)

- Discussion of recent research linking low maternal monitoring and sexual risk taking in adolescence, especially when mothers have mental health symptoms such as depression (Hadley & others, 2011)

- Expanded and updated coverage of adolescents' management of their parents' access to information, including recent research (Laird, Marrero, & Sentse, 2010; Smetana, 2011a, b)

- Description of a recent analysis concluding that the most consistent outcomes of secure attachment in adolescence involve positive peer relations and the development of emotion regulation capacities (Allen & Miga, 2010)

- Coverage of a recent study that revealed the importance of parents acting as "scaffolding" and "safety nets" to support their children's successful transition through emerging adulthood (Schwartz & others, 2011)

- New information about a recent study of mothers' and fathers' parenting styles and their links to emerging adult outcomes (Nelson & others, 2010)

- Discussion of a recent study linking child maltreatment with financial and employment-related difficulties in adulthood (Zielinski, 2009)

- New discussion of E. Mark Cummings and his colleagues' (Cummings & Davies, 2010; Cummings, El-Sheikh, & Kouros, 2009; Cummings & Merrilees, 2009) emotional security theory and its focus on the type of marital conflict that is negative for children's development

- Added commentary about father involvement dropping off more than mother involvement following a divorce, especially fathers of girls

- Inclusion of information about joint custody working best for children when the divorced parents can get along with each other (Parke & Clarke-Stewart, 2011)

- Coverage of recent information about child and adolescent outcomes conceived by new reproductive technologies, which are increasingly used by gay and lesbian adults (Golombok, 2011a, b)
- Coverage of a recent within-family design of families with a biological child and an adopted child indicating only a slight trend in more internalized and externalized problems for adopted children (Glover & others, 2010)
- Discussion of a recent study of improved cognitive development in children who were adopted after they had lived in foster homes and institutions (van den Dries & others, 2010)
- New coverage of the concept of the middle generation more often functioning as a "pivot" generation than a "sandwich" generation (Fingerman & Birditt, 2011a)
- Description of a recent study of how often middle-aged parents provide support to their children who are 18 years and older (Fingerman, Chan, & others, 2011)
- Discussion of recent research linking the transmission of divorce across generations, although this transmission has decreased in recent years (Waldinger & others, 2011)

Chapter 15: Peers and the Sociocultural World

- New material on Judith Smetana's (2008, 2011a, b) research on parents' and adolescents' perceptions that peer relations is the main area in which parents have little authority to dictate adolescents' choices
- Discussion of a recent study of young adolescents' friendships and depression (Brendgen & others, 2010)
- Description of three recent suicides in middle and late childhood and early adolescence that likely were influenced by bullying (Myers, 2010)
- New emphasis on the importance of contexts in the study of bullying (Salmivalli & Peets, 2009; Schwartz & others, 2010)
- Coverage of a recent study of bullies' popularity in the peer group (Veenstra & others, 2010)
- Description of a recent study on peer victimization and the extent of its link to lower academic achievement (Nakamoto & Schwartz, 2010)
- Updated and expanded discussion of social support and aging, including recent research linking a higher level of social support with reduced cognitive decline (Dickinson & others, 2011)
- Coverage of a recent study in which loneliness predicted increased blood pressure four years later in middle-aged and older adults (Hawkley & others, 2010)
- Description of a recent study linking media violence exposure to an increase in relational aggression in children (Gentile, Mathieson, & Crick, 2010)
- New section: "The Electronic Media, Learning, and Children's Development"
- Inclusion of recent research linking early daily TV exposure at 18 months with increased inattention/hyperactivity at 30 months of age (Cheng, Maeda, & others, 2010)

- Discussion of recent research linking the amount of early TV watching with reduced childhood vocalizations (Christakis & others, 2009)
- Substantial updating of media use based on a 2009 national survey of more than 2,000 U.S. adolescents, including comparisons with other previous national surveys to show trends in adolescent media use (Rideout, Foehr, & Roberts, 2010)
- Description of a recent national survey of trends in adolescents' use of social media, including dramatic increases in social networking and text messaging, and declines in tweeting and blogging (Lenhart & others, 2010)
- Updated coverage of social networking, with Facebook surpassing Google as the most visited Web site in 2010
- New commentary about text messaging now being the main way that adolescents prefer to connect with their friends (Lenhart & others, 2010)
- Inclusion of recent research on links between children's cyber aggression and negative peer relations outcomes (Schoffstall & Cohen, 2011)
- Description of a recent study of parenting predictors of adolescent media use (Padilla-Walker & Coyne, 2011)
- Discussion of recent research on frequency of computer use in older adults and cognitive functioning (Tun & Lachman, 2010)
- Updated information about the percentage of children living in poverty (Childstats.gov, 2010)
- Discussion of a recent study linking early and persistent poverty to lower cognitive functioning in 5-year-old children (Schoon & others, 2011)
- Updated coverage of poverty statistics for female-headed households and for ethnic groups (Federal Interagency Forum on Child and Family Statistics, 2010)
- Inclusion of recent research on outcomes of 9- to 19-year-old African American boys after experiencing the New Hope antipoverty program (McLoyd & others, 2011)
- Updated data on the percentage of older adults living in poverty (U.S. Census Bureau, 2010b)
- Expanded and updated coverage of variations in ethnic minority families' adaptations to stress (Gauvain & Parke, 2010)
- Expanded and updated material on immigrant families and their bicultural orientation including recent research by Ross Parke and his colleagues (2011) on immigrant Mexican American families
- New discussion of immigrant adolescents as cultural brokers for their parents (Villanueva & Buriel, 2010)

Chapter 16: Schools, Achievement, and Work

- Expanded and updated discussion of developmentally appropriate education's characteristics and goals (Barbarin & Miller, 2009; Bredekamp, 2011)
- New coverage of recent studies of the influence of Project Head Start on children's cognitive, language, and

- math skills and achievement (Hindman & others, 2010; Puma & others, 2010)

- New discussion of extracurricular activities that highlights the positive aspects of these activities on adolescent development (Barber, Stone, & Eccles, 2010; Mahoney, Parente, & Zigler, 2010)

- Updated coverage of school dropout rates, including a new Figure 16.1 that shows dropout rates by gender and ethnicity as well as the significant decline in Latino dropouts in the first decade of the twenty-first century (National Center for Education Statistics, 2010b)

- Updated data on the percentage of college students who feel overwhelmed with what they have to do (Pryor & others, 2009)

- Updated statistics on the percentage of students with various disabilities that receive special education services in U.S. schools (National Center for Education Statistics, 2010a)

- Expanded coverage of learning disabilities, including new information about dysgraphia and dyscalculia

- Updated discussion of the role of neurotransmitters in ADHD to include dopamine (Zhou & others, 2010)

- New material on recent research using animated faces and emotions to improve autistic children's ability to recognize faces, including a new Figure 16.6 (Baron-Cohen & others, 2007)

- Expanded discussion of schools in low-income areas, including several characteristics of teachers in these areas that can reduce the quality of education experiences (Eccles & Roeser, 2011)

- New commentary about Ryan and Deci's (2009) description of teachers who create circumstances for students to engage in self-determination as autonomy-supportive teachers

- New coverage of Carol Dweck's recent research and ideas about improving students' growth mindset by teaching them about the brain's plasticity and how the brain changes when you put considerable effort into learning (Blackwell & others, 2007; Dweck & Master, 2009)

- New material about Carol Dweck's recent development of computer modules, called "Brainology," that explain how the brain works and how through work and effort students can make their brains work better (Blackwell & Dweck, 2008; Dweck & Master, 2009)

- Description of a recent study of positive developmental outcomes for adolescents whose parents have high self-efficacy (Steca & others, 2011)

- New discussion of personal goals and their importance in students' motivation (Wigfield & Cambria, 2010)

- Coverage of a recent large-scale longitudinal study focused on the importance of academic resources at home, especially in African American or low-SES students' achievement (Xia, 2010)

- Inclusion of recent international comparisons of 15-year-olds' reading, math, and science achievement, including a new Figure 16.8 (OECD, 2010b)

- Discussion of recent reanalysis of data from earlier research on number of hours working part-time in adolescence and adolescent problems (Monahan, Lee, & Steinberg, 2011)

- Updated statistics on the percentage of college students who work while going to college (National Center for Education Statistics, 2010a)

- New section on unemployment, including information about the recent banking financial meltdown and recession

- Updated gender and ethnicity data on the U.S. labor force projected through 2016 (Occupational Outlook Handbook, 2010–2011)

- Expanded commentary about older adults increasingly seeking a type of bridge employment that permits a gradual rather than a sudden movement out of the work context (Bowen, Noack, & Staudinger, 2011)

- Coverage of a recent study that revealed different predictors for men's and women's psychological well-being after retirement (Kubicek & others, 2011)

Chapter 17: Death, Dying, and Grieving

- Inclusion of a recent Dutch study of euthanasia, including the percentage of dying persons who requested it and the percentage whose request was granted (Onwuteaka-Philipsen & others, 2010)

- Update on the countries and states in the U.S. allowing euthanasia (Smets & others, 2010; Watson, 2009)

- Added new information that what we know about death, dying, and grieving is based on older adults because older adults account for approximately two-thirds of the 2 million deaths each year in the United States

- New material on research studies indicating that rather than perceiving themselves to be invulnerable, many adolescents believe that they will experience an early death (Fischhoff & others, 2010)

- Updated description of the percentage of adolescents who are seriously considering a suicide attempt (MMWR, 2010)

- Description of a recent study using data from the National Longitudinal Study of Adolescent Health that found a number of risks for suicidal behavior (Thompson, Kuruwita, & Foster, 2009)

- Discussion of recent research from the National Longitudinal Study of Adolescent Health indicating that parental loss predicted an increase in suicide attempts one year later but not seven years later (Thompson & Light, 2011)

- Description of a recent study on alcohol, depression, and suicide attempts in adolescence (Schilling & others, 2009)

- Inclusion of recent research on suicide attempts by young Latinas (Zayas & others, 2010)

- Updated information about suicide in older adults and comparison of suicidal behavior in older adults with suicidal behavior in adolescents (Demircin & others, 2011)

- Coverage of a recent study indicating that perceived burdensomeness may be a contributing factor in suicide attempts by older adults (Corna & others, 2010)

- Description of recent research on aspects of death most likely to be linked to prolonged grief (Fujisawa & others, 2010)

- New information about the percentage of women and men 65 years of age and older who are widowed in the United States (Administration on Aging, 2009)

- Coverage of a recent large-scale study that found a link between loss of a spouse and risk of psychiatric visits as well as earlier death in individuals 75 years of age and older (Moller & others, 2011)

- Updated statistics and projections on the percentage of corpses being cremated in the U.S. (Cremation Association of North America, 2011)

ACKNOWLEDGMENTS

I very much appreciate the support and guidance provided to me by many people at McGraw-Hill. Mike Sugarman, publisher, has brought a wealth of publishing knowledge and vision to bear on improving my texts. Allison McNamara, senior editor, deserves special mention for the superb work she has done as the new editor for this book. The senior development editor, Cara Labell, and development editor, Elisa Adams, have done an excellent job of editing the manuscript and handling the page-by-page changes to this new edition. Sarah Kiefer, editorial coordinator, has done a very competent job of obtaining reviewers and handling many editorial chores. Julia Flohr, marketing manager, has contributed in numerous positive ways to this book. Janet Tilden did a superb job as the book's copy editor. Brett Coker and Melanie Field did a terrific job coordinating the book's production.

I also want to thank my wife, Mary Jo, our children, Tracy and Jennifer, and our grandchildren, Jordan, Alex, and Luke, for their wonderful contributions to my life and for helping me to better understand the marvels and mysteries of life-span development.

Reviewers

I owe a special gratitude to the reviewers who provided detailed feedback about the book.

Expert Consultants

Life-span development has become an enormous, complex field, and no single author can possibly be an expert in all aspects of it. To solve this problem, in the fourth, fifth, and now in this sixth edition, I have sought the input of leading experts in many different areas of life-span development. These experts have provided me with detailed recommendations of new research to include. The panel of experts is literally a *Who's Who* in the field of life-span development. The experts' photographs and biographies appear on pp. xv–xvii.

General Text Reviewers

I also owe a great deal of thanks to the instructors teaching the life-span course who have provided feedback about the book. Many of the changes in *A Topical Approach to Life-Span Development*, Sixth Edition, are based on their input. For their suggestions, I thank the following individuals:

Reviewers for the Sixth Edition

Katherine Adams, *Valdosta State University*
Tracie Blumentritt, *University of Wisconsin—La Crosse*
Janet Boseovski, *University of North Carolina—Greensboro*
Jerri Edwards, *University of South Florida—Tampa*
Suzanne Gibson, *Meridian Community College*
Jim Hanson, *Grand View University*
Alisha Janowsky, *University of Central Florida*
Larry Kollman, *North Area Iowa Community College—Mason City*
Monica McCoy, *Converse College*
Debbie Palmer, *University of Wisconsin—Stevens Point*
Laura Pannell, *Itawamba Community College*
Peter Phipps, *Dutchess Community College*
Mary Kay Reed, *York College of Pennsylvania*
Janet Reis, *University of Illinois—Champaign*
Jerry Snead, *Coastal Carolina Community College*
Karina Sokol, *Glendale Community College*

Reviewers for Previous Editions

Anora Ackerson, *Kalamazoo Community College;* **Randy Allen**, *Barton Community College;* **Denise M. Arehart**, *University of Colorado—Denver;* **Harriet Bachner**, *Northeastern State University;* **Andrea Backschneider**, *University of Houston;* **Catherine E. Barnard**, *Kalamazoo Valley Community College;* **Terra Bartee**, *Cisco Community College;* **Sheri Bauman**, *University of Arizona;* **Jay Belsky**, *Birkbeck College, University of London;* **James E. Birren**, *University of California—Los Angeles;* **Tracie L. Blumentritt**, *University of Wisconsin—La Crosse;* **John Bonvillian**, *University of Virginia;* **Janet Boseovski**, *University of North Carolina—Greensboro;* **Brenda Butterfield**, *University of Minnesota—Duluth;* **Ann Calhoun-Sauls**, *Belmont Abbey College;* **Silvia Canetto**, *Colorado State University;* **Rick Chandler**, *Itawamba Community College;* **Andrea D. Clements**, *East Tennessee State University;* **Sunshine Corwan**, *University of Central Oklahoma;* **Gregory Cutler**, *Bay de Noc Community College;* **Scott Delys**, *North Central Texas College;* **Susanne Denham**, *George Mason University;* **Kimberly DuVall**, *James Madison University;* **Marion A. Eppler**, *East Carolina University;* **Carolyn Fallahi**, *Central Connecticut State University;* **Dan P. Fawaz**, *Georgia Perimeter College;* **E. Richard Ferraro**, *University of North Dakota;* **Fan Flovell**, *Eastern Kentucky University;* **James Forbes**, *Angelo State University;* **Tom Frangicetto**, *Northampton Community College;* **James Garbarino**, *Cornell University;* **Janet Gebelt**, *University of Portland;* **Gilbert Gottlieb**, *University of North Carolina—Chapel Hill;* **Trione Grayson**, *Florida Community College at Jacksonsville, South Campus;* **Elena Grigorenko**, *Yale University;* **James Guinee**, *University of Central Arkansas;* **Yvette Harris**, *Miami (Ohio) University;* **Carol H. Hoare**, *George Washington University;* **Scott Hofer**, *Pennsylvania State University;* **La Tishia Horrell**, *Ivy Tech Community College;* **William Hoyer**, *Syracuse University;* **Fergus Hughes**, *University of Wisconsin;* **Mary P. Hughes Stone**, *San Francisco State University;* **Janet Shibley Hyde**, *University of Wisconsin—Madison;* **Alisah Janowsky**, *University of Central Florida;* **Emily J. Johnson**, *University of Wisconsin—La Crosse;* **Seth Kalichman**, *University of Connecticut;* **Robert Kastenbaum**, *Emeritus, Arizona State University;* **Kevin Keating**, *Broward Community College;* **Rachel Keen**, *University of Virginia;* **Sue Kelley**, *Lycoming College;* **Melanie Killian**, *University of Maryland;* **Suzanne G. Krinsky**, *University of Southern Colorado;* **Kathleen Lawler**, *University of Tennessee;* **Richard P. Lanthier**, *George Washington University;* **Gary Leka**, *University of Texas—Pan American;* **Gloria Lopez**, *Sacramento City College;* **Salvador Macias III**, *University of South Carolina;* **James Marcia**, *Simon Fraser University;* **Carole Martin**, *Colorado College;* **Gabriela Martorell**, *Portland State University;* **Linda Mayes**, *Yale University;* **Lara Mayeux**, *University of Oklahoma—Norman;* **Katrina McDaniel**, *Barton College;* **Sharon McNeely**, *Northeastern Illinois University;* **Gigliana Meltzi**, *New York University;* **Patricia A. Mills**, *Miami University;* **Daniel K. Mroczek**, *Fordham University;* **Winnie Mucherah**, *Ball State University;* **Bridget Murphy-Kelsey**, *University of Oklahoma;* **Charles Nelson**, *Harvard University;* **Margaret M. Norwood**, *Thomas Nelson Community College;* **Lois Oestreich**, *Salt Lake Community College;* **Pamela Balls Organista**, *University of San Francisco;* **Rob Palkovitz**, *University of Delaware;* **Crystal Park**, *University of Connecticut;* **Denise Park**, *University of Texas at Dallas;* **Ross Parke**, *University of California—Riverside;* **Scott Peterson**, *Cameron University;* **Warren Phillips**, *Iowa State University;* **Janet Polivy**, *University of Toronto;* **James S. Previte**, *Victor Valley College;* **Janet Reis**, *University of Illinois—Urbana;* **Madeline Rex-Lear**, *University of Texas—Arlington;* **Elizabeth Rodriguez**, *Salt Lake City Community College;* **Theresa Sawyer**, *Carroll Community College;* **Kim Schrenk**, *Montana State University;* **Pamela Schuetze**, *Buffalo State College;* **Matthew Scullin**, *West Virginia University;* **Rebecca Shiner**, *Colgate University;* **Thomas D. Spencer**, *San Francisco State University;* **Robert J. Sternberg**, *University of Colorado;* **Robert B. Stewart, Jr.**, *Oakland University;* **Pam Terry**, *Gordon College;* **Ross Thompson**, *University of California—Davis;* **Jonathan Tudge**, *University of North Carolina—Greensboro;* **Robin Valeri**, *St. Bonaventure University;* **Kay Walsh**, *James Madison University;* **Allan Wigfield**, *University of Maryland;* **Clarissa Willis**, *Arkansas Technical University;* **Linda M. Woolf**, *Webster University;* **Dawn Young**, *Boissier Parish Community College*

INSTRUCTOR AND STUDENT RESOURCES

The resources listed here may accompany *A Topical Approach to Life-Span Development*, Sixth Edition. Please contact your McGraw-Hill representative for details concerning policies, prices, and availability.

For the Instructor

Connect Psychology   What if . . .

- You could recreate the one-on-one experience of working through difficult concepts in office hours with every one of your students without having to invest any office-hour time to do so?
- You could see at a glance how well each of your students (or sections) was performing in each segment of your course?
- You had all of the assignments and resources for your course pre-organized by learning objective and with point-and-click flexibility?

Over the course of developing *A Topical Approach to Life-Span Development*, we asked these questions and many more. And we did not stop at simply asking questions. We visited with faculty across the country and also observed you doing what you do to prepare and deliver your courses. We observed students as they worked through assignments and studied for exams. The result of these thousands of hours of research and development is a state-of-the-art learning environment tool that bolsters student performance at the same time that it makes instructors' lives easier and more efficient. To experience this environment for yourself, please visit www.mcgraw-hillconnect.com.

Create   Craft your teaching resources to match the way you teach! With McGraw-Hill Create, www.mcgrawhillcreate.com, you can easily rearrange chapters, combine material from other content sources, and quickly upload content you have written like your course syllabus or teaching notes. Find the content you need in Create by searching through thousands of leading McGraw-Hill textbooks. Arrange your book to fit your teaching style. Create even allows you to personalize your book's appearance by selecting the cover and adding your name, school, and course information. Order a Create book and you'll receive a complimentary print review copy within five business days or a complimentary electronic review copy (eComp) via email in about one hour. Go to www.mcgrawhillcreate.com today and register. Experience how McGraw-Hill Create empowers you to teach your students your way.

Blackboard   McGraw-Hill Higher Education and Blackboard have teamed up. What does this mean for you?

- **Your life, simplified.** Now you and your students can access McGraw-Hill's Connect and Create right from within your Blackboard course—all with one single sign-on. Say goodbye to the days of logging in to multiple applications.

- **Deep integration of content and tools.** Not only do you get single sign-on with Connect and Create, you also get deep integration of McGraw-Hill content and content engines right in Blackboard. Whether you're choosing a book for your course or building Connect assignments, all the tools you need are right where you want them—inside of Blackboard.

- **Seamless gradebooks.** Are you tired of keeping multiple gradebooks and manually synchronizing grades into Blackboard? We thought so. When a student completes an integrated Connect assignment, the grade for that assignment automatically (and instantly) feeds your Blackboard grade center.

- **A solution for everyone.** Whether your institution is already using Blackboard or you just want to try Blackboard on your own, we have a solution for you. McGraw-Hill and Blackboard can now offer you easy access to industry-leading technology and content, whether your campus hosts it or we do. Be sure to ask your local McGraw-Hill representative for details.

Tegrity   Tegrity Campus is a service that makes class time available all the time by automatically capturing every lecture in a searchable format for students to review when they study and complete assignments. With a simple one-click start and stop process, you capture all computer screens and corresponding audio. Students replay any part of any class with easy-to-use browser-based viewing on a PC or Mac.

Educators know that the more students can see, hear, and experience class resources, the better they learn. With Tegrity Campus, students quickly recall key moments by using Tegrity Campus's unique search feature. This search helps students efficiently find what they need, when they need it across an entire semester of class recordings. Help turn all your students' study time into learning moments immediately supported by your lecture.

The Online Learning Center   The instructor side of the Online Learning Center at http://www.mhhe.com/ contains the Instructor's Manual, Test Bank files, PowerPoint slides, Image Gallery, and other valuable material to help you design and enhance your course. Ask your local McGraw-Hill representative for your password.

- **Instructor's Manual** *Edited by Larry Kollman, North Iowa Area Community College.* Each chapter of the Instructor's Manual is introduced by a Resources Overview. This fully integrated tool helps instructors more easily locate and choose among the many resources available for the course by linking each element of the Instructor's Manual to a particular teaching topic within the chapter. These elements include lecture suggestions, classroom activities, personal applications, research project ideas, video suggestions, and handouts.

- **Test Bank and Computerized Test Bank** *Edited by Alisha Janowsky, University of Central Florida.* By increasing the rigor of the Test Bank development process, McGraw-Hill aims to raise the bar for student assessment. Over 3,000 multiple-choice and short-answer questions and five to ten essay questions per chapter were prepared by a coordinated team of subject matter experts. Each question and set of possible answers has been methodically vetted by the team for accuracy, clarity, effectiveness, and accessibility, and each is annotated for level of difficulty, Bloom's taxonomy, and corresponding coverage in the text. Organized by chapter, the questions are designed to test factual, applied, and conceptual understanding and are keyed to Bloom's taxonomy. The test bank is compatible with McGraw-Hill's computerized testing program, EZ Test, and most Course Management systems.

- **PowerPoint Slides** *Edited by Larry Kollman, North Iowa Area Community College.* These presentations cover the key points of each chapter and include charts and graphs from the text. They can be used as is, or you may modify them to meet your specific needs.

McGraw-Hill's Visual Asset Database for Life-Span Development ("VAD")

McGraw-Hill's Visual Assets Database for Life-Span Development (VAD 2.0) (www.mhhe.com/vad) is an online database of videos for use in the developmental psychology classroom, created specifically for instructors. You can customize classroom presentations by downloading the videos to your computer and showing the videos on their own or insert them into your course cartridge or PowerPoint presentations. All of the videos are available with or without captions. Ask your McGraw-Hill representative for access information.

For the Student

Adaptive Learning System This adaptive learning system is an unparalleled, intelligent learning system based on cognitive mapping that *diagnoses* your students' knowledge of a particular subject and then creates an individualized learning path geared toward student success in your course. It offers individualized assessment by delivering appropriate learning material in the form of questions at the right time, helping students attain mastery of the content. Whether the system is assigned by you or used independently by students as a study tool, the results can be recorded in an easy-to-use grade report that allows you to measure student progress at all times and coach your students to success.

As an added benefit, all content covered in this adaptive diagnostic tool is tied to learning objectives for your course so that you can use the results as evidence of subject mastery. This tool also provides a personal study plan that allows the student to estimate the time it will take and number of questions required to learn the subject matter. Your students will learn faster, study more efficiently, and retain more knowledge when using *A Topical Approach to Life-Span Development.*

Milestones Video Program Our new assessable video-based program tracks human development through each major life stage. Starting from infancy, students will watch each baby grow and achieve the major developmental milestones such as balance, development of fine motor control, and social interactions. The program continues through adulthood, capturing attitudes toward issues such as family, sexuality, and death and dying.

McGraw-Hill Contemporary Learning Series *Annual Editions: Human Development* This reader is a collection of articles on topics related to the latest research and thinking in human development. Annual Editions are updated regularly and include useful features such as a topic guide, an annotated table of contents, unit overviews, and a topical index.

Taking Sides: Clashing Views on Controversial Issues in Life-Span Development Current controversial issues are presented in a debate-style format designed to stimulate student interest and develop critical thinking skills. Each issue is thoughtfully framed with an issue summary, an issue introduction, and a postscript.

CourseSmart CourseSmart is a new way to find and buy eTextbooks. At CourseSmart you can save up to 50 percent off the cost of a print textbook, reduce your impact on the environment, and gain access to powerful Web tools for learning. CourseSmart has the largest selection of eTextbooks available anywhere, offering thousands of the most commonly adopted textbooks from a wide variety of higher education publishers. CourseSmart eTextbooks are available in one standard online reader with full text search, notes and highlighting, and e-mail tools for sharing notes between classmates. For further details contact your sales representative or go to www.coursesmart.com.

A TOPICAL APPROACH TO LIFE-SPAN DEVELOPMENT

Sixth Edition

All the world's a stage,
And all the men and women merely players;
They have their exits and their entrances,
And one man in his time plays many parts.

—WILLIAM SHAKESPEARE
English Playwright, 17th Century

The Life-Span Perspective

This book is about human development—its universal features, its individual variations, its nature. Every life is distinct, a new biography in the world. Examining the shape of life-span development allows us to understand it better. *A Topical Approach to Life-Span Development* is about the rhythm and meaning of people's lives, about turning mystery into understanding, and about weaving a portrait of who each of us was, is, and will be. In Section 1, you will read "Introduction" (Chapter 1).

preview

This book is a window into the journey of human development—your own and that of every other member of the human species. Every life is distinct, a new biography in the world. Examining the shape of life-span development helps us to understand it better. In this first chapter, we explore what it means to take a life-span perspective on development, examine the nature of development, discuss theories of development, and outline how science helps us to understand it.

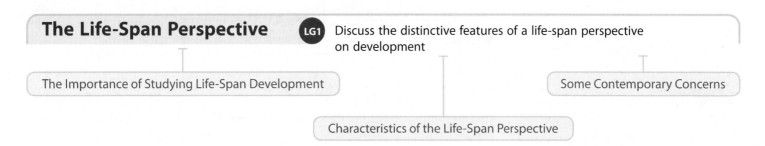

The Life-Span Perspective — **LG1** Discuss the distinctive features of a life-span perspective on development

The Importance of Studying Life-Span Development

Some Contemporary Concerns

Characteristics of the Life-Span Perspective

Each of us develops partly like all other individuals, partly like some other individuals, and partly like no other individuals. Most of the time, our attention is directed to an individual's uniqueness. But as humans, we have all traveled some common paths. Each of us—Leonardo da Vinci, Joan of Arc, George Washington, Martin Luther King, Jr., and you—walked at about 1 year, engaged in fantasy play as a young child, and became more independent as a youth. Each of us, if we live long enough, will experience hearing problems and the death of family members and friends. This is the general course of our **development**—the pattern of movement or change that begins at conception and continues through the human life span.

In this section, we explore what is meant by the concept of development and why the study of life-span development is important. We outline the main characteristics of the life-span perspective and discuss various sources of contextual influences. In addition, we examine some contemporary concerns in life-span development.

THE IMPORTANCE OF STUDYING LIFE-SPAN DEVELOPMENT

How might people benefit from examining life-span development? Perhaps you are, or will be, a parent or a teacher. If so, responsibility for children is, or will be, a part of your everyday life. The more you learn about them, the better you can deal with them. Perhaps you hope to gain some insight about your own history—as an infant, a child, an adolescent, or an adult. Perhaps you want to know more about what your life will be like as you move through the adult years—as a middle-aged adult or as an adult in old age, for example. Or perhaps you have just stumbled upon this course, thinking that it sounded intriguing and that the study of the human life span might raise some provocative issues. Whatever your reasons, you will discover that the study of life-span development is filled with intriguing information about who we are, how we came to be this way, and where our future will take us.

Most development involves growth, but it also includes decline and dying. In exploring development, we examine the life span from the point of conception until the time when life—at least, life as we know it—ends. You will see yourself as an infant, as a child, and as an adolescent, and be stimulated to think about how those years influenced the kind of individual you are today. And you will see yourself as a young adult, as a middle-aged adult, and as an adult in old age, and be motivated

development The pattern of movement or change that begins at conception and continues through the human life span.

to think about how your experiences today will influence your development through the remainder of your adult years.

CHARACTERISTICS OF THE LIFE-SPAN PERSPECTIVE

Although growth and development are dramatic during the first two decades of life, development is not something that happens only to children and adolescents. The traditional approach to the study of development emphasizes extensive change from birth to adolescence (especially during infancy), little or no change during adulthood, and decline in old age. But a great deal of change does occur in the five or six decades after adolescence. The life-span perspective emphasizes developmental change throughout adulthood as well as childhood (Schaie, 2011; Staudinger & Gluck, 2011).

The recent increase in human life expectancy has contributed to the popularity of the life-span approach to development. The upper boundary of the human life span (based on the oldest age documented) is 122 years, as indicated in Figure 1.1; this maximum life span of humans has not changed since the beginning of recorded history. What has changed is *life expectancy:* the average number of years that a person born in a particular year can expect to live (Martin, 2011). During the twentieth century alone, life expectancy in the United States increased by 30 years, thanks to improvements in sanitation, nutrition, and medicine (see Figure 1.2). As we end the first decade of the twenty-first century, the life expectancy in the United States is 78 years of age (Centers for Disease Control and Prevention, 2010). Today, for most individuals in developed countries, childhood and adolescence represent only about one-fourth of their lives.

The belief that development occurs throughout life is central to the **life-span perspective** on human development, but this perspective has other characteristics as well. According to life-span development expert Paul Baltes (1939–2006), the life-span perspective views development as lifelong, multidimensional, multidirectional, plastic, multidisciplinary, and contextual, and as a process that involves growth, maintenance, and regulation of loss (Baltes, 1987, 2003; Baltes, Lindenberger, & Staudinger, 2006). In Baltes' view, it is important to understand that development is constructed through biological, sociocultural, and individual factors working together. Let's look at each of these characteristics.

Development Is Lifelong   In the life-span perspective, early adulthood is not the endpoint of development; rather, no age period dominates development. Researchers increasingly study the experiences and psychological orientations of adults at different points in their lives. Later in this chapter, we consider the age periods of development and their characteristics.

Development Is Multidimensional   At every age, your body, your mind, your emotions, and your relationships change and affect each other. Development has biological, cognitive, and socioemotional dimensions. Within each of these dimensions are many components—for example, attention, memory, abstract thinking, speed of processing information, and social intelligence are just a few of the components of the cognitive dimension.

Development Is Multidirectional   Throughout life, some dimensions or components of a dimension expand and others shrink. For example, when one language (such as English) is acquired early in development, the capacity for acquiring second and third languages (such as Spanish and Chinese) decreases later in development, especially after early childhood (Levelt, 1989). During adolescence, as individuals establish romantic relationships, their time spent with friends may decrease. During late adulthood, older adults might become wiser by being able

Species (common name)	Maximum Life Span (years)
Human	122
Galápagos turtle	100+
Indian elephant	70
Chinese alligator	52
Golden eagle	46
Gorilla	39
Common toad	36
Domestic cat	27
Domestic dog	20
Vampire bat	13
House mouse	3

FIGURE 1.1

MAXIMUM RECORDED LIFE SPAN FOR DIFFERENT SPECIES. Our only competitor for the maximum recorded life span is the Galápagos turtle.

What characterizes the life-span perspective of development?

to call on experience to guide their intellectual decision making, but they perform more poorly on tasks that require speed in processing information (Ardelt, 2011; Karelitz, Jarvin, & Sternberg, 2010; Staudinger & Gluck, 2011).

Development Is Plastic   Developmentalists debate how much *plasticity* people have in various dimensions at different points in their development. Plasticity means the capacity for change. For example, can you still improve your intellectual skills when you are in your seventies or eighties? Or might these intellectual skills be fixed by the time you are in your thirties, so that further improvement is impossible? Researchers have found that the cognitive skills of older adults can be improved through training and development of better strategies (Schaie, 2011; Stine-Morrow & Basak, 2011). However, possibly we possess less capacity for change when we become old (Salthouse, 2010). The search for plasticity and its constraints is a key element on the contemporary agenda for developmental research (Park & Bischof, 2011; Sroufe, Coffino, & Carlson, 2010).

Developmental Science Is Multidisciplinary   Psychologists, sociologists, anthropologists, neuroscientists, and medical researchers all share an interest in unlocking the mysteries of development through the life span. How do your heredity and health limit your intelligence? Do intelligence and social relationships change with age in the same way around the world? How do families and schools influence intellectual development? These are examples of research questions that cut across disciplines.

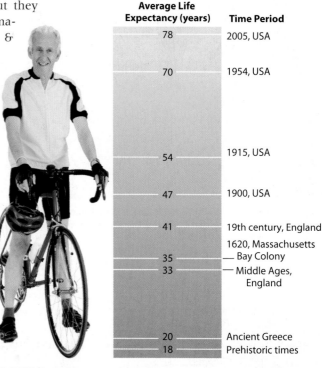

Average Life Expectancy (years)	Time Period
78	2005, USA
70	1954, USA
54	1915, USA
47	1900, USA
41	19th century, England
35	1620, Massachusetts Bay Colony
33	Middle Ages, England
20	Ancient Greece
18	Prehistoric times

FIGURE **1.2**

HUMAN LIFE EXPECTANCY AT BIRTH FROM PREHISTORIC TO CONTEMPORARY TIMES. It took 5,000 years to extend human life expectancy from 18 to 41 years of age.

Development Is Contextual   All development occurs within a context, or setting. Contexts include families, neighborhoods, schools, peer groups, churches, university laboratories, cities, countries, and so on. Each of these settings is influenced by historical, economic, social, and cultural factors (Kitayama & Uskul, 2011).

Contexts, like individuals, change. Thus, individuals are changing beings in a changing world. As a result of these changes, contexts exert three types of influences (Baltes, 2003): (1) normative age-graded influences, (2) normative history-graded influences, and (3) nonnormative or highly individualized life events. Each of these types can have a biological or an environmental impact on development. **Normative age-graded influences** are similar for individuals in a particular age group. These influences include biological processes such as puberty and menopause. They also include sociocultural or environmental processes such as beginning formal education (usually at about age 6 in most cultures) and retirement (which takes place in the fifties and sixties in most cultures).

Normative history-graded influences are common to people of a particular generation because of historical circumstances. For example, in their youth, American baby boomers shared experiences that included the Cuban missile crisis, the assassination of John F. Kennedy, and the Beatles invasion. Other examples of normative history-graded influences include economic, political, and social upheavals such as the Great Depression of the 1930s, World War II during the 1940s, the civil rights and women's rights movements of the 1960s and 1970s, the terrorist attacks of 9/11/2001, as well as the integration of computers, cell phones, and iPods into everyday life in recent decades (Schaie, 2010, 2011; Schaie & Willis, 2012; Yang, 2011). Long-term changes in the genetic and cultural makeup of a population (due to immigration or changes in fertility rates) are also part of normative historical change.

Paul Baltes, a leading architect of the life-span perspective of development, conversing with one of the long-time research participants in the Berlin Aging Study that he directs. She joined the study in the early 1990s and has participated six times in extensive physical, medical, psychological, and social assessments. In her professional life, she was a practicing medical doctor.

life-span perspective The perspective that development is lifelong, multidimensional, multidirectional, plastic, multidisciplinary, and contextual; involves growth, maintenance, and regulation of loss; and is constructed through biological, sociocultural, and individual factors working together.

normative age-graded influences Influences that are similar for individuals in a particular age group.

normative history-graded influences Influences that are common to people of a particular generation because of historical circumstances.

Nonnormative life events, such as Hurricane Katrina in August 2005, are unusual circumstances that have a major impact on a person's life.

Nonnormative life events are unusual occurrences that have a major impact on an individual's life. These events do not happen to all people, and when they do occur they can influence people in different ways. Examples include experiencing the death of a parent when one is still a child, becoming pregnant in early adolescence, surviving a fire that destroys one's home, winning the lottery, or getting an unexpected career opportunity.

Development Involves Growth, Maintenance, and Regulation of Loss Baltes and his colleagues (2006) assert that achieving mastery of life often involves conflicts and competition among three goals of human development: growth, maintenance, and regulation of loss. As individuals age into middle and late adulthood, the maintenance and regulation of loss in their capacities shift their attention away from growth. Thus, a 75-year-old man might aim not to improve his memory or his golf swing but to maintain his independence and merely to continue playing golf.

Development Is a Co-construction of Biology, Culture, and the Individual Development is a co-construction of biological, cultural, and individual factors working together (Baltes, Reuter-Lorenz, & Rösler, 2006). For example, the brain shapes culture, but it is also shaped by culture and the experiences that individuals have or pursue. In terms of individual factors, we can go beyond what our genetic inheritance and environment have given us. We can author a unique developmental path by actively choosing from the environment the things that optimize our lives (Rathunde & Csikszentmihalyi, 2006).

SOME CONTEMPORARY CONCERNS

Children learn to love when they are loved

Pick up a newspaper or magazine and you might see headlines like these: "Political Leanings May Be Written in the Genes," "Mother Accused of Tossing Children into Bay," "Gender Gap Widens," "FDA Warns About ADHD Drug," "Heart Attack Deaths Higher in Black Patients," "Test May Predict Alzheimer Disease." Researchers using the life-span perspective are examining these and many other topics of contemporary concern. The roles that health and well-being, parenting, education, and sociocultural contexts play in life-span development, as well as how social policy is related to these issues, are a particular focus of this textbook.

Health and Well-Being Health professionals today recognize the power of lifestyles and psychological states in health and well-being (Hahn, Payne, & Lucas, 2011; Insel & Roth, 2012). In every chapter of this book, issues of health and well-being are integrated into our discussion.

Parenting and Education Can two gay men raise a healthy family? Are children harmed if both parents work outside the home? Are U.S. schools failing to teach children how to read and write and calculate adequately? We hear many questions like these related to pressures on the contemporary family and the problems of U.S. schools (Cunningham & Allington, 2011; Gosselin, 2010; Parke & Clarke-Stewart, 2011). In later chapters, we analyze child care, the effects of divorce, parenting styles, intergenerational relationships, early childhood education, relationships between childhood poverty and education, bilingual education, new educational efforts to improve lifelong learning, and many other issues related to parenting and education.

Sociocultural Contexts and Diversity Health, parenting, and education—like development itself—are shaped by their sociocultural context (Tamis-LeMonda &

- - - - - - - - - - - - - - ▶

developmental **connection**

Parenting. Which parenting style is most often linked with positive child outcomes? Chapter 14, p. 462

nonnormative life events Unusual occurrences that have a major impact on an individual's life.

Two Korean-born children on the day they became United States citizens. Asian American and Latino children are the fastest-growing immigrant groups in the United States. *How diverse are the students in your life-span development class? How are their experiences in growing up likely similar to or different from yours?*

Around the world women too often are treated as burdens rather than assets in the political process. *What can be done to strengthen women's roles in the political process?*

Doly Akter, age 17, lives in a slum in Dhaka, Bangladesh, where sewers overflow, garbage rots in the streets, and children are undernourished. Nearly two-thirds of young women in Bangladesh get married before they are 18. Doly recently organized a club supported by UNICEF in which girls go door-to-door to monitor the hygiene habits of households in their neighborhood. The monitoring has led to improved hygiene and health in the families. Also, her group has managed to stop several child marriages by meeting with parents and convincing them that it is not in their daughter's best interests. When talking with parents in their neighborhoods, the girls in the club emphasize the importance of staying in school and how this will improve their daughters' future. Doly says that the girls in her UNICEF group are far more aware of their rights than their mothers ever were (UNICEF, 2007).

McFadden, 2010). To analyze this context, four concepts are especially useful: culture, ethnicity, socioeconomic status, and gender.

Culture encompasses the behavior patterns, beliefs, and all other products of a particular group of people that are passed on from generation to generation. Culture results from the interaction of people over many years. A cultural group can be as large as the United States or as small as an isolated Appalachian town. Whatever its size, the group's culture influences the behavior of its members (Shiraev, 2011). **Cross-cultural studies** compare aspects of two or more cultures. The comparison provides information about the degree to which development is similar, or universal, across cultures, or instead is culture-specific (Kitayama & Uskul, 2011; Zhang & Sternberg, 2011).

Ethnicity (the word *ethnic* comes from the Greek word for "nation") is rooted in cultural heritage, nationality, race, religion, and language. African Americans, Latinos, Asian Americans, Native Americans, European Americans, and Arab Americans are examples of broad ethnic groups in the United States. Diversity exists within each ethnic group (Bennett, 2011; Jackson, 2011).

The sociocultural context of the United States has become increasingly diverse in recent years. Its population includes a greater variety of cultures and ethnic groups than ever before. This changing demographic tapestry promises not only the richness that diversity produces but also difficult challenges in extending the American dream to all individuals (Koppelman & Goodhart, 2011).

Socioeconomic status (SES) refers to a person's position within society based on occupational, educational, and economic characteristics. Socioeconomic status implies certain inequalities. Differences in the ability to control resources and to participate in society's rewards produce unequal opportunities (Reno & Veghte, 2011; Whitfield, Thorpe, & Szanton, 2011).

Gender refers to the characteristics of people as males and females. Few aspects of our development are more central to our identity and social relationships than gender (Eagly & Wood, 2011; Matlin, 2012; Meyer, 2011).

Social Policy **Social policy** is a government's course of action designed to promote the welfare of its citizens. Values, economics, and politics all shape a nation's

culture The behavior, patterns, beliefs, and all other products of a group of people that are passed on from generation to generation.

cross-cultural studies Comparison of one culture with one or more other cultures. These provide information about the degree to which development is similar, or universal, across cultures, and the degree to which it is culture-specific.

ethnicity A characteristic based on cultural heritage, nationality characteristics, race, religion, and language.

socioeconomic status (SES) Classification of a person's position in society based on occupational, educational, and economic characteristics.

gender The characteristics of people as females or males.

social policy A government's course of action designed to promote the welfare of its citizens.

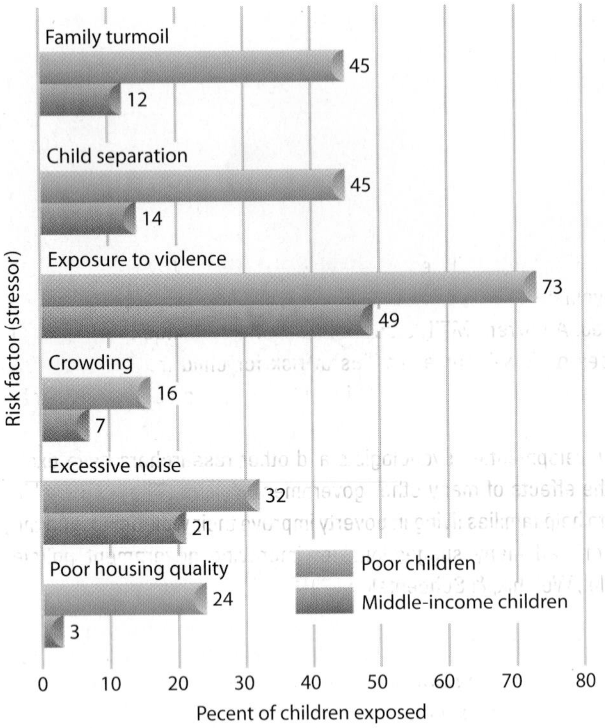
Risk factor (stressor)
Family turmoil
45
12
Child separation
45
14
Exposure to violence
73
49
Crowding
16
7
Excessive noise
32
21
Poor housing quality
24
3
Poor children
Middle-income children
0
10
20
30
40
50
60
70
80
Pecent of children exposed

FIGURE **1.3**

EXPOSURE TO SIX STRESSORS AMONG POOR AND MIDDLE-INCOME CHILDREN. One study analyzed the exposure to six stressors among poor children and middle-income children (Evans & English, 2002). Poor children were much more likely to face each of these stressors.

social policy. Out of concern that policy makers are doing too little to protect the well-being of children and older adults, life-span researchers are increasingly undertaking studies that they hope will lead to the enactment of effective social policy (Giunta, 2010; Phillips & Lowenstein, 2011).

Statistics such as infant mortality rates, mortality among children under 5, and the percentage of children who are malnourished or living in poverty provide benchmarks for evaluating how well children are doing in a particular society. For many years, Marian Wright Edelman, a tireless advocate of children's rights, has pointed out that indicators like these place the United States at or near the lowest rank for industrialized nations in the treatment of children.

Children who grow up in poverty represent a special concern (Huston & Bentley, 2010). In 2008, 19 percent of U.S. children were living in families with incomes below the poverty line (Childstats.gov, 2010). This is an increase from 2001 (16.2 percent) but down from a peak of 22.7 percent in 1993. As indicated in Figure 1.3, one study found that a higher percentage of U.S. children in poor families than in middle-income families were exposed to family turmoil, separation from a parent, violence, crowding, excessive noise, and poor housing (Evans & English, 2002). One study also revealed that the greater the number of years children spent living in poverty, the higher were their physiological indices of stress (Evans & Kim, 2007).

The U.S. figure of 17.4 percent of children living in poverty is much higher than child poverty rates in other industrialized nations. For example, Canada has a child poverty rate of 9 percent and Sweden has a rate of 2 percent.

Edelman says that parenting and nurturing the next generation of children are our society's most important functions and that we need to take them more seriously than we have in the past. To read about efforts to improve the lives of children through social policies, see the *Connecting Development to Life* on the next page.

At the other end of the life span, the well-being of older adults also creates policy issues (Reno & Veghte, 2011; Stirling, 2011). Key concerns are escalating

developmental **connection**

Environment. An increasing number of studies are showing that positive outcomes can be achieved through intervention in the lives of children living in poverty. Chapter 15, p. 516

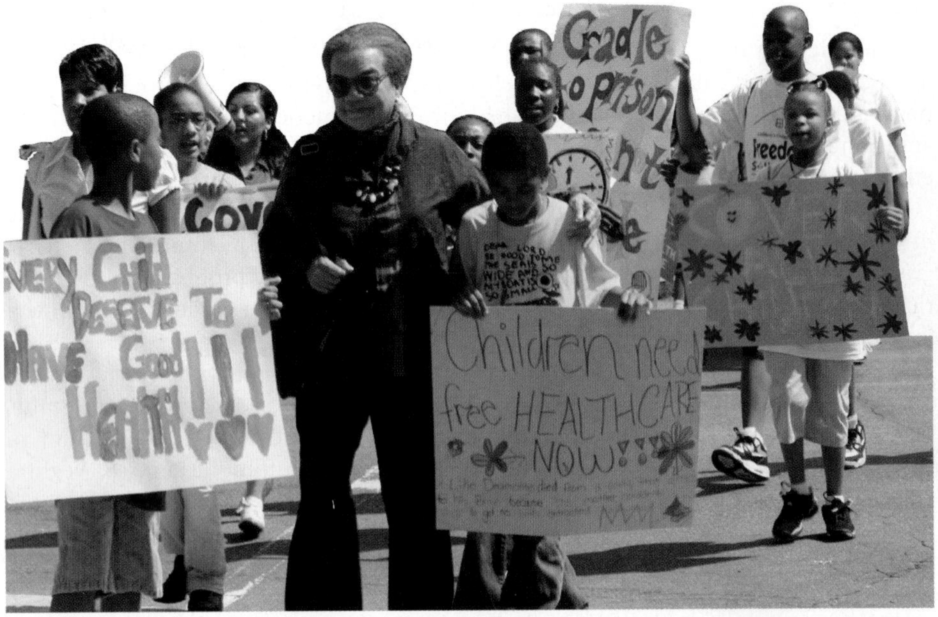
free HEALTHCARE
NOW!!!

Marian Wright Edelman, president of the Children's Defense Fund (shown here advocating for health care), has been a tireless advocate of children's rights and has been instrumental in calling attention to the needs of children. *What are some of these needs?*

Improving Family Policy

In the United States, the national government, state governments, and city governments all play a role in influencing the well-being of children (Benson & Scales, 2011). When families neglect or seriously endanger a child's well-being, governments often step in to help. At the national and state levels, policy makers have debated for decades whether helping poor parents ends up helping their children as well. Researchers are providing some answers by examining the effects of specific policies (Huston & Bentley, 2010).

For example, the Minnesota Family Investment Program (MFIP) was designed in the 1990s primarily to influence the behavior of adults—specifically, to move adults off the welfare rolls and into paid employment. A key element of the program was its guarantee that adults participating in the program would receive more income if they worked than if they did not. When the adults' income rose, how did that affect their children? A study of the effects of MFIP found that increases in the incomes of working poor parents were linked with

benefits for their children (Gennetian & Miller, 2002). The children's achievement in school improved, and their behavior problems decreased. A current MFIP study is examining the influence of specific services on low-income families at risk for child maltreatment and other negative outcomes for children (Minnesota Family Investment Program, 2009).

Developmental psychologists and other researchers have examined the effects of many other government policies. They are seeking ways to help families living in poverty improve their well-being, and they have offered many suggestions for improving government policies (Sandler, Wolchik, & Schoenfelder, 2011).

How does the life-span perspective support this and other research on the role government should play in improving the well-being of children?

health-care costs and the access of older adults to adequate health care (Gorin, 2010; Herd, Robert, & House, 2011). One study found that the health-care system fails older adults in many areas (Wenger & others, 2003). For example, older adults received the recommended care for general medical conditions such as heart disease only 52 percent of the time; they received appropriate care for undernourishment and Alzheimer disease only 31 percent of the time.

These concerns about the well-being of older adults are heightened by two facts. First, the number of older adults in the United States is growing dramatically, as Figure 1.4 shows. Second, many of these older Americans are likely to need

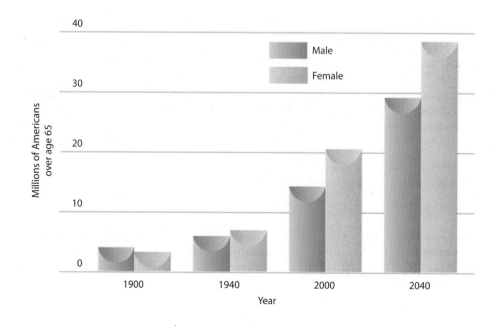

FIGURE 1.4

THE AGING OF AMERICA. The number of Americans over 65 has grown dramatically since 1900 and is projected to increase further from the present to the year 2040. A significant increase will also occur in the number of individuals in the 85-and-over group. Centenarians—persons 100 years of age or older—are the fastest-growing age group in the United States, and their numbers are expected to swell in the coming decades (Perls, 2007).

society's help. Compared with earlier decades, U.S. adults today are less likely to be married, more likely to be childless, and more likely to be living alone. As the older population continues to expand in the twenty-first century, an increasing number of older adults will be without either a spouse or children—traditionally the main sources of support for older adults (Stroebe, Schut, & Boerner, 2010). These individuals will need social relationships, networks, and supports (Antonucci & others, 2010).

Review Connect Reflect

LG1 Discuss the distinctive features of a life-span perspective on development

Review

- What is meant by the concept of development? Why is the study of life-span development important?
- What are eight main characteristics of the life-span perspective? What are three sources of contextual influences?
- What are some contemporary concerns in life-span development?

Connect

- In other courses and throughout your life you have learned that no two people are exactly alike. How might the life-span perspective explain this observation?

Reflect *Your Own Personal Journey of Life*

- Imagine what your development would have been like in a culture that offered fewer or distinctly different choices. How might your development have been different if your family had been significantly richer or poorer than it was when you were growing up?

The Nature of Development

LG2 Identify the most important processes, periods, and issues in development

- Biological, Cognitive, and Socioemotional Processes
- The Significance of Age
- Periods of Development
- Developmental Issues

In this section, we explore what is meant by developmental processes and periods, as well as variations in the way age is conceptualized. We examine key developmental issues, how they describe development, and strategies we can use to evaluate them.

A chronicle of the events in any person's life can quickly become a confusing and tedious array of details. Two concepts help provide a framework for describing and understanding an individual's development: developmental processes and periods of development.

BIOLOGICAL, COGNITIVE, AND SOCIOEMOTIONAL PROCESSES

At the beginning of this chapter, we defined development as the pattern of change that begins at conception and continues through the life span. The pattern is complex because it is the product of biological, cognitive, and socioemotional processes (see Figure 1.5).

Biological Processes   **Biological processes** produce changes in an individual's physical nature. Genes inherited from parents, the development of the brain, height and weight gains, changes in motor skills, nutrition, exercise, the hormonal changes of puberty, and cardiovascular decline are all examples of biological processes that affect development.

Cognitive Processes   **Cognitive processes** refer to changes in the individual's thought process, intelligence, and language. Watching a colorful mobile swinging above the crib, putting together a two-word sentence, memorizing a poem, imagining what it would be like to be a movie star, and solving a crossword puzzle all involve cognitive processes.

Socioemotional Processes   **Socioemotional processes** involve changes in the individual's relationships with other people, changes in emotions, and changes in personality. An infant's smile in response to a parent's touch, a toddler's aggressive attack on a playmate, a school-age child's development of assertiveness, an adolescent's joy at the senior prom, and the affection of an elderly couple all reflect the role of socioemotional processes in development.

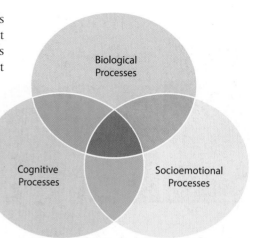

FIGURE 1.5

PROCESSES INVOLVED IN DEVELOPMENTAL CHANGES. Biological, cognitive, and socioemotional processes interact as individuals develop.

Connecting Biological, Cognitive, and Socioemotional Processes   Biological, cognitive, and socioemotional processes are inextricably intertwined (Diamond, 2009; Diamond, Casey, & Munakata, 2011). Consider a baby smiling in response to a parent's touch. This response depends on biological processes (the physical nature of touch and responsiveness to it), cognitive processes (the ability to understand intentional acts), and socioemotional processes (the act of smiling often reflects a positive emotional feeling, and smiling helps to connect us in positive ways with other human beings). Nowhere is the connection across biological, cognitive, and socioemotional processes more obvious than in two rapidly emerging fields:

- *Developmental cognitive neuroscience*, which explores links between development, cognitive processes, and the brain (Diamond, Casey, & Munakata, 2011; Johnson & de Haan, 2012; Park & Bischof, 2011)
- *Developmental social neuroscience*, which examines connections between socioemotional processes, development, and the brain (Bell, Greene, & Wolfe, 2010)

In many instances, biological, cognitive, and socioemotional processes are bidirectional. For example, biological processes can influence cognitive processes and vice versa. Thus, although usually we study the different processes of development (biological, cognitive, and socioemotional) in separate locations, keep in mind that we are talking about the development of an integrated individual with a mind and body that are interdependent.

developmental **connection**

Brain Development. Might changes in the development of the adolescent brain be related to teens' mood swings and increased risk taking? Chapter 3, p. 104

PERIODS OF DEVELOPMENT

The interplay of biological, cognitive, and socioemotional processes produces the periods of the human life span (see Figure 1.6). *A developmental period* refers to a time frame in a person's life that is characterized by certain features. For the purposes of organization and understanding, we commonly describe development in terms of these periods. The most widely used classification of developmental periods involves the eight-period sequence shown in Figure 1.6. Approximate age ranges are listed for the periods to provide a general idea of when a period begins and ends.

The prenatal period is the time from conception to birth. It involves tremendous growth—from a single cell to an organism complete with brain and behavioral capabilities—and takes place in approximately a nine-month period.

biological processes Processes that produce changes in an individual's physical nature.

cognitive processes Processes that involve changes in an individual's thought, intelligence, and language.

socioemotional processes Processes that involve changes in an individual's relationships with other people, emotions, and personality.

| Prenatal period (conception to birth) | Infancy (birth to 18–24 months) | Early childhood (2–5 years) | Middle and late childhood (6–11 years) | Adolescence (10–12 to 18–21 years) | Early adulthood (20s to 30s) | Middle adulthood (40s to 50s) | Late adulthood (60s–70s to death) |

Processes of Development

FIGURE **1.6**

PROCESSES AND PERIODS OF DEVELOPMENT. The unfolding of life's periods of development is influenced by the interaction of biological, cognitive, and socioemotional processes.

> We reach backward
> to our parents and forward
> to our children, and through their
> children to a future we will never see,
> but about which we need to care.
>
> —CARL JUNG
> *Swiss Psychiatrist, 20th Century*

Infancy is the developmental period from birth to 18 or 24 months. Infancy is a time of extreme dependence upon adults. During this period, many psychological activities—language, symbolic thought, sensorimotor coordination, and social learning, for example—are just beginning.

Early childhood is the developmental period from the end of infancy to age 5 or 6. This period is sometimes called the "preschool years." During this time, young children learn to become more self-sufficient and to care for themselves, develop school readiness skills (following instructions, identifying letters), and spend many hours in play with peers. First grade typically marks the end of early childhood.

Middle and late childhood is the developmental period from about 6 to 11 years of age, approximately corresponding to the elementary school years. During this period, the fundamental skills of reading, writing, and arithmetic are mastered. The child is formally exposed to the larger world and its culture. Achievement becomes a more central theme of the child's world, and self-control increases.

Adolescence is the developmental period of transition from childhood to early adulthood, entered at approximately 10 to 12 years of age and ending at 18 to 21 years of age. Adolescence begins with rapid physical changes—dramatic gains in height and weight, changes in body contour, and the development of sexual characteristics such as enlargement of the breasts, growth of pubic and facial hair, and deepening of the voice. At this point in development, the pursuit of independence and an identity are prominent. Thought is more logical, abstract, and idealistic. More time is spent outside the family.

Early adulthood is the developmental period that begins in the late teens or early twenties and lasts through the thirties. It is a time of establishing personal and economic independence, career development, and, for many, selecting a mate, learning to live with someone in an intimate way, starting a family, and rearing children.

Middle adulthood is the developmental period from approximately 40 years of age to about 60. It is a time of expanding personal and social involvement and responsibility; of assisting the next generation in becoming competent, mature individuals; and of reaching and maintaining satisfaction in a career.

Late adulthood is the developmental period that begins in the sixties or seventies and lasts until death. It is a time of life review, retirement, and adjustment to new social roles involving decreasing strength and health. Late adulthood has the longest span of any period of development, and—as noted earlier—the number of people in this age group has been increasing dramatically. As a result, life-span developmentalists have been paying more attention to differences within late adulthood (Staudinger & Jacobs, 2011). Paul Baltes and Jacqui Smith (2003) argue that a major change takes place in older adults' lives as they become the "oldest old," on average at about 85 years of age. For example, the "young old" (classified as 65 through 84 in this analysis) have substantial potential for physical and cognitive fitness, retain much of their cognitive capacity, and can develop strategies to cope with the gains and losses of aging. In contrast, the oldest old (85 and older) show considerable loss in cognitive skills, experience an increase in chronic stress, and are more frail (Baltes & Smith, 2003). Nonetheless, as we see in later chapters, considerable variation exists in how much the oldest old retain their capabilities (Bishop & others, 2010). As you will see in the *Connecting with Research* interlude, contexts, including time of day, play an important role in how well older adults perform.

THE SIGNIFICANCE OF AGE

In the earlier description of developmental periods, an approximate age range was linked with each period. But there are also variations in the capabilities of individuals who are the same age, and we have seen how changes with age can be exaggerated. How important is age when we try to understand an individual?

Age and Happiness   Is one age in life better than another? An increasing number of studies indicate that at least in the United States adults are happier as they age. For example, a recent study of more than 300,000 U.S. adults revealed that psychological well-being increased after the age of 50 years (Stone & others, 2010). In this study, specific aspects of negative affect showed different age trends. When individuals were asked about affect experienced yesterday, stress and anger declined sharply from the early twenties, worry was elevated during middle age, then declined, and sadness showed little change from 18 to 85 years of age.

Consider also a recent U.S. study of approximately 28,000 individuals from 18 to 88 that revealed happiness increased with age (Yang, 2008). For example, about 33 percent were very happy at 88 years of age compared with only about 24 percent in their late teens and early twenties. Why might older people report being happier and more satisfied with their lives than younger people? Despite the increase in physical problems and losses older adults experience, they are more content with what they have in their lives, have better relationships with the people who matter to them, are less pressured to achieve, have more time for leisurely pursuits, and have many years of experience that may help them adapt better to their circumstances with wisdom than younger adults do (Cornwell, Schumm, & Laumann, 2008; Ram & others, 2008). Also in the study, baby boomers (those born from 1946 to 1964) reported being less happy than individuals born earlier—possibly because they are not lowering their aspirations and idealistic hopes as they age

"This is the path to adulthood. You're here."
© Robert Weber/The New Yorker Collection/
www.cartoonbank.com

One's children's children's children. Look back to us as we look to you; we are related by our imaginations. If we are able to touch, it is because we have imagined each other's existence, our dreams running back and forth along a cable from age to age.

—ROGER ROSENBLATT
American Writer, 20th Century

Is There a Best Time of Day to Conduct Research?

Laura Helmuth (2003) described how researchers are finding that certain testing conditions have exaggerated age-related declines in performance in older adults. Optimum testing conditions are not the same for young adults as they are for older adults. Most researchers conduct their studies in the afternoon, a convenient time for researchers and undergraduate participants. Traditional-aged college students in their late teens and early twenties are often more alert and function more optimally in the afternoon, but about 75 percent of older adults are "morning people," performing at their best early in the day (Helmuth, 2003).

Lynn Hasher and her colleagues (2001) tested the memory of college students 18 to 32 years of age and community volunteers 58 to 78 years of age in the late afternoon (about 4 to 5 p.m.) and in the morning (about 8 to 9 a.m.). Regardless of the time of day, the younger college students performed better than the older adults on the memory tests, which involved recognizing sentences from a story and memorizing a list of words. However, when the participants took the memory tests in the morning rather than in the late afternoon, the age difference in performance decreased considerably (see Figure 1.7).

The relevance of information also affects memory. Thomas Hess and his colleagues (2003) asked younger adults (18 to 30 years of age) and older adults (62 to 84 years of age) to listen to a drawn-out description that was identified as either someone's experiences on a first job or their experiences while searching for a retirement home. The younger adults remembered the details of both circumstances. However, the older adults showed a keen memory for the retirement-home search but not for the first-job experience.

In short, researchers have found that age differences in memory are robust when researchers ask for information that doesn't matter much, but when older adults are asked about information that is rele-

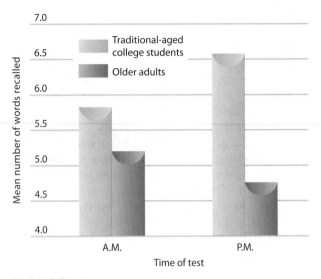

FIGURE **1.7**

MEMORY, AGE, AND TIME OF DAY TESTED (A.M. OR P.M.). In one study, traditional-aged college students performed better than older adults in both the a.m. and the p.m. Note, however, that the memory of the older adults was better when they were tested in the morning than in the afternoon, whereas the memory of the traditional-aged college students was not as good in the morning as it was in the afternoon (Hasher & others, 2001).

vant to their lives, differences in the memory of younger and older adults often decline considerably (Hasher, 2003). Thus, the type of information selected by researchers may produce an exaggerated view of declines in memory with age.

What other factors besides time of day or information tested do you think might affect research results in a study of cognitive differences between two age groups?

as did earlier generations. Because growing older is a certain outcome of living, it is good to know that we are likely to be happier as older adults than when we were younger.

Now that you have read about age variations in life satisfaction, think about how satisfied you are with your life. To help you answer this question, complete the items in Figure 1.8, which presents the most widely used measure in research on life satisfaction (Diener, 2011).

How old would you be if you didn't know how old you were?

—SATCHEL PAIGE

American Baseball Pitcher, 20th Century

Conceptions of Age   Chronological age—the number of years that have elapsed since birth—is not the only way of measuring age. Age has been conceptualized

(*Left*) Pam McSwain, 60, competing in the Senior Olympics in Memphis, Tennessee in 2009; (*right*) a sedentary, overweight middle-aged man. *Even if Pam McSwain's chronological age is older, might her biological age be younger than the middle-aged man's?*

not just as chronological age but also as biological age, psychological age, and social age (Hoyer & Roodin, 2009). *Biological age* is a person's age in terms of biological health. Determining biological age involves knowing the functional capacities of a person's vital organs. One person's vital capacities may be better or worse than those of others of comparable age. The younger the person's biological age, the longer the person is expected to live, regardless of chronological age.

Psychological age is an individual's adaptive capacities compared with those of other individuals of the same chronological age. Thus, older adults who continue to learn, are flexible, cope effectively with stress, and think clearly are engaging in more adaptive behaviors than their chronological age-mates who don't engage in these behaviors (Schaie, 2011). Reflecting the importance of psychological age, a longitudinal study of more than 1,200 individuals across seven decades revealed that the personality trait of conscientiousness (being organized, careful, and disciplined, for example) predicted lower mortality (frequency of death) risk from childhood through late adulthood (Martin, Friedman, & Schwartz, 2007).

Social age refers to connectedness with others and the social roles individuals adopt. Individuals who have better social relationships with others are happier with their lives and are likely to live longer (Carstensen & others, 2011).

From a life-span perspective, an overall age profile of an individual involves not just chronological age but also biological age, psychological age, and social age. For example, a 70-year-old man (chronological age) might be in good physical health (biological age), be experiencing memory problems and not be coping well with the demands placed on him by his wife's recent hospitalization (psychological age), and have a number of friends with whom he regularly plays golf (social age).

Below are five statements that you may agree or disagree with. Using the 1–7 scale below, indicate your agreement with each item by placing the appropriate number on the line preceding that item. Please be open and honest in your responding.

Scale
7 Strongly agree
6 Agree
5 Slightly agree
4 Neither agree nor disagree
3 Slightly disagree
2 Disagree
1 Strongly disagree

Response	Statement
_____	In most ways my life is close to my ideal.
_____	The conditions of my life are excellent.
_____	I am satisfied with my life.
_____	So far I have gotten the important things I want in life.
_____	If I could live my life over, I would change almost nothing.
_____	Total score

Scoring	
31–35	Extremely satisfied
26–30	Satisfied
21–25	Slightly satisfied
20	Neutral
15–19	Slightly dissatisfied
10–14	Dissatisfied
5–9	Extremely dissatisfied

FIGURE **1.8**

HOW SATISFIED AM I WITH MY LIFE?

Source: Diener, E., Emmons, R. A., Larson, R. J., & Griffin, S. (1985). The Satisfaction with Life Scale, *Journal of Personality Assessment, 49*, 71–75.

DEVELOPMENTAL ISSUES

Is your own journey through life marked out ahead of time, or can your experiences change your path? Are the experiences that take place early in your journey more important than later ones? Is your journey more like taking an elevator up a sky-scraper with distinct stops along the way or more like cruising down a river with smoother ebbs and flows? These questions point to three issues about the nature of development: the roles played by nature and nurture, by stability and change, and by continuity and discontinuity.

Nature and Nurture   The **nature-nurture issue** involves the extent to which development is influenced by nature and by nurture. Nature refers to an organism's biological inheritance, nurture to its environmental experiences.

According to those who emphasize the role of nature, just as a sunflower grows in an orderly way—unless flattened by an unfriendly environment—so too the human grows in an orderly way. An evolutionary and genetic foundation produces commonalities in growth and development (Buss, 2012; Cosmides, 2012). We walk before we talk, speak one word before two words, grow rapidly in infancy and less so in early childhood, experience a rush of sex hormones in puberty, reach the peak of our physical strength in late adolescence and early adulthood, and then physically decline. Proponents of the importance of nature acknowledge that extreme environments—those that are psychologically barren or hostile—can depress development. However, they believe that basic growth tendencies are genetically programmed into humans (Kremen & Lyons, 2011; Raven, 2011).

By contrast, others emphasize the importance of nurture, or environmental experiences, in development (Grusec, 2011). Experiences run the gamut from the individual's biological environment (nutrition, medical care, drugs, and physical accidents) to the social environment (family, peers, schools, community, media, and culture).

Stability and Change   Is the shy child who hides behind the sofa when visitors arrive destined to become a wallflower at college dances, or might the child become a sociable, talkative individual? Is the fun-loving, carefree adolescent bound to have difficulty holding down a 9-to-5 job as an adult? These questions reflect the **stability-change issue,** which involves the degree to which early traits and characteristics persist through life or change.

Many developmentalists who emphasize stability in development argue that stability is the result of heredity and possibly early experiences in life. Developmentalists who emphasize change take the more optimistic view that later experiences can produce change. Recall that in the life-span perspective, plasticity—the potential for change—exists throughout the life span.

----▶

developmental **connection**

Nature Versus Nurture. Can specific genes be linked to specific environmental experiences? Chapter 2, p. 60

What is the nature of the early- and later-experience issue in development?

----▶

developmental **connection**

Personality. Is personality more stable at some points in adult development than at others? Chapter 11, p. 356

nature-nurture issue Debate about whether development is primarily influenced by nature or nurture. Nature refers to an organism's biological inheritance, nurture to its environmental experiences. The "nature proponents" claim biological inheritance is the more important influence on development; the "nurture proponents" claim that environmental experiences are more important.

stability-change issue Debate as to whether and to what degree we become older renditions of our early experience (stability) or whether we develop into someone different from who we were at an earlier point in development (change).

continuity-discontinuity issue Debate that focuses on the extent to which development involves gradual, cumulative change (continuity) or distinct stages (discontinuity).

The roles of early and later experience are an aspect of the stability-change issue that has long been hotly debated (Kagan, 2010; Schaie, 2011). Some argue that unless infants experience warm, nurturant caregiving in the first year or so of life, their development will never be optimal (Sroufe, Coffino, & Carlson, 2010). The later-experience advocates see children as malleable throughout development, with sensitive caregiving playing an equally important role in later childhood as it does in infancy (Antonucci & others, 2010; Fingerman & Birditt, 2011).

Continuity and Discontinuity   When developmental change occurs, is it gradual or abrupt? Think about your own development for a moment. Did you gradually become the person you are? Or did you experience sudden, distinct changes in your growth? For the most part, developmentalists who emphasize nurture describe development as a gradual, continuous process. Those who emphasize nature often describe development as a series of distinct stages.

The **continuity-discontinuity issue** focuses on the degree to which development involves either gradual, cumulative change (continuity) or distinct stages (discontinuity). In terms of continuity, as the oak grows from seedling to giant oak, it becomes more and more an oak—its development is continuous (see Figure 1.9). Similarly, a child's first word, though seemingly an abrupt, discontinuous event, is actually the result of weeks and months of growth and practice. Puberty might seem abrupt, but it is a gradual process that occurs over several years.

In terms of discontinuity, as an insect grows from a caterpillar to a chrysalis to a butterfly, it passes through a sequence of stages in which change differs qualitatively rather than quantitatively. Similarly, at some point a child moves from not being able to think abstractly about the world to being able to do so. This is a qualitative, discontinuous change in development rather than a quantitative, continuous change.

Evaluating the Developmental Issues   Most life-span developmentalists acknowledge that development is not all nature or all nurture, not all stability or all change, and not all continuity or all discontinuity (Kopp, 2011; Staudinger & Gluck, 2011). Nature and nurture, stability and change, continuity and discontinuity characterize development throughout the human life span.

Although most developmentalists do not take extreme positions on these three important issues, there is spirited debate regarding how strongly development is influenced by each of them (Buss, 2012; Schaie, 2011).

Continuity

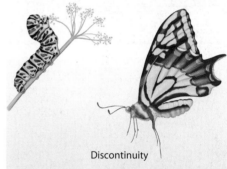

Discontinuity

FIGURE 1.9

CONTINUITY AND DISCONTINUITY IN DEVELOPMENT. *Is our development like that of a seedling gradually growing into a giant oak? Or is it more like that of a caterpillar suddenly becoming a butterfly?*

Theories of Development ⓛⓖ③ Describe the main theories of human development

- Psychoanalytic Theories
- Behavioral and Social Cognitive Theories
- Ecological Theory
- Cognitive Theories
- Ethological Theory
- An Eclectic Theoretical Orientation

Science refines everyday thinking.

—**ALBERT EINSTEIN**
German-born American Physicist, 20th Century

Signmund Freud, the pioneering architect of psychoanalytic theory. *How did Freud portray the organization of an individual's personality?*

theory An interrelated, coherent set of ideas that helps to explain phenomena and make predictions.

hypotheses Specific assumptions and predictions that can be tested to determine their accuracy.

psychoanalytic theories Theories that describe development as primarily unconscious and heavily colored by emotion. Behavior is merely a surface characteristic, and the symbolic workings of the mind must be analyzed to understand behavior. Early experiences with parents are emphasized.

Erikson's theory Theory that proposes eight stages of human development. Each stage consists of a unique developmental task that confronts individuals with a crisis that must be resolved.

How can we answer questions about the roles of nature and nurture, stability and change, and continuity and discontinuity in development? How can we determine, for example, whether special care can repair the harm inflicted by child neglect or whether memory loss in older adults can be prevented? The scientific method is the best tool we have to answer such questions.

The *scientific method* is essentially a four-step process: (1) conceptualize a process or problem to be studied, (2) collect research information (data), (3) analyze data, and (4) draw conclusions.

In step 1, when researchers are formulating a problem to study, they often draw on theories and develop hypotheses. A **theory** is an interrelated, coherent set of ideas that helps to explain phenomena and make predictions. It may suggest **hypotheses,** which are specific assertions and predictions that can be tested. For example, a theory on mentoring might state that sustained support and guidance from an adult make a difference in the lives of children from impoverished backgrounds because the mentor gives the children opportunities to observe and imitate the behavior and strategies of the mentor.

This section outlines key aspects of five theoretical orientations to development: psychoanalytic, cognitive, behavioral and social cognitive, ethological, and ecological. Each contributes an important piece to the life-span development puzzle. Although the theories disagree about certain aspects of development, many of their ideas are complementary rather than contradictory. Together they let us see the total landscape of life-span development in all its richness.

PSYCHOANALYTIC THEORIES

Psychoanalytic theories describe development as primarily unconscious (beyond awareness) and heavily colored by emotion. Psychoanalytic theorists emphasize that behavior is merely a surface characteristic and that a true understanding of development requires analyzing the symbolic meanings of behavior and the deep inner workings of the mind. Psychoanalytic theorists also stress that early experiences with parents extensively shape development. These characteristics are highlighted in the main psychoanalytic theory, that of Sigmund Freud (1856–1939).

Freud's Theory As Freud listened to, probed, and analyzed his patients, he became convinced that their problems were the result of experiences early in life. He thought that as children grow up, their focus of pleasure and sexual impulses shifts from the mouth to the anus and eventually to the genitals. As a result, we go through five stages of psychosexual development: oral, anal, phallic, latency, and genital (see Figure 1.10). Our adult personality, Freud (1917) claimed, is determined by the way we resolve conflicts between sources of pleasure at each stage and the demands of reality.

Freud's theory has been significantly revised by a number of psychoanalytic theorists. Many of today's psychoanalytic theorists argue that Freud overemphasized sexual instincts; they place more emphasis on cultural experiences as determinants of an individual's development. Unconscious thought remains a central theme, but thought plays a greater role than Freud envisioned. Next, you will read about the ideas of an important revisionist of Freud's ideas—Erik Erikson.

Oral Stage	Anal Stage	Phallic Stage	Latency Stage	Genital Stage
Infant's pleasure centers on the mouth.	Child's pleasure focuses on the anus.	Child's pleasure focuses on the genitals.	Child represses sexual interest and develops social and intellectual skills.	A time of sexual reawakening; source of sexual pleasure becomes someone outside the family.
Birth to 1½ Years	1½ to 3 Years	3 to 6 Years	6 Years to Puberty	Puberty Onward

FIGURE 1.10

FREUDIAN STAGES. Because Freud emphasized sexual motivation, his stages of development are known as *psychosexual stages*. In his view, if the need for pleasure at any stage is either undergratified or overgratified, an individual may become *fixated*, or locked in, at that stage of development.

Erikson's Psychosocial Theory Erik Erikson recognized Freud's contributions but stressed that Freud misjudged some important dimensions of human development. For one thing, Erikson (1950, 1968) said we develop in psychosocial stages, rather than in psychosexual stages as Freud maintained. According to Freud, the primary motivation for human behavior is sexual in nature; according to Erikson, it is social and reflects a desire to affiliate with other people. According to Freud, our basic personality is shaped in the first five years of life; according to Erikson, developmental change occurs throughout the life span. Thus, in terms of the early-versus-later-experience issue described earlier in the chapter, Freud viewed early experiences as far more important than later experiences, whereas Erikson emphasized the importance of both early and later experiences.

In **Erikson's theory,** eight stages of development unfold as we go through life (see Figure 1.11). At each stage, a unique developmental task confronts individuals with a crisis that must be resolved. According to Erikson, this crisis is not a catastrophe but a turning point marked by both increased vulnerability and enhanced potential. The more successfully individuals resolve these crises, the healthier their development will be.

Trust versus mistrust is Erikson's first psychosocial stage, which is experienced in the first year of life. Trust in infancy sets the stage for a lifelong expectation that the world will be a good and pleasant place to live.

Autonomy versus shame and doubt is Erikson's second stage. This stage occurs in late infancy and toddlerhood (1 to 3 years). After gaining trust in their caregivers, infants begin to discover that their behavior is their own. They start to assert their sense of independence or autonomy. They realize their will. If infants and toddlers are restrained too much or punished too harshly, they are likely to develop a sense of shame and doubt.

Initiative versus guilt, Erikson's third stage of development, occurs during the preschool years. As preschool children encounter a widening social world, they face new challenges that require active, purposeful, responsible behavior. Feelings of guilt may arise, though, if the child is irresponsible and is made to feel too anxious.

Industry versus inferiority is Erikson's fourth developmental stage, occurring approximately in the elementary school years. Children now need to direct their energy toward mastering knowledge and intellectual skills. The negative outcome is that the child may develop a sense of inferiority—feeling incompetent and unproductive.

During the adolescent years individuals face finding out who they are, what they are all about, and where they are going in life. This is Erikson's fifth developmental stage, identity versus identity confusion. If adolescents explore roles in a healthy manner and arrive at a positive path to follow in life, they achieve a positive identity; if they do not, identity confusion reigns.

Intimacy versus isolation is Erikson's sixth developmental stage, which individuals experience during the early adulthood years. At this time, individuals face the

Erikson's Stages	Developmental Period
Integrity versus despair	Late adulthood (60s onward)
Generativity versus stagnation	Middle adulthood (40s, 50s)
Intimacy versus isolation	Early adulthood (20s, 30s)
Identity versus identity confusion	Adolescence (10 to 20 years)
Industry versus inferiority	Middle and late childhood (elementary school years, 6 years to puberty)
Initiative versus guilt	Early childhood (preschool years, 3 to 5 years)
Autonomy versus shame and doubt	Infancy (1 to 3 years)
Trust versus mistrust	Infancy (first year)

FIGURE 1.11

ERIKSON'S EIGHT LIFE-SPAN STAGES. Like Freud, Erikson proposed that individuals go through distinct, universal stages of development. Thus, in terms of the continuity-discontinuity issue discussed in this chapter, both favor the discontinuity side of the debate. Notice that the timing of Erikson's first four stages is similar to that of Freud's stages. *What are the implications of saying that people go through stages of development?*

Erik Erikson with his wife, Joan, an artist. Erikson generated one of the most important developmental theories of the 20th century. *Which stage of Erikson's theory are you in? Does Erikson's description of this stage characterize you?*

Jean Piaget, the famous Swiss developmental psychologist, changed the way we think about the development of children's minds. *What are some key ideas in Piaget's theory?*

Piaget's theory Theory stating that children actively construct their understanding of the world and go through four stages of cognitive development.

developmental task of forming intimate relationships. If young adults form healthy friendships and an intimate relationship with another, intimacy will be achieved; if not, isolation will result.

Generativity versus stagnation, Erikson's seventh developmental stage, occurs during middle adulthood. By generativity Erikson means primarily a concern for helping the younger generation to develop and lead useful lives. The feeling of having done nothing to help the next generation is stagnation.

Integrity versus despair is Erikson's eighth and final stage of development, which individuals experience in late adulthood. During this stage, a person reflects on the past. If the person's life review reveals a life well spent, integrity will be achieved; if not, the retrospective glances likely will yield doubt or gloom—the despair Erikson described.

We further examine Erikson's theory in Chapter 11, "The Self, Identity, and Personality."

Evaluating Psychoanalytic Theories Contributions of psychoanalytic theories include an emphasis on a developmental framework, family relationships, and unconscious aspects of the mind. These theories have been criticized, however, for a lack of scientific support, too much emphasis on sexual underpinnings, and an image of people that is viewed as too negative.

COGNITIVE THEORIES

Whereas psychoanalytic theories stress the importance of the unconscious, cognitive theories emphasize conscious thoughts. Three important cognitive theories are Piaget's cognitive developmental theory, Vygotsky's sociocultural cognitive theory, and information-processing theory.

Piaget's Cognitive Developmental Theory **Piaget's theory** states that children go through four stages of cognitive development as they actively construct their understanding of the world. Two processes underlie this cognitive construction of the world: organization and adaptation. To make sense of our world, we organize our experiences. For example, we separate important ideas from less important ideas, and we connect one idea to another. In addition to organizing our observations and experiences, we adapt, adjusting to new environmental demands (Miller, 2011).

Jean Piaget (1954) also proposed that we go through four stages in understanding the world (see Figure 1.12). Each age-related stage consists of a distinct way of thinking, a *different* way of understanding the world. Thus, according to Piaget, the child's cognition is *qualitatively* different in one stage compared with another. What are Piaget's four stages of cognitive development?

The *sensorimotor stage*, which lasts from birth to about 2 years of age, is the first Piagetian stage. In this stage, infants construct an understanding of the world by coordinating sensory experiences (such as seeing and hearing) with physical, motoric actions—hence the term *sensorimotor*.

The *preoperational stage*, which lasts from approximately 2 to 7 years of age, is Piaget's second stage. In this stage, children begin to go beyond simply connecting sensory information with physical action and represent the world with words, images, and drawings. However, according to Piaget, preschool children still lack the ability to perform what he calls *operations*, which are internalized mental actions that allow children to do mentally what they previously could only do physically. For example, if you imagine putting two sticks together to see whether they would be as long as another stick, without actually moving the sticks, you are performing a concrete operation.

The *concrete operational stage*, which lasts from approximately 7 to 11 years of age, is the third Piagetian stage. In this stage, children can perform operations that involve objects, and they can reason logically when the reasoning can be applied to specific or concrete examples. For instance, concrete operational thinkers cannot

Sensorimotor Stage	Preoperational Stage	Concrete Operational Stage	Formal Operational Stage
The infant constructs an understanding of the world by coordinating sensory experiences with physical actions. An infant progresses from reflexive, instinctual action at birth to the beginning of symbolic thought toward the end of the stage.	The child begins to represent the world with words and images. These words and images reflect increased symbolic thinking and go beyond the connection of sensory information and physical action.	The child can now reason logically about concrete events and classify objects into different sets.	The adolescent reasons in more abstract, idealistic, and logical ways.
Birth to 2 Years of Age	**2 to 7 Years of Age**	**7 to 11 Years of Age**	**11 Years of Age Through Adulthood**

FIGURE **1.12**

PIAGET'S FOUR STAGES OF COGNITIVE DEVELOPMENT. According to Piaget, how a child thinks—not how much the child knows—determines the child's stage of cognitive development.

imagine the steps necessary to complete an algebraic equation, which is too abstract for thinking at this stage of development.

The *formal operational stage*, which appears between the ages of 11 and 15 and continues through adulthood, is Piaget's fourth and final stage. In this stage, individuals move beyond concrete experiences and think in abstract and more logical terms. As part of thinking more abstractly, adolescents develop images of ideal circumstances. They might think about what an ideal parent is like and compare their parents to this ideal standard. They begin to entertain possibilities for the future and are fascinated with what they can become. In solving problems, they become more systematic, developing hypotheses about why something is happening the way it is and then testing these hypotheses. We will examine Piaget's cognitive developmental theory further in Chapter 6, "Cognitive Developmental Approaches."

Vygotsky's Sociocultural Cognitive Theory

Like Piaget, the Russian developmentalist Lev Vygotsky (1896–1934) maintained that children actively construct their knowledge. However, Vygotsky (1962) gave social interaction and culture far more important roles in cognitive development than Piaget did. **Vygotsky's theory** is a sociocultural cognitive theory that emphasizes how culture and social interaction guide cognitive development.

Vygotsky portrayed the child's development as inseparable from social and cultural activities (Daniels, 2011). He argued that cognitive development involves learning to use the inventions of society, such as language, mathematical systems, and memory strategies. Thus, in one culture, children might learn to count with the help of a computer; in another, they might learn by using beads. According to Vygotsky, children's social interaction with more-skilled adults and peers is indispensable to their cognitive development (Gauvain & Parke, 2010). Through this interaction, they learn to use the tools that will help them adapt and be successful

Lev Vygotsky was born the same year as Piaget, but he died much earlier, at the age of 37. There is considerable interest today in Vygotsky's sociocultural cognitive theory of child development. *What are some key characteristics of Vygotsky's theory?*

Vygotsky's theory Sociocultural cognitive theory that emphasizes how culture and social interaction guide cognitive development.

in their culture. In Chapter 6, "Cognitive Developmental Approaches," we further examine ideas about learning and teaching that are based on Vygotsky's theory.

The Information-Processing Theory   **Information-processing theory** emphasizes that individuals manipulate information, monitor it, and strategize about it. Unlike Piaget's theory, but like Vygotsky's theory, information-processing theory does not describe development as stage-like. Instead, according to this theory, individuals develop a gradually increasing capacity for processing information, which allows them to acquire increasingly complex knowledge and skills (Halford & Andrews, 2011).

Robert Siegler (2007), a leading expert on children's information processing, states that thinking is information processing. In other words, when individuals perceive, encode, represent, store, and retrieve information, they are thinking. Siegler emphasizes that an important aspect of development is learning good strategies for processing information. For example, becoming a better reader might involve learning to monitor the key themes of the material being read. In Chapter 7, "Information Processing," we explore the information-processing approach in greater depth.

Evaluating Cognitive Theories   Contributions of cognitive theories include a positive view of development and an emphasis on the active construction of understanding. Criticisms include skepticism about the pureness of Piaget's stages and insufficient attention given to individual variations.

BEHAVIORAL AND SOCIAL COGNITIVE THEORIES

Behaviorism essentially holds that we can study scientifically only what we can directly observe and measure. Out of the behavioral tradition grew the belief that development is observable behavior that we can learn through experience with the environment (Klein, 2009). In terms of the continuity-discontinuity issue discussed earlier in this chapter, the behavioral and social cognitive theories emphasize continuity in development and argue that development does not occur in stage-like fashion. Let's explore two versions of behaviorism: Skinner's operant conditioning and Bandura's social cognitive theory.

Skinner's Operant Conditioning   According to B. F. Skinner (1904–1990), through *operant conditioning* the consequences of a behavior produce changes in the probability of the behavior's occurrence. A behavior followed by a rewarding stimulus is more likely to recur, whereas a behavior followed by a punishing stimulus is less likely to recur. For example, when an adult smiles at a child after the child has done something, the child is more likely to engage in that behavior again than if the adult gives the child a disapproving look.

In Skinner's (1938) view, such rewards and punishments shape development. For Skinner the key aspect of development is behavior, not thoughts and feelings. He emphasized that development consists of the pattern of behavioral changes that are brought about by rewards and punishments. For example, Skinner would say that shy people learned to be shy as a result of experiences they had while growing up. It follows that modifications in an environment can help a shy person become more socially oriented.

Bandura's Social Cognitive Theory   Some psychologists agree with the behaviorists' notion that development is learned and is influenced strongly by environmental interactions. However, unlike Skinner, they also see cognition as important

B. F. Skinner was a tinkerer who liked to make new gadgets. The younger of his two daughters, Deborah, was raised in Skinner's enclosed Air-Crib, which he invented because he wanted to control her environment completely. The Air-Crib was sound-proofed and temperature controlled. Debbie, shown here as a child with her parents, is currently a successful artist, is married, and lives in London. *What do you think about Skinner's Air-Crib?*

information-processing theory Theory emphasizing that individuals manipulate information, monitor it, and strategize about it. Central to this theory are the processes of memory and thinking.

social cognitive theory Theoretical view that behavior, environment, and cognition are the key factors in development.

in understanding development. **Social cognitive theory** holds that behavior, environment, and cognition are the key factors in development.

American psychologist Albert Bandura (1925–) is the leading architect of social cognitive theory. Bandura (2001, 2010a, b) emphasizes that cognitive processes have important links with the environment and behavior. His early research program focused heavily on *observational learning* (also called *imitation,* or *modeling*), which is learning that occurs through observing what others do. For example, a young boy might observe his father yelling in anger and treating other people with hostility; with his peers, the young boy later acts very aggressively, showing the same characteristics as his father's behavior. Social cognitive theorists stress that people acquire a wide range of behaviors, thoughts, and feelings through observing others' behavior and that these observations form an important part of life-span development.

What is *cognitive* about observational learning in Bandura's view? He proposes that people cognitively represent the behavior of others and then sometimes adopt this behavior themselves.

Bandura's (2001, 2010a, b) model of learning and development includes three elements: behavior, the person/cognition, and the environment. An individual's confidence that he or she can control his or her success is an example of a person factor; strategies are an example of a cognitive factor. As shown in Figure 1.13, behavior, person/cognition, and environmental factors operate interactively.

Further discussion of Bandura's social cognitive theory appears in Chapter 16, "Schools, Achievement, and Work."

Albert Bandura has been one of the leading architects of social cognitive theory. *How does Bandura's theory differ from Skinner's?*

Evaluating Behavioral and Social Cognitive Theories   Contributions of the behavioral and social cognitive theories include an emphasis on scientific research and environmental determinants of behavior. These theories have been criticized for deemphasizing the role of cognition (Skinner) and giving inadequate attention to developmental changes.

developmental **connection**

Achievement. Bandura emphasizes that self-efficacy is a key person/cognitive factor in achievement. Chapter 16, p. 543

ETHOLOGICAL THEORY

Ethology stresses that behavior is strongly influenced by biology, is tied to evolution, and is characterized by critical or sensitive periods. These are specific time frames during which, according to ethologists, the presence or absence of certain experiences has a long-lasting influence on individuals.

European zoologist Konrad Lorenz (1903–1989) helped bring ethology to prominence. In his best-known research, Lorenz (1965) studied the behavior of greylag geese, which will follow their mothers as soon as they hatch. Lorenz separated the eggs laid by one goose into two groups. One group he returned to the goose to be hatched by her. The other group was hatched in an incubator. The goslings in the first group performed as predicted. They followed their mother as soon as they hatched. However, those in the second group, which saw Lorenz when they first hatched, followed him everywhere, as though he were their mother. Lorenz marked the goslings and then placed both groups under a box. Mother goose and "mother" Lorenz stood aside as the box lifted. Each group of goslings went directly to its "mother." Lorenz called this process *imprinting,* the rapid, innate learning that involves attachment to the first moving object that is seen.

John Bowlby (1969, 1989) illustrated an important application of ethological theory to human development. Bowlby stressed that attachment to a caregiver over the first year of life has important consequences throughout the life span. In his view, if this attachment is positive and secure, the individual will likely develop positively in childhood and adulthood. If the attachment is negative and insecure, life-span development will likely not be optimal. In Chapter 10, "Emotional Development," we explore the concept of infant attachment in much greater detail.

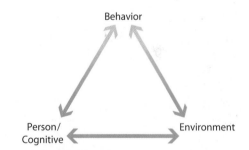

Behavior

Person/
Cognitive   Environment

FIGURE **1.13**

BANDURA'S SOCIAL COGNITIVE MODEL. The arrows illustrate how relations between behavior, person/cognitive, and environment are reciprocal rather than one way. *Person/cognitive* refers to cognitive processes (for example, thinking and planning) and personal characteristics (for example, believing that you can control your experiences).

ethology Theory stressing that behavior is strongly influenced by biology, is tied to evolution, and is characterized by critical or sensitive periods.

Konrad Lorenz, a pioneering student of animal behavior, is followed through the water by three imprinted greylag geese. Describe Lorenz's experiment with the geese. *Do you think his experiment would have the same results with human babies? Explain.*

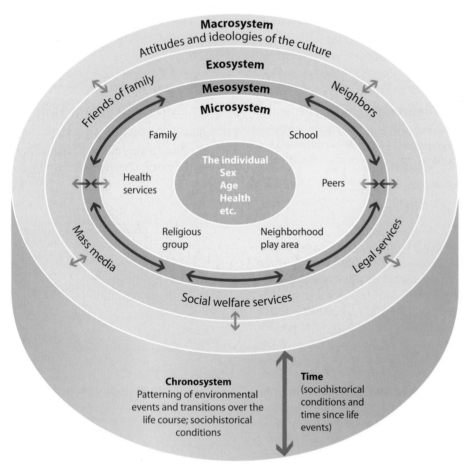

FIGURE **1.14**

BRONFENBRENNER'S ECOLOGICAL THEORY OF DEVELOPMENT. Bronfenbrenner's ecological theory consists of five environmental systems: microsystem, mesosystem, exosystem, macrosystem, and chronosystem.

Bronfenbrenner's ecological theory
Bronfenbrenner's environmental systems theory that focuses on five environmental systems: microsystem, mesosystem, exosystem, macrosystem, and chronosystem.

In Lorenz's view, imprinting needs to take place at a certain, very early time in the life of the animal, or else it will not take place. This point in time is called a *critical period*. A related concept is that of a *sensitive period*, and an example of this is the time during infancy when, according to Bowlby, attachment should occur in order to promote optimal development of social relationships.

Another theory that emphasizes biological foundations of development—evolutionary psychology—is presented in Chapter 2, "Biological Beginnings," along with views on the role of heredity in development. In addition, we examine a number of biological theories of aging in Chapter 3, "Physical Development and Biological Aging."

Contributions of ethological theory include its focus on the biological and evolutionary basis of development and its use of careful observations in naturalistic settings. Ethological theory has been criticized for its overemphasis on biological foundations and lack of flexibility regarding the concepts of critical and sensitive periods.

ECOLOGICAL THEORY

While ethological theory stresses biological factors, ecological theory emphasizes environmental factors. One ecological theory that has important implications for understanding life-span development was created by Urie Bronfenbrenner (1917–2005).

Bronfenbrenner's ecological theory (1986, 2004; Bronfenbrenner & Morris, 1998, 2006) holds that development reflects the influence of several environmental systems. The theory identifies five environmental systems: microsystem, mesosystem, exosystem, macrosystem, and chronosystem (see Figure 1.14).

The *microsystem* is the setting in which the individual lives. Contexts within it include the person's family, peers, school, and neighborhood. It is in the microsystem that the most direct interactions with social agents take place—with parents, friends, and teachers, for example. The individual is not a passive recipient of experiences in these settings, but someone who helps to construct the settings.

The *mesosystem* involves relations between microsystems or connections between contexts. Examples are the relationship of family experiences to school experiences, school experiences to church experiences, and family experiences to peer experiences. For example, children whose parents have rejected them may have difficulty developing positive relations with teachers.

The *exosystem* consists of links between the individual's immediate context and a social setting in which the individual does not play an active role. For example, a husband's or child's experience at home may be influenced by a mother's experiences at work. The mother might receive a promotion that requires more travel, which might increase conflict with the husband and change patterns of interaction with the child.

The *macrosystem* involves the culture in which individuals live. Remember from earlier in the chapter that culture refers to the behavior patterns, beliefs, and all other products of a group of people that are passed on from generation to generation. Remember also that cross-cultural studies—the comparison of one culture with one or more other cultures—provide information about the generality of development.

The *chronosystem* consists of the patterning of environmental events and transitions over the life course, as well as sociohistorical circumstances. For example, divorce is one transition. Researchers have found that the negative effects of divorce on children often peak in the first year after the divorce (Hetherington, 1993, 2006). By two years after the divorce, family interaction is more stable. As an example of sociohistorical circumstances, consider how the opportunities for women to pursue a career have increased since the 1960s.

Bronfenbrenner (2004; Bronfenbrenner & Morris, 2006) subsequently added biological influences to his theory, describing it as a bioecological theory. Nonetheless, it is still dominated by ecological, environmental contexts (Ceci, 2000).

Contributions of the theory include its systematic examination of macro and micro dimensions of environmental systems, and its attention to connections between environmental systems. A further contribution of Bronfenbrenner's theory is an emphasis on a range of social contexts beyond the family, such as neighborhood, religious community, school, and workplace, as influential in children's development (Gauvain & Parke, 2010; Parke & Clarke-Stewart, 2011). The theory has been criticized for giving inadequate attention to the influence of biological and cognitive factors.

AN ECLECTIC THEORETICAL ORIENTATION

No single theory described in this chapter can explain entirely the rich complexity of life-span development, but each has contributed to our understanding of development. Psychoanalytic theory best explains the workings of the unconscious mind. Erikson's theory best describes the changes that occur in adult development. Piaget's, Vygotsky's, and the information-processing views provide the most complete description of cognitive development. The behavioral and social cognitive and ecological theories have been the most adept at examining the environmental determinants of development. The ethological theories have highlighted biology's role and the importance of sensitive periods in development.

In short, although theories can be helpful guides, relying on a single theory to explain development probably would be a mistake. This book instead takes an **eclectic theoretical orientation**—rather than following a single theoretical approach, it selects from each theory whatever is considered its best features. Figure 1.15 compares the main theoretical perspectives in terms of how they view important developmental issues in children's development.

▬ ▬ ▬ ▬ ▬ ▬ ▬ ▬ ▬ ▬ ▬ ➤

developmental **connection**

Peers. How are parent-child relationships linked to children's peer relations? Chapter 15, p. 488

Urie Bronfenbrenner developed ecological theory, a perspective that is receiving increased attention today. His theory emphasizes the importance of both micro and macro dimensions of the environment in which the child lives.

eclectic theoretical orientation An orientation that does not follow any one theoretical approach, but rather selects from each theory whatever is considered best in it.

THEORY	ISSUES	
	Continuity/discontinuity, early versus later experiences	**Biological and environmental factors**
Psychoanalytic	Discontinuity between stages—continuity between early experiences and later development; early experiences very important; later changes in development emphasized in Erikson's theory	Freud's biological determination interacting with early family experiences; Erikson's more balanced biological-cultural interaction perspective
Cognitive	Discontinuity between stages in Piaget's theory; continuity between early experiences and later development in Piaget's and Vygotsky's theories; no stages in Vygotsky's theory or information-processing theory	Piaget's emphasis on interaction and adaptation; environment provides the setting for cognitive structures to develop; information-processing view has not addressed this issue extensively but mainly emphasizes biological-environmental interaction
Behavioral and social cognitive	Continuity (no stages); experience at all points of development important	Environment viewed as the cause of behavior in both views
Ethological	Discontinuity but no stages; critical or sensitive periods emphasized; early experiences very important	Strong biological view
Ecological	Little attention to continuity/discontinuity; change emphasized more than stability	Strong environmental view

FIGURE **1.15**
A COMPARISON OF THEORIES AND ISSUES IN LIFE-SPAN DEVELOPMENT

Review *Connect* Reflect

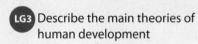 Describe the main theories of human development

Review

- How can theory and hypotheses be defined? What are the four steps of the scientific method? What are two main psychoanalytic theories? What are some contributions and criticisms of the psychoanalytic theories?
- What are three main cognitive theories? What are some contributions and criticisms of the cognitive theories?
- What are two main behavioral and social cognitive theories? What are some contributions and criticisms of the behavioral and social cognitive theories?
- What is the nature of ethological theory? What are some contributions and criticisms of the theory?

- What characterizes ecological theory? What are some contributions and criticisms of the theory?
- What is an eclectic theoretical orientation?

Connect

- In this section you learned about cognitive theories and social cognitive theories. What do these theories have in common? How are they different?

Reflect *Your Own Personal Journey of Life*

- Which of the life-span theories do you think best explains your own development? Why?

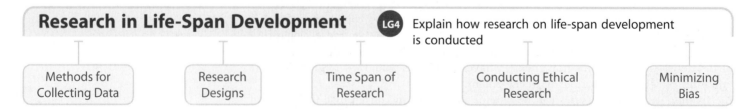

Research in Life-Span Development

LG4 Explain how research on life-span development is conducted

| Methods for Collecting Data | Research Designs | Time Span of Research | Conducting Ethical Research | Minimizing Bias |

If they follow an eclectic orientation, how do scholars and researchers determine that one feature of a theory is somehow better than another? The scientific method discussed earlier in this chapter provides the guide. Through scientific research, they can test and refine the features of theories.

Generally, research in life-span development is designed to test hypotheses, which in some cases are derived from the theories just described. Through research, theories are modified to reflect new data, and occasionally new theories arise.

METHODS FOR COLLECTING DATA

Whether we are interested in studying attachment in infants, the cognitive skills of children, or social relationships in older adults, we can choose from several ways of collecting data. Here we consider the measures most often used, beginning with observation.

Observation Scientific observation requires an important set of skills (Jackson, 2011). For observations to be effective, they have to be systematic. We have to have some idea of what we are looking for. We have to know whom we are observing, when and where we will observe, how we will make our observations, and how we will record them.

What are some important strategies in conducting observational research with children?

Where should we make our observations? We have two choices: the laboratory and the everyday world.

When we observe scientifically, we often need to control certain factors that determine behavior but are not the focus of our inquiry (Stangor, 2011). For this reason, some research in life-span development is conducted in a **laboratory,** a controlled setting where many of the complex factors of the "real world" are absent. For example, suppose you want to observe how children react when they see other people act aggressively. If you observe children in their homes or schools, you have no control over how much aggression the children observe, what kind of aggression they see, which people they see acting aggressively, or how other people treat the children. In contrast, if you observe the children in a laboratory, you can control these and other factors and therefore have more confidence about how to interpret your observations (Langston, 2011).

Laboratory research does have some drawbacks, however, including the following:

- It is almost impossible to conduct research without the participants knowing they are being studied.
- The laboratory setting is unnatural and therefore can cause the participants to behave unnaturally.
- People who are willing to come to a university laboratory may not fairly represent groups from diverse cultural backgrounds.
- People who are unfamiliar with university settings may be intimidated by the laboratory atmosphere.

Naturalistic observation provides insights that we sometimes cannot achieve in the laboratory (Gravetter & Forzano, 2012). **Naturalistic observation** means observing behavior in real-world settings, making no effort to manipulate or control the situation. Life-span researchers conduct naturalistic observations at sporting events, child-care centers, schools, work settings, malls, and other places people live in and frequent.

Naturalistic observation was used in one study that focused on conversations in a children's science museum (Crowley & others, 2001). When visiting exhibits at the science museum, parents were three times as likely to engage boys as girls in explanatory talk. This finding suggests a gender bias that encourages boys more than girls to be interested in science (see Figure 1.16).

Survey and Interview Sometimes the best and quickest way to get information about people is to ask them for it. One technique is to *interview* them directly. A

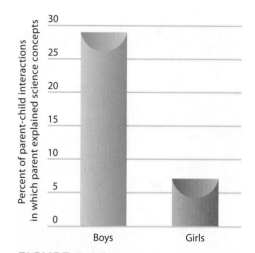

FIGURE **1.16**

PARENTS' EXPLANATIONS OF SCIENCE TO SONS AND DAUGHTERS AT A SCIENCE MUSEUM. In a naturalistic observation study at a children's science museum, parents were three times more likely to explain science to boys than to girls (Crowley & others, 2001). The gender difference occurred regardless of whether the father, the mother, or both parents were with the child, although the gender difference was greatest for fathers' science explanations to sons and daughters.

laboratory A controlled setting from which many of the complex factors of the "real world" have been removed.

naturalistic observation Observing behavior in real-world settings.

Mahatma Gandhi was the spiritual leader of India in the middle of the 20th century. Erik Erikson conducted an extensive case study of Gandhi's life to determine what contributed to his identity development. *What are some limitations of the case study approach?*

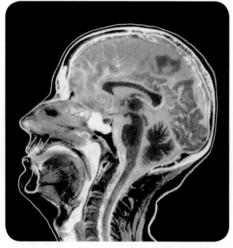

This fMRI scan of a 51-year-old male shows atrophy in the cerebral cortex of the brain, which occurs in various disorders including stroke and Alzheimer disease. The area of the upper cerebral cortex (where higher-level brain functioning such as thinking and planning occur) is colored dark red. Neuroimaging techniques such as the fMRI are helping researchers to learn more about how the brain functions as people develop and age, as well as what happens to the brain when aging diseases such as stroke and Alzheimer disease are present.

standardized test A test with uniform procedures for administration and scoring. Many standardized tests allow a person's performance to be compared with the performance of other individuals.

case study An in-depth look at a single individual.

related method is the survey—sometimes referred to as a *questionnaire*—which is especially useful when information from many people is needed (Babble, 2011). A standard set of questions is used to obtain people's self-reported attitudes or beliefs about a particular topic. In a good survey, the questions are clear and unbiased, allowing respondents to answer unambiguously.

Surveys and interviews can be used to study a wide range of topics from religious beliefs to sexual habits to attitudes about gun control to beliefs about how to improve schools. Surveys and interviews may be conducted in person, over the telephone, and over the Internet.

One problem with surveys and interviews is the tendency of participants to answer questions in a way that they think is socially acceptable or desirable rather than to say what they truly think or feel (Jackson, 2011). For example, on a survey or in an interview some individuals might say that they do not take drugs even though they do.

Standardized Test A **standardized test** has uniform procedures for administration and scoring. Many standardized tests allow a person's performance to be compared with that of other individuals; thus, they provide information about individual differences among people (Gregory, 2011). One example is the Stanford-Binet intelligence test, which is described in Chapter 8, "Intelligence." Your score on the Stanford-Binet test tells you how your performance compares with that of thousands of other people who have taken the test.

One criticism of standardized tests is that they assume a person's behavior is consistent and stable, although personality and intelligence—two primary targets of standardized testing—can vary with the situation. For example, a person may perform poorly on a standardized intelligence test in an office setting but score much higher at home, where he or she is less anxious.

Case Study A **case study** is an in-depth look at a single individual. Case studies are performed mainly by mental health professionals when, for either practical or ethical reasons, the unique aspects of an individual's life cannot be duplicated and tested in other individuals. A case study provides information about one person's experiences; it may focus on nearly any aspect of the subject's life that helps the researcher understand the person's mind, behavior, or other attributes. In later chapters, we discuss vivid case studies, such as that of Michael Rehbein, who had much of the left side of his brain removed at 7 years of age to end severe epileptic seizures.

A case study can provide a dramatic, in-depth portrayal of an individual's life, but we must be cautious when generalizing from this information. The subject of a case study is unique, with a genetic makeup and personal history that no one else shares. In addition, case studies involve judgments of unknown reliability. Researchers who conduct case studies rarely check to see if other professionals agree with their observations or findings.

Physiological Measures Researchers are increasingly using physiological measures when they study development at different points in the life span (Nelson, 2011). For example, as puberty unfolds, the blood levels of certain hormones increase. To determine the nature of these hormonal changes, researchers analyze blood samples from adolescent volunteers (Susman & Dorn, 2009).

Another physiological measure that is increasingly being used is neuroimaging, especially *functional magnetic resonance imaging* (fMRI), in which electromagnetic waves are used to construct images of a person's brain tissue and biochemical activity (Reuter-Lorenz & Park, 2011). We will have much more to say about neuroimaging and other physiological measures in later chapters.

RESEARCH DESIGNS

In conducting research on life-span development, in addition to having a method for collecting data, you also need a research design. There are three main types of research designs: descriptive, correlational, and experimental.

Descriptive Research   All of the data-collection methods that we have discussed can be used in **descriptive research,** which aims to observe and record behavior. For example, a researcher might observe the extent to which people are altruistic or aggressive toward each other. By itself, descriptive research cannot prove what causes some phenomenon, but it can reveal important information about people's behavior (McMillan & Schumacher, 2010; Stake, 2010).

Correlational Research   In contrast with descriptive research, correlational research goes beyond describing phenomena; it provides information that will help us to predict how people will behave. In **correlational research,** the goal is to describe the strength of the relationship between two or more events or characteristics. The more strongly the two events are correlated (or related or associated), the more effectively we can predict one event from the other (Levin & Fox, 2011).

For example, to find out whether children of permissive parents have less self-control than other children, you would need to carefully record observations of parents' permissiveness and their children's self-control. You might observe that the higher a parent was in permissiveness, the lower the child was in self-control. You would then analyze these data statistically to yield a numerical measure, called a **correlation coefficient,** a number based on a statistical analysis that is used to describe the degree of association between two variables. The correlation coefficient ranges from +1.00 to −1.00. A negative number means an inverse (reversed) relation. In the example just given, you might find an inverse correlation between permissive parenting and children's self-control, with a coefficient of, say, −.30. By contrast, you might find a positive correlation of +.30 between parental monitoring of children and children's self-control.

The higher the correlation coefficient (whether positive or negative), the stronger the association between the two factors. A correlation of 0 means that there is no association between the factors. A correlation of −.40 is stronger than a correlation of +.20 because we disregard whether the correlation is positive or negative in determining the strength of the correlation.

A caution is in order, however. Correlation does not equal causation (Heiman, 2011). The correlational finding just mentioned does not mean that permissive parenting necessarily causes low self-control in children. It could mean that, but it also could mean that a child's lack of self-control caused the parents to throw up their arms in despair and give up trying to control the child. It also could mean that other factors, such as heredity or poverty, caused the correlation between permissive parenting and low self-control in children. Figure 1.17 illustrates these possible interpretations of correlational data.

Experimental Research   To study causality, researchers turn to experimental research. An **experiment** is a carefully regulated procedure in which one or more factors believed to influence the behavior being studied are manipulated while all other factors are held constant. If the behavior under study changes when a factor is manipulated, the manipulated factor has caused the behavior to change. In other words, the experiment has demonstrated cause and effect. The cause is the factor that was manipulated. The effect is the behavior that changed because of the manipulation. Nonexperimental research methods (descriptive and correlational research) cannot establish cause and effect because they do not involve manipulating factors in a controlled way (Mitchell & Jolley, 2010).

descriptive research A type of research that aims to observe and record behavior.

correlational research A type of research that strives to describe the strength of the relationship between two or more events or characteristics.

correlation coefficient A number based on a statistical analysis that is used to describe the degree of association between two variables.

experiment Carefully regulated procedure in which one or more factors believed to influence the behavior being studied are manipulated while all other factors are held constant.

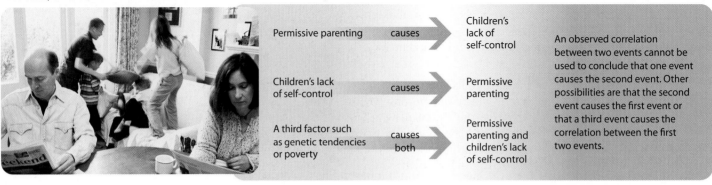

Observed Correlation: As permissive parenting increases, children's self-control decreases.

Possible explanations for this observed correlation

Permissive parenting → **causes** → Children's lack of self-control

Children's lack of self-control → **causes** → Permissive parenting

A third factor such as genetic tendencies or poverty → **causes both** → Permissive parenting and children's lack of self-control

An observed correlation between two events cannot be used to conclude that one event causes the second event. Other possibilities are that the second event causes the first event or that a third event causes the correlation between the first two events.

FIGURE **1.17**
POSSIBLE EXPLANATIONS OF CORRELATIONAL DATA

Independent and Dependent Variables Experiments include two types of changeable factors, or variables: independent and dependent. An *independent variable* is a manipulated, influential, experimental factor. It is a potential cause. The label "independent" is used because this variable can be manipulated independently of other factors to determine its effect. An experiment may include one independent variable or several of them.

A *dependent variable* is a factor that can change in an experiment, in response to changes in the independent variable. As researchers manipulate the independent variable, they measure the dependent variable for any resulting effect.

For example, suppose that you are conducting a study to determine whether pregnant women could change the breathing and sleeping patterns of their newborn babies by meditating during pregnancy. You might require one group of pregnant women to engage in a certain amount and type of meditation each day while another group would not meditate; the meditation is thus the independent variable. When the infants are born, you would observe and measure their breathing and sleeping patterns. These patterns are the dependent variable, the factor that changes as the result of your manipulation.

Experimental and Control Groups Experiments can involve one or more experimental groups and one or more control groups. An experimental group is a group whose experience is manipulated. A *control group* is a comparison group that is as much like the experimental group as possible and that is treated in every way like the experimental group except for the manipulated factor (independent variable). The control group serves as a baseline against which the effects of the manipulated condition can be compared.

Random assignment is an important principle for deciding whether each participant will be placed in the experimental group or in the control group. Random assignment means that researchers assign participants to experimental and control groups by chance. It reduces the likelihood that the experiment's results will be due to any preexisting differences between groups (Christensen, Johnson, & Turner, 2011). In the example of the effects of meditation by pregnant women on the breathing and sleeping patterns of their newborns, you would randomly assign half of the pregnant women to engage in meditation over a period of weeks (the experimental group) and the other half not to meditate over the same number of weeks (the control group). Figure 1.18 illustrates the nature of experimental research.

TIME SPAN OF RESEARCH

Researchers in life-span development have a special concern with studies that focus on the relation of age to some other variable. They have several options: Researchers can study different individuals of varying ages and compare them or they can study the same individuals as they age over time.

Cross-Sectional Approach The **cross-sectional approach** is a research strategy that simultaneously compares individuals of different ages. A typical cross-sectional study might include three groups of children: 5-year-olds, 8-year-olds, and 11-year-olds. Another study might include a group of 15-year-olds, 25-year-olds, and 45-year-olds. The groups can be compared with respect to a variety of dependent variables: IQ, memory, peer relations, attachment to parents, hormonal changes, and so on. All of these comparisons can be accomplished in a short time. In some studies, data are collected in a single day. Even in large-scale cross-sectional studies with hundreds of subjects, data collection does not usually take longer than several months to complete.

The main advantage of the cross-sectional study is that the researcher does not have to wait for the individuals to grow up or become older. Despite its efficiency, though, the cross-sectional approach has its drawbacks. It gives no information about how individuals change or about the stability of their characteristics. It can obscure the increases and decreases of development—the hills and valleys of growth and development. For example, a cross-sectional study of life satisfaction might reveal average increases and decreases, but it would not show how the life satisfaction of individual adults waxed and waned over the years. It also would not tell us whether the same adults who had positive or negative perceptions of life satisfaction in early adulthood maintained their relative degree of life satisfaction as they became middle-aged or older adults.

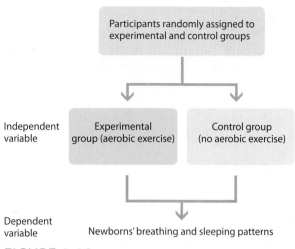

FIGURE 1.18

PRINCIPLES OF EXPERIMENTAL RESEARCH. Imagine that you decide to conduct an experimental study of the effects of aerobic exercise by pregnant women on their newborns' breathing and sleeping patterns. You would randomly assign pregnant women to experimental and control groups. The experimental-group women would engage in aerobic exercise over a specified number of sessions and weeks. The control group would not. Then, when the infants are born, you would assess their breathing and sleeping patterns. If the breathing and sleeping patterns of newborns whose mothers were in the experimental group are more positive than those of the control group, you would conclude that aerobic exercise caused the positive effects.

Longitudinal Approach The **longitudinal approach** is a research strategy in which the same individuals are studied over a period of time, usually several years or more. For example, in a longitudinal study of life satisfaction, the same adults might be assessed periodically over a 70-year time span—at the ages of 20, 35, 45, 65, and 90, for example.

Longitudinal studies provide a wealth of information about vital issues such as stability and change in development and the importance of early experience for later development, but they do have drawbacks (Gibbons, Hedeker, & DuToit, 2010). They are expensive and time consuming. The longer the study lasts, the more participants drop out—they move, get sick, lose interest, and so forth. The participants who remain may be dissimilar to those who drop out, biasing the outcome of the study. Those individuals who remain in a longitudinal study over a number of years may be more responsible and conformity-oriented, for example, or they might have more stable lives.

Cohort Effects A *cohort* is a group of people who are born at a similar point in history and share similar experiences as a result, such as living through the Vietnam War or growing up in the same city around the same time. These shared experiences may produce a range of differences among cohorts. For example, people who were teenagers during World War II are likely to differ from people who were teenagers during the booming 1990s in their educational opportunities and economic status, in how they were raised, and in their attitudes toward sex and religion. In life-span development research, **cohort effects** are due to a person's time of birth, era, or generation but not to actual age.

Cohort effects are important because they can powerfully affect the dependent measures in a study ostensibly concerned with age (Schaie, 2010, 2011). Researchers have shown it is especially important to be aware of cohort effects when assessing adult intelligence (Schaie, 2007). Individuals born at different points in time—such as 1930, 1960, and 1990—have had varying opportunities for education.

cross-sectional approach A research strategy in which individuals of different ages are compared at one time.

longitudinal approach A research strategy in which the same individuals are studied over a period of time, usually several years or more.

cohort effects Effects due to a person's time of birth, era, or generation but not to actual age.

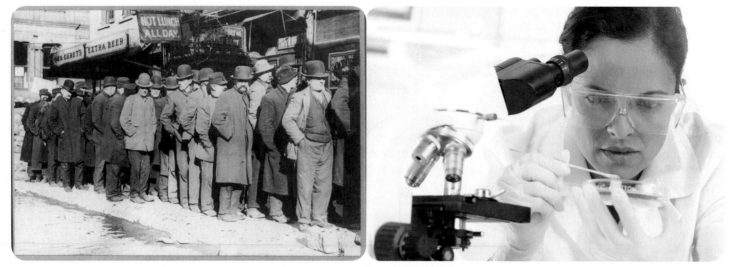

Cohort effects are due to a person's time of birth or generation but not actually to age. Think for a moment about growing up in (a) the Great Depression and (b) today. *How might your development be different depending on which of these time frames has dominated your life? your parents' lives? your grandparents' lives?*

Individuals born in earlier years had less access to education, and this fact may have a significant effect on how this cohort performs on intelligence tests.

Cross-sectional studies can show how different cohorts respond, but they can confuse age changes and cohort effects. Longitudinal studies are effective in studying age changes but only within one cohort.

CONDUCTING ETHICAL RESEARCH

Ethics in research may affect you personally if you ever serve as a participant in a study. In that event, you need to know your rights as a participant and the responsibilities of researchers to assure that these rights are safeguarded.

If you ever become a researcher in life-span development yourself, you will need an even deeper understanding of ethics. Even if you only carry out experimental projects in psychology courses, you must consider the rights of the participants in those projects. A student might think, "I volunteer in a home for the mentally retarded several hours per week. I can use the residents of the home in my study to see if a particular treatment helps improve their memory for everyday tasks." But without proper permissions, the most well-meaning and considerate studies still violate the rights of the participants.

Today, proposed research at colleges and universities must pass the scrutiny of a research ethics committee before the research can begin. In addition, the American Psychological Association (APA) has developed ethics guidelines for its members. The code of ethics instructs psychologists to protect their participants from mental and physical harm. The participants' best interests need to be kept foremost in the researcher's mind (Stangor, 2011). APA's guidelines address four important issues:

1. *Informed consent.* All participants must know what their research participation will involve and what risks might develop. Even after informed consent is given, participants must retain the right to withdraw from the study at any time and for any reason.

2. *Confidentiality.* Researchers are responsible for keeping all of the data they gather on individuals completely confidential and, when possible, completely anonymous.

3. *Debriefing.* After the study has been completed, participants should be informed of its purpose and the methods that were used. In most cases, the experimenter also can inform participants in a general manner beforehand

about the purpose of the research without leading participants to behave in a way they think the experimenter is expecting.

4. *Deception.* In some circumstances, telling the participants beforehand what the research study is about substantially alters the participants' behavior and invalidates the researcher's data. Thus, researchers may deceive the participants about the details of the study. In all cases of deception, however, the psychologist must ensure that the deception will not harm the participants and that the participants will be *debriefed* (told the complete nature of the study) as soon as possible after the study is completed.

MINIMIZING BIAS

Studies of life-span development are most useful when they are conducted without bias or prejudice toward any group of people (Banks, 2010). Of special concern is bias based on gender and bias based on culture or ethnicity.

Gender Bias For most of its existence, our society has had a strong gender bias, a preconceived notion about the abilities of women and men that prevented individuals from pursuing their own interests and achieving their potential (Eagly & Wood, 2011; UNICEF, 2011). Gender bias also has had a less obvious effect within the field of life-span development. For example, it is not unusual for conclusions to be drawn about females' attitudes and behaviors from research conducted with males as the only participants (Matlin, 2012).

Furthermore, when researchers find gender differences, their reports sometimes magnify those differences (Denmark & others, 1988). For example, a researcher might report that 74 percent of the men in a study had high achievement expectations versus only 67 percent of the women and go on to talk about the differences in some detail. In reality, this might be a rather small difference. It also might disappear if the study were repeated, or the study might have methodological problems that don't allow such strong interpretations.

Pam Reid is a leading researcher who studies gender and ethnic bias in development. To read about Pam's interests, see the *Connecting with Careers* profile.

Cultural and Ethnic Bias There is a growing awareness that research on life-span development needs to include more people from diverse ethnic groups (Graham, 2006; Jackson, 2011). Historically, people from ethnic minority groups (African American, Latino, Asian American, and Native American) were excluded from most research in the United States and simply thought of as variations from the norm or average. If minority individuals were included in samples and their scores didn't fit the norm, they were viewed as confounds or "noise" in data and discounted. Given the fact that individuals from diverse ethnic groups were excluded from research on life-span development for so long, we might reasonably conclude that people's real lives are perhaps more varied than research data have indicated in the past.

Researchers also have tended to overgeneralize about ethnic groups (Banks, 2010). **Ethnic gloss** is using an ethnic label such as African American or Latino in a superficial way that portrays an ethnic group as being more homogeneous than it really is (Trimble, 1988). For example, a researcher might describe a research sample like this: "The participants were 60 Latinos." A more complete description of the Latino group might be something like this: "The 60 Latino participants were Mexican Americans from low-income neighborhoods in the southwestern area of Los Angeles. Thirty-six were from homes in which Spanish is the dominant spoken language, 24 from homes in which English is the main spoken language. Thirty were born in the United States, 30 in Mexico. Twenty-eight described themselves as Mexican American, 14 as Mexican, 9 as American, 6 as Chicano, and 3 as Latino." Ethnic gloss can cause researchers to obtain samples of ethnic groups that are not representative of the group's diversity, which can lead to overgeneralization and stereotyping.

ethnic gloss Use of an ethnic label such as African American or Latino in a superficial way that portrays an ethnic group as being more homogeneous than it really is.

Pam Reid, Educational and Development Psychologist

When she was a child, Pam Reid liked to play with chemistry sets. Reid majored in chemistry during college and wanted to become a doctor. However, when some of her friends signed up for a psychology class as an elective she also decided to take the course. She was intrigued by learning about how people think, behave, and develop—so much so that she changed her major to psychology. Reid went on to obtain her Ph.D. in psychology (American Psychological Association, 2003, p. 16).

For a number of years, Reid was professor of education and psychology at the University of Michigan, where she also was a research scientist at the Institute for Research on Women and Gender. Her main focus has been on how children and adolescents develop social skills, with a special interest in the development of African American girls (Reid & Zalk, 2001). In 2004, Reid become Provost and Executive Vice-President at Roosevelt University in Chicago, and in 2007 she became president of Saint Joseph College in Hartford, Connecticut.

Pam Reid (*center*), with students at Saint Joseph College in Hartford, Connecticut, where she is the president of the college.

For more information about what educational psychologists do, see page 42 in the Careers in Life-Span Development appendix.

The growing proportion of minority families in the U.S. population in approaching decades will mainly be due to the immigration of Latino and Asian families. Researchers need "to take into account their acculturation level and generational status of parents and children" and consider how these factors influence family processes and child outcomes (Parke & Buriel, 2006, p. 487). More attention also needs to be given to biculturalism, because the complexity of diversity means that some children of color identify with two or more ethnic groups. And language development research needs to focus more on second-language acquisition (usually English) and bilingualism and how they are linked to school achievement.

Look at these two photographs, one of all non-Latino White males, the other of a diverse group of females and males from different ethnic groups, including some non-Latino White males. Consider a topic in life-span development, such as parenting, love, or cultural values. *If you were conducting research on this topic, might the results of the study be different depending on whether the participants in your study were the individuals in the photograph on the left or the right?*

Review *Connect* Reflect

LG4 Explain how research on life-span development is conducted

Review

- What methods do researchers use to collect data on life-span development?
- What research designs are used to study human development?
- How is research conducted on the time span of people's lives?
- What are researchers' ethical responsibilities to the people they study?
- How can gender, cultural, and ethnic bias affect the outcome of a research study?

Connect

- Earlier in this chapter you read about research on memory decline and age that revealed some potential biases based on the type of information involved and the time of day. How might researchers study memory decline while accounting for such possible biases?

Reflect *Your Own Personal Journey of Life*

- Imagine that you are conducting a research study on the sexual attitudes and behaviors of adolescents. What ethical safeguards should you use in conducting the study?

reach your learning goals

The Life-Span Perspective

 LG1 Discuss the distinctive features of a life-span perspective on development

The Importance of Studying Life-Span Development

- Development is the pattern of change that begins at conception and continues through the human life span. It includes both growth and decline. Studying life-span development helps prepare us to take responsibility for children, gives us insight about our own lives, and gives us knowledge about what our lives will be like as we age.

Characteristics of the Life-Span Perspective

- The life-span perspective includes these basic conceptions: Development is life-long, multidimensional, multidirectional, and plastic; its study is multidisciplinary; it is embedded in contexts; it involves growth, maintenance, and regulation; and it is a co-construction of biological, sociocultural, and individual factors. Three important sources of contextual influences are (1) normative age-graded influences, (2) normative history-graded influences, and (3) nonnormative life events.

Some Contemporary Concerns

- Health and well-being, parenting, education, sociocultural contexts and diversity, and social policy are all areas of contemporary concern that are closely tied to life-span development. Important dimensions of the sociocultural context include culture, ethnicity, socioeconomic status, and gender. There is increasing interest in social policy issues related to children and to older adults.

The Nature of Development

 LG2 Identify the most important processes, periods, and issues in development

Biological, Cognitive, and Socioemotional Processes

- Three key developmental processes are biological, cognitive, and socioemotional. Development is influenced by an interplay of these processes.

Periods of Development

- The life-span is commonly divided into the following periods of development: prenatal, infancy, early childhood, middle and late childhood, adolescence, early adulthood, middle adulthood, and late adulthood. Recently, life-span developmentalists have described the human life span in terms of four ages, with a special focus on the third and fourth ages (young old and oldest old).

The Significance of Age

- An increasing number of studies have found that as adults get older they are happier. We often think of age only in terms of chronological age, but a full evaluation of age requires consideration of chronological, biological, psychological, and social age.

Developmental Issues

- The nature-nurture issue focuses on the extent to which development is mainly influenced by nature (biological inheritance) or nurture (experience). The stability-change issue focuses on the degree to which we become older renditions of our early experience or develop into someone different from who we were earlier in development. A special aspect of the stability-change issue is the extent to which development is determined by early versus later experiences. Developmentalists describe development as continuous (gradual, a cumulative change) or as discontinuous (abrupt, a sequence of stages). Most developmentalists recognize that extreme positions on the nature-nurture, stability-change, and continuity-discontinuity issues are unwise. Despite this consensus, there is still spirited debate on these issues.

Theories of Development

LG3 Describe the main theories of human development

Psychoanalytic Theories

- The scientific method involves four main steps: (1) conceptualize a problem, (2) collect data, (3) analyze data, and (4) draw conclusions. Theory is often involved in conceptualizing a problem. A theory is an interrelated, coherent set of ideas that helps to explain phenomena and to make predictions. Hypotheses are specific assertions and predictions, often derived from theory, that can be tested. According to psychoanalytic theories, development primarily depends on the unconscious mind and is heavily couched in emotion. Freud also argued that individuals go through five psychosexual stages. Erikson's theory emphasizes eight psychosocial stages of development: trust versus mistrust, autonomy versus shame and doubt, initiative versus guilt, industry versus inferiority, identity versus identity confusion, intimacy versus isolation, generativity versus stagnation, and integrity versus despair. Contributions of psychoanalytic theories include an emphasis on a developmental framework, family relationships, and unconscious aspects of the mind. Criticisms include a lack of scientific support for psychoanalytic theories, too much emphasis on sexual underpinnings, and an image of people that is too negative.

Cognitive Theories

- Three main cognitive theories are Piaget's, Vygotsky's, and information processing. Cognitive theories emphasize thinking, reasoning, language, and other cognitive processes. Piaget proposed a cognitive developmental theory in which children use their cognition to adapt to their world. In Piaget's theory, children go through four cognitive stages: sensorimotor, preoperational, concrete operational, and formal operational. Vygotsky's sociocultural cognitive theory emphasizes how culture and social interaction guide cognitive development. The information-processing approach emphasizes that individuals manipulate information, monitor it, and strategize about it. Contributions of cognitive theories include an emphasis on the active construction of understanding and developmental changes in thinking. Criticisms include giving too little attention to individual variations and underrating the unconscious aspects of thought.

Behavioral and Social Cognitive Theories

- Two main behavioral and social cognitive theories are Skinner's operant conditioning and social cognitive theory. In Skinner's operant conditioning, the consequences of a behavior produce changes in the probability of the behavior's occurrence. In social cognitive theory, observational learning is a key aspect of life-span development. Bandura emphasizes reciprocal interactions among person/cognition, behavior, and environment. Contributions of the behavioral and social cognitive theories include an emphasis on scientific research, a focus on environmental factors, and recognition of the importance of person and cognitive factors in social cognitive theory. Criticisms include inadequate attention to developmental changes, too much emphasis on environmental determinants, and (in Skinner's behaviorism) too little attention to cognition.

Ethological Theory

- Ethology stresses that behavior is strongly influenced by biology, is tied to evolution, and is characterized by critical or sensitive periods. Contributions of ethological theory include its focus on the biological and evolutionary basis of development. Criticisms include inflexibility in the concepts of critical and sensitive periods.

Ecological Theory

- Ecological theory emphasizes environmental contexts. Bronfenbrenner's environmental systems view of development proposes five environmental systems: microsystem, mesosystem, exosystem, macrosystem, and chronosystem. Contributions of the theory include a systematic examination of macro- and microdimensions of environmental systems and consideration of sociohistorical influences. Criticisms include inadequate attention to biological factors, as well as a lack of emphasis on cognitive factors.

An Eclectic Orientation

- An eclectic orientation does not follow any one theoretical approach but rather selects from each theory whatever is considered the best in it.

Research in Life-Span Development

LG4 Explain how research on life-span development is conducted

Methods for Collecting Data

- Methods for collecting data about life-span development include observation (in a laboratory or a naturalistic setting), survey (questionnaire) or interview, standardized test, case study, and physiological measures.

Research Designs

- Three main research designs are descriptive, correlational, and experimental. Descriptive research aims to observe and record behavior. The goal of correlational research is to describe the strength of the relationship between two or more events or characteristics. Experimental research involves conducting an experiment, which can determine cause and effect. An independent variable is the manipulated, influential, experimental factor. A dependent variable is a factor that can change in an experiment, in response to changes in the independent variable. Experiments can involve one or more experimental groups and control groups. In random assignment, researchers assign participants to experimental and control groups by chance.

Time Span of Research

- When researchers decide about the time span of their research, they can conduct cross-sectional or longitudinal studies. Life-span researchers are especially concerned about cohort effects.

Conducting Ethical Research

- Researchers' ethical responsibilities include seeking participants' informed consent, ensuring their confidentiality, debriefing them about the purpose and potential personal consequences of participating, and avoiding unnecessary deception of participants.

Minimizing Bias

- Researchers need to guard against gender, cultural, and ethnic bias in research. Every effort should be made to make research equitable for both females and males. Individuals from varied ethnic backgrounds need to be included as participants in life-span research, and overgeneralization about diverse members within a group must be avoided.

key terms

key people

appendix

Careers in Life-Span Development

The field of life-span development offers an amazing breadth of careers that can provide extremely satisfying work. College and university professors teach courses in many areas of life-span development. Teachers impart knowledge, understanding, and skills to children and adolescents. Counselors, clinical psychologists, nurses, and physicians help people of different ages to cope more effectively with their lives and improve their well-being.

These and many other careers related to life-span development offer numerous rewards. By working in the field of life-span development, you can help people to improve their lives, understand yourself and others better, possibly advance the state of knowledge in the field, and have an enjoyable time while you are doing these things. Many careers in life-span development pay reasonably well. For example, psychologists earn well above the median salary in the United States.

If you are considering a career in life-span development, would you prefer to work with infants? children? adolescents? older adults? As you go through this term, try to spend some time with people of different ages. Observe their behavior. Talk with them about their lives. Think about whether you would like to help people of this age in your life's work.

In addition, to find out about careers in life-span development, you might talk with people who work in various jobs. For example, if you have some interest in becoming a school counselor, you can call a school, ask to speak with a counselor, and set up an appointment to discuss the counselor's career and work. If you have an interest in becoming a nurse, call the nursing department at a hospital and set up an appointment to speak with the nursing coordinator about a nursing career.

Another way of exploring careers in life-span development is to work in a related job while you are in college. Many colleges and universities offer internships or other work experiences for students who major in specific fields. Course credit or pay is given for some of these jobs. Take advantage of these opportunities. They can help you decide if this is the right career for you, and they can help you get into graduate school if you decide you want to go.

An advanced degree is not absolutely necessary for some careers in life-span development, but usually you can considerably expand your opportunities (and income) by obtaining a graduate degree. If you think you might want to go to graduate school, talk with one or more professors about your interests, maintain a high grade-point average, take appropriate courses, and realize that you likely will need to take the Graduate Record Examination (GRE) at some point.

Upcoming sections of the text will profile a number of careers in four areas: education/research; clinical/counseling; medical/nursing/physical development; and families/relationships. These are not the only career options in life-span development, but the profiles should give you an idea of the range of opportunities available. The profile for each career will describe the work and address the amount of education required and the nature of the training. The Web site for this book gives more detailed information about these careers in life-span development.

Education/Research

Numerous careers in life-span development involve education or research. The opportunities range from college professor to child-care director to school psychologist.

College/University Professor

Professors teach courses in life-span development at many types of institutions, including research universities with master's or Ph.D. programs in life-span development, four-year colleges with no graduate programs, and community colleges. The courses in life-span development are offered in many different programs and schools, including psychology, education, nursing, child and family studies, social work, and medicine. In addition to teaching at the undergraduate or graduate level (or both), professors may conduct research, advise students or direct their research, and serve on college or university committees. Research is part of a professor's job description at most universities with master's and Ph.D. programs, but some college professors do not conduct research and focus instead on teaching.

Teaching life-span development at a college or university almost always requires a Ph.D. or master's degree. Obtaining a Ph.D. usually takes four to six years of graduate work; a master's degree requires approximately two years. The training involves taking graduate courses, learning to conduct research, and attending and presenting papers at professional meetings. Many graduate students work as teaching or research assistants for professors in an apprenticeship relationship that helps them to become competent teachers and researchers.

Read a profile of a college professor on page 384 in Chapter 12.'

Researcher

Some individuals in the field of life-span development work in research positions. They might work for a university, a government agency such as the National Institute of Mental Health, or private industry. They generate research ideas, plan studies, carry out the research, and usually attempt to publish the research in a scientific journal. A researcher often works in collaboration with other researchers. One researcher might spend much of his or her time in a laboratory; another researcher might work out in the field, such as in schools, hospitals, and so on. Most researchers in life-span development have either a master's degree or Ph.D.

Elementary or Secondary School Teacher

Elementary and secondary school teachers teach one or more subject areas, prepare curriculum, give tests, assign grades, monitor students' progress, conduct parent-teacher conferences, and attend workshops. Becoming an elementary or secondary school teacher requires a minimum of an undergraduate degree. The training involves taking a wide range of courses with a major or concentration in education as well as completion of supervised practice teaching.

Exceptional Children (Special Education) Teacher

Teachers of exceptional children spend concentrated time with children who have a disability such as attention deficit hyperactivity disorder (ADHD), mental retardation, or cerebral palsy,

connecting with careers

Valerie Pang, Professor of Teacher Education

Valerie Pang is a professor of teacher education at San Diego State University and formerly was an elementary school teacher. Like Dr. Pang, many professors of teacher education have a doctorate and have experience in teaching at the elementary or secondary school level.

Pang earned a doctorate at the University of Washington. She has received a Multicultural Educator Award from the National Association of Multicultural Education for her work on culture and equity. She also was given the Distinguished Scholar Award from the American Educational Research Association's Committee on the Role and Status of Minorities in Education.

Pang (2005) believes that competent teachers need to

- Recognize the power and complexity of cultural influences on students.
- Be sensitive to whether their expectations for students are culturally biased.
- Evaluate whether they are doing a good job of seeing life from the perspective of students who come from different cultures.

Valerie Pang is a professor in the School of Education of San Diego State University and formerly an elementary school teacher. Valerie believes it is important for teachers to create a caring classroom that affirms all students.

or they work with children who are gifted. Usually some of their work occurs outside the students' regular classroom and some of it inside the classroom. They work closely with the student's regular classroom teacher and parents to create the best educational program for the student. Teachers of exceptional children often continue their education after obtaining their undergraduate degree and attain a master's degree.

Early Education Educator

Early childhood educators work on college faculties and usually teach in community colleges that award an associate degree in early childhood education. They have a minimum of a master's degree in their field. In graduate school, they take courses in early childhood education and receive supervisory training in child-care or early childhood programs.

Preschool/Kindergarten Teacher

Preschool teachers teach mainly 4-year-old children, and kindergarten teachers primarily teach 5-year-old children. They usually have an undergraduate degree in education, specializing in early childhood education. State certification to become a preschool or kindergarten teacher usually is required.

Family and Consumer Science Educator

Family and consumer science educators may specialize in early childhood education or instruct middle and high school students about such matters as nutrition, interpersonal relationships, human sexuality, parenting, and human development. Hundreds of colleges and universities throughout the United States offer two- and four-year degree programs in family and consumer science. These programs usually require an internship. Additional education courses may be needed to obtain a teaching certificate. Some family and consumer educators go on to graduate school for further training, which provides a background for possible jobs in college teaching or research.

Read a profile of a family and consumer science educator on page 398 in Chapter 12.

Educational Psychologist

Educational psychologists most often teach in a college or university and conduct research in areas of educational psychology such as learning, motivation, classroom management, and assessment. They help train students for positions in educational psychology, school psychology, and teaching. Most educational psychologists have a doctorate in education,

which takes four to six years of graduate work.

Read a profile of an educational psychologist on page 36 in Chapter 1.

School Psychologist

School psychologists focus on improving the psychological and intellectual well-being of elementary, middle/junior, and high school students. They give psychological tests, interview students and their parents, consult with teachers, and may provide counseling to students and their families. They may work in a centralized office in a school district or in one or more schools.

School psychologists usually have a master's or doctoral degree in school psychology. In graduate school, they take courses in counseling, assessment, learning, and other areas of education and psychology.

Gerontologist

Gerontologists usually conduct research in some branch of the federal or state government. They specialize in the study of aging with a particular focus on government programs for older adults, social policy, and delivery of services to older adults. In their research, gerontologists define problems to be studied, collect data, interpret the results, and make recommendations for social policy. Most gerontologists have a master's or doctoral degree and have taken a concentration of coursework in adult development and aging.

Clinical/Counseling

A wide variety of clinical and counseling jobs are linked with life-span development. These range from child clinical psychologist to adolescent drug counselor to geriatric psychiatrist.

Clinical Psychologist

Clinical psychologists seek to help people with psychological problems. They work in a variety of settings, including colleges and universities, clinics, medical schools, and private practice. Some clinical psychologists only conduct psychotherapy; others do psychological assessment and psychotherapy; some also do research. Clinical psychologists may specialize in a particular age group, such as children (child clinical psychologist) or older adults (often referred to as a geropsychologist).

Clinical psychologists have either a Ph.D. (which involves clinical and research training) or a Psy.D. degree (which only involves clinical training). This graduate training usually takes five to seven years and includes courses in clinical psychology and a one-year supervised internship in an accredited setting toward the end of the training. Many geropsychologists pursue a year or two of postdoctoral training. Most states require clinical psychologists to pass a test in order to become licensed in the state and to call themselves clinical psychologists.

Psychiatrist

Psychiatrists obtain a medical degree and then do a residency in psychiatry. Medical school takes approximately four years and the psychiatry residency another three to four years. Unlike most psychologists (who do not go to medical school), psychiatrists can administer drugs to clients. (Recently, several states have given clinical psychologists the right to prescribe drugs.)

Like clinical psychologists, psychiatrists might specialize in working with children (child psychiatry) or with older adults (geriatric psychiatry). Psychiatrists might work in medical schools in teaching and research roles, in medical clinics or hospitals, or in private practice. In addition to administering drugs to help improve the lives of people with psychological problems, psychiatrists also may conduct psychotherapy.

Counseling Psychologist

Counseling psychologists work in the same settings as clinical psychologists and may do psychotherapy, teach, or conduct research. Many counseling psychologists do not do therapy with individuals who have severe mental disorders, such as schizophrenia.

Counseling psychologists go through much the same training as clinical psychologists, although in a graduate program in counseling rather than clinical psychology. Counseling psychologists have either a master's degree or a doctoral degree. They also must go through a licensing procedure. One type of master's degree in counseling leads to the designation of licensed professional counselor.

School Counselor

School counselors help students to cope with adjustment problems, identify their abilities and interests, develop academic plans, and explore career options. The focus of the job depends on the age of the children. High school counselors advise students about vocational and technical training and admissions requirements for college, as well as about taking entrance exams, applying for financial aid, and choosing a major. Elementary school counselors mainly counsel students about social and personal problems. They may observe children in the classroom and at play as part of their work.

School counselors may work with students individually, in small groups, or even in a classroom. They often consult with parents, teachers, and school administrators when trying to help students. School counselors usually have a master's degree in counseling.

Read a profile of a school counselor on page 358 in Chapter 11.

Career Counselor

Career counselors help individuals to identify their best career options and guide them in applying for jobs. They may work in private industry or at a college or university. They usually interview individuals and give them vocational and/or psychological tests to identify appropriate careers that fit their interests and abilities. Sometimes they help individuals to create résumés or conduct mock interviews to help them feel comfortable in a job interview. They might arrange and promote job fairs or other recruiting events to help individuals obtain jobs.

Read a profile of a career counselor on page 548 in Chapter 16.

Rehabilitation Counselor

Rehabilitation counselors work with individuals to identify career options, develop adjustment and coping skills to maximize independence, and resolve problems created by a disability. A master's degree in rehabilitation counseling or guidance or counseling psychology is generally considered the minimum education requirement.

Social Worker

Many social workers are involved in helping people with social or economic problems. They may investigate, evaluate, and attempt to rectify reported cases of abuse, neglect, endangerment, or domestic disputes. They may intervene in families and provide counseling and referral services to individuals and families. Some social workers specialize in a certain area. For example, a medical social worker might coordinate support services provided to people with a long-term disability; family-care social workers often work with families with children or an older adult who needs support services. Social workers often work for publicly funded agencies at the city, state, or national level, although increasingly they work in the private sector in areas such as drug rehabilitation and family counseling.

Social workers have a minimum of an undergraduate degree from a school of social work that includes coursework in sociology and psychology. Some social workers also have a master's or doctoral degree. For example, medical social workers have a master's degree in social work (M.S.W.) and complete graduate coursework and supervised clinical experiences in medical settings.

Drug Counselor

Drug counselors provide counseling to individuals with drug-abuse problems. Some drug counselors specialize in working with adolescents or older adults. They may work on an individual basis with a substance abuser or conduct group therapy. They may work in private practice, with a state or federal government agency, with a company, or in a hospital.

At a minimum, drug counselors complete an associate's or certificate program. Many have an undergraduate degree in substance-abuse counseling, and some have master's and doctoral degrees. Most states provide a certification procedure for obtaining a license to practice drug counseling.

Medical/Nursing/Physical Development

This third main area of careers in life-span development includes a wide range of careers in the medical and nursing areas, as well as jobs that pertain to improving some aspect of a person's physical development.

Obstetrician/Gynecologist

An obstetrician/gynecologist prescribes prenatal and postnatal care, performs deliveries in maternity cases, and treats diseases and

Katherine Duchen Smith, Nurse and Child-Care Health Consultant

Katherine Duchen Smith has a master's degree in nursing and works as a child-care health consultant. She lives in Fort Collins, Colorado, and in 2004 was appointed as the public relations chair of the National Association of Pediatric Nurse Practitioners (NAPNAP), which has more than 6,000 members.

Smith provides health consultation and educational services to child-care centers, private schools, and hospitals. She also teaches in the Regis University Family Nurse Practitioner Program. Smith developed an interest in outreach and public-relations activities during her five-year term as a board member for the Fort Collins Poudre Valley Hospital System. Later, she became the organization's outreach consultant.

As child-care health consultants, nurses might provide telephone consultation and link children, families, or staff with primary care providers. In underserved areas, they might also be asked to administer immunizations, help chronically ill children access specialty care, or develop a comprehensive health promotion or injury prevention program for caregivers and families.

Katherine Duchen Smith (*left*), nurse and child-care health consultant, at a child-care center where she is a consultant.

---

injuries of the female reproductive system. Becoming an obstetrician/gynecologist requires a medical degree plus three to five years of residency in obstetrics/gynecology. Obstetricians may work in private practice, a medical clinic, a hospital, or a medical school.

Pediatrician

A pediatrician monitors infants' and children's health, works to prevent disease or injury, helps children attain optimal health, and treats children with health problems. Pediatricians have earned a medical degree and completed a three- to five-year residency in pediatrics.

Pediatricians may work in private practice, a medical clinic, a hospital, or a medical school. Many pediatricians on the faculty of medical schools also teach and conduct research on children's health and diseases.

Geriatric Physician

Geriatric physicians diagnose medical problems of older adults, evaluate treatment options, and make recommendations for nursing care or other arrangements. They have a medical degree and have specialized in geriatric medicine by doing a three- to five-year residency. Like other doctors, geriatric physicians may work in private practice, a medical clinic,

a hospital, or a medical school. Those in medical school settings may not only treat older adults but also teach future physicians and conduct research.

Neonatal Nurse

Neonatal nurses deliver care to newborn infants. They may work with infants born under normal circumstances or premature and critically ill neonates. A minimum of an undergraduate degree in nursing with a specialization in the newborn is required. This training involves coursework in nursing and the biological sciences, as well as supervised clinical experiences.

Nurse-Midwife

A nurse-midwife formulates and provides comprehensive care to expectant mothers as they prepare to give birth, guides them through the birth process, and cares for them after the birth. The nurse-midwife also may provide care to the newborn, counsel parents on the infant's development and parenting, and provide guidance about health practices. Becoming a nurse-midwife generally requires an undergraduate degree from a school of nursing. A nurse-midwife most often works in a hospital setting.

Pediatric Nurse

Pediatric nurses monitor infants' and children's health, work to prevent disease or injury, and help children attain optimal health. They may work in hospitals, in schools of nursing, or with pediatricians in private practice or at a medical clinic.

Pediatric nurses have a degree in nursing that takes two to five years to complete. They take courses in biological sciences, nursing care, and pediatrics, usually in a school of nursing. They also undergo supervised clinical experiences in medical settings. Some pediatric nurses go on to earn a master's or doctoral degree in pediatric nursing.

Read a profile of a pediatric nurse on page 133 in Chapter 4.

Geriatric Nurse

Geriatric nurses seek to prevent or intervene in the chronic or acute health problems of older adults. They may work in hospitals, nursing homes, schools of nursing, or with geriatric medical specialists or psychiatrists in a medical clinic or in private practice.

Like pediatric nurses, geriatric nurses take courses in a school of nursing and obtain a degree in nursing, which takes from two to five years. They complete courses in biological sciences, nursing care, and mental health as well as supervised clinical training in geriatric settings. They also may obtain a master's or doctoral degree in their specialty.

Read a profile of a geriatric nurse on page 98 in Chapter 3.

Physical Therapist

Physical therapists work with individuals who have a physical problem caused by disease or injury, helping them function as competently as possible. They may consult with other professionals and coordinate services for the individual. Many physical therapists work with people of all ages, although some specialize in working with a specific age group, such as children or older adults.

Physical therapists usually have an undergraduate degree in physical therapy and are licensed by a state. They take courses and experience supervised training in physical therapy.

Occupational Therapist

Occupational therapists initiate the evaluation of clients with various impairments and manage their treatment. They help people regain, develop, and build skills that are important for independent functioning, health, well-being, security, and happiness.

An occupational therapist (OTR) may have an associate, bachelor's, master's, and/or doctoral degree with education ranging from two to six years. Training includes occupational therapy courses in a specialized program. National certification is required, and licensing/registration is mandatory in some states.

Therapeutic/Recreation Therapist

Therapeutic/recreation therapists maintain or improve the quality of life for people with special needs through intervention, leisure education, and recreation. They work in hospitals, rehabilitation centers, local government agencies, and at-risk youth programs, as well as other settings. Becoming a therapeutic/recreation therapist requires an undergraduate degree with coursework in leisure studies and a concentration in therapeutic recreation. National certification is usually required. Coursework in anatomy, special education, and psychology is beneficial.

Audiologist

Audiologists assess and identify the presence and severity of hearing loss, as well as problems in balance. They may work in a medical clinic, with a physician in private practice, in a hospital, or in a medical school.

An audiologist completes coursework and supervised training to earn a minimum of an undergraduate degree in hearing science. Some audiologists also go on to obtain a master's or doctoral degree.

Speech Therapist

Speech therapists identify, assess, and treat speech and language problems. They may work with physicians, psychologists, social workers, and other health-care professionals in a team approach to help individuals with physical or psychological problems that involve speech and language. Some speech therapists specialize in working with individuals of a particular age or people with a particular type of speech disorder.

Speech therapists have a minimum of an undergraduate degree in speech and hearing science or in a type of communications disorder. They may work in private practice, hospitals and medical schools, and government agencies.

Genetic Counselor

Genetic counselors identify and counsel families at risk for genetic disorders. They work as members of a health-care team, providing information and support to families who have members who have genetic defects or disorders or are at risk for a variety of inherited conditions. They also serve as educators and resource people for other health-care professionals and the public. Almost one-half work in university medical centers; one-fourth work in private hospital settings.

Genetic counselors have specialized graduate degrees and experience in medical genetics and counseling. Most enter the field after undergraduate study majoring in such disciplines as biology, genetics, psychology, nursing, public health, or social work.

Read a profile of a genetic counselor on page 59 in Chapter 2.

Families/Relationships

A number of careers and jobs related to lifespan development focus on working with families and relationship problems. These occupations range from home health aide to marriage and family therapist.

Home Health Aide

A home health aide provides services to older adults in the older adults' homes, helping them with basic self-care tasks. No higher education is required for this position. There is brief training by an agency.

Child Welfare Worker

Child protective services in each state employ child welfare workers. They protect children's rights, evaluate any maltreatment, and may have children removed from their homes if necessary. A child social worker has a minimum of an undergraduate degree in social work.

Child Life Specialist

Child life specialists work with children and their families when the child needs to be hospitalized. They monitor the child's activities, seek to reduce the child's stress, and help the child to cope and to enjoy the hospital experience as much as possible. Child life specialists may provide parent education and develop individualized treatment plans based on an assessment of the child's development, temperament, medical plan, and available social supports. Child life specialists have an undergraduate degree. They have taken courses in child development and education and usually have completed additional courses in a child life program.

Marriage and Family Therapist

Marriage and family therapists work on the principle that many individuals who have psychological problems benefit when psychotherapy is provided in the context of a marital or family relationship. Marriage and family therapists may provide marital therapy, couple therapy to individuals in a relationship who are not married, and family therapy to two or more members of a family.

Marriage and family therapists have a master's or a doctoral degree. They complete a training program in graduate school similar to a clinical psychologist's but with a focus on marital and family relationships. In most states, it is necessary to go through a licensing procedure to practice marital and family therapy.

Read a profile of a marriage and family therapist on page 465 in Chapter 14.

Babies are such a nice way to start people.

—DON HEROLD
American Writer, 20th Century

Biological Processes, Physical Development, and Health

The rhythm and meaning of life involve biological foundations. How, from so simple a beginning, can endless forms develop and grow and mature? What was this organism, what is it, and what will it be? In Section 2, you will read and study four chapters: "Biological Beginnings" (Chapter 2), "Physical Development and Biological Aging" (Chapter 3), "Health" (Chapter 4), and "Motor, Sensory, and Perceptual Development" (Chapter 5).

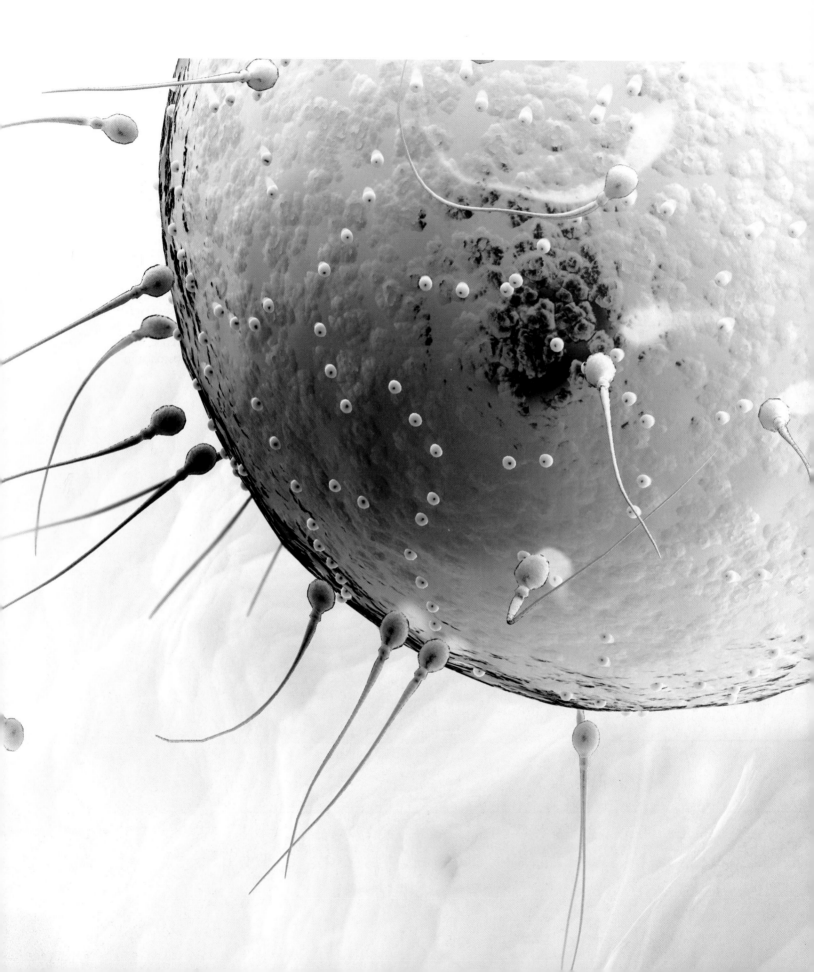

chapter 2 BIOLOGICAL BEGINNINGS

preview

Organisms are not like billiard balls, moved by simple external forces to predictable positions on life's table. Environmental experiences and biological foundations work together to make us who we are. In this chapter, we explore life's biological beginnings and experiences, charting growth from conception through the prenatal period and examining the birth process itself. We will begin our exploration of biological foundations by considering possible evolutionary influences.

The Evolutionary Perspective

 LG1 Discuss the evolutionary perspective on life-span development

- Natural Selection and Adaptive Behavior
- Evolutionary Psychology

From the perspective of evolutionary time, humans are relative newcomers to Earth. As our earliest ancestors left the forest to feed on the savannahs and then to form hunting societies on the open plains, their minds and behaviors changed, and humans eventually became the dominant species on Earth. How did this evolution come about?

NATURAL SELECTION AND ADAPTIVE BEHAVIOR

Charles Darwin (1859) described *natural selection* as the evolutionary process by which those individuals of a species that are best *adapted* to their environment are the ones that are most likely to survive and reproduce. He reasoned that an intense, constant struggle for food, water, and resources must occur among the young of each generation, because many of them do not survive. Those that do survive and reproduce pass on their characteristics to the next generation. Darwin concluded that these survivors are better adapted to their world than are the nonsurvivors (Brooker, 2011; Johnson & Losos, 2010). The best-adapted individuals survive and leave the most offspring. Over the course of many generations, organisms with the characteristics needed for survival make up an increased percentage of the population (Mader, 2011).

EVOLUTIONARY PSYCHOLOGY

Although Darwin introduced the theory of evolution by natural selection in 1859, his ideas have only recently become a popular framework for explaining behavior. Psychology's newest approach, **evolutionary psychology,** emphasizes the importance of adaptation, reproduction, and "survival of the fittest" in shaping behavior. ("Fit" in this sense refers to the ability to bear offspring that survive long enough to bear offspring of their own.) In this view, natural selection favors behaviors that increase reproductive success—that is, the ability to pass your genes to the next generation (Cosmides, 2011; Johnson, 2012).

David Buss (2008, 2012) argues that just as evolution shapes our physical features, such as body shape and height, it also pervasively influences how we make decisions, how aggressive we are, our fears, and our mating patterns. For example, assume that our ancestors were hunters and gatherers on the plains and that men did most of the hunting and women stayed close to home, gathering seeds and plants for food. If you had to walk some distance from your home in an effort to track and slay a fleeing animal, you would need not only certain physical traits but also the ability to perform certain types of spatial thinking. Men born with these

How does the attachment of this Vietnamese baby to its mother reflect the evolutionary process of adaptive behavior?

evolutionary psychology A branch of psychology that emphasizes the importance of adaptation, reproduction, and "survival of the fittest" in shaping behavior.

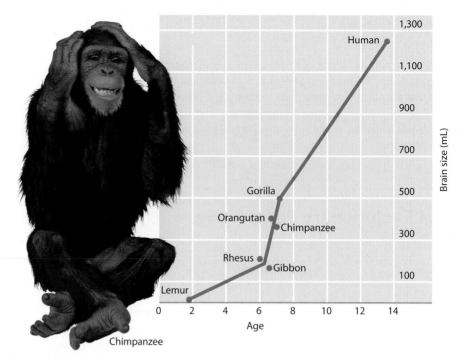

FIGURE **2.1**

THE BRAIN SIZES OF VARIOUS PRIMATES AND HUMANS IN RELATION TO THE LENGTH OF THE CHILDHOOD PERIOD. Compared with other primates, humans have both a larger brain and a longer childhood period. *What conclusions can you draw from the relationship indicated by this graph?*

Children in all cultures are interested in the tools that adults in their cultures use. For example, this 11-month-old boy from the Efe culture in the Democratic Republic of the Congo in Africa is trying to cut a papaya with an *apopau* (a smaller version of a machete). *Might the infant's behavior be evolutionary-based or be due to both biological and environmental conditions?*

developmental **connection**

Life-Span Perspective. Baltes described eight main characteristics of the life-span perspective. Chapter 1, p. 6

traits would be more likely than men without them to survive, to bring home lots of food, and to be considered attractive mates—and thus to reproduce and pass on these characteristics to their children. In other words, these traits would provide a reproductive advantage for males, and over many generations, men with good spatial thinking skills might become more numerous in the population. Critics point out that this scenario might or might not have actually happened.

Evolutionary Developmental Psychology   There is growing interest in using the concepts of evolutionary psychology to understand human development (Bjorklund, 2012; Bjorklund & Pellegrini, 2011). Following are some ideas proposed by evolutionary developmental psychologists (Bjorklund & Pellegrini, 2002).

One important concept is that an extended childhood period evolved because humans require time to develop a large brain and learn the complexity of human societies. Humans take longer to become reproductively mature than any other mammal (see Figure 2.1). During this extended childhood period, they develop a large brain and acquire the experiences needed to become competent adults in a complex society.

Evolved characteristics are not always adaptive in contemporary society. Some behaviors that were adaptive for our prehistoric ancestors may not serve us well today. For example, the food-scarce environment of our ancestors likely led to humans' propensity to gorge when food is available and to crave high-caloric foods, a trait that might lead to an epidemic of obesity when food is plentiful.

Evolution and Life-Span Development   In evolutionary theory, what matters is that individuals live long enough to reproduce and pass on their characteristics (Brooker, 2011; Goodenough & McGuire, 2012). So why do humans live so long after reproduction? Perhaps evolution favored longevity because having older people around improves the survival rates of babies. Possibly having grandparents alive to care for the young while parents were out hunting and gathering food created an evolutionary advantage.

According to life-span developmentalist Paul Baltes (2003), the benefits conferred by evolutionary selection decrease with age. Natural selection has not weeded out many harmful conditions and nonadaptive characteristics that appear among older adults. Why? Natural selection operates primarily on characteristics that are tied to reproductive fitness, which extends through the earlier part of adulthood. Thus, says Baltes, selection primarily operates during the first half of life.

As an example, consider Alzheimer disease, an irreversible brain disorder characterized by gradual deterioration. This disease typically does not appear until age 70 or later. If it were a disease that struck 20-year-olds, perhaps natural selection would have eliminated it eons ago.

Thus, unaided by evolutionary pressures against nonadaptive conditions, we suffer the aches, pains, and infirmities of aging. And, as the benefits of evolutionary selection decrease with age, argues Baltes, the need for culture increases (see Figure 2.2). That is, as older adults weaken biologically, they need culture-based resources such as cognitive skills, literacy, medical technology, and social support. For example, older adults may need help and training from other people to maintain their cognitive skills (Park & Juang, 2010; Reuter-Lorenz & Park, 2011).

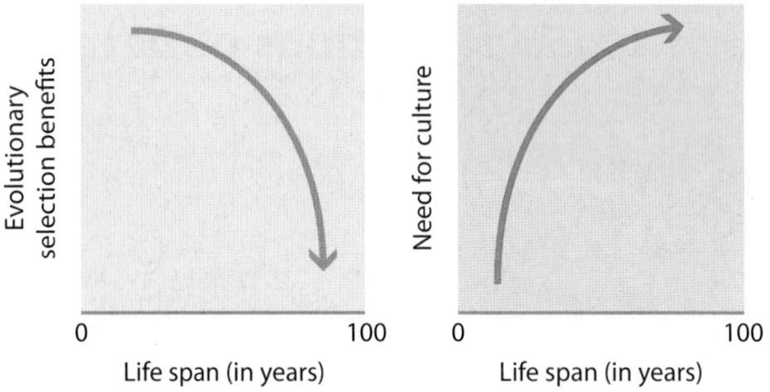

FIGURE 2.2

BALTES' VIEW OF EVOLUTION AND CULTURE ACROSS THE LIFE SPAN. Benefits derived from evolutionary selection decrease as we age, whereas the need for culture increases with age.

Evaluating Evolutionary Psychology   Common criticisms are that much of evolutionary psychology cannot be tested scientifically and that it relies mainly on post-hoc (after the fact) explanations. Another criticism was offered by Albert Bandura (1998), whose social cognitive theory was described in Chapter 1. He acknowledges the influence of evolution on human adaptation but rejects what he calls "one-sided evolutionism," which views social behavior as the product of evolved biology. An alternative is a *bidirectional* view, in which environmental and biological conditions influence each other. In this view, evolutionary pressures created changes in biological structures that allowed the use of tools, which enabled our ancestors to manipulate the environment, constructing new environmental conditions. In turn, environmental innovations produced new selection pressures that led to the evolution of specialized biological systems for consciousness, thought, and language.

In other words, evolution has given us body structures and biological potentialities, but it does not dictate behavior. People have used their biological capacities to produce diverse cultures—aggressive and peaceful; egalitarian and autocratic.

Review Connect Reflect

LG1 Discuss the evolutionary perspective on life-span development

Review

- How can natural selection and adaptive behavior be defined?
- What is evolutionary psychology? What basic ideas about human development are proposed by evolutionary psychologists? How might evolutionary influences have different effects at different points in the life span? How can evolutionary psychology be evaluated?

Connect

- In the section on ethological theory in the preceding chapter, you learned about critical time periods. How does the concept of critical period relate to what you learned about older adults and aging in this section?

Reflect *Your Own Personal Journey of Life*

- Which is more persuasive to you as an explanation of your development: the views of evolutionary psychologists or those of their critics? Why?

Genetic Foundations of Development

LG2 Describe what genes are and how they influence human development

The Collaborative Gene

Genes and Chromosomes

Genetic Principles

Chromosomal and Gene-Linked Abnormalities

Genetic influences on behavior evolved over time and across many species. Our many traits and characteristics that are genetically influenced have a long evolutionary history that is retained in our DNA. In other words, our DNA is not just inherited from our parents; it's also what we've inherited as a species from the species that came before us. Let's take a closer look at DNA and its role in human development.

How are characteristics that suit a species for survival transmitted from one generation to the next? Darwin did not know because genes and the principles of genetics had not yet been discovered. Each of us carries a "genetic code" that we inherited from our parents. Because a fertilized egg carries this human code, a fertilized human egg cannot grow into an egret, eagle, or elephant.

THE COLLABORATIVE GENE

Each of us began life as a single cell weighing about one twenty-millionth of an ounce! This tiny piece of matter housed our entire genetic code—instructions that orchestrated growth from that single cell to a person made of trillions of cells, each containing a replica of the original code. That code is carried by our genes. What are genes and what do they do? For the answer, we need to look into our cells.

The nucleus of each human cell contains **chromosomes,** which are threadlike structures made up of deoxyribonucleic acid, or DNA. **DNA** is a complex molecule that has a double helix shape, like a spiral staircase, and it contains genetic information. **Genes,** the units of hereditary information, are short segments of DNA, as you can see in Figure 2.3. They direct cells to reproduce themselves and to assemble proteins. Proteins, in turn, are the building blocks of cells as well as the regulators that direct the body's processes (Raven, 2011).

Each gene has its own location, its own designated place on a particular chromosome. Today, there is a great deal of enthusiasm about efforts to discover the

---

![arrow]

developmental connection

Biological Processes. A current biological theory of aging emphasizes that changes in the tips of chromosomes play a key role in aging. Chapter 3, p. 117

chromosomes Threadlike structures made up of deoxyribonucleic acid, or DNA.

DNA A complex molecule that has a double helix shape and contains genetic information.

genes Units of hereditary information composed of DNA. Genes direct cells to reproduce themselves and assemble proteins that direct body processes.

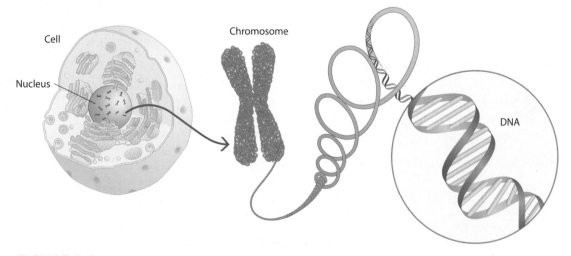

Cell

Chromosome

Nucleus

DNA

FIGURE **2.3**

CELLS, CHROMOSOMES, DNA, AND GENES. (*Left*) The body contains trillions of cells. Each cell contains a central structure, the nucleus. (*Middle*) Chromosomes are threadlike structures located in the nucleus of the cell. Chromosomes are composed of DNA. (*Right*) DNA has the structure of a spiral staircase. A gene is a segment of DNA.

specific locations of genes that are linked to certain functions and to certain diseases (Starr, 2011). An important step in this direction was accomplished when the Human Genome Project completed a preliminary map of the human *genome*—the complete set of developmental instructions for creating proteins that initiate the making of a human organism (Antonarkis, 2009).

One of the big surprises of the Human Genome Project was a report indicating that humans have only about 30,000 genes (U.S. Department of Energy, 2001). More recently, the number of human genes has been revised further downward to approximately 20,500 (Ensembl Human, 2008). Scientists had thought that humans had as many as 100,000 or more genes. They had also maintained that each gene programmed just one protein. In fact, because humans appear to have far more proteins than they have genes, there cannot be a one-to-one correspondence between genes and proteins (Commoner, 2002). Each gene is not translated, in automaton-like fashion, into one and only one protein. A gene does not act independently, as developmental psychologist David Moore (2001) emphasized by titling his book *The Dependent Gene*.

Rather than being a group of independent genes, the human genome consists of many genes that collaborate both with each other and with nongenetic factors inside and outside the body. The collaboration operates at many points. For example, the cellular machinery mixes, matches, and links small pieces of DNA to reproduce the genes, and that machinery is influenced by what is going on around it.

Whether a gene is turned "on," working to assemble proteins, is also a matter of collaboration. The activity of genes (*genetic expression*) is affected by their environment (Gottlieb, 2007). For example, hormones that circulate in the blood make their way into the cell where they can turn genes "on" and "off." And the flow of hormones can be affected by environmental conditions, such as light, day length, nutrition, and behavior. Numerous studies have shown that external events outside of the original cell and the person, as well as events inside the cell, can excite or inhibit gene expression (Gottlieb, 2007). For example, one study revealed that an increase in the concentration of stress hormones such as cortisol produced a fivefold increase in DNA damage (Flint & others, 2007). A recent study also found that exposure to radiation changed the rate of DNA synthesis in cells (Lee & others, 2011).

GENES AND CHROMOSOMES

Genes are not only collaborative, they are enduring. How do genes manage to get passed from generation to generation and end up in all of the trillion cells in the body? The answer lies in three processes that happen at the cellular level: mitosis, meiosis, and fertilization.

Mitosis, Meiosis, and Fertilization All of the cells in your body, except the sperm and egg, have 46 chromosomes arranged in 23 pairs. These cells reproduce by a process called **mitosis**. During mitosis, the cell's nucleus—including the chromosomes—duplicates itself and the cell divides. Two new cells are formed, each containing the same DNA as the original cell, arranged in the same 23 pairs of chromosomes.

However, a different type of cell division—**meiosis**—forms eggs and sperm (or *gametes*). During meiosis, a cell of the testes (in men) or ovaries (in women) duplicates its chromosomes but then divides twice, thus forming four cells, each of which has only half of the genetic material of the parent cell (Johnson, 2012). By the end of meiosis, each egg or sperm has 23 *unpaired* chromosomes.

During **fertilization,** an egg and a sperm fuse to create a single cell, called a **zygote** (see Figure 2.4). In the zygote, the 23 unpaired chromosomes from the egg and the 23 unpaired chromosomes from the sperm combine to form one set of 23 paired chromosomes—one chromosome of each pair from the mother's egg and the other from the father's sperm. In this manner, each parent contributes half of the offspring's genetic material.

A positive result from the Human Genome Project. Shortly after Andrew Gobea was born, his cells were genetically altered to prevent his immune system from failing.

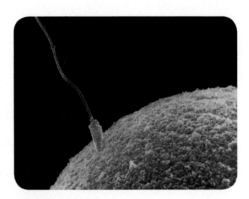

FIGURE **2.4**

A SINGLE SPERM PENETRATING AN EGG AT THE POINT OF FERTILIZATION

mitosis Cellular reproduction in which the cell's nucleus duplicates itself; two new cells are formed, each containing the same DNA as the original cell, arranged in the same 23 pairs of chromosomes.

meiosis A specialized form of cell division that occurs to form eggs and sperm (or gametes).

fertilization A stage in reproduction whereby an egg and a sperm fuse to create a single cell, called a zygote.

zygote A single cell formed through fertilization.

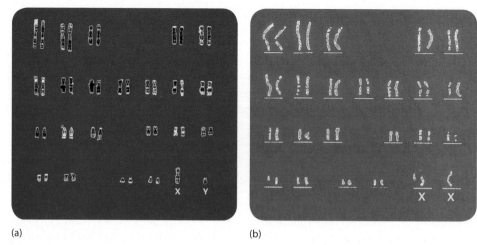

(a)   (b)

FIGURE **2.5**

THE GENETIC DIFFERENCE BETWEEN MALES AND FEMALES. Set (*a*) shows the chromosome structure of a male, and set (*b*) shows the chromosome structure of a female. The last pair of 23 pairs of chromosomes is in the bottom right box of each set. Notice that the Y chromosome of the male is smaller than the X chromosome of the female. To obtain this kind of chromosomal picture, a cell is removed from a person's body, usually from the inside of the mouth. The chromosomes are stained by chemical treatment, magnified extensively, and then photographed.

Figure 2.5 shows 23 paired chromosomes of a male and a female. The members of each pair of chromosomes are both similar and different: Each chromosome in the pair contains varying forms of the same genes, at the same location on the chromosome. A gene for hair color, for example, is located on both members of one pair of chromosomes, in the same location on each. However, one of those chromosomes might carry the gene for blond hair, and the other chromosome in the pair might carry the gene for brown hair.

Do you notice any obvious differences between the chromosomes of the male and the chromosomes of the female in Figure 2.5? The difference lies in the 23rd pair. Ordinarily, in females this pair consists of two chromosomes called X *chromosomes;* in males the 23rd pair consists of an X and a Y chromosome. The presence of a Y chromosome is what makes an individual male.

Sources of Variability   Combining the genes of two parents in offspring increases genetic variability in the population, which is valuable for a species because it provides more characteristics for natural selection to operate on (Raven, 2011). In fact, the human genetic process creates several important sources of variability.

First, the chromosomes in the zygote are not exact copies of those in the mother's ovaries and the father's testes. During the formation of the sperm and egg in meiosis, the members of each pair of chromosomes are separated, but which chromosome in the pair goes to the gamete is a matter of chance. In addition, before the pairs separate, pieces of the two chromosomes in each pair are exchanged, creating a new combination of genes on each chromosome. Thus, when chromosomes from the mother's egg and the father's sperm are brought together in the zygote, the result is a truly unique combination of genes (Goodenough & McGuire, 2012).

Another source of variability comes from DNA (Lewis, 2010). Chance, a mistake by cellular machinery, or damage from an environmental agent such as radiation may produce a *mutated gene*, which is a permanently altered segment of DNA.

Even when their genes are identical, however, people vary. The difference between genotypes and phenotypes helps us to understand this source of variability. All of a person's genetic material makes up his or her **genotype.**

There is increasing interest in studying *susceptibility genes* (Paquette & others, 2010), those that make an individual more vulnerable to specific diseases or

genotype All of a person's actual genetic material.

Calvin and Hobbes

by Bill Watterson

acceleration of aging, and *longevity genes,* those that make an individual less vulnerable to certain diseases and more likely to live to an older age (Bauer & others, 2010; Khabour & Barnawi, 2010); these are aspects of the individual's genotype.

However, not all of the genetic material is apparent in an individual's observed and measurable characteristics. A **phenotype** consists of observable characteristics, including physical characteristics (such as height, weight, and hair color) and psychological characteristics (such as personality and intelligence). For each genotype, a range of phenotypes can be expressed, providing another source of variability (Gottlieb, 2007). An individual can inherit the genetic potential to grow very large, for example, but good nutrition, among other things, will be essential to achieving that potential.

GENETIC PRINCIPLES

What determines how a genotype is expressed to create a particular phenotype? Much is still unknown about the answer to this question. However, a number of genetic principles have been discovered, such as those involving dominant-recessive genes, sex-linked genes, genetic imprinting, and polygenically determined characteristics.

Dominant-Recessive Genes   In some cases, one gene of a pair always exerts its effects; it is *dominant,* overriding the potential influence of the other gene, called the *recessive* gene. This is the principle of *dominant-recessive genes.* A recessive gene exerts its influence only if the two genes of a pair are both recessive. If you inherit a recessive gene for a trait from each of your parents, you will show the trait. If you inherit a recessive gene from only one parent, you may never know you carry the gene. Brown hair, farsightedness, and dimples rule over blond hair, nearsightedness, and freckles in the world of dominant-recessive genes.

Can two brown-haired parents have a blond-haired child? Yes, they can. Suppose that each parent has a dominant gene for brown hair and a recessive gene for blond hair. Since dominant genes override recessive genes, the parents have brown hair, but both are carriers of blondness and pass on their recessive genes for blond hair. With no dominant gene to override them, the recessive genes can make the child's hair blond.

Sex-Linked Genes   Most mutated genes are recessive. When a mutated gene is carried on the X chromosome, the result is called *X-linked inheritance.* It may have very different implications for males and females (Bermejo-Alvarez & others, 2011). Remember that males have only one X chromosome. Thus, if there is an altered, disease-creating gene on the X chromosome, males have no "backup" copy to counter the harmful gene and therefore may carry an X-linked disease. However, females have a second X chromosome, which is likely to be unchanged. As a result, they are not likely to have the X-linked disease. Thus, most individuals who have X-linked diseases are males. Females who have one changed copy of the X gene are known as

phenotype Observable and measurable characteristics of an individual, such as height, hair color, and intelligence.

"carriers," and they usually do not show any signs of the X-linked disease. Hemophilia and fragile X syndrome, which we discuss later in the chapter, are examples of X-linked inheritance diseases (Borjas & others, 2010).

Genetic Imprinting   *Genetic imprinting* occurs when genes have differing effects depending on whether they are inherited from the mother or the father. A chemical process "silences" one member of the gene pair. For example, as a result of imprinting, only the maternally derived copy of a gene might be active, while the paternally derived copy of the same gene is silenced—or vice versa. Only a small percentage of human genes appear to undergo imprinting, but it is a normal and important aspect of development (Wakeling, 2011). When imprinting goes awry, development is disturbed, as in the case of Beckwith-Wiedemann syndrome, a growth disorder, and Wilms tumor, a type of cancer (Barber & others, 2011; Choufani, Shuman, & Weksberg, 2011).

Polygenic Inheritance   Genetic transmission is usually more complex than the simple example we have examined thus far (Engler & Marillonnet, 2011). Few characteristics reflect the influence of only a single gene or pair of genes. Most are determined by the interaction of many different genes; they are said to be *polygenically determined*. Even a simple characteristic such as height, for example, reflects the interaction of many genes as well as the influence of the environment.

The term *gene-gene interaction* is increasingly used to describe studies that focus on the interdependence of two or more genes in influencing characteristics, behavior, diseases, and development (Li & others, 2008). For example, recent studies have documented gene-gene interaction in children's immune system functioning (Reijmerink & others, 2011), asthma (Gu & Zhao, 2011), cancer (Bapal & others, 2010), cardiovascular disease (Jylhava & others, 2009), and arthritis (Chen & others, 2010).

CHROMOSOMAL AND GENE-LINKED ABNORMALITIES

Sometimes abnormalities characterize the genetic process. Some of these abnormalities involve whole chromosomes that do not separate properly during meiosis. Other abnormalities are produced by harmful genes.

Chromosomal Abnormalities   When a gamete is formed, sometimes the sperm or ovum does not have its normal set of 23 chromosomes. The most notable examples involve Down syndrome and abnormalities of the sex chromosomes (see Figure 2.6).

Down Syndrome   An individual with **Down syndrome** has a round face, a flattened skull, an extra fold of skin over the eyelids, a protruding tongue, short limbs, and retardation of motor and mental abilities. The syndrome is caused by the presence of an extra copy of chromosome 21 (Peters & Petrill, 2011). It is not known why the extra chromosome is present, but the health of the male sperm or female ovum may be involved.

Down syndrome appears approximately once in every 700 live births. Women between the ages of 16 and 34 are less likely to give birth to a child with Down syndrome than are younger or older women. African American children are rarely born with Down syndrome.

Sex-Linked Chromosomal Abnormalities   Recall that a newborn normally has either an X and a Y chromosome, or two X chromosomes. Human embryos must

These athletes, several of whom have Down syndrome, are participating in a Special Olympics competition. Notice the distinctive facial features of the individuals with Down syndrome, such as a round face and a flattened skull. *What causes Down syndrome?*

Down syndrome A chromosomally transmitted form of mental retardation, caused by the presence of an extra copy of chromosome 21.

Name	Description	Treatment	Incidence
Down syndrome	An extra chromosome causes mild to severe retardation and physical abnormalities.	Surgery, early intervention, infant stimulation, and special learning programs	1 in 1,900 births at age 20 1 in 300 births at age 35 1 in 30 births at age 45
Klinefelter syndrome (XXY)	An extra X chromosome causes physical abnormalities.	Hormone therapy can be effective	1 in 600 male births
Fragile X syndrome	An abnormality in the X chromosome can cause mental retardation, learning disabilities, or short attention span.	Special education, speech and language therapy	More common in males than in females
Turner syndrome (XO)	A missing X chromosome in females can cause mental retardation and sexual underdevelopment.	Hormone therapy in childhood and puberty	1 in 2,500 female births
XYY syndrome	An extra Y chromosome can cause above-average height.	No special treatment required	1 in 1,000 male births

FIGURE 2.6

SOME CHROMOSOMAL ABNORMALITIES. The treatments for these abnormalities do not necessarily erase the problem but may improve the individual's adaptive behavior and quality of life.

possess at least one X chromosome to be viable. The most common sex-linked chromosomal abnormalities involve the presence of an extra chromosome (either an X or Y) or the absence of one X chromosome in females.

Klinefelter syndrome is a chromosomal disorder in which males have an extra X chromosome, making them XXY instead of XY. Males with this disorder have undeveloped testes, and they usually have enlarged breasts and become tall (Aksglaede & others, 2011). Klinefelter syndrome occurs approximately once in every 800 live male births.

Fragile X syndrome is a chromosomal disorder that results from an abnormality in the X chromosome, which becomes constricted and often breaks (Cornish, Gray, & Rinehart, 2010; Heulens & Kooy, 2011). Mental deficiency frequently is an outcome, but it may take the form of mental retardation, a learning disability, or a short attention span. This disorder occurs more frequently in males than in females, possibly because the second X chromosome in females negates the effects of the abnormal X chromosome (Kuehn, 2011).

Turner syndrome is a chromosomal disorder in females in which either an X chromosome is missing, making the person XO instead of XX, or part of one X chromosome is deleted. Females with Turner syndrome are short in stature and have a webbed neck (Ranke & Lindberg, 2011). They might be infertile and have difficulty in mathematics, but their verbal ability is often quite good. Turner syndrome occurs in approximately 1 of every 2,500 live female births (Kim & others, 2011).

The **XYY syndrome** is a chromosomal disorder in which the male has an extra Y chromosome (Bishop & others, 2011). Early interest in this syndrome focused on the belief that the extra Y chromosome found in some males contributed to aggression and violence. However, researchers subsequently found that XYY males are no more likely to commit crimes than are XY males (Witkin & others, 1976).

Gene-Linked Abnormalities Abnormalities can be produced not only by an uneven number of chromosomes but also by harmful genes (Presson & Jenner, 2008). More than 7,000 such genetic disorders have been identified, although most of them are rare.

Phenylketonuria (PKU) is a genetic disorder in which the individual cannot properly metabolize phenylalanine, an amino acid. It results from a recessive gene and occurs about once in every 10,000 to 20,000 live births. Today, phenylketonuria is easily detected, and it is treated by a diet that prevents an excess accumulation

A boy with fragile X syndrome.

Klinefelter syndrome A chromosomal disorder in which males have an extra X chromosome, making them XXY instead of XY.

fragile X syndrome A chromosomal disorder involving an abnormality in the X chromosome, which becomes constricted and often breaks.

Turner syndrome A chromosomal disorder in females in which either an X chromosome is missing, making the person XO instead of XX, or part of one X chromosome is deleted.

XYY syndrome A chromosomal disorder in which males have an extra Y chromosome.

phenylketonuria (PKU) A genetic disorder in which an individual cannot properly metabolize phenylalanine, an amino acid; PKU is now easily detected—but, if left untreated, results in mental retardation and hyperactivity.

Name	Description	Treatment	Incidence
Cystic fibrosis	Glandular dysfunction that interferes with mucus production; breathing and digestion are hampered, resulting in a shortened life span.	Physical and oxygen therapy, synthetic enzymes, and antibiotics; most individuals live to middle age.	1 in 2,000 births
Diabetes	Body does not produce enough insulin, which causes abnormal metabolism of sugar.	Early onset can be fatal unless treated with insulin.	1 in 2,500 births
Hemophilia	Delayed blood clotting causes internal and external bleeding.	Blood transfusions/injections can reduce or prevent damage due to internal bleeding.	1 in 10,000 males
Huntington's disease	Central nervous system deteriorates, producing problems in muscle coordination and mental deterioration.	Does not usually appear until age 35 or older; death likely 10 to 20 years after symptoms appear.	1 in 20,000 births
Phenylketonuria (PKU)	Metabolic disorder that, left untreated, causes mental retardation.	Special diet can result in average intelligence and normal life span.	1 in 10,000 to 1 in 20,000 births
Sickle-cell anemia	Blood disorder that limits the body's oxygen supply; it can cause joint swelling, as well as heart and kidney failure.	Penicillin, medication for pain, antibiotics, and blood transfusions.	1 in 400 African American children (lower among other groups)
Spina bifida	Neural tube disorder that causes brain and spine abnormalities.	Corrective surgery at birth, orthopedic devices, and physical/medical therapy.	2 in 1,000 births
Tay-Sachs disease	Deceleration of mental and physical development caused by an accumulation of lipids in the nervous system.	Medication and special diet are used, but death is likely by 5 years of age.	1 in 30 American Jews is a carrier.

FIGURE **2.7**
SOME GENE-LINKED ABNORMALITIES

During a physical examination for a college football tryout, Jerry Hubbard, 32, learned that he carried the gene for sickle-cell anemia. Daughter Sara is healthy but daughter Avery (in the print dress) has sickle-cell anemia. *If you were a genetic counselor, would you recommend that this family have more children? Explain.*

sickle-cell anemia A genetic disorder that affects the red blood cells and occurs most often in African Americans.

of phenylalanine (Cotugno & others, 2011; van Spronsen & Enns, 2010). If phenylketonuria is left untreated, however, excess phenylalanine builds up in the child, producing mental retardation and hyperactivity. Phenylketonuria accounts for approximately 1 percent of institutionalized individuals who are mentally retarded, and it occurs primarily in non-Latino Whites.

Sickle-cell anemia, which occurs most often in African Americans, is a genetic disorder that impairs the body's red blood cells. Red blood cells carry oxygen to the body's cells and are usually shaped like a disk. In sickle-cell anemia, a recessive gene causes the red blood cell to become a hook-shaped "sickle" that cannot carry oxygen properly and dies quickly. As a result, the body's cells do not receive adequate oxygen, causing anemia and often early death (Dworkis & others, 2011). About 1 in 400 African American babies is affected by sickle-cell anemia. One in 10 African Americans is a carrier, as is 1 in 20 Latin Americans.

Other diseases that result from genetic abnormalities include cystic fibrosis, diabetes, hemophilia, Huntington disease, spina bifida, and Tay-Sachs disease (Bell & others, 2011; Geborek & Hjelte, 2011). Figure 2.7 provides further information about these diseases. Someday, scientists may identify the origins of these and other genetic abnormalities and discover how to cure them.

Genetic counselors, usually physicians or biologists who are well versed in the field of medical genetics, understand the kinds of problems just described, the odds of encountering them, and helpful strategies for offsetting some of their effects (Clarke & Thirlaway, 2011; Vos & others, 2011). To read about the career and work of a genetic counselor, see the *Connecting with Careers* profile.

Holly Ishmael, Genetic Counselor

Holly Ishmael is a genetic counselor at Children's Mercy Hospital in Kansas City. She obtained an undergraduate degree in psychology from Sarah Lawrence College and a master's degree in genetic counseling from the same college. She uses many of the principles discussed in this chapter in her genetic counseling work.

Ishmael says, "Genetic counseling is a perfect combination for people who want to do something science-oriented, but need human contact and don't want to spend all of their time in a lab or have their nose in a book" (Rizzo, 1999, p. 3).

There are approximately 30 graduate genetic counseling programs in the United States. If you are interested in this profession, you can obtain further information from the National Society of Genetic Counselors at www.nsgc.org.

Holly Ishmael (*left*) in a genetic counseling session.

Review *Connect* Reflect

 Describe what genes are and how they influence human development

Review

- What are genes?
- How are genes passed on?
- What basic principles describe how genes interact?
- What are some chromosomal and gene-linked abnormalities?

Connect

- Would you want to be able to access a full genome analysis of your offspring? Why or why not?

Reflect *Your Own Personal Journey of Life*

- Imagine that you are considering having a child. Would you want to see a genetic counselor to find out about possible genetic risks that might be transmitted to your offspring? Explain.

Heredity and Environment Interaction: The Nature-Nurture Debate

 Explain some of the ways that heredity and environment interact to produce individual differences in development

| Behavior Genetics | Heredity-Environment Correlations | Shared and Nonshared Environmental Influences | The Epigenetic View and Gene × Environment (G × E) Interaction | Conclusions About Heredity-Environment Interaction |

Is it possible to untangle the influence of heredity from that of environment and discover the role of each in producing individual differences in development? When heredity and environment interact, how does heredity influence the environment, and vice versa?

Twin studies compare identical twins with fraternal twins. Identical twins develop from a single fertilized egg that splits into two genetically identical organisms. Fraternal twins develop from separate eggs, making them genetically no more similar than nontwin siblings. *What is the nature of the twin study method?*

BEHAVIOR GENETICS

Behavior genetics is the field that seeks to discover the influence of heredity and environment on individual differences in human traits and development (Silberg, Maes, & Eaves, 2010). To study the influence of heredity on behavior, behavior geneticists often use either twins or adoption situations (Gregory, Ball, & Button, 2011).

In the most common **twin study,** the behavioral similarity of identical twins (who are genetically identical) is compared with the behavioral similarity of fraternal twins. Recall that although fraternal twins share the same womb, they are no more genetically alike than brothers or sisters. Thus, by comparing groups of identical and fraternal twins, behavior geneticists capitalize on the basic knowledge that identical twins are more similar genetically than are fraternal twins. For example, one study found that conduct problems were more prevalent in identical twins than in fraternal twins; the researchers concluded that the study demonstrated an important role for heredity in conduct problems (Scourfield & others, 2004).

However, several issues complicate interpretation of twin studies. For example, perhaps the environments of identical twins are more similar than the environments of fraternal twins. Adults might stress the similarities of identical twins more than those of fraternal twins, and identical twins might perceive themselves as a "set" and play together more than fraternal twins do. If so, the influence of the environment on the observed similarities between identical and fraternal twins might be very significant.

In an **adoption study,** investigators seek to discover whether the behavior and psychological characteristics of adopted children are more like those of their adoptive parents, who have provided a home environment, or more like those of their biological parents, who have contributed their heredity (Loehlin, Horn, & Ernst, 2007). Another form of the adoption study compares adoptive and biological siblings.

HEREDITY-ENVIRONMENT CORRELATIONS

The difficulties that researchers encounter when they interpret the results of twin studies and adoption studies reflect the complexities of heredity-environment interaction. Some of these interactions are *heredity-environment correlations*—that is, individuals' genes may influence the types of environments to which they are exposed. In a sense, individuals "inherit" environments that may be related or linked to genetic "propensities" (Loehlin, 2010). Behavior geneticist Sandra Scarr (1993) described three ways that heredity and environment are correlated (see Figure 2.8):

- **Passive genotype-environment correlations** occur because biological parents, who are genetically related to the child, provide a rearing environment for the child. For example, the parents might have a genetic predisposition to be intelligent and read skillfully. Because they read well and enjoy reading, they provide their children with books to read. The likely outcome is that their children, given their own inherited predispositions from their parents and their book-filled environment, will become skilled readers.

- **Evocative genotype-environment correlations** occur because a child's characteristics elicit certain types of environments. For example, active, smiling children receive more social stimulation than passive, quiet children do. Cooperative, attentive children evoke more pleasant and instructional responses from the adults around them than uncooperative, distractible children do.

- **Active (niche-picking) genotype-environment correlations** occur when children seek out environments that they find compatible and stimulating.

behavior genetics The field that seeks to discover the influence of heredity and environment on individual differences in human traits and development.

twin study A study in which the behavioral similarity of identical twins is compared with the behavioral similarity of fraternal twins.

adoption study A study in which investigators seek to discover whether, in behavior and psychological characteristics, adopted children are more like their adoptive parents, who provided a home environment, or more like their biological parents, who contributed their heredity. Another form of the adoption study compares adoptive and biological siblings.

passive genotype-environment correlations Correlations that exist when the biological parents, who are genetically related to the child, provide a rearing environment for the child.

evocative genotype-environment correlations Correlations that exist when the child's characteristics elicit certain types of environments.

active (niche-picking) genotype-environment correlations Correlations that exist when children seek out environments they find compatible and stimulating.

Heredity-Environment Correlation	Description	Examples
Passive	Children inherit genetic tendencies from their parents, and parents also provide an environment that matches their own genetic tendencies.	Musically inclined parents usually have musically inclined children and they are likely to provide an environment rich in music for their children.
Evocative	The child's genetic tendencies elicit stimulation from the environment that supports a particular trait. Thus genes evoke environmental support.	A happy, outgoing child elicits smiles and friendly responses from others.
Active (niche-picking)	Children actively seek out "niches" in their environment that reflect their own interests and talents and are thus in accord with their genotype.	Libraries, sports fields, and a store with musical instruments are examples of environmental niches children might seek out if they have intellectual interests in books, talent in sports, or musical talents, respectively.

FIGURE 2.8
EXPLORING HEREDITY-ENVIRONMENT CORRELATIONS

Niche-picking refers to finding a setting that is suited to one's abilities. Children select from their surrounding environment some aspects that they respond to, learn about, or ignore. Their active selections of environments are related to their particular genotype. For example, outgoing children tend to seek out social contexts in which to interact with people, whereas shy children don't. Children who are musically inclined are likely to select musical environments in which they can successfully perform their skills. How these "tendencies" come about is discussed shortly under the topic of the epigenetic view.

Scarr notes that the relative importance of the three genotype-environment correlations changes as children develop from infancy through adolescence. In infancy, much of the environment that children experience is provided by adults. Thus, passive genotype-environment correlations are more common in the lives of infants and young children than they are for older children and adolescents who can extend their experiences beyond the family's influence and create their environments to a greater degree.

SHARED AND NONSHARED ENVIRONMENTAL INFLUENCES

Behavior geneticists have argued that to understand the environment's role in differences between people, we should distinguish between shared and nonshared environments. That is, we should consider experiences that children have in common with other children living in the same home, and experiences that are not shared (Burt, McGue, & Iacono, 2010; Cerda & others, 2010).

Shared environmental experiences are siblings' common experiences, such as their parents' personalities or intellectual orientation, the family's socioeconomic status, and the neighborhood in which they live. By contrast, **nonshared environmental experiences** are a child's unique experiences, both within the family and outside the family, that are not shared with a sibling. For example, siblings often have different peer groups, different friends, and different teachers at school.

Behavior geneticist Robert Plomin (2004) has found that shared environment accounts for little of the variation in children's personality or interests. In other

Tennis stars Venus and Serena Williams. *What might be some shared and nonshared environmental experiences they had while they were growing up that contributed to their tennis stardom?*

shared environmental experiences Siblings' common experiences, such as their parents' personalities or intellectual orientation, the family's socioeconomic status, and the neighborhood in which they live.

nonshared environmental experiences The child's own unique experiences, both within the family and outside the family, that are not shared by another sibling; thus, experiences occurring within the family can be part of the "nonshared environment."

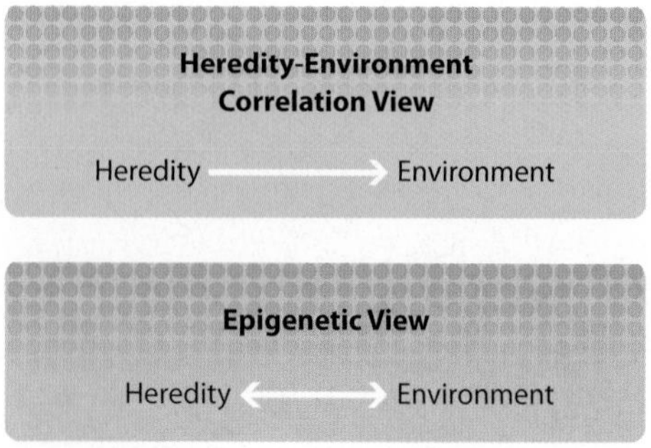

FIGURE **2.9**

**COMPARISON OF THE HEREDITY-
ENVIRONMENT CORRELATION AND
EPIGENETIC VIEWS**

- - - - - - - - - - - - - - - ➤

developmental **connection**

Parenting. Is quantity or quality more important in parenting? Chapter 14, p. 461

epigenetic view Perspective that emphasizes that development is the result of an ongoing, bidirectional interchange between heredity and environment.

gene × environment (g × e) interaction The interaction of a specific measured variation in the DNA and a specific measured aspect of the environment.

words, even though two children live under the same roof with the same parents, their personalities are often very different. Further, Plomin argues that heredity influences the nonshared environments of siblings through the heredity-environment correlations we described earlier. For example, a child who has inherited a genetic tendency to be athletic is likely to spend more time in environments related to sports, whereas a child who has inherited a tendency to be musically inclined is more likely to spend time in environments related to music.

THE EPIGENETIC VIEW AND GENE × ENVIRONMENT (G × E) INTERACTION

In line with the concept of a collaborative gene, Gilbert Gottlieb (2007) proposed an **epigenetic view,** which states that development is the result of an ongoing, bidirectional interchange between heredity and the environment. Figure 2.9 compares the heredity-environment correlation and epigenetic views of development.

Let's look at an example that reflects the epigenetic view. A baby inherits genes from both parents at conception. During prenatal development, toxins, nutrition, and stress can influence some genes to stop functioning while others become stronger or weaker. During infancy, additional environmental experiences, such as toxins, nutrition, stress, learning, and encouragement, continue to modify genetic activity and the activity of the nervous system that directly underlies behavior. Heredity and environment thus operate together—or collaborate—to produce a person's intelligence, temperament, health, ability to pitch a baseball, ability to read, and so on (Gottlieb, 2007; Wright & Christiani, 2010).

An increasing number of researchers are exploring how the interaction between heredity and environment influences development, including interactions that involve specific DNA sequences (Caspi & others, 2011; Goldman & others, 2010; Keers & others, 2011; Rutter & Dodge, 2011). One study found that individuals who have a short version of a genotype labeled 5-HTTLPR (a gene involving the neurotransmitter serotonin) have an elevated risk of developing depression only if they *also* have stressful lives (Caspi & others, 2003). Thus, the specific gene did not link directly to the development of depression, but rather interacted with environmental exposure to stress to predict whether individuals would develop depression; however, some studies have not replicated this finding (Risch & others, 2009). In a recent study, adults who experienced parental loss as young children were more likely to have unresolved attachment as adults only when they had the short version of the 5-HTTLPR gene (Caspers & others, 2009). The long version of the serotonin transporter gene apparently provided some protection and ability to cope better with parental loss. The type of research just described is referred to as **gene × environment (g × e) interaction**—the interaction of a specific measured variation in DNA and a specific measured aspect of the environment (Diamond, 2009; Dodge & Rutter, 2011).

CONCLUSIONS ABOUT HEREDITY-ENVIRONMENT INTERACTION

If an attractive, popular, intelligent girl is elected president of her high school senior class, is her success due to heredity or to environment? Of course, the answer is "both."

The relative contributions of heredity and environment are not additive. That is, we can't say that such-and-such a percentage of nature and such-and-such a percentage of experience make us who we are. Nor is it accurate to say that full genetic expression happens once, at the time of conception or birth, after which we carry our genetic legacy into the world to see how far it takes us. Genes produce proteins throughout the life span, in many different environments. Or they don't produce these proteins, depending in part on how harsh or nourishing those environments are.

The emerging view is that complex behaviors have some *genetic loading* that gives each individual a propensity for a particular developmental trajectory (Goldsmith, 2011; Guo & Tillman, 2009). However, the individual's actual development requires more: a particular environment. And that environment is complex, just like the mixture of genes we inherit (Grusec, 2011; Parke & Clarke-Stewart, 2011). Environmental influences range from the things we lump together under "nurture" (such as parenting, family dynamics, schooling, and neighborhood quality) to biological encounters (such as viruses, birth complications, and even biological events in cells).

Imagine for a moment that there is a cluster of genes that are somehow associated with youth violence. (This example is hypothetical because we don't know of any such combination.) The adolescent who carries this genetic mixture might experience a world of loving parents, regular nutritious meals, lots of books, and a series of competent teachers. Or the adolescent's world might include parental neglect, a neighborhood in which gunshots and crime are everyday occurrences, and inadequate schooling. In which of these environments are the adolescent's genes likely to manufacture the biological underpinnings of criminality?

If heredity and environment interact to determine the course of development, is that all there is to answering the question of what causes development? Are humans completely at the mercy of their genes and their environment as they develop through the life span? Genetic heritage and environmental experiences are pervasive influences on development. But in thinking about what causes development, recall from Chapter 1 our discussion of development as the co-construction of biology, culture, *and* the individual. Not only are we the outcomes of our heredity and the environment we experience, but we also can author a unique developmental path by changing our environment. As one psychologist recently concluded:

> In reality, we are both the creatures and creators of our worlds. We are . . . the products of our genes and environments. Nevertheless, . . . the stream of causation that shapes the future runs through our present choices. . . . Mind matters. . . . Our hopes, goals, and expectations influence our future. (Myers, 2010, p. 168)

> The interaction of heredity and environment is so extensive that to ask which is more important, nature or nurture, is like asking which is more important to a rectangle, height or width.
>
> **—WILLIAM GREENOUGH**
> *Contemporary Developmental Psychologist,*
> *University of Illinois at Urbana*

developmental connection

Life-Span Perspective. An important aspect of the life-span perspective is the co-construction of biology, culture, and the individual. Chapter 1, p. 8

Review Connect Reflect

 LG3 Explain some of the ways that heredity and environment interact to produce individual differences in development

Review

- What is behavior genetics?
- What are three types of heredity-environment correlations?
- What is meant by the concepts of shared and nonshared environmental experiences?
- What is the epigenetic view of development?
- What conclusions can be reached about heredity-environment interaction?

Connect

- Of passive, evocative, and active genotype-environment correlations, which is the best explanation for the similarities discovered between the many sets of adult twins who share characteristics and experiences despite being raised apart?

Reflect *Your Own Personal Journey of Life*

- A friend tells you that she has analyzed her genetic background and environmental experiences and reached the conclusion that environment definitely has had little influence on her intelligence. What would you say to this person about her ability to make this self-diagnosis?

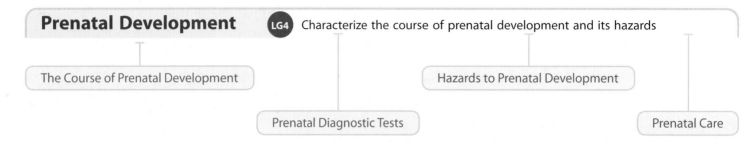

Prenatal Development

LG4 Characterize the course of prenatal development and its hazards

The Course of Prenatal Development

Prenatal Diagnostic Tests

Hazards to Prenatal Development

Prenatal Care

We turn now to a description of how the process of development unfolds from its earliest moment—the moment of *conception*—when two parental cells, with their unique genetic contributions, meet to create a new individual.

Conception occurs when a single sperm cell from a male unites with an ovum (egg) in a female's fallopian tube in a process called fertilization. Over the next few months the genetic code discussed earlier directs a series of changes in the fertilized egg, but many events and hazards will influence how that egg develops and becomes a person.

THE COURSE OF PRENATAL DEVELOPMENT

Prenatal development lasts approximately 266 days, beginning with fertilization and ending with birth. It can be divided into three periods: germinal, embryonic, and fetal.

> The history of man for nine months preceding his birth would, probably, be far more interesting, and contain events of greater moment, than all three score and ten years that follow it.
>
> —SAMUEL TAYLOR COLERIDGE
> *English Poet, Essayist, 19th Century*

The Germinal Period The **germinal period** is the period of prenatal development that takes place in the first two weeks after conception. It includes the creation of the fertilized egg (the *zygote*), cell division, and the attachment of the zygote to the uterine wall.

Rapid cell division by the zygote begins the germinal period. (Recall from earlier in the chapter that this cell division occurs through a process called *mitosis*.) By approximately one week after conception, the differentiation of these cells—their specialization for different tasks—has already begun. At this stage the group of cells, now called the *blastocyst*, consists of an inner mass of cells that will eventually develop into the embryo, and the *trophoblast*, an outer layer of cells that later provides nutrition and support for the embryo. *Implantation*, the attachment of the zygote to the uterine wall, takes place about 10 to 14 days after conception.

The Embryonic Period The **embryonic period** is the period of prenatal development that occurs from two to eight weeks after conception. During the embryonic period, the rate of cell differentiation intensifies, support systems for cells form, and organs appear.

This period begins as the blastocyst attaches to the uterine wall. The mass of cells is now called an *embryo*, and three layers of cells form. The embryo's *endoderm* is the inner layer of cells, which will develop into the digestive and respiratory systems. The *ectoderm* is the outermost layer, which will become the nervous system, sensory receptors (ears, nose, and eyes, for example), and skin parts (hair and nails, for example). The *mesoderm* is the middle layer, which will become the circulatory system, bones, muscles, excretory system, and reproductive system. Every body part eventually develops from these three layers. The endoderm primarily produces internal body parts, the mesoderm primarily produces parts that surround the internal areas, and the ectoderm primarily produces surface parts. **Organogenesis** is the name given to the process of organ formation during the first two months of prenatal development. While they are being formed, the organs are especially vulnerable to environmental influences (Hashimoto-Toril & others, 2011).

As the embryo's three layers form, life-support systems for the embryo develop rapidly. These systems include the amnion, the umbilical cord (both of which develop from the fertilized egg, not the mother's body), and the placenta. The amnion is like

germinal period The period of prenatal development that takes place during the first two weeks after conception; it includes the creation of the zygote, continued cell division, and the attachment of the zygote to the wall of the uterus.

embryonic period The period of prenatal development that occurs from two to eight weeks after conception. During the embryonic period, the rate of cell differentiation intensifies, support systems for the cells form, and organs appear.

organogenesis Process of organ formation that takes place during the first two months of prenatal development.

a bag or an envelope; it contains a clear fluid in which the developing embryo floats. The amniotic fluid provides an environment that is temperature- and humidity-controlled, as well as shockproof. The *umbilical cord*, which contains two arteries and one vein, connects the baby to the placenta. The *placenta* consists of a disk-shaped group of tissues in which small blood vessels from the mother and the offspring intertwine but do not join.

Very small molecules—oxygen, water, salt, and nutrients from the mother's blood, as well as carbon dioxide and digestive wastes from the baby's blood—pass back and forth between the mother and the embryo or fetus (Woolett, 2011). Virtually any drug or chemical substance the pregnant woman ingests can cross the placenta to some degree, unless it is metabolized or altered during passage, or is too large (Eshkoli & others, 2011). A recent study revealed that cigarette smoke weakened and increased the oxidative stress of fetal membranes, from which the placenta develops (Menon & others, 2011). Large molecules that cannot pass through the placental wall include red blood cells and harmful substances, such as most bacteria, maternal wastes, and hormones. The complex mechanisms that govern the transfer of substances across the placental barrier are still not entirely understood (Meschia, 2011).

The Fetal Period The **fetal period,** which lasts about seven months, is the prenatal period that extends from two months after conception until birth in typical pregnancies. Growth and development continue their dramatic course during this time.

Three months after conception, the fetus is about 3 inches long and weighs about 3 ounces. It has become active, moving its arms and legs, opening and closing its mouth, and moving its head. The face, forehead, eyelids, nose, and chin are distinguishable, as are the upper arms, lower arms, hands, and lower limbs. In most cases, the genitals can be identified as male or female. By the end of the fourth month of pregnancy, the fetus has grown to 6 inches in length and weighs 4 to 7 ounces. At this time, a growth spurt occurs in the body's lower parts. For the first time, the mother can feel arm and leg movements.

By the end of the fifth month, the fetus is about 12 inches long and weighs close to a pound. Structures of the skin have formed—toenails and fingernails, for example. The fetus is more active, showing a preference for a particular position in the womb. By the end of the sixth month, the fetus is about 14 inches long and has gained another 6 to 12 ounces. The eyes and eyelids are completely formed, and a fine layer of hair covers the head. A grasping reflex is present and irregular breathing movements occur.

As early as six months of pregnancy (about 24 to 25 weeks after conception), the fetus for the first time has a chance of surviving outside the womb—that is, it is *viable*. Infants that are born early, or between 24 and 37 weeks of pregnancy, usually need help breathing because their lungs are not yet fully mature. By the end of the seventh month, the fetus is about 16 inches long and now weighs about 3 pounds.

During the last two months of prenatal development, fatty tissues develop and the functioning of various organ systems—heart and kidneys, for example—steps up. During the eighth and ninth months, the fetus grows longer and gains substantial weight—about 4 more pounds. At birth, the average American baby weighs 7½ pounds and is about 20 inches long.

In addition to describing prenatal development in terms of germinal, embryonic, and fetal periods, prenatal development also can be divided into equal three-month periods, called *trimesters* (see Figure 2.10). Remember that the three trimesters are not the same as the three prenatal periods we have discussed. The germinal and embryonic periods occur in the first trimester. The fetal period begins toward the end of the first trimester and continues through the second and third trimesters. Viability (the chances of surviving outside the womb) occurs at the beginning of the third trimester.

fetal period The prenatal period of development that begins two months after conception and lasts for seven months, on average.

First trimester (first 3 months)

Conception to 4 weeks

- Is less than $1/10$ inch long
- Beginning development of spinal cord, nervous system, gastrointestinal system, heart, and lungs
- Amniotic sac envelops the preliminary tissues of entire body
- Is called a "zygote"

8 weeks

- Is just over 1 inch long
- Face is forming with rudimentary eyes, ears, mouth, and tooth buds
- Arms and legs are moving
- Brain is forming
- Fetal heartbeat is detectable with ultrasound
- Is called an "embryo"

12 weeks

- Is about 3 inches long and weighs about 1 ounce
- Can move arms, legs, fingers, and toes
- Fingerprints are present
- Can smile, frown, suck, and swallow
- Sex is distinguishable
- Can urinate
- Is called a "fetus"

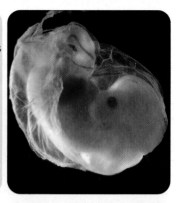

Second trimester (middle 3 months)

16 weeks

- Is about 6 inches long and weighs about 4 to 7 ounces
- Heartbeat is strong
- Skin is thin, transparent
- Downy hair (lanugo) covers body
- Fingernails and toenails are forming
- Has coordinated movements; is able to roll over in amniotic fluid

20 weeks

- Is about 12 inches long and weighs close to 1 pound
- Heartbeat is audible with ordinary stethoscope
- Sucks thumb
- Hiccups
- Hair, eyelashes, eyebrows are present

24 weeks

- Is about 14 inches long and weighs 1 to $1^{1}/2$ pounds
- Skin is wrinkled and covered with protective coating (vernix caseosa)
- Eyes are open
- Waste matter is collected in bowel
- Has strong grip

Third trimester (last 3 months)

28 weeks

- Is about 16 inches long and weighs about 3 pounds
- Is adding body fat
- Is very active
- Rudimentary breathing movements are present

32 weeks

- Is $16^{1}/2$ to 18 inches long and weighs 4 to 5 pounds
- Has periods of sleep and wakefulness
- Responds to sounds
- May assume the birth position
- Bones of head are soft and flexible
- Iron is being stored in liver

36 to 38 weeks

- Is 19 to 20 inches long and weighs 6 to $7^{1}/2$ pounds
- Skin is less wrinkled
- Vernix caseosa is thick
- Lanugo is mostly gone
- Is less active
- Is gaining immunities from mother

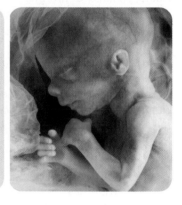

FIGURE 2.10

THE THREE TRIMESTERS OF PRENATAL DEVELOPMENT. Both the germinal and embryonic periods occur during the first trimester. The end of the first trimester as well as the second and third trimesters are part of the fetal period.

The Brain   One of the most remarkable aspects of the prenatal period is the development of the brain (Nelson, 2011). By the time babies are born, they have approximately 100 billion **neurons,** or nerve cells, which handle information processing at the cellular level in the brain. During prenatal development, neurons move to specific locations and start to become connected. The basic architecture of the human brain is assembled during the first two trimesters of prenatal development. Typically, the third trimester of prenatal development and the first two years of postnatal life are characterized by connectivity and functioning of neurons (Nelson, 2011).

As the human embryo develops inside its mother's womb, the nervous system begins forming as a long, hollow tube located on the embryo's back. This pear-shaped *neural tube,* which forms at about 18 to 24 days after conception, develops out of the ectoderm. The tube closes at the top and bottom ends at about 24 days

neurons Nerve cells that handle information processing at the cellular level.

after conception. Figure 2.11 shows that the nervous system still has a tubular appearance six weeks after conception.

Two birth defects related to a failure of the neural tube to close are anencephaly and spina bifida. When fetuses have *anencephaly* (that is, when the head end of the neural tube fails to close), the highest regions of the brain fail to develop and they die in the womb, during childbirth, or shortly after birth (Stoll & others, 2011). *Spina bifida*, an incomplete development of the spinal cord, results in varying degrees of paralysis of the lower limbs. Individuals with spina bifida usually need assistive devices such as crutches, braces, or wheelchairs. A strategy that can help to prevent neural tube defects is for women to take adequate amounts of the B vitamin folic acid, a topic we will discuss later in the chapter (Rasmussen & Clemmensen, 2010). And both maternal diabetes and obesity place the fetus at risk for developing neural tube defects (Yazdy & others, 2010).

In a normal pregnancy, once the neural tube has closed, a massive proliferation of new immature neurons begins to take place at about the fifth prenatal week and continues throughout the remainder of the prenatal period. The generation of new neurons is called *neurogenesis*. At the peak of neurogenesis, it is estimated that as many as 200,000 neurons are being generated every minute.

At approximately 6 to 24 weeks after conception, *neuronal migration* occurs (Nelson, 2011). Cells begin moving outward from their point of origin to their appropriate locations and creating the different levels, structures, and regions of the brain (Cozzi & others, 2010). Once a cell has migrated to its target destination, it must mature and develop a more complex structure.

At about the 23rd prenatal week, connections between neurons begin to form, a process that continues postnatally (Nelson, 2011). We will have much more to say about the structure of neurons, their connectivity, and the development of the infant brain in Chapter 3.

PRENATAL DIAGNOSTIC TESTS

Together with her doctor, a pregnant woman will decide the extent to which she should undergo prenatal testing. A number of tests can indicate whether a fetus is developing normally; these include ultrasound sonography, fetal MRI, chorionic villus sampling, amniocentesis, and maternal blood screening (Du & others, 2011; Nemec & others, 2011). The decision to have a given test depends on several criteria, such as the mother's age, medical history, and genetic risk factors.

An ultrasound test is generally performed 7 weeks into a pregnancy and at various times later in pregnancy. *Ultrasound sonography* is a noninvasive prenatal medical procedure in which high-frequency sound waves are directed into the pregnant woman's abdomen (Cignini & others, 2010). The echo from the sounds is transformed into a visual representation of the fetus's inner structures. This technique can detect many structural abnormalities in the fetus, including microencephaly, a form of mental retardation involving an abnormally small brain; it can also give clues to the baby's sex and indicate whether there is more than one fetus (Masselli & others, 2011). Ultrasound results are available as soon as the images are read by a radiologist.

The development of brain-imaging techniques has led to increasing use of *fetal MRI* to diagnose fetal malformations (Schmid & others, 2011) (see Figure 2.12). MRI (magnetic resonance imaging) uses a powerful magnet and radio waves to generate detailed images of the body's organs and structures. Currently, ultrasound is still the first choice in fetal screening, but fetal MRI can provide more detailed images than ultrasound. In many instances, ultrasound will indicate a possible abnormality and fetal MRI will then be used to obtain a clearer, more detailed image (Mangione & others, 2011). Among the fetal malformations that

Yelyi Nordone, 12, of New York City, casts her line out into the pond during Camp Spifida at Camp Victory, near Millville, Pa., in July 2008. Camp Spifida is a week-long residential camp for children with spina bifida.

developmental **connection**

Brain Development. At birth, infants' brains weigh approximately 25 percent of what they will when adulthood is reached. Chapter 3, p. 101

FIGURE **2.11**

EARLY FORMATION OF THE NERVOUS SYSTEM. The photograph shows the primitive, tubular appearance of the nervous system at six weeks in the human embryo.

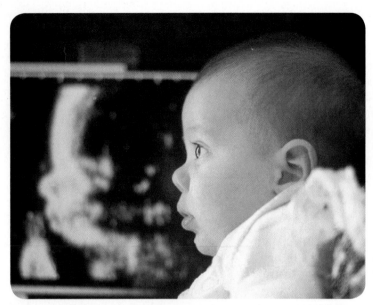

A 6-month-old infant poses with the ultrasound sonography record taken four months into the baby's prenatal development. *What is ultrasound sonography?*

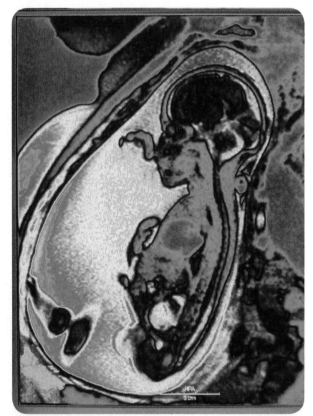

FIGURE **2.12**

A FETAL MRI, WHICH IS INCREASINGLY BEING USED IN PRENATAL DIAGNOSIS OF FETAL MALFORMATIONS

teratogen Any agent that can potentially cause a birth defect or negatively alter cognitive and behavioral outcomes.

fetal MRI may be able to detect better than ultrasound sonography are certain central nervous system, chest, gastrointestinal, genital/urinary, and placental abnormalities (Baysinger, 2010; Nemec & others, 2011; Triulzi, Manganaro, & Volpe, 2011).

At some point between the 10th and 12th weeks of pregnancy, chorionic villus sampling may be used to screen for genetic defects and chromosome abnormalities (Akolekar & others, 2011; Basaran, Basaran, & Topatan, 2011). *Chorionic villus sampling (CVS)* is a prenatal medical procedure in which a tiny tissue sample from the placenta is removed and analyzed. The results are available in about 10 days.

Between the 15th and 18th weeks of pregnancy, *amniocentesis* may be performed. In this procedure, a sample of amniotic fluid is withdrawn by syringe and tested for chromosome or metabolic disorders (Athanasiadis & others, 2011). The later in the pregnancy amniocentesis is performed, the better its diagnostic potential. However, the earlier it is performed, the more useful it is in deciding how to handle a pregnancy when the fetus is found to have a disorder. It may take two weeks for enough cells to grow so that amniocentesis test results can be obtained.

Amniocentesis brings a small risk of miscarriage: about 1 woman in every 200 to 300 miscarries after amniocentesis. Although earlier reports indicated that chorionic villus sampling brings a slightly higher risk of pregnancy loss than amniocentesis, a U.S. study of more than 40,000 pregnancies found that loss rates for CVS decreased from 1998 to 2003 and that there is no longer a difference in pregnancy loss risk between CVS and amniocentesis (Caughey, Hopkins, & Norton, 2006).

During the 16th to 18th weeks of pregnancy, maternal blood screening may be performed. *Maternal blood screening* identifies pregnancies that have an elevated risk for birth defects such as spina bifida and Down syndrome (Ballard, 2011). The current blood test is called the *triple screen* because it measures three substances in the mother's blood. After an abnormal triple screen result, the next step is usually an ultrasound examination. If an ultrasound does not explain the abnormal triple screen results, amniocentesis typically is used.

HAZARDS TO PRENATAL DEVELOPMENT

For most babies, the course of prenatal development goes smoothly. Their mother's womb protects them as they develop. Despite this protection, however, the environment can affect the embryo or fetus in many well-documented ways.

General Principles A **teratogen** is any agent that can potentially cause a birth defect or negatively alter cognitive and behavioral outcomes. The field of study that investigates the causes of birth defects is called *teratology.* Teratogens include drugs, incompatible blood types, environmental pollutants, infectious diseases, nutritional deficiencies, maternal stress, advanced maternal and paternal age, and environmental pollutants.

The dose, the genetic susceptibility, and the time of exposure to a particular teratogen influence both the severity of the damage to an embryo or fetus and the type of defect:

- *Dose* The dose effect is obvious—the greater the dose of an agent, such as a drug, the greater the effect.

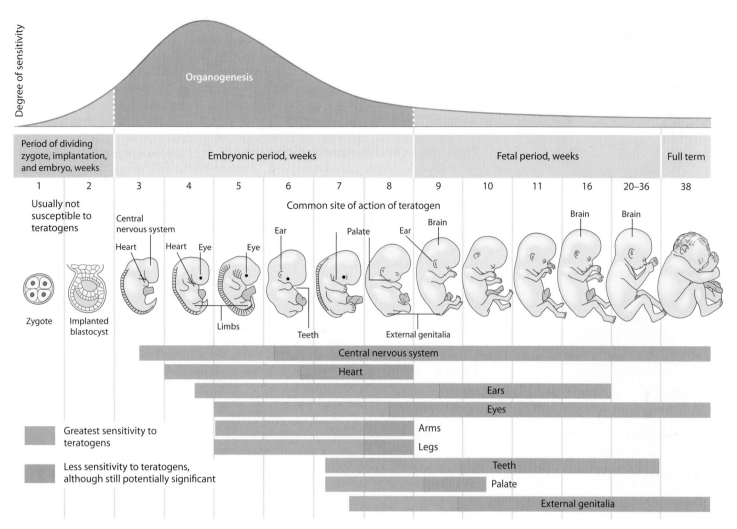

FIGURE **2.13**

TERATOGENS AND THE TIMING OF THEIR EFFECTS ON PRENATAL DEVELOPMENT. The danger of structural defects caused by teratogens is greatest early in embryonic development. The period of organogenesis (red color) lasts for about six weeks. Later assaults by teratogens (blue-green color) mainly occur in the fetal period and instead of causing structural damage are more likely to stunt growth or cause problems of organ function.

- *Genetic Susceptibility* The type or severity of abnormalities caused by a teratogen is linked to the genotype of the pregnant woman and the genotype of the embryo or fetus (Schachter & Kohane, 2011). For example, how a mother metabolizes a particular drug can influence the degree to which the drug effects are transmitted to the embryo or fetus. Differences in placental membranes and placental transport also affect exposure. The extent to which an embryo or fetus is vulnerable to a teratogen may also depend on its genotype. Also, for unknown reasons, male fetuses are far more likely to be affected by teratogens than female fetuses (DiPietro, 2008).

- *Time of Exposure* Teratogens do more damage at some points in development than at others. Damage during the germinal period may even prevent implantation. In general, the embryonic period is more vulnerable than the fetal period (Ortigosa Gomez & others, 2011).

Figure 2.13 summarizes additional information about the effects of time of exposure to a teratogen. The probability of a structural defect is greatest early in the embryonic period, when organs are being formed (Lu & Lu, 2008). Each body structure has its own critical period of formation. Recall from Chapter 1, "Introduction," that a critical period is a fixed time period very early in development during

Fetal alcohol spectrum disorders (FASD) are characterized by a number of physical abnormalities and learning problems. Notice the wide-set eyes, flat cheekbones, and thin upper lip in this child with FASD.

which certain experiences or events can have a long-lasting effect on development. The critical period for the nervous system (week 3) is earlier than that for arms and legs (weeks 4 and 5).

After organogenesis is complete, teratogens are less likely to cause anatomical defects. Instead, exposure during the fetal period is more likely to stunt growth or to create problems in the way organs function. To examine some key teratogens and their effects, let's begin with drugs.

Prescription and Nonprescription Drugs   Prescription drugs that can function as teratogens include antibiotics, such as streptomycin and tetracycline; some antidepressants; certain hormones, such as progestin and synthetic estrogen; and Accutane (often prescribed for acne) (Bayraktar & others, 2010; Teichert & others, 2010). Nonprescription drugs that can be harmful include diet pills and aspirin. Recent research revealed that low doses of aspirin pose no harm to the fetus but that high doses can contribute to maternal and fetal bleeding (James, Brancazio, & Price, 2008; Marret & others, 2010).

Psychoactive Drugs   *Psychoactive drugs* are drugs that act on the nervous system to alter states of consciousness, modify perceptions, and change moods. Examples include caffeine, alcohol, and nicotine, as well as illegal drugs such as cocaine, methamphetamine, marijuana, and heroin.

Caffeine   People often consume caffeine by drinking coffee, tea, or colas, or by eating chocolate. One study revealed that pregnant women who consumed 200 or more milligrams of caffeine a day had an increased risk of miscarriage (Weng, Odouli, & Li, 2008). However, a recent research review found that high amounts of caffeine consumption by pregnant women do not increase the risk of miscarriage, congenital malformations, or growth retardation (Brent, Christian, & Diener, 2011). Nonetheless, the Food and Drug Administration recommends that pregnant women either not consume caffeine or consume it only sparingly.

Alcohol   Heavy drinking by pregnant women can be devastating to offspring (Frost, Gist, & Adriano, 2011). **Fetal alcohol spectrum disorders (FASD)** are a cluster of abnormalities and problems that appear in the offspring of mothers who drink alcohol heavily during pregnancy. The abnormalities include facial deformities and defective limbs, face, and heart (Klingenberg & others, 2010). Most children with FASD have learning problems, and many are below average in intelligence; some are mentally retarded (Dalen & others, 2009). Although mothers of FASD infants are heavy drinkers, many mothers who are heavy drinkers may not have children with FASD or may have one child with FASD and other children who do not have it.

What are some guidelines for alcohol use during pregnancy? Even drinking just one or two servings of beer or wine or one serving of hard liquor a few days a week can have negative effects on the fetus, although it is generally agreed that this level of alcohol use will not cause fetal alcohol spectrum disorders. The U.S. Surgeon General recommends that *no* alcohol be consumed during pregnancy. And research suggests that it may not be wise to consume alcohol at the time of conception. One study revealed that intakes of alcohol by both men and women during the weeks of conception increased the risk of early pregnancy loss (Henriksen & others, 2004).

What are some links between expectant mothers' cigarette smoking and caffeine intake to outcomes for their offspring?

fetal alcohol spectrum disorders (FASD) A cluster of abnormalities that may appear in the offspring of mothers who drink alcohol heavily during pregnancy.

Nicotine   Cigarette smoking by pregnant women can also adversely influence prenatal development, birth, and postnatal development (Blood-Siegfried & Rende, 2010). Preterm births and low birth weights, fetal and neonatal deaths, respiratory problems, sudden infant death syndrome (SIDS, also known as crib death), and cardiovascular problems are all more common among the offspring of mothers who smoked during pregnancy (Beyerlein & others, 2011; Civelek & others, 2011). And a recent meta-analysis indicated that maternal smoking during pregnancy was linked to a modest increase in risk for childhood non-Hodgkin lymphoma (Antonopoulos & others, 2011). Maternal smoking during pregnancy has also been identified as a risk factor for the development of attention deficit hyperactivity disorder in offspring (Knopik, 2009). A recent research review indicates that environmental tobacco smoke, or secondhand smoke, is linked to increased risk of low birth weight in offspring (Leonardi-Bee & others, 2008).

Cocaine Does cocaine use during pregnancy harm the developing embryo and fetus? The most consistent finding is that cocaine exposure during prenatal development is associated with reduced birth weight, length, and head circumference (Gouin & others, 2011). In other studies, prenatal cocaine exposure has been linked to lower arousal, less effective self-regulation, higher excitability, and lower quality of reflexes at 1 month of age (Ackerman, Riggins, & Black, 2010; Lester & others, 2002); impaired motor development at 2 years of age and a slower rate of growth through 10 years of age (Richardson, Goldschmidt, & Willford, 2008); elevated blood pressure at 9 years of age (Shankaran & others, 2010); impaired language development and information processing (Beeghly & others, 2006) and attention deficits (especially in sustained attention) in preschool and elementary school children (Accornero & others, 2007; Ackerman, Riggins, & Black, 2010); increased likelihood of being in a special education program that offers support services (Levine & others, 2008); and increased behavioral problems, especially externalizing problems such as high rates of aggression and delinquency (Minnes & others, 2010; Richardson & others, 2011).

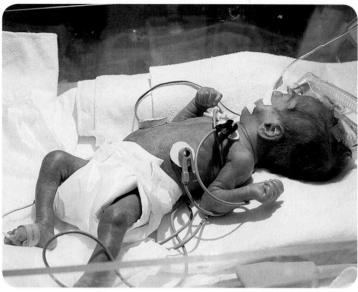

This baby was exposed to cocaine prenatally. *What are some of the possible effects on development of being exposed to cocaine prenatally?*

Some researchers argue that these findings should be interpreted cautiously (Accornero & others, 2006). Why? Because other factors in the lives of pregnant women who use cocaine (such as poverty, malnutrition, and other substance abuse) often cannot be ruled out as possible contributors to the problems found in their children (Hurt & others, 2005; Messiah & others, 2011). For example, cocaine users are more likely than nonusers to smoke cigarettes, use marijuana, drink alcohol, and take amphetamines.

Despite these cautions, the weight of research evidence indicates that children born to mothers who use cocaine are likely to have neurological, medical, and cognitive deficits (Field, 2007; Mayer & Zhang, 2009; Richardson & others, 2011). Cocaine use by pregnant women is never recommended.

Methamphetamine Methamphetamine, like cocaine, is a stimulant, speeding up an individual's nervous system. Babies born to mothers who use methamphetamine, or "meth," during pregnancy are at risk for a number of problems, including high infant mortality, low birth weight, memory deficits, and developmental and behavioral problems (Forrester & Merz, 2007; Piper & others, 2011). A recent study also found that prenatal exposure to meth was linked to less brain activation in a number of areas, especially the frontal lobes, in 7- to 15-year-olds (Roussotte & others, 2011).

Marijuana An increasing number of studies find that marijuana use by pregnant women also has negative outcomes for offspring. For example, a recent study found that prenatal marijuana exposure was related to lower intelligence in children (Goldschmidt & others, 2008). Another study indicated that prenatal exposure to marijuana was linked to marijuana use at 14 years of age (Day, Goldschmidt, & Thomas, 2006). In sum, marijuana use is not recommended for pregnant women.

Heroin It is well documented that infants whose mothers are addicted to heroin show several behavioral difficulties at birth (Steinhausen, Blattmann, & Pfund, 2007). The difficulties include withdrawal symptoms, such as tremors, irritability, abnormal crying, disturbed sleep, and impaired motor control. Many still show behavioral problems at their first birthday, and attention deficits may appear later in development. The most common treatment for heroin addiction, methadone, is associated with very severe withdrawal symptoms in newborns (Blandthorn, Forster, & Love, 2011).

Incompatible Blood Types Incompatibility between the mother's and father's blood types poses another risk to prenatal development. Blood types are created by differences in the surface structure of red blood cells. One type of difference in the surface of red blood cells creates the familiar blood groups—A, B, O, and AB. A second difference creates what is called Rh-positive and Rh-negative blood. If a surface marker, called the *Rh factor*, is present in an individual's red blood cells, the person is said to be Rh-positive; if the Rh-marker is not present, the person is said to be Rh-negative. If a pregnant woman is Rh-negative and her partner is Rh-positive, the fetus may be Rh-positive. If the fetus's blood is Rh-positive and the mother's is Rh-negative, the mother's immune system may produce antibodies that will attack the fetus. The result can be any number of problems, including miscarriage or stillbirth, anemia, jaundice, heart defects, brain damage, or death soon after birth (Moise, 2005).

Generally, the first Rh-positive baby of an Rh-negative mother is not at risk, but with each subsequent pregnancy the risk increases. A vaccine (RhoGAM) may be given to the mother within three days of the child's birth to prevent her body from making antibodies that will attack future Rh-positive fetuses. Also, babies affected by Rh incompatibility can be given blood transfusions before or right after birth.

Maternal Diseases Maternal diseases and infections can produce defects in offspring by crossing the placental barrier, or they can cause damage during birth. Rubella (German measles) is one disease that can cause prenatal defects. Women who plan to have children should have a blood test before they become pregnant to determine whether they are immune to the disease (Dontigny & others, 2008).

Syphilis (a sexually transmitted infection) is more damaging later in prenatal development—four months or more after conception. When syphilis is present at birth, problems can develop in the central nervous system and gastrointestinal tract (Johnson, Erbelding, & Ghanem, 2007). Most states require that pregnant women be given a blood test to detect the presence of syphilis.

Another infection that has received widespread attention recently is genital herpes. Newborns contract this virus when they are delivered through the birth canal of a mother with genital herpes (Nigro & others, 2011). If an active case of genital herpes is detected in a pregnant woman close to her delivery date, a cesarean section (in which the infant is delivered through an incision in the mother's abdomen) can be performed to keep the virus from infecting the newborn.

AIDS is a sexually transmitted infection that is caused by the human immunodeficiency virus (HIV), which destroys the body's immune system. A mother can infect her offspring with HIV/AIDS in three ways: (1) across the placenta during gestation, (2) through contact with maternal blood or fluids during delivery, and (3) through breastfeeding. The transmission of AIDS through breastfeeding is a particular problem in many developing countries (UNICEF, 2011). Babies born to HIV-infected mothers can be (1) infected and symptomatic (show HIV symptoms), (2) infected but asymptomatic (not show HIV symptoms), or (3) not infected at all. An infant who is infected and asymptomatic may still develop HIV symptoms up to 15 months of age.

The more widespread disease of diabetes, characterized by high levels of sugar in the blood, also affects offspring (Huda & others, 2010). A research review indicated that newborns

developmental connection

Conditions, Diseases, Disorders. The greatest incidence of HIV/AIDS occurs in sub-Saharan Africa, where in some areas as many as 30 percent of mothers have HIV; many are unaware that they are infected with the virus. Chapter 12, p. 390

Because the fetus depends entirely on its mother for nutrition, it is important for the pregnant woman to have good nutritional habits. In Kenya, this government clinic provides pregnant women with information about how their diet can influence the health of their fetus and offspring. *What might the information about diet be like?*

with physical defects are more likely to have diabetic mothers than newborns without such defects (Eriksson, 2009). Moreover, women who have gestational diabetes (a condition in which women without previously diagnosed diabetes develop high blood glucose levels during pregnancy) may deliver very large infants (weighing 10 pounds or more), and the infants themselves are at risk for diabetes (Gluck & others, 2009).

Maternal Diet and Nutrition   A developing embryo or fetus depends completely on its mother for nutrition, which comes from the mother's blood. The nutritional status of the embryo or fetus is determined by the mother's total caloric intake as well as her intake of proteins, vitamins, and minerals. Children born to malnourished mothers are more likely than other children to be malformed.

Being overweight before and during pregnancy can also put the embryo or fetus at risk, and an increasing number of pregnant women in the United States are overweight (Poston & others, 2011). A research review concluded that obesity during pregnancy is linked to increased maternal risks of infertility, hypertensive disorders, diabetes, and delivery by cesarean section (Arendas, Qui, & Gruslin, 2008). In this review, obesity during pregnancy put the fetus at increased risk for macrosomia (excessive birth weight), intrauterine fetal death, stillbirth, and admission to the neonatal intensive care unit (NICU).

One aspect of maternal nutrition that is important for normal prenatal development is folic acid, a B-complex vitamin (Rasmussen & Clemmensen, 2010). A recent study of more than 34,000 women who took folic acid either alone or as part of a multivitamin for at least one year prior to conceiving was linked with a 70 percent lower risk of delivering at 20 to 28 weeks and a 50 percent lower risk of delivering at 28 to 32 weeks (Bukowski & others, 2008). Another recent study revealed that toddlers of mothers who did not use folic acid supplements in the first trimester of pregnancy had more behavioral problems (Roza & others, 2010). Also, as we indicated earlier in the chapter, lack of folic acid is related to neural tube defects in offspring (Levene & Chervenak, 2009). The U.S. Department of Health and Human Services (2009) recommends that pregnant women consume a minimum of 400 micrograms of folic acid per day (about twice the amount the average woman gets in one day). Orange juice and spinach are examples of foods that are rich in folic acid.

Emotional States and Stress   When a pregnant woman experiences intense fears, anxieties, and other emotions or negative mood states, physiological changes occur that may affect her fetus (Brunton & Russell, 2011). A mother's stress may also influence the fetus indirectly by increasing the likelihood that the mother will engage in unhealthy behaviors such as taking drugs and receiving poor prenatal care.

High maternal anxiety and stress during pregnancy can have long-term consequences for the offspring (Dunkel Schetter, 2011; Field, 2011). A research review indicated that pregnant women with high levels of stress are at increased risk for having a child with emotional or cognitive problems, attention deficit hyperactivity disorder (ADHD), and language delay (Taige & others, 2007). A recent study of more than 30,000 offspring revealed that across the nine months of pregnancy, their risk of being born preterm was highest when maternal exposure to stress occurred during the fifth and sixth months of pregnancy (Class & others, 2011).

Might maternal depression also have an adverse effect on birth outcomes? Two recent research reviews concluded that maternal depression during pregnancy is linked to preterm birth and low birth weight (Dunkel Schetter, 2011).

Maternal Age   When possible harmful effects on the fetus and infant are considered, two maternal age groups are of special interest: adolescence and 35 years and older (Malizia, Hacker, & Penzias, 2009; Rudang & others, 2011). The mortality rate of infants born to adolescent mothers is double that of infants born to mothers in their twenties. Adequate prenatal care decreases the probability that a child born to

developmental **connection**

Health. What are some key factors that influence whether individuals will become obese? Chapter 4, p. 134

How do pregnant women's emotional states and stress affect prenatal development and birth?

an adolescent girl will have physical problems. However, adolescents are the least likely of women in all age groups to obtain prenatal assistance from clinics and health services.

Maternal age is also linked to the risk that a child will have Down syndrome (Ghosh & others, 2010). A baby with Down syndrome rarely is born to a mother 16 to 34 years of age. However, when the mother reaches 40 years of age, the probability is slightly over 1 in 100 that a baby born to her will have Down syndrome, and by age 50 it is almost 1 in 10. When mothers are 35 years and older, risks also increase for low birth weight, preterm delivery, and fetal death (Mbugua & others, 2009).

We still have much to learn about the effects of the mother's age on pregnancy and childbirth. As women remain active, exercise regularly, and are careful about their nutrition, their reproductive systems may remain healthier at older ages than was thought possible in the past.

What are some of the risks for infants born to adolescent mothers?

Paternal Factors So far, we have discussed how characteristics of the mother—such as drug use, disease, diet and nutrition, age, and emotional states—can influence prenatal development and the development of the child. Might there also be some paternal risk factors? Indeed, there are several. Men's exposure to lead, radiation, certain pesticides, and petrochemicals may cause abnormalities in sperm that lead to miscarriage or diseases such as childhood cancer (Cordier, 2008). The father's smoking during the mother's pregnancy also can cause problems for the offspring. In one study, heavy paternal smoking was associated with the risk of early miscarriage (Venners & others, 2004). This negative outcome may be related to maternal exposure to secondhand smoke.

developmental **connection**

Sexuality. Adolescent pregnancy creates negative developmental trajectories for both mothers and their offspring. Chapter 12, p. 398

An explosion at the Chernobyl nuclear power plant in the Ukraine produced radioactive contamination that spread to surrounding areas. Thousands of infants were born with health problems and deformities as a result of the nuclear contamination, including this boy whose arm did not form. *Other than radioactive contamination, what are some other types of environmental hazards to prenatal development?*

Environmental Hazards Many aspects of our modern industrial world can endanger the embryo or fetus (Wiesel & others, 2011). Some specific hazards to the embryo or fetus include radiation, toxic wastes, and other chemical pollutants.

Women and their physicians should weigh the risk of an X-ray when the woman is or might be pregnant (Baysinger, 2010). However, a routine diagnostic X-ray of a body area other than the abdomen, with the woman's abdomen protected by a lead apron, is generally considered safe (Brent, 2009, 2011).

Despite the multitude of potential hazards during prenatal development, it is important to keep in mind that most of the time prenatal development does not go awry and development proceeds along the positive path that was described at the beginning of the chapter. The *Connecting Development to Life* interlude that follows outlines some of the steps that prospective parents can take to increase the chances for healthy prenatal development.

PRENATAL CARE

Although prenatal care varies enormously from one woman to another, it usually involves a defined schedule of visits for medical care,

A Healthy Pregnancy

A helpful initial strategy for women is to begin preparing for pregnancy before becoming pregnant. Women should consult with their physician about discontinuing any medications that might harm their offspring, including acne medications and tranquilizers. If they smoke or drink alcohol, they need to break these habits before becoming pregnant. It also is wise to reduce caffeine intake and begin taking a multiple vitamin with iron, making sure it has at least 0.4 mg of folic acid. Avoiding fish with high levels of mercury is another good strategy.

In addition to healthy eating, moderate regular exercise is linked with fewer discomforts in pregnancy and an improved sense of wellbeing (Lovelady, 2011; Phelan & others, 2011). For example, one study revealed that regular exercise during the second half of pregnancy reduced the low back pain of expectant mothers (Garshasbi & Faghih Zadeh, 2005). One study found that, compared with sedentary pregnant women, women who engaged in light leisure time physical activity had a 24 percent reduced likelihood of preterm delivery, and those who participated in moderate to heavy leisure time physical activity had a 66 percent reduced risk of preterm delivery (Hegaard & others, 2008). A recent study revealed that exercise during pregnancy improved mothers' perception of their health (Barakat & others, 2011). However, it is important for expectant mothers to avoid overly strenuous exercise because it can increase the probability of bleeding or preterm labor. Walking, swimming, and stretching are among recommended exercises for expectant mothers.

How might a woman's exercise in pregnancy benefit her and her offspring?

Another important aspect of having a healthy pregnancy is to talk with a physician about the use of prenatal tests to assess the health of the developing fetus, a topic that we discussed earlier in this chapter. Another important step in a healthy pregnancy is to obtain early prenatal care, which we will discuss next.

What can society do to ensure that prospective mothers are more aware of the risks if they become pregnant?

which typically includes screening for manageable conditions and treatable diseases that can affect the baby or the mother.

In addition to medical care, prenatal programs often include comprehensive educational, social, and nutritional services. Information about pregnancy, labor, delivery, and caring for the newborn can be especially valuable for first-time mothers (Lowdermilk, Perry, & Cashion, 2011; Murray & McKinney, 2010). Prenatal care is also very important for women in poverty because it links them with other social services (Mattson & Smith, 2011).

An innovative program that is rapidly expanding in the United States is CenteringPregnancy (Steming, 2008). This program is relationship-centered and provides complete prenatal care in a group setting. It replaces traditional 15-minute physician visits with 90-minute peer group support sessions and self-examination led by a physician or certified nurse-midwife. Groups of up to 10 women (and often their partners) meet regularly beginning at 12 to 16 weeks of pregnancy. The sessions emphasize empowering women to play an active role in experiencing a positive pregnancy. A recent study revealed that participants in CenteringPregnancy groups made more prenatal visits, had higher breastfeeding rates, and were more satisfied with their prenatal care than were women in individual care (Klima & others, 2009). In another recent study, high-stress women were randomly assigned to a CenteringPregnancy Plus group, group prenatal care, or standard individual care

A CenteringPregnancy program. This rapidly expanding program alters routine prenatal care by bringing women out of exam rooms and into relationship-oriented groups.

from 18 weeks gestation to birth (Ickovics & others, 2011). The most stressed women in the CenteringPregnancy Plus group showed increased self-esteem and decreased stress and social conflict in their third trimester of pregnancy; their social conflict and depression also were lower at one year postpartum.

Some prenatal programs for parents focus on home visitation (Eckenrode & others, 2010; Issel & others, 2011). Research evaluations indicate that the Nurse Family Partnership created by David Olds and his colleagues (2004, 2007) produces positive results. The Nurse-Family Partnership involves home visits by trained nurses beginning in the second or third trimester of prenatal development. The extensive program consists of approximately 50 home visits beginning during the prenatal period and extending through the child's first two years. The home visits focus on the mother's health, access to health care, parenting, and improvement of the mother's life by providing her with guidance in education, work, and relationships. Research revealed that the Nurse Family Partnership has numerous positive outcomes, including fewer pregnancies, better work circumstances, and stability in relationship partners for the mother, and improved academic success and social development for the child (Olds & others, 2004, 2007).

Review *Connect* Reflect

 LG4 Characterize the course of prenatal development and its hazards

Review

- What is the course of prenatal development? How does the brain develop during the prenatal period?
- What are some prenatal diagnostic tests?
- What are some of the main hazards to prenatal development?
- What types of resources do prenatal care programs provide?

Connect

- In this chapter we've discussed chromosomal and gene-linked abnormalities that can affect prenatal development. How are the symptoms of the related conditions or risks similar to or different from those caused by teratogens or other hazards?

Reflect *Your Own Personal Journey of Life*

- If you are a woman, imagine that you have just found out that you are pregnant. What health-enhancing strategies will you follow through the prenatal period? For others, imagine that you are the partner of a woman who has just found out she is pregnant. What will be your role in increasing the likelihood that the prenatal period will go smoothly?

Birth and the Postpartum Period

LG5 Summarize how birth takes place and describe the nature of the postpartum period

The Birth Process

The Transition from Fetus to Newborn

Low Birth Weight and Preterm Infants

Bonding

The Postpartum Period

> There was a star danced, and under that I was born.
>
> —**WILLIAM SHAKESPEARE**
> *English Playwright, 17th Century*

The long wait for the moment of birth is over, and the infant is about to appear. What happens during childbirth, and what can be done to make the experience a positive one?

Nature writes the basic script for how birth occurs, but parents make important choices about the conditions surrounding birth. We will look first at the sequence of physical steps through which a child is born.

THE BIRTH PROCESS

The birth process occurs in three stages. It may take place in different contexts and in most cases involves one or more attendants.

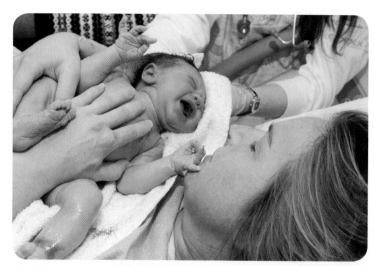

After the long journey of prenatal development, birth takes place. During birth the baby is on a threshold between two worlds. *What is the fetus/newborn transition like?*

Stages of Birth The first stage of the birth process is the longest. Uterine contractions are 15 to 20 minutes apart at the beginning and last up to a minute. These contractions cause the woman's cervix to stretch and open. As the first stage progresses, the contractions come closer together, occurring every two to five minutes. Their intensity increases. By the end of the first stage, contractions dilate the cervix to an opening of about 10 centimeters (4 inches), so that the baby can move from the uterus to the birth canal. For a woman having her first child, the first stage lasts an average of 6 to 12 hours; for subsequent children, this stage typically is much shorter.

The second birth stage begins when the baby's head starts to move through the cervix and the birth canal. It terminates when the baby completely emerges from the mother's body. With each contraction, the mother bears down hard to push the baby out of her body. By the time the baby's head is out of the mother's body, the contractions come almost every minute and last for about a minute. This stage typically lasts approximately 45 minutes to an hour.

Afterbirth is the third stage, during which the placenta, umbilical cord, and other membranes are detached and expelled. This final stage is the shortest of the three birth stages, lasting only minutes.

Childbirth Setting and Attendants In the United States, 99 percent of births take place in hospitals, a figure that has remained constant for several decades (Martin & others, 2005). Who helps a mother during birth varies across cultures. In U.S. hospitals, it has become the norm for fathers or birth coaches to be with the mother throughout labor and delivery. In the East African Nigoni culture, men are completely excluded from the childbirth process. When a woman is ready to give birth, female relatives move into the woman's hut and the husband leaves, taking his belongings (clothes, tools, weapons, and so on) with him. He is not permitted to return until after the baby is born. In some cultures, childbirth is an open, community affair. For example, in the Pukapukan culture in the Pacific Islands, women give birth in a shelter that is open to villagers, who may observe the birth.

In India, a midwife checks on the size, position, and heartbeat of a fetus. Midwives deliver babies in many cultures around the world. *What are some cultural variations in prenatal care?*

Midwives Midwifery is practiced in most countries throughout the world (Byrom & Symon, 2011; Kitzinger, 2011). In Holland, more than 40 percent of babies are delivered by *midwives* rather than by doctors. However, in 2003, 91 percent of U.S. births were attended by physicians, and only 8 percent of women who delivered a baby were attended by a midwife (Martin & others, 2005). Nevertheless, the 8 percent figure for 2003 represents a substantial increase from less than 1 percent in 1975 (Martin & others, 2005). Ninety-five percent of the midwives who delivered babies in the United States in 2003 were certified nurse-midwives.

Doulas In some countries, a doula attends a childbearing woman. *Doula* is a Greek word that means "a woman who helps." A **doula** is a caregiver who provides continuous physical, emotional, and educational support for the mother before, during, and after childbirth. Doulas remain with the parents throughout labor, assessing and responding to their needs. Researchers have found positive

doula A caregiver who provides continuous physical, emotional, and educational support for the mother before, during, and after childbirth.

effects when a doula is present at the birth of a child (Akhavan & Lundgren, 2011; Dahlen, Jackson, & Stevens, 2011).

In the United States, most doulas work as independent providers hired by the expectant parents. Doulas typically function as part of a "birthing team," serving as an adjunct to the midwife or the hospital's obstetric staff.

Methods of Childbirth   U.S. hospitals often allow the mother and her obstetrician a range of options regarding their method of delivery. Key choices involve the use of medication, whether to use any of a number of nonmedicated techniques to reduce pain, and when to have a cesarean delivery.

Medication   Three basic kinds of drugs that are used for labor are analgesia, anesthesia, and oxytocin/pitocin. *Analgesia* is used to relieve pain. Analgesics include tranquilizers, barbiturates, and narcotics such as Demerol.

Anesthesia is used in late first-stage labor and during delivery to block sensation in an area of the body or to block consciousness. There is a trend toward not using general anesthesia, which blocks consciousness, in normal births because general anesthesia can be transmitted through the placenta to the fetus (Lieberman & others, 2005). An *epidural block* is regional anesthesia that numbs the woman's body from the waist down. Researchers are continuing to explore safer drug mixtures for use at lower doses to improve the effectiveness and safety of epidural anesthesia (Balaji, Dhillon, & Russell, 2009).

Oxytocin is a synthetic hormone that is used to stimulate contractions; pitocin is the most widely used oxytocin. The benefits and risks of oxytocin as a part of childbirth continue to be debated (Vasdev, 2008).

Predicting how a drug will affect an individual woman and her fetus is difficult (Lowdermilk, Perry, & Cashion, 2011). A particular drug might have only a minimal effect on one fetus yet have a much stronger effect on another. The drug's dosage is also a factor (Weiner & Buhimschi, 2009). Stronger doses of tranquilizers and narcotics given to decrease the mother's pain potentially have a more negative effect on the fetus than do mild doses. It is important for the mother to assess her level of pain and have a voice in the decision as to whether or not she should receive medication.

Natural and Prepared Childbirth   For a brief time not long ago, the idea of avoiding all medication during childbirth gained favor in the United States. Instead, many women chose to reduce the pain of childbirth through techniques known as natural childbirth and prepared childbirth. Today, at least some medication is used in the typical childbirth, but elements of natural childbirth and prepared childbirth remain popular (Oates & Abraham, 2010).

Natural childbirth is a childbirth method in which no drugs are given to relieve pain or assist in the birth process. The mother and her partner are taught to use breathing methods and relaxation techniques during delivery. French obstetrician Ferdinand Lamaze developed a method similar to natural childbirth that is known as **prepared childbirth,** or the Lamaze method. It includes a special breathing technique to control pushing in the final stages of labor, as well as more detailed education about anatomy and physiology. The Lamaze method has become very popular in the United States. The pregnant woman's partner usually serves as a coach; he attends childbirth classes with her and guides her breathing and relaxation during delivery. In sum, proponents of current prepared childbirth methods conclude that when information and support are provided, women *know* how to give birth.

Other Nonmedicated Techniques to Reduce Pain   The effort to reduce stress and control pain during labor has recently led to an increase in the use of some older and some newer nonmedicated techniques (Kalder & others, 2011; Simkin & Bolding, 2004). These include waterbirth, massage, and acupuncture.

A doula assisting a birth. *What types of support do doulas provide?*

natural childbirth Method attempting to reduce the mother's pain by decreasing her fear through education about childbirth stages and relaxation techniques during delivery.

prepared childbirth Developed by French obstetrician Ferdinand Lamaze, a childbirth strategy similar to natural childbirth but one that teaches a special breathing technique to control pushing in the final stages of labor and provides details about anatomy and physiology.

Waterbirth involves giving birth in a tub of warm water. Some women go through labor in the water and get out for delivery; others remain in the water for delivery. The rationale for waterbirth is that the baby has been in an amniotic sac for many months and that delivery in a similar environment is likely to be less stressful for the baby and the mother (Meyer, Weible, & Woeber, 2010). Mothers get into the warm water when contractions become closer together and more intense. Getting into the water too soon can cause labor to slow or stop. Reviews of research have indicated mixed results for waterbirths (Cluett & Burns, 2009; Pinette, Wax, & Wilson, 2004). A recent study did find that waterbirth was linked with a shorter second stage of labor (Cortes, Basra, & Kelleher, 2011). Waterbirth has been practiced more often in European countries such as Switzerland and Sweden than in the United States in recent decades, but it is increasingly being included in U.S. birth plans.

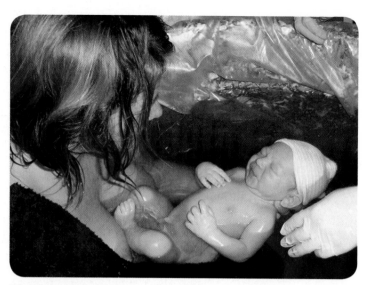

What characterizes the use of waterbirth in delivering a baby?

Massage is increasingly used as a procedure prior to and during delivery (Stager, 2009–2010). Researchers have found that massage can reduce pain and anxiety during labor (Chang, Chen, & Huang, 2006). A recent study revealed that massage therapy reduced pain in pregnant women and alleviated prenatal depression in both parents and improved their relationships (Field, Figueiredo, & others, 2008).

Acupuncture, the insertion of very fine needles into specific locations in the body, is used as a standard procedure to reduce the pain of childbirth in China, although it only recently has begun to be used for this purpose in the United States. Recent research indicates that acupuncture can have positive effects on labor and delivery (Citkovitz & others, 2011).

Cesarean Delivery   Normally, the baby's head comes through the vagina first. But if the baby is in a *breech position*, its buttocks are the first part to emerge from the vagina. In 1 of every 25 deliveries, the baby's head is still in the uterus when the rest of the body is out. Because breech births can cause respiratory problems, if the baby is in a breech position a surgical procedure known as a cesarean delivery is usually performed. In a *cesarean* delivery (or cesarean section), the baby is removed from the uterus through an incision made in the mother's abdomen (Lee, El-Sayed, & Gould, 2008). More cesarean sections are performed in the United States than in any other country in the world. In 2009, 33 percent of babies in the U.S. were cesarean deliveries (Solheim & others, 2011). If the cesarean rate continues to increase at its current pace, more than 50 percent of U.S. babies will be cesarean deliveries. The benefits and risks of cesarean sections continue to be debated (Bangdiwala & others, 2010; Minguez-Milio & others, 2011).

THE TRANSITION FROM FETUS TO NEWBORN

Much of our discussion of birth so far has focused on the mother. However, birth also involves considerable stress for the baby. If the delivery takes too long, the baby can develop *anoxia*, a condition in which the fetus or newborn has an insufficient supply of oxygen. Anoxia can cause brain damage (Davidson & others, 2012).

The baby has considerable capacity to withstand the stress of birth. Large quantities of adrenaline and noradrenaline, hormones that protect the fetus in the event of oxygen deficiency, are secreted in the newborn's body during the birth process (Van Beveren, 2011).

Immediately after birth, the umbilical cord is cut and the baby is on its own. Before birth, oxygen came from the mother via the umbilical cord, but now the baby is self-sufficient and can breathe independently.

Almost immediately after birth, a newborn is taken to be weighed, cleaned up, and tested for signs of developmental problems that might require urgent

Score	0	1	2
Heart rate	Absent	Slow—less than 100 beats per minute	Fast—100–140 beats per minute
Respiratory effort	No breathing for more than one minute	Irregular and slow	Good breathing with normal crying
Muscle tone	Limp and flaccid	Weak, inactive, but some flexion of extremities	Strong, active motion
Body color	Blue and pale	Body pink, but extremities blue	Entire body pink
Reflex irritability	No response	Grimace	Coughing, sneezing and crying

FIGURE **2.14**

THE APGAR SCALE. A newborn's score on the Apgar Scale indicates whether the baby has urgent medical problems. *What are some trends in the Apgar scores of U.S. babies?*

attention (Therrell & others, 2010). The **Apgar Scale** is widely used to assess the health of newborns at one and five minutes after birth. The Apgar Scale evaluates infants' heart rate, respiratory effort, muscle tone, body color, and reflex irritability (see Figure 2.14). An obstetrician or nurse does the evaluation and gives the newborn a score, or reading, of 0, 1, or 2 on each of these five health signs. A total score of 7 to 10 indicates that the newborn's condition is good. A score of 5 indicates that there may be developmental difficulties. A score of 3 or below signals an emergency and warns that the baby might not survive. The Apgar Scale is especially good at assessing the newborn's ability to respond to the stress of delivery and its new environment (Reynolds, 2010). It also identifies high-risk infants who need resuscitation. A recent study revealed that in comparison with children who had a high Apgar score (9 to 10), the risk of developing attention deficit hyperactivity disorder (ADHD) in childhood was 75 percent higher for newborns with a low Apgar score (1 to 4) and 63 percent higher with an Apgar score of 5 to 6 (Li & others, 2011).

Nurses often play important roles in the birth of a baby. To read about the work of a nurse who specializes in the care of women during labor and delivery, see *Connecting with Careers*.

Apgar Scale A widely used method to assess the health of newborns at one and five minutes after birth; it evaluates an infant's heart rate, respiratory effort, muscle tone, body color, and reflex irritability.

low birth weight infants Infants that weigh less than 5½ pounds at birth.

preterm infants Infants born three weeks or more before the pregnancy has reached its full term.

small for date infants Infants whose birth weights are below normal when the length of pregnancy is considered; also called small for gestational age infants. Small for date infants may be preterm or full-term.

LOW BIRTH WEIGHT AND PRETERM INFANTS

Three related conditions pose threats to many newborns: low birth weight, preterm birth, and being small for date. **Low birth weight infants** weigh less than 5½ pounds at birth. *Very low birth weight* newborns weigh under 3 pounds, and *extremely low birth weight* newborns weigh under 2 pounds. **Preterm infants** are born three weeks or more before the pregnancy has reached its full term—in other words, 35 or fewer weeks after conception. **Small for date infants** (also called *small for gestational age infants*) have a birth weight that is below normal when the length of the pregnancy is considered. They weigh less than 90 percent of all babies of the same gestational age. Small for date infants may be preterm or full term. One study found that small for date infants have a 400 percent greater risk of death (Regev & others, 2003).

Linda Pugh, Perinatal Nurse

Perinatal nurses work with childbearing women to support health and growth during the childbearing experience. Linda Pugh, Ph.D., R.N.C., is a perinatal nurse on the faculty at The Johns Hopkins University School of Nursing. She is certified as an inpatient obstetric nurse and specializes in the care of women during labor and delivery. She teaches undergraduate and graduate students, educates professional nurses, and conducts research. In addition, Pugh consults with hospitals and organizations about women's health issues and many of the topics we discuss in this chapter.

Her research interests include nursing interventions with low-income breastfeeding women, discovering ways to prevent and ameliorate fatigue during childbearing, and using breathing exercises during labor.

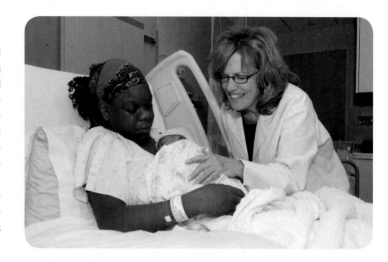

In 2007, 12.7 percent of U.S. infants were born preterm—a 36 percent increase since the 1980s (National Center for Health Statistics, 2009). The increase in preterm birth is likely due to such factors as the increasing number of births to women 35 years of age or older, increasing rates of multiple births, increased management of maternal and fetal conditions (for example, inducing labor preterm if medical technology indicates that it will increase the likelihood of survival), increased rates of substance abuse (tobacco, alcohol), and increased stress (Goldenberg & Culhane, 2007). Ethnic variations characterize preterm birth (Balchin & Steer, 2007). For example, in 2006 the likelihood of being born preterm was 12.8 percent for all U.S. infants, but the rate was 18.5 percent for African American infants (National Center for Health Statistics, 2009).

The incidence of low birth weight varies considerably from country to country. In some countries, such as India and Sudan, where poverty is rampant and the health and nutrition of mothers are poor, the percentage of low birth weight babies reaches as high as 31 percent (see Figure 2.15). In the United States, there has been an increase in low birth weight infants in the last two decades. The U.S. low birth weight rate of 8.2 percent in 2007 is considerably higher than that of many other developed countries (Hamilton & others, 2009). For example, only 4 percent of the infants born in Sweden, Finland, Norway, and Korea are low birth weight, and only 5 percent of those born in New Zealand, Australia, and France are low birth weight.

Recently, there has been considerable interest in the role that progestin might play in reducing preterm births (O'Brien & Lewis, 2009). Recent research indicates that progestin is most effective when it is given to women with a history of previous spontaneous birth at less than 37 weeks (da Fonseca & others, 2009), to women who have a short cervical length of 15 mm or less (da Fonseca & others, 2009), and to women with a singleton rather than twins (Norman & others, 2009).

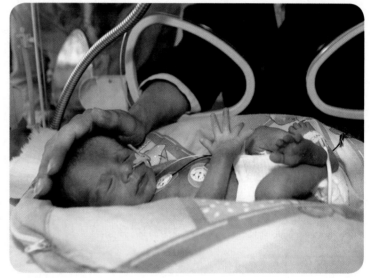

A "kilogram kid," weighing less than 2.3 pounds at birth. *What are some long-term outcomes for weighing so little at birth?*

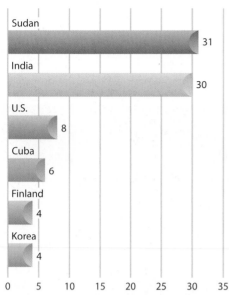

Sudan	31
India	30
U.S.	8
Cuba	6
Finland	4
Korea	4

0   5   10   15   20   25   30   35

Percentage of infants born with low birth weight

FIGURE **2.15**
PERCENTAGE OF INFANTS BORN WITH LOW BIRTH WEIGHT IN SELECTED COUNTRIES

A new mother practicing kangaroo care. *What is kangaroo care?*

---------- ➤

developmental **connection**

Attachment. A classic study with surrogate cloth and wire monkeys demonstrates the important role that touch plays in infant attachment. Chapter 10, p. 319

kangaroo care A way of holding a preterm infant so that there is skin-to-skin contact.

bonding The formation of a close connection, especially a physical bond between parents and their newborn in the period shortly after birth.

Consequences of Low Birth Weight Although most preterm and low birth weight infants are healthy, as a group they have more health and developmental problems than do infants of normal birth weight (Minde & Zelkowitz, 2008). For preterm birth, the terms *extremely preterm* and *very preterm* are increasingly used (Lowdermilk, Perry, & Cashion, 2011). *Extremely preterm infants* are those born less than 28 weeks preterm, and *very preterm infants* are those born at less than 33 weeks of gestational age. A recent Norwegian study indicated that the earlier preterm infants are born, the more likely they will eventually drop out of school (Swamy, Ostbye, & Skjaerven, 2008).

The number and severity of these problems increase when infants are born very early and as their birth weight decreases (Baron & others, 2011; Duncan & others, 2011). Survival rates for infants who are born very early and very small have risen, but with this improved survival rate have come increased rates of severe brain damage (Casey, 2008). Low birth weight children are more likely than their normal birth weight counterparts to develop a learning disability, attention deficit hyperactivity disorder, or breathing problems such as asthma (Anderson & others, 2011; Santo, Portuguez, & Nunes, 2009). Approximately 50 percent of all low birth weight children are enrolled in special education programs.

Nurturing Low Birth Weight and Preterm Infants Two increasingly used interventions in the neonatal intensive care unit (NICU) are kangaroo care and massage therapy. **Kangaroo care** involves skin-to-skin contact in which the baby, wearing only a diaper, is held upright against the parent's bare chest, much as a baby kangaroo is carried by its mother. Kangaroo care is typically practiced for two to three hours per day over an extended time in early infancy.

Why use kangaroo care with preterm infants? Preterm infants often have difficulty coordinating their breathing and heart rate, and the close physical contact with the parent provided by kangaroo care can help stabilize the preterm infant's heartbeat, temperature, and breathing (Nyqvist & others, 2010). Preterm infants who experience kangaroo care also gain more weight than their counterparts who are not given this care (Ahmed & others, 2011). Recent studies also revealed that kangaroo care decreased pain responses in preterm infants (Cong, Ludington-Hoe, & Walsh, 2011; Johnston & others, 2009).

Many preterm infants experience less touch than full-term infants because they are isolated in temperature-controlled incubators (Chia, Sellick, & Gan, 2006). The research of Tiffany Field has led to a surge of interest in the role that massage might play in improving the developmental outcomes for preterm infants. To read about her research, see the *Connecting with Research* interlude.

BONDING

A special component of the parent-infant relationship is **bonding,** the formation of a connection, especially a physical bond between parents and the newborn in the period shortly after birth. In the mid-20th century, U.S. hospitals seemed almost determined to deter bonding. Anesthesia given to the mother during delivery would make the mother drowsy, interfering with her ability to respond to and stimulate the newborn. Mothers and newborns were often separated shortly after delivery, and preterm infants were isolated from their mothers even more than full-term infants were. In recent decades these practices have changed, but to some extent they are still followed in many hospitals.

Do these practices do any harm? Some physicians believe that during the "critical period" shortly after birth the parents and newborn need to form an emotional

connecting with research

How Are Preterm Infants Affected by Touch?

Many preterm infants experience less touch than full-term infants do because they are isolated in temperature-controlled incubators. Research by Tiffany Field and her colleagues (2001, 2007; Diego, Field, & Hernandez-Reif, 2008; Field, Diego, & Hernandez-Reif, 2008, 2010) has led to a surge of interest in the role that massage might play in improving developmental outcomes for preterm infants. In Field's first study in this area, massage therapy consisting of firm stroking with the palms of the hands was given three times per day for 15-minute periods to preterm infants (Field & others, 1986). The massage therapy led to 47 percent greater weight gain than did standard medical treatment. The massaged infants also were more active and alert than preterm infants who were not massaged, and they performed better on developmental tests.

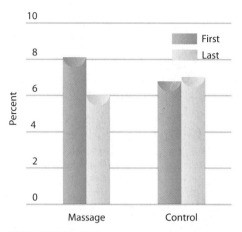

FIGURE **2.16**

PRETERM INFANTS SHOW REDUCED STRESS BEHAVIORS AND ACTIVITY AFTER FIVE DAYS OF MASSAGE THERAPY. *Source:* Hernandez-Reif, Diego, & Field, 2007.

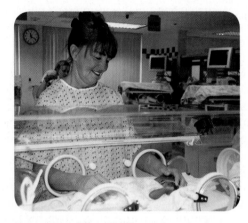

Shown here is Tiffany Field massaging a newborn infant. *What types of infants has massage therapy been shown to help?*

In later studies, Field demonstrated the benefits of massage therapy for infants who faced a variety of problems. For example, preterm infants exposed to cocaine in utero who received massage therapy gained weight and improved their scores on developmental tests (Field, 2001). In one study, preterm infants in a neonatal intensive care unit (NICU) were randomly assigned to a massage therapy group or a control group (Hernandez-Reif, Diego, & Field, 2007). For five consecutive days, the preterm infants in the massage group were given three 15-minute moderate pressure massages. Behavioral observations of the following stress behaviors were made on the first and last days of the study: crying, grimacing, yawning, sneezing, jerky arm and leg movements, startles, and finger flaring. The various stress behaviors were summarized in a composite stress behavior index. As indicated in Figure 2.16, massage had a stress-reducing effect on the preterm infants, which is especially important because they encounter numerous stressors while they are hospitalized.

In a review of the use of massage therapy with preterm infants, Field and her colleagues (2010) concluded that the most consistent findings were two positive results: (1) increased weight gain and (2) discharge from the hospital three to six days earlier.

What results do you think researchers might expect to find if they investigate the effects of massage on full-term infants?

attachment as a foundation for optimal development in years to come (Kennell, 2006; Kennell & McGrath, 1999). Although some research supports this bonding hypothesis (Klaus & Kennell, 1976), a body of research challenges the significance of the first few days of life as a critical period (Bakeman & Brown, 1980; Rode & others, 1981). Indeed, the extreme form of the bonding hypothesis—that the newborn *must* have close contact with the mother in the first few days of life to develop optimally—simply is not true.

developmental **connection**

Attachment. Lorenz demonstrated the importance of early bonding in greylag geese, but the first few days of life are unlikely to be a critical period for bonding in human infants. Chapter 1, p. 25

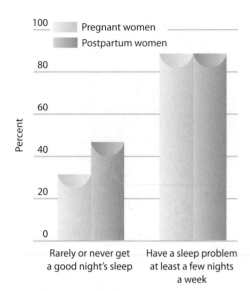

FIGURE **2.17**

SLEEP DEPRIVATION IN PREGNANT AND POSTPARTUM WOMEN

Postpartum blues
Symptoms appear 2 to 3 days after delivery and usually subside within 1 to 2 weeks.

70%

10%

20%

Postpartum depression
Symptoms linger for weeks or months and interfere with daily functioning.

No symptoms

FIGURE **2.18**

POSTPARTUM BLUES AND POSTPARTUM DEPRESSION AMONG U.S. WOMEN. Some health professionals refer to the postpartum period as the "fourth trimester." Though the time span of the postpartum period does not necessarily cover three months, the term "fourth trimester" suggests continuity and the importance of the first several months after birth for the mother.

postpartum period The period after childbirth when the mother adjusts, both physically and psychologically, to the process of childbirth. This period lasts for about six weeks or until her body has completed its adjustment and returned to a near prepregnant state.

postpartum depression A major depressive episode that typically occurs about four weeks after delivery; women with this condition have such strong feelings of sadness, anxiety, or despair that they have trouble coping with daily tasks during the postpartum period.

Nevertheless, the weakness of the bonding hypothesis should not be used as an excuse to keep motivated mothers from interacting with their newborns. Such contact brings pleasure to many mothers and may dispel maternal anxiety about the baby's health and safety. In some cases—including preterm infants, adolescent mothers, and mothers from disadvantaged circumstances—early close contact is key to establishing a climate for improved interaction after the mother and infant leave the hospital.

Many hospitals now offer a *rooming-in* arrangement, in which the baby remains in the mother's room most of the time during its hospital stay. However, if parents choose not to use this rooming-in arrangement, the weight of the research suggests that this decision will not harm the infant emotionally (Lamb, 1994).

THE POSTPARTUM PERIOD

The weeks after childbirth present challenges for many new parents and their offspring. This is the **postpartum period,** the period after childbirth or delivery that lasts for about six weeks or until the mother's body has completed its adjustment and has returned to a nearly prepregnant state. It is a time when the woman adjusts, both physically and psychologically, to the process of childbearing.

Physical Adjustments   A woman's body makes numerous physical adjustments in the first days and weeks after childbirth (Mattson & Smith, 2011). She may have a great deal of energy or feel exhausted and let down. Though these changes are normal, the fatigue can undermine the new mother's sense of well-being and confidence in her ability to cope with a new baby and a new family life.

A concern is the loss of sleep that the primary caregiver experiences during the postpartum period (Montgomery-Downs & others, 2010). In the 2007 Sleep in America survey, a substantial percentage of women reported loss of sleep during pregnancy and in the postpartum period (National Sleep Foundation, 2007) (see Figure 2.17). The loss of sleep can contribute to stress, marital conflict, and impaired decision making (Meerlo, Sgoifo, & Suchecki, 2008).

After delivery, the mother's body undergoes sudden and dramatic changes in hormone production. When the placenta is delivered, estrogen and progesterone levels drop steeply and remain low until the ovaries start producing hormones again.

Involution is the process by which the uterus returns to its prepregnant size five or six weeks after birth. Immediately following birth, the uterus weighs 2 to 3 pounds. By the end of five or six weeks, the uterus weighs 2 to 3½ ounces. Nursing the baby helps contract the uterus at a rapid rate.

Emotional and Psychological Adjustments   Emotional fluctuations are common for mothers in the postpartum period. For some women, emotional fluctuations decrease within several weeks after the delivery, but other women experience more long-lasting emotional swings.

As shown in Figure 2.18, about 70 percent of new mothers in the United States have what are called the *postpartum blues*. About two to three days after birth, they begin to feel depressed, anxious, and upset. These feelings may come and go for several months after the birth, often peaking about three to five days after birth. Even without treatment, these feelings usually go away after one or two weeks.

However, some women develop **postpartum depression,** which involves a major depressive episode that typically occurs about four weeks after delivery. Women with postpartum depression have such strong feelings of sadness, anxiety, or despair that for at least a two-week period they have trouble coping with their daily tasks. Without treatment, postpartum depression may become worse and last for many months (Nolen-Hoeksema, 2011). And many women with postpartum depression don't seek help. For example, one recent study found that 15 percent of the women surveyed had experienced postpartum depression symptoms but less than half had sought help (McGarry & others, 2009). Estimates indicate that 10 to 14 percent of new mothers experience postpartum depression.

Several antidepressant drugs are effective in treating postpartum depression and appear to be safe for breastfeeding women and their infants (Davanzo & others, 2011). Psychotherapy, especially cognitive therapy, also is an effective treatment of postpartum depression for many women (Miller & Larusso, 2011). Also, engaging in regular exercise may help in treating postpartum depression (Daley, MacArthur, & Winter, 2007).

Can a mother's postpartum depression affect the way she interacts with her infant? A recent research review concluded that the interaction difficulties of depressed mothers and their infants occur across cultures and socioeconomic status groups, comprising reduced sensitivity of the mothers and decreased responsiveness on the part of infants (Field, 2010). Several caregiving activities also are compromised, including feeding, sleep routines, and safety practices.

Fathers also undergo considerable adjustment during the postpartum period, even when they work away from home all day. Many fathers feel that the baby comes first and gets all of the mother's attention; some feel that they have been replaced by the baby.

The father's support and caring can play a role in whether the mother develops postpartum depression or not (Dietz & others, 2009; Persson & others, 2011). A recent study revealed that higher support by fathers was related to a lower incidence of postpartum depression in women (Smith & Howard, 2008).

The postpartum period is a time of considerable adjustment and adaptation for both the mother and the father. Fathers can provide an important support system for mothers, especially in helping mothers care for young infants. *What kinds of tasks might the father of a newborn do to support the mother?*

Review *Connect* Reflect

 Summarize how birth takes place and describe the nature of the postpartum period

Review

- What are the three main stages of birth? What are some different birth strategies? What is the transition from fetus to newborn like for the infant?
- What is the transition from fetus to newborn like?
- What are the outcomes for children if they are born preterm or with a low birth weight?
- What is bonding? How is it linked to child outcomes?
- What are some characteristics of the postpartum period?

Connect

- Compare and contrast what you learned about kangaroo care and breast feeding of preterm infants with what you learned about bonding and breast feeding when the mother is suffering from postpartum depression.

Reflect *Your Own Personal Journey of Life*

- If you are a female, which birth strategy do you prefer? Why? If you are a male, how involved would you want to be in helping your partner through pregnancy and the birth of your baby?

The Evolutionary Perspective

 LG1 Discuss the evolutionary perspective on life-span development

Natural Selection and Adaptive Behavior

Evolutionary Psychology

- Natural selection is the process by which those individuals of a species that are best adapted to their environment are more likely to survive and reproduce. Darwin proposed that natural selection fuels evolution. In evolutionary theory, adaptive behavior is behavior that promotes the organism's survival in a natural habitat.

- Evolutionary psychology holds that adaptation, reproduction, and "survival of the fittest" are important in shaping behavior. Ideas proposed by evolutionary developmental psychologists include the view that an extended childhood period is needed to develop a large brain and learn the complexity of human social communities. According to Baltes, the benefits resulting from evolutionary selection decrease with age, mainly because of a decline in reproductive fitness. At the same time, cultural needs increase. Like other theoretical approaches to development, evolutionary psychology has limitations. Bandura rejects "one-sided evolutionism" and argues for a bidirectional link between biology and environment.

Genetic Foundations of Development

 LG2 Describe what genes are and how they influence human development

The Collaborative Gene

Genes and Chromosomes

Genetic Principles

Chromosomal and Gene-Linked Abnormalities

- Short segments of DNA constitute genes, the units of hereditary information that direct cells to reproduce and manufacture proteins. Genes act collaboratively, not independently.

- Genes are passed on to new cells when chromosomes are duplicated during the process of mitosis and meiosis, which are two ways in which new cells are formed. When an egg and a sperm unite in the fertilization process, the resulting zygote contains the genes from the chromosomes in the father's sperm and the mother's egg. Despite this transmission of genes from generation to generation, variability is created in several ways, including the exchange of chromosomal segments during meiosis, mutations, and the distinction between a genotype and a phenotype.

- Genetic principles include those involving dominant-recessive genes, sex-linked genes, genetic imprinting, and polygenic inheritance.

- Chromosomal abnormalities produce Down syndrome, which is caused by the presence of an extra copy of chromosome 21, as well as sex-linked chromosomal abnormalities such as Klinefelter syndrome, fragile X syndrome, Turner syndrome, and XYY syndrome. Gene-linked abnormalities involve harmful genes. Gene-linked disorders include phenylketonuria (PKU) and sickle-cell anemia.

Heredity and Environment Interaction: The Nature-Nurture Debate

 LG3 Explain some of the ways that heredity and environment interact to produce individual differences in development

Behavior Genetics

Heredity-Environment Correlations

- Behavior genetics is the field that seeks to discover the influence of heredity and environment on individual differences in human traits and development. Methods used by behavior geneticists include twin studies and adoption studies.

- In Scarr's heredity-environment correlations view, heredity may influence the types of environments that children experience. She describes three genotype-environment correlations: passive, evocative, and active (niche-picking). Scarr notes that the relative importance of these three genotype-environment correlations changes as children develop.

| Shared and Nonshared Environmental Influences | • Shared environmental experiences refer to siblings' common experiences, such as their parents' personalities and intellectual orientation, the family's socioeconomic status, and the neighborhood in which they live. Nonshared environmental experiences involve the child's unique experiences, both within the family and outside the family, that are not shared with a sibling. Many behavior geneticists argue that differences in the development of siblings are due to nonshared environmental experiences (and heredity) rather than shared environmental experiences. |

The Epigenetic View and Gene × Environment (G × E) Interaction

• The epigenetic view emphasizes that development is the result of an ongoing, bidirectional interchange between heredity and environment. Gene × environment (g × e) interaction involves the interaction of a specific measured variation in DNA and a specific measured aspect of the environment.

Conclusions About Heredity-Environment Interaction

• Complex behaviors have some genetic loading that gives people a propensity for a particular developmental trajectory. However, actual development also requires an environment, and that environment is complex. The interaction of heredity and environment is extensive. Much remains to be discovered about the specific ways that heredity and environment interact to influence development.

Prenatal Development

 LG4 Characterize the course of prenatal development and its hazards

The Course of Prenatal Development

• Prenatal development is divided into three periods: germinal (conception until 10 to 14 days later), which ends when the zygote (a fertilized egg) attaches to the uterine wall; embryonic (two to eight weeks after conception), during which the embryo differentiates into three layers, life-support systems develop, and organ systems begin to form (organogenesis); and fetal (two months after conception until about nine months, or when the infant is born), a time when organ systems have matured to the point at which life can be sustained outside of the womb. By the time babies are born they have approximately 100 billion neurons, or nerve cells. The nervous system begins with the formation of a neural tube at 18 to 24 days after conception. Neurogenesis, proliferation, and migration are three processes that characterize brain development in the prenatal period. The basic architecture of the brain is formed in the first two trimesters of prenatal development.

Prenatal Diagnostic Tests

• Amniocentesis, ultrasound sonography, fetal MRI, chorionic villus sampling, and maternal blood screening are used to determine whether a fetus is developing normally.

Hazards to Prenatal Development

• A teratogen is any agent that can potentially cause a birth defect or negatively alter cognitive and behavioral outcomes. The dose, time of exposure, and genetic susceptibility influence the severity of the damage to an unborn child and the type of defect that occurs. Prescription drugs that can be harmful include antibiotics, some depressants, and certain hormones; nonprescription drugs that can be harmful include diet pills and aspirin. The psychoactive drugs caffeine, alcohol, nicotine, cocaine, methamphetamine, marijuana, and heroin are potentially harmful to offspring. Cigarette smoking by pregnant women also has serious adverse effects on prenatal and child development (such as low birth weight). Incompatibility of the mother's and the father's blood types can be harmful to the fetus. Problems may also result if a pregnant woman has rubella (German measles), syphilis, genital herpes, or AIDS. A developing fetus depends entirely on its mother for nutrition, and it may be harmed if the mother is malnourished, is overweight, or has a diet deficient in folic acid. High anxiety and stress in the mother are linked with less than optimal prenatal and birth outcomes. Maternal age can negatively affect the offspring's development if the mother is an adolescent or if she is 35 or older. Paternal factors also can affect the developing fetus. Radiation is a potential environmental hazard.

Prenatal Care

• Prenatal care programs provide information about teratogens and other prenatal hazards. In addition, various medical conditions are screened for and medical care is given in a defined schedule of visits. Prenatal classes often give information on nutrition, sexuality during pregnancy, and types of birth.

Birth and the Postpartum Period

 LG5 Summarize how birth takes place and describe the nature of the postpartum period

The Birth Process

- Childbirth occurs in three stages. Childbirth strategies involve the childbirth setting and attendants. Methods of delivery include medicated, natural and prepared, and cesarean. An increasing number of nonmedicated techniques, such as waterbirth, are being used to reduce childbirth pain.

The Transition from Fetus to Newborn

- Being born involves considerable stress for the baby, but the baby is well prepared and adapted to handle the stress. For many years, the Apgar Scale has been used to assess the newborn's health.

Low Birth Weight and Preterm Infants

- Low birth weight infants weigh less than 5½ pounds, and they may be preterm or small for date. Although most low birth weight infants are normal and healthy, as a group they have more health and developmental problems than infants of normal birth weight. Kangaroo care and massage therapy have been shown to provide benefits to preterm infants.

Bonding

- Bonding is the formation of a close connection, especially a physical bond between parents and the newborn shortly after birth. Early bonding has not been found to be critical in the development of a competent infant.

The Postpartum Period

- The postpartum period lasts from childbirth until about six weeks after the delivery or until the mother's body has completed its adjustment. The development of postpartum depression is a concern during this period.

key terms

evolutionary psychology 49
chromosomes 52
DNA 52
genes 52
mitosis 53
meiosis 53
fertilization 53
zygote 53
genotype 54
phenotype 55
Down syndrome 56
Klinefelter syndrome 57
fragile X syndrome 57
Turner syndrome 57
XYY syndrome 57

phenylketonuria (PKU) 57
sickle-cell anemia 58
behavior genetics 60
twin study 60
adoption study 60
passive genotype-environment correlations 60
evocative genotype-environment correlations 60
active (niche-picking) genotype-environment correlations 60

shared environmental experiences 61
nonshared environmental experiences 61
epigenetic view 62
gene × environment (g × e) interaction 62
germinal period 64
embryonic period 64
organogenesis 64
fetal period 65
neurons 66
teratogen 68
fetal alcohol spectrum disorders (FASD) 70

doula 77
natural childbirth 78
prepared childbirth 78
Apgar Scale 80
low birth weight infants 80
preterm infants 80
small for date infants 80
kangaroo care 82
bonding 82
postpartum period 84
postpartum depression 84

key people

Charles Darwin 49
David Buss 49
Paul Baltes 51

Albert Bandura 51
David Moore 53
Sandra Scarr 60

Robert Plomin 61
Gilbert Gottlieb 62
David Olds 76

Ferdinand Lamaze 78
Tiffany Field 83

chapter 3

PHYSICAL DEVELOPMENT AND BIOLOGICAL AGING

preview

Think about how much you have changed physically and will continue to change as you age. We come into this life as small beings. But we grow very rapidly in infancy, more slowly in childhood, and once again more rapidly during puberty, and then experience another slow-down. Eventually we decline, but many older adults are still physically robust. In this chapter, we explore changes in body growth, the brain, and sleep across the life span. We also examine longevity and evaluate some fascinating ideas about why we age.

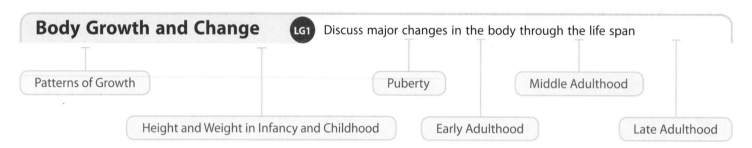

In life's long journey, we go through many bodily changes. We grow up, we grow out, we shrink. The very visible changes in height and weight are accompanied by less visible ones in bones, lungs, and every other organ of the body. These changes will help shape how we think about ourselves, how other people think about us, and what we are capable of thinking, doing, and feeling. Are there strict timelines for these changes? Are they set in our genes? Let's begin by studying some basic patterns of growth and then turn to bodily changes from the time we are infants through the time we are older adults.

PATTERNS OF GROWTH

The **cephalocaudal pattern** is the sequence in which the fastest growth in the human body occurs at the top, with the head. Physical growth in size, weight, and feature differentiation gradually works its way down from the top to the bottom (for example, neck, shoulders, middle trunk, and so on). This same pattern occurs in the head area, because the top parts of the head—the eyes and brain—grow faster than the lower parts, such as the jaw. During prenatal development and early infancy, the head constitutes an extraordinarily large proportion of the total body (see Figure 3.1).

In most cases, sensory and motor development proceeds according to the cephalocaudal pattern. For example, infants see objects before they can control their torso, and they can use their hands long before they can crawl or walk. However, one study contradicted the cephalocaudal pattern by finding that infants reached for toys with their feet before using their hands (Galloway & Thelen, 2004). In this study, infants on average first contacted the toy with their feet when they were 12 weeks old and with their hands when they were 16 weeks old. Thus, contrary to long-standing beliefs, early leg movements can be precisely controlled, some aspects of development that involve reaching do not involve lengthy practice, and early motor behaviors don't always develop in a strict cephalocaudal pattern.

The **proximodistal pattern** is the growth sequence that starts at the center of the body and moves toward the extremities. An example is the early maturation of muscular control of the trunk and arms, compared with that of the hands and fingers. Further, infants use the whole hand as a unit before they can control several fingers.

HEIGHT AND WEIGHT IN INFANCY AND CHILDHOOD

Height and weight increase rapidly in infancy, then take a slower course during the childhood years.

cephalocaudal pattern The sequence in which the fastest growth occurs at the top of the body—the head—with physical growth in size, weight, and feature differentiation gradually working from top to bottom.

proximodistal pattern The sequence in which growth starts at the center of the body and moves toward the extremities.

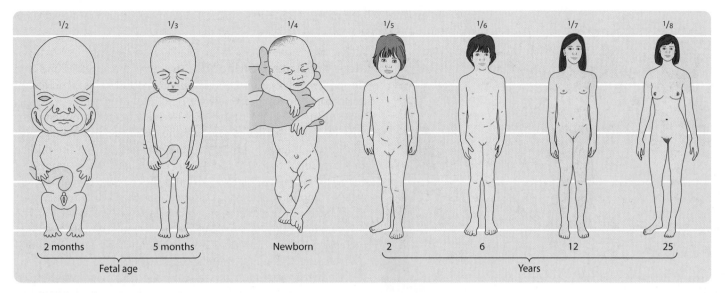

| 1/2 | 1/3 | 1/4 | 1/5 | 1/6 | 1/7 | 1/8 |

| 2 months | 5 months | Newborn | 2 | 6 | 12 | 25 |

Fetal age   Years

FIGURE **3.1**

CHANGES IN PROPORTIONS OF THE HUMAN BODY DURING GROWTH. As individuals develop from infancy through adulthood, one of the most noticeable physical changes is that the head becomes smaller in relation to the rest of the body. The fractions listed refer to head size as a proportion of total body length at different ages.

Infancy The average North American newborn is 20 inches long and weighs 7½ pounds. Ninety-five percent of full-term newborns are 18 to 22 inches long and weigh between 5½ and 10 pounds.

In the first several days of life, most newborns lose 5 to 7 percent of their body weight. Once infants adjust to sucking, swallowing, and digesting, they grow rapidly, gaining an average of 5 to 6 ounces per week during the first month. They have doubled their birth weight by the age of 4 months and have nearly tripled it by their first birthday. Infants grow about 1 inch per month during the first year, reaching approximately 1½ times their birth length by their first birthday. Infants' rate of growth slows considerably in the second year of life (Hockenberry & Wilson, 2011). By 2 years of age, infants weigh approximately 26 to 32 pounds, having gained a quarter to half a pound per month during the second year; now they have reached about one-fifth of their adult weight. The average 2-year-old is 32 to 35 inches tall, which is nearly one-half of adult height.

Early Childhood As the preschool child grows older, the percentage of increase in height and weight decreases with each additional year (Leifer, 2011). Girls are only slightly smaller and lighter than boys during these years. Both boys and girls slim down as the trunks of their bodies lengthen. Although their heads are still somewhat large for their bodies, by the end of the preschool years most children have lost their top-heavy look. Body fat also shows a slow, steady decline during the preschool years. Girls have more fatty tissue than boys; boys have more muscle tissue (McMahon & Stryjewski, 2012).

Growth patterns vary individually (Hockenberry & Wilson, 2011). Think back to your preschool years. This was probably the first time you noticed that some children were taller than you, some shorter; some were fatter, some thinner; some were stronger, some weaker. Much of the variation is due to heredity, but environmental experiences are also involved. A review of the height and weight of children around the world concluded that two important contributors to height differences are ethnic origin and nutrition (Meredith, 1978).

Why are some children unusually short? The culprits are congenital factors (genetic or prenatal problems), growth hormone deficiency, a physical problem that

The bodies of 5-year-olds and 2-year-olds are different from one another. The 5-year-old not only is taller and heavier, but also has a longer trunk and legs than the 2-year-old. *What might be some other physical differences between 2- and 5-year-olds?*

What characterizes children's physical growth in middle and late childhood?

develops in childhood, maternal smoking during pregnancy, or an emotional difficulty (Florin & Ludwig, 2011; Wit, Kiess, & Mullis, 2011).

Middle and Late Childhood   The period of middle and late childhood involves slow, consistent growth. This is a period of calm before the rapid growth spurt of adolescence.

During the elementary school years, children grow an average of 2 to 3 inches a year. At the age of 8, the average girl and the average boy are 4 feet 2 inches tall. During the middle and late childhood years, children gain about 5 to 7 pounds a year. The average 8-year-old girl and the average 8-year-old boy weigh 56 pounds. The weight increase is due mainly to increases in the size of the skeletal and muscular systems, as well as the size of some body organs. Muscle mass and strength gradually increase as "baby fat" decreases in middle and late childhood (Marcdante, Kliegman, & Behrman, 2011).

Changes in proportions are among the most pronounced physical changes in middle and late childhood. Head circumference, waist circumference, and leg length decrease in relation to body height.

PUBERTY

Puberty is a period of rapid physical maturation involving hormonal and bodily changes that take place in early adolescence. In this section, we explore a number of puberty's physical changes and its psychological accompaniments.

Sexual Maturation, Height, and Weight   Think back to the onset of your puberty. Of the striking changes that were taking place in your body, what was the first to occur? Researchers have found that male pubertal characteristics typically develop in this order: increase in penis and testicle size, appearance of straight pubic hair, minor voice change, first ejaculation (which usually occurs through masturbation or a wet dream), appearance of curly pubic hair, onset of maximum growth in height and weight, growth of hair in armpits, more detectable voice changes, and, finally, growth of facial hair. A recent longitudinal study revealed that on average, boys' genital development preceded the development of their pubic hair by about four months (Susman & others, 2010).

What is the order of appearance of physical changes in females? First, for most girls, their breasts enlarge or pubic hair appears. A recent longitudinal study revealed that on average, girls' breast development preceded their pubic hair development by about two months (Susman & others, 2010). Later, hair appears in the armpits. As these changes occur, the female grows in height and her hips become wider than her shoulders. **Menarche**—a girl's first menstruation—comes rather late in the pubertal cycle. Initially, her menstrual cycles may be highly irregular. For the first several years, she may not ovulate every menstrual cycle; some girls do not ovulate at all until a year or two after menstruation begins.

Marked weight gains coincide with the onset of puberty. During early adolescence, girls tend to outweigh boys, but by about age 14 boys begin to surpass girls. Similarly, at the beginning of the adolescent period, girls tend to be as tall as or taller than boys of their age, but by the end of the middle school years most boys have caught up or, in many cases, surpassed girls in height.

As indicated in Figure 3.2, the growth spurt occurs approximately two years earlier for girls than for boys. The mean age at the beginning of the growth spurt in girls is 9; for boys, it is 11. The peak rate of pubertal change occurs at 11½ years for girls and 13½ years for boys. During their growth spurt, girls increase in height about 3½ inches per year, boys about 4 inches.

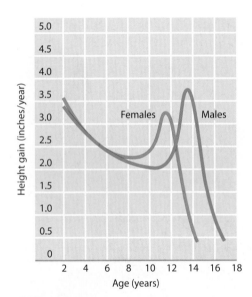

FIGURE **3.2**

PUBERTAL GROWTH SPURT. On average, the peak of the growth spurt during puberty occurs two years earlier for girls (11½) than for boys (13½). *How are hormones related to the growth spurt and to the difference between the average height of adolescent boys and that of girls?* From J. M. Tanner et al., "Standards from Birth to Maturity for Height, Weight, Height Velocity: British Children in 1965" in *Archives of Diseases in Childhood* 41(219), pp. 454–471, 1966. With permission from BMJ Publishing Group Ltd.

puberty A period of rapid physical maturation involving hormonal and bodily changes during early adolescence.

menarche A girl's first menstrual period.

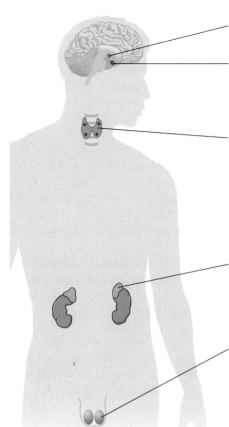

Hypothalamus: A structure in the brain that interacts with the pituitary gland to monitor the bodily regulation of hormones.

Pituitary: This master gland produces hormones that stimulate other glands. It also influences growth by producing growth hormones; it sends gonadotropins to the testes and ovaries and a thyroid-stimulating hormone to the thyroid gland. It sends a hormone to the adrenal gland as well.

Thyroid gland: It interacts with the pituitary gland to influence growth.

Adrenal gland: It interacts with the pituitary gland and likely plays a role in pubertal development, but less is known about its function than about sex glands. Recent research, however, suggests it may be involved in adolescent behavior, particularly for boys.

The gonads, or sex glands: These consist of the testes in males and the ovaries in females. The sex glands are strongly involved in the appearance of secondary sex characteristics, such as facial hair in males and breast development in females. The general class of hormones called estrogens is dominant in females, while androgens are dominant in males. More specifically, testosterone in males and estradiol in females are key hormones in pubertal development.

FIGURE **3.3**

THE MAJOR ENDOCRINE GLANDS INVOLVED IN PUBERTAL CHANGE

Hormonal Changes Behind the first whisker in boys and the widening of hips in girls is a flood of **hormones,** powerful chemical substances secreted by the endocrine glands and carried through the body by the bloodstream. The endocrine system's role in puberty involves the interaction of the hypothalamus, the pituitary gland, and the gonads (see Figure 3.3). The **hypothalamus,** a structure in the brain, is involved with eating and sexual behavior. The **pituitary gland,** an important endocrine gland, controls growth and regulates other glands; among these, the **gonads**—the testes in males, the ovaries in females—are particularly important in giving rise to pubertal changes in the body.

How do the gonads, or sex glands, work? The pituitary gland sends a signal via **gonadotropins** (hormones that stimulate the testes or ovaries) to the appropriate gland to manufacture hormones. These hormones give rise to such changes as the production of sperm in males and menstruation and the release of eggs from the ovaries in females. The pituitary gland, through interaction with the hypothalamus, detects when the optimal level of hormones is reached and maintains it with additional gonadotropin secretion (Kuhn & others, 2010; Susman & Dorn, 2009).

Not only does the pituitary gland release gonadotropins that stimulate the testes and ovaries, but through interaction with the hypothalamus the pituitary gland also secretes hormones that either directly lead to growth and skeletal maturation or produce growth effects through interaction with the thyroid gland, located at the base of the throat.

The concentrations of certain hormones increase dramatically during adolescence (Wankowska & Polkowska, 2010). **Testosterone** is a hormone associated in boys with the development of genitals, increased height, and deepening of the voice. **Estradiol** is a type of estrogen associated in girls with breast, uterine, and skeletal development. In one study, testosterone levels increased eighteenfold in boys but only twofold in girls during puberty; estradiol increased eightfold in girls but only twofold in boys

hormones Powerful chemical substances secreted by the endocrine glands and carried through the body by the bloodstream.

hypothalamus A structure in the brain that is involved with eating and sexual behavior.

pituitary gland An important endocrine gland that controls growth and regulates the activity of other glands.

gonads The sex glands, which are the testes in males and the ovaries in females.

gonadotropins Hormones that stimulate the testes or ovaries.

testosterone A hormone associated in boys with the development of the genitals, increased height, and voice changes.

estradiol A hormone associated in girls with breast, uterine, and skeletal development.

(Nottelmann & others, 1987). Thus, both testosterone and estradiol are present in the hormonal makeup of both boys and girls, but testosterone dominates in male pubertal development, estradiol in female pubertal development (Richmond & Rogol, 2007).

The same influx of hormones that grows hair on a male's chest and increases the fatty tissue in a female's breasts may also contribute to psychological development in adolescence. In one study of boys and girls ranging in age from 9 to 14, a higher concentration of testosterone was present in boys who rated themselves as more socially competent (Nottelmann & others, 1987). However, hormonal effects by themselves do not account for adolescent psychological development (Graber, 2008). For example, in one study, social factors were much better predictors of young adolescent girls' depression and anger than hormonal factors (Brooks-Gunn & Warren, 1989). Behavior and moods also can affect hormones. Stress, eating patterns, exercise, sexual activity, tension, and depression can activate or suppress various aspects of the hormonal system. In sum, the hormone-behavior link is complex (Susman & Dorn, 2009).

Timing and Variations in Puberty

In the United States—where children mature up to a year earlier than children in European countries—the average age of menarche has declined significantly since the mid-nineteenth century. Fortunately, however, we are unlikely to see pubescent toddlers, since what has happened in the past century is likely the result of improved nutrition and health.

Why do the changes of puberty occur when they do, and how can variations in their timing be explained? The basic genetic program for puberty is wired into the species (Stukenborg, Colon, & Soder, 2010). Recently, scientists have begun to conduct molecular genetic studies in an attempt to identify specific genes that are linked to the onset and progression of puberty (Elks & others, 2010; He & others, 2010). However, weight, nutrition, health, stress, and other environmental factors also affect puberty's timing and makeup (Belsky & others, 2010). A number of studies have found that higher weight, especially obesity, is linked with earlier puberty development (Kaplowitz, 2008). For example, a recent study revealed that being overweight or obese was linked with more advanced breast development and pubic hair growth in 8- to 14-year-olds (Christensen & others, 2010). A recent study also revealed that maternal harshness in early childhood was linked to early maturation and to sexual risk taking in adolescence (Belsky & others, 2010).

For most boys, the pubertal sequence may begin as early as age 10 or as late as 13½, and it may end as early as age 13 or as late as 17. Thus, the normal range is wide enough that, given two boys of the same chronological age, one might complete the pubertal sequence before the other one has begun it. For girls, menarche is considered within the normal range if it appears between the ages of 9 and 15.

Psychological Accompaniments of Puberty

What are some links between puberty and psychological characteristics? How do early and late maturation influence adolescents' psychological development?

Body Image One psychological aspect of puberty is certain for both boys and girls: Adolescents are preoccupied with their bodies (Mueller, 2009). Perhaps you looked in the mirror on a daily, and sometimes even hourly, basis to see if you could detect anything different about your changing body. Preoccupation with one's body image is strong throughout adolescence, but it is especially acute during puberty, a time when adolescents are more dissatisfied with their bodies than in late adolescence.

Gender Differences Gender differences characterize adolescents' perceptions of their bodies (Murray, Byrne, & Rieger,

developmental connection

Sexuality. Early sexual experience is one of a number of risk factors in adolescent development. Chapter 12, p. 395

Adolescents show a strong preoccupation with their changing bodies and develop images of what their bodies are like. *Why might adolescent males have more positive body images than adolescent females?*

2010). In general, throughout puberty girls are less happy with their bodies and have more negative body images than boys (Crespo & others, 2010). As pubertal change proceeds, girls often become more dissatisfied with their bodies, probably because their body fat increases (Markey, 2010; Yuan, 2010). In contrast, boys become more satisfied as they move through puberty, probably because their muscle mass increases. The following recent studies shed further light on gender differences in body image during adolescence:

- Adolescent girls placed a higher aesthetic value on body image but had a lower aesthetic satisfaction with their bodies than did adolescent boys (Abbott & Barber, 2010).
- The profile of adolescents with the most positive body images was characterized by health-enhancing behaviors, especially regular exercise (Frisen & Holmqvist, 2010).

Early and Late Maturation   Did you enter puberty early, late, or on time? When adolescents mature earlier or later than their peers, they often perceive themselves differently (Copeland & others, 2010; Graber, Nichols, & Brooks-Gunn, 2010). In the Berkeley Longitudinal Study conducted some years ago, early-maturing boys perceived themselves more positively and had more successful peer relations than did late-maturing boys (Jones, 1965). The findings for early-maturing girls were similar but not as strong as for boys. When the late-maturing boys were in their thirties, however, they had developed a more positive identity than the early-maturing boys had (Peskin, 1967). Perhaps the late-maturing boys had had more time to explore life's options, or perhaps the early-maturing boys continued to focus on their physical status instead of paying attention to career development and achievement.

What are some outcomes of early and late maturation in adolescence?

An increasing number of researchers have found that early maturation increases girls' vulnerability to a number of problems (Graber, Nichols, & Brooks-Gunn, 2010; Westling & others, 2008). Early-maturing girls are more likely to smoke, drink, be depressed, have an eating disorder, struggle for earlier independence from their parents, and have older friends; and their bodies are likely to elicit responses from males that lead to earlier dating and earlier sexual experiences (Wiesner & Ittel, 2002). For example, a recent study revealed that early-maturing girls were more likely to engage in substance abuse and early sexual intercourse (Gaudineau & others, 2010). Another study found that early-maturing girls' higher level of internalizing problems (depression, for example) was linked to their heightened sensitivity to interpersonal stress (Natsuaki & others, 2010). And early-maturing girls are more likely to drop out of high school and to cohabit and marry at younger ages (Cavanagh, 2009). Apparently as a result of their social and cognitive immaturity, combined with early physical development, early-maturing girls are easily lured into problem behaviors, not recognizing the possible long-term effects of these on their development.

A recent longitudinal study revealed that in adolescence early-maturing girls were more likely than on-time or late-maturing girls to engage in a number of problems—self-reported criminality, substance use, and early sexual behavior (Copeland & others, 2010). In emerging adulthood (19 to 21 years of age), functioning of the early-maturing girls improved in some areas; however, early-maturing girls who had exhibited conduct disorders in adolescence were more likely to be depressed in emerging adulthood, and early-maturing girls were more likely to have had many sexual partners.

EARLY ADULTHOOD

After the dramatic physical changes of puberty, the years of early adulthood seem an uneventful time in the body's history. Physical changes during these years may be subtle, but they do continue.

Height remains rather constant during early adulthood. Peak functioning of the body's joints usually occurs in the twenties. Many individuals also reach a peak of

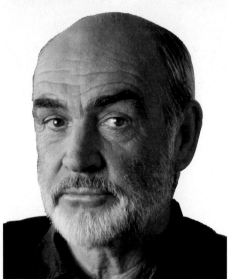

Famous actor Sean Connery as a young adult in his twenties (*top*) and as a middle-aged adult in his fifties (*bottom*). *What are some of the most outwardly noticeable signs of aging in the middle adulthood years?*

climacteric The midlife transition during which fertility declines.

menopause The time in middle age, usually in the late forties or early fifties, when a woman's menstrual periods cease.

muscle tone and strength in their late teens and twenties (Candow & Chilibeck, 2005). However, these may begin to decline in the thirties. Sagging chins and protruding abdomens may also appear for the first time. Muscles start to have less elasticity, and aches may begin to arise in places not felt before.

MIDDLE ADULTHOOD

Like the changes of early adulthood, midlife physical changes are usually gradual. Although everyone experiences some physical change due to aging in the middle adulthood years, the rates of aging vary considerably from one individual to another. Genetic makeup and lifestyle factors play important roles in whether and when chronic diseases will appear. (In Chapter 4, "Health," we explore these diseases.)

Physical Appearance Individuals lose height in middle age, and many gain weight. On average, from 30 to 50 years of age, men lost about ½ inch in height, then lost another ¾ inch from 50 to 70 years of age (Hoyer & Roodin, 2009). The height loss for women can be as much as 2 inches from 25 to 75 years of age. Note that there are large variations in the extent to which individuals become shorter with aging. The decrease in height is due to bone loss in the vertebrae. On average, body fat accounts for about 10 percent of body weight in adolescence; it makes up 20 percent or more in middle age.

Noticeable signs of aging usually are apparent by the forties or fifties. The skin begins to wrinkle and sag because of a loss of fat and collagen in underlying tissues (Farage & others, 2009). Small, localized areas of pigmentation in the skin produce aging spots, especially in areas that are exposed to sunlight, such as the hands and face. The hair thins and grays because of a lower replacement rate and a decline in melanin production.

Since a youthful appearance is stressed in many cultures, many Americans strive to make themselves look younger. Undergoing cosmetic surgery, dyeing hair, purchasing wigs, enrolling in weight reduction programs, participating in exercise regimens, and taking heavy doses of vitamins are common in middle age. Baby boomers have shown a strong interest in plastic surgery and Botox, which may reflect their desire to take control of the aging process (Ascher & others, 2010; Wu, 2010).

Strength, Joints, and Bones The term *sarcopenia* is given to age-related loss of lean muscle mass and strength. After age 50, muscle loss occurs at a rate of approximately 1 to 2 percent per year. A loss of strength especially occurs in the back and legs. Exercise can reduce the decline involved in sarcopenia (Morley & others, 2010; Peterson & Gordon, 2011).

Maximum bone density occurs by the mid to late thirties. From this point on, there is a progressive loss of bone. The rate of bone loss begins slowly but accelerates during the fifties (Burke & others, 2003). Women's rate of bone loss is about twice that of men. By the end of midlife, bones break more easily and heal more slowly (Neer & SWAN investigators, 2010; Ritchie, 2010).

Cardiovascular System The level of cholesterol in the blood increases through the adult years (Khera & Radar, 2010). Cholesterol comes in two forms: LDL (low-density lipoprotein) and HDL (high-density lipoprotein). LDL is often referred to as "bad" cholesterol because when the level of LDL is too high, it sticks to the lining of blood vessels, a condition that can lead to atherosclerosis (hardening of the arteries). HDL is often referred to as "good" cholesterol because when it is high and LDL is low, the risk of cardiovascular disease is lessened. A recent study revealed that a low level of HDL was linked to a higher probability of still being alive at 85 years of age (Rahilly-Tierney & others, 2011). In middle age, cholesterol begins to accumulate on the artery walls, which are thickening. The result is an increased risk of cardiovascular disease. Cholesterol levels are influenced by heredity, but LDL can be reduced and HDL increased by eating food that is low in saturated fat and cholesterol and by exercising regularly (Weissglas-Volkov & Pajukanta, 2010).

Blood pressure, too, usually rises in the forties and fifties, and high blood pressure (hypertension) is linked with an increased rate of mortality (Scalia, Khoo, & O'Neill, 2010). At menopause, a woman's blood pressure rises sharply and usually remains above that of a man through life's later years (Taler, 2009).

An increasing problem in middle and late adulthood that involves the cardiovascular system is the metabolic syndrome, a condition characterized by hypertension, obesity, and insulin resistance (Akintunde & others, 2010). *Metabolic syndrome* often leads to the development of diabetes and cardiovascular disease (Hui & others, 2010). Weight loss and exercise are strongly recommended in the treatment of metabolic syndrome (Touati & others, 2010). A recent study revealed that individuals with metabolic syndrome who were physically active reduced their risk of developing cardiovascular disease (Broekhuizen & others, 2011).

Members of the Masai tribe in Kenya, Africa, can stay on a treadmill for a long time because of their active lives. Incidence of heart disease is extremely low in the Masai tribe, which also can be attributed to their energetic lifestyle.

Lungs   There is little change in lung capacity through most of middle adulthood. However, at about the age of 55, the proteins in lung tissue become less elastic. This change, combined with a gradual stiffening of the chest wall, decreases the lungs' capacity to shuttle oxygen from the air people breathe to the blood in their veins.

For smokers, however, the picture is different and bleaker (Tomiyama & others, 2010). As shown in Figure 3.4, the lung capacity of smokers drops precipitously in middle age. However, if the individuals quit smoking their lung capacity improves, although not to the level of individuals who have never smoked (Williams, 1995).

Sexuality   **Climacteric** is a term used to describe the midlife transition in which fertility declines. **Menopause** is the time in middle age, usually in the late forties or early fifties, when a woman has not had a menstrual period for a full year. The average age at which women have their last period is 52. A small percentage of women—10 percent—go through menopause before 40. Just as puberty has been coming earlier, however, menopause has been coming later (Birren, 2002). Specific causes of the later incidence of menopause have not been documented, but improved nutrition and lower incidence of infectious diseases may be the reasons.

What characterizes metabolic syndrome?

Menopause involves a dramatic decline in the production of estrogen by the ovaries. This decline may produce "hot flashes," nausea, fatigue, and rapid heartbeat, for example. Cross-cultural studies reveal wide variations in the menopause experience (Lerner-Geva & others, 2010). For example, Asian women report fewer hot flashes during menopause than do women in Western societies (Payer, 1991). It is difficult to determine whether these cross-cultural variations are due to genetic, dietary, reproductive, or cultural factors.

Menopause is not the negative experience for most women that it was once thought to be. One study in Taiwan found no significant effect of menopausal transition on women's quality of life (Cheng & others, 2007). However, the loss of fertility is an important marker for women.

Do men go through anything like the menopause that women experience? That is, is there a male menopause? During middle adulthood, most men do not lose their capacity to father children, although there usually is a modest decline in their sexual hormone level and activity (Kohler & others, 2008). Testosterone production begins to decline about 1 percent a year during middle adulthood, and this decline can reduce sexual drive. Sperm count usually shows a slow decline, but men do not lose their fertility.

We will have more to say about the climacteric and the sexual attitudes and behaviors of middle-aged women and men in Chapter 12, "Gender and Sexuality."

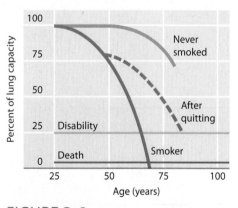

FIGURE **3.4**

THE RELATION OF LUNG CAPACITY TO AGE AND CIGARETTE SMOKING. Lung capacity shows little change through middle age for individuals who have not smoked. However, smoking is linked with reduced lung capacity in middle-aged and older adults. When individuals stop smoking, their lung capacity becomes greater than for those who continue to smoke, but not as great as the lung capacity of individuals who have never smoked.

connecting with careers

Sarah Kagan, Geriatric Nurse

Sarah Kagan is a professor of nursing at the University of Pennsylvania School of Nursing. She provides nursing consultation to patients, their families, nurses, and physicians on the complex needs of older adults related to their hospitalization. She also consults on research and the management of patients who have head and neck cancers. Kagan teaches in the undergraduate nursing program, where she directs the course on "Nursing Care in the Older Adult." In 2003, she was awarded a MacArthur Fellowship for her work in the field of nursing.

In Kagan's own words:

I'm lucky to be doing what I love—caring for older adults and families—and learning from them so that I can share this knowledge and develop or investigate better ways of caring. My special interests in the care of older adults who have cancer allow me the intimate privilege of being with patients at the best and worst times of their lives. That intimacy acts as a beacon—it

Sarah Kagan with a patient.

reminds me of the value I and nursing as a profession contribute to society and the rewards offered in return (Kagan, 2008, p. 1).

For more information about what geriatric nurses do, see page 44 in the Careers in Life-Span Development appendix.

LATE ADULTHOOD

Late adulthood brings an increased risk of physical disability, but there is considerable variability in rates of decline in functioning. Let's explore changes in physical appearance and the cardiovascular system in older adults.

Physical Appearance   The changes in physical appearance that take place in middle adulthood become more pronounced in late adulthood. Most noticeable are facial wrinkles and age spots. Our weight usually drops after we reach 60 years of age, likely because we lose muscle, which also gives our bodies a more "sagging" look. The good news is that exercise and weight lifting can help slow the decrease in muscle mass and improve the older adult's body appearance (Aagaard & others, 2010).

Circulatory System   Significant changes also take place in the circulatory system of older adults (Hotta & Uchida, 2010; Vatner, 2011). In one analysis, 57 percent of 80-year-old men and 60 percent of 81-year-old women had hypertension, and 32 percent of the men and 31 percent of the women had experienced a stroke (Aronow, 2007).

In the past, a 65-year-old with a blood pressure reading of 160/90 would have been told, "For your age, that is normal." Today, most experts on aging recommend that consistent blood pressures above 120/80 should be treated to reduce the risk of heart attack, stroke, or kidney disease (Brennan & others, 2010). A rise in blood pressure with age can be linked with illness, obesity, stress, stiffening of blood vessels, or lack of exercise (Dupree, 2010; Ohta & others, 2010). Various drugs, a healthy diet, and exercise can reduce the risk of cardiovascular disease in older adults (Dupree, 2010).

Geriatric nurses can be especially helpful to older adults who experience acute or chronic illness. To read about the work of one geriatric nurse, see the *Connecting with Careers* profile.

Researchers have found that almost 50 percent of Canadian and American menopausal women have occasional hot flashes, but only one in seven Japanese women do (Lock, 1998). *What factors might account for these variations?*

Review

- What are cephalocaudal and proximodistal patterns?
- How do height and weight change in infancy and childhood?
- What changes characterize puberty?
- What physical changes occur in early adulthood?
- How do people develop physically during middle adulthood?
- What is the nature of physical changes in late adulthood?

Connect

- In this section, you learned that growth spurts in puberty differ for boys and girls. What research methods probably were used to collect such data?

Reflect *Your Own Personal Journey of Life*

- How old were you when you started puberty? How do you think this timing affected your social relationships and development?

The Brain **LG2** Describe how the brain changes through the life span

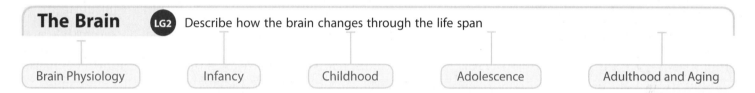

Brain Physiology   Infancy   Childhood   Adolescence   Adulthood and Aging

Until recently, little was known for certain about how the brain changes as we grow and age. Today, dramatic progress is being made in understanding these changes (Nelson, 2011a, b). The study of age-related changes in the brain is one of the most exciting frontiers in science. As we saw in Chapter 2, "Biological Beginnings," remarkable changes already have occurred in the brain during prenatal development. Here we consider the changes in the brain from infancy through late adulthood. Before exploring these developmental changes, let's examine some key structures of the brain and see how they function.

BRAIN PHYSIOLOGY

The brain includes a number of major structures. As we discussed in Chapter 2, "Biological Beginnings," the key components of these structures are neurons—nerve cells that handle information processing.

Structure and Function   Looked at from above, the brain has two halves, or hemispheres (see Figure 3.5). The top portion of the brain, farthest from the spinal cord, is known as the forebrain. Its outer layer of cells, the cerebral cortex, covers it like a thin cap. The cerebral cortex is responsible for about 80 percent of the brain's volume and is critical in perception, thinking, language, and other important functions.

Each hemisphere of the cortex has four major areas, called lobes. Although the lobes usually work together, each has a somewhat different primary function (see Figure 3.6):

- *Frontal lobes* are involved in voluntary movement, thinking, personality, emotion, memory, sustained attention, and intentionality or purpose.
- *Occipital lobes* function in vision.
- *Temporal lobes* have an active role in hearing, language processing, and memory.
- *Parietal lobes* play important roles in registering spatial location, attention, and motor control.

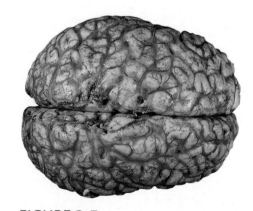

FIGURE **3.5**

THE HUMAN BRAIN'S HEMISPHERES. The two hemispheres of the human brain are clearly seen in this photograph. It is a myth that the left hemisphere is the exclusive location of language and logical thinking or that the right hemisphere is the exclusive location of emotion and creative thinking.

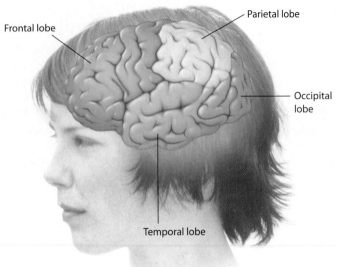

FIGURE **3.6**

THE BRAIN'S FOUR LOBES. Shown here are the locations of the brain's four lobes: frontal, occipital, temporal, and parietal.

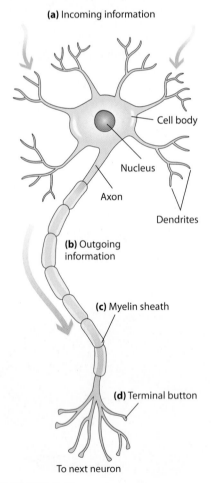

(a) Incoming information

Cell body

Nucleus

Axon

Dendrites

(b) Outgoing information

(c) Myelin sheath

(d) Terminal button

To next neuron

FIGURE **3.7**

THE NEURON. (*a*) The dendrites of the cell body receive information from other neurons, muscles, or glands through the axon. (*b*) Axons transmit information away from the cell body. (*c*) A myelin sheath covers most axons and speeds information transmission. (*d*) As the axon ends, it branches out into terminal buttons.

Deeper in the brain, beneath the cortex, lie other key structures. These include the hypothalamus and the pituitary gland as well as the amygdala, which plays an important role in emotions, and the hippocampus, which is especially important in memory and emotion.

Neurons As we discussed earlier, neurons process information. Figure 3.7 shows some important parts of the neuron, including the axon and dendrites. Basically, an axon sends electrical signals away from the central part of the neuron. At tiny gaps called synapses, the axon communicates with the dendrites of other neurons, which then pass the signals on. The communication in the synapse occurs through the release of chemical substances known as neurotransmitters.

As Figure 3.7 shows, most axons are covered by a myelin sheath, which is a layer of fat cells. The sheath helps impulses travel faster along the axon, increasing the speed and efficiency with which information travels from neuron to neuron in a process called **myelination** (Bartzokis & others, 2010). Myelination also is involved in providing energy to neurons and in communication (Campbell & Mahad, 2011). To some extent, the type of information handled by neurons depends on whether they are in the left or the right hemisphere of the cortex (Phan & Vicario, 2010). Speech and grammar, for example, depend on activity in the left hemisphere in most people; humor and the use of metaphors depend on activity in the right hemisphere (Diaz, Barrett, & Hogstrom, 2011; Pang & others, 2011). This specialization of function in one hemisphere of the cerebral cortex or the other is called **lateralization.** However, most neuroscientists agree that complex functions such as reading or performing music involve both hemispheres (Stroobant, Buijs, & Vingerhoets, 2009). Labeling people as "left-brained" because they are logical thinkers and "right-brained" because they are creative thinkers does not correspond to the way the brain's hemispheres work. For the most part, complex thinking is the outcome of communication between both hemispheres of the brain (van Ettinger-Veenstra & others, 2010).

The degree of lateralization may change as people develop through the human life span. Let's now explore a number of age-related changes in the brain.

INFANCY

As we saw in Chapter 2, "Biological Beginnings," brain development occurs extensively during the prenatal period. The brain's development is also substantial during infancy and later (Nelson, 2011a, b; Zelazo & Lee, 2010).

Because the brain develops so extensively, an infant's head should always be protected from falls or other injuries, and a baby should never be shaken. Shaken baby syndrome, which includes brain swelling and hemorrhaging, affects hundreds of babies in the United States each year (Croucher, 2010; Fanconi & Lips, 2010). A recent analysis found that the father most often was the perpetrator of *shaken baby syndrome,* followed by a child-care provider and a boyfriend of the victim's mother (National Center on Shaken Baby Syndrome, 2008).

Early Experience and the Brain Children who grow up in a deprived environment may have depressed brain activity (Fox, Levitt, & Nelson, 2010; Pollack & others, 2010). As shown in Figure 3.8, a child who grew up in the unresponsive and unstimulating environment of a Romanian orphanage showed considerably depressed brain activity compared with a normal child.

Are the effects of deprived environments reversible? There is reason to think that at least for some individuals the answer is yes (Guzzetta & others, 2008). The brain demonstrates both flexibility and resilience. Consider 14-year-old Michael

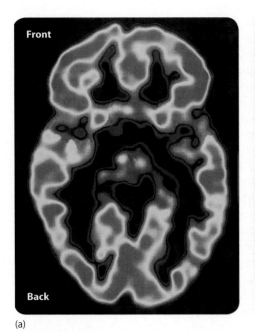

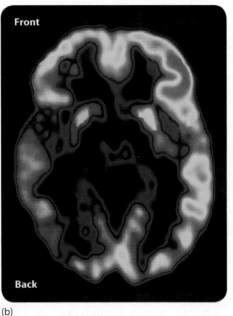

(a)   (b)

FIGURE **3.8**

EARLY DEPRIVATION AND BRAIN ACTIVITY. These two photographs are PET (positron emission tomography) scans—which use radioactive tracers to image and analyze blood flow and metabolic activity in the body's organs. These scans show the brains of (*a*) a normal child and (*b*) an institutionalized Romanian orphan who experienced substantial deprivation since birth. In PET scans, the highest to lowest brain activity is reflected in the colors of red, yellow, green, blue, and black, respectively. As can be seen, red and yellow show up to a much greater degree in the PET scan of the normal child than the deprived Romanian orphan.

FIGURE **3.9**

PLASTICITY IN THE BRAIN'S HEMISPHERES. Michael Rehbein at 14 years of age. Following removal of the left hemisphere of Michael's brain because of uncontrollable seizures, his right hemisphere reorganized to take over the language functions normally carried out by corresponding areas in the left hemisphere of an intact brain.

Rehbein. At age 7, he began to experience uncontrollable seizures—as many as 400 a day. Doctors said the only solution was to remove the left hemisphere of his brain where the seizures were occurring. Recovery was slow, but his right hemisphere began to reorganize and take over functions that normally occur in the brain's left hemisphere, including speech (see Figure 3.9).

Neuroscientists note that what wires the brain—or rewires it, in the case of Michael Rehbein—is repeated experience (Nash, 1997). Each time a baby tries to touch an attractive object or gazes intently at a face, tiny bursts of electricity shoot through the brain, knitting together neurons into circuits. The results are some of the behavioral milestones we discuss in this and other chapters.

In sum, the infant's brain is waiting for experiences to determine how connections are made. Before birth, it appears that genes mainly direct basic wiring patterns. Neurons grow and travel to distant places awaiting further instructions (Nelson, 2011a, b). After birth, the inflowing stream of sights, sounds, smells, touches, language, and eye contact helps shape the brain's neural connections.

Studying the brain's development in infancy is not as easy as it might seem. Even the latest brain-imaging technologies cannot make out fine details in adult brains and cannot be used with babies (Johnson & de Haan, 2010). However, among the researchers who are making strides in finding out more about the brain's development in infancy are Charles Nelson and his colleagues and John Richards and his colleagues (Nelson, 2007, 2011a, b; Moulson & Nelson, 2008; Sheridan & Nelson, 2008; Richards, 2009, 2010; Richards, Reynolds, & Courage, 2010).

Changing Neurons   At birth, the newborn's brain is about 25 percent of its adult weight. By the second birthday, the brain is about 75 percent of its adult weight. Two key developments during these first two years involve the myelin sheath (the layer of fat cells that speeds up the electrical impulse along the axon) and connections between dendrites.

Measuring the Activity in an Infant's Brain. By attaching up to 128 electrodes to a baby's scalp, Charles Nelson and his colleagues have studied the brain's activity in the infant's ability to recognize faces and remember.

myelination The process of encasing axons with a myelin sheath, which helps increase the speed and efficiency of information processing.

lateralization Specialization of function in one hemisphere or the other of the cerebral cortex.

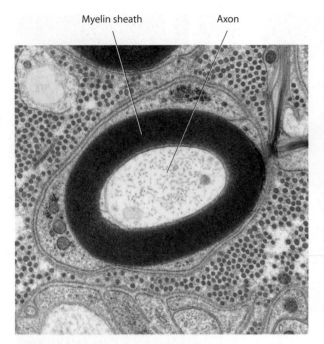

FIGURE **3.10**

A MYELINATED NERVE FIBER. The myelin sheath, shown in brown, encases the axon (white). This image was produced by an electron microscope that magnified the nerve fiber 12,000 times. *What role does myelination play in the brain's development and children's cognition?*

Myelination, the process of encasing axons with a myelin sheath, begins prenatally and continues after birth (see Figure 3.10). Myelination for visual pathways occurs rapidly after birth, being completed in the first six months. Auditory myelination is not completed until 4 or 5 years of age. Some aspects of myelination continue even into adolescence. Indeed, the most extensive changes in myelination in the frontal lobes occur during adolescence (Steinberg, 2008).

Dramatic increases in dendrites and synapses (the tiny gaps between neurons across which neurotransmitters carry information) also characterize the development of the brain in the first two years of life (see Figure 3.11). Nearly twice as many of these connections are made as will ever be used (Huttenlocher & Dabholkar, 1997). The connections that are used become strengthened and survive, while the unused ones are replaced by other pathways or disappear (Faissner & others, 2010; Turrigiano, 2010). That is, connections are "pruned." Figure 3.12 vividly illustrates the growth and later pruning of synapses in the visual, auditory, and prefrontal cortex areas of the brain (Huttenlocher & Dabholkar, 1997). As shown in Figure 3.12, "blooming and pruning" vary considerably by brain region in humans (Gogtay & Thompson, 2010; Thompson & Nelson, 2001).

Changing Structures The areas of the brain do not mature uniformly (Johnson & de Haan, 2012; Nelson, 2011a, b). The frontal lobe is immature in the newborn. As neurons in the frontal lobe become myelinated and interconnected during the first year of life, infants develop an ability to regulate their physiological states (such as sleep) and gain more control over their reflexes. Cognitive skills that require deliberate thinking do not emerge until later (Bell, 2011; Bell & Fox, 1992; Morasch & Bell, 2011). At about 2 months of age, the motor control centers of the brain develop to the point at which infants can suddenly reach out and grab a nearby object. At about 4 months, the neural connections necessary for depth perception begin to form. And at about 12 months, the brain's speech centers are poised to produce one of infancy's magical moments: when the infant utters its first word.

CHILDHOOD

The brain and other parts of the nervous system continue developing through childhood (Diamond, Casey, & Munakata, 2011). These changes enable children to plan their actions, to attend to stimuli more effectively, and to make considerable strides in language development.

FIGURE **3.11**

THE DEVELOPMENT OF DENDRITIC SPREADING. Note the increase in connectedness between neurons over the course of the first two years of life. Reprinted by permission of the publisher from *The Postnatal Development of the Human Cerebral Cortex, Vols. I–VIII*, by J. LeRoy Conel, Cambridge, MA: Harvard University Press, Copyright © 1939, 1941, 1947, 1951, 1955, 1959, 1963, 1967 by the President and Fellows of Harvard College. Copyright © renewed 1967, 1969, 1975, 1979, 1983, 1987, 1991.

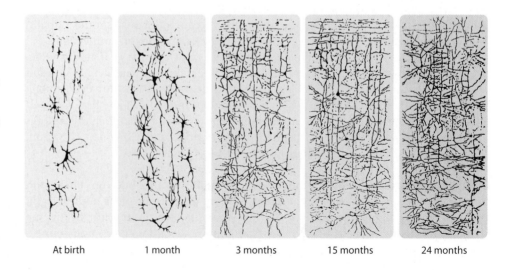

At birth   1 month   3 months   15 months   24 months

During early childhood, the brain and head grow more rapidly than any other part of the body. Figure 3.13 shows how the growth curve for the head and brain advances more rapidly than the growth curve for height and weight. Some of the brain's increase in size is due to myelination and some is due to an increase in the number and size of dendrites. Some developmentalists conclude that myelination is important in the maturation of a number of abilities in children (Abraham & others, 2010). For example, myelination in the areas of the brain related to hand-eye coordination is not complete until about 4 years of age. Myelination in the areas of the brain related to focusing attention is not complete until the end of middle or late childhood.

Still, the brain in early childhood is not growing as rapidly as in infancy. However, the anatomical changes in the child's brain between the ages of 3 and 15 are dramatic. By repeatedly obtaining brain scans of the same children for up to four years, scientists have found that children's brains experience rapid, distinct bursts of growth (Gogtay & Thompson, 2010). The amount of brain material in some areas can nearly double in as little as one year, followed by a drastic loss of tissue as unneeded cells are purged and the brain continues to reorganize itself.

Significant changes in various structures and regions of the brain continue to occur during middle and late childhood. In particular, the brain pathways and circuitry involving the prefrontal cortex, the highest level in the brain, continue to increase in middle and late childhood (Diamond, Casey, & Munakata, 2011). In one study, researchers found less diffusion and more focal activation in the prefrontal cortex from 7 to 30 years of age (Durston & others, 2006). The activation change was accompanied by increased efficiency in cognitive performance, especially in *cognitive control,* which involves flexible and effective control in a number of areas. These areas concern controlling attention, reducing interfering thoughts, inhibiting motor actions, and being cognitively flexible in switching between competing choices (Diamond, Casey, & Munakata, 2011).

Developmental neuroscientist Mark Johnson and his colleagues (2009) have proposed that the prefrontal cortex likely orchestrates the functions of many other brain regions during development. As part of this neural leadership and organizational role, the prefrontal cortex may provide an advantage to neural connections and networks that include the prefrontal cortex. In their view, the prefrontal cortex likely coordinates the best neural connections for solving a problem.

ADOLESCENCE

Until recently, little research has been conducted on developmental changes in the brain during adolescence. Although research in this area is still in its infancy, an increasing number of studies are under way (Blakemore & others, 2010; Van Leijenhorst & others, 2010). Scientists now note that the adolescent's brain is different from the child's brain, and that in adolescence the brain is still growing (Forbes & others, 2010; Paus, 2010).

Earlier we indicated that connections between neurons become "pruned" as children and adolescents develop. Because of this pruning,

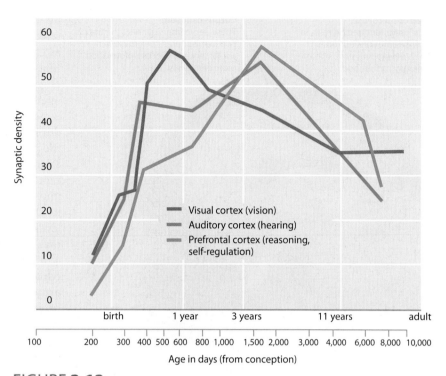

FIGURE **3.12**

SYNAPTIC DENSITY IN THE HUMAN BRAIN FROM INFANCY TO ADULTHOOD. The graph shows the dramatic increase and then pruning in synaptic density for three regions of the brain: visual cortex, auditory cortex, and prefrontal cortex. Synaptic density is believed to be an important indication of the extent of connectivity between neurons.

developmental **connection**

Brain Development. Might some regions of the brain be more closely linked with children's intelligence than others? Chapter 8, p. 252

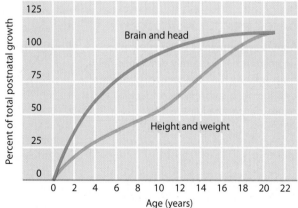

FIGURE **3.13**

GROWTH CURVES FOR THE HEAD AND BRAIN AND FOR HEIGHT AND WEIGHT. The more rapid growth of the brain and head can easily be seen. Height and weight advance more gradually over the first two decades of life.

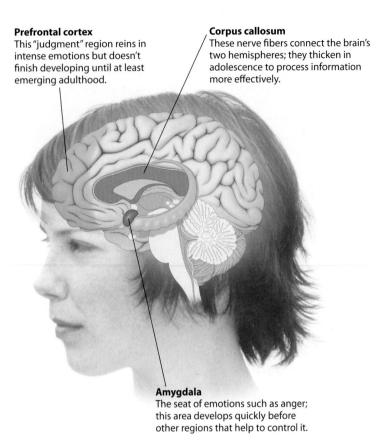

Prefrontal cortex
This "judgment" region reins in intense emotions but doesn't finish developing until at least emerging adulthood.

Corpus callosum
These nerve fibers connect the brain's two hemispheres; they thicken in adolescence to process information more effectively.

Amygdala
The seat of emotions such as anger; this area develops quickly before other regions that help to control it.

FIGURE 3.14
CHANGES IN THE ADOLESCENT BRAIN

developmental connection

Brain Development. Developmental social neuroscience is a recently developed field that focuses on connections between development, socioemotional factors, and neuroscience. Chapter 1, p. 13

corpus callosum A large bundle of axon fibers that connects the brain's left and right hemispheres.

prefrontal cortex The highest level of the frontal lobes that is involved in reasoning, decision making, and self-control.

amygdala A part of the brain's limbic system that is the seat of emotions such as anger.

by the end of adolescence individuals have "fewer, more selective, more effective neuronal connections than they did as children" (Kuhn, 2009, p. 153). And this pruning indicates that the activities adolescents choose to engage in and not to engage in influence which neural connections will be strengthened and which will disappear.

Among the most important structural changes in the brain during adolescence are those involving the corpus callosum, the prefrontal cortex, and the amygdala. The **corpus callosum,** a large bundle of axon fibers that connects the brain's left and right hemispheres, thickens in adolescence, and this thickening improves adolescents' ability to process information. Advances in the development of the **prefrontal cortex**—the highest level of the frontal lobes that is involved in reasoning, decision making, and self-control—continue through the emerging adult years, approximately 18 to 25 years of age, or later (Gogtay & Thompson, 2010; Luciana, 2010). However, the **amygdala**—a part of the brain's limbic system that is the seat of emotions such as anger—matures much earlier than the prefrontal cortex (Casey, Duhoux, & Malter Cohen, 2010). Figure 3.14 shows the locations of the corpus callosum, prefrontal cortex, and amygdala. A study of 137 early adolescents revealed a positive link between the volume of the amygdala and the duration of adolescents' aggressive behavior during interactions with parents (Whittle & others, 2008).

Production of the neurotransmitter dopamine increases in early adolescence, which produces increased reward-seeking and risk-taking (Doremus-Fitzwater, Varlinskaya, & Spear, 2010). In recent research conducted by Laurence Steinberg and his colleagues (Steinberg, 2010, 2011; Albert & Steinberg, 2011a, b; Caufman & others, 2010; O'Brien & others, 2011; Steinberg & others, 2008, 2009), preference for immediate rewards (assessed in such contexts as a gambling task and a video driving game) increased from 14 to 16 years of age and then declined. Also, in Steinberg's (2010, 2011) research, adolescents' belief that the benefits of risk taking outweighed its potential negative outcomes peaked at about 14 to 16 years of age. By contrast, Steinberg and his colleagues (2008, 2009) found that impulse control increased in a linear fashion from preadolescence to emerging adulthood.

The increase in risk taking in adolescence is usually thought to result in negative outcomes. However, there are some aspects of risk taking that benefit adolescents. Being open to new experiences and challenges, even risky ones, can help adolescents to stretch themselves to learn about aspects of the world they would not have encountered if they had shied away from such exploration (Allen & Allen, 2009). In Chapter 6, we will revisit the issue of risk taking in the context of adolescents' sense of invulnerability and recent research that distinguishes between different types of vulnerability (Lapsley & Hill, 2010).

Of course, a major issue is which comes first—biological changes in the brain or experiences that stimulate these changes (Lerner, Boyd, & Du, 2008). Consider a study in which the prefrontal cortex thickened and more brain connections formed when adolescents resisted peer pressure (Paus & others, 2008). Scientists have yet to determine whether the brain changes come first or whether the brain changes are the result of experiences with peers, parents, and others. Once again, we encounter the nature-nurture issue that is so prominent in examining development through the life span.

According to leading expert Jay Giedd (2007, pp. 1–2D), "Biology doesn't make teens rebellious or have purple hair or take drugs. It does not mean you are going to do drugs, but it gives you more of a chance to do that."

Many of the changes in the adolescent brain that have been described involve the rapidly emerging field of *developmental social neuroscience*, which involves connections

Strategies for Helping Adolescents Reduce Their Risk-Taking Behavior

Beginning in early adolescence, individuals seek experiences that create high-intensity feelings. Adolescents like intensity, excitement, and arousal. They are drawn to music videos that shock and bombard the senses. Teenagers flock to horror and slasher movies. They dominate queues waiting to ride high-adrenaline rides at amusement parks. Adolescence is a time when sex, drugs, very loud music, and other high-stimulation experiences take on great appeal. It is a developmental period when an appetite for adventure, a predilection for risks, and desire for novelty and thrills seem to reach naturally high levels. While these patterns of emotional changes are evidence to some degree in most adolescents, it is important to recognize the wide range of individual differences during this period of development (Dahl, 2004, p. 6).

The self-regulatory skills necessary to inhibit risk taking often don't develop until later in adolescence or emerging adulthood (Casey, Duhoux, & Malter Cohen, 2010). And, as we just saw, this gap between the increase in risk-taking behavior and the delay in self-regulation is linked to brain development in the limbic system (involved in pleasure seeking and emotion) taking place earlier than development of the frontal lobes (involved in self-regulation) (Steinberg, 2010, 2011).

It is important for parents, teachers, mentors, and other responsible adults to effectively monitor adolescents' behavior (Fallu & others, 2010; Tobler & Komro, 2010). In many cases, adults decrease their monitoring of adolescents too early, leaving them to cope with tempting situations alone or with friends and peers. When adolescents are in tempting and dangerous situations with minimal adult supervision, their inclination to engage in risk-taking behavior combined with their lack of self-regulatory skills can make them vulnerable to a host of negative outcomes (Sullivan, Childs, & O'Connell, 2010).

How might developmental changes in the brain be involved in adolescent risk taking? What are some strategies for reducing adolescent risk taking?

What does the nature-nurture debate tell us about the influence of adults who monitor adolescents' behavior?

between development, the brain, and socioemotional processes (Casey & others, 2010). For example, consider leading researcher Charles Nelson's (2003) view that, although adolescents are capable of very strong emotions, their prefrontal cortex hasn't adequately developed to the point at which they can control these passions. It is as if their brain doesn't have the brakes to slow down their emotions. Or consider this interpretation of the development of emotion and cognition in adolescents: "early activation of strong 'turbo-charged' feelings with a relatively un-skilled set of 'driving skills' or cognitive abilities to modulate strong emotions and motivations" (Dahl, 2004, p. 18).

Let's further consider the developmental disjunction between the early development of the amygdala and the later development of the prefrontal cortex. This disjunction may account for an increase in risk taking and other problems in adolescence. To read further about risk-taking behavior in adolescence, see the *Connecting Development to Life* interlude.

developmental connection

Cognitive Development. Might developmental changes in the adolescent's brain be linked to adolescents' decision-making skills? Chapter 7, p. 231

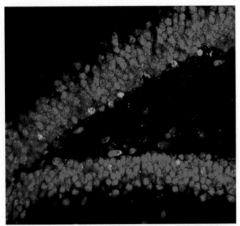

Exercise

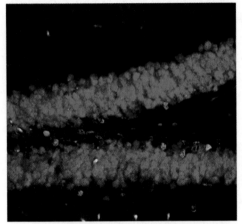

Enriched Environment

FIGURE **3.15**

GENERATING NEW NERVE CELLS IN ADULT

MICE. Researchers have found that exercise (running) and an enriched environment (a larger cage and many toys) can cause brain cells to divide and form new brain cells (Kempermann, van Praag, & Gage, 2000). Cells were labeled with a chemical marker that becomes integrated into the DNA of dividing cells (red). Four weeks later, they were also labeled to mark neurons (nerve cells). As shown here, both the running mice and the mice in an enriched environment had many cells that were still dividing (red) and others that had differentiated into new nerve cells (orange).

neurogenesis The generation of new neurons.

ADULTHOOD AND AGING

Changes in the brain continue during adulthood. Most of the research on the brains of adults, however, has focused on the aging brain of older adults. What are some of the general findings about the aging brain? How much plasticity and adaptability does it retain?

The Shrinking, Slowing Brain   On average, the brain loses 5 to 10 percent of its weight between the ages of 20 and 90. Brain volume also decreases (Sala & others, 2010). One study found that the volume of the brain was 15 percent less in older adults than younger adults (Shan & others, 2005). Scientists are not sure why these changes occur but note they might result from a decrease in dendrites and damage to the myelin sheath that covers axons. The current consensus is that under normal conditions adults are unlikely to lose brain cells per se, or if neuronal loss occurs, it is not substantial (Nelson, 2008; Richard, Taylor, & Greer, 2010).

Some areas shrink more than others. The prefrontal cortex is one area that shrinks with aging, and recent research has linked this shrinkage with a decrease in working memory and other cognitive activities in older adults (Isella & others, 2008).

A general slowing of function in the brain and spinal cord begins in middle adulthood and accelerates in late adulthood (Birren, 2002). Both physical coordination and intellectual performance are affected. For example, after age 70, many adults no longer show a knee jerk and by age 90 most reflexes are much slower (Spence, 1989). The slowing of the brain can impair the performance of older adults on intelligence tests and various cognitive tasks, especially those that are timed (Birren, 2002).

Aging has also been linked to a reduction in the production of some neurotransmitters, including acetylcholine, dopamine, and gamma-aminobutyric acid (GABA). Some researchers conclude that reductions in acetylcholine may be responsible for small declines in memory functioning and even with the severe memory loss associated with Alzheimer disease, which we will discuss in Chapter 4, "Health" (Nyakas & others, 2010). Normal age-related reductions in dopamine may cause problems in planning and carrying out motor activities (Troiano & others, 2010). Severe reductions in the production of dopamine have been linked with age-related diseases characterized by a loss of motor control, such as Parkinson disease (Hanna-Pladdy & Heilman, 2010). GABA helps to control the preciseness of the signal sent from one neuron to another, decreasing "noise," but its production decreases with aging (Pinto & others, 2010).

The Adapting Brain   If the brain were a computer, this description of the aging brain might lead you to think that it could not do much of anything. However, unlike a computer, the brain has remarkable repair capability (Nyberg & Backman, 2011; Reuter-Lorenz & Mikels, 2011). Even in late adulthood, the brain loses only a portion of its ability to function, and the activities older adults engage in can influence the brain's development (Park & Huang, 2010). For example, in a recent fMRI study, higher levels of aerobic fitness were linked with greater volume in the hippocampus, which translates into better memory (Erickson & others, 2009).

Can adults, even aging adults, generate new neurons? Researchers have found that **neurogenesis,** the generation of new neurons, does occur in lower mammalian species, such as mice (Landgren & Curtis, 2010). Also, research indicates that exercise and an enriched, complex environment can generate new brain cells in mice and that stress reduces their survival rate (Kim & others, 2010; Madronal & others, 2010) (see Figure 3.15). And a recent study revealed that coping with stress stimulated hippocampal neurogenesis in adult monkeys (Lyons & others, 2010). Researchers also recently have discovered that if rats are cognitively challenged to learn something, new brain cells survive longer (Shors, 2009).

It also is now accepted that neurogenesis can occur in humans (Lugert & others, 2010). However, researchers have documented neurogenesis only in two brain regions: the hippocampus, which is involved in memory, and the olfactory bulb, which is involved in smell (Arenkiel, 2010; Couillard-Despres, Iglseder, & Aigner, 2011). It also is not known what functions these new brain cells perform, and at this point researchers have documented that they last for only several weeks (Nelson, 2006). Researchers currently are studying factors that might inhibit and promote neurogenesis, including various drugs, stress, and exercise (van Praag, 2009). They also are examining how the grafting of neural stem cells to various regions of the brain, such as the hippocampus, might increase neurogenesis (Taupin, 2011).

Dendritic growth can occur in human adults, possibly even in older adults (Eliasieh, Liets, & Chalupa, 2007). One study compared the brains of adults at various ages (Coleman, 1986). From the forties through the seventies, the growth of dendrites increased. However, in people in their nineties, dendritic growth no longer occurred. This dendritic growth might compensate for the possible loss of neurons through the seventies but not in the nineties. Lack of dendritic growth in older adults could be due to a lack of environmental stimulation and activity.

Changes in lateralization may provide one type of adaptation in aging adults (Angel & others, 2009; Cabeza, Nyberg, & Park, 2009). Recall that lateralization is the specialization of function in one hemisphere of the brain or the other. Using neuroimaging techniques, researchers have found that brain activity in the prefrontal cortex is lateralized less in older adults than in younger adults when they are engaging in cognitive tasks (Cabeza, 2002; Rossi & others, 2005). For example, Figure 3.16 shows that when younger adults are given the task of recognizing words they have previously seen, they process the information primarily in the right hemisphere; older adults are more likely to use both hemispheres (Madden & others, 1999).

The decrease in lateralization in older adults might play a compensatory role in the aging brain. That is, using both hemispheres may improve the cognitive functioning of older adults. Support for this view comes from another study in which older adults who used both brain hemispheres were faster at completing a working memory task than their counterparts who primarily used only one hemisphere (Reuter-Lorenz & others, 2000). However, the decrease in lateralization may be a mere by-product of aging; it may reflect an age-related decline in the brain's ability to specialize functions. In this view, during childhood the brain becomes increasingly differentiated in terms of its functions; as adults become older, this process may reverse. Support for the dedifferentiation view is found in the higher intercorrelations of performance on cognitive tasks in older adults than in younger adults (Baltes & Lindenberger, 1997).

Of course, there are individual differences in how the brain changes in older adults. Consider highly successful businessman 81-year-old T. Boone Pickens, who continues to lead a highly active lifestyle, regularly exercising and engaging in cognitively complex work. Undergoing a recent fMRI in cognitive neuroscientist Denise Park's laboratory, when Pickens was presented various cognitive tasks, instead of both hemispheres being active, Pickens' left hemisphere was dominant, as is true of most younger adults (Helman, 2008). Indeed, as the complexity of the cognitive task increased, the more Pickens used the left hemisphere of his brain (see Figure 3.17). Further indication of variation in the link between brain lateralization and cognitive processing was found in a recent study (Manenti, Cotelli, & Miniussi, 2010). Older adults who performed better on memory tasks showed less asymmetry in the prefrontal cortex than their counterparts who performed more poorly on the tasks.

What kinds of mental activities can help slow brain changes that occur with age? To read about how one group of researchers is seeking to answer this question, see the *Connecting with Research* interlude.

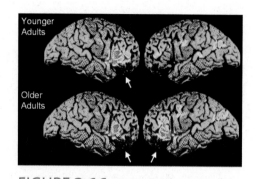

FIGURE **3.16**

THE DECREASE IN BRAIN LATERALIZATION IN OLDER ADULTS. Younger adults primarily used the right prefrontal region of the brain (*top left photo*) during a recall memory task, whereas older adults used both the left and right prefrontal regions (*bottom two photos*).

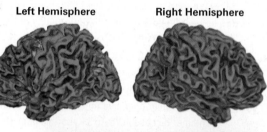

Left Hemisphere   Right Hemisphere

FIGURE **3.17**

INDIVIDUAL DIFFERENCES IN HEMISPHERIC SPECIALIZATION IN OLDER ADULTS. On tough questions—such as "Are 'zombie' and 'unicorn' living or nonliving?"—the red patches indicate that 80-year-old T. Boone Pickens (above, holding a model of the brain) was relying mainly on the left hemisphere of his brain to make a decision. Most older adults show a stronger bilateral activation, using both hemispheres more equally than Pickens, whose lateralization was more characteristic of younger adults.

The Nun Study

The Nun Study, directed by David Snowdon, is an intriguing, ongoing investigation of aging in 678 nuns, many of whom have lived in a convent in Mankato, Minnesota (Snowdon, 1997, 2002, 2003; Tyas & others, 2007). Each of the 678 nuns agreed to participate in annual assessments of their cognitive and physical functioning. They also agreed to donate their brains for scientific research when they die, and they are the largest group of brain donors in the world. Examination of the nuns' donated brains, as well as others, has led neuroscientists to believe that the brain has a remarkable capacity to change and grow, even in old age. The Sisters of Notre Dame in Mankato lead an intellectually challenging life, and brain researchers believe this contributes to their quality of life as older adults and possibly to their longevity.

Findings from the Nun Study so far include:

- Idea density, a measure of linguistic ability assessed early in the adult years (age 22), was linked with higher brain weight, fewer incidences of mild cognitive impairment, and fewer characteristics of Alzheimer disease in 75- to 95-year-old nuns (Riley & others, 2005).
- Positive emotions early in adulthood were linked to longevity (Danner, Snowdon, & Friesen, 2001). Handwritten autobiographies from 180 nuns, composed when they were 22 years of age, were scored for emotional content. The nuns whose early writings had higher scores for positive emotional content were more likely to still be alive at 75 to 95 years of age than their counterparts whose early writings were characterized by negative emotional content.
- Sisters who had taught for most of their lives showed more moderate declines in intellectual skills than those who had spent most of their lives in service-based tasks, a finding supporting the notion that stimulating the brain with intellectual activity keeps neurons healthy and alive (Snowdon, 2002).

This and other research provides hope that scientists will discover ways to tap into the brain's capacity to adapt in order to prevent and treat brain diseases (Creed & Milgram, 2010). For example, scientists might learn more effective ways to help older adults recover from strokes (Landi & Rossini, 2010). Even when areas of the brain are permanently damaged by stroke, new message routes can be created to get around the blockage or to resume the function of that area (Wang & others, 2010).

(a)

(b)

(*a*) Sister Marcella Zachman (*left*) finally stopped teaching at age 97. Now, at 99, she helps ailing nuns exercise their brains by quizzing them on vocabulary or playing a card game called Skip-Bo, at which she deliberately loses. Sister Mary Esther Boor (*right*), also 99 years of age, is a former teacher who stays alert by doing puzzles and volunteering to work the front desk. (*b*) A technician holds the brain of a deceased Mankato nun. The nuns donate their brains for research that explores the effects of stimulation on brain growth.

Although the Nun Study's results are intriguing, an order of nuns is in some ways a self-selected group whose members may come to share many social and environmental characteristics through long years of living together. How might future researchers account for any potential biases in such studies?

Review *Connect* Reflect

LG2 Describe how the brain changes through the life span

Review

- What are the major areas of the brain, and how does it process information?
- How does the brain change during infancy?
- What characterizes the development of the brain in childhood?
- How can the changes in the brain during adolescence be summarized?
- What is the aging brain like?

Connect

- What types of brain research technology can be used to study infants that cannot be used to study them before they are born? Which can be used on adults but not infants? How might these differences in research tools affect our understanding of the human brain across the life span?

Reflect *Your Own Personal Journey of Life*

- If you could interview the Mankato nuns, what would you want to ask them?

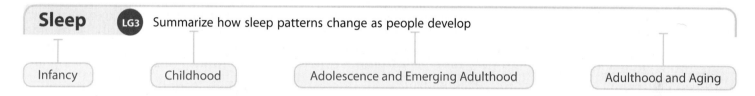

Sleep

LG3 Summarize how sleep patterns change as people develop

| Infancy | Childhood | Adolescence and Emerging Adulthood | Adulthood and Aging |

Sleep restores, replenishes, and rebuilds our brains and bodies. Some neuroscientists maintain that sleep gives neurons that are active while we are awake a chance to shut down and repair themselves (National Institute of Neurological Disorders and Stroke, 2011). How do our sleeping patterns change across the life span?

INFANCY

How much do infants sleep? Can any special problems develop regarding infants' sleep?

> Sleep that knits up the ravelled sleave of care . . . Balm of hurt minds, nature's second course. Chief nourisher in life's feast.
>
> —**WILLIAM SHAKESPEARE**
> *English Playwright, 17th Century*

The Sleep/Wake Cycle   When we were infants, sleep consumed more of our time than it does now. Newborns sleep 16 to 17 hours a day, although some sleep more and others less—the range is from a low of about 10 hours to a high of about 21 hours. Their longest period of sleep is not always between 11 p.m. and 7 a.m. Although total sleep remains somewhat consistent for young infants, their sleep during the day does not always follow a rhythmic pattern. An infant might change from sleeping several long bouts of 7 or 8 hours to three or four shorter sessions only several hours in duration. By about 1 month of age, most infants have begun to sleep longer at night. By 6 months of age, they usually have moved closer to adult-like sleep patterns, spending their longest span of sleep at night and their longest span of waking during the day (Sadeh, 2008).

The most common infant sleep-related problem reported by parents is nighttime waking (Hospital for Sick Children & others, 2010). Surveys indicate that 20 to 30 percent of infants have difficulty going to sleep and staying asleep at night (Sadeh, 2008). A recent study revealed that the mother's emotional availability at bedtime was linked to fewer infant sleep problems, supporting the premise that parents' emotional availability to infants in sleep contexts increases feelings of safety and security, and consequently better-regulated infant sleep (Teti & others, 2010). And a recent study found that a higher involvement of fathers in overall infant care was related to fewer infant sleep problems (Tikotzky, Sadeh, & Glickman-Gavrieli, 2010). However, infant night-time waking problems have

FIGURE **3.18**
SLEEP ACROSS THE HUMAN LIFE SPAN

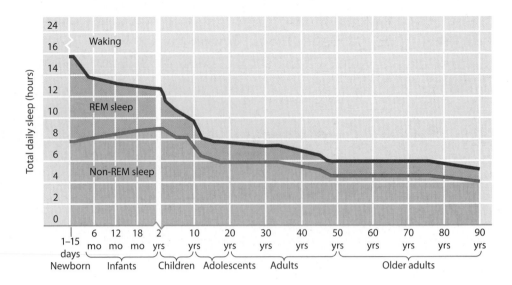

consistently been linked to excessive parental involvement in sleep-related interactions with their infant (Sadeh, 2008). And a recent study revealed that maternal depression during pregnancy, early introduction of solid foods, infant TV viewing, and child-care attendance were related to shorter duration of infant sleep (Nevarez & others, 2010).

REM Sleep   In REM sleep, the eyes flutter beneath closed lids; in non-REM sleep, this type of eye movement does not occur and sleep is quieter. Figure 3.18 shows developmental changes in the average number of total hours spent in REM and non-REM sleep. By the time they reach adulthood, individuals spend about one-fifth of their night in REM sleep, and REM sleep usually appears about one hour after non-REM sleep. However, about half of an infant's sleep is REM sleep, and infants often begin their sleep cycle with REM sleep rather than non-REM sleep (Sadeh, 2008). A much greater amount of time is taken up by REM sleep in infancy than at any other point in the life span. By the time infants reach 3 months of age, the percentage of time they spend in REM sleep falls to about 40 percent, and REM sleep no longer begins their sleep cycle.

Why do infants spend so much time in REM sleep? Researchers are not certain. The large amount of REM sleep may provide infants with added self-stimulation, since they spend less time awake than do older children. REM sleep also might promote the brain's development in infancy (Graven, 2006).

When adults are awakened during REM sleep, they frequently report that they have been dreaming, but when they are awakened during non-REM sleep they are much less likely to report they have been dreaming (Cartwright & others, 2006). Since infants spend more time than adults in REM sleep, can we conclude that they dream a lot? We don't know whether infants dream or not, because they don't have any way of reporting dreams.

Shared Sleeping   Some child experts stress that there are benefits to shared sleeping (as when an infant sleeps in the same bed with its mother). They state that it can promote breast feeding, lets the mother respond more quickly to the baby's cries, and allows her to detect breathing pauses in the baby that might be dangerous (Nelson & others, 2005). Sharing a bed with a mother is common practice in many countries, such as Guatemala and China, whereas in others, such as the United States and Great Britain, most newborns sleep in a crib, either in the same room as the parents or in a separate room.

Shared sleeping remains a controversial issue, with some experts recommending it and others arguing against it, although recently the recommendation trend has been to avoid infant-parent bed sharing, especially until the infant is at least six months of age (McIntosh, Tonkin, & Gunn, 2010; Norton & Grellner, 2010). The American Academy of Pediatrics Task Force on Infant Positioning and SIDS (AAPTFIPS) (2000) recommends against shared sleeping. Its members argue that in some instances bed sharing might lead to sudden infant death syndrome (SIDS), as could be the case if a sleeping mother rolls over on her baby. Recent studies have found that bed sharing is linked with a greater incidence of SIDS, especially when parents smoke (Bajanowski & others, 2007; Senter & others, 2010). And a recent study of two-month-old infants revealed that they had more sleep problems such as disordered breathing when they shared the bed with parents (Kelmanson, 2010).

SIDS **Sudden infant death syndrome (SIDS)** is a condition that occurs when infants stop breathing, usually during the night, and die suddenly without an apparent cause. SIDS remains the highest cause of infant death in the United States with nearly 3,000 infant deaths attributed to it annually (Montagna & Chokroverty, 2011). Risk of SIDS is highest at 2 to 4 months of age (Centers for Disease Control and Prevention, 2011).

Since 1992, the American Academy of Pediatrics (AAP) has recommended that infants be placed to sleep on their backs to reduce the risk of SIDS, and the frequency of prone sleeping among U.S. infants has dropped dramatically (AAPTFIPS, 2000). Researchers have found that SIDS does indeed decrease when infants sleep on their backs rather than their stomachs or sides (Senter & others, 2010). Among the reasons given for prone sleeping being a high-risk factor for SIDS are that it impairs the infant's arousal from sleep and restricts the infant's ability to swallow effectively (Franco & others, 2010; Mitchell, 2009).

In addition to sleeping in a prone position, researchers have found that the following are risk factors for SIDS:

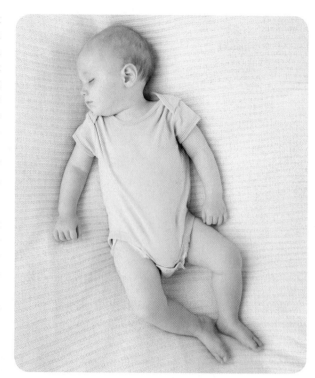

Is this a good sleep position for this 3-month-old infant? Why or why not?

- SIDS is more likely to occur in infants who do not use a pacifier when they go to sleep than in those who do use a pacifier (Jenik & Vain, 2010).
- Low birth weight infants are 5 to 10 times more likely to die of SIDS than are their normal-weight counterparts (Horne & others, 2002).
- Infants whose siblings have died of SIDS are two to four times as likely to die of it (Lenoir, Mallet, & Calenda, 2000).
- Six percent of infants with sleep apnea, a temporary cessation of breathing in which the airway is completely blocked, usually for 10 seconds or longer, die of SIDS (Ednick & others, 2010; McNamara & Sullivan, 2000).
- African American and Eskimo infants are four to six times as likely as all others to die of SIDS (Ige & Shelton, 2004; Kitsantas & Gaffney, 2010).
- SIDS is more common in lower socioeconomic groups (Mitchell & others, 2000).
- SIDS is more common in infants who are passively exposed to cigarette smoke (Dietz & others, 2010).
- SIDS is more common when infants and parents share the same bed (Senter & others, 2010).
- SIDS is more common if infants sleep in soft bedding (McGarvey & others, 2006).
- SIDS is less common when infants sleep in a bedroom with a fan. A recent study revealed that sleeping in a bedroom with a fan lowers the risk of SIDS by 70 percent (Coleman-Phox, Odouli, & Li, 2008).
- SIDS occurs more often in infants with abnormal brain stem functioning involving the neurotransmitter serotonin (Duncan & others, 2010).

sudden infant death syndrome (SIDS) Condition that occurs when an infant stops breathing, usually during the night, and suddenly dies without an apparent cause.

What characterizes children's sleep?

CHILDHOOD

Experts recommend that young children get 11 to 13 hours of sleep each night (National Sleep Foundation, 2011). Most young children sleep through the night and have one daytime nap (Davis, Parker, & Montgomery, 2004).

Following is a sampling of recent research on factors linked to children's sleep problems:

- A national survey indicated that children who do not get adequate sleep are more likely to show depressive symptoms, have problems at school, have a father in poor health, live in a family characterized by frequent disagreements and heated arguments, and live in an unsafe neighborhood than are children who get adequate sleep (Smaldone, Honig, & Byrne, 2007).

- Children who had trouble sleeping in childhood were more likely to have alcohol use problems in adolescence and early adulthood (Wong & others, 2010).

- Sleep problems in early childhood were a subsequent indicator of attention problems that in some cases persisted into early adolescence (O'Callaghan & others, 2010).

- Emotional security in parent-child and marital relationships when children were in the third grade predicted fewer sleep problems when they reached the fifth grade (Keller & El-Sheikh, 2010).

Children can experience a number of sleep problems (Nevsimalova, 2009; Owens & others, 2010). One estimate indicates that more than 40 percent of children experience a sleep problem at some point in their development (Boyle & Cropley, 2004). A recent analysis concluded that chronic sleep disorders that deprive children of adequate sleep may result in impaired brain development (Jan & others, 2010).

ADOLESCENCE AND EMERGING ADULTHOOD

Might changing sleep patterns in adolescence contribute to adolescents' health-compromising behaviors? Recently there has been a surge of interest in adolescent sleep patterns (Dregan & Armstrong, 2010; McHale & others, 2010; Wahlstrom, 2010).

In a recent national survey of youth, only 31 percent of U.S. adolescents got eight or more hours of sleep on an average school night (Eaton & others, 2008). In this study, the percentage of adolescents getting this much sleep on an average school night decreased as they got older (see Figure 3.19). Adolescents who got inadequate sleep (eight hours or less) on school nights were more likely to feel tired or sleepy, act cranky and irritable, fall asleep in school, be in a depressed mood, and drink caffeinated beverages than their counterparts who got optimal sleep (nine or more hours).

Mary Carskadon (2002, 2004, 2005, 2006) has conducted a number of research studies on adolescent sleep patterns. She has found that adolescents sleep an average of 9 hours and 25 minutes when given the opportunity to sleep as long as they like. Most adolescents get considerably less sleep than this, especially during the week. This creates a sleep debt, which adolescents often try to make up on the weekend. Carskadon also has found that older adolescents are often more sleepy during the day than are younger adolescents. She concludes that this was not because of factors such as academic work and social pressures. Rather, her research suggests that adolescents' biological clocks undergo a hormonal phase shift as they get older. This pushes the time of wakefulness to an hour later than when they were young adolescents. Carskadon has found that the shift was caused by a delay in the nightly presence of the hormone *melatonin*, which is produced by the brain's pineal gland in preparation for the body to sleep. Melatonin is secreted at about 9:30 p.m. in younger

FIGURE 3.19

DEVELOPMENTAL CHANGES IN U.S. ADOLESCENTS' SLEEP PATTERNS ON AN AVERAGE SCHOOL NIGHT

Bar graph — Percentage of students who got 8 hours of sleep or more on an average school night: 9th grade 42.3, 10th grade 32.4, 11th grade 24.9, 12th grade 21.8

adolescents but is produced approximately an hour later in older adolescents, which delays the onset of sleep.

Carskadon determined that early school starting times can result in grogginess and lack of attention in class and poor performance on tests. Based on this research, schools in Edina, Minnesota, made the decision to start classes at 8:30 a.m. instead of 7:25 a.m. Discipline problems and the number of students reporting illness or depression have dropped. Test scores in Edina have improved for high school students, but not for middle school students—results that support Carskadon's idea that older adolescents are more affected by earlier school start times than younger adolescents are. Also, a recent study found that just a 30-minute delay in school start time was linked to improvements in adolescents' sleep, alertness, mood, and health (Owens, Belon, & Moss, 2010).

Do sleep patterns change in emerging adulthood? Research indicates that they do (Galambos, Howard, & Maggs, 2011). A recent study revealed that more than 60 percent of college students were categorized as poor-quality sleepers (Lund & others, 2010). In this study, the weekday bedtimes and rise times of first-year college students were approximately 1 hour and 15 minutes later than those of seniors in high school (Lund & others, 2010). However, the first-year college students had later bedtimes and rise times than third- and fourth-year college students, indicating that at about 20 to 22 years of age, a reverse in the timing of bedtimes and rise times occurs. In this study, poor-quality sleep was linked to worse physical and mental health, and the students reported that emotional and academic stress negatively affected their sleep. In another study, the sleep quality of first-year college students was poorer during the months when they experienced the most stress (Galambos, Howard, & Maggs, 2011).

ADULTHOOD AND AGING

It is not only many youth who are getting inadequate sleep. Many adults don't get enough either. The average American adult gets just under seven hours of sleep a night. How much sleep do adults need to function optimally the next day? An increasing number of experts note that eight hours of sleep or more per night are necessary to be at your best the next day. These experts argue that many adults have become sleep deprived (Banks & Dinges, 2008). Work pressures, school pressures, family obligations, and social obligations often lead to long hours of wakefulness and irregular sleep/wake schedules (Dorrian & others, 2008).

Some aspects of sleep become more problematic in middle age (McGee, Caputi, & Iverson, 2010). The total number of hours slept usually remains the same as in early adulthood, but beginning in the forties, wakeful periods are more frequent and there is less of the deepest type of sleep. The amount of time spent lying awake in bed at night begins to increase in middle age, which can produce a feeling of being less rested in the mornings (Abbott, 2003). Sleep problems in middle-aged adults are more common in individuals who take a higher number of prescription drugs, are obese, have cardiovascular disease, or are depressed (Miller & Cappuccio, 2007).

Beginning in middle adulthood and continuing through late adulthood, the timing of sleep also changes. Many older adults go to bed earlier at night and wake up earlier in the morning (Liu & Liu, 2005). Many older adults also take a nap in the afternoon.

Approximately 50 percent of older adults complain of having difficulty sleeping (Neikrug & Ancoli-Israel, 2010). Poor sleep can result in earlier death and is linked to

What are some developmental changes in sleep patterns during adolescence? How might these influence alertness at school?

In Mary Carskadon's sleep laboratory at Brown University, an adolescent girl's brain activity is being monitored. Carskadon (2005) says that in the morning, sleep-deprived adolescents' "brains are telling them it's nighttime . . . and the rest of the world is saying it's time to go to school" (p. 19).

a lower level of cognitive functioning. For example, a recent study found that spending more time in sleep benefited older adults' memory (Aly & Moscovitch, 2010).

Many of the sleep problems of older adults are associated with health problems (Townsend-Roccichelli, Sanford, & VandeWaa, 2010). Here are some strategies to help older adults sleep better at night: avoid caffeine, avoid over-the-counter sleep remedies, stay physically active during the day, stay mentally active, and limit naps.

Review *Connect* Reflect

 Summarize how sleep patterns change as people develop

Review

- How can sleep be characterized in infancy?
- What changes occur in sleep during childhood?
- How does sleep change in adolescence and emerging adulthood?
- What changes in sleep take place during adulthood and aging?

Connect

- How might behavioral theory be applied to help older adults avoid difficulty in sleeping?

Reflect *Your Own Personal Journey of Life*

- How much sleep do you get on a typical night? Do you get enough sleep to function optimally the next day? Explain.

Longevity Explain longevity and the biological aspects of aging

Life Expectancy and Life Span

Centenarians

Biological Theories of Aging

How long do most people live, and what distinguishes people who live a very long time? What is it like to live to a very ripe old age, and why do we age in the first place?

LIFE EXPECTANCY AND LIFE SPAN

We are no longer a youthful society. As more individuals live to older ages, the proportion of individuals at different ages has become increasingly similar. Indeed, the concept of a period called "late adulthood" is a recent one—until the twentieth century, most individuals died before they reached 65. Recall from Chapter 1 that today a much greater percentage of persons live to older ages. However, the life span has remained virtually unchanged since the beginning of recorded history. **Life span** is the upper boundary of life, the maximum number of years an individual can live. The maximum life span of humans is approximately 120 to 125 years of age. *Life expectancy* is the number of years that will probably be lived by the average person born in a specific year. Improvements in medicine, nutrition, exercise, and lifestyle have increased our life expectancy an average of 31 additional years since 1900. The average life expectancy of individuals born today in the United States is 77.9 years (Xu & others, 2010). Sixty-five-year-olds in the United States today can expect to live an average of 18 more years (to 83 years of age) and 85-year-olds can expect to live 6 more years (to 91 years of age) (Xu & others, 2010).

How does the United States fare in life expectancy, compared with other countries around the world? We do considerably better than some,

life span The upper boundary of life, which is the maximum number of years an individual can live. The maximum life span of humans is about 120 years of age.

a little worse than others (Powell, 2009). Japan has the highest life expectancy at birth today (82 years) (Guillot, 2009). Differences in life expectancies across countries are due to factors such as health conditions and medical care throughout the life span.

Life expectancy also differs for various ethnic groups within the United States and for men and women (Xu & others, 2010). For example, the life expectancy of African Americans (73.6) in the United States is five years lower than the life expectancy for non-Latino Whites (78.4). Non-Latino White women have a life expectancy of 80.8, followed by African American women (76.8), non-Latino White men (75.9 years), and African American men (70.0 years).

Today, the overall life expectancy for females is 80.4 years of age, for males 75.4 years of age (Xu & others, 2010). Beginning in the mid-thirties, females outnumber males; this gap widens during the remainder of the adult years. By the time adults are 75 years of age, more than 61 percent of the population is female; for those 85 and over, the figure is almost 70 percent female. Why can women expect to live longer than men? Social factors such as health attitudes, habits, lifestyles, and occupation are probably important (Saint Onge, 2009). For example, men are more likely than women to die from the leading causes of death in the United States, such as cancer of the respiratory system, motor vehicle accidents, cirrhosis of the liver, emphysema, and coronary heart disease (Yoshida & others, 2006). These causes of death are associated with lifestyle. For example, the sex difference in deaths due to lung cancer and emphysema occurs because men tend to be heavier smokers than women.

The sex difference in longevity is also influenced by biological factors (Austad, 2011). In virtually all species, females outlive males. Women have more resistance to infections and degenerative diseases. For example, the female's estrogen production helps to protect her from arteriosclerosis (hardening of the arteries) (Vina & others, 2005). And the additional X chromosome that women carry may be associated with the production of more antibodies to fight off disease.

Frenchwoman Jeanne Louise Calment, who recently died at the age of 122. Greater ages have been claimed, but scientists say the maximum human life span is about 120 to 125.

CENTENARIANS

In industrialized countries, the number of centenarians (individuals 100 years and older) is increasing at a rate of approximately 7 percent each year (Perls, 2007). In the United States, there were only 15,000 centenarians in 1980, a number that had risen to 77,000 in 2000 and is projected to reach more than 800,000 by 2050. The United States has the most centenarians, followed by Japan, China, and England/Wales (Hall, 2008). It is estimated that there are 75 to 100 supercentenarians (individuals 110 years or older) in the United States and about 300 to 450 worldwide (Perls, 2007).

> To me old age is always fifteen years older than I am.
>
> —**Bernard Baruch**
> *American Statesman, 20th Century*

Three participants in the New England Centenarian Study: (*Left*) Adelaide Kruger, age 101, watering her flowers; (*middle*) Waldo McBurney, age 104, active beekeeper, gardener, and runner who has earned five gold medals and set international records in track and field events in his age group; (*right*) Daphne Brann, age 110, voting in an election.

Life Expectancy

This test gives you a rough guide for predicting your longevity. The basic life expectancy for men is age 75, and for women it is 81. Write down your basic life expectancy. If you are in your fifties or sixties, you should add ten years to the basic figure because you have already proved yourself to be a durable individual. If you are over age 60 and active, you can even add another two years.

Decide how each item applies to you and add or subtract the appropriate number of years from your basic life expectancy.

1. Family history

____ Add five years if two or more of your grandparents lived to 80 or beyond.

____ Subtract four years if any parent, grandparent, sister, or brother died of a heart attack or stroke before 50.

____ Subtract two years if anyone died from these diseases before 60.

____ Subtract three years for each case of diabetes, thyroid disorder, breast cancer, cancer of the digestive system, asthma, or chronic bronchitis among parents or grandparents.

2. Marital status

____ If you are married, add four years.

____ If you are over 25 and not married, subtract one year for every unmarried decade.

3. Economic status

____ Add two years if your family income is over $60,000 per year.

____ Subtract three years if you have been poor for the greater part of your life.

4. Physique

____ Subtract one year for every 10 pounds you are overweight.

____ For each inch your girth measurement exceeds your chest measurement deduct two years.

____ Add three years if you are over 40 and not overweight.

5. Exercise

____ Add three years if you exercise regularly and moderately (jogging three times a week).

____ Add five years if you exercise regularly and vigorously (long-distance running three times a week).

____ Subtract three years if your job is sedentary.

____ Add three years if your job is active.

6. Alcohol

____ Add two years if you are a light drinker (one to three drinks a day).

____ Subtract five to ten years if you are a heavy drinker (more than four drinks per day).

____ Subtract one year if you are a teetotaler.

7. Smoking

____ Subtract eight years if you smoke two or more packs of cigarettes per day.

____ Subtract two years if you smoke one to two packs per day.

____ Subtract two years if you smoke less than one pack.

____ Subtract two years if you regularly smoke a pipe or cigars.

8. Disposition

____ Add two years if you are a reasoned, practical person.

____ Subtract two years if you are aggressive, intense, and competitive.

____ Add one to five years if you are basically happy and content with life.

____ Subtract one to five years if you are often unhappy, worried, and often feel guilty.

9. Education

____ Subtract two years if you have less than a high school education.

____ Add one year if you attended four years of school beyond high school.

____ Add three years if you attended five or more years beyond high school.

10. Environment

____ Add four years if you have lived most of your life in a rural environment.

____ Subtract two years if you have lived most of your life in an urban environment.

11. Sleep

____ Subtract five years if you sleep more than nine hours a day.

12. Temperature

____ Add two years if your home's thermostat is set at no more than 68° F.

13. Health care

____ Add three years if you have regular medical checkups and regular dental care.

____ Subtract two years if you are frequently ill.

____ **Your Life Expectancy Total**

FIGURE **3.20**
CAN YOU LIVE TO BE 100?

A disproportionate number of centenarians are women. However, although women are more likely to attain exceptional longevity than men, among centenarians men are likely to be healthier than women (Perls, 2007). Though far fewer in number, male centenarians have better physical and cognitive functioning than their female counterparts (Terry, Sebastian, & others, 2008). One explanation for this gender difference in centenarians' health is that to reach exceptional old age men may need to be in excellent health (Perls, 2007). By contrast, women may be more adaptive in living with illnesses when they are older and thus can reach an exceptional old age in spite of having a chronic disability.

What chance do you have of living to be 100? Genes play an important role in surviving to an extreme old age (Candore, Caruso, & Colonna-Romano, 2010; Sebastiani & others, 2010). As you read in Chapter 2, there is increasing interest in studying *susceptibility genes* (Paquette & others, 2010), which make an individual more vulnerable to specific diseases or acceleration of aging, and *longevity genes,* which make an individual less vulnerable to certain diseases and more likely to live to an older age (Bauer & others, 2010; Khabour & Barnawi, 2010). But as indicated in Figure 3.20, there are also other factors at work, such as family history, health (weight, diet, smoking, and exercise), education, personality, and lifestyle (Barbieri & others, 2009; Luszcz, 2010).

BIOLOGICAL THEORIES OF AGING

Even if we stay remarkably healthy, we begin to age at some point. In fact, life-span experts argue that biological aging begins at birth (Schaie, 2000). What are the biological explanations of aging? Intriguing explanations of why we age are provided by five biological theories: evolutionary, cellular clock, free-radical, mitochondrial, and hormonal stress.

Evolutionary Theory   Recall from Chapter 2 the view that the benefits conferred by evolutionary selection decrease with age. In the evolutionary theory of aging, natural selection has not eliminated many harmful conditions and nonadaptive characteristics in older adults (Austad, 2009; Kittas, 2010; Le Couteur & Simpson, 2011). Why? Because natural selection is linked to reproductive fitness, which is present only in the earlier part of adulthood. For example, consider Alzheimer disease, an irreversible brain disorder that does not appear until late middle adulthood or beyond. In evolutionary theory, if Alzheimer disease had occurred earlier in development, it might have been eliminated many centuries ago.

Cellular Clock Theory   **Cellular clock theory** is Leonard Hayflick's (1977) theory that cells can divide a maximum of about 75 to 80 times and that, as we age, our cells become less capable of dividing. Hayflick found that cells extracted from adults in their fifties to seventies divided fewer than 75 to 80 times. Based on the ways cells divide, Hayflick places the upper limit of the human life-span potential at about 120 to 125 years of age.

In the last decade, scientists have tried to fill in a gap in cellular clock theory (Aviv, 2011; Davioli, Denchi, & de Lange, 2010). Hayflick did not know why cells die. The answer may lie at the tips of chromosomes, at telomeres, which are DNA sequences that cap chromosomes (Sahin & Depinho, 2010; Mather & others, 2011).

Each time a cell divides, the telomeres become shorter and shorter (see Figure 3.21). After about 70 or 80 replications, the telomeres are dramatically reduced and the cell no longer can reproduce. A recent study revealed that healthy centenarians had longer telomeres than unhealthy centenarians (Terry, Nolan, & others, 2008b). Another recent study found that women with higher intakes of vitamins C and E had longer telomeres than women with lower intakes of these vitamins (Xu & others, 2009).

Injecting the enzyme *telomerase* into human cells grown in the laboratory can substantially extend the life of the cells beyond the approximately 70 to 80 normal cell divisions (Aubert & Lansdorp, 2008). However, telomerase is present in approximately 85 percent of cancerous cells and thus may not produce healthy life extension of cells (Fakhoury, Nimmo, & Autexier, 2007). To capitalize on the high presence of telomerase in cancerous cells, researchers currently are investigating gene therapies that inhibit telomerase and lead to the death of cancerous cells while keeping healthy cells alive (Longhese & others, 2010; Zhao & others, 2010). One focus of these gene therapies is on stem cells and their renewal (Zhao, Shay, & Wright, 2011). Telomeres and telomerase are increasingly thought to be key components of the stem cell regeneration process, providing a possible avenue to restrain cancer and delay aging (Barsov, 2011; Flores & Blasco, 2010).

Free-Radical Theory   A second microbiological theory of aging is **free-radical theory,** which states that people age because when cells metabolize energy, the

> To be seventy years young is sometimes far more cheerful and hopeful than to be forty years old.
>
> —Oliver Wendell Holmes, Sr.
> *American Physician, 19th Century*

developmental **connection**

Culture. In Baltes' view, the benefits of evolutionary selection decrease with age and the need for culture increases with age. Chapter 2, p. 51

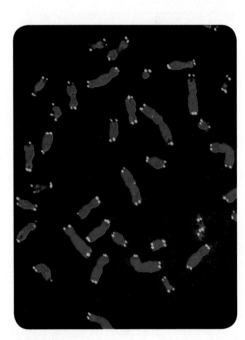

FIGURE **3.21**

TELOMERES AND AGING. The photograph shows actual telomeres lighting up the tips of chromosomes.

cellular clock theory Leonard Hayflick's theory that the number of times human cells can divide is about 75 to 80. As we age, our cells are less able to divide.

free-radical theory A microbiological theory of aging stating that people age because when their cells metabolize energy, they generate waste that includes unstable oxygen molecules, known as free radicals, that damage DNA and other structures.

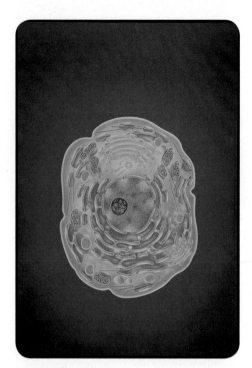

FIGURE **3.22**

MITOCHONDRIA. This color-coded illustration of a typical cell shows mitochondria in green. The illustration also includes the nucleus (pink) with its DNA (brown). *What are ways that changes in mitochondria might be involved in aging?*

by-products include unstable oxygen molecules known as free radicals (Sasaki & others, 2010). The free radicals ricochet around the cells, damaging DNA and other cellular structures (Oliveira & others, 2010; Van Remmen, 2011). The damage can lead to a range of disorders, including cancer and arthritis (Farooqui & Farooqui, 2009). Overeating is linked with an increase in free radicals, and researchers have found that calorie restriction—a diet restricted in calories although adequate in proteins, vitamins, and minerals—reduces the oxidative damage created by free radicals (Keijer & van Schothorst, 2008).

Mitochondrial Theory   There is increasing interest in the role that mitochondria—tiny bodies within cells that supply energy for function, growth, and repair—might play in aging (Brand, 2011) (see Figure 3.22). **Mitochondrial theory** states that aging is due to the decay of mitochondria. It appears that this decay is primarily due to oxidative damage and loss of critical micronutrients supplied by the cell (Vendelbo & Nair, 2011).

How do oxidative damage and loss of nutrients occur? Among the by-products of mitochondrial energy production are the free radicals just described. According to the mitochondrial theory, the damage caused by free radicals initiates a self-perpetuating cycle in which oxidative damage causes impairment of mitochondrial function, which results in the generation of even greater amounts of free radicals. The result is that over time, the affected mitochondria become so inefficient that they cannot generate enough energy to meet cellular needs (McCoy & Cookson, 2011). One study revealed that exercise in older adults increased mitochondrial activity in their cells (Menshikova & others, 2006).

Defects in mitochondria are linked with cardiovascular disease, neurodegenerative diseases such as dementia and Parkinson disease, and decline in liver functioning (Bueler, 2010; Kim, Wei, & Sowers, 2008). However, it is not known whether the defects in mitochondria cause aging or are merely accompaniments of the aging process (Brand, 2011).

Hormonal Stress Theory   The three theories of aging that we have discussed so far—cellular clock, free radical, and mitochondrial—attempt to explain aging at the cellular level. In contrast, **hormonal stress theory** argues that aging in the body's hormonal system can lower resistance to stress and increase the likelihood of disease.

When faced with external challenges, such as stressful situations, the human body adapts by altering internal physiological processes (Almeida & others, 2011). This process of adaptation and adjustment is referred to as *allostasis*. Allostasis is adaptive in the short term; however, continuous accommodation of physiological systems in response to stressors may result in *allostatic load*, a wearing down of body systems due to constant activity (McEwen, 1998).

Normally, when people experience stressors, the body responds by releasing certain hormones. As people age, the hormones stimulated by stress remain at elevated levels longer than when they were younger (Finch, 2011). These prolonged, elevated levels of stress-related hormones are associated with increased risks for many diseases, including cardiovascular disease, cancer, diabetes, and hypertension (Wolkowitz & others, 2010).

A variation of hormonal stress theory has emphasized the contribution of a decline in immune system functioning with aging (Mahbub, Brubaker, & Kovacs, 2011; Shaw & others, 2010). Aging contributes to immune system deficits that give rise to infectious diseases in older adults (Fulop & others, 2010; Okun, Griffioen, & Mattson, 2011). The extended duration of stress and diminished restorative processes in older adults may accelerate the effects of aging on immunity.

Which of these biological theories best explains aging? That question has not yet been answered. It might turn out that all of these biological processes contribute to aging (Miller, 2009).

mitochondrial theory The theory that aging is caused by the decay of the mitochondria, which are tiny cellular bodies that supply energy for cell function, growth, and repair.

hormonal stress theory The theory that aging in the body's hormonal system can lower resistance to stress and increase the likelihood of disease.

Review *Connect* Reflect

LG4 Explain longevity and the biological aspects of aging

Review

- What is the difference between life span and life expectancy? What sex differences exist in longevity?
- What do centenarians have in common?
- What are the four main biological theories of aging?

Connect

- Chapter 1 explained the differences between biological, psychological, and social age. How do biological theories of aging inform these three different conceptions of age?

Reflect *Your Own Personal Journey of Life*

- To what age do you think you will live? Why? To what age would you like to live?

---

reach your **learning goals**

Body Growth and Change

LG1 Discuss major changes in the body through the life span

- Patterns of Growth
- Height and Weight in Infancy and Childhood
- Puberty
- Early Adulthood
- Middle Adulthood
- Late Adulthood

- Human growth follows cephalocaudal (fastest growth occurs at the top) and proximodistal patterns (growth starts at the center of the body and moves toward the extremities).

- Height and weight increase rapidly in infancy and then take a slower course during childhood.

- Puberty is a rapid physical maturation involving hormonal and bodily changes that take place primarily in early adolescence. A number of changes occur in sexual maturation. The growth spurt involves rapid increases in height and weight and occurs about two years earlier for girls than boys. Extensive hormonal changes characterize puberty. Puberty began occurring much earlier in the twentieth century mainly because of improved health and nutrition. The basic genetic program for puberty is wired into the nature of the species, but nutrition, health, and other environmental factors affect puberty's timing and makeup. Adolescents show heightened interest in their bodies and body images. Younger adolescents are more preoccupied with these images than older adolescents. Adolescent girls often have a more negative body image than do adolescent boys. Early maturation often favors boys, at least during early adolescence, but as adults, late-maturing boys have a more positive identity than do early-maturing boys. Early-maturing girls are at risk for a number of developmental problems.

- In early adulthood, height remains rather constant. Many individuals reach their peak of muscle tone and strength in their late teens and twenties; however, these can decline in the thirties.

- In middle adulthood, changes usually are gradual. Visible signs of aging, such as the wrinkling of skin, appear in the forties and fifties. Middle-aged individuals also tend to lose height and gain weight. Strength, joints, and bones show declines in middle age. The cardiovascular system declines in functioning, and at about 55 years of age lung capacity begins to decline, more so in smokers than nonsmokers. The climacteric is a term used to describe the midlife transition in which fertility declines. Menopause is the time in middle age, usually in the later forties or early fifties, when a woman's menstrual periods have ceased. Men do not experience an inability to father children in middle age, although their testosterone level declines.

- In late adulthood, outwardly noticeable physical changes become more prominent, individuals get shorter, and weight often decreases because of muscle loss. The circulatory system declines further.

The Brain

LG2 Describe how the brain changes through the life span

Brain Physiology

- The brain has two hemispheres, each of which has four lobes (frontal, occipital, temporal, and parietal). Throughout the brain, nerve cells called neurons process information. Communication among neurons involves the axon, dendrites, synapses, neurotransmitters, and the myelin sheath. Clusters of neurons, known as neural circuits, work together to handle specific types of information.

Infancy

- Researchers have found that early experience influences the brain's development. Myelination begins prenatally and continues after birth. In infancy, one of the most impressive changes in the brain is the enormous increase in dendrites and synapses. These connections between neurons are overproduced and pruned. Specialization of functioning does occur in the brain's hemispheres, as in language, but for the most part both hemispheres are at work in most complex functions.

Childhood

- During early childhood, the brain and head grow more rapidly than any other part of the body. Researchers have found that dramatic anatomical changes in brain patterns occur from 3 to 15 years of age, often involving spurts of brain activity and growth. In middle and late childhood, focal brain activation increases.

Adolescence

- The corpus callosum, a large bundle of axon fibers that connects the brain's left and right hemispheres, thickens in adolescence, and this thickening improves the adolescent's ability to process information. The prefrontal cortex, the highest level of the frontal lobes that are involved in reasoning, decision making, and self-control, continues to mature through emerging adulthood or later. The amygdala, the part of the limbic system that is the seat of emotions such as anger, matures earlier than the prefrontal cortex. The later development of the prefrontal cortex combined with the earlier maturity of the amygdala may explain the difficulty adolescents have in putting the brakes on their emotional intensity.

Adulthood and Aging

- On average, the brain loses 5 to 10 percent of its weight between the ages of 20 and 90. Brain volume also decreases with aging. Shrinking occurs in some areas of the brain, such as the prefrontal cortex, more than in other areas. A general slowing of function of the central nervous system begins in middle adulthood and increases in late adulthood. A decline in the production of some neurotransmitters is related to aging. Neurogenesis has been demonstrated in lower mammals, but whether it occurs in human adults is still controversial. It appears that dendritic growth can occur in adults. The brain has the capacity to virtually rewire itself to compensate for loss in older adults. Another change is a decrease in brain lateralization in older adults.

Sleep

LG3 Summarize how sleep patterns change as people develop

Infancy

- Newborns sleep about 16 to 17 hours a day. By about 4 months of age, most infants have sleep patterns similar to those of adults. REM sleep occurs more in infancy than in childhood and adulthood. Sleeping arrangements vary across cultures. A special concern is sudden infant death syndrome.

Childhood

- Most young children sleep through the night and have one daytime nap. However, some children develop sleep problems such as persistent nightmares and night terrors.

Adolescence and Emerging Adulthood

- Many adolescents stay up later and sleep longer in the morning than when they were children. Recent interest focuses on biological explanations of these developmental changes in sleep during adolescence and their link to school success. Recent research indicates that a majority of first-year college students have sleep difficulties and that they go to bed even later and get up later than adolescents. However, by the end of college, they have begun to reverse this trend.

Adulthood and Aging

- An increasing concern is that adults do not get enough sleep. In middle age, wakeful periods may interrupt nightly sleep more often. Many older adults go to bed earlier and wake up earlier the next morning. Almost half of older adults report having some insomnia.

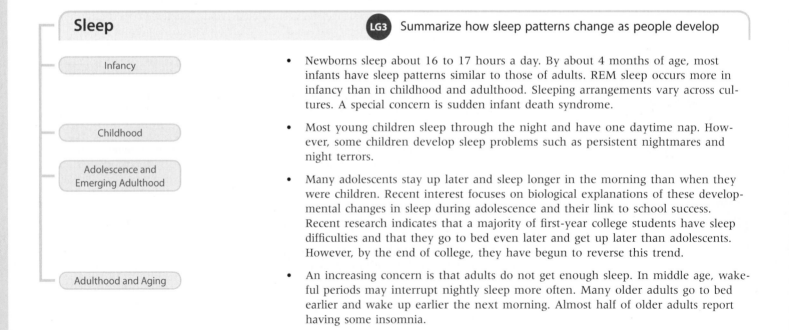

Longevity

 LG4 Explain longevity and the biological aspects of aging

- Life Expectancy and Life Span

- Centenarians

- Biological Theories of Aging

- Life expectancy is the number of years an individual is expected to live when he or she is born. Life span is the maximum number of years any member of a species has been known to live. On the average, females live about five years longer than males do. The sex difference is likely due to biological and social factors. An increasing number of individuals live to be 100 or older.

- Heredity, family history, health, education, personality, and lifestyle are important factors in living to be a centenarian. The ability to cope with stress also is important.

- Five biological theories of the causes of aging are evolutionary, cellular clock, free-radical, mitochondrial, and hormonal stress. The evolutionary theory of aging proposes that natural selection has not eliminated many harmful conditions and nonadaptive characteristics in older adults; thus, the benefits conferred by evolutionary theory decline with age because natural selection is linked to reproductive fitness. Hayflick proposed the cellular clock theory, which states that cells can divide a maximum of about 75 to 80 times and that, as we age, our cells become less capable of dividing. Telomeres are likely involved in explaining why cells lose their capacity to divide. According to free-radical theory, people age because unstable oxygen molecules called free radicals are produced in the cells. According to mitochondrial theory, aging is due to the decay of mitochondria, tiny cellular bodies that supply energy for function, growth, and repair. According to hormonal stress theory, aging in the body's hormonal system can lower resistance to stress and increase the likelihood of disease.

key terms

cephalocaudal pattern 90
proximodistal pattern 90
puberty 92
menarche 92
hormones 93
hypothalamus 93
pituitary gland 93

gonads 93
gonadotropins 93
testosterone 93
estradiol 93
climacteric 97
menopause 97
myelination 100

lateralization 100
corpus callosum 104
prefrontal cortex 104
amygdala 104
neurogenesis 106
sudden infant death
    syndrome (SIDS) 111

life span 114
cellular clock theory 117
free-radical theory 117
mitochondrial
    theory 118
hormonal stress
    theory 118

key people

Charles Nelson 101
John Richards 101

Mark Johnson 103
Laurence Steinberg 104

Mary Carskadon 112
Leonard Hayflick 117

chapter 4   HEALTH

preview

Life is more than just living. It is important to live healthily. As we grow and develop through the life span, we have many opportunities to engage in health-enhancing or health-compromising behaviors, either by our choosing or because of the contexts provided by our caregivers. In this chapter, we will explore many aspects of health, including illness and disease, nutrition and eating behavior, exercise, and substance use.

Health, Illness, and Disease   **LG1** Describe developmental changes in health

Children's Health | Adolescents' Health | Emerging and Young Adults' Health | Health and Aging

Changing patterns of illness have fueled an interest in searching not just for biological causes of health, illness, and disease, but for psychological and socio-cultural causes as well. With these multiple causes in mind, let's now examine changes in health through the human life span.

> Nothing can be changed until it is faced.
>
> —JAMES BALDWIN
> *American Novelist, 20th Century*

CHILDREN'S HEALTH

Many factors affect children's health. In this chapter, we focus on two of the most important influences: prevention and poverty. We will also consider the health impact of immunization, accidents, and access to health care.

Prevention   Although the dangers of many diseases for children have greatly diminished, it is still important for parents to keep their children on a timely immunization schedule (Hammer & others, 2010). The recommended ages for various immunizations are shown in Figure 4.1.

In addition to immunization, another important aspect of preventing health problems in children is to avoid accidents, which are the leading cause of death in children (Powell, Malanchinski, & Sheehan, 2010). Infants need close monitoring as they gain locomotor and manipulative skills, along with a strong curiosity to explore the environment (Betz & Sowden, 2008). Aspiration of foreign objects, suffocation, falls, poisoning, burns, and motor vehicle accidents are among the most common accidents in infancy (Duke & others, 2011).

The status of children's motor, cognitive, and socioemotional development makes their health-care needs unique. For example, think about how the infant's and young child's motor skills are inadequate to ensure their personal safety while riding in an automobile. Adults must take preventive measures to restrain infants and young children in car seats (Durbin & others, 2011). Young children also lack the cognitive skills, including reading ability, to discriminate between safe and unsafe household substances. And they may lack the impulse control to keep from running out into a busy street while chasing a ball or toy.

Caregivers play an important role in children's health (Erkal, 2010; Schnitzer, Covington, & Kruse, 2011). An increasing number of studies reach the conclusion that children are at risk for health problems when they live in homes in which a parent smokes (Bhatt & Smyth, 2011; Constant & others, 2011). For example, children exposed to tobacco smoke in the home are more likely to develop wheezing symptoms and asthma than children in nonsmoking homes (Boldo & others, 2010; Oberg & others, 2011). By driving at safe speeds, decreasing or eliminating drinking—especially before driving—and not smoking around children, caregivers enhance their children's health (Cease, King, & Monroe, 2011; Simonetti & others, 2011).

Age	Immunization
Birth	Hepatitis B
2 months	Diphtheria Polio Influenza
4 months	Diphtheria Polio Influenza
6 months	Diphtheria Influenza
1 year	TB test
15 months	Measles Mumps Rubella Influenza
18 months	Diphtheria Polio
4 to 6 years	Diphtheria Polio
11 to 12 years	Measles Mumps Rubella
14 to 16 years	Tetanus-diphtheria

FIGURE **4.1**

RECOMMENDED IMMUNIZATION SCHEDULE FOR INFANTS AND CHILDREN

developmental connection

Environment. Poverty is linked to many environmental inequities in childhood. Chapter 15, p. 514

Poverty   Of special concern in the United States is the poor health of many young children from low-income families. An estimated 7 percent of U.S. children have no usual source of health care. Approximately 11 million preschool children in the United States are malnourished. Their malnutrition places their health at risk. Many have poor resistance to diseases—including minor ones, such as colds, and major ones, such as influenza.

What is the best way to improve the health of children who live in poverty? Some experts argue that offering medical care is not enough. If you give an antibiotic to a child with a sore throat who then returns to a home where she will be cold and hungry, have you provided good health care? One approach to children's health aims to treat not only medical problems of the individual child but also the conditions of the entire family (Butz & others, 2010). In fact, some programs seek to identify children who are at risk for problems and then try to alter the risk factors in an effort to prevent illness and disease (Miller & others, 2011).

What are some characteristics of adolescents' exercise patterns?

ADOLESCENTS' HEALTH

Adolescence is a critical juncture in the adoption of behaviors relevant to health (Ozer & Irwin, 2009; UNICEF, 2011). Many of the factors linked to poor health habits and early death in the adult years begin during adolescence (Nyaronga & Wickrama, 2009).

Social contexts, including families, peers, schools, neighborhoods, and culture influence adolescent health (Barreto & others, 2011; Wolff & Crockett, 2011). Parents and older siblings can be important models of health-enhancing behaviors. In the National Longitudinal Study of Health, based on data collected from more than 12,000 seventh- through twelfth-graders, youth who did not eat dinner with a parent five or more days a week had dramatically higher rates of smoking cigarettes, using marijuana, getting into fights, and initiating sexual activity (Council of Economic Advisors, 2000). Parental caring and monitoring often combine to produce less risk taking in youth.

Peers also can influence adolescents' health (Heitzler & others, 2010). Adolescents who have a limited capacity to resist dares often engage in risk taking at the urging of their peers. Peer pressure can instigate such health-compromising behaviors as cigarette smoking, substance abuse, early sexual activity, and violence (Ali, Amialchuk, & Dwyer, 2011).

Because adolescents spend so much time in school, it is not surprising that what goes on there can influence their health behavior. Teachers, like parents, can serve as important health role models.

Health experts increasingly recognize that whether adolescents will develop a health problem or be healthy depends primarily on their own behavior (Insel & Roth, 2012). Improving adolescent health involves (1) reducing adolescents' health-compromising behaviors, such as drug abuse, violence, unprotected sexual intercourse, and dangerous driving; and (2) increasing health-enhancing behaviors, such as eating nutritiously, exercising, and wearing seat belts.

developmental connection

Brain Development. Developmental changes in the adolescent's brain may be related to increased risk taking. Chapter 3, p. 104

EMERGING AND YOUNG ADULTS' HEALTH

Emerging adults have more than twice the mortality rate of adolescents (Park & others, 2008) (see Figure 4.2). As indicated in Figure 4.2, males are mainly responsible for the higher mortality rate of emerging adults. Also, compared to adolescents, emerging adults engage in more health-compromising behaviors, have more chronic health problems, are more likely to be obese, and are more likely to have a mental health disorder (Irwin, 2010).

Although emerging adults may know what it takes to be healthy, they often don't apply this information to their own behavior (Furstenberg, 2006). In many cases, emerging adults are not as healthy as they seem (Fatusi & Hindin, 2010).

In emerging and early adulthood, few individuals stop to think about how their personal lifestyles will affect their health later in their adult lives. As young adults, many of us develop a pattern of not eating breakfast, not eating regular meals and relying on snacks as our main food source during the day, eating excessively to the point where we exceed the normal weight for our height, smoking moderately or excessively, drinking moderately or excessively, failing to exercise, and getting by with only a few hours of sleep at night (Cousineau, Goldstein, & Franco, 2005). These lifestyles are associated with poor health, which in turn impairs life satisfaction (Insel & Roth, 2012). In the Berkeley Longitudinal Study—in which individuals were evaluated over a period of 40 years—physical health at age 30 predicted life satisfaction at age 70, more so for men than for women (Mussen, Honzik, & Eichorn, 1982).

HEALTH AND AGING

Aging can bring on new health problems, such as Alzheimer disease. Keep in mind, though, that many older adults are healthy. For example, only 17 percent of U.S. adults from 65 to 74 years of age have a disability. As shown in Figure 4.3, the percentage of Americans without a disability remains above 50 percent until they reach 85 years and older.

Chronic Disorders **Chronic disorders** are characterized by a slow onset and long duration. Chronic disorders are rare in early adulthood, increase in middle adulthood, and become common in late adulthood (Kane, 2007).

The most common chronic disorders in middle age differ for females and males (Austad, 2011). The most common chronic disorders in middle adulthood for U.S. women, in order of prevalence, are arthritis, hypertension, and sinus problems; the most common ones for U.S. men are hypertension, arthritis, hearing impairments, and heart disease. Men have a higher incidence of fatal chronic conditions (such as coronary heart disease, cancer, and stroke); women have a higher incidence of nonfatal ones (such as sinus problems, varicose veins, and bursitis). Older women have higher incidences of arthritis and hypertension and are more likely to have visual problems, but they are less likely to have hearing problems than older men are.

Cancer recently replaced cardiovascular disease as the leading cause of death in U.S. middle-aged adults. The same realignment of causes of death has also occurred in 65- to 74-year-olds, with cancer now the leading cause of death in this age group (National Center for Health Statistics, 2008a, b, c). The decline in cardiovascular disease in middle-aged and older adults has been attributed to improved drugs, decreased rates of smoking, improved diets, and increased exercise (Vatner, 2011).

However, in the 75-to-84 and 85-and-over age groups, cardiovascular disease still is the leading cause of death (National Center for Health Statistics, 2008a, b, c). As individuals age through the late adult years, the older they are the more likely they will die of cardiovascular disease rather than cancer (National Center for Health Statistics, 2008a, b, c).

Even when adults over the age of 65 have a physical impairment, many of them can still carry on their everyday activities or work. Chronic conditions associated with the greatest limitation on work are heart conditions (52 percent), diabetes (34 percent), asthma (27 percent), and arthritis (27 percent).

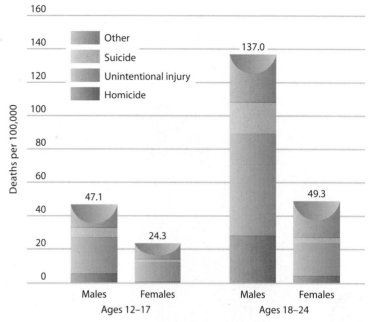

FIGURE **4.2**
MORTALITY RATES OF U.S. ADOLESCENTS AND EMERGING ADULTS

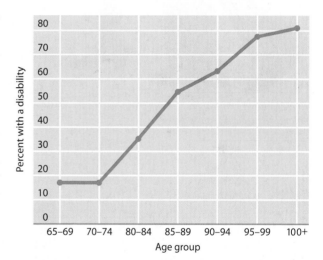

Note: Data for the 75 to 79 age group were unavailable.

FIGURE **4.3**
PERCENTAGE OF U.S. OLDER ADULTS OF DIFFERENT AGES WHO HAVE A DISABILITY

chronic disorders Disorders characterized by slow onset and long duration.

Normal aging involves some loss of bone tissue from the skeleton. However, in some instances loss of bone tissue can become severe. **Osteoporosis** involves an extensive loss of bone tissue. Osteoporosis is the main reason many older adults walk with a marked stoop. Women are especially vulnerable to osteoporosis, the leading cause of broken bones in women (Bessette & others, 2009). Approximately 80 percent of osteoporosis cases in the United States occur in females, 20 percent in males. Almost two-thirds of all women over the age of 60 are affected by osteoporosis. This aging disorder is most common in non-Latina White, thin, and small-framed women.

Osteoporosis is related to deficiencies in calcium, vitamin D, estrogen, and lack of exercise (Dionyssiotis & others, 2010; McCloskey, 2011). To prevent osteoporosis, young and middle-aged women should eat foods rich in calcium, get more exercise, and avoid smoking (Vondracek, 2010). Drugs such as alendronate (Fosamax) can be used to reduce the severity of osteoporosis (Pazaianas & others, 2010). A program of regular exercise has the potential to reduce osteoporosis (Besdine & Wetle, 2010; Forsyth, Quon, & Konkle, 2011).

Health problems that accompany aging also can involve neurological disorders. Next, we examine a neurological disorder in aging that has dramatically increased in recent decades—Alzheimer disease.

Alzheimer Disease **Dementia** is a global term for any neurological disorder in which the primary symptoms involve a deterioration of mental functioning. Individuals with dementia often lose the ability to care for themselves and can lose the ability to recognize familiar surroundings and people, including family members (Cosentino, Brickman, & Manley, 2011). It is estimated that 23 percent of women and 17 percent of men 85 years and older are at risk for developing dementia (Alzheimer's Association, 2010). However, these estimates may be high because of the Alzheimer's Association's lobbying efforts to increase funding for research and treatment facilities. Dementia is a broad category, and it is important that every effort is made to narrow the older adult's disorder and determine a specific cause of the deteriorating mental functioning (Holtzman, Morris, & Goate, 2011).

One form of dementia is **Alzheimer disease**—a progressive, irreversible brain disorder that is characterized by a gradual deterioration of memory, reasoning, language, and eventually, physical function. In 2009, an estimated 5.3 million adults in the United States had Alzheimer disease, and it is projected that 10 million baby boomers will develop Alzheimer disease in their lifetime (Alzheimer's Association, 2010). Figure 4.4 shows the estimated risks for developing Alzheimer disease at different ages for women and men (Alzheimer's Association, 2010). Women are likely to develop Alzheimer disease because they live longer than men and their longer life expectancy increases the number of years during which they can develop it. It is estimated that Alzheimer disease triples the health-care costs of Americans 65 years of age and older (Alzheimer's Association, 2010). Because of the increasing prevalence of Alzheimer disease, researchers have stepped up their efforts to discover the causes of the disease and find more effective ways to treat it (Wouters & others, 2011).

Causes Alzheimer disease involves a deficiency in the important brain messenger chemical acetylcholine, which plays an important role in memory (Alcaro & others, 2010). Also, as Alzheimer disease progresses, the brain shrinks and deteriorates (see Figure 4.5). This deterioration is characterized by the formation of *amyloid plaques* (dense deposits of protein that accumulate in the blood vessels) and *neurofibrillary tangles* (twisted fibers that build up in neurons) (Galimberti & Scarpini, 2010; Galvin, 2011).

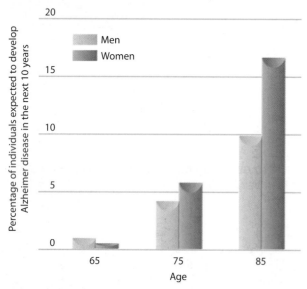

What characterizes osteoporosis? What are some strategies for reducing osteoporosis?

FIGURE **4.4**

ESTIMATED RISKS FOR DEVELOPING ALZHEIMER DISEASE AT DIFFERENT AGES FOR WOMEN AND MEN. *Source:* Alzheimer's Association (2010). 2010 Alzheimer's facts and figures. *Alzheimer's & Dementia, 6,* 158–194.

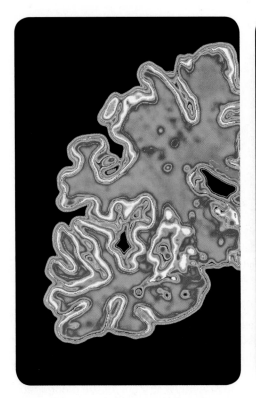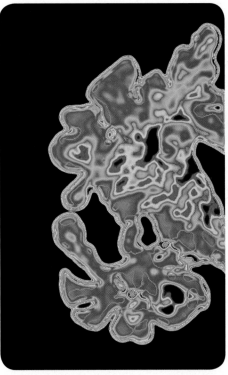

FIGURE **4.5**

TWO BRAINS: NORMAL AGING AND ALZHEIMER DISEASE. The left computer graphic shows a slice of a normal aging brain, the right photograph a slice of a brain ravaged by Alzheimer disease. Notice the deterioration and shrinking in the Alzheimer disease brain.

There is increasing interest in the role that oxidative stress might play in Alzheimer disease (Bonda & others, 2010; Kapogiannis & Mattson, 2011). Oxidative stress occurs when the body's antioxidant defenses don't cope with free-radical attacks and oxidation in the body. Recall from earlier in the chapter that free-radical theory is a major theory of aging.

Although scientists are not certain what causes Alzheimer disease, age is an important risk factor and genes also are likely to play an important role (Bettens, Sleegres, & Van Broeckhoven, 2010; Wilson & others, 2011). The number of individuals with Alzheimer disease doubles every five years after the age of 65. A gene called *apolipoprotein E* (*apoE*), which is linked to increasing presence of plaques and tangles in the brain, could play a role in as many as one-third of the cases of Alzheimer disease (Abrams, Farooq, & Wang, 2011; Vemuri & others, 2010).

Although individuals with a family history of Alzheimer disease are at greater risk, the disease is complex and likely caused by a number of factors, including lifestyles. Researchers are finding that healthy lifestyle factors may lower the risk of Alzheimer disease or delay the onset of the disease. For example, older adults with Alzheimer disease are more likely to have cardiovascular disease than are individuals who do not have Alzheimer disease (Helzner & others, 2009). Recently, more cardiac risk factors have been implicated in Alzheimer disease—obesity, smoking, atherosclerosis, high cholesterol, and lipids (Grammas, 2011; James & Bennett, 2011).

Early Detection and Drug Treatment *Mild cognitive impairment* (*MCI*) represents a transitional state between the cognitive changes of normal aging and very early Alzheimer disease and other dementias. MCI is increasingly recognized as a risk factor for Alzheimer disease. Estimates indicate that as many as 10 to 20 percent of individuals 65 years of age and older have MCI (Alzheimer's Association, 2010). Some individuals with MCI do not go on to develop Alzheimer disease, but MCI is a risk factor for Alzheimer disease.

Distinguishing between individuals who merely have age-associated declines in memory and those with MCI is difficult, as is predicting which individuals with MCI will subsequently develop Alzheimer disease (McEvoy & others, 2011). A recent

developmental **connection**

Memory. A number of changes in memory occur in late adulthood. Chapter 7, p. 224

osteoporosis A disorder that involves an extensive loss of bone tissue and is the main reason many older adults walk with a marked stoop. Women are especially vulnerable to osteoporosis.

dementia A global term for any neurological disorder in which the primary symptom is deterioration of mental functioning.

Alzheimer disease A progressive, irreversible brain disorder characterized by a gradual deterioration of memory, reasoning, language, and eventually, physical function.

Memory loss is a common characteristic of Alzheimer disease. Written reminders, like those shown here, can help individuals with Alzheimer remember daily tasks.

A wife feeding her husband who has Alzheimer disease. *What are some concerns about the family caregivers of individuals with Alzheimer disease?*

research review concluded that fMRI measurement of neuron loss in the medial temporal lobe is a predictor of memory loss and eventually dementia (Vellas & Aisen, 2010). Further, a recent study revealed that amyloid beta—a protein fragment that forms plaques in the brain—was present in the spinal fluid of approximately 75 percent of the individuals with mild cognitive impairment. Every one of the older adults with mild cognitive impairment who had the amyloid beta in their spinal fluid developed Alzheimer disease within 5 years (De Meyer & others, 2010).

Drug Treatment of Alzheimer Disease   Several drugs called cholinesterase inhibitors have been approved by the U.S. Food and Drug Administration to treat Alzheimer disease. They are designed to improve memory and other cognitive functions by increasing levels of acetylcholine in the brain (Emre & others, 2010). Keep in mind, though, that the drugs used to treat Alzheimer disease only slow the downward progression of the disease; they do not treat its cause (Rafii & Aisen, 2009). Also, no drugs have yet been approved by the Federal Drug Administration for the treatment of MCI (Alzheimer's Association, 2010).

Caring for Individuals with Alzheimer Disease   A special concern is caring for Alzheimer patients (Kelsey & others, 2010; Silverstein, Wong, & Brueck, 2010). Health-care professionals emphasize that the family can be an important support system for the Alzheimer patient, but this support can have costs for the family, who can become emotionally and physically drained by the extensive care required for a person with Alzheimer disease (Elliott, Burgio, & Decoster, 2010).

Respite care (services that provide temporary relief for those who are caring for individuals with disabilities, illnesses, or the elderly) has been developed to help people who have to meet the day-to-day needs of Alzheimer patients. This type of care provides an important break from the burden of providing chronic care (de la Cuesta-Benjumea, 2011; Tompkins & Bell, 2009). To read further about individuals who care for Alzheimer patients, see the *Connecting with Research* interlude.

Muhammad Ali, one of the world's leading sports figures, has Parkinson disease.

Parkinson disease A chronic, progressive disease characterized by muscle tremors, slowing of movement, and partial facial paralysis.

Parkinson Disease   Another type of dementia is **Parkinson disease,** a chronic, progressive disease characterized by muscle tremors, slowing of movement, and partial facial paralysis. Parkinson disease is triggered by degeneration of dopamine-producing neurons in the brain (Baydyuk, Nguyen, & Xu, 2011). Dopamine is a neurotransmitter that is necessary for normal brain functioning. Why these neurons degenerate is not known.

The main treatment for Parkinson disease involves administering drugs that enhance the effect of dopamine (dopamine agonists) in the disease's earlier stages and

How Stressful Is Caring for an Alzheimer Patient at Home?

Researchers have recently found that the stress of caring for an Alzheimer patient at home can prematurely age the immune system, putting caregivers at risk for developing age-related diseases (Glaser & Kiecolt-Glaser, 2005; Graham, Christian, & Kiecolt-Glaser, 2006; Mausbach & others, 2007). In one study, 119 older adults who were caring for a spouse with Alzheimer disease or another form of dementia (which can require up to 100 hours a week of time) were compared with 106 older adults who did not have to care for a chronically ill spouse (Kiecolt-Glazer & others, 2003). The age of the older adults upon entry into the study ranged from 55 to 89 with an average age of 70.

Periodically during the six-year study, blood samples were taken and the levels of a naturally produced immune chemical called interleukin-6, or IL-6, were measured. IL-6 increases with age and can place people at risk for a number of illnesses, including cardiovascular disease, type 2 diabetes, frailty, and certain cancers. The researchers found that the levels of IL-6 increased much faster in the Alzheimer caregivers than in the older adults who did not have to care for a critically ill spouse (see Figure 4.6).

Each time IL-6 was assessed by drawing blood, the participants also completed a 10-item perceived stress scale to assess the extent to which they perceived their daily life during the prior week as being "unpredictable, uncontrollable, and overloading" (Kiecolt-Glazer & others, 2003, p. 9091). Participants rated each item from 0 (never) to 4 (very often). Alzheimer caregivers reported greater stress than the noncaregiver controls across each of the six annual assessments.

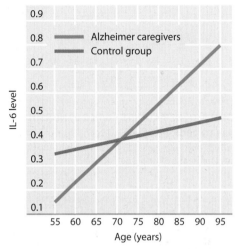

FIGURE **4.6**

COMPARISON OF IL-6 LEVELS IN ALZHEIMER CAREGIVERS AND A CONTROL GROUP OF NONCAREGIVERS. Notice that IL-6 (an immune chemical that places individuals at risk for a number of diseases) increased for both the Alzheimer caregivers and the control group of noncaregivers. However, also note that IL-6 increased significantly more in the Alzheimer caregivers. A higher score for IL-6 reflects a higher level of the immune chemical.

Since family members are especially important in helping Alzheimer patients cope, an important research agenda is to assess the benefits of respite care as well as find other ways to relieve the stress the disease can impose on others. What kinds of studies might help provide some answers? What challenges will researchers face in collecting data?

later administering the drug L-dopa, which is converted by the brain into dopamine (Wood, 2010). However, it is difficult to determine the correct level of dosage of L-dopa, and it loses its efficacy over time (Nomoto & others, 2009). Another treatment for advanced Parkinson disease is deep brain stimulation (DBS), which involves implantation of electrodes within the brain (Kim & others, 2010; Klepitskaya & others, 2011). The electrodes are then stimulated by a pacemaker-like device. Stem cell transplantation and gene therapy offer hope for the future in treating Parkinson disease (Fricker-Gates & Gates, 2010; Tonnesen & others, 2011). Recent research also indicates that certain types of dance, such as the tango, can improve the movement skills of individuals with Parkinson disease (Hackney & Earhart, 2010a, b).

Health Treatment for Older Adults   The development of alternative forms of home and community-based care has decreased the percentage of older adults who

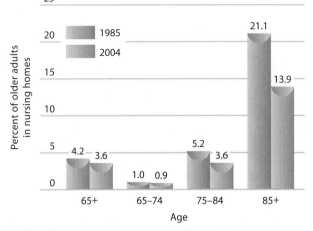

FIGURE 4.7

PERCENT OF U.S. OLDER ADULTS LIVING IN NURSING HOMES: 1985 TO 2004. *Note:* The Lewin Group calculations are based on the 1985 and 2004 National Nursing Home Survey (NNHS), National Center for Health Statistics.

Mathilde Spett (*right*), who is 91 years old, injured herself in a fall but recently graduated from a walker to a cane and learned how to stay on a better diet with the help of home-care aide Marilyn Ferguson (*left*). The demand for home-care aides is predicted to increase dramatically in the next several decades because of the likely doubling of the 65-year-and-older population and older adults' preference for remaining out of nursing homes (Moos, 2007). Not only is it important to significantly increase the number of health-care professionals to treat older adults, it is also very important that they not harbor negative stereotypes of older adults and that they show very positive attitudes toward them.

- - - - - - - - - ➤

developmental connection

Self and Identity. Perceived self-control changes as individuals age. Chapter 11, p. 350

are living in nursing homes (Katz & others, 2009). Still, as older adults age, their probability of being in a nursing home increases (see Figure 4.7). What is the quality of nursing homes and extended-care facilities for older adults? What is the relationship between older adults and health-care providers?

The quality of nursing homes and other extended-care facilities for older adults varies enormously and is a source of ongoing national concern (Eskildsen & Price, 2009). More than one-third of these facilities are seriously deficient. They fail federally mandated inspections because they do not meet the minimum standards for physicians, pharmacists, and various rehabilitation specialists (occupational and physical therapists). Further concerns focus on protecting the patient's right to privacy, providing access to medical information, preventing inappropriate prescriptions, ensuring safety, and preserving lifestyle freedom within the individual's range of mental and physical capabilities (Stafford, Alswayan, & Tenni, 2011).

Because of the inadequate quality of many nursing homes and the escalating costs for nursing home care, many specialists in the health problems of the aged stress that home health care, elder-care centers, and preventive medicine clinics are good alternatives (Katz & others, 2009). They are potentially less expensive than hospitals and nursing homes. They also are less likely to engender the feelings of depersonalization and dependency that occur so often in residents of institutions. Currently, there is an increased demand for home-care workers because of the increased population of older adults and their preference to stay out of nursing homes (Moos, 2007).

In a classic study that focused on the way older adults are cared for in nursing homes, Judith Rodin and Ellen Langer (1977) found that an important factor related to health, and even survival, in a nursing home is the patient's feelings of control and self-determination. A group of elderly nursing home residents were encouraged to make more day-to-day choices and thus feel they had more responsibility for control over their lives. They began to decide such matters as what they ate, when their visitors could come, what movies they saw, and who could come to their rooms. A similar group in the same nursing home was told by the administrator how caring the nursing home was and how much the staff wanted to help, but these elderly nursing home residents were given no opportunities to take more control over their lives. Eighteen months later, the residents who had been given responsibility and control were more alert and active, and said they were happier, than the residents who were encouraged only to feel that the staff would try to satisfy their needs. And the "responsible" or "self-control" group had significantly better improvement in their health than did the "dependent" group. Even more important was the finding that after 18 months only half as many nursing home residents in the "responsibility" group had died as in the "dependent" group (see Figure 4.8). Perceived control over one's environment, then, can literally be a matter of life or death.

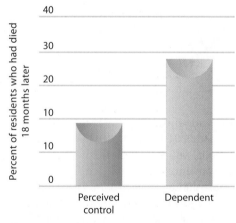

FIGURE 4.8

PERCEIVED CONTROL AND MORTALITY. In the study by Rodin and Langer (1977), nursing home residents who were encouraged to feel more in control of their lives were more likely to be alive 18 months later than those who were treated to feel more dependent on the nursing home staff.

Nutrition and Eating Behavior

LG2 Characterize developmental changes in nutrition and eating behavior

Infancy | Childhood | Adolescence | Adult Development and Aging

Nutritional needs, eating behavior, and related issues vary to some extent across the life span. Let's begin by exploring what takes place with infants.

INFANCY

For infants, the importance of receiving adequate energy and nutrients in a loving and supportive environment cannot be overstated (Schiff, 2011; Wardlaw & Smith, 2011). From birth to 1 year of age, human infants triple their weight and increase their length by 50 percent. Because infants vary in their nutrient reserves, body composition, growth rates, and activity patterns, their nutrient needs vary as well. However, because parents need guidelines, nutritionists recommend that infants consume approximately 50 calories per day for each pound they weigh—more than twice an adult's requirement per pound.

Breast Versus Bottle Feeding For the first four to six months of life, human milk or an alternative formula is the baby's source of nutrients and energy. For years, debate has focused on whether breast feeding is better for the infant than bottle feeding. The growing consensus is that breast feeding is better for the baby's health (Dykes, 2011; Monica & du Plessis, 2011; Silfverdal, 2011). Since the 1970s, breast feeding by U.S. mothers has soared (see Figure 4.9). In 2004, more than two-thirds of U.S. mothers breast fed their newborns, and more than a third breast fed their 6-month-olds. The American Academy of Pediatrics (AAP) and the American Dietetic Association strongly endorse breast feeding throughout the infant's first year (AAP Work Group on Breastfeeding, 1997; James & Dobson, 2005).

What are some of the benefits of breast feeding? The following conclusions have been reached based on the current state of research:

Outcomes of Breast Feeding for the Child

- *Gastrointestinal infections.* Breast fed infants have fewer gastrointestinal infections (Garofalo, 2010; Pfluger & others, 2010).
- *Lower respiratory tract infections.* Breast fed infants have fewer infections of the lower respiratory tract (Ip & others, 2009).

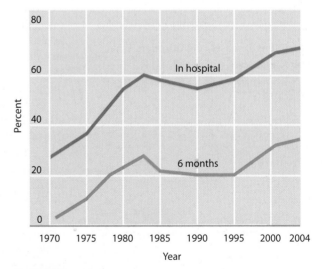

FIGURE **4.9**

TRENDS IN BREAST FEEDING IN THE UNITED STATES: 1970–2004

Human milk or an alternative formula is a baby's source of nutrients for the first four to six months. The growing consensus is that breast feeding is better for the baby's health, although controversy still swirls about the issue of breast feeding versus bottle feeding. *Why is breast feeding strongly recommended by pediatricians?*

- *Allergies.* There is no evidence that breast feeding reduces the risk of allergies in children (Greer & others, 2008). Modest evidence exists for feeding hypoallergenic formulas to susceptible babies if they are not solely breast fed (Greer & others, 2008).
- *Asthma.* Exclusive breast feeding for three months protects against wheezing in babies, but whether it prevents asthma in older children is unclear (Greer & others, 2008).
- *Otitis media.* Breast fed infants are less likely to develop this middle ear infection (Pelton & Leibovitz, 2009).
- *Overweight and obesity.* Consistent evidence indicates that breast fed infants are less likely to become overweight or obese in childhood, adolescence, and adulthood (Lamb & others, 2010).
- *Diabetes.* Breast fed infants are less likely to develop type 1 diabetes in childhood (Ping & Hagopian, 2006) and type 2 diabetes in adulthood (Villegas & others, 2008).
- *SIDS.* Breast fed infants are less likely to experience SIDS (Stuebe, 2009).

In a large-scale research review, no conclusive evidence for the benefits of breast feeding was found for children's cognitive development and cardiovascular system (Agency for Healthcare Research and Quality, 2007).

Outcomes of Breast Feeding for the Mother

- *Breast cancer.* Consistent evidence indicates a lower incidence of breast cancer in women who breast feed their infants (Akbari & others, 2010).
- *Ovarian cancer.* Evidence also reveals a reduction in ovarian cancer in women who breast feed their infants (Stuebe & Schwarz, 2010).
- *Type 2 diabetes.* Some evidence suggests a small reduction in type 2 diabetes in women who breast feed their infants (Stuebe & Schwarz, 2010).

In recent large-scale research reviews, no conclusive evidence could be found for the maternal benefits of breast feeding on return to pre-pregnancy weight, prevention of osteoporosis, and avoidance of postpartum depression (Agency for Healthcare Research and Quality, 2007; Ip & others, 2009).

The AAP Work Group on Breastfeeding (1997) strongly endorses breast feeding throughout the first year of life. Are there circumstances when mothers should not breast feed? Yes, a mother should not breast feed (1) if the mother is infected with HIV or some other infectious disease that can be transmitted through her milk, (2) if she has active tuberculosis, or (3) if she is taking any drug that may not be safe for the infant (Gumbo & others, 2010; Mwiru & others, 2011).

Some women cannot breast feed their infants because of physical difficulties; others feel guilty if they terminate breast feeding early. Mothers may also worry that they are depriving their infants of important emotional and psychological benefits if they bottle feed rather than breast feed. Some researchers have found, however, that there are no psychological differences between breast fed and bottle fed infants (Fergusson, Horwood, & Shannon, 1987; Young, 1990).

A further issue in interpreting the benefits of breast feeding was underscored in a large-scale research review (Ip & others, 2009). While highlighting a number of breast feeding benefits for children and mothers, the report issued a caution about breast feeding research: None of the findings implies causality. Breast versus bottle feeding studies are correlational, not experimental, and women who breast feed are wealthier, older, more educated, and likely more health-conscious than their bottle feeding counterparts—characteristics that could explain why breast fed children are healthier.

developmental **connection**

Conditions, Diseases, and Disorders. What characterizes SIDs? Chapter 3, p. 111

developmental **connection**

Research Methods. How does a correlational study differ from an experimental study? Chapter 1, p. 31

Barbara Deloin, Pediatric Nurse

Barbara Deloin is a pediatric nurse in Denver, Colorado. She practices nursing in the Pediatric Oral Feeding Clinic and is involved in research as part of an irritable infant study for the Children's Hospital in Denver. She also is on the faculty of nursing at the Colorado Health Sciences Center. Deloin previously worked in San Diego, where she was coordinator of the Child Health Program for the County of San Diego.

Her research interests focus on children with special health-care needs, especially high-risk infants and children, and promoting positive parent-child experiences. She is a former president of the National Association of Pediatric Nurse Associates and Practitioners.

For more information about what pediatric nurses do, see page 44 in the Careers in Life-Span Development appendix.

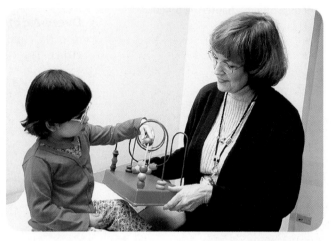

Barbara Deloin, working with a child with special health-care needs.

Pediatric nurses can play an important role in improving the lives of children and advising parents on feeding practices. To read about the work of one pediatric nurse, see the *Connecting with Careers* profile.

CHILDHOOD

Malnutrition continues to be a major threat to millions during the childhood years (Imdad, Sadig, & Bhutta, 2011; Schiff, 2011). Malnutrition and starvation are a daily fact of life for children in many developing countries (UNICEF, 2011). A recent study revealed that two food-assisted maternal and child health programs (both of which emphasized food provision, communication about behavior change, and preventive health services) helped to reduce the impact of economic hardship on stunting of children's growth in Haiti (Donegan & others, 2010).

Poor nutrition also is a special concern in the lives of infants from low-income families in the United States. To address this problem, the WIC (Women, Infants, and Children) program provides federal grants to states for healthy supplemental foods, health-care referrals, and nutrition education for women from low-income families beginning in pregnancy, and to infants and young children up to 5 years of age who are at nutritional risk (Food & Nutrition Service, 2009; WIC New York, 2010). WIC serves approximately 7,500,000 participants in the United States.

Positive influences on infants' and young children's nutrition and health have been found for participants in WIC (Davis, Lazariu, & Sekhobo, 2010; Sekhobo & others, 2010). A recent study

Participants in the WIC program. *What benefits do participants in the WIC program receive?*

developmental connection

Parenting. Some parenting styles are more effective in optimizing children's development than others. Chapter 14, p. 460

What are some trends in the eating habits and weight of young children?

revealed that a WIC program that introduced peer counseling services for pregnant women increased breast feeding initiation by 27 percent (Olson & others, 2010). Another recent study found that entry in the first trimester of pregnancy to the WIC program in Rhode Island reduced maternal cigarette smoking (Brodsky, Viner-Brown, & Handler, 2009).

Overweight Children   Being overweight has become a serious health problem in early childhood (Blake, 2011; Marcdante, Kleigman, & Behrman, 2011; Schiff, 2011). The Centers for Disease Control and Prevention (2011) has established categories for obesity, overweight, and at risk for being overweight. These categories are determined by body mass index (BMI), which is computed by a formula that takes into account height and weight. Children and adolescents whose BMI is at or above the 97th percentile are classified as obese; those whose BMI is at or above the 95th percentile are overweight; and those whose BMI is at or above the 85th percentile are at risk of becoming overweight.

The percentages of young children who are overweight or at risk of becoming overweight in the United States have increased dramatically in recent decades, and these percentages are likely to grow unless changes occur in children's lifestyles (Sorte, Daeschel, & Amador, 2011). A recent study revealed that in 2003–2006, 11 percent of U.S. 2- to 19-year-olds were obese, 16 percent were overweight, and 38 percent were at risk of becoming overweight (Ogden, Carroll, & Flegal, 2008). The good news from this large-scale study is that the percentages in these categories have started to level off rather than increase as they had done in the last several decades. However, a comparison of 34 countries revealed that the United States had the second highest rate of child obesity (Janssen & others, 2005).

The risk that overweight children will continue to be overweight when they are older was documented in a study in which 80 percent of the children who were at risk for being overweight at age 3 were also at risk for being overweight or were overweight at age 12 (Nader & others, 2006). A recent study also revealed that preschool children who were overweight were at significant risk for being overweight/obese at age 12 (Shankaran & others, 2011).

Being overweight in childhood also is linked to being overweight in adulthood. In one study, a high percentage of children who were in the 95th percentile among their peers in terms of weight were likely to remain overweight when they were in their thirties (Guo & others, 2002) (see Figure 4.10). Another study revealed that girls who were overweight in childhood were 11 to 30 times more likely to be obese in adulthood than girls who were not overweight in childhood (Thompson & others, 2007).

Consequences of Obesity   The increase in overweight children in recent decades is cause for great concern because being overweight raises the risk for many medical and psychological problems (Oliver & others, 2010; Raghuveer, 2010). Overweight children are at risk for developing pulmonary problems, such as sleep apnea (which involves upper-airway obstruction), and for having hip problems (Tauman & Gozal, 2006). Diabetes, hypertension (high blood pressure), and elevated blood cholesterol levels also are common in children who are overweight (Amed & others, 2010). Once considered rare in children, hypertension has become increasingly common among overweight

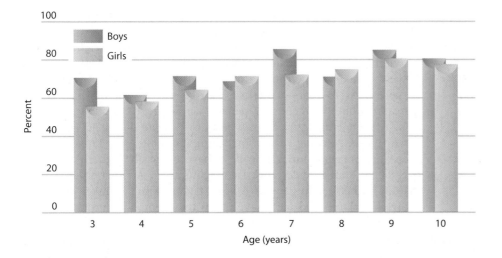

FIGURE **4.10**

RELATION OF BEING OVERWEIGHT IN CHILDHOOD WITH BEING OVERWEIGHT IN ADULTHOOD. *Note:* Data show the chance that children who are in the 95th percentile among their peers in terms of weight are likely to be overweight when they are 35.

children (Genovesi & others, 2010). Social and psychological consequences of being overweight in childhood include low self-esteem, depression, and some exclusion of obese children from peer groups (Gibson & others, 2008; McClure & others, 2010; Rojas & Storch, 2010). A recent study found that the main reason overweight adolescents were depressed was their body dissatisfaction (Mond & others, 2011).

Treatment of Obesity   Many experts recommend a program that includes a combination of diet, exercise, and behavior modification to help children lose weight (Hollar & others, 2010). Exercise is an especially important component of a successful weight-loss program for overweight children (Bond & others, 2010; Cummings & others, 2010).

ADOLESCENCE

Nutrition and being overweight are also key problems among adolescents. A comparison of adolescents in 28 countries found that U.S. adolescents ate more junk food than teenagers in most other countries (World Health Organization, 2000). The National Youth Risk Survey found that U.S. high school students decreased their intake of fruits and vegetables from 1999 through 2007 (Eaton & others, 2008).

The percentage of overweight adolescents and emerging adults increased dramatically in the 1980s, 1990s, and into the early part of the first decade of the twenty-first century. For example, being overweight increased from 11 to 17 percent for U.S. 12- to 19-year-olds from the early 1990s through 2004 (Eaton & others, 2006). However, recent research indicates that a leveling off began occurring about midway through the first decade of the twenty-first century (Ogden, Carroll, & Flegal, 2008). A recent analysis concluded that the leveling off in adolescents being overweight is occurring not only in the United States but also in Europe, Japan, and Australia (Rokholm, Baker, & Sorensen, 2010). In this analysis, the leveling off was less likely to occur in adolescents living in low-income conditions. Despite the recent leveling off in being overweight for some adolescents, overweight and obesity in adolescents remains at epidemic levels.

Being obese in adolescence predicts obesity in emerging adulthood. For example, a recent study of more than 8,000 12- to 21-year-olds found that obese adolescents were more likely to develop severe obesity in emerging adulthood than were overweight or normal weight adolescents (The & others,

These overweight girls and boys are attending a weight-management camp. *What are some trends in the frequency of obesity in U.S. adolescents?*

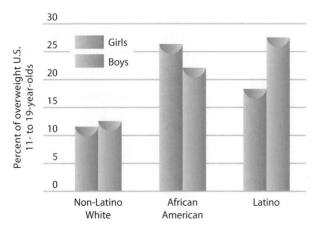

FIGURE **4.11**

PERCENTAGE OF OVERWEIGHT U.S. ADOLESCENT BOYS AND GIRLS IN DIFFERENT ETHNIC GROUPS

2010). And more emerging adults are overweight or obese than are adolescents. A recent longitudinal study tracked more than 1,500 adolescents for 10 years who were classified not overweight, overweight, or obese when they were 14 years of age (Patton & others, 2011). Across the 10-year period, the percentage of overweight individuals increased from 20 percent at 14 years of age to 33 percent at 24 years of age. Obesity increased from 4 percent to 7 percent across the 10 years.

Are there ethnic variations in being overweight during adolescence? A survey by the National Center for Health Statistics (2002) found that African American girls and Latino boys have especially high risks of being overweight during adolescence (see Figure 4.11). Another study revealed that the higher obesity rate for African American girls is linked with a diet higher in calories and fat, as well as with sedentary behavior (Sanchez-Johnsen & others, 2004).

What types of interventions have been successful in reducing overweight in adolescents? One review indicated that a combination of calorie restriction, exercise (walking or biking to school, participating in a regular exercise program), reduction of sedentary activity (watching TV, playing video games), and behavioral therapy (such as keeping weight-loss diaries and receiving rewards for meeting goals) have been moderately effective in helping overweight adolescents lose weight (Fowler-Brown & Kahwati, 2004).

Anorexia Nervosa   **Anorexia nervosa** is an eating disorder that involves the relentless pursuit of thinness through starvation. Anorexia nervosa is a serious disorder that can lead to death (Hebebrand & Bulik, 2011; Knoll, Bulik, & Hebebrand, 2011). Three main characteristics of anorexia nervosa are described below:

- Weighing less than 85 percent of what is considered normal for age and height.
- Having an intense fear of gaining weight. The fear does not decrease with weight loss.
- Having a distorted image of body shape. Even when they are extremely thin, anorexics see themselves as too fat. They never think they are thin enough, especially in the abdomen, buttocks, and thighs. They usually weigh themselves frequently, often take their body measurements, and gaze critically at themselves in mirrors.

Anorexia nervosa typically begins in the early to middle teenage years, often following an episode of dieting and some type of life stress. It is about ten times more likely to characterize females than males. Although most U.S. adolescent girls have been on a diet at some point, slightly less than 1 percent ever develop anorexia nervosa (Walters & Kendler, 1994). When anorexia nervosa does occur in males, the symptoms and other characteristics (such as a distorted body image and family conflict) are usually similar to those reported by females who have the disorder.

Most anorexics are non-Latino White adolescents or young adult females from well-educated, middle- and upper-income families that are competitive and high-achieving. They set high standards, become stressed about not being able to reach the standards, and are intensely concerned about how others perceive them (Liechty, 2010; Woelders & others, 2010). Unable to meet these high expectations, they turn to something they can control: their weight. Problems in family functioning are increasingly being found to be linked to the appearance of anorexia nervosa in adolescent girls (Benninghoven & others, 2007), and recent research reviews indicate that family therapy is often the most effective treatment of adolescent girls with anorexia nervosa (Fisher, Hetrick, & Rushford, 2010; Halmi, 2009).

The fashion image in U.S. culture contributes to the incidence of anorexia nervosa. The media portray thin as beautiful in their choice of fashion models, whom many adolescent girls strive to emulate. And many adolescent girls who strive to be thin hang out together. A recent study of adolescent girls revealed that friends often

anorexia nervosa An eating disorder that involves the relentless pursuit of thinness through starvation.

share similar body image and eating problems (Hutchinson & Rapee, 2007). In this study, an individual girl's dieting and extreme weight-loss behavior could be predicted from her friends' dieting and extreme weight-loss behavior. In addition, social-networking Web sites, such as Facebook, connect thousands of anorexics who are able to share pro-ana (pro-anorexic) information on how to deprive their bodies and become unhealthily thin.

Bulimia Nervosa   Although anorexics control their eating by restricting it, most bulimics cannot. **Bulimia nervosa** is an eating disorder in which the individual consistently follows a binge-and-purge eating pattern. The bulimic goes on an eating binge and then purges by self-inducing vomiting or using a laxative. Although some people binge and purge occasionally and some experiment with it, a person is considered to have a serious bulimic disorder only if the episodes occur at least twice a week for three months.

As with anorexics, most bulimics are preoccupied with food, have a strong fear of becoming overweight, and are depressed or anxious (Speranza & others, 2005). A recent study revealed that bulimics overvalued their body weight and shape, and this overvaluation was linked to higher depression and lower self-esteem (Hrabosky & others, 2007). Unlike anorexics, people who binge and purge typically fall within a normal weight range, a characteristic that makes bulimia more difficult to detect.

Bulimia nervosa typically begins in late adolescence or early adulthood. About 90 percent of the cases are women. Approximately 1 to 2 percent of women are estimated to develop bulimia nervosa. Many women who develop bulimia nervosa were somewhat overweight before the onset of the disorder, and the binge eating often began during an episode of dieting. One study of adolescent girls found that increased dieting, pressure to be thin, exaggerated importance placed on appearance, body dissatisfaction, depression symptoms, low self-esteem, and low social support predicted binge eating two years later (Stice, Presnell, & Spangler, 2002). A recent study of individuals with anorexia nervosa or bulimia nervosa revealed that attachment insecurity was linked with body dissatisfaction, which was a key aspect of predicting and perpetuating these eating disorders (Abbate-Daga & others, 2010). In this study, need for approval was an important predictor of bulimia nervosa. As with anorexia nervosa, about 70 percent of individuals who develop bulimia nervosa eventually recover from the disorder (Agras & others, 2004).

Binge Eating Disorder (BED)   **Binge eating disorder (BED)** involves frequent binge eating but without compensatory behavior like the purging that characterizes bulimics. Because they don't purge, individuals with BED are frequently overweight (Ahrberg & others, 2011). A recent research view indicated that the two best predictors that differentiated BED from other eating disorders were eating in secret and feeling disgust after the episode (White & Grilo, 2011). A recent study also found that individuals with BED showed a more negative pattern of everyday emotions, with anger being the emotion that was most often reported before a binging episode (Zeeck & others, 2011).

Adults in treatment for BED number approximately 1 to 2 million people, and they often say that their binging problems began in childhood or adolescence (New, 2008). Common health risks of BED are those related to being overweight or obese, such as high blood pressure, diabetes, and depression (Araujo, Santos, & Nardi, 2010).

ADULT DEVELOPMENT AND AGING

Nutrition and eating behavior continue to play important roles in adult physical development and health. Among the topics we discuss in this section are obesity, exercising and dieting to lose weight, and links between aging, weight, and nutrition.

Anorexia nervosa has become an increasing problem for adolescent girls and young adult women. *What are some possible causes of anorexia nervosa?*

bulimia nervosa An eating disorder in which the individual consistently follows a binge-and-purge eating pattern.

binge eating disorder (BED) Involves frequent binge eating, but without compensatory behavior like purging that characterizes bulimics.

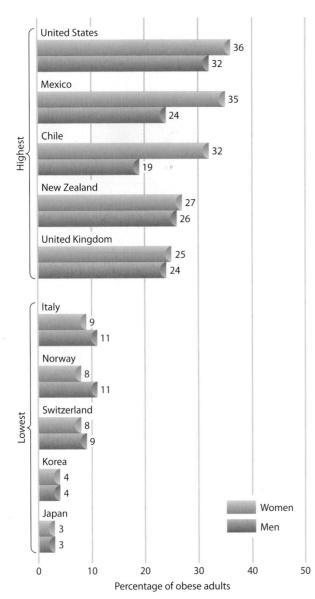

FIGURE **4.12**

COUNTRIES WITH THE HIGHEST AND LOWEST PERCENTAGE OF OBESE ADULTS IN 33 DEVELOPED COUNTRIES. *Source:* OECD (2010). *Obesity and the Economics of Prevention—Fit Not Fat.* Paris, France: OECD.

Obesity Obesity is not only a problem for many children and adolescents but also a serious and pervasive problem for many adults (Wardlaw & Smith, 2011). The prevalence of obesity in U.S. adults increased from 23 percent in the early 1990s to 34 percent in 2008 (Flegal & others, 2010). Also, in 2008, 68 percent of U.S. adults were overweight or obese (Flegal & others, 2010). The National Health and Nutrition Examination Survey (NHANES) recently projected that 86 percent of Americans will be overweight or obese by 2030 if current weight trends continue (Beydoun & Wang, 2009).

A recent international comparison of 33 developed countries revealed that the United States had the highest percentage of obese adults (OECD, 2010). Figure 4.12 shows the developed countries with highest and lowest percentages of obese adults.

Overweight and obesity are linked to increased risk of hypertension, diabetes, and cardiovascular disease (Dallongeville & others, 2011; Uusitupa, Tuomilehto, & Puska, 2011). For individuals who are 30 percent overweight, the probability of dying in middle adulthood increases by about 40 percent. Overweight and obesity also are associated with mental health problems. For example, a recent meta-analysis revealed that overweight women were more likely to be depressed than women who were not overweight, but no significant difference was found for men (de Wit & others, 2010).

What causes obesity? Some individuals do inherit a tendency to be overweight (Kaakinen & others, 2010). Only 10 percent of children who do not have obese parents become obese themselves, whereas 40 percent of children who become obese have one obese parent. Further, 70 percent of children who become obese have two obese parents. Researchers also have documented that animals can be inbred to have a propensity for obesity (Mathes & others, 2010).

Strong evidence of the environment's influence on weight is the doubling of the rate of obesity in the United States since 1900. This dramatic increase in obesity likely is due to greater availability of food (especially food high in fat), energy-saving devices, and declining physical activity (Li & others, 2007).

Exercising and Dieting

The most effective programs for losing weight include exercise (Fahey, Insel, & Roth, 2011; Thompson, Monroe, & Vaughn, 2011). A recent research review concluded that adults who engaged in diet-plus-exercise programs lost more weight than those who relied on diet-only programs (Wu & others, 2009). A recent study of approximately 2,000 U.S. adults found that exercising 30 minutes a day, planning meals, and weighing themselves daily were the main strategies used by successful dieters compared with unsuccessful dieters (Kruger, Blanck, & Gillespie, 2006) (see Figure 4.13). A recent study also revealed that obese adults in a diet program who kept a food diary for six or seven days a week had double the weight loss of obese adults who did not keep a food diary (Hollis & others, 2008).

How effective are diet programs?

Even when diets do produce weight loss, they can place the dieter at risk for other health problems (Cunningham & Hyson, 2006). One main concern focuses on weight cycling—yo-yo dieting—in which the person is in a recurring cycle of weight loss and weight gain (Cifani & others, 2009). Also, liquid diets and other very-low-calorie strategies are linked with gallbladder damage.

With these problems in mind, when overweight people diet and maintain their weight loss, they do become less depressed and reduce their risk for a number of health-impairing disorders (Foster & others, 2010; Mensah & Brown, 2007).

Calorie Restriction and Longevity   Scientists have accumulated considerable evidence that calorie restriction in laboratory animals (in most cases rats) can increase the animals' life span (Marquez, Markus, & Morris, 2010). Animals who are fed diets restricted in calories, although adequate in protein, vitamins, and minerals, live as much as 40 percent longer than animals given unlimited access to food (Jolly, 2005). And chronic problems such as cardiovascular, kidney, and liver disease appear at a later age (Kemnitz, 2011). In addition, recent research indicates that calorie restriction may provide neuroprotection for an aging central nervous system (Contestabile, 2009; Opalach & others, 2010) (see Figure 4.14). For example, a recent study revealed that after older adults engaged in calorie restriction for three months, their verbal memory improved (Witte & others, 2009).

No one knows for certain how calorie restriction works to increase the life span of animals. Some scientists note that it might lower the level of free radicals and reduce oxidative stress in cells (Bloomer & others, 2011). For example, one study found that calorie restriction slowed the age-related increase in oxidative stress (Ward & others, 2005). Others argue that calorie restriction might trigger a state of emergency called "survival mode" in which the body eliminates all unnecessary functions to focus only on staying alive. This survival mode likely is the result of evolution in which calorie restriction allowed animals to survive periods of famine, and thus the genes remain in the genomes of animal and human species today (Chen & Guarente, 2007).

Whether similar very low calorie diets can stretch the human life span is not known (Blagosklonny, 2010). In some instances, the animals in these studies ate 40 percent less than normal. In humans, a typical level of calorie restriction involves a 30 percent decrease, which translates into about 1,120 calories a day for the average woman and 1,540 for the average man.

Do underweight women and men live longer lives? A recent study revealed that women who were 20 pounds or more underweight lived longer even after controlling for smoking, hypertension, alcohol intake, and other factors (Wandell, Carlsson,

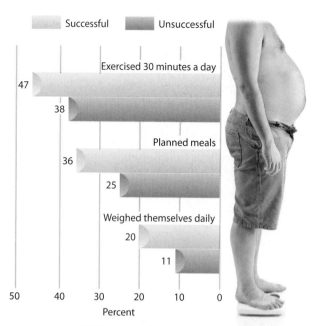

Successful Unsuccessful

Exercised 30 minutes a day
47
38

Planned meals
36
25

Weighed themselves daily
20
11

Percent
50 40 30 20 10 0

FIGURE **4.13**

COMPARISON OF STRATEGIES IN SUCCESSFUL AND UNSUCCESSFUL DIETERS

developmental **connection**

Theories. Evolutionary theory proposes explanations of development and aging. Chapter 2, p. 51; Chapter 3, p. 117

FIGURE **4.14**

CALORIE RESTRICTION IN MONKEYS. Shown here are two male monkeys at the Wisconsin Primate Research Center. Both are 24 years old. The monkey in the left photograph was raised on a calorie-restricted diet, while the monkey in the right photograph was raised on a normal diet. Notice that the monkey on the calorie-restricted diet looks younger; he also has lower glucose and insulin levels. The monkey raised on a normal diet has higher triglycerides and more oxidative damage to his cells.

& Theobald, 2009). In this study, underweight men did not live longer when various factors were controlled.

The Growing Controversy Over Vitamins and Aging For years, most experts on aging and health argued that a balanced diet was all that was needed for successful aging; vitamin supplements were not recommended. However, recent research suggests the possibility that some vitamin supplements—mainly a group called "antioxidants," which includes vitamin C, vitamin E, and beta-carotene—help to slow the aging process and improve the health of older adults.

The theory is that antioxidants counteract the cell damage caused by free radicals, which are produced both by the body's own metabolism and by environmental factors such as smoking, pollution, and bad chemicals in the diet (Obrenovich & others, 2011; Ristow & Zarse, 2010). When free radicals cause damage (oxidation) in one cell, a chain reaction of damage follows. Antioxidants act much like a fire extinguisher, helping to neutralize free-radical activity.

Some research studies find links between the antioxidant vitamins and health (Marko & others, 2007). However, recent large-scale studies of men revealed that taking vitamin C and vitamin E did not prevent cardiovascular disease (Gaziano & others, 2009; Sesso & others, 2008). And another recent study indicated that diet supplementation with vitamins C, E, and beta-carotene had no effect on cancer incidence or cancer death (Lin & others, 2009).

Critics argue that the key experimental studies documenting the effectiveness of the vitamins in slowing the aging process have not been conducted. The studies in this area thus far have been so-called *population studies* that are correlational rather than experimental in nature. Other factors—such as exercise, better health practices, and good nutritional habits—might be responsible for the positive findings about vitamins and aging rather than vitamins themselves.

Review *Connect* Reflect

LG2 Characterize developmental changes in nutrition and eating behavior

Review

- What are some important aspects of nutrition and eating behavior in infancy?
- What are some key nutritional problems in American children?
- How can eating behavior and disorders in adolescence be characterized?
- What are some controversies and issues in nutrition and eating behavior in the adult years?

Connect

- What does the nature versus nurture debate suggest about children's risk of becoming obese?

Reflect *Your Own Personal Journey of Life*

- How good are you at eating nutritiously and healthily? Have your lifestyle and behavior in this area affected your health? Might they affect your health in the future?

Exercise **LG3** Summarize the roles of exercise in child and adult health

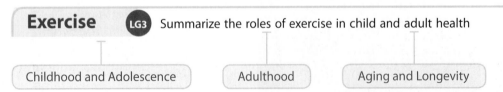

Childhood and Adolescence Adulthood Aging and Longevity

We have seen the important role exercise plays in losing weight. Exercise is linked with many aspects of being physically and mentally healthy. Let's explore the impact of exercise throughout the life span.

How much physical activity should preschool children engage in per day?

CHILDHOOD AND ADOLESCENCE

American children and adolescents are not getting enough exercise (Fahey, Insel, & Roth, 2011; Graham, Holt/Hale, & Parker, 2010; Lumpkin, 2011). Educators and policy makers in the United States and numerous countries around the world, including China, Finland, and Great Britain, have become very concerned about the sedentary lifestyles of many children and adolescents in their countries (Dowda & others, 2009).

Childhood   Because of their activity level and the development of large muscles, especially in the arms and legs, children need daily exercise (Jago & others, 2010). Television watching is linked with low activity and obesity in children (Gable, Chang, & Krull, 2007). A related concern is the dramatic increase in computer use by children. A longitudinal study found that a higher incidence of watching TV in childhood and adolescence was linked with being overweight, being less physically fit, and having higher cholesterol levels at 26 years of age (Hancox, Milne, & Poulton, 2004).

A recent research review concluded that aerobic exercise also increasingly is linked to children's and adolescents' cognitive skills (Best, 2011). Researchers have found that aerobic exercise benefits children's and adolescents' attention, memory, effortful and goal-directed thinking and behavior, and creativity (Budde & others, 2008; Davis & others, 2007, 2011; Ellenberg & St. Louis-Deschenes, 2010; Hillman & others, 2009; Hinkle, Tuckman, & Sampson, 1993; Pesce & others, 2009).

Parents and schools play important roles in children's exercise (Loprinzi & Trost, 2010). Growing up with parents who regularly exercise provides positive models of exercise for children (Crawford & others, 2010). A recent study revealed that mothers were more likely than fathers to limit boys' and girls' sedentary behavior (Edwardson & Gorely, 2010). Another recent study found that school-based physical activity was successful in improving children's fitness and lowering their fat content (Kriemler & others, 2010).

Adolescence   Researchers have found that individuals become less active as they reach and progress through adolescence (Butcher & others, 2008). A recent national study of U.S. 9- to 15-year-olds revealed that almost all 9- and 11-year-olds met the federal government's moderate to vigorous exercise recommendations per day (a minimum of 60 minutes daily), but only 31 percent of 15-year-olds met the recommendations on weekdays, and on weekends only 17 percent met the recommendations (Nader & others, 2008). The recent national study also found that adolescent boys were more likely to engage in moderate to vigorous exercise than girls. Figure 4.15 shows

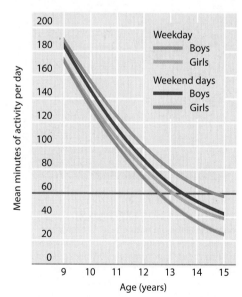

FIGURE **4.15**

AVERAGE AMOUNT OF MODERATE TO VIGOROUS EXERCISE ENGAGED IN BY U.S. 9- TO 15-YEAR-OLDS ON WEEKDAYS AND WEEKENDS. *Note:* The federal government recommends 60 minutes of moderate to vigorous physical activity per day.

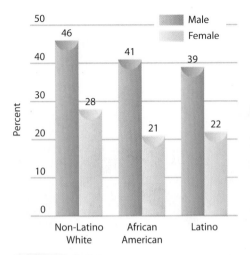

In 2007, Texas became the first state to test students' physical fitness. The student shown here is performing the trunk lift. Other assessments include aerobic exercise, muscle strength, and body fat. Assessments will be done annually.

FIGURE **4.16**

EXERCISE RATES OF U.S. HIGH SCHOOL STUDENTS: GENDER AND ETHNICITY.
Note: Data are for high school students who were physically active doing any kind of physical activity that increased their heart rate and made them breathe hard some of the time for a total of at least 60 minutes a day on five or more of the seven days preceding the survey.

FIGURE **4.17**

THE JOGGING HOG EXPERIMENT. Jogging hogs reveal the dramatic effects of exercise on health. In one investigation, a group of hogs was trained to run approximately 100 miles per week (Bloor & White, 1983). Then, the researchers narrowed the arteries that supplied blood to the hogs' hearts. The hearts of the jogging hogs developed extensive alternate pathways for blood supply, and 42 percent of the threatened heart tissue was salvaged compared with only 17 percent in a control group of nonjogging hogs.

aerobic exercise Sustained activity that stimulates heart and lung functioning.

the average amount of exercise of the U.S. boys and girls from 9 to 15 years of age on weekdays and weekends.

Ethnic differences in exercise participation rates of U.S. adolescents also occur, and these rates vary by gender. As indicated in Figure 4.16, in the National Youth Risk Survey, non-Latino White boys exercised the most, African American girls the least (Eaton & others, 2008).

Screen-based activity (watching television, using computers, talking on the phone, texting, and instant messaging for long hours) may be involved in lower levels of physical fitness in adolescence (Leatherdale, 2010). A recent study revealed that children and adolescents who engaged in the highest amount of daily screen-based activity (TV/video/video game in this study) were less likely to exercise daily (Sisson & others, 2010). In this study, children and adolescents who engaged in low physical activity and high screen-based activity were almost twice as likely to be overweight as their more active, less sedentary counterparts.

Exercise is linked to a number of positive outcomes in adolescence (Powers, Dodd, & Jackson, 2011; van der Heijden & others, 2011). One important outcome is that exercise helps adolescents maintain an appropriate weight. A recent study revealed that low levels of exercise were related to depressive symptoms in young adolescents (Sund, Larsson, & Wichstrom, 2010). And another recent study found that vigorous physical exercise was linked to lower drug use in adolescence (Delisle & others, 2010).

Below are some ways to get children and adolescents to exercise more:

- Improve physical fitness classes in schools.
- Offer more physical activity programs run by volunteers at school facilities.
- Have children plan community and school exercise activities that really interest them.
- Encourage families to focus on physical activity and challenge parents to exercise more.

ADULTHOOD

The benefits of exercise continue in adulthood. Both moderate and intense exercise produce important physical and psychological gains (Hales, 2011). The enjoyment and pleasure we derive from exercise added to its physical benefits make exercise one of life's most important activities (Donatelle, 2011; Shaw, Clark, & Wagenmakers, 2010).

Among the most important health benefits of exercise are reduced risks for obesity, cardiovascular disease, and diabetes (Nagashima & others, 2010; Rider & others, 2010; Walker & others, 2010). Even getting hogs to jog has documented the cardiovascular benefits of exercise (see Figure 4.17).

Although exercise designed to strengthen muscles and bones or to improve flexibility is important to fitness, many health experts stress aerobic exercise. **Aerobic exercise** is sustained activity—jogging, swimming, or cycling, for example—that stimulates heart and lung functioning.

Many health experts recommend that adults engage in 45 minutes or more of moderate physical activity on most, preferably all, days of the week. Most recommend

Exercise

Here are some helpful strategies for building exercise into your life:

- *Reduce TV time.* Heavy TV viewing by college students is linked to poor health (Shields, 2006). Replace some of your TV time with exercise.
- *Chart your progress.* Systematically recording your exercise work-outs will help you to chart your progress. This strategy is especially helpful over the long term.
- *Get rid of excuses.* People make up all kinds of excuses for not exer-cising. A typical excuse is "I don't have enough time." You likely do have enough time.

- *Imagine the alternative.* Ask yourself whether you are too busy to take care of your own health. What will your life be like if you lose your health?
- *Learn more about exercise.* The more you know about exercise, the more you are likely to start an exercise program and continue it.

What kinds of results would you expect to gain from incor-porating these suggestions into your own life? Consider both short- and long-term results.

that you should try to raise your heart rate to at least 60 percent of your maximum heart rate. However, only about one-fifth of adults are active at these recommended levels of physical activity. To read about ways to incorporate regular exercise into your life, see the *Connecting Development to Life* interlude.

AGING AND LONGEVITY

Although we may be in the evening of our lives in late adulthood, we are not meant to live out our remaining years passively. Everything we know about older adults suggests they are healthier and happier the more active they are. Can regular exer-cise lead to a healthier late adulthood and increase longevity? Let's examine several research studies on exercise and aging.

In one study, exercise literally meant a difference in life or death for middle-aged and older adults (Blair, 1990). More than 10,000 men and women were divided into categories of low fitness, medium fitness, and high fitness (Blair & others, 1989). Then they were studied over a period of eight years. As shown in Figure 4.18, sed-entary participants (low fitness) were more than twice as likely to die during the eight-year time span of the study as those who were moderately fit and more than three times as likely to die as those who were highly fit. The positive effects of being physically fit occurred for both men and women in this study. Also, a longitudinal study found that men who exercised regularly at 72 years of age had a 30 percent higher probability of still being alive at 90 years of age than their sedentary coun-terparts (Yates & others, 2008). And a recent study of more than 11,000 women found that low cardiorespiratory fitness was a significant predictor of all-cause mor-tality (Farrell & others, 2010).

Gerontologists increasingly recommend strength training in addition to aerobic activity and stretching for older adults (Peiffer & others, 2010; Peterson & Gordon, 2011). The average person's lean body mass declines with age—about 6.6 pounds of lean muscle are lost each decade during the adult years. The rate of muscle loss accelerates after age 45. Resistance exercise can preserve and possibly increase muscle mass in older adults (Hurley, Hanson, & Sheaff, 2011; Williamson & oth-ers, 2010). A recent meta-analysis revealed that resistance training—especially higher intensity training—was effective in improving older adults' strength and is a viable strategy for reducing muscular weakness associated with aging (Peterson & others, 2010).

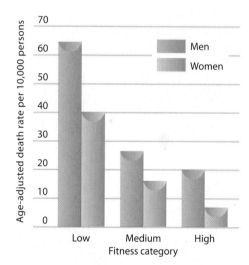

FIGURE **4.18**

PHYSICAL FITNESS AND MORTALITY. In this study of middle-aged and older adults, being moderately fit or highly fit meant that individuals were less likely to die over a period of eight years than their low-fitness (sedentary) counterparts (Blair & others, 1989).

developmental **connection**

Research Methods. What differentiates a longitudinal study from a cross-sectional study? Chapter 1, p. 33

developmental **connection**

Aging. What are telomeres and how are they being investigated in the search for an explanation of why people age? Chapter 3, p. 117

What are some of the benefits of exercise for older adults?

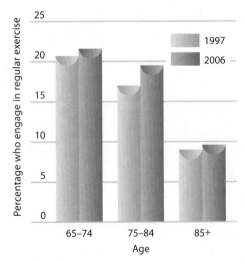

FIGURE **4.19**

REGULAR EXERCISE BY U.S. OLDER ADULTS: 1997 TO 2006

Exercise is an excellent way to maintain health (Lindau & Gavrilova, 2010). The current recommended level of aerobic activity for adults 60 years of age and older is 30 minutes of moderately intense activity, such as brisk walking or riding a stationary bicycle, five or more days a week, and strength training two or more days a week (Der Ananian & Prohaska, 2007).

Researchers continue to document the positive effects of exercise in older adults:

- *Exercise is linked to increased longevity.* In a longitudinal study of Chinese women, those who exercised regularly were less likely to die over approximately a six-year time period (Matthews & others, 2007). In one analysis, energy expenditure by older adults during exercise that burns up at least 1,000 calories a week was estimated to increase life expectancy by about 30 percent, and burning up 2,000 calories a week in exercise was estimated to increase life expectancy by about 50 percent (Lee & Skerrett, 2001).

- *Exercise is related to prevention of common chronic diseases.* Exercise can reduce the risk of developing cardiovascular disease, type 2 diabetes, osteoporosis, stroke, and breast cancer (Aizawa & others, 2010; Marks, Katz, & Smith, 2009; Ryan, 2010).

- *Exercise is associated with improvement in the treatment of many diseases.* When exercise is used as part of the treatment, individuals with these diseases show improvement in symptoms: arthritis, pulmonary disease, congestive heart failure, coronary artery disease, hypertension, type 2 diabetes, obesity, and Alzheimer disease (Coker & others, 2009; Graff-Radford, 2011; Rimmer & others, 2009).

- *Exercise improves older adults' cellular functioning.* Researchers increasingly are finding that exercise improves cellular functioning in older adults (Gielen & others, 2011). For example, two recent studies revealed that telomere length was greater in leukocytes (white blood cells) when older adults engaged in vigorous aerobic activity (Cherkas & others, 2008; La Rocca, Seals, & Pierce, 2010).

- *Exercise improves immune system functioning in older adults* (Maltseva & others, 2011; Walsh & others, 2011). A recent study revealed that following exercise, a number of components of immune system functioning in older adult women improved (Sakamoto & others, 2009).

- *Exercise can optimize body composition and reduce the decline in motor skills as aging occurs.* Exercise can increase muscle mass and bone mass, as well as decrease bone fragility (Hurley, Hanson, & Sheaff, 2011; Liao & others, 2011; Maimoun & Sultan, 2010).

- *Exercise reduces the likelihood that older adults will develop mental health problems and can be effective as part of the treatment of mental health problems.* For example, exercise reduces the likelihood that older adults will develop depression and can be effective in treating depression in older adults (Davidson, 2010; Lavie & Milani, 2011).

- *Exercise is linked to improved brain and cognitive functioning in older adults.* Older adults who exercise show better brain functioning and process information more effectively than older adults who don't exercise (McGregor & others, 2011; Williamson & others, 2009).

Despite the extensive documentation of exercise's power to improve older adults' health and quality of life, a recent national survey revealed that older adults have increased their exercise levels only slightly in recent years (Centers for Disease Control and Prevention, 2008) (see Figure 4.19). Possible explanations of older adults' failure to substantially increase their exercise focus on factors such as chronic illnesses, life crises (such as a spouse's death) that disrupt exercise schedules, embarrassment of being around others who are in better shape (especially if they haven't exercised much earlier in life), and the "why bother?" factor (not believing that exercise will improve their lives much) (Painter, 2008). But it is never too late to start exercising, and older adults can significantly benefit from regular exercise (Farrell & others, 2010; Reibis & others, 2010).

Review *Connect* Reflect

 LG3 Summarize the roles of exercise in child and adult health

Review

- How extensively do U.S. children and adolescents exercise?
- What roles does exercise play in adult health?
- How does exercise influence development in aging adults?

Connect

- Consider what you have learned so far about parents' potential influence on children's health. Do active parents send a different message to their children than sedentary parents do?

Reflect *Your Own Personal Journey of Life*

- Imagine that you have become middle-aged and someone asks you this question: "What would give you the greater advantage: exercising more or eating less?" What would your answer be?

Substance Use   **LG4** Evaluate substance use in adolescence and adulthood

Adolescence and Emerging Adulthood   Substance Use in Older Adults

Besides exercising, another important healthy practice is to not engage in substance abuse (Hart, Ksir, & Ray, 2011; Kinney, 2012). For example, in one longitudinal study, individuals who did not abuse alcohol at age 50 were more likely to still be alive and healthy at 75 to 80 years of age than their counterparts who abused alcohol at age 50 (Vaillant, 2002).

In Chapter 2, "Biological Beginnings," we described the negative effects on the fetus and developing child that can result from substance use by the pregnant mother. Here we examine substance use by adolescents, emerging adults, and older adults.

ADOLESCENCE AND EMERGING ADULTHOOD

Adolescence is a critical time for the onset of substance abuse. Many individuals who abuse drugs begin to do so during the adolescent years. Let's explore some trends in adolescent drug use and then examine drug use in emerging adulthood.

Trends in Adolescent Drug Use   Each year since 1975, Lloyd Johnston and his colleagues at the Institute of Social Research at the University of Michigan have monitored the drug use of America's high school seniors in a wide range of public and private high schools. Since 1991, they also have surveyed drug use by eighth- and tenth-graders. In 2010, the study surveyed more than 46,000 secondary school students in more than 400 public and private schools (Johnston & others, 2011).

According to this study, the proportions of eighth-, tenth-, and twelfth-grade U.S. students who used any illicit drug declined in the late 1990s and the first years of the twenty-first century (Johnston & others, 2011) (see Figure 4.20). The use of drugs among U.S. secondary school students declined in the 1980s but began to increase in the early 1990s (Johnston & others, 2011). In the late 1990s and the early part of the twenty-first century, the proportion of secondary school students reporting the use of any illicit drug has been declining. The overall decline in the

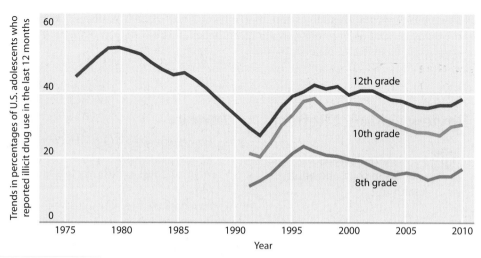

FIGURE **4.20**

TRENDS IN DRUG USE BY U.S. EIGHTH-, TENTH-, AND TWELFTH-GRADE STUDENTS. This graph shows the percentage of U.S. eighth-, tenth-, and twelfth-grade students who reported having taken an illicit drug in the last 12 months from 1991 to 2010, for eighth- and tenth-graders, and from 1975 to 2010, for twelfth-graders (Johnston & others, 2010b, 2011). *Source:* Johnston, L. D., O'Malley, P. M., Bachman, J. G., & Schulenberg, J. E. (2011). *Monitoring the Future national results on adolescent drug use: Overview of key findings,* 2010, Ann Arbor, Mich., Institute for Social Research, The University of Michigan.

use of illicit drugs by adolescents during this time frame is approximately one-third for eighth-graders, one-fourth for tenth-graders, and one-eighth for twelfth-graders. The most notable declines in drug use by U.S. adolescents in the twenty-first century have occurred for LSD, cocaine, cigarettes, sedatives, tranquilizers, and Ecstasy. Marijuana is the illicit drug most widely used in the United States and Europe (Hibell & others, 2004; Johnston & others, 2011). Even with the recent decline in use, the United States still has one of the highest rates of adolescent drug use of any industrialized nation.

As shown in Figure 4.20, in which marijuana is included, an increase in illicit drug use by U.S. adolescents occurred in 2009 and 2010. However, when marijuana use is subtracted from the illicit drug index, no increase in U.S. adolescent drug use occurred in 2009 and 2010 (Johnston & others, 2011).

How extensive is alcohol use by U.S. adolescents? Sizable declines in adolescent alcohol use have occurred in recent years (Johnston & others, 2011). The percentage of U.S. eighth-graders reporting having had any alcohol to drink in the past 30 days fell from a 1996 high of 26 percent to 14 percent in 2010. The 30-day prevalence fell among tenth-graders from 39 percent in 2001 to 29 percent in 2010 and among high school seniors from 72 percent in 1980 to 41 percent in 2010. Binge drinking (defined in the University of Michigan surveys as having five or more drinks in a row in the last two weeks) by high school seniors declined from 41 percent in 1980 to 27 percent in 2010. Binge drinking by eighth- and tenth-graders also has dropped in recent years. A consistent sex difference occurs in binge drinking, with males engaging in this behavior more than females.

Cigarette smoking among U.S. adolescents peaked in 1996 and 1997 and has gradually declined since then (Johnston & others, 2011). Following peak use in 1996, smoking rates for U.S. eighth-graders have fallen by 50 percent. In 2010, the percentages of adolescents who said they had smoked cigarettes in the last 30 days were 19 percent (twelfth grade), 14 percent (tenth grade), and 7 percent (eighth grade).

Cigarette smoking (in which the active drug is nicotine) is one of the most serious yet preventable health problems. Smoking is likely to begin in grades 7 through 9, although sizable portions of youth are still establishing regular smoking habits during high school and college. Risk factors for becoming a regular smoker in adolescence include having a friend who smokes, a weak academic orientation, and low parental support (Tucker, Ellickson, & Klein, 2003).

The Roles of Development, Parents, Peers, and Educational Success A special concern involves adolescents who begin to use drugs early in adolescence or even in childhood (Patrick, Abar, & Maggs, 2009). A longitudinal study of individuals from 8 to 42 years of age also found that early onset of drinking was linked to increased risk of heavy drinking in middle age (Pitkanen, Lyrra, & Pulkkinen, 2005).

Parents play an important role in preventing adolescent drug abuse (Kinney, 2012; Miller & Plant, 2010). Positive relationships with parents and others can reduce adolescents' drug use (Harakeh & others, 2010). Researchers have found that parental monitoring is linked with a lower incidence of drug use (Tobler & Komro, 2010). A recent research review concluded that the more frequently adolescents ate dinner with their family the less likely they were to have substance abuse problems (Sen, 2010). And a recent study revealed that negative interactions with parents were linked to increased adolescent drinking and smoking, while positive identification with parents was related to declines in use of these substances (Gutman & others, 2011). Another study revealed that having friends in their school's social network and having fewer friends who use substances were related to a lower level of substance use by middle school students (Ennett & others, 2006).

Educational success is also a strong buffer for the emergence of drug problems in adolescence. A recent analysis by Jerald Bachman and his colleagues (2008) revealed that early educational achievement considerably reduced the likelihood that adolescents would develop drug problems, including those involving alcohol abuse, smoking, and abuse of various illicit drugs.

Emerging Adults' Drug Use The transition from high school to college may be a critical risk period for alcohol abuse. The large majority of emerging adults recognize that drinking is common among individuals their age and is largely acceptable, even expected by their peers. They also perceive that they get some social and coping benefits from alcohol use and even occasional heavy drinking. A recent study revealed that only 20 percent of college students reported that they abstain from drinking alcohol (Huang & others, 2009).

In 2009, 42 percent of U.S. college students reported having had 5 or more drinks in a row at least once in the last two weeks (Johnston & others, 2010a, b). In the most recent survey, the Institute of Social Research introduced the term *extreme binge drinking* to describe individuals who had 10 or more drinks in a row in the prior two weeks. In 2009 approximately 1 in 7 college students reported drinking this heavily (Johnston & others, 2010a, b).

The effects of heavy drinking take a toll. In a national survey of drinking patterns on 140 campuses, almost half of the binge drinkers reported problems that included missing classes, physical injuries, troubles with police, and having unprotected sex (Wechsler & others, 1994). This survey also found that binge-drinking college students were eleven times more likely to drive after drinking and twice as likely to have unprotected sex as college students who did not binge drink.

Drinking alcohol before going out—called *pregaming*—has become common among college students. A recent study revealed that almost two-thirds of students on one campus had pregamed at least once in a two-week period (DeJong, DeRicco, & Schneider, 2010). Another recent study found that two-thirds of 18- to 24-year-old women on one college pregamed (Read, Merrill, & Bytschkow, 2010). Drinking games, in which the goal is to become intoxicated, also have become common on college campuses (Cameron & others, 2010). Higher levels of alcohol use have been

developmental **connection**

Biological Processes. Early maturation in adolescence is linked with an increased likelihood of substance abuse problems in adolescent girls. Chapter 3, p. 95

What kind of problems are associated with binge drinking in college?

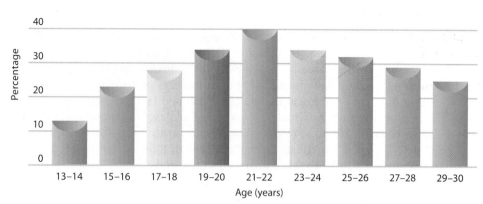

FIGURE **4.21**

BINGE DRINKING IN THE ADOLESCENCE–EARLY ADULTHOOD TRANSITION. Note that the percentage of individuals engaging in binge drinking peaked at 21 or 22 years of age and then began to gradually decline through the remainder of the twenties. Binge drinking was defined as having five or more alcoholic drinks in a row in the past two weeks.

developmental **connection**

Sexuality. When emerging adults drink alcohol, they are most likely to have casual sex. Chapter 12, p. 400

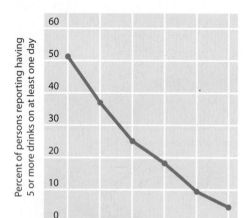

FIGURE **4.22**

AGE AND THE CONSUMPTION OF FIVE OR MORE DRINKS ON AT LEAST ONE DAY IN THE UNITED STATES. The graph shows the considerable decline in having five or more drinks on at least one day as people get older (National Center for Health Statistics, 2002).

consistently linked to higher rates of sexual risk taking, such as engaging in casual sex, sex without contraceptives, and sexual assaults (Lawyer & others, 2010; White & others, 2009).

A special concern is the increase in binge drinking by females during emerging adulthood (Davis & others, 2010; Smith & Berger, 2010). In a national longitudinal study, binge drinking by 19- to 22-year-old women increased from 28 percent in 1995 to 39 percent in 2009 (Johnston & others, 2010a, b).

Fortunately, by the time individuals reach their mid-twenties, many have reduced their use of alcohol and drugs. That is the conclusion reached by Gerald Bachman and his colleagues (2002) in a longitudinal analysis of more than 38,000 individuals (see Figure 4.21). They were evaluated from the time they were high school seniors through their twenties.

Do individuals smoke cigarettes more in emerging adulthood than adolescence? According to a U.S. survey, 18- to 25-year-olds reported a smoking rate that was substantially higher than the rate of 12- to 17-year-olds and higher than the rate of individuals who were 26 years and older (Substance Abuse and Mental Health Services Administration, 2005). Thus, cigarette smoking peaks in emerging adulthood (Park & others, 2006).

SUBSTANCE USE IN OLDER ADULTS

As indicated earlier, alcohol and substance abuse peak in emerging adulthood and then decline somewhat by the mid-twenties. Of course, alcohol and substance abuse continue to raise serious health concerns for many adults in early and middle adulthood (Hart, Ksir, & Ray, 2011).

There also is concern about alcohol and substance abuse in older adults, although a national survey found that binge drinking declines through the late adulthood years (National Center for Health Statistics, 2002) (see Figure 4.22). Indeed, a majority (58 percent) of U.S. adults 65 years and older completely abstain from alcohol, an increase from 38 percent of 45- to 64-year-olds. These declines are usually attributed to increased rates of illness and disease.

Despite these declines in alcohol use, the Substance Abuse and Mental Health Services Administration (2005) has identified substance abuse among older adults as the "invisible epidemic" in the United States. The belief is that substance abuse often goes undetected in older adults, and there is concern about older adults who abuse not only illicit drugs but prescription drugs as well (Segal, 2007). The consequences of abuse—such as depression, inadequate nutrition, congestive heart failure, and frequent falls—may erroneously be attributed to other medical or psychological conditions (Hoyer & Roodin, 2009). As the number of older adults rises, substance abuse is likely to characterize an increasing number of older adults. For older adults who are taking multiple medications, the dangers of substance abuse rise. For example, when combined with tranquilizers or sedatives, alcohol use can impair breathing, produce excessive sedation, and even be fatal.

Despite the concerns about substance abuse in later adulthood, researchers have revealed a protective effect of moderate alcohol use in older adults (Maraldi & others, 2009). One study revealed better physical and mental health, and increased longevity, in older adults who drank moderately compared with those who drank heavily or did not drink at all (Rozzini, Ranhoff, & Trabucchi, 2007). The explanation of moderate drinking's benefits involves better physical and mental performance, being more open to social contacts, and being able to assert mastery over one's life.

What might explain the finding that drinking red wine in moderation is linked to better health and increased longevity?

Researchers have especially found that moderate drinking of red wine is linked to better health and increased longevity (Das, Mukherjee, & Ray, 2010; Queen & Tollefsbol, 2010). Explanation of the benefits of red wine centers on its connection to lowering stress and reducing the risk of coronary heart disease (Angelone & others, 2010; Wu & Hsieh, 2011). Evidence is increasing that a chemical in the skin of red wine grapes—resveratrol—plays a key role in red wine's health benefits (Kaeberlein, 2010; Marquez, Markus, & Morris, 2010). A recent study found that red wine, but not white, killed several lines of cancer cells (Wallenborg & others, 2009). Scientists are exploring how resveratrol might activate SIRT1, an enzyme that is involved in DNA repair and aging (Huber & Superti-Furga, 2011; Lin & others, 2010).

Review Connect Reflect

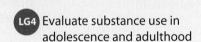 **LG4** Evaluate substance use in adolescence and adulthood

Review

- How extensively do adolescents take drugs? What factors are linked with drug abuse by adolescents? What is the nature of substance use in college students and young adults?
- How can substance use in older adults be described?

Connect

- Research has shown that older adults fare better when they are given more responsibility and control in their lives. In what other age periods is giving individuals more responsibility and control especially important for their development? In what ways is this helpful?

Reflect *Your Own Personal Journey of Life*

- Do you know someone who has a drug problem? If so, describe the nature of the problem. Is the person willing to admit to having a problem?

reach your **learning goals**

Health, Illness, and Disease

LG1 Describe developmental changes in health

Children's Health

- Prevention and poverty are important factors in children's health. Children need timely immunizations. Accident prevention is a key aspect of children's health. Of special concern are children living in poverty, who often are malnourished.

Adolescents' Health

- Adolescence is a critical juncture in health because many health habits—good or bad—still are being formed. Social contexts, including family, peers, and schools, influence the health of adolescents.

Emerging and Young Adults' Health

- Few emerging and young adults have chronic health problems. Many emerging and young adults don't stop to think about how their personal lifestyles will affect their health later in their lives. Emerging adults have double the mortality rate of adolescents.

Health and Aging

- Chronic disorders increase in middle-aged adults and are common in older adults. Osteoporosis is a concern, especially among older women. Various forms of dementia, especially Alzheimer disease, are a major health problem. Another type of dementia is Parkinson disease. A special concern is the quality of nursing homes for older adults and the treatment of older adults in nursing homes.

Nutrition and Eating Behavior

LG2 Characterize developmental changes in nutrition and eating behavior

Infancy

- The importance of adequate energy intake consumed in a loving and supportive environment in infancy cannot be overstated. The growing consensus is that breast feeding is better for the baby's health than bottle feeding. Nutritional supplements can improve infants' cognitive development.

Childhood

- Concerns about nutrition in childhood focus on fat content in diet and obesity. Thirty percent of U.S. children are at risk for being overweight. Obesity increases a child's risk of developing many medical and psychological problems. Poor nutrition in children from low-income families is a special concern.

Adolescence

- Nutrition and being overweight are also key problems among adolescents. Anorexia nervosa, bulimia nervosa, and binge eating disorder can develop in adolescence; most anorexics and bulimics are women.

Adult Development and Aging

- Obesity is a major concern in adulthood, and dieting is pervasive. Calorie restriction is associated with longevity, but a balanced diet is usually recommended for older adults. Controversy surrounds whether antioxidant vitamins can reduce the risk for disease.

Exercise

LG3 Summarize the roles of exercise in child and adult health

Childhood and Adolescence

- Most children and adolescents are not getting nearly enough exercise.

Adulthood

- Both moderate and intense exercise produce physical and psychological advantages, such as lowered risk of heart disease and lowered anxiety.

Aging and Longevity

- Regular exercise in middle-aged and older adults can promote health and increase longevity.

Substance Use

LG4 Evaluate substance use in adolescence and adulthood

Adolescence and
Emerging Adulthood

Substance Use in
Older Adults

- The United States has one of the highest adolescent drug use rates of any industrialized country. Alcohol and cigarette smoking are special concerns. Development, parents, peers, and educational success play important roles in preventing drug abuse in adolescents. Forty percent of U.S. college students say they drink heavily. Substance use peaks in emerging adulthood and then often decreases by the mid-twenties.

- Alcohol use declines in older adults, although abuse is more difficult to detect in older adults than in younger adults. There is concern about older adults who abuse prescription drugs and illicit drugs.

key terms

chronic disorders 125
osteoporosis 126
dementia 126

Alzheimer disease 126
Parkinson disease 128
anorexia nervosa 136

bulimia nervosa 137
binge eating disorder
  (BED) 137

aerobic exercise 142

key people

Judith Rodin and Ellen
  Langer 130

Lloyd Johnston 145

chapter 5

MOTOR, SENSORY, AND PERCEPTUAL DEVELOPMENT

preview

Think about what is required for us to find our way around our environment, to play sports, or to create art. These activities require both active perception and precisely timed motor actions. Neither innate, automatic movements nor simple sensations are enough to let us do the things we take for granted every day. How do we develop perceptual and motor abilities, and what happens to them as we age? In this chapter, we will focus first on the development of motor skills, then on sensory and perceptual development, and finally on the coupling of perceptual-motor skills.

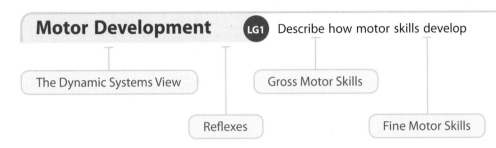

Motor Development **LG1** Describe how motor skills develop

- The Dynamic Systems View
- Reflexes
- Gross Motor Skills
- Fine Motor Skills

Most adults are capable of coordinated, purposive actions of considerable skill, including driving a car, playing golf, and typing effectively on a computer keyboard. Some adults have extraordinary motor skills, such as those involved in winning an Olympic pole vault competition, painting a masterpiece, or performing heart surgery. Look all you want at a newborn infant, and you will observe nothing even remotely approaching these skilled actions. How, then, do the motor behaviors of adults come about?

THE DYNAMIC SYSTEMS VIEW

Developmentalist Arnold Gesell (1934) thought his painstaking observations had revealed how people develop their motor skills. He had discovered that infants and children develop rolling, sitting, standing, and other motor skills in a fixed order and within specific time frames. These observations, said Gesell, show that motor development comes about through the unfolding of a genetic plan, or maturation.

Later studies, however, demonstrated that the sequence of developmental milestones is not as fixed as Gesell indicated and not due as much to heredity as Gesell argued (Adolph, Karasik, & Tamis-LeMonda, 2010; Adolph & Robinson, 2011). In the last two decades, the study of motor development experienced a renaissance as psychologists acquired new insights about how motor skills develop (Spencer, 2009; Thelen & Smith, 1998, 2006). One increasingly influential explanation is dynamic systems theory, proposed by Esther Thelen.

According to **dynamic systems theory,** infants assemble motor skills for perceiving and acting (Thelen & Smith, 2006). To develop motor skills, infants must perceive something in the environment that motivates them to act and then use their perceptions to fine-tune their movements. Motor skills represent pathways to the infant's goals (Clearfield & others, 2009).

How is a motor skill developed, according to this theory? When infants are motivated to do something, they might create a new motor behavior. The new behavior is the result of many converging factors: the development of the nervous system, the body's physical properties and its possibilities for movement, the goal the child is motivated to reach, and the environmental support for the skill (von Hofsten, 2008). For example, babies learn to walk only when maturation of the nervous system allows them to control certain leg muscles, when their legs have grown enough to support their weight, and when they want to move.

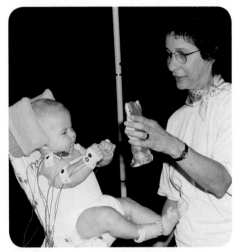

Esther Thelen is shown conducting an experiment to discover how infants learn to control their arms to reach and grasp for objects. A computer device is used to monitor the infant's arm movements and to track muscle patterns. Thelen's research is conducted from a dynamic systems perspective. *What is the nature of this perspective?*

> The experiences of the first three years of life are almost entirely lost to us, and when we attempt to enter into a small child's world, we come as foreigners who have forgotten the landscape and no longer speak the native tongue.
>
> —SELMA FRAIBERG
> *Developmentalist and Child Advocate, 20th Century*

dynamic systems theory A theory proposed by Esther Thelen that seeks to explain how infants assemble motor skills for perceiving and acting.

Mastering a motor skill requires the infant's active efforts to coordinate several components of the skill. Infants explore and select possible solutions to the demands of a new task; they assemble adaptive patterns by modifying their current movement patterns. The first step occurs when the infant is motivated by a new challenge—such as the desire to cross a room—and gets into the "ballpark" of the task demands by taking a couple of stumbling steps. Then, the infant "tunes" these movements to make them smoother and more effective. The tuning is achieved through repeated cycles of action and perception of the consequences of that action. According to the dynamic systems view, even universal milestones, such as crawling, reaching, and walking, are learned through this process of adaptation: Infants modulate their movement patterns to fit a new task by exploring and selecting possible configurations (Adolph & Robinson, 2011; Thelen & Smith, 2006).

To see how dynamic systems theory explains motor behavior, imagine that you offer a new toy to a baby named Gabriel (Thelen & others, 1993). There is no exact program that can tell Gabriel ahead of time how to move his arm and hand and fingers to grasp the toy. Gabriel must adapt to his goal—grasping the toy—and the context. From his sitting position, he must make split-second adjustments to extend his arm, holding his body steady so that his arm and torso don't plow into the toy. Muscles in his arm and shoulder contract and stretch in a host of combinations, exerting a variety of forces. He improvises a way to reach out with one arm and wrap his fingers around the toy.

Thus, according to dynamic systems theory, motor development is not a passive process in which genes dictate the unfolding of a sequence of skills over time (Spencer, 2009). Rather, the infant actively puts together a skill to achieve a goal within the constraints set by the infant's body and environment. Nature and nurture, the infant and the environment, are all working together as part of an ever-changing system.

As we examine the course of motor development, we will see how dynamic systems theory applies to some specific skills. First, though, let's examine how the story of motor development begins with reflexes.

REFLEXES

The newborn is not completely helpless. Among other things, it has some basic reflexes (Pedroso, 2008). For example, the newborn holds its breath and contracts its throat to keep water out. Reflexes allow infants to respond adaptively to their environment before they have had the opportunity to learn.

The rooting and sucking reflexes are important examples. Both have survival value for newborn mammals, who must find a mother's breast to obtain nourishment. The **rooting reflex** occurs when the infant's cheek is stroked or the side of the mouth is touched. In response, the infant turns its head toward the side that was touched in an apparent effort to find something to suck. The **sucking reflex** occurs when newborns suck an object placed in their mouth. This reflex enables newborns to get nourishment before they have associated a nipple with food; it also serves as a self-soothing or self-regulating mechanism.

Another example is the **Moro reflex,** which occurs in response to a sudden, intense noise or movement (see Figure 5.1). When startled, the newborn arches its back, throws back its head, and flings out its arms and legs. Then the newborn rapidly closes its arms and legs. The Moro reflex is believed to be a way of grabbing for support while falling; it would have had survival value for our primate ancestors.

Some reflexes—coughing, sneezing, blinking, shivering, and yawning, for example—persist throughout life. They are as important for the adult as they are for the infant. Other reflexes, though, disappear several months following birth, as the infant's brain matures and voluntary control over many behaviors develops. The rooting and Moro reflexes, for example, tend to disappear when the infant is 3 to 4 months old.

◄ ┅ ┅ ┅ ┅ ┅ ┅ ┅ ┅ ┅ ┅ ┅ ┅ ┅

developmental **connection**

Nature and Nurture. The epigenetic view states that development is an ongoing, bi-directional interchange between heredity and the environment. Chapter 2, p. 62

rooting reflex A newborn's built-in reaction that occurs when the infant's cheek is stroked or the side of the mouth is touched. In response, the infant turns its head toward the side that was touched, in an apparent effort to find something to suck.

sucking reflex A newborn's reaction of sucking an object placed in its mouth. The sucking reflex enables the infant to get nourishment before it has associated a nipple with food.

Moro reflex A startle response that occurs in reaction to a sudden, intense noise or movement. When startled, the newborn arches its back, throws its head back, and flings out its arms and legs. Then the newborn rapidly closes its arms and legs to the center of the body.

grasping reflex A reflex that occurs when something touches an infant's palms. The infant responds by grasping tightly.

gross motor skills Motor skills that involve large-muscle activities, such as walking.

The movements of some reflexes eventually become incorporated into more complex, voluntary actions. One important example is the **grasping reflex,** which occurs when something touches the infant's palms (see Figure 5.1). The infant responds by grasping tightly. By the end of the third month, the grasping reflex diminishes, and the infant shows a more voluntary grasp. As its motor development becomes smoother, the infant will grasp objects, carefully manipulate them, and explore their qualities.

Individual differences in reflexive behavior are soon apparent after birth. For example, the sucking capabilities of newborns vary considerably. Some newborns are efficient at forceful sucking and obtaining milk; others are not as adept and get tired before they are full. Most infants take several weeks to establish a sucking style that is coordinated with the way the mother is holding the infant, the way milk is coming out of the bottle or breast, and the infant's temperament (Blass, 2008).

The old view of reflexes is that they were exclusively genetic, built-in mechanisms that govern the infant's movements. The new perspective on infant reflexes is that they are not automatic or completely beyond the infant's control. For example, infants can control such movements as alternating their legs to make a mobile jiggle or change their sucking rate to listen to a recording (Adolph & Robinson, 2011).

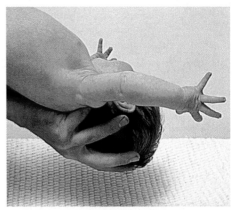

Mono reflex

Grasping reflex

GROSS MOTOR SKILLS

Ask any parents about their baby, and sooner or later you are likely to hear about one or more advances in motor skills, such as "Cassandra just learned to crawl," "Jesse is finally sitting alone," or "Angela took her first step last week." Parents proudly announce such milestones as their children transform themselves from babies unable to lift their heads to toddlers who grab things off the grocery store shelf, chase a cat, and participate actively in the family's social life (Thelen, 2000). These milestones are examples of **gross motor skills,** skills that involve large-muscle activities such as moving one's arms and walking.

FIGURE 5.1
NEWBORN REFLEXES

The Development of Posture   How do gross motor skills develop? As a foundation, these skills require postural control (Adolph & Joh, 2009). For example, to track moving objects, you must be able to control your head in order to stabilize your gaze; before you can walk, you must be able to balance on one leg.

Posture is more than just holding still and straight. Posture is a dynamic process that is linked with sensory information in the skin, joints, and muscles, which tell us where we are in space; in vestibular organs in the inner ear that regulate balance and equilibrium; and in vision and hearing (Thelen & Smith, 2006).

Newborn infants cannot voluntarily control their posture. Within a few weeks, though, they can hold their heads erect, and soon they can lift their heads while prone. By 2 months of age, babies can sit while supported on a lap or an infant seat, but they cannot sit independently until they are 6 or 7 months of age. Standing also develops gradually during the first year of life. By about 8 to 9 months of age, infants usually learn to pull themselves up and hold onto a chair, and they often can stand alone by about 10 to 12 months of age.

Learning to Walk   Locomotion and postural control are closely linked, especially in walking upright (Adolph & Berger, 2011; Adolph & Robinson, 2011). To walk upright, the baby must be able both to balance on one leg as the other is swung forward and to shift the weight from one leg to the other.

Even young infants can make the alternating leg movements that are needed for walking. The neural pathways that control leg alternation are in place from a very early age, even at birth or before. Indeed, researchers have found that alternating leg movements occur during the fetal period and at birth (Adolph & Robinson, 2011).

What are some developmental changes in posture during infancy?

Newly crawling infant

Experienced walker

FIGURE **5.2**

THE ROLE OF EXPERIENCE IN CRAWLING AND WALKING INFANTS' JUDGMENTS OF WHETHER TO GO DOWN A SLOPE.

Source: Karen Adolph (1997)

A baby is an angel whose wings decrease as his legs increase.

—FRENCH PROVERB

If infants can produce forward stepping movements so early, why does it take them so long to learn to walk? The key skills in learning to walk appear to be stabilizing balance on one leg long enough to swing the other forward and shifting the weight without falling. This is a difficult biomechanical problem to solve, and it takes infants about a year to do it.

In learning to locomote, infants discover what kinds of places and surfaces are safe for locomotion (Adolph & Berger, 2011; Adolph & Robinson, 2011). Karen Adolph (1997) investigated how experienced and inexperienced crawling infants and walking infants go down steep slopes (see Figure 5.2). Newly crawling infants, who averaged about 8½ months in age, rather indiscriminately went down the steep slopes, often falling in the process (with an experimenter next to the slope to catch them). After weeks of practice, the crawling babies became more adept at judging which slopes were too steep to crawl down and which ones they could navigate safely. New walkers also could not judge the safety of the slopes, but experienced walkers accurately matched their skills with the steepness of the slopes. They rarely fell downhill, either refusing to go down the steep slopes or going down backward in a cautious manner. Experienced walkers perceptually assessed the situation—looking, swaying, touching, and thinking before they moved down the slope. With experience, both the crawlers and the walkers learned to avoid the risky slopes where they would fall, integrating perceptual information with the development of a new motor behavior. In this research, we again see the importance of perceptual-motor coupling in the development of motor skills. Thus, practice is very important in the development of new motor skills (Adolph & Berger, 2011; Adolph & Robinson, 2011).

The First Year: Motor Development Milestones and Variations Figure 5.3 summarizes important accomplishments in gross motor skills during the first year, culminating in the ability to walk easily. The timing of these milestones, especially the later ones, may vary by as much as two to four months, and experiences can modify the onset of these accomplishments. For example, in the early 1990s, pediatricians began recommending that parents place their babies on their backs when they sleep. Following that instruction, babies who back-sleep began crawling later, typically several weeks later than babies who sleep prone (Davis & others, 1998). Also, some infants do not follow the standard sequence of motor accomplishments (Eaton, 2008). For example, many American infants never crawl on their belly or on their hands and knees. They may discover an idiosyncratic form of locomotion before walking, such as rolling, or they might never locomote until they get upright (Adolph & Robinson, 2011). In Jamaica, approximately one-fourth of babies skip crawling (Hopkins, 1991).

According to Karen Adolph and Sarah Berger (2005), the early view that growth and motor development simply reflect the age-related output of maturation is, at best, incomplete. Rather, infants develop new skills with the guidance of their caregivers in a real-world environment of objects, surfaces, and planes.

Development in the Second Year The motor accomplishments of the first year bring increasing independence, allowing infants to explore their environment more extensively and to initiate interaction with others more readily. In the second year of life, toddlers become more motorically skilled and mobile. Motor activity during the second year is vital to the child's competent development and few restrictions, except for safety, should be placed on their adventures.

By 13 to 18 months, toddlers can pull a toy attached to a string and use their hands and legs to climb up a number of steps. By 18 to 24 months, toddlers can walk quickly or run stiffly for a short distance, balance on their feet in a squat position while playing with objects on the floor, walk backward without losing their balance, stand and kick a ball without falling, stand and throw a ball, and jump in place.

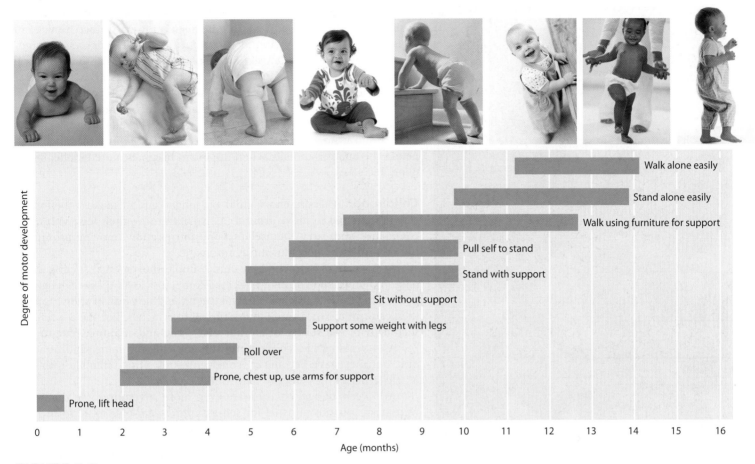

FIGURE **5.3**

MILESTONES IN GROSS MOTOR DEVELOPMENT. The horizontal red bars indicate the range in which most infants reach various milestones in gross motor development.

Can parents give their babies a head start on becoming physically fit and physically talented through structured exercise classes? Most infancy experts recommend against structured exercise classes for babies. But there are other ways to guide infants' motor development. Caregivers in some cultures do handle babies vigorously, and such treatment might advance motor development, as we discuss next.

Cultural Variations in Guiding Infants' Motor Development   Mothers in developing countries tend to stimulate their infants' motor skills more than mothers in more developed countries (Hopkins, 1991). In many African, Indian, and Caribbean cultures, mothers massage and stretch their infants during daily baths (Adolph, Karasik, & Tamis-LeMonda, 2010). Mothers in the Gusii culture of Kenya also encourage vigorous movement in their babies.

Do these cultural variations make a difference in the infant's motor development? When caregivers provide babies with physical guidance by physically handling them in special ways (such as stroking, massaging, or stretching) or by giving them opportunities for exercise, the infants often reach motor milestones earlier than infants whose caregivers have not provided these activities (Adolph, Karasik, & Tamis-LeMonda, 2010). For example, Jamaican mothers expect their infants to sit and walk alone two to three months earlier than English mothers do (Hopkins & Westra, 1990). And in sub-Saharan Africa, traditional practices in many villages involve mothers and siblings engaging babies in exercises, such as frequent exercise for trunk and pelvic muscles (Super & Harkness, 2010).

In Jamaica, mothers massage and stretch their infants' arms and legs. *To what extent do cultural variations in infants' activities influence the time at which they reach motor milestones?*

What are some developmental changes in children's motor development in early childhood and middle and late childhood?

Many forms of restricted movement—such as Chinese sandbags, orphanage restrictions, and failure of caregivers to encourage movement in Budapest—have been found to produce substantial delays in motor development (Adolph, Karasik, & Tamis-LeMonda, 2010). In some rural Chinese provinces, babies are placed in a bag of fine sand, which acts as a diaper and is changed once a day. The baby is left alone, face up, and is visited only when being fed by the mother (Xie & Young, 1999). Some studies of swaddling show slight delays in motor development, but other studies show no delays. Cultures that swaddle infants usually do so before the infant is mobile; when the infant becomes more mobile, swaddling decreases.

Childhood   The preschool child no longer has to make an effort to stay upright and to move around. As children move their legs with more confidence and carry themselves more purposefully, moving around in the environment becomes more automatic.

At 3 years of age, children enjoy simple movements, such as hopping, jumping, and running back and forth, just for the sheer delight of performing these activities. They take considerable pride in showing how they can run across a room and jump all of 6 inches. For the 3-year-old, such activity is a source of considerable pride and accomplishment.

At 4 years of age, children are still enjoying the same kind of activities, but they have become more adventurous. They scramble over low jungle gyms as they display their athletic prowess.

At 5 years of age, children are even more adventuresome than they were at 4. It is not unusual for self-assured 5-year-olds to perform hair-raising stunts on practically any climbing object. They run hard and enjoy races with each other and their parents.

During middle and late childhood, children's motor development becomes much smoother and more coordinated than it was in early childhood. For example, only one child in a thousand can hit a tennis ball over the net at the age of 3, yet by the age of 10 or 11 most children can learn to play the sport. Running, climbing, skipping rope, swimming, bicycle riding, and skating are just a few of the many physical skills elementary school children can master. And, when mastered, these physical skills are a source of great pleasure and a sense of accomplishment. In gross motor skills involving large-muscle activity, boys usually outperform girls.

Organized sports are one way of encouraging children to be active and to develop their motor skills. Schools and community agencies offer programs for children that involve baseball, soccer, football, basketball, swimming, gymnastics, and other sports. For children who participate in them, these programs may play a central role in their lives.

Participation in sports can have both positive and negative consequences for children (Myer & others, 2011). Participation can provide exercise, opportunities to learn how to compete, self-esteem, persistence, and a setting for developing peer relations and friendships (Theokas, 2009). Further, participating in sports reduces the likelihood that children will become obese (Sturm, 2005). A recent study revealed that 10- to 12-year-old girls who participated in extracurricular sports activities for more than 3 hours a week were 59 percent less likely to be overweight or obese than their nonparticipating counterparts (Antonogeorgos &

Parents, Coaches, and Children's Sports

Most sports psychologists stress that it is important for parents to show an interest in their children's sports participation. Most children want their parents to watch them perform in sports. Many children whose parents do not come to watch them play in sporting events feel that their parents do not adequately support them. However, some children become extremely nervous when their parents watch them perform, or they get embarrassed when their parents cheer too loudly or make a fuss. If children request that their parents not watch them perform, parents should respect their children's wishes (Schreiber, 1990).

Parents should compliment their children for their sports performance, and if they don't become overinvolved, they can help their children build their physical skills and help them emotionally—discussing with them how to deal with a difficult coach, how to cope with a tough loss, and how to put in perspective a poorly played game. The following guidelines provided by the Women's Sports Foundation (2001) in its booklet *Parents' Guide to Girls' Sports* can benefit both parents and coaches of all children in sports:

What are some of the possible positive and negative aspects of children's participation in sports?

The Dos

- Make sports fun; the more children enjoy sports, the more they will want to play.
- Remember that it is okay for children to make mistakes; it means they are trying.
- Allow children to ask questions about the sport and discuss the sport in a calm, supportive manner.
- Show respect for the child's sports participation.
- Be positive and convince the child that he or she is making a good effort.
- Be a positive role model for the child in sports.

The Don'ts

- Yell or scream at the child.
- Condemn the child for poor play or continue to bring up failures long after they happen.
- Point out the child's errors in front of others.
- Expect the child to learn something immediately.
- Expect the child to become a pro.
- Ridicule or make fun of the child.
- Compare the child to siblings or to more talented children.
- Make sports all work and no fun.

What developmental theories offer support for the Women's Sports Foundation's assertion that parents should strive to be positive role models for their children in sports?

others, 2011). However, sports also can bring pressure to achieve and win, physical injuries, a distraction from academic work, and unrealistic expectations for success as an athlete (Lerch, Cordes, & Baumeister, 2011; Seto, Statuta, & Solari, 2010). The *Connecting Development to Life* interlude examines the roles of parents and coaches in children's sports.

Adolescence and Adulthood Gross motor skills typically improve during adolescence. Most of us reach our peak physical performance before the age of 30, often between the ages of 19 and 26. This peak occurs both for the average young adult and for outstanding athletes. Even though athletes keep getting better than their predecessors—running faster, jumping higher, and lifting more weight—the age at which they reach their peak performance has remained virtually the same (Schultz & Curnow, 1988). Most swimmers and gymnasts reach their peak in their late teens. Many athletes, including track performers in sprint races (100-, 200-yard dashes),

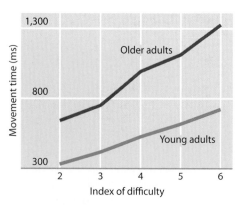

FIGURE **5.4**

MOVEMENT AND AGING. Older adults take longer to move than young adults, and this change occurs across a range of movement difficulty (Ketcham & Stelmach, 2001).

Motor skills decline less in older adults who are active and biologically healthy. *What is the difference between chronological age and biological age?*

developmental **connection**

Health. Exercise is linked to prevention and effective treatment of many diseases. Chapter 4, p. 142

fine motor skills Motor skills that involve finely tuned movements, such as any activity that requires finger dexterity.

peak in their early to mid-twenties. Golfers and marathon runners tend to peak in their late twenties or even early thirties.

After an individual reaches the age of 30, most biological functions begin to decline, although the decline of specific organs can vary considerably. The decline in general biological functioning that begins at about age 30 occurs at a rate of about 0.75 to 1 percent a year. Declines often occur in cardiovascular functioning, muscle strength, bone tissue (especially for females), neural function, balance, and flexibility.

Older adults move more slowly than young adults, and this slowing occurs for movements with a wide range of difficulty (Sakuma & Yamaguchi, 2010) (see Figure 5.4). Even when they perform everyday tasks such as reaching and grasping, moving from one place to another, and continuous movement, older adults tend to move more slowly than they did when they were young (Mollenkopf, 2007).

Adequate mobility is an important aspect of maintaining an independent and active lifestyle in late adulthood (Clark & others, 2010, 2011). Recent research indicates that obesity contributes to mobility limitation in older adults (Jensen & Hsiao, 2010; Vincent, Vincent, & Lamb, 2010). The good news is that regular walking decreases the onset of physical disability in older adults (Newman & others, 2006). Also, a recent study found that a combined program of physical activity and weight loss was linked to preserving mobility in older, obese adults in poor cardiovascular health (Rejeski & others, 2011). And a recent study revealed that it's not just physical exercise and weight loss that are linked to preserving older adults' motor functions; in this study, engaging in social activities protected against loss of motor abilities (Buchman & others, 2009).

Falls are the leading cause of injury deaths among adults who are 65 years and older (National Center for Health Statistics, 2010). Each year, approximately 200,000 adults over the age of 65 (many of them women) fracture a hip in a fall. Half of these older adults die within 12 months, frequently from pneumonia. A recent study revealed that participation in an exercise class once a week for three years reduced the fall risk and the number of falling incidents in older adults who were at high risk for falling (Yokoya, Demura, & Sato, 2009). Another recent study indicated that a lower education level was linked to greater mobility disability in 70- to 79-year-old women (Gregory & others, 2011).

FINE MOTOR SKILLS

Whereas gross motor skills involve large-muscle activity, **fine motor skills** involve finely tuned movements. Buttoning a shirt, typing, or anything that requires finger dexterity demonstrates fine motor skills.

Infancy   Infants have hardly any control over fine motor skills at birth, but newborns do have many components of what will become finely coordinated arm, hand, and finger movements. The onset of reaching and grasping marks a significant achievement in infants' ability to interact with their surroundings (van Hof, van der Kamp, & Savelsbergh, 2008). During the first two years of life, infants refine how they reach and grasp (Keen, 2011). Initially, infants reach by moving their shoulders and elbows crudely, swinging toward an object. Later, when infants reach for an object they move their wrists, rotate their hands, and coordinate their thumb and forefinger. Infants do not have to see their own hands in order to reach for an object (Clifton & others, 1993). Cues from muscles, tendons, and joints, not sight of the limb, guide reaching by 4-month-old infants.

Infants refine their ability to grasp objects by developing two types of grasps. Initially, infants grip with the whole hand, which is called the *palmer grasp*. Later, toward the end of the first year, infants also grasp small objects with their thumb and forefinger, which is called the *pincer grip*. Their grasping system is very flexible.

They vary their grip on an object depending on its size, shape, and texture, as well as the size of their own hands relative to the object's size. Infants grip small objects with their thumb and forefinger (and sometimes their middle finger too), whereas they grip large objects with all of the fingers of one hand or both hands.

Perceptual-motor coupling is necessary for the infant to coordinate grasping (Keen, 2005). Which perceptual system the infant is most likely to use in coordinating grasping varies with age. Four-month-old infants rely greatly on touch to determine how they will grip an object; eight-month-olds are more likely to use vision as a guide (Newell & others, 1989). This developmental change is efficient because vision lets infants preshape their hands as they reach for an object.

Experience plays a role in reaching and grasping. In one study, 3-month-old infants participated in play sessions wearing "sticky mittens"—"mittens with palms that stuck to the edges of toys and allowed the infants to pick up the toys" (Needham, Barrett, & Peterman, 2002, p. 279) (see Figure 5.5). Infants who participated in sessions with the mittens grasped and manipulated objects earlier in their development than a control group of infants who did not receive the "mitten" experience. The experienced infants looked at the objects longer, swatted at them more during visual contact, and were more likely to mouth the objects. In a recent study, 5-month-old infants whose parents trained them to use the sticky mittens for 10 minutes a day over a two-week period showed advances in their reaching behavior at the end of the two weeks (Libertus & Needham, 2010).

Just as infants need to exercise their gross motor skills, they also need to exercise their fine motor skills (Keen, 2011; Needham, 2009). Especially when they can manage a pincer grip, infants delight in picking up small objects. Many develop the pincer grip and begin to crawl at about the same time, and infants at this time pick up virtually everything in sight, especially on the floor, and put the objects in their mouth. Thus, parents need to be vigilant in regularly monitoring what objects are within the infant's reach (Keen, 2005).

Childhood and Adolescence As children get older, their fine motor skills improve (Sveistrup & others, 2008). At 3 years of age, children have had the ability to pick up the tiniest objects between their thumb and forefinger for some time, but they are still somewhat clumsy at it. Three-year-olds can build surprisingly high block towers, each block placed with intense concentration but often not in a completely straight line. When 3-year-olds play with a form board or a simple puzzle, they are rather rough in placing the pieces. Even when they recognize the hole that a piece fits into, they are not very precise in positioning the piece. They often try to force the piece in the hole or pat it vigorously.

By 4 years of age, children's fine motor coordination has become much more precise. Sometimes 4-year-old children have trouble building high towers with blocks because, in their desire to place each of the blocks perfectly, they may upset those already stacked. By age 5, children's fine motor coordination has improved further. Hand, arm, and fingers all move together under better command of the eye. Mere towers no longer interest the 5-year-old, who now wants to build a house or a church, complete with steeple, though adults may still need to be told what each finished project is meant to be.

Increased myelination of the central nervous system is reflected in the improvement of fine motor skills during middle and late childhood. Children use their hands more adroitly as tools. Six-year-olds can hammer, paste, tie shoes, and fasten

A young girl using a pincer grip to pick up puzzle pieces.

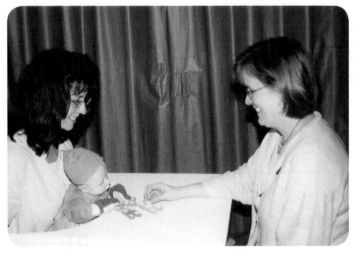

FIGURE **5.5**

INFANTS' USE OF "STICKY MITTENS" TO EXPLORE OBJECTS. Amy Needham and her colleagues (2002) found that "sticky mittens" enhanced young infants' object exploration skills.

clothes. By 7 years of age, children's hands have become steadier. At this age, children prefer a pencil to a crayon for printing, and reversal of letters is less common. Printing becomes smaller. At 8 to 10 years of age, children can use their hands independently with more ease and precision; children can now write rather than print words. Letter size becomes smaller and more even. At 10 to 12 years of age, children begin to show manipulative skills similar to the abilities of adults. The complex, intricate, and rapid movements needed to produce fine-quality crafts or to play a difficult piece on a musical instrument can be mastered. Girls usually outperform boys in fine motor skills.

Adult Development   Fine motor skills may undergo some decline in middle and late adulthood as dexterity decreases, although for most healthy individuals, fine motor skills, such as reaching and grasping, continue to be performed in functional ways. However, pathological conditions may result in weakness or paralysis of an individual's hands, in which case performance of fine motor skills may be impossible.

Review *Connect* Reflect

LG1 Describe how motor skills develop

Review

- What is the dynamic systems view of motor development?
- What are reflexes? What are some reflexes of infants?
- What are gross motor skills, and how do they develop?
- What are fine motor skills? How do fine motor skills develop?

Connect

- How does the development of infants' gross motor skills differ from the development of fine motor skills?

Reflect *Your Own Personal Journey of Life*

- Imagine that you are the parent of a 7-year-old child. How would you evaluate the benefits and drawbacks of allowing him or her to participate in organized competitive sports such as soccer, basketball, or tennis?

Sensory and Perceptual Development

LG2 Outline the course of sensory and perceptual development

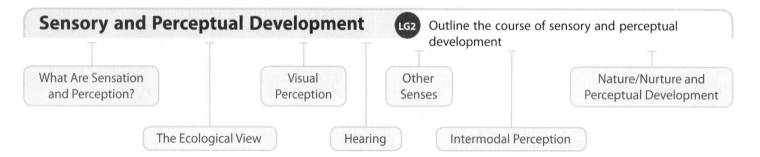

What Are Sensation and Perception?

The Ecological View

Visual Perception

Hearing

Other Senses

Intermodal Perception

Nature/Nurture and Perceptual Development

How do sensations and perceptions develop? Can a newborn see? If so, what can it perceive? What about the other senses—hearing, smell, taste, touch, and pain? What are they like in the newborn, and how do they develop? How do sensation and perception change when adults become older? These are among the intriguing questions that we explore in this section.

WHAT ARE SENSATION AND PERCEPTION?

How does a newborn know that her mother's skin is soft rather than rough? How does a 5-year-old know what color his hair is? How does a 10-year-old know that a firecracker is louder than a cat's meow? Infants and children "know" these things because of information that comes through the senses. Without vision, hearing, touch, taste, smell, and other senses, we would be isolated from the world; we would live in dark silence, a tasteless, colorless, feelingless void.

Sensation occurs when information interacts with sensory *receptors*—the eyes, ears, tongue, nostrils, and skin. The sensation of hearing occurs when waves of pulsating air are collected by the outer ear and conducted through the bones of the inner ear and the *cochlea*, where mechanical vibrations are converted into electrical impulses. Then the electrical impulses move to the *auditory nerve*, which transmits them to the brain. The sensation of vision occurs as rays of light contact the eyes and become focused on the *retina*, where light is converted into electrical impulses. Then the electrical impulses are transmitted by the *optic nerve* to the visual centers of the brain.

Perception is the interpretation of what is sensed. The air waves that contact the ears might be interpreted as noise or as musical sounds, for example. The physical energy transmitted to the retina of the eye might be interpreted as a particular color, pattern, or shape, depending on how it is perceived.

THE ECOLOGICAL VIEW

In recent decades, much of the research on perceptual development in infancy has been guided by the ecological view of Eleanor and James J. Gibson (E. Gibson, 1969, 1989, 2001; J. Gibson, 1966, 1979). They argue that we do not have to take bits and pieces of data from sensations and build up representations of the world in our minds. Instead, our perceptual system can select from the rich information that the environment itself provides.

According to the Gibsons' **ecological view,** we directly perceive information that exists in the world around us. Perception brings us into contact with the environment in order to interact with and adapt to it. Perception is designed for action. Perception gives people such information as when to duck, when to turn their bodies through a narrow passageway, and when to put up their hands to catch something.

In the Gibsons' view, all objects and surfaces have **affordances,** which are opportunities for interaction offered by objects that fit within our capabilities to perform activities. A pot may afford you something to cook with, and it may afford a toddler something to bang. Adults immediately know when a chair is appropriate for sitting, when a surface is safe for walking, or when an object is within reach. We directly and accurately perceive these affordances by sensing information from the environment—the light or sound reflecting from the surfaces of the world—and from our own bodies through muscle receptors, joint receptors, and skin receptors.

An important developmental question is "What affordances can infants or children detect and use?" In one study, for example, when babies who could walk were faced with a squishy waterbed, they stopped and explored it, then chose to crawl rather than walk across it (Gibson & others, 1987). They combined perception and action to adapt to the demands of the task.

Studying the infant's perception has not been an easy task. What do you think some of the research challenges might be? The *Connecting with Research* interlude describes some of the ingenious ways researchers study the infant's perception.

How would you use the Gibsons' ecological theory of perception and the concept of affordance to explain the role that perception is playing in this toddler's activity?

sensation Reaction that occurs when information interacts with sensory receptors—the eyes, ears, tongue, nostrils, and skin.

perception The interpretation of sensation.

ecological view The view proposed by the Gibsons that people directly perceive information in the world around them. Perception brings people in contact with the environment in order to interact with it and adapt to it.

affordances Opportunities for interaction offered by objects that fit within our capabilities to perform activities.

connecting with research

How Do Scientists Study the Newborn's Perception?

Scientists have developed a number of research methods and tools sophisticated enough to examine the subtle abilities of infants and to interpret their complex actions (Bendersky & Sullivan, 2007).

Visual Preference Method

Robert Fantz (1963) was a pioneer in this effort. Fantz made an important discovery that advanced the ability of researchers to investigate infants' visual perception: Infants look at different things for different lengths of time. Fantz placed infants in a "looking chamber," which had two visual displays on the ceiling above the infant's head. An experimenter viewed the infant's eyes by looking through a peephole. If the infant was fixating on one of the displays, the experimenter could see the display's reflection in the infant's eyes. This arrangement allowed the experimenter to determine how long the infant looked at each display. Fantz (1963) found that infants only 2 days old look longer at patterned stimuli, such as faces and concentric circles, than at red, white, or yellow discs. Infants 2 to 3 weeks old preferred to look at patterns—a face, a piece of printed matter, or a bull's-eye—longer than at red, yellow, or white discs (see Figure 5.6). Fantz's research method—studying whether infants can distinguish one stimulus from another by measuring the length of time they attend to different stimuli—is referred to as the **visual preference method.**

Habituation and Dishabituation

Another way that researchers have studied infant perception is to present a stimulus (such as a sight or a sound) a number of times. If the infant decreases its response to the stimulus after several presentations, this change indicates that the infant is no longer interested in looking at the stimulus. If the researcher now presents a new stimulus, the infant's response will recover—an indication that the infant could discriminate between the old and new stimulus (Snyder & Torrence, 2008).

Habituation is the name given to decreased responsiveness to a stimulus after repeated presentations of the stimulus. **Dishabituation** is the recovery of a habituated response after a change in stimulation. Newborn infants can habituate to repeated sights, sounds, smells, or touches (Rovee-Collier, 2004). Among the measures researchers use in habituation studies are sucking behavior (sucking stops when the young infant attends to a novel object), heart and respiration rates, and the length of time the infant looks at an object. Figure 5.7 shows the results of one study of habituation and dishabituation with newborns (Slater, Morison, & Somers, 1988).

High-Amplitude Sucking

To assess an infant's attention to sound, researchers often use a method called *high-amplitude sucking*. In this method, infants are given a non-nutritive nipple to suck, and the nipple is connected to

a sound generating system. Each suck causes a noise to be generated and the infant learns quickly that sucking brings about this noise. At first, babies suck frequently, so the noise occurs often. Then, gradually, they lose interest in hearing repetitions of the same noise and begin to suck

FIGURE **5.6**

FANTZ'S EXPERIMENT ON INFANTS' VISUAL PERCEPTION. (*a*) Infants 2 to 3 weeks old preferred to look at some stimuli more than others. In Fantz's experiment, infants preferred to look at patterns rather than at color or brightness. For example, they looked longer at a face, a piece of printed matter, or a bull's-eye than at red, yellow, or white discs. (*b*) Fantz used a "looking chamber" to study infants' perception of stimuli.

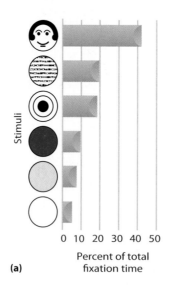

(a)

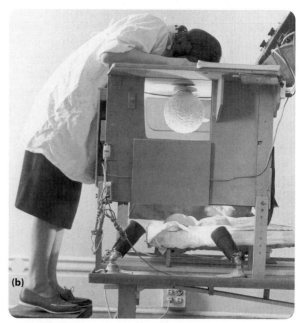

(b)

Habituation

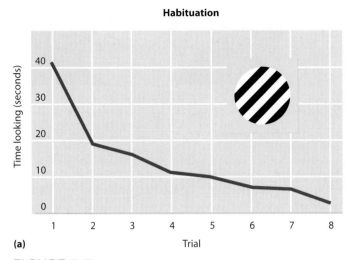

(a)

Dishabituation

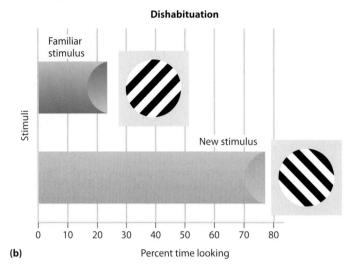

(b)

FIGURE **5.7**

HABITUATION AND DISHABITUATION. In the first part of one study (a), 7-hour-old newborns were shown a stimulus. As indicated, the newborns looked at it an average of 41 seconds when it was first presented to them (Slater, Morison, & Somers, 1988). Over seven more presentations of the stimulus, they looked at it less and less. In the second part of the study (b), infants were presented with both the familiar stimulus to which they had just become habituated and a new stimulus (which was rotated 90 degrees). The newborns looked at the new stimulus three times as much as the familiar stimulus.

less frequently. At this point, the experimenter changes the sound that is being generated. If the babies renew vigorous sucking, we infer that they have discriminated the sound change and are sucking more because they want to hear the interesting new sound. (Menn & Stoel-Gammon, 2009, p. 67)

The Orienting Response

A technique that can be used to determine if an infant can see or hear is the *orienting response,* which involves turning one's head toward a sight or sound. Another technique, *tracking,* measures eye movements that follow (track) a moving object; it can be used to evaluate an infant's early visual ability. A startle response can be used to determine an infant's reaction to a noise (Bendersky & Sullivan, 2007).

Equipment

Technology can facilitate the use of most methods for investigating the infant's perceptual abilities. Videotape equipment allows researchers to investigate elusive

FIGURE **5.8**

AN INFANT WEARING EYE-TRACKING HEADGEAR. Using the ultralight, wireless, head-mounted eye-tracking equipment shown here, researchers can record where infants look while the infants freely locomote. (Source: Courtesy of Dr. Karen Adolph's laboratory, New York University.)

behaviors. High-speed computers make it possible to perform complex data analysis in minutes. Other equipment records respiration, heart rate, body movement, visual fixation, and sucking behavior, which provide clues to what the infant is perceiving. Eye-tracking equipment that assesses the infant's eye movements as the infant tracks an object is increasingly being used in infant perception research (Gredeback, Johnson, & von Hofsten, 2010). Figure 5.8 shows an infant wearing an eye-tracking headgear in a recent study on visually guided motor behavior and social interaction (Franchak & others, 2010).

Scientists have become ingenious at assessing the development of infants, discovering ways to "interview" them even though they cannot yet talk. How might researchers account for any individual differences in infant development in their studies?

FIGURE **5.9**

VISUAL ACUITY DURING THE FIRST MONTHS OF LIFE. The four photographs represent a computer estimation of what a picture of a face looks like to a 1-month-old, 2-month-old, 3-month-old, and 1-year-old (whose visual acuity approximates that of an adult).

VISUAL PERCEPTION

Some important changes in visual perception as we age can be traced to differences in how the eye itself functions over time. These changes in the eye's functioning influence, for example, how clearly we can see an object, whether we can differentiate its colors, at what distances, and in what light. But the differences between what the newborn sees and what a toddler or an adult sees go far beyond those that can be explained by changes in the eye's functioning, as we discuss in this section.

Infancy Psychologist William James (1890/1950) called the newborn's perceptual world a "blooming, buzzing confusion." More than a century later, we can safely say that he was wrong (Johnson, 2011a, b; Slater & others, 2010). Even the newborn perceives a world with some order. That world, however, is far different from the one perceived by the toddler or the adult.

Visual Acuity Just how well can infants see? At birth, the nerves and muscles and lens of the eye are still developing. As a result, newborns cannot see small things that are far away. The newborn's vision is estimated to be 20/240 on the well-known Snellen chart used for eye examinations, which means that a newborn can see at 20 feet what a normal adult can see at 240 feet (Aslin & Lathrop, 2008). In other words, an object 20 feet away is only as clear to the newborn as it would be if it were 240 feet away from an adult with normal vision (20/20). By 6 months of age, though, on average vision is 20/40 (Aslin & Lathrop, 2008).

Infants show an interest in human faces soon after birth (Lee & others, 2011a). Figure 5.9 shows a computer estimation of what a picture of a face looks like to an infant at different ages from a distance of about 6 inches. Infants spend more time looking at their mother's face than a stranger's face as early as 12 hours after being born (Bushnell, 2003). By 3 months of age, infants match voices to faces, distinguish between male and female faces, and discriminate between faces of their own ethnic group and those of other ethnic groups (Kelly & others, 2007, 2009; Liu & others, 2011).

Also, as we discussed in the *Connecting with Research* interlude, young infants can perceive certain patterns. With the help of his "looking chamber," Robert Fantz (1963) revealed that even 2- to 3-week-old infants prefer to look at patterned displays rather than nonpatterned displays. For example, they prefer to look at a normal human face rather than one with scrambled features, and prefer to look at a bull's-eye target or black and white stripes rather than a plain circle.

Color Vision The infant's color vision also improves (Aslin & Lathrop, 2008). By 8 weeks, and possibly by even 4 weeks, infants can discriminate some colors (Kelly, Borchert, & Teller, 1997). By 4 months of age, they have color preferences that mirror those of adults in some cases, preferring saturated colors such as royal blue over pale blue, for example (Bornstein, 1975). A recent study of the reactions to

visual preference method A method developed by Fantz to determine whether infants can distinguish one stimulus from another by measuring the length of time they attend to different stimuli.

habituation Decreased responsiveness to a stimulus after repeated presentations of the stimulus.

dishabituation The recovery of a habituated response after a change in stimulation.

blue, yellow, red, and green hues by 4- to 5-month-old infants revealed that they looked longest at reddish hues and shortest at greenish hues (Franklin & others, 2010). In part, the changes in vision described here reflect maturation. Experience, however, is also necessary for color vision to develop normally (Sugita, 2004).

Perceptual Constancy   Some perceptual accomplishments are especially intriguing because they indicate that the infant's perception goes beyond the information provided by the senses (Johnson, 2011a, b; Slater & others, 2011). This is the case in *perceptual constancy*, in which sensory stimulation is changing but perception of the physical world remains constant. If infants did not develop perceptual constancy, each time they saw an object at a different distance or in a different orientation, they would perceive it as a different object. Thus, the development of perceptual constancy allows infants to perceive their world as stable. Two types of perceptual constancy are size constancy and shape constancy.

Size constancy is the recognition that an object remains the same even though the retinal image of the object changes as you move toward or away from the object. The farther away from us an object is, the smaller its image is on our eyes. Thus, the size of an object on the retina is not sufficient to tell us its actual size. For example, you perceive a bicycle standing right in front of you as smaller than the car parked across the street, even though the bicycle casts a larger image on your eyes than the car does. When you move away from the bicycle, you do not perceive it to be shrinking even though its image on your retinas shrinks; you perceive its size as constant. But what about babies? Do they have size constancy? Researchers have found that babies as young as 3 months of age show size constancy (Bower, 1966; Day & McKenzie, 1973). However, at 3 months of age, a baby's ability is not full-blown. It continues to develop until 10 or 11 years of age (Kellman & Banks, 1998).

Shape constancy is the recognition that an object remains the same shape even though its orientation to us changes. Look around the room you are in right now. You likely see objects of varying shapes, such as tables and chairs. If you get up and walk around the room, you will see these objects from different sides and angles. Even though your retinal image of the objects changes as you walk and look, you will still perceive the objects as the same shape.

Do babies have shape constancy? As with size constancy, researchers have found that babies as young as 3 months of age have shape constancy (Bower, 1966; Day & McKenzie, 1973). Three-month-old infants, however, do not have shape constancy for irregularly shaped objects such as tilted planes (Cook & Birch, 1984).

Perception of Occluded Objects   Look around the context where you are now. You likely see that some objects are partly occluded by other objects that are in front of them—possibly a desk behind a chair, some books behind a computer, or a car parked behind a tree. Do infants perceive an object as complete when it is partly occluded by an object in front of it?

In the first two months of postnatal development, infants don't perceive occluded objects as complete, instead perceiving only what is visible (Johnson, 2011a, b). Beginning at about 2 months of age, infants develop the ability to perceive that occluded objects are whole (Slater & others, 2010). How does perceptual completion develop? In Scott Johnson's (2010a, b, 2011a, b) research, learning, experience, and self-directed exploration via eye movements play key roles in the development of perceptual completion in young infants.

Many of the objects in the world that are occluded appear and disappear behind closer objects, as when you are walking down the street and see cars appear and disappear behind buildings as they move or you move. Can infants predictively track briefly occluded moving objects? They develop the ability to track briefly occluded moving objects at about 3 to 5 months of age (Bertenthal, 2008). A recent study explored 5- to 9-month-old infants' ability to track moving objects that disappeared gradually behind an occluded partition, disappeared abruptly, or imploded (shrank quickly in size) (see Figure 5.10) (Bertenthal, Longo, & Kenny, 2007). In this study,

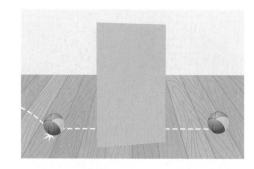

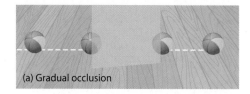
(a) Gradual occlusion

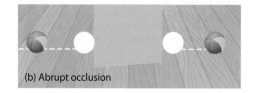
(b) Abrupt occlusion

(c) Implosion

FIGURE 5.10
INFANTS' PREDICTIVE TRACKING OF A BRIEFLY OCCLUDED MOVING BALL

size constancy Recognition that an object remains the same even though the retinal image of the object changes as you move toward or away from the object.

shape constancy Recognition that an object remains the same even though its orientation to us changes.

FIGURE **5.11**

EXAMINING INFANTS' DEPTH PERCEPTION ON THE VISUAL CLIFF.
Eleanor Gibson and Richard Walk (1960) found that most infants would not crawl out on the glass, which, according to Gibson and Walk, indicated that they had depth perception. However, critics point out that the visual cliff is a better indication of the infant's social referencing and fear of heights than of the infant's perception of depth.

the infants were more likely to accurately predict the reappearance of the moving object when it disappeared gradually rather than disappearing abruptly or imploding.

Depth Perception Might infants even perceive depth? To investigate this question, Eleanor Gibson and Richard Walk (1960) constructed a miniature cliff with a drop-off covered by glass in their laboratory. They placed infants on the edge of this visual cliff and had their mothers coax them to crawl onto the glass (see Figure 5.11). Most infants would not crawl out on the glass, choosing instead to remain on the shallow side, an indication that they could perceive depth. However, critics point out that the visual cliff likely is a better test of social referencing and fear of heights than of depth perception.

The 6- to 12-month-old infants in the visual cliff experiment had extensive visual experience. Do younger infants without this experience still perceive depth? Since younger infants do not crawl, this question is difficult to answer. Two- to four-month-old infants show differences in heart rate when they are placed directly on the deep side of the visual cliff instead of on the shallow side (Campos, Langer, & Krowitz, 1970). However, these differences might mean that young infants respond to differences in some visual characteristics of the deep and shallow cliffs, with no actual knowledge of depth. Although researchers do not know exactly how early in life infants can perceive depth, we do know that infants develop the ability to use binocular cues to depth by about 3 to 4 months of age.

Childhood Changes in children's perceptual development continue in childhood (Lee & others, 2011b).Children become increasingly efficient at detecting the boundaries between colors (such as red and orange) at 3 to 4 years of age (Gibson, 1969). When they are about 4 or 5 years old, most children's eye muscles are adequately developed so that they can move their eyes efficiently across a series of letters. Many preschool children are farsighted, unable to see close up as well as they can see far away. By the time they enter the first grade, though, most children can focus their eyes and sustain their attention effectively on close-up objects.

What are the signs of vision problems in children? They include rubbing the eyes, blinking or squinting excessively, appearing irritable when playing games that require good distance vision, shutting or covering one eye, and tilting the head or thrusting it forward when looking at something. A child who shows any of these behaviors should be examined by an ophthalmologist.

After infancy, children's visual expectations about the physical world continue to develop. In one study, 2- to 4½-year-old children were given a task in which the goal was to find a toy ball that had been dropped through an opaque tube (Hood, 1995). As shown in Figure 5.12, if the ball is dropped into the tube at the top right, it will land in the box at the bottom left. However, in this task, most of the 2-year-olds, and even some of the 4-year-olds, persisted in searching in the box immediately beneath the dropping point. For them, gravity ruled and they had failed to perceive the end location of the curved tube.

How do children learn to deal with situations like that in Figure 5.12, and how do they come to understand other laws of the physical world? These questions are addressed by studies of cognitive development, which we discuss in Chapters 6, "Cognitive Developmental Approaches," and 7, "Information Processing."

FIGURE **5.12**

VISUAL EXPECTATIONS ABOUT THE PHYSICAL WORLD. When young children see the ball dropped into the tube, many of them will search for it immediately below the dropping point.

Adulthood Vision changes little after childhood until the effects of aging emerge. With aging, declines in visual acuity, color vision, and depth perception occur. Several diseases of the eye also may emerge in aging adults.

Visual Acuity   **Accommodation of the eye**—the eye's ability to focus and maintain an image on the retina—declines most sharply between 40 and 59 years of age. This loss of accommodation is what is commonly known as *presbyopia*. In particular, middle-aged individuals begin to have difficulty viewing close objects. The eye's blood supply also diminishes, although usually not until the fifties or sixties. The reduced blood supply may decrease the visual field's size and account for an increase in the eye's *blind spot*, the location where the retina does not register any light. And there is some evidence that the retina becomes less sensitive to low levels of illumination (Hughes, 1978). As a result, middle-aged adults begin to have difficulty reading or working in dim light. Presbyopia is correctable with bifocals, reading glasses, laser surgery, or implantation of intraocular lenses (Hantera & others, 2010).

In late adulthood, the decline in vision that began for most adults in early or middle adulthood becomes more pronounced (Dillon & others, 2010). Night driving is especially difficult, to some extent because tolerance for glare diminishes (Babizhayev, Minasyan, & Richer, 2009; Wood & others, 2010). *Dark adaptation* is slower—that is, older individuals take longer to recover their vision when going from a well-lighted room to semidarkness. The area of the visual field becomes smaller, an indication that the intensity of a stimulus in the peripheral area of the visual field needs to be increased if the stimulus is to be seen. Events taking place away from the center of the visual field might not be detected (Fozard & Gordon-Salant, 2001).

This visual decline often can be traced to a reduction in the quality or intensity of light reaching the retina. At 60 years of age, the retina receives only about one-third as much light as it did at 20 years of age (Scialfa & Kline, 2007). In extreme old age, these changes might be accompanied by degenerative changes in the retina, causing severe difficulty in seeing. Large-print books and magnifiers might be needed in such cases.

One extensive study of visual changes in adults found that the age of older adults was a significant factor in how extensively their visual functioning differed from that of younger adults (Brabyn & others, 2001). Beyond 75, and more so beyond age 85, older adults showed significantly worse performance on a number of visual tasks when compared with young adults and older adults in their sixties and early seventies. The greatest decline in visual perception beyond age 75, and especially beyond age 85, involved glare. The older adults, especially those 85 and older, fared much worse in being able to see clearly when glare was present, and they took much longer to recover from glare than did younger adults (see Figure 5.13). For example, whereas young adults recover vision following glare in less than 10 seconds, 50 percent of 90-year-olds have not recovered vision after 1.5 minutes.

Older adults also show a decline in motion sensitivity (Henderson & others, 2010). In terms of practical applications of this decline, researchers have found that compared with younger drivers, older drivers underestimate the time needed for an approaching vehicle to reach their location (Staplin, Lococo, & Sim, 1993). This decline in the accuracy of effortless perceptual guidance means that older adult drivers need to expend cognitive effort when driving, especially when approaching intersections.

Recent research has shown that sensory decline in older adults is linked to a decline in cognitive functioning. One study of individuals in their 70s revealed that visual decline was related to slower speed of processing information, which in turn was associated with greater cognitive decline (Clay & others, 2009).

Color Vision   Color vision also may decline with age in older adults as a result of the yellowing of the lens of the eye (Scialfa & Kline, 2007). This decline is most likely to occur in the green-blue-violet part of the color spectrum. As a result, older adults may have trouble accurately matching closely related colors such as navy socks and black socks.

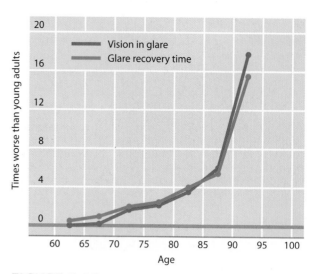

FIGURE 5.13

RATES OF DECLINE IN VISUAL FUNCTIONING RELATED TO GLARE IN ADULTS OF DIFFERENT AGES. Older adults, especially those 85 and older, fare much worse than younger adults in being able to see clearly when glare is present, and their recovery from glare is much slower. These data were collected from a random sample of community-dwelling older adults living in Marin County, California. For each age, the factor by which the group's median performance was worse than normative values for young adults is shown.

What are some concerns about older adults' driving based on changes in visual perception?

developmental connection

Information Processing. Perceptual speed declines in middle adulthood and late adulthood. Chapter 8, p. 261

accommodation of the eye The eye's ability to focus and maintain an image on the retina.

FIGURE **5.14**

MACULAR DEGENERATION. This simulation of the effect of macular degeneration shows how individuals with this eye disease can see their peripheral field of vision but can't clearly see what is in their central visual field.

Depth Perception   As with many areas of perception, depth perception changes little after infancy until adults become older. Depth perception typically declines in late adulthood; thus, it can be difficult for the older adult to determine how close or far away or how high or low something is (Bian & Andersen, 2008). A decline in depth perception can make steps or street curbs difficult to manage.

Diseases of the Eye   Three diseases that can impair the vision of older adults are cataracts, glaucoma, and macular degeneration:

- **Cataracts** are a thickening of the lens of the eye that causes vision to become cloudy, opaque, and distorted (Sugimoto, Kuze, & Uji, 2008). By age 70, approximately 30 percent of individuals experience a partial loss of vision due to cataracts. Initially, cataracts can be treated by glasses; if they worsen, a simple surgical procedure can remove the cloudy lens and replace it with an artificial one (Chung & others, 2009). Diabetes is a risk factor for the development of cataracts (de Fine Olivarius & others, 2011; Grausland, 2011).

- **Glaucoma** damages the optic nerve because of the pressure created by a buildup of fluid in the eye (Fechtner & others, 2010; Lavik, Kuehn, & Kwon, 2011). Approximately 1 percent of individuals in their seventies and 10 percent of those in their nineties have glaucoma, which can be treated with eye drops. If left untreated, glaucoma can ultimately destroy a person's vision (Musch & others, 2009).

- **Macular degeneration** is a disease that causes deterioration of the macula of the retina, which corresponds to the focal center of the visual field (see Figure 5.14). Individuals with macular degeneration may have relatively normal peripheral vision but be unable to see clearly what is right in front of them (Ambati, 2011; Ghosh & others, 2010). Macular degeneration affects 1 in 25 individuals from 66 to 74 years of age and 1 in 6 of those 75 years old and older. If the disease is detected early, it can be treated with laser surgery (Sorensen & Kemp, 2010). However, macular degeneration is difficult to treat and thus a leading cause of blindness in older adults (Lucifero, 2010). A recent study found that macular degeneration was linked to increased risk of falls in adults 77 years and older (Wood & others, 2011).

HEARING

Can the fetus hear? What kind of changes in hearing take place in infancy? When does hearing begin to decline in adulthood?

The Fetus, Infant, and Child   During the last two months of pregnancy, as the fetus nestles in its mother's womb, it can hear sounds such as the mother's voice, music, and so on (Kisilevsky & others, 2009; Morokuma & others, 2008). Two psychologists wanted to find out whether a fetus that heard Dr. Seuss' classic story *The Cat in the Hat* while still in the mother's womb would prefer hearing the story after birth (DeCasper & Spence, 1986). During the last months of pregnancy, sixteen women read *The Cat in the Hat* to their fetuses. Then, shortly after the infants were born, the mothers read aloud either *The Cat in the Hat* or a story with a different rhyme and pace, *The King, the Mice and the Cheese* (which they had not read aloud during prenatal development). The infants sucked on a nipple in a different way when the mothers read the two stories, suggesting that they recognized the pattern and tone of *The Cat in the Hat* (see Figure 5.15). This study illustrates not only that a fetus can hear but also that it has a remarkable ability to learn even before birth.

What kind of changes in hearing take place during infancy? They involve perception of a sound's loudness, pitch, and localization:

- *Loudness.* Immediately after birth, infants cannot hear soft sounds quite as well as adults can; a stimulus must be louder to be heard by a newborn than by an adult (Trehub & others, 1991). For example, an adult can hear a whisper from

cataracts A thickening of the lens of the eye that causes vision to become cloudy, opaque, and distorted.

glaucoma Damage to the optic nerve because of the pressure created by a buildup of fluid in the eye.

macular degeneration A vision problem in the elderly that involves deterioration of the macula of the retina.

(a)   (b)

FIGURE **5.15**

HEARING IN THE WOMB. (*a*) Pregnant mothers read *The Cat in the Hat* to their fetuses during the last few months of pregnancy. (*b*) When they were born, the babies preferred listening to a recording of their mothers reading *The Cat in the Hat,* as evidenced by their sucking on a nipple that produced this recording, rather than another story, *The King, the Mice and the Cheese.*

about 4 to 5 feet away, but a newborn requires that sounds be closer to a normal conversational level to be heard at that distance.

- *Pitch*. Infants are also less sensitive to the pitch of a sound than adults are. Pitch is the perception of the frequency of a sound. A soprano voice sounds high-pitched, a bass voice low-pitched. Infants are less sensitive to low-pitched sounds and are more likely to hear high-pitched sounds (Aslin, Jusczyk, & Pisoni, 1998). By 2 years of age, infants have considerably improved their ability to distinguish sounds with different pitches.

- *Localization*. Even newborns can determine the general location from which a sound is coming, but by 6 months of age they are more proficient at localizing sounds or detecting their origins. Their ability to localize sounds continues to improve during the second year (Saffran, Werker, & Werner, 2006).

Most children's hearing is adequate, but early hearing screening in infancy needs to be conducted (McGrath, Voh, & O'Neil, 2010; Russ & others, 2010). About 1 in 1,000 newborns is deaf and 6 in 1,000 have some degree of hearing loss. Hearing aids or surgery can improve hearing for many of them (Halpin & others, 2010).

Cochlear implants—small, electronic devices that directly stimulate the auditory nerve—are now done routinely for congenitally deaf children, even as early as 12 months of age. Many of the hearing-impaired children who have early cochlear implant surgery show good progress in learning speech and in understanding others' speech, which allows them to function effectively in a hearing world (Asp, Eskilsson, & Berninger, 2011; Bergeson, Houston, & Miyamoto, 2010).

Otitis media is a middle-ear infection that can impair hearing temporarily. If it continues too long, it can interfere with language development and socialization (Casey & others, 2011; Koch & others, 2010). As many as one-third of all U.S. children from birth to 3 years of age have three or more episodes. In some cases, the infection can develop into a more chronic condition in which the middle ear becomes filled with fluid, and this can seriously impair hearing. Treatments for otitis media include antibiotics and placement of a tube in the inner ear to drain fluid (Grevers, 2010; Wald, 2011).

Adulthood and Aging   Few changes in hearing are believed to take place during the adult years until middle adulthood (Feeney & Sanford, 2004). Hearing can start

What are some concerns about adolescents who listen to loud music?

to decline by the age of 40. Sensitivity to high pitches usually declines first. The ability to hear low-pitched sounds does not seem to decline much in middle adulthood, however. Men usually lose their sensitivity to high-pitched sounds sooner than women do, but this sex difference might be due to men's greater exposure to noise in occupations such as mining and automobile work.

Hearing impairment usually does not become much of an impediment until late adulthood (Dillon & others, 2010). Only 19 percent of individuals from 45 to 54 years of age experience some type of hearing problem (Harris, 1975). A recent national survey revealed that 63 percent of adults age 70 years and older had a hearing loss defined as a frequency of more than 25 dB in their better ear (Lin & others, 2011). In this study, hearing aids were used by 40 percent of those with moderate hearing loss. Fifteen percent of the population over the age of 65 is estimated to be legally deaf, usually due to degeneration of the *cochlea*, the primary neural receptor for hearing in the inner ear (Adams, 2009).

Two devices can be used to minimize the problems linked to hearing loss: (1) hearing aids that amplify sound to reduce middle-ear-based conductive hearing loss, and (2) cochlear implants that restore some hearing following neurosensory hearing loss (Lockey, Jennings, & Shaw, 2010; Lu, Litovsky, & Zeng, 2010). Currently, researchers are exploring the use of stem cells as an alternative to the use of cochlear implants (Pandit & others, 2011; Parker, 2011).

Earlier, in the discussion of vision, we considered research on the importance of the age of older adults in determining the degree of their visual decline. Age also is a factor in the degree of hearing decline in older adults (Lavoie, Mehta, & Thornton, 2008). As indicated in Figure 5.16, the declines in vision and hearing are much greater in individuals 75 years and older than in individuals 65 to 74 years of age (Charness & Bosman, 1992).

Older adults often don't recognize that they have a hearing problem, deny that they have one, or accept it as a part of growing old (Fowler & Leigh-Paffenroth, 2007). Older women are more likely to seek treatment for their hearing problem than are older adult men (Fowler & Leigh-Paffenroth, 2007).

Vision impairment and hearing loss among older adults can significantly influence their health and functioning (Huang & Tang, 2010; Schumm & others, 2009). One study found that 20 percent of individuals 70 years and older had both visual and hearing impairment, and the dual impairment was associated with greater difficulty in performing daily activities, such as preparing meals, shopping, and using a telephone (Brennan, Horowitz, & Su, 2005). Another study revealed that individuals 70 years and older with only hearing loss reported that they were less healthy, engaged in fewer activities, and participated less in social roles than their counterparts without sensory loss (Crews & Campbell, 2004). In this study, older adults with only vision loss showed even more impairment in health and functioning than those with only hearing loss, and those with both vision and hearing loss had the greatest

Perceptual System	Young-Old (65 to 74 years)		Old-Old (75 years and older)
Vision	There is a loss of acuity even with corrective lenses. Less transmission of light occurs through the retina (half as much as in young adults). Greater susceptibility to glare occurs. Color discrimination ability decreases.		There is a significant loss of visual acuity and color discrimination, and a decrease in the size of the perceived visual field. In late old age, people are at significant risk for visual dysfunction from cataracts and glaucoma.
Hearing	There is a significant loss of hearing at high frequencies and some loss at middle frequencies. These losses can be helped by a hearing aid. There is greater susceptibility to masking of what is heard by noise.		There is a significant loss at high and middle frequencies. A hearing aid is more likely to be needed than in young-old age.

FIGURE **5.16**
VISION AND HEARING DECLINE IN THE YOUNG-OLD AND THE OLD-OLD

declines in health and functioning. Hearing loss in older adults is also linked to increased depression (Levy, Slade, & Gill, 2006).

OTHER SENSES

As we develop, we not only obtain information about the world from our eyes and our ears but also through sensory receptors in our skin, nose, and tongue.

Touch and Pain Do newborns respond to touch (called tactile stimulation)? Can they feel pain? How does the perception of touch and pain change with age?

Infancy Newborns do respond to touch. A touch to the cheek produces a turning of the head; a touch to the lips produces sucking movements.

Newborns can also feel pain (Gunnar & Quevado, 2007). If and when you have a son and consider whether he should be circumcised, the issue of an infant's pain perception probably will become important to you. Circumcision usually is performed on young boys about the third day after birth. Will your young son experience pain if he is circumcised when he is 3 days old? An investigation by Megan Gunnar and her colleagues (1987) found that newborn infant males cried intensely during circumcision. The circumcised infants also display amazing resiliency. Within several minutes after the surgery, they can nurse and interact in a normal manner with their mothers. And, if allowed to, the newly circumcised newborns drift into a deep sleep, which seems to serve as a coping mechanism.

For many years, doctors performed operations on newborns without anesthesia. This practice was accepted because of the dangers of anesthesia and because of the supposition that newborns do not feel pain. As researchers demonstrated that newborns can feel pain, the practice of operating on newborns without anesthesia is being challenged. Anesthesia now is used in some circumcisions (Taddio, 2008).

Adulthood There has been little research on developmental changes in touch and pain after infancy until the middle and late adulthood years. Changes in touch and pain are associated with aging (Schmader & others, 2010). One study found that older adults could detect touch much less in the lower extremities (ankles, knees, and so on) than in the upper extremities (wrists, shoulders, and so on) (Corso, 1977). For most older adults, though, a decline in touch sensitivity is not problematic (Hoyer & Roodin, 2009).

Older adults are less sensitive to pain and suffer from it less than younger adults do (Gagliese, 2009). Although decreased sensitivity to pain can help older adults cope with disease and injury, it can be harmful if it masks injury or illness that needs to be treated.

Smell Newborns can differentiate odors (Doty & Shah, 2008). The expressions on their faces seem to indicate that they like the way vanilla and strawberry smell but do not like the way rotten eggs and fish smell (Steiner, 1979). In one investigation, 6-day-old infants who were breast fed showed a clear preference for smelling their mother's breast pad rather than a clean breast pad (MacFarlane, 1975) (see Figure 5.17). However, when they were 2 days old, they did not show this preference, an indication that they require several days of experience to recognize this odor.

A decline in sensitivity to odors may occur as early as the twenties, with declines continuing through each subsequent decade of life into the nineties (Margran & Boulton, 2005). Beginning in the sixties, the decrease in sensitivity to smells becomes more noticeable to most people (Hawkes, 2006). A majority of individuals 80 years of age and older experience a significant reduction in smell (Lafreniere & Mann, 2009). A decline in the sense of smell can reduce the ability to detect smoke from a fire.

The decline in the olfactory system can reduce older adults' enjoyment of food and their life satisfaction. If elderly individuals need to be encouraged to eat more, compounds that stimulate the olfactory nerve are sometimes added to food.

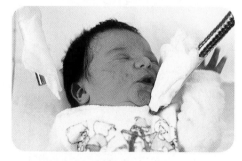

FIGURE **5.17**

NEWBORNS' PREFERENCE FOR THE SMELL OF THEIR MOTHER'S BREAST PAD. In the experiment by MacFarlane (1975), 6-day-old infants preferred to smell their mother's breast pad rather than a clean one that had never been used, but 2-day-old infants did not show the preference, indicating that this odor preference requires several days of experience to develop.

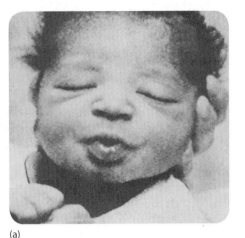 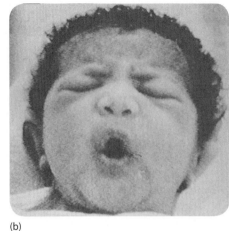 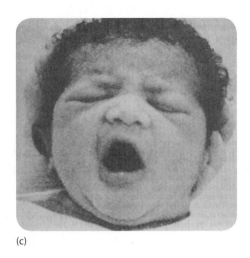

(a)   (b)   (c)

FIGURE **5.18**

NEWBORNS' FACIAL RESPONSES TO BASIC TASTES. Facial expressions elicited by (*a*) a sweet solution, (*b*) a sour solution, and (*c*) a bitter solution.

Taste   Sensitivity to taste is present even before birth (Doty & Shah, 2008). Human newborns learn tastes prenatally through the amniotic fluid and in breast milk after birth (Beauchamp & Mennella, 2009; Mennella, 2009). In one study, even at only 2 hours of age, babies made different facial expressions when they tasted sweet, sour, and bitter solutions (Rosenstein & Oster, 1988) (see Figure 5.18). At about 4 months of age, infants begin to prefer salty tastes, which as newborns they had found to be aversive (Doty & Shah, 2008).

One study found a significant reduction in the ability of older adults to recognize sweet, salty, sour, and bitter tastes (Fukunaga, Uematsu, & Sugimoto, 2005). As with smell, there is less decline in taste in healthy older adults than in unhealthy older adults. However, when even relatively healthy older adults take medications, their taste sensitivity declines (Roberts & Rosenberg, 2006). Many older adults prefer highly seasoned foods (sweeter, spicier, saltier) to compensate for their diminished taste and smell (Hoyer & Roodin, 2009). This preference can lead to increased eating of nonnutritious, highly seasoned "junk food."

Researchers have found that older adults show a greater decline in their sense of smell than in their taste (Schiffman, 2007). Smell, too, declines less in healthy older adults than in their less healthy counterparts.

INTERMODAL PERCEPTION

How is intermodal perception involved in this context in which a boy is listening to headphones while working on a computer?

intermodal perception The ability to integrate information about two or more sensory modalities, such as vision and hearing.

Imagine that you are playing basketball or tennis. You are experiencing many visual inputs—the ball is coming and going, other players are moving around, and so on. However, you are experiencing many auditory inputs as well: the sound of the ball bouncing or being hit, the grunts and groans, and so on. There is good correspondence between much of the visual and auditory information: When you see the ball bounce, you hear a bouncing sound; when a player stretches to hit a ball, you hear a groan. When you look at and listen to what is going on, you do not experience just the sounds or just the sights; you put all these things together. You experience a unitary episode. This is **intermodal perception,** which involves integrating information from two or more sensory modalities, such as vision and hearing. Most perception is intermodal (Bahrick, 2010).

Early, exploratory forms of intermodal perception exist even in newborns (Bahrick & Hollich, 2008). For example, newborns turn their eyes and their head toward the sound of a voice or rattle when the sound is maintained for several seconds (Clifton

& others, 1981), but the newborn can localize a sound and look at an object only in a crude way (Bechtold, Bushnell, & Salapatek, 1979). These early forms of intermodal perception become sharpened with experience in the first year of life (Bremner & others, 2010). In one study, infants as young as 3½ months old looked more at their mother when they also heard her voice and longer at their father when they also heard his voice (Spelke & Owsley, 1979). Thus, even young infants can coordinate visual-auditory information about people.

Can young infants put vision and sound together as precisely as adults do? In the first six months, infants have difficulty connecting sensory input from different modes, but in the second half of the first year they show an increased ability to make this connection mentally.

What roles do nature and nurture play in the infant's perceptual development?

NATURE/NURTURE AND PERCEPTUAL DEVELOPMENT

Now that we have discussed many aspects of perceptual development, let's explore one of developmental psychology's key issues as it relates to perceptual development: the nature-nurture issue. There has been a long-standing interest in how strongly infants' perception is influenced by nature or nurture (Aslin, 2009; Johnson, 2011a, b; Slater & others, 2011). In the field of perceptual development, nature proponents are referred to as *nativists* and those who emphasize learning and experience are called *empiricists*.

In the nativist view, the ability to perceive the world in a competent, organized way is inborn or innate. At the beginning of our discussion of perceptual development, we examined the ecological view of the Gibsons because it has played such a pivotal role in guiding research in perceptual development. In some quarters, the Gibsons' ecological view has been described as leaning toward a nativist explanation of perceptual development because it holds that perception is direct and evolved over time to allow the detection of size and shape constancy, a three-dimensional world, intermodal perception, and so on early in infancy. However, the Gibsons' view is not entirely nativist because they emphasized that perceptual development involves distinctive features that are detected at different ages (Slater & others, 2011). Further, the Gibsons argued that a key question in infant perception is what information is available in the environment and how infants learn to generate, differentiate, and discriminate the information—certainly not a nativist view.

The Gibsons' ecological view is quite different from Piaget's constructivist view (discussed in Chapter 1), which reflects an empiricist approach to explaining perceptual development. According to Piaget, much of perceptual development in infancy must await the development of a sequence of cognitive stages for infants to construct more complex perceptual tasks. Thus, in Piaget's view, the ability to perceive size and shape constancy, a three-dimensional world, intermodal perception, and so on develops later in infancy than the Gibsons envision.

Today, it is clear that an extreme empiricist position on perceptual development is unwarranted. Much of early perception develops from innate (nature) foundations, and the basic foundation of many perceptual abilities can be detected in newborns, whereas others unfold maturationally (Arterberry, 2008). However, as infants develop, environmental experiences (nurture) refine or calibrate many perceptual functions, and they may be the driving force behind some functions. The accumulation of experience with and knowledge about their perceptual world contributes to infants' ability to perceive coherent perceptions of people and things (Johnson, 2011a, b; Slater & others, 2011). Thus, a full portrait of perceptual development includes the influence of nature, nurture, and a developing sensitivity to information (Arterberry, 2008).

developmental connection

Theories. Piaget's theory states that children construct their understanding of the world through four stages of cognitive development. Chapter 1, p. 22; Chapter 6, p. 184

Review

- What are sensation and perception?
- What is the ecological view of perception? What are some research methods used to study infant perception?
- How does vision develop?
- How does hearing develop?
- How do sensitivity to touch and pain develop? How does smell develop? How does taste develop?
- What is intermodal perception, and how does it develop?
- What roles do nature and nurture play in perceptual development?

Connect

- How might the development of vision and hearing contribute to infants' gross motor development?

Reflect *Your Own Personal Journey of Life*

- Imagine that you are the parent of a 1-year-old infant. How would you stimulate your 1-year-old's vision and hearing?

Perceptual-Motor Coupling **LG3** Discuss the connection between perception and action

> The infant is by no means as helpless as it looks and is quite capable of some very complex and important actions.
>
> —**HERB PICK**
> *Contemporary Developmental Psychologist, University of Minnesota*

As we come to the end of this chapter, we return to the important theme of perceptual-motor coupling. The distinction between perceiving and doing has been a time-honored tradition in psychology. However, a number of experts on perceptual and motor development question whether this distinction makes sense (Adolph & Joh, 2009; Bertenthal, 2008; Thelen & Smith, 2006). The main thrust of research in Esther Thelen's dynamic systems approach is to explore how people assemble motor behaviors for perceiving and acting. The main theme of the ecological approach of Eleanor and James J. Gibson is to discover how perception guides action. Action can guide perception, and perception can guide action. Only by moving one's eyes, head, hands, and arms and by moving from one location to another can an individual fully experience his or her environment and learn how to adapt to it. Perception and action are coupled (Corbetta & Snapp-Childs, 2009).

Babies, for example, continually coordinate their movements with perceptual information to learn how to maintain balance, reach for objects in space, and move across various surfaces and terrains (Adolph & Robinson, 2011; Thelen & Smith, 2006). They are motivated to move by what they perceive. Consider the sight of an attractive toy across the room. In this situation, infants must perceive the current state of their bodies and learn how to use their limbs to reach the toy. Although their movements at first are awkward and uncoordinated, babies soon learn to select patterns that are appropriate for reaching their goals.

Equally important is the other part of the perception-action coupling. That is, action educates perception (Adolph & Berger, 2011; Adolph & Robinson, 2011). For example, watching an object while exploring it manually helps infants to discriminate its texture, size, and hardness. Locomoting in the environment teaches babies about how objects and people look from different perspectives, or whether surfaces will support their weight. Individuals perceive in order to move and move in order to perceive. Perceptual and motor development do not occur in isolation from each other but instead are coupled.

How do infants develop new perceptual-motor couplings? Recall from our discussion earlier in this chapter that in the traditional view of Gesell, infants' perceptual-motor development is prescribed by a genetic plan to follow a fixed and sequential

Perception and action are coupled throughout the human life span.

progression of stages in development. The genetic determination view has been replaced by the dynamic systems view that infants learn new perceptual-motor couplings by assembling skills for perceiving and acting. New perceptual-motor coupling is not passively accomplished; rather, the infant actively develops a skill to achieve a goal within the constraints set by the infant's body and the environment (Adolph & Berger, 2011; Adolph & Robinson, 2011).

Driving a car illustrates the coupling of perceptual and motor skills. The decline in perceptual-motor skills in late adulthood makes driving a car difficult for many older adults (Dawson & others, 2010; Vrklijan & others, 2010). Drivers over the age of 65 are involved in more accidents than middle-aged adults because of mistakes such as improper turns, not yielding the right of way, and not obeying traffic signs; their younger counterparts are more likely to have accidents because they are speeding (Sterns, Barrett, & Alexander, 1985; Lavalliere & others, 2011). Older adults can compensate for declines in perceptual-motor skills by driving shorter distances, choosing less congested routes, and driving only in daylight.

Review Connect Reflect

 Discuss the connection between perception and action

Review

- How are perception and action coupled in development?

Connect

- If perception and action are so closely linked, can parents in fact enhance their infants' motor development, or does it always follow its own course?

Reflect *Your Own Personal Journey of Life*

- Describe two examples not given in the text in which perception guides action. Then describe two examples not given in the text in which action guides perception.

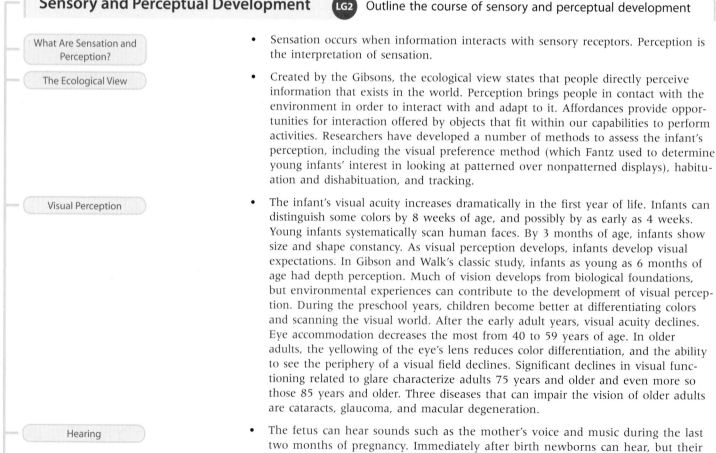

Motor Development

LG1 Describe how motor skills develop

The Dynamic Systems View

- Thelen's dynamic systems theory seeks to explain how motor behaviors are assembled by infants for perceiving and acting. Perception and action are coupled. According to this theory, motor skills are the result of many converging factors, such as the development of the nervous system, the body's physical properties and its movement possibilities, the goal the child is motivated to reach, and environmental support for the skill. In the dynamic systems view, motor development is far more complex than the result of a genetic blueprint.

Reflexes

- Reflexes govern the newborn's movements. They include the sucking, rooting, and Moro reflexes.

Gross Motor Skills

- Gross motor skills involve large-muscle activities. Key skills developed during infancy include control of posture and walking. Gross motor skills improve dramatically in the childhood years. The peak of physical performance often occurs from 19 to 26 years of age. In general, older adults show a slowing of movement.

Fine Motor Skills

- Fine motor skills involve finely tuned motor actions. The onset of reaching and grasping marks a significant accomplishment. Fine motor skills continue to develop through the childhood years and then experience some decline with aging. Neural noise and strategy have been proposed as possible explanations for the slowing of motor behavior in older adults.

Sensory and Perceptual Development

LG2 Outline the course of sensory and perceptual development

What Are Sensation and Perception?

- Sensation occurs when information interacts with sensory receptors. Perception is the interpretation of sensation.

The Ecological View

- Created by the Gibsons, the ecological view states that people directly perceive information that exists in the world. Perception brings people in contact with the environment in order to interact with and adapt to it. Affordances provide opportunities for interaction offered by objects that fit within our capabilities to perform activities. Researchers have developed a number of methods to assess the infant's perception, including the visual preference method (which Fantz used to determine young infants' interest in looking at patterned over nonpatterned displays), habituation and dishabituation, and tracking.

Visual Perception

- The infant's visual acuity increases dramatically in the first year of life. Infants can distinguish some colors by 8 weeks of age, and possibly by as early as 4 weeks. Young infants systematically scan human faces. By 3 months of age, infants show size and shape constancy. As visual perception develops, infants develop visual expectations. In Gibson and Walk's classic study, infants as young as 6 months of age had depth perception. Much of vision develops from biological foundations, but environmental experiences can contribute to the development of visual perception. During the preschool years, children become better at differentiating colors and scanning the visual world. After the early adult years, visual acuity declines. Eye accommodation decreases the most from 40 to 59 years of age. In older adults, the yellowing of the eye's lens reduces color differentiation, and the ability to see the periphery of a visual field declines. Significant declines in visual functioning related to glare characterize adults 75 years and older and even more so those 85 years and older. Three diseases that can impair the vision of older adults are cataracts, glaucoma, and macular degeneration.

Hearing

- The fetus can hear sounds such as the mother's voice and music during the last two months of pregnancy. Immediately after birth newborns can hear, but their sensory threshold is higher than that of adults. Developmental changes in the perception of loudness, pitch, and localization of sound occur during infancy. Most children's hearing is adequate, but one special concern is otitis media. Hearing can start to decline by the age of 40, especially sensitivity to high-pitched sounds. However, hearing impairment usually doesn't become much of an impediment until late adulthood. Hearing aids can diminish hearing problems for many older adults.

Other Senses

- Newborns can respond to touch and feel pain. Sensitivity to pain decreases in late adulthood. Newborns can differentiate odors, and sensitivity to taste is present before birth. Smell and taste may decline in late adulthood, although in healthy individuals the decline is minimal.

Intermodal Perception

- Crude, exploratory forms of intermodal perception—the ability to relate and integrate information from two or more sensory modalities—are present in newborns and become sharpened over the first year of life.

Nature/Nurture and Perceptual Development

- In perception, nature advocates are referred to as nativists and nurture proponents are called empiricists. The Gibsons' ecological view that has guided much of perceptual development research leans toward a nativist approach but still allows for developmental changes in distinctive features. Piaget's constructivist view leans toward an empiricist approach, emphasizing that many perceptual accomplishments must await the development of cognitive stages in infancy. A strong empiricist approach is unwarranted. A full account of perceptual development includes the roles of nature, nurture, and the developing sensitivity to information.

Perceptual-Motor Coupling

 LG3 Discuss the connection between perception and action

- Perception and action often are not isolated but rather are coupled. Action can guide perception and perception can guide action. Individuals perceive in order to move and move in order to perceive.

key terms

dynamic systems theory 153	gross motor skills 155	visual preference method 164	accommodation of the eye 169
rooting reflex 154	fine motor skills 160	habituation 164	cataracts 170
sucking reflex 154	sensation 163	dishabituation 164	glaucoma 170
Moro reflex 154	perception 163	size constancy 167	macular degeneration 170
grasping reflex 155	ecological view 163	shape constancy 167	intermodal perception 174
	affordances 163		

key people

Esther Thelen 153	Eleanor and James J. Gibson 163	William James 166	Richard Walk 168
Karen Adolph 156	Robert Fantz 164	Scott Johnson 167	Megan Gunnar 173

Learning is an ornament in prosperity, a refuge in adversity.

—ARISTOTLE
Greek Philosopher, 4th Century B.C.

Cognitive Processes and Development

Children thirst to know and understand. They construct their own ideas about the world around them and are remarkable for their curiosity, intelligence, and language. And it is always in season for the old to learn. In Section 3, you will read four chapters: "Cognitive Developmental Approaches" (Chapter 6), "Information Processing" (Chapter 7), "Intelligence" (Chapter 8), and "Language Development" (Chapter 9).

chapter 6

COGNITIVE DEVELOPMENTAL APPROACHES

preview

Cognitive developmental approaches place a special emphasis on how individuals actively construct their thinking. They also focus heavily on how thinking changes from one point in development to another. In this chapter, we will focus on the cognitive developmental approaches of Jean Piaget and Lev Vygotsky. We also will explore the possibility that adults think in a qualitatively more advanced way than adolescents do.

Piaget's Theory of Cognitive Development

LG1 Discuss the key processes and four stages in Piaget's theory

- Processes of Development
- Sensorimotor Stage
- Preoperational Stage
- Concrete Operational Stage
- Formal Operational Stage

Poet Nora Perry asks, "Who knows the thoughts of a child?" As much as anyone, Piaget knew. Through careful observations of his own three children—Laurent, Lucienne, and Jacqueline—and observations of and interviews with other children, Piaget changed perceptions of the way children think about the world.

Piaget's theory is a general, unifying story of how biology and experience sculpt cognitive development. Piaget thought that, just as our physical bodies have structures that enable us to adapt to the world, we build mental structures that help us to adapt to the world. *Adaptation* involves adjusting to new environmental demands. Piaget stressed that children actively construct their own cognitive worlds; information is not just poured into their minds from the environment. He sought to discover how children at different points in their development think about the world and how systematic changes in their thinking occur.

> We are born capable of learning.
>
> —**JEAN-JACQUES ROUSSEAU**
> *Swiss-Born French Philosopher, 18th Century*

Piaget is shown here with his family. Piaget's careful observations of his three children—Lucienne, Laurent, and Jacqueline—contributed to the development of his cognitive theory.

PROCESSES OF DEVELOPMENT

What processes do children use as they construct their knowledge of the world? Piaget developed several concepts to answer this question; especially important are schemes, assimilation, accommodation, organization, equilibrium, and equilibration.

Schemes   As the infant or child seeks to construct an understanding of the world, said Piaget (1954), the developing brain creates **schemes.** These are actions or mental representations that organize knowledge. In Piaget's theory, behavioral schemes (physical activities) characterize infancy and mental schemes (cognitive activities) develop in childhood (Lamb, Bornstein, & Teti, 2002). A baby's schemes are structured by simple actions that can be performed on objects, such as sucking, looking, and grasping. Older children have schemes that include strategies and plans for solving problems. By the time we have reached adulthood, we have constructed an enormous number of diverse schemes, ranging from driving a car to balancing a budget to the concept of fairness.

Assimilation and Accommodation   To explain how children use and adapt their schemes, Piaget offered two concepts: assimilation and accommodation. **Assimilation** occurs when children use their existing schemes to deal with new information or experiences. Think about a toddler who has learned the word *car* to identify the family's car. The toddler might call all moving vehicles on roads "cars," including motorcycles and trucks; the child has assimilated these objects to his or her existing scheme. **Accommodation** occurs when children adjust their schemes to take account of new information and experiences. The child soon learns that motorcycles and trucks are

schemes In Piaget's theory, actions or mental representations that organize knowledge.

assimilation Piagetian concept in which children use existing schemes to incorporate new information.

accommodation Piagetian concept of adjusting schemes to fit new information and experiences.

In Piaget's view, what is a scheme? What schemes might this young infant be displaying?

not cars and fine-tunes the category to exclude motorcycles and trucks, accommodating the scheme.

Assimilation and accommodation operate even in very young infants. Newborns reflexively suck everything that touches their lips; they assimilate all sorts of objects into their sucking scheme. By sucking different objects, they learn about their taste, texture, shape, and so on. After several months of experience, though, they construct their understanding of the world differently. Some objects, such as fingers and the mother's breast, can be sucked, and others, such as fuzzy blankets, should not be sucked. In other words, they accommodate their sucking scheme.

Organization   To make sense of their world, said Piaget, children cognitively organize their experiences. **Organization** in Piaget's theory is the grouping of isolated behaviors and thoughts into a higher-order system. Continual refinement of this organization is an inherent part of development. A child who has only a vague idea about how to use a hammer may also have a vague idea about how to use other tools. After learning how to use each one, the child relates these uses, organizing his knowledge.

Equilibration and Stages of Development   Assimilation and accommodation always take the child to a higher ground, according to Piaget. In trying to understand the world, the child inevitably experiences cognitive conflict, or *disequilibrium*. That is, the child is constantly faced with inconsistencies and counterexamples to his or her existing schemes. For example, if a child believes that pouring water from a short and wide container into a tall and narrow container changes the amount of water, then the child might be puzzled by where the "extra" water came from and whether there is actually more water to drink. The puzzle creates disequilibrium; for Piaget, an internal search for equilibrium creates motivation for change. The child assimilates and accommodates, adjusting old schemes, developing new schemes, and organizing and reorganizing the old and new schemes. Eventually, the organization is fundamentally different from the old organization; it is a new way of thinking.

In short, according to Piaget, children constantly assimilate and accommodate as they seek equilibrium. There is considerable movement between states of cognitive equilibrium and disequilibrium as assimilation and accommodation work in concert to produce cognitive change. **Equilibration** is the name Piaget gave to this mechanism by which children shift from one stage of thought to the next.

The result of these processes, according to Piaget, is that individuals go through four stages of development. A different way of understanding the world makes one stage more advanced than another. Cognition is *qualitatively* different in one stage compared with another. In other words, the way children reason at one stage is different from the way they reason at another stage. Figure 6.1 provides a brief description of the four Piagetian stages.

SENSORIMOTOR STAGE

The **sensorimotor stage** lasts from birth to about 2 years of age. In this stage, infants construct an understanding of the world by coordinating sensory experiences (such as seeing and hearing) with physical, motoric actions—hence the term "sensorimotor." At the beginning of this stage, newborns have little more than reflexes with which to work. At the end of the sensorimotor stage, 2-year-olds can produce complex sensorimotor patterns and use primitive symbols.

Substages   Piaget divided the sensorimotor stage into six substages: (1) simple reflexes; (2) first habits and primary circular reactions; (3) secondary circular reactions; (4) coordination of secondary circular reactions; (5) tertiary circular reactions, novelty, and curiosity; and (6) internalization of schemes.

organization Piagetian concept of grouping isolated behaviors and thoughts into a higher-order, more smoothly functioning cognitive system.

equilibration A mechanism that Piaget proposed to explain how children shift from one stage of thought to the next.

sensorimotor stage The first of Piaget's stages, which lasts from birth to about 2 years of age, during which infants construct an understanding of the world by coordinating sensory experiences (such as seeing and hearing) with physical, motoric actions.

Sensorimotor Stage	**Preoperational Stage**	**Concrete Operational Stage**	**Formal Operational Stage**
The infant constructs an understanding of the world by coordinating sensory experiences with physical actions. An infant progresses from reflexive, instinctual action at birth to the beginning of symbolic thought toward the end of the stage.	The child begins to represent the world with words and images. These words and images reflect increased symbolic thinking and go beyond the connection of sensory information and physical action.	The child can now reason logically about concrete events and classify objects into different sets.	The adolescent reasons in more abstract, idealistic, and logical ways.
Birth to 2 Years of Age	**2 to 7 Years of Age**	**7 to 11 Years of Age**	**11 Years of Age Through Adulthood**

FIGURE **6.1**
PIAGET'S FOUR STAGES OF COGNITIVE DEVELOPMENT

Simple reflexes, the first sensorimotor substage, corresponds to the first month after birth. In this substage, sensation and action are coordinated primarily through reflexive behaviors, such as rooting and sucking. Soon the infant produces behaviors that resemble reflexes in the absence of the usual stimulus for the reflex. For example, a newborn will suck a nipple or bottle only when it is placed directly in the baby's mouth or touched to the lips. But soon the infant might suck when a bottle or nipple is only nearby. Even in the first month of life, the infant is initiating action and actively structuring experiences.

First habits and primary circular reactions is the second sensorimotor substage, which develops between 1 and 4 months of age. In this substage, the infant coordinates sensation and two types of schemes: habits and primary circular reactions. A *habit* is a scheme based on a reflex that has become completely separated from its eliciting stimulus. For example, infants in substage 1 suck when bottles are put to their lips or when they see a bottle. Infants in substage 2 might suck even when no bottle is present. A *circular reaction* is a repetitive action.

A *primary circular reaction* is a scheme based on the attempt to reproduce an event that initially occurred by chance. For example, suppose an infant accidentally sucks his fingers when they are placed near his mouth. Later, he searches for his fingers to suck them again, but the fingers do not cooperate because the infant cannot coordinate visual and manual actions.

Habits and circular reactions are stereotyped—that is, the infant repeats them the same way each time. During this substage, the infant's own body remains the infant's center of attention. There is no outward pull by environmental events.

Secondary circular reactions is the third sensorimotor substage, which develops between 4 and 8 months of age. In this substage, the infant becomes more object oriented, moving beyond preoccupation with the self. The infant's schemes are not intentional or goal-directed, but they are repeated because of their consequences. By chance, an infant might shake a rattle. The infant repeats this action for the sake of its fascination. This is a *secondary circular reaction:* an action

I wish I could travel by the road that crosses the baby's mind, and out beyond all bounds; where messengers run errands for no cause between the kingdoms of kings of no history; where reason makes kites of her laws and flies them, and truth sets facts free from its fetters.

—**Rabindranath Tagore**
Bengali Poet and Essayist, 20th Century

This 17-month-old is in Piaget's stage of tertiary circular reactions. *What might the infant do to suggest that she is in this stage?*

repeated because of its consequences. The infant also imitates some simple actions, such as the baby talk or burbling of adults, and some physical gestures. However, the baby imitates only actions that she is already able to produce.

Coordination of secondary circular reactions is Piaget's fourth sensorimotor substage, which develops between 8 and 12 months of age. To progress into this substage, the infant must coordinate vision and touch, hand and eye. Actions become more outwardly directed. Significant changes during this substage involve the coordination of schemes and intentionality. Infants readily combine and recombine previously learned schemes in a coordinated way. They might look at an object and grasp it simultaneously, or they might visually inspect a toy, such as a rattle, and finger it simultaneously, exploring it tactilely. Actions are even more outwardly directed than before. Related to this coordination is the second achievement—the presence of intentionality. For example, infants might manipulate a stick in order to bring a desired toy within reach, or they might knock over one block to reach and play with another one.

Tertiary circular reactions, novelty, and curiosity is Piaget's fifth sensorimotor substage, which develops between 12 and 18 months of age. In this substage, infants become intrigued by the many properties of objects and by the many things that they can make happen to objects. A block can be made to fall, spin, hit another object, and slide across the ground. *Tertiary circular reactions* are schemes in which the infant purposely explores new possibilities with objects, continually doing new things to them and exploring the results. Piaget says that this stage marks the starting point for human curiosity and interest in novelty.

Internalization of schemes is Piaget's sixth and final sensorimotor substage, which develops between 18 and 24 months of age. In this substage, the infant develops the ability to use primitive symbols. For Piaget, a symbol is an internalized sensory image or word that represents an event. Primitive symbols permit the infant to think about concrete events without directly acting them out or perceiving them. Moreover, symbols allow the infant to manipulate and transform the represented events in simple ways. In a favorite Piagetian example, Piaget's young daughter saw a matchbox being opened and closed. Later, she mimicked the event by opening and closing her mouth. This was an obvious expression of her image of the event. A summary of Piaget's six substages of sensorimotor development is shown in Figure 6.2.

FIGURE **6.2**

PIAGET'S SIX SUBSTAGES OF SENSORIMOTOR DEVELOPMENT

Substage	Age	Description	Example
1 Simple reflexes	Birth to 1 month	Coordination of sensation and action through reflexive behaviors.	Rooting, sucking, and grasping reflexes; newborns suck reflexively when their lips are touched.
2 First habits and primary circular reactions	1 to 4 months	Coordination of sensation and two types of schemes: habits (reflex) and primary circular reactions (reproduction of an event that initially occurred by chance). Main focus is still on the infant's body.	Repeating a body sensation first experienced by chance (sucking thumb, for example); then infants might accommodate actions by sucking their thumb differently from how they suck on a nipple.
3 Secondary circular reactions	4 to 8 months	Infants become more object-oriented, moving beyond self-preoccupation; repeat actions that bring interesting or pleasurable results.	An infant coos to make a person stay near; as the person starts to leave, the infant coos again.
4 Coordination of secondary circular reactions	8 to 12 months	Coordination of vision and touch—hand-eye coordination; coordination of schemes and intentionality.	Infant manipulates a stick in order to bring an attractive toy within reach.
5 Tertiary circular reactions, novelty, and curiosity	12 to 18 months	Infants become intrigued by the many properties of objects and by the many things they can make happen to objects; they experiment with new behavior.	A block can be made to fall, spin, hit another object, and slide across the ground.
6 Internalization of schemes	18 to 24 months	Infants develop the ability to use primitive symbols and form enduring mental representations.	An infant who has never thrown a temper tantrum before sees a playmate throw a tantrum; the infant retains a memory of the event, then throws one himself the next day.

 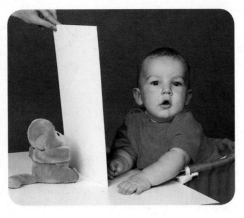

FIGURE **6.3**

OBJECT PERMANENCE. Piaget argued that object permanence is one of infancy's landmark cognitive accomplishments. For this 5-month-old boy, "out-of-sight" is literally out of mind. The infant looks at the toy monkey (*left*), but, when his view of the toy is blocked (*right*), he does not search for it. Several months later, he will search for the hidden toy monkey, an action reflecting the presence of object permanence.

Object Permanence   Imagine how chaotic and unpredictable your life would be if you could not distinguish between yourself and your world. This is what the life of a newborn must be like, according to Piaget. There is no differentiation between the self and world; objects have no separate, permanent existence.

By the end of the sensorimotor period, objects are both separate from the self and permanent. **Object permanence** is the understanding that objects continue to exist even when they cannot be seen, heard, or touched. Acquiring the sense of object permanence is one of the infant's most important accomplishments, according to Piaget.

How can anyone know whether an infant has a sense of object permanence or not? The principal way that object permanence is studied is by watching an infant's reaction when an interesting object disappears (see Figure 6.3). If infants search for the object, it is assumed that they believe it continues to exist.

Object permanence is just one of the basic concepts about the physical world developed by babies. To Piaget, children, even infants, are much like little scientists, examining the world to see how it works. How can this view of children's development be assessed? The *Connecting with Research* interlude describes some of the ways in which adult scientists try to discover what these "baby scientists" are finding out about the world.

Evaluating Piaget's Sensorimotor Stage   Piaget opened up a new way of looking at infants with his view that their main task is to coordinate their sensory impressions with their motor activity. However, the infant's cognitive world is not as neatly packaged as Piaget portrayed it, and some of Piaget's explanations for the cause of change are debated. In the past several decades, sophisticated experimental techniques have been devised to study infants, and there have been a large number of research studies on infant development. Much of the new research suggests that Piaget's view of sensorimotor development needs to be modified (Bauer, Larkino, & Deocampo, 2011; Diamond, Casey, & Munakata, 2011; Johnson, 2011a, b; Quinn, 2011).

The A-Not-B Error   One modification concerns Piaget's claim that certain processes are crucial in transitions from one stage to the next. The data do not always support his explanations. For example, in Piaget's theory, an important feature in the progression into substage 4, *coordination of secondary circular reactions*, is an infant's inclination to search for a hidden object in a familiar location rather than to look

object permanence The Piagetian term for one of an infant's most important accomplishments: understanding that objects continue to exist even when they cannot directly be seen, heard, or touched.

How Do Researchers Study Infants' Understanding of Object Permanence and Causality?

Two accomplishments of infants that Piaget examined were the development of object permanence and the child's understanding of causality. Let's examine two research studies that address these topics.

In both studies, Renée Baillargeon and her colleagues used a research method that involves violation of expectations. In this method, infants see an event happen as it normally would. Then, the event is changed, often in a way that creates a physically impossible event. If infants look longer at the changed event, their reaction indicates they are surprised by it. In other words, it is interpreted to indicate that the infant had certain expectations about the world that were violated.

In one study focused on object permanence, researchers showed infants a toy car that moved down an inclined track, disappeared behind a screen, and then reemerged at the other end, still on the track (Baillargeon & DeVos, 1991) (see Figure 6.4a). After this sequence was repeated several times, something different occurred: A toy mouse was placed behind the tracks but was hidden by the screen while the car rolled by (see Figure 6.4b). This was the "possible" event. Then, the researchers created an "impossible event": The toy mouse was placed on the tracks but was secretly removed after the screen was lowered so that the car seemed to go through the mouse (see Figure 6.4c). In this study, infants as young as 3½ months of age looked longer at the impossible event than at the possible event, an indication that they

were surprised by it. Their surprise suggested that they remembered not only that the toy mouse still existed (object permanence) but where it was located.

Another study focused on the infant's understanding of causality (Kotovsky & Baillargeon, 1994). In this research, a cylinder rolls down a ramp and hits a toy bug at the bottom of the ramp. By 5½ and 6½ months of age, after infants have seen how far the bug will be pushed by a medium-sized cylinder, their reactions indicate that they understand that the bug will roll farther if it is hit by a large cylinder than if it is hit by a small cylinder. Thus, by the middle of the first year of life, these infants understood that the size of a moving object determines how far it will move a stationary object that it collides with.

The research findings discussed in this interlude and other research indicate that infants develop object permanence earlier than Piaget proposed (Baillargeon & others, 2009, 2011). Indeed, as you will see in the next section, a major theme of infant cognitive development today is that infants are more cognitively competent than Piaget envisioned. What methods might researchers use to arrive at this conclusion?

FIGURE **6.4**

USING THE VIOLATION OF EXPECTATIONS METHOD TO STUDY OBJECT PERMANENCE IN INFANTS. If infants looked longer at (*c*) than at (*b*), researchers reasoned that the impossible event in (*c*) violated the infants' expectations and that they remembered that the toy mouse existed.

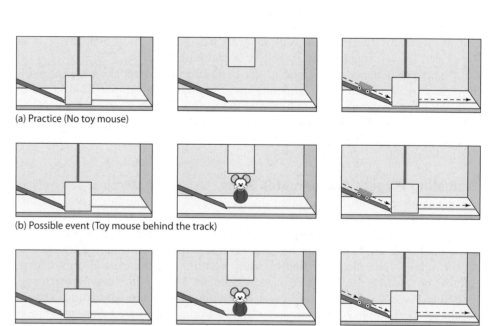

(a) Practice (No toy mouse)

(b) Possible event (Toy mouse behind the track)

(c) Impossible event (Toy mouse on the track)

for the object in a new location. For example, if a toy is hidden twice, initially at location A and subsequently at location B, 8- to 12-month-old infants search initially and correctly at location A. But, when the toy is subsequently hidden at location B, they make the mistake of continuing to search for it at location A. **A-not-B error** (also called AB̄ error) is the term used to describe this common mistake. Older infants are less likely to make the A-not-B error because their concept of object permanence is more complete.

Researchers have found, however, that the A-not-B error does not show up consistently (Sophian, 1985). The evidence indicates that A-not-B errors are sensitive to the delay between hiding the object at B and the infant's attempt to find it (Diamond, 1985). Thus, the A-not-B error might be due to a failure in memory. Another explanation is that infants tend to repeat a previous motor behavior (Clearfield & others, 2006).

Perceptual Development and Expectations   A number of theorists, such as Eleanor Gibson (2001) and Elizabeth Spelke (1991; Spelke & Kinzler, 2009), argue that infants' perceptual abilities are highly developed very early in life. Spelke argues that young infants interpret the world as having predictable occurrences. For example, in Chapter 5, "Motor, Sensory, and Perceptual Development," you read about research that demonstrated the presence of intermodal perception—the ability to coordinate information from two or more sensory modalities, such as vision and hearing—by 3½ months of age, much earlier than Piaget would have predicted (Spelke & Owsley, 1979).

Research also suggests that infants develop the ability to understand how the world works at a very early age (Baillargeon & others, 2011; Quinn, 2011). For example, what kinds of expectations do infants form? Are infants born expecting the world to obey basic physical laws, such as gravity, or if not, then when do they learn about how the world works? Experiments by Elizabeth Spelke (1991, 2000; Spelke & Hespos, 2001) have addressed these questions. She placed babies before a puppet stage and showed them a series of actions that are unexpected if you know how the physical world works—for example, one ball seemed to roll through a solid barrier, another seemed to leap between two platforms, and a third appeared to hang in midair (Spelke, 1979). Spelke measured and compared the babies' looking times for unexpected and expected actions. She concluded that, by 4 months of age, even though infants do not yet have the ability to talk about objects, move around objects, manipulate objects, or even see objects with high resolution, they expect objects to be solid and continuous. However, at 4 months of age, infants do not expect an object to obey gravitational constraints (Spelke & others, 1992). Similarly, research by Renée Baillargeon (1995, 2004; Baillargeon & others, 2011) documents that infants as young as 3 to 4 months expect objects to be *substantial* (in the sense that other objects cannot move through them) and *permanent* (in the sense that objects continue to exist when they are hidden).

In sum, researchers such as Baillargeon and Spelke conclude that infants see objects as bounded, unitary, solid, and separate from their background, possibly at birth or shortly thereafter, but definitely by 3 to 4 months of age— much earlier than Piaget envisioned. Young infants still have much to learn about objects, but the world appears both stable and orderly to them.

The Nature-Nurture Issue   In considering the big issue of whether nature or nurture plays the more important role in infant development, Elizabeth Spelke (Kinzler, Dupoux, & Spelke, 2011; Spelke, 2000; Spelke & Kinzler, 2007, 2009) comes down clearly on the side of nature. Spelke endorses a **core knowledge approach,** which states that infants are born with domain-specific innate knowledge systems. Among these domain-specific knowledge systems are those involving space, number sense, object permanence, and language. Strongly influenced by evolution, the core knowledge domains are theorized to be prewired to allow infants to make sense of their world. After all, Spelke concludes, how could infants possibly grasp the complex

developmental **connection**

Theories. Eleanor Gibson was a pioneer in crafting the ecological perception view of development. Chapter 5, p. 168

A 4-month-old in Elizabeth Spelke's infant perception laboratory is tested to determine whether she knows that an object in motion will not stop in midair. Spelke concluded that at 4 months babies don't expect objects like these balls to obey gravitational constraints, but that they do expect objects to be solid and continuous. Research by Spelke, Renée Baillargeon, and others suggests that infants develop an ability to understand how the world works earlier than Piaget envisioned. However, critics such as Andrew Meltzoff fault their research and conclude there is still controversy about how early some infant cognitive accomplishments occur.

A-not-B error Also called AB̄ error; this occurs when infants make the mistake of selecting the familiar hiding place (A) rather than the new hiding place (B) as they progress into substage 4 in Piaget's sensorimotor stage.

core knowledge approach States that infants are born with domain-specific innate knowledge systems. Among these domain-specific knowledge systems are those involving space, number sense, object permanence, and language.

developmental connection

Nature vs. Nurture. The nature-nurture issue involves the debate about whether development is primarily influenced by nature (biological inheritance) or nurture (environmental experiences). Chapter 1, p. 18; Chapter 2, p. 59

What revisions in Piaget's theory of sensorimotor development do contemporary researchers conclude need to be made?

preoperational stage The second Piagetian developmental stage, which lasts from about 2 to 7 years of age; children begin to represent the world with words, images, and drawings.

operations Reversible mental actions that allow children to do mentally what before they had done only physically.

symbolic function substage The first substage of preoperational thought, occurring roughly between the ages of 2 and 4. In this substage, the young child gains the ability to represent mentally an object that is not present.

world in which they live if they didn't come into the world equipped with core sets of knowledge? In this approach, the innate core knowledge domains form a foundation around which more mature cognitive functioning and learning develop. The core knowledge approach argues that Piaget greatly underestimated the cognitive abilities of infants, especially young infants (Hyde & Spelke, 2011; Kinzler, Dupoux, & Spelke, 2011).

In criticizing the core knowledge approach, British developmental psychologist Mark Johnson (2008) says that the infants Spelke assesses in her research already have accumulated hundreds, and in some cases even thousands, of hours of experience in grasping what the world is about, which gives considerable room for the environment's role in the development of infant cognition (Highfield, 2008). According to Johnson (2008), infants likely come into the world with "soft biases to perceive and attend to different aspects of the environment, and to learn about the world in particular ways." Although debate about the cause and course of infant cognitive development continues, most developmentalists today agree that Piaget underestimated the early cognitive accomplishments of infants and that both nature and nurture are involved in infants' cognitive development.

Conclusions In sum, many researchers conclude that Piaget wasn't specific enough about how infants learn about their world and that infants, especially young infants, are more competent than Piaget thought (Baillargeon & others, 2011; Diamond, Casey, & Munakata, 2011; Johnson, 2011a, b; Quinn, 2011). As they have examined the specific ways that infants learn, the field of infant cognition has become very specialized. There are many researchers working on different questions, with no general theory emerging that can connect all of the different findings (Nelson, 1999). Their theories often are local theories, focused on specific research questions, rather than grand theories like Piaget's (Kuhn, 1998). If there is a unifying theme, it is that investigators in infant development seek to understand more precisely how developmental changes in cognition take place and the big issue of nature and nurture (Aslin, 2009; Bauer, Larkina, & Deocampo, 2011; Quinn, 2011). As they seek to answer more precisely the contributions of nature and nurture to infant development, researchers face the difficult task of determining whether the course of acquiring information, which is very rapid in some domains, is best accounted for by an innate set of biases (that is, core knowledge), or by the extensive input of environmental experiences to which the infant is exposed (Aslin, 2009).

PREOPERATIONAL STAGE

The cognitive world of the preschool child is creative, free, and fanciful. The imagination of preschool children works overtime, and their mental grasp of the world improves. Piaget described the preschool child's cognition as preoperational. What did he mean?

The **preoperational stage,** which lasts from approximately 2 to 7 years of age, is the second Piagetian stage. In this stage, children begin to represent the world with words, images, and drawings. They form stable concepts and begin to reason. At the same time, the young child's cognitive world is dominated by egocentrism and magical beliefs.

Because Piaget called this stage "preoperational," it might sound like an unimportant waiting period. Not so. However, the label *preoperational* emphasizes that the child does not yet perform **operations,** which are reversible mental actions that allow children to do mentally what before they could do only physically. Mentally adding and subtracting numbers are examples of operations. *Preoperational thought* is the beginning of the ability to reconstruct in thought what has been established in

Model of Mountains

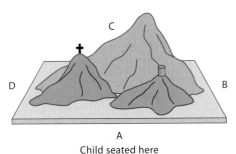

A

Child seated here

Photo 1
(View from A)

Photo 2
(View from B)

Photo 3
(View from C)

Photo 4
(View from D)

FIGURE **6.5**

THE THREE MOUNTAINS TASK. Photo 1 shows the child's perspective from where he or she is sitting. Photos 2, 3, and 4 were taken from different perspectives. For example, Photo 2 shows what the mountains look like to a person sitting at spot B. When asked what a view of the mountains looks like from spot B, the child selects Photo 1, taken from spot A (the child's own view at the time) instead of Photo 2, the correct view.

behavior. It can be divided into two substages: the symbolic function substage and the intuitive thought substage.

The Symbolic Function Substage

The **symbolic function substage** is the first substage of preoperational thought, occurring roughly between the ages of 2 and 4. In this substage, the young child gains the ability to mentally represent an object that is not present. This ability vastly expands the child's mental world (Carlson & Zelazo, 2008; DeLoache, 2011). Young children use scribble designs to represent people, houses, cars, clouds, and so on; they begin to use language and engage in pretend play. However, although young children make distinct progress during this substage, their thought still has important limitations, two of which are egocentrism and animism.

Egocentrism is the inability to distinguish between one's own perspective and someone else's perspective. Piaget and Barbel Inhelder (1969) initially studied young children's egocentrism by devising the three mountains task (see Figure 6.5). The child walks around the model of the mountains and becomes familiar with what the mountains look like from different perspectives and can see that there are different objects on the mountains. The child is then seated on one side of the table on which the mountains are placed. The experimenter moves a doll to different locations around the table, at each location asking the child to select from a series of photos the one photo that most accurately reflects the view that the doll is seeing. Children in the preoperational stage often pick their own view rather than the doll's view. Preschool children frequently show the ability to take another's perspective on some tasks but not others.

Animism, another limitation of preoperational thought, is the belief that inanimate objects have lifelike qualities and are capable of action (Gelman & Opfer, 2004). A young child might show animism by saying, "That tree pushed the leaf off, and it fell down" or "The sidewalk made me mad; it made me fall down." A young child who uses animism fails to distinguish the appropriate occasions for using human and nonhuman perspectives (Opfer & Gelman, 2011).

Possibly because young children are not very concerned about reality, their drawings are fanciful and inventive. Suns are blue, skies are yellow, and cars float on clouds in their symbolic, imaginative world. One 3½-year-old looked at a scribble he had just drawn and described it as a pelican kissing a seal (see Figure 6.6a). The symbolism is simple but strong, like abstractions found in some modern art. Twentieth-century Spanish artist Pablo Picasso commented, "I used to draw like Raphael but it has taken me a lifetime to draw like young children." In the elementary school years, a child's drawings become more realistic, neat, and precise (see Figure 6.6b). Suns are yellow, skies are blue, and cars travel on roads (Winner, 1986).

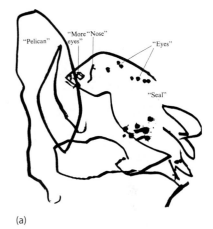

(a)

(b)

FIGURE **6.6**

THE SYMBOLIC DRAWINGS OF YOUNG CHILDREN. (a) A 3½-year-old's symbolic drawing. Halfway into his drawing, the 3½-year-old artist said it was a "pelican kissing a seal." (b) This 11-year-old's drawing is neater and more realistic but also less inventive.

egocentrism The inability to distinguish between one's own and someone else's perspective; an important feature of preoperational thought.

animism A facet of preoperational thought—the belief that inanimate objects have lifelike qualities and are capable of action.

The Intuitive Thought Substage

The **intuitive thought substage** is the second substage of preoperational thought, occurring between approximately 4 and 7 years of age. In this substage, children begin to use primitive reasoning and want to know the answers to all sorts of questions. Consider 4-year-old Tommy, who is at the beginning of the intuitive thought substage. Although he is starting to develop his own ideas about the world he lives in, his ideas are still simple, and he is not very good at thinking things out. He has difficulty understanding events that he knows are taking place but that he cannot see. His fantasized thoughts bear little resemblance to reality. He cannot yet answer the question "What if?" in any reliable way. For example, he has only a vague idea of what would happen if a car were to hit him. He also has difficulty negotiating traffic because he cannot do the mental calculations necessary to estimate whether an approaching car will hit him when he crosses the road.

By the age of 5, children have just about exhausted the adults around them with "why" questions. The child's questions signal the emergence of interest in reasoning and in figuring out why things are the way they are. Following are some samples of the questions children ask during the questioning period of 4 to 6 years of age (Elkind, 1976):

What makes you grow up?

Who was the mother when everybody was a baby?

Why do leaves fall?

Why does the sun shine?

Piaget called this substage *intuitive* because young children seem so sure about their knowledge and understanding yet are unaware of how they know what they know. That is, they know something but know it without the use of rational thinking.

Centration and the Limits of Preoperational Thought

One limitation of preoperational thought is **centration,** a centering of attention on one characteristic to the exclusion of all others. Centration is most clearly evidenced in young children's lack of **conservation,** the awareness that altering an object's or a substance's appearance does not change its basic properties. For example, to adults, it is obvious that a certain amount of liquid stays the same, regardless of a container's shape. But this is not at all obvious to young children. Instead, they are struck by the height of the liquid in the container; they focus on that characteristic to the exclusion of others.

The situation that Piaget devised to study conservation is his most famous task. In the conservation task, children are presented with two identical beakers, each filled to the same level with liquid (see Figure 6.7). They are asked if these beakers have the same amount of liquid, and they usually say yes. Then the liquid from one beaker is poured into a third beaker, which is taller and thinner than the first two. The children are then asked if the amount of liquid in the tall, thin beaker is equal to that which remains in one of the original beakers. Children who are younger than 7 or 8 years old usually say no and justify their answers in terms of the differing height or width of the beakers. Older children usually answer yes and justify their answers appropriately ("If you poured the water back, the amount would still be the same").

In Piaget's theory, failing the conservation-of-liquid task is a sign that children are at the preoperational stage of cognitive development. The failure demonstrates not only centration but also an inability to mentally reverse actions. To understand this concept, see the conservation-of-matter example shown in Figure 6.8. In the row on "matter" you'll see that preoperational children say the longer shape has more clay because they assume that "longer is more." Preoperational children cannot mentally reverse the clay-rolling process to see that the amount of clay is the same in both the shorter ball shape and the longer stick shape.

"I still don't have all the answers, but I'm beginning to ask the right questions." Copyright © Lee Lorenz/The New Yorker Collection/www.cartoonbank.com

intuitive thought substage The second substage of preoperational thought, occurring between approximately 4 and 7 years of age. Children begin to use primitive reasoning and want to know the answers to all sorts of questions.

centration The focusing of attention on one characteristic to the exclusion of all others.

conservation The awareness that altering the appearance of an object or a substance does not change its basic properties.

FIGURE **6.7**

PIAGET'S CONSERVATION TASK. The beaker test is a well-known Piagetian test to determine whether a child can think operationally—that is, can mentally reverse actions and show conservation of the substance. (*a*) Two identical beakers are presented to the child. Then the experimenter pours the liquid from B into C, which is taller and thinner than A or B. (*b*) The child is asked if these beakers (A and C) have the same amount of liquid. The preoperational child says "no." When asked to point to the beaker that has more liquid, the preoperational child points to the tall, thin beaker.

In Figure 6.8 you can see that, in addition to failing the conservation-of-liquid task, preoperational children also fail to conserve number, matter, and length. However, children often vary in their performance on different conservation tasks. Thus, a child might be able to conserve volume but not number.

Some developmentalists do not believe Piaget was entirely correct in his estimate of when children's conservation skills emerge. For example, Rochel Gelman (1969) showed that when the child's attention to relevant aspects of the conservation task is improved, the child is more likely to conserve. Gelman has also demonstrated that attentional training on one dimension, such as number, improves the preschool child's performance on another dimension, such as mass. Thus, Gelman noted that conservation appears earlier than Piaget thought and that attention is especially important in explaining conservation.

Type of Conservation	Initial Presentation	Manipulation	Preoperational Child's Answer
Number	Two identical rows of objects are shown to the child, who agrees they have the same number.	One row is lengthened and the child is asked whether one row now has more objects.	Yes, the longer row.
Matter	Two identical balls of clay are shown to the child. The child agrees that they are equal.	The experimenter changes the shape of one of the balls and asks the child whether they still contain equal amounts of clay.	No, the longer one has more.
Length	Two sticks are aligned in front of the child. The child agrees that they are the same length.	The experimenter moves one stick to the right, then asks the child if they are equal in length.	No, the one on the top is longer.

FIGURE **6.8**

SOME DIMENSIONS OF CONSERVATION: NUMBER, MATTER, AND LENGTH. *What characteristics of preoperational thought do children demonstrate when they fail these conservation tasks?*

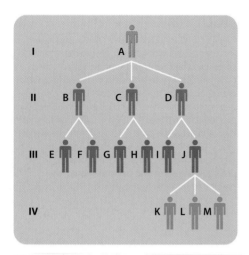

FIGURE **6.9**

CLASSIFICATION: AN IMPORTANT ABILITY IN CONCRETE OPERATIONAL THOUGHT. A family tree of four generations (*I to IV*): The preoperational child has trouble classifying the members of the four generations; the concrete operational child can classify the members vertically, horizontally, and obliquely (up and down and across). For example, the concrete operational child understands that a family member can be a son, a brother, and a father, all at the same time.

concrete operational stage The third Piagetian stage, which lasts from approximately 7 to 11 years of age; children can perform concrete operations, and logical reasoning replaces intuitive reasoning as long as the reasoning can be applied to specific or concrete examples.

seriation The concrete operation that involves ordering stimuli along a quantitative dimension (such as length).

transitivity The ability to logically combine relations to understand certain conclusions. Piaget argued that an understanding of transitivity is characteristic of concrete operational thought.

formal operational stage The fourth and final Piagetian stage, which appears between the ages of 11 and 15; individuals move beyond concrete experiences and think in more abstract and logical ways.

CONCRETE OPERATIONAL STAGE

Piaget proposed that the **concrete operational stage** lasts from approximately 7 to 11 years of age. In this stage, children can perform concrete operations, and they can reason logically as long as reasoning can be applied to specific or concrete examples. Remember that *operations* are mental actions that are reversible, and *concrete operations* are operations that are applied to real, concrete objects. When a child adds two apples together with four apples and concludes that there are now six apples, she is performing a concrete operation.

The conservation tasks described earlier indicate whether children are capable of concrete operations. Concrete operations allow the child to consider several characteristics rather than to focus on a single property of an object. In the clay example, the preoperational child is likely to focus on height or width. The concrete operational child coordinates information about both dimensions.

What other abilities are characteristic of children who have reached the concrete operational stage? One important skill is the ability to classify or divide things into different sets or subsets and to consider their interrelationships. Consider the family tree of four generations that is shown in Figure 6.9 (Furth & Wachs, 1975). This family tree suggests that the grandfather (A) has three children (B, C, and D), each of whom has two children (E through J), and that one of these children (J) has three children (K, L, and M). A child who comprehends the classification system can move up and down a level, across a level, and up and down and across within the system. The concrete operational child understands that person J can at the same time be father, brother, and grandson, for example.

Children who have reached the concrete operational stage are also capable of **seriation,** which is the ability to order stimuli along a quantitative dimension (such as length). To see if students can serialize, a teacher might haphazardly place eight sticks of different lengths on a table. The teacher then asks the students to order the sticks by length. Many young children end up with two or three small groups of "big" sticks or "little" sticks, rather than a correct ordering of all eight sticks. Another mistaken strategy they use is to evenly line up the tops of the sticks but ignore the bottoms. The concrete operational thinker who is capable of seriation simultaneously understands that each stick must be longer than the one that precedes it and shorter than the one that follows it.

Another aspect of reasoning about the relations between classes is **transitivity,** which is the ability to logically combine relations to understand certain conclusions. In this case, consider three sticks (A, B, and C) of differing lengths. A is the longest, B is intermediate in length, and C is the shortest. Does the child understand that, if A is longer than B and B is longer than C, then A is longer than C? In Piaget's theory, concrete operational thinkers who are capable of transitivity do; preoperational thinkers do not.

FORMAL OPERATIONAL STAGE

So far we have studied the first three of Piaget's stages of cognitive development: sensorimotor, preoperational, and concrete operational. What are the characteristics of the fourth and final stage?

The **formal operational stage,** which appears between 11 and 15 years of age, is the fourth and final Piagetian stage. In this stage, individuals move beyond concrete experiences and think in abstract and more logical ways. As part of thinking more abstractly, adolescents develop images of ideal circumstances. They might think about what an ideal parent is like and compare their parents to their ideal standards. They begin to entertain possibilities for the future and are fascinated with what they can be. In solving problems, formal operational thinkers are more systematic and use logical reasoning.

Abstract, Idealistic, and Logical Thinking   The abstract quality of the adolescent's thought at the formal operational level is evident in the adolescent's verbal problem-solving ability. Whereas the concrete operational thinker needs to see the concrete elements A, B, and C to be able to make the logical inference that if A = B and B = C, then A = C, the formal operational thinker can solve this problem merely through verbal presentation.

Another indication of the abstract quality of adolescents' thought is their increased tendency to think about thought itself. One adolescent commented, "I began thinking about why I was thinking about what I was. Then I began thinking about why I was thinking about what I was thinking about what I was." If this sounds abstract, it is, and it characterizes the adolescent's enhanced focus on thought and its abstract qualities.

Accompanying the abstract nature of formal operational thought in adolescence is thought full of idealism and possibilities. Although children frequently think in concrete ways, or in terms of what is real and limited, adolescents begin to engage in extended speculation about ideal characteristics—qualities they desire in themselves and in others. Such thoughts often lead adolescents to compare themselves with others in regard to such ideal standards. And the thoughts of adolescents are often fantasy flights into future possibilities. It is not unusual for the adolescent to become impatient with these newfound ideal standards and to become perplexed over which of many ideal standards to adopt.

As adolescents are learning to think more abstractly and idealistically, they are also learning to think more logically. Children are more likely to solve problems in a trial-and-error fashion. Adolescents begin to think more as a scientist thinks, devising plans to solve problems and systematically testing solutions. They use **hypothetical-deductive reasoning**—that is, they develop hypotheses, or best guesses, and systematically deduce, or conclude, which is the best path to follow in solving the problem.

Assimilation (incorporating new information into existing knowledge) dominates the initial development of formal operational thought, and these thinkers perceive the world subjectively and idealistically. Later in adolescence, as intellectual balance is restored, these individuals accommodate to the cognitive upheaval that has occurred (they adjust to the new information).

Some of Piaget's ideas on formal operational thought are being challenged, however (Keating, 2004; Kuhn, 2009). There is much more individual variation in formal operational thought than Piaget envisioned (Kuhn, 2009). Only about one in three young adolescents is a formal operational thinker. Many American adults never become formal operational thinkers, and neither do many adults in other cultures.

Adolescent Egocentrism   In addition to thinking more logically, abstractly, and idealistically—characteristics of Piaget's formal operational thought stage—in what other ways do adolescents change cognitively? David Elkind (1978) described how adolescent egocentrism governs the way that adolescents think about social matters. **Adolescent egocentrism** is the heightened self-consciousness of adolescents, which is reflected in their belief that others are as interested in them as they are themselves, and in their sense of personal uniqueness and invincibility. Elkind argued that adolescent egocentrism can be dissected into two types of social thinking—imaginary audience and personal fable.

The **imaginary audience** refers to the aspect of adolescent egocentrism that involves feeling one is the center of everyone's attention and sensing that one is on stage. An adolescent boy might think that others are as aware as he is of a few hairs that are out of place. An adolescent girl walks into her classroom and thinks that all eyes are riveted on her complexion. Adolescents especially sense that they are "on stage" in early adolescence, believing they are the main actors and all others are the audience.

According to Elkind, the **personal fable** is the part of adolescent egocentrism that involves an adolescent's sense of personal uniqueness and invincibility. Adolescents' sense of personal uniqueness makes them feel that no one can understand

Might adolescents' ability to reason hypothetically and to evaluate what is ideal versus what is real lead them to engage in demonstrations such as this protest related to better ethical relations? What other causes might be attractive to adolescents' newfound cognitive abilities of hypothetical-deductive reasoning and idealistic thinking?

hypothetical-deductive reasoning Piaget's formal operational concept that adolescents have the cognitive ability to develop hypotheses about ways to solve problems and can systematically deduce which is the best path to follow in solving the problem.

adolescent egocentrism The heightened self-consciousness of adolescents, which is reflected in adolescents' beliefs that others are as interested in them as they are in themselves, and in adolescents' sense of personal uniqueness and invincibility.

imaginary audience That aspect of adolescent egocentrism that involves feeling one is the center of attention and sensing that one is on stage.

personal fable The part of adolescent egocentrism that involves an adolescent's sense of personal uniqueness and invincibility.

> I check my look in the mirror. I wanna change my clothes, my hair, my face.
>
> —**Bruce Springsteen**
> *Contemporary American Rock Star*

Many adolescent girls spend long hours in front of the mirror, depleting cans of hair spray, tubes of lipstick, and jars of cosmetics. *How might this behavior be related to changes in adolescent cognitive and physical development?*

how they really feel. For example, an adolescent girl thinks that her mother cannot possibly sense the hurt she feels because her boyfriend has broken up with her. As part of their effort to retain a sense of personal uniqueness, adolescents might craft stories about themselves that are filled with fantasy, immersing themselves in a world that is far removed from reality. Personal fables frequently show up in adolescent diaries.

One study of sixth- through twelfth-graders revealed that a sense of invincibility was linked to engaging in risky behaviors, such as smoking cigarettes, drinking alcohol, and delinquency, whereas a sense of personal uniqueness was related to depression and suicidal thoughts (Aalsma, Lapsley, & Flannery, 2006). However, some research studies suggest that, rather than perceiving themselves to be invulnerable, many adolescents portray themselves as vulnerable (Reyna & Rivers, 2008). For example, in a recent study, 12- to 18-year-olds were asked about their chance of dying in the next year and prior to age 20 (Fischoff & others, 2010). The adolescents greatly overestimated their chance of dying.

Some researchers have questioned the view that invulnerability is a unitary concept and argued rather that it consists of two dimensions (Duggan & others, 2000; Lapsley & Hill, 2010):

- *Danger invulnerability,* which involves adolescents' sense of indestructibility and tendency to take on physical risks (driving recklessly at high speeds, for example)
- *Psychological invulnerability,* which captures an adolescent's felt invulnerability related to personal or psychological distress (getting one's feelings hurt, for example)

A recent study revealed that adolescents who scored high on a danger invulnerability scale were more likely to engage in juvenile delinquency or substance abuse, or to be depressed (Lapsley & Hill, 2010). In this study, adolescents who scored high on psychological invulnerability were less likely to be depressed, had higher self-esteem, and engaged in better interpersonal relationships. In terms of psychological invulnerability, adolescents often benefit from the normal developmental challenges of exploring identity options, making new friends, asking someone to go out on a date, and learning a new skill. All of these important adolescent tasks involve risk and failure as an option but, if successful, result in enhanced self-image.

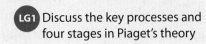

Review *Connect* Reflect

LG1 Discuss the key processes and four stages in Piaget's theory

Review

- What are the key processes in Piaget's theory of cognitive development? What are Piaget's four stages of cognitive development?
- What are the main characteristics of the sensorimotor stage?
- What are the main characteristics of the preoperational stage?
- What are the main characteristics of the concrete operational stage?
- What are the main characteristics of the formal operational stage?

Connect

- In this section, you read that by the age of 6 to 8 months infants have learned to

perceive gravity and support. What aspects of physical development (Chapter 3) and perceptual/motor development (Chapter 5) occurring around this time frame might contribute to infants' exploration and understanding of these concepts?

Reflect *Your Own Personal Journey of Life*

- Do you consider yourself to be a formal operational thinker? Do you still sometimes feel like a concrete operational thinker? Give examples.

Piaget and Education   Evaluating Piaget's Theory

What are some applications of Piaget's theory to education? What are the main contributions and criticisms of Piaget's theory?

PIAGET AND EDUCATION

Piaget was not an educator, but he provided a sound conceptual framework for viewing learning and education. Here are some ideas in Piaget's theory that can be applied to teaching children (Elkind, 1976; Heuwinkel, 1996):

1. *Take a constructivist approach.* Piaget emphasized that children learn best when they are active and seek solutions for themselves. Piaget opposed teaching methods that treat children as passive receptacles. The educational implication of Piaget's view is that, in all subjects, students learn best by making discoveries, reflecting on them, and discussing them, rather than by blindly imitating the teacher or doing things by rote.

2. *Facilitate rather than direct learning.* Effective teachers design situations that allow students to learn by doing. These situations promote students' thinking and discovery. Teachers listen, watch, and question students, to help them gain better understanding.

3. *Consider the child's knowledge and level of thinking.* Students do not come to class with empty minds. They have concepts of space, time, quantity, and causality. These ideas differ from the ideas of adults. Teachers need to interpret what a student is saying and respond in a way that is not too far from the student's level. Also, Piaget suggested that it is important to examine children's mistakes in thinking, not just what they get correct, to help guide them to a higher level of understanding.

4. *Promote the student's intellectual health.* When Piaget came to lecture in the United States, he was asked, "What can I do to get my child to a higher cognitive stage sooner?" He was asked this question so often here compared with other countries that he called it the American question. For Piaget, children's learning should occur naturally. Children should not be pushed and pressured into achieving too much too early in their development, before they are maturationally ready. Some parents spend long hours every day holding up large flash cards with words on them to improve their baby's vocabulary. In the Piagetian view, this is not the best way for infants to learn. It places too much emphasis on speeding up intellectual development, involves passive learning, and will not lead to positive outcomes.

5. *Turn the classroom into a setting of exploration and discovery.* What do actual classrooms look like when the teachers adopt Piaget's views? Several first- and second-grade math classrooms provide some good examples (Kamii, 1985, 1989). The teachers emphasize students' own exploration and discovery. The classrooms are less structured than what we think of as a typical classroom. Workbooks and predetermined assignments are not used. Rather, the teachers observe the students' interests and natural participation in activities to determine what the course of learning will be. For example, a

What are some educational strategies that can be derived from Piaget's theory?

Jean Piaget, the main architect of the field of cognitive development, at age 27.

math lesson might be constructed around counting the day's lunch money or dividing supplies among students. Often, games are prominently used in the classroom to stimulate mathematical thinking. For example, a version of dominoes teaches children about even-numbered combinations. A variation on tic-tac-toe involves replacing Xs and Os with numbers. Teachers encourage peer interaction during the lessons and games because students' different viewpoints can contribute to advances in thinking.

EVALUATING PIAGET'S THEORY

What were Piaget's main contributions? Has his theory withstood the test of time?

Piaget's Contributions   Piaget, the founder of the present field of children's cognitive development, was a giant in the field of developmental psychology (Miller, 2011). Psychologists owe him a long list of masterful concepts of enduring power and fascination: assimilation, accommodation, object permanence, egocentrism, conservation, and others. Psychologists also owe him the current vision of children as active, constructive thinkers (Carpendale, Muller, & Bibok, 2008). And they have a debt to him for creating a theory that has generated a huge volume of research on children's cognitive development.

Piaget also was a genius when it came to observing children. His careful observations showed us inventive ways to discover how children act on and adapt to their world. Piaget showed us some important things to look for in cognitive development, such as the shift from preoperational to concrete operational thinking. He also showed us how children need to make their experiences fit their schemes (cognitive frameworks) yet simultaneously adapt their schemes to fit their experiences. Piaget revealed how cognitive change is likely to occur if the context is structured to allow gradual movement to the next higher level. Concepts do not emerge suddenly, full-blown, but instead develop through a series of partial accomplishments that lead to increasingly comprehensive understanding.

Criticisms of Piaget's Theory   Piaget's theory has not gone unchallenged (Miller, 2011). Questions are raised about estimates of children's competence at different developmental levels, stages, the training of children to reason at higher levels, and culture and education.

Estimates of Children's Competence   Some cognitive abilities emerge earlier than Piaget thought (Bauer, Larkina, & Deocampo, 2011; Meltzoff, 2011; Miller, 2011). For example, as previously noted, some aspects of object permanence emerge earlier than he believed. Even 2-year-olds are nonegocentric in some contexts. When they realize that another person will not see an object, they investigate whether the person is blindfolded or looking in a different direction. Some understanding of the conservation of number has been demonstrated as early as age 3, although Piaget did not think it emerged until 7. Young children are not as uniformly "pre" this and "pre" that (precausal, preoperational) as Piaget thought.

Other cognitive abilities also can emerge later than Piaget thought (Kuhn, 2009, 2011). Many adolescents still think in concrete operational ways or are just beginning to master formal operations. Even many adults are not formal operational thinkers. In sum, recent theoretical revisions highlight more cognitive competencies of infants and young children and more cognitive shortcomings of adolescents and adults (Johnson, 2011a, b; Quinn, 2011).

Stages   In terms of timing and stages, some cognitive abilities have been found to emerge earlier than Piaget had thought, others later (Kuhn, 2011; Quinn, 2011). Recent reviews conclude that the evidence does not support Piaget's view that prior to age 11 children don't engage in abstract thinking and that from 11 years on they do (Kuhn, 2008; Wigfield, Byrnes, & Eccles, 2006). Thus, adolescents' cognitive development is not as stage-like as Piaget thought.

neo-Piagetians Developmentalists who have elaborated on Piaget's theory, emphasizing attention to children's strategies; information-processing speed; the task involved; and division of the problem into more precise, smaller steps.

Effects of Training Some children who are at one cognitive stage (such as pre-operational) can be trained to reason at a higher cognitive stage (such as concrete operational). This discovery poses a problem for Piaget's theory. He argued that such training is only superficial and ineffective, unless the child is at a maturational transition point between the stages (Gelman & Williams, 1998).

Culture and Education Culture and education exert stronger influences on children's development than Piaget maintained (Cole & Packer, 2011; Daniels, 2011). For example, the age at which children acquire conservation skills is related to how much practice their culture provides in these skills. An outstanding teacher and education in the logic of math and science can promote concrete and formal operational thought.

An Alternative View **Neo-Piagetians** argue that Piaget got some things right but that his theory needs considerable revision. They give more emphasis to how children use attention, memory, and strategies to process information (Case, 1987, 1999). They especially stress that a more accurate portrayal of children's thinking requires attention to children's strategies; the speed at which children process information; the specific task involved; and the division of problems into smaller, more precise steps (Morra & others, 2007). In Chapter 7, "Information Processing," we further discuss these aspects of children's thought.

An outstanding teacher and education in the logic of science and mathematics are important cultural experiences that promote the development of operational thought. *Might Piaget have underestimated the roles of culture and schooling in children's cognitive development?*

Review *Connect* Reflect

LG2 Apply Piaget's theory to education, and evaluate Piaget's theory

Review

- How can Piaget's theory be applied to educating children?
- What are some key contributions and criticisms of Piaget's theory?

Connect

- When Piaget developed his theory, research on the development of the child's brain had not yet occurred. After reviewing the discussion of the development of the child's brain in

Chapter 3, describe developmental changes in the brain that might serve as a foundation for the development of Piaget's stages.

Reflect *Your Own Personal Journey of Life*

- How might thinking in formal operational ways rather than concrete operational ways help students to develop better study skills?

Vygotsky's Theory of Cognitive Development

LG3 Identify the main concepts in Vygotsky's theory, and compare it with Piaget's theory

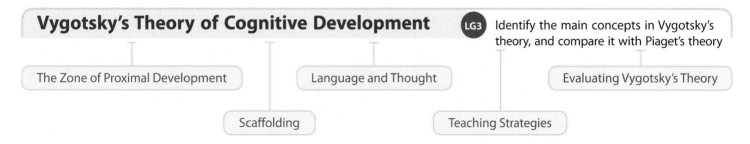

The Zone of Proximal Development

Scaffolding

Language and Thought

Teaching Strategies

Evaluating Vygotsky's Theory

Piaget's theory is a major developmental theory. Another developmental theory that focuses on children's cognition is Vygotsky's theory. Like Piaget, Lev Vygotsky emphasized that children actively construct their knowledge and understanding. In Piaget's theory, children develop ways of thinking and understanding by their actions and interactions with the physical world. In Vygtosky's theory, children are more

Upper limit

Level of additional responsibility
child can accept with assistance
of an able instructor

**Zone of proximal
development (ZPD)**

Lower limit

Level of problem solving
reached on these tasks by
child working alone

FIGURE **6.10**

**VYGOTSKY'S ZONE OF PROXIMAL
DEVELOPMENT.** Vygotsky's zone of proximal
development has a lower limit and an upper limit.
Tasks in the ZPD are too difficult for the child to
perform alone. They require assistance from an adult
or a more-skilled child. As children experience the
verbal instruction or demonstration, they organize
the information in their existing mental structures so
they can eventually perform the skill or task alone.

zone of proximal development (ZPD) Vygotsky's
term for tasks that are too difficult for children to
master alone but can be mastered with guidance
and assistance from adults or more-skilled children.

scaffolding In cognitive development, a term
Vygotsky used to describe the changing level of
support over the course of a teaching session, with
the more-skilled person adjusting guidance to fit
the child's current performance level.

often described as social creatures than in Piaget's theory. They develop their ways of thinking and understanding primarily through social interaction (Daniels, 2011). Their cognitive development depends on the tools provided by society, and their minds are shaped by the cultural context in which they live (Gauvain & Parke, 2010).

We briefly described Vygotsky's theory in Chapter 1. Here we take a closer look at his ideas about how children learn and his view of the role of language in cognitive development.

THE ZONE OF PROXIMAL DEVELOPMENT

Vygotsky's belief in the importance of social influences, especially instruction, to children's cognitive development is reflected in his concept of the zone of proximal development. **Zone of proximal development (ZPD)** is Vygotsky's term for the range of tasks that are too difficult for the child to master alone but that can be learned with guidance and assistance from adults or more-skilled children. Thus, the lower limit of the ZPD is the level of skill reached by the child working independently. The upper limit is the level of additional responsibility the child can accept with the assistance of an able instructor (see Figure 6.10). The ZPD captures the child's cognitive skills that are in the process of maturing and can be accomplished only with the assistance of a more-skilled person (Daniels, 2011). Vygotsky (1962) called these the "buds" or "flowers" of development, to distinguish them from the "fruits" of development, which the child already can accomplish independently.

SCAFFOLDING

Closely linked to the idea of the ZPD is the concept of scaffolding. **Scaffolding** means changing the level of support. Over the course of a teaching session, a more-skilled person (a teacher or advanced peer) adjusts the amount of guidance to fit the child's current performance (Daniels, 2011). When the student is learning a new task, the skilled person may use direct instruction. As the student's competence increases, the person gives less guidance.

Dialogue is an important tool of scaffolding in the zone of proximal development. Vygotsky viewed children as having rich but unsystematic, disorganized, and spontaneous concepts. In a dialogue, these concepts meet with the skilled helper's more systematic, logical, and rational concepts. As a result, the child's concepts become more systematic, logical, and rational. For example, a dialogue might take place between a teacher and a child when the teacher uses scaffolding to help a child understand a concept like "transportation."

LANGUAGE AND THOUGHT

The use of dialogue as a tool for scaffolding is only one example of the important role of language in a child's development. According to Vygotsky, children use speech not only for social communication but also to help them solve tasks. Vygotsky (1962) further believed that young children use language to plan, guide, and monitor their behavior. This use of language for self-regulation is called *private speech*. For Piaget, private speech is egocentric and immature—but for Vygotsky, it is an important tool of thought during the early childhood years (Wertsch, 2008).

Vygotsky said that language and thought initially develop independently of each other and then merge. He emphasized that all mental functions have external, or social, origins. Children must use language to communicate with others before they can focus inward on their own thoughts. Children also must communicate externally and use language for a long period of time before they can make the transition from external to internal speech. This transition period occurs between 3 and 7 years of age and involves talking to oneself. After a while, the self-talk becomes second nature to children, and they can act without verbalizing; at this point, children have internalized their egocentric speech in the form of *inner speech*, which becomes their thoughts (Mercer, 2008).

Vygotsky held that children who use a lot of private speech are more socially competent than those who don't. He argued that private speech represents an early transition in becoming more socially communicative. For Vygotsky, when young children talk to themselves, they are using language to govern their behavior and guide themselves. For example, a child working on a puzzle might say to herself, "Which pieces should I put together first? I'll try those green ones first. Now I need some blue ones. No, that blue one doesn't fit there. I'll try it over here."

Piaget argued that self-talk is egocentric and reflects immaturity. However, researchers have found support for Vygotsky's view that private speech plays a positive role in children's development (Wertsch, 2008). Researchers have found that children use private speech more when tasks are difficult, when they have made errors, and when they are not sure how to proceed (Berk, 1994). They also have revealed that children who use private speech are more attentive and improve their performance more than children who do not use private speech (Berk & Spuhl, 1995).

Lev Vygotsky (1896–1934), shown here with his daughter, reasoned that children's cognitive development is advanced through social interaction with more-skilled individuals embedded in a sociocultural backdrop. *How is Vygotsky's theory different from Piaget's?*

TEACHING STRATEGIES

Vygotsky's theory has been embraced by many teachers and has been successfully applied to education (Daniels, 2011; Gredler, 2009; Holzman, 2009). Here are some ways Vygotsky's theory can be incorporated in classrooms:

1. *Use the child's ZPD in teaching.* Teaching should begin toward the zone's upper limit, so that the child can reach the goal with help and move to a higher level of skill and knowledge. Offer just enough assistance. You might ask, "What can I do to help you?" Or simply observe the child's intentions and attempts and provide support when needed. When the child hesitates, offer encouragement. And encourage the child to practice the skill. You may watch and appreciate the child's practice or offer support when the child forgets what to do.

2. *Use more-skilled peers as teachers.* Remember that it is not just adults who are important in helping children learn. Children also benefit from the support and guidance of more-skilled children.

3. *Monitor and encourage children's use of private speech.* Be aware of the developmental change from externally talking to oneself when solving a problem during the preschool years, to privately talking to oneself in the early elementary school years (Mercer, 2008). In the elementary school years, encourage children to internalize and self-regulate their talk to themselves.

4. *Place instruction in a meaningful context.* Educators today are moving away from abstract presentations of material, instead providing students with opportunities to experience learning in real-world settings. For example, instead of just memorizing math formulas, students work on math problems with real-world implications.

5. *Transform the classroom with Vygotskian ideas.* What does a Vygotskian classroom look like? The Kamehameha Elementary Education Program (KEEP) is based on Vygotsky's theory (Tharp, 1994). The ZPD is the key element of instruction in this program. Children might read a story and then interpret its meaning. Many of the learning activities take place in small groups. All children spend at least 20 minutes each morning in a setting called "Center One." In this context, scaffolding is used to improve children's literary skills. The instructor asks questions, responds to students' queries, and builds on the ideas that students generate. The *Connecting Development to Life* interlude further explores the implications of Vygotsky's theory for children's education.

How can Vygotsky's ideas be applied to educating children?

Tools of the Mind

Tools of the Mind is an early childhood education curriculum that emphasizes children's development of self-regulation and the cognitive foundations of literacy. The curriculum was created by Elena Bodrova and Deborah Leong (2007) and has been implemented in more than 200 classrooms. Most of the children in the Tools of the Mind programs are at risk because of their living circumstances, which in many instances involve poverty and other difficult conditions such as being homeless and having parents with drug problems.

Tools of the Mind is grounded in Vygotsky's (1962) theory with special attention given to cultural tools and developing self-regulation, the zone of proximal development, scaffolding, private speech, shared activity, and play as important activity. In a Tools of the Mind classroom, dramatic play has a central role. Teachers guide children in creating themes that are based on the children's interests, such as treasure hunt, store, hospital, and restaurant. Teachers also incorporate field trips, visitor presentations, videos, and books in the development of children's play. In addition, they help children develop a play plan, which increases the maturity of their play. Play plans describe what the children expect to do in the play period, including the imaginary context, roles, and props to be used. The play plans increase the quality of their play and self-regulation.

Scaffolding writing is another important theme in the Tools of the Mind classroom. Teachers guide children in planning their own message by drawing a line to stand for each word the child says. Children then repeat the message, pointing to each line as they say the word. Then, a child writes on the lines, trying to represent each word with some letters or symbols. Figure 6.11 shows how the scaffolding writing process improved a 5-year-old child's writing over the course of two months.

Research assessments of children's writing in Tools of the Mind classrooms revealed that children in the program have more advanced writing skills than children in other early childhood programs (Bodrova & Leong, 2007) (see Figure 6.11). For example, they write more complex messages, use more words, spell more accurately, show better letter recognition, and have a better understanding of the concept of a sentence.

What educational policy implications do these findings have for children?

(*a*) Five-year-old Aaron's independent journal writing prior to using the scaffolded writing technique.

(*b*) Aaron's journal two months after using the scaffolded writing technique.

FIGURE **6.11**

WRITING PROGRESS OF A 5-YEAR-OLD BOY OVER TWO MONTHS USING THE SCAFFOLDING WRITING PROCESS IN TOOLS OF THE MIND

	Vygotsky	Piaget
Sociocultural Context	Strong emphasis	Little emphasis
Constructivism	Social constructivist	Cognitive constructivist
Stages	No general stages of development proposed	Strong emphasis on stages (sensorimotor, preoperational, concrete operational, and formal operational)
Key Processes	Zone of proximal development, language, dialogue, tools of the culture	Schema, assimilation, accommodation, operations, conservation, classification
Role of Language	A major role; language plays a powerful role in shaping thought	Language has a minimal role; cognition primarily directs language
View on Education	Education plays a central role, helping children learn the tools of the culture	Education merely refines the child's cognitive skills that have already emerged
Teaching Implications	Teacher is a facilitator and guide, not a director; establish many opportunities for children to learn with the teacher and more-skilled peers	Also views teacher as a facilitator and guide, not a director; provide support for children to explore their world and discover knowledge

FIGURE 6.12

COMPARISON OF VYGOTSKY'S AND PIAGET'S THEORIES

EVALUATING VYGOTSKY'S THEORY

Even though their theories were proposed at about the same time, most of the world learned about Vygotsky's theory later than they learned about Piaget's theory, so Vygotsky's theory has not yet been evaluated as thoroughly. Vygotsky's view of the importance of sociocultural influences on children's development fits with the current belief that it is important to evaluate the contextual factors in learning (Gauvain & Parke, 2010).

We already have considered several contrasts between Vygotsky's and Piaget's theories, such as Vygotsky's emphasis on the importance of inner speech in development and Piaget's view that such speech is immature. Although both theories are constructivist, Vygotsky's is a **social constructivist approach,** which emphasizes the social contexts of learning and the construction of knowledge through social interaction.

In moving from Piaget to Vygotsky, the conceptual shift is from the individual to collaboration, social interaction, and sociocultural activity (Holzman, 2009). The endpoint of cognitive development for Piaget is formal operational thought. For Vygotsky, the endpoint can differ, depending on which skills are considered to be the most important in a particular culture. For Piaget, children construct knowledge by transforming, organizing, and reorganizing previous knowledge. For Vygotsky, children construct knowledge through social interaction (Daniels, 2011). The implication of Piaget's theory for teaching is that children need support to explore their world and discover knowledge. The main implication of Vygotsky's theory for teaching is that students need many opportunities to learn with the teacher and more-skilled peers. In both Piaget's and Vygotsky's theories, teachers serve as facilitators and guides, rather than as directors and molders of learning. Figure 6.12 compares Vygotsky's and Piaget's theories.

Criticisms of Vygotsky's theory also have surfaced (Karpov, 2006). Some critics point out that Vygotsky was not specific enough about age-related changes (Gauvain, 2008). Another criticism focuses on Vygotsky not adequately describing how changes in socioemotional capabilities contribute to cognitive development (Gauvain, 2008). Yet another criticism is that he overemphasized the role of language in thinking. Also, his emphasis on collaboration and guidance has potential pitfalls. Might

developmental **connection**

Education. Whether to follow a constructivist or direct instruction approach is a major educational issue. Chapter 16, p. 525

social constructivist approach An emphasis on the social contexts of learning and construction of knowledge through social interaction. Vygotsky's theory reflects this approach.

facilitators be too helpful in some cases, as when a parent becomes too overbearing and controlling? Further, some children might become lazy and expect help when they could have done something on their own.

Review *Connect* Reflect

LG3 Identify the main concepts in Vygotsky's theory, and compare it with Piaget's theory

Review

- What is the zone of proximal development?
- What is scaffolding?
- How did Vygotsky view language and thought?
- How can Vygotsky's theory be applied to education?
- What are some similarities and differences between Vygotsky's and Piaget's theories?

Connect

- As you read in this section, Vygotsky's theory has been applied to education.

Compare the type of education you experienced as a child with the type of education that follows Vygotsky's theory.

Reflect *Your Own Personal Journey of Life*

- Which theory—Piaget's or Vygotsky's—do you think provides a better explanation of your own development as a child? Why?

Cognitive Changes in Adulthood

LG4 Describe cognitive changes in adulthood

- Piaget's View
- Realistic and Pragmatic Thinking
- Reflective and Relativistic Thinking
- Cognition and Emotion
- Is There a Fifth, Postformal Stage?

We have discussed the theories that Piaget and Vygotsky proposed to account for how the cognitive development of children proceeds. Neither, however, had much to say about cognitive development in adulthood. What do developmentalists know about changes in the way that adults think?

PIAGET'S VIEW

Recall that, according to Piaget, the formal operational stage of thought begins at 11 to 15 years of age. During this stage, the final one in Piaget's theory, thinking becomes more abstract, idealistic, and logical than the concrete operational thinking of 7- to 11-year-olds. Of course, young adults have more knowledge than adolescents. But, according to Piaget, adults and adolescents use the same type of reasoning. Adolescents and adults think in qualitatively the same way.

Many individuals don't reach the highest level of their formal operational thinking until adulthood. That is, though many individuals begin to plan and hypothesize about intellectual problems as adolescents, they become more systematic and sophisticated at these skills as young adults. Also, many adults do not think in formal operational ways (Keating, 2004).

REALISTIC AND PRAGMATIC THINKING

Some developmentalists propose that as young adults move into the world of work, their way of thinking does change. One idea is that as they face the constraints of reality that work promotes, their idealism decreases (Labouvie-Vief, 1986).

A related change in thinking was proposed by K. Warner Schaie (1977). He concluded that it is unlikely that adults go beyond the powerful methods of scientific thinking characteristic of the formal operational stage. However, Schaie argued that adults do progress beyond adolescents in their use of intellect. For example, in early adulthood individuals often switch from acquiring knowledge to applying knowledge as they pursue success in their work.

REFLECTIVE AND RELATIVISTIC THINKING

William Perry (1970) also described changes in cognition that take place in early adulthood. He said that adolescents often view the world in terms of polarities—right/wrong, we/they, or good/bad. As youth age into adulthood, they gradually move away from this type of absolutist thinking as they become aware of the diverse opinions and multiple perspectives of others. Thus, in Perry's view, the absolutist, dualistic thinking of adolescence gives way to the reflective, relativistic thinking of adulthood. Other developmentalists also argue that reflective thinking is an important indicator of cognitive change in young adults (Mascalo & Fischer, 2010).

COGNITION AND EMOTION

Gisela Labouvie-Vief and her colleagues (Labouvie-Vief, 2009; Labouvie-Vief, Gruhn, & Studer, 2010) also argue that to understand cognitive changes in adulthood it is

How might emerging and young adults think differently than adolescents?

necessary to consider how emotional maturity might affect cognitive development. They conclude that although emerging and young adults become more aware that emotions influence their thinking, at this point thinking is often swayed too strongly by negative emotions that can produce distorted and self-serving thinking. In their research, a subset of emerging adults who are high in empathy, flexibility, and autonomy are more likely to engage in complex, integrated cognitive-emotional thinking. Labouvie-Vief and her colleagues have found that the ability to think in this cognitively and emotionally balanced, advanced manner increases in the middle adulthood years. Further, they emphasize that in middle age, individuals become more inwardly reflective and less context-dependent in their thinking than they were as young adults. In the work of Labouvie-Vief and her colleagues, we see the effort to discover connections between cognitive and socioemotional development, which was described as an increasing trend in the field of life-span development in Chapter 1.

- - - - - - - - - - - - - - →

developmental **connection**

Cognitive Theory. Links between cognition and emotion are increasingly being studied. Chapter 1, p. 22; Chapter 10, p. 202

IS THERE A FIFTH, POSTFORMAL STAGE?

Some theorists have pieced together these descriptions of adult thinking and have proposed that young adults move into a new qualitative stage of cognitive development, postformal thought (Sinnott, 2003). **Postformal thought** is:

- *Reflective, relativistic, and contextual.* As young adults engage in solving problems, they might think deeply about many aspects of work, politics, relationships, and other areas of life (Labouvie-Vief, 1986). They find that what might be the best solution to a problem at work (with a boss or co-worker) might not be the best solution at home (with a romantic partner). Thus, postformal thought holds that the correct answer to a problem requires reflective thinking and may vary from one situation to another. Some psychologists argue

postformal thought Thinking that is reflective, relativistic, and contextual; provisional; realistic; and influenced by emotions.

What characterizes a possible fifth stage of cognitive development called postformal thought?

that reflective thinking continues to increase and becomes more internal and less contextual in middle age (Labouvie-Vief, Gruhn, & Studer, 2010; Mascalo & Fischer, 2010).

- *Provisional.* Many young adults also become more skeptical about the truth and seem unwilling to accept an answer as final. Thus, they come to see the search for truth as an ongoing and perhaps never-ending process.

- *Realistic.* Young adults understand that thinking can't always be abstract. In many instances, it must be realistic and pragmatic.

- *Recognized as being influenced by emotion.* Emerging and young adults are more likely than adolescents to understand that their thinking is influenced by emotions. However, too often negative emotions produce thinking that is distorted and self-serving at this point in development.

One effort to assess postformal thinking is the 10-item Complex Postformal Thought Questionnaire (Sinnott & Johnson, 1997). Figure 6.13 presents the questionnaire and gives you an opportunity to evaluate your thinking at the postformal level. A recent study found that the questionnaire items reflect three main categories of postformal thinking: (1) Taking into account multiple aspects of a problem or situation; (2) Making a subjective choice in a particular problem situation; and (3) Perceiving underlying complexities in a situation (Cartwright & others, 2009).

A study using the Complex Postformal Thought Questionnaire revealed that college students who had more cross-category friends (based on categories of gender, age, ethnicity, socioeconomic status, and sexual orientation) scored higher on the postformal thought measure than their counterparts who had fewer cross-category

---

Respond to each of the items below in terms of how well they characterize your thinking from 1 = Not True (of Self) to 7 = Very True (of Self).

	Not True 1	2	3	4	5	6	Very True 7
1. I see the paradoxes in life.							
2. I see more than one method that can be used to reach a goal.							
3. I am aware that I can decide which reality to experience at a particular time; but I know that reality is really multi-level and more complicated.							
4. There are many "right" ways to define any life experience; I must make a final decision on how I define the problems of life.							
5. I am aware that sometimes "succeeding" in the everyday world means finding a concrete answer to one of life's problems; but sometimes it means finding a correct path that would carry me through any problems of this type.							
6. Almost all problems can be solved by logic, but this may require different types of "logics."							
7. I tend to see several causes connected with any event.							
8. I see that a given dilemma always has several good solutions.							
9. I realize that I often have several goals in mind, or that life seems to have several goals in mind for me. So I go toward more than one in following my path in life.							
10. I can see the hidden logic in others' solutions to the problem of life, even if I don't agree with their solutions and follow my own path.							

FIGURE **6.13**

COMPLEX POSTFORMAL THOUGHT QUESTIONNAIRE. After you have responded to the items, total your score, which can range from 10 to 70. The higher your score, the more likely you are to engage in postformal thinking.

friends (Galupo, Cartwright, & Savage, 2010). Cross-category friendships likely stimulate individuals to move beyond either/or thinking, critically evaluate stereotypical thinking, and consider alternative explanations.

How strong is the evidence for a fifth, postformal stage of cognitive development? Researchers have found that young adults are more likely to engage in postformal thinking than adolescents are (Commons & Richards, 2003; Commons & others, 1989). But critics argue that research has yet to document that postformal thought is a qualitatively more advanced stage than formal operational thought.

There has been little discussion about whether specific cognitive stages might characterize middle and late adulthood. One candidate for a possible stage is "wisdom," which we discuss in Chapter 8, "Intelligence." In addition, researchers have documented many ways in which specific aspects of cognition change during adulthood, and we discuss those in Chapter 7, "Information Processing."

developmental **connection**

Life-Span Perspective. How might wisdom change as individuals go through the adult years? Chapter 8, p. 262

developmental **connection**

Memory. How does memory change in middle and late adulthood? Chapter 7, p. 224

Review *Connect* Reflect

LG4 Describe cognitive changes in adulthood

Review

- What is Piaget's view of adult cognitive development?
- Do young adults retain the idealism of the formal operational stage?
- What is Perry's view on cognitive changes from adolescence to adulthood?
- What role does emotion play in cognitive changes in emerging and early adulthood?
- What characteristics have been proposed for a fifth, postformal stage of cognitive development?

Connect

- What does Piaget's view of adult cognitive development have in common with his

views about cognitive development in adolescence?

Reflect *Your Own Personal Journey of Life*

- If you are an emerging adult (18 to 25 years of age), what do you think are the most important cognitive changes that have taken place so far in this transition period in your life between adolescence and early adulthood? If you are older, reflect on your emerging adult years and describe what cognitive changes occurred during this time.

reach your **learning goals**

Piaget's Theory of Cognitive Development

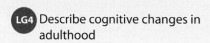

LG1 Discuss the key processes and four stages in Piaget's theory

Processes of Development

- In Piaget's theory, children construct their own cognitive worlds, building mental structures to adapt to their world. Schemes are actions or mental representations that organize knowledge. Behavioral schemes (physical activities) characterize infancy, whereas mental schemes (cognitive activities) develop in childhood. Adaptation involves assimilation and accommodation. Assimilation occurs when children use existing schemes to deal with new information. Accommodation happens when children adjust their schemes to account for new information and experiences. Through organization, children group isolated behaviors into a higher-order, more smoothly functioning cognitive system. Equilibration is a mechanism Piaget proposed to explain how children shift from one cognitive stage to the next. As children experience cognitive conflict in trying to understand the world, they seek equilibrium. The result is equilibration, which brings the child to a new stage of thought. According to Piaget, there are four qualitatively different stages of thought: sensorimotor, preoperational, concrete operational, and formal operational.

- Sensorimotor Stage

- In sensorimotor thought, the first of Piaget's four stages, the infant organizes and coordinates sensations with physical movements. The stage lasts from birth to about 2 years of age. Sensorimotor thought has six substages: simple reflexes; first habits and primary circular reactions; secondary circular reactions; coordination of secondary circular reactions; tertiary circular reactions, novelty, and curiosity; and internalization of schemes. One key aspect of this stage is object permanence, the ability of infants to understand that objects continue to exist even though they are no longer observing them. Another aspect involves infants' understanding of cause and effect. In the past several decades, revisions of Piaget's view have been proposed based on research. For example, researchers have found that a stable and differentiated perceptual world is established earlier than Piaget envisioned.

- Preoperational Stage

- Preoperational thought is the beginning of the ability to reconstruct at the level of thought what has been established in behavior. It involves a transition from a primitive to a more sophisticated use of symbols. In preoperational thought, the child does not yet think in an operational way. The symbolic function substage occurs roughly from 2 to 4 years of age and is characterized by symbolic thought, egocentrism, and animism. The intuitive thought substage stretches from about 4 to 7 years of age. It is called *intuitive* because children seem sure about their knowledge yet are unaware of how they know what they know. The preoperational child lacks conservation and asks a barrage of questions.

- Concrete Operational Stage

- Concrete operational thought occurs roughly from 7 to 11 years of age. During this stage, children can perform concrete operations, think logically about concrete objects, classify things, and reason about relationships among classes of things. Concrete thought is not as abstract as formal operational thought.

- Formal Operational Stage

- Formal operational thought appears between 11 and 15 years of age. Formal operational thought is more abstract, idealistic, and logical than concrete operational thought. Piaget argues that adolescents become capable of engaging in hypothetical-deductive reasoning. But Piaget did not give adequate attention to individual variation in adolescent thinking. Many young adolescents do not think in hypothetical-deductive ways but rather are consolidating their concrete operational thinking. In addition, adolescents develop a special kind of egocentrism that involves an imaginary audience and a personal fable about being unique and invulnerable.

Applying and Evaluating Piaget's Theory

LG2 Apply Piaget's theory to education, and evaluate Piaget's theory

- Piaget and Education

- Piaget was not an educator, but his constructivist views have been applied to teaching. These applications include an emphasis on facilitating rather than directing learning, considering the child's level of knowledge, using ongoing assessment, promoting the student's intellectual health, and turning the classroom into a setting for exploration and discovery.

- Evaluating Piaget's Theory

- We owe to Piaget the field of cognitive development. He was a genius at observing children, and he gave us a number of masterful concepts. Critics, however, question his estimates of competence at different developmental levels, his stage concept, and other ideas. Neo-Piagetians emphasize the importance of information processing.

Vygotsky's Theory of Cognitive Development

 LG3 Identify the main concepts in Vygotsky's theory, and compare it with Piaget's theory

- The Zone of Proximal Development

- Zone of proximal development (ZPD) is Vygotsky's term for the range of tasks that are too difficult for children to master alone but that can be learned with the guidance and assistance of more-skilled adults and peers.

- Scaffolding

- Scaffolding is a teaching technique in which a more-skilled person adjusts the level of guidance to fit the child's current performance level. Dialogue is an important aspect of scaffolding.

- Language and Thought

- Vygotsky argued that language plays a key role in cognition. Language and thought initially develop independently, but then children internalize their egocentric speech in the form of inner speech, which becomes their thoughts. This transition to inner speech occurs between 3 and 7 years of age. Vygotsky's view contrasts with Piaget's view that young children's self-talk is immature and egocentric.

Teaching Strategies

- Applications of Vygotsky's ideas to education include using the child's zone of proximal development and scaffolding, using more-skilled peers as teachers, monitoring and encouraging children's use of private speech, and accurately assessing the zone of proximal development. These practices can transform the classroom and establish a meaningful context for instruction.

Evaluating Vygotsky's Theory

- Like Piaget, Vygotsky emphasized that children actively construct their understanding of the world. Unlike Piaget, he did not propose stages of cognitive development, and he emphasized that children construct knowledge through social interaction. In Vygotsky's theory, children depend on tools provided by the culture, which determines which skills they will develop. Some critics say that Vygotsky overemphasized the role of language in thinking.

Cognitive Changes in Adulthood

 Describe cognitive changes in adulthood

Piaget's View

- Piaget said that formal operational thought, entered at 11 to 15 years of age, is the final cognitive stage, although adults are more knowledgeable than adolescents.

Realistic and Pragmatic Thinking

- Some experts argue that the idealism of Piaget's formal operational stage declines in young adults, being replaced by more realistic, pragmatic thinking.

Reflective and Relativistic Thinking

- Perry said that adolescents often engage in dualistic, absolutist thinking, whereas young adults are more likely to think reflectively and relativistically.

Cognition and Emotion

- Emerging and young adults become more aware that emotions influence their thinking. However, at this point in development, negative emotions often produce distorted and self-serving thinking that interferes with achieving an integrated, complex understanding of the link between cognition and emotion. Nonetheless, a subset of emotionally mature emerging and young adults achieve this understanding.

Is There a Fifth, Postformal Stage?

- Postformal thought is reflective, relativistic, and contextual; provisional; realistic; and influenced by emotions.

key **terms**

key **people**

preview

What do people notice in their environment? What do they remember? And how do they think about it? Questions like these characterize the information-processing approach. Using this approach, which we discuss in this chapter, researchers usually do not describe individuals as being in one stage of cognitive development or another. But they do describe and analyze how the speed of processing information, attention, memory, thinking, and metacognition change over time.

The Information-Processing Approach

LG1 Explain the information-processing approach and its application to development

The Information-Processing Approach and Its Application to Development

Speed of Processing Information

What are some of the basic ideas of the information-processing approach? How does processing information change as individuals develop? How important is speed of processing in development?

> I think, therefore I am.
>
> —**René Descartes**
> *Philosopher, 17th Century*

THE INFORMATION-PROCESSING APPROACH AND ITS APPLICATION TO DEVELOPMENT

As we indicated in Chapter 1, the *information-processing approach* analyzes how individuals manipulate information, monitor it, and create strategies for handling it (Siegler, 2006, 2009). This approach shares some characteristics with the theories of cognitive development that were discussed in Chapter 6, "Cognitive Developmental Approaches." Both those theories and the information-processing approach rejected the behavioral approach that dominated psychology during the first half of the twentieth century. As we discussed in Chapter 1, the behaviorists argued that to explain behavior it is important to examine associations between stimuli and behavior. In contrast, the theories of Piaget and Vygotsky, which were presented in Chapter 6, and the information-processing approach focus on how people think.

Effective information processing involves attention, memory, and thinking (Bjorklund, 2012; Halfor & Andrews, 2011; Schneider, 2011; Zelazo & Muller, 2011). Figure 7.1 is a basic, simplified representation of how information processing works; it omits a great deal and does not indicate the many routes that the flow of information takes. For example, the processes may overlap and not always go in the left-to-right direction indicated in the figure. A number of different processes may be involved in the way memory functions in processing information. The purpose of the model is to get you to begin thinking in a general way about how people process information. In subsequent sections, we consider details about the way people process information and how information processing changes throughout the life span.

Robert Siegler (2006, 2009) emphasizes that *mechanisms of change* are especially important in the advances children make in cognitive development. According to Siegler, three mechanisms work together to create changes in children's cognitive skills: encoding, automaticity, and strategy construction.

developmental **connection**

Theories. In Skinner's behavioral view, it is external rewards and punishment that determine behavior, not thoughts. Chapter 1, p. 24

developmental **connection**

Cognitive Theory. Piaget theorized that cognitive development occurs in four stages: sensorimotor, preoperational, concrete operational, and formal operational. Chapter 6, p. 184

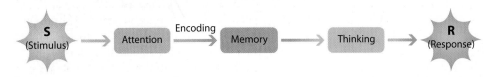

FIGURE 7.1

A BASIC, SIMPLIFIED MODEL OF INFORMATION PROCESSING

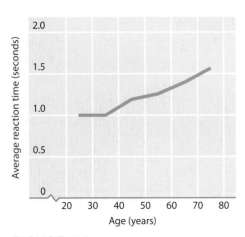

FIGURE **7.2**

THE RELATION OF AGE TO REACTION TIME. In one study, the average reaction time began to slow in the forties, and this decline accelerated in the sixties and seventies (Salthouse, 1994). The task used to assess reaction time required individuals to match numbers with symbols on a computer screen.

encoding The process by which information gets into memory.

automaticity The ability to process information with little or no effort.

strategy construction Creation of new procedures for processing information.

metacognition Cognition about cognition, or "knowing about knowing."

Encoding is the process by which information gets into memory. Changes in children's cognitive skills depend on increased skill at encoding relevant information and ignoring irrelevant information. For example, to a 4-year-old, an *s* in cursive writing is a shape very different from an *s* that is printed. But a 10-year-old has learned to encode the relevant fact that both are the letter *s* and to ignore the irrelevant differences in shape.

Automaticity refers to the ability to process information with little or no effort. Practice allows children to encode increasing amounts of information automatically. For example, once children have learned to read well, they do not think about each letter in a word as a letter; instead, they encode whole words. Once a task is automatic, it does not require conscious effort. As a result, as information processing becomes more automatic, we can complete tasks more quickly and handle more than one task at a time. If you did not encode words automatically but instead read this page by focusing your attention on each letter in each word, imagine how long it would take you to read it.

Strategy construction is the creation of new procedures for processing information. For example, children's reading benefits when they develop the strategy of stopping periodically to take stock of what they have read so far (Schneider, 2011).

In addition, Siegler (2006, 2009) argues that children's information processing is characterized by *self-modification*. That is, children learn to use what they have learned in previous circumstances to adapt their responses to a new situation. Part of this self-modification draws on **metacognition,** which means "knowing about knowing" (Flavell, 2004). One example of metacognition is what children know about the best ways to remember what they have read. Do they know that they will remember what they have read better if they can relate it to their own lives in some way? Thus, in Siegler's application of information processing to development, children play an active role in their own cognitive development.

SPEED OF PROCESSING INFORMATION

A limitation on processing is speed of processing. How fast we process information often influences what we can do with that information. If you are trying to add up in your mind the cost of items you are buying at the grocery store, you need to be able to rapidly compute the sum before you have forgotten the prices of the individual items. If someone gives you a phone message, you want to be able to write it down before the person hangs up or before you have forgotten what the person said.

Researchers have devised a number of ways to assess processing speed. For example, processing speed can be assessed using a *reaction-time* task in which individuals are asked to push a button as soon as they see a stimulus such as a light. Or individuals might be asked to match letters or match numbers with symbols on a computer screen.

Changes in Speed of Processing   There is abundant evidence that the speed with which such tasks are completed improves dramatically across the childhood years (Demetriou, Mouyi, & Spanoudis, 2010). Processing speed continues to improve in early adolescence (Kuhn, 2009). For example, in one study, 10-year-olds were approximately 1.8 times slower at processing information than young adults on such tasks as reaction time, letter matching, mental rotation, and abstract matching (Hale, 1990). Twelve-year-olds were approximately 1.5 times slower than young adults, but 15-year-olds processed information on the tasks as fast as the young adults. Also, a study of 8- to 13-year-old children revealed that processing speed increased with age and, further, that the developmental change in processing speed preceded an increase in working memory capacity (Kail, 2007).

Does processing speed decline in adulthood? In K. Warner Schaie's (1996, 2011) Seattle Longitudinal Study, processing speed began declining in middle adulthood. As Figure 7.2 shows, the slowdown in processing speed continues into late adulthood (Salthouse, 2007, 2012). The decline in processing speed in older adults is likely due to a decline in functioning of the brain and central nervous system (Finch,

Garfield ®   **by Jim Davis**

2009). Recent research indicates that processing speed is an important indicator of the ability of older adults to continue to effectively drive a vehicle (Edwards & others, 2010). One study revealed that older drivers who went through speed of processing training were less likely to stop driving (Edwards, Delahunt, & Mahncke, 2009). Health and exercise can influence the extent to which processing speed declines (Hillman, Erickson, & Kramer, 2008).

Does Processing Speed Matter?   How fast children can process information is linked with their competence in thinking (Demetriou, Mouyi, & Spanoudis, 2010). For example, how fast children can articulate a series of words affects how many words they can store and remember.

For some tasks in everyday life, though, speed of processing information may not be important. For example, the strategies that people learn through experience may compensate for any decline in processing speed with age. In general, though, speed is an important aspect of processing information (Hoyer & Roodin, 2009; Salthouse, 2012).

Review *Connect* Reflect

LG1 Explain the information-processing approach and its application to development

Review

- What is the information-processing approach, and how can it be applied to development?
- How does processing speed change developmentally?

Connect

- How are Piaget's theory and Vygotsky's theory similar to or different from the information-processing approach in explaining how individuals learn and think?

Reflect *Your Own Personal Journey of Life*

- The importance of strategies in processing information was discussed in the section you have just read. What strategies do you use to process information?

Attention   **LG2** Define attention, and outline its developmental changes

| What Is Attention? | Infancy | Childhood and Adolescence | Adulthood |

The world holds a lot of information to perceive. Right now, you are perceiving the letters and words that make up this sentence. Now look around the setting where you are and pick out something to look at other than this book. After that, curl up the toes on your right foot. In each of these circumstances, you engaged in the process of paying attention. What is attention and what effect does it have? How does it change with age?

WHAT IS ATTENTION?

Attention is the focusing of mental resources. Attention improves cognitive processing for many tasks. At any one time, though, people can pay attention to only a limited amount of information.

Individuals can allocate their attention in different ways (Columbo, Kapa, & Curtendale, 2011; Hanania & Smith, 2010). Psychologists have labeled these types of allocation as selective attention, divided attention, sustained attention, and executive attention.

- **Selective attention** is focusing on a specific aspect of experience that is relevant while ignoring others that are irrelevant. Focusing on one voice among many in a crowded room or a noisy restaurant is an example of selective attention. When you switched your attention to the toes on your right foot, you were engaging in selective attention.
- **Divided attention** involves concentrating on more than one activity at the same time. If you are listening to music or the television while you are reading this chapter, you are engaging in divided attention.
- **Sustained attention** is the ability to maintain attention to a selected stimulus for a prolonged period of time. Sustained attention is also called vigilance.
- **Executive attention** involves action planning, allocating attention to goals, error detection and compensation, monitoring progress on tasks, and dealing with novel or difficult circumstances.

This young infant's attention is riveted on the blue toy frog that has just been placed in front of him. His attention involves the processes of habituation and dishabituation. *What characterizes these processes?*

attention Focusing of mental resources.

selective attention Focusing on a specific aspect of experience that is relevant while ignoring others that are irrelevant.

divided attention Concentrating on more than one activity at the same time.

sustained attention The ability to maintain attention to a selected stimulus for a prolonged period of time.

executive attention Cognitive process involving action planning, allocating attention to goals, error detection and compensation, monitoring progress on tasks, and dealing with novel or difficult circumstances.

INFANCY

How effectively can infants attend to something? Even newborns can detect a contour and fixate on it. Older infants scan patterns more thoroughly. By 4 months, infants can selectively attend to an object.

Orienting/Investigative Process Attention in the first year of life is dominated by an *orienting/investigative process* (Posner & Rothbart, 2007a, b). This process involves directing attention to potentially important locations in the environment (that is, *where*) and recognizing objects and their features (such as color and form) (that is, *what*) (Courage & Richards, 2008; Richards, 2011). From 3 to 9 months of age, infants can deploy their attention more flexibly and quickly.

Habituation and Dishabituation Closely linked with attention are the processes of habituation and dishabituation, which we discussed in Chapter 5, "Motor, Sensory, and Perceptual Development" (Kavsek, 2009). If you say the same word or show the same toy to a baby several times in a row, the baby usually pays less attention to it each time. This is *habituation*—decreased responsiveness to a stimulus after repeated presentations of the stimulus. *Dishabituation* is the increase in responsiveness after a change in stimulation.

Infants' attention is often linked to novelty and habituation (Snyder & Torrence, 2008). When an object becomes familiar, attention becomes shorter, making infants more vulnerable to distraction (Oakes, Kannass, & Shaddy, 2002).

Knowing about habituation and dishabituation can help parents interact effectively with infants. Infants respond to changes in stimulation. Wise parents sense when an infant shows an interest and realize that they may have to repeat something many times for the infant to process information. But if the stimulation is repeated often, the infant stops responding to the parent. In parent-infant interaction, it is important for parents to do novel things and to repeat them often until the infant stops responding. The parent stops or changes behaviors when the infant redirects his or her attention (Rosenblith, 1992).

Joint Attention   Another type of attention that is an important aspect of infant development is **joint attention,** in which two or more individuals focus on the same object or event. Joint attention requires (1) an ability to track another's behavior, such as following the gaze of someone; (2) one person directing another's attention; and (3) reciprocal interaction. Early in infancy, joint attention usually involves a caregiver pointing or using words to direct an infant's attention. Emerging forms of joint attention may occur as early as midway through the first year, but it is not until toward the end of the first year that joint attention skills are frequently observed (Kawai & others, 2010). In a study conducted by Rechele Brooks and Andrew Meltzoff (2005), at 10 to 11 months of age infants first began engaging in "gaze following," looking where another person has just looked (see Figure 7.3). And by their first birthday, infants have begun to direct adults' attention to objects that capture their interest (Heimann & others, 2006). A recent study also revealed that the extent to which 9-month-old infants engaged in joint attention was linked to their long-term memory (a one-week delay), possibly because joint attention enhances the relevance of attended items (Kopp & Lindenberger, 2011). Another recent study of 5-month-old infants found that a region of the prefrontal cortex was activated when they engaged in joint attention with another person (Grossmann & Johnson, 2010).

A father and his infant daughter engaging in joint attention. *What about this photograph tells you that joint attention is occurring? Why is joint attention an important aspect of infant development?*

Joint attention plays important roles in many aspects of infant development and considerably increases infants' ability to learn from other people (Carpenter, 2011; Meltzoff, 2011). Nowhere is this more apparent than in observations of interchanges between caregivers and infants as infants are learning language (Tomasello, 2011). When caregivers and infants frequently engage in joint attention, infants say their first word earlier and develop a larger vocabulary (Flom & Pick, 2003).

CHILDHOOD AND ADOLESCENCE

The child's ability to pay attention improves significantly during the preschool years (Hanania & Smith, 2010; Rothbart, 2011). Toddlers wander around, shift attention

joint attention Focus by individuals on the same object or event; requires an ability to track another's behavior, one individual to direct another's attention, and reciprocal interaction.

(a)

(b)

FIGURE **7.3**

GAZE FOLLOWING IN INFANCY. Researcher Rechele Brooks shifts her eyes from the infant to a toy in the foreground (*a*). The infant then follows her eye movement to the toy (*b*). Brooks and colleague Andrew Meltzoff (2005) found that infants begin to engage in this kind of behavior called "gaze following" at 10 to 11 months of age. *Why might gaze following be an important accomplishment for an infant?*

developmental **connection**

Brain Development. One shift in activation of the brain in middle and late childhood is from diffuse, large areas to more focused, smaller areas, which especially involves more focal activation in the prefrontal cortex. Chapter 3, p. 103

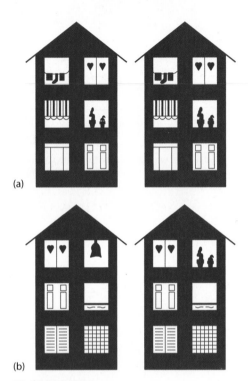

(a)

(b)

FIGURE **7.4**

THE PLANFULNESS OF ATTENTION. In one study, children were given pairs of houses to examine, like the ones shown here (Vurpillot, 1968). For three pairs of houses, what was in the windows was identical (a). For the other three pairs, the windows had different items in them (b). By filming the reflection in the children's eyes, it could be determined what they were looking at, how long they looked, and the sequence of their eye movements. Children under 6 examined only a fragmentary portion of each display and made their judgments on the basis of insufficient information.

developmental **connection**

Culture. A recent survey revealed that when media multitasking is taken into account, 8- to 18-year-olds use media an average of 8 hours a day rather than just 6 hours a day (Roberts & Foehr, 2008). Chapter 15, p. 509

from one activity to another, and seem to spend little time focused on any one object or event. By comparison, the preschool child might be observed watching television for a half hour. However, a recent research study revealed that television watching and video game playing were both linked to attention problems in children (Swing & others, 2010). Young children especially make advances in two aspects of attention—executive attention and sustained attention. Mary Rothbart and Maria Gartstein (2008, p. 332) described why advances in executive and sustained attention are so important in early childhood:

> The development of the . . . executive attention system supports the rapid increases in effortful control in the toddler and preschool years. Increases in attention are due, in part, to advances in comprehension and language development. As children are better able to understand their environment, this increased appreciation of their surroundings helps them to sustain attention for longer periods of time.

In at least two ways, however, the preschool child's control of attention is still deficient:

- *Salient versus relevant dimensions.* Preschool children are likely to pay attention to stimuli that stand out, or are *salient*, even when those stimuli are not relevant to solving a problem or performing a task. For example, if a flashy, attractive clown presents the directions for solving a problem, preschool children are likely to pay more attention to the clown than to the directions. After the age of 6 or 7, children attend more efficiently to the dimensions of the task that are relevant, such as the directions for solving a problem. This change reflects a shift to cognitive control of attention, so that children act less impulsively and reflect more.

- *Planfulness.* Although in general young children's planning improves as part of advances in executive attention, when experimenters ask children to judge whether two complex pictures are the same, preschool children tend to use a haphazard comparison strategy, not examining all of the details before making a judgment. By comparison, elementary-school-age children are more likely to systematically compare the details across the pictures, one detail at a time (Vurpillot, 1968) (see Figure 7.4).

In Central European countries, such as Hungary, kindergarten children participate in exercises designed to improve their attention (Mills & Mills, 2000; Posner & Rothbart, 2007a, b). For example, in one eye-contact exercise, the teacher sits in the center of a circle of children, and each child is required to catch the teacher's eye before being permitted to leave the group. In other exercises created to improve attention, teachers have children participate in stop-go activities during which they have to listen for a specific signal, such as a drumbeat or an exact number of rhythmic beats, before stopping the activity.

Computer exercises also recently have been developed to improve children's attention (Jaeggi, Berman, & Jonides, 2009; Tang & Posner, 2009). For example, one study revealed that five days of computer exercises that involved learning how to use a joystick, working memory, and the resolution of conflict improved the attention of 4- to 6-year-old children (Rueda & others, 2005). In one of the computer games, young children have to move a joystick to keep a cat on the grass and out of the mud, and in another they help a cat find a duck in a pond. Although not commercially available, further information about computer exercises for improving children's attention is available at www.teach-the-brain.org/learn/attention/index.

Preschool children's ability to control and sustain their attention is related to school readiness (Rothbart, 2011). For example, a study of more than 1,000 children revealed that their ability to sustain their attention at 54 months of age was linked to their school readiness (which included achievement and language skills) (NICHD Early Child Care Research Network, 2005). Attention to relevant information increases steadily through the elementary and secondary school years (Davidson, 1996). Processing of irrelevant information decreases in adolescence.

Another important aspect of attention is the ability to shift it from one activity to another as needed. For example, writing a good story requires shifting attention among the competing tasks of forming letters, composing grammar, structuring paragraphs, and conveying the story as a whole. Older children and adolescents are better than younger children at tasks that require shifts of attention.

One trend involving divided attention is adolescents' multitasking, which in some cases involves not just dividing attention between two activities, but even three or more (Bauerlein, 2008). A major influence on the increase in multitasking is the availability of multiple electronic media. Many adolescents have a range of electronic media at their disposal. It is not unusual for adolescents to divide their attention by working on homework while engaging in an instant messaging conversation, surfing the Web, and looking at an iTunes playlist. And a national survey revealed that 50 percent of adolescents made and answered phone calls while driving, and 13 percent (approximately 1.7 million) wrote and/or read text messages while driving (Allstate Foundation, 2005).

Is this multitasking beneficial or distracting? If the key task is at all complex and challenging, such as trying to figure out how to solve a homework problem, multitasking considerably reduces attention to the key task (Myers, 2008).

ADULTHOOD

What happens to attention in adulthood? Attentional skills are often excellent in early adulthood and, of course, the discussion of divided attention and multitasking applies to many adults as well as adolescents. However, in many contexts older adults may not be able to focus on relevant information as effectively as younger adults (Madden, 2007). Consider a study that examined the role that visual attention, involving search, selection, and switching, played in driving risk in older adult drivers (Richardson & Marottoli, 2003). Thirty-five community-dwelling drivers aged 72 and older (mean age, 80) underwent an on-road driving evaluation involving parking lot maneuvers and urban, suburban, and highway driving. They were also given tests of visual attention. The worse their driving, the lower their visual attention score was. Yielding right of way and negotiating safe turns or merges were especially related to visual attention.

A recent study also found that older adults had deficiencies in executive attention (Mahoney & others, 2010). In this study, a lower level of executive attention in older adults was linked to low blood pressure, which likely is related to reduced blood flow to the brain's frontal lobes.

Older adults tend to be less adept at selective attention—focusing on a specific aspect of experience while ignoring others—than younger adults are (Rogers & Fisk, 2001). These age differences are minimal if the task involves a simple search (such as determining whether a target item is present on a computer screen) or if individuals have practiced the task (Kramer & Madden, 2008). As the demands on attention increase, however, the performance of older adults declines (Kramer & Madden, 2008). As long as two competing tasks are reasonably easy, age differences among adults are minimal or nonexistent. However, as competing tasks become more difficult, older adults divide attention less effectively than younger adults (Maciokas & Crognale, 2003).

How well do older adults function on tasks that involve vigilance? On tests of simple vigilance and sustained attention, older adults usually perform as well as younger adults. For example, a recent study revealed that sustained attention increased in early adulthood but remained unchanged thereafter through 77 years of age (Carriere & others, 2010). However, on complex vigilance tasks, older adults' performance usually drops (Bucur & Madden, 2007).

Is multitasking, which involves divided attention, beneficial or distracting?

developmental **connection**

Perception. Researchers study declines in the perceptual skills involved in older adults' driving skills. Chapter 5, p. 169

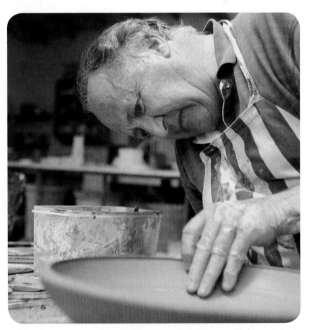

What are some developmental changes in attention in adulthood?

Review

- What is attention? What are three ways that people allocate their attention?
- How does attention develop in infancy?
- How does attention develop in childhood and adolescence?

Connect

- Relate the characteristics of the life-span perspective (Chapter 1) to what you have learned about attention and its developmental changes.

Reflect *Your Own Personal Journey of Life*

- Imagine that you are an elementary school teacher. Devise some strategies to help children pay attention in class.

Memory **LG3** Describe what memory is and how it changes through the life span

What Is Memory? | Infancy | Childhood | Adulthood

Twentieth-century American playwright Tennessee Williams once commented that life is all memory except for that one present moment that goes by so quickly that you can hardly catch it going. But just what is memory?

WHAT IS MEMORY?

Memory is the retention of information over time. Without memory you would not be able to connect what happened to you yesterday with what is going on in your life today. Human memory is truly remarkable when you think of how much information we put into our memories and how much we must retrieve to perform all of life's activities. However, human memory has imperfections that will be discussed shortly.

Processes of Memory Researchers study how information is initially placed in or encoded into memory, how it is retained or stored after being encoded, and how it is found or retrieved for a certain purpose later (see Figure 7.5). Encoding, storage, and retrieval are the basic processes required for memory. Failures can occur in any of these processes. Some part of an event might not be encoded, the mental representation of the event might not be stored, or even if the memory exists, you might not be able to retrieve it.

memory Retention of information over time.

schema theory Theory stating that people mold memories to fit information that already exists in their minds.

Constructing Memory Memories may be inaccurate for a number of reasons (Sabbagh, 2009). Memory is not like a tape recorder or a camera or computer memory. People construct and reconstruct their memories (Gaesser & others, 2011). According to **schema theory,** people mold memories to fit information that already

FIGURE **7.5**

PROCESSING INFORMATION IN MEMORY. As you read about the many aspects of memory in this chapter, think about the organization of memory in terms of these three main activities.

Encoding

Getting information into memory

Storage

Retaining information over time

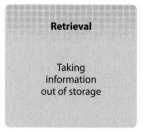

Retrieval

Taking information out of storage

exists in their minds. This process is guided by **schemas,** which are mental frameworks that organize concepts and information. Schemas influence the way people encode, make inferences about, and retrieve information. Often when we retrieve information, we fill in the gaps.

We have schemas for all sorts of information. If a teacher tells your class a story about two men and two women who were involved in a train crash in France, students won't remember every detail of the story and will reconstruct the story with their own particular stamp on it. One student might reconstruct the story by saying they died in a plane crash, another might describe three men and three women, another might say the crash was in Germany, and so on. Such reconstruction and distortion are nowhere more apparent than in clashing testimony given by eyewitnesses at trials.

In sum, schema theory accurately predicts that people don't store and retrieve bits of data in computer-like fashion (Baddeley, Eysenck, & Anderson, 2009). We reconstruct the past rather than take an exact photograph of it, and the mind can distort an event as it encodes and stores impressions of it (Kensinger, 2009).

➡ **developmental connection**

Gender. Gender schema theory emphasizes children's gender schemas that organize the world in terms of male and female. Chapter 12, p. 375

INFANCY

Popular child-rearing expert Penelope Leach (1990) told parents that 6- to 8-month-old babies cannot hold a picture of their mother or father in their mind. However, child development researchers have revealed that infants as young as 3 months of age show a limited type of memory.

First Memories   Carolyn Rovee-Collier (1987, 2007) has conducted research that demonstrates infants can remember perceptual-motor information. In a characteristic experiment, she places a baby in a crib underneath an elaborate mobile and ties one end of a ribbon to the baby's ankle and the other end to the mobile. The baby kicks and makes the mobile move (see Figure 7.6). Weeks later, the baby is returned to the crib, but its foot is not tied to the mobile. The baby kicks, apparently trying to make the mobile move. However, if the mobile's makeup is changed even slightly, the baby doesn't kick. If the mobile is then restored to being exactly as it was when the baby's ankle was tied to it, the baby will begin kicking again. According to Rovee-Collier, even by 2½ months the baby's memory is incredibly detailed.

How well can infants remember? Some researchers such as Rovee-Collier (2007; Rovee-Collier & Barr, 2010) have concluded that infants as young as 2 to 6 months of age can remember some experiences until they are 1½ to 2 years of age. However, critics such as Jean Mandler (2000), a leading expert on infant cognition, argue that the infants in Rovee-Collier's experiments are displaying only implicit memory. **Implicit memory** refers to memory without conscious recollection—memories of skills and routine procedures that are performed automatically. In contrast, **explicit memory** refers to the conscious memory of facts and experiences.

When people think about memory, they are usually referring to explicit memory. Most researchers find that babies do not show explicit memory until the second half of the first year (Bauer, Larkina, & Deocampo, 2011). Then explicit memory improves substantially during the second year of life (Bauer, Larkina, & Deocampo, 2011). In one longitudinal study, infants were assessed several times during their second year (Bauer & others, 2000). Older infants showed more accurate memory and required fewer prompts to demonstrate their memory than younger infants. Researchers have documented that 6-month-olds can remember information for 24 hours but by 20 months of age infants can remember information they encountered 12 months earlier.

In sum, most of young infants' conscious memories are fragile and short-lived, except for memory of perceptual-motor actions, which can be substantial (Mandler,

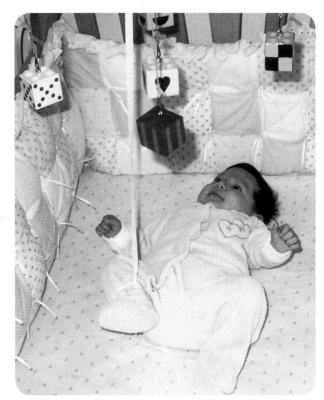

FIGURE 7.6

THE TECHNIQUE USED IN ROVEE-COLLIER'S INVESTIGATION OF INFANT MEMORY. In Rovee-Collier's experiment, operant conditioning was used to demonstrate that infants as young as 2½ months of age can retain information from the experience of being conditioned.

schemas Mental frameworks that organize concepts and information.

implicit memory Memory without conscious recollection—memory of skills and routine procedures that are performed automatically.

explicit memory Conscious memory of facts and experiences.

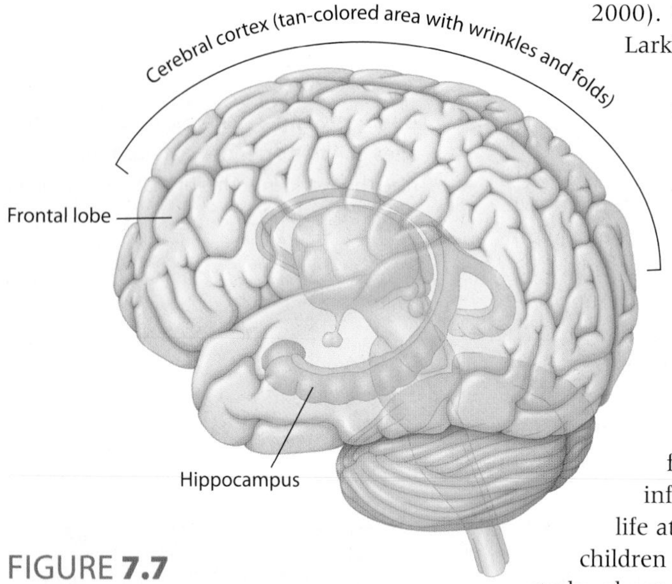

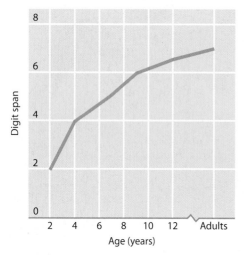

FIGURE **7.7**

KEY BRAIN STRUCTURES INVOLVED IN EXPLICIT MEMORY DEVELOPMENT IN INFANCY

FIGURE **7.8**

DEVELOPMENTAL CHANGES IN MEMORY SPAN. In one study, memory span increased by about three digits from 2 years of age to 7 years of age (Dempster, 1981). By 12 years of age, memory span had increased on average another one and a half digits.

long-term memory A relatively permanent and unlimited type of memory.

short-term memory Retention of information for up to 15 to 30 seconds, without rehearsal of the information. Using rehearsal, individuals can keep the information in short-term memory longer.

2000). Conscious memories improve across the second year of life (Bauer, Larkina, & Deocampo, 2011).

What changes in the brain are linked to infants' memory development? From about 6 to 12 months of age, the maturation of the hippocampus and the surrounding cerebral cortex, especially the frontal lobes, makes the emergence of explicit memory possible (Diamond, Casey, & Munakata, 2011; Nelson, 2011a, b) (see Figure 7.7). Explicit memory continues to improve during the second year as these brain structures further mature and connections between them increase. Less is known about the areas of the brain involved in implicit memory in infancy.

Infantile Amnesia   Do you remember your third birthday party? Probably not. Most adults can remember little if anything from the first three years of their life (Sabbagh, 2009). This is called infantile, or childhood, amnesia. The few reported adult memories of life at age 2 or 3 are at best very sketchy (Neisser, 2004). Elementary school children also do not remember much of their early childhood years. In one study, about three years after leaving preschool, children were much poorer at remembering their former classmates than their teacher was (Lie & Newcombe, 1999). In another study, 10-year-olds were shown pictures of their preschool classmates, and they recognized only about 20 percent of them (Newcombe & Fox, 1994).

What causes infantile amnesia? One reason for the difficulty older children and adults have in recalling events from their infancy and early childhood is the immaturity of the prefrontal lobes of the brain, which are believed to play an important role in memory for events (Boyer & Diamond, 1992).

CHILDHOOD

Children's memory improves considerably after infancy. What are some of the significant strides in memory as children grow older? The progress includes improvements in short-term and long-term memory, as well as the use of strategies.

Short-Term and Working Memory   When people talk about memory, they are usually referring to **long-term memory,** which is relatively permanent and unlimited. When you remember the types of games you enjoyed playing as a child, details of your first date, or characteristics of the life-span perspective (which we discussed in Chapter 1), you are drawing on your long-term memory. But when you remember the word you just read, you are using short-term memory. **Short-term memory** involves the retention of information for up to 15 to 30 seconds, without rehearsal of the information. Using rehearsal, individuals can keep the information in short-term memory longer (Yen, 2008).

Memory Span   Unlike long-term memory, short-term memory has a very limited capacity. One method of assessing that capacity is the memory-span task. You simply hear a short list of stimuli—usually digits—presented at a rapid pace (one per second, for example). Then you are asked to repeat the digits.

Research with the memory-span task suggests that short-term memory increases during childhood. For example, in one investigation, memory span increased from about two digits in 2- to 3-year-old children to about five digits in 7-year-old children. Between 7 and 13 years of age, memory span increased only by one and a half digits (Dempster, 1981) (see Figure 7.8). Keep in mind, though, that individuals have different memory spans.

Why does memory span change with age? Rehearsal of information is important; older children rehearse the digits more than younger children do. Speed of processing information is important, too, especially the speed with which memory items can be identified. For example, one study tested children on their speed at repeating words presented orally (Case, Kurland, & Goldberg, 1982). Speed of repetition was a powerful predictor of memory span. The children who were able to quickly repeat the presented words were also far more likely to have greater memory spans. Indeed, when the speed of repetition was controlled, the 6-year-olds' memory spans were equal to those of young adults.

Working Memory   Short-term memory is like a passive storehouse with shelves to store information until it is moved to long-term memory. Alan Baddeley (1990, 2001, 2007, 2010a, b, 2012) defines **working memory** as a kind of mental "workbench" where individuals manipulate and assemble information when they make decisions, solve problems, and comprehend written and spoken language (see Figure 7.9). Working memory is described as more active and powerful in modifying information than short-term memory.

Working memory is linked to many aspects of children's development (Baddeley, 2010a, b, 2012; Towse & others, 2010). The following three recent studies illustrate the importance of working memory in children's cognitive and language development:

- Working memory and attention control predicted growth in emergent literacy and number skills in young children in low-income families (Welsh & others, 2010).
- Working memory capacity at 9 to 10 years of age predicted foreign language comprehension two years later at 11 to 12 years of age (Andersson, 2010).
- Working memory capacity predicted how many items on a to-be-remembered list that fourth-grade children forgot (Aslan, Zellner, & Bauml, 2010).

Children's Long-Term Memory   Sometimes the long-term memories of preschoolers seem to be erratic, but young children can remember a great deal of information if they are given appropriate cues and prompts. One area in which children's long-term memory is being examined extensively relates to whether young children should be allowed to testify in court (Ceci & others, 2010; Pipe & Salmon, 2009). Increasingly, young children are being allowed to testify, especially if they are the only witnesses to abuse, a crime, and so forth. Several factors influence the accuracy of a young child's memory (Bruck & Ceci, 1999):

- *There are age differences in children's susceptibility to suggestion.* Preschoolers are the most suggestible age group in comparison with older children and adults (Ceci, Papierno, & Kulkofsky, 2007). For example, preschool children are more susceptible to absorbing misleading or incorrect post-event information (Ghetti & Alexander, 2004). Despite these age differences, there is still concern about older children when they are subjected to suggestive interviews (Poole & Lindsay, 1996).
- *There are individual differences in susceptibility.* Some preschoolers are highly resistant to interviewers' suggestions, whereas others immediately succumb to the slightest suggestion (Ceci & others, 2010). A research review concluded that suggestibility is linked to low self-concept, low support from parents, and mothers' insecure attachment in romantic relationships (Bruck & Melnyk, 2004).
- *Interviewing techniques can produce substantial distortions in children's reports about highly salient events.* Children are suggestible not just about peripheral details but also about the central aspects of an event (Ceci & others, 2010; Odegard & others, 2009). Their false claims have been found to persist for at least three months (Ornstein, Gordon, & Larus, 1992). Nonetheless, young children are capable of recalling much that is relevant about an event (Goodman, Batterman-Faunce, & Kenney, 1992). When children do accurately recall an event, the interviewer often has a neutral tone, there is limited use of misleading questions, and there is an absence of any motivation for the child to make a false report (Bruck & Ceci, 1999).

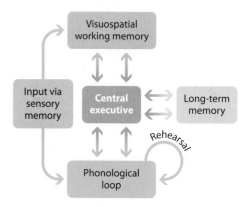

FIGURE **7.9**

WORKING MEMORY. In Baddeley's working memory model, working memory is like a mental workbench, where a great deal of information processing is carried out. Working memory consists of three main components. The phonological loop and visuospatial working memory serve as assistants, helping the central executive do its work. Input from sensory memory goes to the phonological loop, where information about speech is stored and rehearsal takes place, and visuospatial working memory, where visual and spatial information, including imagery, are stored. Working memory is a limited-capacity system, and information is stored there for only a brief time. Working memory interacts with long-term memory, using information from long-term memory in its work and transmitting information to long-term memory for longer storage.

Four-year-old Jennifer Royal was the only eyewitness to one of her playmates' being shot to death. She was allowed to testify in open court and the clarity of her statements helped to convict the gunman. *What are some issues involved in whether young children should be allowed to testify in court?*

working memory A mental "workbench" where individuals manipulate and assemble information when making decisions, solving problems, and comprehending written and spoken language.

In sum, whether a young child's eyewitness testimony is accurate or not may depend on a number of factors such as the type, number, and intensity of the suggestive techniques the child has experienced (Ceci & others, 2010; Pipe & Salmon, 2009). It appears that the reliability of young children's reports has as much to do with the skills and motivation of the interviewer as with any natural limitations on young children's memory (Bruck, Ceci, & Principe, 2006).

Children's long-term memory improves even more as they move into the middle and late childhood years. This advance is especially true when they use the strategies that we describe next.

Strategies   *Strategies* involve the use of mental activities to improve the processing of information (Schneider, 2011). For memory, rehearsing information and organizing are two typical strategies that older children (and adults) use to remember information more effectively. Rehearsal (repetition) works better for short-term memory. Strategies such as organization, elaborating on the information to be remembered, and making it personally relevant, make long-term memory more effective. Preschool children usually do not use strategies such as rehearsal and organization to remember (Flavell, Miller, & Miller, 2002).

Imagery   Creating mental images is another strategy for improving memory. However, using imagery to remember verbal information works better for older children than for younger children (Schneider, 2011).

Elaboration   One important strategy is **elaboration,** which involves engaging in more extensive processing of information. When individuals engage in elaboration, their memory benefits. Thinking of examples and self-reference are effective ways to elaborate information. Thinking about personal associations with information makes the information more meaningful and helps children to remember it. For example, if the word *win* is on a list of words a child is asked to remember, the child might think of the last time she won a bicycle race.

The use of elaboration changes developmentally (Schneider, 2011). Adolescents are more likely than children to use elaboration spontaneously. Elementary school children can be taught to use elaboration strategies on a learning task, but they will be less likely than adolescents to use the strategies on other learning tasks in the future. Nonetheless, verbal elaboration can be an effective strategy even for young elementary school children.

Fuzzy Trace Theory   One theory that emphasizes the reconstructive aspects of memory provides an alternative to strategies in explaining developmental changes in children's memory. Proposed by Charles Brainerd and Valerie Reyna (1993, 2004), **fuzzy trace theory** states that memory is best understood by considering two types of memory representations: (1) verbatim memory trace and (2) gist. The verbatim memory trace consists of the precise details of the information, whereas gist refers to the central idea of the information. When gist is used, fuzzy traces are built up. Although individuals of all ages extract gist, young children tend to store and retrieve verbatim traces. At some point during the early elementary school years, children begin to use gist more and, according to the theory, its use contributes to the improved memory and reasoning of older children because fuzzy traces are more enduring and less likely to be forgotten than verbatim traces (Reyna & Rivers, 2008).

Knowledge   An especially important influence on memory is the knowledge that individuals possess about a specific topic or skill (Nippold,

elaboration Engagement in more extensive processing of information, benefiting memory.

fuzzy trace theory Theory stating that memory is best understood by considering two types of memory representations: verbatim memory trace, and gist. In this theory, older children's better memory is attributed to the fuzzy traces created by extracting the gist of information.

2009). Knowledge influences what people notice and how they organize, represent, and interpret information. This skill, in turn, affects their ability to remember, reason, and solve problems.

One study found that 10- and 11-year-olds who were experienced chess players were able to remember more information about chess pieces than college students who were not chess players (Chi, 1978) (see Figure 7.10). In contrast, the college students were able to remember other stimuli better than the children were. Thus, the children's expertise in chess gave them superior memories, but only in chess.

Teaching Strategies   So far we have described several important strategies adults can adopt when guiding children to remember information more effectively over the long term. These strategies include showing children how to organize information, elaborate the information, and develop images of the information. Another good strategy is to encourage children to understand the material that needs to be remembered rather than rotely memorizing it. Two other strategies adults can use to guide children's retention of memory were recently proposed:

- *Repeat with variation on the instructional information and link early and often.* These are memory development research expert Patricia Bauer's (2009) recommendations to improve children's consolidation and reconsolidation of the information they are learning. Variations on a lesson theme increase the number of associations in memory storage, and linking expands the network of associations in memory storage; both strategies expand the routes for retrieving information from storage.
- *Embed memory-relevant language when instructing children.* Teachers vary considerably in how much they use memory-relevant language that encourages students to remember information. In recent research that involved extensive observations of a number of first-grade teachers in the classroom, Peter Ornstein and his colleagues (Ornstein, Grammar & Coffman, 2010; Ornstein, Haden, & Coffman, 2010; Ornstein & others, 2007, 2010) found that in the time segments observed, the teachers rarely used strategy suggestions or metacognitive (thinking about thinking) questions. In this research, when lower-achieving students were placed in classrooms in which teachers were categorized as "high-mnemonic teachers" who frequently embedded memory-relevant information in their teaching, their achievement increased (Ornstein & others, 2007).

ADULTHOOD

Memory changes during the adult years, but not all memory changes with age in the same way (Barba, Attali, & La Corte, 2010; Nyberg & Backman, 2011; Ornstein & Light, 2010). Let's look first at working memory and processing speed.

Working Memory and Processing Speed   Two important cognitive resources that are linked with aging are working memory and processing speed (Caplan & others, 2011; Delaloye & others, 2009). Remember that working memory is like a mental "workbench" that allows us to manipulate and assemble information (Baddeley, 2010a, b, 2012). Researchers have consistently found declines in working memory during the late adulthood years (Bialystok & Craik, 2010; Ornstein & Light, 2010). Explanation of the decline in working memory in older adults focuses on their less efficient inhibition in preventing irrelevant information from entering working memory and their increased distractibility (Healey & others, 2010).

Also recall from earlier in the chapter that processing speed declines in middle and late adulthood (Deary, Johnson, & Starr, 2010; Salthouse, 2012). Further, the decline in processing speed is linked with a decline in working memory (Chaytor & Schmitter-Edgecombe, 2004).

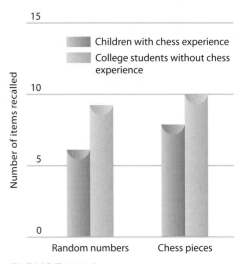

FIGURE **7.10**
MEMORY FOR NUMBERS AND CHESS PIECES

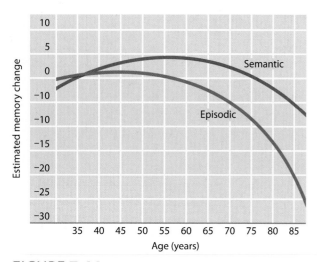

FIGURE **7.11**

CHANGES IN EPISODIC AND SEMANTIC MEMORY IN ADULTHOOD

This older adult woman has forgotten where the keys to her car are. *What type of memory is involved in this situation?*

episodic memory Retention of information about the where and when of life's happenings.

semantic memory A person's knowledge about the world, including fields of expertise, general academic knowledge, and "everyday knowledge" about meanings of words, names of famous individuals, important places, and common things.

source memory The ability to remember where something was learned.

prospective memory Remembering to do something in the future.

Explicit and Implicit Memory   Long-term memory systems include explicit and implicit memory. Recall that *explicit memory* refers to the conscious memory of facts and experiences. Explicit memory is also sometimes called *declarative memory*. Examples of explicit memory include being at a grocery store and remembering that you want to buy something or being able to recall the events of a movie you have seen.

Explicit memory can be subdivided into episodic memory and semantic memory. **Episodic memory** is the retention of information about the where and when of life's happenings. For example, what was it like when your younger sister or brother was born? What happened to you on your first date? What did you eat for breakfast this morning?

Autobiographical memory is the personal recollection of events and facts. Autobiographical memories are stored as episodic memories. A robust finding in autobiographical memory is called the *reminiscence bump,* in which adults remember more events from the second and third decades of their lives than from other decades (Berntsen & Rubin, 2002). The "bump" is found more for positive than negative life events. A recent study revealed support for the reminiscence bump and that these memories were more distinct and more important for identity development (Demiray, Gulgoz, & Bluck, 2009).

Semantic memory is a person's knowledge about the world. It includes a person's fields of expertise (such as knowledge of chess, for a skilled chess player); general academic knowledge of the sort learned in school (such as knowledge of geometry); and "everyday knowledge" about meanings of words, famous individuals, important places, and common things (such as who Nelson Mandela and Mahatma Gandhi are).

Recall that *implicit memory* refers to memory of skills and routine procedures that are performed automatically. (Implicit memory is sometimes referred to as procedural memory.) Examples of implicit memory include unconsciously remembering how to drive a car, swing a golf club, or type on a computer keyboard.

Aging and Explicit Memory   Younger adults have better episodic memory than older adults have (Cansino, 2009; Gaesser & others, 2011). Does semantic memory decline with age? Older adults often take longer to retrieve semantic information, but usually they can ultimately retrieve it. As shown in Figure 7.11, semantic memory continues to increase through the fifties, showing little decline even through the sixties (Rönnlund & others, 2005). Figure 7.11 also shows how the gap between semantic and episodic memory widens during the middle and late adulthood years. In one study, after almost five decades adults picked out their high school classmates with better than 70 percent accuracy (Bahrick, Bahrick, & Wittlinger, 1975). How well do most adults remember the actual subjects they learned in high school, however? In the *Connecting with Research* interlude, we focus on another study that examined the developmental aspects of semantic memory.

Although many aspects of semantic memory are reasonably well preserved in late adulthood, a common memory problem for older adults is the tip-of-the-tongue (TOT) phenomenon, in which individuals can't quite retrieve familiar information but have the feeling that they should be able to retrieve it (Bucur & Madden, 2007). Researchers have found that older adults are more likely to experience TOT states than younger adults (Bucur & Madden, 2007).

Aging and Implicit Memory   Implicit memory is less likely to be adversely affected by aging than explicit memory (Yoon, Cole, & Lee, 2009). Thus, older adults are more likely to forget which items they wanted to buy at the grocery store (unless they wrote them down on a list and took it with them) than they are to forget how

How Well Do Adults Remember What They Learned in High School and College Spanish?

When older adults are assessed for what they learned in high school or college, researchers find neither great durability in memory nor huge deterioration (Salthouse, 1991). In one study, non-Latino adults of various ages in the United States were studied to determine how much Spanish they remembered from classes they had taken in high school or college (Bahrick, 1984). The individuals chosen for the study had used Spanish very little since they initially learned it in high school or college. Not surprisingly, young adults who had taken Spanish classes within the last three years remembered their Spanish best. After that, the deterioration in memory was very gradual (see Figure 7.12). For example, older adults who had studied Spanish 50 years earlier remembered about 80 percent of what young adults did who had studied it in the last three years! The most important factor in the adults' memory of Spanish was not how long ago they had studied it but how well they initially learned it—those who got an A in Spanish 50 years earlier remembered more Spanish than those who got a C when taking Spanish only one year earlier.

What are some of the implications of the research on what adults remember from high school for improving teaching methods in U.S. schools?

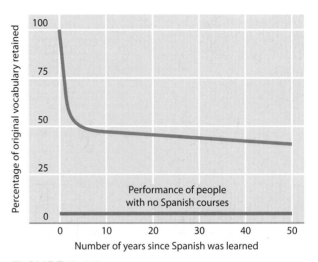

FIGURE **7.12**

MEMORY FOR SPANISH AS A FUNCTION OF AGE SINCE SPANISH WAS LEARNED. An initial steep drop over about a three-year period in remembering the vocabulary learned in Spanish classes occurred. However, there was little dropoff in memory for Spanish vocabulary from three years after taking Spanish classes to 50 years after taking them. Even 50 years after taking Spanish classes, individuals still remembered almost 50 percent of the vocabulary.

to drive a car. Their processing speed may be slower when driving the car, but they can remember how to do it.

Source Memory   **Source memory** is the ability to remember where one learned something. The contexts of source memory might be the physical setting, the emotional context, or the identity of the speaker. Failures of source memory increase with age in the adult years, and they can be embarrassing, as when an older adult forgets who told a joke and retells it to the source (Besken & Gulgoz, 2009; Kuhlmann & Touron, 2011). However, researchers have found that when information is more relevant to older adults, age differences in source memory are less robust (Hasher, 2003).

Prospective Memory   **Prospective memory** involves remembering to do something in the future, such as remembering to take your medicine or remembering to do an errand. Some researchers have found a decline in prospective memory with age (Jacques & Marcovitch, 2010). However, a number of studies show that determining the cause of the decline is complex and depends on such factors as the nature of the task and what is being assessed (Einstein & McDaniel, 2005; Wang, Dew, & Giovanello, 2010). For example, age-related deficits occur more often in time-based tasks (such as remembering to call someone next Friday) than in event-based tasks (remembering to tell your friend to read a particular book the next time you see her).

Prospective memory involves remembering to do something in the future. The older adult woman here is keeping track of what she plans to buy when she goes to a grocery store the next day.

Review

- What is memory? What are memory's processes? What is involved in constructing memory? Can new information alter memories?
- How does memory develop in infancy?
- How does memory change in childhood?
- What are some changes in memory during the adult years?

Connect

- How might the changes in the brain during late adulthood (described in Chapter 3) be linked to the changes in memory in older adults that were just discussed?

Reflect *Your Own Personal Journey of Life*

- What is your earliest memory? Why do you think you can remember this particular situation?

Thinking   **LG4** Characterize thinking and its developmental changes

What Is Thinking?   Childhood   Adolescence   Adulthood

Attention and memory are often steps toward another level of information processing—thinking. What is thinking? How does it change developmentally? What is children's scientific thinking like? Let's explore these questions.

WHAT IS THINKING?

Thinking involves manipulating and transforming information in memory. We think in order to reason, reflect, evaluate ideas, solve problems, and make decisions.

CHILDHOOD

To explore thinking in childhood, we examine these questions: To what extent do infants form concepts and engage in categorization? What is critical thinking and how can it be encouraged in schools? What is cognitive control and how does it change developmentally? What is children's scientific thinking like? How do children solve problems?

> Infants are creating concepts and organizing their world into conceptual domains that will form the backbone of their thought throughout life.
>
> —JEAN MANDLER
> *Contemporary Psychologist, University of California—San Diego*

Concept Formation and Categorization in Infancy   Along with attention, memory, and imitation, concepts are key aspects of infants' cognitive development (Quinn, 2011; Schultz, 2011). **Concepts** are cognitive groupings of similar objects, events, people, or ideas. Without concepts, you would see each object and event as unique; you would not be able to make any generalizations.

Do infants have concepts? Yes, they do, although we do not know just how early concept formation begins (Quinn, 2011; Schultz, 2011).

Using habituation experiments like those described earlier in the chapter, some researchers have found that infants as young as 3 to 4 months of age can group together objects with similar appearances, such as animals (Quinn, 2011). This research capitalizes on the knowledge that infants are more likely to look at a novel object than a familiar object.

Jean Mandler (2004) argues that these early categorizations are best described as *perceptual categorization*. That is, the categorizations are based on similar perceptual features of objects, such as size, color, and movement, as well as parts of objects,

thinking Manipulating and transforming information in memory, in order to reason, reflect, think critically, evaluate ideas and solve problems, and make decisions.

concepts Cognitive groupings of similar objects, events, people, or ideas.

executive functioning An umbrella-like concept that encompasses a number of higher-level cognitive processes linked to the development of the brain's prefrontal cortex. Executive functioning involves managing one's thoughts to engage in goal-directed behavior and to exercise self-control.

such as legs for animals. Mandler (2004) concludes that it is not until about 7 to 9 months of age that infants form *conceptual* categories rather than just making perceptual discriminations between different categories. In one study of 9- to 11-month-olds, infants classified birds as animals and airplanes as vehicles even though the objects were perceptually similar—airplanes and birds with their wings spread (Mandler & McDonough, 1993) (see Figure 7.13).

Further advances in categorization occur during the second year of life (Madole, Oakes, & Rakison, 2011). Many infants' "first concepts are broad and global in nature, such as 'animal' or 'indoor thing.' Gradually, over the first two years these broad concepts become more differentiated into concepts such as 'land animal,' then 'dog,' or to 'furniture,' then 'chair'" (Mandler, 2006, p. 1).

Learning to put things into the correct categories—knowing what makes something one kind of thing rather than another kind of thing, such as what makes a bird a bird, or a fish a fish—is an important aspect of learning. As infant development researcher Alison Gopnik (2010, p. 159) recently pointed out, "If you can sort the world into the right categories—put things in the right boxes—then you've got a big advance on understanding the world."

Do some very young children develop an intense, passionate interest in a specific category of objects or activities? A study of 11-month-old to 6-year-old children confirmed that they do (DeLoache, Simcock, & Macari, 2007). A striking finding was the large gender difference in categories—with an extreme intense interest in particular categories stronger for boys than girls. Categorization of boys' intense interests focused on vehicles, trains, machines, dinosaurs, and balls; girls' intense interests were more likely to involve dress-ups and books/reading (see Figure 7.14). By the time your author's grandson Alex was 2 years old, he already had developed an intense, passionate interest in the category of vehicles. He categorized vehicles into such subcategories as cars, trucks, earthmoving equipment, and buses. In addition to common classifications of cars into police cars, jeeps, taxis, and such, and trucks into fire trucks, dump trucks, and the like, his categorical knowledge of earthmoving equipment included bulldozers and excavators, and he categorized buses into school buses, London buses, and funky Malta buses (retro buses on the island of Malta). By 2½ years of age, Alex developed an intense, passionate interest in categorizing dinosaurs.

In sum, the infant's advances in processing information—through attention, memory, and concept formation—is much richer, more gradual, and less stage-like, and occurs earlier than was envisioned by earlier theorists, such as Piaget (Bauer, Larkina, & Deocampo, 2011; Diamond, Casey, & Munakata, 2011; Johnson, 2011a, b). As leading infant researcher Jean Mandler (2004) concluded, "The human infant shows a remarkable degree of learning power and complexity in what is being learned and in the way it is represented" (p. 304).

Executive Functioning Recently, increasing attention has been directed to the development of children's **executive functioning,** an umbrella-like concept that consists of a number of higher-level cognitive processes linked to the development of the brain's prefrontal cortex. Executive functioning involves managing one's thoughts to engage in

FIGURE **7.13**

CATEGORIZATION IN 9- TO 11-MONTH-OLDS. These are the stimuli used in the study that indicated 9- to 11-month-old infants categorized birds as animals and airplanes as vehicles even though the objects were perceptually similar (Mandler & McDonough, 1993).

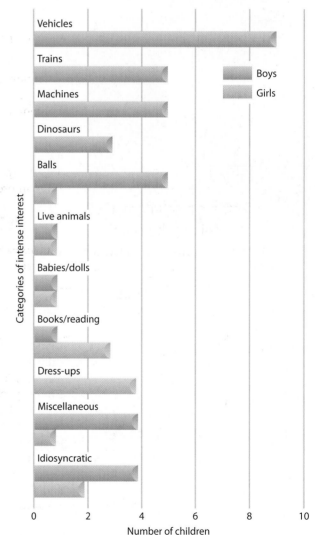

FIGURE **7.14**

CATEGORIZATION OF BOYS' AND GIRLS' INTENSE INTERESTS

The author's grandson Alex at 2 years of age showing his intense, passionate interest in the category of vehicles while playing with a London taxi and a funky Malta bus.

Researcher Stephanie Carlson administers the Less Is More task to a 4-year-old boy. *What were the results of Carlson's research?*

S. GROSS

"For God's sake, think! Why is he being so nice to you?"
© Sam Gross/The New Yorker Collection/ www.cartoonbank.com.

critical thinking Thinking reflectively and productively, and evaluating the evidence.

goal-directed behavior and to exercise self-control. Earlier in this chapter, we described the recent interest in *executive attention*, which comes under the umbrella of executive functioning.

In early childhood, executive functioning especially involves developmental advances in cognitive inhibition (such as inhibiting a strong tendency that is incorrect), cognitive flexibility (such as shifting attention to another item or topic), and goal-setting (such as sharing a toy or mastering a skill like catching a ball) (Beck & others, 2011; Carlson, 2010; Zelazo & Muller, 2011). During early childhood, the relatively stimulus-driven toddler is transformed into a child capable of flexible, goal-directed problem solving that characterizes executive functioning (Zelazo & Muller, 2011).

Stephanie Carlson (2010) has conducted a number of research studies on young children's executive functioning. In one study, Carlson and her colleagues (2005) gave young children a task called Less Is More, in which they are shown two trays of candy—one with five pieces, the other with two—and told that the tray they pick will be given to a stuffed animal seated at the table. Three-year-olds consistently selected the tray with the five pieces of candy, thus giving away more candy than they kept for themselves. However, 4-year-olds were far more likely to choose the tray with only two pieces of candy, keeping five pieces for themselves, and thus inhibiting their impulsiveness far better than the 3-year-olds. In another study, young children were read either *Planet Opposite*—a fantasy book in which everything is turned upside down—or *Fun Town*—a reality-oriented fiction book (Carlson & White, 2011). After being read one of the books, the young children completed the Less Is More task. Sixty percent of the 3-year-olds who heard the *Planet Opposite* story chose the five pieces of candy, as compared with only 20 percent of their counterparts who heard the more straightforward story. The results indicated that learning about a topsy-turvy imaginary world likely helped the young children become more flexible in their thinking.

Researchers have found that advances in executive functioning during the preschool years are linked with school readiness (Bierman & others, 2008). Significant advances in the development of executive functioning occur in middle and late childhood (Diamond, Casey, & Munakata, 2011). One of those cognitive processes is working memory, especially its central executive dimension, which was discussed earlier in this chapter (Baddeley, 2012). Also, advances in cognitive control continue to occur. For example, one study found less diffusion and more focal activation in the prefrontal cortex from 7 to 30 years of age (Durston & others, 2006). The activation change was accompanied by increased efficiency in cognitive performance, especially in *cognitive control*, which involves flexible and effective control in a number of areas. These areas include controlling attention, reducing interfering thoughts, inhibiting motor actions, and being cognitively flexible in switching between competing choices (Diamond, Casey, & Munakata, 2011).

Critical Thinking   Executive functioning also involves being able to think critically. Currently, both psychologists and educators have considerable interest in critical thinking (Bensley & others, 2010; Bonney & Sternberg, 2011; Fairweather & Cramond, 2011; Moore & Stanley, 2010).

Critical thinking involves grasping the deeper meaning of ideas, keeping an open mind about different approaches and perspectives, and deciding for oneself what to believe or do. In this book, the third part of the *Review Connect Reflect* sections challenges you to think critically about a topic or an issue related to the discussion. Thinking critically includes asking not only what happened, but how and why; examining supposed "facts" to determine whether there is evidence to support them; evaluating what other people say rather than immediately accepting it as the truth; and asking questions and speculating beyond what is known to create new ideas and new information.

According to Ellen Langer (2005), *mindfulness*—being alert, mentally present, and cognitively flexible while going through life's everyday activities and tasks—is an

Helen Hadani, Developmental Psychologist, Toy Designer, and LANGO Regional Director

Helen Hadani obtained a Ph.D. from Stanford University in developmental psychology. As a graduate student at Stanford, she worked part-time for Hasbro toys testing its children's software on preschoolers. Her first job after graduate school was with Zowie Entertainment, which was subsequently bought by LEGO. In her work as a toy designer there, Helen conducted experiments and focus groups at different stages of a toy's development, as well as studying the age-effectiveness of the toy. In Helen's words, "Even in a toy's most primitive stage of development . . . you see children's creativity in responding to challenges, their satisfaction when a problem is solved or simply their delight in having fun" (Schlegel, 2000, p. 50).

More recently, she began working for LANGO, a company established on the premise that every American child should learn a foreign language. LANGO uses music, games, and art to help children learn a second language. Helen is currently a regional director for LANGO.

Helen Hadani, a developmental psychologist, with some of the toys and materials for guiding children in learning a second language.

important aspect of thinking critically. Mindful children and adults maintain an active awareness of the circumstances in their life and are motivated to find the best solutions to tasks. Mindful individuals create new ideas, are open to new information, and operate from a single perspective. By contrast, mindless individuals are entrapped in old ideas, engage in automatic behavior, and operate from a single perspective.

In the view of critics such as Jacqueline and Martin Brooks (1993, 2001), few schools teach students to think critically. Schools spend much more time on getting students to give a single correct answer than on encouraging students to come up with new ideas and rethink conclusions. Too often teachers ask students to recite, define, describe, state, and list rather than to analyze, infer, connect, synthesize, criticize, create, evaluate, think, and rethink. As a result, many schools graduate students who think superficially, staying on the surface of problems rather than becoming deeply engaged in meaningful thinking.

To read about one developmental psychologist who used her training in cognitive development to pursue a career in an applied area, see the *Connecting with Careers* profile.

Scientific Thinking Some aspects of thinking are specific to a particular domain, such as mathematics, science, or reading. We explore reading in Chapter 9, "Language Development." Here we examine scientific thinking by children.

Like scientists, children ask fundamental questions about reality and seek answers to problems that seem utterly trivial or unanswerable to other people (such as "Why is the sky blue?"). Do children generate hypotheses, perform experiments, and reach conclusions about their data in ways resembling those of scientists?

Scientific reasoning often is aimed at identifying causal relations. Like scientists, children place a great deal of emphasis on causal mechanisms. Their understanding of how events are caused weighs more heavily in their causal inferences than even such strong influences as whether the cause happened immediately before the effect.

developmental connection

Education. A criticism of the No Child Left Behind legislation is that it does not give adequate attention to the development of critical thinking skills. Chapter 16, p. 526

developmental connection

Exercise. A recent research study found that more physically fit children showed greater cognitive flexibility in intellectual tasks than less physically fit children (Pontifex & others, 2011). Chapter 4, p. 141

Elementary school science teacher Luis Recalde holds up a seaweed specimen in one of the hands-on, high-interest learning contexts he creates for students. Recalde, a fourth- and fifth-grade science teacher at Vincent E. Mauro Elementary School in New Haven, Connecticut, uses every opportunity to make science fascinating and motivating for students to learn. Recalde infuses hands-on science experiences with energy and enthusiasm. To help students get a better sense of what it is like to be a scientist, he brings lab coats to the classroom for students to wear. He holds science fair workshops for teachers and often gives up his vacation time to help students with science projects.

There also are important differences between the reasoning of children and the reasoning of scientists (Kuhn, 2011). Children are more influenced by happenstance events than by an overall pattern (Kuhn, 2011). Often, children maintain their old theories regardless of the evidence (Kuhn, Schauble, & Garcia-Mila, 1992).

Children might go through mental gymnastics trying to reconcile seemingly contradictory new information with their existing beliefs. For example, after learning about the solar system, children sometimes conclude that there are two earths—the seemingly flat world in which they live and the round ball floating in space that their teacher described.

Children also have difficulty designing experiments that can distinguish among alternative causes. Instead, they tend to bias the experiments in favor of whatever hypothesis they began with. Sometimes they see the results as supporting their original hypothesis even when the results directly contradict it. Thus, although there are important similarities between children and scientists in their basic curiosity and in the kinds of questions they ask, there are also important differences in the degree to which they can separate theory and evidence and in their ability to design conclusive experiments (Lehrer & Schauble, 2006).

Too often, the skills scientists use, such as careful observation, graphing, self-regulatory thinking, and knowing when and how to apply one's knowledge to solve problems, are not routinely taught in schools (Duschi & Hamilton, 2011; Peters & Stout, 2011). Children have many concepts that are incompatible with science and reality. Good teachers perceive and understand a child's underlying scientific concepts, then use the concepts as a scaffold for learning. Effective science teaching helps children distinguish between fruitful errors and misconceptions, and detect plainly wrong ideas that need to be replaced by more accurate conceptions (Fraser-Abder, 2011).

It is important for teachers to at a minimum initially scaffold students' science learning, extensively monitor their progress, and ensure that they are learning science content (Duschi & Hamilton, 2011). Thus, in pursuing science investigations, students need to "learn inquiry skills and science content" (Lehrer & Schauble, 2006).

Solving Problems Children face many problems that they must solve in order to adapt effectively, both in school and out of school. Problem solving involves finding an appropriate way to attain a goal. What are some effective ways that children can use strategies to solve problems?

In Michael Pressley's view (Pressley, 2003, 2007), the key to education is helping students learn a rich repertoire of strategies for solving problems. Good thinkers routinely use strategies and effective planning to solve problems. Pressley argues that when children are given instruction about effective strategies, they often can apply strategies that they had not used on their own. Pressley emphasizes that children benefit when the teacher models the appropriate strategy, verbalizes the steps in the strategy, and then guides the children to practice the strategy. Their practice is supported by the teacher's feedback until the children can effectively execute the strategy autonomously.

When instructing children about employing the strategy, the teacher also should explain how using the strategy will benefit them. Children need to be motivated to learn and to use the strategies. Just having children learn a new strategy is usually not enough for them to continue to use it and to transfer the strategy to new situations. For effective maintenance and transfer, children should be encouraged to monitor the effectiveness of the new strategy by comparing their performance on tests and other assessments.

Learning to use strategies effectively often takes time (Schneider, 2011). Initially, it takes time to execute the strategies and to practice them. "Practice" means that children use the effective strategy over and over again until they perform it automatically. To execute the strategies effectively, they need to have the strategies in long-term memory, and extensive practice makes this possible.

Most children benefit from generating a variety of alternative strategies and experimenting with different approaches to a problem, discovering what works well, when, and where. This approach is especially true for children from the middle elementary school grades on, although some cognitive psychologists believe that even young children should be encouraged to practice varying strategies (Siegler, 2006, 2009).

Pressley and his colleagues (Pressley, 2007; Pressley & others, 2001, 2003, 2004) have spent considerable time in recent years observing the use of strategy instruction by teachers and strategy use by students in elementary and secondary school classrooms. They conclude that teachers' use of strategy instruction is far less complete and intense than what is needed for students to learn how to use strategies effectively. They argue that education needs to be restructured so that students are provided with more opportunities to become competent strategic learners.

A final point about strategies is that many strategies depend on prior knowledge (Pressley, 2007). For example, students can't apply organizational strategies to a list of items unless they know the correct categories into which the items fall.

ADOLESCENCE

Deanna Kuhn (2009) recently discussed some important characteristics of adolescents' information processing and thinking. In her view, during the later years of childhood and continuing into adolescence, individuals approach cognitive levels that may or may not be achieved, in contrast with the largely universal cognitive levels that young children attain. By adolescence, considerable variation in cognitive functioning is present across individuals. This variability supports the argument that adolescents are producers of their own development to a greater extent than are children.

> The mind is an enchanting thing.
>
> —MARIANNE MOORE
> *American Poet, 20th Century*

Kuhn (2009) further argues that the most important cognitive change in adolescence is improvement in *executive functioning,* which we discussed earlier in this chapter.

Monitoring and Managing Cognitive Resources It is increasingly thought that executive functioning strengthens during adolescence (Kuhn, 2009). This executive functioning "assumes a role of monitoring and managing the deployment of cognitive resources as a function of a task demands. As a result, cognitive development and learning itself become more effective. . . . Emergence and strengthening of this executive (functioning) is arguably the single most important and consequential intellectual development to occur in the second decade of life" (Kuhn & Franklin, 2006, p. 987).

Attention One illustration of the way in which executive functioning increases in adolescence is its role in determining how attention will be allocated. Controlling attention and reducing interfering thoughts are key aspects of learning and thinking in adolescence and emerging adulthood (Bjorklund, 2012). Distractions that can interfere with attention in adolescence and emerging adulthood may come from the external environment (other students talking while the student is trying to listen to a lecture, or switching one's computer screen to Facebook during a lecture and viewing a new friend request, for example) or intrusive distractions from competing thoughts in the individual's mind. Self-oriented thoughts, such as worry, self-doubt, and intense emotionally-laden concerns, may especially interfere with focusing attention on thinking tasks (Gillig & Sanders, 2011; Walsh, 2011).

Decision Making Adolescence is a time of increased decision making—deciding which friends to choose, which person to date, whether to have sex, buy a car, go to college, and so on (Albert & Steinberg, 2011a, b). How competent are adolescents at making decisions? In some reviews, older adolescents are described as more competent than younger adolescents, who in turn are more competent than children (Keating, 2004). Compared with children, young adolescents are more likely to generate different options, examine a situation from a variety of perspectives, anticipate the consequences of decisions, and consider the credibility of sources.

However, older adolescents' (as well as adults') decision-making skills are far from perfect, and having the capacity to make competent decisions does not guarantee that such decisions will be made in everyday life, where breadth of experience often comes into play (Kuhn, 2009). Most people make better decisions when they are calm rather than emotionally aroused, which often is especially true for adolescents (Steinberg, 2012). Recall from our discussion of brain development in Chapter 3 that adolescents have a tendency to be emotionally intense. Thus, the same adolescent who makes a wise decision when calm may make an unwise decision when emotionally aroused. In the heat of the moment, then, adolescents' emotions may be more likely to overwhelm their decision-making ability.

The social context plays a key role in adolescent decision making (Steinberg, 2012). For example, adolescents' willingness to make risky decisions is more likely to occur in contexts where alcohol, drugs, and other temptations are readily available (Reyna & Rivers, 2008). Recent research reveals that the presence of peers in risk-taking situations increases the likelihood that adolescents will make risky decisions (Albert & Steinberg, 2011a, b). In one study of risk taking involving a simulated driving task, the presence of peers increased an adolescent's decision to engage in risky driving by 50 percent but had no effect on adults (Gardner & Steinberg, 2005). One view is that the presence of peers activates the brain's reward system, especially its dopamine pathways (Albert & Steinberg, 2011a, b).

Adolescents need more opportunities to practice and discuss realistic decision making. Many real-world decisions on matters such as sex, drugs, and daredevil driving occur in an atmosphere of stress that includes time constraints and emotional involvement. One strategy for improving adolescent decision making in such circumstances is to provide more opportunities for them to engage in role playing and group problem solving. Another strategy is for parents to involve adolescents in appropriate decision-making activities.

One proposal to explain effective adolescent decision making is the **dual-process model,** which states that decision making is influenced by two cognitive systems—one analytical and one experiential—that compete with each other (Klaczynski, 2001; Reyna & Farley, 2006). The dual-process model emphasizes that it is the experiential system—monitoring and managing actual experiences—that benefits adolescents' decision making, not the analytical system. In this view, adolescents don't benefit from engaging in reflective, detailed, higher-level cognitive analysis about a decision, especially in high-risk, real-world contexts. In such contexts, adolescents just need to know that there are some circumstances that are so dangerous that they need to be avoided at all costs (Mills, Reyna, & Estrada, 2008). However, some experts on adolescent cognition argue that in many cases adolescents benefit from both analytical and experiential systems (Kuhn, 2009).

How do emotions and social contexts influence adolescents' decision making?

dual-process model Theory stating that decision making is influenced by two cognitive systems—one analytical and one experiential—that compete with each other.

Critical Thinking Among the factors that provide a basis for improvement in critical thinking during adolescence are the following (Keating, 1990):

- Increased speed, automaticity, and capacity of information processing, which free cognitive resources for other purposes;
- Greater breadth of content knowledge in a variety of domains;
- Increased ability to construct new combinations of knowledge;
- A greater range and more spontaneous use of strategies and procedures for obtaining and applying knowledge, such as planning, considering the alternatives, and cognitive monitoring.

ADULTHOOD

Earlier in the chapter, we examined the changes that take place in speed of processing information, attention, and memory during adulthood. Here we continue to focus on changes in executive functioning, including some gains in thinking in the middle adulthood years and some of the challenges that older adults face.

Practical Problem Solving and Expertise Nancy Denney (1986, 1990) observed circumstances such as how young and middle-aged adults handled a landlord who would not fix their stove and what they did if a bank failed to deposit a check. She found that the ability to solve such practical problems improved through the forties and fifties as individuals accumulated practical experience. However, since Denney's research, other studies on everyday problem-solving and decision-making effectiveness across the adult years have been conducted; a meta-analysis of these studies indicated both remained stable in early and middle adulthood, then declined in late adulthood (Thornton & Dumke, 2005). However, in late adulthood, older adults' everyday problem-solving and decision-making effectiveness benefited when individuals were highly educated and the content of the problems involved interpersonal matters. Further, a study revealed that older adults are better at solving emotionally-laden and interpersonal problems than younger adults (Blanchard-Fields, 2007). However, a more recent study revealed that older adults showed less effective decision making on a complex laboratory task that required sustained attention than did younger adults (Isella & others, 2008).

Experience as well as years of learning and effort may bring the rewards of **expertise,** or extensive, highly organized knowledge and understanding of a particular domain. Because it takes so long to attain, expertise often shows up more among middle-aged or older adults than among younger adults (Clancy & Hoyer, 1994; Kim & Hasher, 2005). Individuals may be experts in areas as diverse as physics, art, or knowledge of wine.

Whatever their area of expertise, within that domain experts tend to process information differently from the way novices do (Bransford & others, 2006). Here are some of the characteristics that distinguish experts from novices:

- Experts are more likely to rely on their accumulated experience to solve problems.
- Experts often process information automatically and analyze it more efficiently when solving a problem in their domain than novices do.
- Experts have better strategies and shortcuts to solving problems in their domain than novices do.
- Experts are more creative and flexible in solving problems in their domain than novices are.

Decision Making Despite declines in many aspects of memory, such as working memory and long-term memory, many older adults preserve decision-making skills reasonably well (Healey & Hasher, 2009). In some cases, though, age-related decreases in memory will impair decision making (Brand & Markowitsch, 2010;

Stephen J. Hawking is a world-renowned expert in physics. Hawking authored the best-selling book *A Brief History of Time*. Hawking has a neurological disorder that prevents him from walking or talking. He communicates with the aid of a voice-equipped computer. *What distinguishes experts from novices?*

expertise Having extensive, highly organized knowledge and understanding of a particular domain.

Mata, von Helversen, & Rieskamp, 2010). A recent study revealed that a reduction in effective decision making in risky situations during late adulthood was linked to declines in memory and processing speed (Henninger, Madden, & Huettel, 2010).

However, older adults especially perform well when decision making is not constrained by time pressures and when the decision is meaningful for them (Yoon, Cole, & Lee, 2009).

Education, Work, and Health Education, work, and health are three important influences on the cognitive functioning of older adults (Lachman & others, 2010; Noble & others, 2010). They are also three of the most important factors involved in understanding why cohort effects need to be taken into account in studying the cognitive functioning of older adults. Indeed, cohort effects are very important to consider in the study of cognitive aging. For example, one study of two cohorts tested 16 years apart revealed that at age 74, the average performance on a wide range of cognitive tasks for older adults from the more recent cohort was equal to those of the older adults from the earlier cohort when they were 15 years younger (Zelinski & Kennison, 2007).

Education Successive generations in America's twentieth century were better educated, and this trend continues in the twenty-first century (Lachman & others, 2010). Not only were today's older adults more likely to go to college when they were young adults than were their parents or grandparents, but more older adults are returning to college today to further their education than in past generations. Educational experiences are positively correlated with scores on intelligence tests and information-processing tasks, such as memory exercises (Aiken Morgan, Sims, & Whitfield, 2010). A recent study revealed that older adults with less education had lower cognitive abilities than those with more education (Lachman & others, 2010). However, for older adults with less education, frequently engaging in cognitive activities improved their episodic memory.

Work Successive generations have also had work experiences that include a stronger emphasis on cognitively oriented labor (Elias & Wagster, 2007). Our great-grandfathers and grandfathers were more likely to be manual laborers than were our fathers, who are more likely to be involved in cognitively oriented occupations. As the industrial society continues to be replaced by the information society, younger generations will

How are education, work, and health linked to cognitive functioning in older adults?

have more experience in jobs that require considerable cognitive investment. The increased emphasis on complex information processing in jobs likely enhances an individual's intellectual abilities (Kristjuhan & Taidre, 2010; Schooler, 2007). In one study, substantive complex work was linked with higher intellectual functioning in older adults (Schooler, Mulatu, & Oates, 1999).

Health   Successive generations have also been healthier in late adulthood as better treatments for a variety of illnesses (such as hypertension) have been developed. Many of these illnesses have a negative impact on cognitive functioning (Pressler & others, 2010; Ram & others, 2011). Hypertension has been linked to lower cognitive performance in a number of studies, not only in older adults but also in young and middle-aged adults (Bucur & Madden, 2010; Okonkwo & others, 2010). Thus, some of the decline in intellectual performance found among older adults is likely due to health-related factors rather than to age per se (Flicker, 2010; Williams & Kemper, 2010).

As we saw in Chapter 4, "Health," a number of research studies have found that exercise is linked to improved cognitive functioning (Erickson & others, 2009; Liu-Ambrose & others, 2010). Walking or any other aerobic exercise appears to get blood and oxygen pumping to the brain, which can help people think more clearly (Studenski & others, 2006). A recent research study also revealed that resistance training improved the cognitive functioning of older adults (Liu-Ambrose & others, 2010).

Cognitive Neuroscience and Aging   In Chapter 3, "Physical Development and Biological Aging," we indicated that certain regions of the brain are involved in links between aging and cognitive functioning. In this section, we further explore the substantial increase in interest in the brain's role in aging and cognitive functioning. As we saw in Chapter 1, the field of *developmental cognitive neuroscience* has emerged as the major discipline that studies links between development, the brain, and cognitive functioning (Diamond, Casey, & Munakata, 2011; Phillips & Andres, 2010; Reuter-Lorenz & Park, 2010). This field especially relies on brain-imaging techniques, such as functional magnetic resonance imaging (fMRI) and positron-emission tomography (PET), to reveal the areas of the brain that are activated when individuals are engaging in certain cognitive activities (Charlton & others, 2010; Ystad & others, 2010). For example, as an older adult is asked to encode and then retrieve verbal materials or images of scenes, the older adult's brain activity will be monitored by an fMRI brain scan.

Changes in the brain can influence cognitive functioning, and changes in cognitive functioning can influence the brain (Grady, 2008). For example, aging of the brain's prefrontal cortex may produce a decline in working memory. And when older adults do not regularly use their working memory, neural connections in the prefrontal lobe may atrophy. Further, cognitive interventions that activate older adults' working memory may increase these neural connections.

Although it is in its infancy as a field, the cognitive neuroscience of aging is beginning to uncover some important links between aging, the brain, and cognitive functioning. These include the following:

- Neural circuits in specific regions of the brain's prefrontal cortex decline, and this decline is linked to poorer performance by older adults on complex reasoning tasks, working memory, and episodic memory tasks (Hedden & Gabrielli, 2004) (see Figure 7.15).
- Recall from Chapter 3, "Physical Development and Biological Aging," that older adults are more likely than younger adults to use both hemispheres of the brain to compensate for aging declines in attention, memory, and language (Dennis & Cabeza, 2008).
- Functioning of the hippocampus declines less than the functioning of the frontal lobes in older adults.

⟶ developmental **connection**

Work. Cognitive ability is one of the best predictors of job performance in older adults. Chapter 16, p. 553

⟵ developmental **connection**

Brain Development. A decrease in brain lateralization occurs in older adults when they engage in complex cognitive activities. Chapter 3, p. 107

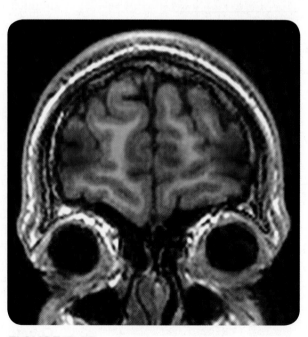

FIGURE 7.15

THE PREFRONTAL CORTEX. Advances in neuroimaging are allowing researchers to make significant progress in connecting changes in the brain with cognitive development. Shown here is an fMRI of the brain's prefrontal cortex. *What links have been found between the prefrontal cortex, aging, and cognitive development?*

- Compared with younger adults, older adults show greater activity in the frontal and parietal regions while they are engaging in tasks that require cognitive control processes such as attention (Grady, 2008).

- Younger adults have better connectivity between brain regions than older adults (Goh, 2011). For example, a recent study revealed that younger adults had more connections between brain activations in frontal, occipital, and hippocampal regions than older adults during a difficult encoding task (Leshikar & others, 2010).

- An increasing number of cognitive and fitness training studies include brain-imaging techniques such as fMRI to assess the results of such training on brain function (Erickson & others, 2011; Ho & others, 2010). In one study, older adults who walked one hour a day three days a week for six months showed increased volume in the frontal and temporal lobes of the brain (Colcombe & others, 2006).

Denise Park and Patricia Reuter-Lorenz (2009) recently proposed a neurocognitive scaffolding view of connections between the aging brain and cognition. In this view, increased activation in the prefrontal cortex with aging reflects an adaptive brain that is compensating for the challenges of declining neural structures and function, and declines in various aspects of cognition, including working memory and long-term memory. Scaffolding involves the use of complementary neural circuits to protect cognitive functioning in an aging brain. Among the factors that can strengthen brain scaffolding are cognitive engagement and exercise.

Use It or Lose It   Changes in cognitive activity patterns might result in disuse and consequent atrophy of cognitive skills (Hughes, 2010; Park & Bischof, 2011). This concept is captured in the expression "use it or lose it." Mental activities that likely benefit the maintenance of cognitive skills in older adults include reading books, doing crossword puzzles, and attending lectures and concerts. "Use it or lose it" also is a significant component of the engagement model of cognitive optimization that emphasizes how intellectual and social engagement can buffer age-related declines in intellectual development (Reuter-Lorenz & Park, 2010). These studies support the "use it or lose it" concept and the engagement model of cognitive optimization:

- When middle-aged and older adults participated in intellectually engaging activities, it served to buffer them against cognitive decline (Hultsch & others, 1999).

- Catholic priests 65 years and older who regularly read books, did crossword puzzles, or otherwise exercised their minds were 47 percent less likely to develop Alzheimer disease than priests who rarely engaged in these activities (Wilson & others, 2002).

- Reading daily was linked to reduced mortality in men in their seventies (Jacobs & others, 2008).

- Older adults indicated how often they participated in six activities—reading, writing, doing crossword puzzles, playing card or board games, having group discussions, and playing music—on a daily basis (Hall & others, 2009). Across the five years of the study, the point at which memory loss accelerated was assessed and it was found that for each additional activity the older adult engaged in, the onset of rapid memory loss was delayed by 18 years. For older adults who participated in 11 activities per week compared to their counterparts who engaged in only 4 activities per week, the point at which accelerated memory decline occurred was delayed by 1.29 years.

Cognitive Training   If an older adult is losing cognitive skills, can those skills be retrained? Two key conclusions can be derived from research: (1) training can improve the cognitive skills of many older adults, but (2) there is some loss in plasticity in late adulthood (Lovden & others, 2010; Ornstein & Light, 2010; Reuter-Lorenz & Mikels, 2011; Stine-Morrow & Basak, 2011). To read further about cognitive training studies with older adults, see the *Connecting Development to Life* interlude on this topic.

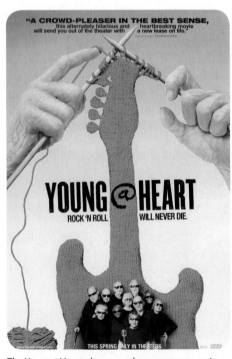

The Young@Heart chorus—whose average age is 80. Young@Heart became a hit documentary in 2008. The documentary displays the singing talents, energy, and optimism of a remarkable group of older adults, who clearly are on the "use it" side of "use it or lose it."

Cognitive Training with Older Adults

What activities are part of successful cognitive training? A seven-year longitudinal study by Sherry Willis and Carolyn Nesselroade (1990) used cognitive training to help adults maintain fluid intelligence (the ability to reason abstractly) with advancing age. The older adults were taught strategies for identifying the rule or pattern required to solve problems. The trainer modeled correct strategies for solving problems. Individuals practiced on training items, received feedback about the correct solutions to practice problems, and participated in group discussion. After this cognitive training, adults in their seventies and eighties performed at a higher level than they had in their late sixties.

A recent study had older adults participate in a 20-week activity called Senior Odyssey, a team-based program involving creative problem solving that is derived from the Odyssey of the Mind program for children and emerging adults (Stine-Morrow & others, 2007). In a field experiment, compared with a control group who did not experience Senior Odyssey, the Senior Odyssey participants showed improved processing speed, somewhat improved creative thinking, and increased mindfulness. As described earlier in the chapter, *mindfulness* includes generating new ideas, remaining open to new information, and being aware of multiple perspectives (Langer, 2007).

Another study trained older adults to increase their processing speed (Ball, Edwards, & Ross, 2007). As a result of the training, older adults increased their processing speed, and the gain was maintained for two years. The benefits of the processing speed training translated into improvements in everyday activities, such as safer driving performance. And in a recent study, older adults who participated in an 8-week memory training program improved their source memory and the training was linked to a thickening of certain areas of the cerebral cortex (Engvig & others, 2010).

Researchers are also finding that improving the physical fitness of older adults can improve their cognitive functioning (Baker & others, 2010; Erickson & Kramer, 2009; Miller & others, 2011). A review of studies revealed that aerobic fitness training improved the planning, scheduling, working memory, resistance to distraction, and processing involving multiple tasks in older adults (Colcombe & Kramer, 2003).

The Stanford Center for Longevity (2011) recently reported on a consensus reached by leading scientists in the field of aging. One of their concerns is the misinformation given to the public touting products to improve the functioning of the mind for which there is no scientific evidence. Nutritional supplements, games, and software products have all been advertised as "magic bullets" to slow the decline of mental functioning and improve the mental ability of older adults. Some of the claims are reasonable but not scientifically tested, and others are unrealistic and implausible. A recent research review of dietary supplements and cognitive aging did indicate that Ginkgo biloba was linked with improvements in some aspects of attention in older adults and

To what extent can training improve the cognitive functioning of older adults?

omega-3 polyunsaturated fatty acids with a reduced risk of age-related cognitive decline (Gorby, Brownell, & Falk, 2010). In this research review, there was no evidence of cognitive improvements in aging adults who consumed ginseng and glucose. Overall, although biologically plausible, research has not provided consistent evidence that such dietary supplements can accomplish major cognitive goals in aging adults over the long term. However, some software-based cognitive training games have been found to improve older adults' cognitive functioning (Lange & others, 2010). Nonetheless, the training games may improve cognitive skills in a laboratory setting but not generalize to gains in the real world.

In sum, some improvements in the cognitive vitality of older adults can be accomplished through cognitive and fitness training (Gross & Rebok, 2011; Kramer & Morrow, 2009; Reuter-Lorenz & Mikels, 2011). However, benefits have not been observed in all studies (Salthouse, 2007). Also, in studying the benefits of cognitive training in older adults, there is a difference in short-term improvement and long-term changes. If older adults' goal is to improve their ability to remember people's names at a forthcoming community meeting, research indicates there is a good chance that this can be accomplished. However, if the goal is to reduce the rate of memory decline over a decade or two in older adults, no intervention has yet been able to document this result (Stanford Center for Longevity, 2011). Further research is needed to determine more precisely which cognitive improvements occur in older adults as a result of training (Margrett & Deshpande-Kamat, 2009).

What effect would you expect such studies to have on older adults' quality of life?

LG4 Characterize thinking and its developmental changes

Review

- What is thinking?
- What characterizes concept formation and categorization in infancy? What is critical thinking? Do children and scientists think in the same ways? What are two important aspects of problem solving?
- What are some changes in thinking during adolescence?
- What are some changes in thinking in adulthood?

Connect

- You've learned that the nature-nurture debate examines the extent to which

development is influenced by nature and by nurture. Which side of the debate would be reflected in the dual-process model that attempts to explain adolescent decision making and the "use it or lose it" view of cognitive aging?

Reflect *Your Own Personal Journey of Life*

- Choose an area in which you consider yourself at least somewhat of an expert. Compare your ability to learn in this field with the ability of a novice.

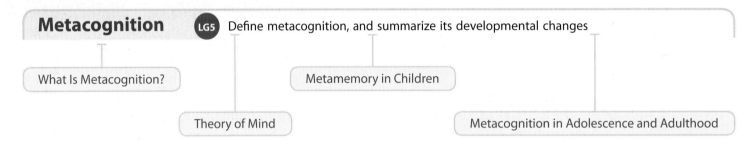

Metacognition

LG5 Define metacognition, and summarize its developmental changes

What Is Metacognition?

Metamemory in Children

Theory of Mind

Metacognition in Adolescence and Adulthood

As you read at the beginning of this chapter, metacognition is "knowing about knowing" (Flavell, 2004). In this section, we examine the role of metacognition in performing cognitive tasks, children's memory abilities, and metacognition in adolescents and adults.

WHAT IS METACOGNITION?

Metacognition can take many forms. It includes knowledge about when and where to use particular strategies for learning or for solving problems. **Metamemory,** individuals' knowledge about memory, is an especially important form of metacognition. Metamemory includes general knowledge about memory, such as knowing that recognition tests (for example, multiple-choice questions) are easier than recall tests (for example, essay questions). It also encompasses knowledge about one's own memory, such as knowing whether you have studied enough for an upcoming test.

Metacognition helps people to perform many cognitive tasks more effectively (Flavell, 2004; Ornstein & Light, 2010). A recent study with college students revealed that metacognition was a key factor in their ability to engage effectively in critical thinking (Magno, 2010). Another study found that metacognition played an important role in adolescents' ability to generate effective hypotheses about solving problems (Kim & Pedersen, 2010). And in yet another study, students were taught metacognitive skills to help them solve math problems (Cardelle-Elawar, 1992). In each of 30 daily lessons involving math story problems, a teacher guided low-achieving students to recognize when they did not know the meaning of a word, did not have all of the information necessary to solve a problem, did not know how to subdivide the problem into specific steps, or did not know how to carry out a computation. After the 30 daily lessons, the students

metamemory Knowledge about memory.

who were given this metacognitive training had better math achievement and more positive attitudes toward math.

THEORY OF MIND

Even young children are curious about the nature of the human mind. They have a **theory of mind,** which refers to awareness of one's own mental processes and the mental processes of others. Studies of theory of mind view the child as "a thinker who is trying to explain, predict, and understand people's thoughts, feelings, and utterances" (Harris, 2006, p. 847). Researchers are increasingly discovering that children's theory of mind is linked to cognitive processes (Wellman, 2011). For example, one study found that theory of mind competence at age 3 is related to a higher level of metamemory at age 5 (Lockl & Schneider, 2007).

Developmental Changes Children's theory of mind changes as they develop through childhood (Gelman, 2009; Wellman, 2011). Some changes occur quite early in development, as we see next.

From 18 months to 3 years of age, children begin to understand three mental states:

- *Perceptions*. By 2 years of age, children recognize that another person will see what's in front of her own eyes instead of what's in front of the child's eyes (Lempers, Flavell, & Flavell, 1977), and by 3 years of age, they realize that looking leads to knowing what's inside a container (Pratt & Bryant, 1990).

- *Emotions*. The child can distinguish between positive (for example, happy) and negative (sad, for example) emotions. A child might say, "Tommy feels bad."

- *Desires*. All humans have some sort of desires. But when do children begin to recognize that someone else's desires may differ from their own? Toddlers recognize that if people want something, they will try to get it. For instance, a child might say, "I want my mommy."

Two- to three-year-olds understand the way that desires are related to actions and to simple emotions. For example, they understand that people will search for what they want and that if they obtain it, they are likely to feel happy, but if they don't they will keep searching for it and are likely to feel sad or angry (Wellman & Woolley, 1990). Children also refer to desires earlier and more frequently than they refer to cognitive states such as thinking and knowing (Bartsch & Wellman, 1995).

One of the landmark developments in understanding others' desires is recognizing that someone else may have different desires from one's own (Wellman, 2011). Eighteen-month-olds understand that their own food preferences may not match the preferences of others—they will give an adult the food to which she says "Yummy!" even if the food is something that the infants detest (Repacholi & Gopnik, 1997). As they get older, they can verbalize that they themselves do not like something but an adult might (Flavell & others, 1992).

Between the ages of 3 and 5, children come to understand that the mind can represent objects and events accurately or inaccurately. The realization that people can have *false beliefs*—beliefs that are not true—develops in a majority of children by the time they are 5 years old (Wellman, Cross, & Watson, 2001) (see Figure 7.16). This point is often described as a pivotal one in understanding the mind—recognizing that beliefs are not just mapped directly into the mind from the surrounding world, but also that different people can have different, and sometimes incorrect, beliefs (Liu & others, 2008). In a classic false-belief task, young children were shown a Band-Aids box and asked what was inside (Jenkins & Astington, 1996). To the children's surprise, the box actually contained pencils. When asked what a child who had never seen the box would think was inside, 3-year-olds typically responded, "Pencils." However, the 4- and 5-year-olds, grinning at the anticipation of the false beliefs of other children who had not seen what was inside the box, were more likely to say "Band-Aids."

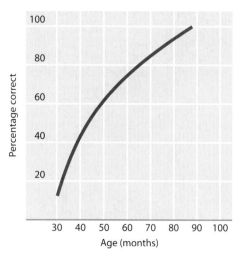

FIGURE **7.16**

DEVELOPMENTAL CHANGES IN FALSE-BELIEF PERFORMANCE. False-belief performance—the child's understanding that a person has a false belief that contradicts reality—dramatically increases from 2½ years of age through the middle of the elementary school years. In a summary of the results of many studies, 2½-year-olds gave incorrect responses about 80 percent of the time (Wellman, Cross, & Watson, 2001). At 3 years 8 months, they were correct about 50 percent of the time and, after that, gave increasingly correct responses.

theory of mind Thoughts about how one's own mental processes work and the mental processes of others.

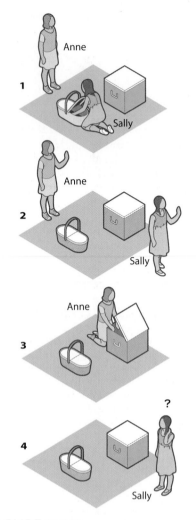

FIGURE **7.17**

THE SALLY AND ANNE FALSE-BELIEF TASK.
In the false-belief task, the skit above in which
Sally has a basket and Anne has a box is shown to
children. Sally places a toy in her basket and then
leaves. While Sally is gone and can't watch, Anne
removes the toy from Sally's basket and places it in
her box. Sally then comes back and the children are
asked where they think Sally will look for her toy.
Children are said to "pass" the false-belief task if
they understand that Sally looks in her basket first
before realizing the toy isn't there.

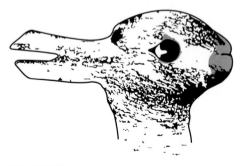

FIGURE **7.18**
AMBIGUOUS LINE DRAWING

In a similar task, children are told a story about Sally and Anne: Sally places a
toy in a basket and then leaves the room (see Figure 7.17). In her absence, Anne
takes the toy from the basket and places it in a box. Children are asked where Sally
will look for the toy when she returns. The major finding is that 3-year-olds tend
to fail false-belief tasks, saying that Sally will look in the box (even though Sally
could not know that the toy has moved to this new location). Four-year-olds and
older children tend to pass the task, correctly saying that Sally will have a "false
belief"—she will think the object is in the basket, even though that belief is now
false. The conclusion from these studies is that children younger than 4 years old
do not understand that it is possible to have a false belief.

However, there are reasons to question the focus on this one supposedly pivotal
moment in the development of a theory of mind. For example, the false-belief task
is a complicated one that involves a number of factors such as the characters in the
story and all of their individual actions (Bloom & German, 2000). Children also have
to disregard their own knowledge in making predictions about what others would
think, which is difficult for young children (Birch & Bloom, 2003). Another important issue is that there is more to understanding the minds of others than this false-
belief task would indicate.

One example of a limitation in 3- to 5-year-olds' understanding the mind is
how they think about thinking. Preschoolers often underestimate when mental
activity is likely occurring. For example, they sometimes think that a person who
is sitting quietly or reading is not actually thinking very much (Flavell, Green, &
Flavell, 1995). Their understanding of their own thinking is also limited. One study
revealed that even 5-year-olds have difficulty reporting their thoughts (Flavell,
Green, & Flavell, 1995). Children were asked to think quietly about the room in
their home where they kept their toothbrushes. Shortly after this direction, many
children denied they had been thinking at all and failed to mention either a tooth-
brush or a bathroom. In another study, when 5-year-olds were asked to try to have
no thoughts at all for about 20 seconds, they reported that they were successful at
doing this (Flavell, Green, & Flavell, 2000). By contrast, most of the 8-year-olds said
they engaged in mental activity during the 20 seconds and reported specific thoughts.

It is only beyond the preschool years—at approximately 5 to 7 years of age—that
children have a deepening appreciation of the mind itself rather than just an understanding of mental states. For example, they begin to recognize that people's behaviors do not necessarily reflect their thoughts and feelings (Flavell, Green, & Flavell,
1993). Not until middle and late childhood do children see the mind as an active
constructor of knowledge or a processing center (Flavell, Green, & Flavell, 1998) and
move from understanding that beliefs can be false to realizing that the same event
can be open to multiple interpretations (Carpendale & Chandler, 1996). For example,
in one study, children saw an ambiguous line drawing (for example, a drawing that
could be seen as either a duck or a rabbit); one puppet told the child she believed
the drawing was a duck while another puppet told the child he believed the drawing
was a rabbit (see Figure 7.18). Before the age of 7, children said that there was one
right answer, and it was not okay for both puppets to have different opinions.

Although most research on children's theory of mind focuses on children around
or before their preschool years, at 7 years of age and beyond there are important
developments in the ability to understand the beliefs and thoughts of others. While
understanding that people may have different interpretations is important, it is also
important to recognize that some interpretations and beliefs may still be evaluated
on the basis of the merits of arguments and evidence (Kuhn, Cheney, & Weinstock,
2000). In early adolescence, children begin to understand that people can have
ambivalent feelings (Harter, 2006). They start to recognize that the same person can
feel both happy and sad about the same event. They also engage in more recursive
thinking: thinking about what other people are thinking about.

Individual Differences   As in other developmental research, there are individual
differences in the ages when children reach certain milestones in their theory of

mind (Wellman, 2011). For example, preschoolers who have more siblings perform better on theory of mind tasks than preschoolers with fewer siblings, especially if they have older siblings (McAlister & Peterson, 2007). Children who talk with their parents about feelings frequently as 2-year-olds show better performance on theory of mind tasks (Ruffman, Slade, & Crowe, 2002), as do children who frequently engage in pretend play (Harris, 2000).

Executive function, which describes several functions (such as inhibition and planning) that are important for flexible, future-oriented behavior, also may be connected to theory of mind development (Doherty, 2008). For example, in one executive function task, children are asked to say the word *night* when they see a picture of a sun, and the word *day* when they see a picture of a moon and stars. Children who perform better at executive function tasks seem also to have a better understanding of theory of mind (Sabbagh & others, 2006).

developmental **connection**

Conditions, Diseases, and Disorders. The current consensus is that autism is a brain dysfunction involving abnormalities in brain structure and neurotransmitters, and that genetic factors play an important role in its occurrence. Chapter 16, p. 536

Theory of Mind and Autism   Another individual difference in understanding the mind involves autism (Wellman, 2011). Approximately 1 in 150 children are estimated to have some type of autism (National Autism Association, 2010). Autism can usually be diagnosed by the age of 3 years, and sometimes earlier. Children with autism show a number of behaviors different from other children their age, including deficits in social interaction and communication as well as repetitive behaviors or interests.

Children and adults with autism have difficulty in social interactions, often described as huge deficits in theory of mind (Adler & others, 2010). These deficits are generally greater than deficits in children the same mental age with mental retardation (Baron-Cohen, 2009, 2011). Researchers have found that autistic children have difficulty in developing a theory of mind, especially in understanding others' beliefs and emotions (Bertoglio & Hendren, 2009). Although children with autism tend to do poorly on reasoning in false-belief tasks, they can perform much better on reasoning tasks requiring an understanding of physical causality (Peterson, 2005).

A young boy with autism. *What are some characteristics of autistic children? What are some deficits in autistic children's theory of mind?*

METAMEMORY IN CHILDREN

Although theory of mind has dominated metacognition research with children in recent years, researchers also have studied children's metamemory (Ornstein & Light, 2010). By 5 or 6 years of age, children usually know that familiar items are easier to learn than unfamiliar ones, that short lists are easier than long ones, that recognition is easier than recall, and that forgetting becomes more likely over time (Lyon & Flavell, 1993). However, in other ways young children's metamemory is limited. They don't understand that related items are easier to remember than unrelated ones or that remembering the gist of a story is easier than remembering information verbatim (Kreutzer, Leonard, & Flavell, 1975). By fifth grade, students understand that gist recall is easier than verbatim recall.

Preschool children also have an inflated opinion of their memory abilities. For example, in one study, a majority of preschool children predicted that they would be able to recall all ten items of a list of ten items. When tested, none of the young children managed this feat (Flavell, Friedrichs, & Hoyt, 1970). As they move through the elementary school years, children give more realistic evaluations of their memory skills (Schneider, 2011).

Preschool children also have little appreciation for the importance of cues for memory, such as "It helps when you can think of an example of it." By 7 or 8 years of age, children better appreciate the importance of cueing for memory.

In general, children's understanding of their memory abilities and their skill in evaluating their performance on memory tasks are relatively poor at the beginning of the elementary school years but improve considerably by 11 to 12 years of age (Bjorklund & Rosenbaum, 2000).

Cognitive developmentalist John Flavell (*left*) is a pioneer in providing insights about children's thinking. Among his many contributions are establishing the field of metacognition and conducting numerous studies in this area, including metamemory and theory of mind studies.

METACOGNITION IN ADOLESCENCE AND ADULTHOOD

Metacognition is increasingly recognized as a very important cognitive skill not only in adolescence but also in emerging adulthood. Compared with children, adolescents have an increased capacity to monitor and manage cognitive resources to effectively meet the demands of a learning task (Kuhn, 2009). This increased metacognitive ability results in improved cognitive functioning and learning. A recent longitudinal study revealed that from 12 to 14 years of age, young adolescents increasingly used metacognitive skills and used them more effectively in math and history classes than in other subjects (van der Stel & Veenman, 2010). For example, 14-year-olds monitored their own text comprehension more frequently and did so more effectively than their younger counterparts. Another recent study documented the importance of metacognitive skills, such as planning, strategizing, and monitoring, in college students' ability to think critically (Magno, 2010).

An important aspect of cognitive functioning and learning is determining how much attention will be allocated to an available resource. Evidence is accumulating that adolescents have a better understanding of how to effectively deploy their attention to different aspects of a task than children do (Kuhn, 2008, 2009). Further, adolescents have a better meta-level understanding of strategies—that is, knowing the best strategy to use and when to use it in performing a learning task.

Keep in mind, though, that there is considerable individual variation in adolescents' metacognition. Indeed, some experts argue that individual variation in metacognition becomes much more pronounced in adolescence than in childhood (Kuhn & Franklin, 2006). Thus, some adolescents are quite good at using metacognition to improve their learning; others are far less effective.

By middle age, adults have accumulated a great deal of metacognitive knowledge. They can draw on this metacognitive knowledge to help them combat a decline in memory skills. For example, they are likely to understand that they need to have good organizational skills and reminders to help combat the decline in memory skills they face.

Older adults tend to overestimate the memory problems they experience on a daily basis. They seem to be more aware of their memory failures than younger adults and become more anxious about minor forgetfulness than younger adults (Hoyer & Roodin, 2009). Researchers have found that in general older adults are as accurate as younger adults in monitoring the encoding and retrieval of information (Hertzog & Dixon, 2005). However, some aspects of monitoring information, such as source memory (discussed earlier in the chapter), decline in older adults (Hertzog & Dixon, 2005; Isingrini, Perrotin, & Souchay, 2008).

Review Connect Reflect

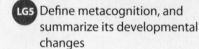 Define metacognition, and summarize its developmental changes

Review

- What is metacognition?
- How does the child's theory of mind change during the preschool years?
- How does metamemory typically change during childhood?
- How does metacognition change in adolescence and adulthood?

Connect

- How is metacognition in children different from metacognition in adolescents?

Reflect *Your Own Personal Journey of Life*

- Take an inventory of your study skills. How might you improve your metacognitive study skills?

The Information-Processing Approach Explain the information-processing approach and its application to development

> The Information-Processing Approach and Its Application to Development

- The information-processing approach analyzes how individuals manipulate information, monitor it, and create strategies for handling it. Attention, memory, and thinking are involved in effective information processing. The computer has served as a model for how humans process information. In the information-processing approach, children's cognitive development results from their ability to overcome processing limitations by increasingly executing basic operations, expanding information-processing capacity, and acquiring new knowledge and strategies. According to Siegler, three important mechanisms of change are encoding (how information gets into memory), automaticity (ability to process information with little or no effort), and strategy construction (creation of new procedures for processing information). Children's information processing is characterized by self-modification, and an important aspect of this self-modification involves metacognition—that is, knowing about knowing.

> Speed of Processing Information

- Processing speed increases across the childhood and adolescent years. Processing speed slows in the middle and late adulthood years. However, strategies that people learn through experience can compensate for age-related decline in speed to some degree.

Attention Define attention, and outline its developmental changes

> What Is Attention?

- Attention is the focusing of mental resources. Four ways that people can allocate their attention are selective attention (focusing on a specific aspect of experience that is relevant while ignoring others that are irrelevant); divided attention (concentrating on more than one activity at the same time); sustained attention (maintaining attention to a selected stimulus for a prolonged period of time; also referred to as vigilance); and executive attention (involving action planning, allocating attention to goals, error detection and compensation, monitoring progress on tasks, and dealing with novel or difficult tasks).

> Infancy

- Even newborns can fixate on a contour, but as they get older they scan a pattern more thoroughly. Attention in the first year of life is dominated by the orienting/investigative process. Attention in infancy often occurs through habituation and dishabituation. Joint attention plays an important role in infant development, especially in the infant's acquisition of language.

> Childhood and Adolescence

- Salient stimuli tend to capture the attention of the preschooler. After 6 or 7 years of age, there is a shift to more cognitive control of attention. Selective attention improves through childhood and adolescence. Multitasking is an example of divided attention, and it can harm adolescents' attention when they are engaging in a challenging task.

> Adulthood

- Attentional skills often are excellent in early adulthood. Older adults are generally less adept than younger adults at selective and divided attention.

Memory Describe what memory is and how it changes through the life span

> What Is Memory?

- Memory is the retention of information over time. Psychologists study the processes of memory: how information is initially placed or encoded into memory, how it is retained or stored, and how it is found or retrieved for a certain purpose later. People construct and reconstruct their memories. Schema theory states that people mold memories to fit the information that already exists in their minds.

- Infants as young as 2 to 6 months of age display implicit memory, which is memory without conscious recollection, as in memory of perceptual-motor skills. However, many experts believe that explicit memory, which is the conscious memory of facts and experiences, does not emerge until the second half of the first year of life. The hippocampus and frontal lobes of the brain are involved in development of memory in infancy. Older children and adults remember little if anything from the first three years of their lives.

- One method of assessing short-term memory (the retention of information for up to 15 to 30 seconds, assuming there is no rehearsal of the information) is with a memory-span task, on which there are substantial developmental changes through the childhood years. Working memory (a kind of "mental workbench" where individuals manipulate and assemble information when they make decisions, solve problems, and comprehend language) is linked to children's reading comprehension and problem solving. Young children can remember a great deal of information if they are given appropriate cues and prompts. Strategies can improve children's memory, and older children are more likely to use these than younger children. Imagery and elaboration are two important strategies. Knowledge is an important influence on memory.

- Younger adults have better episodic memory than older adults do. Older adults have more difficulty retrieving semantic information. Working memory and processing speed decrease in older adults. Explicit memory is more likely to decline in older adults than is implicit memory. Source memory—remembering where one learned something—declines with age. Controversy characterizes whether prospective memory, which is remembering to do something in the future, declines as adults age.

Thinking

LG4 Characterize thinking and its developmental changes

- Thinking involves manipulating and transforming information in memory.

- Mandler argues that it is not until about 7 to 9 months of age that infants form conceptual categories, although we do not know precisely when concept formation begins. Infants' first concepts are broad. Over the first two years of life, these broad concepts gradually become more differentiated. Many infants and young children develop an intense interest in a particular category (or categories) of things. Advances in executive functioning, an umbrella-like concept that encompasses a number of higher-level cognitive processes linked to the development of the prefrontal cortex, occur in early childhood. Executive functioning involves managing one's thoughts to engage in goal-directed behavior and to exercise self-control. Critical thinking involves thinking reflectively and productively, and evaluating evidence. Children and scientists think alike in some ways but differently in others. Children are less influenced by an overall pattern than by happenstance events, and they often cling to old theories despite the evidence. Two important ways of solving problems involve using strategies and using analogies.

- Key changes in information processing occur during adolescence, particularly advances in executive functioning. These changes focus on monitoring and managing cognitive resources, controlling attention and reducing interfering thoughts, making decisions, and exercising critical thinking.

- Everyday problem-solving and decision-making effectiveness remain stable in early and middle adulthood, and then some aspects decline in late adulthood while others may increase. One aspect of cognition that may improve with aging is expertise. In the twentieth and twenty-first centuries, successive generations of older adults have been better educated, have had work experiences that included a stronger emphasis on cognitively oriented labor, and have been healthier. These cohort effects are linked to higher cognitive functioning. There has been considerable increased interest in the cognitive neuroscience of aging that focuses on links between aging, the brain, and cognitive functioning. This field especially relies on fMRI and PET scans to assess brain functioning while individuals are engaging in cognitive tasks. One of the most consistent findings in this field is a decline in the functioning of specific regions in the prefrontal cortex in older adults and links between this decline and poorer performance on complex reasoning, working memory, and episodic memory tasks. Some improvements in the cognitive vitality of older adults can be accomplished through cognitive and fitness training. However, such benefits have not been observed in all studies.

Metacognition

LG5 Define metacognition, and summarize its developmental changes

- What Is Metacognition?
- Theory of Mind
- Metamemory in Children
- Metacognition in Adolescence and Adulthood

- Metacognition is cognition about cognition, or "knowing about knowing."

- Theory of mind is the awareness of one's own mental processes and the mental processes of others. Children begin to understand mental states involving perceptions, desires, and emotions at 2 to 3 years of age and at 4 to 5 years of age realize that people can have false beliefs. It is only beyond the early childhood years that children have a deepening appreciation of the mind itself rather than just understanding mental states. Autistic children have difficulty in developing a theory of mind.

- By 5 to 6 years of age, children usually know that familiar items are easier to learn than unfamiliar ones and that short lists are easier to remember than long ones. By 7 to 8 years of age, children better appreciate the importance of cues for memory.

- Adolescents have an increased capacity to monitor and manage resources to effectively meet the demands of a learning task, although there is considerable individual variation in metacognition during adolescence. Metacognition continues to improve in early adulthood, and many middle-aged individuals have accumulated considerable metacognitive knowledge. Older adults tend to overestimate their everyday memory problems.

key terms

key people

chapter 8 INTELLIGENCE

preview

The concept of intelligence has generated many controversies, including whether intelligence is more strongly influenced by heredity or by environment, whether there is cultural bias in intelligence testing, and whether intelligence tests are misused. We will explore these controversies, as well as the extent to which we have a single intelligence or multiple intelligences, the development of intelligence across the life span, and the extremes of intelligence and creativity.

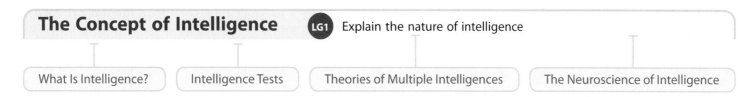

The Concept of Intelligence   **LG1** Explain the nature of intelligence

| What Is Intelligence? | Intelligence Tests | Theories of Multiple Intelligences | The Neuroscience of Intelligence |

Intelligence is one of our most prized possessions. However, even the most intelligent people have not been able to agree on how to define and measure the concept of intelligence.

WHAT IS INTELLIGENCE?

What does the term *intelligence* mean to psychologists? Some experts describe intelligence as the ability to solve problems. Others describe it as the capacity to adapt and learn from experience. Still others argue that intelligence includes characteristics such as creativity and interpersonal skills.

The problem with intelligence is that, unlike height, weight, and age, intelligence cannot be directly measured. We can't peel back a person's scalp and see how much intelligence he or she has. We can evaluate intelligence only *indirectly* by studying and comparing the intelligent acts that people perform.

The primary components of intelligence are similar to the cognitive processes of thinking and memory that we discussed in Chapter 7, "Information Processing." The differences in how we described these cognitive processes in Chapter 7, and how we discuss intelligence, lie in the concepts of *individual differences* and assessment (Deary, 2012). Individual differences are the stable, consistent ways in which people differ from one another. Individual differences in intelligence generally have been measured by intelligence tests designed to tell us whether a person can reason better than others who have taken the test (Neukrug & Fawcett, 2010; Urbina, 2011).

How can intelligence be defined? **Intelligence** is the ability to solve problems and to adapt and learn from experiences. But even this broad definition doesn't satisfy everyone. As you will see shortly, Robert J. Sternberg (2010; 2011a, b) proposes that practical know-how should be considered part of intelligence. In his view, intelligence involves weighing options carefully and acting judiciously, as well as developing strategies to improve shortcomings. Also, a definition of intelligence based on a theory such as Vygotsky's, which we discussed in Chapter 6, "Cognitive Developmental Approaches," would have to include the ability to use the tools of the culture with help from more-skilled individuals. Because intelligence is such an abstract, broad concept, it is not surprising that there are so many different ways to define it.

INTELLIGENCE TESTS

What types of intelligence tests are given to children and adults? What are some contributions and criticisms of intelligence tests?

> What a piece of work is a man! How noble in reason! How infinite in faculty! In form, in moving, how express and admirable! In action how like an angel! In apprehension how like a god!
>
> —**WILLIAM SHAKESPEARE**
> *English Playwright, 17th Century*

developmental connection

Information Processing. The information-processing approach emphasizes how individuals manipulate information, monitor it, and create strategies for handling it. Chapter 7, p. 211

developmental connection

Social Contexts. Vygotsky's theory emphasizes the social contexts of learning and constructing knowledge through social interaction. Chapter 6, p. 199

intelligence The ability to solve problems and to adapt to and learn from experiences.

Alfred Binet constructed the first intelligence test after being asked to create a measure to determine which children could benefit from instruction in France's schools and which could not.

The Binet Tests   In 1904, the French Ministry of Education asked psychologist Alfred Binet to devise a method to determine which students would not profit from typical school instruction. Binet and his student Théophile Simon developed an intelligence test to meet this request. The test consisted of 30 items ranging from the ability to touch one's nose or ear when asked to the ability to draw designs from memory and to define abstract concepts.

Binet stressed that the core of intelligence consists of complex cognitive processes, such as memory, imagery, comprehension, and judgment. In addition, he noted that a developmental approach was crucial for understanding intelligence. He proposed that a child's intellectual ability increases with age. Therefore, he tested potential items and determined the age at which a typical child could answer them correctly. Thus, Binet developed the concept of **mental age (MA),** which is an individual's level of mental development relative to others. For an average child, MA scores correspond to *chronological age (CA),* which is age from birth. A bright child has an MA considerably above CA; a dull child has an MA considerably below CA.

The Binet test has been revised many times to incorporate advances in the understanding of intelligence and intelligence testing. Many revisions were carried out by Lewis Terman, who developed extensive norms and provided detailed, clear instructions for each problem on the test. Terman also applied a concept introduced by William Stern (1912), who coined the term **intelligence quotient (IQ)** to refer to an individual's mental age divided by chronological age multiplied by 100: IQ = MA/CA $\times$ 100.

If a child's mental age, as measured by the Binet test, was the same as the child's chronological age, then the child's IQ score was 100. If the measured mental age was above chronological age, then the IQ score was greater than 100. If mental age was below chronological age, the IQ score was less than 100. Although this scoring system is no longer used, the term IQ is often still used to refer to a score on a standardized intelligence test.

In 2004, the test, now called the Stanford-Binet 5 (Stanford University is where the revisions have been done), was revised to analyze an individual's responses in five content areas: fluid reasoning, knowledge, quantitative reasoning, visual-spatial reasoning, and working memory. A general composite score also is obtained. Today the test is scored by comparing the test-taker's performance with the results achieved by other people of the same age. The average score is set at 100.

The current Stanford-Binet is given to individuals from the age of 2 through adulthood. It includes a wide variety of items, some requiring verbal responses, and others, nonverbal responses. For example, a 6-year-old is expected to complete the verbal task of defining at least six words, such as *orange* and *envelope,* and the nonverbal task of tracing a path through a maze. An adult with average intelligence is expected to define such words as *disproportionate* and *regard,* explain a proverb, and compare the concepts of idleness and laziness.

Over the years, the Stanford-Binet has been given to thousands of children and adults of different ages. By administering the test to large numbers of individuals selected at random from different parts of the United States, researchers have found that the scores approximate a normal distribution (see Figure 8.1). A **normal distribution** is a symmetrical, bell-shaped curve with a majority of the cases falling in the middle of the range of possible scores and few scores appearing toward the extremes of the range. The Stanford-Binet continues to be one of the most widely used individual tests of intelligence.

The Wechsler Scales   Besides the Stanford-Binet, the other most widely used intelligence tests are the Wechsler scales. In 1939, David Wechsler introduced the first of his scales, designed for use with adults (Wechsler, 1939); the current edition is the Wechsler Adult Intelligence Scale—Third Edition (WAIS-III). The Wechsler Intelligence Scale for Children—Fourth Edition (WISC-IV) is designed for children and adolescents between the ages of 6 and 16, and the Wechsler Preschool and

mental age (MA) An individual's level of mental development relative to others.

intelligence quotient (IQ) An individual's mental age divided by chronological age, multiplied by 100; devised in 1912 by William Stern.

normal distribution A symmetrical, bell-shaped curve with a majority of the cases falling in the middle of the possible range of scores and few scores appearing toward the extremes of the range.

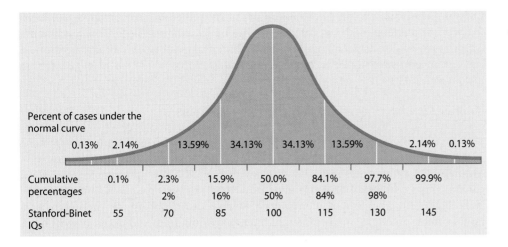

FIGURE **8.1**

THE NORMAL CURVE AND STANFORD-BINET IQ SCORES. The distribution of IQ scores approximates a normal curve. Most of the population falls in the middle range of scores. Notice that extremely high and extremely low scores are very rare. Slightly more than two-thirds of the scores fall between 85 and 115. Only about 1 in 50 individuals has an IQ of more than 130, and only about 1 in 50 individuals has an IQ of less than 70.

Primary Scale of Intelligence—Third Edition (WPPSI–III) is appropriate for children from the ages of 2 years 6 months to 7 years 3 months.

The Wechsler scales not only provide an overall IQ score but also yield several composite scores (for example, the Verbal Comprehension Index, the Working Memory Index, and the Processing Speed Index). These allow the examiner to quickly see whether the individual is strong or weak in different areas of intelligence. Three of the Wechsler subscales (two verbal, one nonverbal) are shown in Figure 8.2.

The Use and Misuse of Intelligence Tests Psychological tests are tools. Like all tools, their effectiveness depends on the knowledge, skill, and integrity of the user. A hammer can be used to build a beautiful kitchen cabinet or it can be used as a weapon of assault. Like a hammer, psychological tests can be used for positive purposes or they can be abused.

Intelligence tests have real-world applications as predictors of school and job success (Deary & others, 2007; Neukrug & Fawcett, 2010). For example, scores on tests of general intelligence are substantially correlated with school grades and achievement test performance, both at the time of the test and years later (Brody, 2007). IQ in the sixth grade correlates about .60 with the number of years of education the individual will eventually obtain (Jencks, 1979).

Intelligence tests are moderately correlated with work performance (Lubinski, 2000). Individuals with higher scores on tests designed to measure general intelligence tend to get higher-paying, more prestigious jobs (Zagorsky, 2007). However, general IQ tests predict only about one-fourth of the variation in job success, with the majority of job success due to motivation, education, and other factors (Wagner & Sternberg, 1986). Further, the correlations between IQ and achievement decrease the longer people work at a job, presumably because as they gain more job experience they perform better (Hunt, 1995).

Thus, although there are correlations between IQ scores and academic achievement and occupational success, many other factors contribute to success in school and at work. These include the motivation to succeed, physical and mental health, and social skills (Sternberg, 2003).

The single number provided by many IQ tests can easily lead to false expectations about an individual (Rosnow & Rosenthal, 1996). Sweeping generalizations are too often made on the basis of an IQ score and can become self-fulfilling prophecies (Weinstein, 2004).

Even though they have limitations, tests of intelligence are among psychology's most widely used tools. To be effective, they should be used

Verbal Subscales

Similarities

A child must think logically and abstractly to answer a number of questions about how things might be similar.

Example: "In what way are a lion and a tiger alike?"

Comprehension

This subscale is designed to measure an individual's judgment and common sense.

Example: "What is the advantage of keeping money in a bank?"

Nonverbal Subscales

Block Design

A child must assemble a set of multicolored blocks to match designs that the examiner shows.
Visual-motor coordination, perceptual organization, and the ability to visualize spatially are assessed.

Example: "Use the four blocks on the left to make the pattern on the right."

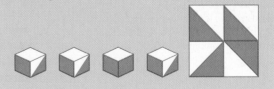

FIGURE **8.2**

SAMPLE SUBSCALES OF THE WECHSLER INTELLIGENCE SCALE FOR CHILDREN—FOURTH EDITION (WISC–IV). The Wechsler includes 11 subscales, 6 verbal and 5 nonverbal. Three of the subscales are shown here. Sample subscales from the Wechsler Intelligence Scale for Children–Fourth Edition (WISC–IV). Copyright © 2004 NCS Pearson, Inc. Reproduced with permission. All rights reserved. "Wechsler Intelligence Scale for Children" and "WISC" are trademarks, in the US and/or other countries, of Pearson Education, Inc. or its affiliates(s).

Robert J. Sternberg, who developed the triarchic theory of intelligence.

in conjunction with other information about an individual. For example, an intelligence test alone should not determine whether a child is placed in a special education or gifted class. The child's developmental history, medical background, performance in school, social competencies, and family experiences should be taken into account as well.

THEORIES OF MULTIPLE INTELLIGENCES

The use of a single score to describe how people perform on intelligence tests implies that intelligence is a general ability, a single trait. Wechsler scales provide scores for a number of intellectual skills, as well as an overall score. Do people have some general mental ability that determines how they perform on all of these tests? Or is intelligence a label for a combination of several distinct abilities? And do conventional intelligence tests measure everything that should be considered part of intelligence? Psychologists disagree about the answers to these questions.

Sternberg's Triarchic Theory   Robert J. Sternberg (1986, 2004, 2010, 2011a, b) notes that traditional IQ tests fail to measure some important dimensions of intelligence. Sternberg proposes a triarchic theory of intelligence involving three main types of intelligence: analytical, creative, and practical.

Sternberg developed the **triarchic theory of intelligence,** which states that intelligence comes in three forms: (1) *analytical intelligence,* which refers to the ability to analyze, judge, evaluate, compare, and contrast; (2) *creative intelligence,* which consists of the ability to create, design, invent, originate, and imagine; and (3) *practical intelligence,* which involves the ability to use, apply, implement, and put ideas into practice.

Sternberg (2011a, b) says that children with different triarchic patterns "look different" in school. Students with high analytic ability tend to be favored in conventional schooling. They often do well under direct instruction, in which the teacher lectures and gives students objective tests. They often are considered to be "smart" students who get good grades, show up in high-level tracks, do well on traditional tests of intelligence and the SAT, and later get admitted to competitive colleges.

In contrast, children who are high in creative intelligence often are not on the top rung of their class. Many teachers have specific expectations about how assignments should be done, and creatively intelligent students may not conform to those expectations. Instead of giving conformist answers, they give unique answers, for which they might get reprimanded or marked down. No teacher wants to discourage creativity, but Sternberg stresses that too often a teacher's desire to increase students' knowledge suppresses creative thinking.

Like children high in creative intelligence, children who are high in practical intelligence often do not relate well to the demands of school. However, many of these children do well outside of the classroom's walls. They may have excellent social skills and good common sense. As adults, some become successful managers, entrepreneurs, or politicians in spite of having undistinguished school records.

Gardner's Theory of Multiple Intelligences   According to Howard Gardner (1983, 1993, 2002), people have multiple intelligences, and IQ tests measure only a few of these. He argues that IQ tests measure verbal, math, and spatial aspects of intelligence while overlooking a number of other abilities. For evidence of the existence of multiple intelligences, Gardner uses information about the ways in which certain cognitive abilities survive particular types of brain damage. He also points to child prodigies and to some individuals who are retarded or autistic but have an extraordinary skill in a particular domain. An example was portrayed by Dustin Hoffman in the movie *Rain Man.* Hoffman's character was autistic but had a remarkable computing ability. In one scene, he helped his brother successfully gamble in Las Vegas by keeping track of all the cards that had been played.

"You're wise, but you lack tree smarts."
© Donald Reilly/ The New Yorker Collection/ www.cartoonbank.com

triarchic theory of intelligence Sternberg's theory that intelligence consists of analytical intelligence, creative intelligence, and practical intelligence.

From Verbal Intelligence to Naturalist Intelligence   Gardner has proposed eight types of intelligence. They are described here, along with examples of the occupations in which they are regarded as strengths (Campbell, Campbell, & Dickinson, 2004):

- *Verbal.* The ability to think in words and use language to express meaning (occupations: authors, journalists, speakers)
- *Mathematical.* The ability to carry out mathematical operations (occupations: scientists, engineers, accountants)
- *Spatial.* The ability to think three-dimensionally (occupations: architects, artists, sailors)
- *Bodily-kinesthetic.* The ability to manipulate objects and be physically adept (occupations: surgeons, craftspeople, dancers, athletes)
- *Musical.* A sensitivity to pitch, melody, rhythm, and tone (occupations: composers, musicians, and sensitive listeners)
- *Interpersonal.* The ability to understand and effectively interact with others (occupations: successful teachers, mental health professionals)
- *Intrapersonal.* The ability to understand oneself (occupations: theologians, psychologists)
- *Naturalist.* The ability to observe patterns in nature and understand natural and human-made systems (occupations: farmers, botanists, ecologists, landscapers)

Howard Gardner, here working with a young child, developed the view that intelligence comes in the forms of these eight kinds of skills: verbal, mathematical, spatial, bodily-kinesthetic, musical, interpersonal, intrapersonal, and naturalist.

Recently, Gardner has considered adding a ninth type of intelligence to his list of multiple intelligences—*existentialist*, which involves exploring and finding meaning in life, especially regarding questions about life, death, and existence.

Gardner notes that each of the eight intelligences can be destroyed by brain damage, that each involves unique cognitive skills, and that each shows up in exaggerated fashion in the gifted and in individuals with mental retardation or autism. According to Gardner, everyone has all of these intelligences but to varying degrees. As a result, we prefer to learn and process information in different ways. People learn best when they can apply their strong intelligences to the task.

Emotional Intelligence   Both Sternberg's and Gardner's theories include one or more categories related to social intelligence. In Sternberg's theory, the category is practical intelligence; in Gardner's theory, they are interpersonal intelligence and intrapersonal intelligence. Another theory that emphasizes interpersonal, intrapersonal, and practical aspects of intelligence is called **emotional intelligence,** which has been popularized by Daniel Goleman (1995) in his book *Emotional Intelligence.* The concept of emotional intelligence was initially developed by Peter Salovey and John Mayer (1990), who define it as the ability to perceive and express emotion accurately and adaptively (such as taking the perspective of others), to understand emotion and emotional knowledge (such as understanding the roles that emotions play in friendship and marriage), to use feelings to facilitate thought (such as being in a positive mood, which is linked to creative thinking), and to manage emotions in oneself and others (such as being able to control one's anger).

Children in the Key School form "pods," in which they pursue activities of special interest to them. Every day, each child can choose from activities that draw on Gardner's eight frames of mind. The school has pods that range from gardening to architecture to gliding to dancing. *What are some of the main ideas of Gardner's theory and its application to education?*

There continues to be considerable interest in the concept of emotional intelligence (Lomas & others, 2011; Mayer & others, 2011; Parker, Keefer, & Wood, 2011; Takeuchi & others, 2011). A recent study of college students revealed that both a general mental abilities test and an emotional intelligence assessment were linked to academic performance, although the general mental abilities test was a better predictor (Song & others, 2010). In this study, emotional intelligence was associated with the quality of peer relations.

Critics argue that emotional intelligence broadens the concept of intelligence too far to be useful and has not been adequately assessed and researched (Matthews, Zeidner, & Roberts, 2006).

emotional intelligence The ability to perceive and express emotions accurately and adaptively, to understand emotion and emotional knowledge, to use feelings to facilitate thought, and to manage emotions in oneself and others.

Gardner	Sternberg	Salovey/Mayer
Verbal Mathematical	Analytical	
Spatial Movement Musical	Creative	
Interpersonal Intrapersonal	Practical	Emotional
Naturalistic		

FIGURE 8.3

COMPARING STERNBERG'S, GARDNER'S, AND SALOVEY/MAYER'S INTELLIGENCES

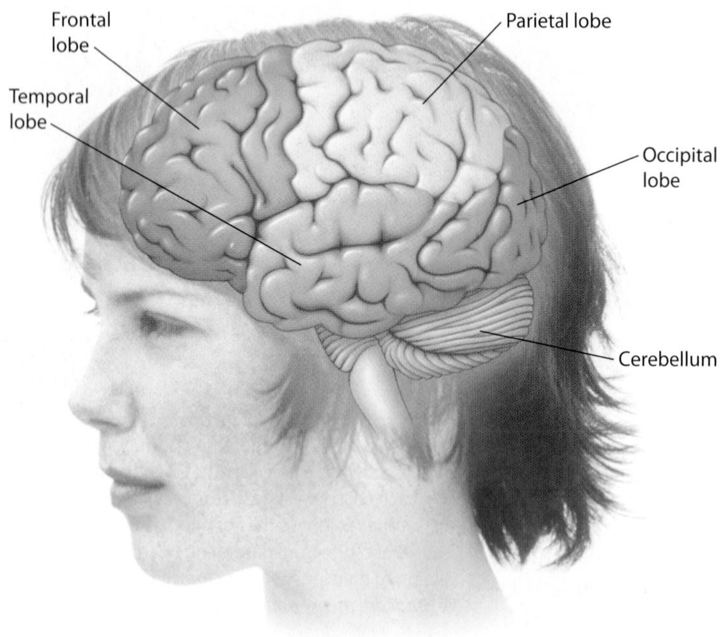

FIGURE 8.4

INTELLIGENCE AND THE BRAIN. Researchers recently have found that a higher level of intelligence is linked to a distributed neural network in the frontal and parietal lobes. To a lesser extent than the frontal/parietal network, the temporal and occipital lobes, as well as the cerebellum, also have been found to have links to intelligence. The current consensus is that intelligence is likely to be distributed across brain regions rather than being localized in a specific region, such as the frontal lobes.

Do People Have One or Many Intelligences? Figure 8.3 provides a comparison of Sternberg's, Gardner's, and Salovey/Mayer's views of intelligence. Notice that Sternberg's view is unique in emphasizing creative intelligence and that Gardner's includes a number of types of intelligence that are not addressed by the other views. These theories of multiple intelligence have much to offer. They have stimulated us to think more broadly about what makes up people's intelligence and competence (Davis & others, 2011; Sternberg, 2011a, b), and they have motivated educators to develop programs that instruct students in different domains.

Theories of multiple intelligences have their critics (Jensen, 2008). Some argue that the research base to support these theories has not yet developed. In particular, some critics say that Gardner's classification seems arbitrary. For example, if musical skills represent a type of intelligence, why don't we also refer to chess intelligence, prize-fighter intelligence, and so on?

A number of psychologists continue to support the concept of general intelligence (Jensen, 2008; Johnson, te Nijenhuis, & Bouchard, 2008). For example, one expert on intelligence, Nathan Brody (2007), argues that people who excel at one type of intellectual task are likely to excel in other intellectual tasks. Thus, individuals who do well at memorizing lists of digits are also likely to be good at solving verbal problems and spatial layout problems. This general intelligence includes abstract reasoning or thinking, the capacity to acquire knowledge, and problem-solving ability (Brody, 2000). Some experts who argue for the existence of general intelligence conclude that individuals also have specific intellectual abilities (Brody, 2007; Chiappe & MacDonald, 2005).

In sum, controversy still characterizes whether it is more accurate to conceptualize intelligence as a general ability, as specific abilities, or as both (Davidson & Kemp, 2011). Sternberg (2011a, b) accepts that there is evidence to support the concept of general intelligence in the kinds of analytical tasks that traditional IQ tests assess but thinks that the range of intellectual tasks those tests measure is too narrow.

THE NEUROSCIENCE OF INTELLIGENCE

In the current era of extensive research on the brain, interest in the neurological underpinnings of intelligence has increased (Deary & others, 2010; Haier, 2011; Preusse & others, 2011). Among the questions about the brain's role in intelligence that are being explored are these: Is having a bigger brain linked to higher intelligence? Is intelligence located in certain brain regions? Is the speed at which the brain processes information linked to intelligence?

Are individuals with bigger brains more intelligent than those with smaller brains? Recent studies using MRI scans to assess total brain volume indicate a moderate correlation (about 1.3 to 1.4) between brain size and intelligence (Carey, 2007; Luders & others, 2009).

Might intelligence be linked to specific regions of the brain? Early consensus was that the frontal lobes are the likely location of intelligence. However, researchers recently have found that intelligence is distributed more widely across brain regions (da Rocha, Rocha, & Massad, 2011; Glascher & others, 2010). The most prominent finding from brain-imaging studies is that a distributed neural network involving the frontal and parietal lobes is related to higher intelligence (Colom & others, 2009, 2010) (see Figure 8.4). Albert Einstein's total brain size was average, but a region of his brain's parietal lobe that is very active in processing math and spatial information was 15 percent larger than average (Witelson, Kigar, & Harvey, 1999). Other brain regions that have been linked to higher intelligence (although at a lower level of significance than the frontal/parietal lobe network) include the temporal and occipital lobes, as well as the cerebellum (Luders & others, 2009).

Examining the neuroscience of intelligence has also led to study of the role that neurological speed might play in intelligence (Waiter & others, 2009). Research results have not been consistent for this possible link, although one study did find that speed of neurological functioning was faster for intellectually gifted children than for children with average intelligence (Liu & others, 2007).

As technological advances allow closer study of the brain's functioning in coming decades, we are likely to see more specific conclusions about the brain's role in intelligence. As this research proceeds, keep in mind that both heredity and environment likely contribute to links between the brain and intelligence, including the connections we discussed between brain size and intelligence.

developmental connection

Information Processing. Speed of processing information declines in middle adulthood and then declines further in late adulthood. Chapter 7, p. 212

Review *Connect* Reflect

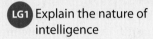 Explain the nature of intelligence

Review

- What is intelligence?
- What are the main individual tests of intelligence? What are some issues in the use and misuse of intelligence tests?
- What theories of multiple intelligence have been developed? Do people have one intelligence or many intelligences? What are some criticisms of the multiple intelligences concept?
- What are some links between the brain and intelligence?

Connect

- What do Sternberg's triarchic theory and Gardner's theory of multiple intelligences

have in common that could be applied in elementary school classrooms?

Reflect *Your Own Personal Journey of Life*

- A CD-ROM is being sold to parents for testing their child's IQ. Several parents tell you that they purchased the CD-ROM and assessed their children's IQ. Why might you want to be skeptical about giving your children an IQ test and interpreting the results yourself?

Controversies and Group Comparisons

LG2 Outline key controversies about differences in IQ scores

The Influence of Heredity and Environment

Group Comparisons and Issues

We have seen that intelligence is a slippery concept with competing definitions, tests, and theories. It is not surprising, therefore, that attempts to understand the concept of intelligence are filled with controversy. In some cases, the controversies arise over comparisons of the intelligence of different groups, such as people from different cultural or ethnic backgrounds.

THE INFLUENCE OF HEREDITY AND ENVIRONMENT

One of the hottest areas in the study of intelligence centers on the extent to which intelligence is influenced by genetics (nature) versus the extent to which it is influenced by environment (nurture) (Martinez, 2010). In Chapter 2, "Biological Beginnings," we indicated how difficult it is to tease apart these influences, but noted that psychologists continue to try to unravel them.

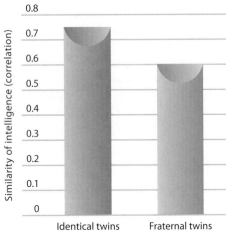

0.8
0.7
0.6
0.5
0.4
0.3
0.2
0.1
0

Similarity of intelligence (correlation)

Identical twins   Fraternal twins

FIGURE **8.5**

CORRELATION BETWEEN INTELLIGENCE TEST SCORES AND TWIN STATUS. The graph represents a summary of research findings that have compared the intelligence test scores of identical and fraternal twins. An approximate .15 difference has been found with a higher correlation for identical twins (.75) and a lower correlation for fraternal twins (.60).

Genetic Influences   To what degree do our genes make us smart? The issue with respect to genetics and intelligence is the degree to which our genes make us smart. A research review found that the difference in the average correlations for identical and fraternal twins was not very high—only .15 (Grigorenko, 2000) (see Figure 8.5).

The concept of **heritability** attempts to tease apart the effects of heredity and environment in a population. Heritability is the portion of the variance in a population that is attributed to genes. The heritability index is computed using correlational techniques. Thus, the highest degree of heritability is 1.00, and correlations of .70 and above suggest a strong genetic influence. A committee of respected researchers convened by the American Psychological Association concluded that by late adolescence, the heritability of intelligence is about .75, which reflects a strong genetic influence (Neisser & others, 1996).

An important point to keep in mind about heritability is that it refers to a specific group (population) rather than to individuals. Researchers use the concept of heritability to try to describe why people differ. Heritability says nothing about why a single individual, like yourself, has a certain intelligence—nor does it say anything about differences between groups.

Most research on heredity and environment does not include environments that differ radically. Thus, it is not surprising that many genetic studies show environment to be a fairly weak influence on intelligence (Fraser, 1995).

The heritability index has several limitations (Sternberg, Kaufman, & Grigorenko, 2008). It is only as good as the data that are entered into its analysis and the interpretations made from it. The data are virtually all from traditional IQ tests, which some experts believe are not always the best indicator of intelligence (Gardner, 2002; Sternberg, 2011a, b). Also, the heritability index assumes that researchers can treat genetic and environmental influences as factors that can be separated, with each part contributing a distinct amount of influence. As we discussed in Chapter 2, "Biological Beginnings," genes and the environment always work together. Genes always exist in an environment, and the environment shapes their activity.

Environmental Influences   Although genetic endowment influences a person's intellectual ability, the environmental experiences of children and adults do make a difference (Grigorenko & Takanishi, 2010; Martinez, 2010). In one study, researchers found that how much parents communicated with their children during the first three years of their lives was correlated with the children's Stanford-Binet IQ scores at age 3 (Hart & Risley, 1995). The more parents communicated with their children, the higher the children's IQs were.

Schooling also influences intelligence (Ceci & Gilstrap, 2000; Cliffordson & Gustafsson, 2008). The biggest effects have been found when large groups of children received no formal education for an extended period, resulting in lower intelligence.

Another possible effect of education can be seen in rapidly increasing IQ test scores around the world (Flynn, 1999, 2007, 2011). IQ scores have been rising so fast that a high percentage of people regarded as having average intelligence in the early 1900s would be considered below average in intelligence today (see Figure 8.6). If a representative sample of today's children took the Stanford-Binet test used in 1932, about one-fourth would be defined as very superior, a label usually accorded to fewer than 3 percent of the population. This worldwide increase in intelligence test scores over a short time frame is called the *Flynn effect* after the researcher who discovered it—James Flynn (1999, 2007, 2011).

Because the change in test scores has taken place in a relatively short period of time, it can't be due to heredity. Rather, it might result from environmental factors such as the exploding quantities of information to which people are exposed and the much higher percentage of the population who receive education. A recent

Students in an elementary school in South Africa. *How might schooling influence the development of children's intelligence?*

heritability The portion of the variance in a population that is attributed to genes.

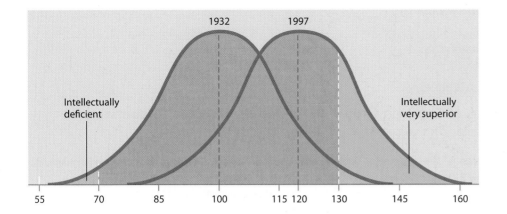

FIGURE **8.6**

THE INCREASE IN IQ SCORES FROM 1932 TO 1997. As measured by the Stanford-Binet test, American children seem to be getting smarter. Scores of a group tested in 1932 fell along a bell-shaped curve with half below 100 and half above. Studies show that if children took that same test today, half would score above 120 on the 1932 scale. Very few of them would score in the "intellectually deficient" end, on the left side, and about one-fourth would rank in the "very superior" range.

analysis indicated that the substantial increase in intelligence scores in recent years may be due to prenatal and early postnatal nutrition (Lynn, 2009). And another recent study revealed that children who have more highly educated (especially college-educated) mothers and/or belong to higher-income families show higher scores on math achievement tests than children who have less-educated mothers and/or belong to lower-income families (Ang, Rodgers, & Wanstrom, 2010).

Keep in mind that environmental influences are complex (Preiss & Sternberg, 2010). Growing up with all the "advantages," for example, does not guarantee success. Children from wealthy families may have easy access to excellent schools, books, travel, and tutoring, but they may take such opportunities for granted and fail to develop the motivation to learn and to achieve. In the same way, "poor" or "disadvantaged" does not automatically equal "doomed." Researchers increasingly are interested in manipulating the early environments of children who are at risk for impoverished intelligence (Gross & others, 2009; Pungello & others, 2010). The emphasis is on prevention rather than remediation. Many low-income parents have difficulty providing an intellectually stimulating environment for their children. Programs that educate parents to be more sensitive caregivers and better teachers, while providing support services such as quality child-care programs, can make a difference in a child's intellectual development (Phillips & Lowenstein, 2011).

A review of the research on early interventions concluded that (1) high-quality center-based interventions improve children's intelligence and school achievement; (2) the effects are strongest for poor children and for children whose parents have little education; (3) the positive benefits continue into adolescence, although the effects are smaller than in early childhood or the beginning of elementary school; and (4) the programs that are continued into elementary school have the most sustained long-term effects (Brooks-Gunn, 2003). Can we actually measure environmental influences on intelligence? To read more, see the *Connecting with Research* interlude.

In sum, there is a consensus among psychologists that both heredity and environment influence intelligence (Grigorenko & Takanishi, 2010; Hunt, 2011; Mandelman & Grigorenko, 2011; Sternberg, 2011a, b). This consensus reflects the nature-nurture issue, which was highlighted in Chapter 1. Recall that the nature-nurture issue focuses on the extent to which development is influenced by nature (heredity) and nurture (environment). Although psychologists agree that intelligence is the product of both nature and nurture, there is still disagreement about how strongly each factor influences intelligence.

The highest-risk children often benefit the most cognitively when they experience early interventions.

—Craig Ramey
Contemporary Psychologist, Georgetown University

developmental **connection**

Nature and Nurture. The epigenetic approach emphasizes the ongoing, bidirectional interaction of heredity and environment. Chapter 2, p. 62

GROUP COMPARISONS AND ISSUES

Group comparisons in intelligence can involve cultures and ethnic groups. We begin by examining cross-cultural comparisons and exploring cultural bias in testing.

Can Early Intervention in the Lives of Children Growing Up in Impoverished Circumstances Improve Their Intelligence?

Each morning a young mother waited with her child for the bus that would take the child to school. The child was only 2 months old, and "school" was an experimental program at the University of North Carolina at Chapel Hill. There the child experienced a number of interventions designed to improve her intellectual development—everything from bright objects dangled in front of her eyes while she was a baby to language instruction and counting activities when she was a toddler (Wickelgren, 1999). The child's mother had an IQ of 40 and could not read signs or determine how much change she should receive from a cashier. Her grandmother had a similarly low IQ.

Today, at age 20, the child's IQ measures 80 points higher than her mother's did when the child was 2 months old. Not everyone agrees that IQ can be affected this extensively, but it is clear that environment can make a substantial difference in a child's intelligence. As behavior geneticist Robert Plomin (1999) has said, even something that is highly heritable (like intelligence) may be malleable through interventions.

The child we just described was part of the Abecedarian Intervention program at the University of North Carolina at Chapel Hill conducted by Craig Ramey and his associates (Campbell, 2007; Ramey & Campbell, 1984; Ramey & Ramey, 1998). They randomly assigned 111 young children from low-income, poorly educated families to either an intervention group, which received full-time, year-round child care along with medical and social work services, or a control group, which received medical and social benefits but no child care. The child-care program included gamelike learning activities aimed at improving language, motor, social, and cognitive skills.

The success of the program in improving IQ was evident by the time the children were 3 years of age. At that age, the experimental group showed normal IQs averaging 101, a 17-point advantage over the control group. Recent follow-up results suggest that the effects are long-lasting. More than a decade later, at 15, children from the intervention group still maintained an IQ advantage of 5 points over the control-group children (97.7 to 92.6) (Campbell, 2007; Campbell & others, 2001; Ramey, Ramey, & Lanzi, 2001). They also did better on standardized tests of reading and math, and were less likely to be held back a year in school. Also, the greatest IQ gains were made by the children whose mothers had especially low IQs—below 70. At age 15, these children showed a 10-point IQ advantage over a group of children whose mothers' IQs were below 70 but who did not experience the child-care intervention.

The Abecedarian intervention study supports other research that has found prevention/intervention rather than later remediation to be important in improving the lives of children growing up in impoverished circumstances (Phillips & Lowenstein, 2011). Thus, it is important to consider the types of environments children experience as they develop, both in the general population and in especially challenging contexts.

"You can't build a hut, you don't know how to find edible roots and you know nothing about predicting the weather. In other words, you do terribly on our I.Q. test." Cartoon by Sidney Harris Copyright © ScienceCartoonsPlus.com.

Cross-Cultural Comparisons Cultures vary in the way they describe what it means to be intelligent (Sternberg, 2011c; Zhang & Sternberg, 2011). People in Western cultures tend to view intelligence in terms of reasoning and thinking skills, whereas people in Eastern cultures see intelligence as a way for members of a community to successfully engage in social roles (Nisbett, 2003).

In a study of the Luo culture in rural Kenya, children who scored highly on a test of knowledge about medicinal herbs—a measure of practical intelligence—tended to score poorly on tests of academic intelligence (Sternberg & others, 2001). These results indicated that practical and academic intelligence can develop independently and may even conflict with each other. They also suggest that the values of a culture may influence the direction in which a child develops. In a cross-cultural context, then, intelligence depends a great deal on environment (Sternberg & Grigorenko, 2008).

Cultural Bias in Testing Many of the early intelligence tests were culturally biased, favoring people who were from urban rather than rural environments, middle socioeconomic status rather than low socioeconomic status, and non-Latino White rather than African American ethnicity (Provenzo, 2002). Also, members of minority groups who do not speak English or who speak nonstandard English are at a disadvantage in trying to understand questions framed in standard English (Gibbs & Huang, 1989).

Researchers have developed **culture-fair tests,** which are intelligence tests that are designed to avoid cultural bias. Two types of culture-fair tests have been developed. The first includes questions that are familiar to people from all socioeconomic and ethnic backgrounds. For example, a child might be asked how a bird and a dog are different, on the assumption that virtually all children are familiar with birds and dogs. The second type of culture-fair test contains no verbal questions.

Why is it so hard to create culture-fair tests? Most tests tend to reflect what the dominant culture thinks is important (Shiraev & Levy, 2010). If tests have time limits, these will bias the test against groups not concerned with time. If languages differ, the same words might have different meanings for different language groups. Even pictures can produce bias because some cultures have less experience than others with drawings and photographs (Anastasi & Urbina, 1996). Within the same culture, different groups could have different attitudes, values, and motivation, and this could affect their performance on intelligence tests. Items that ask why buildings should be made of brick are biased against children who have little or no experience with brick houses. Questions about railroads, furnaces, seasons of the year, distances between cities, and so on can be biased against groups who have less experience than others with these contexts. Because of such difficulties, Robert Sternberg (2011c) concludes that there are no culture-fair tests, but only culture-reduced tests.

Ethnic Comparisons   In the United States, children from African American and Latino families score below children from non-Latino White families on standardized intelligence tests. On the average, African American schoolchildren score 10 to 15 points lower on standardized intelligence tests than non-Latino White schoolchildren do (Brody, 2000; Lynn, 1996). These are *average scores*, however. About 15 to 25 percent of African American schoolchildren score higher than half of non-Latino White schoolchildren do. The reason is that the distribution of scores for African Americans and non-Latino Whites overlap.

As African Americans have gained social, economic, and educational opportunities, the gap between African Americans and non-Latino Whites on standardized intelligence tests has begun to narrow (Ogbu & Stern, 2001). This gap especially narrows in college, where African American and non-Latino White students often experience more similar environments than in the elementary and high school years (Myerson & others, 1998). Also, when children from disadvantaged African American families are adopted into more advantaged middle-socioeconomic-status families, their scores on intelligence tests more closely resemble national averages for middle-socioeconomic-status children than for lower-socioeconomic-status children (Scarr & Weinberg, 1983).

culture-fair tests Intelligence tests that are designed to avoid cultural bias.

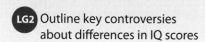

Review *Connect* Reflect

LG2 Outline key controversies about differences in IQ scores

Review

- What evidence suggests genetic influences on IQ scores?
- What evidence suggests environmental influences on IQ scores?
- What do IQ tests tell us about intelligence among people in different cultures and ethnic groups?

Connect

- Apply what you have learned about the nature-nurture debate to possible gender similarities and differences in intelligence. To read about gender's role in intelligence, see Chapter 12, "Gender and Sexuality."

Reflect *Your Own Personal Journey of Life*

- Do you think your performance on standardized tests accurately reflects your intelligence?

How can the intelligence of infants be assessed? Is intelligence stable throughout childhood? Does intelligence decline in older adults, and if so, when and by how much? These are some of the questions we will explore as we examine the development of intelligence.

TESTS OF INFANT INTELLIGENCE

The infant-testing movement grew out of the tradition of IQ testing. However, tests that assess infants are necessarily less verbal than IQ tests for older children. Tests for infants contain far more items related to perceptual-motor development. They also include measures of social interaction. To read about the work of one infant assessment specialist, see the *Connecting with Careers* profile.

The widely used **Bayley Scales of Infant Development** were developed by Nancy Bayley (1969) to assess infant behavior and predict later development. The current version, Bayley-III, has five scales: cognitive, language, motor, socio-emotional, and adaptive (Bayley, 2006). The first three scales are administered directly to the infant, while the latter two are questionnaires given to the caregiver. The Bayley-III also is more appropriate for use in clinical settings than the two previous editions (Lennon & others, 2008).

Bayley Scales of Infant Development Widely used scales, developed by Nancy Bayley, for assessing infant development. The current version, the Bayley-III, has five scales: cognitive, language, motor, socio-emotional, and adaptive; the first three are administered to the infant, the latter two to the caregiver.

connecting with careers

Toosje Thyssen Van Beveren, Infant Assessment Specialist

Toosje Thyssen Van Beveren is a developmental psychologist at the University of Texas Medical Center in Dallas. She has a master's degree in child clinical psychology and a Ph.D. in human development. Currently, Van Beveren is involved in a 12-week program called New Connections, which is a comprehensive intervention for young children who were affected by substance abuse prenatally and for their caregivers.

In the New Connections program, Van Beveren assesses infants' developmental status and progress. She might refer the infants to a speech, physical, or occupational therapist and monitor the infants' services and progress. Van Beveren trains the program staff and encourages them to use the exercises she recommends. She also discusses the child's problems with the primary caregivers, suggests activities, and assists them in enrolling infants in appropriate programs.

During her graduate work at the University of Texas at Dallas, Van Beveren was author John Santrock's teaching assistant in his undergraduate course on life-span development for four years. As a teaching assistant, she attended classes, graded exams, counseled students, and occasionally gave lectures. Each semester, Van Beveren returns to give a lecture on prenatal development and infancy. She also

Toosje Thyssen Van Beveren conducting an infant assessment.

teaches part-time in the psychology department at UT–Dallas. In Van Beveren's words, "My days are busy and full. The work is often challenging. There are some disappointments, but mostly the work is enormously gratifying."

How should a 6-month-old perform on the Bayley cognitive scale? The 6-month-old infant should be able to vocalize pleasure and displeasure, persistently search for objects that are just outside immediate reach, and approach a mirror that is placed in front of the infant by the examiner. By 12 months of age, the infant should be able to inhibit behavior when commanded to do so, imitate words the examiner says (such as *Mama*), and respond to simple requests (such as "Take a drink").

The increasing interest in infant development has produced many new measures, especially tasks that evaluate the ways infants process information (Fagan, 2011). The Fagan Test of Infant Intelligence is increasingly being used (Fagan, 1992). This test focuses on the infant's ability to process information in such ways as encoding the attributes of objects, detecting similarities and differences between objects, forming mental representations, and retrieving these representations. For example, it measures the amount of time babies look at a new object compared with the amount of time they spend looking at a familiar object.

Unlike the Bayley scales, the Fagan test is correlated with measures of intelligence in older children. In fact, evidence is accumulating that measures of habituation and dishabituation are linked to intelligence in childhood, adolescence, and even adulthood. For example, one study revealed that habituation assessed at 3 or 6 months of age was linked to verbal skills and intelligence assessed at 32 months of age (Domsch, Lohaus, & Thomas, 2009). And in another study, selective attention to novelty at 6 to 12 months was positively correlated with intelligence at 21 years of age (Fagan, Holland, & Wheeler, 2007). It is important, however, not to go too far and think that connections between cognitive development in early infancy and later cognitive development are so strong that no discontinuity takes place. As we discussed in Chapters 6 and 7, some important changes in cognitive development occur after infancy.

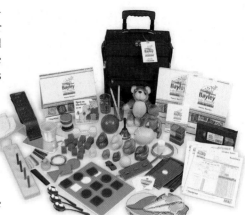

Items in the Bayley-III Scales of Infant Development.

STABILITY AND CHANGE IN INTELLIGENCE THROUGH ADOLESCENCE

A recent longitudinal study examined the intelligence of 200 children from 12 months (using the Bayley scales) to 4 years (using the Stanford-Binet test) of age (Blaga & others, 2009). The results indicated considerable stability from late infancy through the preschool years.

An early study examined correlations between IQ at a number of different ages (Honzik, MacFarlane, & Allen, 1948). There was a strong relation between IQ scores obtained at the ages of 6, 8, and 9 and IQ scores obtained at the age of 10. For example, the correlation between IQ at the age of 8 and IQ at the age of 10 was .88. The correlation between IQ at the age of 9 and IQ at the age of 10 was .90. These figures show a very high relation between IQ scores obtained in these years. The correlation between IQ in the preadolescent years and IQ at the age of 18 was slightly lower but still statistically significant. For example, the correlation between IQ at the age of 10 and IQ at the age of 18 was .70.

What has been said so far about the stability of intelligence has been based on measures of groups of individuals. The stability of intelligence also can be evaluated through studies of individuals. Robert McCall and his associates (McCall, Applebaum, & Hogarty, 1973) studied 140 children between the ages of 2½ and 17. They found that the average range of IQ scores was more than 28 points. The scores of one out of three children changed by as much as 40 points.

What can we conclude about stability and changes in intelligence during childhood? Intelligence test scores can fluctuate dramatically across the childhood years. Intelligence is not as stable as the original intelligence theorists envisioned. Children are adaptive beings. They have the capacity for intellectual change, but they do not become entirely new intelligent beings. In a sense, children's intelligence changes but remains connected with earlier points in development.

developmental **connection**

Life-Span Perspective. The stability-change issue is a major focus of study in the field of life-span development. Chapter 1, p. 18

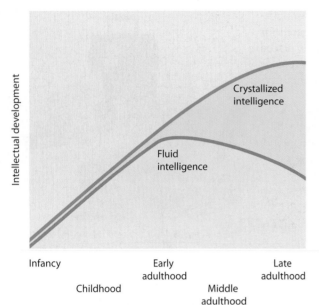

FIGURE **8.7**

FLUID AND CRYSTALLIZED INTELLECTUAL DEVELOPMENT ACROSS THE LIFE SPAN. According to Horn, crystallized intelligence (based on cumulative learning experiences) increases throughout the life span, but fluid intelligence (the ability to perceive and manipulate information) steadily declines from middle adulthood.

K. Warner Schaie (*right*) is one of the leading pioneers in the field of life-span development. He is shown here with two older adults who are actively using their cognitive skills. Schaie's research represents one of the most thorough examinations of how individuals develop and change as they go through the adult years.

crystallized intelligence An individual's accumulated information and verbal skills, which continues to increase with age.

fluid intelligence The ability to reason abstractly, which begins to decline in middle adulthood.

cognitive mechanics The "hardware" of the mind, reflecting the neurophysiological architecture of the brain as developed through evolution. Cognitive mechanics involves the speed and accuracy of the processes involving sensory input, visual and motor memory, discrimination, comparison, and categorization.

INTELLIGENCE IN ADULTHOOD

Does intelligence increase or decrease in adulthood? Might older adults have greater wisdom than younger adults? These are among the questions that we will explore in this section.

Fluid and Crystallized Intelligence John Horn emphasizes that some abilities increase throughout the life span, whereas others steadily decline from middle adulthood onward (Horn, 2007; Horn & Donaldson, 1980). Horn argues that **crystallized intelligence,** an individual's accumulated information and verbal skills, continues to increase throughout the life span. However, he notes that **fluid intelligence,** the ability to reason abstractly, begins to decline in middle adulthood (see Figure 8.7).

Horn's data were collected in a cross-sectional manner. Remember from Chapter 1 that a *cross-sectional study* assesses individuals of different ages at the same point in time. For example, a cross-sectional study might assess the intelligence of groups of 40-, 50-, and 60-year-olds in one evaluation, such as in 1990. The average 40-year-old and the average 60-year-old were born in eras that offered different economic and educational opportunities. For example, as the 60-year-olds grew up they likely had fewer educational opportunities, which probably influenced their scores on intelligence tests. Thus, if we find differences between 40- and 60-year-olds on intelligence tests when they are assessed cross-sectionally, these differences might be due to cohort effects (due to an individual's time of birth or generation but not to age) related to educational differences rather than to age.

In contrast, in a *longitudinal study*, the same individuals are studied over a period of time. Thus, a longitudinal study of intelligence in middle adulthood might consist of giving the same intelligence test to the same individuals when they are 40, when they are 50, and when they are 60 years of age. Whether data are collected cross-sectionally or longitudinally makes a difference in what is found about intellectual decline.

The Seattle Longitudinal Study K. Warner Schaie (1983, 1996, 2000, 2005, 2010, 2011) has conducted an extensive study of intellectual abilities in the adulthood years. Five hundred individuals initially were tested in 1956. New waves of participants are added periodically. The main mental abilities tested in the Seattle Longitudinal Study are as follows:

- *Verbal ability* (ability to understand ideas expressed in words)
- *Verbal memory* (ability to encode and recall meaningful language units, such as a list of words)
- *Numeric ability* (ability to perform simple mathematical computations such as addition, subtraction, and multiplication)
- *Spatial orientation* (ability to visualize and mentally rotate stimuli in two- and three-dimensional space)
- *Inductive reasoning* (ability to recognize and understand patterns and relationships in a problem and use this understanding to solve other instances of the problem)
- *Perceptual speed* (ability to quickly and accurately make simple discriminations in visual stimuli)

As shown in Figure 8.8, the highest level of functioning for four of the six intellectual abilities occurred during the middle adulthood years (Schaie, 2005). For both women and men, performance on verbal ability, verbal memory, inductive reasoning, and spatial orientation peaked in middle age. Only two of the six abilities—numeric ability and perceptual speed—declined in middle age. Perceptual speed showed the earliest decline, beginning in early adulthood.

Notice in Figure 8.8 that decline in functioning for most cognitive abilities began to steepen in the sixties, although the decline in verbal ability did not steepen until the mid-seventies. From the mid-seventies through the late eighties, all cognitive abilities showed considerable decline. When Schaie (1994) assessed intellectual abilities both cross-sectionally and longitudinally, he found decline more likely to occur in the cross-sectional than in the longitudinal assessments. For example, as shown in Figure 8.9, when assessed longitudinally, inductive reasoning increased until toward the end of middle adulthood and then began to show a slight decline. In contrast, when assessed cross-sectionally, inductive reasoning showed a consistent decline during middle adulthood. For the participants in the Seattle Longitudinal Study, middle age was a time of peak performance for both some aspects of crystallized intelligence (verbal ability) and fluid intelligence (spatial orientation and inductive reasoning).

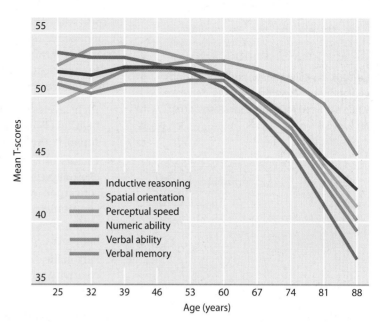

FIGURE **8.8**

LONGITUDINAL CHANGES IN SIX INTELLECTUAL ABILITIES FROM AGE 25 TO AGE 88

Cognitive Mechanics and Cognitive Pragmatics Paul Baltes (1993, 2000, 2003; Baltes, Lindenberger, & Staudinger, 2006) clarified the distinction between those aspects of the aging mind that decline and those that remain stable or even improve. He makes a distinction between "cognitive mechanics" and "cognitive pragmatics," which extends the fluid/crystallized intelligence conceptualization described earlier:

- **Cognitive mechanics** are the "hardware" of the mind and reflect the neurophysiological architecture of the brain developed through evolution. Cognitive mechanics consist of the speed and accuracy of the processes involved in sensory input, attention, visual and motor memory, discrimination, comparison, and categorization. Because of the strong influence of biology, heredity, and health on cognitive mechanics, a decline with aging is likely.

- **Cognitive pragmatics** are the culture-based "software programs" of the mind. Cognitive pragmatics include reading and writing skills, language comprehension, educational qualifications, professional skills, and also the type of knowledge about the self and life skills that help us to master or cope with life. Because of the strong influence of culture on cognitive pragmatics, their improvement into old age is possible. Thus, although cognitive mechanics may decline in old age, cognitive pragmatics may actually improve (see Figure 8.10).

The distinction between cognitive mechanics and cognitive pragmatics is similar to the one between fluid (mechanics) and crystallized (pragmatics) intelligence that was described earlier. Indeed, the similarity is so strong that some experts now use these terms to describe cognitive aging patterns: *fluid mechanics* and *crystallized pragmatics* (Lovden & Lindenberger, 2007).

Wisdom As you just saw, Baltes stresses that wisdom is an important aspect of cognitive pragmatics. Baltes and his colleagues (2006) define **wisdom** as expert knowledge about the practical aspects of life that permits excellent judgment about important matters. This practical knowledge involves exceptional insight about human development and life matters, good judgment, and understanding of how

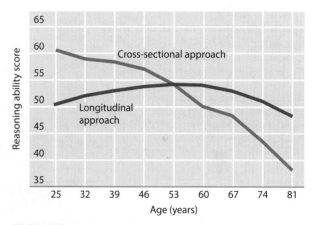

FIGURE **8.9**

CROSS-SECTIONAL AND LONGITUDINAL COMPARISONS OF INDUCTIVE REASONING ABILITY ACROSS THE ADULTHOOD YEARS. In Schaie's research, the cross-sectional approach revealed declining scores with age; the longitudinal approach showed a slight rise of scores in middle adulthood and only a slight decline beginning in the early part of late adulthood.

cognitive pragmatics The culture-based "software" of the mind. Cognitive pragmatics include reading and writing skills, language comprehension, educational qualifications, professional skills, and also the type of self-knowledge and life skills that helps us to master or cope with life.

wisdom Expert knowledge about the practical aspects of life that permits excellent judgment about important matters.

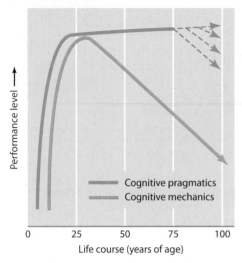

developmental **connection**

Culture. In Baltes' view, for older adults evolutionary selection benefits decrease while the need for culture increases. Chapter 2, p. 51

Performance level →

Cognitive pragmatics
Cognitive mechanics

0   25   50   75   100

Life course (years of age)

FIGURE **8.10**

THEORIZED AGE CHANGES IN COGNITIVE MECHANICS AND COGNITIVE PRAGMATICS.
Baltes argues that cognitive mechanics decline during aging, whereas cognitive pragmatics do not, at least for many people until they become very old. Cognitive mechanics have a biological/genetic foundation; cognitive pragmatics have an experiential/cultural foundation. The broken lines from 75 to 100 years of age indicate possible individual variations in cognitive pragmatics.

to cope with difficult life problems. Thus, wisdom, more than standard conceptions of intelligence, focuses on life's pragmatic concerns and human conditions (Karelitz, Jarvin, & Sternberg, 2010; Staudinger & Gluck, 2011).

In regard to wisdom, Baltes and his colleagues (Baltes & Kunzmann, 2004; Baltes, Lindenberger, & Staudinger, 2006; Baltes & Smith, 2008) have found that:

- High levels of wisdom are rare. Few people, including older adults, attain a high level of wisdom. That only a small percentage of adults show wisdom supports the contention that it requires experience, practice, or complex skills.

- Factors other than age are critical for wisdom to develop to a high level. For example, certain life experiences, such as being trained and working in a field concerned with difficult life problems and having wisdom-enhancing mentors, contribute to higher levels of wisdom. Also, people higher in wisdom have values that are more likely to consider the welfare of others than their own happiness.

- Personality-related factors, such as openness to experience, generativity, and creativity, are better predictors of wisdom than cognitive factors such as intelligence.

A recent study compared college students and older adults on a wisdom scale, which consisted of three dimensions: cognitive, reflective, and affective (Ardelt, 2010, p. 199):

- *Cognitive* scale items measured the absence of cognitive wisdom and included items on not having the ability or being unwilling to understand something thoroughly ("ignorance is bliss," for example), and tending to perceive the world as either/or instead of more complex ("People are either good or bad," for example), and being unaware of ambiguity and uncertainty in life ("There is only one right way to do anything," for example).

- *Reflective* scale items evaluated having the ability and being willing to examine circumstances and issues from different perspectives ("I always try to look at all sides of a problem," for example) and the lack of self-examination and self-insight ("Things often go wrong for me through no fault of my own," for example).

Older adults might not be as quick with their thoughts or behavior as younger people, but wisdom may be an entirely different matter. This older man shares the wisdom of his experience with children at an elementary school. *How is wisdom described by life-span developmentalists?*

- *Affective* scale items assessed positive and caring emotions ("Sometimes I feel a real compassion for everyone," for example) and the lack of those characteristics ("It's not really my problem if others are in trouble and need help," for example).

On the overall wisdom scale that included an assessment of all three dimensions combined, no differences were found between the two age groups. However, older adults who were college educated scored higher on the reflective and affective, but not the cognitive, dimensions of wisdom than the college students.

Review Connect Reflect

 LG3 Discuss the development of intelligence across the human life span

Review

- How is intelligence assessed during infancy?
- How much does intelligence change through childhood and adolescence?
- To what extent does intelligence change as adults age? What is wisdom, and how can it be characterized?

Connect

- In this section, you read about longitudinal and cross-sectional studies of intelligence.

What are the potential advantages and disadvantages that you learned about these two research approaches in Chapter 1?

Reflect *Your Own Personal Journey of Life*

- Think about your parents' and grandparents' intelligence. How might their intelligence have been influenced by cohort effects?

The Extremes of Intelligence and Creativity

 LG4 Describe the characteristics of mental retardation, giftedness, and creativity

Mental Retardation   Giftedness   Creativity

Mental retardation and intellectual giftedness are the extremes of intelligence. Often intelligence tests are used to identify exceptional individuals. We will explore the nature of mental retardation and giftedness, then examine how creativity differs from intelligence.

MENTAL RETARDATION

The most distinctive feature of mental retardation is inadequate intellectual functioning. Long before formal tests were developed to assess intelligence, individuals with mental retardation were identified by a lack of age-appropriate skills in learning and caring for themselves. Once intelligence tests were developed, they were used to identify degrees of mental retardation. But of two individuals with mental retardation who have the same low IQ, one might be married, employed, and involved in the community and the other might require constant supervision in an institution. Such differences in social competence led psychologists to include deficits in adaptive behavior in their definition of mental retardation.

Mental retardation is a condition of limited mental ability in which the individual (1) has a low IQ, usually below 70 on a traditional intelligence test; (2) has difficulty adapting to everyday life; and (3) first exhibits these characteristics by age 18. The age limit is included in the definition of mental retardation because, for example, we don't usually think of a college student who suffers massive brain damage in a car accident, resulting in an IQ of 60, as being "mentally retarded." The low IQ and low adaptiveness should be evident in childhood, not after normal

A child with Down syndrome. *What causes a child to develop Down syndrome? In which major classification of mental retardation does the condition fall?*

mental retardation A condition of limited mental ability in which an individual has a low IQ, usually below 70 on a traditional test of intelligence, and has difficulty adapting to everyday life.

Type of Mental Retardation	IQ Range	Percentage of Mentally Retarded Individuals
Mild	55 to 70	89
Moderate	40 to 54	6
Severe	25 to 39	4
Profound	Below 25	1

FIGURE 8.11

CLASSIFICATION OF MENTAL RETARDATION BASED ON IQ

Classification of Mental Retardation	Level of Support Needed
Intermittent	Supports are provided "as needed." The individual may need episodic or short-term support during life-span transitions (such as job loss or acute medical crisis). Intermittent supports may be low or high intensity when provided.
Limited	Supports are intense and relatively consistent over time. They are time-limited but not intermittent, require fewer staff members, and cost less than more intense supports. These supports likely will be needed for adaptation to the changes involved in the school-to-adult period.
Extensive	Supports are characterized by regular involvement (for example, daily) in at least some setting (such as home or work) and are not time-limited (for example, extended home-living support).
Pervasive	Supports are constant, very intense, and are provided across settings. They may be of a life-sustaining nature. These supports typically involve more staff members and intrusiveness than the other support categories.

FIGURE 8.12

CLASSIFICATION OF MENTAL RETARDATION BASED ON LEVELS OF SUPPORT NEEDED

developmental **connection**

Conditions, Diseases, and Disorders. Down syndrome is caused by the presence of an extra copy of chromosome 21. Chapter 2, p. 56

giftedness Having above-average intelligence (an IQ of 130 or higher) and/or superior talent for something.

functioning is interrupted by damage of some form. About 5 million Americans fit this definition of mental retardation.

There are several ways to define degrees of mental retardation (Hallahan, Kaufmann, Pullen, 2012; Hodapp & others, 2011). Most school systems use the classifications shown in Figure 8.11, in which IQ scores categorize retardation as mild, moderate, severe, or profound.

Note that a large majority of individuals diagnosed with mental retardation fit into the mild category. However, these categories are not perfect predictors of functioning. The American Association of Mental Retardation (1992) developed a different classification based on the degree of support required for a person with mental retardation to function at the highest level. As shown in Figure 8.12, these categories of support are intermittent, limited, extensive, and pervasive.

Some cases of mental retardation have an organic cause. *Organic retardation* is mental retardation caused by a genetic disorder or by brain damage. Down syndrome is one form of organic mental retardation, and it occurs when an extra chromosome is present. Other causes of organic retardation include fragile X syndrome, an abnormality in the X chromosome that was discussed in Chapter 2, "Biological Beginnings"; prenatal malformation; metabolic disorders; and diseases that affect the brain. Most people who suffer from organic retardation have IQs between 0 and 50.

When no evidence of organic brain damage can be found, cases of mental retardation are labeled *cultural-familial retardation*. Individuals with this type of retardation have IQs between 55 and 70. Psychologists suspect that these mental deficits often result from growing up in a below-average intellectual environment. Children who are familially retarded can be identified in schools, where they often fail, need tangible rewards (candy rather than praise), and are highly sensitive to what others expect of them. However, as adults, the familially retarded are usually invisible, perhaps because adult settings don't tax their cognitive skills as sorely. It may also be that the familially retarded increase their intelligence as they move toward adulthood.

GIFTEDNESS

There have always been people whose abilities and accomplishments outshine those of others—the whiz kid in class, the star athlete, the natural musician. People who are **gifted** have high intelligence or superior talent of some kind. An IQ of 130 is often used as the low threshold for giftedness, although this figure is arbitrary. Programs for the gifted in most school systems select children who have intellectual superiority and academic aptitude. They tend to overlook children who are talented in the arts or athletics or who have other special aptitudes (Sternberg, Jarvin, & Grigorenko, 2011; Winner, 2009).

Until recently, giftedness and emotional distress were thought to go hand-in-hand. Virginia Woolf, Sir Isaac Newton, Vincent van Gogh, Anne Sexton, Socrates, and Sylvia Plath all had emotional problems. However, these individuals are the exception rather than the rule. In general, no relation between giftedness and mental disorder has been found. Research supports the conclusion that gifted people tend to be more mature and have fewer emotional problems than others, and to grow up in a positive family climate (Feldhusen, 1999).

Characteristics of Children Who Are Gifted   Aside from their abilities, do children who are gifted have distinctive characteristics? Lewis Terman (1925) conducted an extensive study of 1,500 children whose Stanford-Binet IQs averaged 150. Contrary to the popular myth that children who are gifted are maladjusted, Terman found that they were socially well adjusted.

Ellen Winner (1996) described three criteria that characterize gifted children, whether in art, music, or academic domains:

1. *Precocity.* Gifted children are precocious. They begin to master an area earlier than their peers. Learning in their domain is more effortless for them than for ordinary children. In most instances, these gifted children are precocious because they have an inborn high ability.

2. *Marching to their own drummer.* Gifted children learn in a qualitatively different way from ordinary children. For one thing, they need minimal help from adults to learn. In many cases, they resist explicit instruction. They also often make discoveries on their own and solve problems in unique ways.

3. *A passion to master.* Gifted children are driven to understand the domain in which they have high ability. They display an intense, obsessive interest and an ability to focus. They do not need to be pushed by their parents. They motivate themselves, says Winner.

Art prodigy Alexandra Nechita. *What are some characteristics of gifted children?*

Life Course of the Gifted   As a 10-year-old, Alexandra Nechita (born in 1985) was described as a child prodigy. She paints quickly and impulsively on large canvases, some as large as 5 feet by 9 feet. It is not unusual for her to complete several of these large paintings in a week's time. Her paintings sell for up to $100,000 apiece. When she was only 2 years of age, Alexandra colored in coloring books for hours. She had no interest in dolls or friends. Once she started school, she would start painting as soon as she got home. And she continues to paint—relentlessly and passionately. It is, she says, what she loves to do.

Is giftedness, like Alexandra Nechita's artistic talent, a product of heredity or of environment? Likely both (Sternberg, Jarvin, & Grigorenko, 2011). Individuals who are gifted recall that they had signs of high ability in a specific area at a very young age, prior to or at the beginning of formal training (Howe & others, 1995). This suggests the importance of innate ability in giftedness. However, researchers also have found that individuals with world-class status in the arts, mathematics, science, and sports all report strong family support and years of training and practice (Bloom, 1985). Deliberate practice is an important characteristic of individuals who become experts in a specific domain. For example, in one study, the best musicians engaged in twice as much deliberate practice over their lives as the least successful ones did (Ericsson, Krampe, & Tesch-Römer, 1993).

Do gifted children become gifted and highly creative adults? In Terman's research on children with superior IQs, the children typically became experts in a well-established domain, such as medicine, law, or business. However, they did not become major creators (Winner, 2000). That is, they did not create a new domain or revolutionize an old domain.

One reason that some gifted children do not become gifted adults is that they often have been pushed too hard by overzealous parents and teachers. As a result, they lose their intrinsic (internal) motivation (Winner, 1996, 2006). As adolescents, they may ask themselves, "Who am I doing this for?" If the answer is not for one's self, they may not want to do it anymore. Another reason that gifted children do not become gifted adults is that the criteria for giftedness change— as an adult, an individual has to actually do something special to be labeled gifted.

Margaret (Peg) Cagle with some of the gifted seventh- and eighth-grade math students she teaches at Lawrence Middle School in Chatsworth, California. Cagle especially advocates challenging students who are gifted to take intellectual risks. To encourage collaboration, she often has students work together in groups of four, and frequently tutors students during lunch hour. As 13-year-old Madeline Lewis commented, "If I don't get it one way, she'll explain it another and talk to you about it and show you until you do get it." Cagle says it is important to be passionate about teaching math and open up a world for students that shows them how beautiful learning math can be (Wong Briggs, 2007, p. 6D).

Domain-Specific Giftedness   Individuals who are highly gifted are typically not gifted in many domains, and research on giftedness

A young Bill Gates, founder of Microsoft and now one of the world's richest persons. Like many highly gifted students, Gates was not especially fond of school. He hacked a computer security system when he was 13 and as a high school student, he was allowed to take some college math classes. He dropped out of Harvard University and began developing a plan for what was to become Microsoft Corporation. *What are some ways that schools can enrich the education of such highly talented students as Gates to make it a more challenging, interesting, and meaningful experience?*

- - - - - - - - - - - - - - - - ➤

developmental **connection**

Education. A number of criticisms of the No Child Left Behind policy have been made. Chapter 16, p. 526

creativity The ability to think in novel and unusual ways and to come up with unique solutions to problems.

increasingly focuses on domain-specific developmental trajectories (Horowitz, 2009; Winner, 2009). During the childhood years, the domains in which individuals are gifted usually emerge. Thus, at some point in the childhood years, the child who is to become a gifted artist or the child who is to become a gifted mathematician begins to show expertise in that domain. Regarding domain-specific giftedness, software genius Bill Gates (1998), the founder of Microsoft and one of the world's richest persons, commented that sometimes you have to be careful when you are good at something and resist the urge to think that you will be good at everything. Gates says that because he has been so successful at software development, people expect him to be brilliant in other domains where he is far from being a genius.

Education of Children Who Are Gifted   An increasing number of experts argue that the education of gifted children in the United States requires a significant overhaul (Reis & Renzulli, 2011; Sternberg, Jarvin, & Grigorenko, 2011). Consider the titles of the following books and reports: *Genius Denied: How to Stop Wasting Our Brightest Young Minds* (Davidson & Davidson, 2004) and *A Nation Deceived: How Schools Hold Back America's Brightest Students* (Colangelo, Assouline, & Gross, 2004).

Underchallenged gifted children can become disruptive, skip classes, and lose interest in achieving. Sometimes these children just disappear into the woodwork, becoming passive and apathetic toward school. It is extremely important for teachers to challenge children who are gifted to establish high expectations (Sternberg, Jarvin, & Grigorenko, 2011; Webb & others, 2007; Winner, 2006).

Some educators conclude that the inadequate education of children who are gifted has been compounded by the federal government's No Child Left Behind policy, which seeks to raise the achievement level of students who are not doing well in school at the expense of enriching the education of children who are gifted (Clark, 2008). A number of experts argue that too often children who are gifted are socially isolated and underchallenged in the classroom (Karnes & Stephens, 2008; Sternberg, Jarvin, & Grigorenko, 2011). It is not unusual for them to be ostracized and labeled "nerds" or "geeks." Ellen Winner (1996, 2006) concludes that a child who is truly gifted often is the only child in the room who does not have the opportunity to learn with students of like ability.

Many eminent adults report that school was a negative experience for them, that they were bored and sometimes knew more than their teachers (Bloom, 1985). Winner stresses that American education will benefit when standards are raised for all children. When some children are still underchallenged, she recommends that they be allowed to attend advanced classes in their domain of exceptional ability, such as allowing some especially precocious middle school students to take college classes in their area of expertise. For example, Bill Gates, founder of Microsoft, took college math classes and hacked a computer security system at 13; Yo-Yo Ma, a famous cellist, graduated from high school at 15 and attended Juilliard School of Music in New York City.

CREATIVITY

We have encountered the term "creative" on several occasions in our discussion of giftedness. What does it mean to be creative? **Creativity** is the ability to think about something in novel and unusual ways and come up with unique, good solutions to problems.

Intelligence and creativity are not the same thing (Kaufman & Plucker, 2011; Sternberg, 2011a, b; Sternberg & Kaufman, 2010). Most creative people are quite intelligent, but the reverse is not necessarily true. Many highly intelligent people (as measured by high scores on conventional tests of intelligence) are not very creative. Many highly intelligent people produce large numbers of products, but their output is not necessarily novel.

Why don't IQ scores predict creativity? Creativity requires divergent thinking (Guilford, 1967). **Divergent thinking** produces many answers to the same question. In contrast, conventional intelligence tests require **convergent thinking.** For example, a typical question on a conventional intelligence test is "How many quarters will you get in return for 60 dimes?" There is only one correct answer to this question. In contrast, a question such as "What image comes to mind when you hear the phrase 'sitting alone in a dark room'?" has many possible answers; it calls for divergent thinking.

Steps in the Creative Process   The creative process has often been described as a five-step sequence:

1. *Preparation.* You become immersed in a problem or an issue that interests you and arouses your curiosity.
2. *Incubation.* You churn ideas around in your head. This is the point at which you are likely to make some unusual connections in your thinking.
3. *Insight.* You experience the "Aha!" moment when all pieces of the puzzle seem to fit together.
4. *Evaluation.* Now you must decide whether the idea is valuable and worth pursuing. Is the idea really novel or is it obvious?
5. *Elaboration.* This final step often covers the longest span of time and the hardest work. This is what the famous twentieth-century American inventor Thomas Edison was talking about when he said that creativity is 1 percent inspiration and 99 percent perspiration. Elaboration may require a great deal of perspiration.

Mihaly Csikszentmihalyi (pronounced ME-high CHICK-sent-me-high-ee) (1996) notes that this five-step sequence provides a helpful framework for thinking about how creative ideas are developed. However, he argues that creative people don't always go through the steps in a linear sequence. For example, elaboration is often interrupted by periods of incubation. Fresh insights may appear during incubation, evaluation, and elaboration. And insight might take years or only a few hours. Sometimes the creative idea consists of one deep insight. Other times it's a series of small ones.

Characteristics of Creative Thinkers   Creative thinkers tend to have the following characteristics (Perkins, 1994):

*   *Flexibility and playful thinking.* Creative thinkers are flexible and play with problems, which gives rise to a paradox. Although creativity takes hard work, the work goes more smoothly if you take it lightly (Goleman, Kaufman, & Ray, 1993). When you are joking around, you are more likely to consider any possibility.

*   *Inner motivation.* Creative people often are motivated by the joy of creating. They tend to be less inspired by grades, money, or favorable feedback from others. Thus, creative people are motivated more internally than externally (Runco, 2011).

*   *Willingness to risk.* Creative people make more mistakes than their less imaginative counterparts. It's not that they are less proficient but that they come up with more ideas, more possibilities (Lubart, 2003). They win some, they lose some. For example, the twentieth-century Spanish artist Pablo Picasso created more than 20,000 paintings. Not all of them were masterpieces. Creative thinkers learn to cope with unsuccessful projects and see failure as an opportunity to learn.

*   *Objective evaluation of work.* Contrary to the stereotype that creative people are eccentric and highly subjective, most creative thinkers strive to evaluate their work objectively. They may use established criteria to make this judgment or

What do you mean, "What is it"? It's the spontaneous, unfettered expression of a young mind not yet bound by the restraints of narrative or pictorial representation. Cartoon by Sidney Harris Copyright © ScienceCartoonsPlus.com.

developmental **connection**

Work. Intrinsic motivation requires the internal motivation to do something for its own sake (the activity is an end in itself). Chapter 16, p. 540

divergent thinking Thinking that produces many answers to the same question; characteristic of creativity.

convergent thinking Thinking that produces one correct answer; characteristic of the kind of thinking required on conventional intelligence tests.

rely on the judgments of people they respect. In this manner, they can determine whether further creative thinking will improve their work.

Creativity in Schools A special concern is that children's creative thinking appears to be declining. A study of approximately 300,000 U.S. children and adults found that creativity scores rose until 1990, but since then have been steadily declining (Kim, 2010). Among the likely causes of the creativity decline are the number of hours U.S. children watch TV and play video games instead of engaging in creative activities, as well as the lack of emphasis on creative thinking skills in schools (Beghetto & Kaufman, 2011; Runco, 2011; Sternberg, 2011d). Some countries, though, are placing increasing emphasis on creative thinking in schools. For example, historically, creative thinking has typically been discouraged in Chinese schools. However, Chinese educators are now encouraging teachers to spend more classroom time on creative activities (Plucker, 2010).

An important teaching goal is to help students become more creative (Fairweather & Cramond, 2011; Hennessey, 2011; Sternberg, 2010a). Teachers need to recognize that students will show more creativity in some domains than in others (Runco & Pritzker, 2010). A student who shows creative thinking skills in mathematics may not exhibit these skills in art, for example.

School environments that encourage independent work, are stimulating but not distracting, and make resources readily available are likely to encourage students' creativity. There is mounting concern that the U.S. government's No Child Left Behind legislation has harmed the development of students' creative thinking by focusing attention on memorizing information to ensure high performance on standardized tests (Burke-Adams, 2007; Kaufman & Sternberg, 2007).

Strategies for increasing children's creative thinking include the following:

- *Encourage brainstorming.* **Brainstorming** is a technique in which people are encouraged to come up with creative ideas in a group, play off each other's ideas, and say practically whatever comes to mind that seems relevant to a particular issue. Participants are usually told to hold off from criticizing others' ideas at least until the end of the brainstorming session.

- *Provide environments that stimulate creativity.* Some environments nourish creativity, while others inhibit it. Parents and teachers who encourage creativity often rely

brainstorming Technique in which individuals are encouraged to come up with creative ideas in a group, play off each other's ideas, and say practically whatever comes to mind relevant to a particular issue.

What are some good strategies for guiding children to think more creatively?

on children's natural curiosity. They provide exercises and activities that stimulate children to find insightful solutions to problems, rather than ask a lot of questions that require rote answers. Teachers also encourage creativity by taking students on field trips to locations where creativity is valued. Science, discovery, and children's museums offer rich opportunities to stimulate creativity.

- *Don't overcontrol students.* Teresa Amabile (1993) says that telling children exactly how to do things leaves them feeling that originality is a mistake and exploration is a waste of time. If, instead of dictating which activities they should engage in, you let children select their interests and you support their inclinations, you will be less likely to destroy their natural curiosity (Hennessey, 2011; Hennessey & Amabile, 2010).

- *Encourage internal motivation.* Excessive use of prizes, such as gold stars, money, or toys, can stifle creativity by undermining the intrinsic pleasure students derive from creative activities. Creative children's motivation is the satisfaction generated by the work itself. Competition for prizes and formal evaluations often undermine intrinsic motivation and creativity (Amabile & Hennessey, 1992). However, material rewards should not be eliminated altogether.

- *Build children's confidence.* To expand children's creativity, encourage them to believe in their own ability to create something innovative and worthwhile. Building children's confidence in their creative skills aligns with Bandura's (2010a) concept of self-efficacy—the belief that one can master a situation and produce positive outcomes.

- *Guide children to be persistent and delay gratification.* Most highly successful creative products take years to develop. Most creative individuals work on ideas and projects for months and years without being rewarded for their efforts (Sternberg & Williams, 1996).

- *Encourage children to take intellectual risks.* Creative individuals take intellectual risks and seek to discover or invent something that has never before been discovered or invented (Sternberg & Williams, 1996). They risk spending extensive time on an idea or project that may not work. Creative people are not afraid of failing or getting something wrong (Sternberg, 2011a, b).

- *Introduce children to creative people.* Teachers can invite creative people to their classrooms and ask them to describe what helps them become creative or to demonstrate their creative skills. Writers, poets, musicians, scientists, and many others can bring their props and productions to the class, turning it into a theater for stimulating students' creativity.

You can find out about steps you can take to live a more creative life in the *Connecting Development to Life* interlude on page 270.

developmental connection

Achievement. Self-efficacy is the belief that "I can"; helplessness is the belief that "I cannot." Chapter 16, p. 542

Changes in Adulthood At the age of 30, Thomas Edison invented the phonograph, Hans Christian Andersen wrote his first volume of fairy tales, and Mozart composed *The Marriage of Figaro.* One early study of creativity found that individuals' most creative products were generated in their thirties and that 80 percent of the most important creative contributions were completed by age 50 (Lehman, 1960). More recently, researchers have found that creativity often peaks in the forties before declining (Simonton, 1996). However, any generalization about a relationship between age and creative accomplishments must be qualified by consideration of (1) the size of the decline and (2) differences across domains (Simonton, 1996).

Even though a decline in creative contributions is often found in the fifties and later, the decline is often not great. And a study of artists from 53 to 75 years of age found no age differences in the artists' perceptions of their creativity (Reed, 2005). An impressive array of creative accomplishments have occurred in late adulthood (Tahir & Gruber, 2003). Benjamin Franklin invented the bifocal lens when he

Living a More Creative Life

Leading expert on creativity Mihaly Csik-szentmihalyi (1996) interviewed 90 leading figures in art, business, government, education, and science to learn how creativity works. He discovered that creative people regularly engage in challenges that absorb them. Based on his interviews with some of the most creative people in the world, he concluded that the first step toward a more creative life is to cultivate your curiosity and interest. Here are his recommendations for doing this:

1. *Try to be surprised by something every day.* Maybe it is something you see, hear, or read about. Become absorbed in a lecture or a book. Be open to what the world is telling you. Life is a stream of experiences. Swim widely and deeply in it, and your life will be richer.

2. *Try to surprise at least one person every day.* In a lot of things you do, you have to be predictable and patterned. Do something different for a change. Ask a question you normally would not ask. Invite someone to go to a show or a museum you never have visited.

3. *Write down each day what surprised you and how you surprised others.* Most creative people keep a diary, notes, or lab records to ensure that their experience is not forgotten. Start with a specific task. Each evening, record the most surprising event that occurred that day and your most surprising action. After a few days, reread your notes and reflect on your experiences. After a few weeks, you might see a pattern emerging, one that suggests an area you can explore in greater depth.

4. *When something sparks your interest, follow it.* Usually when something captures your attention, it is short-lived—an idea, a song, a flower. Too often we are too busy to explore the idea, song, or flower further. Or we think these areas are none of our business because we

Leading creativity theorist Mihaly Csikszentmihalyi, in the setting where he gets his most creative ideas.

are not experts about them. Yet the world is our business. We can't know which part of it is best suited to our interests until we make a serious effort to learn as much about as many aspects of it as possible.

5. *Wake up in the morning with a specific goal to look forward to.* Creative people wake up eager to start the day. Why? Not necessarily because they are cheerful, enthusiastic types but because they know that there is something meaningful to accomplish each day, and they can't wait to get started.

6. *Take charge of your schedule.* Figure out which time of the day is your most creative time. Some of us are more creative late at night, others early in the morning. Carve out some time for yourself when your creative energy is at its best.

7. *Spend time in settings that stimulate your creativity.* In Csikszentmihalyi's (1996) research, he gave people an electronic pager and beeped them randomly at different times of the day. When he asked them how they felt, they reported the highest levels of creativity when walking, driving, or swimming. For example, one person said, "I do my most creative thinking when I'm jogging." These activities are semiautomatic in that they take a certain amount of attention while leaving some time free to make connections among ideas. Another setting in which highly creative people report coming up with novel ideas is the half-asleep, half-awake state we are in when we are deeply relaxed or barely awake.

Can the strategies for stimulating creative thinking in children found earlier in this chapter also be used by adults? How do those strategies compare to those discussed here?

---

was 78 years old; Wolfgang von Goethe completed *Faust* when he was in his eighties. After a distinguished career as a physicist, Henri Chevreul switched fields in his nineties to become a pioneer in gerontological research. He published his last research paper just a year prior to his death at the age of 103!

Furthermore, the age at which creativity typically declines varies with the domain involved. In philosophy and history, for example, older adults often show as much creativity as they did when they were in their thirties and forties. In contrast, in lyric poetry, abstract mathematics, and theoretical physics, the peak of creativity is often reached in the twenties or thirties.

Review *Connect* Reflect

LG4 Describe the characteristics of mental retardation, giftedness, and creativity

Review

- What is mental retardation, and what are its causes?
- What makes people gifted?
- What makes people creative?

Connect

- In Chapter 7, "Information Processing," you learned about children's critical-thinking skills and problem-solving strategies. What role, if any, might these play in determining whether or not children become creative thinkers?

Reflect *Your Own Personal Journey of Life*

- How many of the tips in the *Connecting Development to Life* interlude, "Living a More Creative Life," do you practice? In what ways might you benefit from these suggestions, in addition to becoming more creative?

reach your **learning goals**

The Concept of Intelligence

LG1 Explain the nature of intelligence

What Is Intelligence?

- Intelligence consists of the ability to solve problems and to adapt and learn from experiences. A key aspect of intelligence focuses on its individual variations. Traditionally, intelligence has been measured by tests designed to compare people's performance on cognitive tasks.

Intelligence Tests

- Sir Francis Galton is considered the father of mental tests. Alfred Binet developed the first intelligence test and created the concept of mental age. William Stern developed the concept of IQ for use with the Binet test. Revisions of the Binet test are called the Stanford-Binet. The test scores on the Stanford-Binet approximate a normal distribution. The Wechsler scales, created by David Wechsler, are the other main intelligence assessment tool. These tests provide an overall IQ and yield several composite scores, allowing the examiner to identify strengths and weaknesses in different areas of intelligence. Test scores should be only one type of information used to evaluate an individual, not the only criterion. IQ scores can produce unfortunate stereotypes and expectations.

Theories of Multiple Intelligences

- Sternberg's triarchic theory states that there are three main types of intelligence: analytical, creative, and practical. Gardner identifies eight types of intelligence: verbal skills, mathematical skills, spatial skills, bodily-kinesthetic skills, musical skills, interpersonal skills, intrapersonal skills, and naturalist skills. Emotional intelligence is the ability to perceive and express emotion accurately and adaptively, to understand emotion and emotional knowledge, to use feelings to facilitate thought, and to manage emotions in oneself and others. The multiple intelligences approaches have broadened the definition of intelligence and motivated educators to develop programs that instruct students in different domains. Critics maintain that the multiple intelligences theories include factors that really aren't part of intelligence, such as musical skills and creativity. Critics also say that not enough research has been done to support the concept of multiple intelligences.

The Neuroscience of Intelligence

- Interest in discovering links between the brain and intelligence have been stimulated by advances in brain imaging. A moderate correlation has been found between brain size and intelligence. Recent research has revealed a link between a distributed neural network in the frontal and parietal lobes and intelligence. The search for a connection between neural processing speed and intelligence has produced mixed results.

Controversies and Group Comparisons   Outline key controversies about differences in IQ scores

The Influence of Heredity and Environment

- Genetic similarity might explain why identical twins show stronger correlations on intelligence tests than fraternal twins do. Some studies indicate that the IQs of adopted children are more similar to the IQs of their biological parents than to those of their adoptive parents. Many studies show that intelligence has a reasonably strong heritability component. Criticisms of the heritability concept have been made. In recent decades there has been a considerable rise in intelligence test scores around the world—called the Flynn effect—and this supports the role of environment in intelligence. Researchers have found that how much parents talk with their children in the first three years of life is correlated with the children's IQs and that being deprived of formal education lowers IQ scores. Ramey's research revealed the positive effects of educational child care on intelligence.

Group Comparisons and Issues

- Cultures vary in the way they define intelligence. Early intelligence tests favored non-Latino White, middle-socioeconomic-status, urban individuals. Tests may be biased against certain groups that are not familiar with a standard form of English, with the content tested, or with the testing situation. Tests are likely to reflect the values and experience of the dominant culture. In the United States, the average score of African American children is below the average score of non-Latino White children on standardized intelligence tests, but as African Americans have gained economic, social, and educational opportunities, the gap between scores has begun to narrow.

The Development of Intelligence   Discuss the development of intelligence across the human life span

Tests of Infant Intelligence

- The Bayley scales are widely used to assess infant intelligence. The Fagan Test of Infant Intelligence, which assesses how effectively infants process information, is increasingly being used.

Stability and Change in Intelligence Through Adolescence

Intelligence in Adulthood

- Although intelligence is more stable across the childhood and adolescent years than are many other attributes, many children's and adolescents' scores on intelligence tests fluctuate considerably.

- Horn argued that crystallized intelligence continues to increase in middle adulthood, whereas fluid intelligence begins to decline. Schaie found that when assessed longitudinally, inductive reasoning is less likely to decline and more likely to improve than when assessed cross-sectionally in middle adulthood. The highest level of four intellectual abilities (vocabulary, verbal memory, inductive reasoning, and spatial orientation) occurs in middle adulthood. Baltes emphasizes a distinction between cognitive mechanics (the "hardware" of the mind, reflecting the neurophysiological architecture of the brain) and cognitive pragmatics (the culture-based "software" of the mind). Cognitive mechanics are more likely to decline in older adults than are cognitive pragmatics. Wisdom is expert knowledge about the practical aspects of life that permits excellent judgment about important matters. Baltes and his colleagues have found that high levels of wisdom are rare, factors other than age are critical for a high level of wisdom to develop, and personality-related factors are better predictors of wisdom than cognitive factors such as intelligence.

The Extremes of Intelligence and Creativity   Describe the characteristics of mental retardation, giftedness, and creativity

Mental Retardation

- Mental retardation is a condition of limited mental ability in which the individual (1) has a low IQ, usually below 70; (2) has difficulty adapting to everyday life; and (3) has an onset of these characteristics by age 18. Most affected individuals have an IQ in the 55 to 70 range (mild retardation). Mental retardation can have an organic cause (called organic retardation) or be social and cultural in origin if there is no evidence of organic brain damage (called cultural-familial retardation).

Giftedness

- People who are gifted have high intelligence (an IQ of 130 or higher) or some type of superior talent. Three characteristics of gifted children are precocity, marching to their own drummer, and a passion to achieve mastery in their domain. Giftedness is likely a consequence of both heredity and environment. A current concern is the education of children who are gifted.

Creativity

- Creativity is the ability to think about something in novel and unusual ways and come up with unique solutions to problems. Although most creative people are intelligent, individuals with high IQs are not necessarily creative. Creative people tend to be divergent thinkers; traditional intelligence tests measure convergent thinking. Creativity has often been described as occurring in a five-step process: preparation, incubation, insight, evaluation, and elaboration. Characteristics of creative thinkers include flexibility and playful thinking, inner motivation, a willingness to take risks, and interest in objective evaluation. Creativity often peaks in the forties and then declines, but the decline may be slight and the peak age varies across domains. Csikszentmihalyi notes that cultivating curiosity and interest is the first step toward a more creative life.

key terms

intelligence 247
mental age (MA) 248
intelligence quotient (IQ) 248
normal distribution 248
triarchic theory of
    intelligence 250

emotional intelligence 251
heritability 254
culture-fair tests 257
Bayley Scales of Infant
    Development 258
crystallized intelligence 260

fluid intelligence 260
cognitive mechanics 261
cognitive pragmatics 261
wisdom 261
mental retardation 263
giftedness 264

creativity 266
divergent thinking 267
convergent thinking 267
brainstorming 268

key people

Robert J. Sternberg 247
Alfred Binet 248
Théophile Simon 248
David Wechsler 248
Howard Gardner 250

Daniel Goleman 251
Peter Salovey and
    John Mayer 251
James Flynn 254
Robert Plomin 256

Craig Ramey 256
Nancy Bayley 258
Robert McCall 259
John Horn 260
K. Warner Schaie 260

Paul Baltes 261
Lewis Terman 264
Ellen Winner 265
Mihaly Csikszentmihalyi 267

preview

In this chapter, we will tell the remarkable story of language and how it develops. The questions we will explore include these: What is language? What is the course of language development across the life span? What does biology contribute to language? How do different experiences influence language?

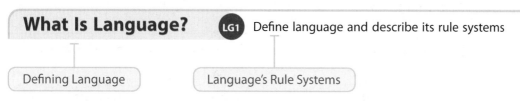

What Is Language?

LG1 Define language and describe its rule systems

Defining Language   Language's Rule Systems

In 1799, a nude boy was observed running through the woods in France. The boy was captured when he was 11 years old. He was called the Wild Boy of Aveyron and was believed to have lived in the woods alone for six years (Lane, 1976). When found, he made no effort to communicate. He never learned to communicate effectively. A modern-day wild child named Genie was discovered in Los Angeles in 1970. Genie had been locked away in almost complete social isolation during her childhood. At age 13, Genie could not speak or stand erect. Sadly, despite intensive intervention, Genie never acquired more than a primitive form of language. Both cases—the Wild Boy of Aveyron and Genie—raise questions about the biological and environmental determinants of language, topics that we will examine later in the chapter. First, though, we need to define language.

> Words not only affect us temporarily; they change us, they socialize us, and they unsocialize us.
>
> —DAVID REISMAN
> *American Social Scientist, 20th Century*

DEFINING LANGUAGE

Language is a form of communication—whether spoken, written, or signed—that is based on a system of symbols. Language consists of the words used by a community and the rules for varying and combining them.

Think how important language is in our everyday lives. We need language to speak with others, listen to others, read, and write. Our language enables us to describe past events in detail and to plan for the future. Language lets us pass down information from one generation to the next and create a rich cultural heritage.

All human languages have some common characteristics. These include infinite generativity and organizational rules. **Infinite generativity** is the ability to produce an endless number of meaningful sentences using a finite set of words and rules. Rules describe the way language works. Let's explore what these rules involve.

Language allows us to communicate with others. *What are some important characteristics of language?*

LANGUAGE'S RULE SYSTEMS

When nineteenth-century American writer Ralph Waldo Emerson said, "The world was built in order and the atoms march in tune," he must have had language in mind. Language is highly ordered and organized (Ambridge & Lieven, 2011; MacWhinney, 2010). The organization involves five systems of rules: phonology, morphology, syntax, semantics, and pragmatics.

Phonology   Every language is made up of basic sounds. **Phonology** is the sound system of the language, including the sounds that are used and how they may be combined (Kuhl & Damasio, 2011; Stoel-Gammon & Sosa, 2010). For example,

language A form of communication, whether spoken, written, or signed, that is based on a system of symbols.

infinite generativity The ability to produce an endless number of meaningful sentences using a finite set of words and rules.

phonology The sound system of a language—includes the sounds used and how they may be combined.

English has the initial consonant cluster *spr* as in *spring,* but no words begin with the cluster *rsp.*

Phonology provides a basis for constructing a large and expandable set of words out of two or three dozen phonemes. A *phoneme* is the basic unit of sound in a language; it is the smallest unit of sound that affects meaning (Stoel-Gammon & Sosa, 2010). For example, in English the sound represented by the letter *p,* as in the words *pot* and *spot,* is a phoneme. The /p/ sound is slightly different in the two words, but this variation is not distinguished in English, and therefore the /p/ sound is a single phoneme. In some languages, such as Hindi, the variations of the /p/ sound represent separate phonemes.

Morphology   **Morphology** refers to the units of meaning involved in word formation. A morpheme is a minimal unit of meaning; it is a word or a part of a word that cannot be broken into smaller meaningful parts. Every word in the English language is made up of one or more morphemes. Some words consist of a single morpheme (for example, *help*), whereas others are made up of more than one morpheme (for example, *helper* has two morphemes, *help* + *er*, with the morpheme -*er* meaning "one who," in this case "one who helps"). Thus, not all morphemes are words by themselves—for example, *pre-*, *tion*, and -*ing* are morphemes.

Just as the rules that govern phonology describe the sound sequences that can occur in a language, the rules of morphology describe the way meaningful units (morphemes) can be combined in words (Tager-Flusberg & Zukowski, 2009). Morphemes have many jobs in grammar, such as marking tense (for example, "she walks" versus "she walked") and number ("she walks" versus "they walk").

Syntax   **Syntax** involves the way words are combined to form acceptable phrases and sentences. If someone says to you, "Bob slugged Tom" or "Bob was slugged by Tom," you know who did the slugging and who was slugged in each case because you have a syntactic understanding of these sentence structures. You also understand that the sentence "You didn't stay, did you?" is a grammatical sentence but that "You didn't stay, didn't you?" is unacceptable and ambiguous.

If you learn another language, English syntax will not get you very far. For example, in English an adjective usually precedes a noun (as in *blue sky*), whereas in Spanish the adjective usually follows the noun (*cielo azul*). Despite the differences in their syntactic structures, however, syntactic systems in all of the world's languages have some common ground (MacWhinney, 2010). For example, no language we know of permits sentences like the following one:

The mouse the cat the farmer chased killed ate the cheese.

It appears that language users cannot process subjects and objects arranged in too complex a fashion in a sentence.

Semantics   **Semantics** refers to the meaning of words and sentences. Every word has a set of semantic features, which are required attributes related to meaning. *Girl* and *women,* for example, share many semantic features, but they differ semantically in regard to age. Words have semantic restrictions on how they can be used in

morphology Units of meaning involved in word formation.

syntax The ways words are combined to form acceptable phrases and sentences.

semantics The meanings of words and sentences.

FRANK & ERNEST: © Thaves/Dist. by United Feature Syndicate, Inc.

Rule System	Description	Examples
Phonology	The sound system of a language. A phoneme is the smallest sound unit in a language.	The word *chat* has three phonemes or sounds: /ch/ /ā/ /t/. An example of phonological rule in the English language is while the phoneme /r/ can follow the phonemes /t/ or /d/ in an English consonant cluster (such as *track* or *drab*), the phoneme /l/ cannot follow these letters.
Morphology	The system of meaningful units involved in word formation.	The smallest sound units that have a meaning are called morphemes, or meaning units. The word *girl* is one morpheme, or meaning unit; it cannot be broken down any further and still have meaning. When the suffix *s* is added, the word becomes *girls* and has two morphemes because the *s* changed the meaning of the word, indicating that there is more than one girl.
Syntax	The system that involves the way words are combined to form acceptable phrases and sentences.	Word order is very important in determining meaning in the English language. For example, the sentence "Sebastian pushed the bike" has a different meaning from "The bike pushed Sebastian."
Semantics	The system that involves the meaning of words and sentences.	Semantics involves knowing the meaning of individual words—that is, vocabulary. For example, semantics includes knowing the meaning of such words as *orange*, *transportation*, and *intelligent*.
Pragmatics	The system of using appropriate conversation and knowledge of how to effectively use language in context.	An example is using polite language in appropriate situations, such as being mannerly when talking with one's teacher. Taking turns in a conversation involves pragmatics.

FIGURE **9.1**
THE RULE SYSTEMS OF LANGUAGE

sentences (Pan & Uccelli, 2009). The sentence *The bicycle talked the boy into buying a candy bar* is syntactically correct but semantically incorrect. The sentence violates our semantic knowledge that bicycles don't talk.

Pragmatics   A final set of language rules involves **pragmatics,** the appropriate use of language in different contexts. Pragmatics covers a lot of territory. When you take turns speaking in a discussion or use a question to convey a command ("Why is it so noisy in here?" "What is this, Grand Central Station?"), you are demonstrating knowledge of pragmatics. You also apply the pragmatics of English when you use polite language in appropriate situations (for example, when talking to one's teacher) or tell stories that are interesting, jokes that are funny, and lies that are convincing. In each of these cases, you are demonstrating that you understand the rules of your culture for adjusting language to suit the context.

Pragmatic rules can be complex and differ from one culture to another (Bryant, 2009). Consider the pragmatics of saying "thank you." Even preschoolers' use of the phrase *thank you* varies with sex, socioeconomic status, and the age of the individual they are addressing. If you were to study the Japanese language, you would come face-to-face with countless pragmatic rules about how to say "thank you" to individuals of various social levels and with various relationships to you.

In this section, we have discussed five important rule systems involved in language. An overview of these rule systems is presented in Figure 9.1.

pragmatics The appropriate use of language in different contexts.

Review *Connect* Reflect

 Define language and describe its rule systems

Review
- What is language?
- What are language's five main rule systems?

Connect
- What have you learned about thinking in childhood that might help explain why Genie and the Wild Boy of Aveyron never learned effective verbal communication skills?

Reflect *Your Own Personal Journey of Life*
- How good are your family members and friends at the pragmatics of language? Describe an example in which one of the individuals showed pragmatic skills and another in which the person did not.

In the thirteenth century, Emperor Frederick II of Germany had a cruel idea. He wanted to know what language children would speak if no one talked to them. He selected several newborns and threatened their caregivers with death if they ever talked to the infants. Frederick never found out what language the children spoke because they all died. As we move forward in the twenty-first century, we are still curious about infants' development of language, although our experiments and observations are, to say the least, far more humane than the evil Frederick's.

INFANCY

Whatever language they learn, infants all over the world follow a similar path in language development. What are some key milestones in this development?

Babbling and Other Vocalizations Long before infants speak recognizable words, they produce a number of vocalizations (Sachs, 2009). The functions of these early vocalizations are to practice making sounds, to communicate, and to attract attention (Lock & Zukow-Goldring, 2010). Babies' sounds go through this sequence during the first year:

- *Crying.* Babies cry even at birth. Crying can signal distress, but—as we discuss in Chapter 10, "Emotional Development"—different types of cries signal different things.
- *Cooing.* Babies first coo at about 2 to 4 months. These gurgling sounds that are made in the back of the throat usually express pleasure during interaction with the caregiver.
- *Babbling.* In the middle of the first year, babies babble—that is, they produce strings of consonant-vowel combinations, such as *ba, ba, ba, ba.*

Gestures Infants start using gestures, such as showing and pointing, at about 8 to 12 months of age. They may wave bye-bye, nod to mean "yes," show an empty cup to ask for more milk, and point to a dog to draw attention to it. Some early gestures are symbolic, as when an infant smacks her lips to indicate food/drink. Pointing is considered by language experts as an important index of the social aspects of language, and it follows this developmental sequence: from pointing without checking on adult gaze to pointing while looking back and forth between an object and the adult (Goldin-Meadow & Iverson, 2010). Lack of pointing is a significant indicator of problems in the infant's communication system (Lock & Zukow-Goldring, 2011). For example, failure to engage in pointing characterizes many autistic children.

A recent study found that parents in high socioeconomic status (SES) families were more likely to use gestures when communicating with their 14-month-old infants (Rowe & Goldin-Meadow, 2009). Further, the infants' use of gestures at 14 months of age in high SES families was linked to a larger vocabulary at 54 months of age.

Recognizing Language Sounds Long before they begin to learn words, infants can make fine distinctions among the sounds of the language (Sachs, 2009). In Patricia Kuhl's (1993, 2000, 2007, 2009, 2011) research, phonemes from languages all over the world are piped through a speaker for infants to hear (see Figure 9.2). A box with a toy bear in it is placed where the infant can

developmental connection

Emotional Development. Three basic cries that infants display are basic cry, anger cry, and pain cry. Chapter 10, p. 305

Long before infants speak recognizable words, they communicate by producing a number of vocalizations and gestures. *At approximately what ages do infants begin to produce different types of vocalizations and gestures?*

see it. A string of identical syllables is played, and then the syllables are changed (for example, *ba ba ba ba*, and then *pa pa pa pa*). If the infant turns its head when the syllables change, the box lights up and the bear dances and drums, rewarding the infant for noticing the change.

Kuhl's research (2007, 2009) has demonstrated that from birth to about 6 months of age, infants are "citizens of the world": They recognize when sounds change most of the time, no matter what language the syllables come from. But over the next six months, infants get even better at perceiving the changes in sounds from their "own" language, the one their parents speak, and they gradually lose the ability to recognize differences that are not important in their own language.

Infants must fish out individual words from the nonstop stream of sound that makes up ordinary speech (Singleton & Ryan, 2009). To do so, they must find the boundaries between words, a task that is very difficult for infants because adults don't pause between words when they speak. Still, infants begin to detect word boundaries by 8 months of age.

First Words   Between about 5 and 12 months of age, infants often indicate their first understanding of words. The infant's first spoken word is a milestone eagerly anticipated by every parent. This event usually occurs between 10 and 15 months of age and at an average of about 13 months. However, long before babies say their first words, they have been communicating with their parents, often by gesturing and using their own special sounds. The appearance of first words is a continuation of this communication process (Berko Gleason, 2009; Hollich, 2011).

A child's first words include those that name important people (*dada*), familiar animals (*kitty*), vehicles (*car*), toys (*ball*), food (*milk*), body parts (*eye*), clothes (*hat*), household items (*clock*), and greeting terms (*bye*). Children often express various intentions with their single words, so that *cookie* might mean "That's a cookie" or "I want a cookie."

The first words of infants can vary across languages. The first words of English-speaking and Romance-language-speaking infants usually are nouns. However, because of the structure of the Korean language, the first words of Korean infants are most often verbs (Choi & Gopnik, 1995).

On average, infants understand about 50 words by 13 months of age, but they can't say that many words until about 18 months (Menyuk, Liebergott, & Schultz, 1995). Thus, in infancy *receptive vocabulary* (words the child understands) considerably exceeds *spoken vocabulary* (words the child uses).

The infant's spoken vocabulary rapidly increases once the first word is spoken (Waxman, 2009). The average 18-month-old can speak about 50 words, but by the age of 2 years can speak about 200 words. This rapid increase in vocabulary that begins at approximately 18 months is called the vocabulary spurt (Bloom, Lifter, & Broughton, 1985).

Like the timing of a child's first word, the timing of the vocabulary spurt varies. Figure 9.3 shows the range for these two language milestones in 14 children (Bloom, 1998). On average, these children said their first word at 13 months and had a

What characterizes the infant's early word learning?

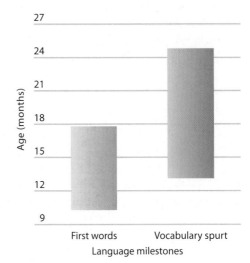

FIGURE **9.3**

VARIATION IN LANGUAGE MILESTONES. *What are some possible explanations for variations in the timing of these milestones?*

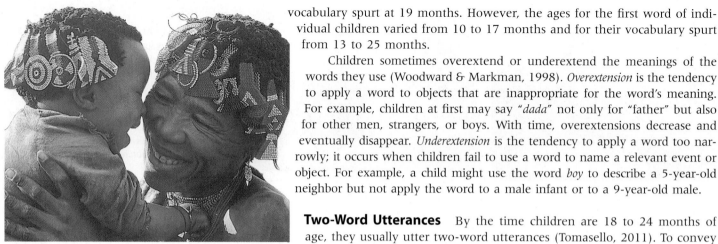

Around the world, most young children learn to speak in two-word utterances, in most cases at about 18 to 24 months of age. *What implications does this have for the biological basis of language?*

Typical Age	Language Milestones
Birth	Crying
2 to 4 months	Cooing begins
5 months	Understands first word
6 months	Babbling begins
7 to 11 months	Change from universal linguist to language-specific listener
8 to 12 months	Uses gestures, such as showing and pointing. Comprehension of words appears
13 months	First word spoken
18 months	Vocabulary spurt starts
18 to 24 months	Uses two-word utterances. Rapid expansion of understanding of words

FIGURE **9.4**

SOME LANGUAGE MILESTONES IN INFANCY. Despite great variations in the language input received by infants, around the world they follow a similar path in learning to speak.

telegraphic speech The use of short, precise words without grammatical markers such as articles, auxiliary verbs, and other connectives.

vocabulary spurt at 19 months. However, the ages for the first word of individual children varied from 10 to 17 months and for their vocabulary spurt from 13 to 25 months.

Children sometimes overextend or underextend the meanings of the words they use (Woodward & Markman, 1998). *Overextension* is the tendency to apply a word to objects that are inappropriate for the word's meaning. For example, children at first may say "*dada*" not only for "father" but also for other men, strangers, or boys. With time, overextensions decrease and eventually disappear. *Underextension* is the tendency to apply a word too narrowly; it occurs when children fail to use a word to name a relevant event or object. For example, a child might use the word *boy* to describe a 5-year-old neighbor but not apply the word to a male infant or to a 9-year-old male.

Two-Word Utterances By the time children are 18 to 24 months of age, they usually utter two-word utterances (Tomasello, 2011). To convey meaning with just two words, the child relies heavily on gesture, tone, and context. The wealth of meaning children can communicate with a two-word utterance includes the following (Slobin, 1972):

- Identification: "See doggie."
- Location: "Book there."
- Repetition: "More milk."
- Nonexistence: "All gone."
- Possession: "My candy."
- Attribution: "Big car."
- Agent-action: "Mama walk."
- Question: "Where ball?"

These examples are from children whose first language is English, German, Russian, Finnish, Turkish, or Samoan.

Notice that the two-word utterances omit many parts of speech and are remarkably succinct. In fact, in every language, a child's first combinations of words have this economical quality; they are telegraphic. **Telegraphic speech** is the use of short and precise words without grammatical markers such as articles, auxiliary verbs, and other connectives. Telegraphic speech is not limited to two words. "Mommy give ice cream" and "Mommy give Tommy ice cream" also are examples of telegraphic speech.

We have discussed a number of language milestones in infancy. Figure 9.4 summarizes the time at which infants typically reach these milestones.

EARLY CHILDHOOD

Toddlers move rather quickly from producing two-word utterances to creating three-, four-, and five-word combinations. Between 2 and 3 years of age, they begin the transition from saying simple sentences that express a single proposition to saying complex sentences.

As young children learn the special features of their own language, there are extensive regularities in how they acquire that specific language (Berko Gleason, 2009). For example, all children learn the prepositions *on* and *in* before other prepositions.

However, some children develop language problems, including speech and hearing problems. To read about an individual who works with children who have speech/language problems, see the *Connecting with Careers* profile.

Understanding Phonology and Morphology During the preschool years, most children gradually become more sensitive to the sounds of spoken words and become increasingly capable of producing all the sounds of their language. By the time children are 3 years of age, they can produce all the vowel sounds and most of the consonant sounds (Stoel-Gammon & Sosa, 2010).

Sharla Peltier, Speech Therapist

A speech therapist is a health professional who works with individuals who have a communication disorder. Sharla Peltier, a speech therapist in Manitoulin, Ontario, Canada, works with Native American children in the First Nations schools. She conducts screenings for speech/language and hearing problems and assesses infants as young as 6 months of age as well as school-aged children. She works closely with community health nurses to identify hearing problems.

Diagnosing problems is only about half of what Peltier does in her work. She especially enjoys treating speech/language and hearing problems. She conducts parent training sessions to help parents understand and help with their children's language problem. As part of this training, she guides parents in communicating more effectively with their children.

Speech therapist Sharla Peltier, helping a young child improve her language and communication skills.

For more information about what speech therapists do, see page 45 in the Careers in Life-Span Development appendix.

By the time children move beyond two-word utterances, they demonstrate a knowledge of morphology rules (Berko Gleason, 2009). Children begin using the plural and possessive forms of nouns (such as *dogs* and *dog's*). They put appropriate endings on verbs (such as *-s* when the subject is third-person singular and *-ed* for the past tense). They use prepositions (such as *in* and *on*), articles (such as *a* and *the*), and various forms of the verb *to be* (such as "I was going to the store"). Some of the best evidence for changes in children's use of morphological rules occurs in their overgeneralization of the rules, as when a preschool child say "foots" instead of "feet," or "goed" instead of "went."

In a classic experiment that was designed to study children's knowledge of morphological rules, such as how to make a plural, Jean Berko (1958) presented preschool children and first-grade children with cards such as the one shown in Figure 9.5. Children were asked to look at the card while the experimenter read aloud the words on the card. Then the children were asked to supply the missing word. This might sound easy, but Berko was interested in the children's ability to apply the appropriate morphological rule—in this case to say "wugs" with the *z* sound that indicates the plural.

Although the children's answers were not perfect, they were much better than they could have attained by chance. What makes Berko's study impressive is that most of the words were made up for the experiment. Thus, the children could not base their responses on remembering past instances of hearing the words. That they could make the plurals or past tenses of words they had never heard before was proof that they knew the morphological rules.

Changes in Syntax and Semantics   Preschool children also learn and apply rules of syntax (Tager-Flusberg & Zukowski, 2009). They show a growing mastery of complex rules for how words should be ordered.

Consider *wh-* questions, such as "Where is Daddy going?" or "What is that boy doing?" To ask these questions properly, the child must know two important differences

FIGURE **9.5**

STIMULI IN BERKO'S CLASSIC STUDY OF CHILDREN'S UNDERSTANDING OF MORPHOLOGICAL RULES. In Jean Berko's study, young children were presented cards such as this one with a "wug" on it. Then the children were asked to supply the missing word and say it correctly.

between *wh-* questions and affirmative statements (for instance, "Mommy is going to work" and "That boy is waiting on the school bus"). First, a *wh-* word must be added at the beginning of the sentence. Second, the auxiliary verb must be inverted—that is, exchanged with the subject of the sentence. Young children learn quite early where to put the *wh-* word, but they take much longer to learn the auxiliary-inversion rule. Thus, preschool children might ask, "Where Daddy is going?" and "What that girl is doing?"

Gains in semantics also characterize early childhood. Vocabulary development is dramatic (Pan & Uccelli, 2009). Some experts have concluded that between 18 months and 6 years of age, young children learn words at the rate of about one new word every waking hour (Gelman & Kalish, 2006)! By the time they enter first grade, it is estimated that children know about 14,000 words (Clark, 1993). However, there are individual variations in children's vocabulary, and children who enter elementary school with a small vocabulary are at risk for developing reading problems (Berninger, 2006).

Why can children learn so many new words so quickly? One possibility is **fast mapping,** which involves children's ability to make an initial connection between a word and its referent after only limited exposure to the word (Woodward, Markman, & Fitzsimmons, 1994). Researchers have found that exposure to words on multiple occasions over several days results in more successful word learning than the same number of exposures in a single day (Childers & Tomasello, 2002).

How might a family's socioeconomic status influence parent-child communication and vocabulary growth in children? To read about this link, see the *Connecting with Research* interlude.

Advances in Pragmatics

Changes in pragmatics also characterize young children's language development (Siegal & Surian, 2010). A 6-year-old is simply a much better conversationalist than a 2-year-old is. What are some of the improvements in pragmatics during the preschool years?

Young children begin to engage in extended discourse (Aktar & Herold, 2008). For example, they learn culturally specific rules of conversation and politeness and become sensitive to the need to adapt their speech in different settings. Their developing linguistic skills and increasing ability to take the perspective of others contribute to their generation of more competent narratives.

As children get older, they become increasingly able to talk about things that are not here (grandma's house, for example) and not now (what happened to them yesterday or might happen tomorrow, for example). A preschool child can tell you what she wants for lunch tomorrow, something that would not have been possible at the two-word stage of language development.

Around 4 to 5 years of age, children learn to change their speech style to suit the situation. For example, even 4-year-old children speak to a 2-year-old differently from the way they speak to a same-aged peer; they use shorter sentences with the 2-year-old. They also speak to an adult differently from the way they speak to a same-aged peer, using more polite and formal language with the adult (Shatz & Gelman, 1973).

Early Literacy

Concern about the ability of U.S. children to read and write has led to a careful examination of preschool and kindergarten children's experiences, with the hope that a positive orientation toward reading and writing can be developed early in life (Jalongo, 2011; Otto, 2010). What should a literacy program for preschool children be like? Instruction should be built on what children already know about oral language, reading, and writing. Further, early precursors of literacy and academic success include language skills, phonological and syntactic knowledge, letter identification, and conceptual knowledge about print and its conventions and

developmental connection

Attention. The ability of children to control and sustain their attention is related to school readiness. Chapter 7, p. 216

Children pick up words as pigeons peas.

—**JOHN RAY**

English Naturalist, 17th Century

What characterizes advances in pragmatics during early childhood?

fast mapping A process that helps to explain how young children learn the connection between a word and its referent so quickly.

connecting with research

What Characteristics of a Family Affect a Child's Language Development?

Socioeconomic status has been linked with how much parents talk to their children and with young children's vocabulary. Betty Hart and Todd Risley (1995) observed the language environments of children whose parents were professionals and children whose parents were on welfare. Compared with the professional parents, the parents on welfare talked much less to their young children, talked less about past events, and provided less elaboration. As indicated in Figure 9.6, the children of the professional parents had a much larger vocabulary at 36 months of age than the children whose parents were on welfare.

Other research has linked how much mothers speak to their infants and the infants' vocabularies. For example, in one study by Janellen Huttenlocher and her colleagues (1991), infants whose mothers spoke more often to them had markedly higher vocabularies. By the second birthday, vocabulary differences were substantial.

However, a study of 1- to 3-year-old children living in low-income families found that the sheer amount of maternal talk was not the best predictor of a child's vocabulary growth (Pan & others, 2005). Rather, it was maternal language and literacy skills that were positively related to the children's vocabulary development. For example, when mothers used a more diverse vocabulary when talking with their children, their children's vocabulary benefited, but their children's vocabulary was not related to the total amount of time mothers spent talking to their children.

Children in low-income families are more likely to have less-educated parents, have inadequate nutrition, live in low-income communities, and attend substandard schools than children in middle- and high-income families (Snow, Burns, & Griffin, 1998). However, living in a

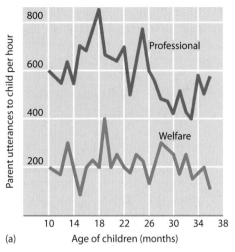
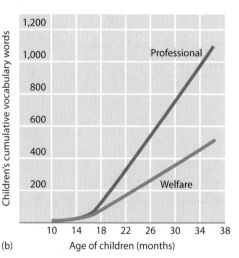

(a) Age of children (months) (b) Age of children (months)

FIGURE **9.6**

LANGUAGE INPUT IN PROFESSIONAL AND WELFARE FAMILIES AND YOUNG CHILDREN'S VOCABULARY DEVELOPMENT. (*a*) In this study (Hart & Risley, 1995), parents from professional families talked with their young children more than parents from welfare families. (*b*) All of the children learned to talk, but children from professional families developed vocabularies that were twice as large as those from welfare families. Thus, by the time children go to preschool, they already have experienced considerable differences in language input in their families and developed different levels of vocabulary that are linked to their socioeconomic context. *Does this study indicate that poverty caused deficiencies in vocabulary development?*

low-income family should not be used as the sole identifier in predicting whether children will have difficulties in language development, such as a low vocabulary and reading problems. If children growing up in low-income families experience effective instruction and support, they can develop effective language skills (Barbarin & Aikens, 2009).

These research studies and others (NICHD Early Child Care Research Network, 2005) demonstrate the important effect that early speech input and poverty can have on the development of a child's language skills.

---

functions (Beatty & Pratt, 2011). Parents and teachers need to provide a supportive environment to help children develop literacy skills (Wagner, 2010). A recent study found that literacy experiences (such as how often the child was read to), the quality of the mother's engagement with her child (such as attempts to cognitively stimulate the child), and provision of learning materials (such as age-appropriate learning materials and books) were important home literacy experiences in low-income families that were linked to the children's language development in positive ways (Rodriguez & others, 2009).

So far, our discussion of early literacy has focused on U.S. children. For example, the extent to which phonological awareness is linked to learning to read effectively varies across language to some extent (McBride-Chang, 2004). For example, one study of second-grade students from Beijing, Hong Kong, Korea, and the United States revealed that phonological awareness may be more important for early reading development in English and Korean than for Chinese (McBride-Chang & others, 2005). Further, rates of dyslexia (severe reading disability) differ across countries and are linked with the spelling and phonetic rules that characterize the language (McBride-Chang & others, 2008). English is one of the more difficult languages because of its irregular spellings and pronunciations. In countries where English is spoken, the rate of dyslexia is higher than in countries where the alphabet script is more phonetically pronounced.

What are some strategies for using books effectively with preschool children? Ellen Galinsky (2010) recently emphasized these strategies:

- *Use books to initiate conversation with young children.* Ask them to put themselves in the places of the characters in the book and to imagine what they might be thinking or feeling.
- *Use what and why questions.* Ask young children to think about what is going to happen next in a story and then to see if it occurs.
- *Encourage children to ask questions about stories.*
- *Choose some books that play with language.* Creative books on the alphabet, including those with rhymes, often interest young children.

MIDDLE AND LATE CHILDHOOD

Upon entering school, children gain new skills that include increasing use of language to talk about things that are not physically present, knowledge of what a word is, and an ability to recognize and talk about sounds (Berko Gleason, 2003). They learn the *alphabetic principle*—the letters of the alphabet represent sounds of the language. As children develop during middle and late childhood, changes in their vocabulary and grammar continue to take place.

Vocabulary, Grammar, and Metalinguistic Awareness During middle and late childhood, children begin to organize their mental vocabulary in new ways. When asked to say the first word that comes to mind when they hear a word, young children typically provide a word that often follows the word in a sentence. For example, when asked to respond to "dog," the young child may say "barks." In response to the word "eat," they may say "lunch." At about 7 years of age, children begin to respond with a word that is the same part of speech as the stimulus word. For example, a child may now respond to the word "dog" with "cat" or "horse." To "eat," they now might say "drink." This type of reply is evidence that children have begun to categorize their vocabulary by parts of speech (Berko Gleason, 2003).

The process of categorizing becomes easier as children increase their vocabulary. Children's vocabulary increases from an average of about 14,000 words at 6 years of age to an average of about 40,000 words by 11 years of age.

Children make similar advances in grammar (Lidz, 2010). During the elementary school years, children's improvement in logical reasoning and analytical skills helps them understand such constructions as the appropriate use of comparatives (*shorter, deeper*) and subjunctives ("If you were president . . ."). During the elementary school years, children become increasingly able to understand and use complex grammar, such as the following sentence: *The boy who kissed his mother wore a hat.* They also learn to use language in a more connected way, producing connected discourse.

These advances in vocabulary and grammar during the elementary school years are accompanied by the development of **metalinguistic awareness,** which is knowledge about language, such as knowing what a preposition is or being able to discuss the sounds of a language. Metalinguistic awareness allows children

developmental **connection**

Conditions, Diseases, and Disorders. Dyslexia is a severe impairment in the ability to read and spell. Chapter 16, p. 534

metalinguistic awareness Knowledge about language.

"to think about their language, understand what words are, and even define them" (Berko Gleason, 2009, p. 4). It improves considerably during the elementary school years (Pan & Uccelli, 2009). Defining words becomes a regular part of classroom discourse, and children increase their knowledge of syntax as they study and talk about the components of sentences such as subjects and verbs (Melzi & Ely, 2009).

Children also make progress in understanding how to use language in culturally appropriate ways—pragmatics (Ariza & Lapp, 2011; Siegel & Surian, 2010). By the time they enter adolescence, most children know the rules for the use of language in everyday contexts—that is, what is appropriate to say and what is inappropriate to say.

Reading   Before learning to read, children learn to use language to talk about things that are not present; they learn what a word is; and they learn how to recognize sounds and talk about them (Berko Gleason, 2003). If they develop a large vocabulary, their path to reading is eased. Children who begin elementary school with a small vocabulary are at risk when it comes to learning to read (Berko Gleason, 2003). Vocabulary development plays an important role in reading comprehension (Cunningham & Allington, 2011).

How should children be taught to read? Currently, debate focuses on the whole-language approach versus the phonics approach (Christie, Enz, & Vukelich, 2011; Otto, 2010; Tompkins, 2011).

The **whole-language approach** stresses that reading instruction should parallel children's natural language learning. In some whole-language classes, beginning readers are taught to recognize whole words or even entire sentences, and to use the context of what they are reading to guess at the meaning of words. Reading materials that support the whole-language approach are whole and meaningful—that is, children are given material in its complete form, such as stories and poems, so that they learn to understand language's communicative function. Reading is connected with listening and writing skills. Although there are variations in whole-language programs, most share the premise that reading should be integrated with other skills and subjects, such as science and social studies, and that it should focus on real-world material. Thus, a class might read newspapers, magazines, or books, and then write about and discuss what they have read.

In contrast, the **phonics approach** emphasizes that reading instruction should teach basic rules for translating written symbols into sounds. Early phonics-centered reading instruction should involve simplified materials. Only after children have learned correspondence rules that relate spoken phonemes to the alphabet letters that are used to represent them should they be given complex reading materials such as books and poems (Fox, 2010, 2012). A recent study revealed that a computer-based phonics program improved first-grade students' reading skills (Savage & others, 2009).

Which approach is better? Research suggests that children can benefit from both approaches, but instruction in phonics needs to be emphasized (Fox & Alexander, 2011). An increasing number of experts in the field of reading now conclude that direct instruction in phonics is a key aspect of learning to read (Cunningham & Allington, 2011).

Beyond the phonics/whole-language issue in learning to read, becoming a good reader includes learning to read fluently (Reutzel & Cooter, 2012; Snowling & Gobel, 2011). Many beginning or poor readers do not recognize words automatically. Their processing capacity is consumed by the demands of word recognition, so they have less capacity to devote to comprehension of groupings of words as phrases or sentences. As their processing of words and passages becomes more automatic, it is said that their reading becomes more *fluent* (Fox & Alexander, 2011). Metacognitive strategies, such as learning to monitor one's reading progress, getting the gist of what is being read, and summarizing, also are fundamental to becoming a good reader (Nash-Ditzel, 2010).

This teacher is helping a student sound out words. Researchers have found that phonics instruction is a key aspect of teaching students to read, especially beginning readers and students with weak reading skills.

developmental connection

Information Processing. Metacognition is cognition about cognition, or knowing about knowing. Chapter 7, p. 238

whole-language approach A teaching approach built on the idea that reading instruction should parallel children's natural language learning. Reading materials should be whole and meaningful.

phonics approach A teaching approach built on the idea that reading instruction should teach basic rules for translating written symbols into sounds.

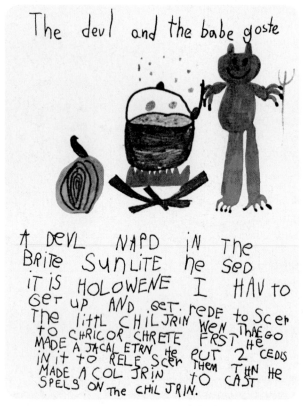

The devl and the babe goste

A DEVL NAPD IN THE
BRITE SUNLITE he SED
IT IS HOLOWENE I HAV to
GET UP AND GET. reDE to SCer
The littL CHILJRIN WEN ThAEGO
to CHRICOR CHRETE FRST He
MADE A JACAL ETRN He PUT 2 CEDLS
in it to RELE SCer THEM ThN He
MADE A COL JRIN to CAST
SPELS ON The CHIL JRIN.

Anna Mudd is the 6-year-old author of "The Devl and the Babe Goste." Anna has been writing stories for at least two years. Her story includes poetic images, sophisticated syntax, and vocabulary that reflect advances in language development. "The Devl and the Babe Goste," from Jean Berko Gleason, *The Development of Language*, 3rd ed. Figure 10.11, p. 336, 1993. Boston: Allyn & Bacon. Reproduced by permission of Pearson Education, Inc.

Writing Children's writing emerges out of their early scribbles, which appear at around 2 to 3 years of age. In early childhood, children's motor skills usually develop to the point that they can begin printing letters. Most 4-year-olds can print their first names. Five-year-olds can reproduce letters and copy several short words. They gradually learn to distinguish the distinctive characteristics of letters, such as whether the lines are curved or straight, open or closed. Through the early elementary grades, many children continue to reverse letters such as *b* and *d* and *p* and *q* (Temple & others, 1993). At this age, if other aspects of the child's development are normal, letter reversals do not predict literacy problems.

As they begin to write, children often invent spellings. Usually they base these spellings on the sounds of words they hear (Spandel, 2009).

Parents and teachers should encourage children's early writing but not be overly concerned about the formation of letters or spelling. Printing errors are a natural part of the child's growth. Corrections of spelling and printing should be selective and made in positive ways that do not discourage the child's writing and spontaneity.

Like becoming a good reader, becoming a good writer takes many years and lots of practice. Children should be given many writing opportunities (Christie, Enz, & Vukelich, 2011; Cunningham & Allington, 2011). As their language and cognitive skills improve with good instruction, so will their writing skills. For example, developing a more sophisticated understanding of syntax and grammar serves as an underpinning for better writing. So do such cognitive skills as organization and logical reasoning. Through the course of the school years, students develop increasingly sophisticated methods of organizing their ideas. In early elementary school, they narrate and describe or write short poems. In late elementary and middle school, they can combine narration with reflection and analysis in projects such as book reports.

There are increasing concerns about students' writing competence (De La Paz & McCutchen, 2011). One study revealed that 70 to 75 percent of U.S. students in grades 4 through 12 are low-achieving writers (Persky, Dane, & Jin, 2003). Two recent studies—one of elementary school teachers, the other of high school teachers—raise concerns about the quality of writing instruction in U.S. schools (Gilbert & Graham, 2010; Kiuhara, Graham, & Hawken, 2009). The teachers in both studies reported that their college courses had inadequately prepared them to teach writing. The fourth- through sixth-grade teachers reported that they taught writing only 15 minutes a day. The high school teachers said that their writing assignments infrequently involved analysis and interpretation, and almost 50 percent of them had not assigned any multiparagraph writing assignments in the span of one month's time.

As with reading, teachers play a critical role in students' development of writing skills (Cunningham & Allington, 2011; Tompkins, 2011). Effective writing instruction provides guidance about planning, drafting, and revising, not only in elementary school but through college (Mayer, 2008). A meta-analysis (use of statistical techniques to combine the results of studies) revealed that the following interventions were the most effective in improving fourth- through twelfth-grade students'

It may have been dark...

It may have been stormy...

One thing, however, was for sure.. It was night.

SOMEHOW, I FEEL THAT COULD BE SHORTENED...

PEANUTS © 1988 Peanuts Worldwide LLC. Dist. by Universal Uclick. Reprinted with permission. All rights reserved.

writing quality: (1) strategy instruction, (2) summarization, (3) peer assistance, and (4) setting goals (Graham & Perin, 2007).

Bilingualism and Second-Language Learning   Are there sensitive periods in learning a second language? That is, if individuals want to learn a second language, how important is the age at which they begin to learn it? For many years, it was claimed that if individuals did not learn a second language prior to puberty they would never reach native-language speakers' proficiency in the second language (Johnson & Newport, 1991). However, recent research indicates a more complex conclusion: Sensitive periods likely vary across different language systems (Thomas & Johnson, 2008). Thus, for late language learners, such as adolescents and adults, new vocabulary is easier to learn than new sounds or new grammar (Neville, 2006). For example, children's ability to pronounce words with a native-like accent in a second language typically decreases with age, with an especially sharp drop occurring after the age of about 10 to 12. Also, adults tend to learn a second language faster than children, but their final level of second-language attainment is not as high as children's. And the way children and adults learn a second language differs somewhat. Compared with adults, children are less sensitive to feedback, less likely to use explicit strategies, and more likely to learn a second language from large amounts of input (Thomas & Johnson, 2008).

Students in the United States are far behind their counterparts in many developed countries in learning a second language. For example, in Russia, schools have 10 grades, called *forms*, which roughly correspond to the 12 grades in American schools. Russian children begin school at age 7 and begin learning English in the third form. Because of this emphasis on teaching English, most Russian citizens under the age of 40 today are able to speak at least some English. The United States is the only technologically advanced Western nation that does not have a national foreign-language requirement at the high school level, even for students in rigorous academic programs.

Some aspects of children's ability to learn a second language are transferred more easily to the second language than others (Pena & Bedore, 2009). Children who are fluent in two languages perform better than their single-language counterparts on tests of control of attention, concept formation, analytical reasoning, cognitive flexibility, and cognitive complexity (Bialystok, 2001, 2007, 2011; Bialystok & Craik, 2010). They also are more conscious of the structure of spoken and written language and better at noticing errors of grammar and meaning, skills that benefit their reading ability (Bialystok, 1997). However, recent research indicates that bilingual children have a smaller vocabulary in each language than monolingual children (Bialystok, 2011).

In the United States, many immigrant children go from being monolingual in their home language to bilingual in that language and in English, only to end up monolingual speakers of English. This is called *subtractive bilingualism*, and it can have negative effects on children, who often become ashamed of their home language.

A current controversy related to bilingualism involves the millions of U.S. children who come from homes in which English is not the primary language (Diaz-Rico, 2012; Oller & Jarmulowicz, 2010). What is the best way to teach these children?

For the last two decades, the preferred strategy has been *bilingual education*, which teaches academic subjects to immigrant children in their native language while slowly teaching English (Haley, 2010; Reiss, 2012). Advocates of bilingual education programs argue that if children who do not know English are taught only in English, they will fall behind in academic subjects. How, they ask, can

A first- and second-grade bilingual English-Cantonese teacher instructing students in Chinese in Oakland, California. *What have researchers found about the effectiveness of bilingual education?*

Salvador Tamayo, Bilingual Education Teacher

Salvador Tamayo teaches bilingual education in the fifth grade at Turner Elementary School in West Chicago. He recently was given a National Educator Award by the Milken Family Foundation for his work in bilingual education. Tamayo especially is adept at integrating technology into his bilingual education classes. He and his students have created several award-winning Web sites about the West Chicago City Museum, the local Latino community, and the history of West Chicago. His students also developed an "I Want to Be an American Citizen" Web site to assist family and community members in preparing for the U.S. Citizenship Test. Tamayo also teaches a bilingual education class at Wheaton College.

Salvador Tamayo, instructing students in his bilingual education class.

7-year-olds learn arithmetic or history taught only in English when they do not speak the language?

Some critics of bilingual programs argue that too often it is thought that immigrant children need only one year of bilingual education. However, in general it takes immigrant children approximately three to five years to develop speaking proficiency and seven years to develop reading proficiency in English (Hakuta, Butler, & Witt, 2001). Also, immigrant children vary in their ability to learn English (Echevarria & Vogt, 2011; Herrera & Murry, 2011). Children who come from lower socioeconomic backgrounds have more difficulty than those from higher socioeconomic backgrounds (Hakuta, 2001). Thus, especially for immigrant children from low socioeconomic backgrounds, more years of bilingual education may be needed than they currently are receiving.

Critics who oppose bilingual education argue that as a result of these programs, the children of immigrants are not learning English, which puts them at a permanent disadvantage in U.S. society. What have researchers found regarding outcomes of bilingual education programs? Drawing conclusions about the effectiveness of bilingual education programs is difficult because of variations across programs in the number of years they are in effect, type of instruction, qualities of schooling other than bilingual education, teachers, children, and other factors. Further, no effectively conducted experiments that compare bilingual education with English-only education in the United States have been conducted (Snow & Kang, 2006). Some experts have concluded that the quality of instruction is more important in determining outcomes than the language in which it is delivered (Lesaux & Siegel, 2003).

Nonetheless, research supports bilingual education because (1) children have difficulty learning a subject when it is taught in a language they do not understand; and (2) when both languages are integrated in the classroom, children learn the second language more readily and participate more actively (Hakuta, 2001, 2005).

To read about the work of one bilingual education teacher, see the *Connecting with Careers* profile.

ADOLESCENCE

Language development during adolescence includes greater sophistication in the use of words. With an increase in abstract thinking, adolescents are much better than children at analyzing the role a word plays in a sentence.

developmental **connection**

Cognitive Theory. According to Piaget, at 11 to 15 years of age a new stage—formal operational thought—emerges that is characterized by thought that is more abstract, idealistic, and logical. Chapter 6, p. 194

Adolescents also develop more subtle abilities with words. They make strides in understanding **metaphor,** which is an implied comparison between unlike things. For example, individuals "draw a line in the sand" to indicate a nonnegotiable position; a political campaign is said to be a marathon, not a sprint; a person's faith is shattered. And adolescents become better able to understand and to use **satire,** which is the use of irony, derision, or wit to expose folly or wickedness. Caricatures are an example of satire. More advanced logical thinking also allows adolescents, from about 15 to 20 years of age, to understand complex literary works.

Most adolescents are also much better writers than children are. They are better at organizing ideas before they write, at distinguishing between general and specific points as they write, at stringing together sentences that make sense, and at organizing their writing into an introduction, body, and concluding remarks.

What are some changes in language development in adolescence?

Everyday speech changes during adolescence "and part of being a successful teenager is being able to talk like one" (Berko Gleason, 2005, p. 9). Young adolescents often speak a **dialect** with their peers that is characterized by jargon and slang (Cave, 2002). A dialect is a variety of language that is distinguished by its vocabulary, grammar, or pronunciation. For example, when meeting a friend, instead of saying hello, a young adolescent might say, "Give me five." Nicknames that are satirical and derisive ("Stilt," "Refrigerator," "Spaz") also characterize the dialect of young adolescents. Such labels might be used to show that one belongs to the group and to reduce the seriousness of a situation (Cave, 2002).

ADULTHOOD AND AGING

Most research on language development has focused on infancy and childhood. It is generally thought that for most of adulthood individuals maintain their language skills.

In the adolescent and adult years, the development of an identity, a sense of who one is, is an important life task. A distinct personal linguistic style is part of one's special identity (Berko Gleason, 2009). Further psychological goals of early adulthood that call for expanded linguistic skills include entering the world of work and establishing intimate relations with others.

Language development during the adult years varies greatly among individuals, depending on such things as level of education and social and occupational roles. Actors, for instance, must learn not only to be heard by large audiences but also to speak the words of others using varying voices and regional dialects. Working people learn the special tones of voice and terminology associated with their own occupational register or code (Berko Gleason, 2005, p. 9).

The vocabulary of individuals often continues to increase throughout most of the adult years, at least until late adulthood (Berko Gleason, 2009). Many older adults "maintain or improve their knowledge of words and word meanings" (Burke & Shafto, 2004, p. 24).

In late adulthood, however, some decrements in language may appear. Among the most common language-related complaints reported by older adults is difficulty in retrieving words to use in conversation and in understanding spoken language in certain contexts (Clark-Cotton & others, 2007). These often involve the *tip-of-the-tongue phenomenon*, in which individuals are confident that they can remember something but just can't quite seem to retrieve it from memory, as described in Chapter 7, "Information Processing" (Thornton & Light, 2006). Older adults also report that in less than ideal listening conditions they can have difficulty in understanding speech. This difficulty is most likely to occur when speech is rapid, when competing stimuli are present (a noisy room, for example), and

What are some differences in the ways older and younger adults communicate?

metaphor An implied comparison between two unlike things.

satire The use of irony, derision, or wit to expose folly or wickedness.

dialect A variety of language that is distinguished by its vocabulary, grammar, or pronunciation.

when they can't see their conversation partner (in a telephone conversation, for example). The difficulty in understanding speech may be due to hearing loss (Gordon-Salant & others, 2006). In general, though, most language skills decline little among older adults who are healthy (Clark-Cotton & others, 2007; Thornton & Light, 2006).

Some aspects of the phonological skills of older adults differ from those of younger adults (Clark-Cotton & others, 2007). Older adults' speech is typically lower in volume, slower, less precisely articulated, and less fluent (more pauses, fillers, repetition, and corrections). Despite these age differences, the speech skills of most older adults are adequate for everyday communication.

Nonlanguage factors may be responsible for some of the decline in language skills that occur in older adults (Obler, 2009). Slower information-processing speed and a decline in working memory, especially in being able to keep information in mind while processing, likely contribute to lowered language efficiency in older adults (Stine-Morrow, Miller, & Hertzog, 2006).

Language does change among individuals with Alzheimer disease (Obler, 2009). (Recall our discussion of Alzheimer disease in Chapter 4, "Health.") Word-finding difficulties are one of the earliest symptoms of Alzheimer disease, but most individuals with Alzheimer disease retain much of their ability to produce well-formed sentences until the late stages of the disease. Nonetheless, they do make more grammatical errors than older adults without Alzheimer disease.

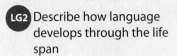

developmental **connection**

Conditions, Diseases, and Disorders. Alzheimer disease is a progressive brain disorder characterized by a gradual deterioration of memory, reasoning, language, and eventually physical function. Chapter 4, p. 126

Review *Connect* Reflect

LG2 Describe how language develops through the life span

Review

- What are some key milestones of language development during infancy?
- How do language skills change during early childhood?
- How does language develop in middle and late childhood?
- How does language develop in adolescence?
- How do language skills change during adulthood and aging?

Connect

- What are some aspects of metacognition (discussed in Chapter 7, "Information

Processing") that might apply to the concept of metalinguistic awareness?

Reflect *Your Own Personal Journey of Life*

- How many languages can you speak and read? If and when you have children, do you want them to learn more than one language while they are young? Explain.

Biological and Environmental Influences

 LG3 Discuss the biological and environmental contributions to language skills

| Biological Influences | Environmental Influences | An Interactionist View of Language |

Broca's area An area of the brain's left frontal lobe that is involved in producing words.

Wernicke's area An area of the brain's left hemisphere that is involved in language comprehension.

We have described how language develops, but we have not explained what makes this amazing development possible. Everyone who uses language in some way "knows" its rules and has the ability to create an infinite number of words and sentences. Where does this knowledge come from? Is it the product of biology? Or is language learned and influenced by experiences?

In the wild, chimps communicate through calls, gestures, and expressions, which evolutionary psychologists believe might be the roots of true language.

← developmental **connection**

Brain Development. Much of our language processing takes place in the brain's left hemisphere. Chapter 3, p. 99

BIOLOGICAL INFLUENCES

Some language scholars view the remarkable similarities in how children acquire language all over the world, despite the vast variation in language input they receive, as strong evidence that language has a biological basis. What role did evolution play in the biological foundations of language?

Evolution and the Brain's Role in Language The ability to speak and understand language requires a certain vocal apparatus as well as a nervous system with certain capabilities. The nervous system and vocal apparatus of humanity's predecessors changed over hundreds of thousands or millions of years. With advances in the nervous system and vocal structures, *Homo sapiens* went beyond the grunting and shrieking of other animals to develop speech. Although estimates vary, many experts hold that humans acquired language about 100,000 years ago, which in evolutionary time represents a very recent acquisition. It gave humans an enormous edge over other animals and increased the chances of human survival (Pinker, 1994).

As further support of the biological foundations of language, there is evidence that specific regions of the brain are predisposed to be used for language (Friederici, Mueller, & Oberecker, 2011). Two regions involved in language were first discovered in studies of brain-damaged individuals: **Broca's area,** a region of the left frontal lobe of the brain that is involved in producing words, and **Wernicke's area,** a region of the brain's left hemisphere that is involved in language comprehension (see Figure 9.7). Damage to either of these areas produces types of **aphasia,** which is a loss or impairment of language processing. Individuals with damage to Broca's area have difficulty producing words correctly; individuals with damage to Wernicke's area have poor comprehension and often produce fluent but incomprehensible speech.

Chomsky's Language Acquisition Device (LAD) Linguist Noam Chomsky (1957) proposed that humans are biologically prewired to learn language at a certain time and in a certain way. He said that children are born into the world with a **language acquisition device (LAD),** a biological endowment that enables the child to detect certain features and rules of language, including phonology, syntax, and semantics. Children are endowed by nature with the ability to detect the sounds of language, for example, and to follow rules such as how to form plurals and ask questions.

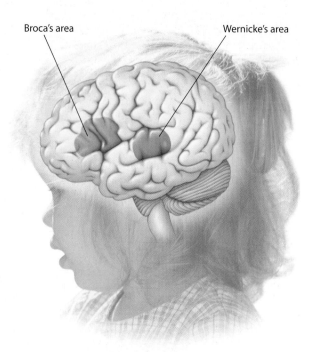

Broca's area   Wernicke's area

FIGURE **9.7**

BROCA'S AREA AND WERNICKE'S AREA.
Broca's area is located in the frontal lobe of the brain's left hemisphere, and it is involved in the control of speech. Wernicke's area is a portion of the left hemisphere's temporal lobe that is involved in understanding language. *How does the role of these areas of the brain relate to lateralization, which was discussed in Chapter 3?*

aphasia A loss or impairment of language processing resulting from damage to Broca's area or Wernicke's area.

language acquisition device (LAD) Chomsky's term that describes a biological endowment that enables the child to detect certain features and rules of language, including phonology, syntax, and semantics.

Chomsky's LAD is a theoretical construct, not a physical part of the brain. Is there evidence for the existence of a LAD? Supporters of the LAD concept cite the uniformity of language milestones across languages and cultures, evidence that children create language even in the absence of well-formed input, and biological substrates of language. But, as we will see, critics argue that even if infants have something like a LAD, it cannot explain the entirety of language acquisition.

ENVIRONMENTAL INFLUENCES

Decades ago, behaviorists opposed Chomsky's hypothesis and argued that language represents nothing more than chains of responses acquired through reinforcement (Skinner, 1957). A baby happens to babble "Ma-ma"; Mama rewards the baby with hugs and smiles; the baby says "Mama" more and more. Bit by bit, said the behaviorists, the baby's language is built up. According to behaviorists, language is a complex learned skill, much like playing the piano or dancing.

There are several problems with the behaviorial view of language learning. First, it does not explain how people create novel sentences—sentences that people have never heard or spoken before. Second, children learn the syntax of their native language even if they are not reinforced for doing so. Social psychologist Roger Brown (1973) spent long hours observing parents and their young children. He found that parents did not directly or explicitly reward or correct the syntax of most children's utterances. That is, parents did not say "good," "correct," "right," "wrong," and so on. Also, parents did not offer direct corrections such as "You should say two shoes, not two shoe." However, as we see shortly, many parents do expand on their young children's grammatically incorrect utterances and recast many of those that have grammatical errors (Bonvillian, 2005).

The behavioral view is no longer considered a viable explanation of how children acquire language. But a great deal of research describes ways in which children's environmental experiences influence their language skills (Berko Gleason & Ratner, 2009). Many language experts argue that a child's experiences, the specific language to be learned, and the context in which learning takes place can strongly influence language acquisition (Goldfield & Snow, 2009).

Language is not learned in a social vacuum. Most children are bathed in language from a very early age (Kuhl, 2011). The Wild Boy of Aveyron, who never learned to communicate effectively, had lived in social isolation for years. If infants do not hear language or don't develop an emotional bond with an adult, the neural connections linked with language and emotion may be weakened (Berko Gleason, 2009).

The support and involvement of caregivers and teachers greatly facilitate a child's language learning (Ariza & Lapp, 2011; Jalongo, 2011). One study found that when mothers immediately smiled and touched their 8-month-old infants after they babbled, the infants subsequently made more complex speechlike sounds than when mothers responded to their infants in a random manner (Goldstein, King, & West, 2003) (see Figure 9.8).

One intriguing component of the young child's linguistic environment is **child-directed speech,** language spoken in a higher pitch than normal with simple words and sentences (Clark, 2009). It is hard to use child-directed speech when not in the presence of a baby. As soon as you start talking to a baby, though, you shift into child-directed speech. Much of this is automatic and something most parents are not aware they are doing. As mentioned previously, even 4-year-olds speak in simpler ways to 2-year-olds than to their 4-year-old friends. Child-directed speech has the important function of capturing the infant's attention and maintaining communication.

FIGURE **9.8**

SOCIAL INTERACTION AND BABBLING. One study focused on two groups of mothers and their 8-month-old infants (Goldstein, King, & West, 2003). One group of mothers was instructed to smile and touch their infants immediately after the babies cooed and babbled; the other group was also told to smile and touch their infants but in a random manner, unconnected to sounds the infants made. The infants whose mothers immediately responded in positive ways to their babbling subsequently made more complex, speechlike sounds, such as *da* and *gu*. The research setting for this study, which underscores how important caregivers are in the early development of language, is shown above.

child-directed speech Language spoken in a higher pitch than normal, with simple words and sentences.

Adults often use strategies other than child-directed speech to enhance the child's acquisition of language, including recasting, expanding, and labeling:

- **Recasting** is rephrasing something the child has said, perhaps turning it into a question or restating the child's immature utterance in the form of a fully grammatical sentence. For example, if the child says, "The dog was barking," the adult can respond by asking, "When was the dog barking?" Effective recasting lets the child indicate an interest and then elaborates on that interest.

- **Expanding** is restating, in a linguistically sophisticated form, what a child has said. For example, a child says, "Doggie eat," and the parent replies, "Yes, the dog is eating."

- **Labeling** is identifying the names of objects. Young children are forever being asked to identify the names of objects. Roger Brown (1968) called this "the original word game" and claimed that much of a child's early vocabulary is motivated by this adult pressure to identify the words associated with objects.

Parents use these strategies naturally and in meaningful conversations. Parents do not (and should not) use any deliberate method to teach their children to talk, even for children who are slow in learning language. Children usually benefit when parents guide their children's discovery of language rather than overloading them with language; "following in order to lead" helps a child learn language. If children are not ready to take in some information, they are likely to tell you (perhaps by turning away). Thus, giving the child more information is not always better.

Infants, toddlers, and young children benefit when adults read books to and with them (shared reading) (Westerlund & Lagerberg, 2008). In one study, reading daily to children at 14 to 24 months of age was positively related to the children's language and cognitive development at 36 months of age (Raikes & others, 2006).

Remember, the encouragement of language development, not drill and practice, is the key. Language development is not a simple matter of imitation and reinforcement. To read further about ways that parents can facilitate children's language development, see the *Connecting Development to Life* interlude.

Our discussion of environmental influences on language development has focused mainly on parents. However, children interact with many other people who can influence their language development, including teachers and peers. A recent study of more than 1,800 4-year-olds focused on ways in which peers might influence children's language development (Mashburn & others, 2009). In this study, peers' expressive language abilities were positively linked with young children's receptive and expressive language development.

AN INTERACTIONIST VIEW OF LANGUAGE

If language acquisition depended only on biology, then Genie and the Wild Boy of Aveyron (discussed at the beginning of the chapter) should have talked without difficulty. A child's experiences influence language acquisition. But we have seen that language does have strong biological foundations. No matter how much you converse with a dog, it won't learn to talk.

An interactionist view emphasizes that both biology and experience contribute to language development (Ambridge & Lieven, 2011; MacWhinney, 2010). This interaction of biology and experience can be seen in the variations in the acquisition of language. Children vary in their ability to acquire language, and this variation cannot be readily explained by differences in environmental input alone. For children who are slow in developing language skills, however, opportunities to talk and be talked with are important. Children whose parents provide them with

> The linguistics problems children have to solve are always embedded in personal and interpersonal contexts.
>
> **—Lois Bloom**
> *Contemporary Psychologist, Columbia University*

recasting Rephrasing a statement that a child has said, perhaps turning it into a question, or restating a child's immature utterance in the form of a fully grammatical sentence.

expanding Restating, in a linguistically sophisticated form, what a child has said.

labeling Identifying the names of objects.

How Parents Can Facilitate Infants' and Toddlers' Language Development

Linguist Naomi Baron (1992) in *Growing Up with Language,* and more recently Ellen Galinsky (2010) in *Mind in the Making,* provided ideas to help parents facilitate their infants' and toddlers' language development. A summary of their ideas follow:

- *Be an active conversational partner.* Talk to your baby from the time it is born. Initiate conversation with the baby. If the baby is in a day-long child-care program, ensure that the baby receives adequate language stimulation from adults.
- *Talk in a slowed-down pace and don't worry about how you sound to other adults when you talk to your baby.* Talking in a slowed-down pace will help your baby detect words in the sea of sounds they experience. Babies enjoy and attend to the high-pitched sound of child-directed speech.
- *Use parent-look and parent-gesture, and name what you are looking at.* When you want your child to pay attention to something, look at it and point to it. Then name it, for example, saying "Look, Alex, there's an airplane."
- *When you talk with infants and toddlers, be simple, concrete, and repetitive.* Don't try to talk to them in abstract, high-level ways and think you have to say something new or different all of the time. Using familiar words often will help them remember the words.
- *Play games.* Use word games like peek-a-boo and pat-a-cake to help infants learn words.
- *Remember to listen.* Since toddlers' speech is often slow and laborious, parents are often tempted to supply words and thoughts for them. Be patient and let toddlers express themselves, no matter how painstaking the process is or how great a hurry you are in.
- *Expand and elaborate language abilities and horizons with infants and toddlers.* Ask questions that encourage answers other than "Yes" and "No." Actively repeat, expand, and recast the utterances. Your toddler might say, "Dada." You could follow with "Where's Dada?" and then you might continue, "Let's go find him."
- *Adjust to your child's idiosyncrasies instead of working against them.* Many toddlers have difficulty pronouncing words and making

It is a good idea for parents to begin talking to their babies at the start. The best language teaching occurs when the talking is begun before the infant becomes capable of intelligible speech. *What are some other guidelines for parents to follow in helping their infants and toddlers develop their language?*

themselves understood. Whenever possible, make toddlers feel that they are being understood.
- *Resist making normative comparisons.* Be aware of the ages at which your child reaches specific milestones (such as the first word, first 50 words), but do not measure this development rigidly against that of other children. Such comparisons can bring about unnecessary anxiety.

The first suggestion for parents of infants is to "be an active conversational partner." What did you learn earlier in this chapter about the amount of conversation mothers have with their infants? Does the amount of conversation or the mother's literacy skills and vocabulary diversity have a stronger positive effect on infants' vocabulary?

a rich verbal environment show many positive benefits (Beatty & Pratt, 2011). Parents who pay attention to what their children are trying to say, expand their children's utterances, read to them, and label things in the environment are providing valuable, if unintentional, benefits (Garcia-Sierra & others, 2011; Howard & others, 2011).

Today, most language acquisition researchers note that children from a wide variety of cultural contexts acquire their native language without explicit teaching. In some cases, they do so even without encouragement. Thus, very few aids are necessary for learning language (Shafer & Garrido-Nag, 2010). However, caregivers greatly facilitate a child's language learning (Beatty & Pratt, 2011).

Review Connect Reflect

 LG3 Discuss the biological and environmental contributions to language skills

Review

- What are the biological foundations of language?
- What are the environmental aspects of language?
- How does an interactionist view describe language?

Connect

- Relate what you learned about the nature-nurture debate in Chapters 1 and 2 to understanding biological and environmental influences on the development of language skills.

Reflect *Your Own Personal Journey of Life*

- If and when you become a parent, how should you respond to your child's grammar when conversing with the child? Will you allow mistakes to continue and assume that your young child will grow out of them, or will you closely monitor your young child's grammar and correct mistakes whenever you hear them? Explain.

reach your **learning goals**

What Is Language?

LG1 Define language and describe its rule systems

Defining Language

Language's Rule Systems

- Language is a form of communication, whether spontaneous, written, or signed, that is based on a system of symbols. Language consists of all the words used by a community and the rules for varying and combining them. Infinite generativity is the ability to produce an endless number of meaningful sentences using a finite set of words and rules.

- The main rule systems of language are phonology, morphology, syntax, semantics, and pragmatics. Phonology is the sound system of a language, including the sounds used and the sound sequences that may occur in the language. Morphology refers to units of meaning in word formation. Syntax is the way words are combined to form acceptable phrases and sentences. Semantics involves the meaning of words and sentences. Pragmatics is the appropriate use of language in different contexts.

How Language Develops

Infancy

- Among the milestones in infant language development are crying (birth), cooing (2 to 4 months), understanding first word (5 months), babbling (6 months), making the transition from universal linguist to language-specific listener (6 to 12 months), using gestures (8 to 12 months), detecting word boundaries (8 months), first word spoken (13 months), vocabulary spurt (18 months), rapid expansion of understanding words (18 to 24 months), and two-word utterances (18 to 24 months).

Early Childhood

- Advances in phonology, morphology, syntax, semantics, and pragmatics continue in early childhood. The transition to complex sentences begins between 2 and 3 years and continues through the elementary school years. Fast mapping provides one explanation for how rapidly young children's vocabulary develops.

Middle and Late Childhood

- In middle and late childhood, children become more analytical and logical in their approach to words and grammar. Current debate involving how to teach children to read focuses on the whole-language approach versus the phonics approach. Researchers have found strong evidence that the phonics approach should be used in teaching children to read but that children also benefit from the whole-language approach. Children's writing emerges out of scribbling. Advances in children's language and cognitive development provide the underpinnings for improved writing. Recent research indicates a complex conclusion about whether there are sensitive periods in learning a second language. Bilingual education aims to teach academic subjects to immigrant children in their native languages while gradually adding English instruction. Researchers have found that bilingualism does not interfere with performance in either language.

Adolescence

- In adolescence, language changes include more effective use of words; improvements in the ability to understand metaphor, satire, and adult literary works; and improvements in writing.

Adulthood and Aging

- For many individuals, knowledge of words and word meanings continues unchanged or may even improve in later adulthood. However, some decline in language skills may occur in retrieving words for use in conversation, in understanding speech, in phonological skills, and in some aspects of discourse. These changes in language skills in older adults likely occur as a consequence of declines in memory or in speed of processing information, or as a result of disease.

Biological and Environmental Influences

 LG3 Discuss the biological and environmental contributions to language skills

Biological Influences

- In evolution, language clearly gave humans an enormous edge over other animals and increased their chances of survival. A substantial portion of language processing occurs in the brain's left hemisphere, with Broca's area and Wernicke's area being important left-hemisphere locations. Chomsky argues that children are born with the ability to detect basic features and rules of language. In other words, they are biologically prepared to learn language with a prewired language acquisition device (LAD).

Environmental Influences

- The behavioral view—that children acquire language as a result of reinforcement—has not been supported. Adults help children acquire language through child-directed speech, recasting, expanding, and labeling. Environmental influences are demonstrated by differences in the language development of children as a consequence of being exposed to different language environments in the home. Parents should talk extensively with an infant, especially about what the baby is attending to.

An Interactionist View of Language

- An interactionist view emphasizes the contributions of both biology and experience in language.

key terms

language 275
infinite generativity 275
phonology 275
morphology 276
syntax 276
semantics 276
pragmatics 277

telegraphic
  speech 280
fast mapping 282
metalinguistic
  awareness 284
whole-language
  approach 285

phonics approach 285
metaphor 289
satire 289
dialect 289
Broca's area 291
Wernicke's area 291
aphasia 291

language acquisition
  device (LAD) 291
child-directed
  speech 292
recasting 293
expanding 293
labeling 293

key people

Patricia Kuhl 278
Jean Berko 281

Betty Hart and Todd Risley 283
Janellen Huttenlocher 283

Ellen Galinsky 284
Noam Chomsky 291

Roger Brown 292
Naomi Baron 294

Generations will depend on the ability of all procreating individuals to face their children.

—ERIK ERIKSON
Danish-Born American Psychoanalyst, 20th Century

Socioemotional Processes and Development

As children develop, they need "the meeting eyes of love." They split the universe into two halves: "me and not me." They juggle the need to curb their will with becoming what they can freely. Children and youth want to fly but discover that first they have to learn to stand and walk and climb and dance. Adolescents try on one face after another, searching for a face of their own. As adults age, they seek satisfaction in their emotional lives and search for the meaning of life. Section 4 contains four chapters: "Emotional Development" (Chapter 10), "The Self, Identity, and Personality" (Chapter 11), "Gender and Sexuality" (Chapter 12), and "Moral Development, Values, and Religion" (Chapter 13).

chapter 10 EMOTIONAL DEVELOPMENT

preview

For many years, emotion was neglected in the study of life-span development. Today, emotion is increasingly important in conceptualizations of development. For example, even as infants, individuals show different emotional styles, display varying temperaments, and begin to form emotional bonds with their caregivers. In this chapter, we study how temperament and attachment change across the human life span. But first, we examine emotion itself, exploring the functions of emotions in people's lives and the development of emotion from infancy through late adulthood.

Exploring Emotion — LG1 Discuss basic aspects of emotion

What Are Emotions? | Regulation of Emotion | Emotional Competence

Imagine your life without emotion. Emotion is the color and music of life, as well as the tie that binds people together. How do psychologists define and classify emotions, and why are they important to development?

WHAT ARE EMOTIONS?

For our purposes, we will define **emotion** as feeling, or affect, that occurs when a person is in a state or an interaction that is important to him or her, especially to his or her well-being. In many instances emotions involve an individual's communication with the world. Although emotion consists of more than communication, in infancy it is the communication aspect that is at the forefront of emotion (Witherington & others, 2011).

When we think about emotions, a few dramatic feelings such as rage or glorious joy spring to mind. But emotions can be subtle as well, such as uneasiness in a new situation or the contentment a mother feels when she holds her baby. Psychologists classify the broad range of emotions in many ways, but almost all classifications designate an emotion as either positive or negative. Positive emotions include enthusiasm, joy, and love. Negative emotions include anxiety, anger, guilt, and sadness.

Emotions are influenced both by biological foundations and by a person's experience. Biology's importance to emotion also is apparent in the changes in a baby's emotional capacities (Bell, Greene, & Wolfe, 2010; Bell & Deater-Deckard, 2007). Certain regions of the brain that develop early in life (such as the brain stem, hippocampus, and amygdala) play a role in distress, excitement, and rage, and even infants display these emotions (Goldsmith, 2011; Kagan, 2010). But, as we discuss later in the chapter, infants only gradually develop the ability to regulate their emotions, and this ability seems tied to the gradual maturation of frontal regions of the cerebral cortex that can exert control over other areas of the brain (Zelazo, Qu, & Kesek, 2010).

Social relationships, in turn, provide the setting for the development of a rich variety of emotions (Thompson, 2010, 2011a, b; Thompson & Goodman, 2011). When toddlers hear their parents quarreling, they often react with distress and inhibit their play. Well-functioning families make each other laugh and may develop a light mood to defuse conflicts. Biological evolution has endowed human beings to be *emotional*, but embeddedness in relationships and culture with others provides diversity in emotional experiences. For example, researchers have found that East

Blossoms are scattered by the wind
And the wind cares nothing, but
The blossoms of the heart,
No wind can touch.

—Youshida Kenko
Buddhist Monk, 14th Century

developmental **connection**

Brain Development. The maturation of the amygdala and prefrontal cortex may be linked to adolescent risk taking. Chapter 3, p. 104

emotion Feeling, or affect, that occurs when a person is engaged in an interaction that is important to him or her, especially to his or her well-being.

How do Japanese mothers handle their infants' and children's emotional development differently from non-Latina White mothers?

Asian infants display less frequent and less positive and negative emotions than non-Latino White infants (Cole & Tan, 2007). Throughout childhood, East Asian parents encourage their children to show emotional reserve rather than to be emotionally expressive (Cole & Tan, 2007). Further, Japanese parents try to prevent children from experiencing negative emotions, whereas non-Latino White mothers more frequently respond after their children become distressed and then help them cope (Rothbaum & Trommsdorff, 2007). In sum, biological evolution has endowed human beings to be emotional, but culture and relationships with others provide diversity in emotional experiences (Eisenberg, 2010; Super & Harkness, 2011; Thompson, 2011b).

REGULATION OF EMOTION

The ability to control one's emotions is a key dimension of development (Denham & others, 2011; Eisenberg, 2010). Emotional regulation consists of effectively managing arousal to adapt and reach a goal (Thompson, 2011c). Arousal involves a state of alertness or activation, which can reach levels that are too high for effective functioning. Anger, for example, often requires regulation.

In infancy and early childhood, regulation of emotion gradually shifts from external sources to self-initiated, internal sources. Also, with increasing age, children are more likely to improve their use of cognitive strategies for regulating emotion, modulate their emotional arousal, become more adept at managing situations to minimize negative emotion, and choose effective ways to cope with stress.

Of course, there are wide variations in children's ability to modulate their emotions (Calkins & Markovitch, 2010; Thompson & Goodman, 2010). Indeed, a prominent feature of adolescents with problems is that they often have difficulty managing their emotions.

Parents can play an important role in helping young children regulate their emotions (Eisenberg, 2010; Grusec, 2011; Thompson & Waters, 2011). Depending on how they talk with their children about emotion, parents can be described as taking an *emotion-coaching* or an *emotion-dismissing* approach (Gottman, 2011). The distinction between these approaches is most evident in the way the parent deals with the child's negative emotions (anger, frustration, sadness, and so on). *Emotion-coaching parents* monitor their children's emotions, view their children's negative emotions as opportunities for teaching, assist them in labeling emotions, and coach them in how to deal effectively with emotions. In contrast, *emotion-dismissing parents* view their role as to deny, ignore, or change negative emotions. Researchers have observed that emotion-coaching parents interact with their children in a less rejecting manner, use more scaffolding and praise, and are more nurturant than are emotion-dismissing parents (Gottman & DeClaire, 1997). Moreover, the children of emotion-coaching parents were better at soothing themselves when they got upset, were more effective in regulating their negative affect, focused their attention better, and had fewer behavior problems than the children of emotion-dismissing parents. A study revealed that having emotion-dismissing parents is linked with children's poor emotion regulation (Lunkenheimer, Shields, & Cortina, 2007).

A problem that parents face is that young children typically don't want to talk about difficult emotional topics, such as being distressed or engaging in negative behaviors. Among the strategies young children use to avoid these conversations is to not talk at all, change the topic, push the parent away, or run away. In a recent study, Ross Thompson and his colleagues (2009) found that young children were more likely to openly discuss difficult emotional circumstances when they were securely attached to their mother and when their mother conversed with them in a way that validated and accepted the child's views.

An emotion-coaching parent. What are some differences in emotion-coaching and emotion-dismissing parents?

EMOTIONAL COMPETENCE

In Chapter 8, we briefly considered the concept of emotional intelligence. Here we examine a closely related concept, *emotional competence*, that focuses on the adaptive nature of emotional experience. Carolyn Saarni (1999; Saarni & others, 2006) notes that becoming emotionally competent involves developing a number of skills in social contexts that include the following:

◄ developmental **connection**

Intelligence. Emotional intelligence involves perceiving and expressing emotions accurately, understanding emotion and emotional knowledge, using feelings to facilitate thought, and managing emotions effectively. Chapter 8, p. 251

Skill	Example
Having awareness of one's emotional states	Being able to differentiate whether one feels sad or anxious
Detecting others' emotions	Understanding when another person is sad rather than afraid
Using the vocabulary of emotion terms in socially and culturally appropriate ways	Appropriately describing a social situation in one's culture when a person is feeling distressed
Having empathic and sympathetic sensitivity to others' emotional experiences	Being sensitive to other people when they are feeling distressed
Recognizing that inner emotional states do not have to correspond to outer expressions	Recognizing that one can feel very angry yet manage one's emotional expression so that it appears more neutral
Adaptively coping with negative emotions by using self-regulatory strategies that reduce the intensity or duration of such emotional states	Reducing anger by walking away from an aversive situation and engaging in an activity that takes one's mind off the aversive situation
Having awareness that the expression of emotions plays a major role in relationships	Knowing that expressing anger toward a friend on a regular basis is likely to harm the friendship
Viewing oneself overall as feeling the way one wants to feel	Striving to cope effectively with the stress in one's life and feeling that one is successfully doing this

As children acquire these emotional competence skills in a variety of contexts, they are more likely to effectively manage their emotions, become resilient in the face of stressful circumstances, and develop more positive relationships (Denham, Bassett, & Wyatt, 2007).

Review *Connect* Reflect

 LG1 Discuss basic aspects of emotion

Review

- How is *emotion* defined?
- What are some developmental changes in the regulation of emotion?
- What constitutes emotional competence, according to Saarni?

Connect

- How similar or different are the concepts of emotional intelligence discussed in Chapter 8, "Intelligence," and the concept of emotional competence described in this chapter?

Reflect *Your Own Personal Journey of Life*

- Think back to your childhood and adolescent years. How effective were you in regulating your emotions? Give some examples. Has your ability to regulate your emotions changed as you have grown older? Explain.

Joy   Sadness

Fear   Surprise

FIGURE **10.1**

EXPRESSION OF DIFFERENT EMOTIONS IN INFANTS

Does an adult's emotional life differ from an adolescent's? Does a young child's emotional life differ from an infant's? Does an infant even have an emotional life? In this section, we consider an overview of the changes in emotion over the life span, looking not only at changes in emotional experience but also at the development of emotional competence.

INFANCY

What are some early developmental changes in emotions? What functions do infants' cries serve? When do infants begin to smile?

Early Emotions   A leading expert on infant emotional development, Michael Lewis (2007, 2008, 2010) distinguishes between primary emotions and self-conscious emotions. **Primary emotions** are emotions that are present in humans and other animals; these emotions appear in the first six months of the human infant's development. Primary emotions include surprise, interest, joy, anger, sadness, fear, and disgust (see Figure 10.1 for infants' facial expressions of some of these early emotions). In Lewis' classification, **self-conscious emotions** require self-awareness that involves consciousness and a sense of "me." Self-conscious emotions include jealousy, empathy, embarrassment, pride, shame, and guilt—most of these occurring for the first time at some point in the second half of the first year through the second year.

Researchers such as Joseph Campos (2005) and Michael Lewis (2007, 2010) debate about how early in the infant and toddler years these emotions first appear and what their sequence is. As an indication of the controversy regarding when certain emotions first are displayed by infants, consider jealousy. Some researchers argue that jealousy does not emerge until approximately 18 months of age (Lewis, 2007), whereas others emphasize that it is displayed much earlier (Draghi-Lorenz, 2007). Some research studies suggest that the appearance of jealousy might occur as early as 6 months of age (Hart & others, 2004). In one study, 6-month-old infants observed their mothers giving attention either to a lifelike baby doll (hugging or gently rocking it, for example) or to a book. When mothers directed their attention to the doll, the infants were more likely to display negative emotions, such as anger and sadness, which may have indicated their jealousy (Hart & Carrington, 2002) (see Figure 10.2). On the other hand, their expressions of anger and sadness simply may have reflected frustration in not being able to have the novel doll to play with.

Debate about the onset of an emotion such as jealousy illustrates the complexity and difficulty of indexing early emotions. That said, some experts on infant socioemotional development, such as Jerome Kagan (2010), conclude that the structural immaturity of the infant brain make it unlikely that emotions that require thought—such as guilt, pride, despair, shame, empathy, and jealousy—can be experienced during the first year. Thus, both Kagan (2010) and Campos

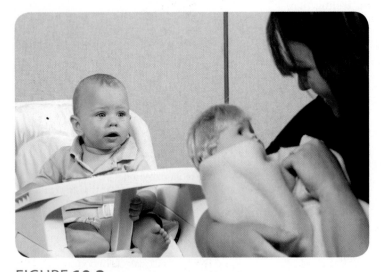

FIGURE **10.2**

IS THIS THE EARLY EXPRESSION OF JEALOUSY? In the study by Hart and Carrington (2002), the researchers concluded that the 6-month old infants who observed their mothers giving attention to a baby doll may indicate the early appearance of jealousy because of the negative emotions—such as anger and sadness—they displayed. However, experts on emotional development, such as Joseph Campos (2009) and Jerome Kagan (2010), argue that emotions such as jealousy don't appear during the first year. *Why do they conclude that jealousy does not occur in the first year?*

(2009) argue that so-called "self-conscious" emotions don't occur until after the first year, which increasingly reflects the view of most developmental psychologists. Thus, in regard to the photograph in Figure 10.2, it is unlikely that the 6-month-old infant is experiencing jealousy.

Emotional Expression and Social Relationships Emotional expressions are involved in infants' first relationships. The ability of infants to communicate emotions permits coordinated interactions with their caregivers and the beginning of an emotional bond between them (Thompson, 2010, 2011a, b). Not only do parents change their emotional expressions in response to infants' emotional expressions, but infants also modify their emotional expressions in response to their parents' emotional expressions. In other words, these interactions are mutually regulated (Bridgett & others, 2009). Because of this coordination, the interactions are described as reciprocal, or synchronous, when all is going well. Sensitive, responsive parents help their infants grow emotionally, whether the infants respond in distressed or happy ways (Thompson & Waters, 2011).

What are some different types of cries?

Cries and smiles are two emotional expressions that infants display when interacting with parents. These are babies' first forms of emotional communication.

Crying Crying is the most important mechanism newborns have for communicating with their world. The first cry verifies that the baby's lungs have filled with air. Cries also may provide information about the health of the newborn's central nervous system. Newborns even tend to respond with cries and negative facial expressions when they hear other newborns cry (Dondi, Simion, & Caltran, 1999).

Babies have at least three types of cries:

- **Basic cry.** A rhythmic pattern that usually consists of a cry, followed by a briefer silence, then a shorter inspiratory whistle that is somewhat higher in pitch than the main cry, then another brief rest before the next cry. Some infancy experts stress that hunger is one of the conditions that incite the basic cry.
- **Anger cry.** A variation of the basic cry in which more excess air is forced through the vocal cords.
- **Pain cry.** A sudden long, initial loud cry followed by breath holding; no preliminary moaning is present. The pain cry is stimulated by a high-intensity stimulus.

Most adults can determine whether an infant's cries signify anger or pain (Zeskind, 2007). Parents can distinguish between the various cries of their own baby better than those of another baby.

Smiling Smiling is critical as a means of developing a new social skill and is a key social signal (Campos, 2009; Witherington & others, 2011). Two types of smiling can be distinguished in infants:

- **Reflexive smile.** A smile that does not occur in response to external stimuli and appears during the first month after birth, usually during sleep.
- **Social smile.** A smile that occurs in response to an external stimulus, typically a face in the case of the young infant. Social smiling occurs as early as 4 to 6 weeks of age in response to a caregiver's voice (Messinger, 2008).

The infant's social smile can have a powerful impact on caregivers (Bates, 2008). Following weeks of endless demands, fatigue, and little reinforcement, an infant starts smiling at them and all of the caregivers' efforts are rewarded.

He who binds to himself a joy
Does the winged life destroy;
But he who kisses the joy as it flies
Lives in eternity's sun rise.

—**WILLIAM BLAKE**
English Poet, 19th Century

primary emotions Emotions that are present in humans and other animals, emerge early in life, and are culturally universal; examples are joy, anger, sadness, fear, and disgust.

self-conscious emotions Emotions that require consciousness and a sense of "me"; they include empathy, jealousy, embarrassment, pride, shame, and guilt, most of which first appear at some point in the second half of the first year through the second year.

basic cry A rhythmic pattern usually consisting of a cry, a briefer silence, a shorter inspiratory whistle that is higher pitched than the main cry, and then a brief rest before the next cry.

anger cry A cry similar to the basic cry but with more excess air forced through the vocal cords.

pain cry A sudden, initial loud cry followed by breath holding, without preliminary moaning.

reflexive smile A smile that does not occur in response to external stimuli. It happens during the month after birth, usually during sleep.

social smile A smile in response to an external stimulus, which, early in development, typically is a face.

FIGURE **10.3**

A 6-MONTH-OLD'S STRONG SMILE. This strong smile reflects the Duchenne marker (eye constriction) and mouth opening.

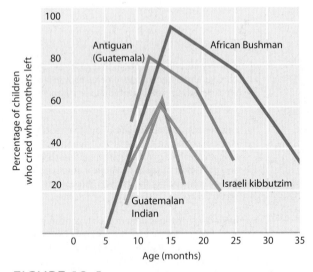

FIGURE **10.4**

SEPARATION PROTEST IN FOUR CULTURES. Note that separation protest peaked at about the same time in all four cultures in this study (13 to 15 months of age) (Kagan, Kearsley, & Zelazo, 1978). However, a higher percentage (100 percent) of infants in an African Bushman culture engaged in separation protest compared to only about 60 percent of infants in Guatemalan Indian and Israeli kibbutzim cultures. *What might explain the fact that separation protest peaks at about the same time in these cultures?* Reprinted by permission of the publisher from *Infancy: Its Place in Human Development*, by Jerome Kagan, Richard B. Kearsley and Philip R. Zelazo, p. 107, Cambridge, MA: Harvard University Press, Copyright © 1978 by the President and Fellows of Harvard College.

Daniel Messinger (2008) has described the developmental course of infant smiling. From 2 to 6 months after birth, infants' social smiling increases considerably, both in self-initiated smiles and in smiles in response to others' smiles. At 6 to 12 months, smiles that couple what is called the Duchenne marker (eye constriction) and mouth opening occur in the midst of highly enjoyable interactions and play with parents (see Figure 10.3). In the second year, smiling continues to occur in such positive circumstances with parents, and in many cases an increase in smiling occurs when interacting with peers. Also in the second year, toddlers become increasingly aware of the social meaning of smiles, especially in their relationship with parents.

Fear One of a baby's earliest emotions is fear, which typically first appears at about 6 months of age and peaks at about 18 months. However, abused and neglected infants can show fear as early as 3 months (Campos, 2005). Researchers have found that infant fear is linked to guilt, empathy, and low aggression at 6 to 7 years of age (Rothbart, 2007).

The most frequent expression of an infant's fear involves **stranger anxiety,** in which an infant shows a fear and wariness of strangers. Stranger anxiety usually emerges gradually. It first appears at about 6 months of age in the form of wary reactions. By age 9 months, the fear of strangers is often more intense, reaching a peak toward the end of the first year of life (Scher & Harel, 2008).

Not all infants show distress when they encounter a stranger. Besides individual variations, whether an infant shows stranger anxiety also depends on the social context and the characteristics of the stranger (Kagan, 2008).

Infants show less stranger anxiety when they are in familiar settings. It appears that when infants feel secure, they are less likely to show stranger anxiety.

In addition to stranger anxiety, infants experience fear of being separated from their caregivers. The result is **separation protest**—crying when the caregiver leaves. Separation protest is initially displayed by infants at approximately 7 to 8 months and peaks at about 15 months (Kagan, 2008). One study revealed that separation protest peaked at about 13 to 15 months in four different cultures (Kagan, Kearsley, & Zelazo, 1978). As indicated in Figure 10.4, the percentage of infants who engaged in separation protest varied across cultures, but the infants reached a peak of protest at about the same age—just before the middle of the second year of life.

Emotional Regulation and Coping Earlier, we discussed some general developmental changes in emotional regulation across the childhood years. Here we examine in detail how infants develop emotional regulation and coping skills.

During the first year of life, the infant gradually develops an ability to inhibit, or minimize, the intensity and duration of emotional reactions (Calkins & Markovitch, 2010). From early in infancy, babies put their thumbs in their mouths to soothe themselves. But at first, infants mainly depend on caregivers to help them soothe their emotions, as when a caregiver rocks an infant to sleep, sings lullabies to the infant, gently strokes the infant, and so on.

Later in infancy, when they become aroused, infants sometimes redirect their attention or distract themselves in order to reduce their arousal. By 2 years of age, toddlers can use language to define their feeling states and the context that is upsetting them (Kopp, 2008). A toddler might say, "Feel bad. Dog scare." This type of communication may allow caregivers to help the child in regulating emotion.

Contexts can influence emotional regulation (Thompson, 2010, 2011b, c). Infants are often affected by fatigue, hunger, time of day, which people are around them, and where they are. Infants must learn to adapt to different contexts that require emotional regulation. Further, new demands appear as the infant becomes older and parents modify their expectations. For example, a parent may take it in stride if a 6-month-old infant screams in a grocery store but may react very differently if a 2-year-old starts screaming.

To soothe or not to soothe—should a crying baby be given attention and soothed, or does this attention spoil the infant? Many years ago, the behaviorist John Watson (1928) argued that parents spend too much time responding to infant crying. As a consequence, he said, parents reward crying and increase its incidence. Some researchers have found that a caregiver's quick, soothing response to crying increased crying (Gewirtz, 1977). However, infancy experts Mary Ainsworth (1979) and John Bowlby (1989) stress that you can't respond too much to infant crying in the first year of life. They argue that a quick, comforting response to the infant's cries is an important ingredient in the development of a strong bond between the infant and caregiver. In one of Ainsworth's studies, infants whose mothers responded quickly when they cried at 3 months of age cried less later in the first year of life (Bell & Ainsworth, 1972).

Controversy still characterizes the question of whether or how parents should respond to an infant's cries. Some developmentalists argue that an infant cannot be spoiled in the first year of life, a view suggesting that parents should soothe a crying infant. This reaction should help infants develop a sense of trust and secure attachment to the caregiver.

EARLY CHILDHOOD

The young child's growing awareness of self is linked to the ability to feel an expanding range of emotions. Young children, like adults, experience many emotions during the course of a day. At times, they also try to make sense of other people's emotional reactions and to control their own emotions.

Expressing Emotions   Recall from our earlier discussion that even young infants experience emotions such as joy and fear, but to experience self-conscious emotions, children must be able to refer to themselves and be aware of themselves as distinct from others (Lewis, 2008, 2010). Pride, shame, embarrassment, and guilt are examples of self-conscious emotions. Self-conscious emotions do not appear to develop until self-awareness appears in the second half of the second year of life.

During the early childhood years, emotions such as pride and guilt become more common (Thompson & Newton, 2011). They are especially influenced by parents' responses to children's behavior. For example, a young child may experience shame when a parent says, "You should feel bad about biting your sister."

Understanding Emotions   Among the most important changes in emotional development in early childhood is an increased understanding of emotion (Denham & others, 2011). During early childhood, young children increasingly understand that certain situations are likely to evoke particular emotions, facial expressions indicate specific emotions, emotions affect behavior, and emotions can be used to influence others' emotions (Cole & others, 2009). In a recent study, young children's emotional understanding was linked to how extensively they engaged in prosocial behavior (Ensor, Spencer, & Hughes, 2010).

Between 2 and 4 years of age, children considerably increase the number of terms they use to describe emotions. During this time, they are also learning about the causes and consequences of feelings (Denham & others, 2011).

When they are 4 to 5 years of age, children show an increased ability to reflect on emotions. They also begin to understand that the same event can elicit different feelings in different people. Moreover, they show a growing awareness that they need to manage their emotions to meet social standards. And, by 5 years of age, most children can accurately determine emotions that are produced by challenging circumstances and describe strategies they might call on to cope with everyday stress (Cole & others, 2009).

Should a crying baby be given attention and soothed, or does this spoil the infant? Should the infant's age, the type of cry, and the circumstances be considered?

A young child expressing the emotion of shame, which occurs when a child evaluates his or her actions as not living up to standards. A child experiencing shame wishes to hide or disappear. *Why is shame called a self-conscious emotion?*

stranger anxiety An infant's fear of and wariness toward strangers; it tends to appear in the second half of the first year of life.

separation protest Reaction that occurs when infants experience a fear of being separated from a caregiver, which results in crying when the caregiver leaves.

MIDDLE AND LATE CHILDHOOD

During middle and late childhood, many children show marked improvement in understanding and managing their emotions. However, in some instances, as when they experience stressful circumstances, their coping abilities can be challenged.

Developmental Changes in Emotion   Here are some important developmental changes in emotions during the middle and late childhood years (Denham, Bassett, & Wyatt, 2007; Denham & others, 2011; Kuebli, 1994; Thompson, 2011b; Wintre & Vallance, 1994):

- *Improved emotional understanding.* Children in elementary school develop an increased ability to understand such complex emotions as pride and shame. These emotions become less tied to the reactions of other people; they become more self-generated and integrated with a sense of personal responsibility. A child may feel a sense of pride about developing new reading skills or shame after hurting a friend's feelings.
- *Marked improvements in the ability to suppress or conceal negative emotional reactions.* Children now sometimes intentionally hide their emotions. Although a boy may feel sad that a friend does not want to play with him, he may decide not to share those feelings with his parents.
- *The use of self-initiated strategies for redirecting feelings.* In the elementary school years, children reflect more about emotional experiences and develop strategies to cope with their emotional lives. Children can more effectively manage their emotions by cognitive means, such as using distracting thoughts. A boy may be excited about his birthday party later in the afternoon, but still be able to concentrate on his schoolwork during the day.
- *An increased tendency to take into fuller account the events leading to emotional reactions.* A fourth-grader may become aware that her sadness today is influenced by her friend's moving to another town last week.
- *Development of a capacity for genuine empathy.* Two girls see another child in distress on the playground and run to the child and ask if they can help.

Coping with Stress   An important aspect of children's lives is learning how to cope with stress (Bonnano, Mancini, & Westphal, 2011; Masten, 2011; Walter & others, 2010). As children get older, they are able to more accurately appraise a stressful situation and determine how much control they have over it. Older children generate more coping alternatives to stressful conditions and use more cognitive coping strategies (Saarni & others, 2006). For example, older children are better than younger children at intentionally shifting their thoughts to something that is less stressful. Older children are also better at reframing, or changing one's perception of a stressful situation. For example, younger children may be very disappointed that their teacher did not say hello to them when they arrived at school. Older children may reframe this type of situation and think, "She may have been busy with other things and just forgot to say hello."

By 10 years of age, most children are able to use these cognitive strategies to cope with stress (Saarni & others, 2006). However, in families that have not been supportive and are characterized by turmoil or trauma, children may be so overwhelmed by stress that they do not use such strategies (Thabet & others, 2009).

Disasters can especially harm children's development and produce adjustment problems. Among the outcomes for children who experience disasters are acute stress reactions, depression, panic disorder, and post-traumatic stress disorder (Bonnano, Mancini, & Westphal, 2011; Masten & Osofksy, 2010). The likelihood that a child will face these problems following a disaster depends on factors such as the nature and severity of the disaster and the type of support available to the child.

Following are descriptions of recent studies of how various aspects of traumatic events and disasters affect children:

- In a study of mothers and their children aged 5 years and younger who were directly exposed to the 9/11 attacks in New York City, the mothers who developed post-traumatic stress disorder (PTSD) and depression were less likely to help their children regulate their emotions and behavior than mothers who were only depressed or only had PTSD (Chemtob & others, 2010). This outcome was linked to their children having anxiety, depression, aggression, and sleep problems.
- A study of the effects of the 2004 tsunami in Sri Lanka found that severe exposure to the tsunami combined with more exposure to other adversities, such as an ongoing war and family violence, was linked to poorer adjustment after the tsunami disaster (Catani & others, 2010).
- A research review revealed that children with disabilities are more likely than children without disabilities to live in poverty conditions, which increases their exposure to hazards and disasters (Peek & Stough, 2010). When a disaster occurs, children with disabilities have more difficulty escaping from the disaster.

What are some effective strategies to help children cope with traumatic events such as Hurricane Katrina in August 2005?

In research on disasters/trauma, the term *dose-response effects* is often used. A widely supported finding in this research area is that the more severe the disaster/trauma (dose), the worse the adaptation and adjustment (response) following the disaster/trauma (Masten & Osofsky, 2010; Obradovic, Shaffer, & Masten, 2011).

Children who have a number of coping techniques have the best chance of adapting and functioning competently in the face of disasters and traumas. Following are some recommendations for helping children cope with the stress of especially devastating events (Gurwitch & others, 2001, pp. 4–11):

- *Reassure children of their safety and security.* This step may need to be taken numerous times.
- *Allow children to retell events and be patient in listening to them.*
- *Encourage children to talk about any disturbing or confusing feelings.* Tell them that these are normal feelings after a stressful event.
- *Help children make sense of what happened.* Children may misunderstand what took place. For example, young children "may blame themselves, believe things happened that did not happen, believe that terrorists are in the school, etc. Gently help children develop a realistic understanding of the event" (p. 10).
- *Protect children from re-exposure to frightening situations and reminders of the trauma.* This strategy includes limiting conversations about the event in front of the children.

ADOLESCENCE

Adolescence has long been described as a time of emotional turmoil (Hall, 1904). Adolescents are not constantly in a state of "storm and stress," but emotional highs and lows do increase during early adolescence (Rosenblum & Lewis, 2003). Young adolescents can be on top of the world one moment and down in the dumps the next. In some instances, the intensity of their emotions seems out of proportion to the events that elicit them (Steinberg, 2011). Young adolescents might sulk a lot, not knowing how to adequately express their feelings. With little or no provocation, they can blow up at their parents or siblings, a response that might reflect the defense mechanism of displacing their feelings onto another person. For some

developmental **connection**

Brain Development. The amygdala, where much of emotion is processed in the brain, matures earlier than the prefrontal cortex in adolescence. Chapter 3, p. 104

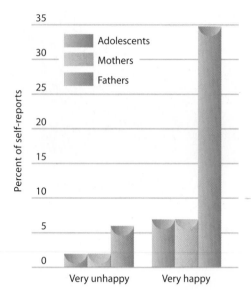

FIGURE **10.5**

SELF-REPORTED EXTREMES OF EMOTION BY ADOLESCENTS, MOTHERS, AND FATHERS USING THE EXPERIENCE SAMPLING METHOD. In the study by Reed Larson and Maryse Richards (1994), adolescents and their mothers and fathers were beeped at random times by researchers using the experience sampling method. The researchers found that adolescents reported more emotional extremes than their parents.

Laura Carstensen (*right*), in a caring relationship with an older woman. Her theory of socioemotional selectivity is gaining recognition as an important way of thinking about developmental changes in adulthood.

socioemotional selectivity theory The theory that older adults become more selective about their social networks. Because they place high value on emotional satisfaction, older adults often spend more time with familiar individuals with whom they have had rewarding relationships.

adolescents, such emotional swings can reflect serious problems. Girls are especially vulnerable to depression in adolescence (Nolen-Hoeksema, 2011). But it is important for adults to recognize that moodiness is a normal aspect of early adolescence, and most adolescents make it through these moody times to become competent adults.

Reed Larson and Maryse Richards (1994) found that adolescents reported more extreme emotions and more fleeting emotions than their parents did. For example, adolescents were five times more likely to report being "very happy" and three times more likely to report being "very unhappy" than their parents (see Figure 10.5). These findings lend support to the perception of adolescents as moody and changeable (Rosenblum & Lewis, 2003).

ADULT DEVELOPMENT AND AGING

Like children, adults adapt more effectively when they are emotionally intelligent—when they are skilled at perceiving and expressing emotion, understanding emotion, using feelings to facilitate thought, and managing emotions effectively. (In Chapter 14, "Families, Lifestyles, and Parenting," we examine a number of aspects of relationships that involve emotions.)

Developmental changes in emotion continue through the adult years (Carstensen & others, 2011). The changes often are characterized by an effort to create lifestyles that are emotionally satisfying, predictable, and manageable by making decisions about an occupation, a life partner, and other circumstances. Of course, not all individuals are successful in these efforts. A key theme of emotional development in adulthood is "the adaptive integration of emotional experience into satisfying daily life and successful relationships with others" (Thompson & Goodvin, 2007, p. 402).

Stereotypes suggest that older adults' emotional landscape is bleak and that most live sad, lonely lives. Researchers have found a different picture (Carstensen, 2009; Charles & Carstensen, 2010). One study of a very large U.S. sample examined emotions at different ages (Mroczek & Kolarz, 1998). Older adults reported experiencing more positive emotion and less negative emotion than younger adults, and positive emotion increased with age in adults at an accelerating rate (see Figure 10.6).

Overall, compared with younger adults, the feelings of older adults mellow. Emotional life is on a more even keel, with fewer highs and lows. It may be that although older adults have less extreme joy, they have more contentment, especially when they are connected in positive ways with friends and family. A recent study revealed that positive emotion increased and negative emotion (except for sadness) decreased from 50 years of age through the mid-80s (Stone & others, 2010). In this study, a pronounced decline in anger occurred from the early 20s and sadness was essentially unchanged from the early 20s through the mid-80s. Another recent study found that aging was linked to more positive overall well-being and greater emotional stability (Carstensen & others, 2011). In this study, adults who experienced more positive than negative emotions were more likely to still be alive over a 13-year period. Other research also indicates that happier people live longer (Frey, 2011). In sum, researchers have found that the emotional life of older adults is more positive than stereotypes suggest (Carstensen & others, 2011; Stone & others, 2010).

One theory developed by Laura Carstensen (1991, 1998, 2006, 2009) stands out as important in thinking about developmental changes in adulthood, especially in older adults. **Socioemotional selectivity theory** states that older adults become more selective about their social networks. Because they place a high value on emotional satisfaction, older adults often spend more time with familiar individuals with whom they have had rewarding relationships. This theory argues that older adults deliberately withdraw from social contact with individuals peripheral to their lives while they maintain or increase contact with close friends and family members with whom they have had enjoyable relationships. This selective narrowing of social interaction maximizes positive emotional experiences and minimizes emotional risks as individuals become older. According to this theory, older adults systematically hone their social networks so that available social partners satisfy their emotional needs.

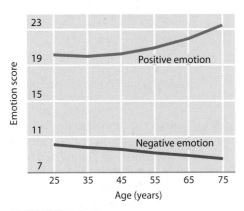

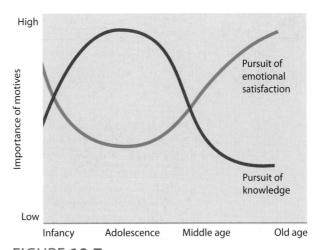

FIGURE **10.6**

CHANGES IN POSITIVE AND NEGATIVE EMOTION ACROSS THE ADULT YEARS. Positive and negative scores had a possible range of 6 to 30 with higher scores reflecting positive emotion and lower scores negative emotion. Positive emotion increased in the middle adulthood and late adulthood years, while negative emotion declined.

FIGURE **10.7**

IDEALIZED MODEL OF SOCIOEMOTIONAL SELECTIVITY THROUGH THE LIFE SPAN. In Carstensen's theory of socioemotional selectivity, the motivation to reach knowledge-related and emotion-related goals changes across the life span.

Is there research to support life-span differences in the composition of social networks? Researchers have found that the social networks of older adults are smaller than those of younger adults (Charles & Carstensen, 2010). In one study of individuals 69 to 104 years of age, the oldest participants had fewer peripheral social contacts than the relatively younger participants but about the same number of close emotional relationships (Lang & Carstensen, 1994).

Socioemotional selectivity theory also focuses on the types of goals that individuals are motivated to achieve (Charles & Carstensen, 2010). According to the theory, motivation for knowledge-related goals starts relatively high in the early years of life, peaks in adolescence and early adulthood, then declines in middle and late adulthood (see Figure 10.7). The trajectory for emotion-related goals is high during infancy and early childhood, declines from middle childhood through early adulthood, and increases in middle and late adulthood. A recent study revealed that younger adults performed better in decision making about health-care choices when they had an information focus (focus on specific attributes, report details about options, then make a choice), whereas older adults did better on these decision-making tasks when they had an emotion focus (focus on emotional reactions to options, report feelings about the options, and then make a choice) (Mikels & others, 2010).

> Recent research paints a distinctly positive picture of aging in the emotional domain.
>
> —LAURA CARSTENSEN
> *Contemporary Psychologist, Stanford University*

Review *Connect* **Reflect**

 Describe the development of emotion through the life span

Review

- How does emotion develop in infancy?
- What characterizes emotional development in early childhood?
- What changes take place in emotion during middle and late childhood?
- How does emotion change in adolescence?
- What are some key aspects of emotional development in adulthood?

Connect

- How might cognitive development (discussed in Chapters 7 and 8) and language development (described in Chapter 9) be linked to the development of emotional regulation and coping in young children?

Reflect *Your Own Personal Journey of Life*

- Imagine that you are the parent of an 8-month-old baby and you are having difficulty getting sufficient sleep because the baby wakes up crying in the middle of the night. How would you deal with this situation?

Do you get upset a lot? Does it take much to get you angry or to make you laugh? Even at birth, babies seem to have different emotional styles. One infant is cheerful and happy much of the time; another baby seems to cry constantly. These tendencies reflect **temperament,** which involves individual differences in behavioral styles, emotions, and characteristic ways of responding. With regard to its link to emotion, temperament refers to individual differences in how quickly the emotion is shown, how strong it is, how long it lasts, and how quickly it fades away (Campos, 2009).

DESCRIBING AND CLASSIFYING TEMPERAMENT

How would you describe your temperament or the temperament of a friend? Researchers have described and classified the temperaments of individuals in different ways. Here we examine three of those ways.

Chess and Thomas' Classification Psychiatrists Alexander Chess and Stella Thomas (Chess & Thomas, 1977; Thomas & Chess, 1991) identified three basic types, or clusters, of temperament:

- An **easy child** is generally in a positive mood, quickly establishes regular routines in infancy, and adapts easily to new experiences.
- A **difficult child** reacts negatively and cries frequently, engages in irregular daily routines, and is slow to accept change.
- A **slow-to-warm-up child** has a low activity level, is somewhat negative, and displays a low intensity of mood.

"Oh, he's cute, all right, but he's got the temperament of a car alarm."
© Barbara Smaller/The New Yorker Collection/www.cartoonbank.com.

What are some ways that developmentalists have classified infants' temperaments? Which classification makes the most sense to you, based on your observations of infants?

In their longitudinal investigation, Chess and Thomas found that 40 percent of the children they studied could be classified as easy, 10 percent as difficult, and 15 percent as slow to warm up. Notice that 35 percent did not fit any of the three patterns. Researchers have found that these three basic clusters of temperament are moderately stable across the childhood years. A recent study revealed that young children with a difficult temperament showed more problems when they experienced low-quality child care and fewer problems when they experienced high-quality child care than did young children with an easy temperament (Pluess & Belsky, 2009).

Kagan's Behavioral Inhibition   Another way of classifying temperament focuses on the differences between a shy, subdued, timid child and a sociable, extraverted, bold child (Asendorph, 2008). Jerome Kagan (2002, 2008, 2010) regards shyness with strangers (peers or adults) as one feature of a broad temperament category called *inhibition to the unfamiliar*. Beginning at about 7 to 9 months, inhibited children react to many aspects of unfamiliarity with initial avoidance, distress, or subdued affect. In Kagan's research, inhibition shows some continuity from infancy through early childhood, although a substantial number of infants who are classified as inhibited become less so by 7 years of age.

What characterizes an inhibited temperament?

Rothbart and Bates' Classification   New classifications of temperament continue to be forged. Mary Rothbart and John Bates (2006) argue that three broad dimensions best represent what researchers have found to characterize the structure of temperament: extraversion/surgency, negative affectivity, and effortful control (self-regulation):

- *Extraversion/surgency* includes "positive anticipation, impulsivity, activity level, and sensation seeking" (Rothbart, 2004, p. 495). Kagan's uninhibited children fit into this category.

- *Negative affectivity* includes "fear, frustration, sadness, and discomfort" (Rothbart, 2004, p. 495). These children are easily distressed; they may fret and cry often. Kagan's inhibited children fit this category.

temperament An individual's behavioral style and characteristic way of responding.

easy child A temperament style in which the child is generally in a positive mood, quickly establishes regular routines, and adapts easily to new experiences.

difficult child A temperament style in which the child tends to react negatively and cry frequently, engages in irregular daily routines, and is slow to accept change.

slow-to-warm-up child A temperament style in which the child has a low activity level, is somewhat negative, and displays a low intensity of mood.

- *Effortful control* (self-regulation) includes "attentional focusing and shifting, inhibitory control, perceptual sensitivity, and low-intensity pleasure" (Rothbart, 2004, p. 495). Infants who are high on effortful control show an ability to keep their arousal from getting too high and have strategies for soothing themselves. By contrast, children low on effortful control are often unable to control their arousal; they become easily agitated and intensely emotional.

The description of temperament categories so far reflects the development of normative capabilities of children, not individual differences in children. The development of these capabilities, such as effortful control, allows individual differences to emerge (Bates, 2008; Bates, Schermerhorn, & Goodnight, 2010). For example, although maturation of the brain's prefrontal lobes must occur for any child's attention to improve and the child to achieve effortful control, some children develop effortful control while others do not. And it is these individual differences in children that are at the heart of temperament (Bates, 2008; Bates, Schermerhorn, & Goodnight, 2010).

BIOLOGICAL FOUNDATIONS AND EXPERIENCE

How does a child acquire a certain temperament? Kagan (2002, 2008, 2010) argues that children inherit a physiology that biases them to have a particular type of temperament. However, through experience they may learn to modify their temperament to some degree (Thompson, Winer, & Goodvin, 2011). For example, children may inherit a physiology that biases them to be fearful and inhibited, but they learn to reduce their fear and inhibition to some degree.

Biological Influences   Physiological characteristics have been linked with different temperaments. In particular, an inhibited temperament is associated with a unique physiological pattern that includes high and stable heart rate, high level of the hormone cortisol, and high activity in the right frontal lobe of the brain (Kagan, 2008). This pattern may be tied to the excitability of the amygdala, a structure of the brain that plays an important role in fear and inhibition. And the development of effortful control is linked to advances in the brain's frontal lobes (Bates, 2008).

What is heredity's role in the biological foundations of temperament? Twin and adoption studies suggest that heredity has a moderate influence on differences in temperament within a group of people (Buss & Goldsmith, 2007).

Developmental Connections in Temperaments   Is temperament in childhood linked with adjustment in adulthood? In one study, children who had an easy temperament at 3 to 5 years of age were likely to be well adjusted as young adults (Chess & Thomas, 1977). In contrast, many children who had a difficult temperament at 3 to 5 years of age were not well adjusted as young adults. Also, other researchers have found that boys with a difficult temperament in childhood are less likely as adults to continue their formal education, whereas girls with a difficult temperament in childhood are more likely to experience marital conflict as adults (Wachs, 2000).

Inhibition is another characteristic of temperament that has been studied extensively (Kagan, 2008, 2010). A recent study revealed that behavioral inhibition at 3 years of age was linked to shyness at age 7 (Volbrecht & Goldsmith, 2010). Also, research indicates that individuals with an inhibited temperament in childhood are less likely as adults to be assertive or to experience social support, and more likely to delay entering a stable job track (Asendorph, 2008).

In sum, these studies reveal some continuity between certain aspects of temperament in childhood and adjustment in early adulthood (Rothbart, 2011; Wachs & Bates, 2011). However, keep in mind that these connections between childhood

developmental **connection**

Nature and Nurture. Twin and adoption studies have been used in the effort to sort out hereditary and environmental influences on development. Chapter 2, p. 60

How is temperament in childhood linked to socioemotional development in adulthood?

temperament and adult adjustment are based on only a small number of studies; more research is needed to verify these linkages.

Developmental Contexts What accounts for the continuities and discontinuities between a child's temperament and an adult's personality? Physiological and hereditary factors likely are involved in continuity. Links between temperament in childhood and personality in adulthood also might vary, depending on the contexts in individuals' experience (Bates, Schermerhorn, & Goodnight, 2010; Wachs & Bates, 2011).

The reaction to an infant's temperament may depend, in part, on culture (Cole & Tan, 2007; Super & Harkness, 2011). For example, behavioral inhibition is more highly valued in China than in North America, and researchers have found that Chinese infants are more inhibited than Canadian infants (Chen & others, 1998). The cultural differences in temperament were linked to parental attitudes and behaviors. Canadian mothers of inhibited 2-year-olds were less accepting of their infants' inhibited temperament, whereas Chinese mothers were more accepting.

In short, many aspects of a child's environment can encourage or discourage the persistence of temperament characteristics (Rothbart & Bates, 2006; Wachs & Bates, 2011). One useful way of thinking about these relationships applies the concept of goodness of fit, which we examine next.

GOODNESS OF FIT AND PARENTING

Goodness of fit refers to the match between a child's temperament and the environmental demands the child must cope with. Some temperament characteristics pose more parenting challenges than others, at least in modern Western societies (Bates, Schermerhorn, & Goodnight,

developmental connection

Culture. Cross-cultural studies seek to determine culture-universal and culture-specific aspects of development. Chapter 1, p. 9

An infant's temperament can vary across cultures. *What do parents need to know about a child's temperament?*

goodness of fit The match between a child's temperament and the environmental demands the child must cope with.

Parenting and the Child's Temperament

What are the implications of temperamental variations for parenting? Although answers to this question necessarily are speculative, these conclusions regarding the best parenting strategies to use in relation to children's temperament were reached by temperament experts Ann Sanson and Mary Rothbart (1995):

- *Attention to and respect for individuality.* One implication is that it is difficult to generate general prescriptions for "good" parenting. A goal might be accomplished in one way with one child and in another way with another child, depending on the child's temperament. Parents need to be sensitive and remain flexible to the infant's signals and needs.

- *Structuring the child's environment.* Crowded, noisy environments can pose greater problems for some children (such as a "difficult child") than others (such as an "easygoing" child). We might also expect that a fearful, withdrawing child would benefit from slower entry into new contexts.

- *The "difficult child" and packaged parenting programs.* Programs for parents often focus on dealing with children who have "difficult" temperaments. In some cases, "difficult child" refers to Thomas and Chess' description of a child who reacts negatively, cries frequently, engages in irregular daily routines, and is slow to accept change. In others, the concept might be used to describe a child who is irritable, displays anger frequently, does not follow directions well, or shows some other negative characteristic. Acknowledging that some children are harder than others to parent is often helpful, and advice on how to handle specific difficult characteristics can be useful. However, whether a specific characteristic is difficult depends on its fit with the environment. To label a child "difficult" has the danger of becoming a self-fulfilling prophecy. If a child is identified as "difficult," people may treat the child in a way that actually elicits "difficult" behavior.

What are some good strategies for parents to adopt when responding to their infant's temperament?

Too often, we pigeonhole children into categories without examining the context (Rothbart, 2011; Rothbart & Bates, 2006). Nonetheless, caregivers need to take children's temperament into account. Research does not yet allow for many highly specific recommendations, but, in general, caregivers should (1) be sensitive to the individual characteristics of the child, (2) be flexible in responding to these characteristics, and (3) avoid applying negative labels to the child.

How does the advice to "structure the child's environment" relate to what you learned about the concept of "goodness of fit"?

2010; Rothbart, 2011). When children are prone to distress, as exhibited by frequent crying and irritability, their parents may eventually respond by ignoring the child's distress or trying to force the child to "behave." In one research study, though, extra support and training for mothers of distress-prone infants improved the quality of mother-infant interaction (van den Boom, 1989).

To read further about some positive strategies for parenting that take into account the child's temperament, see the *Connecting Development to Life* interlude.

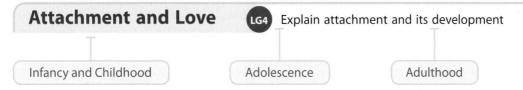

Attachment and Love — **LG4** Explain attachment and its development

Infancy and Childhood   Adolescence   Adulthood

So far, we have discussed how emotions and emotional competence change over the life span. We have also examined the role of emotional style—in effect, we have seen how emotions set the tone of our experiences in life. But emotions also write the lyrics because they are at the core of our relationships with others. Foremost among these relationships is **attachment,** a close emotional bond between two people. In this section, we focus on two types of attachments: the attachment between parents and children and the attachment between romantic partners.

INFANCY AND CHILDHOOD

Before we describe parent-child attachment in detail, we set the stage for its development by exploring the strength of social orientation among infants. We also examine infants' early development of social understanding.

Social Orientation/Understanding   As socioemotional beings, infants show a strong interest in the social world and are motivated to orient to it and understand it. In previous chapters, we described many of the biological and cognitive foundations that contribute to the infant's development of social orientation and understanding. In this chapter we will call attention to relevant biological and cognitive factors as we explore social orientation; locomotion; intention, goal-directed behavior, and cooperation; and social referencing. Discussing biological, cognitive, and social processes together reminds us of an important aspect of development that we considered in Chapter 1: These processes are intricately intertwined (Diamond, Casey, & Munakata, 2011).

Social Orientation   From early in their development, infants are captivated by the social world. As we discussed in our coverage of infant perception in Chapter 5, "Motor, Sensory, and Perceptual Development," young infants stare intently at faces and are attuned to the sounds of human voices, especially those of their caregivers (Ramsey-Rennels & Langlois, 2007). Later, they become adept at interpreting the meaning of facial expressions.

attachment A close emotional bond between two people.

A mother and her baby engaging in face-to-face play. *At what age does face-to-face play usually begin, and when does it typically start decreasing in frequency?*

developmental **connection**

Developmental Theories. The dynamic system view is increasingly used to explain how infants develop. Chapter 5, p. 153

FIGURE **10.8**

THE COOPERATION TASK. The cooperation task consisted of two handles on a box, atop which was an animated musical toy, surreptitiously activated by remote control when both handles were pulled. The handles were placed far enough apart that one child could not pull both handles. The experimenter demonstrated the task, saying, "Watch! If you pull the handles, the doggies will sing" (Brownell, Ramani, & Zerwas, 2006).

Face-to-face play often begins to characterize caregiver-infant interactions when the infant is about 2 to 3 months of age. The focused social interaction of face-to-face play may include vocalizations, touch, and gestures (Leppanen & others, 2007). Such play is part of many mothers' motivation to create a positive emotional state in their infants (Thompson, 2010).

In part because of such positive social interchanges between caregivers and infants, by 2 to 3 months of age infants respond differently to people and objects, showing more positive emotion to people than to inanimate objects such as puppets (Legerstee, 1997). At this age, most infants expect people to react positively when the infants initiate a behavior, such as a smile or a vocalization. This finding has been discovered by use of a method called the *still-face paradigm*, in which the caregiver alternates between engaging in face-to-face interaction with the infant and remaining still and unresponsive (Conradt & Ablow, 2010). As early as 2 to 3 months of age, infants show more withdrawal, negative emotions, and self-directed behavior when their caregivers are still and unresponsive (Adamson & Frick, 2003). The frequency of face-to-face play decreases after 7 months of age as infants become more mobile (Thompson, 2006).

Infants also learn about the social world through contexts other than face-to-face play with a caregiver. Even though infants as young as 6 months of age show an interest in each other, their interaction with peers increases considerably in the second half of the second year. As increasing numbers of U.S. infants experience child care outside the home, they are spending more time in social play with peers. Later in the chapter, we further discuss child care.

Locomotion   Recall from earlier in the chapter how important independence is for infants, especially in the second year of life. As infants develop the ability to crawl, walk, and run, they are able to explore and expand their social world. These newly developed self-produced locomotor skills allow the infant to independently initiate social interchanges on a more frequent basis (Laible & Thompson, 2007). Remember from Chapter 5, "Motor, Sensory, and Perceptual Development," that the development of these gross motor skills is the result of a number of factors, including the development of the nervous system, the goal the infant is motivated to reach, and environmental support for the skill (Adolph & Robinson, 2011).

The infant's and toddler's push for independence also is likely paced by the development of locomotion skills (Campos, 2009). Locomotion is also important for its motivational implications. Once infants have the ability to move in goal-directed pursuits, the reward from these pursuits leads to further efforts to explore and develop skills.

Intention, Goal-Directed Behavior, and Cooperation   Perceiving people as engaging in intentional and goal-directed behavior is an important social cognitive accomplishment that initially occurs toward the end of the first year (Thompson, 2011a). Joint attention and gaze following help the infant to understand that other people have intentions (Meltzoff, 2011; Meltzoff & Brooks, 2009). Recall from Chapter 7, "Information Processing," that *joint attention* occurs when the caregiver and infant focus on the same object or event. By their first birthday, infants have begun to direct the caregiver's attention to objects that capture their interest (Heimann & others, 2006).

One study involved presenting 1- and 2-year-olds with a simple cooperative task that consisted of pulling a lever to get an attractive toy (Brownell, Ramani, & Zerwas, 2006) (see Figure 10.8). Any coordinated actions of the 1-year-olds appeared to be more coincidental than cooperative, whereas the 2-year-olds' behavior was characterized as more actively cooperative efforts to reach a goal. In this study, the infants also were assessed with two social understanding tasks, observation of children's behavior in a joint attention task, and the parents' perceptions of the language the children use about the self and others (Brownell,

Ramani, & Zerwas, 2006). Those with more advanced social understanding were more likely to cooperate. To cooperate, the children had to connect their own intentions with the peer's intentions and put this understanding to use in interacting with the peer to reach a goal.

Social Referencing   Another important social cognitive accomplishment in infancy is developing the ability to "read" the emotions of other people. **Social referencing** is the term used to describe "reading" emotional cues in others to help determine how to act in a specific situation. The development of social referencing helps infants to interpret ambiguous situations more accurately, as when they encounter a stranger and need to know whether or not to fear the person (Kim, Walden, & Knieps, 2010). By the end of the first year, a mother's facial expression—either smiling or fearful—influences whether an infant will explore an unfamiliar environment.

Infants become better at social referencing in the second year of life. At this age, they tend to "check" with their mother before they act; they look at her to see if she is happy, angry, or fearful.

Infants' Social Sophistication and Insight   In sum, researchers are discovering that infants are more socially sophisticated and insightful at younger ages than previously envisioned (Thompson, 2011a, b). Such sophistication and insight are reflected in infants' perceptions of others' actions as intentionally motivated and goal-directed (Brune & Woodward, 2007) and their motivation to share and participate in that intentionality by their first birthday (Carpenter, 2011). The more advanced social cognitive skills of infants could be expected to influence their understanding and awareness of attachment to a caregiver.

What is social referencing? What are some developmental changes in social referencing?

What Is Attachment?   There is no shortage of theories about why infants become attached to a caregiver. Three theorists discussed in Chapter 1—Freud, Erikson, and Bowlby—proposed influential views.

Freud noted that infants become attached to the person or object that provides oral satisfaction. For most infants, this is the mother, since she is most likely to feed the infant. Is feeding as important as Freud thought? A classic study by Harry Harlow (1958) reveals that the answer is no (see Figure 10.9).

social referencing "Reading" emotional cues in others to help determine how to act in a specific situation.

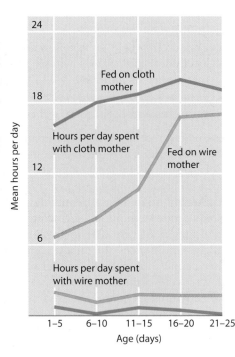

FIGURE **10.9**

CONTACT TIME WITH WIRE AND CLOTH SURROGATE MOTHERS. Regardless of whether the infant monkeys were fed by a wire or a cloth mother, they overwhelmingly preferred to spend contact time with the cloth mother. *How do these results compare with what Freud's theory and Erikson's theory would predict about human infants?*

Harlow removed infant monkeys from their mothers at birth; for six months they were reared by surrogate (substitute) "mothers." One surrogate mother was made of wire, the other of cloth. Half of the infant monkeys were fed by the wire mother, half by the cloth mother. Periodically, the amount of time the infant monkeys spent with either the wire or the cloth mother was computed. Regardless of which mother fed them, the infant monkeys spent far more time with the cloth mother. Even if the wire mother but not the cloth mother provided nourishment, the infant monkeys spent more time with the cloth mother. And when Harlow frightened the monkeys, those "raised" by the cloth mother ran to the mother and clung to it; those raised by the wire mother did not. Whether the mother provided comfort seemed to determine whether the monkeys associated the mother with security. This study clearly demonstrated that feeding is not the crucial element in the attachment process and that contact comfort is important.

Physical comfort also plays a role in Erik Erikson's (1968) view of the infant's development. Recall Erikson's proposal that the first year of life represents the stage of trust versus mistrust. Physical comfort and sensitive care, according to Erikson (1968), are key to establishing a basic trust in infants. The infant's sense of trust, in turn, is the foundation for attachment and sets the stage for a lifelong expectation that the world will be a good and pleasant place to be.

The ethological perspective of British psychiatrist John Bowlby (1969, 1989) also stresses the importance of attachment in the first year of life and the responsiveness of the caregiver. Bowlby stresses that both infants and their primary caregivers are biologically predisposed to form attachments. He argues that the newborn is biologically equipped to elicit attachment behavior. The baby cries, clings, coos, and smiles. Later, the infant crawls, walks, and follows the mother. The immediate result is to keep the primary caregiver nearby; the long-term effect is to increase the infant's chances of survival.

Attachment does not emerge suddenly but rather develops in a series of phases, moving from a baby's general preference for human beings to a partnership with primary caregivers. Following are four such phases based on Bowlby's conceptualization of attachment (Schaffer, 1996):

- *Phase 1: From birth to 2 months.* Infants instinctively direct their attachment to human figures. Strangers, siblings, and parents are equally likely to elicit smiling or crying from the infant.

- *Phase 2: From 2 to 7 months.* Attachment becomes focused on one figure, usually the primary caregiver, as the baby gradually learns to distinguish familiar from unfamiliar people.

- *Phase 3: From 7 to 24 months.* Specific attachments develop. With increased locomotor skills, babies actively seek contact with regular caregivers, such as the mother or father.

- *Phase 4: From 24 months on.* Children become aware of others' feelings, goals, and plans and begin to take these into account in forming their own actions.

Researchers' recent findings that infants are more socially sophisticated and insightful than previously envisioned suggests that some of the characteristics of Bowlby's phase 4, such as understanding the goals and intentions of the attachment figure, appear to be developing in phase 3 as attachment security is taking shape.

Bowlby argued that infants develop an *internal working model* of attachment, a simple mental model of the caregiver, their relationship, and the self as deserving of nurturant care. The infant's internal working model of attachment with the caregiver influences the infant's and later, the child's, subsequent responses to other people. The internal model of attachment also has played a pivotal role in the discovery of links between attachment and subsequent emotion understanding, conscious development, and self-concept. A recent analysis concluded that secure attachment enhances the positive processing of social information (Dykas & Cassidy, 2011).

In Bowlby's model, what are the four phases of attachment?

Strange Situation Ainsworth's observational measure of infant attachment to a caregiver that requires the infant to move through a series of introductions, separations, and reunions with the caregiver and an adult stranger in a prescribed order.

securely attached babies Babies who use the caregiver as a secure base from which to explore the environment.

insecure avoidant babies Babies who show insecurity by avoiding the mother.

insecure resistant babies Babies who might cling to the caregiver, then resist her by fighting against the closeness, perhaps by kicking or pushing away.

insecure disorganized babies Babies who show insecurity by being disorganized and disoriented.

In sum, attachment emerges from the social cognitive advances that allow infants to develop expectations for the caregiver's behavior and to determine the affective quality of their relationship (Thompson, 2010, 2011a). These social cognitive advances include recognizing the caregiver's face, voice, and other features, as well as developing an internal working model of expecting the caregiver to provide pleasure in social interaction and relief from distress.

What is the nature of secure and insecure attachment?

Individual Differences in Attachment   Although attachment to a caregiver intensifies midway through the first year, isn't it likely that the quality of babies' attachment experiences varies? Mary Ainsworth (1979) thought so. Ainsworth created the **Strange Situation,** an observational measure of infant attachment in which the infant experiences a series of introductions, separations, and reunions with the caregiver and an adult stranger in a prescribed order. In using the Strange Situation, researchers hope that their observations will provide information about the infant's motivation to be near the caregiver and the degree to which the caregiver's presence provides the infant with security and confidence.

Based on how babies respond in the Strange Situation, they are described as being securely attached or insecurely attached (in one of three ways) to the caregiver:

- **Securely attached babies** use the caregiver as a secure base from which to explore the environment. When in the presence of their caregiver, securely attached infants explore the room and examine toys that have been placed in it. When the caregiver departs, securely attached infants might protest mildly, and when the caregiver returns these infants reestablish positive interaction with her, perhaps by smiling or climbing on her lap. Subsequently, they often resume playing with the toys in the room.

- **Insecure avoidant babies** show insecurity by avoiding the mother. In the Strange Situation, these babies engage in little interaction with the caregiver, are not distressed when she leaves the room, usually do not reestablish contact with her on her return, and may even turn their back on her. If contact is established, the infant usually leans away or looks away.

- **Insecure resistant babies** often cling to the caregiver and then resist her by fighting against the closeness, perhaps by kicking or pushing away. In the Strange Situation, these babies often cling anxiously to the caregiver and don't explore the playroom. When the caregiver leaves, they often cry loudly and push away if she tries to comfort them on her return.

- **Insecure disorganized babies** are disorganized and disoriented. In the Strange Situation, these babies might appear dazed, confused, and fearful. To be classified as disorganized, babies must show strong patterns of avoidance and resistance or display certain specified behaviors, such as extreme fearfulness around the caregiver.

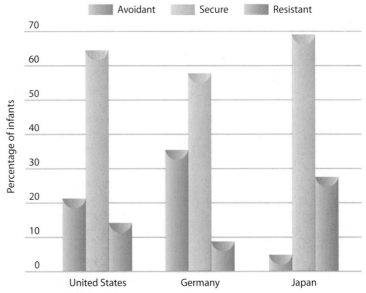

FIGURE **10.10**

CROSS-CULTURAL COMPARISON OF ATTACHMENT. In one study, infant attachment in three countries—the United States, Germany, and Japan—was measured in the Ainsworth Strange Situation (van IJzendoorn & Kroonenberg, 1988). The dominant attachment pattern in all three countries was secure attachment. However, German infants were more avoidant and Japanese infants were less avoidant and more resistant than U.S. infants. *What are some explanations for differences in how German, Japanese, and American infants respond to the Strange Situation?*

Evaluating the Strange Situation   Does the Strange Situation capture important differences among infants? As a measure of attachment, it may be culturally biased. For example, German and Japanese babies often show different patterns of attachment from those of American infants. As illustrated in Figure 10.10, German infants are more likely than U.S. infants to show an avoidant attachment pattern and Japanese infants are less likely than U.S. infants to display this pattern (van IJzendoorn & Kroonenberg, 1988). The avoidant pattern in German babies likely occurs because their caregivers encourage them to be independent (Grossmann & others, 1985). Also as shown in Figure 10.10, Japanese babies are more likely than American babies to be categorized as resistant. This may have more to do with the Strange Situation as a measure of attachment than with attachment insecurity itself. Japanese mothers rarely let anyone unfamiliar with their babies care for them. Thus, the Strange Situation might create considerably more stress for Japanese infants than for American infants, who are more accustomed to separation from their mothers (Miyake, Chen, & Campos, 1985). Even though there are cultural variations in attachment classification, the most frequent classification in every culture studied so far is secure attachment (van IJzendoorn & Kroonenberg, 1988).

Some critics stress that behavior in the Strange Situation—like other laboratory assessments—might not indicate what infants do in a natural environment. But researchers have found that infants' behaviors in the Strange Situation are closely related to how they behave at home in response to separation and reunion with their mothers (Pederson & Moran, 1996). Thus, many infant researchers stress that the Strange Situation continues to show merit as a measure of infant attachment.

Interpreting Differences in Attachment Do individual differences in attachment matter? Ainsworth notes that secure attachment in the first year of life provides an important foundation for psychological development later in life. The securely attached infant moves freely away from the mother but keeps track of where she is through periodic glances. The securely attached infant responds positively to being picked up by others and, when put back down, freely moves away to play. An insecurely attached infant, by contrast, avoids the mother or is ambivalent toward her, fears strangers, and is upset by minor, everyday separations.

If early attachment to a caregiver is important, it should influence a child's social behavior later in development. For some children, early attachments seem to foreshadow later functioning (Fearon & others, 2010; Posada & Kaloustian, 2011). In the extensive longitudinal study conducted by Alan Sroufe and his colleagues (2005; Sroufe, Coffino, & Carlson, 2010), early secure attachment (assessed by the Strange Situation at 12 and 18 months) was linked with positive emotional health, high self-esteem, self-confidence, and socially competent interaction with peers, teachers, camp counselors, and romantic partners through adolescence. Another study found that attachment security at 24 and 36 months was linked to the child's enhanced social problem-solving at 54 months (Raikes & Thompson, 2009). And a recent meta-analysis revealed that disorganized attachment was more strongly linked to externalizing problems (aggression and hostility, for example) than were avoidant and resistant attachment (Fearon & others, 2010).

For some children, though, there is little continuity (Thompson, 2011a). Not all research reveals the power of infant attachment to predict subsequent development. In one longitudinal study, attachment classification in infancy did not predict attachment classification at 18 years of age (Lewis, 1997). In this study, the best predictor of an insecure attachment classification at 18 was the occurrence of parental divorce in the intervening years.

Consistently positive caregiving over a number of years is likely an important factor in connecting early attachment and the child's functioning later in development. Indeed, researchers have found that early secure attachment and subsequent experiences, especially maternal care and life stresses, are linked with children's later behavior and adjustment (Thompson, 2011a).

Some developmentalists note that too much emphasis has been placed on the attachment bond in infancy. Jerome Kagan (2000), for example, emphasizes that infants are highly resilient and adaptive; he argues that they are evolutionarily equipped to stay on a positive developmental course, even in the face of wide variations in parenting. Kagan and others stress that genetic characteristics and temperament play more important roles in a child's social competence than the attachment theorists, such as Bowlby and Ainsworth, are willing to acknowledge (Bakermans-

Kranenburg & others, 2007). For example, if some infants inherit a low tolerance for stress, this, rather than an insecure attachment bond, may be responsible for an inability to get along with peers. A recent study found links between disorganized attachment in infancy, a specific gene, and level of maternal responsiveness. In this study, a disorganized attachment style developed in infancy only when infants had the short version of the serotonin transporter gene—5-*HTTLPR* (Spangler & others, 2009). Infants were not characterized by this attachment style when they had the long version of the gene (Spangler & others 2009). Further, this gene-environment interaction occurred only when mothers showed a low level of responsiveness toward their infants.

Another criticism of attachment theory is that it ignores the diversity of socializing agents and contexts that exists in an infant's world. A culture's value system can influence the nature of attachment (van IJzendoorn & Sagi-Schwartz, 2008). Mothers' expectations for infants to be independent are high in northern Germany, whereas Japanese mothers are more strongly motivated to keep their infants close to them (Grossmann & others, 1985; Rothbaum & others, 2000). Not surprisingly, northern German infants tend to show less distress than Japanese infants when separated from their mother. Also, in some cultures, infants show attachments to many people. Among the Hausa (who live in Nigeria), both grandmothers and siblings provide a significant amount of care for infants (Harkness & Super, 1995). Infants in agricultural societies tend to form attachments to older siblings, who are assigned a major responsibility for younger siblings' care. Researchers recognize the importance of competent, nurturant caregivers in an infant's development (Parke & Clarke-Stewart, 2011). At issue, though, is whether or not secure attachment, especially to a single caregiver, is critical (Lamb, 2010; Thompson, 2009, 2010).

Despite such criticisms, there is ample evidence that security of attachment is important to development (Lamb, 2010; Thompson, 2010, 2011a). Secure attachment in infancy reflects a positive parent-infant relationship and provides the foundation that supports healthy socioemotional development in the years that follow.

Caregiving Styles and Attachment   Is the style of caregiving linked with the quality of the infant's attachment? Securely attached babies have caregivers who are sensitive to their signals and are consistently available to respond to their infants' needs (Bigelow & others, 2010). These caregivers often let their babies have an active part in determining the onset and pacing of interaction in the first year of life. A recent study revealed that maternal sensitivity in responding was linked to infant attachment security (Finger & others, 2009). Another study found that maternal sensitivity in parenting was linked with secure attachment in infants in two different cultures: the United States and Colombia (Posada & others, 2002). Although maternal sensitivity is linked to the development of secure attachment in infancy, however, it is important to note that the relation is not especially strong (Campos, 2009).

How do the caregivers of insecurely attached babies interact with them? Caregivers of avoidant babies tend to be unavailable or rejecting (Posada & Kaloustian, 2011). They often don't respond to their babies' signals and have little physical contact with them. When they do interact with their babies, they may behave in an angry and irritable way. Caregivers of resistant babies tend to be inconsistent; sometimes they respond to their babies' needs, and sometimes they don't. In general, they tend not to be very affectionate with their babies and show little synchrony when interacting with them. Caregivers of disorganized babies often neglect or physically abuse them (Connell-Carrick, 2011; Stonach & others, 2011). In some cases, these caregivers are depressed. In sum, caregivers' interactions with infants influence whether infants are securely or insecurely attached to the caregivers (Sroufe, Coffino, & Carlson, 2010).

Developmental Social Neuroscience and Attachment   In Chapter 1 we described the emerging field of *developmental social neuroscience*, which examines connections between socioemotional processes, development, and the brain. Attachment

developmental **connection**

Nature vs. Nurture. What is involved in gene-environment (G × E) interaction? Chapter 2, p. 62

In the Hausa culture, siblings and grandmothers provide a significant amount of care for infants. *How might these variations in care affect attachment?*

developmental **connection**

Brain Development. Connections are increasingly being made between development, socioemotional processes, and the brain. Chapter 1, p. 13

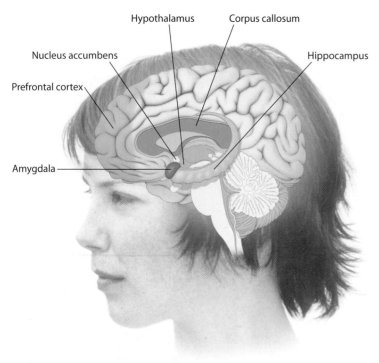

FIGURE 10.11

REGIONS OF THE BRAIN PROPOSED AS LIKELY IMPORTANT IN INFANT-MOTHER ATTACHMENT. This illustration shows the brain's left hemisphere. The corpus callosum is the large bundle of axons that connect the brain's two hemispheres.

is one of the main areas in which theory and research on developmental social neuroscience has focused (Beauchamp & Anderson, 2010; Parsons & others, 2010). These connections of attachment and the brain involve the neuroanatomy of the brain, neurotransmitters, and hormones.

Theory and research on the role of the brain's regions in mother-infant attachment is just emerging (de Haan & Gunnar, 2009). A recent theoretical view proposed that the prefrontal cortex likely has an important role in maternal attachment behavior, as do the subcortical (areas of the brain lower than the cortex) regions of the amygdala (which is strongly involved in emotion) and the hypothalamus (Gonzalez, Atkinson, & Fleming, 2009). An ongoing fMRI longitudinal study is exploring the possibility that different attachment patterns can be distinguished by different patterns of brain activity (Strathearn, 2007).

Research on the role of hormones and neurotransmitters in attachment has emphasized the importance of two neuropeptide hormones—oxytocin and vasopressin—in the formation of the maternal-infant bond (Bales & Carter, 2009). Oxytocin, a mammalian hormone that also acts as a neurotransmitter in the brain, is released during breast feeding and by contact and warmth (Campbell, 2010). Oxytocin is especially thought to be a likely candidate in the formation of infant-mother attachment (Bales & Carter, 2009).

The influence of these neuropeptides on the neurotransmitter dopamine in the nucleus accumbens (a collection of neurons in the forebrain that are involved in pleasure) likely is important in motivating approach to the attachment object (de Haan & Gunnar, 2009). Figure 10.11 shows the regions of the brain we have described that are likely important in infant-mother attachment.

In sum, it is likely that a number of brain regions, neurotransmitters, and hormones are involved in the development of infant-mother attachment. Key candidates for influencing this attachment are connections between the prefrontal cortex, amygdala, and hypothalamus; the neuropeptides oxytocin and vasopressin; and the activity of the neurotransmitter dopamine in the nucleus accumbens.

Mothers and Fathers as Caregivers An increasing number of U.S. fathers stay home full-time with their children (Cohen, 2009; Lamb, 2010). As indicated in Figure 10.12, there was a 300-plus percent increase in stay-at-home fathers in the United States from 1996 to 2006. A large portion of the full-time fathers have career-focused wives who provide most of the family's income. One study revealed that the stay-at-home fathers were as satisfied with their marriage as traditional parents, although they indicated that they missed their daily life in the workplace (Rochlen & others, 2008). In this study, the stay-at-home fathers reported that they tended to be ostracized when they took their children to playgrounds and often were excluded from parent groups.

Can fathers take care of infants as competently as mothers can? Observations of fathers and their infants suggest that fathers have the ability to act as sensitively and responsively as mothers with their infants (Parke & Clarke-Stewart, 2011). Consider the Aka pygmy culture in Africa, where fathers spend as much time interacting with their infants as mothers do (Hewlett, 2000; Hewlett & MacFarlan, 2010). Remember, however, that although fathers can be active, nurturant, involved caregivers with their infants as Aka pygmy fathers do, in many cultures men have not chosen to follow this pattern (Lamb, 2005; Parke & Clarke-Stewart, 2011).

Do fathers behave differently from mothers when interacting with their infants? Maternal interactions usually center on child-care activities—feeding, changing

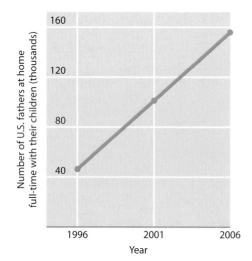

FIGURE 10.12

THE INCREASE IN THE NUMBER OF U.S. FATHERS STAYING AT HOME FULL-TIME WITH THEIR CHILDREN

diapers, bathing. Paternal interactions are more likely to include play (Parke & Clarke-Stewart, 2011). Fathers engage in more rough-and-tumble play than mothers do. They bounce infants, throw them up in the air, tickle them, and so on (Lamb, 2010). Mothers do play with infants, but their play is less physical and arousing than that of fathers.

Child Care   Many U.S. children today experience multiple caregivers. Most do not have a parent staying home to care for them; instead, the children have some type of care provided by others—"child care." Many parents worry that child care will reduce their infants' emotional attachment to them, retard the infants' cognitive development, fail to teach them how to control anger, and allow them to be unduly influenced by their peers. How extensive is child care? Are the worries of these parents justified?

An Aka pygmy father with his infant son. In the Aka culture, fathers were observed to be holding their infants or close to them 47 percent of the time (Hewlett, 1991).

Parental Leave   Today far more young children are in child care than at any other time in history. About 2 million children in the United States currently receive formal, licensed child care, and uncounted millions of children are cared for by unlicensed baby-sitters.

Child-care policies around the world vary in eligibility criteria, leave duration, benefit level, and the extent to which parents take advantage of the policies (Tolani & Brooks-Gunn, 2008). Europe has led the way in creating new standards of parental leave: The European Union (EU) mandated a paid 14-week maternity leave in 1992. In most European countries today, working parents on leave receive from 70 percent of the worker's prior wage to the full wage, and paid leave averages about 16 weeks (Tolani & Brooks-Gunn, 2008). The United States currently allows workers to take up to 12 weeks of unpaid leave to care for a newborn.

Most countries restrict eligibility for maternity benefits to women employed for a minimum time prior to childbirth (Tolani & Brooks-Gunn, 2008). In Denmark, even unemployed mothers are eligible for extended parental leave related to childbirth. In Sweden, parents can take an 18-month job-protected parental leave with benefits allowed to be shared by parents and applied to full-time or part-time work.

How do most fathers and mothers interact differently with infants?

Variations in Child Care   Because the United States does not have a policy of paid leave for child care, child care in the United States has become a major national concern (Belsky, 2009). Many factors influence the effects of child care, including the age of the child, the type of child care, and the quality of the program.

The type of child care varies extensively (Friedman, Melhuish, & Hill, 2011; Phillips & Lowenstein, 2011). Child care is provided in large centers with elaborate facilities and in private homes. Some child-care centers are commercial operations; others are nonprofit centers run by churches, civic groups, and employers. Some child-care providers are professionals; others are mothers who want to earn extra money. Figure 10.13 presents the primary care arrangements for children under 5 years of age with employed mothers (Clarke-Stewart & Miner, 2008).

How are child-care policies in many European countries, such as Sweden, different from those in the United States?

We have all the knowledge necessary to provide absolutely first-rate child care in the United States. What is missing is the commitment and the will.

—EDWARD ZIGLER

Contemporary Developmental Psychologist, Yale University

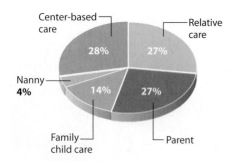

FIGURE 10.13

PRIMARY CARE ARRANGEMENTS IN THE UNITED STATES FOR CHILDREN UNDER 5 YEARS OF AGE WITH EMPLOYED MOTHERS

In the United States, approximately 15 percent of children 5 years of age and younger attend more than one child-care arrangement. A recent study of 2- and 3-year-olds revealed that an increase in the number of child-care arrangements the children experienced was linked to an increase in behavioral problems and a decrease in prosocial behavior (Morrissey, 2009).

What constitutes a high-quality child-care program for infants? In high-quality child care (Clarke-Stewart & Miner, 2008, p. 273):

> . . . caregivers encourage the children to be actively engaged in a variety of activities, have frequent, positive interactions that include smiling, touching, holding, and speaking at the child's eye level, respond properly to the child's questions or requests, and encourage children to talk about their experiences, feelings, and ideas.

High-quality child care also involves providing children with a safe environment, access to age-appropriate toys and participation in age-appropriate activities, and a low caregiver–child ratio that allows caregivers to spend considerable time with children on an individual basis. To read about one individual who provides quality child care to individuals from impoverished backgrounds, see the *Connecting with Careers* profile.

A major, ongoing longitudinal study of U.S. child care was initiated by the National Institute of Child Health and Human Development (NICHD) in 1991. Data were collected on a diverse sample of almost 1,400 children and their families at ten locations across the United States over a period of seven years. Researchers used multiple methods (trained observers, interviews, questionnaires, and testing), and they measured many facets of children's development, including physical health, cognitive development, and socioemotional development. Following are some of the results of what is now referred to as the NICHD Study of Early Child Care and Youth Development, or NICHD SECCYD (NICHD Early Child Care Network, 2001, 2002, 2003, 2004, 2005, 2006).

- *Patterns of use.* Many families placed their infants in child care very soon after the child's birth, and there was considerable instability in the child-care arrangements. By 4 months of age, nearly three-fourths of the infants had entered some form of nonmaternal child care. Almost half of the infants were

connecting with careers

Wanda Mitchell, Child-Care Director

Wanda Mitchell is the Center Director of the Hattie Daniel's Day Care Center in Wilson, North Carolina. Her responsibilities include directing the operation of the center, which involves creating and maintaining an environment in which young children can learn effectively, and for ensuring that the center meets state licensing requirements. Wanda obtained her undergraduate degree from North Carolina A & T University, majoring in Child Development. Prior to her current position, she had been an education coordinator for Project Head Start and an instructor at Wilson Technical Community College. Describing her work, Wanda says, "I really enjoy working in my field. This is my passion. After graduating from college, my goal was to advance in my field."

Wanda Mitchell, child-care director, working with some of the children at her center.

cared for by a relative when they first entered care; only 12 percent were enrolled in child-care centers. Low-income families were more likely than more affluent families to use child care, but infants from low-income families who were in child care averaged as many hours as other income groups. In the preschool years, mothers who were single, those with more education, and families with higher incomes used more hours of center-based care than other families. Minority families and mothers with less education used more hours of care by relatives.

What are some important findings from the national longitudinal study of child care conducted by the National Institute of Child Health and Human Development?

- *Quality of care.* Evaluations of quality of care were based on characteristics such as group size, child–adult ratio, physical environment, caregiver characteristics (such as formal education, specialized training, and child-care experience), and caregiver behavior (such as sensitivity to children). An alarming conclusion is that a majority of the child care in the first three years of life was of unacceptably low quality. Positive caregiving by non-parents in child-care settings was infrequent—only 12 percent of the children studied experienced positive nonparental child care (such as positive talk and language stimulation)! Further, infants from low-income families experienced lower quality of child care than infants from higher-income families. When quality of caregivers' care was high, children performed better on cognitive and language tasks, were more cooperative with their mothers during play, showed more positive and skilled interaction with peers, and had fewer behavior problems. Caregiver training and good child–staff ratios were linked with higher cognitive and social competence when children were 54 months of age. A recent study revealed that higher-quality child care from birth to 4½ years of age was linked to higher cognitive-academic achievement at 15 years of age (Vandell & others, 2010). In this study, early high-quality care also was related to youth reports of less externalizing behavior (lower rates of delinquency, for example).

- *Amount of child care.* In general, when children spent 30 hours or more per week in child care, their development was less than optimal (Ramey, 2005). In a recent study, more hours of early non-relative child care was related to higher levels of risk taking and impulsivity at 15 years of age (Vandell & others, 2010)

- *Family and parenting influences.* The influence of families and parenting was not weakened by extensive child care. Parents played a significant role in helping children to regulate their emotions. Especially important parenting influences were being sensitive to children's needs, being involved with children, and cognitively stimulating them. Indeed, parental sensitivity has been the most consistent predictor of a secure attachment, with child-care experiences being relevant in many cases only when mothers engage in insensitive parenting (Friedman, Melhuish, & Hill, 2011). An important point about the extensive NICHD research is that findings show that family factors are considerably stronger and more consistent predictors of a wide variety of child outcomes than are child-care experiences (such as quality, quantity, and type).

- *Home and Child-Care Settings.* The worst outcomes for children occur when both home and child-care settings are of poor quality. For example, a recent study involving the NICHD SECCYD data revealed that worse socioemotional outcomes (higher levels of problem behavior, lower levels of prosocial behavior) for children occurred when they experienced both home and child-care environments that conferred risk (Watamura & others, 2011).

What are some strategies parents can follow in regard to child care? Child-care expert Kathleen McCartney (2003, p. 4) offered this advice:

- *Recognize that the quality of your parenting is a key factor in your child's development.*
- *Make decisions that will improve the likelihood you will be good parents.* "For some this will mean working full-time"—for personal fulfillment, income, or both. "For others, this will mean working part-time or not working outside the home."
- *Monitor your child's development.* "Parents should observe for themselves whether their children seem to be having behavior problems." They need to talk with their child-care providers and their pediatrician about their child's behavior.
- *Take some time to find the best child care.* Observe different child-care facilities and be certain that you like what you see. "Quality child care costs money, and not all parents can afford the child care they want. However, state subsidies, and other programs like Head Start, are available for families in need."

ADOLESCENCE

Relationships between parents and children continue to be important into the adolescent years. But the adolescent's emotions may become more involved with people outside the family, especially with romantic partners. What do psychologists know about these relationships?

Attachment to Parents   The initial interest in attachment focused on infants and their caregivers. Developmentalists have recently begun to explore the role of secure attachment and related concepts, such as connectedness to parents, during adolescence (Shomaker & Furman, 2009). Secure attachment to parents in adolescence facilitates the adolescent's social competence and well-being, as reflected in such characteristics as self-esteem, emotional adjustment, and physical health. Recent research indicated that the most consistent outcomes of secure attachment in adolescence are positive peer relations and emotional regulation (Allen & Miga, 2010). In other recent research, Joseph Allen and his colleagues (2009) also found that adolescents who were securely attached at 14 years of age were more likely to report that they were in an exclusive relationship, comfortable with intimacy in relationships, and attaining increased financial independence at 21 years of age.

Dating and Romantic Relationships   Adolescents not only have attachments to their parents. Dating and romantic relationships also can lead to attachment. Adolescents spend considerable time either dating or thinking about dating, which has gone far beyond its original courtship function to become a form of recreation, a source of status and achievement, and a setting for learning about close relationships. One function of dating, though, continues to be mate selection.

Types of Dating and Developmental Changes   Three stages characterize the development of romantic relationships in adolescence (Connolly & McIsaac, 2009):

- *Entry into romantic attractions and affiliations at about 11 to 13 years of age.* This initial stage is triggered by puberty. From 11 to 13, adolescents become intensely interested in romance, and it dominates many conversations with same-sex friends. Developing a crush on someone is common, and the crush often is shared with a same-sex friend. Young adolescents may or may not interact with the individual who is the object of their infatuation. When dating occurs, it usually takes place in a group setting.
- *Exploring romantic relationships at approximately 14 to 16 years of age.* At this point in adolescence, two types of romantic involvement occur: casual dating and group dating. Casual dating emerges between individuals who are mutually attracted. These dating experiences are often short-lived, last a few months at

best, and usually endure for only a few weeks. *Dating in groups* is common and reflects embeddedness in the peer context. Friends often act as a third-party facilitator of a potential dating relationship by communicating their friend's romantic interest and confirming whether this attraction is reciprocated.

- *Consolidating dyadic romantic bonds at about 17 to 19 years of age.* At the end of the high school years, more serious romantic relationships develop. This is characterized by strong emotional bonds more closely resembling those in adult romantic relationships. These bonds often are more stable and enduring than earlier bonds, typically lasting one year or more.

What are dating relationships like in adolescence?

Two variations on these stages in the development of romantic relationships in adolescence involve early and late bloomers (Connolly & McIsaac, 2009). Early bloomers include 15 to 20 percent of 11- to 13-year-olds who say that they currently are in a romantic relationship and 35 percent who indicate that they have had some prior experience in romantic relationships. Late bloomers comprise approximately 10 percent of 17- to 19-year-olds who say that they have had no experience with romantic relationships and another 15 percent who report that they have not engaged in any romantic relationships that lasted more than four months.

In their early exploration of romantic relationships, today's adolescents often find comfort in numbers and begin hanging out together in heterosexual groups. Sometimes they just hang out at someone's house or get organized enough to get someone to drive them to a mall or a movie. Indeed, peers play an important role in adolescent romantic relationships. One study also found that young adolescents increase their participation in mixed-gender peer groups (Connolly & others, 2004). This participation was "not explicitly focused on dating but rather brought boys and girls together in settings in which heterosocial interaction might occur but is not obligatory" (p. 201).

Dating and Adjustment   Researchers have linked dating and romantic relationships with various measures of how well adjusted adolescents are (Collins, Welsh, & Furman, 2009). For example, a recent study of 200 tenth-graders revealed that the more romantic experiences they had, the more they reported higher levels of social acceptance, friendship competence, and romantic competence—however, having more romantic experience also was linked with a higher level of substance use, delinquency, and sexual behavior (Furman, Low, & Ho, 2009). Also, among adolescent girls but not adolescent males, having an older romantic partner was linked with an increase in depressive symptoms, largely influenced by an increase in substance use (Haydon & Halpern, 2010). Dating and romantic relationships at an early age can be especially problematic (Connolly & McIsaac, 2009). Researchers have found that early dating and "going with" someone are linked with adolescent pregnancy and problems at home and school (Florsheim, Moore, & Edgington, 2003).

developmental **connection**

Sexuality. Early sexual intercourse is linked with a number of negative developmental outcomes. Chapter 12, p. 395

Sociocultural Contexts and Dating   The sociocultural context is a strong influence on adolescents' dating patterns. Values and religious beliefs of various cultures often dictate the age at which dating begins, how much freedom in dating is allowed, whether dates must be chaperoned by adults or parents, and the roles of males and females in dating. For example, Latino and Asian American cultures have more conservative standards regarding adolescent dating than does the Anglo-American culture.

Dating may be a source of cultural conflict for many adolescents whose families come from cultures in which dating begins at a late age with little freedom, especially for adolescent girls. One study found that Asian American adolescents were less likely to have been involved in a romantic relationship in the past 18 months than African American or Latino adolescents (Carver, Joyner, & Udry, 2003). In another study, Latina young adults in the midwestern United States reflected on their dating experiences during adolescence (Raffaelli & Ontai, 2001). They said that their parents placed strict boundaries on their romantic involvement. As a result, the young women recalled that their adolescent dating experiences were filled with tension and conflict. Over half of the Latinas engaged in "sneak dating" without their parents' knowledge.

ADULTHOOD

Attachment and romantic relationships continue to be very important aspects of close relationships in adulthood. Let's explore attachment first, then different types of love.

Attachment   Earlier in this chapter, we discussed the importance of attachment in childhood and adolescence (Posada & Kaloustian, 2011; Sroufe, Coffino, & Carlson, 2010). How do these earlier patterns of attachment and adults' attachment styles influence the lives of adults?

Although relationships with romantic partners differ from those with parents, romantic partners fulfill some of the same needs for adults as parents do for their children (Mikulincer & others, 2010). Recall that *securely attached* infants are defined as those who use the caregiver as a secure base from which to explore the environment (Cassidy, 2008). Similarly, adults may count on their romantic partners to be a secure base to which they can return and obtain comfort and security in stressful times (Zeifman & Hazan, 2008).

Do adult attachment patterns with partners reflect childhood attachment patterns with parents? In a retrospective study, Cindy Hazan and Phillip Shaver (1987) revealed that young adults who were securely attached in their romantic relationships were more likely to describe their early relationship with their parents as securely attached. In a longitudinal study, infants who were securely attached at 1 year of age were securely attached 20 years later in their adult romantic relationships (Steele & others, 1998). However, in another longitudinal study, links between early attachment styles and later attachment styles were lessened by stressful and disruptive experiences, such as the death of a parent or instability of caregiving (Lewis, Feiring, & Rosenthal, 2000).

How are attachment patterns in childhood linked to relationships in early adulthood? How is attachment in adulthood assessed?

Hazan and Shaver (1987) measured attachment styles using the following brief assessment:

Read each paragraph and then place a check mark next to the one that best describes your interactions with others:

_____ **1.** I find it relatively easy to get close to others and I am comfortable depending on them and having them depend on me. I don't worry about being abandoned or about someone getting too close to me.

_____ **2.** I am somewhat uncomfortable being close to others. I find it difficult to trust them completely and to allow myself to depend on them. I get nervous when anyone gets too close to me and it bothers me when someone tries to be more intimate with me than I feel comfortable with.

_____ **3.** I find that others are reluctant to get as close as I would like. I often worry that my partner doesn't really love me or won't want to stay with me. I want to get very close to my partner, and this sometimes scares people away.

What are some key dimensions of attachment in adulthood, and how are they related to relationship patterns and well-being?

These items correspond to three attachment styles—secure attachment (option 1 in the list) and two insecure attachment styles (avoidant—option 2, and anxious—option 3):

- **Secure attachment style.** Securely attached adults have positive views of relationships, find it easy to get close to others, and are not overly concerned with, or stressed out about, their romantic relationships. These adults tend to enjoy sexuality in the context of a committed relationship and are less likely than others to have one-night stands.

- **Avoidant attachment style.** Avoidant individuals are hesitant about getting involved in romantic relationships and once in a relationship tend to distance themselves from their partner.

- **Anxious attachment style.** These individuals demand closeness, are less trusting, and are more emotional, jealous, and possessive.

The majority of adults (about 60 to 80 percent) describe themselves as securely attached, and not surprisingly adults prefer having a securely attached partner (Zeifman & Hazan, 2009).

Researchers are studying links between adults' current attachment styles and many aspects of their lives (Mikulincer & others, 2010). For example, securely attached adults are more satisfied with their close relationships than insecurely attached adults, and the relationships of securely attached adults are more likely to be characterized by trust, commitment, and longevity (Feeney & Monin, 2008). A recent study of 18- to 25-year-olds revealed that attachment security predicted the perceived quality of romantic relationships (Holland & Roisman, 2010). Another recent study found that attachment-anxious individuals showed strong ambivalence toward a romantic partner (Mikulincer & others, 2010). Also, a study of 18- to 20-year-olds revealed that recent secure attachment to parents was linked to ease in forming friendships in college (Parade, Leerkes, & Blankson, 2010). A national survey indicated that insecure attachment in adults was associated with the development of disease and chronic illness, especially cardiovascular problems such as high blood pressure, heart attack, and stroke (McWilliams & Bailey, 2010). And a research review of 10,000 adult attachment interviews found that attachment insecurity was related to depression (Bakermans-Kranenburg & van IJzendoorn, 2009).

Recent research reviews conclude that attachment insecurity places couples at risk for relationship problems (Mikulincer & Shaver, 2008; Shaver & Mikulincer, 2012). For example, when an anxious individual is paired with an avoidant individual, the anxious partner's needs and demands frustrate the avoidant partner's preference for distance in the relationship; the avoidant partner's need for distance

secure attachment style An attachment style that describes adults who have positive views of relationships, find it easy to get close to others, and are not overly concerned or stressed out about their romantic relationships.

avoidant attachment style An attachment style that describes adults who are hesitant about getting involved in romantic relationships and, once in a relationship, tend to distance themselves from their partner.

anxious attachment style An attachment style that describes adults who demand closeness, are less trusting, and are more emotional, jealous, and possessive.

causes stress for the anxious partner's need for closeness. The result: Both partners are unhappy in the relationship, and the anxious-avoidant pairing can produce abuse or violence when a partner criticizes or tries to change the other's behavior. Researchers also have found that when both partners have an anxious attachment pattern, the pairing usually produces dissatisfaction with the marriage and can lead to a mutual attack and retreat in the relationship (Feeney & Monin, 2008). When both partners have an anxious attachment style, they feel misunderstood and rejected, excessively dwell on their own insecurities, and seek to control the other's behavior (Shaver & Mikulincer, 2012).

If you have an insecure attachment style, are you stuck with it and does it doom you to have problematic relationships? Attachment categories are somewhat stable in adulthood, but adults do have the capacity to change their attachment thinking and behavior. It also is important to note that although attachment insecurities are linked to relationship problems, attachment style makes only a moderate-size contribution to relationship functioning and that other factors such as communication skills, effectively dealing with conflict, friendship, and personality traits such as conscientiousness and emotional instability contribute to relationship satisfaction and success (Shaver & Mikulincer, 2012).

Romantic Love Think for a moment about songs and books that hit the top of the charts. Chances are, they're about love. Poets, playwrights, and musicians through the ages have lauded the fiery passion of romantic love—and lamented the searing pain when it fails. **Romantic love** is also called *passionate love* or *eros*; it has strong components of sexuality and infatuation, and it often predominates in the early part of a love relationship.

Well-known love researcher Ellen Berscheid (1988) says that romantic love is what we mean when we say that we are "in love" with someone. It is romantic love, she stresses, that we need to understand if we are to learn what love is all about. According to Berscheid, sexual desire is the most important ingredient of romantic love. We discuss sexuality in more detail in Chapter 12, "Gender and Sexuality."

Romantic love includes a complex intermingling of emotions—fear, anger, sexual desire, joy, and jealousy, for example. Obviously, some of these emotions are a source of anguish. One study found that romantic lovers were more likely than friends to be the cause of depression (Berscheid & Fei, 1977).

Recently, romantic attraction has not only taken place in person but also over the Internet. More than 16 million individuals in the United States and 14 million in China have tried online matchmaking (Masters, 2008). Some critics argue that online romantic relationships lose the interpersonal connection, whereas others emphasize that the Internet may benefit shy or anxious individuals who find it difficult to meet potential partners in person (Holmes, Little, & Welsh, 2009). One problem with online matchmaking is that many individuals misrepresent their characteristics, such as how old they are, how attractive they are, and their occupation. Despite such dishonesty, researchers have found that romantic relationships initiated on the Internet are more likely than relationships established in person to last for more than two years (Bargh & McKenna, 2004).

Affectionate Love Love is more than just passion. **Affectionate love,** also called companionate love, is the type of love that occurs when individuals desire to have the other person near and have a deep, caring affection for the person.

There is a growing belief that as love matures, passion tends to give way to affection (Sternberg & Sternberg, 2010). One investigation interviewed 102 happily married couples in early (average age 28), middle (average age 45), and late (average age 65) adulthood to explore the nature of age and sex differences in satisfying love relationships (Reedy, Birren, & Schaie, 1981). As indicated in Figure 10.14, communication and sexual intimacy were more important in early adulthood, and feelings of emotional security and loyalty were more important in later-life love

Love is a canvas furnished by nature and embroidered by imagination.

—Voltaire
French Essayist, 18th Century

developmental **connection**

Sexuality. At the beginning of emerging adulthood, more than 60 percent of individuals have experienced sexual intercourse. Chapter 12, p. 395

romantic love Also called passionate love, or *eros*, this type of love has strong components of sexuality and infatuation, and it often predominates in the early part of a love relationship.

affectionate love Also called companionate love, this type of love occurs when individuals desire to have another person near and have a deep, caring affection for the person.

triangular theory of love Sternberg's theory that love includes three components or dimensions—passion, intimacy, and commitment.

relationships. Young adult lovers also rated communication as more characteristic of their love than their older counterparts. Aside from the age differences, however, there were some striking similarities in the nature of satisfying love relationships. At all ages, emotional security was ranked as the most important factor in love, followed by respect, communication, help and play behaviors, sexual intimacy, and loyalty. The findings in this research also suggested that women believe emotional security is more important in love than men do.

Sternberg's Triangular Theory of Love

Clearly, there is more to satisfying love relationships than sex (Berscheid, 2010). One theory of love that captures this idea was proposed by Robert J. Sternberg (1988). His **triangular theory of love** states that love has three main components or dimensions—passion, intimacy, and commitment (see Figure 10.15):

- *Passion*, as described earlier, is physical and sexual attraction to another.
- *Intimacy* is the emotional feelings of warmth, closeness, and sharing in a relationship.
- *Commitment* is our cognitive appraisal of the relationship and our intent to maintain the relationship even in the face of problems.

According to Sternberg, if passion is the only ingredient (with intimacy and commitment low or absent), we are merely experiencing infatuation. This might happen in an affair or a one-night stand. But varying combinations of the dimensions of love create three qualitatively different types of love:

- A relationship marked by intimacy and commitment but low or lacking in passion is called *affectionate love,* a pattern often found among couples who have been married for many years.
- If passion and commitment are present but intimacy is not, Sternberg calls the relationship *fatuous love,* as when one person worships another from a distance.
- If passion, intimacy, and commitment are all strong, the result is *consummate love*, the fullest type of love.

Falling Out of Love

The collapse of a close relationship may feel tragic. In the long run, however, our happiness and personal development may benefit from getting over being in love and ending a close relationship.

In particular, falling out of love may be wise if you are obsessed with a person who repeatedly betrays your trust; if you are involved with someone who is draining you emotionally or financially; or if you are desperately in love with someone who does not return your feelings.

Being in love when love is not returned can lead to depression, obsessive thoughts, sexual dysfunction, inability to work effectively, difficulty in making new friends, and self-condemnation. Thinking clearly in such relationships is often difficult, because they are so colored by arousing emotions.

Some people get taken advantage of in relationships (Duck, 2011; Metts & Cupach, 2007). For example, without either person realizing it, a relationship can evolve in a way that creates dominant and submissive roles. Detecting this pattern is an important step toward learning either to reconstruct the relationship or to end it if the problems cannot be worked out. What other types of personal growth can follow romantic relationship breakups? To find out more about this aspect of relationships, see the *Connecting with Research* interlude.

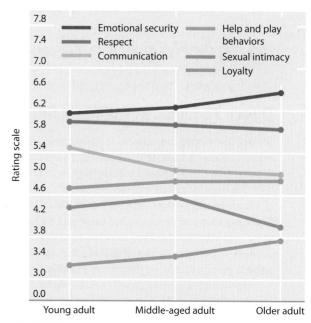

FIGURE **10.14**

CHANGES IN SATISFYING LOVE RELATIONSHIPS ACROSS THE ADULT YEARS. In the investigation by Reedy, Birren, and Schaie (1981), emotional security was the most important factor in love at all ages. Sexual intimacy was more important in early adulthood, whereas emotional security and loyalty were more important in the love relationships of older adults. Young adult lovers also rated communication as more important in a love relationship than their older counterparts.

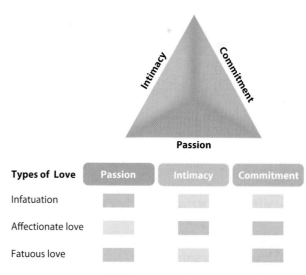

FIGURE **10.15**

STERNBERG'S TRIANGLE OF LOVE. Sternberg identified three dimensions that shape the experience we call love: passion, intimacy, and commitment. Various combinations of the three dimensions produce particular types of love.

Does a Romantic Relationship Breakup Present an Opportunity for Personal Growth?

Studies of romantic breakups have mainly focused on their negative aspects (Frazier & Cook, 1993; Kato, 2005). Few studies have examined the possibility that a romantic breakup might lead to positive changes.

One study assessed the personal growth that can follow the breakup of a romantic relationship (Tashiro & Frazier, 2003). The participants were 92 undergraduate students who had experienced a relationship breakup in the past nine months. They were asked to describe "what positive changes, if any, have happened as a result of your breakup that might serve to improve your future romantic relationships" (p. 118).

Self-reported positive growth was common following a romantic breakup. Changes were categorized in terms of personal, relational,

and environmental changes. The most commonly reported types of growth were personal changes, which included feeling stronger and more self-confident, more independent, and better off emotionally. Relational positive changes included gaining relational wisdom, and environmental positive changes included having better friendships because of the breakup. Figure 10.16 provides examples of these positive changes. Women reported more positive growth than did men.

What other aspects of romantic dissolution might be interesting to study?

FIGURE **10.16**

EXAMPLES OF POSITIVE CHANGES IN THE AFTERMATH OF A ROMANTIC BREAKUP

Change Category	Examples of Frequently Mentioned Responses
Personal positives	1. "I am more self-confident." 2. "Through breaking up I found I could handle more on my own." 3. "I didn't always have to be the strong one, it's okay to cry or be upset without having to take care of him."
Relational positives	1. "Better communication." 2. "I learned many relationship skills that I can apply in the future (for example, the importance of saying you're sorry)." 3. "I know not to jump into a relationship too quickly."
Environmental positives	1. "I rely on my friends more. I forgot how important friends are when I was with him." 2. "Concentrate on school more: I can put so much more time and effort toward school." 3. "I believe friends' and family's opinions count—will seek them out in future relationships."

Review *Connect* Reflect

 LG4 Explain attachment and its development

Review

- What is attachment? How does attachment develop in infancy and childhood? How are caregiving styles related to attachment? How is child care related to children's development?
- How does attachment develop in adolescence? What is the nature of dating and romantic relationships in adolescence?
- What are attachment and love like across the adulthood years?

Connect

- How is attachment similar or different in infancy and adolescence?

Reflect *Your Own Personal Journey of Life*

- How would you describe your attachment style? Why do you think you developed this attachment style?

reach your **learning goals**

Exploring Emotion

What Are Emotions?

Regulation of Emotion

Emotional Competence

LG1 Discuss basic aspects of emotion

- Emotion is feeling, or affect, that expresses the pleasantness or unpleasantness of a person's state; it occurs when a person is engaged in an interaction that is important to him or her, especially to his or her well-being. Emotions can be classified as positive or negative and vary in intensity. Darwin described the evolutionary basis of emotions, and today psychologists note that emotions, especially facial expressions of emotions, have a biological foundation. Facial expressions of emotion are similar across cultures but display rules are not culturally universal. Biological evolution endowed humans to be emotional, but culture and relationships with others provides diversity in emotional experiences.

- The ability to control one's emotions is a key dimension of development. Emotional regulation consists of effectively managing arousal to adapt and reach a goal. In infancy and early childhood, regulation of emotion gradually shifts from external sources to self-initiated, internal sources. Also with increasing age, children are more likely to increase their use of cognitive strategies for regulating emotion, modulate their emotional arousal, become more adept at managing situations to minimize negative emotion, and choose effective ways to cope with stress. Emotion-coaching parents have children who engage in more effective self-regulation of their emotions than do emotion-dismissing parents.

- Saarni argues that becoming emotionally competent involves developing a number of skills such as being aware of one's emotional states, discerning others' emotions, adaptively coping with negative emotions, and understanding the role of emotions in relationships.

Development of Emotion

Infancy

Early Childhood

Middle and Late Childhood

Adolescence

LG2 Describe the development of emotion through the life span

- Infants display a number of emotions early in the first six months, including sadness, surprise, interest, joy, fear, and anger—although researchers debate the onset and sequence of these emotions. Lewis distinguishes between primary emotions and self-conscious emotions. Crying is the most important mechanism newborns have for communicating with their world. Babies have at least three types of cries—basic, anger, and pain cries. Controversy surrounds the question of whether babies should be soothed when they cry, although increasingly experts recommend immediately responding in a caring way in the first year. Social smiling in response to a caregiver's voice occurs as early as 4 weeks of age. Two fears that infants develop are stranger anxiety and separation from a caregiver (which is reflected in separation protest).

- Young children's range of emotions expands during early childhood as they increasingly experience self-conscious emotions such as pride, shame, and guilt. Between 2 and 4 years of age, children use an increasing number of terms to describe emotion and learn more about the causes and consequences of feelings. At 4 to 5 years of age, children show an increased ability to reflect on emotions and understand that a single event can elicit different emotions in different people.

- In middle and late childhood, children show a growing awareness about controlling and managing emotions to meet social standards. Also in this age period, they show improved emotional understanding, markedly improve their ability to suppress or conceal negative emotions, use self-initiated strategies for redirecting feelings, have an increased tendency to take into fuller account the events that lead to emotional reactions, and develop a genuine capacity for empathy.

- As individuals go through early adolescence, they are less likely to report being very happy. Moodiness is a normal aspect of early adolescence. Although pubertal change is associated with an increase in negative emotions, hormonal influences are often small, and environmental experiences may contribute more to the emotions of adolescence than hormonal changes.

- Older adults are better at controlling their emotions than younger adults are, and older adults experience more positive and less negative emotions than younger adults do. An important theory regarding developmental changes in emotion during adulthood, especially late adulthood, is Carstensen's socioemotional selectivity theory. Knowledge-related and emotion-related goals change across the life span; emotion-related goals become more important when individuals get older.

Temperament

LG3 Characterize variations in temperament and their significance

Describing and Classifying Temperament

Biological Foundations and Experience

Goodness of Fit and Parenting

- Temperament is an individual's behavioral style and characteristic way of emotional responding. Developmentalists are especially interested in the temperament of infants. Chess and Thomas classified infants as (1) easy, (2) difficult, or (3) slow to warm up. Kagan argues that inhibition to the unfamiliar is an important temperament category. Rothbart and Bates' view of temperament emphasizes this classification: (1) extraversion/surgency, (2) negative affectivity, and (3) effortful control (self-regulation).

- Physiological characteristics are associated with different temperaments, and a moderate influence of heredity has been found in studies of the heritability of temperament. Children inherit a physiology that biases them to have a particular type of temperament, but through experience they learn to modify their temperament style to some degree. Very active young children are likely to become outgoing adults. In some cases, a difficult temperament is linked with adjustment problems in early adulthood. The link between childhood temperament and adult personality depends in part on context, which helps shape the reaction to a child and thus the child's experiences. For example, the reaction to a child's temperament depends in part on the child's culture.

- Goodness of fit refers to the match between a child's temperament and the environmental demands the child must cope with. Goodness of fit can be an important aspect of a child's adjustment. Although research evidence is sketchy at this time, some general recommendations are that caregivers should (1) be sensitive to the individual characteristics of the child, (2) be flexible in responding to these characteristics, and (3) avoid negative labeling of the child.

Attachment and Love

LG4 Explain attachment and its development

Infancy and Childhood

- Infants show a strong interest in the social world and are motivated to understand it. Infants orient to the social world early in their development. Face-to-face play with a caregiver begins to occur at about 2 to 3 months of age. Newly developed self-produced locomotion skills significantly expand the infant's ability to initiate social interchanges and explore its social world more independently. Perceiving people as engaging in intentional and goal-directed behavior is an important social cognitive accomplishment that occurs toward the end of the first year. Social referencing increases in the second year of life.

    Attachment is a close emotional bond between two people. In infancy, contact comfort and trust are important in the development of attachment. Bowlby's ethological theory stresses that the caregiver and the infant are biologically predisposed to form an attachment. Attachment develops in four phases during infancy. Securely attached babies use the caregiver, usually the mother, as a secure base from which to explore the environment.

    Three types of insecure attachment are avoidant, resistant, and disorganized. Ainsworth created the Strange Situation, an observational measure of attachment. Ainsworth notes that secure attachment in the first year of life provides an important foundation for psychological development later in life. The strength of the link between early attachment and later development has varied somewhat across studies.

    Some critics argue that attachment theorists have not given adequate attention to genetics and temperament. Other critics stress that they have not adequately taken into account the diversity of social agents and contexts.

Adult Development and Aging

Cultural variations in attachment have been found, but in all cultures studied to date secure attachment is the most common classification. Caregivers of secure babies are sensitive to the babies' signals and are consistently available to meet their needs. Caregivers of avoidant babies tend to be unavailable or rejecting. Caregivers of resistant babies tend to be inconsistently available to their babies and usually are not very affectionate. Caregivers of disorganized babies often neglect or physically abuse their babies.

The mother's primary role when interacting with the infant is caregiving; the father's is playful interaction. More U.S. children are in child care now than at any earlier point in history. The quality of child care is uneven, and child care remains a controversial topic. Quality child care can be achieved and seems to have few adverse effects on children. In the NICHD child-care study, infants from low-income families were more likely to receive the lowest quality of care. Also, higher quality of child care was linked with fewer child problems.

Adolescence

- Securely attached adolescents show more competent behavior than their insecurely attached counterparts, with the most consistent outcomes involving positive peer relations and emotional regulation. Dating, or thinking about dating, becomes an important aspect of many adolescents' lives. Early dating is associated with developmental problems. Culture can exert a powerful influence on dating.

Adulthood

- Three adult attachment styles are insecure attachment, avoidant attachment, and anxious attachment. Attachment styles in early adulthood are linked with a number of relationship patterns and developmental outcomes. For example, securely attached adults often show more positive relationship patterns than insecurely attached adults. Also, adults with avoidant and anxious attachment styles tend to be more depressed and have more relationship problems than securely attached adults. Romantic love and affectionate love are two important types of love. Romantic love tends to be more important in early adulthood; affectionate love is more likely to be important in later-life love relationships. Sternberg proposed a triangular theory of love that focuses on different combinations of (1) passion, (2) intimacy, and (3) commitment. The collapse of a close relationship can be traumatic, but for some individuals it results in increased self-confidence, relational wisdom, and being better off emotionally. For most individuals, falling out of love is painful and emotionally intense.

key terms

emotion 301	separation protest 306	attachment 317	secure attachment style 331
primary emotions 304	socioemotional selectivity theory 310	social referencing 319	avoidant attachment style 331
self-conscious emotions 304		Strange Situation 321	
basic cry 305	temperament 312	securely attached babies 321	anxious attachment style 331
anger cry 305	easy child 312	insecure avoidant babies 321	
pain cry 305	difficult child 312	insecure resistant babies 321	romantic love 332
reflexive smile 305	slow-to-warm-up child 312		affectionate love 332
social smile 305		insecure disorganized babies 321	triangular theory of love 333
stranger anxiety 306	goodness of fit 315		

key people

Ross Thompson 302	John Bowlby 307	Mary Rothbart and John Bates 313	Cindy Hazan and Phillip Shaver 330
Carolyn Saarni 303	Reed Larson and Maryse Richards 310	Harry Harlow 319	Ellen Berscheid 332
Joseph Campos 304	Laura Carstensen 310	Erik Erikson 320	Robert J. Sternberg 333
Michael Lewis 304	Alexander Chess and Stella Thomas 312	Mary Ainsworth 321	
Daniel Messinger 306		Alan Sroufe 322	
John Watson 307	Jerome Kagan 313	Kathleen McCartney 328	
Mary Ainsworth 307			

THE SELF, IDENTITY, AND PERSONALITY

preview

Think about yourself for a few moments. Who are you? What are you like as a person? This chapter seeks to answer such questions by exploring the self, identity, and personality. We will examine these dimensions of people at different points in the human life span, from infancy through late adulthood.

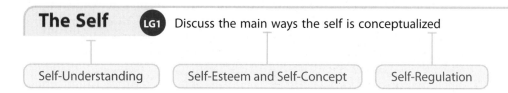

The Self **LG1** Discuss the main ways the self is conceptualized

Self-Understanding   Self-Esteem and Self-Concept   Self-Regulation

What do we mean by the concepts of self, identity, and personality? Here are the definitions, and as you will see, there is considerable overlap among them:

- The **self** consists of all of the characteristics of a person.
- **Identity** is who a person is, representing a synthesis and integration of self-understanding.
- **Personality** refers to the enduring personal characteristics of individuals. Personality is usually viewed as the broadest of the three domains and as encompassing the other two (self and identity).

Theorists and researchers who focus on the self usually argue that the self is the central aspect of the individual's personality and that the self lends an integrative dimension to our understanding of different personality characteristics (Thompson & Goodman, 2011; Thompson, Winer, & Goodvin, 2011). Several aspects of the self have been studied more than others. These include self-understanding, self-esteem, and self-concept. Let's now turn our attention to how these aspects of the self develop across the human life span.

> When I say "I," I mean something absolutely unique and not to be confused with any other.
>
> —UGO BETTI,
> *Italian Playwright, 20th Century*

SELF-UNDERSTANDING

What is self-understanding? **Self-understanding** is the cognitive representation of the self, the substance of self-conceptions. For example, an 11-year-old boy understands that he is a student, a boy, a football player, a family member, a video game lover, and a rock music fan. A 13-year-old girl understands that she is a middle school student, in the midst of puberty, a girl, a soccer player, a student council member, and a movie fan. Self-understanding is based, in part, on roles and membership categories (Harter, 2006). It provides the underpinnings for the development of identity. How does self-understanding develop across the life span?

Infancy   Studying the self in infancy is difficult mainly because infants cannot tell us how they experience themselves. Infants cannot verbally express their views of the self. They also cannot understand complex instructions from researchers.

A rudimentary form of self-recognition—being attentive and positive toward one's image in a mirror—appears as early as 3 months of age (Mascolo & Fischer, 2007). However, a central, more complete index of self-recognition—the ability to recognize one's physical features—does not emerge until the second year (Thompson, 2006).

One ingenious strategy to test infants' visual self-recognition is the use of a mirror technique, in which first an infant's mother puts a dot of rouge on the infant's nose. Then an observer watches to see how often the infant touches its nose. Next, the infant is placed in front of a mirror, and observers detect whether nose touching increases. Why does this matter? The idea is that increased nose

self All of the characteristics of a person.

identity Who a person is, representing a synthesis and integration of self-understanding.

personality The enduring personal characteristics of individuals.

self-understanding The individual's cognitive representation of the self, the substance of self-conceptions.

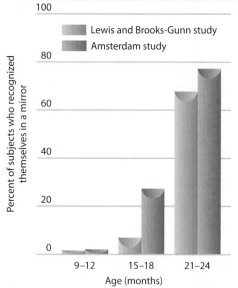

FIGURE **11.1**

THE DEVELOPMENT OF SELF-RECOGNITION IN INFANCY. The graph shows the findings of two studies in which infants less than 1 year of age did not recognize themselves in the mirror. A slight increase in the percentage of infant self-recognition occurred around 15 to 18 months of age. By 2 years of age, a majority of children recognized themselves. *Why do researchers study whether infants recognize themselves in a mirror?*

touching indicates that the infant recognizes the self in the mirror and is trying to touch or rub off the rouge because the rouge violates the infant's view of the self. Increased touching indicates that the infant realizes that it is the self in the mirror but that something is not right since the real self does not have a dot of rouge on it.

Figure 11.1 displays the results of two investigations that used the mirror technique. The researchers found that before they were 1 year old, infants did not recognize themselves in the mirror (Amsterdam, 1968; Lewis & Brooks-Gunn, 1979). Signs of self-recognition began to appear among some infants when they were 15 to 18 months old. By the time they were 2 years old, most children recognized themselves in the mirror. In sum, infants begin to develop a self-understanding called self-recognition at approximately 18 months of age (Hart & Karmel, 1996).

In one study, biweekly assessments from 15 to 23 months of age were conducted (Courage, Edison, & Howe, 2004). Self-recognition gradually emerged over this time, first appearing in the form of mirror recognition, followed by use of the personal pronoun "me" and then by recognizing a photo of themselves. These aspects of self-recognition are often referred to as the first indications of toddlers' understanding of the mental state of "me"—"that they are objects in their own mental representation of the world" (Lewis, 2005, p. 363).

Late in the second year and early in the third year, toddlers show other emerging forms of self-awareness that reflect a sense of "me" (Laible & Thompson, 2007). For example, they refer to themselves by saying "Me big"; they label internal experiences such as emotions; they monitor themselves, as when a toddler says, "Do it myself"; and they say that things are theirs (Bullock & Lutkenhaus, 1990; Fasig, 2000). A recent study revealed that it is not until the second year that infants develop a conscious awareness of their own bodies (Brownell & others, 2009). This developmental change in body awareness marks the beginning of children's representation of their own three-dimensional body shape and appearance, providing an early step in the development of their self-image and identity (Brownell, 2009).

Early Childhood   Recent research studies have revealed that young children are more psychologically aware—of themselves and others—than used to be thought (Carpendale & Lewis, 2010; Hughes & Ensor, 2010; Thompson, Winer, & Goodvin, 2011). This increased psychological awareness reflects young children's expanding psychological sophistication.

Self-Understanding   Because children can verbally communicate, research on self-understanding in childhood is not limited to visual self-recognition, as it is during infancy. Mainly through interviews, researchers have probed many aspects of children's self-understanding. Here are five main characteristics of self-understanding in young children:

- *Confusion of self, mind, and body*. Young children generally confuse self, mind, and body. Most young children conceive of the self as part of the body, which usually means the head. For them, the self can be described along many material dimensions, such as size, shape, and color.

- *Concrete descriptions*. Preschool children mainly think of themselves and define themselves in concrete terms. A young child might say, "I know my ABC's," "I can count," and "I live in a big house" (Harter, 2006). Although young children mainly describe themselves in terms of concrete, observable features and action tendencies, at about 4 to 5 years of age, as they hear others use psychological trait and emotion terms, they begin to include these in their own self-descriptions (Thompson, 2006). Thus, in a self-description, a 4-year-old might say, "I'm not scared. I'm always happy."

- *Physical descriptions*. Young children also distinguish themselves from others through many physical and material attributes. Says 4-year-old Sandra, "I'm different from Jennifer because I have brown hair and she has blond hair."

Says 4-year-old Ralph, "I am different from Hank because I am taller, and I am different from my sister because I have a bicycle."

- *Active descriptions.* The active *dimension* is a central component of the self in early childhood. For example, preschool children often describe themselves in terms of activities such as play.

- *Unrealistic positive overestimations.* Self-evaluations during early childhood are often unrealistically positive and represent an overestimation of personal attributes (Harter, 2006). A young child might say, "I know all of my ABC's" but does not; or might comment, "I'm never scared," which is not the case. These unrealistic positive overestimations of the self occur because young children (1) have difficulty in differentiating their desired and actual competence, (2) cannot yet generate an ideal self that is distinguished from a real self, and (3) rarely engage in *social comparison*—how they compare with others. Young children's self-evaluations also reflect an inability to recognize that they can possess opposite attributes, such as "good" and "bad" or "nice" and "mean" (Harter, 2006).

Young children's self-descriptions are typically unrealistically positive, as reflected in the comment of the 4-year-old above who says he is always happy, which he is not (Harter, 2006). These occur because the children don't yet distinguish between their desired competence and their actual competence, tend to confuse ability and effort (thinking that differences in ability can be changed as easily as can differences in effort), don't engage in spontaneous social comparison of their abilities with those of others, and tend to compare their present abilities with what they could do at an earlier age (which usually makes their abilities look quite good).

What characterizes young children's self-understanding?

Understanding Others   Children also make advances in their understanding of others in early childhood (Lewis & Carpendale, 2011; Thompson, Winer, & Goodvin, 2011; Schneider & others, 2011). As we saw in Chapter 7, young children's theory of mind includes understanding that other people have emotions and desires. And, at about 4 to 5 years, children not only start describing themselves in terms of psychological traits, but they also begin to perceive others in terms of psychological traits. Thus, a 4-year-old might say, "My teacher is nice."

Something important for children to develop is an understanding that people don't always give accurate reports of their beliefs (Mills, Elashi, & Archacki, 2011). Researchers have found that even 4-year-olds realize that people may make statements that aren't true to obtain what they want or to avoid trouble (Lee & others, 2002). For example, one study revealed that 4- and 5-year-olds were increasingly skeptical of another child's claim to be sick when the children were informed that the child was motivated to avoid having to go to camp (Gee & Heyman, 2007).

Another important aspect of understanding others involves understanding joint commitments. A recent study revealed that 3-year-olds, but not 2-year-olds, recognized when an adult is committed and when they themselves are committed to joint activity that involves obligation to a partner (Grafenhain & others, 2009).

Both the extensive theory of mind research (discussed in Chapter 7) and the recent research on young children's social understanding underscore that young children are not as *egocentric* as Piaget envisioned (Sokol & others, 2010). A leading expert on children's socioemotional development, Ross Thompson (2009), recently commented on how amazed he is that Piaget's concept of egocentrism has become so ingrained in people's thinking about young children, given the fact that the current research on social awareness in infancy and early childhood is so dissonant with Piaget's egocentrism concept.

Young children are more psychologically aware of themselves and others than used to be thought. Some children are better than others at understanding people's feelings and desires, and to some degree, these individual differences are influenced by conversations caregivers have with young children about feelings and desires.

Individual differences characterize young children's social understanding (Lewis & Carpendale, 2011). Some young children are better than others at understanding what people are feeling and what they desire, for example. To some degree, these individual differences are linked to conversations caregivers have with young children about other people's feelings and desires, and children's opportunities to observe others talking about people's feelings and desires. For example, a mother might say to a 3-year-old, "You should think about Raphael's feelings next time before you hit him."

Middle and Late Childhood   Children's self-understanding becomes more complex during middle and late childhood. And their social understanding, especially in taking the perspective of others, also increases.

Self-Understanding   Five key changes characterize the increased complexity in children's self-understanding in middle and late childhood:

- *Psychological characteristics and traits.* In middle and late childhood, especially from 8 to 11 years of age, children increasingly describe themselves in terms of psychological characteristics and traits, in contrast with the more concrete self-descriptions of younger children. Older children are more likely to describe themselves as "*popular, nice, helpful, mean, smart,* and *dumb*" (Harter, 2006, p. 526).

  - *Social descriptions.* In middle and late childhood, children begin to include social aspects such as references to social groups in their self-descriptions (Harter, 2006). For example, children might describe themselves as Girl Scouts, as Catholics, or as someone who has two close friends.

  - *Social comparison.* Children's self-understanding in middle and late childhood includes increasing reference to social comparison (Harter, 2006). That is, elementary-school-age children increasingly think about what they can do in comparison with others.

  - *Real self and ideal self.* In middle and late childhood, children begin to distinguish between their real and ideal selves (Harter, 2006). This change involves differentiating their actual competencies from those they aspire to have and think are the most important.

  - *Realistic.* In middle and late childhood, children's self-evaluations become more realistic (Harter, 2006). This change may occur because of increased social comparison and perspective taking.

What are some changes in children's understanding of others in middle and late childhood?

Understanding Others   Earlier we described the advances and limitations of young children's understanding of others. In middle and late childhood, children show an increase in **perspective taking,** the ability to assume other people's perspectives and understand their thoughts and feelings. In Robert Selman's (1980) view, at about 6 to 8 years of age, children begin to understand that others may have a perspective because some people have more access to information. Then, he says, in the next several years, children become aware that each individual is aware of the other's perspective and that putting one's self in the other's place is a way of judging the other person's intentions, purposes, and actions.

Perspective taking is especially thought to be important in whether children develop prosocial or antisocial attitudes and behavior. In terms of prosocial behavior, taking another's perspective improves children's likelihood of understanding and sympathizing with others when they are distressed or in need. A recent study revealed that in children characterized as being emotionally reactive, good perspective-taking skills were linked to being able to regain a neutral emotional state after being emotionally aroused (Bengtsson & Arvidsson, 2011). In this study, children who made gains in perspective-taking skills reduced their emotional reactivity over a two-year period.

perspective taking The ability to assume another person's perspective and understand his or her thoughts and feelings.

Executive functioning is at work in perspective taking (Galinsky, 2010). Among the executive functions called on when young children engage in perspective taking are cognition inhibition (controlling one's own thoughts to consider the perspective of others) and cognitive flexibility (seeing situations in different ways).

In middle and late childhood, children also become more skeptical of others' claims. Earlier, we indicated that even 4-year-old children show some skepticism of others' claims. In middle and late childhood, children become increasingly wary of some sources of information about psychological traits. For example, in one study, 10- to 11-year-olds were more likely to reject other children's self-reports that they were smart and honest than were 6- to 7-year-olds (Heyman & Legare, 2005). The more psychologically sophisticated 10- to 11-year-olds also showed a better understanding than the 6- to 7-year-olds that others' self-reports may involve socially desirable tendencies.

Adolescence   The development of self-understanding in adolescence is complex and involves a number of aspects of the self (Harter, 1998, 2006). The tendency to compare themselves with others continues to increase in the adolescent years. However, when asked whether they engage in social comparison, most adolescents deny it because they are aware that it is somewhat socially undesirable to do so.

Self-Understanding   Let's examine other ways in which the adolescent's self-understanding differs from the child's:

- *Abstract and idealistic thinking.* Remember from our discussion of Piaget's theory of cognitive development in Chapter 6, "Cognitive Developmental Approaches," that many adolescents begin to think in more *abstract* and *idealistic* ways. When asked to describe themselves, adolescents are more likely than children to use abstract and idealistic labels. Consider 14-year-old Laurie's abstract description of herself: "I am a human being. I am indecisive. I don't know who I am." Also consider her idealistic description of herself: "I am a naturally sensitive person who really cares about people's feelings. I think I'm pretty good looking."

- *Self-consciousness.* Adolescents are more likely than children to be *self-conscious* about and preoccupied with their self-understanding. This self-consciousness and self-preoccupation reflect adolescent egocentrism, which we discussed in Chapter 6.

- *Contradictions within the self.* As adolescents begin to differentiate their concept of the self into multiple roles in different relationship contexts, they sense potential contradictions between their differentiated selves (Harter, 2006). An adolescent might use this self-description: "I'm moody *and* understanding, ugly *and* attractive, bored *and* inquisitive, caring *and* uncaring, and introverted *and* fun-loving" (Harter, 1986). Young adolescents tend to view these opposing characteristics as contradictory, which can cause internal conflict. However, older adolescents and emerging adults begin to understand why an individual can possess opposing characteristics and integrate these opposing self-labels into their emerging identity (Harter, 2006).

- *The fluctuating self.* The adolescent's self-understanding fluctuates across situations and across time (Harter, 2006). The adolescent's self continues to be characterized by instability until the adolescent constructs a more unified theory of self, usually not until late adolescence or even early adulthood.

- *Real and ideal selves.* The adolescent's emerging ability to construct ideal selves in addition to actual ones can be perplexing and agonizing to the adolescent. In one view, an important aspect of the ideal or imagined self is the possible self—what individuals might become, what they would like to become, and what they are afraid of (Markus & Kitayama, 2010; Markus & Nurius, 1986). Thus, adolescents' **possible selves** include both what adolescents hope to be

developmental **connection**

Cognitive Processes. Executive functioning is an umbrella-like concept that encompasses a number of higher-level cognitive processes linked to the development of the brain's prefrontal cortex. Executive functioning involves managing one's thoughts to engage in goal-directed behavior and to exercise self-control. Chapter 7, p. 227

developmental **connection**

Cognitive Theory. In Piaget's fourth stage of cognitive development, thought becomes more abstract, idealistic, and logical. Chapter 6, p. 194

How does self-understanding change in adolescence?

possible selves What adolescents hope to become as well as what they dread they will become.

What characterizes adolescents' possible selves?

and what they dread they will become. The attributes of future positive selves (getting into a good college, being admired, having a successful career) can direct future positive states. The attributes of future negative selves (being unemployed, being lonely, not getting into a good college) can identify what is to be avoided.

• *Self-integration.* In late adolescence and emerging adulthood, self-understanding becomes more integrative, with the disparate parts of the self more systematically pieced together (Harter, 2006). Older adolescents are more likely to detect inconsistencies in their earlier self-descriptions as they attempt to construct a general theory of self, an integrated sense of identity.

Adulthood As individuals move into the traditional college-age years and make the transition from adolescence to adulthood, they begin to engage in more self-reflection about what they want to do with their lives. The extended schooling that takes place in developed countries like the United States and Japan provides time for further self-reflection and understanding of one's self.

> Know thyself, for once we know ourselves, we may learn how to care for ourselves, but otherwise we never shall.
>
> —**Socrates**
> *Greek Philosopher, 5th Century B.C.*

Self-Awareness An aspect of self-understanding that becomes especially important in early adulthood is *self-awareness*—that is, how much a young adult is aware of his or her psychological makeup, including strengths and weaknesses. Many individuals do not have very good awareness of their psychological makeup and skills. For example, how aware is the person that she or he is a good or bad listener, uses the best strategies to solve personal problems, and is assertive rather than aggressive or passive in resolving conflicts? Awareness of strengths and weaknesses in these and many other aspects of life is an important dimension of self-understanding throughout the adult years, and early adulthood is a time when individuals can benefit considerably from improving some of their weaknesses.

Possible Selves Another aspect of self-understanding that is important in the adult years involves *possible selves*. Recall that possible selves are what individuals might become, what they would like to become, and what they are afraid of becoming (Hoppmann & others, 2007). Adults in their twenties mention many possible selves that they would like to become and might become. Some of these are unrealistic, such as being happy all of the time and being very rich. As individuals get older, they often describe fewer possible selves and portray them in more concrete and realistic ways. By middle age, individuals frequently describe their possible selves in terms of areas of their life in which they already have performed, such as "being good at my work" or "having a good marriage" (Cross & Markus, 1991). Also, for some individuals, as middle-aged adults, their possible selves center on attaining hoped-for selves, such as acquiring material possessions, but as older adults, they become more concerned with maintaining what they have and preventing or avoiding health problems and dependency (Smith, 2009).

Many individuals continue to revise their possible selves as they go through the adult years. This ability to revise possible selves and adapt them to find a better match between desired and achieved goals may be an important aspect of maintaining positive self-esteem and psychological well-being as individuals get older (Bengtson, Reedy, & Gordon, 1985).

Life Review Another important aspect of self-understanding in adulthood is the *life review*. Life review is prominent in Erikson's final stage of integrity versus despair. Life review involves looking back at one's life experiences, evaluating them, interpreting them, and often reinterpreting them. As the past marches in review, the older adult surveys it, observes it, and reflects on it. Reconsideration of previous experiences and their meaning occurs, often

What characterizes self-awareness and possible selves in young adults?

with revision or expanded understanding taking place. This reorganization of the past may provide a more valid picture for the individual, providing new and significant meaning to one's life. It may also help prepare the individual for death, in the process reducing fear.

One aspect of life review involves identifying and reflecting on not only the positive aspects of one's life but also on regrets as part of developing a mature wisdom and self-understanding The hope is that by examining not only the positive aspects of one's life, but also what an individual has regretted doing, a more accurate vision of the complexity of one's life and possibly increased life satisfaction will be attained (King & Hicks, 2007).

Some clinicians use *reminiscence therapy* with their older clients. Reminiscence therapy involves discussing past activities and experiences with another individual or group. The therapy may include the use of photographs, familiar items, and video/audio recordings (Peng & others, 2009). Researchers have found that reminiscence therapy improves the mood of older adults (Fiske, Wetherell, & Gatz, 2009). For example, a recent study of institutionalized older adults found that reminiscence therapy increased their life satisfaction and decreased their depression and loneliness (Chiang & others, 2010). And another recent study revealed that a life-review course, "Looking for Meaning," reduced the depressive symptoms of middle-aged and older adults (Pot & others, 2010).

Successful aging, though, doesn't mean thinking about the past all of the time. In one study, older adults who were obsessed about the past were less well adjusted than older adults who integrated their past and present (Wong & Watt, 1991).

What characterizes a life review in late adulthood?

SELF-ESTEEM AND SELF-CONCEPT

High self-esteem and a positive self-concept are important characteristics of children's and adults' well-being (Kaplan, 2009). **Self-esteem** refers to global evaluations of the self. Self-esteem is also referred to as *self-worth*, or *self-image*. For example, a person may perceive that she or he is not merely a person but a *good* person. Of course, not all people have an overall positive image of themselves. **Self-concept** refers to domain-specific evaluations of the self. Individuals can make self-evaluations in many domains of their lives—academic, athletic, appearance, and so on. In sum, *self-esteem* refers to global self-evaluations, *self-concept* to domain-specific evaluations (Harter, 2006).

Investigators sometimes use the terms *self-esteem* and *self-concept* interchangeably and don't always precisely define them (Donnellan & Robins, 2009). However, the distinction between self-esteem as global self-evaluation and self-concept as domain-specific self-evaluation should help you keep the terms straight.

Issues in Self-Esteem Is self-esteem related to school and adult job performance? There are "only modest correlations between school performance and self-esteem, and these correlations do not indicate that high self-esteem causes good performance" (Baumeister & others, 2003, p. 1). Attempts to increase students' self-esteem have not produced improvements in academic performance (Davies & Brember, 1999).

How is self-esteem related to school performance?

In some studies, adult job performance is linked to self-esteem, but the correlations vary greatly and the direction of the causation is not clear (Baumeister & others, 2003). Occupational success might lead to higher self-esteem, but the opposite might occur.

Is self-esteem related to happiness? Self-esteem is strongly related to happiness, and it seems likely that high self-esteem increases happiness, whereas depression lowers it (Baumeister & others, 2003; Van Voorhees & others, 2008).

self-esteem The global evaluative dimension of the self. Self-esteem is also referred to as self-worth, or self-image.

self-concept Domain-specific evaluations of the self.

Domain	Harter's U.S. Samples	Other Countries
Physical appearance	.65	.62
Scholastic competence	.48	.41
Social acceptance	.46	.40
Behavioral conduct	.45	.45
Athletic competence	.33	.30

FIGURE **11.2**

CORRELATIONS BETWEEN GLOBAL SELF-ESTEEM AND DOMAINS OF COMPETENCE. *Note:* The correlations shown are the average correlations computed across a number of studies. The other countries in this evaluation were England, Ireland, Australia, Canada, Germany, Italy, Greece, the Netherlands, and Japan. Recall from Chapter 1 that correlation coefficients can range from −1.00 to +1.00. The correlations between physical appearance and global self-esteem (.65 and .62) are moderately high.

Is self-esteem related to physical appearance? Self-esteem is related to perceived physical appearance. For example, researchers have found that in adolescence, global self-esteem is correlated more strongly with physical appearance than scholastic competence, social acceptance, behavioral conduct, and athletic competence (Harter, 1999) (see Figure 11.2). This association between perceived physical appearance is not confined to adolescence but holds across the life span from early childhood through middle age (Harter, 1999, 2006).

Is self-esteem linked to depression? A large number of studies have found that individuals with low self-esteem report that they feel more depressed than individuals with high self-esteem (Baumeister & others, 2003). Low self-esteem has also been implicated in suicide attempts and anorexia nervosa (Fenzel, 1994).

Does self-esteem in adolescence foreshadow adjustment and competence in adulthood? A New Zealand longitudinal study assessed self-esteem at 11, 13, and 15 years of age and adjustment and competence of the same individuals when they were 26 years old (Trzesniewski & others, 2006). The results revealed that adults characterized by poorer mental and physical health, worse economic prospects, and higher levels of criminal behavior were more likely to have had low self-esteem in adolescence than their better-adjusted, more competent adult counterparts.

An important point needs to be made about much of the research on self-esteem: It is correlational rather than experimental. Remember from Chapter 1 that correlation does not equal causation. Thus, if a correlational study finds an association between self-esteem and depression, it could be equally likely that depression causes low self-esteem or low self-esteem causes depression.

Developmental Changes   One cross-sectional study assessed the self-esteem of a very large, diverse sample of 326,641 individuals ranging from 9 to 90 years of age (Robins & others, 2002). About two-thirds of the participants were from the United States. The individuals were asked to respond to the item "I have high self-esteem" on a scale from 1 to 5 with 1 meaning "strongly agree" and 5 meaning "strongly disagree." Self-esteem decreased in adolescence, increased in the twenties, leveled off in the thirties, rose in the fifties and sixties, and then dropped in the seventies and eighties (see Figure 11.3). In most age periods, the self-esteem of males was higher than the self-esteem of females. Let's now explore developmental changes in self-esteem in more detail.

Childhood and Adolescence   Researchers have found that the accuracy of self-evaluations increases across the elementary school years (Harter, 2006). Young children

FIGURE **11.3**

SELF-ESTEEM ACROSS THE LIFE SPAN. One cross-sectional study found that self-esteem was high in childhood, dropped in adolescence, increased through early and middle adulthood, then dropped in the seventies and eighties (Robins & others, 2002). More than 300,000 individuals were asked the extent to which they have high self-esteem on a 5-point scale, with 5 being "Strongly Agree" and 1 being "Strongly Disagree."

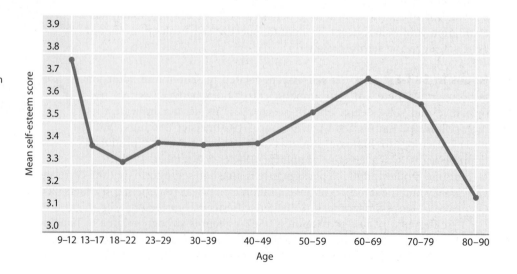

tend to provide inflated views of themselves, but by about 8 years of age most children give more realistic appraisals of their skills (Harter, 2006). For example, older elementary school children who report a positive self-image of themselves in sports indeed are the ones who are reported by peers to be good at athletics.

Adolescents in general have long been described as having low self-esteem (Robins & others, 2002). However, the majority of adolescents actually have a positive self-image. In an extensive cross-cultural study, Daniel Offer and his colleagues (1988) sampled the self-images of adolescents around the world—in the United States, Australia, Bangladesh, Hungary, Israel, Italy, Japan, Taiwan, Turkey, and West Germany. Almost three-fourths of the adolescents had a healthy self-image.

Researchers have found that after 13 years of age, girls' self-esteem increases.

Some researchers note that gender differences in self-esteem emerge by early adolescence, and these were found in the study just described (Robins & others, 2002). Girls and boys enter first grade with roughly equivalent levels of self-esteem. Yet some research studies have shown that by the middle school years girls' self-esteem is significantly lower than boys' (American Association of University Women, 1992). For example, a recent study confirmed that male adolescents have higher self-esteem than do female adolescents (McLean & Breen, 2009).

However, other researchers caution that the self-esteem of girls is only slightly lower than boys' and still in the positive range (Harter, 2006; Kling & others, 1999). Researchers also have found that after age 13, girls' self-esteem increases through the remainder of adolescence and in emerging adulthood (Baldwin & Hoffman, 2002).

A current concern is that too many of today's college students grew up receiving empty praise and as a consequence have inflated self-esteem (Graham, 2005; Stipek, 2005). Too often they were given praise for performance that was mediocre or even poor. Now in college, they may have difficulty handling competition and criticism. The title of a book, *Dumbing Down Our Kids: Why American Children Feel Good About Themselves But Can't Read, Write, or Add* (Sykes, 1995), vividly captured the theme that many U.S. children's academic problems stem from unmerited praise as part of an effort to prop up their self-esteem.

Adulthood Are there differences in the self-esteem of young, middle-aged, and older adults? In the self-esteem study described earlier, self-esteem dropped in late adulthood (Robins & others, 2002). However, some researchers have not found any differences in self-esteem across the age periods of adulthood (McGue, Hirsch, & Lykken, 1993).

Given that older adults have more physical problems, why wouldn't they have lower self-esteem than young or middle-aged adults? One possible reason is that many older adults don't interpret their "losses" as negatively, and don't become as emotionally upset, as younger adults would (Carstensen & Freund, 1994). For example, being asked to retire at age 63 may not be nearly as devastating as being fired from a job at 40. Furthermore, as we saw in Chapter 10, Laura Carstensen (1998, 2008) argues that knowledge-related goals decrease in older adults, whereas emotion-related goals increase. And many older adults have the ability to reach their emotion-related goals of honing their social network to spend most of their time with the people with whom they have enjoyed satisfying close relationships in the past (Scheibe & Carstensen, 2010). Finally, many older adults choose to compare themselves with other older adults rather than younger adults, which can help them maintain their positive self-image (Brandstädter, 1999).

Why might self-esteem decline for some older adults? Explanations include deteriorating physical health and negative societal attitudes toward older adults, although these factors were not examined in the large-scale study just described. Researchers have found that in late adulthood, being widowed, institutionalized, or

Even when older adults have physical problems, other aspects of their lives, such as spending time with people whose company they enjoy, can help to buffer any decline in their self-esteem.

physically impaired, having a low religious commitment, and experiencing a decline in health are linked to low self-esteem (Giarrusso & Bengtson, 2007).

Strategies for Increasing Self-Esteem   What are some good strategies for increasing self-esteem? Five ways to improve self-esteem are (1) identify the causes of low self-esteem and the domains of competence important to the self, (2) provide emotional support and opportunities for social approval, (3) take responsibility for one's own self-esteem, (4) achieve goals, and (5) develop effective coping strategies.

Identifying sources of self-esteem—that is, competence in domains important to the self—is critical to improving self-esteem. Susan Harter (1990) points out that the self-esteem enhancement programs of the 1970s and 1980s, in which self-esteem itself was the target and individuals were encouraged to simply feel good about themselves, were ineffective. Rather, Harter notes that intervention must occur at the level of the *causes* of self-esteem if the individual's self-esteem is to improve significantly. Individuals have the highest self-esteem when they perform competently in domains that are important to them. Therefore, people should be encouraged to identify and value areas of competence.

Emotional support and social approval also powerfully influence self-esteem. Some children with low self-esteem come from conflicted families or conditions in which they experienced abuse or neglect—situations in which support was unavailable. In some cases, alternative sources of support can be implemented either informally through the encouragement of a teacher, a coach, or another significant adult or, more formally, through programs such as Big Brothers and Big Sisters. As peer approval becomes increasingly important during adolescence, peer support is an important influence on the adolescent's self-esteem.

Developing self-confidence and believing that one has the ability to do what it takes to improve self-esteem are other good strategies. Although it is helpful to have the social support and emotional approval of others, it is also very important to take the initiative to increase one's own self-esteem.

Achievement can also improve an individual's self-esteem (Baumeister & others, 2003). For example, self-esteem can be enhanced by the straightforward teaching of skills to individuals. People develop higher self-esteem because they know the important tasks to accomplish goals and they realize that by carrying out these tasks they are more likely to reach their goals.

Self-esteem often increases when individuals face a problem and try to cope with it rather than avoid it (Frydenberg, 2008). When coping prevails, the individual often faces problems realistically, honestly, and nondefensively. This process leads to favorable self-evaluative thoughts, which then lead to self-generated approval and higher self-esteem. The converse is true of low self-esteem. Unfavorable self-evaluations trigger denial, deception, and avoidance in an attempt to disavow that which has already been glimpsed as true. This process leads to self-generated disapproval as a form of feedback to the self about personal adequacy.

SELF-REGULATION

Self-regulation involves the ability to control one's behavior without having to rely on others' help. Self-regulation includes the self-generation and cognitive monitoring of thoughts, feelings, and behaviors in order to reach a goal. An individual might develop better self-control in the physical, cognitive, or socioemotional domain than in other domains.

Throughout most of the life span, individuals who engage in self-regulation are better achievers and are more satisfied with their lives than their counterparts who let external factors dominate their lives (Schunk, 2012). For example, researchers have found that, compared with low-achieving students, high-achieving students engage in greater self-regulation. They do this by setting more specific learning goals, using more strategies to learn and adapt, self-monitoring more, and more systematically evaluating their progress toward a goal (Schunk, 2012).

How can parents help children develop higher self-esteem?

The living self has one purpose only: to come into its own fullness of being, as a tree comes into full blossom, or a bird into spring beauty, or a tiger into luster.

—D. H. LAWRENCE
English Author, 20th Century

self-regulation The ability to control one's behavior without having to rely on others for help.

Infancy and Early Childhood In Chapter 10, we discussed the importance of children learning to regulate their emotions as they develop. Emotional regulation is an important aspect of the overall development of self-regulation (Geldhof, Little, & Colombo, 2010; Thompson & Goodman, 2011). How do other aspects of self-regulation develop? Claire Kopp (1982, 1987, 2008) described a sequence for its development early in life. Initially, beginning at about 12 to 18 months of age, infants depend completely on caregivers for reminder signals about acceptable behaviors. At this age, infants begin to show compliance with caregivers' demands. For example, a parent might say, "No. Don't touch!" And the infant doesn't touch.

The next phase of developing self-regulation takes place at approximately 2 to 3 years of age. At this point, children begin to comply with the caregiver's expectations in the absence of external monitoring by the caregiver. Thus, most 2- to 3-year-old children are aware of where they may and may not play and which objects they may and may not touch if they are at home, on a playground, or in the homes of friends and relatives.

Nonetheless, at these young ages, there are clear limitations on self-regulation (Thompson & Goodman, 2011). Given a strong stimulus, such as a ball rolling down the street or the motivation to explore an interesting place, toddlers often ignore safety or exhortations. Also, only rudimentary aspects of delaying gratification are present at these early ages. For example, when 2-year-olds are confronted with an unexpected delay (such as not being able to go outside and play), they often whine and beg to engage in the activity. But there are clear signs of advances in self-initiated regulation, as when young children announce a toy cleanup without prompting from caregivers.

Preschoolers become better at self-control, learning how to resist temptation and giving themselves instructions that keep them focused (Thompson, 2006). Thus, toward the end of the preschool years, children might say to themselves, "No. I can't do that. I'm working," in response to a temptation to stop working and do something else, like play with an attractive toy.

Middle/Late Childhood and Adolescence One of the most important aspects of the self in middle and late childhood is the increased capacity for self-regulation (Veenman, 2011). This increased capacity is characterized by deliberate efforts to manage one's behavior, emotions, and thoughts that lead to increased social competence and achievement (Eisenberg, Spinrad, & Eggum, 2010; Winne & Nesbit, 2010). For example, a recent study revealed that children from low-income families who had a higher level of self-regulation made better grades in school than their counterparts who had a lower level of self-regulation (Buckner, Mezzacappa, & Beardslee, 2009). Another recent study found that self-control increased from 4 to 10 years of age and that high self-control was linked to lower levels of deviant behavior (Vazsonyi & Huang, 2010).

How does self-regulation change during childhood and adolescence?

The increased capacity for self-regulation is linked to developmental advances in the brain's prefrontal cortex, which was discussed in Chapter 3 (Diamond, Casey, & Munakata, 2011). In that discussion, increased focal activation in the prefrontal cortex was linked to improved cognitive control. Such cognitive control includes self-regulation.

Few studies of self-regulation have focused on adolescents. On the one hand, advances in cognitive skills (logical thinking, for example), increased introspection, and the greater independence of adolescence might lead to increased self-control. Also, advances in cognitive abilities provide adolescents with a better understanding of the importance of delaying gratification for something desirable (such as a good grade in a class) rather than seeking immediate gratification (listening to rock music rather than studying). On the other hand, an increased sense of invincibility (which can lead to risk taking) and social comparison might produce less self-control.

developmental connection

Information Processing. Cognitive control (inhibition and flexibility) increases from childhood through early adulthood. Chapter 7, p. 212

According to selective optimization with compensation theory, what characterizes successful aging?

Adulthood Self-control plays an important role in adult development (Geldhof, Little, & Colombo, 2010). For example, higher levels of self-control are linked to better health and adjustment (Lachman, Neupert, & Agrigoroaei, 2011).

Self-control increases in early adulthood and on into the middle adult years (Gatz & Karel, 1993). Researchers have found a decline in perceived self-control in cognitive functioning in older adults (Bertrand & Lachman, 2003).

Although older adults are aware of age-related losses, most still effectively maintain a sense of self-control. The negative effects of age-typical problems, such as a decline in physical and cognitive skills and an increase in illness, may be buffered by a flexible, accommodating control style (Brandstädter & Renner, 1990).

Selective Optimization with Compensation **Selective optimization with compensation theory** states that successful aging is linked with three main factors: selection, optimization, and compensation (SOC). The theory states that individuals can produce new resources and allocate them effectively to tasks they want to master (Baltes & Smith, 2008). Selection is based on the concept that older adults have a reduced capacity and a loss of functioning, which require a reduction in performance in most life domains such as memory and physical skills. Optimization suggests that it is possible to maintain performance in some areas through continued practice and the use of new technologies. Examples might include doing crossword puzzles to maintain memory skills and exercising to optimize strength. Compensation becomes relevant when life tasks require a level of capacity beyond the current level of the older adult's performance potential. Older adults especially need to compensate in circumstances with high mental or physical demands, such as when thinking about and memorizing new material very rapidly, reacting quickly when driving a car, or running fast. When older adults develop an illness, the need for compensation increases.

Selective optimization with compensation theory was proposed by Paul Baltes and his colleagues (Baltes, 2003; Baltes, Lindenberger, & Staudinger, 2006; Baltes & Smith, 2006). They describe the life of the pianist Arthur Rubinstein (1887–1982) to illustrate their theory. When he was interviewed at 80 years of age, Rubinstein said that three factors were responsible for his ability to maintain his status as an admired concert pianist into old age. First, he mastered the weakness of old age by reducing the scope of his performances and playing fewer pieces (which reflects selection). Second, he spent more time at practice than earlier in his life (which reflects optimization). Third, he used special strategies, such as slowing down before fast segments, thus creating the image of faster playing (which reflects compensation).

The process of selective optimization with compensation is likely to be effective whenever people pursue successful outcomes. What makes SOC attractive to researchers in aging is that it makes explicit how individuals can manage and adapt to losses. By using SOC, they can continue to live satisfying lives, although in a more restricted manner. Loss is a common dimension of old age, although there are wide variations in the nature of the losses involved. Because of this individual variation, the specific form of selection, optimization, and compensation will likely vary depending on the person's life history, pattern of interests, values, health, skills, and resources. To read about some strategies for effectively engaging in selective optimization with compensation, see the *Connecting Development to Life* interlude.

In Baltes' view (2003; Baltes & Smith, 2008), the selection of domains and life priorities is an important aspect of development. Life goals and priorities likely vary across the life course for most people. For many individuals, it is not just the sheer attainment of goals, but rather the attainment of *meaningful* goals, that makes life satisfying. In one study, younger adults were more likely to assess their well-being in terms of accomplishments and careers, whereas older adults were more likely to

selective optimization with compensation theory The theory that successful aging is related to three factors: selection, optimization, and compensation.

Strategies for Effectively Engaging in Selective Optimization with Compensation

What are some good strategies that aging adults can engage in to attain selective optimization with compensation? According to Paul Baltes and his colleagues (Baltes, Lindenberger, & Staudinger, 2006; Freund & Baltes, 2002), the following strategies are likely to be effective:

Selection Strategies

- Focus on the most important goal at a particular time.
- Think about what you want in life, and commit yourself to one or two major goals.
- To reach a particular goal, you may need to abandon other goals.

Optimization Strategies

- Keep working on what you have planned until you are successful.
- Persevere and keep trying until you reach your goal.

- When you want to achieve something, you may need to be patient until the right moment arrives.

Compensation

- When things don't go the way they used to, search for other ways to achieve what you want.
- If things don't go well for you, be willing to let others help you.
- When things don't go as well as in the past, keep trying other ways until you can achieve results that are similar to what you accomplished earlier in your life.

Which of the selection, optimization, and compensation strategies have you used? Which of the strategies would you benefit from using more?

---

link well-being with good health and the ability to accept change. And, as you read in Chapter 10, in our discussion of socioemotional selectivity theory, emotion-related goals become increasingly important for older adults (Carstensen, 2008; Charles & Carstensen, 2010).

In one cross-sectional study, the personal life investments of 25- to 105-year-olds were assessed (Staudinger, 1996) (see Figure 11.4). From 25 to 34 years of age,

FIGURE **11.4**

DEGREE OF PERSONAL LIFE INVESTMENT AT DIFFERENT POINTS IN LIFE. Shown here are the top four domains of personal life investment at different points in life. The highest degree of investment is listed at the top (for example, work was the highest personal investment from 25 to 34 years of age, family from 35 to 84, and health from 85 to 105).

participants said that they personally invested more time in work, friends, family, and independence, in that order. From 35 to 54 and 55 to 65 years of age, family became more important than friends to them in terms of their personal investment. Little changed in the rank ordering of persons 70 to 84 years old, but for participants 85 to 105 years old, health became the most important personal investment. Thinking about life showed up for the first time on the most important list for those who were 85 to 105 years old.

Review Connect Reflect

LG1 Discuss the main ways the self is conceptualized

Review

- How can the terms *self*, *identity*, and *personality* be defined? What is self-understanding, and how does it develop?
- What are self-esteem and self-concept, and how do they develop? How is self-esteem related to performance, initiative, and happiness? Is there a dark side to high self-esteem? What are some ways to increase self-esteem?
- What is self-regulation, and how does it develop?

Connect

- How might the life reflection of older adults differ from the life reflection of individuals in middle adulthood?

Reflect *Your Own Personal Journey of Life*

- If a psychologist had interviewed you when you were 8 years old, 14 years old, and again today, would your self-understanding and self-esteem have been different at each of these ages?

Identity

LG2 Explain the key facets of identity development

What Is Identity?   Some Contemporary Thoughts on Identity   Family Influences

Erikson's View   Developmental Changes   Ethnic Identity

Who am I? What am I all about? What am I going to do with my life? What is different about me? How can I make it on my own? These questions reflect the search for an identity. By far the most comprehensive and provocative theory of identity development is Erik Erikson's. In this section, we examine his views on identity and some contemporary thoughts on identity. We also discuss research on how identity develops and how social contexts influence that development.

What are some important dimensions of identity?

WHAT IS IDENTITY?

Identity is a self-portrait composed of many pieces, including these:

- The career and work path the person wants to follow (vocational/career identity)
- Whether the person is conservative, liberal, or middle-of-the-road (political identity)
- The person's spiritual beliefs (religious identity)
- Whether the person is single, married, divorced, and so on (relationship identity)
- The extent to which the person is motivated to achieve and is intellectually active (achievement, intellectual identity)

- Whether the person is heterosexual, homosexual, or bisexual (sexual identity)
- Which part of the world or country a person is from and how intensely the person identifies with his or her cultural heritage (cultural/ethnic identity)
- The kinds of things a person likes to do, which can include sports, music, hobbies, and so on (interests)
- The individual's personality characteristics, such as being introverted or extraverted, anxious or calm, friendly or hostile, and so on (personality)
- The individual's body image (physical identity)

ERIKSON'S VIEW

Questions about identity surface as common, virtually universal, concerns during adolescence. Some decisions made during adolescence might seem trivial: whom to date, whether or not to break up, which major to study, whether to study or play, whether or not to be politically active, and so on. Over the years of adolescence, however, such decisions begin to form the core of what the individual is all about as a human being—what is called his or her identity.

It was Erik Erikson (1950, 1968) who first understood the importance of identity questions to understanding adolescent development. Identity is now believed to be a key aspect of adolescent development because of Erikson's masterful thinking and analysis. His ideas reveal rich insights into adolescents' thoughts and feelings, and reading one or more of his books is worthwhile. A good starting point is *Identity: Youth and Crisis* (1968). Other works that portray identity development are *Young Man Luther* (1962) and *Gandhi's Truth* (1969).

Erikson's theory was introduced in Chapter 1. Recall that his fifth developmental stage, which individuals experience during adolescence, is **identity versus identity confusion.** During this time, said Erikson, adolescents are faced with deciding who they are, what they are all about, and where they are going in life. These questions about identity occur throughout life, but they become especially important for adolescents. Erikson maintains that adolescents face an overwhelming number of choices. As they gradually come to realize that they will be responsible for themselves and their own lives, adolescents search for what those lives are going to be.

The search for an identity during adolescence is aided by a **psychosocial moratorium,** which is Erikson's term for the gap between childhood security and adult autonomy. During this period, society leaves adolescents relatively free of responsibilities, which allows them to try out different identities. Adolescents in effect search their culture's identity files, experimenting with different roles and personalities. They may want to pursue one career one month (lawyer, for example) and another career the next month (doctor, actor, teacher, social worker, or astronaut, for example). They may dress neatly one day, sloppily the next. This experimentation is a deliberate effort on the part of adolescents to find out where they fit into the world. Most adolescents eventually discard undesirable roles.

Youth who successfully cope with conflicting identities emerge with a new sense of self that is both refreshing and acceptable. Adolescents who do not successfully resolve this identity crisis suffer what Erikson calls identity confusion. The confusion takes one of two courses: Individuals withdraw, isolating themselves from peers and family, or they immerse themselves in the world of peers and lose their identity in the crowd.

SOME CONTEMPORARY THOUGHTS ON IDENTITY

Contemporary views of identity development suggest that it is a lengthy process, in many instances more gradual and less cataclysmic than Erikson's term *crisis* implies

Erik Erikson

"Who are you?" said the caterpillar. Alice replied rather shyly, "I—I hardly know, sir, just at present—at least I know who I was when I got up this morning, but I must have changed several times since then."

—LEWIS CARROLL
English Writer, 19th Century

identity versus identity confusion Erikson's fifth stage of development, which occurs during the adolescent years; adolescents are faced with finding out who they are, what they are all about, and where they are going in life.

psychosocial moratorium Erikson's term for the gap between childhood security and adult autonomy that adolescents experience as part of their identity exploration.

(Moshman, 2011; Syed, 2011). Resolution of the identity issue during adolescence and emerging adulthood does not mean that identity will be stable through the remainder of one's life. An individual who develops a healthy identity is flexible and adaptive, open to changes in society, in relationships, and in careers. This openness ensures numerous reorganizations of identity throughout the individual's life.

Identity formation neither happens neatly, nor is it usually cataclysmic. At the bare minimum, it involves commitment to a vocational direction, an ideological stance, and a sexual orientation. Synthesizing the components of identity can be a long, drawn-out process, with many negations and affirmations of various roles. Identity development gets done in bits and pieces. Decisions are not made once and for all, but must be made again and again. While the decisions might seem trivial at the time—whom to date, whether or not to have sexual intercourse, to break up, to take drugs; whether to go to college or get a job, to study or play, to be politically active or not—over the years, they begin to form the core of what an individual is all about.

What are some contemporary thoughts about identity formation and development?

DEVELOPMENTAL CHANGES

Although questions about identity may be especially important during adolescence and emerging adulthood, identity formation neither begins nor ends during these years (McAdams & Cox, 2011). It begins with the appearance of attachment, the development of the sense of self, and the emergence of independence in infancy; the process reaches its final phase with a life review and integration in old age. What is important about identity development in adolescence, especially late adolescence, is that for the first time, physical development, cognitive development, and socioemotional development advance to the point at which the individual can sort through and synthesize childhood identities and identifications to construct a viable path toward adult maturity.

Identity Statuses   How do individual adolescents go about the process of forming an identity? Eriksonian researcher James Marcia (1980, 1994) notes that Erikson's theory of identity development contains four *statuses* of identity, or ways of resolving the identity crisis: identity diffusion, identity foreclosure, identity moratorium, and identity achievement. What determines an individual's identity status? Marcia classifies individuals based on the existence or extent of their crisis or commitment (see Figure 11.5). **Crisis** is defined as a period of identity development during which the individual explores alternatives. Most researchers use the term *exploration* rather than crisis. **Commitment** is personal investment in identity.

The four statuses of identity are as follows:

- **Identity diffusion** is the status of individuals who have not yet experienced a crisis or made any commitments. Not only are they undecided about occupational and ideological choices, but they are also likely to show little interest in such matters.

- **Identity foreclosure** is the status of individuals who have made a commitment but have not experienced a crisis. This occurs most often when parents hand down commitments to their adolescents, usually in an authoritarian way, before adolescents have had a chance to explore different approaches, ideologies, and vocations on their own.

Has the person made a commitment?

		Yes	**No**
Has the person explored meaningful alternatives regarding some identity question?	**Yes**	Identity Achievement	Identity Moratorium
	No	Identity Foreclosure	Identity Diffusion

FIGURE **11.5**

MARCIA'S FOUR STATUSES OF IDENTITY

crisis A period of identity development during which the individual is exploring alternatives.

commitment A personal investment in identity.

identity diffusion Marcia's term for the status of individuals who have not yet experienced a crisis (explored meaningful alternatives) or made any commitments.

identity foreclosure Marcia's term for the status of individuals who have made a commitment but have not experienced a crisis.

- **Identity moratorium** is the status of individuals who are in the midst of a crisis but whose commitments are either absent or only vaguely defined.
- **Identity achievement** is the status of individuals who have undergone a crisis and have made a commitment.

Let's explore some examples of Marcia's identity statuses. Thirteen-year-old Sarah has neither begun to explore her identity in any meaningful way nor made an identity commitment; she is *identity diffused*. Eighteen-year-old Tim's parents want him to be a medical doctor, so he is planning on majoring in premedicine in college and has not explored other options; he is *identity foreclosed*. Nineteen-year-old Sasha is not quite sure what life paths she wants to follow, but she recently went to the counseling center at her college to find out about different careers; she is in *identity moratorium* status. Twenty-one-year-old Marcelo extensively explored several career options in college, eventually getting his degree in science education, and is looking forward to his first year of teaching high school students; he is *identity achieved*. These examples focused on the career dimension of identity, but keep in mind that identity has a number of dimensions.

Marcia's approach has been sharply criticized by some researchers who conclude that it oversimplifies Erikson's concepts of crisis and commitment and doesn't examine them deeply enough (Coté, 2009).

One way that researchers are examining identity changes in depth is by using a *narrative approach*. This involves asking individuals to tell their life stories and then evaluating the extent to which their stories are meaningful and integrated (McLean & Pasupathi, 2010; Syed, 2010, 2011). The term *narrative identity* "refers to the stories people construct and tell about themselves to define who they are for themselves and others. Beginning in adolescence and young adulthood, our narrative identities are the stories we live by" (McAdams, Josselson, & Lieblich, 2006, p. 4). A recent study using the narrative identity approach revealed that between the ages of 11 and 18, boys increasingly engaged in thinking about the meaningfulness of their lives, especially meaning related to changes in the self (McLean, Breen, & Fournier, 2010).

Early Adolescence to Adulthood   During early adolescence, most youth are primarily in the identity statuses of *diffusion, foreclosure,* or *moratorium*. According to Marcia (1987, 1996), at least three aspects of the young adolescent's development are important to identity formation. Young adolescents must be confident that they have parental support, must have an established sense of industry, and must be able to take a self-reflective stance toward the future.

A recent study of 1,200 Dutch 12- to 20-year-olds revealed that the majority of adolescents don't often experience identity conflicts and their identity development proceeds more smoothly than is commonly thought (Meeus & others, 2010). In this study, though, approximately 1 in 8 adolescents struggled with identity conflicts throughout adolescence.

Researchers have developed a consensus that the key changes in identity are most likely to take place in emerging adulthood, the period from about 18 to 25 years of age, not adolescence (Juang & Syed, 2010; Swanson, 2010). A recent study found that as individuals aged from early adolescence to emerging adulthood, they increasingly engaged in in-depth exploration of their identity (Klimstra & others, 2010). Alan Waterman (1985, 1992) has found that from the years preceding high school through the last few years of college, the number of individuals who are identity achieved increases, whereas the number of individuals who are identity diffused decreases. Many young adolescents are identity diffused. College upperclassmen are more likely than high school students or college freshmen to be identity achieved.

Why might college produce some key changes in identity? Increased complexity in the reasoning skills of college students combined with a wide range of new

identity moratorium Marcia's term for the status of individuals who are in the midst of a crisis, but whose commitments are either absent or vaguely defined.

identity achievement Marcia's term for the status of individuals who have undergone a crisis and have made a commitment.

How does identity change in emerging adulthood?

experiences that highlight contrasts between home and college and between themselves and others stimulate them to reach a higher level of integrating various dimensions of their identity (Phinney, 2008).

A recent meta-analysis of 124 studies revealed that during adolescence and emerging adulthood, identity moratorium status rose steadily to age 19 and then declined; identity achievement rose across late adolescence and emerging adulthood; and foreclosure and diffusion statuses declined across the high school years but fluctuated in the late teens and emerging adulthood (Kroger, Martinussen, & Marcia, 2010). The studies also found that a large portion of individuals were not identity achieved by the time they reached their twenties.

Resolution of the identity issue during adolescence and emerging adulthood does not mean that identity will be stable through the remainder of life (McAdams & Cox, 2011). Many individuals who develop positive identities follow what are called "MAMA" cycles; that is, their identity status changes from *m*oratorium to *a*chievement to *m*oratorium to *a*chievement (Marcia, 1994). These cycles may be repeated throughout life (Francis, Fraser, & Marcia, 1989). Marcia (2002) points out that the first identity is just that—it is not, and should not be expected to be, the final product.

Researchers have shown that identity consolidation—the process of refining and enhancing the identity choices that are made in emerging adulthood—continues well into early adulthood and possibly into the early part of middle adulthood (Kroger, 2007). Further, as individuals move from early to middle adulthood they become more certain about their identity. For example, a longitudinal study of college women found that identity certainty increased from the thirties through the fifties (Stewart, Ostrove, & Helson, 2001).

> As long as one keeps searching, the answers come.
>
> **—Joan Baez**
> *American Folk Singer, 20th Century*

developmental **connection**

Attachment. Even while adolescents seek autonomy, attachment to parents is important; secure attachment in adolescence is linked to a number of positive outcomes. Chapter 10, p. 328

individuality Characteristic consisting of two dimensions: self-assertion, the ability to have and communicate a point of view; and separateness, the use of communication patterns to express how one is different from others.

FAMILY INFLUENCES

Parents are important figures in the adolescent's development of identity (Cooper, 2011). For example, one study found that poor communication between mothers and adolescents, as well as persistent conflicts with friends, was linked to less positive identity development (Reis & Youniss, 2004). Catherine Cooper and her colleagues (Cooper, 2011; Cooper, Behrens, & Trinh, 2009; Cooper & Grotevant, 1989) have found that a family atmosphere that promotes *both* individuality and connectedness is important to the adolescent's identity development:

- **Individuality** consists of two dimensions: self-assertion, which is the ability to have and communicate a point of view; and separateness, which is the use of communication patterns to express how one is different from others.

- **Connectedness** also consists of two dimensions: mutuality, which involves sensitivity to and respect for others' views; and permeability, which involves openness to others' views.

ETHNIC IDENTITY

Throughout the world, ethnic minority groups have struggled to maintain their ethnic identities while blending in with the dominant culture (Erikson, 1968; Liu & others, 2009). **Ethnic identity** is an enduring aspect of the self that includes a sense of membership in an ethnic group, along with the attitudes and feelings related to that membership (Phinney, 2006). Thus, for adolescents from ethnic minority groups, the process of identity formation has an added dimension: the choice between two or more sources of identification—their own ethnic group and the mainstream, or dominant, culture (Seaton, 2010; Syed, 2011). Many adolescents resolve this choice by developing a *bicultural identity*. That is, they identify in some ways with their ethnic group and in other ways with the majority culture (Cooper, 2011; Phinney & Baldelomar, 2011). A study of Mexican American and Asian American college students found that they identified both with the American mainstream culture and with their culture of origin (Devos, 2006).

Time is another aspect of the context that influences ethnic identity. The indicators of identity often differ for each succeeding generation of immigrants (Phinney, 2006; Phinney & Baldelomar, 2011). First-generation immigrants are likely to be secure in their identities and unlikely to change much; they may or may not develop a new identity. The degree to which they begin to feel "American" appears to be related to whether or not they learn English, develop social networks beyond their ethnic group, and become culturally competent in their new country. Second-generation immigrants are more likely to think of themselves as "American"—possibly because citizenship is granted at birth. For second-generation immigrants, ethnic identity is likely to be linked to retention of their ethnic language and social networks. In the third and later generations, the issues become more complex. Broad social factors may affect the extent to which members of this generation retain their ethnic identities. For example, media images may influence whether members of an ethnic group will continue to identify with their group and retain parts of its culture. Discrimination may force people to see themselves as cut off from the majority group and encourage them to seek the support of their own ethnic culture.

The immediate contexts in which ethnic minority youth live also influence their identity development (Rivas-Drake, 2011; Syed & Azmitia, 2010). In the United States, many ethnic minority youth live in pockets of poverty, are exposed to drugs, gangs, and crime, and interact with youth and adults who have dropped out of school or are unemployed. Support for developing a positive identity is scarce. In such settings, programs for youth can make an important contribution to identity development (Cooper, 2011).

Researchers are also increasingly finding that a positive ethnic identity is related to positive outcomes for ethnic minority adolescents (Umana-Taylor, Updegraff, & Gonzales-Bracken, 2010). One study indicated that Navajo adolescents' positive ethnic heritage was linked to higher self-esteem, school connectedness, and social functioning (Jones & Galliher, 2007). Another study found that exploration was an important aspect of establishing a secure sense of one's ethnic identity, which in turn was linked to a positive attitude toward one's own group and other groups (Whitehead & others, 2009). In another study, ethnic identity was linked to adjustment in adolescents primarily by fostering a positive sense of meaning (Kiang & Fuligni, 2010). In this study, Asian American adolescents reported engaging in a search for meaning in life more than non-Latino White and Latino adolescents. To read about one individual who guides Latino adolescents in developing a positive identity, see the *Connecting with Careers* profile.

Michelle Chin, age 16: "Parents do not understand that teenagers need to find out who they are, which means a lot of experimenting, a lot of mood swings, a lot of emotions and awkwardness. Like any teenager, I am facing an identity crisis. I am still trying to figure out whether I am a Chinese American or an American with Asian eyes."

How do social contexts influence adolescents' ethnic identity?

connectedness Characteristic consisting of two dimensions: mutuality, sensitivity to and respect for others' views; and permeability, openness to others' views.

ethnic identity An enduring aspect of the self that includes a sense of membership in an ethnic group, along with the attitudes and feelings related to that membership.

Armando Ronquillo, High School Counselor

Armando Ronquillo is a high school counselor and admissions advisor at Pueblo High School in a low-income area of Tucson, Arizona. More than 85 percent of the students have a Latino background. Ronquillo was named the top high school counselor in the state of Arizona for the year 2000.

Ronquillo especially works with Latino students to guide them in developing a positive identity. He talks with them about their Latino background and what it's like to have a bicultural identity—preserving important aspects of their Latino heritage but also pursuing what is important to be successful in the contemporary culture of the United States.

Ronquillo believes that helping students stay in school and getting them to think about the lifelong opportunities provided by a college education will benefit their identity development. He also works with parents to help them understand that their child going to college is doable and affordable.

Armando Ronquillo counseling a Latina high school student about college.

For more information about what school counselors do, see page 43 in the Careers in Life-Span Development appendix.

Review Connect Reflect

LG2 Explain the key facets of identity development

Review

- What does an identity involve?
- What is Erikson's view of identity?
- What are some contemporary thoughts on identity?
- What are the four identity statuses, and how do they change developmentally?
- How does the family influence identity?
- What characterizes ethnic identity?

Connect

- Connect the concept of adolescents' "possible selves" to Erikson's view of

adolescence as a time of identity versus identity confusion.

Reflect *Your Own Personal Journey of Life*

- Do you think your parents influenced your identity development? If so, how?

Personality   **LG3**   Describe personality and its development in adulthood

Trait Theories and the Big Five Factors of Personality

Views on Adult Personality Development

Generativity

Stability and Change

Earlier in the chapter, *personality* was defined as the enduring personal characteristics of individuals. Personality psychologists use many strategies to better understand the enduring characteristics of individuals. Some of them study the entire personality of

Openness	**C**onscientiousness	**E**xtraversion	**A**greeableness	**N**euroticism (emotional stability)
• Imaginative or practical	• Organized or disorganized	• Sociable or retiring	• Softhearted or ruthless	• Calm or anxious
• Interested in variety or routine	• Careful or careless	• Fun-loving or somber	• Trusting or suspicious	• Secure or insecure
• Independent or conforming	• Disciplined or impulsive	• Affectionate or reserved	• Helpful or uncooperative	• Self-satisfied or self-pitying

FIGURE 11.6

THE BIG FIVE FACTORS OF PERSONALITY. Each of the broad supertraits encompasses more narrow traits and characteristics. Use the acronym OCEAN to remember the Big Five personality factors (openness, conscientiousness, extraversion, agreeableness, neuroticism).

individuals; some come up with a list of traits that best describe individuals; others zero in on specific traits or characteristics, such as being introverted or extraverted.

In Chapter 1, we considered several major personality theories—psychoanalytic theories and the social cognitive theory of Albert Bandura. You might wish to review those theories at this time. Here our exploration of personality focuses on trait theory, several views of personality development in adulthood, and studies of stability and change in personality during adulthood.

TRAIT THEORIES AND THE BIG FIVE FACTORS OF PERSONALITY

Trait theories state that personality consists of broad dispositions, called traits, that tend to produce characteristic responses. In other words, people can be described in terms of the basic ways they behave, such as whether they are outgoing or friendly or whether they are dominant and assertive. Although trait theorists disagree about which traits make up personality, they agree that traits are the fundamental units and building blocks of personality (Olson & Hergenhahn, 2011).

One trait theory that has received considerable attention is the **Big Five factors of personality,** the view that personality is made up of openness to experience, conscientiousness, extraversion, agreeableness, and neuroticism (see Figure 11.6). (Notice that if you create an acronym from these trait names, you will get the word *OCEAN.*) A number of research studies point toward these five factors as important dimensions of personality (Costa & McCrae, 1995; McCrae & Costa, 2006).

Consider recent research on the Big Five factors and adolescent development. The Big Five factor of conscientiousness has emerged as a key predictor of adjustment and competence (Roberts & others, 2009). One study of the Big Five factors revealed that conscientiousness was the best predictor of both high school and college grade-point average (Noftle & Robins, 2007). Another study found that adolescents who did not have substance abuse problems or conduct problems were higher in conscientiousness than their counterparts who had these problems (Anderson & others, 2007).

The trait theories have identified a number of characteristics that are important to consider when attempting to understand an individual's personality (Berecz, 2009). The trait approach also has led to advances in the assessment of personality through the development of numerous personality tests. However, some psychologists note that the trait approach gives too little attention to environmental factors and puts too much emphasis on stability. These criticisms initially were leveled by social cognitive theorist Walter Mischel (1968). Mischel argued that personality often changes according to the situation. Thus, an individual may behave very differently at a party from the way he would in the library.

Today, most personality psychologists believe that personality is a product of *trait-situation interaction*. In other words, both traits and situational (context) factors

An adolescent with a high level of conscientiousness organizes his daily schedule and plans how to use his time effectively. *What are some characteristics of conscientiousness? How is it linked to adolescents' competence?*

trait theories Theories emphasizing that personality consists of broad dispositions, called traits, which tend to produce characteristic responses.

Big Five factors of personality The view that personality is made up of openness to experience, conscientiousness, extraversion, agreeableness, and neuroticism.

Era of late adulthood:
60 to ?

Late adult transition: Age 60 to 65

Culminating life structure for middle adulthood:
55 to 60

Age 50 transition:
50 to 55

Entry life structure for middle adulthood:
45 to 50

Middle adult transition: Age 40 to 45

Culminating life structure for early adulthood:
33 to 40

Age 30 transition:
28 to 33

Entry life structure for early adulthood:
22 to 28

Early adult transition: Age 17 to 22

FIGURE 11.7

LEVINSON'S PERIODS OF ADULT DEVELOPMENT. According to Levinson, adulthood has three main stages, which are surrounded by transition periods. Specific tasks and challenges are associated with each stage.

must be considered to understand personality (Burger, 2011). Also, some people are more consistent on some traits and other people are consistent on other traits.

VIEWS ON ADULT PERSONALITY DEVELOPMENT

Two important views on adult development are the stage-crisis view and the life-events approach. In examining these approaches, we discuss the extent to which adults experience a midlife crisis and consider how life events influence the individual's development.

The Stage-Crisis View   Erikson's theory, which we discussed earlier, is a stage-crisis view. Here we describe the view of Daniel Levinson and examine the concept of a midlife crisis.

Levinson's Seasons of a Man's Life   In *The Seasons of a Man's Life*, clinical psychologist Daniel Levinson (1978) reported the results of extensive interviews with 40 middle-aged men. The interviews were conducted with hourly workers, business executives, academic biologists, and novelists. Levinson bolstered his conclusions with information from the biographies of famous men and the development of memorable characters in literature. Although Levinson's major interest focused on midlife change, he described a number of stages and transitions in the life span, which are shown in Figure 11.7.

Levinson emphasizes that developmental tasks must be mastered at each of these stages. In early adulthood, the two major tasks to be mastered are exploring the possibilities for adult living and developing a stable life structure. Levinson sees the twenties as a *novice phase* of adult development. At the end of one's teens, a transition from dependence to independence should occur. This transition is marked by the formation of a dream—an image of the kind of life the youth wants to have, especially in terms of a career and marriage. The novice phase is a time of reasonably free experimentation and of testing the dream in the real world.

From about the ages of 28 to 33, the man goes through a transition period in which he must face the more serious question of determining his goals. During the thirties, he usually focuses on family and career development. In the later years of this period, he enters a phase of Becoming One's Own Man (or BOOM, as Levinson calls it). By age 40, he has reached a stable location in his career, has outgrown his earlier, more tenuous attempts at learning to become an adult, and now must look forward to the kind of life he will lead as a middle-aged adult.

According to Levinson, the change to middle adulthood lasts about five years (ages 40 to 45) and requires the adult male to come to grips with four major conflicts that have existed in his life since adolescence: (1) being young versus being old, (2) being destructive versus being constructive, (3) being masculine versus being feminine, and (4) being attached to others versus being separated from them. Seventy to eighty percent of the men Levinson interviewed found the midlife transition tumultuous and psychologically painful, as many aspects of their lives came into question. According to Levinson, the success of the midlife transition rests on how effectively the individual reduces the polarities and accepts each of them as an integral part of his being.

The original Levinson data included no females. However, Levinson (1987, 1996) subsequently reported that his stages, transitions, and the crisis of middle age hold for females as well as males.

Midlife Crises   Levinson (1978) views midlife as a crisis, believing that the middle-aged adult is suspended between the past and the future, trying to cope with this gap that threatens life's continuity. George Vaillant (1977) concludes that just as adolescence is a time for detecting parental flaws and discovering the truth about childhood, the forties are a decade of reassessing and recording the truth about the adolescent and adulthood years. However, whereas Levinson sees midlife as a crisis, Vaillant notes that only a minority of adults experience a midlife crisis:

> Just as pop psychologists have reveled in the not-so-common high drama of adolescent turmoil, also the popular press, sensing good copy, had made all too much of the mid-life crisis. The term *mid-life crisis* brings to mind some variation of the renegade minister who leaves behind four children and the congregation that loved him in order to drive off in a magenta Porsche with a 25-year-old striptease artiste. As with adolescent turmoil, mid-life crises are much rarer in community samples. (pp. 222–223)

Vaillant's study—called the Grant Study—involved a follow-up of Harvard University men in their early thirties and in their late forties who initially had been interviewed as undergraduates. Other research has also found that midlife is not characterized by pervasive crises. For example, a longitudinal study of 2,247 individuals found few midlife crises (McCrae & Costa, 1990). The emotional well-being of these individuals did not significantly decrease during their middle-aged years (see Figure 11.8). In fact, some studies have documented psychological gains among middle-aged adults. For example, one study revealed that individuals from 40 to 60 years of age were less nervous and worried than those under 40. The middle-aged adults reported a growing sense of control in their work as well as increased financial security, greater environmental mastery (the ability to handle daily responsibilities), and more autonomy than their younger counterparts.

Adult development experts have become virtually unanimous in their belief that midlife crises have been exaggerated (Lachman & Kranz, 2010; Pudrovska, 2009). In sum, (1) the stage theories place too much emphasis on crises in development, especially midlife crises; and (2) there often is considerable individual variation in the way people experience the stages, a topic that we turn to next.

Individual Variations   Stage theories especially focus on the universals of adult personality development. They try to pin down stages that all individuals go through in their adult lives. These theories do not adequately address individual variations in adult development. In an extensive study of a random sample of 500 men at midlife, it was concluded that there is extensive individual variation among men (Farrell & Rosenberg, 1981). In the individual variations view, middle-aged adults interpret, shape, alter, and give meaning to their lives (Arpanantikul, 2004).

It also is important to recognize how some individuals may experience a midlife crisis in some contexts of their lives but not others (Lachman, 2004). Thus, turmoil and stress may characterize one area of a person's life (such as work) while things are going smoothly in another context (such as family).

Researchers have found that in one-third of the cases in which individuals have reported having a midlife crisis, the crisis is triggered by life events such as a job loss, financial problems, or illness (Wethington, Kessler, & Pixley, 2004). Let's now further explore the role of life events in midlife development.

The Life-Events Approach   An alternative to the stage approach to adult development is the life-events approach (Serido, 2009). In the early version of the life-events approach, life events were viewed as taxing circumstances for individuals, forcing them to change their personality (Holmes & Rahe, 1967). Such events as the death of a spouse, divorce, marriage, and so on were believed to involve varying degrees of stress, and therefore likely to influence the individual's development.

Today's life-events approach is more sophisticated (Cui & Vaillant, 1996; Hultsch & Plemons, 1979). The **contemporary life-events approach** emphasizes that how life events influence the individual's development depends not only on the event but also on mediating factors (physical health and family supports, for example), the individual's adaptation to the life event (appraisal of the threat and coping

> Mid-life crises are greatly exaggerated in America.
>
> —George Vaillant
> *Contemporary Psychologist, Harvard University*

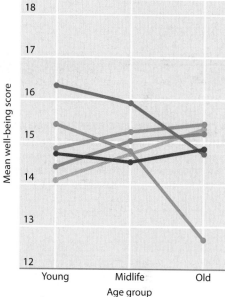

FIGURE 11.8

AGE AND WELL-BEING. In one study, six dimensions of well-being (self-acceptance, positive relations, personal growth, purpose in life, environmental mastery, and autonomy) were assessed in three different age groups of individuals (young adults, middle-aged adults, and older adults) (Keyes & Ryff, 1998). An increase or little change in most of the dimensions of well-being occurred during middle adulthood.

contemporary life-events approach Approach emphasizing that how a life event influences the individual's development depends not only on the event but also on mediating factors, the individual's adaptation to the life event, the life-stage context, and the sociohistorical context.

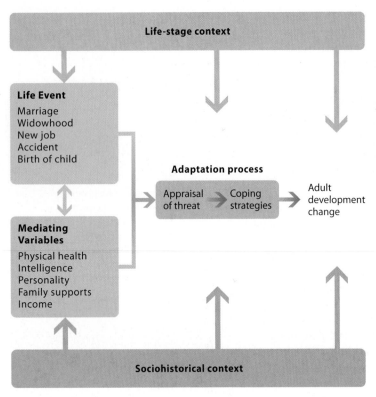

FIGURE 11.9

A CONTEMPORARY LIFE-EVENTS FRAMEWORK FOR INTERPRETING ADULT DEVELOPMENTAL CHANGE. According to the contemporary life-events approach, the influence of a life event depends on the event itself, on mediating variables, on the life-stage and sociohistorical context, and on the individual's appraisal of the event and coping strategies.

strategies, for example), the life-stage context, and the socio-historical context (see Figure 11.9).

Consider how the life event of divorce might affect personality. A divorce is likely to be more stressful for individuals who are in poor health and have little family support. One individual may perceive it as highly stressful (less adaptive) rather than a challenge while another may develop coping strategies to effectively deal with it (more adaptive). And a divorce may be more stressful after many years of marriage when adults are in their fifties than when they have been married only several years and are in their twenties (an example of life-stage context). Finally, adults may be able to cope more effectively with divorce today than several decades ago because divorce has become more commonplace and accepted in today's society (an example of sociohistorical context).

Though the life-events approach is a valuable addition to understanding adult development, it has its drawbacks. One drawback is that the life-events approach places too much emphasis on change. It does not adequately recognize the stability that, at least to some degree, characterizes adult development. Another drawback is that it may not be life's major events that are the primary sources of stress, but our daily experiences (Almeida & others, 2011; Piazza & others, 2010). Enduring a boring but tense job or living in poverty does not show up on scales of major life events. Yet the everyday pounding from these conditions can add up to a highly stressful life and eventually illness. Greater insight into the source of life's stresses might come from focusing more on daily hassles and daily uplifts (McIntosh, Gillanders, & Rodgers, 2010; O'Connor & others, 2009). Researchers have found that young and middle-aged adults experience a greater daily frequency of stressors than older individuals (Almeida & Horn, 2004). In a recent study, healthy older adult women 63 to 93 years of age reported their daily experiences over the course of one week (Charles & others, 2010). In this study, the older the women were, the fewer stressors and less frequent negative affect they reported.

The manner in which different stressors affect health varies—life events often produce prolonged arousal whereas daily stressors are linked to spikes in arousal (Piazza & others, 2010). Consider caring for a spouse who has Alzheimer disease. In this case, a life event (spouse diagnosed with an incurable disease) produces chronic stress for the caregiver, which also is linked to the daily stressors involved in caring for the individual.

GENERATIVITY

Erikson (1968) argues that middle-aged adults face the issue of **generativity versus stagnation,** which is the name Erikson gave to the seventh stage in his life-span theory. Generativity encompasses adults' desire to leave a legacy of themselves to the next generation. By contrast, stagnation (sometimes called "self-absorption") develops when individuals sense that they have done nothing for the next generation.

Does research support Erikson's theory that generativity is an important dimension of middle age? Yes, it does (McAdams & Cox, 2011). In George Vaillant's (2002) longitudinal studies of aging, in middle age, generativity (defined in this study as "taking care of the next generation") was more strongly related than intimacy to whether individuals would have an enduring and happy marriage at 75 to 80 years of age. One participant in Vaillant's studies said, "From twenty to thirty I learned how to get along with my wife. From thirty to forty I learned how to be a success at my job, and at forty to fifty I worried less about myself and more about the children" (p. 114).

developmental connection

Life-Span Perspective. Erikson's early adulthood stage is intimacy versus isolation, and his late adulthood stage is integrity versus despair. Chapter 1, p. 21

generativity versus stagnation The seventh stage in Erikson's life-span theory; it encompasses adults' desire to leave a legacy of themselves to the next generation.

Other research also supports Erikson's (1968) view on the importance of generativity in middle. In one study, Carol Ryff (1984) examined the views of women and men at different ages and found that middle-aged adults especially were concerned about generativity. In a longitudinal study of Smith College women, the desire for generativity increased as the participants aged from their thirties to their fifties (Stewart, Ostrove, & Helson, 2001) (see Figure 11.10). And in a recent study, generativity was strongly linked to middle-aged adults' positive social engagement in contexts such as family life and community activities (Cox & others, 2010).

Middle-aged adults can develop generativity in a number of ways (Kotre, 1984). Through biological generativity, adults conceive and give birth to an infant. Through parental generativity, adults provide nurturance and guidance to children. Through work generativity, adults develop skills that are passed down to others. And through cultural generativity, adults create, renovate, or conserve some aspect of culture that ultimately survives.

STABILITY AND CHANGE

Recall from Chapter 1 that an important issue in life-span development is the extent to which individuals show stability in their development versus the extent to which they change. A number of longitudinal studies have assessed stability and change in the personality of individuals at different points in their lives (Hopwood & others, 2011; McAdams & Olson, 2010; Roberts & Mroczek, 2008). A common finding is that, in most cases, the less time between measurements of personality characteristics, the more stability they show. Thus, if we measure a person's introversion/extraversion at the age of 20 and then again at age 30, we are likely to find more stability than if we assess the person at the age of 20 and then again at age 40.

Costa and McCrae's Baltimore Study   Earlier we discussed the Big Five factors in personality as an important trait theory. Paul Costa and Robert McCrae (1998; McCrae & Costa, 2006) have studied the Big Five factors in approximately a thousand college-educated women and men from 20 to 96 years of age. Longitudinal data collection initially began in the 1950s to the mid-1960s on people of varying ages and is ongoing. Costa and McCrae found a great deal of stability across the adult years in the Big Five personality factors—openness to experience, conscientiousness, extraversion, agreeableness, and neuroticism. However, recent studies have found age differences in the Big Five factors across the life span. Research on individuals from 16 years of age to the mid-eighties revealed that extraversion and openness decreased with age, whereas agreeableness increased with age (Donnellan & Lucas, 2008). In this study, conscientiousness peaked in middle age. Another study found that conscientiousness continued to develop in late adulthood (Roberts, Walton, & Bogg, 2005).

A meta-analysis of personality stability and change organized according to the Big Five framework included 92 longitudinal studies spanning 10 to 101 years of age (Roberts, Walton, & Viechtbauer, 2006):

- Results for extraversion were complex until it was subdivided into social dominance (assertiveness, dominance) and social vitality (talkativeness, sociability). Social dominance increased from adolescence through middle adulthood, whereas social vitality increased in adolescence and then decreased in early and late adulthood.

- Agreeableness and conscientiousness increased in early and middle adulthood.

- Neuroticism decreased in early adulthood.

- Openness to experience increased in adolescence and early adulthood and then decreased in late adulthood.

Might some Big Five factors be related to how long older adults live? To find out, read the *Connecting with Research* interlude.

Generativity

Feeling needed by people

Effort to ensure that young people get their chance to develop

Influence in my community or area of interest

A new level of productivity or effectiveness

Appreciation and awareness of older people

Having a wider perspective

Interest in things beyond my family

Identity certainty

A sense of being my own person

Excitement, turmoil, confusion about my impulses and potential (reversed)

Coming near the end of one road and not yet finding another (reversed)

Feeling my life is moving well

Searching for a sense of who I am (reversed)

Wishing I had a wider scope to my life (reversed)

Anxiety that I won't live up to opportunities (reversed)

Feeling secure and committed

FIGURE **11.10**

ITEMS USED TO ASSESS GENERATIVITY AND IDENTITY CERTAINTY. These items were used to assess generativity and identity certainty in the longitudinal study of Smith College women (Stewart, Ostrove, & Helson, 2001). In the assessment of identity certainty, five of the items involved reversed scoring. For example, if an individual scored high on the item "Searching for a sense of who I am," it was an indication of identity uncertainty rather than identity certainty.

Are Personality Traits Related to Longevity?

Researchers have found that some personality traits are associated with the mortality of older adults (Mroczek, Spiro, & Griffin, 2006; Noftle & Fleeson, 2010). In one study, 883 older Catholic clergy were given the NEO Five-Factor Inventory that assesses the Big Five factors in personality (Wilson & others, 2004). The clergy were followed for five years, during which 182 of the 883 clergy died. At the beginning of the study, the average age of the clergy was 75, and 69 percent of them were women. Risk of death nearly doubled in clergy with a high score on neuroticism (90th percentile) compared with a low score (10th percentile) and was halved in clergy who were very high in conscientiousness compared with those who were very low. Results for extraversion were mixed, whereas agreeableness and openness were not related to mortality.

Why might a high score on neuroticism and a low score on conscientiousness lead to an earlier death? Researchers have found that high-neuroticism older adults react more emotionally to stressful circumstances than their low-neuroticism counterparts (Mroczek, Spiro, & Griffin, 2006). Over many years, high neuroticism may elevate harmful stress hormones and produce physical damages to the cardiovascular system, thus contributing to mortality. By contrast, individuals who score high on conscientiousness engage in more healthy behaviors than those who score low. For example, low-conscientiousness individuals engage in more risky behaviors, such as excessive drinking and impulsive behaviors that lead to fatal accidents. It also has been proposed that they tend to have less healthy diets and are less likely to exercise regularly than high-conscientiousness individuals (Mroczek, Spiro, & Griffin, 2006).

A longitudinal study of more than 1,200 individuals across seven decades revealed that the Big Five personality factor of conscientiousness predicted lower mortality risk from childhood through late adulthood (Martin, Friedman, & Schwartz, 2007). Another longitudinal study recently

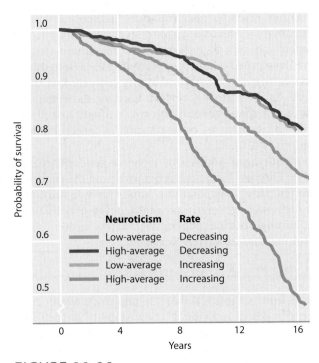

FIGURE **11.11**

LINK BETWEEN NEUROTICISM AND SURVIVAL IN AGING MEN. *Note:* At the beginning of the study, the men were 43 to 91 years old. During the 18-year period of the study, 30 percent of the participants died, with more than 70 percent of the deaths due to cardiovascular disease and cancer.

underscored the importance of the link between neuroticism and mortality in a sample of more than 1,600 aging men (Mroczek & Spiro, 2007). A high level of neuroticism and an increasing level of neuroticism were related to lower survival across an 18-year period (see Figure 11.11).

What type of studies might researchers conduct to identify personality traits such as conscientiousness and neuroticism in an effort to increase longevity?

Berkeley Longitudinal Studies   Most longitudinal studies indicate that neither extreme stability nor extreme change characterizes most people's personality as they go through the adult years. One of the longest-running inquiries is the series of analyses called the Berkeley Longitudinal Studies. Initially, more than 500 children and their parents were studied in the late 1920s and early 1930s. The book *Present and Past in Middle Life* (Eichorn & others, 1981) profiles these individuals as they became middle-aged.

The results from early adolescence through a portion of midlife did not support either extreme in the debate over whether personality is characterized by stability or change. Some characteristics were more stable than others, however. The most stable characteristics were the degree to which individuals were intellectually oriented, self-confident, or open to new experiences. The characteristics that changed the most included the extent to which the individuals were nurturant or hostile and whether they had good self-control.

John Clausen (1993), one of the researchers in the Berkeley Longitudinal Studies, holds that too much attention has been given to discontinuities for all members of the human species, as exemplified in the adult stage theories. Rather, he stresses that some people experience recurrent crises and change a great deal over the life course, whereas others have more stable, continuous lives and change far less.

Helson's Mills College Studies   Another longitudinal investigation of adult personality development was conducted by Ravenna Helson and her colleagues (Helson, 1997; Helson & Wink, 1992; Roberts, Helson, & Klohnen, 2002). They initially studied 132 women who were seniors at Mills College in California in the late 1950s. In 1981, when the women were 42 to 45 years old, they were studied again.

Helson and her colleagues distinguished three main groups among the Mills women: family-oriented (participants who had children), career-oriented (whether or not they also wanted families), and those who followed neither path (women without children who pursued only low-level work). Despite their different college profiles and their diverging life paths, the women in all three groups experienced some similar psychological changes over their adult years. However, the women in the third group changed less than those committed to career or family.

During their early forties, many of the women shared the concerns that stage theorists such as Levinson found in men: concern for young and old, introspectiveness, interest in roots, and awareness of limitations and death. However, the researchers in the Mills College Study concluded that rather than being in a midlife crisis, what the Mills women experienced was midlife *consciousness*. They also indicated that commitment to the tasks of early adulthood—whether to a career or family (or both)—helped women learn to control their impulses, develop interpersonal skills, become independent, and work hard to achieve goals. Women who did not commit themselves to one of these lifestyle patterns faced fewer challenges and did not develop as fully as the other women (Rosenfeld & Stark, 1987). In the Mills study, some women moved toward becoming "pillars of society" in their early forties to early fifties (Helson & Wink, 1992).

George Vaillant's Studies   George Vaillant (2002) has conducted three longitudinal studies of adult development and aging: (1) a sample of 268 socially advantaged Harvard graduates born about 1920 (called the "Grant Study"); (2) a sample of 456 socially disadvantaged inner-city men born about 1930; and (3) a sample of 90 middle-SES, intellectually gifted women born about 1910. These individuals have been assessed numerous times (in most cases every two years), beginning in the 1920s to 1940s and continuing today for those still living. The main assessments involve extensive interviews with the participants, their parents, and teachers.

Vaillant categorized 75- to 80-year-olds as "happy-well," "sad-sick," or "dead." He used data collected from these individuals when they were 50 years of age to predict which categories they were likely to end up in at 75 to 80 years of age. Alcohol abuse and smoking at age 50 were the best predictors of which individuals would be dead at 75 to 80 years of age. Other factors at age 50 were linked with being in the "happy-well" category at 75 to 80 years of age: getting regular exercise; avoiding being overweight; being well educated; having a stable marriage; being future-oriented; being thankful and forgiving; empathizing with others; being active with other people; and having good coping skills. Wealth and income at age 50 were not linked with being in the "happy-well" category at 75 to 80 years of age. The results for one of Vaillant's studies, the Grant Study of Harvard men, are shown in Figure 11.12.

What characterized the development of women in Ravenna Helson's Mills College Study?

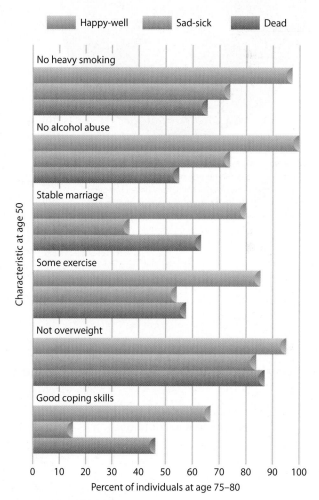

FIGURE 11.12

LINKS BETWEEN CHARACTERISTICS AT AGE 50 AND HEALTH AND HAPPINESS AT AGE 75 TO 80. In a longitudinal study, the characteristics shown above at age 50 were related to whether individuals were happy-well, sad-sick, or dead at age 75 to 80 (Vaillant, 2002).

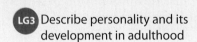

developmental **connection**

Life-Span Perspective. The extent to which development is characterized by stability and/or change is one of life-span development's key issues. Chapter 1, p. 18

At age 55, actor Jack Nicholson said "I feel exactly the same as I've always felt: a slightly reined-in voracious beast." Nicholson felt his personality had not changed much. Some others might think they have changed more. *How much does personality change and how does it stay the same through adulthood?*

Conclusions What can we conclude about stability and change in personality development during the adult years? According to a recent research review by leading researchers Brent Roberts and Daniel Mroczek (2008), there is increasing evidence that personality traits continue to change during the adult years, even into late adulthood. However, in the recent meta-analysis of 92 longitudinal studies described earlier, the greatest change in personality traits occurred in early adulthood—from about 20 to 40 years of age (Roberts, Walton, & Viechtbauer, 2006).

Thus, people show more stability in their personality when they reach midlife than when they were younger adults (McAdams & Olson, 2010). These findings support what is called a cumulative *personality model* of personality development, which states that with time and age people become more adept at interacting with their environment in ways that promote increased stability in personality (Caspi & Roberts, 2001).

This does not mean that change is absent throughout middle and late adulthood. Ample evidence shows that social contexts, new experiences, and sociohistorical changes can affect personality development, but the changes in middle and late adulthood are usually not as great as in early adulthood (Mroczek, Spiro, & Griffin, 2006).

In general, changes in personality traits across adulthood also occur in a positive direction (George, 2010; Staudinger & Jacobs, 2010). Over time, "people become more confident, warm, responsible, and calm" (Roberts & Mroczek, 2008, p. 33). Such positive changes equate with becoming more socially mature.

In sum, recent research contradicts the old view that stability in personality begins to set in at about 30 years of age (McAdams & Olson, 2010; Roberts & others, 2009). Although there are some consistent developmental changes in the personality traits of large numbers of people, at the individual level people can show unique patterns of personality traits, and these patterns often reflect life experiences related to themes of their specific developmental period (Roberts & Mroczek, 2008). For example, researchers have found that individuals who are in a stable marriage and a solid career track become more socially dominant, conscientious, and emotionally stable as they go through early adulthood (Roberts & Wood, 2006). And, for some of these individuals, there is greater change in their personality traits than for other individuals (Roberts & Mroczek, 2008).

Review Connect Reflect

LG3 Describe personality and its development in adulthood

Review

- What are trait theories? What are the Big Five factors of personality?
- What are some views of adult development of personality?
- What is Erikson's view of middle-aged adults?
- What are some major longitudinal studies of adult personality development, and what implications do they have for the stability/change issue?

Connect

- This section discussed four different longitudinal studies. What are the pros and cons of using a longitudinal study to collect data (as discussed in Chapter 1)?

Reflect *Your Own Personal Journey of Life*

- Think about the Big Five factors of personality for a few moments. Using the Big Five factors, describe your own personality.

reach your **learning goals**

The Self

LG1 Discuss the main ways the self is conceptualized

Self-Understanding

- There is considerable overlap in the concepts of self, identity, and personality. Self consists of all characteristics of a person, identity is who a person is, and personality comprises the enduring personal characteristics of individuals. Self-understanding is the cognitive representation of the self, the substance of self-conceptions. Developmental changes in self-understanding include the construction of the self in infancy in terms of self-recognition and transformations in self-understanding in childhood (including perspective taking). Self-understanding in early childhood is characterized by confusion of self, mind, and body; concrete, physical, and active descriptions; and unrealistic positive overestimations. Young children display more sophisticated self-understanding and understanding of others than was previously thought. Self-understanding in middle and late childhood involves an increase in the use of psychological characteristics and traits, social descriptions, and social comparison; distinction between the real and ideal self; and an increase in realistic self-evaluations. Social understanding also increases in middle and late childhood, especially in taking the perspective of others. Self-definition in adolescence is more abstract and idealistic, involves more contradictions within the self, is more fluctuating, includes concern about the real self versus the ideal self, is characterized by increased self-consciousness, and is more integrative. Developments in adulthood include expanded self-awareness, revision of possible selves, and life reviews of older adults.

Self-Esteem and Self-Concept

- Self-esteem refers to global evaluations of the self; it is also called self-worth and self-image. Self-concept consists of domain-specific evaluations of the self. Self-esteem can change over time, and low self-esteem is linked with depression. The accuracy of self-evaluations increases across the elementary school years. Some studies have found that self-esteem decreases in adolescence, but overall, most adolescents still have positive self-esteem. Important aspects of self-esteem include the degree to which it is linked to performance. This varies, as there are only moderate correlations with school performance and varying correlations with job performance; individuals with high self-esteem have greater initiative and this can produce positive or negative outcomes. Self-esteem is strongly correlated with happiness, but there is a dark side to high self-esteem in that some individuals who have high self-esteem are conceited and narcissistic. Five ways to increase self-esteem are through (1) identifying the causes of low self-esteem and the domains of competence important to the self, (2) providing emotional support and social approval, (3) taking responsibility for self-esteem, (4) achieving goals, and (5) developing effective coping strategies.

Self-Regulation

- Self-regulation involves the ability to control one's behavior without having to rely on others' help. Two-year-olds may show rudimentary forms of self-regulation, but many preschoolers show increased self-regulation. Elementary-school-aged children increase their self-regulation. In adolescence, some changes may increase self-regulation, while others decrease it. Self-control increases in early and middle adulthood. Self-regulation may vary by domain. For example, older adults often show less self-regulation in the physical domain than younger adults. Baltes proposed the selective optimization with compensation theory of self-regulation. Many older adults show a remarkable ability to engage in self-regulation despite encountering losses.

Identity

LG2 Explain the key facets of identity development

What Is Identity?

- Identity is a self-portrait with many pieces, including vocational/career identity, political identity, religious identity, relationship identity, sexual identity, and cultural/ethnic identity.

Erikson's View

- Identity versus identity confusion is Erikson's fifth developmental stage, which individuals experience during the adolescent years. At this time, adolescents examine who they are, what they are all about, and where they are going in life. Erikson describes the psychosocial moratorium between childhood dependence and adult independence that adolescents experience, which promotes identity exploration.

Some Contemporary Thoughts on Identity

- In the contemporary view, identity development is more gradual than Erikson's term *crisis* implies, is extraordinarily complex, neither begins nor ends with adolescence, and emphasizes multiple identities.

Developmental Changes

- According to Marcia, various combinations of crisis and commitment produce four identity statuses: identity diffused, identity foreclosed, identity moratorium, and identity achieved. A number of experts stress that the key developmental changes in identity occur in the late teens and early twenties. "MAMA" (moratorium-achievement-moratorium-achievement) cycles may continue throughout adulthood.

Family Influences

- Adolescents' identity development advances when their relationship with their parents includes both individuality and connectedness.

Ethnic Identity

- Ethnic identity may present special issues for members of ethnic minority groups, and they may confront these issues for the first time in adolescence. A positive ethnic identity is increasingly linked to positive outcomes for ethnic minority adolescents.

Personality

LG3 Describe personality and its development in adulthood

Trait Theories and the Big Five Factors of Personality

- Trait theories state that personality consists of broad dispositions, called traits, that tend to produce characteristic responses. One trait theory that has received considerable attention is the Big Five factors of personality, which consist of openness to experience, conscientiousness, extraversion, agreeableness, and neuroticism. Today most psychologists stress that personality is a product of trait-situation interaction.

Views on Adult Personality Development

- Two of the important adult developmental views are the stage-crisis view and the life-events approach. Levinson's and Erikson's theories are stage-crisis views. Midlife crises do not occur nearly as much as the stereotype suggests. What does arise is a midlife consciousness that focuses on such matters as how to adapt to aging. The life-events approach argues that life events and how people adapt to them are important in understanding adult development. There is considerable variation in how people go through the adult stages of development and in how they experience and adapt to life events.

Generativity

- Erikson argues that middle-aged adults face a significant issue in life—generativity versus stagnation—which is the name he gave to the seventh stage in his life-span theory. Generativity encompasses adults' desire to leave a legacy of themselves to the next generation.

Stability and Change

- Four longitudinal studies that have addressed stability and change in adult development are Costa and McCrae's Baltimore Study, the Berkeley Longitudinal Studies, Helson's Mills College Study, and Vaillant's studies. The longitudinal studies have shown both stability and change in adult personality development. The cumulative personality model states that with time and age personality becomes more stable. Change in personality traits occurs more in early adulthood than middle and late adulthood, but a number of aspects of personality do continue to change after early adulthood. Change in personality traits across adulthood occurs in a positive direction, reflecting social maturity. At the individual level, changes in personality are often linked to life experiences related to a specific developmental period. Some people change more than others.

key terms

self 339
identity 339
personality 339
self-understanding 339
perspective taking 342
possible selves 343
self-esteem 345
self-concept 345

self-regulation 348
selective optimization
    with compensation
    theory 350
identity versus identity
    confusion 353
psychosocial
    moratorium 353

crisis 354
commitment 354
identity diffusion 354
identity foreclosure 354
identity moratorium 355
identity achievement 355
individuality 356
connectedness 357

ethnic identity 357
trait theories 359
Big Five factors of
    personality 359
contemporary life-events
    approach 361
generativity versus
    stagnation 362

key people

Ross Thompson 341
Robert Selman 342
Susan Harter 348
Claire Kopp 349
Paul Baltes 350

Erik Erikson 353
James Marcia 354
Alan Waterman 355
Walter Mischel 359
Daniel Levinson 360

George Vaillant 361
Paul Costa and
    Robert McCrae 363
John Clausen 365

Ravenna Helson 365
Brent Roberts and
    Daniel Mroczek 366

chapter 12 GENDER AND SEXUALITY

chapter outline

preview

As females and males, human beings are involved in the existence and continuation of life. Gender and sexuality—our lives as females and males—are important aspects of human development and are the topics of this chapter.

Biological, Social, and Cognitive Influences on Gender

LG1 Explain biological, social, and cognitive influences on gender

- Biological Influences
- Social Influences
- Cognitive Influences

Gender refers to the characteristics of people as males and females. **Gender identity** involves a sense of one's own gender, including knowledge, understanding, and acceptance of being male or female (Egan & Perry, 2001; Pasterski, Golombok, & Hines, 2011). **Gender roles** are sets of expectations that prescribe how females or males should think, act, and feel. During the preschool years, most children increasingly act in ways that match their culture's gender roles. **Gender-typing** refers to acquisition of a traditional masculine or feminine role. For example, fighting is more characteristic of a traditional masculine role and crying is more characteristic of a traditional feminine role.

One aspect of gender identity involves knowing whether you are a boy or a girl (Martin & Ruble, 2010). Until recently, it was thought that this aspect of gender identity emerged at about 2½ years. However, a recent longitudinal study that explored the acquisition of gender labels in infancy and their implications for gender-typed play revealed that gender identity likely emerges before 2 years of age (Zosuls & others, 2009). In this study, infants began using gender labels on average at 19 months of age, with girls beginning to use gender labels earlier than boys. This gender difference became present at 17 months of age and increased at 21 months of age. Use of gender labels was linked to gender-typed play, indicating that knowledge of gender categories may affect gender-typing earlier than 2 years of age.

A recent study revealed that sex-typed behavior (boys playing with cars and girls with jewelry, for example) increased during the preschool years, and children engaging in the most sex-typed behavior during the preschool years were still doing so at 8 years of age (Golombok & others, 2008).

> We are born twice over; the first time for existence, the second time for life; once as human beings and later as men or as women.
>
> —JEAN-JACQUES ROUSSEAU
> *French-Born Swiss Philosopher, 18th Century*

BIOLOGICAL INFLUENCES

It was not until the 1920s that researchers confirmed the existence of human sex chromosomes, the genetic material that determines our sex. Humans normally have 46 chromosomes, arranged in pairs. A 23rd pair with two X-shaped chromosomes produces a female. A 23rd pair with an X chromosome and a Y chromosome produces a male.

Hormones   In Chapter 3, we discussed the two classes of hormones that have the most influence on gender: estrogens and androgens. Both estrogens and androgens occur in females and males, but in very different concentrations.

Estrogens primarily influence the development of female physical sex characteristics and help regulate the menstrual cycle. Estrogens are a general class of hormones. An example of an important estrogen is estradiol. In females, estrogens are produced mainly by the ovaries.

gender The characteristics of people as females or males.

gender identity Involves a sense of one's own gender, including knowledge, understanding, and acceptance of being male or female.

gender role A set of expectations that prescribe how females or males should think, act, or feel.

gender-typing Acquisition of a traditional masculine or feminine role.

estrogens A class of sex hormones—an important one of which is estradiol—that primarily influences the development of female sex characteristics and helps regulate the menstrual cycle.

◄─ ■ ■ ■ ■ ■ ■ ■ ■ ■ ■ ■

developmental connection

Biological Processes. Hormones are powerful chemical substances secreted by the endocrine glands and carried through the body by the bloodstream. Chapter 3, p. 93

◄─ ■ ■ ■ ■ ■ ■ ■ ■ ■ ■ ■

developmental connection

Biological Processes. Figure 2.5 shows the genetic difference in males and females; in the 23rd pair of chromosomes, the male's Y chromosome is smaller than the female's X chromosome. Chapter 2, p. 54

androgens A class of sex hormones—an important one of which is testosterone—that primarily promotes the development of male genitals and secondary sex characteristics.

Androgens primarily promote the development of male genitals and secondary sex characteristics. One important androgen is testosterone. Androgens are produced by the adrenal glands in males and females, and by the testes in males.

During the first few weeks of gestation, female and male embryos look alike. Male sex organs start to differ from female sex organs when a gene on the Y chromosome directs a small piece of tissue in the embryo to turn into testes. Once the tissue has turned into testes, they begin to secrete testosterone. Because in females there is no Y chromosome, the tissue turns into ovaries. To explore biological influences on gender, researchers have studied individuals who are exposed to unusual levels of sex hormones early in development (Pasterski, Golombok, & Hines, 2011). Here are four examples of the problems that may occur as a result (Lippa, 2005, pp. 122–124, 136–137):

- *Congenital adrenal hyperplasia (CAH).* Some girls have this condition, which is caused by a genetic defect. Their adrenal glands enlarge, resulting in abnormally high levels of androgens. Although CAH girls are XX females, they vary in how much their genitals look like male or female genitals. Their genitals may be surgically altered to look more like those of a typical female. Although CAH girls usually grow up to think of themselves as girls and women, they are less content with being a female and show a stronger interest in being a male than non-CAH girls (Berenbaum & Bailey, 2003; Ehrhardt & Baker, 1974; Hall & others, 2004). They like sports and enjoy playing with boys and boys' toys. CAH girls usually don't like typical girl activities such as playing with dolls and wearing makeup.

- *Androgen-insensitive males.* Because of a genetic error, a small number of XY males don't have androgen cells in their bodies. Their bodies look female, they develop a female gender identity, and they usually are sexually attracted to males.

- *Pelvic field defect.* A small number of newborns have a disorder called pelvic field defect, which in boys involves a missing penis. These XY boys have normal amounts of testosterone prenatally but usually are castrated just after being born and raised as females. One study revealed that despite the efforts by parents to rear them as girls, most of the XY children insisted that they were boys (Reiner & Gearhart, 2004). Apparently, normal exposure to androgens prenatally had a stronger influence on their gender identity than being castrated and raised as girls.

- *Early loss of penis and sexual reassignment.* In an intriguing case, one of two identical twin boys lost his penis due to an errant circumcision. The twin who lost his penis was surgically reassigned to be a girl and reared as a girl. Bruce (the real name of the boy) became "Brenda." Early indications were that the sex reassignment had positive outcomes (Money, 1975), but later it was concluded that "Brenda" had not adjusted well to life as a girl (Diamond & Sigmundson, 1997). As a young adult, Brenda became David and lived as a man with a wife and adopted children (Colapinto, 2000). Tragically in 2004, when David was 38 years old, he committed suicide.

Although sex hormones alone, of course, do not determine behavior, researchers have found links between sex hormone levels and certain behaviors. The most established effects of testosterone on humans involve aggressive behavior and sexual behavior (Hyde & DeLamater, 2011). Levels of testosterone are correlated with sexual behavior in boys during puberty (Udry & others, 1985). And a recent study revealed that a higher fetal testosterone level measured from amniotic fluid was linked to increased male-typical play, such as increased aggression, in 6- to 10-year-old boys and girls (Auyeung & others, 2009).

The Evolutionary Psychology View   In Chapter 2, we described the approach of evolutionary psychology, which emphasizes that adaptation during the evolution of humans produced psychological differences between males and females (Buss, 2012). Evolutionary psychologists argue that primarily because of their differing roles in reproduction, males and females faced different pressures in primeval environments when the human species was evolving. In particular, because having multiple sexual liaisons improves the likelihood that males will pass on their genes, natural selection favored males who adopted short-term mating strategies. These males competed with other males to acquire more resources in order to access females. Therefore, say evolutionary psychologists, males evolved dispositions that favor violence, competition, and risk taking.

In contrast, according to evolutionary psychologists, females' contributions to the gene pool were improved by securing resources for their offspring, which was promoted by obtaining long-term mates who could support a family. As a consequence, natural selection favored females who devoted effort to parenting and chose mates who could provide their offspring with resources and protection. Females developed preferences for successful, ambitious men who could provide these resources (Buss, 2012).

Critics of evolutionary psychology argue that its hypotheses are backed by speculations about prehistory, not evidence, and that in any event people are not locked into behavior that was adaptive in the evolutionary past. Critics also claim that the evolutionary view pays little attention to cultural and individual variations in gender differences (Brannon, 2012).

SOCIAL INFLUENCES

Many social scientists do not locate the cause of psychological gender differences in biological dispositions. Rather, they argue that these differences are due to social experiences. Three theories that reflect this view have been influential.

Alice Eagly (2001, 2010) proposed **social role theory,** which states that psychological gender differences result from the contrasting roles of women and men. In most cultures around the world, women have less power and status than men do, and they control fewer resources (UNICEF, 2011). Compared with men, women perform more domestic work, spend fewer hours in paid employment, receive lower pay, and are more thinly represented in the highest levels of organizations. In Eagly's view, as women adapted to roles with less power and less status in society, they showed more cooperative, less dominant profiles than men. Thus, the social hierarchy and division of labor are important causes of gender differences in power, assertiveness, and nurture.

The **psychoanalytic theory of gender** stems from Sigmund Freud's view that the preschool child develops a sexual attraction to the opposite-sex parent. At 5 or 6 years of age, the child renounces this attraction because of anxious feelings. Subsequently, the child identifies with the same-sex parent, unconsciously adopting the same-sex parent's characteristics. However, developmentalists do not hold that gender development proceeds as Freud proposed. Children become gender-typed much earlier than 5 or 6 years of age, and they become masculine or feminine even when the same-sex parent is not present in the family.

The social cognitive approach discussed in Chapter 1 provides an alternative explanation of how children develop gender-typed behavior (see Figure 12.1). According to the **social cognitive theory of gender,** children's gender development occurs through observation and imitation, and through the rewards and punishments children experience for gender-appropriate and gender-inappropriate behavior (Bussey & Bandura, 1999).

Parents, by action and example, influence their children's and adolescents' gender development (Blakemore, Berenbaum, & Liben, 2009). Parents often use rewards and punishments to teach their daughters to be feminine ("Karen, you are being a good girl when you play gently with your doll") and their sons to be masculine ("Keith, a boy as big as you is not supposed to cry").

developmental connection

Biological Processes. Evolutionary psychology emphasizes the importance of adaptation, reproduction, and "survival of the fittest" in shaping behavior. Chapter 2, p. 49

Sex differences are adaptations to the differing restrictions and opportunities that a society provides for its men and women.

—**ALICE EAGLY**
Contemporary Psychologist, Northwestern University

developmental connection

Theories. Freud proposed that individuals go through five stages of psychosocial development. Chapter 1, p. 21

developmental connection

Social Cognitive Theory. Social cognitive theory holds that behavior, environment, and person (cognitive) factors are the key aspects of development. Chapter 1, p. 25

social role theory Eagly's theory that psychological gender differences are caused by the contrasting social roles of women and men.

psychoanalytic theory of gender Theory that stems from Freud's view that preschool children develop a sexual attraction to the opposite-sex parent, then at 5 or 6 years of age renounce the attraction because of anxious feelings, subsequently identifying with the same-sex parent and unconsciously adopting the same-sex parent's characteristics.

social cognitive theory of gender The idea that children's gender development occurs through observation and imitation of gender behavior, as well as through the rewards and punishments children experience for behaviors believed to be appropriate or inappropriate for their gender.

Theory	Processes	Outcome
Psychoanalytic theory	Sexual attraction to opposite-sex parent at 3 to 5 years of age; anxiety about sexual attraction and subsequent identification with same-sex parent at 5 to 6 years of age	Gender behavior similar to that of same-sex parent
Social cognitive theory	Rewards and punishments of gender-appropriate and -inappropriate behavior by adults and peers; observation and imitation of models' masculine and feminine behavior	Gender behavior

FIGURE **12.1**

PARENTS INFLUENCE THEIR CHILDREN'S GENDER DEVELOPMENT BY ACTION AND EXAMPLE

"How is it gendered?"
© Edward Koren/The New Yorker Collection/
www.cartoonbank.com.

Mothers and fathers often interact differently with their children and adolescents. Mothers are more involved with their children and adolescents than are fathers, although fathers increase the time they spend in parenting when they have sons, and they are less likely to become divorced when they have sons (Diekmann & Schmidheiny, 2004; Galambos, Berenbaum, & McHale, 2009). Mothers' interactions with their children and adolescents often center on caregiving and teaching activities, whereas fathers' interactions often involve leisure activities (Galambos, Berenbaum, & McHale, 2009).

Parents frequently interact differently with sons and daughters, and these gendered interactions that begin in infancy usually continue through childhood and adolescence. In reviewing research on this topic, Phyllis Bronstein (2006) reached these conclusions:

- *Mothers' socialization strategies.* In many cultures, mothers socialize their daughters to be more obedient and responsible than their sons. They also place more restrictions on daughters' autonomy.

- *Fathers' socialization strategies.* Fathers pay more attention to sons than daughters, engage in more activities with sons, and put forth more effort to promote sons' intellectual development.

Thus, according to Bronstein (2006, pp. 269–270), "Despite an increased awareness in the United States and other Western cultures of the detrimental effects of gender stereotyping, many parents continue to foster behaviors and perceptions that are consonant with traditional gender role norms."

Children also learn about gender from observing other adults in the neighborhood and in the media (Brannon, 2012). As children get older, peers become increasingly important. Peers extensively reward and punish gender behavior (Leaper & Bigler, 2011). For example, when children play in ways that the culture says are sex-appropriate, they tend to be rewarded by their peers. Those who engage in activities that are considered sex-inappropriate tend to be criticized or abandoned by their peers. It is generally more accepted for girls to act more like boys than it is for boys to act more like girls; thus, use of the term *tomboy* to describe masculine girls is often thought of as less derogatory than the term *sissy* to describe feminine boys (Pasterski, Golombok, & Hines, 2011).

From 4 to about 12 years of age, children spend a large majority of their free play time exclusively with others of their own sex (Maccoby, 2002). What kind of socialization takes place in these same-sex play groups? In one study, researchers observed preschoolers over a period of six months (Martin & Fabes, 2001). The more time boys spent interacting with other boys, the more their activity level, rough-and-tumble play, and sex-typed choice of toys and games increased, and the less time boys spent near adults. By contrast, the more time the preschool girls

What role does gender play in children's peer relations?

spent interacting with other girls, the more their activity level and aggression decreased, and the more their girl-type play activities and time spent near adults increased. After watching elementary school children repeatedly play in same-sex groups, two researchers characterized the playground as "gender school" (Luria & Herzog, 1985). Continuing in adolescence and the adulthood years through late adulthood, friendships also mainly consist of same-sex peers (Mehta & Strough, 2009, 2010).

COGNITIVE INFLUENCES

Observation, imitation, rewards, and punishment—these are the mechanisms by which gender develops, according to social cognitive theory. Interactions between the child and the social environment are viewed as the main keys to gender development. Some critics who adopt a cognitive approach argue that this explanation pays too little attention to the child's own mind and understanding, portraying the child as passively acquiring gender roles (Martin, Ruble, & Szkrybalo, 2002).

One influential cognitive theory is **gender schema theory,** which states that gender-typing emerges as children gradually develop gender schemas of what is gender-appropriate and gender-inappropriate in their culture (Martin & Ruble, 2010). A *schema* is a cognitive structure, a network of associations that guide an individual's perceptions. A *gender schema* organizes the world in terms of female and male. Children are internally motivated to perceive the world and to act in accordance with their developing schemas. Bit by bit, children pick up what is gender-appropriate and gender-inappropriate in their culture, using this information to develop gender schemas that shape how they perceive the world and what they remember. Children are motivated to act in ways that conform to these gender schemas. Thus, gender schemas fuel gender-typing. How effectively do gender schemas extend to young children's judgments about occupations, for instance? For more information on this topic, see the *Connecting with Research* interlude.

In sum, cognitive factors contribute to the way children think and act as males and females (Martin & Ruble, 2010). Through biological, social, and cognitive processes, children develop their gender attitudes and behaviors (Blakemore, Berenbaum, & Liben, 2009).

gender schema theory The theory that gender-typing emerges as children gradually develop gender schemas of what is gender-appropriate and gender-inappropriate in their culture.

connecting with research

What Are Young Children's Gender Schemas About Occupations?

In one study, researchers interviewed children 3 to 7 years old about 10 traditionally masculine occupations (airplane pilot, car mechanic) and feminine occupations (clothes designer, secretary), using questions such as these (Levy, Sadovsky, & Troseth, 2000):

- *Example of a traditionally masculine occupation item.* An airplane pilot is a person who "flies airplanes for people." Who do you think would do the best job as an airplane pilot, a man or a woman?
- *Example of a traditionally feminine occupation item.* A clothing designer is a person "who draws up and makes clothes for people." Who do you think would do the best job as a clothes designer, a man or a woman?

As indicated in Figure 12.2, the children had well-developed gender schemas, in this case reflected in stereotypes, of occupations. They "viewed men as more competent than women in masculine occupations, and rated women as more competent than men in feminine occupations" (p. 993). Also, "girls' ratings of women's competence at feminine occupations were substantially higher than their ratings of men's competence at masculine occupations. Conversely, boys' ratings of men's competence at masculine occupations were considerably greater than their ratings of women's competence at feminine occupations" (p. 1002). These findings demonstrate that children as young as 3 to 4 years of age have strong gender schemas regarding the perceived competencies of men and women in gender-typed occupations.

The researchers also asked the children to select from a list of emotions how they would feel if they grew up to have each of the 10 occupations. Girls said they would be happy with the feminine occupations and angry or disgusted with the masculine occupations. As expected, boys reversed their choices, saying they would be happy if they grew up to have the masculine occupations but angry and disgusted with the feminine occupations. However, the boys' emotions were more intense (more angry and disgusted) in desiring to avoid the feminine occupations than girls in wanting to avoid the masculine occupations. This finding supports other research that indicates gender roles often constrict boys more than girls (Matlin, 2012).

Children in this study were at the height of gender stereotyping. Most older children, adolescents, and adults become more flexible about occupational roles (Leaper & Bigler, 2011). What does our understanding of this flexibility suggest about the role of education in reducing gender-based stereotypes?

FIGURE **12.2**

CHILDREN'S JUDGMENTS ABOUT THE COMPETENCE OF MEN AND WOMEN IN GENDER-STEREOTYPED OCCUPATIONS

	Boy	Girl
"Masculine Occupations"		
Percentage who judged men more competent	87	70
Percentage who judged women more competent	13	30
"Feminine Occupations"		
Percentage who judged men more competent	35	8
Percentage who judged women more competent	64	92

Review **Connect** Reflect

 LG1 Explain biological, social, and cognitive influences on gender

Review

- What is gender? What are some components of gender?
- How does biology influence gender?
- How do cognitive factors influence gender development?

Connect

- Compare biological, social, and cognitive influences on gender.

Reflect *Your Own Personal Journey of Life*

- Which theory of gender development do you think best explains your gender development? Explain. What might an eclectic view of gender development be like? (You might want to review the discussion of an eclectic theoretical view in Chapter 1.)

Gender Stereotypes, Similarities, and Differences

LG2 Discuss gender stereotypes, similarities, and differences

Gender Stereotyping

Gender Similarities and Differences

To what extent do real behavioral differences exist between males and females? Are many of the reported differences just stereotypes?

GENDER STEREOTYPING

Gender stereotypes are general impressions and beliefs about females and males. For example, men are powerful; women are weak. Men make good physicians; women make good nurses. Men are good with numbers; women are good with words. Women are emotional; men are not. All of these are stereotypes. They are generalizations about a group that reflect widely held beliefs. Recent research has found that gender stereotypes are, to a great extent, still present in today's world, in the lives of both children and adults (Best, 2010; Leaper & Bigler, 2011). Researchers also have found that boys' gender stereotypes are more rigid than girls' (Blakemore, Berenbaum, & Liben, 2009).

Traditional Masculinity and Femininity   A classic study in the early 1970s assessed which traits and behaviors college students believed were characteristic of females and which they believed were characteristic of males (Broverman & others, 1972). The traits associated with males were labeled *instrumental:* they included characteristics such as being independent, aggressive, and power-oriented. The traits associated with females were labeled *expressive:* they included characteristics such as being warm and sensitive.

Thus, the instrumental traits associated with males suited them for the traditional masculine role of going out into the world as the breadwinner. The expressive traits associated with females paralleled the traditional feminine role of being the sensitive, nurturing caregiver in the home. These roles and traits, however, are not just different; they also are unequal in terms of social status and power. The traditional feminine characteristics are childlike, suitable for someone who is dependent and subordinate to others. The traditional masculine characteristics suit one to deal competently with the wider world and to wield authority.

Developmental Changes in Gender Stereotyping   Earlier we described how young children stereotype occupations as being "masculine" or "feminine." When do children begin to engage in gender stereotyping? In one study, gender stereotyping by children was present even in 2-year-olds, but increased considerably by 4 years of age (Gelman, Taylor, & Nguyen, 2004).

Gender stereotyping continues to change during middle and late childhood and adolescence (Martin & Ruble, 2010). A recent study of 3- to 10-year-old U.S. children revealed that girls and older children used a higher percentage of gender stereotypes (Miller & others, 2009). In this study, appearance stereotypes were more prevalent on the part of girls, whereas activity (sports, for example) and trait (aggressive, for example) stereotyping was more commonly engaged in by boys. During middle and late childhood, children expanded the range and extent of their gender stereotyping in areas such as occupations, sports, and school tasks. In early adolescence, gender stereotyping might increase again, a topic we will address shortly. By late adolescence, gender attitudes become more flexible.

First imagine that this is a photograph of a baby girl. *What expectations would you have for her?* Then imagine that this is a photograph of a baby boy. *What expectations would you have for him?*

gender stereotypes General impressions and beliefs about females and males.

GENDER SIMILARITIES AND DIFFERENCES

What is the reality behind gender stereotypes? Let's examine some of the differences between the sexes, keeping in mind the following:

- The differences are averages and do not apply to all females or all males.
- Even when gender differences occur, there often is considerable overlap between males and females.
  - The differences may be due primarily to biological factors, sociocultural factors, or both.

First, we examine physical similarities and differences, and then we turn to cognitive and socioemotional similarities and differences.

Physical Similarities and Differences   We could devote pages to describing physical differences between the average man and the average woman. For example, women have about twice the body fat of men, most of it concentrated around breasts and hips. In males, fat is more likely to go to the abdomen. On the average, males grow to be 10 percent taller than females. Androgens (the "male" hormones) promote the growth of long bones; estrogens (the "female" hormones) stop such growth at puberty.

Many physical differences between men and women are tied to health. From conception onward, females have a longer life expectancy than males, and females are less likely than males to develop physical or mental disorders. Females are more resistant to infection, and their blood vessels are more elastic than males'. Males have higher levels of stress hormones, which cause faster clotting and higher blood pressure.

Just how much does gender matter when it comes to brain structure and activity? Among the differences that have been discovered are the following:

- One part of the hypothalamus involved in sexual behavior tends to be larger in men than in women (Swaab & others, 2001).
- An area of the parietal lobe that functions in visuospatial skills tends to be larger in males than in females (Frederikse & others, 2000).
- The areas of the brain involved in emotional expression tend to show more metabolic activity in females than in males (Gur & others, 1995).
- Female brains are smaller than male brains, but female brains have more folds; the larger folds (called convolutions) allow more surface brain tissue within the skulls of females than males (Luders & others, 2004).

Although some gender differences in brain structure and function have been found, many of these differences are small or research results are inconsistent regarding the differences. Also, when gender differences in the brain have been revealed, in many cases they have not been directly linked to psychological differences (Blakemore, Berenbaum, & Liben, 2009). Although research on gender differences in the brain is still in its infancy, it is likely that there are far more similarities than differences in the brains of females and males (Hyde, 2007). Similarities and differences in the brains of males and females could be due to evolution and heredity, as well as experiences.

What are some developmental changes in children's gender stereotyping? What are some cautions in interpreting gender differences?

Cognitive Similarities and Differences   No gender differences occur in overall intellectual ability, but in some cognitive areas gender differences do appear (Blakemore, Berenbaum, & Liben, 2009; Galambos, Berenbaum, & McHale, 2009). Some gender experts, such as Janet Shibley Hyde (2007), stress that the cognitive differences between females and males have been exaggerated. For example, Hyde points out that there usually is considerable overlap in the distributions of female and male scores on visuospatial tasks (see Figure 12.3). However, some researchers have found that males have better visuospatial skills than females (Blakemore, Berenbaum, & Liben, 2009). Despite equal participation in the National Geography Bee, in most years all 10 finalists have been boys (Liben, 1995). Also, a research review concluded that boys have better visuospatial skills than girls (Halpern & others, 2007).

A recent very large-scale study of more than 7 million U.S. students in grades 2 through 11 revealed no differences in math scores for boys and girls (Hyde & others, 2008). And a recent meta-analysis found no gender differences in math for adolescents (Lindberg & others, 2010).

In the most recent National Assessment of Educational Progress (2005, 2007) reports, girls scored significantly higher than boys in literacy skills, although boys scored slightly higher than girls in math. For example, in reading skills, 41 percent of girls reached the proficient level (compared with 29 percent of boys), and in writing skills, 32 percent of girls were proficient (compared with 16 percent of boys).

With regard to school achievement, girls earn better grades and complete high school at a higher rate than boys (Halpern, 2006). Males are more likely than females to be assigned to special/remedial education classes. Girls are more likely to be engaged with academic material, be attentive in class, put forth more academic effort, and participate more in class than boys are (DeZolt & Hull, 2001).

Socioemotional Similarities and Differences Are "men from Mars" and "women from Venus"? Perhaps the gender differences that most fascinate people are those regarding how males and females relate to each other as people. For just about every imaginable socioemotional characteristic, researchers have examined whether there are differences between males and females. Here we examine just two that have been closely studied: (1) aggression and (2) emotion and its regulation.

One of the most consistent gender differences is that boys are more physically aggressive than girls. The difference occurs in all cultures and appears very early in children's development (Baillargeon & others, 2007). The difference in physical aggression is especially pronounced when children are provoked.

Although boys are consistently more physically aggressive than girls, might girls show as much or more verbal aggression, such as yelling, than boys? When verbal aggression is examined, gender differences typically disappear or aggression is even more pronounced in girls (Eagly & Steffen, 1986).

Recently, increased interest has been directed toward *relational aggression*, which involves harming someone by manipulating a relationship (Crick & others, 2009; Kistner & others, 2010). Relational aggression includes such behaviors as trying to make others dislike a certain individual by spreading malicious rumors about the person (Underwood, 2011). Relational aggression increases in middle and late childhood (Dishion & Piehler, 2009). Mixed findings have characterized research on whether girls show more relational aggression than boys, but one consistency in findings is that relational aggression comprises a greater percentage of girls' overall aggression than is the case for boys (Putallaz & others, 2007). And a recent research review revealed that girls engage in more relational aggression than boys in adolescence but not in childhood (Smith, Rose, & Schwartz-Mette, 2010).

Gender differences occur in some aspects of emotion (Hertenstein & Keltner, 2010). Females express emotion more openly than males, are better than males at decoding emotion, smile more, cry more, and are happier (Brody & Hall, 2008; Gross, Frederickson, & Levenson, 1994; LaFrance, Hecht, & Paluck, 2003). Males report experiencing and expressing more anger than females (Kring, 2000). Girls also are better at reading others' emotions and more likely to show empathy than are boys (Blakemore, Berenbaum, & Liben, 2009).

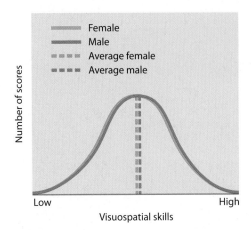

FIGURE **12.3**

VISUOSPATIAL SKILLS OF MALES AND FEMALES. Notice that, although an average male's visuospatial skills are higher than an average female's, scores for the two sexes almost entirely overlap. Not all males have better visuospatial skills than all females—the overlap indicates that, although the average male score is higher, many females outperform most males on such tasks.

"So according to the stereotype, you can put two and two together, but I can read the handwriting on the wall."
Copyright © 1994 Joel Pett. Reprinted by permission.

What gender differences characterize aggression?

An important skill is to be able to regulate and control one's emotions and behavior (Eisenberg, Spinrad, & Eggum, 2010; Thompson & Goodman, 2011). Boys usually show less self-regulation than girls (Blakemore, Berenbaum, & Liben, 2009). This low self-control can translate into behavior problems.

Researchers have found that girls are more "people oriented" and boys are more "things oriented" (Galambos, Berenbaum, & McHale, 2009). In a recent research review, this conclusion was supported by findings that girls spend more time in relationships, while boys spend more time alone, playing video games, and playing sports; that girls work at part-time jobs that are people-oriented such as waitressing and babysitting, while boys are more likely to take part-time jobs that involve manual labor and using tools; and girls are interested in careers that are more people-oriented, such as teaching and social work, while boys are more likely to be interested in object-oriented careers, such as mechanics and engineering (Perry & Pauletti, 2011).

Gender Controversy   Controversy continues about the extent of gender differences and what might cause them (Brannon, 2012; Priess & Lindberg, 2011a). As we saw earlier, evolutionary psychologists such as David Buss (2012) argue that gender differences are extensive and caused by the adaptive problems people have faced across their evolutionary history. Alice Eagly (2001, 2010) also concludes that gender differences are substantial but reaches a very different conclusion about their cause. She traces gender differences to social conditions that have resulted in women having less power and controlling fewer resources than men do.

By contrast, Janet Shibley Hyde (2007) concludes that gender differences have been greatly exaggerated, with these comparisons being especially fueled by popular books such as John Gray's (1992) *Men Are from Mars, Women Are from Venus* and Deborah Tannen's (1990) *You Just Don't Understand*. She argues that the research indicates females and males are similar on most psychological factors. In a research review, Hyde (2005) summarized the results of 44 meta-analyses of gender differences and similarities. A *meta-analysis* is a statistical analysis that combines the results of many different studies. Gender differences in most areas—including math ability and communication—were either nonexistent or small. Gender differences in physical aggression were moderate. The largest difference occurred on motor skills (favoring males), followed by sexuality (males masturbate more and are more likely to endorse sex in a casual, uncommitted relationship) and physical aggression (males are more physically aggressive than are females).

Hyde's summary of meta-analyses is unlikely to quiet the controversy about gender differences and similarities, but further research should continue to provide a basis for more accurate judgments on this topic.

Gender in Context   In thinking about gender, it is important to consider the context of behavior (Best, 2010; Blakemore, Berenbaum, & Liben, 2009). Gender behavior often varies across contexts. Consider helping behavior. Males are more likely to help in contexts in which a perceived danger is present and they feel competent to help (Eagly & Crowley, 1986). For example, males are more likely than females to help a person who is stranded by the roadside with a flat tire; automobile problems are an area about which many males feel competent. In contrast, when the context involves volunteering time to help a child with a personal problem, females are more likely to help than males are, because there is little danger present and females feel more competent at nurturing. In many cultures, girls show more caregiving behavior than boys do.

Context is also relevant to gender differences in the display of emotions (Shields, 1998). Consider anger. Males are more likely to show anger toward strangers, especially other males, when they think they have been challenged. Males also are more likely than females to turn their anger into aggressive action, especially when their culture endorses such action (Tavris & Wade, 1984).

In many cultures around the world, traditional gender roles continue to guide the behavior of males and females (UNICEF, 2011). In China and Iran, for instance,

In China, females and males are usually socialized to behave, feel, and think differently. The old patriarchal traditions of male supremacy have not been completely uprooted. Chinese women still make considerably less money than Chinese men do, and, in rural China (such as here in the Lixian Village of Sichuan), male supremacy still governs many women's lives.

developmental connection

Nature and Nurture. Bronfenbrenner's ecological theory emphasizes the importance of contexts; in his theory, the macrosystem includes cross-cultural comparisons. Chapter 1, p. 26

it is still widely accepted for males to engage in dominant behavior and females to behave in subordinate ways. Many Western cultures, such as the United States, have become more flexible about gender behavior and allow for more diversity. For example, although a girl's father might promote traditional femininity, her friends might engage in many traditionally masculine activities, and her teachers might encourage her to be assertive.

In the United States, the cultural backgrounds of children and adolescents influence how boys and girls will be socialized. In one study, Latino and Latina adolescents were socialized differently as they were growing up (Raffaelli & Ontai, 2004). Latinas experienced far greater restrictions than Latinos in having curfews, interacting with members of the other sex, getting a driver's license, getting a job, and being involved in after-school activities.

Review Connect Reflect

LG2 Discuss gender stereotypes, similarities, and differences

Review

- What is gender stereotyping, and how extensive is it?
- What are some physical, cognitive, and socioemotional differences between men and women?

Connect

- Compare cognitive and socioemotional similarities and differences based on gender. What are your conclusions?

Reflect *Your Own Personal Journey of Life*

- How do your gender behavior and thoughts stack up against the similarities and differences in gender we discussed?
- Are gender roles more flexible for boys or for girls?

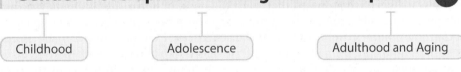

Gender Development Through the Life Span

LG3 Describe the development of gender through the life span

Childhood   Adolescence   Adulthood and Aging

In this section we will focus further on gender-related developmental changes in the childhood years. In addition, we will look at some changes that take place in adolescence and adulthood, including the influence of gender roles in adolescence and some of the ways in which gender might be linked with aging.

CHILDHOOD

The amount, timing, and intensity of gender socialization differs for girls and boys (Beal, 1994). Boys receive earlier and more intense gender socialization than girls do. The social cost of deviating from the expected male role is higher for boys than is the cost for girls of deviating from the expected female role, in terms of peer rejection and parental disapproval. Imagine a girl who is wearing a toy holster, bandanna, and cowboy hat, running around in the backyard pretending to herd cattle. Now imagine a boy who is wearing a flowered hat, ropes of pearls, and lipstick, pretending to cook dinner on a toy stove. Which of these do you have a stronger reaction to—the girl's behavior or the boy's? Probably the boy's. Researchers have found that "effeminate" behavior in boys elicits more negative reactions than does "masculine" behavior in girls (Martin, 1990).

Boys might have a more difficult time learning the masculine gender role because male models are less accessible to young children and messages from adults about the male role are not always consistent. For example, most mothers and

Are gender roles more flexible for boys or for girls?

developmental **connection**

Biological Processes. Girls enter puberty approximately two years earlier than boys, with pubertal change peaking on average at age 11½ in girls and 13½ in boys. Chapter 3, p. 92

gender-intensification hypothesis The view that psychological and behavioral differences between boys and girls become greater during early adolescence because of increased socialization pressures to conform to traditional gender roles.

teachers would like boys to behave in masculine ways, but also to be neat, well mannered, and considerate. However, fathers and peers usually want boys to behave in another way—independent and engaging in rough-and-tumble play. The mixed messages make it difficult for boys to figure out how to act.

Although gender roles have become more flexible in recent years, the flexibility applies more for girls than for boys (Beal, 1994). Girls can now safely be ambitious, competitive, and interested in sports, but relatively few adults are equally supportive of boys' being gentle, interested in fashion, and motivated to sign up for ballet classes. Instrumental traits and masculine gender roles may be evolving into a new norm for everyone.

Concern about the ways boys are being brought up has been called a "national crisis of boyhood" by William Pollack (1999) in his book *Real Boys*. Pollack says that little has been done to change what he calls the "boy code." The boy code tells boys they should not show their feelings and should act tough, says Pollack. Boys learn the boy code in many contexts—sandboxes, playgrounds, schoolrooms, camps, hangouts—and are taught the code by parents, peers, coaches, teachers, and other adults. Pollack, as well as many others, argues that boys would benefit from being socialized to express their anxieties and concerns and to better regulate their aggression.

ADOLESCENCE

Early adolescence is another transitional point that seems to be especially important in gender development. Young adolescents have to cope with the enormous changes of puberty. These changes are intensified by their expanding cognitive abilities, which make them acutely aware of how they appear to others. Relations with others change extensively as dating begins and sexuality is experienced.

As females and males experience the physical and social changes of early adolescence, they must come to terms with new definitions of their gender roles (Belansky & Clements, 1992; Priess & Lindberg, 2011a, b). During early adolescence, individuals develop the adult, physical aspects of their sex. Some theorists and researchers have proposed that, with the onset of puberty, girls and boys experience an intensification of gender-related expectations. Puberty might signal to socializing others—parents, peers, and teachers, for example—that the adolescent is beginning to approach adulthood and therefore should begin to act more in ways that resemble the stereotypical female or male adult. The **gender-intensification hypothesis** states that psychological and behavioral differences between boys and girls become greater during early adolescence because of increased pressures to conform to traditional masculine and feminine gender roles (Galambos, 2004; Hill & Lynch, 1983).

Some researchers have reported evidence of gender intensification in early adolescence (Hill & Lynch, 1983). However, a recent longitudinal study of individuals from 7 to 19 years of age revealed stable gender differences in activity interests by the decline in both male- and female-typed activity interests across this age range (McHale & others, 2009). And another recent study found no evidence for intensification in masculinity or femininity in young adolescents (Priess, Lindberg, & Hyde, 2009). The jury is still out on the validity of the gender-intensification hypothesis, but recent research has raised questions about its accuracy (Galambos, Berenbaum, & McHale, 2009; Priess & Lindberg, 2011b).

Gender intensification may create special problems for boys. Adopting a strong masculine role in adolescence is increasingly being found to be associated with problem behaviors. Joseph Pleck (1995) argues that what has defined traditional masculinity includes behaviors that do not have social approval but nonetheless validate the adolescent boy's masculinity. That is, in the male adolescent culture, male adolescents perceive that they will be thought of as more masculine if they engage in premarital sex, drink alcohol, take drugs, and participate in delinquent activities. A recent study revealed that both boys and girls who engaged in extreme gender-typed (hyper-gender) behaviors had lower levels of school engagement and school attachment (Ueno & McWilliams, 2010).

ADULTHOOD AND AGING

How might women's and men's development vary as they go through their adult years? How might gender be linked with aging?

Gender and Communication Stereotypes about differences in men's and women's attitudes toward communication and about differences in how they communicate with each other have spawned countless cartoons and jokes. Are the supposed differences real?

When Deborah Tannen (1990) analyzed the talk of women and men, she found that many wives complained about their husbands that "He doesn't listen to me anymore" and "He doesn't talk to me anymore." Lack of communication, although high on women's lists of reasons for divorce, is mentioned much less often by men.

Communication problems between men and women may come in part from differences in their preferred ways of communicating. Tannen distinguishes *rapport talk* from *report talk*. **Rapport talk** is the language of conversation; it is a way of establishing connections and negotiating relationships. **Report talk** is talk that is designed to give information; this category of communication includes public speaking. According to Tannen, women enjoy rapport talk more than report talk, and men's lack of interest in rapport talk bothers many women. In contrast, men prefer to engage in report talk. Men hold center stage through verbal performances such as telling stories and jokes. They learn to use talk as a way to get and keep attention.

How extensive are gender differences in communication? Research has yielded somewhat mixed results. Recent studies do reveal some gender differences (Anderson, 2006). One study of a sampling of students' e-mails found that people could guess the writer's gender two-thirds of the time (Thompson & Murachver, 2001). Another study revealed that women make 63 percent of phone calls and when talking to another woman stay on the phone longer (7.2 minutes) than men do when talking with other men (4.6 minutes) (Smoreda & Licoppe, 2000). However, meta-analyses suggest that overall gender differences in communication are small in both children and adults (Hyde, 2005; Leaper & Smith, 2004).

Women's Development Tannen's analysis of women's preference for rapport talk suggests that women place a high value on relationships and focus on nurturing their connections with others. This view echoes some ideas of Jean Baker Miller (1986), who has been an important voice in stimulating the examination of psychological issues from a female perspective. Miller argues that when researchers examine what women have been doing in life, a large part of it is active participation in the development of others. In Miller's view, women often try to interact with others in ways that will foster the other person's development along many dimensions—emotional, intellectual, and social.

Most experts stress that it is important for women not only to maintain their competency in relationships but to be self-motivated, too (Brabek & Brabek, 2006). As Harriet Lerner (1989) concludes in her book *The Dance of Intimacy*, it is important for women to bring to their relationships nothing less than a strong, assertive, independent, and authentic self. She emphasizes that competent relationships are those in which the separate "I-ness" of both persons can be appreciated and enhanced while the partners remain emotionally connected with each other.

In sum, Miller, Tannen, and other gender experts such as Carol Gilligan note that women are more relationship-oriented than men—and that this relationship

What are some gender differences in communication?

rapport talk The language of conversation; a way to establish connections and negotiate relationships; preferred by women.

report talk Language designed to give information, including public speaking; preferred by men.

Cynthia de las Fuentes, College Professor and Counseling Psychologist

Cynthia de las Fuentes is a professor at Our Lady of the Lake University in San Antonio. She obtained her undergraduate degree in psychology and her doctoral degree in counseling psychology at the University of Texas in Austin. Among the courses she teaches are the psychology of women, Latino psychology, and counseling theories.

Dr. de las Fuentes is president of the Division of the Psychology of Women in

Cynthia de las Fuentes.

the American Psychological Association. "'Many young women,' she says, 'take for granted that the women's movement has accomplished its goals—like equal pay for women, or reproductive rights—and don't realize that there is still work to be done.' ... She's interested in learning about people's intersecting identities, like female and Latina, and how the two work together"

(Winerman, 2005, pp. 66–67) For more information about what college professors do, see page 41 in the Careers in Life-Span Development appendix.

---

developmental connection

Peers. How is adult friendship different among female friends, male friends, and cross-gender friends? Chapter 15, p. 498

Tom Cruise (*left*) played Jerry Maguire in the movie *Jerry Maguire* with 6-year-old Ray, son of Jerry's love interest. The image of nurturing and nurtured males was woven throughout the movie. Jerry's relationship with Ray was a significant theme in the movie. It is through the caring relationship with Ray that Jerry makes his first genuine movement toward emotional maturity. The boy is guide to the man (Shields, 1998). Many experts on gender stress that men and boys would benefit from engaging in more nurturant behaviors.

orientation should be valued more highly in our culture than it currently is. Critics of this view of gender differences in relationships contend that it is too stereotypical (Hyde, 2007; Matlin, 2012). They argue that there is greater individual variation in the relationship styles of men and women than this view acknowledges (Brabek & Brabek, 2006).

In the field of the psychology of women, there is increased interest in women of color. To read about the work and views of one individual in this field, see the *Connecting with Careers* profile.

Men's Development The male of the species—what is he really like? What are his concerns? According to Joseph Pleck's (1995) *role-strain view*, male roles are contradictory and inconsistent. Men not only experience stress when they violate men's roles, they also are harmed when they do act in accord with men's roles. Here are some of the areas where men's roles can cause considerable strain (Levant, 2001):

- *Health.* Men live 8 to 10 years less than women do. They have higher rates of stress-related disorders, alcoholism, car accidents, and suicide. Men are more likely than women to be the victims of homicide. In sum, the male role is hazardous to men's health.

- *Male-female relationships.* Too often, the male role involves expectations that men should be dominant, powerful, and aggressive and should control women. "Real men," according to many traditional definitions of masculinity, look at women in terms of their bodies, not their minds and feelings, have little interest in rapport talk and relationships, and do not consider women equal to men in work or many other aspects of life. Thus, the traditional view of the male role encourages men to disparage women, be violent toward women, and refuse to have equal relationships with women.

- *Male-male relationships.* Too many men have had too little interaction with their fathers, especially fathers who are positive role models. Nurturing and being sensitive to others have been considered aspects of the female role, not the male role. And the male role emphasizes competition rather than cooperation. All of these aspects of the male role have left men with inadequate positive, emotional connections with other males.

To reconstruct their masculinity in more positive ways, Ron Levant (2001) suggests that every man should (1) reexamine his beliefs about manhood, (2) separate out the valuable aspects of the male role, and (3) get rid of those parts of the masculine role that are destructive. All of these involve becoming more "emotionally intelligent"—that is, becoming more emotionally self-aware, managing emotions more effectively, reading emotions better (one's own emotions and others'), and being motivated to improve close relationships.

Gender and Aging   Do our gender roles change when we become older adults? Some developmentalists maintain there is decreasing femininity in women and decreasing masculinity in men when they reach the late adulthood years (Gutmann, 1975). The evidence suggests that older men do become more *feminine*—nurturant, sensitive, and so on—but it appears that older women do not necessarily become more *masculine*—assertive, dominant, and so on (Turner, 1982). A longitudinal study revealed that as men entered their 60s, they endorsed more feminine items, which increased their classification as *androgynous* (combination of masculine and feminine traits) (Hyde, Krajnik, & Skuldt-Niederberger, 1991).

In a more recent cross-sectional study of individuals from 12 to 80 years and older, men in their 70s were more likely than adolescents and younger men to endorse androgynous traits (Strough & others, 2007). Also in this study, women in their 80s and older were less likely than younger and middle-aged women to endorse masculine and androgynous traits. Keep in mind that cohort effects are especially important to consider in areas such as gender roles. As sociohistorical changes take place and are assessed more frequently in life-span investigations, what were once perceived to be age effects may turn out to be cohort effects (Jackson, Govia, & Sellers, 2011; Schaie, 2010, 2011). For example, in the study described above (Strough & others, 2007), the early-adult and middle-aged women were "baby boomers," likely influenced by the women's movement as they were growing up and developing their identity. However, the oldest-old women likely had already established their gender identity when the women's movement began, which might explain why they were less likely than younger women to endorse masculine and androgynous traits.

A possible double jeopardy also faces many women—the burden of both ageism and sexism (Meyer & Parker, 2011; UNICEF, 2006). In developing countries, the poverty rate for older adult females is almost double that of older adult males.

Not only is it important to be concerned about older women's double jeopardy of ageism and sexism, but special attention also needs to be devoted to female ethnic minority older adults (Jackson, Govia, & Sellers, 2011; Leifheit-Limson & Levy, 2009). Many, but not all, immigrant ethnic groups traditionally have relegated the woman's role to family maintenance. Many important decisions may be made by a woman's husband or parents, and she is often not expected to seek an independent career or enter the workforce unless the family is in dire financial need.

Some ethnic minority groups may define an older woman's role as unimportant, especially if she is unable to contribute financially. However, in some ethnic minority groups, an older woman's social status improves. For example, older African American women can express their own needs and can be given status and power in the community. Despite their positive status in the African American family and the African American culture, African American women over the age of 70 are the poorest population group in the United States. Three of five older African American women live alone; most of them are widowed. The low incomes of older African American women translate into less than adequate access to health care. Substantially lower incomes for African American older women are related to the kinds of jobs they hold. Frequently these jobs are not covered by Social Security or, in the case of domestic service, the income of these women is not reported, even when reporting is legally required.

A portrayal of older African American women in cities reveals some of their survival strategies. They highly value the family as a system of mutual support and aid, adhere to the American work ethic, and view religion as a source of strength.

A special concern is the stress faced by African American elderly women. *What are some ways they cope with stress?*

developmental **connection**

Culture. Aging presents special challenges for ethnic minority individuals. Chapter 15, p. 519

In sum, older African American women have faced considerable stress in their lives (Locher & others, 2005). In dealing with this stress, they have shown remarkable adaptiveness, resilience, responsibility, and coping skills. However, many older African American women would benefit considerably from improved support.

Review *Connect* Reflect

LG3 Describe the development of gender through the life span

Review

- What are some developmental changes in gender in childhood?
- How does gender development change during adolescence?
- How does gender development change during adulthood?

Connect

- Relate this chapter's gender-intensification hypothesis to what you learned about identity development in adolescence in Chapter 11. What are your conclusions?

Reflect *Your Own Personal Journey of Life*

- How have your gender attitudes and behavior changed since childhood? Are the changes mainly age changes or do they reflect cohort effects?

Exploring Sexuality

LG4 Characterize influences on sexuality, the nature of sexual orientation, and some sexual problems

Biological and Cultural Factors

Sexual Orientation

Sexually Transmitted Infections

Forcible Sexual Behavior and Sexual Harassment

Now that we have studied the gender aspects of being female and male, let's turn our attention to the sexual aspects. To explore sexuality, we examine biological and cultural factors, sexual orientation, sexually transmitted infections, and forcible sexual behavior and sexual harassment.

BIOLOGICAL AND CULTURAL FACTORS

We don't need sex for everyday survival the way we need food and water, but we do need it for the survival of the species. With this important role of sex in mind, let's examine some biological and cultural factors involved in sexuality.

Biological Factors   In our discussion of gender, we identified two main classes of sex hormones: estrogens (which primarily promote the development of female physical sex characteristics) and androgens (which mainly promote the development of male physical sex characteristics). The pituitary gland in the brain monitors hormone levels but is itself regulated by the hypothalamus. The pituitary gland sends out a signal to the testes or ovaries to manufacture a hormone; then the pituitary gland, through interaction with the hypothalamus, detects when the optimal level of the hormone is reached and maintains this level.

As we move from lower to higher animals, the role of hormones becomes less clear, especially in females. For human males, higher androgen levels are associated with sexual motivation and orgasm frequency (Knussmann, Christiansen, & Couwenbergs, 1986). Nonetheless, sexual behavior is so individualized in humans that it is difficult to specify the effects of hormones.

Cultural Factors   Sexual motivation also is influenced by cultural factors (Hock, 2010). The range of sexual values across cultures is substantial. Some cultures consider sexual pleasures "weird" or "abnormal." Consider the people who live on the small island of Ines Beag off the coast of Ireland. They are some of the most sexually repressed people in the world. They know nothing about tongue kissing or hand stimulation of the penis, and they detest nudity. For both females and males, premarital sex is out of the question (Messinger, 1971).

In contrast, consider the Mangaian culture in the South Pacific. In Mangaia, young boys are taught about masturbation and are encouraged to engage in it as much as they like. At age 13, the boys undergo a ritual that initiates them into sexual manhood. First, their elders instruct them about sexual strategies, including how to help their female partner have orgasms. Then, two weeks later, the boy has intercourse with an experienced woman who helps him hold back ejaculation until she can achieve orgasm with him. By the end of adolescence, Mangaians have sex virtually every day.

As reflected in the behavior of the people in these two different cultures, our sexual motivation is influenced by **sexual scripts.** These are stereotyped patterns of expectancies for how people should behave sexually (Regenerus & Uecker, 2011). Two well-known sexual scripts are the traditional religious script and the romantic script. In the **traditional religious script,** sex is accepted only within marriage. Extramarital sex is taboo, especially for women. Sex means reproduction and sometimes affection. In the **romantic script,** sex is synonymous with love. If we develop a relationship with someone and fall in love, it is acceptable to have sex with the person whether or not we are married.

You probably are familiar with some sex differences in sexual scripts. Females tend to link sexual intercourse with love more than males do, and males are more likely to emphasize sexual conquest. Some sexual scripts involve a double standard; for example, it is okay for male adolescents to have sex but not females, and if the female gets pregnant it's her fault for not using contraception.

SEXUAL ORIENTATION

Obtaining accurate information about such a private activity as sexual behavior is not easy (Carroll, 2010). The best information currently available comes from what is often referred to as the 1994 Sex in America survey. In this well-designed, comprehensive study of American adults' sexual patterns, Robert Michael and his colleagues (1994) interviewed more than 3,000 people from 18 to 59 years of age who were randomly selected, a sharp contrast from earlier samples that were based on unrepresentative groups of volunteers.

Heterosexual Attitudes and Behavior   Here are some of the key findings from the 1994 Sex in America survey:

- Americans tend to fall into three categories: One-third have sex twice a week or more, one third a few times a month, and one-third a few times a year or not at all.
- Married (and cohabiting) couples have sex more often than noncohabiting couples (see Figure 12.4).
- Most Americans do not engage in kinky sexual acts. When asked about their favorite sexual acts, the vast majority (96 percent) said that vaginal sex was "very" or "somewhat" appealing. Oral sex was in third place, after an activity that many have not labeled a sexual act—watching a partner undress.
- Adultery is clearly the exception rather than the rule. Nearly 75 percent of the married men and 85 percent of the married women in the survey indicated that they had never been unfaithful.
- Men think about sex far more often than women do—54 percent of the men said they thought about it every day or several times a day, whereas 67 percent of the women said they thought about it only a few times a week or a few times a month.

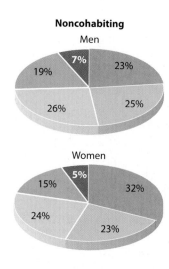

Noncohabiting

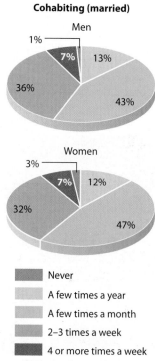

Cohabiting (married)

- Never
- A few times a year
- A few times a month
- 2–3 times a week
- 4 or more times a week

FIGURE 12.4

THE SEX IN AMERICA SURVEY. The percentages show noncohabiting and cohabiting (married) males' and females' responses to the question "How often have you had sex in the past year?" in a 1994 survey (Michael & others, 1994). *What was one feature of the Sex in America survey that made it superior to most surveys of sexual behavior?*

sexual scripts Stereotyped patterns of expectancies for how people should behave sexually.

traditional religious script View that sex is acceptable only within marriage; extramarital sex is taboo, especially for women; and sex means reproduction and sometimes affection.

romantic script Sex is synonymous with love; if we develop a relationship with someone and fall in love, it is acceptable to have sex with the person whether we are married or not.

In sum, one of the most powerful messages in the 1994 survey was that Americans' sexual lives are more conservative than was previously believed. Although 17 percent of the men and 3 percent of the women said they had had sex with at least 21 partners, the overall impression from the survey was that sexual behavior is ruled by marriage and monogamy for most Americans.

How extensive are gender differences in sexuality? A recent meta-analysis revealed that men reported having slightly more sexual experiences and more permissive attitudes than women regarding most aspects of sexuality (Peterson & Hyde, 2010). For the following factors, stronger differences were found: Men said that they engaged more often in masturbation, pornography use, and casual sex, and they expressed more permissive attitudes about casual sex than their female counterparts.

Given all the media and public attention directed toward the negative aspects of sexuality—such as adolescent pregnancy, sexually transmitted infections, rape, and so on—it is important to underscore that research strongly supports the role of sexuality in well-being (Brody, 2010). For example, in a recent Swedish study frequency of sexual intercourse was strongly linked to life satisfaction for both women and men (Brody & Costa, 2009).

Sources of Sexual Orientation   Until the end of the nineteenth century, it was generally believed that people were either heterosexual or homosexual. Today, it is more accepted to view sexual orientation not as an either/or proposition but as a continuum from exclusive male-female relations to exclusive same-sex relations (Crooks & Baur, 2011; Kelly, 2011). Some individuals are also **bisexual,** being sexually attracted to people of both sexes.

In the Sex in America survey, 2.7 percent of the men and 1.3 percent of the women reported having had same-sex relations in the past year (Michael & others, 1994). Why are some individuals lesbian, gay, or bisexual (LGB) and others heterosexual? Speculation about this question has been extensive (Diamond & Savin-Willliams, 2011; Yarber, Sayad, & Strong, 2010).

All people, regardless of their sexual orientation, have similar physiological responses during sexual arousal and seem to be aroused by the same types of tactile stimulation. Investigators typically find no differences between LGBs and heterosexuals in a wide range of attitudes, behaviors, and adjustments (Peplau & Fingerhut, 2007).

Recently, researchers have explored the possible biological basis of same-sex relations. The results of hormone studies have been inconsistent (Gooren, 2006). If gay males are given male sex hormones (androgens), their sexual orientation doesn't change. Their sexual desire merely increases. A very early prenatal critical period might influence sexual orientation. In the second to fifth months after conception, exposure of the fetus to hormone levels characteristic of females might cause the individual (male or female) to become attracted to males (Ellis & Ames, 1987). If this critical-period hypothesis turns out to be correct, it would explain why clinicians have found that sexual orientation is difficult, if not impossible, to modify.

Researchers have also examined genetic influences on sexual orientation by studying twins. A recent Swedish study of almost 4,000 twins found that only about 35 percent of the variation in homosexual behavior in men and 19 percent in women could be explained by genetic differences (Langstrom & others, 2010). This result suggests that although genes likely play a role in sexual orientation, they are not the only factor (King, 2011).

An individual's sexual orientation—same-sex, heterosexual, or bisexual—is most likely determined by a combination of genetic, hormonal, cognitive, and environmental factors (Hyde & DeLamater, 2011; King, 2011). Most experts on same-sex relations believe that no one factor alone causes sexual orientation and that the relative weight of each factor can vary from one individual to the next.

What are some similarities and differences in lesbian and gay relationships?

bisexuality Sexual attraction to people of both sexes.

Attitudes and Behavior of Lesbians and Gays   Many gender differences that appear in heterosexual relationships occur in same-sex relationships (Diamond,

Fagundes, & Butterworth, 2010; Savin-Williams, 2011). For example, like heterosexual women, lesbians have fewer sexual partners than gays, and lesbians have less permissive attitudes about casual sex outside a primary relationship than gays (Peplau & Fingerhut, 2007).

According to psychologist Laura Brown (1989), lesbians and gays experience life as a minority in a dominant, majority culture. For lesbians and gays, developing a *bicultural identity* creates new ways of defining themselves. Brown believes that lesbians and gays adapt best when they don't define themselves in polarities, such as trying to live in an encapsulated lesbian or gay world completely divorced from the majority culture or completely accepting the dictates and biases of the majority culture. A special concern is discrimination and prejudice toward sexual minority individuals (Saewyc, 2011).

SEXUALLY TRANSMITTED INFECTIONS

Sexually transmitted infections (STIs) are diseases that are primarily contracted through sex—penile-vaginal intercourse as well as oral-genital and anal-genital sex. STIs affect about one of every six U.S. adults (National Center for Health Statistics, 2010b). Among the most prevalent STIs are bacterial infections—such as gonorrhea, syphilis, and chlamydia—and STIs caused by viruses—such as AIDS (acquired immune deficiency syndrome), genital herpes, and genital warts. Figure 12.5 describes these sexually transmitted infections.

sexually transmitted infections (STIs) Diseases that are contracted primarily through sexual contact, including oral-genital contact, anal-genital contact, and vaginal intercourse.

STI	Description/cause	Incidence	Treatment
Gonorrhea	Commonly called the "drip" or "clap." Caused by the bacterium *Neisseria gonorrhoeae*. Spread by contact between infected moist membranes (genital, oral-genital, or anal-genital) of two individuals. Characterized by discharge from penis or vagina and painful urination. Can lead to infertility.	500,000 cases annually in U.S.	Penicillin, other antibiotics
Syphilis	Caused by the bacterium *Treponema pallidum*. Characterized by the appearance of a sore where syphilis entered the body. The sore can be on the external genitals, vagina, or anus. Later, a skin rash breaks out on palms of hands and bottom of feet. If not treated, can eventually lead to paralysis or even death.	100,000 cases annually in U.S.	Penicillin
Chlamydia	A common STI named for the bacterium *Chlamydia trachomatis*, an organism that spreads by sexual contact and infects the genital organs of both sexes. A special concern is that females with chlamydia may become infertile. It is recommended that adolescent and young adult females have an annual screening for this STI.	About 3 million people in U.S. annually.	Antibiotics
Genital herpes	Caused by a family of viruses with different strains. Involves an eruption of sores and blisters. Spread by sexual contact.	One of five U.S. adults	No known cure but antiviral medications can shorten outbreaks
AIDS	Caused by a virus, the human immunodeficiency virus (HIV), which destroys the body's immune system. Semen and blood are the main vehicles of transmission. Common symptoms include fevers, night sweats, weight loss, chronic fatigue, and swollen lymph nodes.	More than 300,000 cumulative cases of HIV virus in U.S. 25–34-year-olds; epidemic incidence in sub-Saharan countries	New treatments have slowed the progression from HIV to AIDS; no cure
Genital warts	Caused by the human papillomavirus, which does not always produce symptoms. Usually appear as small, hard painless bumps in the vaginal area, or around the anus. Very contagious. Certain high-risk types of this virus cause cervical cancer and other genital cancers. May recur despite treatment. A new HPV preventive vaccine, Gardasil, has been approved for girls and women 9–26 years of age.	About 5.5 million new cases annually; considered the most common STI in the U.S.	A topical drug, freezing, or surgery

FIGURE **12.5**
SEXUALLY TRANSMITTED INFECTIONS

A youth group presents a play in the local marketplace in Morogoro, Tanzania. The play is designed to educate the community about HIV and AIDS.

A 13-year-old boy pushes his friends around in his barrow during his break from his work as a barrow boy in a sub-Saharan Africa community. He became the breadwinner in the family because both of his parents died of AIDS.

No single disease has had a greater impact on sexual behavior, or created more public fear in the last several decades, than infection with the human immunodeficiency virus (HIV) (Crooks & Baur, 2011). HIV is a virus that destroys the body's immune system. Once infected with HIV, the virus breaks down and overpowers the immune system, which leads to AIDS. An individual sick with AIDS has such a weakened immune system that a common cold can be life-threatening.

Through 2007, 580,146 cases of AIDS in 20- to 39-year-olds had been reported in the United States (National Center for Health Statistics, 2010a). In 2007, male-male sexual contact continued to be the most frequent AIDS transmission category (National Center for Health Statistics, 2010a). Because of education and the development of more effective drug treatments, deaths due to HIV/AIDS have begun to decline in the United States (National Center for Health Statistics, 2010a).

Globally, the total number of individuals living with HIV was 33 million in 2007, with 22 million of these individuals with HIV living in sub-Saharan Africa (UNAIDS, 2009). Approximately half of all new HIV infections around the world occur in the 15- to 24-year-old age category (Campbell, 2009).

What are some good strategies for protecting against HIV and other sexually transmitted infections? They include:

- *Knowing your own and your partner's risk status.* Anyone who has had previous sexual activity with another person might have contracted an STI without being aware of it. Spend time getting to know a prospective partner before you have sex. Use this time to inform the other person of your STI status and inquire about your partner's. Remember that many people lie about their STI status.

- *Obtaining medical examinations.* Many experts recommend that couples who want to begin a sexual relationship have a medical checkup to rule out STIs before they engage in sex. If cost is an issue, contact your campus health service or a public health clinic.

- *Having protected, not unprotected, sex.* When correctly used, latex condoms help to prevent many STIs from being transmitted. Condoms are most effective in preventing gonorrhea, syphilis, chlamydia, and HIV. They are less effective against the spread of herpes.

- *Not having sex with multiple partners.* One of the best predictors of getting an STI is having sex with multiple partners. Having more than one sex partner elevates the likelihood that you will encounter an infected partner.

FORCIBLE SEXUAL BEHAVIOR AND SEXUAL HARASSMENT

Too often, sex involves the exercise of power. Here we briefly look at three of the problems that may result: two types of rape and sexual harassment.

Rape **Rape** is forcible sexual intercourse with a person who does not give consent. Legal definitions of rape differ from state to state. For example, in some states, husbands are not prohibited from forcing their wives to have intercourse, although this has been challenged in several of those states.

Because victims may be reluctant to suffer the consequences of reporting rape, the actual number of incidences is not easily determined (Carroll, 2010). Rape occurs most often in large cities, where it has been reported that 8 of every 10,000 women 12 years and older are raped each year. Nearly 200,000 rapes are reported each year in the United States. Although most victims of rape are women, rape of men does occur (McLean, Balding, & White, 2005). Men in prisons are especially vulnerable to rape, usually by heterosexual males who use rape as a means of establishing their dominance and power.

A recent national study found that 7.4 percent of U.S. ninth- through twelfth-grade students reported that they had been physically forced to have intercourse against their will (Eaton & others, 2010). In this study, 10.5 percent of the female students and 4.5 percent of the male students reported having been forced to have sexual intercourse.

Why does rape of females occur so often in the United States? Among the causes given are that males are socialized to be sexually aggressive, to regard women as inferior beings, and to view their own pleasure as the most important objective in sexual relations (Beech, Ward, & Fisher, 2006). Researchers have found that male rapists share the following characteristics: Aggression enhances their sense of power or masculinity; they are angry at women in general; and they want to hurt and humiliate their victims. A recent study revealed that a higher level of men's sexual narcissism (assessed by these factors: sexual exploitation, sexual entitlement, low sexual empathy, and sexual skill) was linked to a greater likelihood that they would engage in sexual aggression (Wildman & McNulty, 2010). A recent study also revealed that regardless of whether or not the victim was using substances, sexual assault was more likely to occur when the offender was using substances (Brecklin & Ullman, 2010).

Rape is a traumatic experience for the victims and those close to them (Jordan, Campbell, & Follingstad, 2010). As victims strive to get their lives back to normal, they may experience depression, fear, anxiety, and increased substance use for months or years (Herrera & others, 2006). Sexual dysfunctions, such as reduced sexual desire and an inability to reach orgasm, occur in 50 percent of female rape victims (Sprei & Courtois, 1988). Recovery depends on the victim's coping abilities, psychological adjustments prior to the assault, and social support (Kelly, 2011). Parents, partner, and others close to the victim can provide important support for recovery, as can mental health professionals (Littleton, 2010).

An increasing concern is **date or acquaintance rape,** which is coercive sexual activity directed at someone with whom the victim is at least casually acquainted

What are some characteristics of date or acquaintance rape?

rape Forcible sexual intercourse, oral sex, or anal sex with a person who does not give consent. Legal definitions of rape differ from state to state.

date or acquaintance rape Coercive sexual activity directed at someone with whom the victim is at least casually acquainted.

(Alleyne & others, 2011; Carroll, 2010). By some estimates, one in three adolescent girls will be involved in a controlling, abusive relationship before she graduates from high school, and two-thirds of college freshman women report having been date raped or having experienced an attempted date rape at least once (Watts & Zimmerman, 2002). About two-thirds of college men admit that they fondle women against their will, and half admit to forcing sexual activity.

A number of colleges and universities describe the *red zone* as a period of time early in the first year of college when women are at especially high risk for unwanted sexual experiences. A recent study revealed that first-year women were more at risk for unwanted sexual experiences, especially early in the fall term, than second-year women (Kimble & others, 2008).

Sexual Harassment **Sexual harassment** is a manifestation of power of one person over another. It takes many forms—from inappropriate sexual remarks and physical contact (patting, brushing against one's body) to blatant propositions and sexual assaults. Millions of women experience sexual harassment each year in work and educational settings (Best & others, 2010; Das, 2009). Sexual harassment of men by women also occurs but to a far lesser extent than sexual harassment of women by men.

In a survey of 2,000 college women, 62 percent reported having experienced sexual harassment while attending college (American Association of University Women, 2006). Most of the college women said that the sexual harassment involved noncontact forms such as crude jokes, remarks, and gestures. However, almost one-third said that the sexual harassment was physical in nature.

Sexual harassment can result in serious psychological consequences for the victim. A study of almost 1,500 college women revealed that when they had been sexually harassed they reported increases in psychological distress, physical illness, and disordered eating (Huerta & others, 2006).

The elimination of such exploitation requires the improvement of work and academic environments. These types of improvements help to provide equal opportunities for people to develop a career and obtain an education in a climate free of sexual harassment (Hunes & Davis, 2009).

sexual harassment Sexual persecution that can take many forms—from sexist remarks and physical contact (patting, brushing against someone's body) to blatant propositions and sexual assaults.

Review *Connect* Reflect

LG4 Characterize influences on sexuality, the nature of sexual orientation, and some sexual problems

Review

- How do biology and culture influence sexuality?
- What is the nature of heterosexual and homosexual attitudes and behavior?
- What are some common sexually transmitted infections? What are some good strategies for protecting against STIs?
- What is the nature of forcible sexual behavior and sexual harassment?

Connect

- How might our acceptance of sexual scripts be linked to ethnic identity as described in Chapter 11?

Reflect *Your Own Personal Journey of Life*

- Have you ever experienced (or unwittingly committed) an act of sexual harassment?

Sexuality Through the Life Span   Summarize how sexuality develops through the life span

| Childhood | Adolescence and Emerging Adulthood | Adult Development and Aging |

So far we have discussed a number of aspects of human sexuality. Now, let's explore sexuality at different points in development, beginning with childhood.

CHILDHOOD

Most psychologists doubt Freud's claim that preschool children have a strong sexual attraction to the parent of the other sex. But what are some aspects of child sexuality?

A majority of children engage in some sex play, usually with friends or siblings (Crooks & Baur, 2011). Child sex play includes exhibiting or inspecting the genitals. Much of this child sex play is likely motivated by curiosity. There does not appear to be any link between such sexual play and sexual adjustment in adolescence or adulthood.

As the elementary school years progress, sex play with others usually declines, although romantic interest in peers may be present. Curiosity about sex remains high in the elementary school years, and children may ask many questions about reproduction and sexuality (Gordon & Gordon, 1989). However, the main surge in sexual interest takes place not in childhood but in early adolescence.

ADOLESCENCE AND EMERGING ADULTHOOD

Adolescence is a critical juncture in the development of sexuality as pubertal changes unfold and individuals develop a sexual identity. And emerging adulthood provides further opportunities for individuals to explore the sexual aspects of their lives.

Adolescence   Adolescence is a time of sexual exploration and experimentation, of sexual fantasies and realities, of incorporating sexuality into one's identity. Adolescents have an almost insatiable curiosity about sexuality. They think about whether they are sexually attractive, how to do sex, and what the future holds for their sexual lives. The majority of adolescents eventually manage to develop a mature sexual identity, but most experience times of vulnerability and confusion (Tolman & McClleland, 2011).

Adolescence is a bridge between the asexual child and the sexual adult. Every society gives some attention to adolescent sexuality. In some societies, adults clamp down and protect adolescent females from males by chaperoning them. Other societies promote very early marriage. Yet others allow some sexual experimentation.

In the United States, children and adolescents learn a great deal about sex from television (Bersamin & others, 2010; Strasburger, 2010). The messages come from TV commercials, which use sex to sell just about everything, as well as from the content of TV shows. A research review concluded that adolescents who view more sexual content on TV are likely to initiate sexual intercourse earlier than their peers who view less sexual content on TV (Brown & Strasburger, 2007).

The American Academy of Pediatrics (2010) recently issued a policy statement on sexuality, contraception, and the media. It pointed out that television, film, music, and the Internet are all becoming increasingly explicit, yet information about abstinence, sexual responsibility, and birth control rarely is included in these media outlets. A recent study revealed that adolescents who reported ever visiting a sexually explicit Web site were more sexually permissive and were more likely to have had multiple lifetime sexual partners, had more than one sexual partner in the last three months, and used alcohol or other substances at their last sexual encounter than their counterparts who reported having never visited a sexually explicit Web site (Braun-Courville & Rojas, 2009).

Developing a Sexual Identity   Mastering emerging sexual feelings and forming a sense of sexual identity is a multifaceted and lengthy process (Diamond & Savin-Williams, 2011; Savin-Williams, 2011). It involves learning to manage sexual feelings (such as sexual arousal and attraction), developing new forms of intimacy, and learning the skills to regulate sexual behavior to avoid undesirable consequences. An adolescent's sexual identity is influenced by *social norms* related

> Sexual arousal emerges as a new phenomenon in adolescence, and it is important to view sexuality as a normal aspect of adolescent development.
>
> —**SHIRLEY FELDMAN**
> *Contemporary Psychologist, Stanford University*

developmental **connection**

Technology. Media influences on adolescents and emerging adults include the digitally mediated social environment. Chapter 15, p. 511

What are some developmental pathways of same-sex attraction in adolescence?

to sex—the extent to which adolescents perceive that their peers are having sex, using protection, and so on. These social norms have important influences on adolescents' sexual behavior. For example, one study revealed that when adolescents perceived that their peers were sexually permissive, the adolescents had a higher rate of initiating sexual intercourse and engaging in risky sexual practices (Potard, Courtois, & Rusch, 2008). An individual's sexual identity also can be linked to other developing identities, which were discussed in Chapter 11.

An adolescent's sexual identity involves activities, interests, styles of behavior, and an indication of sexual orientation (whether an individual has same-sex or other-sex attractions) (Buzwell & Rosenthal, 1996; Diamond & Savin-Williams, 2011). For example, some adolescents have a high anxiety level about sex, others a low level. Some adolescents are strongly aroused sexually, others less so. Some adolescents are very active sexually, others not at all. Some adolescents are sexually inactive in response to their strong religious upbringing, while others attend church regularly but their religious training does not inhibit their sexual activity (Thorton & Camburn, 1989).

developmental **connection**

Identity. Identity can be conceptualized in terms of identity statuses: diffused, foreclosed, moratorium, and achievement. Chapter 11, p. 354

It is commonly believed that most gay and lesbian individuals quietly struggle with same-sex attractions in childhood, do not engage in heterosexual dating, and gradually recognize that they are gay or lesbian in mid to late adolescence (Diamond & Savin-Williams, 2011; Savin-Williams, 2011). Many youth do follow this developmental pathway, but others do not. For example, many youth have no recollection of same-sex attractions and experience a more abrupt sense of their same-sex attraction in late adolescence (Savin-Williams, 2006). Researchers also have found that the majority of adolescents with same-sex attractions also experience some degree of other-sex attractions (Garofalo & others, 1999). Even though some adolescents who are attracted to same-sex individuals fall in love with these individuals, others claim that their same-sex attractions are purely physical (Diamond & Savin-Williams, 2011).

In sum, gay and lesbian youth have diverse patterns of initial attraction, often have bisexual attractions, and may have physical or emotional attraction to same-sex individuals but do not always fall in love with them (Diamond & Savin-Williams, 2011; Savin-Williams, 2011).

The Timing and Frequency of Adolescent Sexual Behaviors The timing of sexual initiation varies by country as well as by gender and other socioeconomic characteristics. In one cross-cultural study, among females, the proportion having first intercourse by age 17 ranged from 72 percent in Mali to 47 percent in the United States and 45 percent in Tanzania (Singh & others, 2000). The percentage of males who had their first intercourse by age 17 ranged from 76 percent in Jamaica to 64 percent in the United States and 63 percent in Brazil. Within the United States, male, African American, and inner-city adolescents report being the most sexually active, whereas Asian American adolescents have the most restrictive sexual timetable (Feldman, Turner, & Araujo, 1999).

A recent study examined the role that acculturation might play in Latino adolescents' sexual behavior (McDonald, Manlove, & Ikamullah, 2009). Fewer first-generation Latino adolescents engaged in sexual intercourse before 18 years of age, and fewer first- and second-generation Latino adolescents used contraceptives consistently at 17 years of age than third-generation Latino adolescents. Thus, as acculturation proceeded, the sexual behavior of the Latino adolescents began to more closely resemble that of non-Latino White adolescents—earlier sexual initiation and increased condom use.

What is the current profile of sexual activity of adolescents? In a U.S. national survey conducted in 2009, 62 percent of twelfth-graders reported having had sexual intercourse compared with 32 percent of ninth-graders (Eaton & others, 2010). By age 20, 77 percent of U.S. youth have engaged in sexual intercourse (Dworkin & Santelli, 2007). Nationally, 49 percent of twelfth-graders, 40 percent of eleventh-graders, 29 percent of tenth-graders, and 21 percent of ninth-graders recently reported they were sexually active (Eaton & others, 2010).

What trends in adolescent sexual activity have occurred in the last two decades? From 1991 to 2009, fewer adolescents reported having ever had sexual intercourse, currently being sexually active, having had sexual intercourse before the age of 13, and having had sexual intercourse with 4 or more persons during their lifetime, as shown in Figure 12.6 (Eaton & others, 2010).

Until very recently, at all grade levels, adolescent males were more likely than adolescent females to report having had sexual intercourse and being sexually active. However, in the 2009 national survey, a higher percentage of twelfth-grade females (65 percent) reported having had sexual intercourse than twelfth-grade males (60 percent); a higher percentage of ninth-grade males (34 percent) still reported having had sexual intercourse than ninth-grade females (29 percent) (Eaton & others, 2010). Adolescent males are more likely than their female counterparts to describe sexual intercourse as an enjoyable experience.

Ages of sexual initiation vary by ethnic group in the United States (Santelli, Abraido-Lanza, & Melnikas, 2009). In a recent national U.S. survey of ninth- to twelfth-graders, 67 percent of African Americans, 51 percent of Latinos, and 43 percent of non-Latino Whites said they had ever experienced sexual intercourse (Eaton & others, 2010). In this study, 15 percent of African Americans (compared with 7 percent of Latinos and 3 percent of non-Latino Whites) said they had their first sexual experience before 13 years of age. Other research indicates that Asian American adolescents engage in sexual intercourse later than adolescents from other groups (Feldman, Turner, & Araujo, 1999).

Recent research indicates that oral sex is now a common occurrence among U.S. adolescents (Song & Halpern-Felsher, 2010). In a national survey, 55 percent of U.S. 15- to 19-year-old boys and 54 percent of girls said they had engaged in oral sex (National Center for Health Statistics, 2002).

Sexual Risk Factors in Adolescence Many adolescents are not emotionally prepared to handle sexual experiences, especially in early adolescence. Early sexual activity is linked with risky behaviors such as drug use, delinquency, and school-related problems (Jayakody & others, 2011; Yi & others, 2010). In a longitudinal study of people from 10 to 25 years of age, early sexual intercourse and affiliation with deviant peers were linked to substance-use disorders in emerging adulthood (Cornelius & others, 2007). A recent study of adolescents in five countries, including the United States, found that substance use was related to early sexual intercourse (Madkour & others, 2010). Another recent study revealed that alcohol use, early menarche, and poor parent-child communication were linked to early sexually intimate behavior in girls (Hipwell & others, 2011).

In addition to having sex in early adolescence, other risk factors for sexual problems in adolescence include contextual factors such as socioeconomic status (SES) and poverty, family/parenting and peer factors, and school-related influences (Van Ryzin & others, 2010). The percentage of sexually active young adolescents is higher in low-income areas of inner cities (Silver & Bauman, 2006). A recent study revealed that neighborhood poverty concentrations predicted 15- to 17-year-old girls' and boys' ages of sexual initiation (Cubbin & others, 2010).

A number of family factors are linked to sexuality outcomes for adolescents. A recent research review indicated that the following aspects of connectedness predicted sexual and reproductive health outcomes for youth: family connectedness,

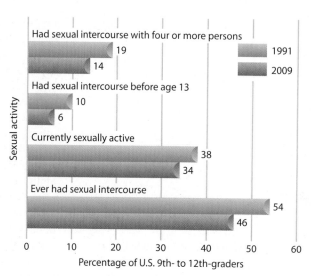

FIGURE **12.6**

SEXUAL ACTIVITY OF U.S. ADOLESCENTS FROM 1991 TO 2009. *Source:* Eaton, D. K., & others (2010). Youth risk behavior surveillance—United States 2009. *MMWR Surveillance Summary, 59*(5), 1–142.

parent-adolescent communication about sexuality, parental monitoring, and partner connectedness (Markham & others, 2010). Also, having older sexually active siblings or pregnant/parenting teenage sisters places adolescent girls at risk for pregnancy (Miller, Benson, & Galbraith, 2001). Further, recent research indicated that associating with more deviant peers in early adolescence was related to having more sexual partners at age 16 (Lansford & others, 2010). And a recent research review found that school connectedness was linked to positive sexuality outcomes (Markham & others, 2010).

Cognitive factors are increasingly implicated in sexual risk taking in adolescence (Fantasia, 2008). Two such factors are attention problems and self-regulation (the ability to control one's emotions and behavior). A longitudinal study revealed that attention problems and high rates of aggressive disruptive behavior at school entry increased the risk of multiple problem behaviors (school maladjustment, antisocial behavior, and substance use) in middle school, which in turn was linked to early initiation of sexual activity (Schofield & others, 2008). Another longitudinal study found that weak self-regulation at 8 to 9 years of age and risk proneness (tendency to seek sensation and make poor decisions) at 12 to 13 years of age set the stage for sexual risk taking at 16 to 17 years of age (Crockett, Raffaelli, & Shen, 2006).

Might adolescents' spirituality protect them from negative sexual outcomes? A recent research review concluded that *spirituality* (being spiritual, religious, or believing in a higher power, for example) was linked to positive sexual outcomes. Adolescents in this category were less likely to intend to have sex, were not as likely to engage in early sex, tended to have sex less frequently, and were not as likely to become pregnant as adolescents without a spiritual orientation (House & others, 2010).

A recent effort to develop a strategy reducing negative outcomes for adolescent sexuality focuses on positive youth development (PYD) (Lerner & others, 2011; Lewin-Bizan, Bowers, & Lerner, 2011). PYD programs seek to strengthen adolescents' relationships and skills and help them develop a more positive future outlook by enhancing academic, economic, and volunteer activities. An increasing number of efforts utilizing a PYD focus to improve sexual outcomes in adolescence are being implemented (Catalano, Gavin, & Markham, 2010; Gavin & others, 2010; House & others, 2010; Markham & others, 2010).

Contraceptive Use Sexual intercourse is a normal activity necessary for procreation, but if appropriate safeguards are not taken it brings the risk of unintended pregnancy and sexually transmitted infections (Kelly, 2011; Welch, 2011). Both of these risks can be reduced significantly by using certain forms of contraception, particularly condoms (Breheny & Stephens, 2004).

Are adolescents increasingly using condoms? A recent national study revealed a substantial increase in the proportion of U.S. high school students reporting the use of a contraceptive the last time they had sexual intercourse— 61 percent in 2009 compared with 46 percent in 1991 (Eaton & others, 2010). However, in this study, condom use by U.S. adolescents did not significantly change between 2003 and 2009.

Many sexually active adolescents still do not use contraceptives, or they use them inconsistently (Tschann & others, 2010). In 2009, 34 percent of sexually active adolescents said they had not used a condom the last time they had sexual intercourse (Eaton & others, 2010). Younger adolescents are less likely than older adolescents to take contraceptive precautions.

Sexually Transmitted Infections Earlier, we described sexually transmitted infections. Here we focus on their incidence among adolescents. Every year more than 3 million American adolescents (about one-fourth of those who are sexually

developmental connection

Development of the Self. One of the most important aspects of the self in middle and late childhood is the increased capacity for self-regulation. Chapter 11, p. 349

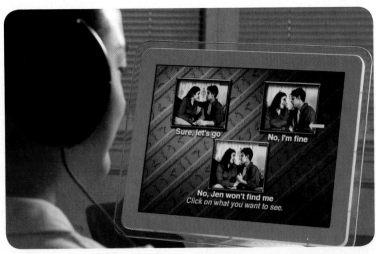

An adolescent participates in an interactive video session developed by Julie Downs and her colleagues at the Department of Social and Decision Making Sciences at Carnegie Mellon University. The videos help adolescents evaluate their responses and decisions in high-risk sexual contexts.

experienced) acquire an STI (Centers for Disease Control and Prevention, 2008). In a single act of unprotected sex with an infected partner, a teenage girl has a 1 percent risk of getting infected with HIV, a 30 percent risk of acquiring genital herpes, and a 50 percent chance of contracting gonorrhea. In some areas of the United States, as many as 25 percent of sexually active adolescents have contracted chlamydia. Adolescents have a higher incidence of gonorrhea and of chlamydia than young adults.

As we discussed earlier, a special concern is the high incidence of AIDS in sub-Saharan Africa (Renju & others, 2011; UNICEF, 2011). Adolescent girls in many African countries are vulnerable to being infected with HIV by adult men. Approximately six times as many adolescent girls as boys have AIDS in these countries, whereas in the United States adolescent males are more likely to have AIDS than their female counterparts (Centers for Disease Control and Prevention, 2008). In Kenya, 25 percent of 15- to 19-year-old girls are HIV-positive compared with 4 percent of the boys.

Adolescent Pregnancy   In cross-cultural comparisons, the United States continues to have one of the highest adolescent pregnancy and childbearing rates in the industrialized world, despite a considerable decline in the 1990s (Cooksey, 2009). The U.S. adolescent pregnancy rate is eight times as high as in the Netherlands. This dramatic difference exists in spite of the fact that U.S. adolescents are no more sexually active than their counterparts in the Netherlands.

Despite the negative comparisons of the United States with many other developed countries, there have been some encouraging trends in U.S. adolescent pregnancy rates. In 2004, births to adolescent girls fell to a record low (Child Trends, 2006). In fact, the rate of births to adolescent girls has dropped 30 percent since 1991. Reasons for these declines include increased contraceptive use and fear of sexually transmitted infections such as AIDS (Joyner, 2009). However, the U.S. adolescent birth rate increased by 5 percent in 2005 and 2006, although it resumed its downward trend in 2007 and 2008, as shown in Figure 12.7 (Hamilton, Martin, & Ventura, 2010).

Latina adolescents are more likely than African American and non-Latina White adolescents to become pregnant (Child Trends, 2008; Santelli, Abraido-Lanza, & Melnikas, 2009) (see Figure 12.7). Latinas also have had the smallest recent declines in adolescent pregnancy and birth rates among ethnic groups in the United States (Ventura & others, 2008). Latina and African American adolescent girls who have a child are also more likely to have a second child than are non-Latino White adolescent girls (Rosengard, 2009). And daughters of teenage mothers are at risk for teenage childbearing, thus perpetuating an intergenerational cycle. A study using data from the National Longitudinal Survey of Youth revealed that daughters of teenage mothers were 66 percent more likely to become teenage mothers themselves (Meade, Kershaw, & Ickovics, 2008). In this study, risks that increased the

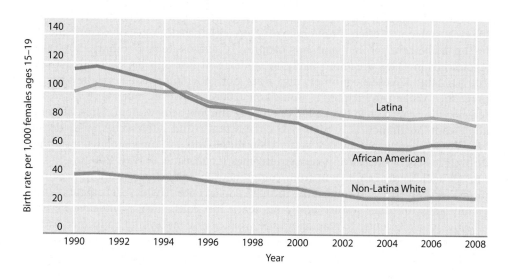

FIGURE 12.7

U.S. ADOLESCENT BIRTH RATE BY ETHNICITY, 1990 TO 2008. *Source:* Child Trends (2008, July). *Facts at a Glance.* Washington, DC: Author.

Lynn Blankenship, Family and Consumer Science Educator

Lynn Blankenship is a family and consumer science educator. She has an undergraduate degree in this area from the University of Arizona. She has taught for more than 20 years, the last 14 at Tucson High Magnet School.

Blankenship was awarded the Tucson Federation of Teachers Educator of the Year Award for 1999–2000 and the Arizona Association of Family and Consumer Science Teacher of the Year in 1999.

Blankenship especially enjoys teaching life skills to adolescents. One of her favorite activities is having students care for an automated baby that imitates the needs of real babies. She says that this program has a profound impact on students because the baby must be cared for around the clock for the duration of the assignment. Blankenship also coordinates real-world work experiences and training for students in several child-care facilities in the Tucson area.

Lynn Blankenship (*center*) with students carrying their automated babies.

For more information about what family and consumer science educators do, see page 42 in the Careers in Life-Span Development appendix.

---

developmental connection

Culture. The high school dropout rate for Latino adolescents is higher than any other ethnic group, except Native American adolescents. Chapter 16, p. 531

---

likelihood the daughters of the teenage mothers would become pregnant included low parental monitoring and poverty.

The consequences of America's high adolescent pregnancy rate are cause for great concern (Sieving & others, 2011). Adolescent pregnancy creates health risks for both the baby and the mother. Infants born to adolescent mothers are more likely to have low birth weights—a prominent factor in infant mortality—as well as neurological problems and childhood illness (Malamitsi-Puchner & Boutsikou, 2006). Adolescent mothers often drop out of school. Although many adolescent mothers resume their education later in life, they generally do not catch up economically with women who bear children in their twenties. A longitudinal study revealed that these characteristics of adolescent mothers were related to their likelihood of having problems as emerging adults: a history of school problems, delinquency, hard substance use, and mental health problems (Oxford & others, 2006).

Though the consequences of America's high adolescent pregnancy rate are cause for great concern, it often is not pregnancy alone that leads to negative consequences for an adolescent mother and her offspring (Cavazos-Rehg & others, 2010a, b). Adolescent mothers are more likely to come from low-SES backgrounds (Joyner, 2009). Many adolescent mothers also were not good students before they became pregnant (Malamitsi-Puchner & Boutsikou, 2006). However, not every adolescent female who bears a child lives a life of poverty and low achievement. Thus, although adolescent pregnancy is a high-risk circumstance and adolescents who do not become pregnant generally fare better than those who do, some adolescent mothers do well in school and have positive outcomes (Leadbeater & Way, 2000).

All adolescents can benefit from comprehensive sexuality education, beginning prior to adolescence and continuing through adolescence (Hyde & DeLamater, 2011). Family and consumer science educators teach life skills, such as effective decision making, to adolescents. To read about the work of one family and consumer science educator, see the *Connecting with Careers* profile. And to learn more about ways to reduce adolescent pregnancy, see the *Connecting Development to Life* interlude.

Reducing Adolescent Pregnancy

One strategy for reducing adolescent pregnancy, called the Teen Outreach Program (TOP), focuses on engaging adolescents in volunteer community service and stimulates discussions that help adolescents appreciate the lessons they learn through volunteerism (Dryfoos & Barkin, 2006). In one study, 695 adolescents in grades 9 to 12 were randomly assigned to either a Teen Outreach group or a control group (Allen & others, 1997). They were assessed at both program entry and program exit nine months later. The rate of pregnancy was substantially lower for the Teen Outreach adolescents. These adolescents also had a lower rate of school failure and academic suspension.

Girls, Inc., includes four programs that are designed to increase adolescent girls' motivation to avoid pregnancy until they are mature enough to make responsible decisions about motherhood (Roth & others, 1998). Growing Together, a series of five two-hour workshops for mothers and adolescents, and Will Power/Won't Power, a series of six two-hour sessions that focus on assertiveness training, are for 12- to 14-year-old girls. For older adolescent girls, Taking Care of Business provides nine sessions that emphasize career planning and provide information about sexuality, reproduction, and contraception. Health Bridge coordinates health and education services—girls can participate in this program as one of their club activities. Girls who participated in these programs were less likely to get pregnant than girls who did not participate (Girls, Inc., 1991).

Currently, a major controversy in sex education is whether schools should have an abstinence-only program or a program that emphasizes contraceptive knowledge. Two research reviews found that abstinence-only programs did not delay the initiation of sexual intercourse and did not reduce HIV-risk behaviors (Kirby, Laris, & Rolleri, 2007; Underhill, Montgomery, & Operario, 2007). Further, one study revealed that adolescents who experienced comprehensive sex education were less likely to report adolescent pregnancies than those who were given abstinence-only sex education or no education (Kohler, Manhart, & Lafferty, 2008).

These are not adolescent mothers, but rather adolescents who are participating in the Teen Outreach Program (TOP), which engages adolescents in volunteer community service. These adolescents are serving as volunteers in a child-care center for crack babies. Researchers have found that such volunteer experiences can reduce the rate of adolescent pregnancy.

Some sex education programs are starting to include abstinence-plus sexuality, an approach that promotes abstinence as well as contraceptive use (Realini & others, 2010).

A number of leading experts on adolescent sexuality now conclude that sex education programs that emphasize contraceptive knowledge do not increase the incidence of sexual intercourse and are more likely to reduce the risk of adolescent pregnancy and sexually transmitted infections than abstinence-only programs (Constantine, 2008; Eisenberg & others, 2008; Hyde & DeLamater, 2011). What additional research might help expand the reach of such programs?

Emerging Adulthood   At the beginning of emerging adulthood (age 18), surveys indicate that slightly more than 60 percent of individuals have experienced sexual intercourse, but by the end of emerging adulthood (age 25), most individuals have had sexual intercourse (Lefkowitz & Gillen, 2006). Also, the average age of marriage in the United States is currently 27 for males and 26 for females (Popenoe, 2009). Thus, emerging adulthood is a time frame during which most individuals are both sexually active and unmarried (Lefkowitz & Gillen, 2006; Regenerus & Uecker, 2011).

Patterns of heterosexual behavior for males and females in emerging adulthood include the following (Lefkowitz & Gillen, 2006):

- Males have a greater number of casual sexual partners, and females report being more selective about their choice of a sexual partner.

What are some characteristics of sexual patterns in emerging adulthood?

• Approximately 60 percent of emerging adults have had sexual intercourse with only one individual in the past year, but compared with young adults in their late twenties and thirties, emerging adults are more likely to have had sexual intercourse with two or more individuals.

• Although emerging adults have sexual intercourse with more individuals than young adults, they have sex less frequently. Approximately 25 percent of emerging adults report having sexual intercourse only a couple of times a year or not at all (Michael & others, 1994).

• Casual sex is more common in emerging adulthood than in young adulthood (Regenerus & Uecker, 2011). One study indicated that 30 percent of emerging adults said they had "hooked up" with someone and had sexual intercourse during college (Paul, McManus, & Hayes, 2000).

What are some predictors of risky heterosexual behavior in emerging adults, such as engaging in casual and unprotected sexual intercourse? Some research findings indicate the following (Lefkowitz & Gillen, 2006):

• Individuals who became sexually active in adolescence engage in more risky sexual behaviors in emerging adulthood than do their counterparts who delayed their sexual debuts until emerging adulthood (Capaldi & others, 2002).

• Emerging adults who are more religious have had fewer sexual partners and engaged in less risky sexual behaviors than have their less religious counterparts (Lefkowitz, Boone, & Shearer, 2004).

• When emerging adults drink alcohol, they are more likely to have casual sex and less likely to discuss possible risks (Cooper, 2002). A recent study also found that emerging adult women who engaged in casual sex were more likely to report having depressive symptoms than were emerging adult men (Grello, Welsh, & Harper, 2006).

ADULT DEVELOPMENT AND AGING

Earlier in our coverage of sexual orientation, we examined a number of basic ideas about heterosexual and gay/lesbian attitudes and behavior. Much of what we said there applied to young adults. Here we focus on changes in middle adulthood and late adulthood.

Middle Adulthood   What kind of changes characterize the sexuality of women and men as they go through middle age? **Climacteric** is a term used to describe the midlife transition in which fertility declines.

Menopause   **Menopause** is the time in middle age, usually during the late forties or early fifties, when a woman's menstrual periods cease. The average age at which U.S. women have their last period is 51 (Wise, 2006). However, there is a large variation in the age at which menopause occurs—from 39 to 59 years of age. Later menopause is linked with increased risk of breast cancer (Mishra & others, 2009).

Perimenopause is the transitional period from normal menstrual periods to no menstrual periods at all, which often takes up to 10 years. Perimenopause is most common in the forties but can occur in the thirties (Prior & Hitchcock, 2011). One study of 30- to 50-year-old women found that depressed feelings, headaches, moodiness, and palpitations were the perimenopausal symptoms that these women most frequently discussed with health-care providers (Lyndaker & Hulton, 2004). Lifestyle factors such as whether women are overweight, smoke, drink heavily, or exercise regularly during perimenopause influence their future health status, such as whether they develop cardiovascular disease or chronic illnesses (ESHRE Capri Workshop Group, 2011).

In menopause, production of estrogen by the ovaries declines dramatically, and this decline produces uncomfortable symptoms in some women—"hot flashes,"

climacteric The midlife transition in which fertility declines.

menopause The complete cessation of a woman's menstruation, which usually occurs during the late forties or early fifties.

perimenopause The transitional period from normal menstrual periods to no menstrual periods at all, which often takes up to 10 years.

nausea, fatigue, and rapid heartbeat, for example. A recent study revealed that increased estradiol and improved sleep, but not hot flashes, predicted enhanced mood in women during their menopausal transition (Joffe & others, 2011).

Cross-cultural studies also reveal wide variations in the menopause experience (Anderson & Yoshizawa, 2007; Lerner-Geva & others, 2010). For example, hot flashes are uncommon in Mayan women (Beyene, 1986). Asian women report fewer hot flashes than women in Western societies (Payer, 1991). It is difficult to determine the extent to which these cross-cultural variations are due to genetic, dietary, reproductive, or cultural factors.

Menopause overall is not the negative experience for most women it was once thought to be (Henderson, 2011; Weissmiller, 2009). Most women do not have severe physical or psychological problems related to menopause. For example, a recent research review concluded that there is no clear evidence that depressive disorders occur more often during menopause than at other times in a woman's reproductive life (Judd, Hickey, & Bryant, 2011).

However, the loss of fertility is an important marker for women—it means that they have to make final decisions about having children. Women in their thirties who have never had children sometimes speak about being "up against the biological clock" because they cannot postpone choices about having children much longer.

Until recently, hormone replacement therapy was often prescribed as treatment for unpleasant side effects of menopause. *Hormone replacement therapy (HRT)* augments the declining levels of reproductive hormone production by the ovaries (Studd, 2010; Yang & Reckelhoff, 2011). HRT can consist of various forms of estrogen, and usually a progestin. A study of HRT's effects was halted as evidence emerged that participants who were receiving HRT faced an increased risk of stroke (National Institutes of Health, 2004). Recent analyses confirmed that combined estrogen and progestin hormone therapy poses an increased risk of cardiovascular disease (Toh & others, 2010). Recent research studies on HRT have revealed that coinciding with the decreased use of HRT, research is mixed regarding the incidence of breast cancer (Baber, 2011; Chlebowski & others, 2010; Howell & Evans, 2011).

The National Institutes of Health recommends that women with a uterus who are currently taking hormones should consult with their doctor to determine whether they should continue the treatment. If they are taking HRT for short-term relief of symptoms, the benefits may outweigh the risks. However, the evidence of risks associated with HRT suggests that long-term hormone therapy should be seriously reevaluated (Warren, 2007). Consequently, many middle-aged women are seeking alternatives to HRT such as regular exercise, dietary supplements, herbal remedies, relaxation therapy, acupuncture, and nonsteroidal medications (Holloway, 2010).

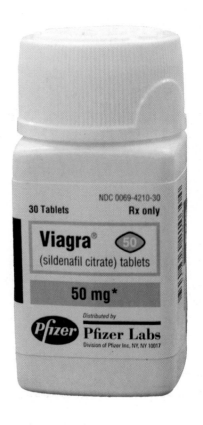

Hormonal Changes in Middle-Aged Men

Hormonal Changes in Middle-Aged Men   Do men go through anything like the menopause that women experience? That is, is there a male menopause? During middle adulthood, most men do not lose their capacity to father children, although there usually is a modest decline in their sexual hormone level and activity (Yassin & others, 2011). They experience hormonal changes in their fifties and sixties, but nothing like the dramatic drop in estrogen that women experience. Testosterone production begins to decline about 1 percent a year during middle adulthood, and sperm count usually shows a slow decline, but men do not lose their fertility in middle age. What has been referred to as "male menopause," then, probably has less to do with hormonal change than with the psychological adjustment men must make when they are faced with declining physical energy and with family and work pressures. Testosterone therapy has not been found to relieve such symptoms, suggesting that they are not induced by hormonal change.

The gradual decline in men's testosterone levels in middle age can reduce their sexual drive (Goel & others, 2009). Their erections are less full and less frequent, and men require more stimulation to achieve them. Researchers once attributed these changes to psychological factors, but increasingly they find that as many as

75 percent of the erectile dysfunctions in middle-aged men stem from physiological problems. Smoking, diabetes, hypertension, elevated cholesterol levels, and lack of exercise are at fault in many erectile problems in middle-aged men (Heidelbaugh, 2010; La Vignera & others, 2011; Shin, Pregenzer, & Gardin, 2011).

Erectile dysfunction (ED) is a common condition in aging men, being present in approximately 50 percent of men 40 to 70 years of age (Berookhim & Bar-Chama, 2011). Treatment for men with erectile dysfunction has focused on the drug Viagra and on similar drugs, such as Levitra and Cialis (Alberson & others, 2011; Sperling & others, 2010). Viagra works by allowing increased blood flow into the penis, which produces an erection. Its success rate is in the 60 to 85 percent range (Claes & others, 2010).

How frequently do middle-aged U.S. adults engage in sexual intercourse?

Sexual Attitudes and Behavior   Although the ability of men and women to function sexually shows little biological decline in middle adulthood, sexual activity usually occurs on a less frequent basis than in early adulthood (Welch, 2011). Career interests, family matters, decreased energy levels, and routine may contribute to this decline (Avis & others, 2009).

In the Sex in America survey (described earlier in this chapter), the frequency of having sex was greatest for individuals aged 25 to 29 years old (47 percent had sex twice a week or more) and dropped off for individuals in their fifties (23 percent of 50- to 59-year-old males said they had sex twice a week or more, while only 14 percent of the females in this age group reported this frequency) (Michael & others, 1994). Note, though, that the Sex in America survey may underestimate the frequency of sexual activity of middle-aged adults because the data were collected prior to the widespread use of erectile dysfunction drugs such as Viagra.

Living with a spouse or partner makes all the difference in whether people engage in sexual activity, especially for women over 40 years of age. In one study conducted by the MacArthur Foundation, 95 percent of women in their forties with partners said that they had been sexually active in the last six months, compared with only 53 percent of those without partners (Brim, 1999). By their fifties, 88 percent of women living with a partner had been sexually active in the last six months, but only 37 percent of those who were neither married nor living with someone reported having had sex in the last six months.

A recent large-scale study of U.S. adults 40 to 80 years of age found that early ejaculation (26 percent) and erectile difficulties (22 percent) were the most common sexual problems of older men, whereas lack of sexual interest (33 percent) and lubrication difficulties (21 percent) were the most common sexual problems of older women (Laumann & others, 2009).

Late Adulthood   Aging does induce some changes in human sexual performance, more so in men than in women (Bouman, 2008). Orgasm becomes less frequent in males, occurring in every second to third act of intercourse rather than every time. More direct stimulation usually is needed to produce an erection. From 65 to 80 years of age, approximately one out of four men has serious problems getting or keeping erections; for those over 80 years of age, the percentage rises to one out of two men (Butler & Lewis, 2002). Even when intercourse is impaired by infirmity, other relationship needs persist, among them closeness, sensuality, and being valued as a man or a woman (Bouman, 2008).

An interview study of more than 3,000 adults 57 to 85 years of age revealed that many older adults are sexually active as long as they are healthy (Lindau & others, 2007) (see Figure 12.8). Sexual activity did decline through the later years of life: 73 percent of 57- to 64-year-olds, 53 percent of 65- to 74-year-olds, and 26 percent of 75- to 85-year-olds reported that they were sexually active. Even in the sexually active oldest

FIGURE 12.8

SEXUAL ACTIVITY IN OLDER ADULTS WITH A PARTNER

(Bar graph) Percentage of older adults who reported sexual activity with a partner in the previous 12 months, by age group (57–64, 65–74, 75–85), comparing Men and Women.

group (75 to 85), more than 50 percent said they still had sex at least two to three times a month. Fifty-eight percent of sexually active 65- to 74-year-olds and 31 percent of 75- to 85-year-olds said they engaged in oral sex. As with middle-aged and younger adults, older adults who did not have a partner were far less likely to be sexually active than those who had a partner. For older adults with a partner who reported not having sex, the main reason was poor health, especially the male partner's physical health.

As indicated in Figure 12.8, older women had a lower rate of sexual activity than did men. Indeed, a challenge for a sexually inter-ested older woman is not having a partner. At 70 years of age, only about 35 percent of women have a partner compared with approx-imately 70 percent of men. Many older women's husbands have died, and many older men are with younger women.

At this point, we have discussed many aspects of sexuality, but we have not examined three influential factors: an individual's morality, values, and religion. In Chapter 13, we will explore these topics.

What are some characteristics of sexuality in older adults? How does sexual activity change as older adults go through the late adulthood period?

Review Connect Reflect

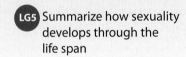 Summarize how sexuality develops through the life span

Review

- What is the nature of child sexuality?
- How do adolescents develop a sexual identity? How does sexual behavior develop? What are some risk factors for sexual problems during adolescence? What are some patterns of behavior for emerging adults?
- How does sexuality change in middle adulthood? How does sexuality change in late adulthood?

Connect

- In this section you read that the production of estrogen by the ovaries declines dramatically in menopause. What did you learn in Chapter 3 about the role of estradiol, a type of estrogen, in puberty?

Reflect *Your Own Personal Journey of Life*

- How would you describe your sexual identity? What contributed to this identity?

reach your **learning goals**

Biological, Social, and Cognitive Influences on Gender

 Explain biological, social, and cognitive influences on gender

Biological Influences

- Gender refers to the characteristics of people as males and females. Key aspects of gender include gender roles and gender-typing (the process by which children acquire the thoughts, feelings, and behaviors that are considered appropriate for their gender). Biological influences on gender include heredity, hormones, and evo-lution. The 23rd pair of chromosomes with two X-shaped chromosomes produces a female; a 23rd pair with an X and a Y chromosome produces a male. Estrogens primarily influence the development of female physical sex characteristics and help regulate the menstrual cycle. Androgens primarily promote the development of male genitals and secondary sex characteristics. To explore biological influences on gender, researchers have studied individuals who are exposed to unusual levels of sex hormones early in prenatal development. Evolutionary psychology argues that adaptation during the evolution of humans produced psychological differences between males and females.

Social Influences

- Three theories have been influential in arguing that psychological differences between the genders are due to social factors. Social role theory states that gender differences result from the contrasting roles of women and men. The psychoanalytic theory of gender stems from Freud's view that the preschool child develops a sexual attraction to the opposite-sex parent, then at 5 or 6 years of age renounces the attraction because of anxious feelings, subsequently identifies with the same-sex parent and unconsciously adopts the characteristics of the same-sex parent. The social cognitive theory of gender states that children learn about gender through observation and imitation and through reward and punishment for gender-appropriate and gender-inappropriate behavior.

Cognitive Influences

- Gender schema theory states that gender-typing emerges as children gradually develop gender schemas of what is gender-appropriate and gender-inappropriate in their culture.

Gender Stereotypes, Similarities, and Differences

LG2 Discuss gender stereotypes, similarities, and differences

Gender Stereotyping

- Gender stereotypes are general impressions and beliefs about males and females. Gender stereotypes are widespread. Gender stereotyping changes developmentally; it is present even at 2 years of age but increases considerably in early childhood. In middle and late childhood, children become more flexible in their gender attitudes, but gender stereotyping may increase again in early adolescence. By late adolescence, gender attitudes are often more flexible.

Gender Similarities and Differences

- There are a number of physical differences in males and females, small or nonexistent cognitive differences, and some socioemotional differences (males are more physically aggressive and active, but engage in less emotional self-regulation; females show a stronger interest in relationships; and females are more people-oriented, boys more object-oriented). Controversy continues to occur regarding how extensive gender differences are and what causes the differences. Gender in context is an important concept—gender behavior often varies across contexts, not only within a particular culture but also across cultures.

Gender Development Through the Life Span

LG3 Describe the development of gender through the life span

Childhood

- Children form many ideas about what the sexes are like from about 1½ to 3 years of age. The amount, timing, and intensity of gender socialization are different for girls and for boys. Boys receive earlier and more intense gender socialization than girls do.

Adolescence

- During early adolescence, females and males must come to terms with new definitions of their gender roles as they experience the extensive changes of puberty. There is continued controversy about whether all young adolescents experience gender intensification.

Adulthood and Aging

- Many experts argue that it is important for women to retain their relationship strengths but also to put more energy into self-development. Tannen stresses that many women prefer rapport talk and many men prefer report talk. Men have been successful at achieving, but the male role involves considerable strain. There is diversity in men's experiences, just as there is in women's. Men seem to become more nurturant and sensitive when they get older, but the evidence about whether women tend to become more assertive and dominant when they are older is mixed.

Exploring Sexuality

 LG4 Characterize influences on sexuality, the nature of sexual orientation, and some sexual problems

Biological and Cultural Factors

- The role of hormones in human sexual behavior is difficult to specify. Sexual motivation is also influenced by cultural factors. Sexual scripts in cultures influence sexual behavior. In some sexual scripts, females link sexual intercourse with love more than do males, the female is to blame if she becomes pregnant, and males tend to emphasize sexual conquest.

Sexual Orientation

- An individual's sexual preference—heterosexual, homosexual, or bisexual—likely is the result of a combination of genetic, hormonal, cognitive, and environmental factors. In the 1994 Sex in America survey, Americans' sexual lives were reported to be more conservative than in earlier surveys. Sexual orientation is generally viewed as a continuum. Regardless of sexual orientation, most people emphasize the importance of trust, affection, and shared interests in a relationship.

Sexually Transmitted Infections

- Sexually transmitted infections (STIs) are contracted primarily through sexual contact. The STI that has received the most attention in recent years is AIDS. Gonorrhea, syphilis, chlamydia, genital herpes, and HPV are among the most common STIs. Some good strategies for protecting against STIs include knowing your own and your partner's risk status; obtaining screening for STIs; having protected, not unprotected, sex; and not having sex with multiple partners.

Forcible Sexual Behavior and Sexual Harassment

- Rape is forcible sexual intercourse, oral sex, or anal sex with a person who does not give consent. Rape usually produces traumatic reactions in its victims. Sexual harassment occurs when one person uses his or her power over another individual in a sexual manner.

Sexuality Through the Life Span

 LG5 Summarize how sexuality develops through the life span

Childhood

- A majority of children engage in some sex play, usually with siblings of friends. Their motivation is probably mainly curiosity, and there does not appear to be a link between sex play and adolescent or adult sexual adjustment.

Adolescence and Emerging Adulthood

- Adolescence is a time of sexual exploration and sexual experimentation. Mastering emerging sexual feelings and forming a sense of sexual identity are two challenges of the period. Gay and lesbian youth have diverse patterns of initial attraction, often have bisexual attractions, and may experience same-sex emotional or physical attractions. National U.S. data indicate that by age 19, four out of five individuals have had sexual intercourse. A dramatic increase in oral sex has occurred in adolescence, although many adolescents are unaware of the health risks associated with oral sex. Risk factors for sexual problems include early sexual activity, engaging in delinquency and excessive drinking, living in a low-SES neighborhood, ineffective parenting, and having an older sibling who engages in sex. Contraceptive use by adolescents is increasing. About one in four sexually experienced adolescents acquires a sexually transmitted infection (STI). America's adolescent pregnancy rate is high but has been decreasing in recent years. Emerging adults have sexual intercourse less frequently than young adults; males have more casual sexual partners and are less selective than females in their partner choice; and by the end of emerging adulthood, most have had sexual intercourse.

Adult Development and Aging

- Menopause usually occurs during the late forties or early fifties. Perimenopause, the transition from normal menstrual periods to no menstrual periods at all, often takes up to 10 years. Hormone replacement therapy (HRT) augments the declining levels of reproductive hormone production by the ovaries. HRT consists of various forms of estrogen, and usually progestin. Although HRT reduces many short-term symptoms of menopause, its long-term use is no longer recommended by the National Institutes of Health because of its association with increased risks of coronary heart disease and stroke. Men do not experience an inability to father children in middle age, although their testosterone level drops. In late adulthood, sexual changes do occur, more so for men than for women.

key terms

gender 371
gender identity 371
gender role 371
gender-typing 371
estrogens 371
androgens 372
social role theory 373
psychoanalytic theory of gender 373

social cognitive theory of gender 373
gender schema theory 375
gender stereotypes 377
gender-intensification hypothesis 382
rapport talk 383
report talk 383
sexual scripts 387

traditional religious script 387
romantic script 387
bisexuality 388
sexually transmitted infections (STIs) 389
rape 391
date or acquaintance rape 391

sexual harassment 392
climacteric 400
menopause 400
perimenopause 400

key people

Alice Eagly 373
Sigmund Freud 373
Phyllis Bronstein 374

Janet Shibley Hyde 380
Deborah Tannen 380
Joseph Pleck 382

Jean Baker Miller 383
Harriet Lerner 383
Ron Levant 385

Robert Michael 387
Laura Brown 389

chapter 13

MORAL DEVELOPMENT, VALUES, AND RELIGION

preview

Just as a person's emotional life and sexual life change with age, a person's moral life and spiritual life also develop through the life span. In this chapter we examine how moral development proceeds. We also explore how people go beyond questions of right and wrong to search for values, religion, spirituality, and meaning at different points in their lives.

Domains of Moral Development   **LG1** Discuss theory and research on moral thought, behavior, feeling, and personality

- What Is Moral Development?
- Moral Thought
- Moral Behavior
- Moral Feeling
- Moral Personality

Moral development has been a topic of great concern to societies, communities, and families. It is also one of the oldest topics of interest to those who are curious about human nature. Philosophers and theologians have talked about it and written about it for many centuries. In the twentieth century, psychologists began theorizing about and studying moral development.

WHAT IS MORAL DEVELOPMENT?

Moral development involves changes in thoughts, feelings, and behaviors regarding standards of right and wrong. Moral development has an *intrapersonal* dimension, which regulates a person's activities when she or he is not engaged in social interaction, and an *interpersonal* dimension, which regulates social interactions and arbitrates conflict (Walker, 2004, 2006). To understand moral development, we need to consider four basic questions:

> First, how do individuals *reason* or *think* about moral decisions?
> Second, how do individuals actually *behave* in moral circumstances?
> Third, how do individuals *feel* about moral matters?
> Fourth, what characterizes an individual's moral *personality*?

As we consider these four domains in the following sections, keep in mind that thoughts, behaviors, feelings, and personality often are interrelated. For example, if the focus is on an individual's behavior, it is still important to evaluate the person's reasoning. Also, emotions can distort moral reasoning. And moral personality encompasses thoughts, behavior, and feeling.

MORAL THOUGHT

How do individuals think about what is right and wrong? Are children able to evaluate moral questions in the same way that adults can? Jean Piaget had some thoughts about these questions. So did Lawrence Kohlberg.

Piaget's Theory   Interest in how children think about moral issues was stimulated by Piaget (1932), who extensively observed and interviewed children from the ages of 4 through 12. Piaget watched children play marbles to learn how they used and thought about the game's rules. He also asked children about ethical issues—theft, lies, punishment, and justice, for example. Piaget concluded that children go through two distinct stages in how they think about morality.

- From 4 to 7 years of age, children display **heteronomous morality,** the first stage of moral development in Piaget's theory. Children think of justice and rules as unchangeable properties of the world, removed from the control of people.

Piaget extensively observed and interviewed 4- to 12-year-old children as they played games to learn how they used and thought about the games' rules.

moral development Changes in thoughts, feelings, and behaviors regarding standards of right and wrong.

heteronomous morality (Piaget) The first stage of moral development in Piaget's theory, occurring at 4 to 7 years of age. Justice and rules are conceived of as unchangeable properties of the world, removed from the control of people.

- From 7 to 10 years of age, children are in a transition showing some features of the first stage of moral reasoning and some features of the second stage, autonomous morality.
- From about 10 years of age and older, children show **autonomous morality.** They become aware that rules and laws are created by people, and in judging an action, they consider the actor's intentions as well as the consequences.

Because young children are heteronomous moralists, they judge the rightness or goodness of behavior by considering its consequences, not the intentions of the actor. For example, to the heteronomous moralist, breaking twelve cups accidentally is worse than breaking one cup intentionally. As children develop into moral autonomists, intentions assume paramount importance.

The heteronomous thinker also believes that rules are unchangeable and are handed down by all-powerful authorities. When Piaget suggested to young children that they use new rules in a game of marbles, they resisted. By contrast, older children—moral autonomists—accept change and recognize that rules are merely convenient conventions, subject to change.

The heteronomous thinker also believes in **immanent justice,** the concept that if a rule is broken, punishment will be meted out immediately. The young child believes that a violation is connected automatically to its punishment. Thus, young children often look around worriedly after doing something wrong, expecting inevitable punishment. Immanent justice also implies that if something unfortunate happens to someone, the person must have transgressed earlier. Older children, who are moral autonomists, recognize that punishment occurs only if someone witnesses the wrongdoing and that, even then, punishment is not inevitable.

How do these changes in moral reasoning occur? Piaget argued that, as children develop, they become more sophisticated in thinking about social matters, especially about the possibilities and conditions of cooperation. Piaget stressed that this social understanding comes about through the mutual give-and-take of peer relations. In the peer group, where others have power and status similar to the child's, plans are negotiated and coordinated, and disagreements are reasoned about and eventually settled. Parent-child relations, in which parents have the power and children do not, are less likely to advance moral reasoning, because rules are often handed down in an authoritarian way.

Kohlberg's Theory

A second major perspective on moral development was proposed by Lawrence Kohlberg (1958, 1986). Piaget's cognitive stages of development serve as the underpinnings for Kohlberg's theory, but Kohlberg suggested that there are six stages of moral development. These stages, he argued, are universal. Development from one stage to another, said Kohlberg, is fostered by opportunities to take the perspective of others and to experience conflict between one's current stage of moral thinking and the reasoning of someone at a higher stage.

Kohlberg arrived at his view after 20 years of using a unique interview with children. In the interview, children are presented with a series of stories in which characters face moral dilemmas. The following is the most popular Kohlberg dilemma:

> In Europe a woman was near death from a special kind of cancer. There was one drug that the doctors thought might save her. It was a form of radium that a druggist in the same town had recently discovered. The drug was expensive to make, but the druggist was charging ten times what the drug cost him to make. He paid $200 for the radium and charged $2,000 for a small dose of the drug. The sick woman's husband, Heinz, went to everyone he knew to borrow the money, but he could only get together $1,000, which is half of what it cost. He told the druggist that his wife was dying and asked him to sell it cheaper or let him pay later. But the druggist said, "No, I discovered the drug, and I am going to make money from it." So Heinz got desperate and broke into the man's store to steal the drug for his wife. (Kohlberg, 1969, p. 379)

developmental **connection**

Cognitive Theory. In which of Piaget's cognitive stages is a 5-year-old heteronomous thinker likely to be? Chapter 6, p. 190

How is this child's moral thinking likely to be different about stealing a cookie depending on whether he is in Piaget's heteronomous or autonomous stage?

Lawrence Kohlberg.

autonomous morality The second stage of moral development in Piaget's theory, displayed by children about 10 years of age and older. At this stage, children become aware that rules and laws are created by people and that in judging an action they should consider the actor's intentions as well as the consequences.

immanent justice Belief that if a rule is broken, punishment will be meted out immediately.

LEVEL 1	LEVEL 2	LEVEL 3
Preconventional Level	**Conventional Level**	**Postconventional Level**
Stage 1 Punishment and Obedience Orientation *Children obey because adults tell them to obey. People base their moral decisions on fear of punishment.* **Stage 2** Individualism, Purpose, and Exchange *Individuals pursue their own interests but let others do the same. What is right involves equal exchange.*	**Stage 3** Mutual Interpersonal Expectations, Relationships, and Interpersonal Conformity *Individuals value trust, caring, and loyalty to others as a basis for moral judgments.* **Stage 4** Social System Morality *Moral judgments are based on understanding and the social order, law, justice, and duty.*	**Stage 5** Social Contract or Utility and Individual Rights *Individuals reason that values, rights, and principles undergird or transcend the law.* **Stage 6** Universal Ethical Principles *The person has developed moral judgments that are based on universal human rights. When faced with a dilemma between law and conscience, a personal, individualized conscience is followed.*

FIGURE 13.1
KOHLBERG'S THREE LEVELS AND SIX STAGES OF MORAL DEVELOPMENT

This story is one of 11 that Kohlberg devised to investigate the nature of moral thought. After reading the story, the interviewee answers a series of questions about the moral dilemma. Should Heinz have stolen the drug? Was stealing it right or wrong? Why? Is it a husband's duty to steal the drug for his wife if he can get it no other way? Would a good husband steal? Did the druggist have the right to charge that much when there was no law setting a limit on the price? Why or why not?

The Kohlberg Stages   Based on the answers interviewees gave for this and other moral dilemmas, Kohlberg identified three levels of moral thinking, each of which is characterized by two stages (see Figure 13.1). A key concept in understanding progression through the levels and stages is that people's morality becomes more internal or mature. That is, their reasons for their moral decisions or values begin to go beyond the external or superficial reasons they gave when they were younger. Let's further examine Kohlberg's stages.

Preconventional reasoning is the lowest level of moral reasoning, said Kohlberg. At this level, good and bad are interpreted in terms of external rewards and punishments.

- *Stage 1.* **Heteronomous morality** is the first stage in preconventional reasoning. At this stage, moral thinking is tied to punishment. For example, children think that they must obey because they fear punishment for disobedience.
- *Stage 2.* **Individualism, instrumental purpose, and exchange** is the second stage of preconventional reasoning. At this stage, individuals reason that pursuing their own interests is the right thing to do, but they let others do the same. Thus, they think that what is right involves an equal exchange. They reason that if they are nice to others, others will be nice to them in return.

Conventional reasoning is the second, or intermediate, level in Kohlberg's theory of moral development. At this level, individuals apply certain standards, but they are the standards set by others, such as parents or the government.

- *Stage 3.* **Mutual interpersonal expectations, relationships, and interpersonal conformity** is Kohlberg's third stage of moral development. At this stage, individuals value trust, caring, and loyalty to others as a basis of moral judgments. Children and adolescents often adopt their parents' moral standards at this stage, seeking to be thought of by their parents as a "good girl" or a "good boy."

preconventional reasoning The lowest level in Kohlberg's theory of moral development. The individual's moral reasoning is controlled primarily by external rewards and punishments.

heteronomous morality (Kohlberg) The first stage of preconventional reasoning in Kohlberg's theory, in which moral thinking is tied to punishment.

individualism, instrumental purpose, and exchange The second Kohlberg stage of preconventional reasoning. At this stage, individuals pursue their own interests but also let others do the same.

conventional reasoning The second, or intermediate, level in Kohlberg's theory of moral development. At this level, individuals abide by the standards of others such as parents or the laws of society.

mutual interpersonal expectations, relationships, and interpersonal conformity Kohlberg's third stage of moral development. At this stage, individuals value trust, caring, and loyalty to others as a basis of moral judgments.

- *Stage 4.* **Social systems morality** is the fourth stage in Kohlberg's theory of moral development. At this stage, moral judgments are based on understanding the social order, law, justice, and duty. For example, adolescents may reason that in order for a community to work effectively, it needs to be protected by laws that are adhered to by its members.

Postconventional reasoning is the highest level in Kohlberg's theory of moral development. At this level, the individual recognizes alternative moral courses, explores the options, and then decides on a personal moral code.

- *Stage 5.* **Social contract or utility and individual rights** is the fifth Kohlberg stage. At this stage, individuals reason that values, rights, and principles undergird or transcend the law. A person evaluates the validity of actual laws and social systems in terms of the degree to which they preserve and protect fundamental human rights and values.

- *Stage 6.* **Universal ethical principles** is the sixth and highest stage in Kohlberg's theory of moral development. At this stage, the person has developed a moral standard based on universal human rights. When faced with a conflict between law and conscience, the person reasons that conscience should be followed, even though the decision might bring risk.

Kohlberg noted that these levels and stages occur in a sequence and are age related: before age 9, most children use level 1, preconventional reasoning based on external rewards and punishments, when they consider moral choices. By early adolescence, their moral reasoning is increasingly based on the application of standards set by others. Most adolescents reason at stage 3, with some signs of stages 2 and 4. By early adulthood, a small number of individuals reason in postconventional ways.

What evidence supports this description of development? A 20-year longitudinal investigation found that use of stages 1 and 2 decreased with age (Colby & others, 1983). Stage 4, which did not appear at all in the moral reasoning of 10-year-olds, was reflected in the moral thinking of 62 percent of the 36-year-olds. Stage 5 did not appear until age 20 to 22 and never characterized more than 10 percent of the individuals.

Thus, the moral stages appeared somewhat later than Kohlberg initially envisioned, and reasoning at the higher stages, especially stage 6, was rare. Although stage 6 has been removed from the Kohlberg moral judgment scoring manual, it still is considered to be theoretically important in the Kohlberg scheme of moral development.

Influences on the Kohlberg Stages

What factors influence movement through Kohlberg's stages? Although moral reasoning at each stage presupposes a certain level of cognitive development, Kohlberg argued that advances in children's cognitive development did not ensure development of moral reasoning. Instead, moral reasoning also reflects children's experiences in dealing with moral questions and moral conflict.

Several investigators have tried to advance individuals' levels of moral development by having a model present arguments that reflect moral thinking one stage above the individuals' established levels. This approach applies the concepts of equilibrium and conflict that Piaget used to explain cognitive development. By presenting arguments slightly beyond the children's level of moral reasoning, the researchers created a disequilibrium that motivated the children to restructure their moral thought. The upshot of studies using this approach is that virtually any plus-stage discussion, for any length of time, seems to promote more advanced moral reasoning (Walker, 1982).

Kohlberg noted that peer interaction is a critical part of the social stimulation that challenges children to change their moral reasoning. Whereas adults characteristically impose rules and regulations on children, the give-and-take among peers gives children an opportunity to take the perspective of another person and to

social systems morality The fourth stage in Kohlberg's theory of moral development. Moral judgments are based on understanding the social order, law, justice, and duty.

postconventional reasoning The highest level in Kohlberg's theory of moral development. At this level, the individual recognizes alternative moral courses, explores the options, and then decides on a personal moral code.

social contract or utility and individual rights The fifth Kohlberg stage of moral development. At this stage, individuals reason that values, rights, and principles undergird or transcend the law.

universal ethical principles The sixth and highest stage in Kohlberg's theory of moral development. Individuals develop a moral standard based on universal human rights.

Both Piaget and Kohlberg argued that peer relations are a critical part of the social stimulation that challenges children to advance their moral reasoning. The mutual give-and-take of peer relations provides children with role-taking opportunities that give them a sense that rules are generated democratically.

generate rules democratically. Kohlberg stressed that in principle, encounters with any peers can produce perspective-taking opportunities that may advance a child's moral reasoning.

Kohlberg's Critics   Kohlberg's theory provoked debate, research, and criticism (Gibbs, 2010; Narváez, 2010a, b; Walker & Frimer, 2011). Key criticisms involve the link between moral thought and moral behavior, the roles of culture and the family in moral development, and the significance of concern for others.

Moral Thought and Moral Behavior   Kohlberg's theory has been criticized for placing too much emphasis on moral thought and not enough emphasis on moral behavior (Walker, 2004). Moral reasons can sometimes be a shelter for immoral behavior. Corrupt CEOs and politicians endorse the loftiest of moral virtues in public before their own behavior is exposed. Whatever the latest public scandal, you will probably find that the culprits displayed virtuous thoughts but engaged in immoral behavior. No one wants a nation of cheaters and thieves who can reason at the postconventional level. The cheaters and thieves may know what is right yet still do what is wrong. Heinous actions can be cloaked in a mantle of moral virtue.

developmental connection

Culture. Cross-cultural studies provide information about the degree to which children's development is universal, or similar, across cultures or is culture-specific. Chapter 15, p. 507

Culture and Moral Reasoning   Kohlberg emphasized that his stages of moral reasoning are universal, but some critics claim his theory is culturally biased (Gibbs, 2010; Miller, 2007). Both Kohlberg and his critics may be partially correct. One review of 45 studies in 27 cultures around the world, mostly non-European, provided support for the universality of Kohlberg's first four stages (Snarey, 1987). As Kohlberg predicted, individuals in diverse cultures developed through these four stages in sequence. A more recent research review revealed support for the qualitative shift from stage 2 to stage 3 across cultures (Gibbs & others, 2007). Stages 5 and 6, however, have not been found in all cultures (Gibbs & others, 2007; Snarey, 1987). Furthermore, Kohlberg's scoring system does not recognize the higher-level moral reasoning of certain cultures, and thus that moral reasoning is more culture-specific than Kohlberg envisioned (Snarey, 1987).

A recent study explored links between culture, mindset, and moral judgment (Narváez & Hill, 2010). In this study, a higher level of multicultural experience was linked to open mindedness (being cognitively flexible), a growth mindset (perceiving that one's qualities can change and improve through effort), and higher moral judgment.

Families and Moral Development   Kohlberg argued that family processes are essentially unimportant in children's moral development. As noted earlier, he argued that parent-child relationships usually provide children with little opportunity for give-and-take or perspective taking. Rather, Kohlberg said that such opportunities are more likely to be provided by children's peer relations.

Did Kohlberg underestimate the contribution of family relationships to moral development? Most developmentalists emphasize that parents play more important roles in children's moral development than Kohlberg envisioned (Thompson, 2009). They stress that parents' communication with children, their discipline techniques, and many other aspects of parent-child relationships influence children's moral development—we will have more to discuss about this topic later in the chapter. Nonetheless, most developmentalists agree with Kohlberg, and Piaget, that peers play an important role in moral development.

Carol Gilligan. *What is Gilligan's view of moral development?*

Gender and the Care Perspective   The most publicized criticism of Kohlberg's theory has come from Carol Gilligan (1982, 1992, 1996), who argues that Kohlberg's theory reflects a gender bias. According to Gilligan, Kohlberg's theory is based on a male norm that puts abstract principles above relationships and concern for others and sees the individual as standing alone and independently making moral decisions.

It puts justice at the heart of morality. In contrast with Kohlberg's **justice perspective,** Gilligan argues for a **care perspective,** which is a moral perspective that views people in terms of their connectedness with others and emphasizes interpersonal communication, relationships with others, and concern for others. According to Gilligan, Kohlberg greatly underplayed the care perspective, perhaps because he was a male, because most of his research was with males rather than females, and because he used male responses as a model for his theory.

In extensive interviews with girls from 6 to 18 years of age, Gilligan and her colleagues found that girls consistently interpret moral dilemmas in terms of human relationships and base these interpretations on listening and watching other people (Gilligan, 1992; Gilligan & others, 2003). However, a meta-analysis (a statistical analysis that combines the results of many different studies) casts doubt on Gilligan's claim of substantial gender differences in moral judgment (Jaffee & Hyde, 2000). And a recent analysis concluded that girls' moral orientations are "somewhat more likely to focus on care for others than on abstract principles of justice, but they can use both moral orientations when needed (as can boys . . .)" (Blakemore, Berenbaum, & Liben, 2009, p 132).

Social Conventional Reasoning   Some theorists and researchers argue that Kohlberg did not adequately distinguish between moral reasoning and social conventional reasoning (Helwig & Turiel, 2011; Smetana, 2011). **Social conventional reasoning** focuses on conventional rules that have been established by social consensus in order to control behavior and maintain the social system. The rules themselves are arbitrary, such as using a fork at meals and raising your hand in class before speaking.

In contrast, moral reasoning focuses on ethical issues and rules of morality. Unlike conventional rules, moral rules are not arbitrary. They are obligatory, widely accepted, and somewhat impersonal (Helwig & Turiel, 2011). Rules pertaining to lying, cheating, stealing, and physically harming another person are moral rules because violation of these rules affronts ethical standards that exist apart from social consensus and convention. Moral judgments involve concepts of justice, whereas social conventional judgments are concepts of social organization.

Recently, a distinction also has been made between moral and conventional issues, which are viewed as legitimately subject to adult social regulation, and personal issues, which are more likely subject to the child's or adolescent's independent decision making and personal discretion (Helwig & Turiel, 2011). Personal issues include control over one's body, privacy, and choice of friends and activities. Thus, some actions belong to a *personal* domain, not governed by moral strictures or social norms.

MORAL BEHAVIOR

What are the basic processes responsible for moral behavior? What is the nature of self-control and resistance to temptation? How do social cognitive theorists view moral development?

Basic Processes   The processes of reinforcement, punishment, and imitation have been invoked to explain how individuals learn certain responses and why their responses differ from one another (Grusec, 2006). When individuals are reinforced for behavior that is consistent with laws and social conventions, they are likely to repeat that behavior. When provided with models who behave morally, individuals are likely to adopt their actions. Finally, when individuals are punished for immoral behaviors, those behaviors can be eliminated, but at the expense of sanctioning punishment by its very use and of causing emotional side effects for the individual.

← ------- developmental **connection**

Gender. Janet Shibley Hyde concluded that many views and studies of gender exaggerate differences. Chapter 12, p. 380

How does social conventional reasoning differ from moral reasoning? What are some examples of social conventional reasoning?

justice perspective A moral perspective that focuses on the rights of the individual; individuals independently make moral decisions.

care perspective The moral perspective of Carol Gilligan; views people in terms of their connectedness with others and emphasizes interpersonal communication, relationships with others, and concern for others.

social conventional reasoning Focuses on conventional rules established by social consensus and convention, as opposed to moral reasoning, which stresses ethical issues.

These general conclusions come with some important qualifiers. The effectiveness of reward and punishment depends on the consistency and timing with which they are administered. The effectiveness of modeling depends on the characteristics of the model and the cognitive skills of the observer.

Behavior is situationally dependent. Thus, individuals do not consistently display moral behavior in different situations. How consistent is moral behavior? In a classic investigation of moral behavior, one of the most extensive ever conducted, Hugh Hartshorne and Mark May (1928–1930) observed the moral responses of 11,000 children who were given the opportunity to lie, cheat, and steal in a variety of circumstances—at home, at school, at social events, and in athletics. A completely honest or a completely dishonest child was difficult to find. Situation-specific behavior was the rule. Children were more likely to cheat when their friends put pressure on them to do so and when the chance of being caught was slim. However, other analyses suggest that although moral behavior is influenced by situational determinants, some children are more likely than others to cheat, lie, and steal (Burton, 1984).

In further support of the situational determinants of morality, in a recent study, very few 7-year olds were willing to donate any money after watching a UNICEF film on children suffering from poverty (van IJzendoorn & others, 2010). However, after gentle probing by an adult, most children were willing to donate some of their money.

Resistance to Temptation and Self-Control   When pressures mount for individuals to cheat, lie, or steal, it is important to ask whether they have developed the ability to resist temptation and to exercise self-control (Grusec, 2006). Walter Mischel (1974) argues that self-control is strongly influenced by cognitive factors. Researchers have shown that children can instruct themselves to be more patient and, in the process, show more self-control.

Social Cognitive Theory   The role of cognitive factors in resistance to temptation and self-control illustrates ways in which cognitions mediate the link between environmental experiences and moral behavior (Grusec, 2006). The relationships between these three elements—environment, cognition, and behavior—are highlighted by social cognitive theorists. The **social cognitive theory of morality** emphasizes a distinction between an individual's moral competence (the ability to perform moral behaviors) and moral performance (performing those behaviors in specific situations) (Mischel & Mischel, 1975). *Moral competencies* include what individuals are capable of doing, what they know, their skills, their awareness of moral rules and regulations, and their cognitive ability to construct behaviors. Moral competence is the outgrowth of cognitive-sensory processes. *Moral performance*, or behavior, however, is determined by motivation and the rewards and incentives to act in a specific moral way.

Albert Bandura (2002) also stresses that moral development is best understood by considering a combination of social and cognitive factors, especially those involving self-control. He proposed that in developing a moral self, individuals adopt standards of right and wrong that serve as guides and deterrents for conduct. In this self-regulatory process, people monitor their conduct and the conditions under which it occurs, judge it in relation to moral standards, and regulate their actions by the consequences they apply to themselves. They do things that provide them satisfaction and a sense of self-worth. They refrain from behaving in ways that violate their moral standards because such conduct will bring self-condemnation. Self-sanctions keep conduct in line with internal standards. Thus, in Bandura's view, self-regulation rather than abstract reasoning is the key to positive moral development.

MORAL FEELING

Think about a time when you did something you sensed was wrong. Did it affect you emotionally? Maybe you had a twinge of guilt. And when you gave someone

◀ - - - - - - - - - - - -

developmental **connection**

Social Cognitive Theory. What are the main themes of Bandura's social cognitive theory? Chapter 1, p. 24

social cognitive theory of morality The theory that distinguishes between moral competence—the ability to produce moral behaviors—and moral performance—performing those behaviors in specific situations.

a gift, you might have felt joy. What role do emotions play in moral development, and how do these emotions develop?

Psychoanalytic Theory

According to Sigmund Freud, guilt and the desire to avoid feeling guilty are the foundation of moral behavior. In Freud's theory, the *superego* is the moral branch of personality. The superego consists of two main components: the ego ideal and the conscience. The **ego ideal** rewards the child by conveying a sense of pride and personal value when the child acts according to ideal standards approved by the parents. The **conscience** punishes the child for behaviors disapproved by the parents, making the child feel guilty and worthless.

How does the superego and hence guilt develop? According to Freud, children fear losing their parents' love and being punished for their unacceptable sexual wishes toward the opposite-sex parent. To reduce anxiety, avoid punishment, and maintain parental affection, children identify with the same-sex parent. Through this identification, children *internalize* the parent's standards of right and wrong, which reflect societal prohibitions, and hence develop their superego. Also, the child turns inward the hostility that was previously aimed externally at the same-sex parent. This inwardly directed hostility is then experienced self-punitively (and unconsciously) as guilt. In the psychoanalytic account of moral development, children conform to societal standards to avoid guilt. In this way, self-control replaces parental control.

Freud's claims regarding the formation of the ego ideal and conscience cannot be verified. However, researchers can examine the extent to which children feel guilty when they misbehave. Grazyna Kochanska and her colleagues (Kochanska & Aksan, 2007; Kochanska & others, 2002, 2005, 2008; Kochanska, Koenig, & others, 2010) have conducted a number of studies that explore children's conscience development. In a recent research review of children's conscience, she concluded that young children are aware of right and wrong, have the capacity to show

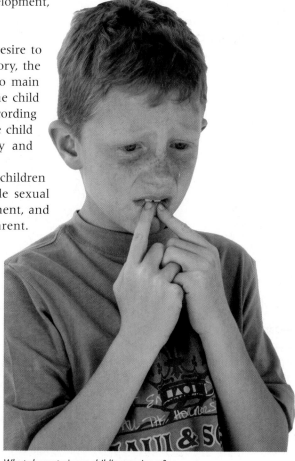

What characterizes a child's conscience?

empathy toward others, experience guilt, indicate discomfort following a transgression, and are sensitive to violating rules (Kochanska & Aksan, 2007). In one study, Kochanska and her colleagues (2002) observed 106 preschool children in laboratory situations in which they were led to believe that they had damaged valuable objects. In these mishaps, the behavioral indicators of guilt that were coded by observers included avoiding gaze (looking away or down), body tension (squirming, backing away, hanging head down, covering face with hands), and distress (looking uncomfortable, crying). Girls expressed more guilt than boys did. Children with a more fearful temperament expressed more guilt. Children of mothers who used power-oriented discipline (such as spanking, slapping, and yelling) displayed less guilt. In another study, young children with a history of stronger internalization of both parents' rules were more competent and better socialized (Kochanska, Woodard, & others, 2010).

Empathy

Positive feelings, such as empathy, contribute to the child's moral development (Grusec, Hastings, & Almas, 2011; Prinz, 2009; Roth-Hanania, Davidov, & Zahn-Waxler, 2011). Feeling **empathy** means reacting to another's feelings with an emotional response that is similar to the other's feelings (Damon, 1988). To empathize is not just to sympathize; it is to put oneself in another's place emotionally.

Although empathy is an emotional state, it has a cognitive component—the ability to discern another's inner psychological states, or what we have previously discussed as *perspective taking* (Eisenberg & others, 2002; Maxwell & DesRoches, 2010). Infants have the capacity for some purely empathic responses, but for effective moral action, children must learn to identify a wide range of emotional states in others and to anticipate what kinds of action will improve another person's emotional state.

ego ideal The component of the superego that rewards the child by conveying a sense of pride and personal value when the child acts according to ideal standards approved by the parents.

conscience The component of the superego that punishes the child for behaviors disapproved of by parents by making the child feel guilty and worthless.

empathy Reacting to another's feelings with an emotional response that is similar to the other's feelings.

FIGURE **13.2**

DAMON'S DESCRIPTION OF DEVELOPMENTAL CHANGES IN EMPATHY

Age Period	Nature of Empathy
Early infancy	Characterized by global empathy, the young infant's empathic response does not distinguish between feelings and needs of self and others.
1 to 2 years of age	Undifferentiated feelings of discomfort at another's distress grow into more genuine feelings of concern, but infants cannot translate realization of others' unhappy feelings into effective action.
Early childhood	Children become aware that every person's perspective is unique and that someone else may have a different reaction to a situation. This awareness allows the child to respond more appropriately to another person's distress.
10 to 12 years of age	Children develop an emergent orientation of empathy for people who live in unfortunate circumstances—the poor, the handicapped, and the socially outcast. In adolescence, this newfound sensitivity may give a humanitarian flavor to the individual's ideological and political views.

developmental **connection**

Social Cognitive Development. In Robert Selman's view, perspective taking is a key aspect of whether children develop prosocial or antisocial attitudes and behavior. Chapter 11, p. 342

What are the milestones in children's development of empathy? According to an analysis by child developmentalist William Damon (1988), changes in empathy take place in early infancy, at 1 to 2 years of age, in early childhood, and at 10 to 12 years of age.

Global empathy is the young infant's empathic response in which clear boundaries between the feelings and needs of the self and those of another have not yet been established. For example, one 11-month-old infant fought off her own tears, sucked her thumb, and buried her head in her mother's lap after she had seen another child fall and hurt himself. Not all infants cry every time someone else is hurt, though. Many times, an infant will stare at another's pain with curiosity. Although global empathy is observed in some infants, it does not consistently characterize all infants' behavior.

When they are 1 to 2 years of age, infants may feel genuine concern for the distress of other people but only when they reach early childhood can they respond appropriately to another person's distress. This ability depends on children's new awareness that people have different reactions to situations. By late childhood, they may begin to feel empathy for the unfortunate. To read further about Damon's description of the developmental changes in empathy from infancy through adolescence, see Figure 13.2.

The Contemporary Perspective on the Role of Emotion in Moral Development We have seen that classical psychoanalytic theory emphasizes the power of unconscious guilt in moral development but that other theorists, such as Damon, emphasize the role of empathy. Today, many child developmentalists believe that both positive feelings—such as empathy, sympathy, admiration, and self-esteem—and negative feelings—such as anger, outrage, shame, and guilt—contribute to children's moral development (Malti & Latzko, 2010). When strongly experienced, these emotions influence children to act in accord with standards of right and wrong.

Such emotions as empathy, shame, guilt, and anxiety over other people's violations of standards are present early in development and undergo developmental change throughout childhood and beyond (Damon, 1988). These emotions provide a natural base for children's acquisition of moral values, motivating them to pay close attention to moral events (Thompson, 2009). However, moral emotions do not operate in a vacuum to build a child's moral awareness, and they are not sufficient in themselves to generate moral responses. They do not give the "substance" of moral regulation—the rules, values, and standards of behavior that children need to understand and act on. Moral emotions are inextricably interwoven with the cognitive and social aspects of children's development (Malti & Latzko, 2010; Narváez, 2010b).

MORAL PERSONALITY

So far we have examined three key dimensions of moral development: thoughts, behavior, and feelings. Recently, there has been a surge of interest in a fourth dimension: personality (Frimer & others, 2011; Narváez & Lapsley, 2009; Walker, Frimer, & Dunlop, 2011). Thoughts, behavior, and feelings can all be involved in an individual's moral personality. For many years, skepticism characterized the likelihood that a set of moral characteristics or traits could be discovered that would constitute a core of moral personality. Much of this skepticism stemmed from the results of Hartshorne and May's (1928–1930) classic study, and Walter Mischel's (1968) social learning theory and research, which argued that situations trump traits when attempts are made to predict moral behavior. Mischel's (2004) subsequent research and theory and Bandura's (2010) social cognitive theory have emphasized the importance of "person" factors while still recognizing situational variation. Until recently, though, there has been little interest in studying what might constitute a moral personality. Three aspects of moral personality that have recently been emphasized are (1) moral identity, (2) moral character, and (3) moral exemplars.

Moral Identity A central aspect of the recent interest in the role of personality in moral development focuses on **moral identity.** Individuals have a moral identity when moral notions and commitments are central to their life (Aquino, McFerran, & Laven, 2011). In this view, behaving in a manner that violates this moral commitment places the integrity of the self at risk (Narváez & Lapsley, 2009).

Recently, Darcia Narváez (2010b) concluded that a mature moral individual cares about morality and being a moral person. For these individuals, moral responsibility is central to their identity. Mature moral individuals engage in moral metacognition, including moral self-monitoring and moral self-reflection. Moral self-monitoring involves monitoring one's thoughts and actions related to moral situations, and engaging in self-control when it is needed. Moral self-reflection encompasses critical evaluations of one's self-judgments and efforts to minimize bias and self-deception.

Moral Character James Rest (1995) argued that moral character has not been adequately emphasized in moral development. In Rest's view, *moral character* involves having the strength of your convictions, persisting, and overcoming distractions and obstacles. If individuals don't have moral character, they may wilt under pressure or fatigue, fail to follow through, or become distracted and discouraged, and fail to behave morally. Moral character presupposes that the person has set moral goals and that achieving those goals involves the commitment to act in accord with those goals. Rest (1995) also concluded that motivation has not been adequately emphasized in moral development. In Rest's view, *moral motivation* involves prioritizing moral values over other personal values.

Lawrence Walker (2002) has studied moral character by examining people's conceptions of moral excellence. Among the moral virtues people emphasize are "honesty, truthfulness, and trustworthiness, as well as those of care, compassion, thoughtfulness, and considerateness. Other salient traits revolve around virtues of dependability, loyalty, and conscientiousness" (Walker, 2002, p. 74). In Walker's perspective, these aspects of moral character provide a foundation for positive social relationships and functioning.

Moral Exemplars **Moral exemplars** are people who have lived exemplary lives. Moral exemplars have a moral personality, identity, character, and set of virtues that reflect moral excellence and commitment (Walker & Frimer, 2009, 2011; Walker, Frimer, & Dunlop, 2011).

One study examined the personality of exemplary young adults to determine what characterized their moral excellence (Matsuba & Walker, 2004). Forty young adults were nominated by executive directors of a variety of social organizations (such as Big Brothers, AIDS Society, and Ronald McDonald House) as moral exemplars based on

◄ ━ ━ ━ ━ ━ ━ ━ ━ ━ ┐

developmental **connection**

Identity. According to James Marcia, what are the four statuses of identity development? Chapter 11, p. 354

moral identity The aspect of personality that is present when individuals have moral notions and commitments that are central to their lives.

moral exemplars People who have a moral personality, identity, character, and set of virtues that reflect moral excellence and commitment.

Rosa Parks (*left photo,* sitting in the front of a bus after the U.S. Supreme Court ruled that segregation was illegal on her city's bus system) and Andrei Sakharov (*right photo*) are moral exemplars. Parks (1913–2005), an African American seamstress in Montgomery, Alabama, became famous for her quiet, revolutionary act of not giving up her bus seat to a non-Latino White man in 1955. Her heroic act is cited by many historians as the beginning of the modern civil rights movement in the United States. Across the next four decades, Parks continued to work for progress in civil rights. Sakharov (1921–1989) was a Soviet physicist who spent several decades designing nuclear weapons for the Soviet Union and came to be known as the father of the Soviet hydrogen bomb. However, later in his life he became one of the Soviet Union's most outspoken critics and worked relentlessly to promote human rights and democracy.

their extraordinary moral commitment to these social organizations. They were compared with 40 young adults matched in age, education, and other variables who were attending a university. The moral exemplars were more advanced in moral reasoning, further along in developing an identity, and more likely to be in close relationships.

Review Connect Reflect

LG1 Discuss theory and research on moral thought, behavior, feeling, and personality

Review

- What is moral development?
- What are Piaget's and Kohlberg's theories of moral development? What are some criticisms of Kohlberg's theory? What is social conventional reasoning?
- What processes are involved in moral behavior? What is the social cognitive theory of moral development?
- How are moral feelings related to moral development?
- What characterizes moral personality?

Connect

- In Chapter 7 you learned about the concept of joint attention. How is that similar to or different from the concept of perspective taking you learned about here?

Reflect *Your Own Personal Journey of Life*

- Which of the four approaches—cognitive, psychoanalytic, behavioral/social cognitive, and personality—we have discussed do you think best describes the way you have developed morally? Explain.

Contexts of Moral Development

LG2 Explain how parents and schools influence moral development

Parenting   Schools

So far, we have examined the four principal domains of moral development—thoughts, behaviors, feelings, and personality. We saw that both Piaget and Kohlberg noted that peer relations exert an important influence on moral development. What other contexts play a role in moral development? In particular, what are the roles of parents and schools?

PARENTING

Both Piaget and Kohlberg held that parents do not provide unique or essential inputs to children's moral development. Parents, in their view, are responsible for providing role-taking opportunities and cognitive conflict, but peers play the primary role in moral development. Research reveals that both parents and peers contribute to children's moral maturation (Walker, Hennig, & Krettenauer, 2000).

In Ross Thompson's (2006, 2009) view, young children are moral apprentices, striving to understand what is moral. They can be assisted in this quest by the "sensitive guidance of adult mentors in the home who provide lessons about morality in everyday experiences" (Thompson, 2009). Among the most important aspects of the relationship between parents and children that contribute to children's moral development are relational quality, proactive strategies, and conversational dialogue.

Relational Quality Parent-child relationships introduce children to the mutual obligations of close relationships that involve warmth and responsibility (Laible & Thompson, 2007; Thompson, 2009). Parents' obligations include engaging in positive caregiving and guiding children to become competent human beings. Children's obligations include responding appropriately to parents' initiatives and maintaining a positive relationship with parents.

In terms of relationship quality, secure attachment may play an important role in children's moral development. A secure attachment can place the child on a positive path for internalizing parents' socializing goals and family values. In one study, secure attachment in infancy was linked to early conscience development (Laible & Thompson, 2000). And in a recent study, early secure attachment defused a maladaptive trajectory toward antisocial outcomes (Kochanska, Barry, & others, 2010). In another recent study, securely attached children's willing, cooperative stance was linked to positive future socialization outcomes, such as internalizing mothers' prohibitions and a lower incidence of externalizing problems (high level of aggression, for example) (Kochanska, Woodard, & others, 2010).

developmental **connection**

Attachment. Securely attached infants use the caregiver as a secure base from which to explore the environment. Chapter 10, p. 321

Proactive Strategies An important parenting strategy is to proactively avert potential misbehavior by children before it takes place (Thompson, McGinley, & Meyer, 2006). With younger children, being proactive means using diversion, such as distracting their attention or moving them to alternative activities. With older children, being proactive may involve talking with them about values that the parents deem important. Transmitting these values can help older children and adolescents to resist temptations that inevitably emerge in contexts such as peer relations and the media that can be outside the scope of direct parental monitoring.

Conversational Dialogue Conversations related to moral development can benefit children whether they occur as part of a discipline encounter or outside the encounter in the everyday stream of parent-child interaction (Thompson, 2009). The conversations can be planned or spontaneous and can focus on topics such as past events (for example, a child's prior misbehavior or positive moral conduct), shared future events (for example, going somewhere that may involve a temptation and requires positive moral behavior), and immediate events (for example, talking with the child about a sibling's tantrums). Even when they are not intended to teach a moral lesson or explicitly encourage better moral judgment, such conversations can contribute to children's moral development.

Parenting Recommendations One research review concluded that, in general, children who behave morally tend to have parents who (Eisenberg & Valiente, 2002, p. 134):

- Are warm and supportive rather than punitive.
- Provide opportunities for the children to learn about others' perspectives and feelings.
- Involve children in family decision making and in the process of thinking about moral decisions.

What are some aspects of relationships between parents and children that contribute to children's moral development?

- Model moral behaviors and thinking themselves, and provide opportunities for their children to do so.
- Provide information about what behaviors are expected and why.
- Foster an internal rather than an external sense of morality.

Parents who show this configuration of behaviors likely foster in their children concern and caring about others, and create a positive parent-child relationship. A recent study found that adolescents' moral motivation was positively linked to the quality of their relationship with their parents (Malti & Buchmann, 2010). Another recent study revealed that dimensions of authoritative parenting (such as a combination of responsiveness, autonomy-granting, and demandingness) predicted an increase in adolescents' moral identity (Hardy & others, 2010).

In addition, parenting recommendations based on Ross Thompson's (2009; Laible & Thompson, 2007; Thompson, McGinley, & Meyer, 2006) analysis of parent-child relations suggest that children's moral development is likely to benefit when there are mutual parent-child obligations involving warmth and responsibility, when parents use proactive strategies, and when parents engage children in conversational dialogue.

SCHOOLS

No matter how parents treat their children at home, they may feel that they have little control over a great deal of their children's moral education. Children spend extensive time away from their parents at school, and the time spent can influence children's moral development (Narváez & Lapsley, 2009).

The Hidden Curriculum   More than 80 years ago, educator John Dewey (1933) recognized that even when schools do not have specific programs in moral education, they provide moral education through a "hidden curriculum." The **hidden curriculum** is conveyed by the moral atmosphere that is a part of every school. The moral atmosphere is created by school and classroom rules, the moral orientation of teachers and school administrators, and text materials. Teachers serve as models of ethical or unethical behavior (Sanger, 2008). Classroom rules and peer relations at school transmit attitudes about cheating, lying, stealing, and consideration of others. And through its rules and regulations, the school administration infuses the school with a value system.

Recently, increased attention has been directed to the role of classroom and school climate as part of the hidden curriculum. Darcia Narváez (2010a) argues that attention should be given to the concept of "sustaining climates." In her view, a sustaining classroom climate is more than a positive learning environment and more than a caring context. Sustaining climates involve focusing on students' sense of purpose, social engagement, community connections, and ethics. In sustaining classroom and school climates, students learn skills for flourishing and reaching their potential and help others to do so as well.

Character Education   Currently 40 of 50 states have mandates regarding **character education,** a direct education approach that involves teaching students a basic moral literacy to prevent them from engaging in immoral behavior and doing harm to themselves or others (Carr, 2008). The argument is that behaviors such as lying, stealing, and cheating are wrong, and students should be taught this throughout their education (Davidson, Lickona, & Khmelkov, 2008).

Every school should have an explicit moral code that is clearly communicated to students. Any violations of the code should be met with sanctions. Instruction in specified moral concepts, such as cheating, can take the form of example and definition, class discussions and role playing, or rewards for students exhibiting proper behavior. More recently, an emphasis on the importance of encouraging students to develop a care perspective that involves considering others' feelings and helping

hidden curriculum The pervasive moral atmosphere that characterizes every school.

character education A direct moral education program in which students are taught moral literacy to prevent them from engaging in immoral behavior.

others has been accepted as a relevant aspect of character education (Noddings, 2008; Roberts, 2010).

Lawrence Walker (2002) argues that it is important for character education to involve more than a listing of moral virtues on a classroom wall. Instead, he emphasizes that children and adolescents need to participate in critical discussions of values; they need to discuss and reflect on how to incorporate virtues into their daily lives. Walker also advocates exposing children to moral exemplars worthy of emulating and getting them to participate in community service. The character education approach reflects the moral personality domain of moral development discussed earlier in the chapter.

Values Clarification A second approach to providing moral education is **values clarification**—that is, helping people to clarify what their lives mean and what is worth working for. Unlike character education, which tells students what their values should be, values clarification encourages students to define their own values and understand the values of others (Williams & others, 2003).

Advocates of values clarification say it is value-free. However, critics argue that its content offends community standards and that the values-clarification exercises fail to stress the right behavior.

Cognitive Moral Education A third approach to moral education, **cognitive moral education,** is based on the belief that students should learn to value such things as democracy and justice as their moral reasoning develops. Kohlberg's theory has served as the foundation for a number of cognitive moral education programs. In a typical program, high school students meet in a semester-long course to discuss a number of moral issues. The instructor acts as a facilitator rather than as a director of the class. The goal is that students will develop more advanced notions of concepts such as cooperation, trust, responsibility, and community (Power & Higgins-D'Alessandro, 2008).

Service Learning **Service learning** is a form of education that promotes social responsibility and service to the community. In service learning, adolescents engage in activities such as tutoring, helping older adults, working in a hospital, assisting at a child-care center, or cleaning up a vacant lot to make a play area. An important goal of service learning is that adolescents become less self-centered and more strongly motivated to help others (Hart, Matsuba, & Atkins, 2008). Service learning is often more effective when two conditions are met (Nucci, 2006): (1) students are given some degree of choice in the service activities in which they participate, and (2) students are provided opportunities to reflect about their participation.

Jewel Cash, seated next to her mother, participating in a crime-watch meeting at a community center. She is an exemplar of teenage community involvement. The mayor of Boston says she is "everywhere." Jewel recently swayed a neighborhood group to support her proposal for a winter jobs program. A junior at Boston Latin Academy, she was raised in one of Boston's housing projects by her mother, a single parent. Today she is a member of the Boston Student Advisory Council, mentors children, volunteers at a women's shelter, and is a member of a neighborhood crime-watch organization. (*Source:* Silva, 2005)

Service learning takes education out into the community (Davidson & others, 2010; Zaff & others, 2010). Adolescent volunteers tend to be extraverted, committed to others, and have a high level of self-understanding (Eisenberg & Morris, 2004). Also, one study revealed that adolescent girls participated in service learning more than adolescent boys (Webster & Worrell, 2008).

Researchers have found that service learning benefits adolescents in a number of ways (Zaff & others, 2010). These improvements in adolescent development related to service learning include higher grades in school, increased goal setting, higher self-esteem, an improved sense of empowerment to make a difference for others, and an increased likelihood that they will serve as volunteers in the future. In one study, 74 percent of African American and 70 percent of Latino adolescents said that service-learning programs could have a "fairly or very big effect" on keeping students from dropping out of school (Bridgeland, Dilulio, & Wulsin, 2008).

An analysis revealed that 26 percent of U.S. public high schools require students to participate in service learning (Metz & Youniss, 2005). The benefits of service

values clarification A moral education program in which students are helped to clarify what their lives are for and what is worth working for. Students are encouraged to define their own values and understand others' values.

cognitive moral education A moral education program based on the belief that students should learn to value things like democracy and justice as their moral reasoning develops; Kohlberg's theory has been the basis for many of the cognitive moral education programs.

service learning A form of education that promotes social responsibility and service to the community.

learning, for both the volunteer and the recipient, suggest that more adolescents should be required to participate in such programs (Enfield & Collins, 2008; Zaff & others, 2010).

Cheating   A moral education concern is whether students cheat and how to handle the cheating if it is discovered (Anderman & Anderman, 2010). Academic cheating can take many forms, including plagiarism, using "cheat sheets" during an exam, copying from a neighbor during a test, purchasing papers, and falsifying lab results. A 2006 survey revealed that 60 percent of secondary school students said they had cheated on a test in school during the past year, and one-third of the students reported that they had plagiarized information from the Internet in the past year (Josephson Institute of Ethics, 2006).

Why do students cheat? Among the reasons students give for cheating are pressure to get high grades, time constraints, poor teaching, and lack of interest (Stephens, 2008). In terms of poor teaching, "students are more likely to cheat when they perceive their teacher to be incompetent, unfair, and uncaring" (Stephens, 2008, p. 140).

Why do students cheat? What are some strategies teachers can adopt to prevent cheating?

A long history of research also implicates the power of the situation in determining whether students cheat (Hartshorne & May, 1928–1930; Vandehey, Diekhoff, & LaBeff, 2007). For example, students are more likely to cheat when they are not being closely monitored during a test; when they know their peers are cheating; when they know that another student has cheated without being caught; and when student scores are made public (Anderman & Murdock, 2007; Carrell, Malmstrom, & West, 2008; Harmon, Lambrinos, & Kennedy, 2008).

Certain personality traits also are linked to cheating. For example, a recent study revealed that college students who engaged in academic cheating were characterized by the personality traits of low conscientiousness and low agreeableness (Williams, Nathanson, & Paulhus, 2010).

Among the strategies for decreasing academic cheating are preventive measures such as making sure students are aware of what constitutes cheating, explaining the consequences if they do cheat, closely monitoring students' behavior while they are taking tests, and emphasizing the importance of being a moral, responsible individual who practices academic integrity. In promoting academic integrity, many colleges have instituted an honor code that emphasizes self-responsibility, fairness, trust, and scholarship. However, few secondary schools have developed honor codes. The Center for Academic Integrity (www.academicintegrity.org/) has extensive materials available to help schools develop academic integrity policies.

An Integrative Approach   Darcia Narváez (2006, 2008, 2010a, b) emphasizes an *integrative approach* to moral education that encompasses both the reflective moral thinking and commitment to justice advocated in Kohlberg's approach, and developing a particular moral character as advocated in the character education approach. She highlights the Child Development Project as an excellent example of an integrative moral education approach. In the Child Development Project, students are given multiple opportunities to discuss other students' experiences, which inspires empathy and perspective taking, and they participate in exercises that encourage them to reflect on their own behaviors in terms of values such as fairness and social responsibility (Battistich, 2008; Solomon, Watson, & Battistich, 2002). Adults coach students in ethical decision making and guide them in becoming more caring individuals. Students experience a caring community, not only in the classroom but also in after-school activities and through parental involvement in the program. Research evaluations of the Child Development Project indicate that it is related to an improved sense of community, an increase in prosocial behavior, better interpersonal understanding, and an increase in social problem solving (Battistich, 2008; Solomon & others, 1990).

Another integrative moral education program that is being implemented is called *integrative ethical education* (Narváez, 2006, 2008, 2010a, b; Narváez & others, 2004). This program builds on the concept of expertise discussed in Chapter 7. The goal is to turn moral novices into moral experts by educating students about four ethical skills that moral experts possess: ethical sensitivity, ethical judgment, ethical focus, and ethical action (Narváez, 2010a).

Review Connect Reflect

 LG2 Explain how parents and schools influence moral development

Review

- What are some effective parenting strategies for advancing children's moral development?
- What is the hidden curriculum? What are some contemporary approaches to moral education?

Connect

- What parenting strategies might best prevent students from cheating?

Reflect *Your Own Personal Journey of Life*

- How do you think your parents influenced your moral development?

Prosocial and Antisocial Behavior

 LG3 Describe the development of prosocial and antisocial behavior

| Prosocial Behavior | Antisocial Behavior |

Service learning encourages positive moral behavior. This behavior is not just moral behavior but behavior that is intended to benefit other people, and psychologists call it *prosocial behavior* (Eisenberg & others, 2009). Of course, people have always engaged in antisocial behavior as well. In this section, we take a closer look at prosocial and antisocial behavior, focusing on how they develop.

PROSOCIAL BEHAVIOR

Caring about the welfare and rights of others, feeling concern and empathy for them, and acting in a way that benefits others are all components of prosocial behavior (Grusec & Sherman, 2011). What motivates this behavior, and how does it develop in children?

> It is one of the beautiful compensations of this life that no one can sincerely try to help another without helping himself.
>
> —**CHARLES DUDLEY WARNER**
> *American Essayist, 19th Century*

Altruism and Reciprocity   The purest forms of prosocial behavior are motivated by **altruism,** an unselfish interest in helping another person. Human acts of altruism are plentiful. Think of the hardworking laborer who places $5 in a Salvation Army kettle, the volunteers at homeless shelters, the person who donates a kidney so someone else can live. Altruism is found throughout the human world. It is also taught by every widely practiced religion in the world—Christianity, Judaism, Islam, Hinduism, Buddhism. The circumstances most likely to evoke altruism are empathy for an individual in need or a close relationship between the benefactor and the recipient (Batson, 1989).

altruism An unselfish interest in helping another person.

How does children's sharing change from the preschool to the elementary school years?

The notion of *reciprocity*, which is the obligation to return a favor with a favor, pervades human interactions all over the world. Fund-raisers try to exploit the norm of reciprocity when they send free calendars or other knick-knacks in the mail, hoping that you'll feel obligated to reciprocate with a donation to their cause. People feel guilty when they do not reciprocate, and they may feel angry if someone else does not reciprocate. Reciprocity or altruism may motivate many important prosocial behaviors, including sharing.

Sharing and Fairness   William Damon (1988) described a developmental sequence by which sharing develops in children. Most sharing during the first three years of life is done for nonempathetic reasons, such as for the fun of the social play ritual or out of imitation. Then, at about 4 years of age, a combination of empathetic awareness and adult encouragement produces a sense of obligation on the part of the child to share with others. Most 4-year-olds are not selfless saints, however. Children believe they have an obligation to share but do not necessarily think they should be as generous to others as they are to themselves. Neither do their actions always support their beliefs, especially when they covet an object. What is important developmentally is that the child has developed a belief that sharing is an obligatory part of a social relationship and involves a question of right and wrong. These early ideas about sharing set the stage for giant strides that children make in the years that follow.

By the start of the elementary school years, children begin to express more complicated notions of what is fair. Throughout history, varied definitions of fairness have been used as the basis for distributing goods and resolving conflicts. These definitions involve the principles of equality, merit, and benevolence—*equality* means that everyone is treated the same; *merit* means giving extra rewards for hard work, a talented performance, or other laudatory behavior; *benevolence* means giving special consideration to individuals in a disadvantaged condition.

Equality is the first of these principles used regularly by elementary school children. It is common to hear 6-year-old children use the word *fair* as synonymous with *equal* or *same*. By the mid to late elementary school years, children also believe that equity means special treatment for those who deserve it—a belief that applies the principles of merit and benevolence.

Parental advice and prodding certainly foster standards of sharing, but the give-and-take of peer requests and arguments provides the most immediate stimulation of sharing. Parents can set examples that children carry into their interactions and communication with peers, but parents are not present during all of their children's peer exchanges. The day-to-day construction of fairness standards is done by children in collaboration and negotiation with each other. Over the course of many years and thousands of encounters, children's understanding of concepts such as equality, merit, benevolence, and compromise deepens. With this understanding comes a greater consistency and generosity in children's sharing (Damon, 1988).

How does prosocial behavior change through childhood and adolescence? Prosocial behavior occurs more often in adolescence than in childhood, although examples of caring for others and comforting someone in distress occur even during the preschool years (Grusec, Hastings, & Almas, 2011).

Are there different types of prosocial behavior? In a recent study, Gustavo Carlo and his colleagues (2010, pp. 340–341) investigated this question and confirmed the presence of six types of prosocial behavior in young adolescents:

- altruism ("One of the best things about doing charity work is that it looks good.")
- public ("Helping others while I'm being watched is when I work best.")
- emotional ("I usually help others when they are very upset.")
- dire ("I tend to help people who are hurt badly.")
- anonymous ("I prefer to donate money without anyone knowing.")
- compliant ("I never wait to help others when they ask for it.")

In this study, adolescent girls reported more emotional, dire, compliant, and altruistic behavior than did boys while boys engaged in more public prosocial behavior. Parental monitoring was positively related to emotional, dire, and compliant behavior but not the other types of behavior. Compliant, anonymous, and altruistic prosocial behavior were positively related to religiosity.

Research on prosocial behavior is often conceptualized in a global and unidimensional manner. The study by Carlo and others (2010) illustrates the important point that in thinking about and studying prosocial behavior it is important to consider its dimensions.

Two other aspects of prosocial behavior are forgiveness and gratitude. **Forgiveness** is an aspect of prosocial behavior that occurs when the injured person releases the injurer from possible behavioral retaliation (Klatt & Enright, 2009). In one investigation, individuals from the fourth grade through college and adulthood were asked questions about forgiveness (Enright, Santos, & Al-Mabuk, 1989). The individuals were especially swayed by peer pressure in their willingness to forgive others. A recent study of older adults revealed that women were more likely to forgive than men, individuals were more likely to forgive family members than non-family members, and forgiveness was more likely to be extended to people who were still alive than those who were dead (Hantman & Cohen, 2010).

Gratitude is a feeling of thankfulness and appreciation, especially in response to someone doing something kind or helpful (Grant & Gino, 2010). A recent study of young adolescents revealed that gratitude was linked to a number of positive aspects of development, including satisfaction with one's family, optimism, and prosocial behavior (Froh, Yurkewicz, & Kashdan, 2009).

Gender and Prosocial Behavior Are there gender differences in prosocial behavior during childhood and adolescence? Research concludes that there are (Eisenberg & others, 2009; Grusec, Hastings, & Almas, 2011). For example, across childhood and adolescence, females engage in more prosocial behavior than males. The largest gender difference occurs for kind and considerate behavior with a smaller difference for sharing.

Altruism and Volunteerism in Older Adults A study of 21,000 individuals 50 to 79 years of age in 21 countries revealed that one-third give back to society, saying that they volunteer now or have volunteered in the past (HSBC Insurance, 2007). In this study, about 50 percent who volunteer reported that they do so for at least one-half day each week. And a recent large-scale U.S. study revealed that volunteering steadily increased from 57 years of age to 85 years of age (Cornwell, Laumann, & Schumm, 2008).

A common perception is that older adults need to be given help rather than give help themselves. However, researchers recently have found that when older adults engage in altruistic behavior and volunteering they benefit from these activities (Morrow-Howell, 2010; Tang & others, 2010). One study followed 423 older adult couples for five years (Brown & others, 2003). At the beginning of the study, the couples were asked about the extent to which they had given or received emotional or practical help in the past year. Five years later, those who said they had helped others were half as likely to have died. One possible reason for this finding is that helping others may reduce the output of stress hormones, which improves cardiovascular health and strengthens the immune system. A recent study of adults 65 years of age and older who were institutionalized and had functional limitations revealed that an increased risk of dying over a six-year period occurred only for those who never or almost never volunteered (Okun & others, 2010).

Researchers also have found that volunteering as an older adult is associated with a number of positive outcomes (Morrow-Howell, 2010). An early study of

Ninety-eight-year-old volunteer Iva Broadus plays cards with 10-year-old DeAngela Williams in Dallas, Texas. Iva recently was recognized as the oldest volunteer in the Big Sister program in the United States. Iva says that the card-playing helps to keep her memory and thinking skills good and can help DeAngela's as well. *What are some other positive outcomes of volunteering as an older adult?*

forgiveness An aspect of prosocial behavior that occurs when the injured person releases the injurer from possible behavioral retaliation.

gratitude A feeling of thankfulness and appreciation, especially in response to someone's doing something kind or helpful.

individuals 65 years and older found that volunteer workers were more satisfied with their lives than nonvolunteers and were less depressed and anxious (Hunter & Linn, 1980). In another study, being a volunteer as an older adult was associated with more positive affect and less negative affect (Greenfield & Marks, 2004). Among the reasons for the positive outcomes of volunteering are its provision of constructive activities and productive roles, social integration, and enhanced meaningfulness.

ANTISOCIAL BEHAVIOR

Most children and adolescents at one time or another act out or do things that are destructive or troublesome for themselves or others. If these behaviors occur often, psychiatrists diagnose them as conduct disorders. If these behaviors result in illegal acts by juveniles, society labels them *delinquents*. Both problems are much more common in males than in females (Farrington, 2009; Thio, 2010).

Conduct Disorder   **Conduct disorder** refers to age-inappropriate actions and attitudes that violate family expectations, society's norms, and the personal or property rights of others. Children with conduct problems show a wide range of rule-violating behaviors, from swearing and temper tantrums to severe vandalism, theft, and assault.

As part of growing up, most children and youth break the rules from time to time—they fight, skip school, break curfew, steal, and so on. As many as 50 percent of the parents of 4- to 6-year-old children report that their children steal, lie, disobey, or destroy property at least some of the time (Achenbach, 1997). Most of these children show a decrease in antisocial behavior from 4 to 18 years of age, but adolescents who are referred to psychological clinics for therapy still show high rates of antisocial behavior (Achenbach, 1997).

It has been estimated that about 5 percent of children show serious conduct problems. These children are often described as showing an *externalizing*, or *undercontrolled*, pattern of behavior. Children who show this pattern often are impulsive, overactive, and aggressive and engage in delinquent actions.

Conduct problems in children are best explained by a confluence of causes, or risk factors, operating over time (Conduct Problems Prevention Research Group, 2011; Dodge & McCourt, 2010). These include possible genetic inheritance of a difficult temperament, ineffective parenting, and living in a neighborhood where violence is the norm.

Juvenile Delinquency   Closely linked with conduct disorder is **juvenile delinquency,** which refers to actions taken by an adolescent in breaking the law or engaging in behavior that is considered illegal. Like other categories of disorders, juvenile delinquency is a broad concept; legal infractions range from littering to murder. Because the adolescent technically becomes a juvenile delinquent only after being judged guilty of a crime by a court of law, official records do not accurately reflect the number of illegal acts juvenile delinquents commit.

Frequency   Estimates of the number of juvenile delinquents in the United States are sketchy, but FBI statistics indicate that at least 2 percent of all youth are involved in juvenile court cases. U.S. government statistics reveal that eight of ten cases of juvenile delinquency involve males (Snyder & Sickmund, 1999). In the last two decades, however, there has been a greater increase in female delinquency than in male delinquency (Snyder & Sickmund, 1999). For both male and female delinquents, rates for property offenses are higher than rates for other offenses (such as offenses against persons, drug offenses, and public order offenses). Arrests for delinquency are much higher for adolescent males than for adolescent females.

Developmental Changes and Pathways   As adolescents become emerging adults, do their rates of delinquency and crime change? Recent analyses indicate that theft,

What are some characteristics of conduct disorder?

conduct disorder Age-inappropriate actions and attitudes that violate family expectations, society's norms, and the personal or property rights of others.

juvenile delinquency Actions taken by an adolescent in breaking the law or engaging in illegal behavior.

property damage, and physical aggression decrease from 18 to 26 years of age (Schulenberg & Zarrett, 2006). The peak ages for property damage are 16 to 18 years for males and 15 to 17 years for females. However, the peak ages for violence are 18 to 19 years for males and 19 to 21 years for females (Farrington, 2004).

A distinction is made between early-onset (before age 11) and late-onset (after age 11) antisocial behavior. Early-onset antisocial behavior is associated with more negative developmental outcomes than late-onset antisocial behavior (Schulenberg & Zarrett, 2006). Early-onset antisocial behavior is more likely to persist into emerging adulthood and is associated with more mental health and relationship problems (Roisman, Aguilar, & Egeland, 2004; Stouthamer-Loeber & others, 2004).

In the Pittsburgh Youth Study, a longitudinal study focused on more than 1,500 inner-city boys, three developmental pathways to delinquency were as follows (Loeber, Burke, & Pardini, 2009; Loeber & Farrington, 2001; Stouthamer-Loeber & others, 2002):

- *Authority conflict.* Youth on this pathway showed stubbornness prior to age 12, then moved on to defiance and avoidance of authority.
- *Covert.* This pathway included minor covert acts, such as lying, followed by property damage and moderately serious delinquency, then serious delinquency.
- *Overt.* This pathway included minor aggression followed by fighting and violence.

One issue in juvenile justice is whether an adolescent who commits a crime should be tried as an adult (Steinberg, 2009). In one study, trying adolescent offenders as adults increased rather than reduced their crime rate (Myers, 1999). The study evaluated more than 500 violent youth in Pennsylvania, which has adopted a "get tough" policy. Although these 500 offenders had been given harsher punishments than a comparison group retained in juvenile court, they were more likely to be rearrested—and rearrested more quickly—for new offenses once they were returned to the community. These results suggest that the price of short-term public safety attained by prosecuting juveniles as adults may be to increase the number of criminal offenses over the long run.

One individual whose goal is to reduce juvenile delinquency and help at-risk adolescents cope more effectively with their lives is Rodney Hammond. To read about his work, see the *Connecting with Careers* profile.

Causes of Delinquency   What causes delinquency? Many causes have been proposed, including heredity, identity problems, community influences, and family experiences. Erik Erikson (1968), for example, notes that adolescents whose development has restricted them from acceptable social roles or made them feel that they cannot measure up to the demands placed on them may choose a negative identity. Adolescents with a negative identity may find support for their delinquent image among peers, reinforcing the negative identity. For Erikson, delinquency is an attempt to establish an identity, although a negative one.

Although delinquency is less exclusively a phenomenon of lower socioeconomic status today than it was in the past, some characteristics of lower-class culture might promote delinquency (Grunwald & others, 2010). The norms of many lower-SES peer groups and gangs are antisocial, or counterproductive, to the goals and norms of society at large. Getting into and staying out of trouble are prominent features of life for some adolescents in low-income neighborhoods. Adolescents from low-income backgrounds may sense that they can gain attention and status by performing antisocial actions. Furthermore, adolescents in communities with high crime rates observe many models who engage in criminal activities. Quality schooling, educational funding, and organized neighborhood activities may be lacking in these communities. A recent study revealed that engaged parenting and mothers' social network support were linked to a lower level of delinquency in low-income families

Rodney Hammond, Health Psychologist

Rodney Hammond described how his college experiences influenced his choice of career: "When I started as an undergraduate at the University of Illinois Champaign-Urbana, I hadn't decided on my major. But to help finance my education, I took a part-time job in a child development research program sponsored by the psychology department. There, I observed inner-city children in settings designed to enhance their learning. I saw first-hand the contribution psychology can make, and I knew I wanted to be a psychologist" (American Psychological Association, 2003, p. 26).

Rodney Hammond went on to obtain a doctorate in school and community psychology with a focus on children's development. For a number of years, he trained clinical psychologists at Wright State University in Ohio and directed a program to reduce violence in ethnic minority youth. There, he and his associates taught at-risk youth how to use social skills to effectively manage conflict and to recognize situations that could lead to violence. Today, Hammond is director of Violence Prevention at the Centers for Disease Control and Prevention in Atlanta. Hammond says that if you are interested in people and problem solving, psychology is a wonderful way to put the two together. (*Source:* American Psychological Association, 2003, pp. 26–27)

Rodney Hammond

---

developmental **connection**

Parenting. A neglectful parenting style is linked with low levels of self-control in children. Chapter 14, p. 462

What are some factors that influence whether adolescents will become delinquents?

(Ghazarian & Roche, 2010). And another recent study found that youth whose families had experienced repeated poverty were more than twice as likely to be delinquent at 14 and 21 years of age (Najman & others, 2010).

Certain characteristics of family support systems are also associated with delinquency. Parents of delinquents are less skilled in discouraging antisocial behavior and in encouraging skilled behavior than are parents of nondelinquents. Parental monitoring of adolescents is especially important in determining whether an adolescent becomes a delinquent (Laird & others, 2008). For example, a study of families living in high-risk neighborhoods revealed that parents' lack of knowledge of their young adolescents' whereabouts was linked to whether the adolescents engaged in delinquency later in adolescence (Lahey & others, 2008). Another study revealed that maternal monitoring was linked to a lower incidence of delinquency in Latino girls (Loukas, Suizzo, & Prelow, 2007). And a recent study found that early parental monitoring in adolescence and ongoing parental support were linked to a lower incidence of criminal behavior in emerging adulthood (Johnson & others, 2011).

Rare are the studies that actually demonstrate in an experimental design that changing parenting practices in childhood is related to a lower incidence of juvenile delinquency in adolescence. However, one recent study by Marion Forgatch and her colleagues (2009) randomly assigned divorced mothers with sons to an experimental group (mothers received extensive parenting training) and a control group (mothers received no parenting training) when their sons were in the first to third grades. The parenting training consisted of 14 parent group meetings that especially focused on improving parenting practices with their sons (skill encouragement, limit setting, monitoring, problem solving, and positive involvement). Best practices for emotion regulation, managing interparental conflict, and talking with children about divorce also were included in the sessions. Improved parenting practices and reduced contact with deviant peers were linked with lower rates

connecting with research

Does Intervention Reduce Juvenile Delinquency?

Fast Track is an intervention that attempts to lower the risk of juvenile delinquency and other problems (Conduct Problems Prevention Research Group, 2007, 2010a, b, 2011; Dodge & McCourt, 2010; Jones & others, 2010; Miller & others, 2011). Schools in four areas (Durham, North Carolina; Nashville, Tennessee; Seattle, Washington; and rural central Pennsylvania) were identified as high risk based on neighborhood crime and poverty data. Researchers screened more than 9,000 kindergarten children in the four schools and randomly assigned 891 of the highest-risk and moderate-risk children to intervention or control conditions. The average age of the children when the intervention began was 6.5 years of age.

The 10-year intervention consisted of behavior management training of parents, social cognitive skills training of children, reading tutoring, home visitations, mentoring, and a revised classroom curriculum that was designed to increase socioemotional competence and decrease aggression. Outcomes were assessed in the third, sixth, and ninth grades for the following behavioral problems:

- *Conduct disorder* (multiple instances of behaviors such as truancy, running away, fire setting, cruelty to animals, breaking and entering, and excessive fighting across a six-month period)
- *Oppositional defiant disorder* (an ongoing pattern of disobedient, hostile, and defiant behavior toward authority figures)

- *Attention deficit hyperactivity disorder* (having one or more of these characteristics over a period of time: inattention, hyperactivity, and impulsivity)
- *Any externalizing disorder* (presence of any of the three disorders previously described)
- *Self-reported antisocial behavior* (a list of 34 behaviors, such as skipping school, stealing, and attacking someone with an intent to hurt the person)

The extensive intervention was successful only for children and adolescents who were identified as the highest risk in kindergarten, and it resulted in lowering their incidence of conduct disorder, attention deficit hyperactivity disorder, any externalized disorder, and antisocial behavior. Positive outcomes for the intervention occurred as early as the third grade and continued through the ninth grade. For example, in the ninth grade the intervention reduced the likelihood that the highest-risk kindergarten children would develop conduct disorder by 75 percent, attention deficit hyperactivity disorder by 53 percent, and any externalized disorder by 43 percent.

Recently, data have been reported through age 19 (Miller & others, 2011). Findings indicate that the comprehensive Fast Track intervention was successful in reducing youth arrest rates (Conduct Problems Prevention Research Group, 2010a).

What might be some other strategies for intervening in the lives of high-risk children to reduce their likelihood of become juvenile delinquents?

of delinquency in the experimental group than in the control group at a nine-year follow-up assessment.

An increasing number of studies have found that siblings can have a strong influence on delinquency (Bank, Burraston, & Snyder, 2004). In one study, high levels of hostile sibling relationships and older sibling delinquency were linked with younger sibling delinquency in both brother pairs and sister pairs (Slomkowski & others, 2001).

Having delinquent peers increases the risk of becoming delinquent. For example, a recent study found that peer rejection and having deviant friends at 7 to 13 years of age were linked with increased delinquency at 14 to 15 years of age (Vitaro, Pedersen, & Brendgen, 2007).

Cognitive factors, such as low self-control, low intelligence, and lack of sustained attention, are also implicated in delinquency. For example, one study revealed that low-IQ serious delinquents were characterized by low self-control (Koolhof & others, 2007).

Does intervening in the lives of children who show early conduct problems help reduce their delinquency risk in adolescence? See the *Connecting with Research* interlude to find out how researchers have tried to answer this question.

Review *Connect* Reflect

LG3 Describe the development of prosocial and antisocial behavior

Review

- How is altruism defined? How does prosocial behavior develop?
- What is conduct disorder? What are key factors in the development of juvenile delinquency?

Connect

- Compare the development of prosocial and antisocial behavior in children. What are your conclusions?

Reflect *Your Own Personal Journey of Life*

- Did you commit acts of delinquency as an adolescent? Most adolescents commit one or more juvenile delinquent acts but don't become habitual juvenile delinquents. Reflect on your experiences of either committing juvenile offenses or not committing them, and then review the discussion of likely causes of juvenile delinquency and apply them to your development.

Values, Religion, Spirituality, and Meaning in Life

LG4 Characterize the development of values, religion, spirituality, and meaning in life

Values | Religion and Spirituality | Meaning in Life

James Garbarino (1999) has interviewed a number of young killers. He concludes that nobody really knows precisely why a tiny minority of youth kill, but that the cause might be a lack of a spiritual center. In many of the youth killers he interviewed, Garbarino found a spiritual or emotional emptiness in which the youth sought meaning in the dark side of life. Are spirituality and religion important in your life? How much time have you spent thinking about the meaning of life? What are your values?

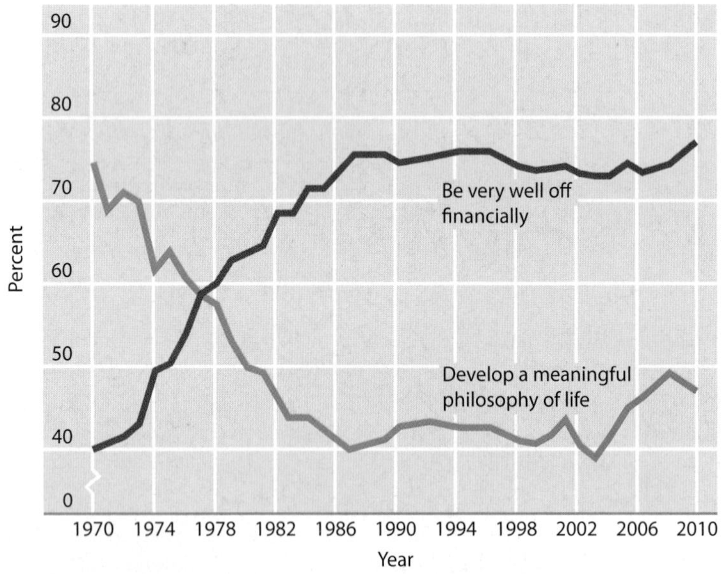

FIGURE **13.3**

CHANGING FRESHMAN LIFE GOALS, 1970 TO 2010. In the last three decades, a significant change has occurred in freshman students' life goals. A far greater percentage of today's college freshmen state that an "essential" or "very important" life goal is to be well-off financially, and far fewer state that developing a meaningful philosophy of life is an "essential" or a "very important" life goal.

VALUES

Values are beliefs and attitudes about the way things should be. They involve what is important to us. We attach value to all sorts of things: politics, religion, money, sex, education, helping others, family, friends, career, recognition, self-respect, and so on. We carry with us values that influence our thoughts, feelings, and actions. One way to measure what people value is to ask them what their goals are. Over the past four decades, traditional-aged college students have shown an increased concern for personal well-being and a decreased concern for the well-being of others, especially for the disadvantaged (Pryor & others, 2010). As shown in Figure 13.3, today's college freshmen are more strongly motivated to be well-off financially and less motivated to develop a meaningful philosophy of life than were their counterparts of 20 or even 10 years ago. In 2010, 77 percent of students viewed becoming well-off financially as an "essential" or a "very important" objective compared with only 42 percent in 1971.

values Beliefs and attitudes about the way things should be.

There are, however, some signs that U.S. college students are shifting toward a stronger interest in the welfare of society. In the survey just described, interest in developing a meaningful philosophy of life increased from 39 percent to 47 percent of U.S. freshmen from 2001 through 2010 (Pryor & others, 2010) (see Figure 13.3). Also in this survey, the percentage of college freshmen who said the chances are very good that they will participate in volunteer or community service programs increased from 18 percent in 1990 to 32 percent in 2010 (Pryor & others, 2010).

Our discussion of values corresponds to William Damon's (2008) view proposed in *The Path to Purpose: Helping Children Find Their Calling in Life*. Damon concluded that a major difficulty confronting today's youth is their lack of a clear sense of what they want to do with their lives—that too many youth are essentially "rudderless." Damon (2008, p. 8) found that only about 20 percent of 12- to 22-year-olds in the United States expressed "a clear vision of where they want to go, what they want to accomplish in life, and why." He argues that their goals and values too often focus on the short term, such as getting a good grade on a test this week and finding a date for a dance, rather than developing a plan for the future based on positive values. The types of questions that adults can pose to youth to guide them in the direction of developing more purposeful values include "What's most important in your life? Why do you care about those things? . . . What does it mean to be a good person?" (Damon, 2008, p. 135).

RELIGION AND SPIRITUALITY

In Damon's (2008) view, one long-standing source for discovering purpose in life is religion. Religion and spirituality play important roles in the lives of many people around the world (Scarlett & Warren, 2010).

Can religion and spirituality be distinguished? Recent analysis by Pamela King and her colleagues (2011) provides the following distinctions:

- **Religion** is an organized set of beliefs, practices, rituals, and symbols that increases an individual's connection to a sacred or transcendent other (God, higher power, or ultimate truth).
- **Religiousness** refers to the degree of affiliation with an organized religion, participation in its prescribed rituals and practices, connection with its beliefs, and involvement in a community of believers.
- **Spirituality** involves experiencing something beyond oneself in a transcendent manner and living in a way that benefits others and society.

What developmental changes characterize the influence of religion, religiousness, and spirituality in people's lives?

Childhood, Adolescence, and Emerging Adulthood   Societies use many methods—such as Sunday schools, parochial education, and parental teaching—to ensure that people will carry on a religious tradition. In a recent national study, 63 percent of parents with children at home said they pray or read Scripture with their children and 60 percent reported that they send their children to religious education programs (Pew Research Center, 2008). Does this religious socialization work? In many cases it does (Paloutzian, 2000).

In general, individuals tend to adopt the religious teachings of their upbringing. For instance, individuals who are Catholics by the time they are 25 years of age, and who were raised as Catholics, likely will continue to be Catholics throughout their adult years. If a religious change or reawakening occurs, it is most likely to take place during adolescence. However, it is important to consider the quality of the parent-adolescent relationship (Ream & Savin-Williams, 2003). Adolescents who have a positive relationship with their parents or are securely attached to them are likely to adopt the religious orientation of their parents (Dudley, 1999). Adolescents who have a negative relationship with their parents or are insecurely attached to them may disaffiliate from religion or seek religion-based attachments that are missing in their family system (Streib, 1999).

Religious issues are important to many adolescents and emerging adults, but in the twenty-first century, a downturn in religious interest among college students

Nina Vasan founded ACS Teens, a nationwide group of adolescent volunteers who support the efforts of the American Cancer Society (ACS). Nina's organization has raised hundreds of thousands of dollars for cancer research, helped change state tobacco laws, and conducted a number of cancer control programs. She created a national letter-writing campaign to obtain volunteers, established a Web site and set up an e-mail network, started a newsletter, and arranged monthly phone calls to communicate ideas and plan projects.

In Nina's words: ". . . I realized that teenagers like myself could make a big difference in the fight against cancer. I knew that the best way to help was to start a teen organization. . . . To be a beneficial part of the human race, it is essential and fundamental to give back to the community and others." (Vasan, 2002, p. 1)

Nina Vasan's work on behalf of cancer involved pursuing a purpose. She says that the success of her work involving cancer far outweighs the many honors she has been awarded (Damon, 2008).

religion An organized set of beliefs, practices, rituals, and symbols that increases an individual's connection to a sacred or transcendent other (God, higher power, or higher truth).

religiousness The degree of affiliation with an organized religion, participation in prescribed rituals and practices, connection with its beliefs, and involvement in a community of believers.

spirituality Experiencing something beyond oneself in a transcendent manner and living in a way that benefits others and society.

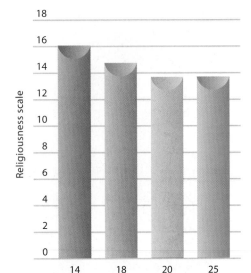

FIGURE **13.4**

DEVELOPMENTAL CHANGES IN RELIGIOUSNESS FROM 14 TO 25 YEARS OF AGE. *Note:* The religiousness scale ranged from 0 to 32, with higher scores indicating stronger religiousness.

has occurred. In the 2009 study of American freshmen described in our discussion of values, 75 percent said they attended a religious service frequently or occasionally during their senior year in high school, down from a high of 85 percent in 1997 (Pryor & others, 2010). Further, in 2009, almost three times as many first-year students (22 percent) reported not having a religious preference as did first-year students in 1978 (8 percent).

A recent developmental study revealed that religiousness declined from 14 to 20 years of age in the United States (Koenig, McGue, & Iacono, 2008) (see Figure 13.4). In this study, religiousness was assessed with items such as frequency of prayer, frequency of discussing religious teachings, frequency of deciding moral actions for religious reasons, and the overall importance of religion in everyday life. As indicated in Figure 13.4, more change in religiousness occurred from 14 to 18 years of age than from 20 to 25 years of age. Also, attending religious services was highest at 14 years of age, declining from 14 to 18 years of age and increasing at 20 years of age. More change occurred in attending religious services than in religiousness. And a recent study found that across the first three semesters of college, students were less likely to attend religious services or engage in religious activities (Stoppa & Lefkowitz, 2010).

Analysis of the World Values Survey of 18- to 24-year-olds revealed that emerging adults in less developed countries were more likely to be religious than their counterparts in more developed countries (Lippman & Keith, 2006). For example, emerging adults' reports of religion being very important in their lives ranged from a low of 0 in Japan to 93 percent in Nigeria, and belief in God ranged from a low of 40 percent in Sweden to a high of 100 percent in Pakistan.

Religion and Cognitive Development Adolescence and emerging adulthood can be especially important junctures in religious development (Scarlett & Warren, 2010). Even if children have been indoctrinated into a religion by their parents, because of advances in their cognitive development adolescents and emerging adults may question what their own religious beliefs truly are.

Many of the cognitive changes thought to influence religious development involve Piaget's cognitive developmental theory, which we discussed in Chapter 6. More so than in childhood, adolescents think abstractly, idealistically, and logically. The increase in abstract thinking lets adolescents consider various ideas of religious and spiritual concepts. For example, an adolescent might ask how a loving God can possibly exist given the extensive suffering of many people in the world (Good & Willoughby, 2008). Adolescents' increased idealistic thinking provides a foundation for thinking about whether religion provides the best route to a better, more ideal world than the present. And adolescents' increased logical reasoning gives them the ability to develop hypotheses and systematically sort through different answers to spiritual questions (Good & Willoughby, 2008).

Religion and Identity Development During adolescence and emerging adulthood, especially emerging adulthood, identity development becomes a central focus (Coté, 2009; Erikson, 1968). Adolescents and emerging adults look for answers to questions like these: "Who am I? What am I all about as a person? What kind of life do I want to lead?" As part of their search for identity, adolescents and emerging adults begin to grapple in more sophisticated, logical ways with such questions as "Why am I on this planet? Is there really a God or higher spiritual being, or have I just been believing what my parents and the church imprinted in my mind? What really are my religious views?" An analysis of the link between identity and spirituality concluded that adolescence and

How does religious thinking change in adolescence? How is religion linked to adolescents' health?

adulthood can serve as gateways to a spiritual identity that "transcends, but not necessarily excludes, the assigned religious identity in childhood" (Templeton & Eccles, 2006, p. 261).

The Positive Role of Religion in Adolescents' Lives   Researchers have found that various aspects of religion are linked with positive outcomes for adolescents (King & Roeser, 2009; Mellor & Freeborn, 2010). A recent study revealed that a higher level of church engagement (based on years of attendance, choice in attending, and participation in activities) was related to higher grades for male adolescents (Kang & Romo, 2010). Churchgoing may benefit students because religious communities encourage socially acceptable behavior, which includes doing well in school. Churchgoing also may benefit students because churches often offer positive role models for students.

Religion also plays a role in adolescents' health and whether they engage in problem behaviors (King & Roeser, 2009). In a national random sample of more than 2,000 11- to 18-year-olds, those who were higher in religiosity were less likely to smoke, drink alcohol, use marijuana, be truant from school, engage in delinquent activities, and be depressed than their low-religiosity counterparts (Sinha, Cnaan, & Gelles, 2007). A recent study of ninth- through twelfth-graders revealed that more frequent religious attendance in one grade predicted lower levels of substance abuse in the next grade (Good & Willoughby, 2010). And a recent study found that parents' religiosity was linked to a lower level of adolescents' risky sexual behavior, in part by adolescents hanging out with less sexually permissive peers (Landors & others, 2011).

Many religious adolescents also internalize their religion's message about caring and concern for people. For example, in one survey, religious youth were almost three times as likely to engage in community service as nonreligious youth (Youniss, McLellan, & Yates, 1999).

developmental **connection**

Identity. In addition to religious/spiritual identity, what are some other identity components? Chapter 11, p. 352

developmental **connection**

Sexuality. In Chapter 12, recent research was discussed that indicated spirituality was linked to a number of positive adolescent sexual outcomes (House & others, 2010). Chapter 12, p. 396

Many children and adolescents show an interest in religion, and many religious institutions created by adults (such as this Muslim school in Malaysia) are designed to introduce them to religious benefits and ensure that they will carry on a religious tradition.

What roles do religion and spirituality play in the lives of middle-aged adults?

Adulthood and Aging   What roles do religion and spirituality play in the lives of adults? Is religion related to adults' health? Is there a point in adult development at which understanding of the meaning of life increases? How do religious beliefs affect the lives of older adults?

Religion and Spirituality in Adulthood   How religious are Americans? A recent national poll of more than 35,000 U.S. adults revealed the following: 92 percent said they believe in God, 75 percent reported that they pray at least weekly and 58 percent said they pray every day, 56 percent said that religion is very important, and 39 percent indicated that they attend religious services at least weekly (Pew Research Center, 2008). In the MacArthur Study of Midlife Development, more than 70 percent of U.S. individuals surveyed said they are religious and consider spirituality a major part of their lives (Brim, 1999).

Gender and ethnic differences characterize religious interest and participation. Females have consistently shown a stronger interest in religion than males have (Idler, 2006). Compared with men, they participate more in both organized and personal forms of religion, are more likely to believe in a higher power or presence, and are more likely to feel that religion is an important dimension of their lives. Regarding ethnicity, African Americans and Latinos show higher rates of religious participation than non-Latino White Americans (Idler, 2006).

> Religion enlightens,
> terrifies, subdues; it gives faith,
> inflicts remorse, inspires resolutions,
> and inflames devotion.
>
> —HENRY NEWMAN
> *English Churchman and Writer, 19th Century*

In thinking about religion and adult development, it is important to consider individual differences. Religion is a powerful influence in some adults' lives, whereas it plays little or no role in others' lives (Myers, 2000). Further, the influence of religion in people's lives may change as they develop. In John Clausen's (1993) longitudinal investigation, some individuals who had been strongly religious in their early-adult years became less so in middle age; others became more religious in middle age.

Religion and Health   How might religion be linked to physical health? Some cults and religious sects encourage behaviors that are damaging to health, such as ignoring sound medical advice (Williams & Sternthal, 2007). For individuals in the religious mainstream, researchers increasingly are finding that religion is positively linked to health (McCullough & Willoughby, 2009). Researchers have found that religious commitment helps to moderate blood pressure and hypertension, and that religious attendance is linked to a reduction in hypertension (Gillum & Ingram, 2007). Also, a number of studies have confirmed a positive association between religious participation and longevity (Oman & Thoresen, 2006).

Why might religion promote physical health? There are several possible answers (Hill & Butter, 1995):

- *Lifestyle issues.* For example, religious individuals have lower drug use than their nonreligious counterparts (Gartner, Larson, & Allen, 1991).

- *Social networks.* Well-connected individuals have fewer health problems (Benjamins & Finlayson, 2007). Religious groups, meetings, and activities provide social connectedness for individuals.

- *Coping with stress.* Religion offers a source of comfort and support when individuals are confronted with stressful events (Park, 2009).

Why might religion be linked to physical health?

Gabriel Dy-Liacco, Pastoral Counselor

Gabriel Dy-Liacco is a pastoral counselor at the Pastoral Counseling and Consultation Centers of Greater Washington, D.C. He obtained his Ph.D. in pastoral counseling from Loyola College in Maryland and also has experience as a psychotherapist in a substance-abuse program, military family center, psychiatric clinic, and community mental health center. As a pastoral counselor, he works with adolescents and adults on the aspects of life that they show the most concern about—psychological, spiritual, or the interface of both. Having lived in Peru, Japan, and the Philippines, he brings considerable multicultural experience to the counseling setting. Dr. Dy-Liacco also is a professor in the Graduate School of Psychology and Counseling at Regent University in the Washington, D.C., area.

Religious counselors often advise people about mental health and coping. To read about the work of one religious counselor, see the *Connecting with Careers* profile. In the *Connecting Development to Life* interlude that follows, we further explore links between religion and coping.

Religion in Older Adults In many societies around the world, older adults are the spiritual leaders in their churches and communities. For example, in the Catholic Church, more popes have been elected in their eighties than in any other 10-year period of the human life span.

The religious patterns of older adults have increasingly been studied (Vahia & others, 2011a, b). A recent study revealed that religious attendance at least weekly compared with never was linked to a lower risk of mortality (Gillum & others, 2008). Another study revealed that African American and Caribbean Black older adults reported higher levels of religious participation, religious coping, and spirituality than non-Latino White older adults (Taylor, Chatters, & Jackson, 2007). And in a recent study, older adults who reported having a higher level of spirituality had more resilience in the face of stressful and difficult circumstances (Vahia & others, 2011).

In one study of individuals from their early thirties through their late sixties and early seventies, a significant increase in spirituality occurred between late middle adulthood (mid-fifties/early sixties) and late adulthood (late sixties/mid-seventies) (Wink & Dillon, 2002) (see Figure 13.5). The spirituality of women increased more than that of men. In this study, spirituality in late adulthood was linked with religiosity in early adulthood (thirties). This finding supports the idea that early religious involvement predisposes individuals to further spiritual development.

Individuals over 65 years of age are more likely than younger people to say that religious faith is the most significant influence in their lives, that they try to put religious faith into practice, and that they attend religious services (Gallup & Bezilla, 1992). A recent study of more than 500 African Americans 55 to 105 years of age revealed that they had a strong identification with religious institutions and high levels of attendance and participation in religious activities (Williams, Keigher, & Williams, 2010).

Is religion related to a sense of well-being and life satisfaction in old age? In one study, older adults' self-esteem was highest when they had a strong religious commitment and lowest when they had little religious commitment (Krause, 1995). In another study, older adults who derived a sense of meaning in life from religion had higher levels of life satisfaction, self-esteem, and optimism (Krause, 2003).

Religion can meet some important psychological needs in older adults, helping them to face impending death, to find and maintain a sense of meaningfulness in

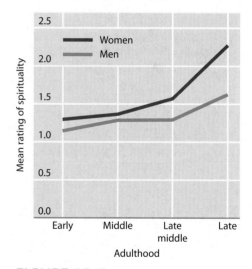

FIGURE **13.5**

LEVEL OF SPIRITUALITY IN FOUR ADULT AGE PERIODS. In a longitudinal study, the spirituality of individuals in four different adult age periods—early (thirties), middle (forties), late middle (mid-fifties/early sixties), and late (late sixties/early seventies) adulthood—was assessed (Wink & Dillon, 2002). Based on responses to open-ended questions in interviews, the spirituality of the individuals was coded on a 5-point scale with 5 being the highest level of spirituality and 1 the lowest.

Religion and Coping

Is religion linked to individuals' ability to cope with stress? Some psychologists have categorized prayer and religious commitment as defensive coping strategies, arguing that they are less effective in helping individuals cope than are life-skill, problem-solving strategies. However, religious coping often benefits individuals during times of high stress. For example, a recent study found that coping styles that relied on collaboration with others and turning to religious groups were more strongly related to improved psychological adjustment than a self-directed coping style (Ross & others, 2009).

A recent interest in linking religion and coping focuses on **meaning-making coping,** which involves drawing on beliefs, values, and goals to change the meaning of a stressful situation, especially in times of high levels of stress such as when a loved one dies. In Crystal Park's (2005, 2007, 2009, 2010, 2011) view, individuals who are religious experience more disruption of their beliefs, values, and goals immediately after the death of a loved one than do individuals who are not religious. Eventually, though, individuals who are religious often show better adjustment to the loss. Initially, religion is linked with more depressed feelings about a loved one's death. Over time, however, as religious

How is religion linked to the ability to cope with stress?

individuals search for meaning in their loss, the depressed feelings lessen. Thus, religion can serve as a meaning system through which bereaved individuals are able to reframe their loss and even find avenues of personal growth. A recent study revealed that personal religiosity decreased the negative effects of a spouse's death on the psychological well-being of widowed individuals (Momtaz & others, 2010).

In sum, various dimensions of religiousness can help some individuals cope more effectively with their lives (George, 2009; Park, 2009). Religious beliefs can shape a person's psychological perception of pain or disability. Religious cognitions can play an important role in maintaining hope and stimulating motivation toward recovery. Because of its effectiveness in reducing distress, religious coping can help prevent denial of the problem and thus facilitate early recognition and more appropriate health-seeking behavior. Religion also can forestall the development of anxiety and depression disorders by promoting communal or social interaction. Houses of religious worship are a readily available, acceptable, and inexpensive source of support for many individuals, especially the elderly. The socialization provided by religious organizations can help prevent isolation and loneliness (Koenig & Larson, 1998).

How would you explain successful coping strategies in those who are not religious?

life, and to accept the inevitable losses of old age (Koenig, 2004). Socially, the religious community can serve many functions for older adults, such as social activities, social support, and the opportunity to assume teaching and leadership roles.

MEANING IN LIFE

Austrian psychiatrist Viktor Frankl's mother, father, brother, and wife died in the concentration camps and gas chambers in Auschwitz, Poland. Frankl survived the concentration camp and went on to write about meaning in life. In his book, *Man's Search for Meaning*, Frankl (1984) emphasized each person's uniqueness and the finiteness of life. He believed that examining the finiteness of our existence and the certainty of death adds meaning to life. If life were not finite, said Frankl, we could spend our life doing just about whatever we pleased because time would continue forever.

meaning-making coping Drawing on beliefs, values, and goals to change the meaning of a stressful situation, especially in times of high levels of stress such as when a loved one dies.

Frankl said that the three most distinct human qualities are spirituality, freedom, and responsibility. Spirituality, in his view, does not have a religious underpinning. Rather, it refers to a human being's uniqueness—to spirit, philosophy, and mind. Frankl proposed that people need to ask themselves such questions as why they exist, what they want from life, and what is the meaning of their life.

It is in middle adulthood that individuals begin to be faced with death more often, especially the deaths of parents and other older relatives. Also faced with less time in their life, many individuals in middle age begin to ask and evaluate the questions that Frankl proposed. And, as we indicated in the discussion of religion and coping, meaning-making coping is especially helpful in times of chronic stress and loss.

Researchers are increasingly studying the factors involved in a person's exploration of meaning in life and whether developing a sense of meaning in life is linked to positive developmental outcomes. Many individuals state that religion played an important role in increasing their exploration of meaning in life (Krause, 2008, 2009). Studies also suggest that individuals who have found a sense of meaning in life are more physically healthy and happier, and experience less depression, than their counterparts who report that they have not discovered meaning in life (Debats, 1990; Krause, 2009).

Roy Baumeister and Kathleen Vohs (2002, pp. 610–611) argue that the quest for a meaningful life can be understood in terms of four main needs for meaning that guide how people try to make sense of their lives:

What characterizes the search for meaning in life?

- *Need for purpose.* "Present events draw meaning from their connection with future events." Purposes can be divided into (1) goals and (2) fulfillments. Life can be oriented toward a future anticipated state, such as living happily ever after or being in love.

- *Need for values.* This "can lend a sense of goodness or positive characterization of life and justify certain courses of action. Values enable people to decide whether certain acts are right or wrong." Frankl's (1984) view of meaning in life emphasized value as the main form of meaning that people need.

- *Need for a sense of efficacy.* This involves the "belief that one can make a difference. A life that had purposes and values but no efficacy would be tragic. The person might know what is desirable but could not do anything with that knowledge." With a sense of efficacy, people believe that they can control their environment, which has positive physical and mental health benefits (Bandura, 2010).

- *Need for self-worth.* Most individuals want to be "good, worthy persons. Self-worth can be pursued individually, such as" finding out that one is very good at doing something, or collectively, as when people find self-esteem from belonging to a group or category of people.

Review *Connect* Reflect

LG4 Characterize the development of values, religion, spirituality, and meaning in life

Review

- What are values? How are the values of U.S. college students changing?
- How do individuals experience religion and spirituality at different points in the life span?
- How do people seek meaning in life?

Connect

- How might the search for meaning in life connect with what you learned in Chapter 11 about developmental personality changes in adults, especially in middle age?

Reflect *Your Own Personal Journey of Life*

- What characterizes your quest for a meaningful life?

Domains of Moral Development

 LG1 Discuss theory and research on moral thought, behavior, feeling, and personality

What Is Moral Development?

- Moral development involves changes in thoughts, feelings, and behaviors regarding right and wrong. Moral development has intrapersonal and interpersonal dimensions.

Moral Thought

- Piaget distinguished between the heteronomous morality of younger children and the autonomous morality of older children. Kohlberg developed a provocative theory of moral reasoning. He argued that development of moral reasoning consists of three levels—preconventional, conventional, and postconventional—and six stages (two at each level). Kohlberg argued that these stages were age related. Influences on the Kohlberg stages include cognitive development, imitation and cognitive conflict, peer relations, and perspective taking. Criticisms of Kohlberg's theory have been made, especially by Gilligan, who advocates a stronger care perspective. Other criticisms focus on the inadequacy of moral reasoning to predict moral behavior, culture and family influences, and the assessment of moral reasoning. A distinction can be made between moral reasoning and social conventional reasoning, which concerns social consensus and conventions.

Moral Behavior

- The processes of reinforcement, punishment, and imitation have been used to explain the acquisition of moral behavior, but they provide only a partial explanation. Situational variability is stressed by behaviorists. Cognitions can play a role in resistance to temptation and self-control. Social cognitive theory of morality emphasizes a distinction between moral competence and moral performance.

Moral Feeling

- In Freud's theory, the superego is the moral branch of personality. The superego consists of the ego ideal and the conscience. According to Freud, guilt is the foundation of children's moral behavior. Empathy is an important aspect of moral feelings, and it changes developmentally. In the contemporary perspective, both positive and negative feelings contribute to moral development.

Moral Personality

- Recently, there has been a surge of interest in studying moral personality. This interest has focused on moral identity, moral character, and moral exemplars. People who have a moral identity value moral notions and commitments to such an extent that behaving in a manner that violates this moral commitment would place the integrity of the self at risk. Moral character involves having the strength of your convictions, and persisting and overcoming distractions and obstacles. Moral character also means having certain virtues, such as honesty, truthfulness, loyalty, and compassion. Moral exemplars' identity, character, and virtues reflect moral commitment and excellence.

Contexts of Moral Development

 LG2 Explain how parents and schools influence moral development

Parenting

- Warmth and responsibility in mutual obligations of parent-child relationships provide important foundations for the child's positive moral growth. Moral development can be advanced by these parenting strategies: being warm and supportive rather than punitive; providing opportunities to learn about others' perspectives and feelings; involving children in family decision making; modeling moral behaviors; averting misbehavior before it takes place; and engaging in conversational dialogue related to moral development.

Schools

- The hidden curriculum, initially described by Dewey, is the moral atmosphere of every school. Contemporary approaches to moral education include character education, values clarification, cognitive moral education, service learning, and integrative ethical education. Cheating is a moral education concern and can take many forms. Various situational aspects influence whether students will cheat or not.

Prosocial and Antisocial Behavior

 Describe the development of prosocial and antisocial behavior

Prosocial Behavior

- Altruism, which is an unselfish interest in helping another person, and reciprocity often motivate prosocial behaviors (behaviors intended to help others) such as sharing. Damon described a sequence by which children develop their understanding of fairness and come to share more consistently. Peers play a key role in this development. Altruism is linked to having a longer life. Volunteering is associated with higher life satisfaction, less depression and anxiety, better physical health, and more positive affect and less negative affect.

Antisocial Behavior

- Conduct disorder involves age-inappropriate actions and attitudes that violate family expectations, society's norms, and the personal or property rights of others. The disorder is more common in boys than in girls. Juvenile delinquency refers to actions taken by an adolescent in breaking the law or engaging in illegal behavior. In the Pittsburgh Youth Study, pathways to delinquency included conflict with authority, minor covert acts followed by property damage and more serious acts, and overt acts of minor aggression followed by fighting and violence. Associating with peers and friends who are delinquents, low parental monitoring, ineffective discipline, having an older sibling who is a delinquent, living in an urban, high-crime area, having low self-control, and having low intelligence are also linked with delinquency,

Values, Religion, Spirituality, and Meaning in Life

 Characterize the development of values, religion, spirituality, and meaning in life

Values

- Values are beliefs and attitudes about the way people think things should be. Over the last four decades, traditional-age college students have shown an increased interest in personal well-being and a decreased interest in the welfare of others.

Religion and Spirituality

- Distinctions have been made between the concepts of religion, religiousness, and spirituality. Many children, adolescents, and emerging adults show an interest in religion, and religious institutions are designed to introduce them to religious beliefs. Cognitive changes—such as increases in abstract, idealistic, and logical thinking—in adolescence increase the likelihood adolescents will seek a better understanding of religion and spirituality. As part of their search for identity, many adolescents and emerging adults begin to grapple with more complex aspects of religion. A downturn in religious interest among college students has occurred. When adolescents have a positive relationship with parents or are securely attached to them, they often adopt their parents' religious beliefs. Various aspects of religion are linked with positive outcomes in adolescent development. Religion is an important dimension of many American adults' lives as well as the lives of people around the world. Females tend to have a stronger interest in religion than males do. Although some people in certain religious sects try to avoid using medical treatment, individuals in the religious mainstream generally enjoy a positive or neutral link between religion and physical health. Religious interest often increases in late adulthood.

Meaning in Life

- Frankl argued that people need to face the finiteness of their life in order to understand life's meaning. Faced with the death of older relatives and less time to live themselves, middle-aged adults increasingly examine life's meaning. Baumeister described four main needs that guide how people try to make sense of their lives: (1) need for purpose, (2) need for values, (3) need for a sense of efficacy, and (4) need for self-worth.

key terms

key people

Generations will depend on the ability of every procreating individual to face his children.

—**ERIK ERIKSON**
American Psychotherapist, 20th Century

Social Contexts of Development

As children develop, their small world widens and they discover new contexts and people. As they grow through childhood, their parents still cradle their lives, but their lives also are shaped by successive choirs of peers and friends. Parents can give adolescents both roots and wings. When some adults become parents, they recognize for the first time how much effort their parents put into rearing them. In recent decades, increasing numbers of adults have chosen to get married later or not at all. As people age, they come to sense that the generations of living things pass in a short while, and, like runners, they pass on the torch of life. Section 5 contains three chapters: "Families, Lifestyles, and Parenting" (Chapter 14), "Peers and the Sociocultural World" (Chapter 15), and "Schools, Achievement, and Work" (Chapter 16).

chapter 14

FAMILIES, LIFESTYLES, AND PARENTING

preview

Love and attachment are two aspects of family life that we discussed in Chapter 10. Beyond these emotional ties, what else goes on in families that influences development? And how do the choices that adults make about family life affect their development and the development of their children? These are some of the questions that we will consider in this chapter.

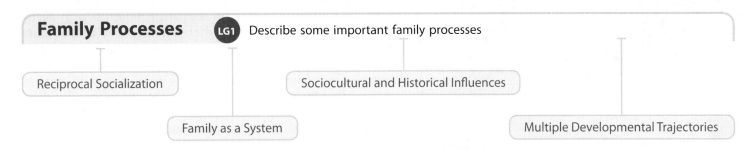

Family Processes **LG1** Describe some important family processes

- Reciprocal Socialization
- Family as a System
- Sociocultural and Historical Influences
- Multiple Developmental Trajectories

As we examine the family and other social contexts of development, think back to Urie Bronfenbrenner's (1986, 2004; Bronfenbrenner & Morris, 2006) ecological theory, which we discussed in Chapter 1. Recall that Bronfenbrenner analyzes the social contexts of development in terms of five environmental systems:

- The *microsystem*, or the setting in which the individual lives, such as a family, the world of peers, schools, work, and so on
- The *mesosystem*, which consists of links between microsystems, such as the connection between family processes and peer relations
- The *exosystem*, which consists of influences from another setting (such as parents' work) that the individual does not experience directly
- The *macrosystem*, or the culture in which the individual lives, such as an ethnic group or a nation
- The *chronosystem*, or sociohistorical circumstances, such as the increased numbers of working mothers, divorced parents, stepparent families, gay and lesbian parents, and multiethnic families in the United States in the last 30 to 40 years

RECIPROCAL SOCIALIZATION

Socialization between parents and children is not a one-way process. Parents do socialize children, but socialization in families is reciprocal (Gauvain & Parke, 2010; Manongdo & Garcia, 2011; Parke & Clarke-Stewart, 2011). **Reciprocal socialization** is socialization that is bidirectional; children socialize parents just as parents socialize children. These reciprocal interchanges and mutual influence processes are sometimes referred to as *transactional* (Sameroff, 2009).

For example, the interaction of mothers and their infants is sometimes symbolized as a dance in which successive actions of the partners are closely coordinated. This coordinated dance can assume the form of synchrony—that is, each person's behavior depends on the partner's previous behavior. Or the interaction can be reciprocal in a precise sense, in which the actions of the partners can be matched, as when one partner imitates the other or when there is mutual smiling. An important example of early synchronized interaction is mutual

developmental **connection**

Environment. An important contribution of Bronfenbrenner's ecological theory is its focus on a range of social contexts that influence the child's development. Chapter 1, p. 26

Children socialize parents just as parents socialize children.

reciprocal socialization Socialization that is bidirectional in that children socialize parents just as parents socialize children.

How does the game of peek-a-boo reflect the concept of scaffolding?

gaze or eye contact. In one study, the mother and infant engaged in a variety of behaviors while they looked at each other; by contrast, when they looked away from each other, the rate of such behaviors dropped considerably (Stern & others, 1977). In another study, synchrony in parent-child relationships was positively related to children's social competence (Harrist, 1993).

Another example of synchronization occurs in *scaffolding*, which means adjusting the level of guidance to fit the child's performance, as we discussed in Chapter 6 (Melzi, Schick, & Kennedy, 2011). The parent responds to the child's behavior with scaffolding, which in turn affects the child's behavior. For example, in the game peek-a-boo, parents initially cover their babies, then remove the covering, and finally register "surprise" at the babies' reappearance. As infants become more skilled at peek-a-boo, they gradually do some of the covering and uncovering. Parents try to time their actions in such a way that the infant takes turns with the parent. In addition to peek-a-boo, pat-a-cake and "so-big" are other caregiver games that exemplify scaffolding and turn-taking sequences.

Scaffolding can be used to support children's efforts at any age. A recent study of Hmong families living in the United States revealed that maternal scaffolding of young children's problem solving the summer before kindergarten, especially in the form of cognitive support, predicted the children's reasoning skills in kindergarten (Stright, Herr, & Neitzel, 2009).

FAMILY AS A SYSTEM

As a social system, the family can be thought of as a constellation of subsystems defined in terms of generation, gender, and role. Divisions of labor among family members define particular subunits, and attachments define others. Each family member is a participant in several subsystems—some dyadic (involving two people) and some polyadic (involving more than two people). The father and child represent one dyadic subsystem, the mother and father another; the mother-father-child represent one polyadic subsystem, the mother and two siblings another.

These subsystems interact with and influence each other (Carlson & others, 2011; Fosco & Grych, 2010). Thus, as Figure 14.1 illustrates, marital relations, parenting, and infant/child behavior can have both direct and indirect effects on each other (Belsky, 1981). The link between marital relationships and parenting has recently received increased attention. The most consistent findings are that compared with unhappily married parents, happily married parents are more sensitive, responsive, warm, and affectionate toward their children (Grych, 2002).

Researchers have found that promoting marital satisfaction often leads to good parenting. The marital relationship is an important support for parenting (Cox & others, 2008). When parents report more intimacy and better communication in their marriage, they are more affectionate with their children (Grych, 2002). Thus, marriage-enhancement programs may end up improving parenting and helping children. Programs that focus on parenting skills might also benefit from including attention to the participants' marriages.

SOCIOCULTURAL AND HISTORICAL INFLUENCES

Family development does not occur in a social vacuum. Important sociocultural and historical influences affect family processes, which reflect Bronfenbrenner's concepts of the macrosystem and chronosystem (Bronfenbrenner & Morris, 2006). Both great upheavals such as war, famine, or mass immigration and subtle transitions in ways of life may stimulate changes in families (Elder & Shanahan, 2006). One example is the effect on U.S. families of the Great Depression of the 1930s. During its height,

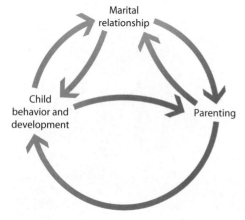

Marital relationship

Child behavior and development

Parenting

FIGURE **14.1**

INTERACTION BETWEEN CHILDREN AND THEIR PARENTS: DIRECT AND INDIRECT EFFECTS

the Depression produced economic deprivation, adult discontent, and depression about living conditions. It also increased marital conflict, inconsistent child rearing, and unhealthy lifestyles—heavy drinking, demoralized attitudes, and health disabilities—especially in fathers (Elder, 1980).

A major change in families in the last several decades has been the dramatic increase in the immigration of Latino and Asian families into the United States (Cheah & Yeung, 2011; Gold & Amthor, 2011). Immigrant families often experience stressors uncommon to or less prominent among longtime residents, such as language barriers, dislocations and separations from support networks, the dual struggle to preserve identity and to acculturate, and changes in SES status (Chen & others, 2011). We further discuss some ethnic variations in families later in this chapter and then examine these variations more extensively in Chapter 15.

Subtle changes in a culture have significant influences on the family (Weisner, 2011). Such changes include the longevity of older adults, movement to urban and suburban areas, television, computers, and the Internet, and a general dissatisfaction and restlessness.

Early in the twentieth century, middle-aged and older adults were often closely linked to the family (Mead, 1978). Today, older parents may have lost some of their socializing role in the family as many of their children moved considerable distances away. However, as we see later in the chapter, in the twenty-first century an increasing number of grandparents are raising their grandchildren.

In the twentieth century, many families moved from farms and small towns to urban and suburban settings (Mead, 1978). In the small towns and farms, individuals were surrounded by lifelong neighbors, relatives, and friends. Today, neighborhood and extended-family support systems are not nearly as prevalent. Families now move all over the country, often uprooting children from a school and peer group they have known for a considerable length of time. And it is not unusual for this type of move to occur every several years, as one or both parents are transferred from job to job.

The media and technology also play a major role in the changing family (Charness, Fox, & Mitchum, 2011; Cotton, McCullough, & Adams, 2011; Padilla-Walker & Coyne, 2011). Many children who watch television or work on computers find that parents are too busy working to share this experience with them. Children increasingly experience a world in which their parents are not participants. Instead of interacting in neighborhood peer groups, children come home after school and watch television or log on to a computer. Among the historical changes related to computers, consider the dramatic increase in young people's participation on Internet social networking sites (Pew Research Center, 2010a, b).

developmental connection

Family. Many families who have immigrated to the United States in recent decades, such as Mexican Americans and Asian Americans, come from collectivist cultures in which family obligation is strong. Chapter 15, p. 508

developmental connection

Family. Recent research indicates that children's and adolescents' media use has increased dramatically in the last decade. Chapter 15, p. 509

Two important changes in families are the increased mobility of families and the increase in media use. *What are some other changes?*

Another change in families has been an increase in general dissatisfaction and restlessness (Mead, 1978). The result of such restlessness and the tendency to divorce and remarry has been a hodgepodge of family structures, with far greater numbers of divorced and remarried families than ever before. Later in the chapter, we will discuss in greater detail these aspects of the changing social world of the child and the family.

MULTIPLE DEVELOPMENTAL TRAJECTORIES

The concept of **multiple developmental trajectories** refers to the fact that adults follow one trajectory or pattern of development and children another one (Parke & Buriel, 2006). How adult and child developmental trajectories mesh is important for understanding the timing of entry into various family tasks. Adult developmental trajectories include timing of entry into cohabitation, marriage, or parenthood; child developmental trajectories include timing of child care and entry into middle school. The timing of some family tasks and changes is planned, such as reentry into the workforce or delaying parenthood, whereas the timing of others is not, such as job loss or divorce (Parke & Buriel, 2006).

multiple developmental trajectories Adults follow one trajectory or pattern of development and children another one.

Review *Connect* Reflect

LG1 Describe some important family processes

Review

- What characterizes reciprocal socialization?
- How does the family function as a system?
- How do sociocultural and historical circumstances influence families?
- What is meant by the concept of multiple developmental trajectories?

Connect

- In Chapter 12 you learned about mothers' and fathers' socialization strategies.

Compare this view of parenting with this section's description of reciprocal socialization.

Reflect *Your Own Personal Journey of Life*

- Reflect for several moments on your own family as you were growing up, and give some examples of the family processes discussed in this section as you experienced them in your own family.

The Diversity of Adult Lifestyles

LG2 Discuss the diversity of adult lifestyles and how they influence people's lives

Single Adults — Cohabiting Adults — Married Adults — Divorced Adults — Remarried Adults — Gay and Lesbian Adults

A striking social change in recent decades has been the decreased stigma attached to individuals who do not maintain what were long considered conventional families. Adults today choose many lifestyles and form many types of families (Benokratis, 2011; Kunz & Kunz, 2011). They live alone, cohabit, marry, divorce, or live with someone of the same sex.

In a recent book, *The Marriage-Go-Round*, sociologist Andrew Cherlin (2009) concluded that the U.S. has more marriages and remarriages, more divorces, and more short-term cohabiting (living together) relationships than most countries. Combined, these lifestyles create more turnover and movement in and out of relationships in the United States than in virtually any other country. Let's explore these varying relationship lifestyles.

SINGLE ADULTS

Recent decades have seen a dramatic rise in the percentage of single adults. Recent data (2009) indicate that for the first time in history the proportion of individuals 25 to 34 years of age who have never been married (46 percent) exceeded those who were married (45 percent) (U.S. Census Bureau, 2010). The increasing number of single adults is the result of rising rates of cohabitation and a trend toward postponing marriage.

Even when singles enjoy their lifestyles and are highly competent individuals, they often are stereotyped (Koropeckyj-Cox, 2009). Stereotypes associated with being single range from the "swinging single" to the "desperately lonely, suicidal" single. Of course, most single adults are somewhere between these extremes.

Common challenges faced by single adults may include forming intimate relationships with other adults, confronting loneliness, and finding a niche in a society that is marriage-oriented. Bella DePaulo (2006, 2011) argues that society has a widespread bias against unmarried adults that is seen in everything from missed perks in jobs to deep social and financial prejudices.

Advantages of being single include having time to make decisions about one's life course, time to develop personal resources to meet goals, freedom to make autonomous decisions and pursue one's own schedule and interests, opportunities to explore new places and try out new things, and privacy.

Once adults reach the age of 30, they may face increasing pressure to settle down and get married. This is when many single adults make a conscious decision to marry or to remain single. A national survey revealed that a higher percentage of singles (58 percent) reported having experienced extreme stress in the past month than married (52 percent) and divorced individuals (48 percent) (American Psychological Association, 2007).

A recent U.S. survey of more than 5,000 single adults 21 years and older revealed that men are now more interested in love, marriage, and children than their counterparts in earlier generations (Match.com, 2011). In this study, today's women desire more independence in their relationships than their mothers did. Across every age group, more women than men reported that they want to pursue their own interests, have personal space, have their own bank account, have regular nights out with girlfriends, and take vacations on their own. Keep in mind, though, that this survey consisted of single adults on an Internet matchmaking site and thus was far from being a random sample of single adults.

Approximately 8 percent of all individuals in the United States who reach the age of 65 have never been married. Contrary to the popular stereotype, older adults who have never been married seem to have the least difficulty coping with loneliness in old age. Many of them discovered long ago how to live autonomously and how to become self-reliant.

COHABITING ADULTS

Cohabitation refers to living together in a sexual relationship without being married. Cohabitation has undergone considerable changes in recent years (Goodwin, Mosher, & Chandra, 2010). As indicated in Figure 14.2, there has been a dramatic increase in the number of cohabiting U.S. couples since 1970 with more than 75 percent cohabiting prior to getting married (Popenoe, 2009). And the upward trend shows no sign of letting up—from 3.8 million cohabiting couples in 2000 to 6.5 million cohabiting couples in 2007. Cohabiting rates are even higher in some countries—in Sweden, for example, cohabitation before marriage is virtually universal (Stokes & Raley, 2009).

Some couples view their cohabitation not as a precursor to marriage but as an ongoing lifestyle. These couples do not want the official aspects of marriage. In the United States, cohabiting arrangements tend to be short-lived, with one-third lasting less than a year (Hyde & DeLamater, 2011). Fewer than 1 out of 10 lasts five years. Of course, it is easier to dissolve a cohabitation relationship than to divorce.

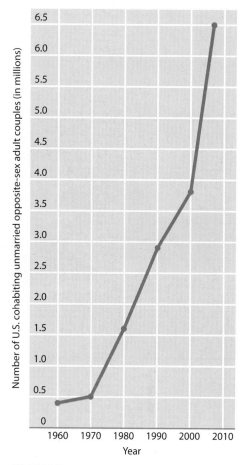

FIGURE **14.2**

THE INCREASE IN COHABITATION IN THE UNITED STATES. Since 1970, there has been a dramatic increase in the number of unmarried adults living together in the United States.

cohabitation Living together in a sexual relationship without being married.

What are some potential advantages and disadvantages of cohabitation?

Couples who cohabit face certain problems (Rhoades, Stanley, & Markman, 2009). Disapproval by parents and other family members can place emotional strain on the cohabiting couple. Some cohabiting couples have difficulty owning property jointly. Legal rights involving the dissolution of the relationship are less clear than in a divorce. A recent study also revealed that cohabiting women experience elevated higher risk of partner violence than married women do (Brownridge, 2008).

Cohabitation and Marital Stability/Happiness If a couple lives together before they marry, does cohabiting help or harm their chances of later having a stable and happy marriage? The majority of studies have found lower rates of marital satisfaction and higher rates of divorce in couples who lived together before getting married (Whitehead & Popenoe, 2003).

What might explain the finding that cohabiting is linked with divorce more than not cohabiting? The most frequently given explanation is that the less traditional lifestyle of cohabitation may attract less conventional individuals who are not great believers in marriage in the first place. An alternative explanation is that the experience of cohabiting changes people's attitudes and habits in ways that increase their likelihood of divorce.

Recent research has provided clarification of cohabitation outcomes. One meta-analysis found the negative link between cohabitation and marital instability did not hold up when only cohabitation with the eventual marital partner was examined, indicating that these cohabitors may attach more long-term positive meaning to living together (Jose, O'Leary, & Moyer, 2010). Another study also revealed that for first marriages, cohabiting with the spouse without first being engaged was linked to more negative interaction and a higher probability of divorce than cohabiting after engagement (Stanley & others, 2010). In contrast, premarital cohabitation prior to a second marriage placed couples at risk for divorce regardless of whether they were engaged. Also, a recent analysis indicated that cohabiting does not have a negative effect on marriage if the couple did not have any previous live-in lovers and did not have children prior to the marriage (Cherlin, 2009).

Cohabiting Older Adults An increasing number of older adults cohabit (Noel-Miller, 2011). In 1960, hardly any older adults cohabited. Today, approximately 4 percent of older adults cohabit (Brown, Lee, & Bulanda, 2006). It is expected that the number of cohabiting older adults will increase even further as more baby boomers turn 65 and bring their historically nontraditional values about love, sex, and relationships to late adulthood.

In many cases, cohabiting by older adults is more for companionship than for love. In other cases, for example, when one partner faces the potential for expensive care, a couple may decide to maintain their assets separately and thus not marry. One study found that older adults who cohabited had a more positive, stable relationship than younger adults who cohabited, although older adults who cohabited were less likely to make plans to marry their partner (King & Scott, 2005).

MARRIED ADULTS

Until about 1930, stable marriage was widely accepted as the endpoint of adult development. In the last 70 to 80 years, however, personal fulfillment both inside and outside marriage has emerged as a goal that competes with marital stability. The changing norm of male-female equality in marriage and increasingly high expectations for what a marital relationship should be have produced marital relationships that are more fragile and intense than they were earlier in the twentieth century (Hoelter, 2009).

Marital Trends In recent years, marriage rates in the United States have declined (Waite, 2009). From 2007 to 2009, the marriage rate continued to drop (National

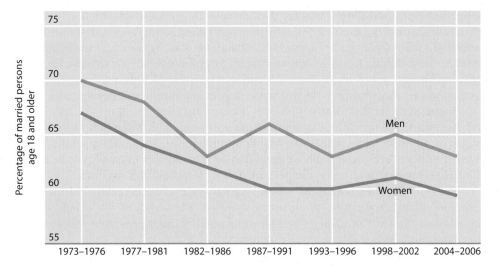

FIGURE **14.3**

PERCENTAGE OF MARRIED PERSONS AGE 18 AND OLDER WITH "VERY HAPPY" MARRIAGES

Center for Vital Statistics, 2010). Currently, slightly over 50 percent of Americans are married, down from 70 percent in 1960 (Pew Research Center, 2010a).

More adults are remaining single longer, with 27 percent of U.S. adults currently having never married (Pew Research Center, 2010a). In 2007, the U.S. average age for a first marriage climbed to 27.5 years for men and 25.6 years for women, higher than at any other point in history (U.S. Census Bureau, 2008). In 1980, the average age for a first marriage in the United States was 24 years for men and 21 years for women. In addition, the increase in cohabitation and a slight decline in the percentage of divorced individuals who remarry contribute to the decline in marriage rates in the United States (Stokes & Raley, 2009).

Despite the decline in marriage rates, the United States is still a marrying society (Popenoe, 2009). Currently, about 70 percent of Americans have been married at least once (U.S. Census Bureau, 2010). In a recent national poll, more than 40 percent of Americans under 30 think marriage is headed for extinction, yet only 5 percent of those young adults said they didn't want to get married (Pew Research Center, 2010a). In a recent analysis, Andrew Cherlin (2009) explained these findings as reflecting marriage's impact as a way to show friends and family that you have a successful social life.

How happy are people who do marry? As indicated in Figure 14.3, the percentage of married individuals in the U.S. who said their marriages were "very happy" declined from the 1970s through the early 1990s, increased around the turn of the century, but recently began to decrease again (Popenoe, 2009). Notice in Figure 14.3 that married men consistently report being happier than married women.

Social Contexts Contexts within a culture and across cultures are powerful influences on marriage. A U.S. study found that although poor communication was rated as a relatively severe problem regardless of household income, it was rated as most severe in high-income households (Karney, Garvin, & Thomas, 2003) (see Figure 14.4). By contrast, drugs and infidelity were rated as more severe problems in low-income households.

Many aspects of marriage vary across cultures. For example, as part of China's efforts to control population growth, a 1981 law set the minimum age for marriage at 22 years for males and 20 for females.

The traits that people look for in a marriage partner vary around the world. In one large-scale study of 9,474 adults from 37 cultures on six continents and five islands, people varied most regarding how much they

> When two people are under the influence of the most violent, most insane, most delusive, and most transient of passions, they are required to swear that they will remain in that excited, abnormal, and exhausting condition continuously until death do them part.
>
> —GEORGE BERNARD SHAW
> *Irish Playwright, 20th Century*

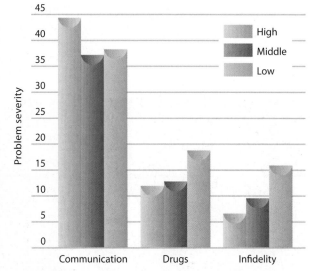

FIGURE **14.4**

SEVERITY OF SPECIFIC RELATIONSHIP PROBLEMS IN LOW-, MIDDLE-, AND HIGH-INCOME HOUSEHOLDS

valued chastity—desiring a marital partner with no previous experience in sexual intercourse (Buss & others, 1990). Chastity was the most important characteristic in selecting a marital partner in China, India, Indonesia, Iran, Taiwan, and the Palestinian Arab culture. Adults from Ireland and Japan placed moderate importance on chastity. In contrast, adults in Sweden, Finland, Norway, the Netherlands, and Germany generally said that chastity was not important in selecting a marital partner.

Domesticity is also valued in some cultures and not in others. In this study, adults from the Zulu culture in South Africa, Estonia, and Colombia placed a high value on housekeeping skills in their marital preference. By contrast, adults in the United States, Canada, and all Western European countries except Spain said that housekeeping skill was not an important trait in selecting their partner.

Religion plays an important role in marital preferences in many cultures. For example, Islam stresses the honor of the male and the purity of the female. It also emphasizes the woman's role in childbearing, child rearing, educating children, and instilling the Islamic faith in their children.

International comparisons of marriage also reveal that individuals in Scandinavian countries marry later than Americans, whereas their counterparts in many African, Asian, and Latin American countries marry younger (Waite, 2009). In Denmark, for example, almost 80 percent of the women and 90 percent of the men aged 20 to 24 have never been married. In Hungary, less than 40 percent of the women and 70 percent of the men the same age have never been married. In Scandinavian countries, cohabitation is popular among young adults; however, most Scandinavians eventually marry (Popenoe, 2008). In Sweden, on average, women delay marriage until they are 31, men until they are 33. Some countries, such as Hungary, encourage early marriage and childbearing to offset declines in the population. Like Scandinavian countries, Japan has a high proportion of unmarried young people. However, rather than cohabiting as the Scandinavians do, unmarried Japanese young adults tend to live with their parents before marrying.

What Makes Marriages Work   John Gottman (1994; Gottman & Gottman, 2009; Gottman & Silver, 1999; Gottman & others, 1998) has been studying married couples' lives since the early 1970s. He uses many methods to analyze what makes marriages work. Gottman interviews couples about the history of their marriage, their philosophy about marriage, and how they view their parents' marriages. He videotapes them talking with each other about how their day went and evaluates what they say about the good and bad times of their marriages. Gottman also uses physiological measures to measure their heart rate, blood flow, blood pressure, and immune functioning moment by moment. He checks back with the couples every year to see how their marriage is faring. Gottman's research represents the most extensive assessment of marital relationships available. Currently he and his colleagues are following 700 couples in seven studies.

(a)

(b)

(c)

(*a*) In Scandinavian countries, cohabitation is popular; only a small percentage of 20- to 24-year-olds are married. (*b*) Islam stresses male honor and female purity. (*c*) Japanese young adults live at home longer with their parents before marrying than young adults in most other countries.

In his research, Gottman has identified the following factors as important predictors of success in marriage:

- *Establishing love maps.* Individuals in successful marriages have personal insights and detailed maps of each other's life and world. They aren't psychological strangers. In good marriages, partners are willing to share their feelings with each other. They use these "love maps" to express not only their understanding of each other but also their fondness and admiration.
- *Nurturing fondness and admiration.* In successful marriages, partners sing each other's praises. More than 90 percent of the time, when couples put a positive spin on their marriage's history, the marriage is likely to have a positive future.
- *Turning toward each other instead of away.* In good marriages, spouses are adept at turning toward each other regularly. They see each other as friends. This friendship doesn't keep arguments from occurring, but it can prevent differences from overwhelming the relationship. In these good marriages, spouses respect each other and appreciate each other's points of view despite disagreements.
- *Letting your partner influence you.* Bad marriages often involve one spouse who is unwilling to share power with the other. Although power-mongering is more common in husbands, some wives also show this trait. A willingness to share power and to respect the other person's view is a prerequisite to compromising. A study revealed that equality in decision making was one of the main factors that predicted positive marriage quality (Amato & others, 2007).
- *Overcoming gridlock.* One partner wants the other to attend church, the other is an atheist. One partner is a homebody, the other wants to go out and socialize a lot. Such problems often produce gridlock. Gottman stresses that the key to ending gridlock is not to solve the problem but to move from gridlock to dialogue and to be patient.
- *Creating shared meaning.* The more that partners can speak candidly and respectfully with each other, the more likely it is that they will create shared meaning in their marriage. This also includes sharing goals with one's spouse and working together to achieve each other's goals.

John Gottman, who has conducted extensive research on what makes marriages work.

> Unlike most approaches to helping couples, mine is based on knowing what makes marriages succeed rather than fail.
>
> —**JOHN GOTTMAN**
> *Contemporary Psychologist, University of Washington*

In a provocative book titled *Marriage, a History*, Stephanie Coontz (2005) concluded that marriages in America today are fragile not because Americans have become self-centered and career-minded but because expectations for marriage have become unrealistically high compared with previous generations. However, she states that many marriages today are better than in the past, citing the increase in marriages that are equitable, loving, intimate, and protective of children. To make a marriage work, she emphasizes (as does Gottman) that partners need to develop a deep friendship, show respect for each other, and embrace commitment.

Premarital Education   Premarital education occurs in a group and focuses on relationship advice. Might premarital education improve the quality of a marriage and possibly reduce the chances that the marriage will end in divorce? Researchers have found that it can (Halford, Markman, & Stanley, 2008; Owen & others, 2011). For example, a survey of more than 3,000 adults revealed that premarital education was linked to a higher level of marital satisfaction and commitment to a spouse, a lower level of destructive marital conflict, and a 31 percent lower likelihood of divorce (Stanley & others, 2006). The premarital education programs in the study ranged from several hours to 20 hours, with a median of 8 hours. It is recommended that premarital education begin approximately six months to a year before the wedding. A recent study revealed that individuals in second marriages are less likely to get premarital education than those in first marriages (Doss & others, 2009). In this study, for both first and second marriages, individuals who received premarital education had a lower risk of subsequent marital distress and divorce.

What makes marriages work? What are the benefits of having a good marriage?

The Benefits of a Good Marriage Are there any benefits to having a good marriage? Yes. Individuals who are happily married live longer, healthier lives than those who are either divorced or unhappily married (Choi & Marks, 2011; Waite, 2009). One study indicated that the longer women were married, the less likely they were to develop a chronic health condition and that the longer men were married, the lower their risk of developing a disease (Dupre & Meadows, 2007). A recent study of U.S. adults 50 years and older also revealed that a lower portion of adult life spent in marriage was linked to an increased likelihood of dying at an earlier age (Henretta, 2010). Further, an unhappy marriage can shorten a person's life by an average of four years (Gove, Style, & Hughes, 1990).

Marriage in Middle and Late Adulthood What is marriage like for middle-aged adults? How does marriage change in late adulthood?

Middle Adulthood Even some marriages that were difficult and rocky during early adulthood turn out to be better adjusted during middle adulthood (Wickrama & others, 2004). Although the partners may have lived through a great deal of turmoil, they eventually discover a deep and solid foundation on which to anchor their relationship. In middle adulthood, the partners may have fewer financial worries, less housework and chores, and more time with each other. Partners who engage in mutual activities usually view their marriage as more positive at this time.

In midlife, most individuals who are married voice considerable satisfaction with being married. In one large-scale study of individuals in middle adulthood, 72 percent of those who were married said their marriage was either "excellent" or "very good" (Brim, 1999). Possibly by middle age, many of the worst marriages already have dissolved.

Might relationship skills in emerging adulthood predict marital adjustment in middle age? A longitudinal study revealed that individuals with higher levels of emotional intimacy skills in their early 20s were more likely to have well-adjusted marriages in middle age than their counterparts with lower levels of intimacy skills in their 20s (Boden, Fischer, & Niehuis, 2010).

What are some adaptations that many married older adults need to make?

Grow old along with me!
The best is yet to be,
The last of life,
For which the first was made.

—ROBERT BROWNING
English Poet, 19th Century

Late Adulthood In 2009, 56 percent of U.S. adults over 65 years of age were married (U.S. Census Bureau, 2010). Individuals who are in a marriage or a partnership in late adulthood are usually happier, are less distressed, and live longer than those who are single (Peek, 2009). One study found that older adults were more satisfied with their marriages than were young and middle-aged adults (Bookwala & Jacobs, 2004). Indeed, the majority of older adults evaluate their marriages as happy or very happy (Huyck, 1995). A recent study of octogenerians revealed that marital satisfaction helped to protect their happiness from daily fluctuations in perceived health (Waldinger & Schulz, 2010). Also, a longitudinal study of adults 75 years of age and older revealed that individuals who were married were less likely to die during a seven-year time span (Rasulo, Christensen, & Tomassini, 2005).

DIVORCED ADULTS

Divorce has become an epidemic in the United States (Hoelter, 2009). However, the divorce rate declined in recent decades after peaking at 5.1 divorces per 1,000 people in 1981 and had declined by 2009 to 3.6 divorces per 1,000 people (National Center for Vital Statistics, 2010). Still, the United States has one of the highest divorce rates in the world.

Individuals in some groups have a higher incidence of divorce (Amato, 2010). Youthful marriage, low educational level, low income, not having a religious affiliation, having parents who are divorced, and having a baby before marriage are factors that are associated with increased rates of divorce (Hoelter, 2009). And characteristics of one's partner that increase the likelihood of divorce include alcoholism, psychological problems, domestic violence, infidelity, and inadequate division of household labor (Hoelter, 2009).

Earlier, we indicated that researchers have not been able to pin down a specific age that is the best time to marry in order to reduce the likelihood of divorce. However, if a divorce is going to occur, it usually takes place early in a marriage; most occur in the fifth to tenth years of marriage (National Center for Health Statistics, 2000) (see Figure 14.5). This timing may reflect an effort by partners in troubled marriages to stay in the marriage and try to work things out. If after several years these efforts have not improved the relationship, they may then seek a divorce.

Even those adults who initiated their divorce go through challenges after a marriage dissolves (Eidar-Avidan, Haj-Yahia, & Greenbaum, 2009). Both divorced women and divorced men complain of loneliness, diminished self-esteem, anxiety about the unknowns in their lives, and difficulty in forming satisfactory new intimate relationships.

The stress of separation and divorce places both men and women at risk for psychological and physical difficulties (Kulik & Heine-Cohen, 2011). Separated and divorced women and men have higher rates of psychiatric disorders, admission to psychiatric hospitals, clinical depression, alcoholism, and psychosomatic problems, such as sleep disorders, than do married adults (Breslau & others, 2011; Keyes, Hatzenbuehler, & Hasin, 2011). One analysis of more than 8,000 51- to 61-year-olds revealed that divorce was associated with an increase in chronic health problems (Waite, 2005).

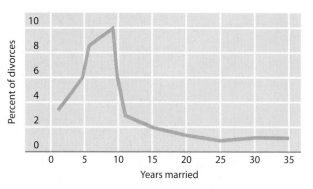

FIGURE **14.5**

THE DIVORCE RATE IN RELATION TO NUMBER OF YEARS MARRIED. Shown here is the percentage of divorces as a function of how long couples have been married. Notice that most divorces occur in the early years of marriage, peaking in the fifth to tenth years of marriage.

Coping with Divorce   Psychologically, one of the most common characteristics of divorced adults is difficulty in trusting someone else in a romantic relationship. Following a divorce, though, people's lives can take diverse turns (Tashiro, Frazier, & Berman, 2006). Strategies for divorced adults include the following (Hetherington & Kelly, 2002):

- Think of divorce as a chance to grow personally and to develop more positive relationships.
- Make decisions carefully. The consequences of your decisions regarding work, lovers, and children may last a lifetime.
- Focus more on the future than the past. Think about what is most important to help you go forward in your life, and then set some challenging goals and plan how to reach them.
- Use your strengths and resources to cope with difficulties.
- Don't expect to be successful and happy in everything you do. "The road to a more satisfying life is bumpy and will have many detours" (p. 109).
- Remember that "you are never trapped by one pathway. Most of those who were categorized as defeated immediately after divorce gradually moved on to a better life, but moving onward usually requires some effort" (p. 109).

Divorced Middle-Aged and Older Adults   A survey by AARP (2004) of more than 1 million 40- to 79-year-olds who were divorced at least once in their forties, fifties, or sixties found that staying married because of their children was by far the main reason many people took so long to become divorced. Despite the worry and stress involved in going through the divorce process, three in four of the divorcees said they had made the right decision to dissolve their marriage and reported a positive outlook on life. Sixty-six percent of the divorced women said they had initiated the divorce, compared with only 41 percent of the divorced men. The divorced women were much more afraid of having financial problems (44 percent)

What are some strategies for coping with divorce?

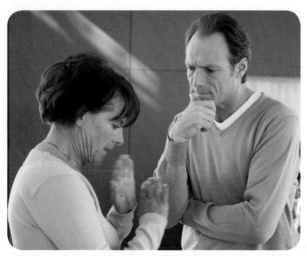

What are some ways that divorce might be more positive or more negative in middle adulthood than in early adulthood?

than the divorced men were (11 percent). Following are the main reasons these middle-aged and older adults cited for their divorce:

Main Causes for Women

- Verbal, physical, or emotional abuse (23 percent)
- Alcohol or drug abuse (18 percent)
- Cheating (17 percent)

Main Causes for Men

- No obvious problems, just fell out of love (17 percent)
- Cheating (14 percent)
- Different values, lifestyles (14 percent)

In 2008, 13 percent of women and 10 percent of men 65 years and older in the United States were divorced or separated (U.S. Census Bureau, 2010). Many of these individuals were divorced or separated before they entered late adulthood (Carr & Pudrovska, 2011). The majority of divorced older adults are women, due to their greater longevity. Men are more likely to remarry, thus removing themselves from the pool of divorced older adults (Peek, 2009). Divorce is far less common among older adults than younger adults, likely reflecting cohort effects rather than age effects since divorce was somewhat rare when current cohorts of older adults were young (Peek, 2009).

There are social, financial, and physical consequences of divorce for older adults (Carr & Pudrovska, 2011; Dare, 2011). Divorce can weaken kinship ties when it occurs in later life, especially in the case of older men. Divorced older women are less likely to have adequate financial resources than married older women, and older adults who are divorced have more health problems than those who are not (Bennett, 2006).

REMARRIED ADULTS

Adults who remarry usually do so rather quickly, with approximately 50 percent remarrying within three years after they initially divorce (Sweeney, 2009, 2010). Men remarry sooner than women. Men with higher incomes are more likely to remarry than their counterparts with lower incomes. Remarriage occurs sooner for partners who initiate a divorce (especially in the first several years after divorce and for older women) than for those who do not initiate it (Sweeney, 2009, 2010).

Adjustment Evidence on the benefits of remarriage is mixed. Remarried families are more likely to be unstable than first marriages, with divorce more likely to occur—especially in the first several years of the remarried family—than in first marriages (Waite, 2009). Adults who get remarried have a lower level of mental health (higher rates of depression, for example) than adults in first marriages, but remarriage often improves the financial status of remarried adults, especially women (Waite, 2009). Researchers have found that remarried adults' marital relationship is more egalitarian and more likely to be characterized by shared decision making than first marriages (Waite, 2009). Remarried wives also report that they have more influence on financial matters in their new family than do wives in first marriages (Waite, 2009). The complex histories and multiple relationships make adjustment difficult in a stepfamily (Pann & Crosbie-Burnett, 2005). Only one-third of stepfamily couples stay married.

Why do remarried adults find it so difficult to stay married? For one thing, many remarry not for love but for financial reasons, for help in rearing children, and for a reduction in loneliness. They also might carry into the stepfamily negative patterns that produced failure in an earlier marriage. Remarried couples also experience more stress in rearing children than do parents in never-divorced families (Ganong, Coleman, & Hans, 2006).

Among the strategies that can help remarried couples cope with the stress of living in a stepfamily are these (Visher & Visher, 1989):

- *Have realistic expectations.* Allow time for loving relationships to develop, and look at the complexity of the stepfamily as a challenge to overcome.
- *Develop new positive relationships within the family.* Create new traditions and ways of dealing with difficult circumstances. Allocation of time is especially important because so many people are involved. The remarried couple needs to allot some time for each person to spend alone.

Remarriage and Aging   Rising divorce rates, increased longevity, and better health have led to an increase in remarriage by older adults. What happens when an older adult wants to remarry or does remarry? Researchers have found that some older adults perceive negative social pressure about their decision to remarry (McKain, 1972). These negative sanctions range from raised eyebrows to rejection by adult children. However, the majority of adult children support the decision of their older adult parents to remarry. Researchers have found that remarried parents and step-parents provide less financial and emotional support to adult stepchildren than do parents in first marriages (White, 1994).

GAY AND LESBIAN ADULTS

The legal and social context of marriage creates barriers to breaking up that do not usually exist for same-sex partners (Biblarz & Savci, 2010; Rostosky & others, 2010). But in other ways, researchers have found that gay and lesbian relationships are similar—in their satisfactions, loves, joys, and conflicts—to heterosexual relationships (Crooks & Baur, 2011). For example, like heterosexual couples, gay and lesbian couples need to find the balance of romantic love, affection, autonomy, and equality that is acceptable to both partners (Hope, 2009). And like heterosexual couples, many gay and lesbian couples are creating families that include children.

Lesbian couples especially place a high priority on equality in their relationships. Indeed, some researchers have found that gay and lesbian couples are more flexible in their gender roles than heterosexual individuals are (Marecek, Finn, & Cardell, 1988). And a recent study of couples revealed that over the course of ten years of cohabitation, partners in gay and lesbian relationships showed a higher average level of relationship quality than heterosexual couples (Kurdek, 2008).

What are some characteristics of lesbian and gay relationships?

There are a number of misconceptions about gay and lesbian couples (Diamond, Fagundes, & Butterworth, 2010; Diamond & Savin-Williams, 2011). Contrary to stereotypes, one partner is masculine and the other feminine in only a small percentage of gay and lesbian couples. Only a small segment of the gay population has a large number of sexual partners, and this is uncommon among lesbians. Furthermore, researchers have found that gay and lesbian couples prefer long-term, committed relationships (Fingerhut & Peplau, 2012). About half of committed gay couples do have an open relationship that allows the possibility of sex (but not affectionate love) outside of the relationship. Lesbian couples usually do not have this type of relationship.

Review Connect Reflect

LG2 Discuss the diversity of adult lifestyles and how they influence people's lives

Review

- What characterizes single adults?
- What are the lives of cohabiting adults like?
- What are some key aspects of the lives of married adults?
- How does divorce affect adults?
- What are the lives of remarried adults like?
- What characterizes the lifestyles of gay and lesbian adults?

Connect

- What did you learn in Chapter 12 about the sexual attitudes and behaviors of lesbians and gays?

Reflect *Your Own Personal Journey of Life*

- Which type of lifestyle are you living today? What do you think are its advantages and disadvantages? If you could have a different lifestyle, which one would it be? Why?

Parenting

LG3 Characterize parenting and how it affects children's development

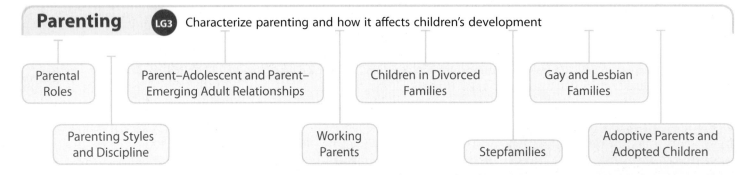

Just as there are diverse lifestyles that adults can adopt, so are there diverse styles of parenting and diverse types of parents. Before we examine these diverse styles and types, let's explore the roles of parents.

> I looked on child rearing not only as a work of love and duty but as a profession that was fully as interesting and challenging as any honorable profession in the world and one that demanded the best that I could bring to it.
>
> —**ROSE KENNEDY**
>
> *U.S. Public Figure, Philanthropist; 20th Century*

PARENTAL ROLES

Many adults plan when to be parents and consider how parenting will fit with their economic situation. For others, the discovery that they are about to become parents is a startling surprise. In either event, the prospective parents may have mixed emotions and romantic illusions about having a child. The needs and expectations of parents have stimulated many myths about parenting.

Currently, there is a tendency to have fewer children. The number of one-child families is increasing. Is there a best time to have children? What are some of the restrictions individuals face when they become parents? These are some of the questions we now consider.

Timing of Parenthood   As with marriage, the age at which individuals have children has been increasing. In 2005, the average age at which women gave birth for the first time was a record high 25.2 years of age, up from 21 years of age in 2001 (Joint Economic Committee, 2007). As birth control has become common practice, many individuals choose when they will have children and how many children they will raise. They are not only marrying later but also having children later or not at all. The percentage of 40- to 44-year-old U.S. women who remain childless increased from 10 percent in 1976 to 20 percent in 2006 (U.S. Census Bureau, 2008).

What are some of the advantages of having children early or late? Some of the advantages of having children early (in the twenties) are these: (1) the parents are likely to have more physical energy—for example, they can cope better with such matters as getting up in the middle of the night with infants and waiting up until adolescents come home at night; (2) the mother is likely to have fewer medical problems with pregnancy and childbirth; and (3) the parents may be less likely to build up expectations for their children, as do many couples who have waited many years to have children.

There are also advantages to having children later (in the thirties): (1) the parents will have had more time to consider their goals in life, such as what they want from their family and career roles; (2) the parents will be more mature and will be able to benefit from their experiences to engage in more competent parenting; and (3) the parents will be better established in their careers and have more income for child-rearing expenses.

The Transition to Parenting   Whether people become parents through pregnancy, adoption, or stepparenting, they face disequilibrium and must adapt (Dew & Wilcox, 2011; Perry-Jenkins & Claxton, 2011). In a longitudinal investigation of couples from late pregnancy until 3½ years after the baby was born, most couples enjoyed more positive marital relations before the baby was born than after (Cowan & Cowan, 2000, 2009). Still, almost one-third showed an increase in marital satisfaction. Some couples said that the baby had both brought them closer together and moved them farther apart; being parents enhanced their sense of themselves and gave them a new, more stable identity as a couple. Babies opened men up to a concern with intimate relationships, and the demands of juggling work and family roles stimulated women to manage family tasks more efficiently and pay attention to their own personal growth. A recent study revealed that when new mothers had low marital satisfaction it often was linked to reductions in quality time spent with husbands and perception of unfairness in housework (Dew & Wilcox, 2011).

The Bringing Baby Home project is a workshop for new parents that emphasizes strengthening the couple's relationship, understanding and becoming acquainted with the baby, resolving conflict, and developing parenting skills (Gottman, Gottman, & Shapiro, 2009). Evaluations of the project revealed that participants were better able to work together as parents, fathers were more involved with their baby and sensitive to the baby's behavior, and mothers had a lower incidence of postpartum depression symptoms, and their babies showed better overall development than the babies of participants in a control group (Gottman, 2008; Shapiro & Gottman, 2005).

What characterizes the transition to parenting?

Parents as Managers of Children's Lives   Parents can play important roles as managers of children's opportunities, as monitors of their lives, and as social initiators and arrangers (Parke & Buriel, 1998, 2006). An important developmental task of childhood and adolescence is to learn how to make competent decisions in an increasingly independent manner. To help children and adolescents reach their full potential, an important parental role is to be an effective manager—one who finds information, makes contacts, helps structure choices, and provides guidance. Parents

Janis Keyser (*right*), conducting a parenting workshop.

Janis Keyser, Parent Educator

Janis Keyser is a parent educator who also teaches in the Department of Early Childhood Education at Cabrillo College in California. In addition to teaching college classes and conducting parenting workshops, she has coauthored a book with Laura Davis (Davis & Keyser, 1997), titled *Becoming the Parent You Want to Be: A Sourcebook of Strategies for the First Five Years.*

Keyser writes as an expert on the iVillage Web site (www .parentsplace.com) and coauthors a nationally syndicated parenting column, "Growing Up, Growing Together." She is the mother of three, stepmother of five, grandmother of twelve, and great-grandmother of six.

> We never know the love of our parents until we have become parents.
>
> —HENRY WARD BEECHER
> *American Clergyman, 19th Century*

developmental **connection**

Moral Development. Families have an important influence on whether adolescents engage in acts of juvenile delinquency. Chapter 13, p. 428

who fulfill this important managerial role help children and adolescents to avoid pitfalls and to work their way through the myriad choices and decisions they face.

Parents can serve as regulators of opportunities for their children's social contact with peers, friends, and adults. From infancy through adolescence, mothers are more likely than fathers to have a managerial role in parenting. In infancy, this might involve taking a child to a doctor and arranging for child care; in early childhood, it might involve a decision about which preschool the child should attend; in middle and late childhood, it might include directing the child to take a bath, to match their clothes and wear clean clothes, and to put away toys; in adolescence, it could involve participating in a parent-teacher conference and subsequently managing the adolescent's homework activity.

A key aspect of the managerial role of parenting is effective monitoring, which is especially important as children move into the adolescent years (Amsel & Smetana, 2011; Smetana, 2010, 2011a, b). Monitoring includes supervising an adolescent's choice of social settings, activities, and friends. As we saw in Chapter 13, a lack of adequate parental monitoring is the parental factor that is related to juvenile delinquency more than any other. One study revealed that low parental monitoring was linked to adolescents' sexual risk taking, especially when mothers had mental health symptoms such as depression (Hadley & others, 2011).

A recent interest involving parental monitoring focuses on adolescents' voluntary disclosure, especially about their activities. Attention is being paid to adolescents' management of their parents' access to information, especially disclosing or concealing strategies about their activities (Amsel & Smetana, 2011; Keijsers & Laird, 2010). Researchers have found that adolescents' disclosure to parents about their whereabouts, activities, and friends is linked to positive adolescent adjustment (Laird, Marrero, & Sentse, 2010; Smetana, 2010, 2011a, b).

To read about one individual who helps parents become more effective in managing their children's lives, see the *Connecting with Careers* profile.

PARENTING STYLES AND DISCIPLINE

A few years ago, there was considerable interest in Mozart CDs that were marketed with the promise that playing them would enrich infants' and young children's

Calvin and Hobbes

by Bill Watterson

WHAT ASSURANCE DO I HAVE THAT YOUR PARENTING ISN'T SCREWING ME UP?

brains. Some of the parents who bought them probably thought, "I don't have enough time to spend with my children so I'll just play these intellectual CDs and then they won't need me as much." Similarly, one-minute bedtime stories have been marketed for parents to read to their children (Walsh, 2000). There are one-minute bedtime bear books, puppy books, and so on. Parents who buy them know it is good for them to read to their children, but they don't want to spend a lot of time doing it. Behind the popularity of these products is an unfortunate theme that suggests that parenting can be done quickly, with little or no inconvenience (Sroufe, 2000).

What is wrong with these quick-fix approaches to parenting? Good parenting takes time and effort (Chen, 2009a, b; Holden, Vittrup, & Rosen, 2011). You can't do it in a minute here and a minute there. You can't do it with CDs.

Of course, it's not just the quantity of time parents spend with children that is important for children's development—the quality of the parenting is clearly important (Brumariu & Kerns, 2011; Russell, 2011). To understand variations in parenting, let's consider the styles parents use when they interact with their children, how they discipline their children, and coparenting.

> Parenting is a very important profession, but no test of fitness for it is ever imposed in the interest of children.
>
> —GEORGE BERNARD SHAW
> *Irish Playwright, 20th Century*

Baumrind's Parenting Styles Diana Baumrind (1971) argues parents should be neither punitive nor aloof. Rather, they should develop rules for their children and be affectionate with them. She has described four types of parenting styles:

- **Authoritarian parenting** is a restrictive, punitive style in which parents exhort the child to follow their directions and respect their work and effort. The authoritarian parent places firm limits and controls on the child and allows little verbal exchange. For example, an authoritarian parent might say, "You will do it my way or else." Authoritarian parents also might spank the child frequently, enforce rules rigidly but not explain them, and show rage toward the child. Children of authoritarian parents are often unhappy, fearful, and anxious about comparing themselves with others, fail to initiate activity, and have weak communication skills. Sons of authoritarian parents may behave aggressively (Hart & others, 2003).

- **Authoritative parenting** encourages children to be independent but still places limits and controls on their actions. Extensive verbal give-and-take is allowed, and parents are warm and nurturant toward the child. An authoritative parent might put his arm around the child in a comforting way and say, "You know you should not have done that. Let's talk about how you can handle the situation better next time." Authoritative parents show pleasure and support in response to children's constructive behavior. They also expect

authoritarian parenting A restrictive, punitive style in which parents exhort the child to follow their directions and to respect their work and effort. Firm limits are placed on the child, and little verbal exchange is allowed.

authoritative parenting A style that encourages children to be independent but still places limits and controls on children's actions; extensive verbal give-and-take is allowed, and parents are warm and nurturant toward the child.

	Accepting, responsive	Rejecting, unresponsive
Demanding, controlling	Authoritative	Authoritarian
Undemanding, uncontrolling	Indulgent	Neglectful

FIGURE **14.6**

CLASSIFICATION OF PARENTING STYLES. The four types of parenting styles (authoritative, authoritarian, indulgent, and neglectful) involve the dimensions of acceptance and responsiveness, on the one hand, and demand and control on the other. For example, authoritative parenting involves being both accepting/responsive and demanding/controlling.

neglectful parenting A style in which the parent is very uninvolved in the child's life.

indulgent parenting A style in which parents are very involved with their children but place few demands or controls on them.

mature, independent, and age-appropriate behavior by children. Children whose parents are authoritative are often cheerful, self-controlled, self-reliant, and achievement-oriented; they tend to maintain friendly relations with peers, cooperate with adults, and cope well with stress.

- **Neglectful parenting** is a style in which the parent is very uninvolved in the child's life. Children whose parents are neglectful develop the sense that other aspects of the parents' lives are more important than they are. These children tend to be socially incompetent. Many have poor self-control and don't handle independence well. They frequently have low self-esteem, are immature, and may be alienated from the family. In adolescence, they may show patterns of truancy and delinquency.

- **Indulgent parenting** is a style in which parents are highly involved with their children but place few demands or controls on them. Such parents let their children do what they want. The result is that the children never learn to control their own behavior and always expect to get their way. Some parents deliberately rear their children in this way because they believe the combination of warm involvement and few restraints will produce a creative, confident child. However, children whose parents are indulgent rarely learn respect for others and tend to have difficulty controlling their behavior. They might be domineering, egocentric, and noncompliant, and have difficulties in peer relations.

These four classifications of parenting involve combinations of acceptance and responsiveness on the one hand and demand and control on the other (Maccoby & Martin, 1983). How these dimensions combine to produce authoritarian, authoritative, neglectful, and indulgent parenting is shown in Figure 14.6.

Parenting Styles in Context Do the benefits of authoritative parenting transcend the boundaries of ethnicity, socioeconomic status, and household composition? Although some exceptions have been found, evidence linking authoritative parenting with competence on the part of the child occurs in research across a wide range of ethnic groups, social strata, cultures, and family structures (Steinberg, Blatt-Eisengart, & Cauffman, 2006).

Other research with ethnic groups suggests that some aspects of the authoritarian style may be associated with positive child outcomes (Parke & Buriel, 2006). Elements of the authoritarian style may take on different meanings and have different effects depending on the context. For example, Asian American parents often continue aspects of traditional Asian child-rearing practices that have sometimes been described as authoritarian. The parents exert considerable control over their children's lives. However, Ruth Chao (2005, 2007; Chao & Otsuki-Clutter, 2011; Chao & Tseng, 2002) argues that the style of parenting used by many Asian American parents is distinct from the domineering control of the authoritarian style. Instead, Chao argues that the control reflects concern and involvement in their children's lives and is best conceptualized as a type of training. The high academic achievement of Asian American children may be a consequence of their "training" parents (Stevenson & Zusho, 2002). In recent research involving Chinese American adolescents and their parents, parental control was endorsed as were the Confucian parental goals of perseverance, working hard in school, obedience, and being sensitive to parents' wishes (Russell, Crockett, & Chao, 2010).

An emphasis on requiring respect and obedience is also associated with the authoritarian style, but in Latino child rearing this focus may be positive rather than punitive. Rather than suppressing the child's development, it may encourage the development of a different type of self. Latino child-rearing practices encourage the development of a self and identity that is embedded in the family and requires respect and obedience (Dixon, Graber, & Brooks-Gunn, 2008). Furthermore, many Latino families have several generations living together and helping each other (Zinn & Wells, 2000). In these circumstances, emphasizing respect and obedience by children may be part of maintaining a harmonious home and may be important in the formation of the child's identity.

Even physical punishment, another characteristic of the authoritarian style, may have varying effects in different contexts. African American parents are more likely than non-Latino White parents to use physical punishment (Deater-Deckard & Dodge, 1997). However, the use of physical punishment has been linked with increased externalized child problems (such as acting out and high levels of aggression) in non-Latino White families but not in African American families. One explanation of this finding points to the need for African American parents to enforce rules in the dangerous environments in which they are more likely to live (Harrison-Hale, McLoyd, & Smedley, 2004). In this context, requiring obedience to parental authority may be an adaptive strategy to keep children from engaging in antisocial behavior that can have serious consequences for the victim or the perpetrator. As we will see, though, overall the use of physical punishment in disciplining children raises many concerns.

Further Thoughts on Parenting Styles   Several caveats about parenting styles are in order. First, the parenting styles do not capture the important themes of reciprocal socialization and synchrony. Keep in mind that children socialize parents, just as parents socialize children (Parke & Clarke-Stewart, 2011). Second, many parents use a combination of techniques rather than a single technique, although one technique may be dominant. Although consistent parenting is usually recommended, the wise parent may sense the importance of being more permissive in certain situations, more authoritarian in others, and yet more authoritative in others. Moreover, parenting styles often are talked about as if both parents have the same style, but this is not always the case. Also, some critics argue that the concept of parenting style is too broad and that more research needs to be conducted to "unpack" parenting styles by studying the influence of various components of the styles (Maccoby, 2007). For example, is parental monitoring more important than warmth in predicting child and adolescent outcomes?

Punishment   Use of corporal (physical) punishment is legal in every state in the United States. A national survey of U.S. parents with 3- and 4-year-old children found that 26 percent of parents reported spanking their children frequently, and 67 percent reported yelling at their children frequently (Regalado & others, 2004). A cross-cultural comparison found that individuals in the United States were among those with the most favorable attitudes toward corporal punishment and were most likely to remember it being used by their parents (see Figure 14.7) (Curran & others, 2001).

A research review concluded that corporal punishment by parents is associated with higher levels of immediate compliance and aggression by the children (Gershoff, 2002). The review also found that corporal punishment is linked to lower levels of moral internalization and mental health (Gershoff, 2002). A recent study in six countries revealed that mothers' use of physical punishment was linked to high rates of aggression in their children (Gershoff & others, 2010). Another study also discovered that a history of harsh physical discipline was related to adolescent depression and externalized problems, such as juvenile delinquency (Bender & others, 2007).

According to Ruth Chao, what type of parenting style do many Asian American parents use?

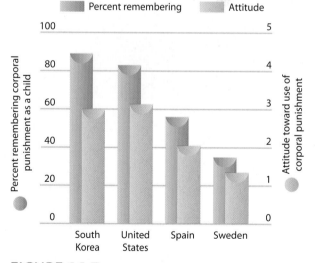

FIGURE **14.7**
CORPORAL PUNISHMENT IN DIFFERENT COUNTRIES.
A 5-point scale was used to assess attitudes toward corporal punishment with scores closer to 1 indicating an attitude against its use and scores closer to 5 suggesting an attitude favoring its use. *Why are studies of corporal punishment correlational studies, and how does that affect their usefulness?*

Are Marital Conflict, Individual Hostility, and the Use of Physical Punishment Linked?

A longitudinal study assessed couples across the transition to parenting to investigate possible links between marital conflict, individual adult hostility, and the use of physical punishment with young children (Kanoy & others, 2003). Before the birth of the first child, the level of marital conflict was observed in a marital problem-solving discussion; answers to questionnaires regarding individual characteristics were also obtained. Thus, these characteristics of the couples were not influenced by characteristics of the child. When the children were 2 and 5 years old, the couples were interviewed about the frequency and intensity of their physical punishment of the children. At both ages, the parents' level of marital conflict was again observed in a marital problem-solving discussion.

The researchers found that both hostility and marital conflict were linked with the use of physical punishment. Individuals with high rates of hostility on the prenatal measures used more frequent and more severe physical punishment with their children. The same was evident for marital conflict—when marital conflict was high, both mothers and fathers were more likely to use physical punishment in disciplining their young children.

If parents who have a greater likelihood of using physical punishment can be identified in prenatal classes, these families could be encouraged to use other forms of discipline before they develop a pattern of physically punishing their children. How might counselors help prevent this pattern from developing?

How do most child psychologists recommend handling a child's misbehavior?

What are some reasons for avoiding spanking or similar punishments? They include the following:

- When adults punish a child by yelling, screaming, or spanking, they are presenting children with out-of-control models for handling stressful situations. Children may imitate this behavior.
- Punishment can instill fear, rage, or avoidance. For example, spanking the child may cause the child to avoid being near the parent and to fear the parent.
- Punishment tells children what not to do rather than what to do. Children should be given feedback, such as "Why don't you try this?"
- Parents might unintentionally become so aroused when they are punishing the child that they become abusive (Durrant, 2008).

Most child psychologists recommend handling misbehavior by reasoning with the child, especially explaining the consequences of the child's actions for others. *Time out,* in which the child is removed from a setting that offers positive reinforcement, can also be effective.

Debate about the effects of punishment on children's development continues (Grusec, 2011; Knox, 2010). A research review of 26 studies concluded that only severe or predominant use of spanking, not mild spanking, compared unfavorably with alternative discipline practices (Larzelere & Kuhn, 2005). There are few longitudinal studies of punishment and few studies that distinguish adequately between moderate and heavy use of punishment. Thus, in the view of some experts, it is still difficult to determine whether the effects of physical punishment are harmful to children's development, although such a view might be distasteful to some individuals (Grusec, 2011). It is nonetheless clear that when physical punishment involves abuse, it can be very harmful to children's development, as discussed later in this chapter (Cicchetti & Toth, 2011).

Considering the family as a system (as discussed earlier in this chapter), what connections might be found between marital relationships and parenting practices? To read about a family systems study involving marital conflict and the use of physical punishment, see the *Connecting with Research* interlude.

Darla Botkin, Marriage and Family Therapist

Darla Botkin is a marriage and family therapist who teaches, conducts research, and engages in marriage and family therapy. She is on the faculty of the University of Kentucky. Botkin obtained a bachelor's degree in elementary education with a concentration in special education and then went on to receive a master's degree in early childhood education. She spent the next six years working with children and their families in a variety of settings, including child care, elementary school, and Head Start. These experiences led Darla to recognize the interdependence of the developmental settings that children and their parents experience (such as home, school, and work). She returned to graduate school and obtained a Ph.D. in family studies from the University of Tennessee. She then became a faculty member in the Family Studies program at the University of Kentucky. Completing further coursework and clinical training in marriage and family therapy, she became certified as a marriage and family therapist.

Botkin's current interests include working with young children in family therapy, understanding gender and ethnic issues in family therapy, and exploring the role of spirituality in family wellness.

Darla Botkin (*left*), conducting a family therapy session.

For more information about what marriage and family therapists do, see page 45 in the Careers in Life-Span Development appendix.

Coparenting The relationship between marital conflict and the use of punishment highlights the importance of **coparenting,** which is the support that parents provide one another in jointly raising a child. Poor coordination between parents, undermining of the other parent, lack of cooperation and warmth, and disconnection by one parent are conditions that place children at risk for problems (Solmeyer & others, 2011; Talbot, Baker, & McHale, 2009). For example, one study revealed that coparenting influenced young children's effortful control above and beyond maternal and paternal parenting by themselves (Karreman & others, 2008). And a recent study found that greater father involvement in young children's play was linked to an increase in supportive coparenting (Jia & Schoppe-Sullivan, 2011).

Parents who do not spend enough time with their children or who have problems in child rearing can benefit from counseling and therapy. To read about the work of marriage and family therapist Darla Botkin, see the *Connecting with Careers* profile.

What characterizes coparenting?

Child Maltreatment Unfortunately, punishment sometimes leads to the abuse of infants and children (Cicchetti, 2011, 2012; Cicchetti & Toth, 2011). In 2007, approximately 794,000 U.S. children were found to be victims of child abuse (U.S. Department of Health and Human Services, 2009). Nearly 80 percent of these children were abused by a parent or parents. Laws in many states now require physicians and teachers to report suspected cases of child abuse, yet many cases go unreported, especially those involving battered infants.

coparenting The support that parents provide one another in jointly raising a child.

GRANT HILL
Phoenix Suns

TAMIA
Recording Artist

We're with
the band

We're wearing the blue wristband because it's time to
prevent child abuse. To get with the band or learn more, visit
www.preventchildabuse.org

Prevent Child Abuse
America

This print ad was created by Prevent Child Abuse America to make people aware of its national blue wristband campaign. The campaign's goal is to educate people about child-abuse prevention and encourage them to support the organization.

child abuse The term used most often by the public and many professionals to refer to both abuse and neglect.

child maltreatment The term increasingly used by developmentalists that refers to abuse and neglect, but also includes diverse conditions.

physical abuse Abuse characterized by the infliction of physical injury by punching, beating, kicking, biting, burning, shaking, or otherwise harming a child.

child neglect Failure to provide for a child's basic needs, including physical, educational, or emotional needs.

sexual abuse Fondling a child's genitals, intercourse, incest, rape, sodomy, exhibitionism, and commercial exploitation through prostitution or the production of pornographic materials.

emotional abuse Acts or omissions by parents or other caregivers that have caused, or could cause, serious behavioral, cognitive, or emotional problems.

Whereas the public and many professionals use the term **child abuse** to refer to both abuse and neglect, developmentalists increasingly use the term **child maltreatment** (Cicchetti, 2010, 2011, 2012). This term does not have quite the emotional impact of the term *abuse* and acknowledges that maltreatment includes diverse conditions.

Types of Child Maltreatment   The four main types of child maltreatment are physical abuse, child neglect, sexual abuse, and emotional abuse (National Clearinghouse on Child Abuse and Neglect, 2004):

- **Physical abuse** is characterized by the infliction of physical injury as a result of punching, beating, kicking, biting, burning, shaking, or otherwise harming a child. The parent or other person may not have intended to hurt the child; the injury may have resulted from excessive physical punishment (Milot & others, 2010).

- **Child neglect** is characterized by failure to provide for the child's basic needs (Newton & Vandeven, 2010). Neglect can be physical (abandonment, for example), educational (allowing chronic truancy, for example), or emotional (marked inattention to the child's needs, for example). Child neglect is by far the most common form of child maltreatment. In every country where relevant data have been collected, neglect occurs up to three times as often as abuse (Benoit, Coolbear, & Crawford, 2008).

- **Sexual abuse** includes fondling a child's genitals, intercourse, incest, rape, sodomy, exhibitionism, and commercial exploitation through prostitution or the production of pornographic materials (Bahali & others, 2010). In many cases of sexual abuse, there are no outward physical signs of abuse, unlike in incidences of physical abuse.

- **Emotional abuse** (psychological/verbal abuse/mental injury) includes acts or omissions by parents or other caregivers that have caused, or could cause, serious behavioral, cognitive, or emotional problems (van Harmelen & others, 2010).

Although any of these forms of child maltreatment may be found separately, they often occur in combination. Emotional abuse is almost always present when other forms are identified.

The Context of Abuse   No single factor causes child maltreatment (Cicchetti & Toth, 2011). A combination of factors, including the culture, neighborhood, family, and development, likely contribute to child maltreatment (Prinz & others, 2009).

The extensive violence that takes place in American culture is reflected in the occurrence of violence in the family (Durrant, 2008). A regular diet of violence appears on television screens, and parents often resort to power assertion as a disciplinary technique. In China, where physical punishment is rarely used to discipline children, the incidence of child abuse is reported to be very low.

The family itself is obviously a key part of the context of abuse (Shin, Hong, & Hazen, 2010). The interactions of all family members should be considered, regardless of who performs the violent acts against the child (Kim & Cicchetti, 2004). For example, even though the father may be the one who physically abuses the child, contributions by the mother, the child, and siblings also should be evaluated.

Were parents who abuse children abused by their own parents? About one-third of parents who were abused when they were young abuse their own children (Cicchetti & Toth, 2006, 2011). Thus, some, but not a majority, of parents are locked into an intergenerational transmission of abuse (Dixon, Browne, & Hamilton-Giachritsis, 2005).

Developmental Consequences of Abuse   Among the consequences of child maltreatment in childhood and adolescence are poor emotion regulation, attachment problems, problems in peer relations, difficulty in adapting to school, and other psychological problems such as depression and delinquency (Cicchetti & Toth, 2011; Trickett & Negriff, 2011). As shown in Figure 14.8, maltreated young children in foster care were more likely to show abnormal stress hormone levels than middle-SES young children living with their birth family (Gunnar & Fisher, 2006). In this study, the abnormal stress hormone levels were mainly present in the foster children who experienced neglect, best described as "institutional neglect" (Fisher, 2005). Adolescents who experienced abuse or neglect as children are more likely than adolescents who were not maltreated as children to engage in violent romantic relationships, delinquency, sexual risk taking, and substance abuse (Wekerle & others, 2009).

Later, during the adult years, individuals who were maltreated as children often have difficulty establishing and maintaining healthy intimate relationships (Dozier, Stovall-McClough, & Albus, 2009). As adults, maltreated children are also at higher risk for violent behavior toward other adults—especially dating partners and marital partners—as well as for substance abuse, anxiety, and depression (Kennedy, 2009). A recent study also revealed that adults who experienced child maltreatment were at increased risk for financial and employment-related difficulties (Zielinski, 2009).

An important strategy for avoiding these problems is to prevent child maltreatment (Cicchetti, 2010, 2011, 2012; Cicchetti & Toth, 2011; Corso & Fertig, 2010). In one study of maltreating mothers and their 1-year-olds, two treatments were effective in reducing child maltreatment: (1) home visitation that emphasized improved parenting, coping with stress, and increased support for the mother; and (2) psychotherapy that focused on improving maternal-infant attachment (Cicchetti, Toth, & Rogusch, 2005).

PARENT–ADOLESCENT AND PARENT–EMERGING ADULT RELATIONSHIPS

Even the best parents may find their relationship with their child strained during adolescence, yet attachment to parents is an important aspect of adolescent development. As individuals become emerging adults, their relationship with their parents changes.

Parent-Adolescent Relationships   Important aspects of parent-adolescent relationships include autonomy/attachment and conflict. First, we explore the young adolescent's push for autonomy.

Autonomy and Attachment   The young adolescent's push for autonomy and responsibility puzzles and angers many parents. Parents see their teenager slipping from their grasp. They may have an urge to assert stronger control as the adolescent seeks autonomy and responsibility. Heated emotional exchanges may ensue, with either side calling names, making threats, and doing whatever seems necessary to gain control. Most parents anticipate that their teenager will have some difficulty adjusting to the changes that adolescence brings, but few parents can imagine and predict just how strong an adolescent's desires will be to spend time with peers or how much adolescents will want to show that it is they—not their parents—who are responsible for their successes and failures.

The ability to attain autonomy and gain control over one's behavior in adolescence is acquired through appropriate adult reactions to the adolescent's desire for control (McElhaney & others, 2009). At the onset of adolescence, the average individual does not have the knowledge to make mature decisions in all areas of life. As the adolescent pushes for autonomy, the wise adult relinquishes control in those areas in which the adolescent can make reasonable decisions but continues to guide the adolescent to make reasonable decisions in areas in which the adolescent's knowledge is more limited. Gradually, adolescents acquire the ability to make mature decisions on their own (Laursen & Collins, 2009). In a recent study, young adolescents' perception that their parents promoted more psychological autonomy

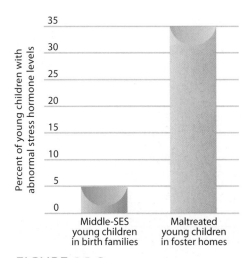

FIGURE **14.8**

ABNORMAL STRESS HORMONE LEVELS IN YOUNG CHILDREN IN DIFFERENT TYPES OF REARING CONDITIONS

When I was a boy of 14, my father was so ignorant I could hardly stand to have the man around. But when I got to be 21, I was astonished at how much he had learnt in 7 years.

—**Mark Twain**
American Writer and Humorist, 19th Century

and less psychological control predicted fewer depressive symptoms two years later (Sher-Censor, Parke, & Coltrane, 2010).

Gender differences characterize autonomy-granting in adolescence, with boys being given more independence than girls are. In one study, this was especially true in those U.S. families with a traditional gender-role orientation (Bumpus, Crouter, & McHale, 2001). Also, Latino parents are more likely to protect and monitor daughters more closely than sons, in comparison with parents in non-Latino White families (Allen & others, 2008).

Cultural differences also characterize adolescent autonomy. In one study, U.S. adolescents sought autonomy earlier than did Japanese adolescents (Rothbaum & others, 2000). In the transition to adulthood, Japanese youth are less likely to live outside the home than Americans are (Hendry, 1999).

Even while adolescents seek autonomy, parent-child attachment remains important (Rothbaum & Trommsdorff, 2007). Mothers maintain closer emotional ties with adolescents, especially daughters, than fathers do (Collins & Steinberg, 2006).

Recall from Chapter 10 that one of the most widely discussed aspects of socioemotional development in infancy is secure attachment to caregivers. In the past decade, researchers have explored whether secure attachment also might be an important element in adolescents' relationships with their parents (Laursen & Collins, 2009; Rosenthal & Kobak, 2010). For example, Joseph Allen and his colleagues (2009) found that adolescents who were securely attached at age 14 were more likely to report at age 21 that they were in an exclusive relationship, comfortable with intimacy in relationships, and moving toward financial independence. In a recent analysis, it was concluded that the most consistent outcomes of secure attachment in adolescence involve positive peer relations and development of the adolescent's emotion regulation capacities (Allen & Miga, 2010).

Parent-Adolescent Conflict   Although attachment to parents may remain strong during adolescence, the connectedness is not always smooth (Harold, Colarossi, & Mercier, 2007). Early adolescence is a time when conflict with parents escalates (Laursen & Collins, 2009). Much of the conflict involves the everyday events of family life, such as keeping a bedroom clean, dressing neatly, getting home by a certain time, and not talking incessantly on the phone. The conflicts rarely involve major dilemmas such as drugs and delinquency.

The increased conflict in early adolescence may be due to a number of factors: the biological changes of puberty, cognitive changes involving increased idealism and logical reasoning, social changes focused on independence and identity, maturational changes in parents, and expectations that are violated by parents and adolescents (Collins & Steinberg, 2006). Adolescents compare their parents with an ideal standard and then criticize their flaws. Many parents see their adolescent changing from a compliant child to someone who is noncompliant, oppositional, and resistant to parental standards. Also, early-maturing adolescents experience more conflict with their parents than do adolescents who mature late or on time (Collins & Steinberg, 2006).

It is not unusual to hear parents of young adolescents ask, "Is it ever going to get better?" Things usually do get better as adolescents move from early to late adolescence. Conflict with parents often escalates during early adolescence, remains somewhat stable during the high school years, and then lessens as the adolescent reaches 17 to 20 years of age. Parent-adolescent relationships become more positive if adolescents go away to college than if they stay at home and attend college (Sullivan & Sullivan, 1980).

The everyday conflicts that characterize parent-adolescent relationships may serve a positive function. These minor disputes and negotiations facilitate the adolescent's transition from being dependent on parents to becoming an autonomous individual. For example, in one

What strategies can parents use to guide adolescents in effectively handling their increased motivation for autonomy?

developmental **connection**

Attachment. Securely attached infants use the caregiver as a secure base from which to explore the environment. Chapter 10, p. 321

Conflict with parents increases in early adolescence. *What is the nature of this conflict in a majority of American families?*

Old Model		New Model
Autonomy, detachment from parents; parent and peer worlds are isolated Intense, stressful conflict throughout adolescence; parent-adolescent relationships are filled with storm and stress on virtually a daily basis		Attachment and autonomy; parents are important support systems and attachment figures; adolescent-parent and adolescent-peer worlds have some important connections Moderate parent-adolescent conflict is common and can serve a positive developmental function; conflict greater in early adolescence

FIGURE 14.9

OLD AND NEW MODELS OF PARENT-ADOLESCENT RELATIONSHIPS

study, adolescents who expressed disagreement with their parents explored identity development more actively than did adolescents who did not express disagreement with their parents (Cooper & others, 1982). One way for parents to cope with the adolescent's push for independence and identity is to recognize that adolescence is a decade-long transitional period in the journey to adulthood, rather than an overnight accomplishment. Recognizing that conflict and negotiation can serve a positive developmental function can further tone down parental hostility. Understanding parent-adolescent conflict, though, is not simple (Riesch & others, 2003).

In sum, the old model of parent-adolescent relationships suggested that parent-adolescent conflict is intense and stressful throughout adolescence. The new model emphasizes that most parent-adolescent conflict is moderate rather than intense and that the moderate conflict can serve a positive function. Figure 14.9 summarizes the old and new models of parent-adolescent relationships, which include changes in thinking about attachment and autonomy.

Still, a high degree of conflict characterizes some parent-adolescent relationships. According to one estimate, parents and adolescents engage in prolonged, intense, repeated, unhealthy conflict in about one in five families (Montemayor, 1982). In other words, 4 to 5 million American families encounter serious, highly stressful parent-adolescent conflict. And this prolonged, intense conflict is associated with a number of adolescent problems—movement out of the home, juvenile delinquency, school dropout, pregnancy and early marriage, membership in religious cults, and drug abuse (Brook & others, 1990). In a recent study of Latino families, higher levels of conflict with either the mother or the father were linked to higher levels of adolescent boys' and girls' internalizing (depression, for example) and externalizing (delinquency, for example) behaviors (Crean, 2008). In this study, conflict with the mother was especially detrimental for Latina girls.

Conclusions We have seen that parents play very important roles in adolescent development. Although adolescents are moving toward independence, they still need to stay connected with families (Laursen & Collins, 2009; Smetana, 2010, 2011a, b). Competent adolescent development is most likely when adolescents have parents who show them warmth and mutual respect, demonstrate sustained interest in their lives, recognize and adapt to their cognitive and socioemotional development, communicate expectations for high standards of conduct and achievement, and display constructive ways of dealing with problems and conflict (Small, 1990). These ideas coincide with Diana Baumrind's (1971, 1991) authoritative parenting style.

Emerging Adults' Relationships with Their Parents

For the most part, emerging adults' relationships with their parents improve when they leave home. They often grow closer psychologically to their parents and share more with them than they did before they left home (Arnett, 2007). However,

Stacey Christensen, age 16: "I am lucky enough to have open communication with my parents. Whenever I am in need or just need to talk, my parents are there for me. My advice to parents is to let your teens grow at their own pace, be open with them so that you can be there for them. We need guidance; our parents need to help but not be too overwhelming."

Doonesbury

BY GARRY TRUDEAU

What are some strategies that can benefit the relationship between emerging adults and their parents?

challenges in the parent–emerging adult relationship involve the emerging adult's possessing adult status in many areas while still depending on parents in some manner (Aquilino, 2006; Fingerman, Cheng, & others, 2011; Swartz & others, 2011). Many emerging adults can make their own decisions about where to live, whether to stay in college, which lifestyle to adopt, whether to get married, and so on. At the same time, parents often provide support for their emerging adult children even after they leave home. This might be accomplished through loans and monetary gifts for education or purchase of a car, financial contributions to living arrangements, and emotional support.

In successful emerging adulthood, individuals separate from their parents without cutting off ties completely or fleeing to some substitute emotional refuge. Complete cutoffs from parents rarely solves emotional problems. Emerging adulthood is a time for young people to sort out emotionally what they will take along from the family of origin, what they will leave behind, and what they will create.

The vast majority of studies of parenting have focused on outcomes for children and adolescents and have involved mothers rather than fathers. A recent study revealed that parents act as "scaffolding" and "safety nets" to support their children's successful transition through emerging adulthood (Swartz & others, 2011). Another recent study examined mothers' and fathers' parenting styles with their emerging adult children (Nelson & others, 2010). An authoritative parenting style (defined in this study as high responsiveness, low control) by both mothers and fathers was linked with positive outcomes in emerging adult children (high self-worth and high social acceptance, and low depression, for example). The most negative outcomes for emerging adult children (low self-worth, high depression, and high anxiety, for example) were related to a controlling-indulgent style (low responsiveness, high control) on the part of both mothers and fathers. High control by parents may be especially detrimental with emerging adults who are moving toward more autonomy as they leave their parents' home. Negative outcomes for emerging adult children also resulted from an uninvolved parenting style (low responsiveness, low control) on the part of both mothers and fathers. The most positive outcomes for emerging adult children involved having fathers who parented with an authoritative style.

WORKING PARENTS

More than one of every two U.S. mothers with a child under the age of 5 is in the labor force; more than two of every three with a child from 6 to 17 years of age work outside the home. Maternal employment is a part of modern life, but its effects continue to be debated.

Most research on parental work has focused on young children and the mother's employment (Brooks-Gunn, Han, & Waldfogel, 2010). However, the effects of working parents involves the father as well as the mother when such matters as work schedules and work-family stress are considered (O'Brien & Moss, 2010;

---

developmental **connection**

Social Contexts. Research consistently shows that family factors are considerably better at predicting children's developmental outcomes than are child-care experiences. Chapter 10, p. 327

Parke & Clarke-Stewart, 2011). Recent research indicates that what matters for children's development is the nature of parents' work rather than whether one parent works outside the home (Goodman & others, 2011; Han, 2009; Parke & Clarke-Stewart, 2011).

Work can produce positive and negative effects on parenting (Crouter & McHale, 2005). Ann Crouter (2006) described how parents bring their experiences at work into their homes. She concluded that parents who have poor working conditions, such as long hours, overtime work, stressful work, and lack of autonomy at work, are likely to be more irritable at home and engage in less effective parenting than their counterparts who have better work conditions in their jobs. A consistent finding is that children (especially girls) of working mothers engage in less gender stereotyping and have more egalitarian views of gender (Goldberg & Lucas-Thompson, 2008).

CHILDREN IN DIVORCED FAMILIES

Divorce rates changed dramatically in the United States and many countries around the world during the late twentieth century (Amato & Dorius, 2010). The U.S. divorce rate increased enormously in the 1960s and 1970s but has declined since the 1980s. However, the divorce rate in the United States is still much higher than in most other countries.

It is estimated that 40 percent of children born to married parents in the United States will experience their parents' divorce (Hetherington & Stanley-Hagan, 2002). Let's examine some important questions about children in divorced families:

How does work affect parenting?

Are children better adjusted in intact, never-divorced families than in divorced families? Most researchers agree that children from divorced families show poorer adjustment than their counterparts in nondivorced families (Hetherington, 2006; Lansford, 2009; Wallerstein, 2008) (see Figure 14.10). Those who have experienced multiple divorces are at greater risk. Children in divorced families are more likely than children in nondivorced families to have academic problems, to show externalized problems (such as acting out and delinquency) and internalized problems (such as anxiety and depression), to be less socially responsible, to have less competent intimate relationships, to drop out of school, to become sexually active at an early age, to take drugs, to associate with antisocial peers, to have low self-esteem, and to be less securely attached as young adults (Lansford, 2009). One study revealed that adolescent girls with divorced parents were especially vulnerable to developing symptoms of depression (Oldehinkel & others, 2008). Nonetheless, keep in mind that a majority of children in divorced families do not have significant adjustment problems (Ahrons, 2007). One study found that 20 years after their parents had divorced when they were children, approximately 80 percent of adults concluded that their parents' decision to divorce had been a wise one (Ahrons, 2004).

Note that marital conflict may have negative consequences for children in the context of marriage or divorce (Cummings & Davies, 2010). A longitudinal study revealed that conflict in nondivorced families was associated with emotional problems in children (Amato, 2006). Indeed, many of the problems that children from divorced homes experience begin during the predivorce period, a time when parents are often in active conflict with each other. Thus, when children from divorced homes show problems, the problems may be due not only to the divorce, but also to the marital conflict that led to it (Thompson, 2008).

E. Mark Cummings and his colleagues (Cummings & Davies, 2010; Cummings, El-Sheikh, & Kouros, 2009; Cummings & Kouros, 2008; Cummings & Merrilees, 2009; Schermerhorn, Chow, & Cummings, 2010) have proposed *emotion security theory*, which has its roots in attachment theory and states that children appraise

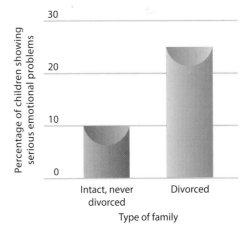

FIGURE **14.10**

DIVORCE AND CHILDREN'S EMOTIONAL PROBLEMS. In Hetherington's research, 25 percent of children from divorced families showed serious emotional problems compared with only 10 percent of children from intact, never-divorced families. However, keep in mind that a substantial majority (75 percent) of the children from divorced families did not show serious emotional problems.

marital conflict in terms of their sense of security and safety in the family. These researchers make a distinction between marital conflict that is negative for children (such as hostile emotional displays and destructive conflict tactics) and marital conflict that can be positive for children (such as marital disagreement that involves a calm discussion of each person's perspective and working together to reach a solution).

Should parents stay together for the sake of the children?

Whether parents should stay in an unhappy or conflicted marriage for the sake of their children is one of the most commonly asked questions about divorce (Deutsch & Pruett, 2009; Hetherington, 2006; Ziol-Guest, 2009). If the stresses and disruptions in family relationships associated with an unhappy, conflictual marriage that erode the well-being of children are reduced by the move to a divorced, single-parent family, divorce can be advantageous. However, if the diminished resources and increased risks associated with divorce also are accompanied by inept parenting and sustained or increased conflict, not only between the divorced couple but also among the parents, children, and siblings, the best choice for the children would be that an unhappy marriage be retained (Hetherington & Stanley-Hagan, 2002). It is difficult to determine how these "ifs" will play out when parents either remain together in an acrimonious marriage or become divorced.

How much do family processes matter in divorced families?

In divorced families, family processes matter a great deal (Hetherington, 2006; Lansford, 2009; Parke & Clarke-Stewart, 2011; Sigal & others, 2011). When the divorced parents have a harmonious relationship and use authoritative parenting, the adjustment of adolescents is improved (Hetherington, 2006). When the divorced parents can agree on child-rearing strategies and can maintain a cordial relationship with each other, frequent visits by the noncustodial parent usually benefit the child (Fabricius & others, 2010). Following a divorce, father involvement with children drops off more than mother involvement, especially for fathers of girls. Also, a recent study in divorced families revealed that an intervention focused on improving the mother-child relationship was linked to improvements in relationship quality that increased children's coping skills over the short term (6 months) and long term (6 years) (Velez & others, 2011).

What factors influence an individual child's vulnerability to suffering negative consequences as a result of living in a divorced family?

Among the factors involved in the child's risk and vulnerability are the child's adjustment prior to the divorce, as well as the child's personality and temperament, and the custody situation (Hetherington, 2006). Children whose parents later divorce show poorer adjustment before the breakup (Amato & Booth, 1996). Children who are socially mature and responsible, who show few behavioral problems, and who have an easy temperament are better able to cope with their parents' divorce. Children with a difficult temperament often have problems coping with their parents' divorce (Hetherington, 2006). Joint custody works best for children when the parents can get along with each other (Parke & Clarke-Stewart, 2011).

What role does socioeconomic status play in the lives of children in divorced families?

Custodial mothers experience the loss of about one-fourth to one-half of their predivorce income, in comparison with a loss of only one-tenth by custodial fathers (Emery, 1999). This income loss for divorced mothers is accompanied by increased workloads, high rates of job instability, and residential moves to less desirable neighborhoods with inferior schools (Sayer, 2006).

What concerns are involved in whether parents should stay together for the sake of the children or become divorced?

> As marriage has become a more optional, less permanent institution in contemporary America, children and adolescents are encountering stresses and adaptive challenges associated with their parents' marital transitions.
>
> —E. MAVIS HETHERINGTON
> *Contemporary Psychologist, University of Virginia*

Communicating with Children About Divorce

Ellen Galinsky and Judy David (1988) developed a number of guidelines for communicating with children about divorce:

- *Explain the separation.* As soon as daily activities in the home make it obvious that one parent is leaving, tell the children. If possible, both parents should be present when children are told about the separation to come. The reasons for the separation are very difficult for young children to understand. No matter what parents tell children, children can find reasons to argue against the separation. It is extremely important for parents to tell the children who will take care of them and to describe the specific arrangements for seeing the other parent.

- *Explain that the separation is not the child's fault.* Young children often believe their parents' separation or divorce is their own fault. Therefore, it is important to tell children that they are not the cause of the separation. Parents need to repeat this point a number of times.

- *Explain that it may take time to feel better.* Tell young children that it's normal not to feel good about what is happening and that many other children feel this way when their parents become separated. It is also okay for divorced parents to share some of their emotions with children, by saying something like "I'm having a hard time since the separation just like you, but I know it's going to get better after a while." Such statements are best kept brief and should not criticize the other parent.

- *Keep the door open for further discussion.* Tell your children to come to you any time they want to talk about the separation. It is healthy for children to express their pent-up emotions in discussions with their parents and to learn that the parents are willing to listen to their feelings and fears.

- *Provide as much continuity as possible.* The less children's worlds are disrupted by the separation, the easier their transition to a single-parent family will be. This guideline means maintaining the rules already in place as much as possible. Children need parents who care enough not only to give them warmth and nurturance but also to set reasonable limits.

- *Provide support for your children and yourself.* After a divorce or separation, parents are as important to children as before the divorce or separation. Divorced parents need to provide children with as much support as possible. Parents function best when other people are available to give them support as adults and as parents. Divorced parents can find people who provide practical help and with whom they can talk about their problems.

How well do these strategies complement E. Mavis Hetherington's six strategies for divorced adults, discussed earlier in this chapter?

In sum, many factors affect how divorce influences a child's development (Hetherington, 2006). To read about some strategies for helping children cope with the divorce of their parents, see the *Connecting Development to Life* interlude.

STEPFAMILIES

Not only are parents divorcing more, they are also getting remarried more (Ganong, Coleman, & Jamison, 2011). The number of remarriages involving children has grown steadily in recent years. About half of all children whose parents divorce will have a stepparent within four years of parental separation. However, divorces occur at a 10 percent higher rate in remarriages than in first marriages (Cherlin & Furstenberg, 1994).

In some cases, the stepfamily may have been preceded by the death of the spouse. However, by far the largest number of stepfamilies are preceded by divorce rather than death.

Three common types of stepfamily structure are (1) stepfather, (2) stepmother, and (3) blended or complex. In stepfather families, the mother typically had custody of the children and remarried, introducing a stepfather into her children's lives. In stepmother families, the father usually had custody and remarried, introducing a stepmother into his children's lives. In a blended or complex stepfamily, both parents bring children from previous marriages to live in the newly formed stepfamily.

How does living in a stepfamily influence a child's development?

In E. Mavis Hetherington's (2006) most recent longitudinal analyses, children and adolescents who had been in a simple stepfamily (stepfather or stepmother) for a number of years were adjusting better than in the early years of the remarried family and were functioning well in comparison with children and adolescents in conflicted nondivorced families and children and adolescents in complex (blended) stepfamilies. More than 75 percent of the adolescents in long-established simple stepfamilies described their relationships with their stepparents as "close" or "very close." Hetherington (2006) concluded that in long-established simple stepfamilies, adolescents seem eventually to benefit from the presence of a stepparent and the resources provided by the stepparent.

Children often have better relationships with their custodial parents (mothers in stepfather families, fathers in stepmother families) than with stepparents (Santrock, Sitterle, & Warshak, 1988). Also, children in simple families (stepmother, stepfather) often show better adjustment than their counterparts in complex (blended) families (Anderson & others, 1999; Hetherington & Kelly, 2002).

As in divorced families, children in stepfamilies show more adjustment problems than children in nondivorced families (Hetherington & Kelly, 2002). The adjustment problems are similar to those found among children of divorced parents—academic problems and lower self-esteem, for example (Anderson & others, 1999). However, it is important to recognize that a majority of children in stepfamilies do not have problems. In one analysis, 25 percent of children from stepfamilies showed adjustment problems compared with 10 percent in intact, never-divorced families (Hetherington & Kelly, 2002). Adolescence is an especially difficult time for the formation of a stepfamily (Anderson & others, 1999). This may occur because becoming part of a stepfamily exacerbates normal adolescent concerns about identity, sexuality, and autonomy.

GAY AND LESBIAN PARENTS

Increasingly, gay and lesbian couples are creating families that include children (Patterson, 2009; Patterson & Wainright, 2010) (see Figure 14.11). Approximately 33 percent of lesbian couples and 23 percent of gay couples are parents (Patterson, 2004). There may be more than 1 million gay and lesbian parents in the United States today.

An important aspect of gay and lesbian families with children is the sexual identity of parents at the time of a child's birth or adoption (Patterson, 2009). The largest group of children with gay and lesbian parents are likely those who were born in the context of heterosexual relationships, with one or both parents only later identifying themselves as gay or lesbian. Gay and lesbian parents may be single or they may have same-gender partners. In addition, gays and lesbians are increasingly choosing parenthood through donor insemination or adoption. Researchers have found that the children created through new reproductive technologies—such as in vitro fertilization—are as well adjusted as their counterparts conceived by natural means (Golombok, 2011a, b; Golombok & Tasker, 2010).

Another issue focuses on custody arrangements for adolescents. Many gays and lesbians have lost custody of their adolescents to heterosexual spouses following divorce. For this reason, many gay fathers and lesbian mothers are noncustodial parents.

Researchers have found few differences in children growing up with gay fathers and lesbian mothers and children growing up with heterosexual parents (Patterson & Wainright, 2010). For example, children growing up in gay or lesbian families are just as popular with their peers, and there are no differences in the adjustment and mental health of children living in these families when they are compared with children in heterosexual families (Hyde & DeLamater, 2011). Also, the overwhelming majority of children growing up in a gay or lesbian family have a heterosexual orientation (Golombok & Tasker, 2010).

Percentage of same-sex couples

- 1990
- 2000

Gay couples with children

Lesbian couples with children

FIGURE **14.11**

PERCENTAGE OF GAY AND LESBIAN COUPLES WITH CHILDREN: 1990 AND 2000.
Why do you think more lesbian couples have children than gay couples?

developmental **connection**

Sexuality. Regardless of sexual orientation, most males and females emphasize the importance of affection, trust, and shared interests in a relationship. Chapter 12, p. 405

ADOPTIVE PARENTS AND ADOPTED CHILDREN

Another variation in the type of family in which children live involves adoption, the social and legal process by which a parent-child relationship is established between persons unrelated at birth (Cohen & others, 2008; Rosnati, Montirosso, & Barni, 2008). As we see next, an increase in diversity has characterized the adoption of children in the United States in recent years.

The Increased Diversity of Adopted Children and Adoptive Parents A number of changes have characterized adoptive children and adoptive parents in the last three to four decades (Brodzinsky & Pinderhughes, 2002). In the first half of the twentieth century, most U.S. adopted children were healthy, non-Latino White infants who were adopted at birth or soon after; however, in recent decades as abortion became legal and contraception increased, fewer of these infants became available for adoption. Increasingly, U.S. couples adopted a much wider diversity of children—from other countries, from other ethnic groups, children with physical and/or mental problems, and children who had been neglected or abused.

Changes also have characterized adoptive parents in the last three to four decades (Brodzinsky & Pinderhughes, 2002). In the first half of the twentieth century, most adoptive parents were from non-Latino White middle or upper socioeconomic status backgrounds who were married and did not have any type of disability. However, in recent decades, increased diversity has characterized adoptive parents. Many adoption agencies today have no income requirements for adoptive parents and now allow adults from a wide range of backgrounds to adopt children, including single adults, gay and lesbian adults, and older adults.

Do these changes matter? They open opportunities for many children and many couples, but possible effects of changes in the characteristics of parents on the outcomes for children are still unknown. For example, in one study, adopted adolescents were more likely to have problems if the adoptive parents had low levels of education (Miller & others, 2000). In another study, international adoptees showed fewer behavior problems and were less likely to be using mental health services than domestic adoptees (Juffer & van IJzendoorn, 2005). More research is needed before definitive conclusions can be reached about the changing demographic characteristics of adoption.

The changes in adoption practice over the last several decades make it difficult to generalize about the average adopted child or average adoptive parent. As we see next, though, some researchers have provided useful comparisons between adopted children and nonadopted children and their families.

Developmental Outcomes for Adopted and Nonadopted Children How do adopted children fare after they are adopted? Children who are adopted very early in their lives are more likely to have positive outcomes than children adopted later in life (Bernard & Dozier, 2008).

In general, adopted children and adolescents are more likely to experience psychological and school-related problems than nonadopted children (Bernard & Dozier, 2008). For example, a meta-analysis (a statistical procedure that combines the results of a number of studies) revealed that adoptees were far more likely to be using mental health services than their nonadopted counterparts (Juffer & van IJzendoorn, 2005). Adopted children also showed more behavior problems than nonadoptees, but this difference was small. A recent large-scale study found that adopted children are more likely to have a learning disability than are nonadopted children (Altarac & Saroha, 2007).

Research that contrasts adopted and nonadopted adolescents has also found positive characteristics among the adopted adolescents. For example, in one study, although adopted adolescents were more likely than nonadopted adolescents to use illicit drugs and to engage in delinquent behavior, the adopted adolescents were also less likely to be withdrawn and more likely to engage in more prosocial behavior, such as being altruistic, caring, and supportive of others (Sharma, McGue, & Benson, 1996).

An increasing number of Hollywood celebrities are adopting children from developing countries. Actress Angelina Jolie (*above*) with her adopted children, carrying adopted daughter Zahara with adopted sons Maddox and Pax alongside them.

What are some strategies for parenting adopted children at different points in their development?

In short, the vast majority of adopted children (including those adopted at older ages, transracially, and across national borders) adjust well, and their parents report considerable satisfaction with their decision to adopt (Brodzinsky & Pinderhughes, 2002; Castle & others, 2010). A research review of 88 studies also revealed no difference in the self-esteem of adopted and nonadopted children, as well as no differences between transracial and same-race adoptees (Juffer & van IJzendoorn, (2007).

Most studies of adopted and nonadopted children compare different families (adoptive and nonadoptive). A recent study used a different strategy: studying families in which the parents were raising their biological offspring along with an adopted child (Glover & others, 2010). Findings similar to studies of between-family comparisons occurred with only a slight (but nonsignificant) trend for adopted children to show more internalized (depression, for example) and externalized (antisocial behavior, for example) problems.

In other comparisons, adopted children fare much better than children raised in long-term foster care or in an institutional environment (Bernard & Dozier, 2008). A recent study of infants in China revealed that their cognitive development improved two to six months following their adoption from foster homes and institutions (van den Dries & others, 2010).

Parenting Adopted Children   Many of the keys to effectively parenting adopted children are no different from those for effectively parenting biological children: be supportive and caring; be involved and monitor the child's behavior and whereabouts; be a good communicator; and help the child learn to develop self-control. However, parents of adopted children face some unique circumstances (Fontenot, 2007; Wolfgram, 2008). They need to recognize the differences involved in adoptive family life, communicate about these differences, show respect for the birth family, and support the child's search for self and identity.

Because many children begin to ask where they came from when they are about 4 to 6 years old, this is a natural time to begin talking in simple ways to children about their adoption status (Warshak, 2008). Some parents (although not as many as in the past) decide not to tell their children about the adoption. This secrecy may create psychological risks for the child if he or she later finds out about the adoption.

Review *Connect* Reflect

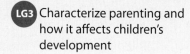 **LG3** Characterize parenting and how it affects children's development

Review

- What are some parental roles?
- What are four main parenting styles? Which parenting style is most often linked with children's social competence? Is physical punishment a wise choice by parents? Does coparenting have positive effects on children? What is the nature of child maltreatment?
- How can parent–adolescent relationships and parent–emerging adult relationships be described?
- What are the effects of working parents on children's development?
- How does divorce affect children's development?
- What influence does growing up in a stepfamily have on children's development?
- What characterizes gay and lesbian parenting?

- How do the lives of adoptive parents and adopted children differ from the lives of nonadoptive parents and nonadopted children?

Connect

- How does what you learned about working parents in this chapter connect with the discussion of child care in Chapter 10, "Emotional Development"?

Reflect *Your Own Personal Journey of Life*

- What characterized your relationship with your parents during middle school and high school? Has your relationship with your parents changed since then? Does it involve less conflict? What do you think are the most important aspects of parenting adolescents competently?

Other Family Relationships

LG4 Explain other aspects of family relationships

| Sibling Relationships and Birth Order | Grandparenting and Great-Grandparenting | Intergenerational Relationships |

As important as child-parent relationships are to children's development, other family relationships are also important. Here we briefly examine sibling relationships, grandparenting and great-grandparenting, and intergenerational relationships.

SIBLING RELATIONSHIPS AND BIRTH ORDER

What are sibling relationships like? How extensively does birth order influence behavior?

Sibling Relationships Approximately 80 percent of American children have one or more siblings—that is, sisters and brothers (Dunn, 2007). If you grew up with siblings, you probably have a rich memory of aggressive, hostile interchanges. Siblings in the presence of each other when they are 2 to 4 years of age, on average, have a conflict once every 10 minutes, and then the conflicts decrease somewhat from 5 to 7 years of age (Kramer, 2006). What do parents do when they encounter siblings having a verbal or physical confrontation? One study revealed that they do one of three things: (1) intervene and try to help them resolve the conflict, (2) admonish or threaten them, or (3) do nothing at all (Kramer & Perozynski, 1999). Of interest is that in families with two siblings 2 to 5 years of age, the most frequent parental reaction is to do nothing at all. A recent review concluded that sibling relationships in adolescence are not as close as, are not as intense as, and are more egalitarian than in childhood (East, 2009).

Negative aspects of sibling relationships, such as high conflict, are linked to negative outcomes for children and adolescents. The negative outcomes can develop not only through conflict but also through direct modeling of a sibling's behavior, as when a younger sibling has an older sibling who has poor study habits and engages in delinquent behavior. By contrast, close and supportive sibling relationships can buffer the negative effects of stressful circumstances in children's and adolescents' lives.

Laurie Kramer (2006), who had conducted a number of research studies on siblings, says that not intervening and letting sibling conflict escalate is not a good strategy. She developed a program titled "More Fun with Sisters and Brothers," which teaches 4- to 8-year-old siblings social skills for developing positive interactions (Kramer & Radey, 1997). Among the social skills taught in the program are how to appropriately initiate play, how to accept and refuse invitations to play, how to take another's perspective, how to deal with angry feelings, and how to manage conflict.

However, conflict is only one of the many dimensions of sibling relations (Howe, Ross, & Recchia, 2011). Sibling relationships include helping, sharing, teaching, fighting, and playing, and siblings can act as emotional supports, rivals, and communication partners. One study found that adolescent siblings spent an average of 10 hours a week together, with an average of 12 percent of that time spent in constructive time (creative activities such as art, music, and hobbies; sports; religious activities; and games) and 25 percent in nonconstructive time (watching TV and hanging out) (Tucker, McHale, & Crouter, 2003).

Judy Dunn (2007), a leading expert on sibling relationships, described three important characteristics of sibling relationships:

What characterizes children's sibling relationships?

- *Emotional quality of the relationship.* Intense positive and negative emotions are often expressed by siblings toward each other. Many children and adolescents have mixed feelings toward their siblings.

- *Familiarity and intimacy of the relationship.* Siblings typically know each other very well, and this intimacy suggests that they can either provide support or tease and undermine each other, depending on the situation.
- *Variation of the relationship.* Some siblings describe their relationships more positively than others. Thus, there is considerable variation in sibling relationships. We've indicated that many siblings have mixed feelings about each other, but some children and adolescents mainly describe their sibling in warm, affectionate ways, whereas others primarily talk about how irritating and mean a sibling is.

Do parents usually favor one sibling over others—and if so, does it make a difference in an adolescent's development? One study of 384 adolescent sibling pairs revealed that 65 percent of their mothers and 70 percent of their fathers showed favoritism toward one sibling (Shebloski, Conger, & Widaman, 2005). When favoritism of one sibling occurred, it was linked to lower self-esteem and sadness in the less-favored sibling.

In some instances, siblings may be stronger socializing influences on the child than parents are (Cicirelli, 1994). Someone close in age to the child—such as a sibling—may be able to understand the child's problems and communicate more effectively than parents can. In dealing with peers, coping with difficult teachers, and discussing such taboo subjects as sex, siblings may have more influence than parents.

Is sibling interaction the same around the world? In industrialized societies, such as the United States, parents tend to delegate responsibility for younger siblings to older siblings primarily to give the parents freedom to pursue other activities. However, in nonindustrialized countries, such as Kenya, the older sibling's role as a caregiver to younger siblings has much more importance. In industrialized countries, the older sibling's caregiving role is often discretionary; in nonindustrialized countries, it is more obligatory (Cicirelli, 1994).

Birth Order   Whether a child has older or younger siblings has been linked to development of certain personality characteristics. For example, one review concluded that "firstborns are the most intelligent, achieving, and conscientious, while later-borns are the most rebellious, liberal, and agreeable" (Paulhus, 2008, p. 210). Compared with later-born children, firstborn children have also been described as more adult-oriented, helpful, conforming, and self-controlled. However, when such birth-order differences are reported, they often are small.

What might account for even small differences related to birth order? Proposed explanations usually point to variations in interactions with parents and siblings associated with being in a specific position in the family. This is especially true in the case of the firstborn child (Teti, 2001). The oldest child is the only one who does not have to share parental love and affection with other siblings—until another sibling comes along. An infant requires more attention than an older child; thus the firstborn sibling receives less attention after the newborn arrives. Does this result in conflict between parents and the firstborn? In one research study, mothers became more negative, coercive, and restraining and played less with the firstborn following the birth of a second child (Dunn & Kendrick, 1982).

What is the only child like? The popular conception is that the only child is a "spoiled brat," with such undesirable characteristics as dependency, lack of self-control, and self-centered behavior. But researchers present a more positive portrayal of the only child. Only children often are achievement-oriented and display a desirable personality, especially in comparison with later-borns and children from large families (Falbo & Poston, 1993).

So far, our discussion suggests that birth order might be a strong predictor of behavior. However, an increasing number of family researchers stress that when all of the factors that influence behavior are considered, birth order by itself shows limited ability to predict behavior.

The one-child family is becoming much more common in China because of the strong motivation to limit the population growth in the People's Republic of China. The policy is still relatively new, and its effects on children have not been fully examined. *In general, though, what have researchers found the only child to be like?*

Think about some of the other important factors in children's lives beyond birth order that influence their behavior. They include heredity, models of competency or incompetency that parents present to children on a daily basis, peer influences, school influences, socioeconomic factors, sociohistorical factors, and cultural variations. When someone says firstborns are always like this but last-borns are always like that, the person is making overly simplistic statements that do not adequately take into account the complexity of influences on a child's development.

Sibling Relationships in Adulthood Sibling relationships persist over the entire life span for most adults (Bedford, 2009). Eighty-five percent of today's adults have at least one living sibling. Sibling relationships in adulthood may be extremely close, apathetic, or highly rivalrous. The majority of sibling relationships in adulthood have been found to be close (Cicirelli, 2009). Those siblings who are psychologically close to each other in adulthood tended to be that way in childhood. It is rare for sibling closeness to develop for the first time in adulthood (Dunn, 1984). A recent study revealed that adult siblings often provide practical and emotional support to each other (Voorpostel & Blieszner, 2008).

GRANDPARENTING AND GREAT-GRANDPARENTING

The increase in longevity is influencing the nature of grandparenting (Szinovacz, 2009). In 1900 only 4 percent of 10-year-old children had four living grandparents but in 2000 that figure had risen to more than 40 percent. And in 1990 only about 20 percent of children at 30 years of age had living grandparents, a figure that is projected to increase to 80 percent in 2020 (Hagestad & Uhlenberg, 2007). Further increases in longevity are likely to support this trend in the future, although the current trend in delaying childbearing is likely to undermine it (Szinovacz, 2009).

Grandparent Roles Grandparents play important roles in the lives of many grandchildren (Oberlander, Black, & Starr, 2007). Many adults become grandparents for the first time during middle age. Researchers have consistently found that grandmothers have more contact with grandchildren than do grandfathers (Watson, Randolph, & Lyons, 2005). Perhaps women tend to define their role as grandmothers as part of their responsibility for maintaining ties between family members across generations. Men may have fewer expectations about the grandfather role and see it as more voluntary.

Three prominent meanings are attached to being a grandparent (Neugarten & Weinstein, 1964). For some older adults, being a grandparent is a source of biological reward and continuity. For others, being a grandparent is a source of emotional self-fulfillment, generating feelings of companionship and satisfaction that may have been missing in earlier adult-child relationships. And for yet others, being a grandparent is a remote role.

The grandparent role may have different functions in different families, in different ethnic groups and cultures, and in different situations (Szinovacz, 2009). For example, in one study of White, African American, and Mexican American grandparents and grandchildren, the Mexican American grandparents saw their grandchildren more frequently, provided more support for the grandchildren and their parents, and had more satisfying relationships with their grandchildren (Bengtson, 1985). And in a study of three generations of families in Chicago, grandmothers had closer relationships with their children and grandchildren and gave more personal advice than grandfathers did (Hagestad, 1985).

The Changing Profile of Grandparents An increasing number of U.S. grandchildren live with their grandparents (Silverstein, 2009). In 1980, 2.3 million grandchildren lived with their grandparents, but in 2005 that figure had reached 6.1 million (U.S. Census Bureau, 2006). Divorce, adolescent pregnancies, and drug use by parents are the main reasons that grandparents are thrust

What is the changing profile of grandparents in the United States?

At the beginning of the twentieth century, the three-generation family was common, but now the four-generation family is common as well. Thus, an increasing number of grandparents are also great-grandparents. The four-generation family shown here is the Jordans—author John Santrock's mother-in-law, daughter, granddaughter, and wife.

back into the "parenting" role they thought they had shed. A recent study revealed that grandparent involvement was linked with better adjustment when it occurred in single-parent and stepparent families than in two-parent biological families (Attar-Schwartz & others, 2009).

Grandparents who are full-time caregivers for grandchildren are at elevated risk for health problems, depression, and stress (Silverstein, 2009). Caring for grandchildren is linked with these problems in part because full-time grandparent caregivers are often characterized by low-income, minority status, and by not being married (Minkler & Fuller-Thompson, 2005). Grandparents who are part-time caregivers are less likely to have the negative health portrait that full-time grandparent caregivers have. In a recent study of part-time grandparent caregivers, few negative effects on grandparents were found (Hughes & others, 2007).

As divorce and remarriage have become more common, a special concern of grandparents is visitation privileges with their grandchildren. In the last 10 to 15 years, more states have passed laws giving grandparents the right to petition a court for visitation privileges with their grandchildren, even if a parent objects. Whether such forced visitation rights for grandparents are in the child's best interest is still being debated.

Great-Grandparenting Because of increased longevity, more grandparents today than in the past are also great-grandparents. At the turn of the previous century, the three-generation family was common, but now the four-generation family is common. One contribution of great-grandparents is to transmit family history by telling their children, grandchildren, and great-grandchildren where the family came from, what their members achieved, what they endured, and how their lives changed over the years (Harris, 2002).

There has been little research on great-grandparenting. One study examined the relationship between young adults and their grandparents and great-grandparents (Roberto & Skoglund, 1996). The young adults interacted with and participated in more activities with their grandparents than with their great-grandparents. They also perceived their grandparents to have a more defined role and to be more influential in their lives than great-grandparents.

INTERGENERATIONAL RELATIONSHIPS

Family is important to most people. When 21,000 adults aged 40 to 79 in 21 countries were asked, "When you think of who you are, you think mainly of _____,"

Middle-aged and older adults around the world show a strong sense of family responsibility. A recent study of middle-aged and older adults in 21 countries revealed that the strongest intergenerational ties were in Saudi Arabia.

63 percent said "family," 9 percent said "religion," and 8 percent said "work" (HSBC Insurance, 2007). In this study, in all 21 countries, middle-aged and older adults expressed a strong feeling of responsibility between generations in their family, with the strongest intergenerational ties indicated in Saudi Arabia, India, and Turkey. More than 80 percent of the middle-aged and older adults reported that adults have a duty to care for their parents (and parents-in-law) in time of need later in life.

Adults in midlife play important roles in the lives of the young and the old (Fingerman & Birditt, 2011; Martini & Busseri, 2010). Middle-aged adults share their experience and transmit values to the younger generation. They may be launching children and experiencing the empty nest, adjusting to having grown children return home, or becoming grandparents. They also may be giving or receiving financial assistance, caring for a widowed or sick parent, or adapting to being the oldest generation after both parents have died.

Middle-aged adults have been described as the "sandwich," "squeezed," or "overload" generation because of the responsibilities they have for their adolescent and young adult children on the one hand and their aging parents on the other (Etaugh & Bridges, 2010; Pudrovska,

2009). However, an alternative view is that in the United States, a "sandwich" generation, in which the middle generation cares for both grown children and aging parents simultaneously, occurs less often than a "pivot" generation, in which the middle generation alternates attention between the demands of grown children and aging parents (Fingerman & Birditt, 2011).

Many middle-aged adults experience considerable stress when their parents become very ill and die. One survey found that when adults enter midlife, 41 percent have both parents alive, but that 77 percent leave midlife with no parents alive (Bumpass & Aquilino, 1994). A recent study revealed that middle-aged parents are more likely to provide support to their grown children than to their parents (Fingerman, Chan, & others, 2011). When middle-aged adults' parents have a disability, their support for their aging parents increases.

A valuable service that adult children can perform is to coordinate and monitor services for an aging parent who becomes disabled. This might involve locating a nursing home and monitoring its quality, procuring medical services, arranging public service assistance, and handling finances. In some cases, adult children provide direct assistance with daily living, including such activities as eating, bathing, and dressing. Even less severely impaired older adults may need help with shopping, housework, transportation, home maintenance, and bill paying.

In most cases researchers have found that relationships between aging parents and their children are usually characterized by ambivalence (Birditt, Fingerman, & Zarit, 2010; Davey & others, 2009; Fingerman & Birditt, 2011; Fingerman & others, 2008). Perceptions include love, reciprocal help, and shared values on the positive side and isolation, family conflicts and problems, abuse, neglect, and caregiver stress on the negative side.

With each new generation, personality characteristics, attitudes, and values are replicated or changed. As older family members die, their biological, intellectual, emotional, and personal legacies are carried on in the next generation. Their children become the oldest generation and their grandchildren the second generation. As adult children become middle-aged, they often develop more positive perceptions of their parents (Field, 1999). Both similarity and dissimilarity across generations are found. For example, similarity between parents and an adult child is most noticeable in religion and politics, least in gender roles, lifestyle, and work orientation.

The following studies provide further evidence of the importance of intergenerational relationships in development:

- The motivation of adult children to provide social support to their older parents was linked with earlier family experiences (Silverstein & others, 2002). Children who spent more time in shared activities with their parents and were given more financial support by them earlier in their lives provided more support to their parents when they became older.
- Children of divorce were disproportionately more likely to end their own marriage than were children from intact, never divorced families, although the transmission of divorce across generations has declined in recent years (Wolfinger, 2011).
- Adult children of divorce who were classified as securely attached were less likely to divorce in the early years of their marriage than their insecurely attached counterparts (Crowell, Treboux, & Brockmeyer, 2009).
- Parents who smoked early and often, and persisted in becoming regular smokers, were more likely to have adolescents who became smokers (Chassin & others, 2008).

The generations of living things pass in a short time, and like runners hand on the torch of life.

—LUCRETIUS
Roman Poet, 1st Century B.C.

What is the nature of intergenerational relationships?

Gender differences also characterize intergenerational relationships (Etaugh & Bridges, 2010). Women have an especially important role in connecting family relationships across generations. Women's relationships across generations are typically closer than other family bonds (Merrill, 2009). In one study, mothers and their daughters had much closer relationships during their adult years than mothers and sons, fathers and daughters, and fathers and sons (Rossi, 1989). Also in this study, married men were more involved with their wives' kin than with their own. And maternal grandmothers and maternal aunts were cited twice as often as their counterparts on the paternal side of the family as the most important or loved relative. Also, a recent study revealed that mothers' intergenerational ties were more influential for grandparent-grandchild relationships than fathers' (Monserud, 2008).

Review *Connect* Reflect

LG4 Explain other aspects of family relationships

Review

- How do siblings interact with each other? How is birth order linked with developmental outcomes?
- What is the nature of grandparenting and great-grandparenting?
- How do intergenerational relationships influence development?

Connect

- Connect what you learned about longevity in Chapter 3 to this chapter's discussion of grandparenting and great-grandparenting.

Reflect *Your Own Personal Journey of Life*

- Do you have a sibling(s)? If so, what is your relationship like? Has it changed over the years? If you don't have a sibling, how do you think your life would have been different with one or more siblings?

reach your **learning goals**

Family Processes

LG1 Describe some important family processes

Reciprocal Socialization

Family as a System

Sociocultural and Historical Influences

Multiple Developmental Trajectories

- Reciprocal socialization is socialization that is bidirectional; children socialize parents just as parents socialize children. Synchrony and scaffolding are two important types of reciprocal socialization.

- The family system consists of subsystems defined by generation, gender, and role. These subsystems interact with each other and can have direct and indirect effects on each other.

- Sociocultural and historical contexts influence families, reflecting Bronfenbrenner's concepts of macrosystem and chronosystem. Both great upheavals such as war and subtle transitions in ways of life may influence families. A major change in families in the last several decades has been the extensive immigration of Latino and Asian families into the United States.

- Adults follow one developmental trajectory and children another one. How these trajectories mesh is important for understanding timing of entry into various family tasks.

The Diversity of Adult Lifestyles

LG2 Discuss the diversity of adult lifestyles and how they influence people's lives

Single Adults

- Being single has become an increasingly prominent lifestyle. There are advantages and disadvantages to being single, autonomy being one of the advantages. Intimacy, loneliness, and finding a positive identity in a marriage-oriented society are concerns of single adults. Approximately 8 percent of 65-year-old adults have never been married. Many of them cope effectively with loneliness in old age.

Cohabiting Adults

- Cohabitation is an increasingly prevalent lifestyle for many adults that offers some advantages as well as problems. Cohabitation does not lead to greater marital happiness but rather to no differences or differences, suggesting that it is not good for a marriage. An increasing number of older adults cohabit, in many cases more for companionship than for love.

Married Adults

- Even though adults are remaining single longer and the divorce rate is high, Americans still show a strong predilection for marriage. The age at which individuals marry, expectations about what the marriage will be like, and the developmental course of marriage vary not only over time within a culture, but also across cultures. John Gottman has conducted extensive research on what makes marriages work. In his research, the following factors are among the most important for having a good marriage: establishing love maps, nurturing fondness and admiration, turning toward each other instead of away, letting your partner influence you, overcoming gridlock, and creating shared meaning. Premarital education is associated with positive relationship outcomes. The benefits of marriage include better physical and mental health and a longer life. A majority of middle-aged adults who are married say their marriage is very good or excellent. The time from retirement until death is sometimes called the final stage in the marital process. Married older adults are often happier than single older adults.

Divorced Adults

- The U.S. divorce rate increased dramatically in the twentieth century but began to decline in the 1980s. Divorce is complex and emotional. In the first year following divorce, a disequilibrium in the divorced adult's behavior occurs, but by several years after the divorce, more stability has been achieved. The divorced displaced homemaker may encounter excessive stress; however, men do not go through a divorce unscathed. There are social, financial, and physical consequences of divorce for older adults.

Remarried Adults

- Divorced adults remarry on average within four years of their divorce. Stepfamilies are complex and adjustment is difficult. Only about one-third of stepfamily couples stay remarried. Rising divorce rates, increased longevity, and better health have led to an increase in remarriage by older adults.

Gay and Lesbian Adults

- One of the most striking findings about gay and lesbian couples is how similar they are to heterosexual couples—for example, gay and lesbian couples prefer committed, long-term relationships and work to find a balance of romantic love, affection, and autonomy. There are many misconceptions about gay and lesbian adults.

Parenting

LG3 Characterize parenting and how it affects children's development

Parental Roles

- Currently, there is a trend toward having fewer children and choosing when to have children. The transition to parenting involves a great deal of adaptation for many people. A key aspect of being a competent parent is effectively managing children's lives.

Parenting Styles and Discipline

- Authoritarian, authoritative, neglectful, and indulgent are four main parenting styles. Authoritative parenting is the style most often associated with children's social competence. Physical punishment is widely used by U.S. parents, but there are a number of reasons why it is not a good choice. Coparenting can have positive effects on children's development if it is accompanied by parental warmth and cooperation. The four main types of child maltreatment are physical abuse, child neglect, sexual abuse, and emotional abuse. An understanding of child abuse requires information about cultural, familial, and community influences. Child maltreatment places the child at risk for a number of developmental problems.

Parent–Adolescent and Parent–Emerging Adult Relationships

- Adolescents seek to be independent, but secure attachment to parents is positive for development. Conflict with parents often increases in adolescence but usually is moderate rather than severe. An increasing number of emerging adults are returning home to live with their parents, often for economic reasons. Both emerging adults and their parents need to adapt when emerging adults return home to live.

Working Parents

- In general, having both parents employed full-time outside the home has not been shown to have negative effects on children. However, the nature of parents' work can affect the quality of their parenting.

Children in Divorced Families

- Overall, divorce is linked with adjustment problems in children, but not for all children. Whether parents should stay together for the sake of the children is a difficult question to answer. Family processes, such as harmony between parents, quality of parenting, and support systems, matter in the development of children of divorced parents. So does socioeconomic status.

Stepfamilies

- Children in stepparent families have more problems than their counterparts in nondivorced families. Adolescence is an especially difficult time for remarriage of parents to occur. Restabilization takes longer in stepfamilies than in divorced families.

Gay and Lesbian Parents

- Researchers have found few differences between children growing up with gay or lesbian parents and children growing up with heterosexual parents.

Adoptive Parents and Adopted Children

- Although adopted children and adolescents have more problems than their non-adopted counterparts, the vast majority of adopted children adapt effectively. When adoption occurs very early in development, the outcomes for the child are improved. Because of the dramatic changes that have occurred in adoption in recent decades, it is difficult to generalize about characteristics of the average adopted child or average adoptive family.

Other Family Relationships

LG4 Explain other aspects of family relationships

Sibling Relationships and Birth Order

- Siblings interact with each other in positive and negative ways. Birth order is related in certain ways to child characteristics, but some critics argue that birth order is not a good predictor of behavior. Sibling relationships persist over the entire life span for most adults.

Grandparenting and Great-Grandparenting

- There are different grandparent roles and styles. Grandmothers spend more time with grandchildren than grandfathers do, and the grandmother role involves greater expectations for maintaining ties across generations than the grandfather role. The profile of grandparents is changing because of factors such as divorce and remarriage. An increasing number of U.S. grandchildren live with their grandparents.. Because of increased longevity, more grandparents today are also great-grandparents. One contribution of great-grandparents is their knowledge of family history.

Intergenerational Relationships

- Family members usually maintain contact across generations. Mothers and daughters have the closest relationships. The middle-aged generation, which has been called the "sandwich" or "squeezed" generation, plays an important role in linking generations.

key **terms**

key **people**

chapter 15 · PEERS AND THE SOCIOCULTURAL WORLD

preview

The social worlds outside the family play important roles in life-span development. As we go through life, we interact with a convoy of people through peer relations, friendships, cliques, and support systems in many different cultural worlds.

Peer Relations in Childhood and Adolescence **LG1** Discuss peer relations in childhood and adolescence

- Exploring Peer Relations
- Peer Statuses
- Bullying
- Gender and Peer Relations
- Adolescent Peer Relations

As children grow older, peer relations consume increasing amounts of their time. In some cases, these relations are positive influences, in others negative.

EXPLORING PEER RELATIONS

Some important questions involving peer relations are the following: What are the functions of a child's peer group? How are peer relations and adult-child relations linked? What are some developmental changes in peer relations during childhood? What role does social cognition play in peer relations? How is emotional regulation involved in peer relations?

Functions of Peer Groups **Peers** are individuals of about the same age or maturity level. Peer groups provide a source of information and comparison about the world outside the family. Children receive feedback about their abilities from their peer group. They evaluate what they do in terms of whether it is better than, as good as, or worse than what other children do. It is hard to do this comparison at home because siblings are usually older or younger.

Both Jean Piaget (1932) and Harry Stack Sullivan (1953) stressed that children learn reciprocity through interaction with their peers. Children explore the meanings of fairness and justice by working through disagreements with peers. They also learn to be keen observers of peers' interests and perspectives in order to smoothly integrate themselves into ongoing peer activities.

Of course, peer influences can be negative as well as positive (Dishion & Tipsord, 2011; Hymel & others, 2011). Being rejected or overlooked by peers leads some children to feel lonely or hostile. Further, rejection and neglect by peers are related to an individual's subsequent mental health and criminal problems. Withdrawn children who are rejected by peers or victimized and lonely are at risk for depression. Children who are aggressive with their peers are at risk for developing a number of problems, including delinquency and dropping out of school (Prinstein, Brechwald, & Cohen, 2011). Peers can also undermine parental values and control (Masten, 2005).

Keep in mind that the influences of peer experiences vary according to the type of peer experience, developmental status, and outcome (such as achievement, delinquency, depression, and so on) (Brechwald & Prinstein, 2011; Brown & others, 2008; Hartup, 2008). "Peers" and "peer group" are global concepts. For example, "peer group" might refer to acquaintances, clique, neighborhood associates, a friendship network, or an activity group (Brown, 1999).

What are some functions of peer group?

peers Individuals who share the same age or maturity level.

Adult-Child and Peer Relations Parents may influence their children's peer relations in many ways, both direct and indirect (Reich & Vandell, 2011). Parents affect their children's peer relations through their interactions with their children, how they manage their children's lives, and the opportunities they provide their children. A recent study revealed that warmth, advice giving, and provision of opportunities by mothers and fathers were linked to children's social competence (high prosocial behavior, low aggression), and subsequently to social acceptance (being well liked by peers and teachers) one year later (McDowell & Parke, 2009).

Basic lifestyle decisions by parents—their choices of neighborhoods, churches, schools, and their own friends—largely determine the pool from which their children select possible friends. These choices in turn affect which children their children meet, their purpose in interacting, and eventually which children become their friends.

Researchers also have found that children's peer relations are linked to attachment security and parents' marital quality (Ross & Howe, 2009). Early attachments to caregivers provide a connection to children's peer relations not only by creating a secure base from which children can explore social relationships beyond the family but also by conveying a working model of relationships (Hartup, 2009).

Do these results indicate that children's peer relations always are wedded to parent-child relationships? Although parent-child relationships influence children's subsequent peer relations, children also learn other modes of relating through their relationships with peers. For example, rough-and-tumble play occurs mainly with other children, not in parent-child interaction. In times of stress, children often turn to parents, not peers, for support. In parent-child relationships, children learn how to relate to authority figures. With their peers, children are likely to interact on a much more equal basis and to learn a mode of relating based on mutual influence.

Some researchers have found that parents and adolescents perceive that parents have little authority over adolescents' choices in some areas but more authority over choices in other areas. For example, Judith Smetana's (2002, 2008, 2011a, b) research has revealed that both parents and adolescents view peer relations as an arena in which parents have little authority to dictate adolescents' choices, in contrast with moral, religious, and educational arenas in which parents are perceived to have more authority.

Peer Contexts Peer interaction is influenced by contexts, which can include the type of peer the individual interacts with—such as an acquaintance, a crowd, a clique, a friend, a romantic partner—and the situation or location where they interact—such as a school, neighborhood, community center, dance, religious setting, sporting event, and so on, as well as the culture in which the individual lives (Brown & Larson, 2009; Dishion & Tipsord, 2011; Ladd, Kochenderfer-Ladd, & Rydell, 2011; Rubin & others, 2011). As they interact with peers in these various contexts,

developmental **connection**

Attachment. Securely attached infants use the caregiver as a secure base from which to explore their environment. Chapter 10, p. 321

What are some examples of how social contexts and individual difference factors influence adolescents' peer relations?

individuals are likely to encounter different messages and different opportunities to engage in adaptive or maladaptive behavior that can influence their development (Brechwald & Prinstein, 2011).

Individual Difference Factors Individual differences among peers also are important considerations in understanding peer relations (Brechwald & Prinstein, 2011). Among the wide range of individual differences that can affect peer relations are personality traits, such as how shy or outgoing an individual is. For example, a very shy individual is more likely than a gregarious individual to be neglected by peers and have anxiety about introducing himself or herself to new peers. One individual difference factor that has been found to impair peer relations is the trait of negative emotionality, which involves a relatively low threshold for experiencing anger, fear, anxiety, and irritation. For example, one recent study revealed that adolescents characterized by negative emotionality tended to engage in negative interpersonal behavior when interacting with a friend or a romantic partner (Hatton & others, 2008). Other individual differences include how open the individual is to peer influence and the status/power of the individual and the status/power of the other peer or peer group (Brown & others, 2008). Being in a subordinate social position decreases the likelihood the individual will influence other peers but increases the probability that the individual will be open to peer influence.

Developmental Changes in Childhood Around the age of 3, children already prefer to spend time with same-sex rather than opposite-sex playmates, and this preference increases in early childhood. During these same years, the frequency of peer interaction, both positive and negative, picks up considerably (Hartup, 1983). Although aggressive interaction and rough-and-tumble play increase, the proportion of aggressive exchanges, compared with friendly exchanges, decreases. Many preschool children spend considerable time in peer interaction just playing, conversing with peers, trying out roles, and negotiating rules (Rubin, Bukowski, & Parker, 2006). In early childhood, children distinguish between friends and nonfriends (Howes, 2009). For most young children, a friend is someone to play with. Young preschool children are more likely than older children to have friends of different gender and ethnicity (Howes, 2009).

What are some developmental changes in peer relations during childhood?

As children enter the elementary school years, reciprocity becomes especially important in peer interchanges. Children play games, function in groups, and cultivate friendships. Until about 12 years of age, their preference for same-sex groups increases. The amount of time children spend in peer interaction also rises during middle and late childhood and adolescence. Researchers estimate that the percentage of time spent in social interaction with peers increases from approximately 10 percent at 2 years of age to more than 30 percent in middle and late childhood (Rubin, Bukowski, & Parker, 2006). Other changes in peer relations as children move through middle and late childhood involve an increase in the size of their peer group and peer interaction that is less closely supervised by adults (Rubin, Bukowski, & Parker, 2006).

Social Cognition A boy accidentally trips and knocks another boy's soft drink out of his hand. That boy misinterprets the encounter as hostile, which leads him to retaliate aggressively against the boy who tripped. Through repeated encounters of this kind, the aggressive boy's classmates come to perceive him as habitually acting in inappropriate ways.

What are some aspects of social cognition that are involved in getting along with peers?

◄ - - - - - - - - - - - - - -

developmental connection

Social Cognition. Social cognition refers to the processes involved in understanding the world around us, especially how we think and reason about others. Chapter 11, p. 341

This example demonstrates the importance of social cognition—thoughts about social matters, such as the aggressive boy's interpretation of an encounter as hostile and his classmates' perception of his behavior as inappropriate (Fontaine & others, 2010). Children's social cognition about their peers becomes increasingly important for understanding peer relationships in middle and late childhood. Of special interest are the ways in which children process information about peer relations and their social knowledge (Lansford & others, 2010).

Kenneth Dodge (1983) argues that children go through five steps in processing information about their social world. They decode social cues, interpret, search for a response, select an optimal response, and enact. Dodge has found that aggressive boys are more likely to perceive another child's actions as hostile when the child's intention is ambiguous. And, when aggressive boys search for cues to determine a peer's intention, they respond more rapidly, less efficiently, and less reflectively than do nonaggressive children. These are among the social cognitive factors believed to be involved in children's conflicts.

Social knowledge also is involved in children's ability to get along with peers (Lewis & Carpendale, 2011). They need to know what goals to pursue in poorly defined or ambiguous situations, how to initiate and maintain a social bond, and what scripts to follow to get other children to be their friends. For example, as part of the script for getting friends, it helps to know that making positive comments to the peer will make the peer like the child more.

Regulation of Emotion and Peer Relations Emotions play a strong role in determining whether a child's peer relationships are successful (Bukowski, Buhrmester, & Underwood, 2011; Denham & others, 2011). Moody and emotionally negative children are often rejected by their peers, whereas emotionally positive children are often popular (Stocker & Dunn, 1990). The ability to modulate one's emotions is an important skill that benefits children in their relationships with peers (Denham & others, 2011).

PEER STATUSES

Which children are likely to be popular with their peers and which ones are disliked? Developmentalists address these and similar questions by examining sociometric status, a term that describes the extent to which children are liked or disliked by their peer group (Cillessen & Bellmore, 2011; Hymel & others, 2011). Sociometric status is typically assessed by asking children to rate how much they like or dislike each of their classmates. Or it may be assessed by asking children to nominate the children they like the most and those they like the least.

Developmentalists have distinguished five peer statuses (Wentzel & Asher, 1995):

- **Popular children** are frequently nominated as a best friend and are rarely disliked by their peers.
- **Average children** receive an average number of both positive and negative nominations from their peers.
- **Neglected children** are infrequently nominated as a best friend but are not disliked by their peers.
- **Rejected children** are infrequently nominated as someone's best friend and are actively disliked by their peers.
- **Controversial children** are frequently nominated both as someone's best friend and as being disliked.

Popular children have a number of social skills that contribute to their being well liked (Asher & McDonald, 2009). Researchers have found that popular children give out reinforcements, listen carefully, maintain open lines of communication with peers, are happy, control their negative emotions, show enthusiasm and concern for others, and are self-confident without being conceited (Hartup, 1983; Rubin, Bukowski, & Parker, 2006).

Neglected children engage in low rates of interaction with their peers and are often described as shy by peers. The goal of many training programs for neglected children is to help them attract attention from their peers in positive ways and to hold that attention by asking questions, by listening in a warm and friendly way, and by saying things about themselves that relate to the peers' interests. They also are taught to enter groups more effectively.

What are some statuses that children have with their peers?

Rejected children often have more serious adjustment problems than those who are neglected. One study found that in kindergarten, children who were rejected by their peers were less likely to engage in classroom participation, more likely to express a desire to avoid school, and more likely to report being lonely than children who were accepted by their peers (Buhs & Ladd, 2002). The combination of being rejected by peers and being aggressive especially forecasts problems (Dishion & Piehler, 2009; Hymel & others, 2011).

John Coie (2004, pp. 252–253) gave three reasons why aggressive peer-rejected boys have problems in social relationships:

- "First, the rejected, aggressive boys are more impulsive and have problems sustaining attention. As a result, they are more likely to be disruptive of ongoing activities in the classroom and in focused group play.
- Second, rejected, aggressive boys are more emotionally reactive. They are aroused to anger more easily and probably have more difficulty calming down once aroused. Because of this they are more prone to become angry at peers and attack them verbally and physically. . . .
- Third, rejected children have fewer social skills in making friends and maintaining positive relationships with peers."

Not all rejected children are aggressive (Rubin & others, 2011). Although aggression and its related characteristics of impulsiveness and disruptiveness underlie rejection about half the time, approximately 10 to 20 percent of rejected children are shy.

> Peer rejection contributes to subsequent problems of adaptation, including antisocial behavior.
>
> —**JOHN COIE**
> *Contemporary Psychologist, Duke University*

popular children Children who are frequently nominated as a best friend and are rarely disliked by their peers.

average children Children who receive an average number of both positive and negative nominations from their peers.

neglected children Children who are infrequently nominated as a best friend but are not disliked by their peers.

rejected children Children who are infrequently nominated as a best friend and are actively disliked by their peers.

controversial children Children who are frequently nominated both as someone's best friend and as being disliked.

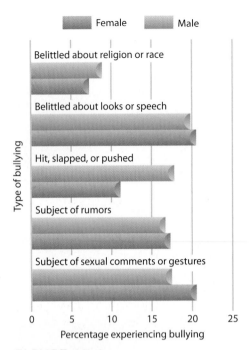

Female   Male

Belittled about religion or race

Belittled about looks or speech

Hit, slapped, or pushed

Subject of rumors

Subject of sexual comments or gestures

Type of bullying

0   5   10   15   20   25

Percentage experiencing bullying

FIGURE **15.1**

BULLYING BEHAVIORS AMONG U.S. YOUTH.
This graph shows the type of bullying most often experienced by U.S. youth. The percentages reflect the extent to which bullied students said that they had experienced a particular type of bullying. In terms of gender, note that when they were bullied, boys were more likely to be hit, slapped, or pushed than girls were.

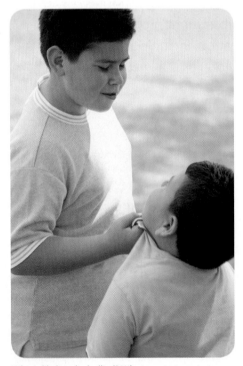

Who is likely to be bullied? What are some outcomes of bullying?

How can rejected children be trained to interact more effectively with their peers? Rejected children may be taught to more accurately assess whether the intentions of their peers are negative (Fontaine & others, 2010). They may be asked to engage in role playing or to discuss hypothetical situations involving negative encounters with peers, such as when a peer cuts into a line ahead of them. In some programs, children are shown videotapes of appropriate peer interaction and asked to draw lessons from what they have seen (Ladd, Buhs, & Troop, 2004).

BULLYING

Significant numbers of students are victimized by bullies (Espelage, Holt, & Poteat, 2010; Salmivalli, Peets, & Hodges, 2011). In a national survey of more than 15,000 students in grades 6 through 10, nearly one of every three students said that they had experienced occasional or frequent involvement as a victim or perpetrator in bullying (Nansel & others, 2001). In this study, bullying was defined as verbal or physical behavior intended to disturb someone less powerful (see Figure 15.1). Boys are more likely to be bullies than girls, but gender differences regarding victims of boys is less clear (Salmivalli & Peets, 2009).

Who is likely to be bullied? In the study just described, boys and younger middle school students were most likely to be affected (Nansel & others, 2001). Children who said they were bullied reported more loneliness and difficulty in making friends, while those who did the bullying were more likely to have low grades and to smoke and drink alcohol. Researchers have found that anxious, socially withdrawn, and aggressive children are often the victims of bullying (Hanish & Guerra, 2004). Anxious and socially withdrawn children may be victimized because they are nonthreatening and unlikely to retaliate if bullied, whereas aggressive children may be the targets of bullying because their behavior is irritating to bullies (Rubin, Bukowski, & Parker, 2006).

Social contexts also influence bullying (Schwartz & others, 2010). Recent research indicates that 70 to 80 percent of victims and their bullies are in the same school classroom (Salmivalli & Peets, 2009). Classmates are often aware of bullying incidents and in many cases witness bullying. The larger social context of the peer group plays an important role in bullying (Salmivalli, Peets, & Hodges, 2011). In many cases, bullies torment victims to gain higher status in the peer group and bullies need others to witness their power displays. Many bullies are not rejected by the peer group. In one study, bullies were only rejected by peers for whom they were a potential threat (Veenstra & others, 2010). In another study, bullies often affiliated with each other or in some cases maintained their position in the popular peer group (Witvliet & others, 2010).

What are the outcomes of bullying? One study indicated that bullies and their victims in adolescence were more likely to experience depression and engage in suicide ideation and attempt suicide than their counterparts who were not involved in bullying (Brunstein Klomek & others, 2007). A recent meta-analysis of 33 studies revealed a small but significant link between peer victimization and lower academic achievement (Nakamoto & Schwartz, 2010). Another study revealed that bullies, victims, or those who were both bullies and victims had more health problems (such as headaches, dizziness, sleep problems, and anxiety) than their counterparts who were not involved in bullying (Srabstein & others, 2006). Recently, bullying has been linked to suicides in which an 8-year-old jumped out of a two-story building in Houston; a 13-year-old boy hanged himself in Houston; and teenagers harassed a girl so mercilessly that she killed herself in Massachusetts.

What leads some children to become bullies and others to fall victim to bullying? To read further about bullying, see the *Connecting with Research* interlude.

Extensive interest is being directed to preventing and treating bullying and victimization (Guerra & Williams, 2010; Salmivalli, Peets, & Hodges, 2011; Singh,

How Are Perspective Taking and Moral Motivation Linked to Bullying?

A recent study explored the roles that perspective taking and moral motivation play in the lives of bullies, bully-victims, victims, and prosocial children (Gasser & Keller, 2009):

- *Bullies* are highly aggressive toward other children but are not victims of bullying.
- *Bully-victims* not only are highly aggressive toward other children but also are the recipients of other children's bullying.
- *Victims* are passive, non-aggressive respondents to bullying.
- *Prosocial children* engage in such positive behaviors as sharing, helping, comforting, and empathizing.

Teacher and peer ratings in 34 classrooms of 7- and 8-year-old students were used to classify 212 boys and girls into the aforementioned four categories. On a five-point scale (from never to several times a week), teachers rated (1) how often the child bullied others and (2) how often the child was bullied. The ratings focused on three types of bullying and being victimized: physical, verbal, and excluding others. On a four-point scale (from not applicable to very clearly applicable), teachers also rated children's prosocial behavior on three items: "willingly shares with others," "comforts others if necessary," and "empathizes with others." Peer ratings assessed children's nominations of which children in the classroom acted as bullies, were victimized by bullies, and engaged in prosocial behavior. Combining the teacher and peer ratings after eliminating those that did not agree on which children were bullies, victims, or prosocial children, the final sample consisted of 49 bullies, 80 bully-victims, 33 victims, and 50 prosocial children.

Children's perspective-taking skills were assessed using theory of mind tasks, and moral motivation was examined by interviewing children about aspects of right and wrong in stories about children's transgressions. In one theory of mind task, children were tested to see whether they understood that people may have false beliefs about another individual. In another theory of mind task, children were assessed to determine whether they understood that people sometimes hide their emotions by showing emotions that differ from what they really feel. A moral interview also was conducted in which children were told four moral transgression stories (with content about being unwilling to share with a classmate, stealing sweets from a classmate, hiding a victim's shoes, and verbally bullying a victim) and then asked to judge whether the acts were right or wrong and how the participants in the stories likely felt.

The results of the study indicated that only bully-victims—but not bullies—were deficient in perspective taking. Further analysis revealed that both aggressive groups of children—bullies and bully-victims—had a deficiency in moral motivation. The analyses were consistent with a portrait of bullies as socially competent and knowledgeable in terms of perspective-taking skills and being able to effectively interact with peers. However, bullies use this social knowledge for their own manipulative purposes. The analysis also confirmed the picture of the bully as being morally insensitive.

How can researchers ensure that results that might help prevent bullying are properly applied in school settings (and not, for instance, used to label potential bullies or segregate potential victims)?

Orpinas, & Horne, 2010; Vernberg & Biggs, 2010). A research review revealed mixed results for school-based intervention (Vreeman & Carroll, 2007). School-based interventions vary greatly, ranging from involving the whole school in an antibullying campaign to providing individualized social skills training. One of the most promising bullying intervention programs has been created by Dan Olweus. This program focuses on 6- to 15-year-olds with the goal of decreasing opportunities and rewards for bullying. School staff are instructed in ways to improve peer relations and make schools safer. When properly implemented, the program reduces bullying by 30 to 70 percent (Olweus, 2003).

GENDER AND PEER RELATIONS

We know that boys are far more likely to be involved in bullying than girls are. Indeed, there is increasing evidence that gender plays an important role in peer relations, as we saw in Chapter 12 (Blakemore, Berenbaum, & Liben, 2009; Bukowski, Buhrmester, & Underwood, 2011; Coyne, Nelson, & Underwood, 2011).

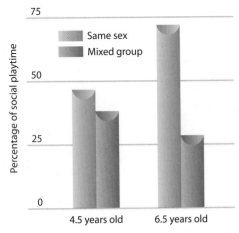

FIGURE **15.2**

DEVELOPMENTAL CHANGES IN PERCENTAGE OF TIME SPENT IN SAME-SEX AND MIXED-GROUP SETTINGS. Observations of children show that they are more likely to play in same-sex than mixed-sex groups. This tendency increases between 4 and 6 years of age.

Gender influences the composition of children's groups, their size, and the interaction within groups (Maccoby, 2002):

- *Gender composition.* Around the age of 3, children already prefer to spend time with same-sex playmates. From 4 to 12 years of age, this preference for playing in same-sex groups increases (see Figure 15.2).
- *Group size.* From about 5 years of age onward, boys tend to associate in larger clusters than girls do. Girls are more likely than boys to play in groups of two or three.
- *Interaction in same-sex groups.* Boys are more likely to participate in organized group games than girls are. They also are more likely to engage in rough-and-tumble play, competition, conflict, ego displays, risk taking, and dominance seeking. And, more than girls' groups, boys' groups seek to attain a group goal (Benenson, Apostolaris, & Parnass, 1997). By contrast, girls are more likely to engage in "collaborative discourse."

ADOLESCENT PEER RELATIONS

Unlike children, whose groups are usually informal collections of friends or neighborhood acquaintances, adolescents are often members of formal and heterogeneous groups, including adolescents who may not be friends and neighborhood acquaintances. Adolescent groups are also more likely than child groups to include boys and girls.

Do these and other peer groups matter? Yes, they do. Researchers have found that the standards of peer groups and the influence of crowds and cliques become increasingly important during adolescence (Brown & others, 2008).

Peer Pressure Young adolescents conform more to peer standards than children do. Around the eighth and ninth grades, conformity to peers—especially to their antisocial standards—peaks (Brechwald & Prinstein, 2011; Brown & Larson, 2009). At this point, adolescents are most likely to go along with a peer to steal hubcaps off a car, draw graffiti on a wall, or steal cosmetics from a store counter. One study found that U.S. adolescents are more likely than Japanese adolescents to put pressure on their peers to resist parental influence (Rothbaum & others, 2000). Adolescents are more likely to conform to their peers when they are uncertain about their social identity and when they are in the presence of someone they perceive to have higher status than they do (Prinstein & Dodge, 2010; Prinstein & others, 2009).

What characterizes peer pressure in adolesence? What characterizes adolescent cliques? How are they different from crowds?

cliques Small groups that range from 2 to 12 individuals and average about 5 to 6 individuals. Clique members usually are of the same age and same sex and often engage in similar activities, such as belonging to a club or participating in a sport.

crowds The crowd is a larger group than a clique. Adolescents usually are members of a crowd based on reputation and may not spend much time together. Many crowds are defined by the activities in which adolescents engage.

Cliques and Crowds Cliques and crowds assume more important roles in the lives of adolescents than in the lives of children (Brown & Dietz, 2009). **Cliques** are small groups that range from 2 to about 12 individuals and average about 5 to 6 individuals. The clique members are usually of the same sex and about the same age.

Cliques can form because adolescents engage in similar activities, such as being in a club or on a sports team. Some cliques also form because of friendship. Several adolescents may form a clique because they have spent time with each other, share mutual interests, and enjoy each other's company. Not necessarily friends, they often develop a friendship if they stay in the clique. What do adolescents do in cliques? They share ideas and hang out together. Often they develop an in-group identity in which they believe that their clique is better than other cliques.

Crowds are larger than cliques and less personal. Adolescents are usually members of a crowd based on reputation, and they may or may not spend much time together. Many crowds are defined by the activities adolescents engage in (such as "jocks" who are good at sports or "druggies" who take drugs).

Review *Connect* Reflect

LG1 Discuss peer relations in childhood and adolescence

Review

- What are peers, and what are the functions of peer groups? What are Piaget's and Sullivan's views on peers? How are the worlds of parents and peers distinct but coordinated? What is the developmental course of peer relations in childhood? How is social cognition involved in peer relations? What role does emotional regulation play in peer relations?
- Describe five types of peer statuses.
- What is the nature of bullying?
- How is gender involved in children's peer relations?
- How do adolescent peer groups differ from child peer groups? What are peer pressure and conformity like in adolescence? How are cliques and crowds involved in adolescent development? What are some cultural variations in adolescent peer relations?

Connect

- In Chapter 13 you read that most developmentalists agree that peers play an important role in the development of moral reasoning. Of the five peer status groups you learned about in this section of the chapter, in which one(s) do you think children would have the least opportunity to fully develop their moral reasoning capacities and why?

Reflect *Your Own Personal Journey of Life*

- Think back to your childhood and adolescent years. Which peer status would you use to describe yourself? How important do you think your peer status was in your development?

Friendship

LG2 Explain the role of friendship through the life span

Functions of Friendship

Friendship During Adolescence and Emerging Adulthood

Friendship During Childhood

Adult Friendship

The world of peers is one of varying acquaintances; we interact with some people we barely know, and with others we know well, every day. It is to the latter type—friends—that we now turn.

FUNCTIONS OF FRIENDSHIP

Why are friendships important? They serve the following functions (Gottman & Parker, 1987):

- *Companionship*. Friendship provides a familiar partner and playmate, someone who is willing to spend time with us and join in collaborative activities.
- *Stimulation*. Friendship provides interesting information, excitement, and amusement.
- *Ego support*. Friendship provides the expectation of support, encouragement, and feedback, which helps us maintain an impression of ourselves as competent, attractive, and worthwhile individuals.
- *Social comparison*. Friendship provides information about where we stand vis-à-vis others and how we are doing.
- *Affection and intimacy*. Friendship provides a warm, close, trusting relationship with another individual. **Intimacy in friendships** is characterized by self-disclosure and the sharing of private thoughts. Research reveals that intimate friendships may not appear until early adolescence (Berndt & Perry, 1990).

intimacy in friendship Self-disclosure and the sharing of private thoughts.

Appropriate and Inappropriate Strategies for Making Friends

Here are some strategies that adults can recommend to children and adolescents for making friends (Wentzel, 1997):

- *Initiate interaction.* Learn about a friend: Ask for his or her name, age, favorite activities. Use these prosocial overtures: Introduce yourself, start a conversation, and invite him or her to do things.
- *Be nice.* Show kindness, be considerate, and compliment the other person.
- *Engage in prosocial behavior.* Be honest and trustworthy: Tell the truth, keep promises. Be generous, share, and be cooperative.
- *Show respect for yourself and others.* Have good manners, be polite and courteous, and listen to what others have to say. Have a positive attitude and personality.
- *Provide social support.* Show you care.

And here are some inappropriate strategies for making friends that adults can recommend that children and adolescents avoid using (Wentzel, 1997):

- *Be psychologically aggressive.* Show disrespect and have bad manners. Use others, be uncooperative, don't share, ignore others, gossip, and spread rumors.
- *Present yourself negatively.* Be self-centered, snobby, conceited, and jealous; show off, care only about yourself. Be mean, have a bad attitude, be angry, throw temper tantrums, and start trouble.
- *Behave antisocially.* Be physically aggressive, yell at others, pick on them, make fun of them, be dishonest, tell secrets, and break promises.

These suggestions were developed for adults to recommend to children. Do you think there is any period of the life span in which they would not be appropriate? Are some more effective in some periods of the life span than in others? If so, which ones and why?

FRIENDSHIP DURING CHILDHOOD

Children's friendships are typically characterized by similarity (referred to as homophily, the tendency to associate with similar others). Similarity is a central aspect of friendship that may or may not be beneficial (Prinstein & Dodge, 2008). Throughout childhood, friends are more similar than dissimilar in terms of age, sex, ethnicity, and many other factors. Friends often have similar attitudes toward school, similar educational aspirations, and closely aligned achievement orientations.

Although having friends can be a developmental advantage, not all friendships are alike (Bukowski, Buhrmester, & Underwood, 2011; Erath & others, 2010). People differ in the company they keep—that is, who their friends are. Developmental advantages occur when children have friends who are socially skilled, supportive, and oriented toward academic achievement (Crosnoe & others, 2008). However, it is not developmentally advantageous to have coercive, conflict-ridden, and poor-quality friendships (Hartup, 2009). To read about strategies for helping children develop friendships, see the *Connecting Development to Life* interlude.

FRIENDSHIP DURING ADOLESCENCE AND EMERGING ADULTHOOD

How are adolescent friendships different from childhood friendships? What characterizes friendship in emerging adulthood?

What characterizes children's friendships?

Adolescence For most children, being popular with their peers is a strong motivator. The focus of their peer relations is on being liked by classmates and being included in games or lunchroom conversations. Beginning in early adolescence, however, teenagers typically prefer to have a smaller number of friendships that are more intense and intimate than those of young children.

Harry Stack Sullivan (1953) has been the most influential theorist in the study of adolescent friendships. Sullivan argued that friends are also important in shaping the development of children and adolescents. Everyone, said Sullivan, has basic social needs, such as the need for secure attachment, playful companionship, social acceptance, intimacy, and sexual relations. Whether or not these needs are fulfilled largely determines our emotional well-being. For example, if the need for playful companionship goes unmet, then we become bored and depressed; if the need for social acceptance is not met, we suffer a lowered sense of self-worth.

During adolescence, said Sullivan, friends become increasingly important in meeting social needs. In particular, Sullivan argued that the need for intimacy intensifies during early adolescence, motivating teenagers to seek out close friends. If adolescents fail to forge such close friendships, they often experience loneliness and a reduced sense of self-worth.

Many of Sullivan's ideas have withstood the test of time. For example, adolescents report disclosing intimate and personal information to their friends more often than do younger children (Buhrmester, 1998) (see Figure 15.3). Adolescents also say they depend more on friends than on parents to satisfy their needs for companionship, reassurance of worth, and intimacy. The ups and downs of experiences with friends shape adolescents' well-being (Berndt, 2002).

Are the friendships of adolescent girls more intimate than the friendships of adolescent boys? Girls' friendships in adolescence are more likely to focus on intimacy; boys' friendships tend to emphasize power and excitement (Blakemore, Berenbaum, & Liben, 2009; Rose & Smith, 2009). Boys may discourage one another from openly disclosing their problems because self-disclosure is not considered masculine (Maccoby, 1998).

A recent study of third- through ninth-graders, though, revealed that one aspect of girls' social support in friendship may have costs as well as benefits (Rose, Carlson, & Waller, 2007). In the study, girls' co-rumination (as reflected in excessively discussing problems) predicted not only an increase in positive friendship quality but also an increase in further co-rumination as well as an increase in depressive and anxiety symptoms. One implication of the research is that some girls who are vulnerable to developing internalized problems may go undetected because they have supportive friendships.

The study just described indicates that the characteristics of an adolescent's friends can influence whether the friends have a positive or negative influence on the adolescent. Consider a recent study which revealed that friends' grade-point average was an important positive attribute (Cook, Deng, & Morgano, 2007). Friends' grade-point average was a consistent predictor of positive school achievement and also was linked to a lower level of negative behavior in areas such as drug abuse and acting out. Another recent study found that taking math courses in high school, especially for girls, was strongly linked to the achievement of their best friends (Crosnoe & others, 2008). And as we saw in Chapter 13, having delinquent peers and friends greatly increases the risk of becoming delinquent (Bukowski, Motzoi, & Meyer, 2009). Further, not having a close relationship with a best friend, having less contact with friends, having friends who are depressed, and experiencing peer rejection all increase depressive tendencies in adolescents (Brendgen & others, 2010).

Although most adolescents develop friendships with individuals who are close to their own age, some adolescents become best friends with younger or older individuals. Do older friends encourage adolescents to engage in delinquent behavior or early sexual behavior? Adolescents who interact with older youth do engage in these behaviors more frequently, but it is not known whether the older youth guide younger adolescents toward deviant behavior or whether the younger adolescents

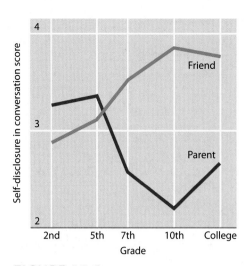

FIGURE **15.3**

DEVELOPMENTAL CHANGES IN SELF-DISCLOSING CONVERSATIONS. Self-disclosing conversations with friends increased dramatically in adolescence while declining in an equally dramatic fashion with parents. However, self-disclosing conversations with parents began to pick up somewhat during the college years. The measure of self-disclosure involved a 5-point rating scale completed by the children and youth with a higher score representing greater self-disclosure. The data shown represent the means for each age group.

were already prone to deviant behavior before they developed the friendship with the older youth (Billy, Rodgers, & Udry, 1984). A study also revealed that over time from the sixth through tenth grades girls were more likely to have older male friends, which places some girls on a developmental trajectory for engaging in problem behavior (Poulin & Pedersen, 2007).

Emerging Adulthood   Many aspects of friendship are the same in emerging adulthood as they were in adolescence. One difference was found, however, in a longitudinal study (Collins & van Dulmen, 2006). Close relationships—between friends, family members, and romantic partners—were more integrated and similar in emerging adulthood than they were in adolescence. Also in this study, the number of friendships declined from the end of adolescence through emerging adulthood.

Another research study indicated that best friendships often decline in satisfaction and commitment in the first year of college (Oswald & Clark, 2003). In this study, maintaining communication with high school friends and keeping the same best friends across the transition to college lessened the decline.

> A man's growth is seen in the successive choirs of his friends.
>
> —RALPH WALDO EMERSON
> *American Author and Poet, 19th Century*

ADULT FRIENDSHIP

As in childhood, adult friends tend to be similar in a number of ways. Among the similarities in friendship during the adult years are occupational status, ethnicity, age, marital status, income, education, gender, and religion (Rawlins, 2009).

Gender Differences   As in the childhood and adolescent years, there are gender differences in adult friendships. Women have more close friends than men do, and their friendships are more intimate (Wood, 2011, 2012). When adult female friends get together, they often talk, whereas adult male friends are more likely to engage in activities, especially outdoors. Thus, the adult male pattern of friendship often involves keeping one's distance while sharing useful information. When women talk with their friends, they expect to be able to express their feelings, reveal their weaknesses, and discuss their problems. They anticipate that their friends will listen at length and be sympathetic. In contrast, men are less likely to talk about their weaknesses with their friends, and they want practical solutions to their problems rather than sympathy (Tannen, 1990). Also, adult male friendships are more competitive than those of women (Sharkey, 1993). For example, male friends disagree with each other more. Keep in mind, however, that these differences in same-sex adult friendship tend to be small (Sabini, 1995).

<-- - - - - - - - - -

developmental connection

Gender. Deborah Tannen emphasizes gender differences in report talk and rapport talk. Chapter 12, p. 383

How is adult friendship different among female friends, male friends, and cross-gender friends?

What about female-male friendship? Cross-gender friendships are more common among adults than among elementary school children, but not as common as same-gender friendships (Wood, 2011, 2012). Cross-gender friendships can provide both opportunities and problems. The opportunities involve learning more about common feelings and interests and shared characteristics, as well as acquiring knowledge and understanding of beliefs and activities that historically have been typical of the other gender.

Problems can arise in cross-gender friendships because of different expectations. For example, a woman might expect sympathy from a male friend but might receive a directive solution rather than a shoulder to cry on (Tannen, 1990). Another problem that can plague adult cross-gender friendship is unclear sexual boundaries, which can produce tension and confusion (Swain, 1992).

Friendship in Late Adulthood In early adulthood, friendship networks expand as new social connections are made away from home. In late adulthood, new friendships are less likely to be forged, although some adults do seek out new friendships, especially following the death of a spouse (Zettel-Watson & Rook, 2009).

Aging expert Laura Carstensen and her colleagues (1998, 2009; Carstensen, Mikels, & Mather, 2006; Charles & Carstensen, 2010) concluded that people choose close friends over new friends as they grow older. And as long as they have several close people in their network, they seem content, says Carstensen. Supporting Carstensen's view, recall the study described in Chapter 10 in which, compared with younger adults, older adults said they tended to experience less intense positive emotions with new friends and equal levels of positive emotions with established friends (Charles & Piazza, 2007) (see Figure 15.4).

The following three studies document the importance of friendship in older adults:

- Friendships were more important than family relationships in predicting mental health in adults 60 years and older (Fiori, Antonucci, & Cortina, 2006).
- Older adults 75 years of age and older with close ties with friends were less likely to die across a seven-year age span (Rasulo, Christensen, & Tomassini, 2005). The findings were stronger for women than for men.
- Unmarried older adults embedded in a friend-focused network fared better physically and psychologically than unmarried older adults in a restricted network with little friend contact (Fiori, Smith, & Antonucci, 2007).

FIGURE 15.4

HAPPINESS OF YOUNGER ADULTS AND OLDER ADULTS WITH NEW AND ESTABLISHED FRIENDS. *Note:* The happiness scale ranged from 0 to 6 with participants rating how intensely they experienced happiness (0 = not at all, 6 = extremely intense). Older adults mean age 71; younger adults mean age 23.

What are some characteristics of older adults' friendships?

Play and Leisure **LG3** Describe the developmental aspects of play and leisure

Childhood   Adolescence   Adulthood

Peers and friends often engage in play and enjoy leisure activities together. Let's explore the developmental aspects of play and leisure.

CHILDHOOD

An extensive amount of peer interaction during childhood involves play; however, social play is but one type of play. **Play** is a pleasurable activity that is engaged in for its own sake.

Play's Functions Play is an important aspect of the child's development (Lillard, Pinkham, & Smith, 2011; Power, 2011). Theorists have focused on different aspects of play and highlighted a long list of functions.

According to Freud and Erikson, play helps the child master anxieties and conflicts. Because tensions are relieved in play, the child can better cope with life's problems. Play permits the child to work off excess physical energy and to release pent-up tensions. Therapists use **play therapy** both to allow the child to work off frustrations and to analyze the child's conflicts and ways of coping with them. Children may feel less threatened and be more likely to express their true feelings in the context of play.

Piaget (1962) maintained that play advances children's cognitive development. At the same time, he said that children's cognitive development *constrains* the way they play. Play permits children to practice their competencies and skills in a relaxed, pleasurable way. Piaget thought that cognitive structures need to be exercised, and play provides the perfect setting for this exercise. For example, children who have just learned to add or multiply begin to play with numbers in different ways as they perfect these operations, laughing as they do so.

Vygotsky (1962) also considered play to be an excellent setting for cognitive development. He was especially interested in the symbolic and make-believe aspects of play, as when a child substitutes a stick for a horse and rides the stick as if it were a horse. For young children, the imaginary situation is real. Parents should encourage such imaginary play, because it advances the child's cognitive development, especially creative thought. Both Piaget and Vygotsky described play as the work of the child.

Daniel Berlyne (1960) described play as exciting and pleasurable in itself because it satisfies our exploratory drive. This drive involves curiosity and a desire for information about something new or unusual. Play is a means whereby children can safely explore and seek out new information. Play encourages exploratory behavior by offering children the possibilities of novelty, complexity, uncertainty, surprise, and incongruity.

An increasing concern is that the large number of hours children spend with electronic media, such as television and computers, takes time away from play (Linn, 2008). An important agenda for parents is to include ample time for play in their children's lives.

Types of Play The contemporary perspective on types of play emphasizes

---

developmental connection

Education. The child-centered kindergarten emphasizes the education of the whole child and the importance of play in young children's development. Chapter 16, p. 527

> You are troubled at seeing him spend his early years in doing nothing. What! Is it nothing to be happy? Is it nothing to skip, to play, to run about all day long? Never in his life will he be so busy as now.
>
> —**JEAN-JACQUES ROUSSEAU**
> *Swiss-Born French Philosopher, 18th Century*

developmental connection

Cognitive Development. Vygotsky emphasized that children mainly develop their ways of thinking and understanding through social interaction. Chapter 6, p. 199

play A pleasurable activity that is engaged in for its own sake.

play therapy Therapy that lets children work off frustrations while therapists analyze their conflicts and coping methods.

both cognitive and social aspects of play (Sumaroka & Bornstein, 2008). Among the most widely studied types of children's play today are sensorimotor and practice play, pretense/symbolic play, social play, constructive play, and games.

Sensorimotor and Practice Play **Sensorimotor play** is behavior by infants to derive pleasure from exercising their sensorimotor schemes. The development of sensorimotor play follows Piaget's description of sensorimotor thought, which we discussed in Chapter 6. Infants initially engage in exploratory and playful visual and motor transactions in the second quarter of the first year of life. By the end of the third quarter, infants begin to select novel objects for exploration and play, especially responsive objects, such as toys that make noise or bounce. At 12 months of age, infants enjoy making things work and exploring cause and effect.

Practice play involves the repetition of behavior when new skills are being learned or when physical or mental mastery and coordination of skills are required for games or sports. Sensorimotor play, which often involves practice play, is primarily confined to infancy, whereas practice play can be engaged in throughout life. During the preschool years, children frequently engage in practice play. Although practice play declines in the elementary school years, practice play activities such as running, jumping, sliding, twirling, and throwing balls or other objects are frequently observed on the playgrounds at elementary schools.

A preschool "superhero" at play.

Pretense/Symbolic Play **Pretense/symbolic play** occurs when the child transforms aspects of the physical environment into symbols. Between 9 and 30 months of age, children increase their use of objects in symbolic play. They learn to transform objects—substituting them for other objects and acting toward them as if they were these other objects (Smith, 2007). For example, a preschool child treats a table as if it were a car and says, "I'm fixing the car," as he grabs a leg of the table.

Many experts on play consider the preschool years the "golden age" of symbolic/pretense play that is dramatic or sociodramatic in nature. This type of make-believe play often appears at about 18 months of age and reaches a peak at 4 to 5 years of age, then gradually declines.

Some child psychologists conclude that pretense/symbolic play is an important aspect of young children's development and often reflects advances in their cognitive development, especially as an indication of symbolic understanding (Lillard, Pinkham, & Smith, 2011). For example, Catherine Garvey (2000) and Angeline Lillard (2006) emphasize that hidden in young children's pretend play narratives are capacities for role-taking, balancing of social roles, metacognition (thinking about thinking), testing of the reality-pretense distinction, and numerous nonegocentric capacities that reveal the remarkable cognitive skills of young children.

Social Play **Social play** is play that involves interaction with peers. Social play increases dramatically during the preschool years (Power, 2011). Social play includes varied interchanges such as turn taking, conversations about numerous topics, social games and routines, and physical play (Sumaroka & Bornstein, 2008). Social play often involves a high degree of pleasure on the part of the participants (Sumaroka & Bornstein, 2008).

Constructive Play **Constructive play** combines sensorimotor/practice play with symbolic representation. Constructive play occurs when children engage in the self-regulated creation of a product or a solution (Sawyer & DeZutter, 2007). Constructive play increases in the preschool years as symbolic play increases and sensorimotor play decreases. In the preschool years, some practice play is replaced by constructive play. For example, instead of moving their fingers around and around in finger paint (practice play), children are more likely to draw the outline of a house or a person in the paint (constructive play). Constructive play is also a frequent form of play in the elementary school years, both within and outside the classroom.

sensorimotor play Behavior by infants to derive pleasure from exercising their sensorimotor schemes.

practice play Play that involves repetition of behavior when new skills are being learned or when mastery and coordination of skills are required for games or sports.

pretense/symbolic play Play that occurs when a child transforms aspects of the physical environment into symbols.

social play Play that involves interaction with peers.

constructive play Combination of sensorimotor/practice play with symbolic representation.

In the elementary school years, children increasingly play games such as hopscotch.

Games Games are activities that are engaged in for pleasure and have rules. Often they involve competition. Preschool children may begin to participate in social games that involve simple rules of reciprocity and turn taking. However, games take on a much stronger role in the lives of elementary school children.

In sum, play ranges from an infant's simple exercise of a new sensorimotor talent to a preschool child's riding a tricycle to an older child's participation in organized games. Note that children's play can involve a combination of the play categories we have discussed. For example, social play can be sensorimotor (rough-and-tumble), symbolic, or constructive.

ADOLESCENCE

Leisure refers to the pleasant times when individuals are free to pursue activities and interests of their own choosing—hobbies, sports, or reading, for example. How much leisure time do U.S. adolescents have compared with adolescents in other countries? How do U.S. adolescents use their leisure time?

Figure 15.5 indicates that U.S. adolescents spend more time in leisure activities than do adolescents in other industrialized countries (Larson & Verma, 1999). About 40 to 50 percent of U.S. adolescents' waking hours (not counting summer vacations) is spent in leisure activities compared with 25 to 35 percent in East Asia and 35 to 45 percent in Europe. Whether this additional leisure time is a liability or an asset for U.S. adolescents, of course, depends on how they use it.

The largest amounts of U.S. adolescents' free time are spent using the media and playing, hanging out, and engaging in unstructured leisure activities, often with friends. U.S. adolescents spend more time in voluntary structured activities—such as sports, hobbies, and organizations—than East Asian adolescents do.

developmental **connection**

Culture. In the research of Harold Stevenson and his colleagues, the longer students were in school, the wider the gap was between Asian and U.S. students in math achievement. Chapter 16, p. 546

Activity	Nonindustrial, Unschooled Populations	Postindustrial, Schooled Populations		
		United States	**Europe**	**East Asia**
TV viewing	Insufficient data	1.5 to 2.5 hours	1.5 to 2.5 hours	1.5 to 2.5 hours
Talking	Insufficient data	2 to 3 hours	Insufficient data	45 to 60 minutes
Sports	Insufficient data	30 to 60 minutes	20 to 80 minutes	0 to 20 minutes
Structured voluntary activities	Insufficient data	10 to 20 minutes	10 to 20 minutes	0 to 10 minutes
Total free time	4 to 7 hours	6.5 to 8.0 hours	5.5 to 7.5 hours	4.0 to 5.5 hours

games Activities that are engaged in for pleasure and include rules.

leisure The pleasant times when individuals are free to pursue activities and interests of their own choosing.

Note: The estimates in the table are averaged across a 7-day week, including weekdays and weekends. The data for nonindustrial, unschooled populations come primarily from rural peasant populations in developing countries.

FIGURE **15.5**

AVERAGE DAILY LEISURE TIME OF ADOLESCENTS IN DIFFERENT REGIONS OF THE WORLD

According to Reed Larson (2001), in terms of optimal development U.S. adolescents may have too much unstructured time because when adolescents are allowed to choose what they do with their time, they typically engage in unchallenging leisure activities such as hanging out and watching TV. Although relaxation and social interaction are important aspects of adolescence, it seems unlikely that spending large numbers of hours per week in unchallenging activities fosters development. Structured voluntary activities may provide more promise for adolescent development than unstructured time, especially if adults give responsibility to adolescents, challenge them, and provide competent guidance in these activities (Mahoney, Larson, & Eccles, 2004). A recent study revealed support for Larson's view that structured activities can improve adolescents' initiative (Watts & Caldwell, 2010).

How do U.S. adolescents spend their time differently from European and East Asian adolescents?

ADULTHOOD

As adults, not only must we learn how to work well, but we also need to learn how to relax and enjoy leisure (Iwasaki, 2008). In an analysis of what U.S. adults regret the most, not engaging in more leisure was one of the top six regrets (Roese & Summerville, 2005).

Leisure can be an especially important aspect of middle adulthood (Mannell, 2000). By middle adulthood, more money is available to many individuals, and there may be more free time and paid vacations. In short, midlife changes may produce expanded opportunities for leisure. For many individuals, middle adulthood is the first time in their lives when they have the opportunity to diversify their interests.

In one study, 12,338 men 35 to 57 years of age were assessed each year for five years regarding whether they took vacations or not (Gump & Matthews, 2000). Then, the researchers examined the medical and death records over nine years for men who lived for at least a year after the last vacation survey. Compared with those who never took vacations, men who went on annual vacations were 21 percent less likely to die over the nine years and 32 percent less likely to die of coronary heart disease. The qualities that lead men to avoid taking a vacation tend to promote heart disease, such as not trusting anyone to fill in while they are gone or fearing that they will get behind in they work and someone will replace them. These are behaviors that sometimes have been described as part of the Type A behavioral pattern.

Adults at midlife need to begin preparing psychologically for retirement. Participating in constructive and fulfilling leisure activities in middle adulthood is an important part of this preparation (Kelly, 1996). If adults develop leisure activities that they can continue into retirement, the transition from work to retirement can be less stressful.

How much leisure activity do older adults get? A recent national study revealed that more than half of U.S. adults 60 years and older spend no time in leisure activities (Hughes, McDowell, & Brody, 2008). In this study, 27 percent of the older adults participated in 2½ hours or more of leisure time activities per week. Older adults who were male, younger, non-Latino White, had a higher income status and education, were married, and reported being in better health were more likely to engage in leisure activities.

Sigmund Freud once commented that the two things adults need to do well to adapt to society's demands are to work and to love. To his list we add "to play." In our fast-paced society, it is all too easy to get caught up in the frenzied, hectic pace of our achievement-oriented work world and ignore leisure and play. *Imagine your life as a middle-aged adult. What would be the ideal mix of work and leisure? What leisure activities do you want to enjoy as a middle-aged adult?*

Aging and the Social World   **LG4** Summarize the social aspects of aging

Social Theories of Aging

Stereotyping of Older Adults

Social Support and Social Integration

Successful Aging

What happens to our social world when get older? Does it shrink? Do we become more selective and spend more time with our closest friends? How do social experiences influence the aging process? In this section we'll explore some theories of aging that give social experiences an important role.

SOCIAL THEORIES OF AGING

In Chapter 10, we discussed *socioemotional selectivity theory*, which states that older adults become more selective about their social networks and often seek greater emotional quality in relationships with friends and family. Researchers have found extensive support for socioemotional selectivity theory (Charles & Carstensen, 2010). Let's consider two other social theories of aging.

Disengagement theory states that to cope effectively, older adults should gradually withdraw from society. This theory was proposed half a century ago (Cumming & Henry, 1961). In this view, older adults develop increasing self-preoccupation, lessen emotional ties with others, and show decreasing interest in society's affairs. By following these strategies of disengagement, it was thought that older adults would enjoy enhanced life satisfaction. This theory generated a storm of protest and met with a quick death. We present it because of its historical relevance. Although not formally proposed until 1961, it summarized the prevailing beliefs about older adults in the first half of the twentieth century.

Activity theory states that the more active and involved older adults are, the more likely they will be satisfied with their lives. Thus, activity theory is the exact opposite of disengagement theory. Researchers have found strong support for activity theory, beginning in the 1960s and continuing into the twenty-first century (Neugarten, Havighurst, & Tobin, 1968). One longitudinal study found that a greater overall activity level (which included social activities such as visiting relatives or friends, solitary activities such as hobbies, and productive activities such as volunteer work and gardening) at the beginning of the study was related to greater happiness, better physical and cognitive functioning, and reduced mortality six years later

developmental **connection**

Social Contexts. Socioemotional selectivity theory also focuses on the types of goals individuals are motivated to achieve as they go through the adult years. Chapter 10, p. 310

disengagement theory The theory that, to cope effectively, older adults should gradually withdraw from society; this theory is no longer supported.

activity theory The theory that the more active and involved older adults are, the more likely they are to be satisfied with their lives.

(Menec, 2003). In sum, when older adults are active, energetic, and productive, they age more successfully and are happier than if they disengage from society.

STEREOTYPING OF OLDER ADULTS

Social participation by older adults is often discouraged by **ageism,** which is prejudice against others because of their age, especially prejudice against older adults (Leifheit-Limson & Levy, 2009). Older adults are often perceived as incapable of thinking clearly, learning new things, enjoying sex, contributing to the community, or holding responsible jobs. Many older adults face painful discrimination and might be too polite or timid to attack it (Cunningham, 2004). Because of their age, older adults might not be hired for new jobs or might be eased out of old ones; they might be shunned socially; and they might be edged out of their family life.

Ageism is widespread (Hummert, 2011). One study found that men were more likely to negatively stereotype older adults than were women (Rupp, Vodanovich, & Crede, 2005). Research indicates that the most frequent form of ageism is disrespect for older adults, followed by assumptions about ailments or frailty caused by age (Palmore, 2004). However, the increased number of adults living to older ages has led to active efforts to improve society's image of older adults, obtain better living conditions for older adults, and gain political clout to address issues involving this group.

One-hundred-year-old He Jingming, demonstrating his calligraphy skills in China. *How does his behavior contradict stereotyping of older adults?*

SOCIAL SUPPORT AND SOCIAL INTEGRATION

Social support and social integration play important roles in the physical and mental health of older adults (Antonucci, Birditt, & Ajrouch, 2011; Antonucci & others, 2010; Levitt & Cici-Gokaltun, 2011). In the *social convoy* model of social relations, individuals go through life embedded in a personal network of individuals to whom they give, and from whom they receive, social support (Antonucci & others, 2010; Levitt & Ceci-Gokaltun, 2011). Social support can help individuals of all ages cope more effectively (Griffiths & others, 2007). For older adults, social support is related to their physical and mental health (Cheng, Lee, & Chow, 2010). It is linked with a reduction in symptoms of disease, with the ability to meet one's own health-care needs, and increased longevity (Rook & others, 2007). A higher level of social support also is related to a lower probability of an older adult being institutionalized and depressed (Heard & others, 2011; Richardson & others, 2011). Further, a recent study revealed that older adults who experienced a higher level of social support showed later cognitive decline than their counterparts with a lower level of social support (Dickinson & others, 2011).

What role does social support play in the health of older adults?

Social integration also plays an important role in the lives of many older adults (Antonucci, Birditt, & Ajrouch, 2011; Fingerman, Brown, & Blieszner, 2011). Remember from our earlier discussion of socioemotional selectivity

ageism Prejudice against other people because of their age, especially prejudice against older adults.

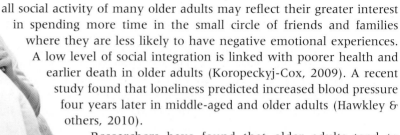

theory that many older adults choose to have fewer peripheral social contacts and more emotionally positive contacts with friends and family (Carstensen & others, 2011; Charles & Carstensen, 2010). Thus, a decrease in the overall social activity of many older adults may reflect their greater interest in spending more time in the small circle of friends and families where they are less likely to have negative emotional experiences. A low level of social integration is linked with poorer health and earlier death in older adults (Koropeckyj-Cox, 2009). A recent study found that loneliness predicted increased blood pressure four years later in middle-aged and older adults (Hawkley & others, 2010).

Researchers have found that older adults tend to report being less lonely than younger adults and less lonely than would be expected based on their circumstances (Schnittker, 2007). Their reports of feeling less lonely than younger adults likely reflect their more selective social networks and greater acceptance of loneliness in their lives (Koropeckyj-Cox, 2009).

What characterizes social integration in the lives of older adults?

SUCCESSFUL AGING

For too long, the positive dimensions of late adulthood were ignored (Stirling, 2011). Throughout this book, we have called attention to the positive aspects of aging. In fact, examining the positive aspects of aging is an important trend in life-span development that is likely to benefit future generations of older adults (Carstensen & others, 2011; Depp & Jeste, 2010). There are many robust, healthy older adults. With a proper diet, an active lifestyle, mental stimulation and flexibility, positive coping skills, good social relationships and support, and the absence of disease, many abilities can be maintained or in some cases even improved as we get older (Lachman & others, 2010). Even when individuals develop a disease, improvements in medical technology mean that increasing numbers of older adults can continue to lead active, constructive lives.

Being active is especially important to successful aging (Erickson & Kramer, 2009). Older adults who exercise regularly, get out and go to meetings, participate in church activities, and go on trips are more satisfied with their lives than their counterparts who disengage from society (James & others, 2011; Peterson & Gordon, 2011). Older adults who are emotionally selective, optimize their choices, and compensate effectively for losses increase their chances of aging successfully (Charles, 2011; Staudinger & Jacobs, 2010).

John Glenn's space mission is emblematic of our rethinking of older adults in terms of successful aging.

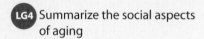

Review *Connect* Reflect

LG4 Summarize the social aspects of aging

Review

- What are three social theories of aging?
- How extensively are older adults stereotyped?
- What roles do social support and social integration play in the development of older adults?
- What are some important aspects of successful aging?

Connect

- Connect the research in Chapter 14 on intergenerational relationships

with this section's discussion of successful aging.

Reflect *Your Own Personal Journey of Life*

- Consider your parents, grandparents, and possibly even great-grandparents who are still alive. How have their social lives changed as they have aged?

Personal relations with friends and other peers form only part of the social world outside the family that influences development. As we have seen throughout this book, development is also influenced by the sociocultural context. Here we take a closer look at three aspects of that context: culture, socioeconomic status, and ethnicity.

CULTURE

Recall from Chapter 1 that **culture** refers to the behavior, patterns, beliefs, and all other products of a group of people that are passed on from generation to generation. It results from the interaction between people and their environment over many years. Also remember from Chapter 1 that **cross-cultural studies** compare aspects of two or more cultures. The comparison provides information about the degree to which development is similar, or universal, across cultures, or is instead culture-specific.

A recent study revealed that from the beginning of the seventh grade through the end of the eighth grade, U.S. adolescents valued academics less and their motivational behavior also decreased (Wang & Pomerantz, 2009). By contrast, the value placed on academics by Chinese adolescents did not change across this time frame and their motivational behavior was sustained. In Chapter 16, we discuss in greater detail the higher math and science achievement of Asian children in comparison with U.S. children.

The concept of culture is broad; it includes many components and can be analyzed in many ways (Shiraev & Levy, 2010). Cross-cultural expert Richard Brislin (1993) described a number of characteristics of culture:

- Culture is made up of ideals, values, and assumptions about life that guide people's behavior.
- Culture consists of those aspects of the environment that people make.
- Culture is transmitted from generation to generation, with responsibility for the transmission resting on the shoulders of parents, teachers, and community leaders.
- When their cultural values are violated or their cultural expectations are ignored, people react emotionally.
- It is not unusual for people to accept a cultural value at one point in their lives and reject it at another point. For example, rebellious adolescents and young adults might accept a culture's values and expectations after having children of their own.

Classical research by American psychologist Donald Campbell and his colleagues (Brewer & Campbell, 1976; Campbell & LeVine, 1968) revealed that people in all cultures tend to

- think that what happens in their culture is "natural" and "correct" and that what happens in other cultures is "unnatural" and "incorrect";
- perceive their cultural customs as universally valid—that is, conclude that "what is good for us is good for everyone";
- behave in ways that favor their cultural group; and
- feel hostile toward other cultural groups.

developmental connection

Theories. In Bronfenbrenner's ecological theory, the macrosystem is the environmental system that involves the influence of culture on children's development. Chapter 1, p. 27

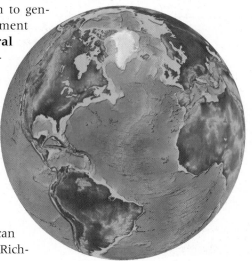

What is culture? How does it influence people's lives?

culture The behavior, patterns, beliefs, and all other products of a group of people that are passed on from generation to generation.

cross-cultural studies Studies that compare aspects of two or more cultures to provide information about the degree to which development is similar or universal across the cultures, or is instead culture-specific.

Individualistic	Collectivistic
Focuses on individual.	Focuses on groups.
Self is determined by personal traits independent of groups; self is stable across contexts.	Self is defined by in-group terms; self can change with context.
Private self is more important.	Public self is most important.
Personal achievement, competition, power are important.	Achievement is for the benefit of the in-group; cooperation is stressed.
Cognitive dissonance is frequent.	Cognitive dissonance is infrequent.
Emotions (such as anger) are self-focused.	Emotions (such as anger) are often relationship based.
People who are the most liked are self-assured.	People who are the most liked are modest, self-effacing.
Values: pleasure, achievement, competition, freedom.	Values: security, obedience, in-group harmony, personalized relationships.
Many casual relationships.	Few, close relationships.
Save own face.	Save own and other's face.
Independent behaviors: swimming, sleeping alone in room, privacy.	Interdependent behaviors: co-bathing, co-sleeping.
Relatively rare mother-child physical contact.	Frequent mother-child physical contact (such as hugging, holding).

FIGURE 15.6

CHARACTERISTICS OF INDIVIDUALISTIC AND COLLECTIVISTIC CULTURES

ethnocentrism The tendency to consider one's own group superior to other groups.

individualism Giving priority to personal goals rather than to group goals; emphasizing values that serve the self, such as feeling good, obtaining personal distinction through achievement, and preserving independence.

collectivism Emphasizing values that serve the group by subordinating personal goals to preserve group integrity, supporting interdependence of members, and promoting harmonious relationships.

In other words, people in all cultures tend to display **ethnocentrism,** the tendency to consider one's own group superior to others.

The Relevance of Culture for the Study of Life-Span Development Global interdependence is an inescapable reality (Shiraev & Levy, 2010). Children, adolescents, and adults are not just citizens of one country; they are citizens of the world—a world that, through advances in transportation and technology, has become increasingly connected. By better understanding cultures around the world, we may be able to interact more effectively with each other and make this planet a more hospitable, peaceful place (Chen & others, 2011; Kitayama & Uskul, 2011; Koppelman & Goodhart, 2011).

Individualism and Collectivism What cultural differences are significant in life-span development? One finding in cross-cultural research is that cultures around the world tend to take two very different orientations to life and social relations. That is, cultures tend to emphasize either individualism or collectivism:

- **Individualism** involves giving priority to personal goals rather than to group goals; it emphasizes values that serve the self, such as feeling good, obtaining personal distinction through achievement, and preserving independence.
- **Collectivism** emphasizes values that serve the group by subordinating personal goals to preserve group integrity, supporting interdependence of the members, and promoting harmonious relationships.

Figure 15.6 summarizes some of the main characteristics of individualistic and collectivistic cultures. Many Western cultures, such as those of the United States, Canada, Great Britain, and the Netherlands, are described as individualistic; many Eastern cultures, such as those of China, Japan, India, and Thailand, are described as collectivistic.

Many of the assumptions about contemporary ideas in fields like life-span development were developed in individualistic cultures (Triandis, 1994, 2001, 2007). Consider the flurry of self-terms in psychology that have an individualistic focus: *self-actualization, self-awareness, self-efficacy, self-reinforcement, self-criticism, self-serving, selfishness,* and *self-doubt* (Lonner, 1988).

Self-conceptions are related to culture. In one study, American and Chinese college students completed 20 sentences beginning with "I am _____" (Trafimow, Triandis, & Goto, 1991). As indicated in Figure 15.7, the American college students were much more likely than the Chinese students to describe themselves with personal traits ("I am assertive," for example), than to identify themselves by their group affiliations ("I am a member of the math club," for example).

Some social scientists note that many problems in Western cultures are intensified by the Western cultural emphasis on individualism. The rates of suicide, drug abuse, crime, teenage pregnancy, divorce, child abuse, and mental disorders are higher in individualistic cultures than in collectivistic ones.

Critics of the concept of individualistic and collectivistic cultures argue that these terms are too broad and simplistic, especially with globalization increasing (Greenfield, 2009). Regardless of their cultural background, people need both a positive sense of self and connectedness to others to develop fully as human beings. Carolyn Tamis-LeMonda and her colleagues (2008) emphasize that in many families, children are not reared in environments that uniformly endorse either individualistic or collectivistic values, thoughts, and actions. Rather, in many families, children are "expected to be quiet, assertive, respectful, curious, humble, self-assured, independent, dependent, affectionate, or reserved depending on the situation, people present, children's age, and social-political and economic circles."

Technology, the Media, and Culture   If the amount of time spent in an activity is any indication of its importance, there is no doubt that media play important roles in children's and adolescents' lives (Brown & Bobkowski, 2011). To better understand various aspects of U.S. children's and adolescents' media use, the Kaiser Family Foundation has funded three national surveys in 1999, 2004, and 2009. The 2009 survey included more than 2,000 8- to 18-year-olds and documented that children's and adolescents' media use has increased dramatically in the last decade (Rideout, Foehr, & Roberts, 2010). Today's youth live in a world in which they are encapsulated by media. In this survey, in 2009, 8- to 11-year-olds used media 5 hours and 29 minutes a day, but 11- to 14-year-olds used media an average of 8 hours and 40 minutes a day and 15- to 18-year-olds an average of 7 hours and 58 minutes a day (see Figure 15.8). Thus, daily media use jumps more than 3 hours in early adolescence. The largest increases in media use in early adolescence are for TV viewing and videogaming. TV use by youth increasingly has involved watching TV on the Internet, an iPod/MP3 player, or on a cell phone. As indicated in Figure 15.8, listening to music and using computers also increase considerably among 11- to 14-year-old adolescents. Based on the 2009 survey, adding up the daily media use figures to obtain weekly media use leads to the staggering levels of more than 60 hours a week of media use by 11- to 14-year-olds and almost 56 hours a week by 15- to 18-year-olds.

A major trend in the use of technology is the dramatic increase in media multitasking (Brown & Bobkowski, 2011). In the 2009 survey, when the amount of time spent multitasking was included in computing media use, 11- to 14-year-olds spent nearly 12 hours a day (as compared with almost 9 hours a day when multitasking was not included) exposed to media (Rideout, Foehr, & Roberts, 2010). In this survey, 39 percent of seventh- to twelfth-graders said "most of the time" they use two or more media concurrently, such as surfing the Web while listening to music. In some cases, media multitasking—such as text messaging, listening to an iPod, and updating a YouTube site—is engaged in at the same time as doing homework. It is hard to imagine that this allows a student to do homework efficiently, although there is little research on media multitasking. A recent study that compared heavy and light media multitaskers revealed that heavy media multitaskers were more susceptible to interference from irrelevant information (Ophir, Nass, & Wagner, 2009).

Mobile media, such as cell phones and iPods, are mainly driving the increased media use by adolescents. For example, in the 2004 survey, only 18 percent of youth owned an iPod or MP3 player, but in 2009, 76 percent owned them; in 2004, 39 percent owned a cell phone, a figure that jumped to 66 percent in 2009 (Rideout, Foehr, & Roberts, 2010).

Television   Few developments during the second half of the twentieth century had a greater impact on children than television (Lever-Duffy & McDonald, 2011; Maloy & others, 2011). Many children spend more time in front of the television set than they do with their parents. Although it is only one of the many mass media that affect children's behavior, television may be the most influential. The persuasive capabilities of television are staggering. The 20,000 hours of television watched by the time the average American adolescent graduates from high school are greater than the number of hours spent in the classroom.

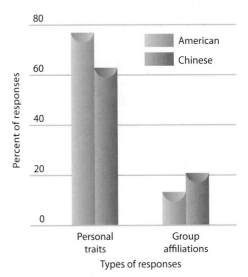

FIGURE **15.7**

AMERICAN AND CHINESE SELF-CONCEPTIONS. College students from the United States and China completed 20 "I am _____" sentences. Both groups filled in personal traits more than group affiliations. However, the Chinese students filled in the blanks with group affiliations more often than the U.S. students did.

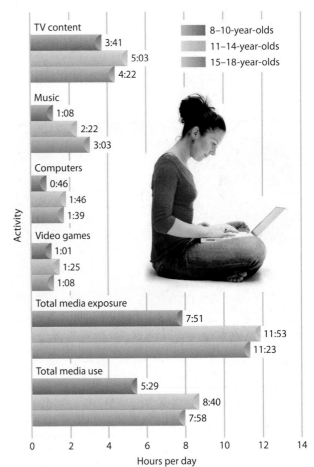

FIGURE **15.8**

DEVELOPMENTAL CHANGES IN THE AMOUNT OF TIME U.S. 8-TO 18-YEAR-OLDS SPEND WITH DIFFERENT TYPES OF MEDIA

"Mrs. Horton, could you stop by school today?"
Copyright © 1981 Martha F. Campbell. Reprinted by permission.

Television can have positive or negative effects on children's and adolescents' development. Television can have a positive influence by presenting motivating educational programs, increasing children's and adolescents' information about the world beyond their immediate environment, and providing models of prosocial behavior (Schmidt & Vandewater, 2008; Wilson, 2008). However, television can have a negative influence on children and adolescents by making them passive learners, distracting them from doing homework, teaching them stereotypes, providing them with violent models of aggression, and presenting them with unrealistic views of the world (Murray & Murray, 2008). Further, as we saw in Chapter 4, researchers have found that a high level of TV viewing is linked to a greater incidence of obesity in children and adolescents (Escobar-Chaves & Anderson, 2008).

A recent research review concluded that children and adolescents who experience a heavy media diet of violence are more likely to perceive the world as a dangerous place and to view aggression as more acceptable than their counterparts who see media violence less frequently (Wilson, 2008). Also, another recent research review concluded that there is strong evidence that media violence is a risk factor for aggressive behavior but less evidence linking it to juvenile delinquency and crime (Escobar-Chaves & Anderson, 2008). Much of the media violence described in these two recent research reviews comes from television, but as we see next, it also includes violent video games.

Violent video games, especially those that are highly realistic, also raise concerns about their effects on children and adolescents (Barlett, Anderson, & Swing, 2009). Correlational studies indicate that children and adolescents who extensively play violent electronic games are more aggressive and more likely to engage in delinquent acts than their counterparts who spend less time playing the games or do not play them at all (Anderson, Gentile, & Buckley, 2007; Carnagey, Anderson, & Bushman, 2007).

A recent study revealed a link between media violence exposure and both physical aggression and relational aggression in third- to fifth-grade students (Gentile, Mathieson, & Crick, 2010). In this study, the link with relational aggression was stronger for girls than for boys.

How might playing violent video games be related to adolescent aggression?

The Electronic Media, Learning, and Children's Development   The effects of electronic media on children depends on how old children are and the type of media involved. A recent research review reached the following conclusions about infants and young children (Kirkorian, Wartella, & Anderson, 2008):

- *Infancy.* Learning from electronic media is difficult for infants and toddlers, and they learn much more easily from direct experiences with people.
- *Early childhood.* At about 3 years of age, children can learn from electronic media with educational material if the media use effective strategies, such as repeating concepts a number of times, using images and sounds that get young children's attention, and use children's rather than adults' voices. However, the vast majority of media young children experience is entertainment rather than education oriented.

The American Academy of Pediatrics (2001) has recommended that children under 2 years of age not watch television because it likely reduces direct interactions with parents. One study found that the more hours 1- and 3-year-olds watched TV per day, the more likely they were to have attention problems at 7 years of age (Christakis & others, 2004), and a recent study also revealed that daily TV exposure at 18 months was linked to increased inattention/hyperactivity at 30 months of age (Cheng & others, 2010). A recent study of 2- to 48-month-olds indicated that each hour of audible TV was linked to a reduction in child vocalizations (Christakis & others, 2009), and another study revealed that 8- to 16-month-olds who viewed baby DVDs/videos had poor language development (Zimmerman, Christakis, & Meltzoff, 2007).

The more children and adolescents watch TV, the lower their school achievement (Comstock & Scharrer, 2006). Why might TV watching be negatively linked to children's achievement? Three possibilities involve interference, displacement, and self-defeating tastes/preferences (Comstock & Scharrer, 2006). In terms of interference, having a television on while doing homework can distract children while they are doing cognitive tasks such as homework. In terms of displacement, television can take away time and attention from engaging in achievement-related tasks, such as homework, reading, writing, and mathematics.

Technology and Digitally Mediated Communication   Culture involves change, and nowhere is that change greater than in the technological revolution individuals are experiencing with increased use of computers and the Internet (Maloy & others, 2011). Society still relies on some basic non-technological competencies—for example, good communication skills, positive attitudes, and the ability to solve problems and to think deeply and creatively. But how people pursue these competencies is changing in ways and at a speed that few people had to cope with in previous eras. For youth to be adequately prepared for tomorrow's jobs, technology needs to become an integral part of their lives (Lever-Duffy & McDonald, 2011).

The digitally mediated social environment of youth includes e-mail, instant messaging, social networking sites such as Facebook, chat rooms, videosharing and photosharing, multiplayer online computer games, and virtual worlds. The remarkable increase in the popularity of Facebook was reflected in its recent replacement of Google in 2010 as the most frequently visited Internet site. Most of these digitally mediated social interactions began on computers but more recently have also shifted to cell phones, especially smartphones (Valkenburg & Peter, 2011).

What have researchers found about TV watching by infants?

A national survey revealed dramatic increases in adolescents' use of social media and text messaging (Lenhart & others, 2010). In 2009, nearly three-fourths of U.S. 12- to 17-year-olds reported that they used social networking sites. Eighty-one percent of 18- to 24-year-olds had created a profile on a social networking site and 31 percent of them visited a social networking site at least several times a day. More emerging adult women visited a social networking site several times a day (33 percent) than did their male counterparts (24 percent).

Text messaging has now become the main way that adolescents connect with their friends, surpassing face-to-face contact, e-mail, instant messaging, and voice calling (Lenhart & others, 2010). However, voice mailing is the primary way that most adolescents prefer for connecting with parents.

Special concerns have emerged about children's and adolescents' access to information on the Internet, which has been largely unregulated. Youth can access adult sexual material, instructions for making bombs, and other information that is inappropriate for them.

Another concern is peer bullying and harassment on the Internet (called *cyberbullying*) (Sontag & others, 2011; Valkenburg & Peter, 2011). A recent survey found that peer bullying offline and online was the most frequent type of threat that children and adolescents encountered (Palfrey & others, 2009). And a recent study of third- to sixth-graders revealed that engaging in cyber aggression was related to loneliness, lower self-esteem, fewer mutual friendships, and lower peer popularity (Schoffstall & Cohen, 2011). Information about preventing cyberbullying can be found at www.stopcyberbullying.org/.

A recent study of college students—mean age 20 years old—found that when the Internet was used for shopping, entertainment, and pornography, negative outcomes resulted: higher level of drinking and drug use, greater number of sexual partners, worse relationships with friends and parents, and lower self-worth; however, when college students used the Internet for schoolwork, positive outcomes included a lower level of drug use and higher self-worth (Padilla-Walker & others, 2010).

What characterizes the online social environment of adolescents?

Clearly, the Internet is a technology that needs parents to monitor and regulate adolescents' use of it. Consider Bonita Williams, who began to worry about how obsessed her 15-year-old daughter, Jade, had become with MySpace (Kornblum, 2006). She became even more concerned when she discovered that Jade was posting suggestive photos of herself and giving her cell phone number to people in different parts of the United States. She grounded her daughter, blocked MySpace at home, and moved Jade's computer from her bedroom into the family room.

The following recent studies explored the role of parents in guiding adolescents' use of the Internet and media:

- Parents' high estimates of online dangers were not matched by their low rates of setting limits and monitoring their adolescents' online activities (Rosen, Cheever, & Carrier, 2008). Also in this study, adolescents who perceived that their parents had an indulgent parenting style (high warmth and involvement but low levels of strictness and supervision) reported engaging in the most risky online behavior, such as meeting someone in person whom they had initially contacted on the Internet.

- Both maternal and paternal authoritative parenting predicted proactive monitoring of adolescent media use, including restriction of certain media from adolescent use and parent-adolescent discussion of exposure to questionable media content (Padilla-Walker & Coyne, 2011).

- Problematic mother-adolescent (age 13) relationships (such as insecure attachment and autonomy conflicts) predicted emerging adults' preference for online communication and greater probability of forming a relationship of poor quality with someone they met online (Szwedo, Mikami, & Allen, 2011).

The Internet and Aging Adults The Internet plays an increasingly important role in providing access to information and communication for adults as well as youth (Cresci, Yarandi, & Morrell, 2010). How well are older adults keeping up with changes in technology? Older adults are less likely to have a computer in their home and less likely to use the Internet than younger adults, but older adults are the fastest-growing segment of Internet users (Czaja & others, 2006). Older adults log more time on the Internet (an average of 8.3 hours per week), visit more Web sites, and spend more money on the Internet than their younger adult counterparts do. They are especially interested in learning to use e-mail and going online for health information (Westlake & others, 2007). Increasing numbers of older adults use e-mail to communicate with relatives. As with children and younger adults, cautions about the inconsistent accuracy of Internet information—particularly in areas such as health care—should be kept in mind (Cutler, 2009).

Links between older adults' use of technology and their cognitive development are being studied. A recent study found that frequent computer use was linked to higher performance on cognitive tasks in older adults (Tun & Lachman, 2010). And researchers are examining the role that video games might have in maintaining or improving older adults' cognitive skills (Charness, Fox, & Mitchum, 2011). For example, a recent research study found that a lengthy 40-hour video game training program improved older adults' attention and memory (Smith & others, 2009).

Aging and Culture Culture plays an important role in aging (Gold & Amthor, 2011). What promotes a good old age in most cultures? What factors are associated with whether older adults are accorded a position of high status in a culture? Seven factors are most likely to predict high status for the elderly in a culture (Sangree, 1989):

- Older persons have valuable knowledge.
- Older persons control key family/community resources.

Are older adults keeping up with changes in technology?

- Older persons are permitted to engage in useful and valued functions as long as possible.
- There is role continuity throughout the life span.
- Age-related role changes involve greater responsibility, authority, and advisory capacity.
- The extended family is a common family arrangement in the culture, and the older person is integrated into the extended family.
- In general, respect for older adults is greater in collectivistic cultures (such as China and Japan) than in individualistic cultures (such as the United States). However, some researchers are finding that this collectivistic/individualistic difference in respect for older adults is not as strong as it used to be and that in some cases older adults in individualistic cultures receive considerable respect (Antonucci, Vandewater, & Lansford, 2000).

SOCIOECONOMIC STATUS AND POVERTY

Analyzing cultures represents just one way to understand the social context of life-span development. Another approach focuses on inequalities present in every society (Govia, Jackson, & Sellers, 2011). That is, how do people in a particular society differ in their access to economic, social, and psychological resources, and how do these differences affect their development through life?

What Is Socioeconomic Status? Socioeconomic status (SES) refers to a grouping of people with similar occupational, educational, and economic characteristics. Generally, members of a society have (1) occupations that vary in prestige, and some individuals have more access than others to higher-status occupations; (2) different levels of educational attainment, and some individuals have more access than others to better education; (3) different economic resources; and (4) different degrees of power to influence a community. These differences go together. That is, people with prestigious occupations tend also to have higher levels of educational attainment, more economic resources, and more power. These differences in the ability to control resources and to participate in society's rewards produce unequal opportunities for people (Entwisle, Alexander, & Olson, 2010; Lynch & Brown, 2011). Socioeconomic differences are a "proxy for material, human, and social capital within and beyond the family" (Huston & Ripke, 2006, p. 425).

The number of different socioeconomic statuses depends on the community's size and complexity. In most investigators' descriptions of socioeconomic status, two broad categories—low SES and middle SES—are used, although as many as five categories are delineated. Sometimes low SES is described as low-income, working class, or blue collar; sometimes middle SES is described as middle-income, managerial, or white collar. Examples of low-SES occupations are factory worker and maintenance worker. Examples of middle-SES occupations include manager and professional careers (doctor, lawyer, teacher, accountant, and so on).

Cultures differ in the amount of prestige they give to older adults. In Navajo culture, older adults are especially treated with respect because of their wisdom and extensive life experiences. *What are some other factors that are linked with respect for older adults in a culture?*

What characterizes socioeconomic variations in neighborhoods?

Socioeconomic Variations in Neighborhoods and Families A parent's SES is likely linked to the neighborhoods in which children live and the schools they attend (Chen, Howard, & Brooks-Gunn, 2011). Such variations in neighborhood settings can influence children's adjustment (Conger & Conger, 2008).

Neighborhood crime and isolation have been linked with low self-esteem and psychological distress in children (Roberts, Jacobson, & Taylor, 1996). Further, schools in low-income neighborhoods have fewer resources than schools in

socioeconomic status (SES) A grouping of people with similar occupational, educational, and economic characteristics.

higher-income neighborhoods, and they are more likely to have more students with lower achievement test scores and low rates of graduation with small percentages of students going to college (Garbarino & Asp, 1981).

In America and most Western cultures, differences have been found in child rearing among different SES groups (Hoff, Laursen, & Tardiff, 2002, p. 246):

- "Lower-SES parents (1) are more concerned that their children conform to society's expectations, (2) create a home atmosphere in which it is clear that parents have authority over children," (3) use physical punishment more in disciplining their children, and (4) are more directive and less conversational with their children.

- "Higher-SES parents (1) are more concerned with developing children's initiative" and ability to delay gratification, (2) "create a home atmosphere in which children are more nearly equal participants and in which rules are discussed as opposed to being laid down" in an authoritarian manner, (3) are less likely to use physical punishment, and (4) are less directive and more conversational with their children.

Nevertheless, a sizable portion of children from low-SES backgrounds are very competent and perform well in school; some perform better than many middle-SES students. When children from low-SES backgrounds achieve well in school, it is not unusual to find a parent or parents making special sacrifices to provide the conditions that contribute to academic success.

So far we have focused on the challenges that many adolescents from low-income families face. However, research by Suniya Luthar and her colleagues (Ansary & Luthar, 2009; Luthar, 2006; Luthar & Goldstein, 2008) found that adolescents from affluent families also face challenges. In her research, adolescents from affluent families are vulnerable to high rates of substance abuse. Also, in the affluent families she has studied, males tend to have more adjustment difficulties than females, with affluent female adolescents being more likely to attain superior levels of academic success.

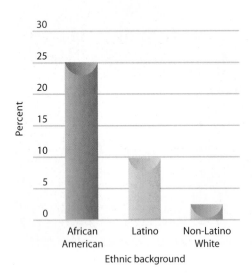

◄ - - - - - - - - - - - - -

developmental connection

Environment. Reducing the poverty level and improving the lives of children living in poverty are important goals of U.S. social policy. Chapter 1, p. 10

Note: A distressed neighborhood is defined by high levels (at least one standard deviation above the mean) of (1) poverty; (2) female-headed families; (3) high school dropouts; (4) unemployment; and (5) reliance on welfare.

FIGURE 15.9

PERCENTAGES OF YOUTH UNDER 18 WHO ARE LIVING IN DISTRESSED NEIGHBORHOODS

Poverty When sixth-graders in a poverty-stricken area of St. Louis were asked to describe a perfect day, one boy said he would erase the world, then he would sit and think. Asked if he wouldn't rather go outside and play, the boy responded, "Are you kidding, out there?" (Children's Defense Fund, 1992). The world is a dangerous and unwelcoming place for too many of America's children, especially those who live in poverty (Children's Defense Fund, 2011). Some children are resilient and cope with the challenges of poverty without any major setbacks, but too many struggle unsuccessfully (Santiago & others, 2011; Williams & Hazell, 2011). Each child of poverty who reaches adulthood unhealthy, unskilled, or alienated keeps our nation from being as competent and productive as it can be (Children's Defense Fund, 2011; Park, Fertig, & Allison, 2011).

Poverty Rates In 2008, 19 percent of children under 18 years of age were living in families with incomes below the poverty line (Childstats.gov, 2010). This is an increase from 2001 (16.2 percent) but a decrease from a peak of 22.7 percent in 1993. The U.S. figure of 19 percent of children living in poverty is much higher than the rates in other industrialized nations. For example, Canada has a child poverty rate of 9 percent and Sweden has a rate of 2 percent.

Poverty in the United States is demarcated along ethnic lines. In 2008, 22 percent of African Americans and 21 percent of Latinos lived in poverty, compared with only 8 percent of non-Latino Whites (U.S. Census Bureau, 2011). Compared with non-Latino White children, ethnic minority children are more likely to experience persistent poverty over many years and live in isolated poor neighborhoods where social supports are minimal and threats to positive development abundant (Jarrett, 1995) (see Figure 15.9).

(*Left*) Children playing in Nueva Era, a low-income area on the outskirts of Nuevo Laredo, Mexico. (*Right*) Two boys who live in a poverty section of the South Bronx in New York City. *How does poverty affect the development of children like these?*

Psychological Ramifications of Poverty   Poor children are often exposed to poor health conditions, inadequate housing and homelessness, less effective schools, environmental toxins, and violence (Borjas, 2011; Park, Fertig, & Allison, 2011). What are the psychological ramifications of living in poverty? First, the poor are often powerless. At work, they rarely are the decision makers; rules are handed down to them. Second, the poor are often vulnerable to disaster. They are not likely to be given notice before they are laid off from work, and they usually do not have financial resources to fall back on when problems arise. Third, their alternatives are restricted. Only a limited number of jobs are open to them. Even when alternatives are available, the poor might not know about them or be prepared to make a wise decision, because of inadequate education and inability to read well. Fourth, being poor means having less prestige.

One review concluded that compared with their economically more advantaged counterparts, poor children experience widespread environmental inequities (Evans, 2004). For example, as we saw in Chapter 1, one study found that a higher percentage of children in poor families than in middle-income families were exposed to family turmoil, separation from a parent, violence, crowding, excessive noise, and poor housing (Evans & English, 2002).

Persistent and long-standing poverty can have especially damaging effects on children (McLoyd & others, 2009). One study revealed that the more years children spent in poverty, the more their physiological indices of stress were elevated (Evans & Kim, 2007). And a recent study found that persistent economic hardship as well as very early poverty was linked to lower cognitive functioning in children at 5 years of age (Schoon & others, 2011).

Vonnie McLoyd (*right*) has conducted a number of important investigations of the roles of poverty, ethnicity, and unemployment in children's and adolescents' development. She has found that economic stressors often diminish children's and adolescents' belief in the utility of education and their achievement strivings.

Feminization of Poverty   The term **feminization of poverty** refers to the fact that far more women than men live in poverty. A special concern is the high percentage of children and adolescents growing up in mother-headed households in poverty (Leon-Guerrero, 2009). In 2008, 36.5 percent of female-headed families lived in poverty compared with only 6.4 percent of married-couple families (Federal Interagency Forum on Child and Family Statistics, 2010).

Vonnie McLoyd (1998) concluded that because poor, single mothers are more distressed than their middle-SES counterparts are, they tend to show lower levels of support, nurturance, and involvement with their children. Among the reasons

feminization of poverty The fact that far more women than men live in poverty. Women's lower income, divorce, infrequent awarding of alimony, and poorly enforced child support by fathers—which usually leave women with less money than they and their children need to adequately function—are the likely causes.

What are some characteristics of older U.S. adults living in poverty conditions?

for the high poverty rate of single mothers are women's low pay, infrequent awarding of alimony payments, and poorly enforced child support by fathers (Graham & Beller, 2002).

Families and Poverty One study documented the important links among economic well-being, parenting behavior, and social adjustment (Mistry & others, 2002). Lower levels of economic well-being and elevated perceptions of economic pressure were linked with parenting behavior. Distressed parents reported feeling less effective and capable in disciplining their children and were observed to be less affectionate in parent-child interactions. In turn, less optimal parenting predicted lower teacher ratings of children's social behavior and higher ratings of behavior problems.

Benefits provided to low-income parents may have positive outcomes for children (Phillips & Lowenstein, 2011; Sandler & others, 2011). For example, the Minnesota Family Investment Program (MFIP) was primarily designed to improve the lives of adults—specifically, to move adults off the welfare rolls and into paid employment. A key element of the program was that it guaranteed that adults who participated in the program would receive more money if they worked than if they did not. When the adults' income rose, how did it affect their children? A study of the effects of MFIP found that increases in the incomes of working poor parents were linked with benefits for their children (Gennetian & Miller, 2002). The children's achievement in school improved, and their behavior problems decreased.

Might intervention with families of children living in poverty improve children's school performance? In an experimental study, Aletha Huston and her colleagues (2006) evaluated the effects on adolescent development of a program called New Hope, which is designed to increase parental employment and reduce family poverty. They randomly assigned families with 6- to 10-year-old children living in poverty to the New Hope program and a control group. New Hope offered adults living in poverty who were employed 30 or more hours a week benefits that were designed to increase family income (a wage supplement that ensured that net income increased as parents earned more) and to provide work supports through subsidized child care (for any child under age 13) and health insurance. Management services were provided to New Hope participants to assist them in job searches and other needs. The New Hope program was available to the experimental group families for 3 years (until the children were 9 to 13 years old). Five years after the program began and 2 years after it had ended, the program's effects on the children were examined when they were 11 to 16 years old. Compared to adolescents in the control group, New Hope adolescents were more competent at reading, had better school performance, were less likely to be in special education classes, had more positive social skills, and were more likely to be in formal after-school arrangements. New Hope parents reported better psychological well-being and a greater sense of self-efficacy in managing their adolescents than parents in the control group did. In a further assessment, the influence of the New Hope program on adolescents and emerging adults 9 to 19 years after they left the program was evaluated (McLoyd & others, 2011). Positive outcomes especially occurred for African American males, who were more optimistic about their future employment and career prospects.

SES, Poverty, and Aging Another group of special concern consists of older adults who are poor (Reno & Veghte, 2011). Researchers have found that poverty in late adulthood is linked to an increase in physical and mental health problems (Herd, Robert, & House, 2011). Poverty also is linked to lower levels of physical and cognitive fitness in older adults (Basta & others, 2008). And one study revealed that low SES increases the risk of earlier death in older adults (Krueger & Chang, 2008).

Census data suggest that the overall number of older people living in poverty has declined since the 1960s, but in 2008, 9.7 percent of older adults in the U.S. still were living in poverty (U.S. Census Bureau, 2010). In 2008, almost twice as many U.S. women 65 years and older (11.9 percent) lived in poverty as did their male counterparts (U.S. Census Bureau, 2010).

Many older adults are understandably concerned about their income (Reno & Veghte, 2011). Social Security is the largest contributor to the income of older Americans (38 percent), followed by assets, earnings, and pensions. There is a special concern about poverty in older women and the role of Social Security in providing a broad economic safety net for them (Lynch & Brown, 2011; Meyer & Parker, 2011).

ETHNICITY

As our discussion of poverty and aging indicated, differences in SES often overlap with ethnic differences. The United States is a showcase for these differences because it has been a great magnet for people from many ethnic groups. Cultural heritages from every continent have connected and mixed here (Cheah & Yeung, 2011). Native Americans, European Americans, African Americans, Latinos, Chinese Americans, and other groups have retained parts of their culture of origin, lost other parts, and seen some elements transformed as they became part of the mainstream culture.

Immigration Relatively high rates of minority immigration have contributed to growth in the proportion of ethnic minorities in the U.S. population (Cheah & Yeung, 2011; Grigorenko & Takanishi, 2010). And this growth of ethnic minorities is expected to continue throughout the twenty-first century. The United States is more ethnically diverse than ever before (Banks, 2010). Ninety-three languages are spoken in Los Angeles alone.

Asian Americans are expected to be the fastest-growing ethnic group of adolescents, with a growth rate of almost 600 percent by 2100. Latino adolescents are projected to increase almost 400 percent by 2100. Figure 15.10 shows the actual numbers of adolescents in different ethnic groups in the year 2000, as well as the numbers projected through 2100. Notice that by 2100, Latino adolescents are expected to outnumber non-Latino White adolescents.

Immigrants often experience special stressors (Landale, Thomas, & Van Hook, 2011). These include language barriers, separations from support networks, changes in SES, and the struggle both to preserve ethnic identity and to adapt to the majority culture (Grigorenko & Takanishi, 2010).

Parents and children may be at different stages of acculturation, the process of adapting to the majority culture. The result may be conflict over cultural values (Greder & Allen, 2007). One study examined values in immigrant (Vietnamese, Armenian, and Mexican) and nonimmigrant families (African American and European American) (Phinney, 1996). In all groups, parents endorsed family obligations more than adolescents did, and the differences between generations generally increased with time spent in the United States.

Ethnicity and Families Families within different ethnic groups in the United States differ in their size, structure, composition, reliance on kinship networks, and levels of income and education (Umana-Taylor, 2009). Large

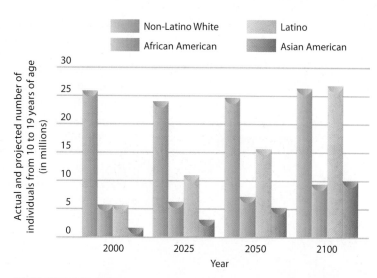

FIGURE **15.10**

ACTUAL AND PROJECTED NUMBER OF U.S. ADOLESCENTS AGED 10 TO 19, 2000 TO 2100. In 2000, there were more than 25 million non-Latino White adolescents 10 to 19 years of age in the United States, whereas the numbers for ethnic minority groups were substantially lower. However, projections for 2025 through 2100 reveal dramatic increases in the number of Latino and Asian American adolescents to the point at which in 2100 it is projected that there will be more Latino than non-Latino White adolescents in the United States and more Asian American than African American adolescents.

Latino immigrants in the Rio Grande Valley, Texas. *What are some characteristics of the families who have recently immigrated to the United States?*

and extended families are more common among minority groups than among the non-Latino White majority. For example, 19 percent of Latino families have three or more children, compared with 14 percent of African American and 10 percent of non-Latino White families. African American and Latino children interact more with their grandparents, aunts, uncles, cousins, and more distant relatives than do non-Latino White children.

Single-parent families are more common among African Americans and Latinos than among non-Latino White Americans (Hattery & Smith, 2007). In comparison with two-parent households, single parents often have more limited resources of time, money, and energy. Ethnic minority parents also are less educated and more likely to live in low-income circumstances than their non-Latino White counterparts. Still, many impoverished ethnic minority families manage to find ways to raise competent children (Gamble & Modry-Mandell, 2008).

Poverty contributes to the stressful life experiences of many ethnic minority children (McLoyd & others, 2009, 2011). But even when they are not poor, economic advantage does not enable ethnic minority children to escape entirely the prejudice and discrimination directed at them (Harwood & others, 2002). Although middle-SES ethnic minority children have more resources available to counter the destructive influences of prejudice and discrimination, they still cannot completely avoid the pervasive influence of negative stereotypes about ethnic minority groups.

Vonnie McLoyd (1990) concluded that ethnic minority children experience a disproportionate share of the adverse effects of poverty and unemployment in America today. Thus, many ethnic minority children experience a double disadvantage: (1) prejudice and discrimination because of their ethnic minority status, and (2) the stressful effects of poverty. Some aspects of home life can help protect ethnic minority children from injustice. The community and the family can filter out destructive racist messages, and parents can present alternative frames of reference to those presented by the majority. The extended family also can serve as an important buffer to stress (Harris & Graham, 2007; Hayashino & Chopra, 2009).

Research indicates that many members of families that have recently immigrated to the United States adopt a bicultural orientation, selecting characteristics of the U.S. culture that help them to survive and advance, while still retaining aspects of their culture of origin (Cheah & Yeung, 2011; Cooper, 2011). Immigration also involves cultural brokering, which has increasingly occurred in the United States as children and adolescents serve as mediators (cultural and linguistic) for their immigrant parents (Villanueva & Buriel, 2010).

In adopting characteristics of the U.S. culture, Latino families are increasingly embracing the importance of education (Cooper, 2011). Although their school dropout rates have remained higher than for other ethnic groups, toward the end of the first decade of the twenty-first century they declined considerably (National Center for Education Statistics, 2010). Ross Parke and his colleagues (2011) have found that Latino families are retaining a strong commitment to family when they immigrate to the United States despite facing challenges advancing economically. For example, divorce rates for Latino families are lower than for non-Latino White families of similar socioeconomic status.

Of course, individual families vary, and how ethnic minority families deal with stress depends on many factors (Gauvain & Parke, 2010). Whether the parents are native-born or immigrants, how long the family has been in the United States, its socioeconomic status, and its national origin all make a difference (Govia, Jackson, & Sellers, 2011; Lynch & Brown, 2011). The characteristics of the family's social context also influence its adaptation. What are the attitudes toward the family's ethnic group within its neighborhood or city? Can the family's children attend good schools? Are there community groups that welcome people

What characterizes families in different ethnic groups in the United States?

Consider the flowers of a garden: though differing in kind, color, form, and shape, yet, inasmuch as they are refreshed by the waters of one spring, revived by the breath of one wind, invigorated by the rays of one sun, this diversity increases their charm and adds to their beauty. . . . How unpleasing to the eye if all the flowers and plants, the leaves and blossoms, the fruits, the branches, and the trees of that garden were all the same shape and color! Diversity of hues, form, and shape enriches and adorns the garden and heightens its effect.

—ABDU'L BAHA

Persian Bahá'í Religious Leader, 19th/20th Century

Norma Thomas, Social Work Professor and Administrator

Norma Thomas.

Dr. Norma Thomas has worked for more than three decades in the field of aging. She obtained her undergraduate degree in social work from Pennsylvania State University and her doctoral degree in social work from the University of Pennsylvania. Thomas' activities are varied. Earlier in her career, as a social work practitioner, she provided services to older adults of color in an effort to improve their lives. She currently is a professor and academic administrator at Widener University in Chester, Pennsylvania, a fellow of the Institute of Aging at the University of Pennsylvania, and the chief executive officer and cofounder of the Center on Ethnic and Minority Aging (CEMA). CEMA was formed to provide research, consultation, training, and services to benefit aging individuals of color, their families, and their communities. Thomas has created numerous community service events that benefit older adults of color, especially African Americans and Latinos. She has also been a consultant to various national, regional, and state agencies in her effort to improve the lives of aging adults of color.

from the family's ethnic group? Do members of the family's ethnic group form community groups of their own?

Ethnicity and Aging Of special concern are ethnic minority older adults, especially African Americans and Latinos, who are overrepresented in poverty statistics (U.S. Census Bureau, 2010). Comparative information about African Americans, Latinos, and non-Latino Whites indicates a possible double jeopardy for elderly ethnic minority individuals. They face problems related to both ageism and racism. One study of more than 4,000 older adults found that African Americans perceived more discrimination than non-Latino Whites (Barnes & others, 2004). Both the wealth and the health of ethnic minority older adults decrease more rapidly than for elderly non-Latino Whites (Jackson, Govia, & Sellers, 2011). Older ethnic minority individuals are more likely to become ill but less likely to receive treatment (Hinrichsen, 2006). They also are more likely to have a history of less education, longer periods of unemployment, worse housing conditions, and shorter life expectancies than their older non-Latino White counterparts (Himes, Hogan, & Eggebeen, 1996). And many ethnic minority workers never enjoy the Social Security and Medicare benefits to which their earnings contribute, because they die before reaching the age of eligibility for benefits (Ciol & others, 2008).

Despite the stress and discrimination older ethnic minority individuals face, many of these older adults have developed coping mechanisms that allow them to survive in the dominant non-Latino White world (Kingston & Bartholomew, 2009). Extension of family networks helps older minority group individuals cope with the bare essentials of living and gives them a sense of being loved (Antonucci, Vandewater, & Lansford, 2000). Churches in African American and Latino communities provide avenues for meaningful social participation, feelings of power, and a sense of internal satisfaction (Hill & others, 2006). And residential concentrations of ethnic minority groups give their older members a sense of belonging. Thus, it is important to consider individual variations in the lives of aging minorities. To read about one individual who is providing help for aging minorities, see the *Connecting with Careers* profile.

Review

- How can culture, cross-cultural comparisons, and individualism/collectivism be defined? What are some outcomes of the increase in media use? How is culture related to development?
- What is socioeconomic status? How are socioeconomic status and poverty linked to development?
- What is ethnicity? How is ethnicity involved in development? What are some important aspects of ethnicity to recognize?

Connect

- Compare what you learned in this section about the digitally mediated world of children and adolescents with the chapter's earlier discussion of the importance of play. What are your conclusions?

Reflect *Your Own Personal Journey of Life*

- No matter how well intentioned people are, their life circumstances likely have given them some prejudices. If they don't have prejudices toward people with different cultural and ethnic backgrounds, other kinds of people may bring out prejudices in them. For example, prejudices can be developed about people who have certain religious or political convictions, people who are unattractive or too attractive, people with a disability, and people who live in a nearby town. As a parent or teacher, how would you attempt to reduce children's prejudices?

reach your **learning goals**

Peer Relations in Childhood and Adolescence

 LG1 Discuss peer relations in childhood and adolescence

Exploring Peer Relations

- Peers are individuals who are at about the same age or maturity level. Peers provide a means of social comparison and a source of information about the world outside the family. Good peer relations may be necessary for normal social development. The inability to "plug in" to a social network is associated with a number of problems. Peer relations can be both positive and negative. Piaget and Sullivan stressed that peer relations provide the context for learning the reciprocal aspects of relationships. Healthy family relations usually promote healthy peer relations. Parents can model or coach their children in ways of relating to peers. Parents' choices of neighborhoods, churches, schools, and their own friends influence the pool from which their children might select possible friends. Rough-and-tumble play occurs mainly in peer relations rather than in parent-child relations. In times of stress, children usually turn to parents rather than peers. Peer relations have a more equal basis than parent-child relations. Contexts and individual difference factors influence peer relations. The frequency of peer interaction, both positive and negative, increases in the preschool years. Children spend even more time with peers in the elementary and secondary school years. Social information-processing skills and social knowledge are important dimensions of social cognition in peer relations. Emotional regulation plays an important role in determining whether a child's peer relationships are successful.

Peer Statuses

- Popular children are frequently nominated as a best friend and are rarely disliked by their peers. Average children receive an average number of both positive and negative nominations from their peers. Neglected children are infrequently nominated as a best friend but are not disliked by their peers. Rejected children are infrequently nominated as a best friend and are actively disliked by their peers.

Controversial children are frequently nominated both as a best friend and as being disliked by peers.

- Significant numbers of students are bullied, and bullying can result in short-term and long-term negative effects for the victim. Anxious, withdrawn children and aggressive children often are victims of bullying, and boys are far more likely to be involved in bullying than girls are.

- Gender is linked to peer relations in several ways. From 4 to 12 years of age, preference for playing in same-sex groups increases. Boys' groups are larger than girls', and they participate in more organized games than girls do. Boys are more likely to engage in rough-and-tumble play, competition, ego displays, risk taking, and dominance, whereas girls are more likely to engage in collaborative discourse. Peers play more important roles in adolescents' lives in some cultures than in others, with some countries restricting adolescents' access to peers, especially for girls.

- Child groups are less formal and less heterogeneous than adolescent groups; child groups are also more likely to have same-sex participants. The pressure to conform to peers is strong during adolescence, especially during the eighth and ninth grades. Cliques and crowds assume more importance in the lives of adolescents than in the lives of children. Membership in certain crowds—especially jocks and populars—is associated with increased self-esteem. Independents also show high self-esteem.

Friendship

LG2 Explain the role of friendship through the life span

- The functions of friendship include companionship, stimulation, ego support, social comparison, and intimacy/affection.

- Throughout childhood and adolescence, friends are generally similar—in terms of age, sex, ethnicity, and many other factors. Although having friends is usually a developmental advantage, the quality of friendships varies and having a coercive, conflict-ridden friendship can be harmful.

- Sullivan argued that there is a dramatic increase in the psychological importance of intimacy of close friends in adolescence. Friendships are important sources of support for adolescents. Research findings generally support his view. The friendships of adolescent girls are more intimate than those of adolescent boys. Adolescents who become friends with older individuals engage in more deviant behaviors than their counterparts with same-age friends. Many aspects of friendship are the same in emerging adulthood as in adolescence, although the transition to college can bring changes in friendship.

- Friendships play an important role in adult development, especially in providing emotional support. Female, male, and female-male friendships often have different characteristics. Regardless of age, friendship is an important aspect of relationships. In old age, there often is more change in male than in female friendships.

Play and Leisure

LG3 Describe the developmental aspects of play and leisure

- The functions of play include affiliation with peers, tension release, advances in cognitive development, and exploration. The contemporary perspective emphasizes both social and cognitive aspects of play. The most widely studied types of play include sensorimotor and practice play, pretense/symbolic play, social play, constructive play, and games.

- Leisure refers to the pleasant times when individuals are free to pursue activities and interests of their own choosing—hobbies, sports, or reading, for example. U.S. adolescents have more discretionary time than do adolescents in other industrialized countries, but they often fill this time with unchallenging activities such as hanging out and watching television. U.S. adolescents spend more time in voluntary unstructured activities—such as hobbies, sports, and organizations—than do East Asian adolescents. Some scholars argue that U.S. adolescents have too much unstructured discretionary time that should be replaced with more challenging activities.

Adulthood

- As adults, we not only need to learn to work well, but we also need to learn to enjoy leisure. Midlife may be an especially important time for leisure because of expanded free time, because of the availability of more money to many individuals, and because of the need for psychological preparation for an active retirement.

Aging and the Social World

LG4 Summarize the social aspects of aging

Social Theories of Aging

- Disengagement theory, in which older adults gradually withdraw from society, has not held up, but socioemotional selectivity theory and activity theory are viable theories of aging.

Stereotyping of Older Adults

- There is extensive stereotyping of older adults, and ageism is a common occurrence.

Social Support and Social Integration

- Social support is an important aspect of helping people cope with stress. Older adults usually have less integrated social networks and engage in less social activity than their younger counterparts, although these findings may be influenced by cohort effects.

Successful Aging

- Increasingly, the positive aspects of aging are being studied. Factors that are linked with successful aging include an active lifestyle, positive coping skills, good social relationships and support, and self-efficacy.

Sociocultural Influences

LG5 Evaluate sociocultural influences on development

Culture

- Culture refers to the behavior, patterns, beliefs, and all other products of a group of people that are passed on from generation to generation. Cross-cultural comparisons involve the comparison of one culture with one or more cultures to gain information about the degree to which aspects are universal or culture-specific. One way that the influence of culture has been studied is to characterize cultures as individualistic (giving priority to personal rather than group goals) or collectivistic (emphasizing values that serve the group). Many experts argue that exposure to television violence is linked to increased aggression. Heavy TV watching is linked to lower school achievement. Children and youth also spend substantial amounts of time on the Internet. Large numbers of adolescents and college students engage in social networking on Facebook. Although older adults are less likely to have a computer and use the Internet than younger adults, they are the fastest-growing age segment of Internet users. Respect for the aged may vary across cultures. Factors that predict high status for older adults across cultures range from the perception that they have valuable knowledge to the belief that they serve useful functions.

Socioeconomic Status and Poverty

- Socioeconomic status (SES) is the grouping of people with similar occupational, educational, and economic characteristics. The neighborhoods and families of children have SES characteristics that are related to children's development. Parents from low-SES families are more concerned that their children conform to society's expectations, have an authoritarian parenting style, use physical punishment more in disciplining their children, and are more directive and less conversational with their children than higher-SES parents. Poverty is defined by economic hardship. The subculture of the poor is often characterized not only by economic hardship but also by social and psychological difficulties. Persistent, long-lasting poverty especially has adverse effects on children's development. Older adults who live in poverty are a special concern.

- Ethnicity is based on cultural heritage, nationality characteristics, race, religion, and language. Immigration brings a number of challenges as children adapt to their new culture. Although not all ethnic minority families are poor, poverty contributes to the stress of many ethnic minority families and between ethnic minority groups and the non-Latino White majority. African American and Latino children are more likely than non-Latino White American children to live in single-parent families and larger families and to have extended family connections. A special concern involves ethnicity and aging.

key terms

peers 487
popular children 491
average children 491
neglected children 491
rejected children 491
controversial children 491
cliques 494
crowds 494

intimacy in friendship 495
play 500
play therapy 500
sensorimotor play 501
practice play 501
pretense/symbolic
   play 501
social play 501

constructive play 501
games 502
leisure 502
disengagement
   theory 504
activity theory 504
ageism 505
culture 507

cross-cultural studies 507
ethnocentrism 508
individualism 508
collectivism 508
socioeconomic status
   (SES) 513
feminization of
   poverty 515

key people

Judy Smetana 488
Kenneth Dodge 490
John Coie 491
Harry Stack Sullivan 497

Daniel Berlyne 500
Catherine Garvey 501
Angeline Lillard 501
Reed Larson 503

Richard Brislin 507
Donald Campbell 507
Suniya Luthar 514
Vonnie McLoyd 515

Aletha Huston 516
Ross Parke 518

chapter 16 · SCHOOLS, ACHIEVEMENT, AND WORK

preview

This chapter is about becoming educated, achieving, and working. We will begin the chapter by exploring the importance of schools in development and then examine many aspects of a topic that is closely linked to success in school and life—achievement. The final section of the chapter focuses on key aspects of career development, the role of work across the life span, and retirement as a help or a hindrance to our development.

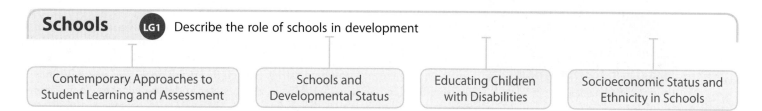

Schools **LG1** Describe the role of schools in development

| Contemporary Approaches to Student Learning and Assessment | Schools and Developmental Status | Educating Children with Disabilities | Socioeconomic Status and Ethnicity in Schools |

We have discussed many aspects of schools throughout this book but especially in Section 3. Recall our coverage of applications of Piaget's and Vygotsky's theories to education in Chapter 6, strategies for encouraging children's critical thinking in schools in Chapter 7, applications of Gardner's and Sternberg's theories of intelligence to education in Chapter 8, and bilingual education in Chapter 9. Among the topics related to schools that we explore here are contemporary approaches to student learning, education for individuals at different developmental levels, educating children with disabilities, and socioeconomic status and ethnicity in schools.

developmental **connection**

Cognitive Theory. Piaget's and Vygotsky's theories can be applied to children's education. Chapter 6, p. 203

CONTEMPORARY APPROACHES TO STUDENT LEARNING AND ASSESSMENT

Because there are so many approaches to education, controversy swirls about the best way to teach children (Arends, 2012; Powell, 2012). There also is considerable interest in finding the best way to hold schools and teachers accountable for whether children are learning (Popham, 2011).

The whole art of teaching is the art of awakening the natural curiosity of young minds.

—**ANATOLE FRANCE**
French Novelist, 20th Century

Constructivist and Direct Instruction Approaches   The **constructivist approach** is learner centered, and it emphasizes the importance of individuals actively constructing their knowledge and understanding with guidance from the teacher. In the constructivist view, teachers should not attempt to simply pour information into children's minds. Rather, children should be encouraged to explore their world, discover knowledge, reflect, and think critically with careful monitoring and meaningful guidance from the teacher (Eby, Herrell, & Jordan, 2011). The constructivist belief is that for too long in American education children have been required to sit still, be passive learners, and rotely memorize irrelevant as well as relevant information. Today, constructivism may include an emphasis on collaboration—children working with each other in their efforts to know and understand (Slavin, 2011).

By contrast, the **direct instruction approach** is structured and teacher centered. It is characterized by teacher direction and control, high teacher expectations for students' progress, maximum time spent by students on academic tasks, and efforts by the teacher to keep negative affect to a minimum. An important goal in the direct instruction approach is maximizing student learning time (Borich, 2011; Cruickshank, Jenkins, & Metcalf, 2012).

Advocates of the constructivist approach argue that the direct instruction approach turns children into passive learners and does not adequately challenge them to think in critical and creative ways (Arends, 2012; Fraser, 2011). The direct

Is this classroom more likely constructivist or direct instruction? Explain.

constructivist approach A learner-centered approach that emphasizes the individual's active, cognitive construction of knowledge and understanding with guidance from the teacher.

direct instruction approach A teacher-centered approach characterized by teacher direction and control, high expectations for students' progress, and maximum time spent on academic tasks.

instruction enthusiasts say that the constructivist approaches do not give enough attention to the content of a discipline, such as history or science. They also believe that the constructivist approaches are too relativistic and vague.

Some experts in educational psychology believe that many effective teachers use both a constructivist *and* a direct instruction approach rather than using either exclusively (Bransford & others, 2006). Further, some circumstances may call more for a constructivist approach, others for a direction instruction approach. For example, experts increasingly recommend an explicit, intellectually engaging direct instruction approach when teaching students with a reading or a writing disability (Berninger, 2006).

Accountability   Since the 1990s, the U.S. public and governments at every level have demanded increased accountability from schools. One result has been the spread of state-mandated tests to measure just what students have or have not learned (Popham, 2011; Russell & Arisian, 2012). Many states have identified objectives for students in their state and created tests to measure whether students are meeting those objectives. This approach became national policy in 2002 when the No Child Left Behind (NCLB) legislation was signed into law.

Advocates argue that statewide standardized testing will have a number of positive effects. These include improved student performance; more time teaching the subjects that are tested; high expectations for all students; identification of poorly performing schools, teachers, and administrators; and improved confidence in schools as test scores rise.

Critics argue that the NCLB legislation is doing more harm than good (Yell & Drasgow, 2009). One criticism stresses that using a single test as the sole indicator of students' progress and competence presents a very narrow view of students' skills (Lewis, 2007). This criticism is similar to the one leveled at IQ tests, which we described in Chapter 8. To assess student progress and achievement, many psychologists and educators emphasize that a number of measures should be used, including tests, quizzes, projects, portfolios, classroom observations, and so on. Also, the tests used as part of NCLB don't measure creativity, motivation, persistence, flexible thinking, and social skills (Stiggins, 2008). Critics point out that teachers end up spending far too much class time "teaching to the test" by drilling students and having them memorize isolated facts at the expense of teaching that focuses on thinking skills, which students need for success in life (Pressley, 2007). Also, some individuals are concerned that in the era of No Child Left Behind policy there is a neglect of students who are gifted in the effort to raise the achievement level of students who are not doing well (Clark, 2008).

Consider also the following: Each state is allowed to establish different criteria for what constitutes passing or failing grades on tests designated for NCLB inclusion. An analysis of NCLB data indicated that almost every fourth-grade student in Mississippi knows how to read but only half of Massachusetts' students do (Birman & others, 2007). Clearly, Mississippi's standards for passing the reading test are far below those of Massachusetts. In the recent analysis of state-by-state comparisons, many states have taken the safe route by choosing a low passing score. Thus, while one of NCLB's goals was to raise standards for achievement in U.S. schools, apparently allowing states to set their own standards likely has lowered achievement standards.

What are some of the most important purposes of standardized tests?

Despite such criticisms, the U.S. Department of Education is committed to implementing No Child Left Behind, and schools are making accommodations to meet the requirement of this law. Indeed, most educators support high expectations and high standards of excellence for students and teachers. At issue, however, is whether the tests and procedures mandated by NCLB are the best means of achieving these high standards (Darling-Hammond, 2011; Nitko & Brookhart, 2011; Witte, 2012).

SCHOOLS AND DEVELOPMENTAL STATUS

Let's now explore how schools work at different developmental levels of students. We will begin with early childhood education.

Early Childhood Education How do early education programs treat children, and how do the children fare? Our exploration of early childhood education focuses on variations in programs, education for children who are disadvantaged, and some controversies in early childhood education.

Variations in Early Childhood Education There are many variations in the way young children are educated (Follari, 2011; Morrison, 2011, 2012). The foundation of early childhood education is the child-centered kindergarten.

Nurturing is a key aspect of the **child-centered kindergarten,** which emphasizes the education of the whole child and concern for his or her physical, cognitive, and socioemotional development (Segal & others, 2012). Instruction is organized around the child's needs, interests, and learning styles. Emphasis is on the process of learning, rather than what is learned (Jalongo & Isenberg, 2012). The child-centered kindergarten honors three principles: (1) Each child follows a unique developmental pattern; (2) young children learn best through firsthand experiences with people and materials; and (3) play is extremely important in the child's total development. *Experimenting, exploring, discovering, trying out, restructuring, speaking,* and *listening* are frequent activities in excellent kindergarten programs. Such programs are closely attuned to the developmental status of 4- and 5-year-old children.

What are some characteristics of the child-centered kindergarten?

Montessori schools are patterned on the educational philosophy of Maria Montessori (1870–1952), an Italian physician-turned-educator who at the beginning of the twentieth century crafted a revolutionary approach to young children's education. The **Montessori approach** is a philosophy of education in which children are given considerable freedom and spontaneity in choosing activities. They are allowed to move from one activity to another as they desire. The teacher acts as a facilitator rather than a director. The teacher shows the child how to perform intellectual activities, demonstrates interesting ways to explore curriculum materials, and offers help when the child requests it. "By encouraging children to make decisions from an early age, Montessori programs seek to develop self-regulated problem solvers who can make choices and manage their time effectively" (Hyson, Copple, & Jones, 2006, p. 14). The number of Montessori schools in the United States has expanded dramatically in recent years, from one school in 1959 to 355 schools in 1970 to more than 4,000 today.

Larry Page and Sergey Brin, founders of the highly successful Internet search engine, Google, said that their early years at Montessori schools were a major factor in their success (International Montessori Council, 2006). During an interview with Barbara Walters, they said they learned how to be self-directed and self-starters at Montessori (ABC News, 2005). They commented that Montessori experiences encouraged them to think for themselves and allowed them the freedom to develop their own interests.

Some developmental psychologists favor the Montessori approach, but others believe that it neglects children's socioemotional development. For example, although the Montessori approach fosters independence and the development of cognitive skills, it deemphasizes verbal interaction between the teacher and child and between peers. Montessori's critics also argue that it restricts imaginative play and that its heavy reliance on self-corrective materials may not adequately allow for creativity and for a variety of learning styles.

Many educators and psychologists conclude that preschool and young elementary school children learn best through active, hands-on teaching methods such as games and dramatic play. They know that children develop at varying rates and that

child-centered kindergarten Education that involves the whole child by considering both the child's physical, cognitive, and socioemotional development and the child's needs, interests, and learning styles.

Montessori approach An educational philosophy in which children are given considerable freedom and spontaneity in choosing activities and are allowed to move from one activity to another as they desire.

schools need to allow for these individual differences. They also argue that schools should focus on supporting children's socioemotional development as well as their cognitive development. Educators refer to this type of schooling as **developmentally appropriate practice (DAP),** which is based on knowledge of the typical development of children within a particular age span (age appropriateness), as well as on the uniqueness of the individual child (individual appropriateness). DAP emphasizes the importance of creating settings that encourage children to be active learners and reflect children's interests and capabilities (Bredekamp, 2011; Kostelnik, Soderman, & Whiren, 2011). Desired outcomes for DAP include thinking critically, working cooperatively, solving problems, developing self-regulatory skills, and enjoying learning. The emphasis in DAP is on the process of learning rather than on its content (Barbarin & Miller, 2009; Bredekamp, 2011).

Do developmentally appropriate educational practices improve young children's development? Some researchers have found that young children in developmentally appropriate classrooms are likely to feel less stress, be more motivated, be more socially skilled, have better work habits, be more creative, have better language skills, and demonstrate better math skills than children in developmentally inappropriate classrooms (Hart & others, 2003). However, not all studies find DAP to have significant positive effects (Hyson, Copple, & Jones, 2006). Among the reasons that it is difficult to generalize about research on developmentally appropriate education is that individual programs often vary, and developmentally appropriate education is an evolving concept. Recent changes in the concept have given more attention to how strongly academic skills should be emphasized and how they should be taught.

Education for Young Children Who Are Disadvantaged   For many years, U.S. children from low-income families did not receive any education before they entered the first grade. Often when they began first grade they were already several steps behind their classmates in readiness to learn. In the summer of 1965, the federal government began an effort to break the cycle of poverty and poor education for young children through **Project Head Start.** Head Start is a compensatory program designed to give children from low-income families the opportunity to acquire skills and experiences that are important for success in school (Zigler & Styfco, 2010). After almost half a century, Head Start continues to be the largest federally funded program for U.S. children, with almost 1 million children enrolled in it annually (Hagen & Lamb-Parker, 2008). In 2007, 3 percent of Head Start children were 5 years old, 51 percent were 4 years old, 36 percent were 3 years old, and 10 percent were under age 3 (Administration for Children & Families, 2008).

Early Head Start was established in 1995 to serve children from birth to age 3. In 2007, half of all new funds appropriated for Head Start programs were used for the expansion of Early Head Start. Researchers have found these programs to have positive effects (Hoffman & Ewen, 2007).

Head Start programs are not all created equal. One estimate is that 40 percent of the 1,400 Head Start programs are of questionable quality (Zigler & Styfco, 1994). More attention needs to be given to developing consistently high-quality Head Start programs (Chambers, Cheung, & Slavin, 2006). One person who is strongly motivated to make Head Start a valuable learning experience for young children from disadvantaged backgrounds is Yolanda Garcia. To read about her work, see the *Connecting with Careers* profile.

Evaluations support the positive influence of quality early childhood programs on both the cognitive and social worlds of disadvantaged young children (Phillips & Lowenstein, 2011). A recent national evaluation of Head Start revealed that the program had a positive influence on the language and cognitive development of the 3- and 4-year-olds (Puma & others, 2010). However, by the end of the first grade, there were few lasting outcomes. One exception was a larger vocabulary for those who went to Head Start as 4-year-olds and better oral comprehension for those who went to Head Start as 3-year-olds. Another recent study found that when young

developmentally appropriate practice (DAP) Education that focuses on the typical developmental patterns of children (age appropriateness) and the uniqueness of each child (individual appropriateness). Such practice contrasts with developmentally inappropriate practice, which has an academic, direct instruction emphasis focused largely on abstract paper-and-pencil activities, seatwork, and rote/drill practice activities.

Project Head Start Compensatory education designed to provide children from low-income families the opportunity to acquire skills and experiences important for school success.

Yolanda Garcia, Director of Children's Services, Head Start

Yolanda Garcia has been the director of the Children's Services Department of the Santa Clara, California, County Office of Education since 1980. As director, she is responsible for managing child development programs for 2,500 3- to 5-year-old children in 127 classrooms. Her training includes two master's degrees, one in public policy and child welfare from the University of Chicago and another in education administration from San Jose State University.

Garcia has served on many national advisory committees that have resulted in improvements in the staffing of Head Start programs. Most notably, she served on the Head Start Quality Committee that recommended the development of Early Head Start and revised performance standards for Head Start programs. Garcia currently is a member of the American Academy of Science Committee on the Integration of Science and Early Childhood Education.

Yolanda Garcia, Director of Children's Services/Head Start, working with a Head Start child in Santa Clara, California.

children initially began Head Start, they were well below their more academically advantaged peers in literacy and math (Hindman & others, 2010). However, by the end of the first grade, the Head Start children were on par with national averages in literacy and math.

One high-quality early childhood education program (although not a Head Start program) is the Perry Preschool program in Ypsilanti, Michigan, a two-year preschool program that includes weekly home visits from program personnel. In analyses of the long-term effects of the program, adults who had been in the Perry Preschool program were compared with a control group of adults from the same background who had not received the enriched early childhood education (Schweinhart & others, 2005; Weikert, 1993). Those who had been in the Perry Preschool program had fewer teen pregnancies and higher high school graduation rates, and at age 40 they were more likely to be in the workforce, own a home, and have a savings account, and they'd also had fewer arrests.

Controversy Over Curriculum A current controversy in early childhood education involves what the curriculum for early childhood education should be (Barbarin & Miller, 2009; Bredekamp, 2011; Marion, 2010). On one side are those who advocate a child-centered, constructivist approach much like that emphasized by the National Association for the Education of Young Children (NAEYC), along the lines of developmentally appropriate practice. On the other side are those who advocate an academic, direct-instruction approach.

In reality, many high-quality early childhood education programs include both academic and constructivist approaches. Many education experts such as Lilian Katz (1999), however, worry about academic approaches that place too much pressure on young children to achieve and don't provide opportunities to actively construct knowledge. Competent early childhood programs should focus on both cognitive development *and* socioemotional development, not exclusively on cognitive development (Bredekamp, 2011; NAEYC, 2009).

What are two controversies in early childhood education?

As children make the transition to elementary school, they interact and develop relationships with new and significant others. School provides them with a rich source of new ideas to shape their sense of self.

Elementary School For many children, entering the first grade signals a change from being a "home-child" to being a "school-child"—a situation in which they experience new roles and obligations. Children take up the new role of being a student, interact, develop new relationships, adopt new reference groups, and develop new standards by which to judge themselves. School provides children with a rich source of new ideas to shape their sense of self.

Too often early schooling proceeds mainly on the basis of negative feedback. For example, children's self-esteem in the later part of elementary school is lower than it is in the earlier part, and older children rate themselves as less smart, less good, and less hardworking than do younger ones (Eccles, 2003).

Educating Adolescents What is the transition from elementary to middle or junior high school like? What are the characteristics of effective schools for adolescents?

The Transition to Middle or Junior High School The transition to middle school or junior high school can be stressful (Anderman & Anderman, 2010; Bellmore & others, 2011). Why? The transition takes place at a time when many changes—in the individual, in the family, and in school—are occurring simultaneously. These changes include puberty and related concerns about body image; the emergence of at least some aspects of formal operational thought, including accompanying changes in social cognition; increased responsibility and decreased dependency on parents; change to a larger, more impersonal school structure; change from one teacher to many teachers and from a small, homogeneous set of peers to a larger, more heterogeneous set of peers; and an increased focus on achievement and performance and their assessment. Also, when students make the transition to middle or junior high school, they experience the **top-dog phenomenon,** moving from being the oldest, biggest, and most powerful students in the elementary school to being the youngest, smallest, and least powerful students in the middle or junior high school. A recent study in North Carolina schools revealed that sixth-grade students attending middle schools were far more likely to be cited for discipline problems than their counterparts who were attending elementary schools (Cook & others, 2008).

The transition from elementary to middle or junior high school occurs at the same time as a number of other developmental changes. *What are some of these other developmental changes?*

There can also be positive aspects to the transition to middle or junior high school. Students are more likely to feel grown up, have more subjects from which to select, have more opportunities to spend time with peers and locate compatible friends, and enjoy increased independence from direct parental monitoring. They also may be more challenged intellectually by academic work.

Effective Schools for Young Adolescents Educators and psychologists worry that junior high and middle schools have become watered-down versions of high schools, mimicking their curricular and extracurricular schedules. Critics argue that these schools should offer activities that reflect a wide range of individual differences in biological and psychological development among young adolescents (Casas, 2011). The Carnegie Foundation (1989) issued an extremely negative evaluation of U.S. middle schools. It concluded that most young adolescents attended massive, impersonal schools, learned from irrelevant curricula, trusted few adults in school, and lacked access to health care and counseling. It recommended that the nation develop smaller "communities" or "houses" to lessen the impersonal nature of large middle schools; have lower student-to-counselor ratios (10 to 1 instead of several hundred

top-dog phenomenon The circumstance of moving from the top position in elementary school to the youngest, smallest, and least powerful position in middle or junior high school.

to 1); involve parents and community leaders in schools; develop new curricula; have teachers team teach in more flexibly designed curriculum blocks that integrate several disciplines; boost students' health and fitness with more in-school physical education programs; and help students who need public health care to get it. In sum, many of the Carnegie Foundation's recommendations have not been implemented, and middle schools throughout the nation continue to need a major redesign if they are to be effective in educating adolescents (Eccles & Roeser, 2009).

High School Just as there are concerns about U.S. middle school education, so are there concerns about U.S. high school education (Smith, 2009). Critics stress that many high schools foster passivity and that schools should create a variety of pathways for students to achieve an identity. Many students graduate from high school with inadequate reading, writing, and mathematical skills; of these, many go on to college and have to enroll in remediation classes there. Other students drop out of high school and do not have skills that will allow them to obtain decent jobs, much less to be informed citizens.

Adolescents in U.S. schools usually have a wide array of extracurricular activities they can participate in beyond their academic courses. These activities include such diverse activities as sports, academic clubs, band, drama, and math clubs. Researchers have found that participation in extracurricular activities is linked to higher grades, greater school engagement, less likelihood of dropping out of school, improved probability of going to college, higher self-esteem, and lower rates of depression, delinquency, and substance abuse (Barber, Stone, & Eccles, 2010; Mahoney, Parente, & Zigler, 2010). Adolescents benefit from a breadth of extracurricular activities more than focusing on a single extracurricular activity.

In the second half of the twentieth century and the first several years of the twenty-first century, U.S. high school dropout rates declined (National Center for Education Statistics, 2010). In the 1940s, more than half of U.S. 16- to 24-year-olds had dropped out of school; by 2008, this figure had decreased to 8 percent. The dropout rate of Latino adolescents remains high, although it has been decreasing in the twenty-first century (from 28 percent in 2000 to 18 percent in 2008). The lowest dropout rate in 2008 occurred for Asian American adolescents (3.2 percent), followed by non-Latino White adolescents (6.2 percent), African American adolescents (10.4 percent), then Latino adolescents (19 percent). Native American adolescents also have a high dropout rate, although government statistics for this ethnic group have not been adequately assessed.

Gender differences characterize U.S. dropout rates, with males more likely to drop out than females (10.4 versus 7.9 percent) (data for 2008) (National Center for Education Statistics, 2010). The gender gap in dropout rates is especially large for Latino adolescents (21.9 versus 15 percent). Figure 16.1 shows the dropout rates of 16- to 24-year-olds by ethnicity and gender in 2008.

Students drop out of school for many reasons (Jimerson, 2009). In one study, almost 50 percent of the dropouts cited school-related reasons for leaving school, such as not liking school or being expelled or suspended (Rumberger, 1995). Twenty percent of the dropouts (but 40 percent of the Latino students) cited economic reasons for leaving school. One-third of the female students dropped out for personal reasons, such as pregnancy or marriage. A recent study revealed that when children's parents were involved in their school in middle and late childhood and when parents and adolescents had good relationships in early adolescence, a positive trajectory toward academic success was the likely outcome

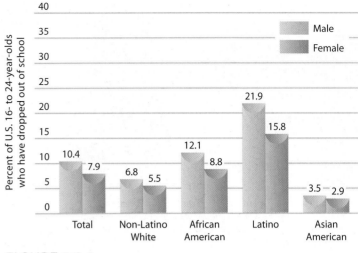

FIGURE **16.1**

SCHOOL DROPOUT RATES OF U.S. 16- TO 24-YEAR-OLDS BY GENDER AND ETHNICITY

Students in the technology training center at Wellpinit Elementary/ High School located on the Spokane Indian Reservation in Washington. An important educational goal is to increase the high school graduation rate of Native American adolescents.

These adolescents are participating in the "I Have a Dream" (IHAD) Program, a comprehensive, long-term dropout prevention program that has been very successful. *What are some other strategies for reducing high school dropout rates?*

(Englund, Egeland, & Collins, 2008). By contrast, those who had poor relationships with their parents were more likely to drop out of high school despite doing well academically and behaviorally.

"I Have a Dream" (IHAD) is an innovative comprehensive, long-term dropout prevention program administered by the National "I Have a Dream" Foundation in New York. Since the National IHAD Foundation was created in 1986, it has grown to comprise more than 180 projects in 64 cities and 27 states serving more than 15,000 children ("I Have a Dream" Foundation, 2010). Local IHAD projects around the country "adopt" entire grades (usually the third or fourth) from public elementary schools, or corresponding age cohorts from public housing developments. These children—"Dreamers"—are then provided with a program of academic, social, cultural, and recreational activities throughout their elementary, middle school, and high school years. When participants complete high school, IHAD provides the tuition assistance necessary for them to attend a state or local college or vocational school.

The IHAD program was created in 1981, when philanthropist Eugene Lang made an impromptu offer of college tuition to a class of graduating sixth-graders at P.S. 121 in East Harlem. Evaluations of IHAD programs have found dramatic improvements in grades, test scores, and school attendance, as well as a reduction in behavioral problems of Dreamers. In a recent analysis of the I Have a Dream program in Houston, 91 percent of the participants received passing grades in reading/English, 83 percent said they liked school, 98 percent said getting good grades is important to them, 100 percent said they plan to graduate from high school, and 94 percent reported they plan to go to college ("I Have a Dream" Foundation, 2010).

College and Adult Education   Going to college offers many practical benefits, even beyond an education. The more education individuals have, the more income they will earn (*Occupational Outlook Handbook*, 2010–2011). Also, individuals with a college education live two years longer on the average than their counterparts who only graduate from high school. What is the transition to college like? Are adults seeking more education than in the past?

The transition from high school to college often involves positive as well as negative features. In college, students are likely to feel grown up, be able to spend more time with peers, have more opportunities to explore different lifestyles and values, and enjoy greater freedom from parental monitoring. However, college involves a larger, more impersonal school structure and an increased focus on achievement and its assessment. *What was your transition to college like?*

Transition to College   Just as the transition from elementary school to middle or junior high school involves change and possible stress, so does the transition from high school to college. The two transitions have many parallels. Going from being a senior in high school to being a freshman in college replays the top-dog phenomenon of transferring from the oldest and most powerful group of students to the youngest and least powerful group of students that occurred earlier as adolescence began. For many students, the transition from high school to college involves movement to a larger, more impersonal school structure; interaction with peers from more diverse geographical and sometimes more diverse ethnic backgrounds; and increased focus on achievement and its assessment. And like the transition from elementary to middle or junior high school, the transition from high school to college can involve positive features. Students are more likely to feel grown up, have more subjects from which to select, have more time to spend with peers, have more opportunities to explore different lifestyles and values, enjoy greater independence from parental monitoring, and be challenged intellectually by academic work (Santrock & Halonen, 2009).

Today's college students experience more stress and are more depressed than in the past, according to a national study of more than 300,000 freshmen at more than 500 colleges and universities (Pryor & others, 2009). In 2009, 27 percent (up from 16 percent in 1985) said they frequently "felt overwhelmed with what I have to do." College females were more than twice as likely as their male counterparts

(37 to 17 percent, respectively) to say that they felt overwhelmed with all they had to do. And college freshmen in 2009 indicated that they felt more depressed than their counterparts from the 1980s had indicated. The pressure to succeed in college, get a great job, and make lots of money were pervasive concerns of these students.

What makes college students happy? One study of 222 undergraduates compared the upper 10 percent of college students who were very happy with average and very unhappy college students (Diener & Seligman, 2002). The very happy college students were highly social, more extraverted, and had stronger romantic and social relationships than the less happy college students, who spent more time alone (see Figure 16.2).

Adult Education   An increasing number of adults older than the traditional college age go to school (Smith & Reio, 2007). *Adult education* refers to all forms of schooling and learning in which adults participate. Adult education includes literacy training, community development, university credit programs, on-the-job training, and continuing professional education (Comings, 2007). Institutions that offer education to adults include colleges, libraries, museums, government agencies, businesses, and churches.

In 1985, individuals over the age of 25 represented 45 percent of the enrollment in credit courses in the United States. At the beginning of the twenty-first century, that figure is now slightly over 50 percent. A large and expanding number of college students are adults who pursue education and advanced degrees on a part-time basis (Smith & Reio, 2007). The increase in adult education is a result of increased leisure time for some individuals and the need to update information and skills for others. Some older adults simply take educational courses because they enjoy learning and want to keep their minds active.

Women represent the majority of adult learners—almost 60 percent. In the 35-and-over age group, women constitute an even greater percentage of the enrollment in adult education—almost 70 percent. Some of these women devoted their early adult lives to parenting and decided to go back to school to enter a new career.

Going back to a classroom after being away from school for a long time can be stressful. However, returning students should realize that they bring a wealth of experience to college and should feel good about the contributions they can make.

EDUCATING CHILDREN WITH DISABILITIES

So far we have discussed schools as they are experienced by the majority of U.S. students. But 13.4 percent of all children from 3 to 21 years of age in the United States receive special education or related services (National Center for Education Statistics, 2010). Figure 16.3 shows the four largest groups of students with a disability who were served by federal programs during the 2006–2007 school year (National Center for Education Statistics, 2010). As indicated in Figure 16.3, students with a learning disability were by far the largest group of students with a disability to be given special education, followed by children with speech or language impairments, mental retardation, and emotional disturbance.

Learning Disabilities   The U.S. government defines whether a child should be classified as having a learning disability in the following way: A child with a **learning disability** has difficulty in learning that involves understanding or using spoken or written language, and the difficulty can appear in listening, thinking, reading, writing, and spelling. A learning disability also may involve difficulty in doing mathematics.

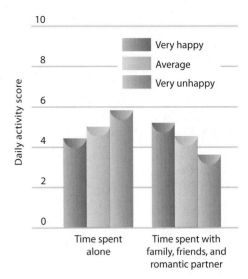

FIGURE **16.2**

DAILY ACTIVITY SELF-RATINGS AND COLLEGE STUDENTS' HAPPINESS. In this study of undergraduates, the daily activity scores reflect mean times with 0 representing no time and 8 reflecting 8 hours per day (Diener & Seligman, 2002). Students were classified as very happy, average, or very unhappy based on their self-ratings.

Many immigrants to the United States, such as this Spanish-speaking woman enrolled in an English class, take adult education classes. *What are some trends in adult education?*

learning disabilities Disabilities in which children experience difficulty in learning that involves understanding or using spoken or written language; the difficulty can appear in listening, thinking, reading, writing, and spelling. A learning disability also may involve difficulty in doing mathematics. To be classified as a learning disability, the learning problem is not primarily the result of visual, hearing, or motor disabilities; mental retardation; emotional disorders; or environmental, cultural, or economic disadvantage.

Disability	Percentage of All Children in Public Schools
Learning disabilities	5.2
Speech and language impairments	3.0
Mental retardation	1.1
Emotional disturbance	0.9

FIGURE 16.3

U.S. CHILDREN WITH A DISABILITY WHO RECEIVE SPECIAL EDUCATION SERVICES. Figures are for the 2007–2008 school year and represent the four categories with the highest number and percentage of children. Both learning disability and attention deficit hyperactivity disorder are combined in the learning disabilities category (National Center for Education Statistics, 2010).

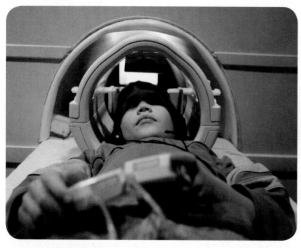

FIGURE 16.4

BRAIN SCANS AND LEARNING DISABILITIES. An increasing number of studies are using MRI brain scans to examine the brain pathways involved in learning disabilities. Shown here is 9-year-old Patrick Price, who has dyslexia. Patrick is going through an MRI scanner disguised by drapes to look like a child-friendly castle. Inside the scanner, children must lie virtually motionless as words and symbols flash on a screen, and they are asked to identify them by clicking different buttons.

attention deficit hyperactivity disorder (ADHD) A disability in which children consistently show one or more of the following characteristics: (1) inattention, (2) hyperactivity, and (3) impulsivity.

To be classified as a learning disability, the learning problem is not primarily the result of visual, hearing, or motor disabilities; mental retardation; emotional disorders; or due to environmental, cultural, or economic disadvantage.

About three times as many boys as girls are classified as having a learning disability. Among the explanations for this gender difference are a greater biological vulnerability among boys and *referral bias.* That is, boys are more likely to be referred by teachers for treatment because of troublesome behavior.

Approximately 80 percent of children with a learning disability have a reading problem (Shaywitz, Gruen, & Shaywitz, 2007). Three types of learning disabilities are dyslexia, dysgraphia, and discalculia:

- *Dyslexia* is a category reserved for individuals who have a severe impairment in their ability to read and spell (Anderson & Meir-Hedde, 2011).

- *Dysgraphia* is a learning disability that involves difficulty in handwriting (Rosenblum, Aloni, & Josman, 2010). Children with dysgraphia may write very slowly, their writing products may be virtually illegible, and they may make numerous spelling errors because of their inability to match up sounds and letters.

- *Dyscalculia,* also known as developmental arithmetic disorder, is a learning disability that involves difficulty in math computation (Rykhlevskaia & others, 2010).

The precise causes of learning disabilities have not yet been determined (Rosenberg, Westling, & McLeskey, 2011). To reveal any regions of the brain that might be involved in learning disabilities, researchers use brain-imaging techniques, such as magnetic resonance imaging (Shaywitz, Lyon, & Shaywitz, 2006) (see Figure 16.4). This research indicates that it is unlikely that learning disabilities reside in a single, specific brain location. More likely, learning disabilities are due to problems in integrating information from multiple brain regions or subtle difficulties in brain structures and functions.

Interventions with children who have a learning disability often focus on improving reading ability (Bursuck & Damer, 2011). Intensive instruction over a period of time by a competent teacher can help many children (Berninger, 2006; Waber, 2010).

Attention Deficit Hyperactivity Disorder (ADHD) **Attention deficit hyperactivity disorder (ADHD)** is a disability in which children consistently show one or more of the following characteristics over a period of time: (1) inattention, (2) hyperactivity, and (3) impulsivity. Children who are inattentive have such difficulty focusing on any one thing that they may get bored with a task after only a few minutes—or even seconds. Children who are hyperactive show high levels of physical activity, seeming to be almost constantly in motion. Children who are impulsive have difficulty curbing their reactions; they do not do a good job of thinking before they act. Depending on the characteristics that children with ADHD display, they can be diagnosed as (1) ADHD with predominantly inattention, (2) ADHD with predominantly hyperactivity/impulsivity, or (3) ADHD with both inattention and hyperactivity/impulsivity.

The number of children diagnosed and treated for ADHD has increased substantially in recent decades. The disorder is diagnosed as much as four to nine times as often in boys as in girls. There is controversy, however, about the increased diagnosis of ADHD (Stolzer, 2009). Some experts attribute the increase mainly to heightened awareness of the disorder; others are concerned that many children are being incorrectly diagnosed (Parens & Johnston, 2009).

Definitive causes of ADHD have not been found. However, a number of causes have been proposed (Faraone & Mick, 2010). Some children likely inherit

Many children and adults show impulsive behavior, such as this boy who is jumping out of his seat and throwing a paper airplane at classmates. *What is the best way for teachers to handle such situations?*

a tendency to develop ADHD from their parents (Durston, 2010). Other children likely develop ADHD because of damage to their brain during prenatal or post-natal development (Lindblad & Hjern, 2010). Among early possible contributors to ADHD are cigarette and alcohol exposure during prenatal development and low birth weight (Knopik, 2009).

As with learning disabilities, the development of brain-imaging techniques is lead-ing to a better understanding of ADHD (Hoeksema & others, 2010). One study revealed that peak thickness of the cerebral cortex occurred three years later (10.5 years) in children with ADHD than in children without ADHD (peak at 7.5 years) (Shaw & others, 2007). The delay was more prominent in the prefrontal regions of the brain that are especially important in attention and planning (see Figure 16.5). Researchers also are exploring the roles that various neurotransmitters, such as serotonin and dopamine, might play in ADHD (Rondou, Haegeman, & Van Craenenbroeck, 2010; Zhou & others, 2010).

Stimulant medication such as Ritalin or Adderall (which has fewer side effects than Ritalin) is effective in improving the attention of many children with ADHD, but it usually does not improve their attention to the same level as children who do not have ADHD (Stray, Ellertsen, & Stray, 2010). A recent meta-analysis con-cluded that behavior management treatments are effective in reducing the effects of ADHD (Fabiano & others, 2009). Researchers have often found that a combination of medication (such as Ritalin) and behavior management improves the behavior of children with ADHD better than medication alone or behavior management alone, although not in all cases (Parens & Johnston, 2009).

Autism Spectrum Disorders   **Autism spectrum disorders (ASDs),** also called pervasive developmental disorders, range from the more severe disorder called *autis-tic disorder* to the milder disorder called *Asperger syndrome*. Autism spectrum disorders are characterized by problems in social interaction, problems in verbal and nonver-bal communication, and repetitive behaviors (Boutot & Myles, 2011; Hall, 2009). Children with these disorders may also show atypical responses to sensory experi-ences (National Institute of Mental Health, 2008). Autism spectrum disorders can often be detected in children as young as 1 to 3 years of age.

Recent estimates of autism spectrum disorders indicate that they are increasing in occurrence or are increasingly being detected and labeled (Neal, 2009). These disorders were once thought to affect only 1 in 2,500 individuals, but today's

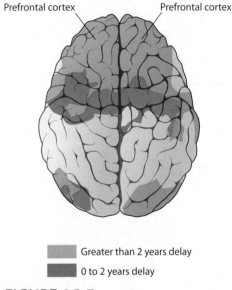

Prefrontal cortex   Prefrontal cortex

■ Greater than 2 years delay

■ 0 to 2 years delay

FIGURE **16.5**

REGIONS OF THE BRAIN IN WHICH CHILDREN WITH ADHD HAD A DELAYED PEAK IN THE THICKNESS OF THE CEREBRAL CORTEX.
Note: The greatest delays occurred in the prefrontal cortex.

developmental **connection**

Conditions, Diseases, and Disorders. Au-tistic children have difficulty in developing a theory of mind, especially in understand-ing others' beliefs and emotions. Chap-ter 7, p. 241

autism spectrum disorders (ASDs) Also called pervasive developmental disorders, these range from the severe disorder labeled autistic disorder to the milder disorder called Asperger syndrome. Children with these disorders are characterized by problems in social interaction, verbal and nonverbal communication, and repetitive behaviors.

What characterizes autism spectrum disorders?

estimates suggest that they occur in about 1 in 150 individuals (Centers for Disease Control and Prevention, 2010).

Autistic disorder is a severe developmental autism spectrum disorder that has its onset in the first three years of life and includes deficiencies in social relationships; abnormalities in communication; and restricted, repetitive, and stereotyped patterns of behavior.

Asperger syndrome is a relatively mild autism spectrum disorder in which the child has relatively good verbal language skills, milder nonverbal language problems, and a restricted range of interests and relationships (Bennett & others, 2008). Children with Asperger syndrome often engage in obsessive repetitive routines and preoccupations with a particular subject. For example, a child may be obsessed with baseball scores or railroad timetables.

What causes the autism spectrum disorders? The current consensus is that autism is a brain dysfunction with abnormalities in brain structure and neurotransmitters (Anderson & others, 2009). Genetic factors likely play a role in the development of the autism spectrum disorders (El-Fishawy & State, 2010; Shen & others, 2010). A recent study revealed that mutations—missing or duplicated pieces of DNA on chromosome 16—can raise a child's risk of developing autism 100-fold (Weiss & others, 2008). There is no evidence that family socialization causes autism. Mental retardation is present in some children with autism; others show average or above-average intelligence (Hoekstra & others, 2010).

Boys are four times as likely to have autism spectrum disorders as girls are (Gong & others, 2009). Expanding on autism's male linkage, Simon Baron-Cohen (2008, 2009, 2011) recently argued that autism reflects an extreme male brain, especially indicative of males' less effective ability to show empathy and read facial expressions

FIGURE **16.6**

A SCENE FROM THE DVD ANIMATIONS USED IN A STUDY BY BARON-COHEN AND OTHERS (2007). *What did they do to improve autistic children's ability to read facial expressions?* © Crown copyright MMVI, www.thetransporters.com, courtesy of Changing Media Development.

and gestures. In an attempt to improve these skills in 4- to 8-year-old autistic boys, Baron-Cohen and his colleagues (2007) produced a number of animations on a DVD that put faces with different emotions on toy trains and tractor characters in a boy's bedroom (see Figure 16.6) (see www.thetransporters.com for a look at a number of the facial expression animations in addition to the one shown in Figure 16.6). After the autistic children watch the animations 15 minutes every weekday for one month, their ability to recognize real faces in a different context equaled that of children without autism.

Children with autism benefit from a well-structured classroom, individualized instruction, and small-group instruction. Behavior modification techniques are sometimes effective in helping autistic children learn (Boutot & Myles, 2011; Kasari & Lawton, 2010). A recent research review concluded that when behavior modifications are intensely provided and used early in the autistic child's life, they are more effective than when used intermittently and later in life (Howlin, Magiati, & Charman, 2009).

autistic disorder A severe autism spectrum disorder that has its onset in the first three years of life and includes deficiencies in social relationships; abnormalities in communication; and restricted, repetitive, and stereotyped patterns of behavior.

Asperger syndrome A relatively mild autism spectrum disorder in which the child has relatively good verbal language skills, milder nonverbal language problems, and a restricted range of interests and relationships.

Educational Issues Until the 1970s most U.S. public schools either refused enrollment to children with disabilities or inadequately served them. This changed in 1975 when Public Law 94-142, the Education for All Handicapped Children Act, required that all students with disabilities be given a free, appropriate public education. In 1990, Public Law 94-142 was recast as the Individuals with Disabilities Education Act (IDEA). IDEA was amended in 1997 and then reauthorized in 2004 and renamed the Individuals with Disabilities Education Improvement Act.

IDEA spells out broad mandates for services to children with disabilities of all kinds (Friend, 2011; Hallahan, Kauffman, & Pullen, 2012). These services include evaluation and eligibility determination, appropriate education and an individualized education plan (IEP), and education in the least restrictive environment (LRE).

An **individualized education plan (IEP)** is a written statement that spells out a program that is specifically tailored for a student with a disability. The **least restrictive environment (LRE)** is a setting that is as similar as possible to the one in which children who do not have a disability are educated. This provision of the IDEA has given a legal basis to efforts to educate children with a disability in the regular classroom (Smith & others, 2012). The term **inclusion** describes educating a child with special educational needs full-time in the regular classroom (Boyle & Provost, 2012; Friend & Bursuck, 2012).

Many legal changes regarding children with disabilities have been extremely positive (Kavale & Spaulding, 2011; Rosenberg, Westling, & McLeskey, 2011). Compared with several decades ago, far more children today are receiving competent, specialized services. For many children, inclusion in the regular classroom, with modifications or supplemental services, is appropriate. However, some leading experts on special education argue that some children with disabilities may not benefit from inclusion in the regular classroom (Hallahan, Kauffman, & Pullen, 2012). James Kauffman and his colleagues, for example, advocate a more individualized approach that does not necessarily involve full inclusion but allows options such as special education outside the regular classroom with trained professionals and adapted curricula (Kauffman, McGee, & Brigham, 2004). They go on to say, "we sell students with disabilities short when we pretend that they are not different from typical students. We make the same error when we pretend that they must *not* be expected to put forth extra effort if they are to learn to do some things—or learn to do something in a different way" (p. 620). Like general education, special education should challenge students with disabilities to become all they can be.

IDEA mandates free, appropriate education for all children. *What services does IDEA mandate for children with disabilities?*

SOCIOECONOMIC STATUS AND ETHNICITY IN SCHOOLS

Children from low-income, ethnic minority backgrounds have more difficulties in school than do their middle-socioeconomic-status, non-Latino White counterparts. Why? Critics argue that schools have not done a good job of educating low-income, ethnic minority students to overcome the barriers to their achievement (Nieto & Bode, 2012; Spring, 2012). And recent comparisons of student achievement indicate that U.S. students have lower achievement in math and science than students in a number of countries, especially those in East Asia (TIMMS, 2008).

The Education of Students from Low-Income Backgrounds Many children in poverty face problems that present barriers to their learning (Borjas, 2011; Chen, Howard, & Brooks-Gunn, 2011). They might have parents who don't set high educational standards for them, who are incapable of reading to them, or who don't have enough money to pay for educational materials and experiences, such as books and trips to zoos and museums. They might be malnourished or live in areas where crime and violence are a way of life. One study revealed that neighborhood disadvantage (involving characteristics such as low neighborhood income and high unemployment) was linked to less consistent, less stimulating, and more punitive parenting, and ultimately to negative child outcomes such as behavioral problems and low verbal ability (Kohen & others, 2008). Another study revealed that the longer children experienced poverty the more detrimental the poverty was to their cognitive development (Najman & others, 2009).

Compared with schools in higher-income areas, schools in low-income areas are more likely to have more students with low achievement test scores, low graduation rates, and small percentages of students going to college; they are more likely to have young teachers with less experience, larger proportions of noncredentialed or nonqualified teachers, and substitute teachers regularly filling in to teach; they are more likely to encourage rote learning; and they are less likely to provide adequate

developmental **connection**

Environment. Socioeconomic differences are a proxy for material, human, and social capital within and beyond the family (Huston & Ripke, 2006). Chapter 15, p. 513

individualized education plan (IEP) A written statement that spells out a program tailored to a child with a disability. The plan should be (1) related to the child's learning capacity, (2) specially constructed to meet the child's individual needs and not merely a copy of what is offered to other children, and (3) designed to provide educational benefits.

least restrictive environment (LRE) A setting that is as similar as possible to the one where children without a disability are educated.

inclusion Education of a child with special educational needs full-time in the regular classroom.

Jill Nakamura, teaching in her first-grade classroom. Jill teaches in a school located in a high-poverty area. She visits students at home early in the school year in an effort to connect with them and develop a partnership with their parents. "She holds a daily afternoon reading club for students reading below grade level.... In one school year (2004), she raised the percent of students reading at or above grade level from 29 percent to 76 percent" (Wong Briggs, 2004, p. 6D).

support for English-language learners (Eccles & Roeser, 2011; Entwisle, Alexander, & Olson, 2010). Too few schools in low-income neighborhoods provide students with environments that are conducive to learning (Koppelman & Goodhart, 2011). Many of the schools' buildings and classrooms are old and crumbling. In sum, far too many schools in low-income neighborhoods provide students with environments that are not conducive to effective learning (Cheah & Yeung, 2011).

Ethnicity in Schools More than one-third of all African American and almost one-third of all Latino students attend schools in the 47 largest city school districts in the United States, compared with only 5 percent of all White and 22 percent of all Asian American students. Many of these inner-city schools are still segregated, are grossly underfunded, and do not provide adequate opportunities for children to learn effectively. Thus, the effects of socioeconomic status (SES) and the effects of ethnicity are often intertwined (Banks, 2010; Bennett, 2011).

Even outside inner-city schools, school segregation remains a factor in U.S. education (Koppelman & Goodhart, 2011). Almost one-third of all African American and Latino students attend schools in which 90 percent or more of the students are from minority groups (Banks, 2008).

The school experiences of students from different ethnic groups vary considerably (Banks, 2010; Spring, 2012). African American and Latino students are much less likely than non-Latino White or Asian American students to be enrolled in academic, college preparatory programs and are much more likely to be enrolled in remedial and special education programs. Asian American students are far more likely than other ethnic minority groups to take advanced math and science courses in high school. African American students are twice as likely as Latinos, Native Americans, or Whites to be suspended from school.

Following are some strategies for improving relationships among ethnically diverse students:

In *The Shame of the Nation,* Jonathan Kozol (2005) criticized the inadequate quality and lack of resources in many U.S. schools, especially those in the poverty areas of inner cities that have high concentrations of ethnic minority children. Kozol praises teachers like Angela Lively (*above*), who keeps a box of shoes in her Indianapolis classroom for students in need.

- *Turn the class into a jigsaw classroom.* When Elliot Aronson was a professor at the University of Texas at Austin, the school system contacted him for ideas on how to reduce the increasing racial tension in classrooms. Aronson (1986) developed the concept of a "jigsaw classroom," in which students from different cultural backgrounds are placed in a cooperative group in which they have to construct different parts of a project to reach a common goal. Aronson used the term *jigsaw* because he saw the technique as much like a group of students cooperating to put different pieces together to complete a jigsaw puzzle. How might this work? Team sports, drama productions, and musical performances are examples of contexts in which students cooperatively participate to reach a common goal.

- *Encourage students to have positive personal contact with diverse other students.* Contact alone does not do the job of improving relationships with diverse others. For example, busing ethnic minority students to predominantly non-Latino White schools, or vice versa, has not reduced prejudice or improved interethnic relations (Minuchin & Shapiro, 1983). What matters is what happens after children get to school. Especially beneficial in improving interethnic relations is sharing one's worries, successes, failures, coping strategies, interests, and other personal information with people of other

James Comer, Child Psychiatrist

James Comer grew up in a low-income neighborhood in East Chicago, Indiana, and credits his parents with leaving no doubt about the importance of education. He obtained a B.A. degree from Indiana University. He went on to obtain a medical degree from Howard University College of Medicine, a Master of Public Health degree from the University of Michigan School of Public Health, and psychiatry training at the Yale University School of Medicine's Child Study Center. He currently is the Maurice Falk Professor of Child Psychiatry at the Yale University Child Study Center and an associate dean at the Yale University Medical School. During his years at Yale, Comer has concentrated his career on promoting a focus on child development as a way of improving schools. His efforts in support of healthy development of young people are known internationally.

Dr. Comer perhaps is best known for the founding of the School Development program in 1968, which promotes the collaboration of parents, educators, and community to improve social, emotional, and academic outcomes for children. His concept of teamwork is currently improving the educational environment in more than 600 schools throughout the United States.

James Comer is shown with some of the inner-city African American children who attend a school that became a better learning environment because of Comer's intervention.

ethnicities. When this sharing happens, people tend to look at others as individuals rather than as members of a homogeneous group.

- *Encourage students to engage in perspective taking.* Exercises and activities that help students see others' perspectives can improve interethnic relations. These help students "step into the shoes" of peers who are culturally different and feel what it is like to be treated in fair or unfair ways.

- *Reduce bias.* Teachers can reduce bias by displaying images of children from diverse ethnic and cultural groups, selecting play materials and classroom activities that encourage cultural understanding, helping students resist stereotyping, and working with parents.

- *View the school and community as a team.* James Comer (2004, 2006, 2010) emphasizes that a community, team approach is the best way to educate children. Three important aspects of the Comer Project for Change are (1) a governance and management team that develops a comprehensive school plan, assessment strategy, and

What are some features of a jigsaw classroom?

staff development plan; (2) a mental health or school support team; and (3) a parents' program. Comer holds that the entire school community should have a cooperative rather than an adversarial attitude. The Comer program is currently operating in more than 600 schools in 26 states. To read further about James Comer's work, see the *Connecting with Careers* profile.

Achievement   **LG2** Explain the key aspects of achievement

Extrinsic and Intrinsic Motivation

Mastery Motivation and Mindset

Self-Efficacy

Goal Setting, Planning, and Self-Monitoring

Expectations

Ethnicity and Culture

Life is a gift . . . Accept it.

Life is a puzzle . . . Solve it.

Life is an adventure . . . Dare it.

Life is an opportunity . . . Take it.

Life is a mystery . . . Unfold it.

Life is a mission . . . Fulfill it.

Life is a struggle . . . Face it.

Life is a goal . . . Achieve it.

—AUTHOR UNKNOWN

In any classroom, whoever the teacher is and whatever approach is used, some children achieve more than others. Why? Among the reasons for variations in achievement are characteristics of the child and sociocultural contexts related to motivation.

EXTRINSIC AND INTRINSIC MOTIVATION

The behavioral perspective emphasizes the importance of extrinsic motivation. **Extrinsic motivation** involves doing something to obtain something else (the activity is a means to an end). Extrinsic motivation is often influenced by external incentives such as rewards and punishments. For example, a student may study for a test in order to obtain a good grade.

Whereas the behavioral perspective emphasizes extrinsic motivation in achievement, the cognitive perspective stresses the importance of intrinsic motivation. **Intrinsic motivation** involves the internal motivation to do something for its own sake (the activity is an end in itself). For example, a student may study hard for a test because he or she enjoys the content of the course.

Parental intrinsic/extrinsic motivational practices are linked to children's motivation. In one study, children had higher intrinsic motivation in math and science from 9 to 17 years of age when their parents engaged in task-intrinsic practices (encouraging children's pleasure and engagement in learning) than when their parents engaged in task-extrinsic practices (providing external rewards and consequences contingent on children's performance) (Gottfried & others, 2009).

Let's first consider the intrinsic motivation of self-determination and personal choice. Next, we identify some developmental changes in intrinsic and extrinsic motivation as students move up the educational ladder. Finally, we draw some conclusions about intrinsic and extrinsic motivation.

Self-Determination and Choice   One view of intrinsic motivation emphasizes that students want to believe that they are doing something because of their own will, not because of external success or rewards (Deci, Koestner, & Ryan, 2001). Students' internal motivation and intrinsic interest in school tasks increase when

extrinsic motivation Doing something to obtain something else (the activity is a means to an end).

intrinsic motivation Doing something for its own sake; involves factors such as self-determination and opportunities to make choices.

Calvin and Hobbes

by Bill Watterson

they have opportunities to make choices and take responsibility for their learning (Stipek, 2002). In one study, students who were given some choice of activities and when to do them, and were encouraged to take personal responsibility for their behavior, had higher achievement gains and were more likely to graduate from high school than a control group (deCharms, 1984). The architects of self-determination theory, Richard Ryan and Edward Deci (2009), refer to teachers who create circumstances for students to engage in self-determination as *autonomy-supportive teachers.*

Developmental Shifts in Intrinsic and Extrinsic Motivation   Many psychologists and educators stress that it is important for children to develop intrinsic motivation as they grow older. However, as students move from the early elementary school years to the high school years, intrinsic motivation tends to drop (Harter, 1996). In one study, the biggest drop in intrinsic motivation and largest increase in extrinsic motivation occurred between the sixth and seventh grades (Harter, 1981).

Jacquelynne Eccles and her colleagues (Eccles, 2004; Eccles & Roeser, 2009; Wigfield & others, 2006) identified some specific changes in the school context that help to explain the decline in intrinsic motivation. Middle and junior high schools are more impersonal, more formal, more evaluative, and more competitive than elementary schools. Students compare themselves more with other students because they are increasingly graded in terms of their relative performance on assignments and standardized tests.

Conclusions About Intrinsic and Extrinsic Motivation   An overwhelming conclusion of motivation research is that teachers should encourage students to become intrinsically motivated (Eccles & Roeser, 2010). Similarly, teachers should create learning environments that promote students' cognitive engagement and self-responsibility for learning (Anderman & Anderman, 2010). That said, the real world includes both intrinsic and extrinsic motivation, and too often intrinsic and extrinsic motivation have been pitted against each other as polar opposites. In many aspects of students' lives, both intrinsic and extrinsic motivation are at work (Cameron & Pierce, 2008). Further, both intrinsic and extrinsic motivation can operate simultaneously. Thus, a student may work hard in a course because she enjoys the content and likes learning about it (intrinsic) and because she wants to earn a good grade (extrinsic) (Schunk, 2012). Keep in mind, though, that many educational psychologists suggest that extrinsic motivation by itself is not a good strategy.

MASTERY MOTIVATION AND MINDSET

The increasingly competitive, impersonal atmosphere of middle schools obviously does not discourage all students. To some, these characteristics represent a challenge.

The student:

- Says "I can't"
- Doesn't pay attention to teacher's instructions
- Doesn't ask for help, even when it is needed
- Does nothing (for example, stares out the window)
- Guesses or answers randomly without really trying
- Doesn't show pride in successes
- Appears bored, uninterested
- Is unresponsive to teacher's exhortations to try
- Is easily discouraged
- Doesn't volunteer answers to teacher's questions
- Maneuvers to get out of or to avoid work (for example, has to go to the nurse's office)

FIGURE 16.7

BEHAVIORS THAT SUGGEST A HELPLESS ORIENTATION

mastery orientation A perspective in which one is task-oriented—concerned with learning strategies and the process of achievement rather than the outcome.

helpless orientation An orientation in which one seems trapped by the experience of difficulty and attributes one's difficulty to a lack of ability.

performance orientation An orientation in which one focuses on winning, rather than on achievement outcome; happiness is thought to result from winning.

mindset The cognitive view individuals develop for themselves that either is fixed or involves growth.

How students typically respond to challenges has a lot to do with how much they achieve (Dweck, 2011; Meece & Eccles, 2009). Becoming cognitively engaged and self-motivated to improve are reflected in individuals with mastery motivation. These individuals also have a growth mindset—a belief that they can produce positive outcomes if they put forth the effort.

Mastery Motivation   Carol Dweck and her colleagues (Dweck & Elliott, 1983; Dweck, Mangels, & Good, 2004; Murphy & Dweck, 2011) have found that individuals respond in two distinct ways to difficult or challenging circumstances. People who display a **mastery orientation** are task-oriented—instead of focusing on their ability, they concentrate on learning strategies and the process of achievement rather than the outcome. Those with a **helpless orientation** seem trapped by the experience of difficulty, and they attribute their difficulty to lack of ability. They frequently say such things as "I'm not very good at this," even though they might earlier have demonstrated their ability through many successes. And, once they view their behavior as failure, they often feel anxious, and their performance worsens even further. Figure 16.7 describes some behaviors that might reflect helplessness (Stipek, 2002).

In contrast, mastery-oriented individuals often instruct themselves to pay attention, to think carefully, and to remember strategies that have worked for them in previous situations. They frequently report feeling challenged and excited by difficult tasks, rather than being threatened by them (Anderman & Anderman, 2010; Murphy & Dweck, 2011). A study revealed that seventh- to eleventh-grade students' mastery goals were linked to how much effort they put forth in mathematics (Chouinard, Karsenti, & Roy, 2007).

Another issue in motivation involves whether to adopt a mastery or a performance orientation. Individuals with a **performance orientation** are focused on winning, rather than on achievement outcome, and believe that happiness results from winning. Does this focus mean that mastery-oriented individuals do not like to win and that performance-oriented individuals are not motivated to experience the self-efficacy that comes from being able to take credit for one's accomplishments? No. A matter of emphasis or degree is involved, though. For mastery-oriented individuals, winning isn't everything; for performance-oriented individuals, skill development and self-efficacy take a backseat to winning.

The U.S. government's No Child Left Behind Act (NCLB) emphasizes testing and accountability. Although NCLB may motivate some teachers and students to work harder, motivation experts worry that it encourages a performance rather than a mastery motivation orientation on the part of students (Schunk, Pintrich, & Meece, 2008).

A final point needs to be made about mastery and performance goals: They are not always mutually exclusive. Students can be both mastery- and performance-oriented, and researchers have found that mastery goals combined with performance goals often benefit students' success (Anderman & Anderman, 2010; Schunk, 2012).

Mindset   Carol Dweck's (2006, 2007, 2012) most recent analysis of motivation for achievement stresses the importance of developing a **mindset,** which she defines as the cognitive view individuals develop for themselves. She concludes that individuals have one of two mindsets: (1) a *fixed mindset*, in which they believe that their qualities are carved in stone and cannot change; or (2) a *growth mindset*, in which they believe their qualities can change and improve through their effort. A fixed mindset is similar to a helpless orientation; a growth mindset is much like having mastery motivation.

In *Mindset*, Dweck (2006) argued that individuals' mindsets influence whether they will be optimistic or pessimistic, shape their goals and how hard they will strive to reach those goals, and affect many aspects of their lives, including achievement and success in school and sports. Dweck says that mindsets begin to be shaped as children and adolescents interact with parents, teachers, and coaches, who themselves have either a fixed mindset or a growth mindset.

Dweck and her colleagues (Blackwell & Dweck, 2008; Blackwell & others, 2007; Dweck, 2011; Dweck & Master, 2009) recently incorporated information about the brain's plasticity into their effort to improve students' motivation to achieve and succeed. In one study, they assigned two groups of students to eight sessions of either (1) study skills instruction or (2) study skills instruction plus information about the importance of developing a growth mindset (called *incremental theory* in the research) (Blackwell & others, 2007). One of the exercises in the growth mindset group was titled "You Can Grow Your Brain," and it emphasized that the brain is like a muscle that can change and grow as it gets exercise and develops new connections. Students were informed that the more you challenge your brain to learn, the more your brain cells grow. Both groups had a pattern of declining math scores prior to the intervention. Following the intervention, scores of the group who had received only the study skills instruction continued to decline, but the group that received the combination of study skills instruction plus the growth mindset emphasis reversed the downward trend and improved their math achievement.

A screen from Carol Dweck's Brainology program, which is designed to cultivate children's growth mindset.

In other work, Dweck has been creating a computer-based workshop, "Brainology," to teach students that their intelligence can change (Blackwell & Dweck, 2008). Students experience six modules about how the brain works and how the students can make their brain improve. After being tested in 20 New York City schools recently, students strongly endorsed the value of the computer-based brain modules. Said one student, "I will try harder because I know that the more you try the more your brain knows" (Dweck & Master, 2009, p. 137).

SELF-EFFICACY

Albert Bandura (1997, 2001, 2009, 2010a), whose social cognitive theory was described in Chapter 1, stresses that a critical factor in whether or not students achieve is **self-efficacy**, the belief that one can master a situation and produce favorable outcomes. Self-efficacy is the belief that "I can"; helplessness is the belief that "I cannot." Students with high self-efficacy endorse statements such as "I know that I will be able to learn the material in this class" and "I expect to be able to do well at this activity."

Dale Schunk (2012) has applied the concept of self-efficacy to many aspects of students' achievement. In his view, self-efficacy influences a student's choice of activities. Students with low self-efficacy for learning may avoid many learning tasks, especially those that are challenging. By contrast, those with high self-efficacy eagerly work at learning tasks (Schunk, Pintrich, & Meece, 2008). High-self-efficacy students are more likely than low-self-efficacy students to expend effort and persist longer at a learning task.

Children's and adolescents' development is influenced by their parents' self-efficacy. A recent study revealed a number of positive developmental outcomes, including more daily opportunities for optimal functioning, better peer relations, and fewer problems, for children and adolescents whose parents had high self-efficacy (Steca & others, 2011).

GOAL SETTING, PLANNING, AND SELF-MONITORING

Self-efficacy and achievement improve when individuals set goals that are specific, proximal, and challenging (Anderman & Anderman, 2010; Schunk, 2012). A nonspecific, fuzzy goal is "I want to be successful." A more concrete, specific goal is "I want to make the honor roll by the end of the semester."

Students can set both long-term (distal) and short-term (proximal) goals. It is okay for individuals to set some long-term goals, such as "I want to graduate from high school" or "I want to go to college," but they also need to create short-term goals,

developmental connection

Cognitive Theory. Social cognitive theory holds that behavior, environment, and person/cognitive factors are the key influences on development. Chapter 1, p. 24

They can because they think they can.

—VIRGIL

Roman Poet, 1st Century B.C.

self-efficacy The belief that one can master a situation and produce favorable outcomes.

which are steps along the way. "Getting an A on the next math test" is an example of a short-term, proximal goal. So is "Doing all of my homework by 4 p.m. Sunday."

Another good strategy is to set challenging goals (Anderman & Anderman, 2010). A challenging goal is a commitment to self-improvement. Strong interest and involvement in activities are sparked by challenges. Goals that are easy to reach generate little interest or effort. However, goals should be optimally matched to the individual's skill level. If goals are unrealistically high, the result will be repeated failures that lower the individual's self-efficacy.

Another good strategy is to develop personal goals about desired and undesired future circumstances (Ford & Smith, 2007; Wigfield & Cambria, 2010). Personal goals can be a key aspect of an individual's motivation for coping and dealing with life's challenges and opportunities (Maehr & Zusho, 2009).

It is not enough just to set goals. In order to achieve, it also is important to plan how to reach those goals. Being a good planner means managing time effectively, setting priorities, and being organized.

Individuals should not only plan their next week's activities but also monitor how well they are sticking to their plan. Once engaged in a task, they need to monitor their progress, judge how well they are doing on the task, and evaluate the outcomes to regulate what they do in the future (Wigfield & others, 2006). High-achieving children are often self-regulatory learners (Perry & Rahim, 2011; Schunk, 2011). For example, high-achieving children monitor their learning and systematically evaluate their progress toward a goal more than low-achieving students do. Encouraging children to monitor their learning conveys the message that they are responsible for their own behavior and that learning requires their active, dedicated participation (Wigfield, Klauda, & Cambria, 2011).

EXPECTATIONS

Expectations play important roles in children's and adolescents' achievement. These expectations involve not only the expectations of children and adolescents themselves but also the expectations of parents, teachers, and other adults.

How hard students will work can depend on how much they expect to accomplish. If they expect to succeed, they are more likely to work hard to reach a goal than if they expect to fail. Jacquelynne Eccles (2007) defined expectations for students' success as beliefs about how well they will do on upcoming tasks, in either the immediate or long-term future (Wigfield & others, 2006). Three aspects of ability beliefs, according to Eccles, are students' beliefs about how good they are at a particular activity, how good they are in comparison with other individuals, and how good they are in relation to their performance in other activities.

How hard students work also depends on the *value* they place on the goal (Wigfield & Cambria, 2010). Indeed, the combination of expectancy and value has been the focus of a number of efforts to better understand students' achievement motivation. In Eccles' (2007) model, students' expectancies and values are assumed to directly influence their performance, persistence, and task choice.

Researchers have found that parents' expectations are linked with children's and adolescents' academic achievement (Burchinal & others, 2002). One longitudinal study revealed that children whose mothers had higher academic expectations for them in the first grade were more likely to reach a higher level of educational attainment in emerging adulthood (age 23) than children whose mothers had lower expectations for them in the first grade (Englund & others, 2004).

Too often parents attempt to protect children's and adolescents' self-esteem by setting low standards (Graham, 2005; Stipek, 2005). In reality, it is more beneficial to set standards that challenge them and expect performance at the highest levels they are capable of achieving.

Teachers' expectations also are important influences on children's achievement (Rubie-Davies, 2011). In an observational study of twelve classrooms, teachers with

A student and a teacher at Langston Hughes Elementary School in Chicago, a school whose teachers have high expectations for students. *How do teachers' expectations influence students' achievement?*

developmental **connection**

Culture. Ethnicity refers to characteristics rooted in cultural heritage, including nationality, race, religion, and language. Chapter 1, p. 9; Chapter 15, p. 517

high expectations spent more time providing a framework for students' learning, asked higher-level questions, and were more effective in managing students' behavior than teachers with average and low expectations (Rubie-Davies, 2007).

ETHNICITY AND CULTURE

How do ethnicity and culture influence children's achievement? Of course, diversity exists within every group in terms of achievement. But Americans have been especially concerned about two questions related to ethnicity and culture. First, does their ethnicity deter ethnic minority children from high achievement in school? And second, is there something about American culture that accounts for the poor performance of U.S. children in math and science?

Ethnicity   As we discussed in Chapter 15, analyzing the effects of ethnicity in the United States is complicated by the fact that a disproportionate number of ethnic minorities have low socioeconomic status. Disentangling the effects of SES and ethnicity can be difficult, and many investigations overlook the socioeconomic status of ethnic minority students. In many instances, when ethnicity and socioeconomic status are investigated, socioeconomic status predicts achievement better than ethnicity does. Students from middle- and upper-income families fare better than their counterparts from low-income backgrounds in a host of achievement situations—for example, expectations for success, achievement aspirations, and recognition of the importance of effort (Wigfield & others, 2006). A recent longitudinal study revealed that African American children or children from low-income families benefited more than children from higher-income families when they did homework more frequently, had Internet access at home, and had a community library card (Xia, 2010).

Sandra Graham (1986, 1990) has conducted a number of studies that reveal stronger socioeconomic status than ethnic differences in achievement. She is struck by how consistently middle-income African American students, like their non-Latino White middle-income counterparts, have high achievement expectations and understand that failure is usually due to a lack of effort. An especially important factor in the lower achievement of students from low-income families regardless of their ethnic background is lack of adequate resources, such as an up-to-date computer in the home or even a computer at all, to support students' learning (Schunk, Pintrich, & Meece, 2008).

Cross-Cultural Comparisons   Since the early 1990s, the poor performance of American children and adolescents in math and science has become well publicized. In a recent large-scale international comparison of 15-year-olds in 65 countries, the top five scores in reading, math, and science were held by Asian countries (Shanghai-China, South Korea, Singapore, Hong Kong-China, and Taipei-China), with the exception of 15-year-olds from Finland being third in reading and second in science (OECD, 2010). Shanghai-China 15-year-olds held first place among the 65 countries in all three academic areas. In this study, U.S. 15-year-olds placed seventeenth in reading, thirty-second in math, and twenty-third in science. The international rankings for reading and math are shown in Figure 16.8.

Why do U.S. students fare so poorly in mathematics? In the *Connecting with Research* interlude, you can read about Harold Stevenson's efforts to find an answer.

UCLA educational psychologist Sandra Graham is shown talking with adolescent boys about motivation. She has conducted a number of studies which reveal that middle-socioeconomic-status African American students—like their White counterparts—have high achievement expectations and attribute success to internal factors such as effort rather than external factors such as luck.

Reading		Mathematics	
1. China: Shanghai	556	1. China: Shanghai	600
2. Korea	539	2. Singapore	562
3. Finland	536	3. China: Hong Kong	555
4. China: Hong Kong	533	4. Korea	546
5. Singapore	526	5. Chinese Taipei	543
6. Canada	524	6. Finland	541
7. New Zealand	521	7. Liechtenstein	536
8. Japan	520	8. Switzerland	534
9. Australia	515	9. Japan	529
10. Netherlands	508	10. Canada	527
11. Belgium	506	11. Netherlands	526
12. Norway	503	12. China: Macao	525
13. Estonia	501	13. New Zealand	519
14. Switzerland	501	14. Belgium	515
15. Iceland	500	15. Australia	514
16. Poland	500	16. Germany	513
17. United States	500	17. Estonia	512
18. Liechtenstein	499	18. Iceland	507
19. Germany	497	19. Denmark	503
20. Sweden	497	20. Slovenia	501
21. France	496	21. Norway	498
22. Ireland	496	22. France	497
23. Chinese Taipei	495	23. Slovak Republic	497
24. Denmark	495	24. Austria	496
25. Hungary	494	25. OECD average	496
26. United Kingdom	494	26. Poland	495
27. OECD average	493	27. Sweden	494
28. Portugal	489	28. Czech Republic	493
29. China: Macao	487	29. United Kingdom	492
30. Italy	486	30. Hungary	490
31. Latvia	484	31. Luxembourg	489
32. Greece	483	32. United States	487

FIGURE **16.8**

INTERNATIONAL COMPARISONS OF 15-YEAR-OLDS' READING AND MATH SCORES. *Source:* OECD (2010). *Strong performers and successful reformers in education: Lessons from PISA for the United States.* Paris, France: OECD.

Why Do U.S. Students Underperform in Math?

Harold Stevenson has been conducting research on children's learning for five decades. His research has explored the reasons for the poor performance of American students. Stevenson and his colleagues (Stevenson, 1995, 2000; Stevenson, Hofer, & Randel, 1999; Stevenson & others, 1990) have completed five cross-cultural comparisons of students in the United States, China, Taiwan, and Japan. In these studies, Asian students consistently outperform American students. Furthermore, the longer the students are in school, the wider the gap becomes between Asian and American students—the lowest difference is in the first grade, the highest in the eleventh grade (the highest grade studied).

To learn more about the reasons for these large cross-cultural differences, Stevenson and his colleagues spent thousands of hours observing in classrooms, as well as interviewing and surveying teachers, students, and parents. They found that the Asian teachers spent more of their time teaching math than did the American teachers. For example, more than one-fourth of total classroom time in the first grade was spent on math instruction in Japan, compared with only one-tenth of the time in the U.S. first-grade classrooms. Also, the Asian students were in school an average of 240 days a year, compared with 178 days in the United States.

In addition, differences were found between the Asian and American parents. The American parents had much lower expectations for their children's education and achievement than did the Asian parents. Also, the American parents were more likely to believe that their children's math achievement

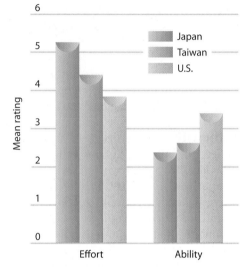

FIGURE **16.9**

MOTHERS' BELIEFS ABOUT THE FACTORS RESPONSIBLE FOR CHILDREN'S MATH ACHIEVEMENT IN THREE COUNTRIES. In one study, mothers in Japan and Taiwan were more likely to believe that their children's math achievement was due to effort rather than innate ability, while U.S. mothers were more likely to believe their children's math achievement was due to innate ability (Stevenson, Lee, & Stigler, 1986). If parents believe that their children's math achievement is due to innate ability and their children are not doing well in math, the implication is that they are less likely to think their children will benefit from putting forth more effort.

Asian grade schools intersperse studying with frequent periods of activities. This approach helps children maintain their attention and likely makes learning more enjoyable. Shown here are Japanese fourth-graders making wearable masks. *What are some differences in the way children in many Asian countries are taught compared with children in the United States?*

was due to innate ability, while the Asian parents were more likely to say that their children's math achievement was the consequence of effort and training (see Figure 16.9). The Asian students were more likely to do math homework than were the American students, and the Asian parents were far more likely to help their children with their math homework than were the American parents (Chen & Stevenson, 1989).

How would you turn the research of Stevenson and his colleagues into recommendations for U.S. teachers and parents?

Review

- What are intrinsic motivation and extrinsic motivation? How are they related to achievement?
- How are mastery, helpless, and performance orientations linked with achievement?
- What is self-efficacy, and how is it related to achievement?
- Why are goal setting, planning, and self-monitoring important in achievement?
- How are expectations involved in an individual's achievement motivation?
- How do cultural, ethnic, and socioeconomic variations influence achievement?

Connect

- One of Carol Dweck's exercises in the growth-mindset group was titled "You Can Grow Your Brain." Can you actually grow your brain? What physical changes, if any, are still occurring in the brain in middle and late childhood and in adolescence? You might want to review the discussion of the brain in middle and late childhood and adolescence in Chapter 3, "Physical Development and Biological Aging," to help you answer these questions.

Reflect *Your Own Personal Journey of Life*

- Think about several of your own past schoolmates who showed low motivation in school. Why do you think they behaved that way? What teaching strategies might have helped them?

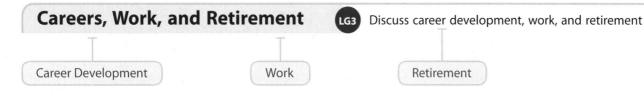

Careers, Work, and Retirement

LG3 Discuss career development, work, and retirement

Career Development   Work   Retirement

The quality of schooling children experience and the achievement orientation they develop provide the foundation for career success and work when they become adults. Choosing a career, developing in a career, working, and coping with retirement—these are important themes in adulthood.

CAREER DEVELOPMENT

When you were a child, what were your thoughts about a career? How did your thinking about careers change as you became an adolescent? What are your thoughts now?

Developmental Changes Many children have idealistic fantasies about what they want to be when they grow up. For example, many young children want to be superheroes, sports stars, or movie stars. In the high school years, they often have begun to think about careers on a somewhat less idealistic basis. In their late teens and early twenties, their career decision making has usually turned more serious as they explore different career possibilities and zero in on the career they want to enter. In college, this focus often means choosing a major or specialization that is designed to lead to work in a specific field. By their early and mid-twenties, many individuals have completed their education or training and started to enter a full-time occupation. From the mid-twenties through the remainder of early adulthood, individuals often seek to establish their emerging career in a particular field. They may work hard to move up the career ladder and improve their financial standing.

Phyllis Moen (2009a) recently described the *career mystique*, ingrained cultural beliefs that engaging in hard work for long hours through adulthood will produce a path to status, security, and happiness. That is, many individuals have an ideal concept of a career path toward achieving the American dream by upward mobility

"Your son has made a career choice, Mildred. He's going to win the lottery and travel a lot." Copyright © 2011; reprinted courtesy of Bunny Hoest.

Grace Leaf, College/Career Counselor

Grace Leaf is a counselor at Spokane Community College in Washington. She has a master's degree in educational leadership and is working toward a doctoral degree in educational leadership at Gonzaga University in Spokane, Washington. Her job involves teaching, orientation for international students, advising individuals and groups, and doing individual and group career planning. Leaf tries to connect students with their own goals and values and helps them design an educational program that fits their needs and visions.

For more information about what career counselors do, see page 43 in the Careers in Life-Span Development appendix.

Grace Leaf, counseling college students at Spokane Community College about careers.

"Did you think the ladder of success would be straight up?"
© Joseph Farris/ The Yorker Collection/www.cartoonbank.com

through occupational ladders. However, the lockstep career mystique has never been a reality for many individuals, especially ethnic minority individuals, women, and poorly educated adults. Further, the career mystique has increasingly become a myth for many individuals in middle-income occupations as global outsourcing of jobs and the 2007–2009 recession have meant reduced job security for millions of Americans.

Monitoring the Occupational Outlook   As you explore the type of work you are likely to enjoy and in which you can succeed, it is important to be knowledgeable about different fields and companies. Occupations may have many job openings one year but few in another year as economic conditions change. Thus, it is critical to keep up with the occupational outlook in various fields. An excellent source for doing this is the U.S. government's *Occupational Outlook Handbook*, which is revised every two years.

According to the 2010–2011 handbook, service industries, especially health services, professional and business services, and education are projected to account for the most new jobs in the next decade. Projected job growth varies widely by educational requirements. Jobs that require a college degree are expected to grow the fastest. Most of the highest-paying occupations require a college degree. To read about the work of one individual who advises college students about careers, see the *Connecting with Careers* profile.

WORK

Work is one of the most important activities in people's lives. Our developmental coverage of work begins with adolescence and concludes with late adulthood.

Work in Adolescence   One of the greatest changes in adolescents' lives in recent years has been the increased number of adolescents who work part-time and still attend school on a regular basis. Our discussion of adolescents and work focuses on the sociohistorical context of adolescent work and the advantages and disadvantages of part-time work.

Even though education keeps many of today's youth from holding full-time jobs, it has not prevented them from working part-time while going to school (Staff, Messersmith, & Schulenberg, 2009). In 1940, only 1 of 25 tenth-grade males attended school and simultaneously worked part-time. In the 1970s, the number had increased to 1 in 4. Today, it is estimated that 80 to 90 percent of adolescents are employed at some point during high school (Staff, Messersmith, & Schulenberg, 2009). As adolescents go from the eighth to the twelfth grade, their likelihood of working and the average number of hours they work during the school year increase (Staff, Messersmith, & Schulenberg, 2009). In the eighth through tenth grades, the majority of students don't work in paid employment during the school year, but in the twelfth grade only one-fourth don't engage in paid employment during the school year. Almost 10 percent of employed twelfth-graders work more than 30 hours per week during the school year.

What are some advantages and disadvantages of part-time work during adolescence?

Overall, the weight of the evidence suggests that spending large amounts of time in paid labor has limited developmental benefits for youth, and for some it is associated with risky behavior and costs to physical health (Larson, Wilson, & Rickman, 2009; Staff, Messersmith, & Schulenberg, 2009). For example, one research study found that it was not just working that affected adolescents' grades—more important was how long they worked (Greenberger & Steinberg, 1986). Tenth-graders who worked more than 14 hours a week suffered a drop in grades. Eleventh-graders worked up to 20 hours a week before their grades dropped. When adolescents spend more than 20 hours per week working, there is little time to study for tests and to complete homework assignments. In addition, working adolescents felt less involved in school, were absent more, and said that they did not enjoy school as much as their nonworking counterparts did. Adolescents who worked long hours also were more frequent users of alcohol and marijuana.

A recent reanalysis of the data in Greenberger and Steinberg's 1986 study included a better-matched control group of students who did not work. Even with the more careful matching of groups, adolescents in the tenth and eleventh grades who worked more than 20 hours a week were less engaged in school and showed increased substance abuse and delinquency (Monahan, Lee, & Steinberg, 2011). For adolescents who cut back their part-time work hours to 20 hours a week or less, negative outcomes disappeared.

Some youth, though, are engaged in challenging work activities, are provided constructive supervision by adults, and experience favorable work conditions (Staff, Messersmith, & Schulenberg, 2009). For example, work may benefit adolescents in low-income, urban contexts by providing them with economic benefits and adult monitoring. These may increase school engagement and decrease delinquency.

Work in Emerging Adulthood The work patterns of emerging adults have changed over the last 100 years (Hamilton & Hamilton, 2006, 2009). As an increasing number of emerging adults have participated in higher education, many leave home and begin their careers at later ages. Changing economic conditions have made the job market more competitive for emerging adults and increased the demand for more highly skilled workers (Gauthier & Furstenberg, 2005).

A diversity of school and work patterns characterizes emerging adults (Borges & others, 2008; Hamilton & Hamilton, 2009). Some emerging adults are going to college full-time; others are working full-time. Some emerging adults work full-time immediately after high school, others after they graduate from college. Many emerging adults who attend college drop out and enter the workforce before they complete their degree; some of these individuals return to college later. Some emerging adults are attending two-year colleges, others four-year colleges; and some are working part-time while going to college but others are not.

Working During College

The percentage of full-time U.S. college students who were employed increased from 34 percent in 1970 to 47 percent in 2008 (down from a peak of 52 percent in 2000) (National Center for Education Statistics, 2010). In this recent survey, 81 percent of part-time U.S. college students were employed.

Working can pay or help offset some costs of schooling, but working also can restrict students' opportunities to learn. For those who identified themselves primarily as students, one national study found that as the number of hours worked per week increased, their grades suffered (National Center for Education Statistics, 2002) (see Figure 16.10). Thus, college students need to carefully examine whether the number of hours they work is having a negative impact on their college success.

Of course, jobs also can contribute to a student's education. More than 1,000 colleges in the United States offer *cooperative (co-op) programs,* which are paid apprenticeships in specific fields. (You may not be permitted to participate in a co-op program until your junior year.) Other useful opportunities for working while going to college include internships and part-time or summer jobs relevant to your field of study. In a national survey of employers, almost 60 percent said their entry-level college hires had co-op or internship experience (Collins, 1996). Participating in these work experiences can be a key factor in whether you land the job you want when you graduate.

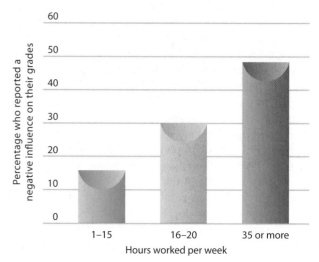

FIGURE **16.10**

THE RELATION OF HOURS WORKED PER WEEK IN COLLEGE TO GRADES. Among students working to pay for school expenses, 16 percent of those working 1 to 15 hours per week reported that working negatively influenced their grades (National Center for Education Statistics, 2002). Thirty percent of college students who worked 16 to 20 hours a week said the same, as did 48 percent who worked 35 hours or more per week.

As unpaid internships become more common, some students complain that they are merely a way for organizations to obtain free labor. How can student interns ensure that they have a rewarding experience in spite of not being paid?

These emerging adults are college graduates who have started their own business. Emerging adults follow a diversity of work and educational pathways. *What are some of these variations in education and work that characterize emerging adults?*

The nature of the transition from school to work in emerging adulthood is strongly influenced by the individual's level of education (Hamilton & Hamilton, 2009). In the last two decades, the job market for emerging adults with only a high school education has worsened. The MacArthur Foundation Research Network on Emerging Adults recently concluded that for emerging adults who don't go to college, the problem is not jobs but a lack of good jobs (Settersten, Furstenberg, & Rumbaut, 2005). The Research Network also stated that community colleges are an underutilized resource for connecting high schools and employers. A special concern is the large number of students who begin their college education in a community college but don't finish it (Horn & Nevill, 2006).

What about work during college? To read about the pluses and minuses of working during college, see the *Connecting Development to Life* interlude.

Work in Adulthood   Both Sigmund Freud and the Russian Count Leo Tolstoy described love and work as the two most important things that adults need to do well. We discussed love in Chapter 10, "Emotional Development." Let's now explore work in the adult years.

The Work Landscape   Do you work to live or live to work? Most individuals spend about one-third of their lives at work. In one survey, 35 percent of Americans worked 40 hours a week, but 18 percent worked 51 hours or more per week (Center for Survey Research at the University of Connecticut, 2000). Only 10 percent worked less than 30 hours a week.

Work defines people in fundamental ways (Bowen, Noack, & Staudinger, 2011; Rix, 2011). It is an important influence on their financial standing, housing, the way they spend their time, where they live, their friendships, and their health (Hodson, 2009; Shirom & others, 2011). Some people define their identity through their work. Work also creates a structure and rhythm to life that is often missed when individuals do not work for an extended period. When unable to work, many individuals experience emotional distress and low self-esteem.

What are some characteristics of work settings linked with employees' stress?

An important consideration regarding work is how stressful it is (Burgard, 2009). A recent national survey of U.S. adults revealed that 55 percent indicated they were less productive because of stress (American Psychological Association, 2007). In this study, 52 percent reported that they had considered or made a career decision, such as looking for a new job, declining a promotion, or quitting a job, because of stress in the workplace (American Psychological Association, 2007). In this survey, main sources of stress included low salaries (44 percent), lack of advancement opportunities (42 percent), uncertain job expectations (40 percent), and long hours (39 percent).

Many adults hold changing expectations about work, yet employers often aren't meeting their expectations (Grzywacz, 2009; Moen, 2009a, b). For example, current policies and practices often were designed for a single-breadwinner (male) workforce and an industrial economy, making these policies and practices out of step with a workforce of women and men, and of single parents and dual earners. Many workers today want flexibility and greater control over the duration and timing of their work, and yet most employers offer little flexibility, even though policies like flextime may be "on the books."

Unemployment   Unemployment produces stress regardless of whether the job loss is temporary, cyclical, or permanent (Romans, Cohen, & Forte, 2010). Problems with banks and the economic recession toward the end of the first decade of the twenty-first century have produced very high unemployment rates, especially in the United States. Researchers have found unemployment is related to increased rates of physical problems (such as heart attack and stroke), mental problems (such as depression and anxiety) (Nultman-Shwartz & Gadot, 2011), marital difficulties, and homicide (Gallo & others, 2006). A 15-year longitudinal study of more than 24,000 adults found that life satisfaction dropped considerably following unemployment and increased after becoming reemployed but did not completely return to the same level of life satisfaction previous to being unemployed (Lucas & others, 2004). Another study also revealed that immune system functioning declined with unemployment and increased with new employment (Cohen & others, 2007).

Stress comes not only from a loss of income and the resulting financial hardships but also from decreased self-esteem (Audhoe & others, 2010; Beutel & others, 2010). Individuals who cope best with unemployment have financial resources to rely on, often savings or the earnings of other family members. The support of understanding,

The economic recession that hit in 2007 resulted in millions of Americans losing their jobs, such as the individuals in line here waiting to apply for unemployment benefits in June 2009, in Chicago. *What are some of the potential negative outcomes of the stress caused by job loss?*

adaptable family members also helps individuals to cope with unemployment. Job counseling and self-help groups can provide practical advice on job searching, résumé writing, and interviewing skills, and also can lend emotional support.

As more women have worked outside the home, how has the division of responsibility for work and family changed?

Dual-Career Couples Dual-career couples may have special problems finding a balance between work and the rest of life (Moen, 2009a, b). If both partners are working, who cleans up the house or calls the repairman or takes care of the other endless details involved in maintaining a home? If the couple has children, who is responsible for making sure that the children get to school or to piano practice; who writes the notes to approve field trips or attends parent-teacher conferences or schedules dental appointments?

Although single-earner married families still make up a sizable minority of families, the number of two-earner couples has increased considerably in recent decades. A recent projection indicates that women's share of the U.S. labor force will increase through 2016 (*Occupational Outlook Handbook*, 2010–2011). As more U.S. women work outside the home, the division of responsibility for work and family has changed: (1) U.S. husbands are taking increased responsibility for maintaining the home; (2) U.S. women are taking increased responsibility for breadwinning; and (3) U.S. men are showing greater interest in their families and parenting.

Many jobs have been designed for single earners, usually a male breadwinner, without taking account of family responsibilities and the realities of people's actual lives. Consequently, many dual-earner couples engage in a range of adaptive strategies to coordinate their work and manage the family side of the work-family equation (Moen, 2009b). Researchers have found that even though couples may strive for gender equality in dual-earner families, gender inequalities still persist (Cunningham, 2009). For example, women still do not earn as much as men in the same jobs, and this inequity means that gender divisions in how much time each partner spends in paid work, homemaking, and caring for children continue. Thus, dual-earner career decisions often are made in favor of men's greater earning power and women spending more time than men in homemaking and caring for children (Moen, 2009b).

Careers and Work in Middle Adulthood The role of work—whether a person works in a full-time career, in a part-time job, as a volunteer, or as a homemaker—is central during middle age. Middle-aged adults may reach their peak in position and earnings but also be saddled with financial burdens from rent or mortgage, child care, medical bills, home repairs, college tuition, or bills from nursing homes for care of an elderly parent.

The progression of career trajectories in middle age is diverse, with some individuals having stable careers, whereas others move in and out of the labor force, experiencing layoffs and unemployment (Lachman, 2004). Middle-aged adults also may experience age discrimination in some job situations. Finding a job in midlife may be difficult because technological advances may render the midlife worker's skills outdated.

Some midlife career changes are the consequence of losing one's job; others are self-motivated (Moen, 1998; Moen & Spencer, 2006). Among the work issues that some people face in midlife are recognizing limitations in career progress, deciding whether to change jobs or careers, considering whether to rebalance family and work, and planning for retirement (Sterns & Huyck, 2001).

Work in Late Adulthood The percentage of older U.S. adult men still working or returning to work has been increasing since the early 1990s. As more women have entered the workforce, the percentage of older adult women still working also has increased. Figure 16.11 shows the increase in the percentage of men and women

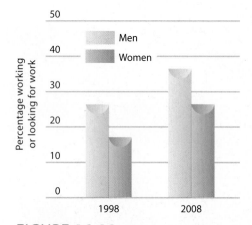

FIGURE **16.11**

PERCENTAGE OF 65- TO 69-YEAR-OLD U.S. MEN AND WOMEN WORKING OR LOOKING FOR WORK IN 1998 AND 2008

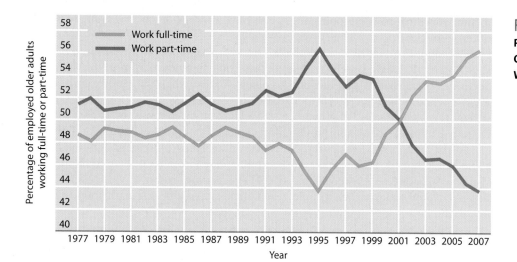

65 to 69 years old still working or looking for work in 1998 and 2008 (U.S. Bureau of Labor Statistics, 2008).

Since the mid-1990s, a significant shift has occurred in the percentage of older adults working part-time or full-time (U.S. Bureau of Labor Statistics, 2008). As shown in Figure 16.12, after 1995, of the adults 65 and older in the workforce, those engaging in full-time work rose substantially and those working part-time decreased considerably. This significant rise in full-time employment likely reflects the increasing number of older adults who realize that they may not have adequate money to fund their retirement (Rix, 2011; Williamson, 2011). Older adults are increasingly seeking some type of bridge employment that permits a gradual rather than a sudden movement out of the work context (Bowen, Noack, & Staudinger, 2011).

Cognitive ability is one of the best predictors of job performance in older adults. And older workers have lower rates of absenteeism, fewer accidents, and increased job satisfaction compared with their younger counterparts (Warr, 1994). Thus the older worker can be of considerable value to a company, above and beyond the older worker's cognitive competence. Changes in federal law now allow individuals over the age of 65 to continue working (Shore & Goldberg, 2005). Also, remember from our discussion in Chapter 7, "Information Processing," that substantively complex work is linked with a higher level of intellectual functioning (Schooler, 2007). In sum, a cognitively stimulating work context promotes successful aging (Bowen, Noack, & Staudinger, 2011; Hertzog & others, 2009).

In sum, age affects many aspects of work. Nonetheless, many studies of work and aging—such as evaluation of hiring and performance—have yielded inconsistent results. Important contextual factors—such as age composition of departments or applicant pools, occupations, and jobs—all affect decisions about older workers. It also is important to recognize that ageist stereotypes of workers and of tasks can limit older workers' career opportunities and can encourage early retirement or other forms of downsizing that adversely affect older workers (Finkelstein & Farrell, 2007).

RETIREMENT

How is retirement in the United States similar to and different from retirement in other countries? What factors predict whether individuals will adapt well to retirement?

Retirement in the United States and Other Countries What are some life paths that retired individuals follow? Do many people return

Ninety-two-year-old Russell "Bob" Harrell (*right*) puts in 12-hour days at Sieco Consulting Engineers in Columbus, Indiana. A highway and bridge engineer, he designs and plans roads. James Rice (age 48), a vice president of client services at Sieco, says that Bob wants to learn something new every day and that he has learned many life lessons from being around him. Harrell says he is not planning on retiring. *What are some variations in work and retirement in older adults?*

to the workforce at some point after they have retired? What is retirement like in other countries?

The option to retire is a twentieth-century phenomenon in the United States (Rix, 2011). It exists largely thanks to the implementation in 1935 of the Social Security system, which gives benefits to older workers when they retire. On average, today's workers will spend 10 to 15 percent of their lives in retirement. A recent survey revealed that as baby boomers move into their sixties, they expect to delay retirement longer than their parents or grandparents did (Frey, 2007).

In the past, when most people reached an accepted retirement age—usually at some point during their sixties—retirement meant a one-way exit from full-time work to full-time leisure (Williamson, 2011). Leading expert Phyllis Moen (2007) described how today, when people reach their sixties, the life path they follow is less clear:

- Some don't retire—they continue in their career jobs.
- Some retire from their career work and then take up a new and different job.
- Some retire from career jobs but do volunteer work.
- Some retire from a postretirement job and go on to yet another job.
- Some move in and out of the workforce, so they never really have a "career" job from which they retire.
- Some who are in poor health move to a disability status and eventually into retirement.
- Some who are laid off define it as "retirement."

Increasingly both spouses are in the workforce and both expect to retire. Historically retirement has been a male transition, but today more and more couples have to plan two retirements—his and hers (Moen, Kelly, & Magennis, 2008).

Approximately 7 million retired Americans return to work after they have retired (Putnam Investments, 2006). On average, retired adults return to the labor force four years after retirement (Hardy, 2006). In many instances, these postretirement jobs pay much less than their preretirement jobs did. In one study of older adults who returned to work, approximately two-thirds said they were happy they had done so, whereas about one-third indicated they were forced to go back to work to meet financial needs (Putnam Investments, 2006).

Just as the life path after individuals reach retirement age may be varied, so are their reasons for working (Rix, 2011). For example, some older adults who reach retirement age work for financial reasons, others to stay busy, and yet others "to give back" (Moen, 2007).

Work and Retirement Around the World   A large-scale study of 21,000 individuals aged 40 to 79 in 21 countries examined patterns of work and retirement (HSBC Insurance, 2007). On average, 33 percent of individuals in their sixties and 11 percent in their seventies were still in some kind of paid employment. In this study, 19 percent of those in their seventies in the United States were still working. As indicated in Figure 16.13, a substantial percentage of individuals expect to continue working as long as possible before retiring (HSBC Insurance, 2007).

In the study of work and retirement in 21 countries, Japanese retirees missed the work slightly more than they expected and the money considerably less than they expected (HSBC Insurance, 2007). U.S. retirees missed both the work and the money slightly less than they expected. German retirees were the least likely to miss the work, Turkish and Chinese retirees the most likely to miss it. Regarding the money, Japanese and Chinese retirees were the least likely to miss it, Turkish retirees the most likely to miss it.

Early retirement policies were introduced by many companies in the 1970s and 1980s with an intent to make room for younger workers.

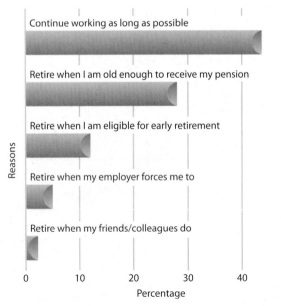

FIGURE **16.13**

RESPONSES GIVEN BY PEOPLE WHO WERE ASKED WHEN THEY EXPECT TO RETIRE FROM WORK

However, in the recent survey, there was some indication that an increasing number of adults are beginning to reject the early retirement option as they hear about people who retired and then regretted it. In the 21-country study, on average only 12 percent of individuals in their forties and fifties expected to take early retirement, whereas 16 percent in their sixties and seventies had taken early retirement. Only in Germany, South Korea, and Hong Kong did a higher percentage of individuals expect earlier retirement than in the past.

Adjustment to Retirement   Retirement is a process, not an event (Moen, 2007). Much of the research on retirement has been cross-sectional rather than longitudinal and has focused on men rather than women. One study found that men had higher morale when they had retired within the last two years compared with men who had been retired for longer periods of time (Kim & Moen, 2002). Another study revealed that retired married and remarried women reported being more satisfied with their lives and in better health than retired women who were widowed, separated, divorced, or had never been married (Price & Joo, 2005). One study indicated that women spend less time planning for retirement than men do (Jacobs Lawson, Hershey, & Neukam, 2005). And a recent study revealed that a higher level of financial assets and job satisfaction were more strongly linked to men's higher psychological well-being in retirement, while preretirement social contacts were more strongly related to women's psychological well-being in retirement (Kubicek & others, 2011).

In the recent cross-national study, to what extent did Japanese retirees miss the work and the money in comparison with U.S. retirees?

Older adults who adjust best to retirement are healthy, have adequate income, are active, are better educated, have an extended social network including both friends and family, and usually were satisfied with their lives before they retired (Raymo & Sweeney, 2006). Older adults with inadequate income and poor health, and those who must adjust to other stress that occurs at the same time as retirement, such as the death of a spouse, have the most difficult time adjusting to retirement (Reichstadt & others, 2007). A study also found that individuals who had difficulty adjusting to retirement had a strong attachment to work, including full-time jobs and a long work history, lack of control over the transition to retirement, and low self-efficacy (van Solinge & Henkens, 2005).

The U.S. retirement system is in transition (Williamson, 2011). Following are the results of a 2007 survey on retirement (Helman, VanDerhei, & Copeland, 2007):

- Half of the workers were not confident about their pension benefits.
- Many workers count on benefits that won't be there when they retire.
- Workers often don't heed advice about retirement even when they are provided the advice.
- Workers overestimate long-term care coverage.
- Most workers' savings are modest.
- Many workers know little about the Social Security income they will receive when they retire.

What are some keys to adjusting effectively in retirement?

Flexibility is also a key factor in whether individuals adjust well to retirement (Shultz & Adams, 2007). When people retire, they no longer have the structured environment they had when they were working, so they need to be flexible and discover and pursue their own interests (Eisdorfer, 1996). Cultivating interests and friends unrelated to work improves adaptation to retirement (Zarit & Knight, 1996).

Planning and then successfully carrying out the plan is an important aspect of adjusting well in retirement (Williamson, 2011). A special concern in retirement planning involves women, who are likely to live longer than men and more likely to live alone (less likely to remarry and more likely to be widowed) (Moen, 2007).

Individuals who view retirement planning only in terms of finances don't adapt as well to retirement as those who have a more balanced retirement plan (Birren, 1996). It is important not only to plan financially for retirement but to consider other areas of life as well (Sener, Terzioglu, & Karabulut, 2007). In addition to financial planning, questions individuals need to ask about retirement include: What am I going to do with my leisure time? What am I going to do to stay active? What am I going to do socially? What am I going to do to keep my mind active?

Review *Connect* Reflect

LG3 Discuss career development, work, and retirement

Review

- What is involved in developing a career?
- What are some key aspects of work?
- What characterizes retirement?

Connect

- In Chapter 15 you learned that U.S. adolescents spend more time in unstructured leisure activities than East Asian adolescents do. How might establishing challenging lifelong leisure activities in adolescence benefit an individual at retirement age?

Reflect *Your Own Personal Journey of Life*

- At what age would you like to retire? Or would you prefer to continue working as long as you are healthy? At what age did your father and/or mother retire, if they are no longer working? How well did they adjust to retirement?

---

reach your **learning goals**

Schools

LG1 Describe the role of schools in development

Contemporary Approaches to Student Learning and Assessment

- Contemporary approaches to student learning include the direct instruction approach and the constructivist approach. Today, many effective teachers use *both* a constructivist approach and a direct instruction approach. Increased concern by the public and government in the United States has produced extensive state-mandated testing, which has both strengths and weaknesses and is controversial. The most visible example of the increased state-mandated testing is the No Child Left Behind federal legislation.

Schools and Developmental Status

- The child-centered kindergarten emphasizes the education of the whole child, with special attention to individual variation, the process of learning, and the importance of play in development. The Montessori approach allows children to choose from a range of activities while teachers serve as facilitators. Developmentally appropriate practice focuses on the typical patterns of children (age appropriateness) and the uniqueness of each child (individual appropriateness). Such practice contrasts with developmentally inappropriate practice, which ignores the concrete, hands-on approach to learning. The U.S. government has tried to break the poverty cycle with programs such as Head Start. Model programs have been shown to have positive effects on children who live in poverty. Controversy characterizes early childhood education curricula. On the one side are the child-centered, constructivist advocates; on the other are those who advocate a direct instruction, academic approach. A special concern is that early elementary school education proceeds too much on the basis of providing negative feedback to children. The transition from elementary school to middle or junior high school can be stressful. Successful schools for young adolescents focus on individual differences, show a deep concern for what is known about early adolescence, and emphasize social as well as cognitive development. There are concerns about dropping out of school and improving the high school experience. The transition to college can involve a number of positive and negative experiences.

Educating Children with Disabilities

- An estimated 14 percent of U.S. children receive special education or related services. Slightly less than 45 percent of students with disabilities are classified as having a learning disability. In the federal government classification, this category includes attention deficit hyperactivity disorder, or ADHD. Children with learning disabilities have difficulty in learning that involves understanding or using spoken or written language, and the difficulty can appear in listening, thinking, reading, writing, and spelling. A learning disability also may involve difficulty in doing mathematics. To be classified as a learning disability, the learning problem is not primarily the result of visual, hearing, or motor disabilities; mental retardation; emotional disorders; or environmental, cultural, or economic disadvantage. Dyslexia is a category of learning disabilities that involves a severe impairment in the ability to read and spell. Attention deficit hyperactivity disorder (ADHD) is a disability in which individuals consistently show problems in one or more of these areas: (1) inattention, (2) hyperactivity, and (3) impulsivity. ADHD has been increasingly diagnosed. Autism is a severe disorder with an onset in the first three years of life, and it involves abnormalities in social relationships and communication. It also is characterized by repetitive behaviors. The current consensus is that autism involves an organic brain dysfunction. Autism spectrum disorders (ASD) is an increasingly popular term that refers to a broad range of autism disorders including the classical, severe form of autism, as well as Asperger syndrome. In 1975, Public Law 94-142, the Education for All Handicapped Children Act, required that all children with disabilities be given a free, appropriate public education. This law was renamed the Individuals with Disabilities Education Act (IDEA) in 1990 and updated in 2004. IDEA includes requirements that children with disabilities receive an individualized education plan (IEP), which is a written plan that spells out a program tailored to the child, and that they be educated in the least restrictive environment (LRE), which is a setting that is as similar as possible to the one in which children without disabilities are educated. The trend is toward the use of inclusion, although some aspects of inclusion have recently been criticized.

Socioeconomic Status and Ethnicity in Schools

- Children living in poverty face problems at home and at school that present barriers to learning. The school experiences of children from different ethnic groups vary considerably. A number of strategies can be adopted to improve relationships with diverse others.

Achievement

 Explain the key aspects of achievement

Extrinsic and Intrinsic Motivation

- Extrinsic motivation involves doing something to obtain something else (a means to an end). Intrinsic motivation involves the internal motivation to do something for its own sake (an end in itself). Overall, most experts recommend that teachers create a classroom climate in which students are intrinsically motivated to learn. One view of intrinsic motivation emphasizes its self-determining characteristics. Giving students some choice and providing opportunities for personal responsibility increase intrinsic motivation. When rewards are used, they should convey information about task mastery rather than external control. Researchers have found that as students move from the early elementary school years to high school, their intrinsic motivation declines, especially during the middle school years. Intrinsic motivation is typically favored by educational psychologists, although in many aspects of achievement, both intrinsic and extrinsic factors are at work.

Mastery Motivation and Mindset	• A mastery orientation is preferred over helpless or performance orientations in achievement situations. Mindset is the cognitive view, either fixed or growth, that individuals develop for themselves. Dweck argues that a key aspect of optimal development is guiding children and adolescents to develop a growth mindset.
Self-Efficacy	• Self-efficacy is the belief that one can master a situation and produce positive outcomes. Bandura stresses that self-efficacy is a critical factor that determines whether students will achieve. Schunk argues that self-efficacy influences a student's choice of tasks, with low-efficacy students avoiding many learning tasks.
Goal Setting, Planning, and Self-Monitoring	• Setting specific, proximal (short-term), and challenging goals benefits students' self-efficacy and achievement. Being a good planner means managing time effectively, setting priorities, and being organized. Self-monitoring is a key aspect of self-regulation that benefits student learning.
Expectations	• Students' expectations for success and the value they place on what they want to achieve influence their motivation. The combination of expectancy and value has been the focus of a number of efforts to understand students' achievement motivation. Individuals benefit when their parents, teachers, and other adults have high expectations for their achievement.
Ethnicity and Culture	• In most investigations, socioeconomic status predicts achievement better than ethnicity. U.S. children do more poorly on math and science achievement tests than children in Asian countries such as China, Taiwan, and Japan.

Careers, Work, and Retirement

 LG3 Discuss career development, work, and retirement

Career Development	• Many young children have idealistic fantasies about a career. In the late teens and early twenties, their career thinking has usually become more serious. By their early to mid-twenties, many individuals have started in a career. In the remainder of early adulthood, they seek to establish their career and start moving up the career ladder. Service-producing industries will account for the most jobs in America in the next decade. Jobs that require a college education will be the fastest growing and highest paying.
Work	• Work defines people in fundamental ways and is a key aspect of their identity. Most individuals spend about one-third of their adult lives at work. People often become stressed if they are unable to work, but work also can produce stress, as when there is a heavy workload and time pressure. Working part-time during adolescence can have advantages or disadvantages, although working too many hours harms students' grades. Working during college can have negative outcomes when students work long hours, or positive outcomes when students participate in co-op programs, internships, or part-time or summer work relevant to their field of study. The work patterns of emerging adults have changed over the last 100 years, and diverse school and work patterns now characterize emerging adults. The nature of the transition from school to work is strongly influenced by the individual's educational level. Many emerging adults change jobs, which can involve searching or floundering. Unemployment produces stress regardless of whether the job loss is temporary, cyclical, or permanent. The increasing number of women who work in careers outside the home has led to new work-related issues. There has been a considerable increase in the time men spend in household work and child care. For many people, midlife is a time of reflection, assessment, and evaluation of their current work and what they plan to do in the future. Midlife job or career changes can be self-motivated or forced on individuals. Some individuals continue a life of strong work productivity throughout late adulthood. An increasing number of older U.S. men and women are working and since the mid-1990s there has been a substantial rise in the percentage of older adults who work full-time and a considerable decrease in the percentage of older adults who work part-time.

Retirement

- A retirement option for older workers is a late-twentieth-century phenomenon in the United States. The United States has extended the mandatory retirement age upward, and efforts have been made to reduce age discrimination in work-related circumstances. The pathways individuals follow when they reach retirement age today are less clear than in the past. Individuals who are healthy, have adequate income, are active, are better educated, have an extended social network of friends and family, and are satisfied with their lives before they retire adjust best to retirement.

key terms

key people

Years following years steal something every day:
At last they steal us from ourselves away.

—**ALEXANDER POPE**
English Poet, 18th Century

Endings

Our life ultimately ends—when we approach life's grave sustained and soothed

with unfaltering trust or rave at the close of day; when at last years steal us from

ourselves, and when we are linked to our children's children's children by an invis-

ible cable that runs from age to age. This final section contains one chapter:

"Death, Dying, and Grieving" (Chapter 17).

chapter 17 DEATH, DYING, AND GRIEVING

preview

In this final chapter of the book, we will explore many aspects of death and dying. Among the questions that we will ask are these: What characterizes the death system and its cultural and historical contexts? How can death be defined? What are some links between development and death? How do people face their own death? How do individuals cope with the death of someone they love?

> Sustained and soothed by
> an unfaltering trust, approach
> thy grave, Like one who wraps the
> drapery of his couch, About him,
> and lies down to pleasant dreams.
>
> —**William Cullen Bryant**
> *American Poet, 19th Century*

The Death System and Cultural Contexts

 LG1 Describe the death system and its cultural and historical contexts

- The Death System and Its Cultural Variations
- Changing Historical Circumstances

Every culture has a death system, and variations in this death system occur across cultures. Also, when, where, and how people die have changed historically in the United States.

THE DEATH SYSTEM AND ITS CULTURAL VARIATIONS

Robert Kastenbaum (2004, 2007, 2009) emphasizes that a number of components compose the *death system* in any culture. The components include:

- *People*. Because death is inevitable, everyone is involved with death at some point, either their own death or the deaths of others. Some individuals have a more systematic role with death, such as those who work in the funeral industry or belong to the clergy, as well as people who work in life-threatening contexts, such as firefighters and the police.
- *Places or contexts*. These include hospitals, funeral homes, cemeteries, hospices, battlefields, and memorials (such as the Vietnam Veterans Memorial Wall in Washington, D.C.).
- *Times*. Death involves times or occasions—such as Memorial Day in the United States and the Day of the Dead in Mexico—which are set aside to honor those who have died. Also, anniversaries of disasters such as D-Day in World War II, 9/11/2001, and Hurricane Katrina in 2005, as well as the 2004 tsunami in Southeast Asia that took approximately 100,000 lives, are times when those who died are remembered in special ways such as ceremonies.
- *Objects*. Many objects in a culture are associated with death, including caskets and various black objects such as clothes, arm bands, and hearses.
- *Symbols*. Symbols such as a skull and crossbones, as well as last rites in the Catholic religion and various religious ceremonies, are connected to death.

Kastenbaum (2004, 2007, 2009) also argues that the death system serves certain functions in a culture. These functions include *issuing warnings and predictions* (by such providers as weather-forecasting services and the media, laboratories that analyze test results, and doctors that communicate with patients and their families); *preventing death* (by such people as firefighters, the police, physicians, and researchers who work to

These children's parents died when they were swept away by the tsunami in Indonesia in 2004. The death system includes times such as the 2004 tsunami. *What are some other components of the death system?*

A body lies in the flooded streets of New Orleans in the aftermath of Hurricane Katrina.

improve safety and find cures for diseases); *caring for the dying* (by various health professionals such as physicians and nurses, as well as in places where dying individuals are cared for, such as hospitals or hospices); *disposing of the dead* (removal of the body, embalming or cremation, and so on); *social consolidation after death* (coping and adapting by family members and friends of the deceased, who often need support and counseling); *making sense of the death* (how people in the society try to understand death); and *killing* (when, how, and for what reasons people in the culture can be killed, such as criminals, and whether the death penalty should be given to some individuals). Figure 17.1 describes the functions of the death system in the context of Hurricane Katrina in 2005 (Kastenbaum, 2007, 2009).

What are some cultural variations in the death system? To live a full life and to die with glory were the prevailing goals of the ancient Greeks. Individuals are more conscious of death in times of war, famine, and plague. Whereas Americans are conditioned from early in life to live as though they were immortal, in much of the world this fiction cannot be maintained. Death crowds the streets of Calcutta in daily overdisplay, as it does the scrubby villages of Africa's Sahel. Children live with the ultimate toll of malnutrition and disease, mothers lose as many babies as survive into adulthood, and it is rare that a family remains intact for many years. Even in peasant areas where life is better, and health and maturity may be reasonable expectations, the presence of dying people in the house, the large attendance at funerals, and the daily contact with aging adults prepare the young for death and provide them with guidelines on how to die. By contrast, in the United States it is not uncommon to reach adulthood without having seen someone die.

Most societies throughout history have had philosophical or religious beliefs about death, and most societies have a ritual that deals with death (Bruce, 2007). Death may be seen as a punishment for one's sins, an act of atonement, or a judgment of a just God. For some, death means loneliness; for others, death is a quest for happiness. For still others, death represents redemption, a relief from the trials and tribulations of the earthly world. Some embrace death and welcome it; others abhor and fear it. For those who welcome it, death may be seen as the fitting end to a fulfilled life. From this perspective, how we depart from earth is influenced by how we have lived.

In most societies, death is not viewed as the end of existence—although the biological body has died, the spiritual body is believed to live on. This religious perspective is favored by most Americans as well (Gowan, 2003). Cultural variations in attitudes toward death include belief in reincarnation, which is an important aspect of the Hindu and Buddhist religions (Dillon, 2003). In the Gond culture of India, death is believed to be caused by magic and demons. The members of the Gond culture react angrily to death. In the Tanala culture of Madagascar, death is believed to be caused by natural forces. The members of the Tanala culture show a much more peaceful reaction to death than their counterparts in the Gond culture. Figure 17.2 shows a ritual associated with death in South Korea.

In many ways, we in the United States are death avoiders and death deniers (Gold, 2011). This denial can take many forms:

- The tendency of the funeral industry to gloss over death and fashion lifelike qualities in the dead

Death System Function	Hurricane Katrina
Warnings and predictions	Long-standing recognition of vulnerability; clear advance warning of impending disaster.
Preventing death	The hurricane itself could not be prevented; loss of life, social disorganization, and massive property destruction could have been sharply reduced by better advanced planning and emergency response.
Caring for the dying	Medical care was interrupted and undermined by damage to hospitals and communications.
Disposing of the dead	Recovering bodies was delayed, and there were major problems in identifying bodies.
Social consolidation after death	Community cohesiveness and support was negatively impacted by evacuation, scattering of family members, and limited response by overwhelmed human service agencies.
Making sense of death	There was intense criticism of government agencies, whose alleged failures contributed to death and destruction.
Killing	The media reported spikes in lethal violence after the hurricane, but those reports were later found to be inaccurate.

FIGURE **17.1**
HURRICANE KATRINA AND DEATH SYSTEM FUNCTIONS

- The adoption of euphemistic language for death—for example, exiting, passing on, never say die, and good for life, which implies forever
- The persistent search for a fountain of youth
- The rejection and isolation of the aged, who may remind us of death
- The adoption of the concept of a pleasant and rewarding afterlife, suggesting that we are immortal
- The medical community's emphasis on prolonging biological life rather than on diminishing human suffering

FIGURE **17.2**

A RITUAL ASSOCIATED WITH DEATH. Family memorial day at the national cemetery in Seoul, South Korea.

CHANGING HISTORICAL CIRCUMSTANCES

One historical change involves the age group that death most often strikes. Two hundred years ago, almost one of every two children died before the age of 10, and one parent died before children grew up. Today, death occurs most often among older adults (Carr, 2009). Life expectancy has increased from 47 years for a person born in 1900 to 78 years for someone born today (U.S. Census Bureau, 2011). In 1900, most people died at home, cared for by their family. As our population has aged and become more mobile, a larger number of older adults die apart from their families (Carr, 2009). In the United States today, more than 80 percent of all deaths occur in institutions or hospitals. The care of a dying older person has shifted away from the family and minimized our exposure to death and its painful surroundings.

developmental **connection**

Life Expectancy. The upper boundary of the human life span is 122 years of age (based on the oldest age documented). Chapter 1, p. 6

Review *Connect* Reflect

LG1 Describe the death system and its cultural and historical contexts

Review

- What characterizes the death system in a culture? What are some cultural variations in the death system?
- What are some changing sociohistorical circumstances regarding death?

Connect

- You just read about how changes in life expectancy over time have affected the experience of death. In Chapter 1, "Introduction," and Chapter 3, "Physical Development and Biological Aging," what did you learn about life expectancy and life span?

Reflect *Your Own Personal Journey of Life*

- How extensively have death and dying been discussed in your family? Explain.

Defining Death and Life/Death Issues

 Evaluate issues in determining death and decisions regarding death

Issues in Determining Death   Decisions Regarding Life, Death, and Health Care

Is there one point in the process of dying that is *the* point at which death takes place, or is death a more gradual process? What are some decisions individuals can make about life, death, and health care?

ISSUES IN DETERMINING DEATH

Twenty-five years ago, determining whether someone was dead was simpler than it is today. The end of certain biological functions—such as breathing and blood pressure, and the rigidity of the body (rigor mortis)—were considered to be clear signs of death. In the past several decades, defining death has become more complex (Hooyman & Kiyak, 2011; Zamperetti & Bellomo, 2009).

Brain death is a neurological definition of death, which states that a person is brain dead when all electrical activity of the brain has ceased for a specified period of time. A flat EEG (electroencephalogram) recording for a specified period of time is one criterion of brain death. The higher portions of the brain often die sooner than the lower portions. Because the brain's lower portions monitor heartbeat and respiration, individuals whose higher brain areas have died may continue breathing and have a heartbeat. The definition of brain death currently followed by most physicians includes the death of both the higher cortical functions and the lower brain stem functions (Truog, 2008).

Some medical experts argue that the criteria for death should include only higher cortical functioning. If the cortical death definition were adopted, then physicians could claim a person is dead who has no cortical functioning, even though the lower brain stem is functioning. Supporters of the cortical death policy argue that the functions we associate with being human, such as intelligence and personality, are located in the higher cortical part of the brain. They believe that when these functions are lost, the "human being" is no longer alive.

DECISIONS REGARDING LIFE, DEATH, AND HEALTH CARE

In cases of catastrophic illness or accidents, patients might not be able to respond adequately to participate in decisions about their medical care. To prepare for this situation, some individuals make choices earlier.

Natural Death Act and Advance Directive   For many patients in a coma, it has not been clear what their wishes regarding termination of treatment might be if they still were conscious. Recognizing that terminally ill patients might prefer to die rather than linger in a painful or vegetative state, the organization "Choice in Dying" created the *living will*. This document is designed to be filled in while the individual can still think clearly; it expresses the person's desires regarding extraordinary medical procedures that might be used to sustain life when the medical situation becomes hopeless (Henrikson, 2010; Racine & others, 2010).

Physicians' concerns over malpractice suits and the efforts of people who support the living will concept have produced natural death legislation in many states. For example, California's Natural Death Act permits individuals who have been diagnosed by two physicians as terminally ill to sign an *advance directive,* which states that life-sustaining procedures shall not be used to prolong their lives when death is imminent. An advance directive must be signed while the individual still is able to think clearly (Westphal & McKee, 2009).

Euthanasia   Euthanasia ("easy death") is the act of painlessly ending the lives of individuals who are suffering from an incurable disease or severe disability (Karlsson, Milberg, & Strang, 2011; Sorta-Bilajac & others, 2011). Sometimes euthanasia is called "mercy killing." Distinctions are made between two types of euthanasia: passive and active. **Passive euthanasia** occurs when a person is allowed to die by withholding available treatment, such as withdrawing a life-sustaining device. For example, this might involve turning off a respirator or a heart-lung machine. **Active euthanasia** occurs when death is deliberately induced, as when a lethal dose of a drug is injected (Fass & Fass, 2011). A recent Dutch study of almost 7,000 dying persons revealed that only 7 percent requested passive or active euthanasia, and of those who requested, approximately one-third of the requests were granted (Onwuteaka-Philipsen & others, 2010).

Technological advances in life-support devices raise the issue of quality of life (Facciorusso & others, 2011; Yun & others, 2011). Nowhere was this more apparent

brain death A neurological definition of death—an individual is dead when all electrical activity of the brain has ceased for a specified period of time.

euthanasia The act of painlessly ending the lives of persons who are suffering from incurable diseases or severe disabilities; sometimes called "mercy killing."

passive euthanasia The withholding of available treatments, such as life-sustaining devices, allowing the person to die.

active euthanasia Death induced deliberately, as by injecting a lethal dose of a drug.

hospice A program committed to making the end of life as free from pain, anxiety, and depression as possible. The goals of hospice contrast with those of a hospital, which are to cure disease and prolong life.

palliative care Emphasized in hospice care; involves reducing pain and suffering and helping individuals die with dignity.

in the highly publicized case of Terri Schiavo, who suffered severe brain damage related to cardiac arrest and a lack of oxygen to the brain (Givens & Mitchell, 2009). She went into a coma and spent 15 years in a vegetative state. Across the 15 years, whether passive euthanasia should be implemented, or whether she should be kept in the vegetative state with the hope that her condition might change for the better, was debated between family members and eventually at a number of levels in the judicial system. At one point toward the end of her life in early spring 2005, a judge ordered her feeding tube be removed. However, subsequent appeals led to its reinsertion twice. The feeding tube was removed a third and final time on March 18, 2005, and she died 13 days later. Withholding the life-support system allowed Terri Schiavo to die from passive euthanasia.

Terri Schiavo (*right*) shown with her mother in an undated photo. *What issues does the Terri Schiavo case raise?*

Should individuals like Terri Schiavo be kept alive in a vegetative state? The trend is toward acceptance of passive euthanasia in the case of terminally ill patients (Seay, 2011; Truog, 2008). However, a recent study revealed that family members were reluctant to have their relatives disconnected from a ventilator but rather wanted an escalation of treatment for them (Sviri & others, 2009). In this study, most of the individuals said that in similar circumstances they would not want to be chronically ventilated or resuscitated.

The most widely publicized cases of active euthanasia involve "assisted suicide." Jack Kevorkian, a Michigan physician, assisted a number of terminally ill patients in ending their lives. After a series of trials, Kevorkian was convicted in the state of Michigan of second-degree murder and served eight years in prison.

Active euthanasia is a crime in most countries and in all states in the United States except two—Oregon and Washington. In 1994, the state of Oregon passed the Death with Dignity Act, which allows active euthanasia. Through 2001, 91 individuals were known to have died by active euthanasia in Oregon. In January 2006, the U.S. Supreme Court upheld Oregon's active euthanasia law. Active euthanasia is legal in the Netherlands, Belgium, Luxembourg, and Uruguay (Smets & others, 2010; Watson, 2009).

Dr. Jack Kevorkian assisted a number of people in Michigan to end their lives through active euthanasia. *Where do you stand on the use of active euthanasia?*

Needed: Better Care for Dying Individuals

Too often, death in America is lonely, prolonged, and painful. Scientific advances sometimes have made dying harder by delaying the inevitable. Also, even though painkillers are available, too many people experience severe pain during the last days and months of life (Alonso-Babarro & others, 2010; Cassell & Rich, 2010). Many health-care professionals have not been trained to provide adequate end-of-life care or to understand its importance.

Care providers are increasingly interested in helping individuals experience a "good death" (Goodie & McGlory, 2010; Toledo-Pereyra, 2010). One view is that a good death involves physical comfort, support from loved ones, acceptance, and appropriate medical care. For some individuals, a good death involves accepting one's impending death and not feeling like a burden to others (Carr, 2009).

Hospice is a program committed to making the end of life as free from pain, anxiety, and depression as possible (Berry, 2010). Whereas a hospital's goals are to cure illness and prolong life, hospice care emphasizes **palliative care,** which involves reducing pain and suffering and helping individuals die with dignity (Bruera & others, 2010; Chan & Webster, 2010). Hospice-care professionals work together to treat the dying person's symptoms, make the individual as comfortable as possible, show interest in the person and the person's family, and help everyone involved cope with death (Ireland, 2010; Kahana, Kahana, & Wykle, 2010).

Today more hospice programs are home-based, a blend of institutional and home care designed to humanize the end-of-life experience for the dying person. To read about the work of a home hospice nurse, see the *Connecting with Careers* profile.

What characterizes hospice care?

Kathy McLaughlin, Home Hospice Nurse

Kathy McLaughlin is a home hospice nurse in Alexandria, Virginia. She provides care for individuals with terminal cancer, Alzheimer disease, and other diseases. There currently is a shortage of home hospice nurses in the United States.

Kathy says that she has seen too many people dying in pain, away from home, hooked up to needless machines. In her work as a home hospice nurse, she comments, "I know I'm making a difference. I just feel privileged to get the chance to meet this person who is not going to be around much longer. I want to enjoy the moment with this person. And I want them to enjoy the moment. They have great stories. They are better than novels" (McLaughlin, 2003, p. 1).

Hospice nurses like Kathy McLaughlin care for terminally ill patients and seek to make their remaining days of life as pain-free and comfortable as possible. They typically spend several hours a day in the terminally ill patient's home, serving not just as a medical caregiver but also as an emotional caregiver. Hospice nurses usually coordinate the patient's care through an advising physician.

A hospice nurse must be a registered nurse (RN) who is also certified as a hospice worker. The educational requirement is an under-

Kathy McLaughlin checks the vital signs of Kathryn Francis, 86, who is in an advanced stage of Alzheimer disease.

graduate degree in nursing; some hospice nurses also have graduate degrees in nursing. To be a certified hospice nurse requires a current license as an RN, a minimum of two years of experience as an RN in hospice-nursing settings, and passing an exam administered by the National Board for the Certification of Hospice Nurses.

Review *Connect* Reflect

LG2 Evaluate issues in determining death and decisions regarding death

Review

- What are some issues regarding the determination of death?
- What are some decisions to be made regarding life, death, and health care?

Connect

- In this section you learned that hospices try to provide adequate pain management for dying patients. What did you learn about older adults in Chapter 5, "Motor, Sensory, and Perceptual Development," that might help them deal with pain better than younger adults?

Reflect *Your Own Personal Journey of Life*

- Have you signed an advance directive (living will)? Why or why not?

A Developmental Perspective on Death

LG3 Discuss death and attitudes about it at different points in development

Causes of Death

Attitudes Toward Death at Different Points in the Life Span

Suicide

Today in the United States, the deaths of older adults account for approximately two-thirds of the 2 million deaths that occur each year. Thus, what we know about death, dying, and grieving mainly is based on information about older adults.

Youthful death is far less common. When, where, and how people die have changed historically in the United States (Leming & Dickinson, 2011).

CAUSES OF DEATH

Death can occur at any point in the human life span. Death can occur during pre-natal development through miscarriages or stillborn births. Death can also occur during the birth process or in the first few days after birth, which usually happens because of a birth defect or because infants have not developed adequately to sustain life outside the uterus. In Chapter 3 we discussed *sudden infant death syndrome* (SIDS), in which infants stop breathing, usually during the night, and die without apparent cause (Goldwater, 2011). SIDS currently is the leading cause of infant death in the United States, with the risk highest at 2 to 4 months of age (NICHD, 2011).

In childhood, death occurs most often because of accidents or illness. Acciden-tal death in childhood can be the consequence of such things as an automobile accident, drowning, poisoning, fire, or a fall from a high place. Major illnesses that cause death in children are heart disease, cancer, and birth defects.

Compared with childhood, death in adolescence is more likely to occur because of motor vehicle accidents, suicide, and homicide. Many motor vehicle accidents that cause death in adolescence are alcohol-related. We will examine suicide in greater depth shortly.

Older adults are more likely to die from chronic diseases, such as heart disease and cancer, whereas younger adults are more likely to die from accidents. Older adults' diseases often incapacitate before they kill, which produces a course of dying that slowly leads to death. Of course, many young and middle-aged adults die of illnesses such as heart disease and cancer.

ATTITUDES TOWARD DEATH AT DIFFERENT POINTS IN THE LIFE SPAN

The ages of children and adults influence the way they experience and think about death (Silverman & Kelly, 2009; Torbic, 2011). A mature, adult-like conception of death includes an understanding that death is final and irreversible, that death rep-resents the end of life, and that all living things die. Most researchers have found that as children grow, they develop a more mature approach to death (Hayslip & Hansson, 2003).

Childhood   Most researchers note that infants do not have even a rudimentary concept of death. However, as infants develop an attachment to a caregiver, they can experience loss or separation and an accompanying anxiety. But young children do not perceive time the way adults do. Even brief separations may be experienced as total losses. For most infants, the reappearance of the caregiver provides a con-tinuity of existence and a reduction of anxiety. We know very little about the infant's actual experiences with bereavement, although the loss of a parent, especially if the caregiver is not replaced, can negatively affect the infant's health.

Even children 3 to 5 years of age have little or no idea of what death means. They may confuse death with sleep or ask in a puzzled way, "Why doesn't it move?" Preschool-aged children rarely get upset by the sight of a dead animal or by being told that a person has died. They believe that the dead can be brought back to life spontaneously by magic or by giving them food or medical treatment. Young chil-dren often believe that only people who want to die, or who are bad or careless, actually die. They also may blame themselves for the death of someone they know well, illogically reasoning that the event may have happened because they disobeyed the person who died.

Sometime in the middle and late childhood years more realistic perceptions of death develop. In one early investigation of children's perception of death, children 3 to 5 years of age denied that death exists, children 6 to 9 years of age believed

developmental connection

Conditions, Diseases, and Disorders. Nearly 3,000 deaths of infants a year in the United States are attributed to SIDS. Chap-ter 3, p. 111

Three- to nine-year-old children with their mother visiting their father's grave in Kenya. *What are some developmental changes in children's conceptions of death?*

that death exists but happens to only some people, and children 9 years of age and older recognized death's finality and universality (Nagy, 1948). In a review of research on children's conception of death, it was concluded that children probably do not view death as universal and irreversible until about 9 years of age (Cuddy-Casey & Orvaschel, 1997). Most children under 7 do not see death as likely. Those who do see it as likely perceive it as reversible.

An expert on death and dying, Robert Kastenbaum (2007) takes a different view on developmental dimensions of death and dying. He notes that even very young children are acutely aware of and concerned about *separation* and *loss*, just as attachment theorist John Bowlby (1980) pointed out. Kastenbaum also says that many children work hard at trying to understand death. Thus, instead of viewing young children as having illogical perceptions of death, Kastenbaum thinks a more accurate stance is to view them as having concerns about death and striving to understand it.

The death of a parent is especially difficult for children. When a child's parent dies, the child's school performance and peer relationships often worsen. For some children, as well as adults, a parent's death can be devastating and result in a hypersensitivity about death, including a fear of losing others close to the individual. In some cases, loss of a sibling can result in similar negative outcomes. However, a number of factors, such as the quality of the relationship and type of the death (whether due to an accident, long-standing illness, suicide, or murder, for example), can influence the individual's development following the death of a person close to the individual.

Most psychologists stress that honesty is the best strategy in discussing death with children. Treating the concept as unmentionable is thought to be an inappropriate strategy, yet most of us have grown up in a society in which death is rarely discussed.

developmental connection

Cognitive Development. In Piaget's theory, adolescents think more abstractly, idealistically, and logically than do children. Chapter 6, p. 194

In addition to honesty, what other strategies can be adopted in discussing death with children? The best response to the child's query about death might depend on the child's maturity level. For example, a preschool child requires a less elaborate explanation than an older child. Death can be explained to preschool children in simple physical and biological terms. Actually, what young children need more than elaborate explanations of death is reassurance that they are loved and will not be abandoned. Regardless of children's ages, adults should be sensitive and sympathetic, encouraging them to express their own feelings and ideas.

Adolescence Adolescents develop more abstract conceptions of death than children do. For example, adolescents describe death in terms of darkness, light, transition, or nothingness (Wenestam & Wass, 1987). They also develop religious and philosophical views about the nature of death and whether there is life after death.

Recall from Chapter 11 the concepts of adolescent egocentrism and personal fable—adolescents' preoccupation with themselves and their belief that they are invincible and unique. Thus, it is not unusual for some adolescents to think that they are somehow immune to death and that death is something that happens to other people but not to them. However, as we indicated in Chapter 11, some research studies suggest that rather than perceiving themselves to be invulnerable, adolescents tend to portray themselves as vulnerable to experiencing a premature death (Fischoff & others, 2010).

Adulthood There is no evidence that a special orientation toward death develops in early adulthood. An increase in consciousness about

What are children's and adolescents' attitudes about death? What are some good strategies for helping children and adolescents understand death?

death accompanies individuals' awareness that they are aging, which usually intensifies in middle adulthood. In our discussion of middle adulthood, we considered that midlife is a time when adults begin to think more about how much time is left in their lives. Researchers have found that middle-aged adults actually fear death more than do young adults or older adults (Kalish & Reynolds, 1976). Older adults, though, think about death more and talk about it more in conversation with others than do middle-aged and young adults. They also have more direct experience with death as their friends and relatives become ill and die (Hayslip & Hansson, 2003). Older adults are forced to examine the meanings of life and death more frequently than are younger adults.

How might older adults' attitudes about death differ from those of younger adults?

Younger adults who are dying often feel cheated more than do older adults who are dying (Kalish, 1987). Younger adults are more likely to think they have not had the opportunity to do what they want to do with their lives. Younger adults perceive they are losing what they might achieve; older adults perceive they are losing what they have.

In older adults, one's own death may take on an appropriateness it lacked in earlier years. Some of the increased thinking and conversing about death, and an increased sense of integrity developed through a positive life review, may help older adults accept death. Older adults are less likely to have unfinished business than are younger adults. They usually do not have children who need to be guided to maturity, their spouses are more likely to be dead, and they are less likely to have work-related projects that require completion. Lacking such anticipations, death may be less emotionally painful to them. Even among older adults, however, attitudes toward death vary (Whitbourne & Meeks, 2011).

SUICIDE

What are some of the factors that place people at risk for suicide? They include serious physical illnesses, mental disorders, feelings of hopelessness, social isolation, failure in school and work, loss of loved ones, serious financial difficulties, drug use, and a prior suicide attempt (Lapierre & others, 2011; Rhodes & Bethell, 2008; Swahn & others, 2011).

There are cultural differences in suicide (Hjelmeland, 2011; Shah, 2008). The highest rate of suicide for males is in Lithuania (68 per 100,000 population); the lowest is in the Dominican Republic (0 per 100,000 population). The highest rate of suicide for females is in Sri Lanka (17 per 100,000 population) and China; the lowest rate (0 per 100,000 population) occurs in several Caribbean islands, including Aruba and Barbados, and in several Middle Eastern countries, including Egypt and Jordan (World Health Organization, 2009). The United States' rate of suicide is 18 per 100,000 population for males, 4.5 per 100,000 for females.

Adolescence Suicide behavior is rare in childhood but escalates in adolescence and then increases further in emerging adulthood (Park & others, 2006). Suicide is the third leading cause of death in 10- to 19-year-olds today in the United States (U.S. Census Bureau, 2010). After increasing to high levels in the 1990s, suicide rates in adolescents have declined in recent years. Emerging adults have triple the suicide rate of adolescents (Park & others, 2006).

Although a suicide threat should always be taken seriously, far more adolescents contemplate or attempt it unsuccessfully than actually commit it. In a national study, in 2009, 14 percent of U.S. high school students said that they had seriously considered or attempted suicide in the last 12 months (MMWR, 2010). Females were more likely to attempt suicide than males, but males were more likely to succeed in committing suicide. Males use more lethal means, such as guns, in their suicide attempts, whereas adolescent females are more likely to cut their wrists or take an overdose of sleeping pills—methods less likely to result in death.

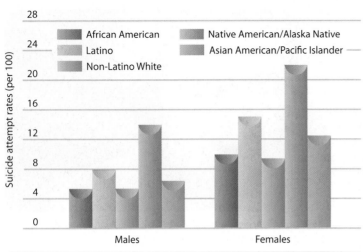

FIGURE **17.3**

SUICIDE ATTEMPTS BY U.S. ADOLESCENTS FROM DIFFERENT ETHNIC GROUPS. *Note:* Data shown are for one-year rates of self-reported suicide attempts.

The suicidal behavior of adolescents varies not only by gender, but also by ethnicity Hjelmeland, 2011). As shown in Figure 17.3, Native American/Alaska Native adolescent females are the most likely and African American males the least likely to attempt suicide (Goldston & others, 2008). However, Native American/Alaska Native adolescents are the most likely and non-Latino White females the least likely to actually commit suicide (Goldston & others, 2008). A major risk factor in the high rate of suicide attempts by NA/AN adolescents is their elevated rate of alcohol abuse.

Distal, or earlier, experiences often are involved in suicide attempts as well (Shah & Bhandarkar, 2011). The adolescent may have a long-standing history of family instability and unhappiness. Just as a lack of affection and emotional support, high control, and pressure for achievement by parents during childhood are related to adolescent depression, such combinations of family experiences also are likely to show up as distal factors in adolescents' suicide attempts.

What is the psychological profile of the suicidal adolescent? Suicidal adolescents often have depressive symptoms. Although not all depressed adolescents are suicidal, depression is the most frequently cited factor associated with adolescent suicide (Nrugham, Holen, & Sund, 2010; Thompson & Light, 2011). A sense of hopelessness, low self-esteem, and high self-blame also are associated with adolescent suicide (O'Donnell & others, 2004). The following studies document a number of factors linked with adolescent suicide attempts:

- Perception of being overweight increased the risk of suicide ideation and attempts by adolescent girls but not boys (Dave & Rashad, 2009).

- Adolescents who used alcohol while they were sad or depressed were at risk for making a suicide attempt (Schilling & others, 2009).

- Data from the National Longitudinal Study of Adolescent Health indicated that the following were indicators of suicide risk: depressive symptoms, a sense of hopelessness, engaging in suicidal ideation, having a family background of suicidal behavior, and having friends with a history of suicidal behavior (Thompson, Kuruwita, & Foster, 2009).

- Another analysis based on the National Longitudinal Study of Adolescent Health also found that parental loss predicted an increase in suicide attempts one year later but not seven years later (Thompson & Light, 2011).

- Frequent, escalating stress, especially at home, was linked with suicide attempts in young Latinas (Zayas & others, 2010).

In some instances, suicides in adolescence occur in clusters. That is, when one adolescent commits suicide, other adolescents who find out about it also commit suicide. Such "copycat" suicides raise the issue of whether or not suicides should be reported in the media; a news report might plant the idea of committing suicide in other adolescents' minds.

Adulthood and Aging U.S. suicide rates remain reasonably stable during early and middle adulthood, then increase in late adulthood (see Figure 17.4) (U.S. Census Bureau, 2008). Older non-Latino White men are more likely to commit suicide than any other group (Garand & others, 2006). One study found that African Americans are less likely to commit suicide than non-Latino Whites, but African Americans commit suicide at a younger age (median age of 34 years compared with 44 years for non-Latino Whites) (Garlow, Purselle, & Heninger, 2005). For all adult age groups (as for adolescents), males are more likely to commit suicide than are females (Fung & Chan, 2011; Schrijvers, Bollen, & Sabbe, 2011). The older adult most likely to commit suicide is a male who lives alone, has lost his spouse, and is experiencing failing health (Heisel, 2006). A recent study revealed that perceiving oneself as burdensome also may be a contributing factor in suicide attempts by older adults (Corna & others, 2010).

Are there factors that distinguish between individuals who just think about suicide and those who actually attempt it? A study of more than 7,000 adults revealed that suicide attempters were more likely than suicide ideators to be unemployed, have poor health, and have relationship problems (Fairweather & others, 2006).

Older adults are more likely to plan their suicide than adolescents, while impulsivity is more likely to be involved in adolescent suicide behavior (Demircin & others, 2011). Older adults also are more likely to actually commit suicide than are adolescents, with one in four attempts by older adults resulting in death (Demircin & others, 2011). A surviving spouse is especially at risk for depression or suicide (De Leo, 2002).

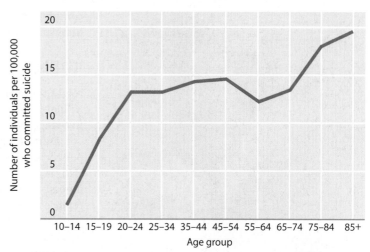

FIGURE 17.4

U.S. RATES OF SUICIDE IN DIFFERENT AGE GROUPS

Review *Connect* Reflect

 Discuss death and attitudes about it at different points in development

Review

- What are some developmental changes in the cause of death?
- What are some attitudes about death at different points in development?
- Why do people commit suicide? What are some links of suicide to development?

Connect

- In this section you learned that children 3 to 5 years of age often believe the dead can be brought back to life spontaneously, by magic or by giving them food or medical treatment. During which of Piaget's stages of development is a child's cognitive world dominated by egocentrism and magical beliefs?

Reflect *Your Own Personal Journey of Life*

- What is your current attitude about death? Has it changed since you were an adolescent? If so, how?

Facing One's Own Death

 Explain the psychological aspects involved in facing one's own death and the contexts in which people die

Kübler-Ross' Stages of Dying   Perceived Control and Denial   The Contexts in Which People Die

Knowledge of death's inevitability permits us to establish priorities and structure our time accordingly. As we age, these priorities and structurings change in recognition of diminishing future time. Values concerning the most important uses of time also change. For example, when asked how they would spend six remaining months of life, younger adults described such activities as traveling and accomplishing things they previously had not done; older adults described more inner-focused activities—contemplation and meditation, for example (Kalish & Reynolds, 1976).

Most dying individuals want an opportunity to make some decisions regarding their own life and death (Kastenbaum, 2007). Some individuals want to

> Man is the only animal that finds his own existence a problem he has to solve and from which he cannot escape. In the same sense man is the only animal who knows he must die.
>
> —ERICH FROMM
> *American Psychotherapist, 20th Century*

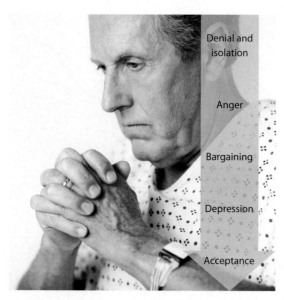

FIGURE 17.5

KÜBLER-ROSS' STAGES OF DYING. According to Elisabeth Kübler-Ross, we go through five stages of dying: denial and isolation, anger, bargaining, depression, and acceptance. *Does everyone go through these stages, or go through them in the same order? Explain.*

denial and isolation Kübler-Ross' first stage of dying, in which the dying person denies that she or he is really going to die.

anger Kübler-Ross' second stage of dying, in which the dying person's denial gives way to anger, resentment, rage, and envy.

bargaining Kübler-Ross' third stage of dying, in which the dying person develops the hope that death can somehow be postponed.

depression Kübler-Ross' fourth stage of dying, in which the dying person perceives the certainty of her or his death. A period of depression or preparatory grief may appear.

acceptance Kübler-Ross' fifth stage of dying, in which the dying person develops a sense of peace, an acceptance of her or his fate, and, in many cases, a desire to be left alone.

complete unfinished business; they want time to resolve problems and conflicts and to put their affairs in order.

KÜBLER-ROSS' STAGES OF DYING

Might there be a sequence of stages we go through as we face death? Elisabeth Kübler-Ross (1969) divided the behavior and thinking of dying persons into five stages: denial and isolation, anger, bargaining, depression, and acceptance.

Denial and isolation is Kübler-Ross' first stage of dying, in which the person denies that death is really going to take place. The person may say, "No, it can't be me. It's not possible." This is a common reaction to terminal illness. However, denial is usually only a temporary defense. It is eventually replaced with increased awareness when the person is confronted with such matters as financial considerations, unfinished business, and worry about the welfare of surviving family members.

Anger is Kübler-Ross' second stage of dying, in which the dying person recognizes that denial can no longer be maintained. Denial often gives way to anger, resentment, rage, and envy. The dying person's question is "Why me?" At this point, the person becomes increasingly difficult to care for as anger may become displaced and projected onto physicians, nurses, family members, and even God. The realization of loss is great, and those who symbolize life, energy, and competent functioning are especially salient targets of the dying person's resentment and jealousy.

Bargaining is Kübler-Ross' third stage of dying, in which the person develops the hope that death can somehow be postponed or delayed. Some persons enter into bargaining or negotiation—often with God—as they try to delay their death. Psychologically, the person is saying, "Yes, me, but . . ." In exchange for a few more days, weeks, or months of life, the person promises to lead a reformed life dedicated to God or to the service of others.

Depression is Kübler-Ross' fourth stage of dying, in which the dying person perceives the certainty of his or her death. At this point, a period of depression or preparatory grief may appear. The dying person may become silent, refuse visitors, and spend much of the time crying or grieving. This behavior is normal and is an effort to disconnect the self from love objects. Attempts to cheer up the dying person at this stage should be discouraged, says Kübler-Ross, because the dying person has a need to contemplate impending death.

Acceptance is Kübler-Ross' fifth stage of dying, in which the person develops a sense of peace, an acceptance of one's fate, and—in many cases—a desire to be left alone. In this stage, feelings and physical pain may be virtually absent. Kübler-Ross describes this fifth stage as the end of the dying struggle, the final resting stage before death. A summary of Kübler-Ross' dying stages is presented in Figure 17.5.

What is the current evaluation of Kübler-Ross' theory about the stages of dying? According to Robert Kastenbaum (2007, 2009), there are some problems with Kübler-Ross' approach:

- The existence of the five-stage sequence has not been demonstrated by either Kübler-Ross or independent research.
- The stage interpretation neglected the patients' situations, including relationship support, specific effects of illness, family obligations, and institutional climate in which they were interviewed.

Despite these limitations, Kübler-Ross' pioneering efforts were important in calling attention to those who are attempting to cope with life-threatening illnesses. She did much to encourage attention to the quality of life for dying persons and their families.

Because of the criticisms of Kübler-Ross' stages, some psychologists prefer to describe them not as stages but as potential reactions to dying. At any one moment, a number of emotions may wax and wane. Hope, disbelief, bewilderment, anger, and acceptance may come and go as individuals try to make sense of what is happening to them.

In facing their own death, some individuals struggle until the end, desperately trying to hang on to their lives. Acceptance of death never comes for them. Some psychologists note that the harder individuals fight to avoid the inevitable death they face and the more they deny it, the more difficulty they will have in dying peacefully and in a dignified way; other psychologists argue that not confronting death until the end may be adaptive for some individuals (Lifton, 1977).

The extent to which people have found meaning and purpose in their lives is linked with how they approach death (Carr, 2009). A recent study revealed that individuals with a chronic, life-threatening illness—congestive heart failure—were trying to understand meaning in life (Park & others, 2008). Another study of 160 individuals with less than three months to live revealed that those who had found purpose and meaning in their lives felt the least despair in the final weeks, whereas dying individuals who saw no reason for living were the most distressed and wanted to hasten death (McClain, Rosenfeld, & Breitbart, 2003). In this and other studies, spirituality helped to buffer dying individuals from severe depression (Smith, McCullough, & Poll, 2003).

Do individuals become more spiritual as they get closer to death? A recent study of more than 100 patients with advanced congestive heart failure who were studied at two times six months apart found that as the patients perceived they were closer to death, they became more spiritual (Park, 2008).

developmental **connection**

Religion. Religion can fulfill some important psychological needs in older adults, helping them face impending death and accept the inevitable losses of old age. Chapter 13, p. 435

PERCEIVED CONTROL AND DENIAL

Perceived control may work as an adaptive strategy for some older adults who face death. When individuals are led to believe they can influence and control events—such as prolonging their lives—they may become more alert and cheerful. Remember from Chapter 4, "Health," that giving nursing home residents options for control improved their attitudes and increased their longevity (Rodin & Langer, 1977).

Denial also may be a fruitful way for some individuals to approach death. It can be adaptive or maladaptive. Denial can be used to avoid the destructive impact of shock by delaying the necessity of dealing with one's death. Denial can insulate the individual from having to cope with intense feelings of anger and hurt—however, if denial keeps us from having a life-saving operation, it clearly is maladaptive. Denial is neither good nor bad; its adaptive qualities need to be evaluated on an individual basis.

THE CONTEXTS IN WHICH PEOPLE DIE

For dying individuals, the context in which they die is important (Hooyman & Kiyak, 2011). More than 50 percent of Americans die in hospitals, and nearly 20 percent die in nursing homes. Some people spend their final days in isolation and fear. An increasing number of people choose to die in the humane atmosphere of hospice care.

Hospitals offer several important advantages to the dying individual—for example, professional staff members are readily available, and the medical technology present may prolong life. But a hospital may not be the best place for many people to die. Most individuals say they would rather die at home. Many feel, however, that they will be a burden at home, that there is limited space there, and that dying at home may alter relationships. Individuals who are facing death also worry about the competency and availability of emergency medical treatment if they remain at home.

Review

- What are Kübler-Ross' five stages of dying? What conclusions can be reached about them?
- What roles do perceived control and denial play in facing one's own death?
- What are the contexts in which people die?

Connect

- In this section you learned that the extent to which people have found meaning and

purpose in their lives is linked with the way they approach death. In Chapter 13, "Moral Development, Values, and Religion," what did Roy Baumeister and Kathleen Vohs say are the four main needs for meaning that guide how people try to make sense of their lives?

Reflect *Your Own Personal Journey of Life*

- How do you think you will psychologically handle facing your own death?

Coping with the Death of Someone Else

LG5 Identify ways to cope with the death of another person

- Communicating with a Dying Person
- Grieving
- Making Sense of the World
- Losing a Life Partner
- Forms of Mourning

Loss can come in many forms in our lives—divorce, a pet's death, loss of a job—but no loss is greater than that which comes through the death of someone we love and care for: a parent, child, sibling, spouse, relative, or friend. In the ratings of life's stresses that require the most adjustment, death of a spouse is given the highest number. How should we communicate with a dying individual? How do we cope with the death of someone we love?

COMMUNICATING WITH A DYING PERSON

Most psychologists stress that it is best for dying individuals to know that they are dying and that significant others know they are dying so they can interact and communicate with each other on the basis of this mutual knowledge. What are some of the advantages of this open awareness for the dying individual? First, dying individuals can close their lives in accord with their own ideas about proper dying. Second, they may be able to complete some plans and projects, can make arrangements for survivors, and can participate in decisions about a funeral and burial. Third, dying individuals have the opportunity to reminisce, to converse with others who have been important in their life, and to end life conscious of what life has been like. And fourth, dying individuals have more understanding of what is happening within their bodies and what the medical staff is doing to them (Kalish, 1981). In the *Connecting Development to Life* interlude, you can read further about effective communication strategies with a dying person.

GRIEVING

Grief is a complex emotional state that is an evolving process with multiple dimensions. Our exploration of grief focuses on dimensions of grieving and how coping may vary with the type of death.

Communicating with a Dying Person

Effective strategies for communicating with a dying person include these:

1. Establish your presence, be at the same eye level; don't be afraid to touch the dying person—dying individuals are often starved for human touch.
2. Eliminate distraction—for example, ask whether it is okay to turn off the TV. Realize that excessive small talk can be a distraction.
3. Dying individuals who are very frail often have little energy. If the dying person you are visiting is very frail, you may not want to visit for very long.
4. Don't insist that the dying person feel acceptance about death if he or she wants to deny the reality of the situation; on the other hand, don't insist on denial if the dying individual indicates acceptance.
5. Allow the dying person to express guilt or anger; encourage the expression of feelings.
6. Don't be afraid to ask the person what the expected outcome for the illness is. Discuss alternatives, unfinished business.
7. Sometimes dying individuals don't have access to other people. Ask the dying person whether there is anyone he or she would like to see whom you can contact.
8. Encourage the dying individual to reminisce, especially if you have memories in common.

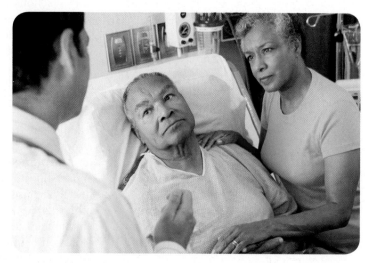

What are some good strategies for communicating with a dying person?

9. Talk with the individual when she or he wishes to talk. If this is impossible, make a later appointment and keep it.
10. Express your regard for the dying individual. Don't be afraid to express love, and don't be afraid to say good-bye.

How would you adjust these strategies if the dying person were very young or very old?

Dimensions of Grieving **Grief** is the emotional numbness, disbelief, separation anxiety, despair, sadness, and loneliness that accompany the loss of someone we love. An important dimension of grief is pining for the lost person. Pining or yearning reflects an intermittent, recurrent wish or need to recover the lost person. Another important dimension of grief is separation anxiety, which not only includes pining and preoccupation with thoughts of the deceased person but also focuses on places and things associated with the deceased, as well as crying or sighing. Grief may also involve despair and sadness, which include a sense of hopelessness and defeat, depressive symptoms, apathy, loss of meaning for activities that used to involve the person who is gone, and growing desolation (Buglass, 2010; Chiambretto & others, 2010).

These feelings occur repeatedly shortly after a loss. As time passes, pining and protest over the loss tend to diminish, although episodes of depression and apathy may remain or increase. The sense of separation anxiety and loss may continue to the end of one's life, but most of us emerge from grief's tears, turning our attention once again to productive tasks and regaining a more positive view of life (Lund & others, 2009).

The grieving process is more like a roller-coaster ride than an orderly progression of stages with clear-cut time frames. The ups and downs of grief often involve

> Everyone can master grief but he who has it.
>
> **—WILLIAM SHAKESPEARE**
> *English Playwright, 17th Century*

grief The emotional numbness, disbelief, separation anxiety, despair, sadness, and loneliness that accompany the loss of someone we love.

What are some different types of grief?

rapidly changing emotions, meeting the challenges of learning new skills, detecting personal weaknesses and limitations, creating new patterns of behavior, and forming new friendships and relationships. For most individuals, grief becomes more manageable over time, with fewer abrupt highs and lows (Maciejewski & others, 2007). But many grieving spouses report that even though time has brought some healing, they have never gotten over their loss. They have just learned to live with it.

An estimated 80 to 90 percent of survivors experience normal or uncomplicated grief reactions that include sadness and even disbelief or considerable anguish. By six months after their loss, they accept it as a reality, are more optimistic about the future, and function competently in their everyday lives. However, six months after their loss, approximately 10 to 20 percent of survivors have difficulty moving on with their life, feel numb or detached, believe their life is empty without the deceased, and feel that the future has no meaning.

The latter type of grief reaction has been referred to as complicated grief (Dell'osso & others, 2011; Guldin & others, 2011; Sung & others, 2011). However, leading expert Holly Prigerson and her colleagues (Boelen & Prigerson, 2007; Givens & others, 2011; Maciejewski & others, 2011) recently have advocated use of the term **prolonged grief** to describe this type of grief that involves enduring despair and is still unresolved over an extended period of time. Prolonged grief usually has negative consequences for physical and mental health (Collier, 2011; Hauksdottir & others, 2010; Kersting & others, 2011). A person who loses someone he or she was emotionally dependent on is often at greatest risk for developing prolonged grief (Johnson & others, 2007; Zisook & others, 2010). A recent study revealed that prolonged grief was more likely to occur when individuals had lost their spouse, lost a loved one unexpectedly, or spent time with the deceased every day in the last week of the person's life (Fujisawa & others, 2010). One study found that therapy focused on motivational interviewing, emotion coping, and communication skills was effective in reducing prolonged grief (Zuckoff & others, 2006). Also, recent research indicated that African Americans experienced more prolonged grief than non-Latino Whites (Goldsmith & others, 2008).

Another type of grief is **disenfranchised grief,** which describes an individual's grief over a deceased person that is a socially ambiguous loss that can't be openly mourned or supported (Hendry, 2009). Examples of disenfranchised grief include a relationship that isn't socially recognized such as an ex-spouse, a hidden loss such as an abortion, and circumstances of the death that are stigmatized such as death because of AIDS. Disenfranchised grief may intensify an individual's grief because it cannot be publicly acknowledged. This type of grief may be hidden or repressed for many years, only to be reawakened by later deaths.

Dual-Process Model of Coping with Bereavement   The **dual-process model** of coping with bereavement consists of two main dimensions: (1) loss-oriented stressors and (2) restoration-oriented stressors (Stroebe, Schut, & Stroebe, 2005). Loss-oriented stressors focus on the deceased individual and can include grief work and both positive and negative reappraisal of the loss. A positive reappraisal of the loss might include acknowledging that death brought relief at the end of suffering, whereas a negative reappraisal might involve yearning for the loved one and rumination about the death. Restoration-oriented stressors involve the secondary stressors that emerge as indirect outcomes of bereavement. They can include a changing identity (such as from "wife" to "widow") and mastering skills (such as dealing with finances). Restoration rebuilds "shattered assumptions about the world and one's own place in it."

In the dual-process model, effective coping with bereavement often involves an oscillation between coping with loss and coping with restoration. Earlier models often emphasized a sequence of coping with loss through such strategies as grief work as an initial phase, followed by restoration efforts. However, in the dual-process model, coping with loss and engaging in restoration can be carried out concurrently (Richardson, 2007). According to this model, the person coping with

prolonged grief Grief that involves enduring despair and is still unresolved over an extended period of time.

disenfranchised grief Grief involving a deceased person that is a socially ambiguous loss that can't be openly mourned or supported.

dual-process model A model of coping with bereavement that emphasizes oscillation between loss-oriented stressors and restoration-oriented stressors.

death might be involved in grief group therapy while settling the affairs of the loved one. Oscillation might occur in the short term during a specific day as well as across weeks, months, and even years. Although loss and restoration coping can occur concurrently, over time there often is an initial emphasis on coping with loss followed by greater emphasis on restoration.

Coping and Type of Death   The impact of death on surviving individuals is strongly influenced by the circumstances under which the death occurs (Gold, 2011; Smith & others, 2009). Deaths that are sudden, untimely, violent, or traumatic are likely to have more intense and prolonged effects on surviving individuals and make the coping process more difficult for them. Such deaths often are accompanied by post-traumatic stress disorder (PTSD) symptoms, such as intrusive thoughts, flashbacks, nightmares, sleep disturbance, problems in concentrating, and others. The death of a child can be especially devastating and extremely difficult for parents (Harper & others, 2011; Meert & others, 2011).

In sum, people grieve in a variety of ways (Carr, 2009). Thus, there is no one right, ideal way to grieve. There are many different ways to feel about a deceased person and no set series of stages that the bereaved must pass through to become well adjusted. What is needed is an understanding that healthy coping with the death of a loved one involves growth, flexibility, and appropriateness within a cultural context.

developmental **connection**

Stress and Coping. Meaning-making coping includes drawing on beliefs, values, and goals to change the meaning of a stressful situation, especially in times of chronic stress as when a loved one dies. Chapter 13, p. 436

MAKING SENSE OF THE WORLD

One beneficial aspect of grieving is that it stimulates many individuals to try to make sense of their world (Carr, 2009; Park, 2009, 2010, 2011). A common occurrence is to go over again and again all of the events that led up to the death. In the days and weeks after the death, the closest family members share experiences with each other, sometimes reminiscing about family experiences. A recent study revealed that finding meaning in the death of a spouse was linked to a lower level of anger during bereavement (Kim, 2009).

Each individual may offer a piece of death's puzzle. "When I saw him last Saturday, he looked as though he were rallying," says one family member. "Do you think it might have had something to do with his sister's illness?" remarks another. "I doubt it, but I heard from an aide that he fell going to the bathroom that morning," comments yet another. "That explains the bruise on his elbow," says the first individual. "No wonder he told me that he was angry because he could not seem to do anything right," chimes in a fourth family member. So it goes in the attempt to understand why someone who was rallying on Saturday was dead on Wednesday.

When a death is caused by an accident or a disaster, the effort to make sense of it is pursued more vigorously. As added pieces of news come trickling in, they are integrated into the puzzle. The bereaved want to put the death into a perspective that they can understand—divine intervention, a curse from a neighboring tribe, a logical sequence of cause and effect, or whatever it may be.

LOSING A LIFE PARTNER

In 2008 in the United States, 14 percent of men and 42 percent of women age 65 and older were widowed (Administration on Aging, 2009). Those left behind after the death of an intimate partner often suffer profound grief and often endure financial loss, loneliness, increased physical illness, and psychological disorders, including depression. A recent study of widowed individuals 75 years and older found that loss of a spouse increases the likelihood of psychiatric visits and an earlier death (Moller & others, 2011).

Mary Assanful (*front right,* with other former restaurant workers) worked at Windows on the World restaurant located in the World Trade Center and lost her job because of the terrorist attacks of 9/11/2001. Three years later, Mary was still unemployed and regularly had nightmares. She and several other former coworkers were planning to open a restaurant near Ground Zero. They hoped the new restaurant would honor those who died and provide renewed focus and meaning for their still-unsettled lives. Mary says that working on this new project had calmed her mind somewhat.

How Is Widowhood Related to Women's Physical and Mental Health?

A three-year longitudinal study of more than 130,000 women 50 to 79 years of age in the United States, as part of the Women's Health Initiative, examined the relation of widowhood to physical and mental health, health behaviors, and health outcomes (Wilcox & others, 2003). Women were categorized as (1) remaining married, (2) transitioning from married to widowed, (3) remaining widowed, and (4) transitioning from widowed to married. Widows were further subdivided into the recently widowed (widowed for less than one year) and longer-term widowed (widowed for more than one year).

The measures used to assess the older women's health were:

- *Physical health.* Blood pressure was assessed after five minutes of quiet rest using the average of two readings with 30 seconds between the readings. Hypertension was defined as more than 140/90. Body mass index (BMI) was calculated and used to determine whether a woman was obese. A health survey assessed physical function and health status.

- *Mental health.* Depressive symptoms were assessed by a six-item depression scale, with participants rating the frequency of their depressed thoughts during the past week. The participant's self-report of antidepressant medicine use was also obtained. Information about social functioning and mental health was based on participants' responses on the Social Functioning Scale (Ware, Kosinski, & Dewey, 2000).

- *Health behaviors.* Dietary behaviors were assessed with a modified version of the National Cancer Institute Health Habits and History Questionnaire. Participants also were asked if they smoked tobacco

and, if so, how much. To assess physical activity, participants were asked how often they walked outside the home each week and the extent to which they engaged in strenuous or moderate exercise. To assess health-care use, they were asked whether they had visited their doctor in the past year.

- *Health outcomes.* Cardiovascular disease and cancer occurrences were assessed annually and any overnight hospitalizations were noted.

At the beginning of the three-year study, married women reported better physical and mental health, and better health in general, than widowed women. Women who remained married over the three-year period of the study showed stability in mental health, recent widows experienced marked impairments in mental health, and longer-term widows showed stability or slight improvements in mental health. Both groups of widows (recent and longer term) reported more unintentional weight loss across the three years.

These findings underscore the resilience of older women and their capacity to reestablish connections but point to the need for services that strengthen social support for those who have difficulty during the transition from marriage to widowhood. How might the study's specific findings be applied to new or improved social services for widowed women?

Surviving spouses seek to cope with the loss of their spouse in various ways (Gold, 2011: Hahn & others, 2011; Park, 2011). In one study, widowed individuals were more likely to intensify their religious and spiritual beliefs following the death of a spouse, and this increase was linked with a lower level of grief (Brown & others, 2004). Another study revealed that finding meaning in the death of a spouse was linked to a lower level of anger during bereavement (Kim, 2009).

Many widows are lonely and benefit considerably from social support (Ha & Ingersoll-Dayton, 2011). The poorer and less educated they are, the lonelier they tend to be. The bereaved are also at increased risk for many health problems (Mechakra-Tahiri & others, 2010). How might you expect widowhood to affect a woman's physical and mental health, for instance? The following *Connecting with Research* interlude examines how research has investigated this link.

Optimal adjustment after a death depends on various factors (Gold, 2011; Schulz, Hebert, & Boerner, 2008). Women do better than men largely because, in our society, women are responsible for the emotional life of a couple, whereas men usually manage the finances and material goods (Fry, 2001). Thus, women have better networks of friends, closer relationships with relatives, and experience in taking care of themselves psychologically (Antonucci & others, 2010; Whitbourne & Meeks, 2011). Older widows do better than younger widows, perhaps because the death of a partner is more expected for older women. For their part, widowers usually have more money than widows do, and they are far more likely to remarry.

One study found that psychological and religious factors—such as personal meaning, optimism, the importance of religion, and access to religious support— were related to the psychological well-being of older adults following the loss of a spouse (Fry, 2001). Other studies have indicated that religiosity and coping skills are related to well-being following the loss of a spouse in late adulthood (Whitbourne & Meeks, 2011; Wortmann & Park, 2008).

Two recent studies revealed that volunteering and helping behavior improved the well-being of widowed individuals. In one study, volunteering following spousal loss helped to protect against depressive symptoms and increased self-efficacy (Li, 2007). In another study, following spousal loss, engaging in helping behavior (providing instrumental support to others) was linked to an accelerated decline in the helper's depressive symptoms 6 to 18 months following spousal loss (Brown & others, 2008).

For either widows or widowers, social support helps them adjust to the death of a spouse (Bennett, 2009; Gold, 2011). The Widow-to-Widow program, begun in the 1960s, provides support for newly widowed women. Volunteer widows reach out to other widows, introducing them to others who may have similar problems, leading group discussions, and organizing social activities. The program has been adopted by the AARP and disseminated throughout the United States as the Widowed Person's Service. The model has since been adopted by numerous community organizations to provide support for those going through a difficult transition.

FORMS OF MOURNING

One decision facing the bereaved is what to do with the body. In the United States, in 2007, 66 percent of corpses were disposed of by burial, 34 percent by cremation— a significant increase from 15 percent in 1985 (Cremation Association of North America, 2011). Projections indicate that by 2015, 44 percent of corpses will be cremated (Cremation Association of North America, 2011). Cremation is more popular in the Pacific region of the United States, less popular in the South. Cremation also is more popular in Canada than in the United States and most popular of all in Japan and many other Asian countries. In the United States, the trend is away

A widow with the urn containing the remains of her husband, who was killed while working in Iraq. *What are some factors that are related to the adjustment of a widow after the death of her husband?*

developmental connection

Community. For older adults, social support is linked with a reduction in the symptoms of disease and mortality. Chapter 15, p. 505

A funeral in the United States.

A crowd gathered at a cremation ceremony in Bali, Indonesia, balancing decorative containers on their heads.

from public funerals and displaying the dead body in an open casket and toward private funerals followed by a memorial ceremony (Callahan, 2009)

The funeral industry has been the source of controversy in recent years. Funeral directors and their supporters argue that the funeral provides a form of closure to the relationship with the deceased, especially when there is an open casket. Their critics claim that funeral directors are just trying to make money and that embalming is grotesque. One way to avoid being exploited during bereavement is to purchase funeral arrangements in advance.

In some cultures, a ceremonial meal is held after death; in others, a black armband is worn for one year following a death. The family and the community have important roles in mourning in some cultures. Two of those cultures are the Amish and traditional Judaism (Worthington, 1989).

The Amish are a conservative group with approximately 80,000 members in the United States, Ontario, and several small settlements in South and Central America. The Amish live in a family-oriented society in which family and community support is essential for survival. Today, they live at the same unhurried pace as did their ancestors, using horses instead of cars and facing death with the same steadfast faith as their forebears. At the time of death, close neighbors assume the responsibility of notifying others of the death. The Amish community handles virtually all aspects of the funeral.

A funeral procession of horse-drawn buggies on their way to the burial of five young Amish girls who were murdered in October 2006. A remarkable aspect of their mourning involved the outpouring of support and forgiveness they gave to the widow of the murderer.

Meeting in a Jewish graveyard.

The funeral service is held in a barn in warmer months and in a house during colder months. Calm acceptance of death, influenced by a deep religious faith, is an integral part of the Amish culture. Following the funeral, a high level of support is given to the bereaved family for at least a year. Visits to the family, special scrapbooks and handmade items for the family, new work projects started for the widow, and quilting days that combine fellowship and productivity are among the supports given to the bereaved family. A profound example of the Amish culture's religious faith and acceptance of death occurred after Charles Roberts shot and killed five Amish schoolgirls and then apparently took his own life in October 2006 in the small town of Nickel Mines in Bart Township, Pennsylvania. Soon after the murders and suicide, members of the Amish community visited his widow and offered their support and forgiveness.

The family and community also have specific and important roles in mourning in traditional Judaism. The program of mourning is divided into graduated time periods, each with its appropriate practices. The observance of these practices is required of the spouse and the immediate blood relatives of the deceased. The first period is aninut, the period between death and burial—which must take place within one day. The next two periods make up avelut, or mourning proper. The first of these is shivah, a period of seven days, which commences with the burial. It is followed by sheloshim, the 30-day period following the burial, including shivah. At the end of sheloshim, the mourning process is considered over for all but one's parents. For parents, mourning continues for 11 months, although observances are minimal.

The seven-day period of the shivah is especially important in traditional Judaism. The mourners, sitting together as a group through an extended period, have an opportunity to project their feelings to the group as a whole. Visits from others during shivah may help the mourner deal with feelings of guilt. After shivah, the mourner is encouraged to resume normal social interaction. In fact, it is customary for the mourners to walk together a short distance as a symbol of their return to society. In its entirety, the elaborate mourning system of traditional Judaism is designed to promote personal growth and to reintegrate the individual into the community.

We have arrived at the end of this book. I hope this book and course have been a window to the life span of the human species and a window to your own personal journey in life.

Our study of the human life span has been long and complex. You have read about many physical, cognitive, and socioemotional changes that take place from conception through death. This is a good time to reflect on what you have learned. Which theories, studies, and ideas were especially interesting to you? What did you learn about your own development?

I wish you all the best in the remaining years of your journey though the human life span.

Review Connect Reflect

LG5 Identify ways to cope with the death of another person

Review

- What are some strategies for communicating with a dying person?
- What is the nature of grieving?
- How is making sense of the world a beneficial outcome of grieving?
- What are some characteristics and outcomes of losing a life partner?
- What are some forms of mourning? What is the nature of the funeral?

Connect

- In this section you learned that one advantage of knowing you are dying is

that you have the opportunity to reminisce. Which of Erikson's stages of development involves reflecting on the past and either piecing together a positive life review or concluding that one's life has not been well spent?

Reflect *Your Own Personal Journey of Life*

- What are considered appropriate forms of mourning in the culture in which you live?

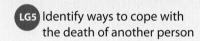

reach your **learning goals**

The Death System and Cultural Contexts

LG1 Describe the death system and its cultural and historical contexts

The Death System and Its Cultural Variations

- In Kastenbaum's view, every culture has a death system that involves people, places, times, objects, and symbols. He also argues that the death system serves certain functions in a culture that include issuing warnings and predictions, preventing death, caring for the dying, disposing of the dead, attaining social consolidation after the death, making sense of the death, and killing. Most societies throughout history have had philosophical or religious beliefs about death, and most societies have rituals that deal with death. Most cultures do not view death as the end of existence—spiritual life is thought to continue. The United States has been described as more of a death-denying and death-avoiding culture than most cultures.

Changing Historical Circumstances

- When, where, and why people die have changed historically. Today, death occurs most often among older adults. More than 80 percent of all deaths in the United States now occur in a hospital or other institution; our exposure to death in the family has been minimized.

Defining Death and Life/Death Issues Evaluate issues in determining death and decisions regarding death

Issues in Determining Death

- Twenty-five years ago, determining whether someone was dead was simpler than it is today. Brain death is a neurological definition of death which states that a person is brain dead when all electrical activity of the brain has ceased for a specified period of time. Medical experts debate whether this should include both the higher and lower brain functions or just the higher cortical functions. Most physicians use the cessation of brain function (both higher and lower) as a standard for determining death.

Decisions Regarding Life, Death, and Health Care

- Decisions regarding life, death, and health care can involve whether to have a living will, euthanasia, and hospice care. Living wills and advance directives are increasingly being used. Euthanasia is the act of painlessly ending the life of a person who is suffering from an incurable disease or disability. Distinctions are made between active and passive euthanasia. Hospice care emphasizes reducing pain and suffering rather than prolonging life.

A Developmental Perspective on Death Discuss death and attitudes about it at different points in development

Causes of Death

- Although death is more likely to occur in late adulthood, it can come at any point in development. In children and younger adults, death is more likely to occur because of accidents; in older adults, death is more likely to occur because of chronic diseases.

Attitudes Toward Death at Different Points in the Life Span

- Infants do not have a concept of death. Preschool children also have little or no concept of death. Preschool children sometimes blame themselves for a person's death. During the elementary school years, children develop a more realistic orientation toward death. Most psychologists stress that honesty is the best strategy for helping children cope with death. Death may be glossed over in adolescence. Adolescents have more abstract, philosophical views of death than children do. There is no evidence that a special orientation toward death emerges in early adulthood. Middle adulthood is a time when adults show a heightened consciousness about death and death anxiety. The deaths of some persons, especially children and younger adults, are often perceived to be more tragic than those of others, such as very old adults, who have had an opportunity to live a long life. Older adults often show less death anxiety than middle-aged adults, but older adults experience and converse about death more. Attitudes about death may vary considerably among adults of any age.

Suicide

- Among the factors that place people at risk for suicide are serious physical illnesses, feelings of hopelessness, social isolation, failure in school and work, loss of loved ones, serious financial difficulties, and depression. Suicide behavior is rare in childhood but escalates in adolescence. Both earlier and later experiences can influence suicide. U.S. suicide rates remain rather stable in early and middle adulthood, then increase in late adulthood.

Facing One's Own Death

 LG4 Explain the psychological aspects involved in facing one's own death and the contexts in which people die

Kübler-Ross' Stages of Dying

- Kübler-Ross proposed five stages of dying: denial and isolation, anger, bargaining, depression, and acceptance. Not all individuals go through the same sequence. Critics emphasize that many individuals don't go through the stages in the order she proposed.

Perceived Control and Denial

- Perceived control and denial may work together as an adaptive orientation for the dying individual. Denial can be adaptive or maladaptive, depending on the circumstances.

The Contexts in Which People Die

- Most deaths in the United States occur in hospitals; this has advantages and disadvantages. Most individuals say they would rather die at home, but they worry that they will be a burden and they are concerned about the lack of medical care.

Coping with the Death of Someone Else

 LG5 Identify ways to cope with the death of another person

Communicating with a Dying Person

- Most psychologists recommend an open communication system with the dying. Communication should not dwell on pathology or preparation for death but should emphasize the dying person's strengths.

Grieving

- Grief is the emotional numbness, disbelief, separation, anxiety, despair, sadness, and loneliness that accompany the loss of someone we love. Grief is multidimensional and in some cases may last for years. Prolonged grief involves enduring despair that is still unresolved after an extended period of time. In the dual-process model of coping with bereavement, oscillation occurs between two dimensions: loss-oriented stressors and restoration-oriented stressors. Grief and coping vary with the type of death. There are cultural variations in grieving.

Making Sense of the World

- The grieving process may stimulate individuals to strive to make sense out of their world; each individual may contribute a piece to death's puzzle.

Losing a Life Partner

- Usually the most difficult loss is the death of a spouse. The bereaved are at risk for many health problems, although there are variations in the distress experienced by a surviving spouse. Social support benefits widows and widowers.

Forms of Mourning

- Forms of mourning vary across cultures. Approximately 66 percent of corpses are disposed of by burial, 34 percent by cremation. An important aspect of mourning in many cultures is the funeral. In recent years, the funeral industry has been the focus of controversy. In some cultures, a ceremonial meal is held after death.

key terms

brain death 566	hospice 567	bargaining 574	prolonged grief 578
euthanasia 566	palliative care 567	depression 574	disenfranchised grief 578
passive euthanasia 566	denial and isolation 574	acceptance 574	dual-process model 578
active euthanasia 566	anger 574	grief 577	

key people

Robert Kastenbaum 563   Elisabeth Kübler-Ross 574   Holly Prigerson 578

glossary

A

acceptance Kübler-Ross' fifth stage of dying, in which the dying person develops a sense of peace, an acceptance of her or his fate, and, in many cases, a desire to be left alone.

accommodation Piagetian concept of adjusting schemes to fit new information and experiences.

accommodation of the eye The eye's ability to focus and maintain an image on the retina.

active euthanasia Death induced deliberately, as by injecting a lethal dose of a drug.

active (niche-picking) genotype-environment correlations Correlations that exist when children seek out environments they find compatible and stimulating.

activity theory The theory that the more active and involved older adults are, the more likely they are to be satisfied with their lives.

adolescent egocentrism The heightened self-consciousness of adolescents, which is reflected in adolescents' beliefs that others are as interested in them as they are in themselves, and in adolescents' sense of personal uniqueness and invincibility.

adoption study A study in which investigators seek to discover whether, in behavior and psychological characteristics, adopted children are more like their adoptive parents, who provided a home environment, or more like their biological parents, who contributed their heredity. Another form of the adoption study compares adoptive and biological siblings.

aerobic exercise Sustained activity that stimulates heart and lung functioning.

affectionate love Also called companionate love, this type of love occurs when individuals desire to have another person near and have a deep, caring affection for the person.

affordances Opportunities for interaction offered by objects that fit within our capabilities to perform activities.

ageism Prejudice against other people because of their age, especially prejudice against older adults.

altruism An unselfish interest in helping another person.

Alzheimer disease A progressive, irreversible brain disorder characterized by a gradual deterioration of memory, reasoning, language, and eventually, physical function.

amygdala A part of the brain's limbic system that is the seat of emotions such as anger.

androgens A class of sex hormones—an important one of which is testosterone—that primarily promotes the development of male genitals and secondary sex characteristics.

anger Kübler-Ross' second stage of dying, in which the dying person's denial gives way to anger, resentment, rage, and envy.

anger cry A cry similar to the basic cry but with more excess air forced through the vocal cords.

animism A facet of preoperational thought—the belief that inanimate objects have lifelike qualities and are capable of action.

anorexia nervosa An eating disorder that involves the relentless pursuit of thinness through starvation.

A-not-B error Also called $A\overline{B}$ error; this occurs when infants make the mistake of selecting the familiar hiding place (A) rather than the new hiding place (B) as they progress into substage 4 in Piaget's sensorimotor stage.

anxious attachment style An attachment style that describes adults who demand closeness, are less trusting, and are more emotional, jealous, and possessive.

Apgar Scale A widely used method to assess the health of newborns at one and five minutes after birth; it evaluates an infant's heart rate, respiratory effort, muscle tone, body color, and reflex irritability.

aphasia A loss or impairment of language processing resulting from damage to Broca's area or Wernicke's area.

Asperger syndrome A relatively mild autism spectrum disorder in which the child has relatively good verbal language skills, milder nonverbal language problems, and a restricted range of interests and relationships.

assimilation Piagetian concept in which children use existing schemes to incorporate new information.

attachment A close emotional bond between two people.

attention Focusing of mental resources.

attention deficit hyperactivity disorder (ADHD) A disability in which children consistently show one or more of the following characteristics: (1) inattention, (2) hyperactivity, and (3) impulsivity.

authoritarian parenting A restrictive, punitive style in which parents exhort the child to follow their directions and to respect their work and effort. Firm limits are placed on the child, and little verbal exchange is allowed.

authoritative parenting A style that encourages children to be independent but still places limits and controls on children's actions; extensive verbal give-and-take is allowed, and parents are warm and nurturant toward the child.

autism spectrum disorders (ASDs) Also called pervasive developmental disorders, these range from the severe disorder labeled autistic disorder to the milder disorder called Asperger syndrome. Children with these disorders are characterized by problems in social interaction, verbal and nonverbal communication, and repetitive behaviors.

autistic disorder A severe autism spectrum disorder that has its onset in the first three years of life and includes deficiencies in social relationships; abnormalities in communication; and restricted, repetitive, and stereotyped patterns of behavior.

automaticity The ability to process information with little or no effort.

autonomous morality The second stage of moral development in Piaget's theory, displayed by children about 10 years of age and older. At this stage, children become aware that rules and laws are created by people and that in judging an action they should consider the actor's intentions as well as the consequences.

average children Children who receive an average number of both positive and negative nominations from their peers.

avoidant attachment style An attachment style that describes adults who are hesitant about getting involved in romantic relationships and, once in a relationship, tend to distance themselves from their partner.

B

bargaining Kübler-Ross' third stage of dying, in which the dying person develops the hope that death can somehow be postponed.

basic cry A rhythmic pattern usually consisting of a cry, a briefer silence, a shorter inspiratory whistle that is higher pitched than the main cry, and then a brief rest before the next cry.

Bayley Scales of Infant Development Widely used scales, developed by Nancy Bayley, for assessing infant development. The current version, the Bayley-III, has five scales: cognitive, language, motor, socioemotional, and adaptive; the first three are administered to the infant, the latter two to the caregiver.

behavior genetics   The field that seeks to discover the influence of heredity and environment on individual differences in human traits and development.

Big Five factors of personality   The view that personality is made up of openness to experience, conscientiousness, extraversion, agreeableness, and neuroticism.

binge eating disorder (BED)   Involves frequent binge eating, but without compensatory behavior like purging that characterizes bulimics.

biological processes   Processes that produce changes in an individual's physical nature.

bisexuality   Sexual attraction to people of both sexes.

bonding   The formation of a close connection, especially a physical bond between parents and their newborn in the period shortly after birth.

brain death   A neurological definition of death—an individual is dead when all electrical activity of the brain has ceased for a specified period of time.

brainstorming   Technique in which individuals are encouraged to come up with creative ideas in a group, play off each other's ideas, and say practically whatever comes to mind relevant to a particular issue.

Broca's area   An area of the brain's left frontal lobe that is involved in producing words.

Bronfenbrenner's ecological theory
Bronfenbrenner's environmental systems theory that focuses on five environmental systems: microsystem, mesosystem, exosystem, macrosystem, and chronosystem.

bulimia nervosa   An eating disorder in which the individual consistently follows a binge-and-purge eating pattern.

C

care perspective   The moral perspective of Carol Gilligan; views people in terms of their connectedness with others and emphasizes interpersonal communication, relationships with others, and concern for others.

case study   An in-depth look at a single individual.

cataracts   A thickening of the lens of the eye that causes vision to become cloudy, opaque, and distorted.

cellular clock theory   Leonard Hayflick's theory that the number of times human cells

can divide is about 75 to 80. As we age, our cells are less able to divide.

centration   The focusing of attention on one characteristic to the exclusion of all others.

cephalocaudal pattern   The sequence in which the fastest growth occurs at the top of the body—the head—with physical growth in size, weight, and feature differentiation gradually working from top to bottom.

character education   A direct moral education program in which students are taught moral literacy to prevent them from engaging in immoral behavior.

child abuse   The term used most often by the public and many professionals to refer to both abuse and neglect.

child-centered kindergarten   Education that involves the whole child by considering both the child's physical, cognitive, and socioemotional development and the child's needs, interests, and learning styles.

child-directed speech   Language spoken in a higher pitch than normal, with simple words and sentences.

child maltreatment   The term increasingly used by developmentalists that refers to abuse and neglect, but also includes diverse conditions.

child neglect   Failure to provide for a child's basic needs, including physical, educational, or emotional needs.

chromosomes   Threadlike structures made up of deoxyribonucleic acid, or DNA.

chronic disorders   Disorders characterized by slow onset and long duration.

climacteric   The midlife transition during which fertility declines.

cliques   Small groups that range from 2 to 12 individuals and average about 5 to 6 individuals. Clique members usually are of the same age and same sex and often engage in similar activities, such as belonging to a club or participating in a sport.

cognitive mechanics   The "hardware" of the mind, reflecting the neurophysiological architecture of the brain as developed through evolution. Cognitive mechanics involves the speed and accuracy of the processes involving sensory input, visual and motor memory, discrimination, comparison, and categorization.

cognitive moral education   A moral education program based on the belief that students should learn to value things like democracy and justice as their moral reasoning develops; Kohlberg's theory has been the basis for many of the cognitive moral education programs.

cognitive pragmatics   The culture-based "software" of the mind. Cognitive pragmatics

include reading and writing skills, language comprehension, educational qualifications, professional skills, and also the type of self-knowledge and life skills that helps us to master or cope with life.

cognitive processes   Processes that involve changes in an individual's thought, intelligence, and language.

cohabitation   Living together in a sexual relationship without being married.

cohort effects   Effects due to a person's time of birth, era, or generation but not to actual age.

collectivism   Emphasizing values that serve the group by subordinating personal goals to preserve group integrity, supporting interdependence of members, and promoting harmonious relationships.

commitment   A personal investment in identity.

concepts   Cognitive groupings of similar objects, events, people, or ideas.

concrete operational stage   The third Piagetian stage, which lasts from approximately 7 to 11 years of age; children can perform concrete operations, and logical reasoning replaces intuitive reasoning as long as the reasoning can be applied to specific or concrete examples.

conduct disorder   Age-inappropriate actions and attitudes that violate family expectations, society's norms, and the personal or property rights of others.

connectedness   Characteristic consisting of two dimensions: mutuality, sensitivity to and respect for others' views; and permeability, openness to others' views.

conscience   The component of the superego that punishes the child for behaviors disapproved of by parents by making the child feel guilty and worthless.

conservation   The awareness that altering the appearance of an object or a substance does not change its basic properties.

constructive play   Combination of sensorimotor/practice play with symbolic representation.

constructivist approach   A learner-centered approach that emphasizes the individual's active, cognitive construction of knowledge and understanding with guidance from the teacher.

contemporary life-events approach   Approach emphasizing that how a life event influences the individual's development depends not only on the event but also on mediating factors, the individual's adaptation to the life event, the life-stage context, and the sociohistorical context.

continuity-discontinuity issue Debate that focuses on the extent to which development involves gradual, cumulative change (continuity) or distinct stages (discontinuity).

controversial children Children who are frequently nominated both as someone's best friend and as being disliked.

conventional reasoning The second, or intermediate, level in Kohlberg's theory of moral development. At this level, individuals abide by the standards of others such as parents or the laws of society.

convergent thinking Thinking that produces one correct answer; characteristic of the kind of thinking required on conventional intelligence tests.

coparenting The support that parents provide one another in jointly raising a child.

core knowledge approach States that infants are born with domain-specific innate knowledge systems. Among these domain-specific knowledge systems are those involving space, number sense, object permanence, and language.

corpus callosum A large bundle of axon fibers that connects the brain's left and right hemispheres.

correlational research A type of research that strives to describe the strength of the relationship between two or more events or characteristics.

correlation coefficient A number based on a statistical analysis that is used to describe the degree of association between two variables.

creativity The ability to think in novel and unusual ways and to come up with unique solutions to problems.

crisis A period of identity development during which the individual is exploring alternatives.

critical thinking Thinking reflectively and productively, and evaluating the evidence.

cross-cultural studies Comparison of one culture with one or more other cultures. These provide information about the degree to which development is similar, or universal, across cultures, and the degree to which it is culture-specific.

cross-cultural studies Studies that compare aspects of two or more cultures to provide information about the degree to which development is similar or universal across the cultures, or is instead culture-specific.

cross-sectional approach A research strategy in which individuals of different ages are compared at one time.

crowds The crowd is a larger group than a clique. Adolescents usually are members of a crowd based on reputation and may not spend much time together. Many crowds are defined by the activities in which adolescents engage.

crystallized intelligence An individual's accumulated information and verbal skills, which continues to increase with age.

culture The behavior, patterns, beliefs, and all other products of a group of people that are passed on from generation to generation.

culture-fair tests Intelligence tests that are designed to avoid cultural bias.

D

date or acquaintance rape Coercive sexual activity directed at someone with whom the victim is at least casually acquainted.

dementia A global term for any neurological disorder in which the primary symptom is deterioration of mental functioning.

denial and isolation Kübler-Ross' first stage of dying, in which the dying person denies that she or he is really going to die.

depression Kübler-Ross' fourth stage of dying, in which the dying person perceives the certainty of her or his death. A period of depression or preparatory grief may appear.

descriptive research A type of research that aims to observe and record behavior.

development The pattern of movement or change that begins at conception and continues through the human life span.

developmentally appropriate practice (DAP) Education that focuses on the typical developmental patterns of children (age appropriateness) and the uniqueness of each child (individual appropriateness). Such practice contrasts with developmentally inappropriate practice, which has an academic, direct instruction emphasis focused largely on abstract paper-and-pencil activities, seatwork, and rote/drill practice activities.

dialect A variety of language that is distinguished by its vocabulary, grammar, or pronunciation.

difficult child A temperament style in which the child tends to react negatively and cry frequently, engages in irregular daily routines, and is slow to accept change.

direct instruction approach A teacher-centered approach characterized by teacher direction and control, high expectations for students' progress, and maximum time spent on academic tasks.

disenfranchised grief Grief involving a deceased person that is a socially ambiguous loss that can't be openly mourned or supported.

disengagement theory The theory that, to cope effectively, older adults should gradually withdraw from society; this theory is no longer supported.

dishabituation The recovery of a habituated response after a change in stimulation.

divergent thinking Thinking that produces many answers to the same question; characteristic of creativity.

divided attention Concentrating on more than one activity at the same time.

DNA A complex molecule that has a double helix shape and contains genetic information.

doula A caregiver who provides continuous physical, emotional, and educational support for the mother before, during, and after childbirth.

Down syndrome A chromosomally transmitted form of mental retardation, caused by the presence of an extra copy of chromosome 21.

dual-process model A model of coping with bereavement that emphasizes oscillation between loss-oriented stressors and restoration-oriented stressors.

dual-process model Theory stating that decision making is influenced by two cognitive systems—one analytical and one experiential—that compete with each other.

dynamic systems theory A theory proposed by Esther Thelen that seeks to explain how infants assemble motor skills for perceiving and acting.

E

easy child A temperament style in which the child is generally in a positive mood, quickly establishes regular routines, and adapts easily to new experiences.

eclectic theoretical orientation An orientation that does not follow any one theoretical approach, but rather selects from each theory whatever is considered best in it.

ecological view The view proposed by the Gibsons that people directly perceive information in the world around them. Perception brings people in contact with the environment in order to interact with it and adapt to it.

egocentrism The inability to distinguish between one's own and someone else's perspective; an important feature of preoperational thought.

ego ideal The component of the superego that rewards the child by conveying a sense of pride and personal value when the child acts according to ideal standards approved by the parents.

elaboration Engagement in more extensive processing of information, benefiting memory.

embryonic period The period of prenatal development that occurs from two to eight weeks after conception. During the embryonic period, the rate of cell differentiation intensifies, support systems for the cells form, and organs appear.

emotion Feeling, or affect, that occurs when a person is engaged in an interaction that is important to him or her, especially to his or her well-being.

emotional abuse Acts or omissions by parents or other caregivers that have caused, or could cause, serious behavioral, cognitive, or emotional problems.

emotional intelligence The ability to perceive and express emotions accurately and adaptively, to understand emotion and emotional knowledge, to use feelings to facilitate thought, and to manage emotions in oneself and others.

empathy Reacting to another's feelings with an emotional response that is similar to the other's feelings.

encoding The process by which information gets into memory.

epigenetic view Perspective that emphasizes that development is the result of an ongoing, bidirectional interchange between heredity and environment.

episodic memory Retention of information about the where and when of life's happenings.

equilibration A mechanism that Piaget proposed to explain how children shift from one stage of thought to the next.

Erikson's theory Theory that proposes eight stages of human development. Each stage consists of a unique developmental task that confronts individuals with a crisis that must be resolved.

estradiol A hormone associated in girls with breast, uterine, and skeletal development.

estrogens A class of sex hormones—an important one of which is estradiol—that primarily influences the development of female sex characteristics and helps regulate the menstrual cycle.

ethnic gloss Use of an ethnic label such as African American or Latino in a superficial way that portrays an ethnic group as being more homogeneous than it really is.

ethnic identity An enduring aspect of the self that includes a sense of membership in an ethnic group, along with the attitudes and feelings related to that membership.

ethnicity A characteristic based on cultural heritage, nationality characteristics, race, religion, and language.

ethnocentrism The tendency to consider one's own group superior to other groups.

ethology Theory stressing that behavior is strongly influenced by biology, is tied to evolution, and is characterized by critical or sensitive periods.

euthanasia The act of painlessly ending the lives of persons who are suffering from incurable diseases or severe disabilities; sometimes called "mercy killing."

evocative genotype-environment correlations Correlations that exist when the child's characteristics elicit certain types of environments.

evolutionary psychology A branch of psychology that emphasizes the importance of adaptation, reproduction, and "survival of the fittest" in shaping behavior.

executive attention Cognitive process involving action planning, allocating attention to goals, error detection and compensation, monitoring progress on tasks, and dealing with novel or difficult circumstances.

executive functioning An umbrella-like concept that encompasses a number of higher-level cognitive processes linked to the development of the brain's prefrontal cortex. Executive functioning involves managing one's thoughts to engage in goal-directed behavior and to exercise self-control.

expanding Restating, in a linguistically sophisticated form, what a child has said.

experiment Carefully regulated procedure in which one or more factors believed to influence the behavior being studied are manipulated while all other factors are held constant.

expertise Having extensive, highly organized knowledge and understanding of a particular domain.

explicit memory Conscious memory of facts and experiences.

extrinsic motivation Doing something to obtain something else (the activity is a means to an end).

F

fast mapping A process that helps to explain how young children learn the connection between a word and its referent so quickly.

feminization of poverty The fact that far more women than men live in poverty. Women's lower income, divorce, infrequent awarding of alimony, and poorly enforced child support by fathers—which usually leave women with less money than they and their children need to adequately function—are the likely causes.

fertilization A stage in reproduction whereby an egg and a sperm fuse to create a single cell, called a zygote.

fetal alcohol spectrum disorders (FASD) A cluster of abnormalities that may appear in the offspring of mothers who drink alcohol heavily during pregnancy.

fetal period The prenatal period of development that begins two months after conception and lasts for seven months, on average.

fine motor skills Motor skills that involve finely tuned movements, such as any activity that requires finger dexterity.

fluid intelligence The ability to reason abstractly, which begins to decline in middle adulthood.

forgiveness An aspect of prosocial behavior that occurs when the injured person releases the injurer from possible behavioral retaliation.

formal operational stage The fourth and final Piagetian stage, which appears between the ages of 11 and 15; individuals move beyond concrete experiences and think in more abstract and logical ways.

fragile X syndrome A chromosomal disorder involving an abnormality in the X chromosome, which becomes constricted and often breaks.

free-radical theory A microbiological theory of aging stating that people age because when their cells metabolize energy, they generate waste that includes unstable oxygen molecules, known as free radicals, that damage DNA and other structures.

fuzzy trace theory Theory stating that memory is best understood by considering two types of memory representations: verbatim memory trace, and gist. In this theory, older children's better memory is attributed to the fuzzy traces created by extracting the gist of information.

G

games Activities that are engaged in for pleasure and include rules.

gender The characteristics of people as females or males.

gender identity Involves a sense of one's own gender, including knowledge, understanding, and acceptance of being male or female.

gender-intensification hypothesis The view that psychological and behavioral differences between boys and girls become greater during early adolescence because of increased socialization pressures to conform to traditional gender roles.

gender role   A set of expectations that prescribe how females or males should think, act, or feel.

gender schema theory   The theory that gender-typing emerges as children gradually develop gender schemas of what is gender-appropriate and gender-inappropriate in their culture.

gender stereotypes   General impressions and beliefs about females and males.

gender-typing   Acquisition of a traditional masculine or feminine role.

gene × environment (g × e) interaction   The interaction of a specific measured variation in the DNA and a specific measured aspect of the environment.

generativity versus stagnation   The seventh stage in Erikson's life-span theory; it encompasses adults' desire to leave a legacy of themselves to the next generation.

genes   Units of hereditary information composed of DNA. Genes direct cells to reproduce themselves and assemble proteins that direct body processes.

genotype   All of a person's actual genetic material.

germinal period   The period of prenatal development that takes place during the first two weeks after conception; it includes the creation of the zygote, continued cell division, and the attachment of the zygote to the wall of the uterus.

giftedness   Having above-average intelligence (an IQ of 130 or higher) and/or superior talent for something.

glaucoma   Damage to the optic nerve because of the pressure created by a buildup of fluid in the eye.

gonadotropins   Hormones that stimulate the testes or ovaries.

gonads   The sex glands, which are the testes in males and the ovaries in females.

goodness of fit   The match between a child's temperament and the environmental demands the child must cope with.

grasping reflex   A reflex that occurs when something touches an infant's palms. The infant responds by grasping tightly.

gratitude   A feeling of thankfulness and appreciation, especially in response to someone's doing something kind or helpful.

grief   The emotional numbness, disbelief, separation anxiety, despair, sadness, and loneliness that accompany the loss of someone we love.

gross motor skills   Motor skills that involve large-muscle activities, such as walking.

H

habituation   Decreased responsiveness to a stimulus after repeated presentations of the stimulus.

helpless orientation   An orientation in which one seems trapped by the experience of difficulty and attributes one's difficulty to a lack of ability.

heritability   The portion of the variance in a population that is attributed to genes.

heteronomous morality (Kohlberg)   The first stage of preconventional reasoning in Kohlberg's theory, in which moral thinking is tied to punishment.

heteronomous morality (Piaget)   The first stage of moral development in Piaget's theory, occurring at 4 to 7 years of age. Justice and rules are conceived of as unchangeable properties of the world, removed from the control of people.

hidden curriculum   The pervasive moral atmosphere that characterizes every school.

hormonal stress theory   The theory that aging in the body's hormonal system can lower resistance to stress and increase the likelihood of disease.

hormones   Powerful chemical substances secreted by the endocrine glands and carried through the body by the bloodstream.

hospice   A program committed to making the end of life as free from pain, anxiety, and depression as possible. The goals of hospice contrast with those of a hospital, which are to cure disease and prolong life.

hypothalamus   A structure in the brain that is involved with eating and sexual behavior.

hypotheses   Specific assumptions and predictions that can be tested to determine their accuracy.

hypothetical-deductive reasoning   Piaget's formal operational concept that adolescents have the cognitive ability to develop hypotheses about ways to solve problems and can systematically deduce which is the best path to follow in solving the problem.

I

identity   Who a person is, representing a synthesis and integration of self-understanding.

identity achievement   Marcia's term for the status of individuals who have undergone a crisis and have made a commitment.

identity diffusion   Marcia's term for the status of individuals who have not yet experienced a crisis (explored meaningful alternatives) or made any commitments.

identity foreclosure   Marcia's term for the status of individuals who have made a commitment but have not experienced a crisis.

identity moratorium   Marcia's term for the status of individuals who are in the midst of a crisis, but whose commitments are either absent or vaguely defined.

identity versus identity confusion   Erikson's fifth stage of development, which occurs during the adolescent years; adolescents are faced with finding out who they are, what they are all about, and where they are going in life.

imaginary audience   That aspect of adolescent egocentrism that involves feeling one is the center of attention and sensing that one is on stage.

immanent justice   Belief that if a rule is broken, punishment will be meted out immediately.

implicit memory   Memory without conscious recollection—memory of skills and routine procedures that are performed automatically.

inclusion   Education of a child with special educational needs full-time in the regular classroom.

individualism   Giving priority to personal goals rather than to group goals; emphasizing values that serve the self, such as feeling good, obtaining personal distinction through achievement, and preserving independence.

individualism, instrumental purpose, and exchange   The second Kohlberg stage of preconventional reasoning. At this stage, individuals pursue their own interests but also let others do the same.

individuality   Characteristic consisting of two dimensions: self-assertion, the ability to have and communicate a point of view; and separateness, the use of communication patterns to express how one is different from others.

individualized education plan (IEP)   A written statement that spells out a program tailored to a child with a disability. The plan should be (1) related to the child's learning capacity, (2) specially constructed to meet the child's individual needs and not merely a copy of what is offered to other children, and (3) designed to provide educational benefits.

indulgent parenting   A style in which parents are very involved with their children but place few demands or controls on them.

infinite generativity   The ability to produce an endless number of meaningful sentences using a finite set of words and rules.

information-processing theory   Theory emphasizing that individuals manipulate information, monitor it, and strategize about it. Central to this theory are the processes of memory and thinking.

insecure avoidant babies Babies who show insecurity by avoiding the mother.

insecure disorganized babies Babies who show insecurity by being disorganized and disoriented.

insecure resistant babies Babies who might cling to the caregiver, then resist her by fighting against the closeness, perhaps by kicking or pushing away.

intelligence The ability to solve problems and to adapt to and learn from experiences.

intelligence quotient (IQ) An individual's mental age divided by chronological age, multiplied by 100; devised in 1912 by William Stern.

intermodal perception The ability to integrate information about two or more sensory modalities, such as vision and hearing.

intimacy in friendship Self-disclosure and the sharing of private thoughts.

intrinsic motivation Doing something for its own sake; involves factors such as self-determination and opportunities to make choices.

intuitive thought substage The second substage of preoperational thought, occurring between approximately 4 and 7 years of age. Children begin to use primitive reasoning and want to know the answers to all sorts of questions.

J

joint attention Focus by individuals on the same object or event; requires an ability to track another's behavior, one individual to direct another's attention, and reciprocal interaction.

justice perspective A moral perspective that focuses on the rights of the individual; individuals independently make moral decisions.

juvenile delinquency Actions taken by an adolescent in breaking the law or engaging in illegal behavior.

K

kangaroo care A way of holding a preterm infant so that there is skin-to-skin contact.

Klinefelter syndrome A chromosomal disorder in which males have an extra X chromosome, making them XXY instead of XY.

L

labeling Identifying the names of objects.

laboratory A controlled setting from which many of the complex factors of the "real world" have been removed.

language A form of communication, whether spoken, written, or signed, that is based on a system of symbols.

language acquisition device (LAD) Chomsky's term that describes a biological endowment that enables the child to detect certain features and rules of language, including phonology, syntax, and semantics.

lateralization Specialization of function in one hemisphere or the other of the cerebral cortex.

learning disabilities Disabilities in which children experience difficulty in learning that involves understanding or using spoken or written language; the difficulty can appear in listening, thinking, reading, writing, and spelling. A learning disability also may involve difficulty in doing mathematics. To be classified as a learning disability, the learning problem is not primarily the result of visual, hearing, or motor disabilities; mental retardation; emotional disorders; or environmental, cultural, or economic disadvantage.

least restrictive environment (LRE) A setting that is as similar as possible to the one where children without a disability are educated.

leisure The pleasant times when individuals are free to pursue activities and interests of their own choosing.

life span The upper boundary of life, which is the maximum number of years an individual can live. The maximum life span of humans is about 120 years of age.

life-span perspective The perspective that development is lifelong, multidimensional, multidirectional, plastic, multidisciplinary, and contextual; involves growth, maintenance, and regulation of loss; and is constructed through biological, sociocultural, and individual factors working together.

longitudinal approach A research strategy in which the same individuals are studied over a period of time, usually several years or more.

long-term memory A relatively permanent and unlimited type of memory.

low birth weight infants Infants that weigh less than 5½ pounds at birth.

M

macular degeneration A vision problem in the elderly that involves deterioration of the macula of the retina.

mastery orientation A perspective in which one is task-oriented—concerned with learning strategies and the process of achievement rather than the outcome.

meaning-making coping Drawing on beliefs, values, and goals to change the meaning of a stressful situation, especially in times of high levels of stress such as when a loved one dies.

meiosis A specialized form of cell division that occurs to form eggs and sperm (or gametes).

memory Retention of information over time.

menarche A girl's first menstrual period.

menopause The time in middle age, usually in the late forties or early fifties, when a woman's menstrual periods cease.

mental age (MA) An individual's level of mental development relative to others.

mental retardation A condition of limited mental ability in which an individual has a low IQ, usually below 70 on a traditional test of intelligence, and has difficulty adapting to everyday life.

metacognition Cognition about cognition, or "knowing about knowing."

metalinguistic awareness Knowledge about language.

metamemory Knowledge about memory.

metaphor An implied comparison between two unlike things.

mindset The cognitive view individuals develop for themselves that either is fixed or involves growth.

mitochondrial theory The theory that aging is caused by the decay of the mitochondria, which are tiny cellular bodies that supply energy for cell function, growth, and repair.

mitosis Cellular reproduction in which the cell's nucleus duplicates itself; two new cells are formed, each containing the same DNA as the original cell, arranged in the same 23 pairs of chromosomes.

Montessori approach An educational philosophy in which children are given considerable freedom and spontaneity in choosing activities and are allowed to move from one activity to another as they desire.

moral development Changes in thoughts, feelings, and behaviors regarding standards of right and wrong.

moral exemplars People who have a moral personality, identity, character, and set of virtues that reflect moral excellence and commitment.

moral identity The aspect of personality that is present when individuals have moral notions and commitments that are central to their lives.

Moro reflex A startle response that occurs in reaction to a sudden, intense noise or movement. When startled, the newborn arches its back, throws its head back, and flings out its arms and legs. Then the newborn rapidly closes its arms and legs to the center of the body.

morphology   Units of meaning involved in word formation.

multiple developmental trajectories   Adults follow one trajectory or pattern of development and children another one.

mutual interpersonal expectations, relationships, and interpersonal conformity   Kohlberg's third stage of moral development. At this stage, individuals value trust, caring, and loyalty to others as a basis of moral judgments.

myelination   The process of encasing axons with a myelin sheath, which helps increase the speed and efficiency of information processing.

N

natural childbirth   Method attempting to reduce the mother's pain by decreasing her fear through education about childbirth stages and relaxation techniques during delivery.

naturalistic observation   Observing behavior in real-world settings.

nature-nurture issue   Debate about whether development is primarily influenced by nature or nurture. Nature refers to an organism's biological inheritance, nurture to its environmental experiences. The "nature proponents" claim biological inheritance is the more important influence on development; the "nurture proponents" claim that environmental experiences are more important.

neglected children   Children who are infrequently nominated as a best friend but are not disliked by their peers.

neglectful parenting   A style in which the parent is very uninvolved in the child's life.

neo-Piagetians   Developmentalists who have elaborated on Piaget's theory, emphasizing attention to children's strategies; information-processing speed; the task involved; and division of the problem into more precise, smaller steps.

neurogenesis   The generation of new neurons.

neurons   Nerve cells that handle information processing at the cellular level.

nonnormative life events   Unusual occurrences that have a major impact on an individual's life.

nonshared environmental experiences   The child's own unique experiences, both within the family and outside the family, that are not shared by another sibling; thus, experiences

occurring within the family can be part of the "nonshared environment."

normal distribution   A symmetrical, bell-shaped curve with a majority of the cases falling in the middle of the possible range of scores and few scores appearing toward the extremes of the range.

normative age-graded influences   Influences that are similar for individuals in a particular age group.

normative history-graded influences   Influences that are common to people of a particular generation because of historical circumstances.

O

object permanence   The Piagetian term for one of an infant's most important accomplishments: understanding that objects continue to exist even when they cannot directly be seen, heard, or touched.

operations   Reversible mental actions that allow children to do mentally what before they had done only physically.

organization   Piagetian concept of grouping isolated behaviors and thoughts into a higher-order, more smoothly functioning cognitive system.

organogenesis   Process of organ formation that takes place during the first two months of prenatal development.

osteoporosis   A disorder that involves an extensive loss of bone tissue and is the main reason many older adults walk with a marked stoop. Women are especially vulnerable to osteoporosis.

P

pain cry   A sudden, initial loud cry followed by breath holding, without preliminary moaning.

palliative care   Emphasized in hospice care; involves reducing pain and suffering and helping individuals die with dignity.

Parkinson disease   A chronic, progressive disease characterized by muscle tremors, slowing of movement, and partial facial paralysis.

passive euthanasia   The withholding of available treatments, such as life-sustaining devices, allowing the person to die.

passive genotype-environment correlations   Correlations that exist when the biological parents, who are genetically related to the child, provide a rearing environment for the child.

peers   Individuals who share the same age or maturity level.

perception   The interpretation of sensation.

performance orientation   An orientation in which one focuses on winning, rather than on achievement outcome; happiness is thought to result from winning.

perimenopause   The transitional period from normal menstrual periods to no menstrual periods at all, which often takes up to 10 years.

personal fable   The part of adolescent egocentrism that involves an adolescent's sense of personal uniqueness and invincibility.

personality   The enduring personal characteristics of individuals.

perspective taking   The ability to assume another person's perspective and understand his or her thoughts and feelings.

phenotype   Observable and measurable characteristics of an individual, such as height, hair color, and intelligence.

phenylketonuria (PKU)   A genetic disorder in which an individual cannot properly metabolize phenylalanine, an amino acid; PKU is now easily detected—but, if left untreated, results in mental retardation and hyperactivity.

phonics approach   A teaching approach built on the idea that reading instruction should teach basic rules for translating written symbols into sounds.

phonology   The sound system of a language—includes the sounds used and how they may be combined.

physical abuse   Abuse characterized by the infliction of physical injury by punching, beating, kicking, biting, burning, shaking, or otherwise harming a child.

Piaget's theory   Theory stating that children actively construct their understanding of the world and go through four stages of cognitive development.

pituitary gland   An important endocrine gland that controls growth and regulates the activity of other glands.

play   A pleasurable activity that is engaged in for its own sake.

play therapy   Therapy that lets children work off frustrations while therapists analyze their conflicts and coping methods.

popular children   Children who are frequently nominated as a best friend and are rarely disliked by their peers.

possible selves   What adolescents hope to become as well as what they dread they will become.

postconventional reasoning   The highest level in Kohlberg's theory of moral development. At this level, the individual recognizes alternative moral courses, explores the options, and then decides on a personal moral code.

postformal thought Thinking that is reflective, relativistic, and contextual; provisional; realistic; and influenced by emotions.

postpartum depression A major depressive episode that typically occurs about four weeks after delivery; women with this condition have such strong feelings of sadness, anxiety, or despair that they have trouble coping with daily tasks during the postpartum period.

postpartum period The period after childbirth when the mother adjusts, both physically and psychologically, to the process of childbirth. This period lasts for about six weeks or until her body has completed its adjustment and returned to a near prepregnant state.

practice play Play that involves repetition of behavior when new skills are being learned or when mastery and coordination of skills are required for games or sports.

pragmatics The appropriate use of language in different contexts.

preconventional reasoning The lowest level in Kohlberg's theory of moral development. The individual's moral reasoning is controlled primarily by external rewards and punishments.

prefrontal cortex The highest level of the frontal lobes that is involved in reasoning, decision making, and self-control.

preoperational stage The second Piagetian developmental stage, which lasts from about 2 to 7 years of age; children begin to represent the world with words, images, and drawings.

prepared childbirth Developed by French obstetrician Ferdinand Lamaze, a childbirth strategy similar to natural childbirth but one that teaches a special breathing technique to control pushing in the final stages of labor and provides details about anatomy and physiology.

pretense/symbolic play Play that occurs when a child transforms aspects of the physical environment into symbols.

preterm infants Infants born three weeks or more before the pregnancy has reached its full term.

primary emotions Emotions that are present in humans and other animals, emerge early in life, and are culturally universal; examples are joy, anger, sadness, fear, and disgust.

Project Head Start Compensatory education designed to provide children from low-income families the opportunity to acquire skills and experiences important for school success.

prolonged grief Grief that involves enduring despair and is still unresolved over an extended period of time.

prospective memory Remembering to do something in the future.

proximodistal pattern The sequence in which growth starts at the center of the body and moves toward the extremities.

psychoanalytic theories Theories that describe development as primarily unconscious and heavily colored by emotion. Behavior is merely a surface characteristic, and the symbolic workings of the mind must be analyzed to understand behavior. Early experiences with parents are emphasized.

psychoanalytic theory of gender Theory that stems from Freud's view that preschool children develop a sexual attraction to the opposite-sex parent, then at 5 or 6 years of age renounce the attraction because of anxious feelings, subsequently identifying with the same-sex parent and unconsciously adopting the same-sex parent's characteristics.

psychosocial moratorium Erikson's term for the gap between childhood security and adult autonomy that adolescents experience as part of their identity exploration.

puberty A period of rapid physical maturation involving hormonal and bodily changes during early adolescence.

R

rape Forcible sexual intercourse, oral sex, or anal sex with a person who does not give consent. Legal definitions of rape differ from state to state.

rapport talk The language of conversation; a way to establish connections and negotiate relationships; preferred by women.

recasting Rephrasing a statement that a child has said, perhaps turning it into a question, or restating a child's immature utterance in the form of a fully grammatical sentence.

reciprocal socialization Socialization that is bidirectional in that children socialize parents just as parents socialize children.

reflexive smile A smile that does not occur in response to external stimuli. It happens during the month after birth, usually during sleep.

rejected children Children who are infrequently nominated as a best friend and are actively disliked by their peers.

religion An organized set of beliefs, practices, rituals, and symbols that increases an individual's connection to a sacred or transcendent other (God, higher power, or higher truth).

religiousness The degree of affiliation with an organized religion, participation in prescribed rituals and practices, connection with its beliefs, and involvement in a community of believers.

report talk Language designed to give information, including public speaking; preferred by men.

romantic love Also called passionate love, or *eros*, this type of love has strong components of sexuality and infatuation, and it often predominates in the early part of a love relationship.

romantic script Sex is synonymous with love; if we develop a relationship with someone and fall in love, it is acceptable to have sex with the person whether we are married or not.

rooting reflex A newborn's built-in reaction that occurs when the infant's cheek is stroked or the side of the mouth is touched. In response, the infant turns its head toward the side that was touched, in an apparent effort to find something to suck.

S

satire The use of irony, derision, or wit to expose folly or wickedness.

scaffolding In cognitive development, a term Vygotsky used to describe the changing level of support over the course of a teaching session, with the more-skilled person adjusting guidance to fit the child's current performance level.

schemas Mental frameworks that organize concepts and information.

schema theory Theory stating that people mold memories to fit information that already exists in their minds.

schemes In Piaget's theory, actions or mental representations that organize knowledge.

secure attachment style An attachment style that describes adults who have positive views of relationships, find it easy to get close to others, and are not overly concerned or stressed out about their romantic relationships.

securely attached babies Babies who use the caregiver as a secure base from which to explore the environment.

selective attention Focusing on a specific aspect of experience that is relevant while ignoring others that are irrelevant.

selective optimization with compensation The theory that successful aging is related to three factors: selection, optimization, and compensation.

self All of the characteristics of a person.

self-concept Domain-specific evaluations of the self.

self-conscious emotions Emotions that require consciousness and a sense of "me"; they include empathy, jealousy, embarrassment, pride, shame, and guilt, most of which first appear at some point in the second half of the first year through the second year.

self-efficacy The belief that one can master a situation and produce favorable outcomes.

self-esteem The global evaluative dimension of the self. Self-esteem is also referred to as self-worth, or self-image.

self-regulation The ability to control one's behavior without having to rely on others for help.

self-understanding The individual's cognitive representation of the self, the substance of self-conceptions.

semantic memory A person's knowledge about the world, including fields of expertise, general academic knowledge, and "everyday knowledge" about meaning of words, names of famous individuals, important places, and common things.

semantics The meanings of words and sentences.

sensation Reaction that occurs when information interacts with sensory receptors—the eyes, ears, tongue, nostrils, and skin.

sensorimotor play Behavior by infants to derive pleasure from exercising their sensorimotor schemes.

sensorimotor stage The first of Piaget's stages, which lasts from birth to about 2 years of age, during which infants construct an understanding of the world by coordinating sensory experiences (such as seeing and hearing) with physical, motoric actions.

separation protest Reaction that occurs when infants experience a fear of being separated from a caregiver, which results in crying when the caregiver leaves.

seriation The concrete operation that involves ordering stimuli along a quantitative dimension (such as length).

service learning A form of education that promotes social responsibility and service to the community.

sexual abuse Fondling a child's genitals, intercourse, incest, rape, sodomy, exhibitionism, and commercial exploitation through prostitution or the production of pornographic materials.

sexual harassment Sexual persecution that can take many forms—from sexist remarks and physical contact (patting, brushing against someone's body) to blatant propositions and sexual assaults.

sexually transmitted infections (STIs) Diseases that are contracted primarily through sexual contact, including oral-genital contact, anal-genital contact, and vaginal intercourse.

sexual scripts Stereotyped patterns of expectancies for how people should behave sexually.

shape constancy Recognition that an object remains the same even though its orientation to us changes.

shared environmental experiences Siblings' common experiences, such as their parents' personalities or intellectual orientation, the family's socioeconomic status, and the neighborhood in which they live.

short-term memory Retention of information for up to 15 to 30 seconds, without rehearsal of the information. Using rehearsal, individuals can keep the information in short-term memory longer.

sickle-cell anemia A genetic disorder that affects the red blood cells and occurs most often in African Americans.

size constancy Recognition that an object remains the same even though the retinal image of the object changes as you move toward or away from the object.

slow-to-warm-up child A temperament style in which the child has a low activity level, is somewhat negative, and displays a low intensity of mood.

small for date infants Infants whose birth weights are below normal when the length of pregnancy is considered; also called small for gestational age infants. Small for date infants may be preterm or full-term.

social cognitive theory Theoretical view that behavior, environment, and cognition are the key factors in development.

social cognitive theory of gender The idea that children's gender development occurs through observation and imitation of gender behavior, as well as through the rewards and punishments children experience for behaviors believed to be appropriate or inappropriate for their gender.

social cognitive theory of morality The theory that distinguishes between moral competence—the ability to produce moral behaviors—and moral performance—performing those behaviors in specific situations.

social constructivist approach An emphasis on the social contexts of learning and construction of knowledge through social interaction. Vygotsky's theory reflects this approach.

social contract or utility and individual rights The fifth Kohlberg stage of moral development. At this stage, individuals reason that values, rights, and principles undergird or transcend the law.

social conventional reasoning Focuses on conventional rules established by social consensus and convention, as opposed to moral reasoning, which stresses ethical issues.

social play Play that involves interaction with peers.

social policy A government's course of action designed to promote the welfare of its citizens.

social referencing "Reading" emotional cues in others to help determine how to act in a specific situation.

social role theory Eagly's theory that psychological gender differences are caused by the contrasting social roles of women and men.

social smile A smile in response to an external stimulus, which, early in development, typically is a face.

social systems morality The fourth stage in Kohlberg's theory of moral development. Moral judgments are based on understanding the social order, law, justice, and duty.

socioeconomic status (SES) A grouping of people with similar occupational, educational, and economic characteristics.

socioemotional processes Processes that involve changes in an individual's relationships with other people, emotions, and personality.

socioemotional selectivity theory The theory that older adults become more selective about their social networks. Because they place high value on emotional satisfaction, older adults often spend more time with familiar individuals with whom they have had rewarding relationships.

source memory The ability to remember where something was learned.

spirituality Experiencing something beyond oneself in a transcendent manner and living in a way that benefits others and society.

stability-change issue Debate as to whether and to what degree we become older renditions of our early experience (stability) or whether we develop into someone different from who we were at an earlier point in development (change).

standardized test A test with uniform procedures for administration and scoring. Many standardized tests allow a person's performance to be compared with the performance of other individuals.

stranger anxiety An infant's fear of and wariness toward strangers; it tends to appear in the second half of the first year of life.

Strange Situation Ainsworth's observational measure of infant attachment to a caregiver that requires the infant to move through a series of introductions, separations, and reunions with the caregiver and an adult stranger in a prescribed order.

strategy construction Creation of new procedures for processing information.

sucking reflex A newborn's reaction of sucking an object placed in its mouth. The sucking reflex enables the infant to get nourishment before it has associated a nipple with food.

sudden infant death syndrome (SIDS) Condition that occurs when an infant stops breathing, usually during the night, and suddenly dies without an apparent cause.

sustained attention The ability to maintain attention to a selected stimulus for a prolonged period of time.

symbolic function substage The first substage of preoperational thought, occurring roughly between the ages of 2 and 4. In this substage, the young child gains the ability to represent mentally an object that is not present.

syntax The ways words are combined to form acceptable phrases and sentences.

T

telegraphic speech The use of short, precise words without grammatical markers such as articles, auxiliary verbs, and other connectives.

temperament An individual's behavioral style and characteristic way of responding.

teratogen Any agent that can potentially cause a birth defect or negatively alter cognitive and behavioral outcomes.

testosterone A hormone associated in boys with the development of the genitals, increased height, and voice changes.

theory An interrelated, coherent set of ideas that helps to explain phenomena and make predictions.

theory of mind Thoughts about how one's own mental processes work and the mental processes of others.

thinking Manipulating and transforming information in memory, in order to reason, reflect, think critically, evaluate ideas and solve problems, and make decisions.

top-dog phenomenon The circumstance of moving from the top position in elementary school to the youngest, smallest, and least powerful position in middle or junior high school.

traditional religious script View that sex is acceptable only within marriage; extramarital sex is taboo, especially for women; and sex means reproduction and sometimes affection.

trait theories Theories emphasizing that personality consists of broad dispositions, called traits, which tend to produce characteristic responses.

transitivity The ability to logically combine relations to understand certain conclusions. Piaget argued that an understanding of transitivity is characteristic of concrete operational thought.

triangular theory of love Sternberg's theory that love includes three components of dimensions—passion, intimacy, and commitment.

triarchic theory of intelligence Sternberg's theory that intelligence consists of analytical intelligence, creative intelligence, and practical intelligence.

Turner syndrome A chromosomal disorder in females in which either an X chromosome is missing, making the person XO instead of XX, or part of one X chromosome is deleted.

twin study A study in which the behavioral similarity of identical twins is compared with the behavioral similarity of fraternal twins.

U

universal ethical principles The sixth and highest stage in Kohlberg's theory of moral development. Individuals develop a moral standard based on universal human rights. Both Piaget and Kohlberg argued that peer relations are a critical part of the social stimulation that challenges children to advance their moral reasoning. The mutual give-and-take of peer relations provides children with role-taking opportunities that give them a sense that rules are generated democratically.

V

values Beliefs and attitudes about the way things should be.

values clarification A moral education program in which students are helped to clarify what their lives are for and what is worth working for. Students are encouraged to define their own values and understand others' values.

visual preference method A method developed by Fantz to determine whether infants can distinguish one stimulus from another by measuring the length of time they attend to different stimuli.

Vygotsky's theory Sociocultural cognitive theory that emphasizes how culture and social interaction guide cognitive development.

W

Wernicke's area An area of the brain's left hemisphere that is involved in language comprehension.

whole-language approach A teaching approach built on the idea that reading instruction should parallel children's natural language learning. Reading materials should be whole and meaningful.

wisdom Expert knowledge about the practical aspects of life that permits excellent judgment about important matters.

working memory A mental "workbench" where individuals manipulate and assemble information when making decisions, solving problems, and comprehending written and spoken language.

X

XYY syndrome A chromosomal disorder in which males have an extra Y chromosome.

Z

zone of proximal development (ZPD) Vygotsky's term for tasks that are too difficult for children to master alone but can be mastered with guidance and assistance from adults or more-skilled children.

zygote A single cell formed through fertilization.

references

A

Aagaard, P., Suetta, C., Casserotti, P., Magnusson, S. P., & Kjaer, M. (2010). Role of the nervous system in sarcopenia and muscle atrophy with aging: Strength training as a countermeasure. *Scandinavian Journal of Medicine & Science in Sports, 20,* 49–64.

Aalsma, M., Lapsley, D. K., & Flannery, D. (2006). Narcissism, personal fables, and adolescent adjustment. *Psychology in the Schools, 43,* 481–491.

AARP. (2004). *The divorce experience: A study of divorce at midlife and beyond.* Washington, DC: Author.

Abbate-Daga, G., & others. (2010). Attachment insecurity, personality, and body dissatisfaction in eating disorders. *Journal of Nervous and Mental Disease, 198,* 520–524.

Abbott, A. (2003). Restless nights, listless days. *Nature, 4235,* 896–898.

Abbott, B. D., & Barber, B. L. (2010). Embodied image: Gender differences in functional and aesthetic body image among Australian adolescents. *Body Image, 7,* 22–31.

ABC News. (2005, December 12). Larry Page and Sergey Brin. Retrieved June 24, 2006, from www.Montessori.org/enews/barbara Walters.html

Abraham, H., & others. (2010). Myelination in the human hippocampal formation from midgestation to adulthood. *International Journal of Developmental Neuroscience, 28,* 401–410.

Abrams, A. J., Farooq, A., & Wang, G. (2011, in press). S-Nitrosylation of ApoE in Alzheimer's disease. *Biochemistry.*

Accornero, V. H., Amado, A. J., Morrow, C. E., Xue, L., Anthony, J. C., & Bandstra, E. S. (2007). Impact of prenatal cocaine exposure on attention and response inhibition as assessed by continuous performance tests. *Journal of Developmental and Behavioral Pediatrics, 28,* 195–205.

Achenbach, T. M. (1997). What is normal? What is abnormal? Developmental perspectives on behavioral and emotional problems. In S. S. Luthar, J. A. Burack, D. Cicchetti, & J. R. Weisz (Eds.), *Developmental psychopathology: Perspectives on adjustment, risk, and disorder.* New York: Cambridge University Press.

Ackerman, J. P., Riggins, T., & Black, M. M. (2010). A review of the effects of prenatal cocaine exposure among school-aged children. *Pediatrics, 125,* 554–565.

Adams, J. C. (2009). Immunocytochemical traits of type IV fibrocytes and their possible relation to cochlear function and pathology. *Journal of the Association for Research in Otolaryngology, 10,* 369–382.

Adamson, L., & Frick, J. (2003). The still face: A history of a shared experimental paradigm. *Infancy, 4,* 451–473.

Adler, N., Nadler, B., Eviater, Z., & Shamay-Tsoory, S. G. (2010). The relationship between theory of mind and autobiographical memory in high-functioning autism and Asperger syndrome. *Psychiatry, 178,* 214–216.

Administration for Children and Families. (2008). *Statistical fact sheet, fiscal year 2008.* Washington, DC: Author.

Administration on Aging. (2009). *A profile of older Americans: 2009.* Washington, DC: U.S. Department of Health and Human Services.

Adolph, K. E. (1997). Learning in the development of infant locomotion. *Monographs of the Society for Research in Child Development, 62* (3, Serial No. 251).

Adolph, K. E., & Berger, S. E. (2005). Physical and motor development. In M. H. Bornstein & M. E. Lamb (Eds.), *Developmental psychology* (5th ed.). Mahwah, NJ: Erlbaum.

Adolph, K. E., & Berger, S. E. (2011). Development of the motor system. In H. Pashler & others (Eds.), *Encyclopedia of the mind.* Thousand Oaks, CA: Sage.

Adolph, K. E., & Joh, A. S. (2009). Multiple learning mechanisms in the development of action. In A. Needham & A. Woodward (Eds.), *Learning and the infant mind.* New York: Oxford University Press.

Adolph, K. E., Karasik, L. B., & Tamis-LeMonda, C. S. (2010). Moving between cultures: Cross-cultural research on motor development. In M. Bornstein & L. R. Cote (Eds.), *Handbook of cross-cultural developmental science, Vol. 1, Domains of development across cultures.* Clifton, NJ: Psychology Press.

Adolph, K. E., & Robinson, S. R. R. (2011). The road to walking: What learning to walk tells us about development. In P. Zelazo (Ed.), *Oxford handbook of developmental psychology.* New York: Oxford University Press.

Agency for Healthcare Research and Quality. (2007). *Evidence report/Technology assessment Number 153: Breastfeeding and maternal and health outcomes in developed countries.* Rockville, MD: U.S. Department of Health and Human Services.

Agras, W. S., & others. (2004). Report of the National Institutes of Health workshop on overcoming barriers to treatment research in anorexia nervosa. *International Journal of Eating Disorders, 35,* 509–521.

Ahmed, S., & others. (2011, in press). Community kangaroo mother care: Implementation and potential for neonatal survival and health in very low-income settings. *Journal of Perinatology.*

Ahrberg, M., Trojca, D., Nasrawi, N., & Vocks, S. (2011, in press). Body image disturbance in binge eating disorder: A review. *European Eating Disorders Review.*

Ahrons, C. (2004). *We're still family.* New York: Harper Collins.

Ahrons, C. R. (2007). Family ties after divorce: Long-term implications for children. *Family Process, 46,* 53–65.

Aiken Morgan, A., Sims, R. C., & Whitfield, K. E. (2010). Cardiovascular health and education as sources of individual variability in cognitive aging among African Americans. *Journal of Aging and Health, 22*(4), 477–503.

Ainsworth, M. D. S. (1979). Infant-mother attachment. *American Psychologist, 34,* 932–937.

Aizawa, K., Shoemaker, J. K., Overend, T. J., & Petrella, R. J. (2010). Longitudinal changes in central artery stiffness with lifestyle modification, washout, and drug treatment in individuals at risk for cardiovascular disease. *Metabolic Syndrome and Related Disorders, 8*(4), 323–329.

Akbari, A., & others. (2010). Parity and breastfeeding are preventive measures against breast cancer in Iranian women. *Breast Cancer, 18*(1), 51–55.

Akhavan, S., & Lundgren, I. (2011, in press). Midwives' experiences of doula support for immigrant women in Sweden—A qualitative study. *Midwifery.*

Akintunde, A. A., Ayodele, O. E., Akinwusi, P. O., & Opadijo, G. O. (2010). Metabolic syndrome: Comparison of occurrence using three definitions in hypertensive patients. *Clinical and Medical Research, 9*(1): 26–31.

Akolekar, R., Brown, S., Flack, N., Bilardo, C. M., & Nicolaides, K. H. (2011). Prediction of miscarriage and stillbirth at 11–13 weeks and the contribution of chorionic villus sampling. *Prenatal Diagnosis, 31,* 38–45.

Aksglaede, L., Skakkebaek, N. E., Almstrup, K., & Juul, A. (2011, in press). Clinical and biological parameters in 166 boys, adolescents, and adults with non-mosaic Klinefelter syndrome: A Copenhagen experience. *Acta Pediatrica.*

Aktar, N., & Herold, K. (2008). Pragmatic development. In M. M. Haith & J. B. Benson (Eds.), *Encyclopedia of infant and early childhood development.* New York: Elsevier.

Alberson, M., Mwamukonda, K. B., Shindel, A. W., & Lue, T. F. (2011). Evaluation and treatment of erectile dysfunction. *Medical Clinics of North America, 95,* 201–212.

Albert, D., & Steinberg, L. (2011a). Judgment and decision making in adolescence. *Journal of Research on Adolescence, 21,* 211–224.

Albert, D., & Steinberg, L. (2011b). Peer influences on adolescent risk behavior. In M. Bardo, D. Fishbein, & R. Milich (Eds.), *Inhibitory control and drug abuse prevention: From research to translation*. New York: Springer.

Alcaro, S., & others. (2010). Simple choline esters as potential anti-Alzheimer agents. *Current Pharmaceutical Design, 16,* 692–697.

Ali, M. M., Amialchuk, A., & Dwyer, D. S. (2011). The social contagion effect of marijuana use among adolescents. *PLoS One, 6,* e16183.

Allen, J. P., & Allen, C. W. (2009). *Escaping the endless adolescence.* New York: Ballantine.

Allen, J. P., & Miga, E. M. (2010). Attachment in adolescence: A move to the level of emotion regulation. *Journal of Social and Personal Relationships, 27*(2), 181–190.

Allen, J. P., & others. (2009, April). *Portrait of the secure teen as an adult.* Paper presented at the meeting of the Society for Research in Child Development, Denver.

Allen, J. P., Philliber, S., Herring, S., & Kuperminc, G. P. (1997). Preventing teen pregnancy and academic failure: Experimental evaluation of a developmentally-based approach. *Child Development, 68,* 729–742.

Allen, M., Svetaz, M. V., Hardeman, R., & Resnick, M. D. (2008, February). *What research tells us about Latino parenting practices and their relationship to youth sexual behavior.* The National Campaign to Prevent Teen and Unplanned Pregnancy. Retrieved December 2, 2008, from www.TheNationalCampaign.org

Alleyne, B., Coleman-Cowger, V. H., Crown, L., Gibbons, M. A., & Vines, L. N. (2011). The effects of dating violence, substance use, and risky sexual behavior among a diverse sample of Illinois youth. *Journal of Adolescence, 34,* 11–18.

Allstate Foundation. (2005). *Teen driving— Chronic: A report on the state of teen driving.* Northbrook, IL: Author.

Almeida, D. M., & Horn, M. C. (2004). Is daily life more stressful during middle adulthood? In C. D. Ryff & R. C. Kessler (Eds.), *A portrait of midlife in the United States.* Chicago: University of Chicago Press.

Almeida, D. M., Piazza, J. R., Stawski, R. S., & Klein, L. C. (2011). The speedometer of life: Stress, health, and aging. In K. W. Schaie & S. L. Willis (Eds.), *Handbook of the psychology of aging* (7th ed.). New York: Elsevier.

Alonso-Babarro, A., Varela-Cerdeira, M. A., Rodriguez-Barrientos, R., & Bruera, E. (2010, February 3). At-home palliative sedation for end-of-life cancer patients. *Palliative Medicine.*

Altarac, M., & Saroha, E. (2007). Life prevalence of learning disability among U.S. children. *Pediatrics, 119*(Suppl. 1), S77–S83.

Alvarez, A., & del Rio, P. (2007). Inside and outside the zone of proximal development: An eco-functional reading of Vygotsky. In H. Daniels, J. Wertsch, & M. Cole (Eds.), *The Cambridge companion to Vygotsky.* New York: Cambridge University Press.

Aly, M., & Moscovitch, M. (2010). The effects of sleep on episodic memory in older and younger adults. *Memory, 18,* 327–334.

Alzheimer's Association. (2010). *Alzheimer's disease facts and figures.* Chicago: Alzheimer's Association.

Amabile, T. M., (1993). (Commentary). In D. Goleman, P. Kaufman, & M. Ray (Eds.), *The creative spirit.* New York: Plume.

Amabile, T. M., & Hennessey, B. A. (1992). The motivation for creativity in children. In A. K. Boggiano & T. S. Pittman (Eds.), *Achievement and motivation.* New York: Cambridge University Press.

Amato, P. R. (2006). Marital discord, divorce, and children's well-being: Results from a 20-year longitudinal study of two generations. In A. Clarke-Stewart & J. Dunn (Eds.), *Families count.* New York: Cambridge University Press.

Amato, P. R. (2010). Research on divorce: Continuing trends and new developments. *Journal of Marriage and the Family, 72*(3), 650–666.

Amato, P. R., & Booth, A. (1996). A prospective study of divorce and parent-child relationships. *Journal of Marriage and the Family, 58,* 356–365.

Amato, P. R., Booth, A., Johnson, D. R., & Rogers, S. J. (2007). *Alone together: How marriage in America is changing.* Cambridge, MA: Harvard University Press.

Amato, P. R., & Dorius, C. R. (2010). Fathers, children, and divorce. In M. E. Lamb (Ed.), *The role of the father in child development* (5th ed.). New York: Wiley.

Ambati, J. (2011). Age-related macular degeneration and the other double helix. *Investigative Ophthalmology and Visual Science, 52,* 2166–2169.

Ambridge, B., & Lieven, E. V. M. (2011). *Child language acquisition.* New York: Cambridge University Press.

Amed, S., Daneman, D., Mahmud, F. H., & Hamilton, J. (2010). Type 2 diabetes in children and adolescents. *Expert Review of Cardiovascular Therapy, 8,* 393–406.

American Academy of Pediatrics. (2001). Committee on Public Education: Children, adolescents, and television. *Pediatrics, 107,* 423–426.

American Academy of Pediatrics. (2010). Policy statement—sexuality, contraception, and the media. *Pediatrics, 126,* 576–582.

American Academy of Pediatrics Task Force on Infant Positioning and SIDS. (2000). Changing concepts of sudden infant death syndrome. *Pediatrics, 105,* 650–656.

American Academy of Pediatrics Work Group on Breastfeeding. (1997). Breastfeeding and the use of human milk. *Pediatrics, 100,* 1035–1039.

American Association of University Women. (1992). *How schools shortchange girls: A study of major findings on girls and education.* Washington, DC: Author.

American Association of University Women. (2006). *Drawing the line: Sexual harassment on campus.* Washington, DC: Author.

American Association on Mental Retardation, Ad Hoc Committee on Terminology and Classification. (1992). *Mental retardation* (9th ed.). Washington, DC: Author.

American Psychological Association. (2003). *Psychology: Scientific problem solvers.* Washington, DC: Author.

American Psychological Association. (2007). *Stress in America.* Washington, DC: Author.

Amsel, E., & Smetana, J. G. (Eds.). (2011, in press). *Adolescent vulnerabilities and opportunities: Constructivist and development perspectives.* New York: Cambridge University Press.

Amsterdam, B. K. (1968). *Mirror behavior in children under two years of age.* Unpublished doctoral dissertation, University of North Carolina, Chapel Hill.

Anastasi, A., & Urbina, S. (1996). *Psychological testing* (7th ed.). Upper Saddle River, NJ: Prentice-Hall.

Anderman, E. M., & Anderman, L. H. (2010). *Classroom motivation.* Upper Saddle River, NJ: Prentice Hall.

Anderman, E. M., & Murdock, T. B. (Eds.). (2007). *Psychology of academic cheating.* San Diego: Academic Press.

Anderson, B. M., & others. (2009). Examination of associations of genes in the serotonin system to autism. *Neurogenetics, 10,* 209–216.

Anderson, C. A., Gentile, D. A., & Buckley, K. E. (2007). *Violent video game effects on children and adolescents.* New York: Oxford University Press.

Anderson, D. J., & Yoshizawa, T. (2007). Cross-cultural comparisons of the health-related quality of life in Australian and Japanese women: The Australian and Japanese Midlife Women's Health study. *Menopause, 35,* 18–38.

Anderson, E., Greene, S. M., Hetherington, E. M., & Clingempeel, W. G. (1999). The dynamics of parental remarriage. In E. M. Hetherington (Ed.), *Coping with divorce, single parenting, and remarriage.* Mahwah, NJ: Erlbaum.

Anderson, K. G., Tapert, S. F., Moadab, I., Crowley, T. J., & Brown, S. A. (2007). Personality risk profile for conduct disorder and substance use disorders in youth. *Addictive Behaviors, 32,* 2377–2382.

Anderson, P. A. (2006). The evolution of biological sex differences in communication. In K. Dindia & D. J. Canary (Eds.), *Sex differences and similarities in communication.* Mahwah, NJ: Erlbaum.

Anderson, P. J., & others. (2011). Attention problems in a representative sample of extremely preterm/extremely low birth weight children. *Developmental Neuropsychology, 36,* 57–73.

Anderson, P. L., & Meier-Hedde, R. (2011). *International case studies of dyslexia.* New York: Routledge.

Andersson, U. (2010). The contribution of working memory capacity to foreign language comprehension in children. *Memory, 18*(4), 458–472.

Ang, S., Rodgers, J. L., & Wanstrom, L. (2010). The Flynn effect within subgroups in the U.S.: Gender, race, income, education, and urbanization differences in the NYLS-children data. *Intelligence, 38,* 367–384.

Angel, L., Fay, S., Bourazzaoui, B., Granjon, L., & Isingrini, M. (2009). Neural correlates of cued recall in young and older adults: An event-related potential study. *Neuroreport, 20,* 75–79.

Angelone, T., & others. (2010, in press). Distinct signaling mechanisms are involved in the dissimilar myocardial and coronary effects elicited by quercetin and myricetin, two red wine flavonols. *Nutrition, Metabolism, and Cardiovascular Diseases.*

Ansary, N. S., & Luthar, S. S. (2009). Distress and academic achievement among adolescents of affluence: A study of externalizing and internalizing problem behaviors and school performance. *Development and Psychopathology, 21,* 319–341.

Antonarakis, S. E. (2009). Whole genome association studies: What have we learned and where do we go from here? *Annual Review of Genomics and Human Genetics* (Vol. 10). Palo Alto, CA: Annual Reviews.

Antonogeorgos, G., & others. (2011). Association of extracurricular sports participation with obesity in Greek children. *Journal of Sports Medicine and Physical Fitness, 51,* 121–127.

Antonopoulos, C., & others. (2011, in press). Maternal smoking during pregnancy and childhood lymphoma: A meta-analysis. *International Journal of Cancer.*

Antonucci, T. C., Birditt, K. S., & Ajrouch, K. (2011). Convoys of social relations: Past, present, and future. In K. L. Fingerman, C. A. Berg, J. Smith, & T. C. Antonucci (Eds.), *Handbook of life-span development.* New York: Springer.

Antonucci, T. C., Fiori, K. L., Birditt, K., & Jackey, L. M. H. (2010). Convoys of social relations: Integrating life-span and life-course perspectives. In R. M. Lerner, W. F. Overton, A. M. Freund, & M. E. Lamb (Eds.), *Handbook of life-span development.* New York: Wiley.

Antonucci, T. C., Vandewater, E. A., & Lansford, J. E. (2000). Adulthood and aging: Social processes and development. In A. Kazdin (Ed.), *Encyclopedia of psychology.* New York: American Psychological Association and Oxford University Press.

Aquilino, W. S. (2006). Family relationships and support systems in emerging adulthood. In J. J. Arnett & J. L. Tanner (Eds.), *Emerging adults in America.* Washington, DC: American Psychological Association.

Aquino, K., McFerran, B., & Laven, M. (2011). Moral identity and the experience of moral elevation in response to acts of uncommon goodness. *Journal of Personality and Social Behavior, 100,* 703–718.

Araujo, D. M., Santos, G. F., & Nardi, A. E. (2010). Binge eating disorder and depression: A systematic review. *World Journal of Biological Psychiatry, 11*(2, Pt 2), 199–207.

Ardelt, M. (2010). Are older adults wiser than college students? A comparison of two age cohorts. *Journal of Adult Development, 17,* 193–207.

Ardelt, M. (2011). Wisdom, age, and well-being. In K. W. Schaie & S. L. Willis (Eds.), *Handbook of the psychology of aging* (7th ed.). New York: Elsevier.

Arendas, K., Qui, Q., & Gruslin, A. (2008). Obesity in pregnancy: Pre-conceptual to postpartum consequences. *Journal of Obstetrics and Gynecology Canada, 30,* 477–488.

Arends, R. I. (2012). *Learning to teach* (9th ed.). New York: McGraw-Hill.

Arenkiel, B. R. (2010). Adult neurogenesis supports short-term olfactory memory. *Journal of Neurophysiology, 102*(6), 2925–2937.

Ariza, E. N. W., & Lapp, S. I. (2011). *Literacy, language, and culture.* Boston: Allyn & Bacon.

Arnett, J. J. (2007). Socialization in emerging adulthood. In J. E. Grusec & P. D. Hastings (Eds.), *Handbook of socialization.* New York: Guilford.

Aronow, W. S. (2007). Cardiovascular system. In J. E. Birren (Ed.), *Encyclopedia of gerontology* (2nd ed.). San Diego: Academic Press.

Aronson, E. (1986, August). *Teaching students things they think they already know about: The case of prejudice and desegregation.* Paper presented at the meeting of the American Psychological Association, Washington, DC.

Arpanantikul, M. (2004). Midlife experiences of Thai women. *Journal of Advanced Nursing, 47,* 49–56.

Arterberry, M. E. (2008). Perceptual development. In M. M. Haith & J. B. Benson (Eds.), *Encyclopedia of infant and early childhood development.* Oxford, UK: Elsevier.

Ascher, B., & others. (2010). International consensus recommendations on the aesthetic usage of botulinum toxin type A (Speywood Unit)—Part I: Upper facial wrinkles. *Journal of the European Academy of Dermatology, 24*(11), 178–184.

Asendorph, J. B. (2008). Shyness. In M. M. Haith & J. B. Benson (Eds.), *Encyclopedia of infant and early childhood development.* Oxford, UK: Elsevier.

Asher, S. R., & McDonald, K. L. (2009). The behavior basis of acceptance, rejection, and perceived popularity. In K. H. Rubin, W. M. Bukowski, & B. Laursen (Eds.), *Handbook of peer interactions, relationships, and groups.* New York: Guilford.

Aslan, A., Zellner, M., & Bauml, K. H. (2010). Working memory capacity predicts listwise directed forgetting in adults and children. *Memory, 18*(4), 442–450

Aslin, R. N. (2009). The role of learning in cognitive development. In A. Woodward & A. Needham (Eds.), *Learning and the infant mind.* New York: Oxford University Press.

Aslin, R. N., Jusczyk, P. W., & Pisoni, D. B. (1998). Speech and auditory processing during infancy: Constraints on and precursors to language. In W. Damon (Ed.), *Handbook of child psychology* (5th ed., Vol. 2). New York: Wiley.

Aslin, R. N., & Lathrop, A. L. (2008). Visual perception. In M. M. Haith & J. B. Benson (Eds.), *Encyclopedia of infant and early childhood development.* Oxford, UK: Elsevier.

Asp, F., Eskilsson, G., & Berninger, E. (2011, in press). Horizontal sound localization in children with bilateral cochlear implants: Effects of auditory experience and age at implantation. *Otology and Neurotology.*

Athanasiadis, A. P., & others. (2011, in press). Correlation of 2nd trimester amniotic fluid amino acid profile with gestational age and estimated fetal weight. *Journal of Maternal-Fetal and Neonatal Medicine.*

Attar-Schwartz, S., Tan, J. P., Buchanan, A., Flouri, E., & Griggs, J. (2009). Grandparenting and adolescent adjustment in two-parent biological, lone-parent, and step-families. *Journal of Family Psychology, 23*(1), 67–75.

Aubert, G., & Lansdorp, P. M. (2008). Telomeres and aging. *Physiological Review, 88,* 557–579.

Audhoe, S. S., Hoving, J. L., Sluiter, J. K., & Frings-Dresen, M. H. (2010). Vocational interventions for unemployed: Effects on work participation and mental distress. A systematic review. *Journal of Occupational Rehabilitation, 20,* 1–13.

Austad, S. (2009). Making sense of biological theories of aging. In V. L. Bengtson, D. Gans, N. M. Putney, & M. Silverstein (Eds.), *Handbook of theories of aging* (2nd ed.). New York: Springer.

Austad, S. (2011). Sex differences in aging. In E. J. Masoro & S. Austad (Eds.), *Handbook of the biology of aging* (7th ed.). New York: Elsevier.

Auyeung, B., & others. (2009). Fetal testosterone predicts sexually differentiated childhood behavior in girls and boys. *Psychological Science, 20,* 144–148.

Avis, N. E., & others. (2009). Longitudinal changes in sexual functioning as women transition through menopause: Results from the Study of Women's Health Across the Nation. *Menopause, 16,* 425–426.

Aviv, A. (2011). The role of telomere biology in aging. In E. Masoro & S. Austad (Eds.), *Handbook of the biology of aging* (7th ed.). New York: Elsevier.

B

Babble, E. R. (2011). *The basics of social research* (5th ed.). Boston: Cengage.

Baber, R. (2011). Breast cancer in postmeno-pausal women after hormone therapy. *Journal of the American Medical Association, 305,* 466.

Babizhayev, M. A., Minasyan, H., & Richer, S. P. (2009) Cataract halos: A driving hazard in aging populations: Implications of the Halometer DG test for assessment of intraocular light scatter. *Applied Ergonomics, 40,* 545–553.

Bachman, J. G., O'Malley, P. M., Schulenberg, J. E., Johnston, L. D., Bryant, A. L., & Merline, A. C. (2002). *The decline in substance use in young adulthood.* Mahwah, NJ: Erlbaum.

Bachman, J. G., O'Malley, P. M., Schulenberg, J. E., Johnston, L. D., Freedman-Doan, P., & Messermith, E. E. (2008). *The education-drug use connection.* Clifton, NJ: Psychology Press.

Backhans, M. C., & Hemmingsson, T. (2011, in press). Unemployment and mental health—who is (not) affected? *European Journal of Public Health.*

Baddeley, A. D. (1990). *Human memory: Theory and practice.* Boston: Allyn & Bacon.

Baddeley, A. D. (2001). *Is working memory still working?* Paper presented at the meeting of the American Psychological Association, San Francisco.

Baddeley, A. D. (2007). *Working memory, thought and action.* New York: Oxford University Press.

Baddeley, A. D. (2010a). Working memory. *Current Biology, 20,* 136–140.

Baddeley, A. D. (2010b). Long-term and working memory: How do they interact? In L. Backman & L. Nyberg (Eds.), *Memory, aging, and the brain.* New York: Psychology Press.

Baddeley, A. D. (2012). Prefatory. *Annual Review of Psychology* (Vol. 63). Palo Alto, CA: Annual Reviews.

Baddeley, A. D., Eysenck, M., & Anderson, M. (2009). *Memory.* New York: Psychology Press.

Bahali, K., Akcan, R., Tahiroglu, A. Y., & Avci, A. (2010). Child sexual abuse: Seven years in practice. *Journal of Forensic Sciences, 55*(3), 633–636.

Bahrick, H. P. (1984). Semantic memory content in permastore: Fifty years of memory for Spanish learned in school. *Journal of Experimental Psychology: General, 113,* 1–35.

Bahrick, H. P., Bahrick, P. O., & Wittlinger, R. P. (1975). Fifty years of memory for names and faces: A cross-sectional approach. *Journal of Experimental Psychology: General, 104,* 54–75.

Bahrick, L. E. (2010). Intermodal perception and selective attention to intersensory redundancy: Implications for social development and autism. In J. G. Bremner & T. D. Wachs (Eds.), *Wiley-Blackwell handbook of infant development* (2nd ed.). New York: Wiley.

Bahrick, L. E., & Hollich, G. (2008). Intermodal perception. In M. M. Haith & J. B. Benson (Eds.), *Encyclopedia of infant and early childhood development.* Oxford, UK: Elsevier.

Baillargeon, R. (1995). The object concept revisited: New directions in the investigation of infants' physical knowledge. In C. E. Granrud (Ed.), *Visual perception and cognition in infancy.* Hillsdale, NJ: Erlbaum.

Baillargeon, R. (2004). The acquisition of physical knowledge in infancy: A summary in eight lessons. In U. Goswami (Ed.), *Blackwell handbook of childhood cognitive development.* Malden, MA: Blackwell.

Baillargeon, R., & DeVos, J. (1991). Object permanence in young children: Further evidence. *Child Development, 62*(1991), 1227–1246.

Baillargeon, R., Li, J., Gertner, Y., & Wu, D. (2011). How do infants reason about physical events? In U. Goswami (Ed.), *Wiley-Blackwell handbook of childhood cognitive development* (2nd ed.). New York: Wiley.

Baillargeon, R., Li, J., Ng, W., & Yuan, S. (2009). A new account of infants' physical reasoning. In A. Woodward & A. Needham (Eds.), *Learning and the infant mind* (pp. 66–116). New York: Oxford University Press.

Baillargeon, R. H., & others. (2007). Gender difference in physical aggression: A prospective population-based survey of children before and after two years of age. *Developmental Psychology, 43,* 13–26.

Bajanowski, T., & others. (2007). Nicotine and cotinine in infants dying from sudden infant death syndrome. *International Journal of Legal Medicine, 122,* 23–28.

Bakeman, R., & Brown, J. V. (1980). Early interaction: Consequences for social and mental development at three years. *Child Development, 51,* 437–447.

Baker, L. D., & others. (2010). Effects of aerobic exercise on mild cognitive impairment: A controlled trial. *Archives of Neurology, 67,* 71–79.

Bakermans-Kranenburg, M. J., & van IJzendoorn, M. H. (2009). The first 10,000 adult attachment interviews: Distributions of adult attachment representations in clinical and non-clinical groups. *Attachment and Human Development, 11,* 223–263.

Bakermans-Kranenburg, M. J., Breddels-Van Bardewijk, F., Juffer, M. K., Velderman, M. H., & van IJzendoorn, M. H. (2007). Insecure mothers with temperamentally reactive infants. In F. Juffer, M. J. Bakermans-Kranenburg, & M. H. van IJzendoorn (Eds.), *Promoting positive parenting.* Mahwah, NJ: Erlbaum.

Balaji, P., Dhillon, P., & Russell, I. F. (2009). Low-dose epidural top up for emergency cesarean delivery: A randomized comparison of levobupivacaine versus lidocaine/epinephrine/ fentanyl. *International Journal of Obstetric Anesthesia, 18,* 335–341.

Balchin, L., & Steer, P. J. (2007). Race, prematurity, and immaturity. *Early Human Development, 83,* 749–754.

Baldwin, S. A., & Hoffman, J. P. (2002). The dynamics of self-esteem: A growth-curve analysis. *Journal of Youth and Adolescence, 31,* 101–113.

Bales, K. L., & Carter, C. S. (2009). Neuroendocrine mechanisms of social bonds and child-parent attachment, from the child's perspective. In M. de Haan & M. R. Gunnar (Eds.), *Handbook of developmental social neuroscience.* New York: Guilford.

Ball, K., Edwards, J. D., & Ross, L. A. (2007). The impact of speed of process training on cognitive and everyday functions. *Journals of Gerontology B: Psychological Sciences and Social Sciences, 62,* P19–P31.

Ballard, S. (2011). Blood tests for investigating maternal well-being. 4. When nausea and vomiting in pregnancy becomes pathological: Hyperemesis gravidarum. *Practicing Midwife, 14,* 37–41.

Baltes, P. B. (1987). Theoretical propositions of life-span developmental psychology: On the dynamics between growth and decline. *Developmental Psychology, 23,* 611–626.

Baltes, P. B. (1993). The aging mind: Potentials and limits. *Gerontologist, 33,* 580–594.

Baltes, P. B. (2000). Life-span developmental theory. In A. Kazdin (Ed.), *Encyclopedia of psychology.* New York: Oxford University Press.

Baltes, P. B. (2003). On the incomplete architecture of human ontogeny: Selection, optimization, and compensation as foundation of developmental theory. In U. M. Staudinger & U. Lindenberger (Eds.), *Understanding human development.* Boston: Kluwer.

Baltes, P. B., & Kunzmann, U. (2004). The two faces of wisdom: Wisdom as a general theory of knowledge and judgment about excellence in mind and virtue vs. wisdom as everyday realization in people and products. *Human Development, 47,* 290–299.

Baltes, P. B., & Lindenberger, U. (1997). Emergence of a powerful connection between sensory and cognitive functions across the adult life span: A new window to the study of cognitive aging? *Psychology and Aging, 12,* 12–21.

Baltes, P. B., Lindenberger, U., & Staudinger, U. M. (2006). Lifespan theory in developmental psychology. In W. Damon & R. Lerner (Eds.), *Handbook of child psychology* (6th ed.). New York: Wiley.

Baltes, P. B., Reuter-Lorenz, P., & Rösler, F. (Eds.). (2006). *Lifespan development and the brain.* New York: Cambridge University Press.

Baltes, P. B., & Smith, J. (2003). New frontiers in the future of aging: From successful aging of the young to the dilemmas of the fourth age. *Gerontology, 49,* 123–135.

Baltes, P. B., & Smith, J. (2008). The fascination of wisdom: Its nature, ontogeny, and function. *Perspectives on Psychological Science, 3,* 56–64.

Bandura, A. (1997). *Self-efficacy.* New York: W. H. Freeman.

Bandura, A. (1998, August). *Swimming against the mainstream: Accentuating the positive aspects of humanity.* Paper presented at the meeting of the American Psychological Association, San Francisco.

Bandura, A. (2001). Social cognitive theory. *Annual Review of Psychology* (Vol. 52). Palo Alto, CA: Annual Reviews.

Bandura, A. (2002). Selective moral disengagement in the exercise of moral agency. *Journal of Moral Education, 31,* 101–119.

Bandura, A. (2009). Social and policy impact of social cognitive theory. In M. Mark, S. Donaldson, & B. Campbell (Eds.), *Social psychology and program/policy evaluation.* New York: Guilford.

Bandura, A. (2010a). Self-efficacy. In D. Matsumoto (Ed.), *Cambridge dictionary of psychology.* New York: Cambridge University Press.

Bandura, A. (2010b). Self-reinforcement. In D. Matsumoto (Ed.), *Cambridge dictionary of psychology.* New York: Cambridge University Press.

Bangdiwala, S. I., & others. (2010). NIH consensus development conference draft statement on vaginal birth after cesarean: New insights. *Obstetrics & Gynecology: 115*(6), 1279–1295.

Bank, L., Burraston, B., & Snyder, J. (2004). Sibling conflict and ineffective parenting as predictors of adolescent boys' antisocial behavior and peer difficulties: Additive and interactive effects. *Journal of Research on Adolescence, 14,* 99–125.

Banks, J. A. (2008). *Introduction to multicultural education* (4th ed.). Boston: Allyn & Bacon.

Banks, J. A. (Ed.). (2010). *Routledge international handbook of multicultural education.* New York: Routledge.

Banks, S., & Dinges, D. F. (2008). Behavioral and physiological consequences of sleep restriction. *Journal of Clinical Sleep Medicine, 15,* 519–528.

Bapal, S. A., Krishnan, A., Ghanate, A. D., Kusumbe, A. P., & Kaira, R. S. (2010). Gene expression: Protein interaction systems network modeling identifies transformation-associated molecules and pathways in ovarian cancer. *Cancer Research, 70,* 4809.

Barakat, R., & others. (2011, in press). Exercise during pregnancy improves maternal health perception: A randomized controlled trial. *American Journal of Obstetrics and Gynecology.*

Barba, G. D., Attali, E., & La Corte, V. (2010). Confabulation in healthy aging is related to interference of overlearned, semantically similar information on episodic memory recall. *Journal of Clinical and Experimental Neuropsychology, 32*(6), 655–660.

Barbarin, O., & Aikens, N. (2009). Supporting parental practices in the language and literacy development of young children. In O. Barbarin & H. Wasik (Eds.), *Handbook of child development and education.* New York: Guilford.

Barbarin, O. A., & Miller, K. M. (2009). Developmental science and early education: An introduction. In O. A. Barbarin & B. H. Wasik (Eds.), *Handbook of child development and early education.* New York: Oxford University Press.

Barber, B., Stone, M., & Eccles, J. (2010). Protect, prepare, support, and engage: The roles of school-based extracurricular activities in students' development. In J. Meece & J. Eccles (Eds.), *Handbook of research on schools, schooling, and human development.* New York: Routledge.

Barber, T. D., & others. (2011, in press). Wilms Tumor: Preoperative risk factors identified for intraoperative tumor spill. *Journal of Urology.*

Barbieri, M., Bocardi, V., Papa, M., & Paolisso, G. (2009). Metabolic journey to healthy longevity. *Hormone Research, 71*(Suppl. 1), S24–S27.

Bargh, J. A., & McKenna, K. Y. A. (2004). The Internet and social life. *Annual Review of Psychology* (Vol. 55). Palo Alto, CA: Annual Reviews.

Barlett, C. P., Anderson, C. A., & Swing, E. L. (2009). Video game effects confirmed, suspected and speculative: A review of the evidence. *Simulation and Gaming, 40,* 377–403.

Barnes, L. L., Mendes de Leon, C. F., Wilson, R. S., Bienias, J. L., Bennett, D. A., & Evans, D. A. (2004). Racial difference in perceived discrimination in a community population of older Blacks and Whites. *Journal of Aging and Health, 16,* 315–317.

Baron, I. S., Erickson, K., Ahronovich, M. D., Baker, R., & Litman, F. R. (2011). Neuropsychological and behavioral outcomes of extremely low birth weight at age three. *Developmental Neuropsychology, 36,* 5–21.

Baron, N. S. (1992). *Growing up with language.* Reading, MA: Addison-Wesley.

Baron-Cohen, S. (2008). Autism, hyper-systematizing, and truth. *Quarterly Journal of Experimental Psychology, 61,* 64–75.

Baron-Cohen, S. (2009). Autism: The empathizing-systematizing (E-S) theory. *Annals of the New York Academy of Sciences, 1156,* 68–80.

Baron-Cohen, S. (2011). The empathizing-systematizing (E-S) theory of autism: A cognitive developmental account. In U. Goswami (Ed.), *Wiley-Blackwell handbook of childhood cognitive development* (2nd ed.). New York: Wiley-Blackwell.

Baron-Cohen, S., Golan, O., Chapman, E., & Granader, Y. (2007). Transported to a world of emotions. *The Psychologist, 20,* 76–77.

Barreto, S. M., & others. (2011, in press). Contextual factors associated with smoking among Brazilian adolescents. *Journal of Epidemiology and Community Health.*

Barsov, E. V. (2011). Telomerase and primary T cells: Biology and immortalization for adaptive immunotherapy. *Immunotherapy, 3,* 407–421.

Bartsch, K., & Wellman, H. M. (1995). *Children talk about the mind.* New York: Oxford University Press.

Bartzokis, G., & others. (2010). Lifespan trajectory of myelin integrity and maximum motor speed. *Neurobiology of Aging, 31,* 1554–1562.

Basaran, A., Basaran, M., & Topatan, B. (2011, in press). Chorionic villus sampling and the risk of preeclampsia: A systematic review and meta-analysis. *Archives of Gynecology and Obstetrics.*

Basta, N. E., Matthews, F. E., Chatfield, M. D., Byrnes, C., & MRC-FFAS. (2008). Community-level socio-economic status and cognitive and functional impairment in the older population. *European Journal of Public Health, 18,* 48–54.

Bates, J. E. (2008). Unpublished review of J. W. Santrock's *Children,* 11th ed. (New York: McGraw-Hill).

Bates, J. E., Schermerhorn, A. C., & Goodnight, J. A. (2010). Temperament and personality through the life span. In A. Freund, M. Lamb, & R. M. Lerner (Eds.), *Handbook of life-span development.* New York: Wiley.

Batson, C. D. (1989). Personal values, moral principles, and the three-path model of prosocial motivation. In N. Eisenberg & J. Reykowski (Eds.), *Social and moral values.* Hillsdale, NJ: Erlbaum.

Battistich, V. A. (2008). The Child Development Project: Creating caring school communities. In L. Nucci & D. Narváez (Eds.), *Handbook of moral and character education.* Clifton, NJ: Psychology Press.

Bauer, J., & others. (2010). Comparative transcriptional profiling identifies takeout as a gene that regulates life span. *Aging, 2,* 298–310.

Bauer, P. J. (2009). Neurodevelopmental changes in infancy and beyond: Implications for learning and memory. In O. A. Barbarin & B. H. Wasik (Eds.), *Handbook of child development and early education.* New York: Oxford University Press.

Bauer, P. J., Larkina, M., & Deocampo, J. (2011). Early memory development. In U. Goswami (Ed.), *Wiley-Blackwell handbook of childhood cognitive development* (2nd ed.). New York: Wiley-Blackwell.

Bauer, P. J., Wenner, J. A., Dropik, P. L., & Wewerka, S. S. (2000). Parameters of remembering and forgetting in the transition from infancy to early childhood. *Monographs of the Society for Research in Child Development, 65* (4, Serial No. 263).

Bauerlein, M. (2008). *The dumbest generation: How the digital age stupefies young Americans and jeopardizes our future (Or, don't trust anyone under 30).* New York: Tarcher.

Baumeister, R. F., Campbell, J. D., Krueger, J. I., & Vohs, K. D. (2003). Does high self-esteem cause better performance, interpersonal success, happiness, or healthier lifestyles? *Psychological Science in the Public Interest, 4*(1), 1–44.

Baumeister, R. F., & Vohs, K. D. (2002). The pursuit of meaningfulness in life. In C. R. Snyder & S. J. Lopez (Eds.), *Handbook of positive psychology.* New York: Oxford University Press.

Baumrind, D. (1971). Current patterns of parental authority. *Developmental Psychology Monographs, 4*(I, Pt. 2).

Baumrind, D. (1991). Effective parenting during the early adolescent transition. In P. A. Cowan & E. M. Hetherington (Eds.), *Advances in family research* (Vol. 2). Hillsdale, NJ: Erlbaum.

Baydyuk, M., Nguyen, M. T., & Xu, B. (2011, in press). Chronic deprivation of TrkB signaling leads to selective late-onset nigrostriatal dopaminergic degeneration. *Experimental Neurology.*

Bayley, N. (1969). *Manual for the Bayley Scales of Infant Development.* New York: Psychological Corporation.

Bayley, N. (2006). *Bayley Scales of Infant and Toddler Development* (3rd ed.). San Antonio: Harcourt Assessment.

Bayraktar, M. R., Ozerol, I. H., Gucluer, N., & Celik, O. (2010). Prevalence and antibiotic susceptibility: *Mycoplasma hominis* and *Ureaplasma urealyticum* in pregnant women. *International Journal of Infectious Diseases, 14,* e90–e95.

Baysinger, C. L. (2010). Imaging during pregnancy. *Anesthesia and Analgesia, 110,* 863–867.

Beal, C. R. (1994). *Boys and girls: The development of gender roles.* New York: McGraw-Hill.

Beatty, J. J., & Pratt, L. (2011). *Early literacy in preschool and kindergarten* (3rd ed.). Boston: Allyn & Bacon.

Beauchamp, G., & Mennella, J. A. (2009). Early flavor learning and its impact on later feeding behavior. *Journal of Pediatric Gastroenterology and Nutrition, 48*(Suppl. 1), S25–S30.

Beauchamp, M. H., & Anderson, V. (2010). SOCIAL: An integrative framework for the development of social skills. *Psychological Bulletin, 136,* 39–64.

Bechtold, A. G., Bushnell, E. W., & Salapatek, P. (1979, April). *Infants' visual localization of visual and auditory targets.* Paper presented at the meeting of the Society for Research in Child Development, San Francisco.

Beck, C. T. (2006). Postpartum depression: It isn't just the blues. *American Journal of Nursing, 106,* 40–50.

Beck, D. M., Schaefer, C., Pang, K., & Carlson, S. M. (2011, in press). Executive functioning in preschool children: Test-retest reliability. *Journal of Cognition and Development.*

Bedford, V. H. (2009). Sibling relationships: Adulthood. In D. Carr (Eds.), *Encyclopedia of the life course and human development.* Boston: Gale Cengage.

Beech, A. R., Ward, T., & Fisher, D. (2006). The identification of sexual or violent motivations in men who assault women: Implications for treatment. *Journal of Interpersonal Violence, 21,* 1635–1653.

Beeghly, M., & others. (2006). Prenatal cocaine exposure and children's language functioning at 6 and 9.5 years: Moderating effects of child age, birthweight, and gender. *Journal of Pediatric Psychology, 31,* 98–115.

Beghetto, R. A., & Kaufman, J. C. (Eds.). (2011). *Nurturing creativity in the classroom.* New York: Cambridge University Press.

Belansky, E. S., & Clements, P. (1992, March). *Adolescence: A crossroads for gender-role transcendence or gender-role intensification.* Paper presented at the meeting of the Society for Research on Adolescence, Washington, DC.

Bell, C. J., & others. (2011, in press). Carrier testing for severe childhood recessive diseases by next-generation sequencing. *Science Translational Medicine.*

Bell, M. A. (2011, in press). A psychobiological perspective on working memory performance at 8 months of age. *Child Development.*

Bell, M. A., & Deater-Deckard, K. (2007). Biological systems and the development of self-regulation: Integrating behavior, genetics, and psychopathology. *Journal of Development & Behavioral Pediatrics, 28,* 409–420.

Bell, M. A., & Fox, N. A. (1992). The relations between frontal brain electrical activity and cognitive development during infancy. *Child Development, 63,* 1142–1163.

Bell, M. A., Greene, D. R., & Wolfe, C. D. (2010). Psychobiological mechanisms of cognition-emotion integration in early development. In S. D. Calkins & M. A. Bell (Eds.), *Child development at the intersection of emotion and cognition.* Washington, DC: American Psychological Association.

Bell, S. M., & Ainsworth, M. D. S. (1972.). Infant crying and maternal responsiveness. *Child Development, 43,* 1171–1190.

Bellmore, A., Villarreal, V. M., & Ho, A. Y. (2011, in press). Staying cool across the first year of middle school. *Journal of Youth and Adolescence.*

Belsky, J. (1981). Early human experience: A family perspective. *Developmental Psychology, 17,* 3–23.

Belsky, J. (2009). Classroom composition, childcare history, and social development: Are childcare effects disappearing or spreading? *Social Development, 18,* 230–238.

Belsky, J., Steinberg, L., Houts, R. M., Halpern-Felsher, B. L., & NICHD Early Child Care Research Network. (2010). The development of reproductive strategy in females: Early maternal harshness—earlier menarche—increased sexual risk taking. *Developmental Psychology, 46,* 120–128.

Bender, H. L., & others. (2007). Use of harsh discipline and developmental outcomes in adolescence. *Development and Psychopathology, 19,* 227–242.

Bendersky, M., & Sullivan, M. W. (2007). Basic methods in infant research. In A. Slater & M. Lewis (Eds.), *Introduction to infant development* (2nd ed.). New York: Oxford University Press.

Benenson, J. F., Apostolaris, N. H., & Parnass, J. (1997). Age and sex differences in dyadic and group interaction. *Developmental Psychology, 33,* 538–543.

Bengtson, V. L. (1985). Diversity and symbolism in grandparental roles. In V. L. Bengtson & J. Robertson (Eds.), *Grandparenthood.* Newbury Park, CA: Sage.

Bengtson, V. L., Reedy, M. N., & Gordon, C. (1985). Aging and self-conceptions: Personality processes and social contexts. In J. E. Birren & K. W. Schaie (Eds.), *Handbook of the psychology of aging.* New York: Van Nostrand Reinhold.

Bengtsson, H., & Arvidsson, A. (2011). The impact of developing social perspective-taking skills on emotionality in middle and late childhood. *Social Development, 20,* 353–375.

Benjamins, M. R., & Finlayson, M. (2007). Using religious services to improve health: Findings from a sample of middle-aged and older adults with multiple sclerosis. *Journal of Aging and Health, 19,* 537–553.

Bennett, C. I. (2011a). *Comprehensive multicultural education.* Boston: Allyn & Bacon.

Bennett, C. I. (2011b). *Perspectives on human differences.* Boston: Allyn & Bacon.

Bennett, K. M. (2006). Does marital status and marital status change predict physical health in older adults? *Psychological Medicine, 36,* 1313–1320.

Bennett, K. M. (2009). Widowhood. In D. Carr (Ed.), *Encyclopedia of the life course and human development.* Boston: Gale Cengage.

Bennett, T., & others. (2008). Differentiating autism and Asperger syndrome on the basis of language delay or impairment. *Journal of Autism and Developmental Disorders, 38,* 616–625.

Benninghoven, D., Tetsch, N., Kunzendorf, S., & Jantschek, G. (2007). Body image in patients with eating disorders and their mothers, and the role of family functioning. *Comprehensive Psychiatry, 48,* 118–123.

Benoit, D., Coolbear, J., & Crawford, A. (2008). Abuse, neglect, and maltreatment of infants. In M. M. Haith & J. B. Benson (Eds.), *Encyclopedia of infant and early childhood development.* Oxford, UK: Elsevier.

Benokratis, N. (2011). *Marriage and families* (7th ed.). Upper Saddle River, NJ: Pearson.

Bensley, D. A., Crowe, D. S., Bernhardt, P., Buckner, C., & Allman, A. L (2010). Teaching and assessing critical thinking skills for argument analysis in psychology. *Teaching of Psychology, 37,* 91–96.

Benson, P. L., & Scales, P. C. (2011, in press). Thriving and sparks: Development and emergence of new core concepts in positive youth development. In R. J. R. Levesque (Ed.), *Encyclopedia of adolescence.* New York: Springer.

Berecz, J. M. (2009). *Theories of personality.* Boston: Allyn & Bacon.

Berenbaum, S. A., & Bailey, J. M. (2003). Effects on gender identity of prenatal androgens and genital appearance: Evidence from girls with congenital adrenal hyperplasia. *Journal of Clinical Endocrinology and Metabolism, 88,* 1102–1106.

Bergeson, T. R., Houston, D. M., & Miyamoto, R. T. (2010). Effect of congenital hearing loss and cochlear implantation on audiovisual speech perception in infants and children. *Restorative Neurology and Neuroscience, 28,* 157–165.

Berk, L. E. (1994). Why children talk to themselves. *Scientific American, 271*(5), 78–83.

Berk, L. E., & Spuhl, S. T. (1995). Maternal interaction, private speech, and task performance in preschool children. *Early Childhood Research Quarterly, 10,* 145–169.

Berko, J. (1958). The child's learning of English morphology. *Word, 14,* 150–177.

Berko Gleason, J. (2003). Unpublished review of J. W. Santrock's *Life-span development,* 9th ed. (New York: McGraw-Hill).

Berko Gleason, J. (2005). The development of language: An overview. In J. Berko Gleason &

N. B. Ratner (Eds.), *The development of language* (6th ed.). Boston: Allyn & Bacon.

Berko Gleason, J. (2009). The development of language: An overview. In J. Berko Gleason & N. B. Ratner (Eds.), *The development of language* (7th ed.). Boston: Allyn & Bacon.

Berko Gleason, J., & Ratner, N. B. (Eds.). (2009). *The development of language* (7th ed.). Boston: Allyn & Bacon.

Berlyne, D. E. (1960). *Conflict, arousal, and curiosity.* New York: McGraw-Hill.

Bermejo-Alvarez, P., Rizos, D., Lonergan, P., & Adan, A. G. (2011, in press). 181 transcripted sexual dimorphism in autosomal genes on bovine day 14 embryos. *Reproduction, Fertility, and Development.*

Bernard, K., & Dozier, M. (2008). Adoption and foster placement. In M. M. Haith & J. B. Benson (Eds.), *Encyclopedia of infant and early childhood development.* Oxford UK: Elseiver.

Berndt, T. J. (2002). Friendship quality and social development. *Current Directions in Psychological Science, 11,* 7–10.

Berndt, T. J., & Perry, T. B. (1990). Distinctive features and effects of early adolescent friendships. In R. Montemayor (Ed.), *Advances in adolescent research.* Greenwich, CT: JAI Press.

Berninger, V. W. (2006). Learning disabilities. In W. Damon & R. Lerner (Eds.), *Handbook of child psychology* (6th ed.). New York: Wiley.

Berntsen, D., & Rubin, D. C. (2002). Emotionally charged autobiographical memories across the life span: The role of happy, sad, traumatic, and involuntary memories. *Psychology and Aging, 17,* 636–652.

Berookhim, B. M., & Bar-Charma, N. (2011). Medical implications of erectile dysfunction. *Medical Clinics of North America, 95,* 213–221.

Berry, J. L. (2010). Hospice and heart disease: Missed opportunities. *Journal of Pain and Palliative Care Pharmacotherapy, 24,* 125–128.

Bersamin, M. M., Bourdeau, B., Fisher, D. A., & Grube, J. W. (2010). Television use, sexual behavior, and relationship status at last oral sex and vaginal intercourse. *Sexuality and Culture, 14,* 157–168.

Berscheid, E. (1988). Some comments on love's anatomy: Or, whatever happened to old-fashioned lust? In R. J. Sternberg (Ed.), *Anatomy of love.* New Haven, CT: Yale University Press.

Berscheid, E. (2010). Love in the fourth dimension. *Annual Review of Psychology* (Vol. 61). Palo Alto, CA: Annual Reviews.

Berscheid, E., & Fei, J. (1977). Sexual jealousy and romantic love. In G. Clinton & G. Smith (Eds.), *Sexual jealousy.* Englewood Cliffs, NJ: Prentice-Hill.

Bertenthal, B. I. (2008). Perception and action. In M. M. Haith & J. B. Benson (Eds.), *Encyclopedia of infant and early childhood development.* Oxford, UK: Elseiver.

Bertenthal, B. I., Longo, M. R., & Kenny, S. (2007). Phenomenal permanence and the development of predictive tracking in infancy. *Child Development, 78,* 350–363.

Bertoglio, K., & Hendren, R. L. (2009). New developments in autism. *Psychiatric Clinics of North America, 32,* 1–14.

Bertrand, R. M., & Lachman, M. E. (2003). Personality development in adulthood and old age. In I. B. Weiner (Ed.), *Handbook of psychology* (Vol. VI). New York: Wiley.

Besdine, R. W., & Wetle, T. F. (2010). Improving health for elderly people: An international health promotion and disease prevention agenda. *Aging: Clinical and Experimental Research, 22,* 219–230.

Besken, M., & Gulgoz, S. (2009). Reliance on schemas in source memory: Age differences and similarities of schemas. *Neuropsychology, Development, and Cognition. Section B: Aging, Neuropsychology, and Cognition, 16,* 1–2.

Bessette, L., Jean, S., Davison, K. S., Roy, S., Ste-Marie, L. G., & Brown, J. P. (2009). Factors influencing the treatment of osteoporosis following fragility fracture. *Osteoporosis International, 20,* 1911–1919.

Best, C. L., Smith, D. W., Raymond, J. R., Greenberg, R. S., & Crouch, R. K. (2010). Preventing and responding to complaints of sexual harassment in an academic health center: A 10-year review from the Medical University of South Carolina. *Academic Medicine, 85,* 721–727.

Best, D. L. (2010). Gender. In M. H. Bronstein (Ed.), *Handbook of cultural developmental science.* New York: Psychology Press.

Best, J. R. (2011, in press). Effects of physical activity on children's executive function: Contributions of experimental research on aerobic exercise. *Developmental Review.*

Bettens, K., Sleegers, K., & Van Broeckhoven, C. (2010). Current status on Alzheimer disease molecular genetics: From past, to present, to future. *Human Molecular Genetics, 19*(R1), R4–R11.

Betz, C., & Sowden, L. (2008). *Mosby's pediatric nursing reference* (6th ed.). Oxford, UK: Elsevier.

Beutel, M. E., Glaesmer, H., Wiltink, J., Marian, H., & Brahler, E. (2010). Life satisfaction, anxiety, depression, and resilience across the life span of men. *Aging Male, 13,* 32–39.

Beydoun, M. A., & Wang, Y. (2009). Gender-ethnic disparity in BMI and waist circumference distribution shifts in U.S. adults. *Obesity, 17,* 169–176.

Beyene, Y. (1986). Cultural significance and physiological manifestations of menopause: A biocultural analysis. *Culture, Medicine and Psychiatry, 10,* 47–71.

Beyerlein, A., & others. (2011, in press). Is low birth weight in the causal pathway of the association between maternal smoking in pregnancy and higher BMI in the offspring? *European Journal of Epidemiology.*

Bhatt, J. M., & Smyth, A. R. (2011). The management of pre-school wheeze. *Pediatric Respiratory Review, 12,* 70–77.

Bialystok, E. (1997). Effects of bilingualism and biliteracy on children's emerging concepts of print. *Developmental Psychology, 33,* 429–440.

Bialystok, E. (2001). *Bilingualism in development: Language, literacy, and cognition.* New York: Cambridge University Press.

Bialystok, E. (2007). Acquisition of literacy in preschool children: A framework for research. *Language Learning, 57,* 45–77.

Bialystok, E. (2011). *Becoming bilingual: Emergence of cognitive outcomes of bilingualism in immersion education.* Paper presented at the meeting of the Society for Research in Child Development, Montreal.

Bialystok, E., & Craik, F. I. M. (2010a). Cognitive and linguistic progressing in the bilingual mind. *Current Directions in Psychological Science, 19,* 19–23.

Bialystok, E., & Craik, F. I. M. (2010b). Structure and process in life-span cognitive development. In W. F. Overton & R. H. Lerner (Eds.), *Handbook of life-span development.* New York: Wiley.

Bian, Z., & Andersen, G. J. (2008). Aging and the perceptual organization of 3-D scenes. *Psychology and Aging, 23,* 342–352.

Biblarz, T. J., & Savci, E. (2010). Lesbian, gay, bisexual, and transgender families. *Journal of Marriage and the Family, 72*(3), 480–497.

Bierman, K. L., & others. (2008). Executive functions and school readiness intervention: Impact, moderation, and mediation in the Head Start-REDI Program. *Development and Psychopathology, 20,* 821–843.

Bigelow, A. W., & others. (2010). Maternal sensitivity throughout infancy: Continuity and relation to attachment security. *Infant Behavior and Development, 33,* 50–60.

Billy, J. O. G., Rodgers, J. L., & Udry, J. R. (1984). Adolescent sexual behavior and friendship choice. *Social Forces, 62,* 653–678.

Birch, S., & Bloom, P. (2003). Children are cursed: An asymmetric bias in mental state attribution. *Psychological Science, 14,* 283–286.

Birditt, K. S., Fingerman, K. L., & Zarit, S. H. (2010). Adult children's problems and successes: Implications for intergenerational ambivalence. *Journals of Gerontology B: Psychological Sciences, 65*(2), 145–153.

Birman, B. F., & others. (2007). *State and local implementation of the "No Child Left Behind Act." Volume II—Teacher quality under "NCLB": Interim report.* Jessup, MD: U.S. Department of Education.

Birren, J. E. (Ed.). (1996). *Encyclopedia of gerontology.* San Diego: Academic Press.

Birren, J. E. (2002). Unpublished review of J. W. Santrock's *Life-span development,* 9th ed. (New York: McGraw-Hill).

Bishop, A. J., & others. (2010). Predicting happiness among centenarians. *Gerontology, 56,* 88–92.

Bishop, D. V., & others. (2011, in press). Autism, language, and communication in children with sex chromosome trisomies. *Archives of Disease in Childhood.*

Bjorklund, D. F. (2012). *Children's thinking* (8th ed.). Boston: Cengage.

Bjorklund, D. F., & Pellegrini, A. D. (2002). The origins of human nature. New York: Oxford University Press.

Bjorklund, D. F., & Pellegrini, A. D. (2011). Evolutionary perspectives on social development. In P. K. Smith & C. H. Hart (Eds.), *Wiley-Blackwell handbook of childhood social development* (2nd ed.). New York: Wiley.

Bjorklund, D. F., & Rosenbaum, K. (2000). Middle childhood: Cognitive development. In A. Kazdin (Ed.), *Encyclopedia of psychology.* New York: Oxford University Press.

Blackwell, L. S., & Dweck, C. S. (2008). *The motivational impact of a computer-based program that teaches how the brain changes with learning.* Unpublished manuscript, Department of Psychology, Stanford University, Palo Alto, CA.

Blackwell, L. S., Trzesniewski, K. H., & Dweck, C. S. (2007). Implicit theories of intelligence predict achievement across an adolescent transition: A longitudinal study and an intervention. *Child Development, 78,* 246–263.

Blaga, O. M., Shaddy, D. J., Anderson, C. J., Kannass, K. N., Little, T. D., & Colombo, J. (2009). Structure and continuity of intellectual development in early childhood. *Intelligence, 37,* 106–113.

Blagosklonny, M. V. (2010). Calorie restriction: Decelerating mTOR-driven aging from cells to organisms (including humans). *Cell Cycle, 9,* 683–688.

Blair, B. L., & Fletcher, A. C. (2011, in press). "The only 13-year-old on planet Earth without a cell phone": Meanings of cell phones in adolescents' lives. *Journal of Adolescent Research.*

Blair, S. N. (1990, January). Personal communication. Aerobics Institute, Dallas.

Blair, S. N., Kohl, H. W., Paffenbarger, R. S., Clark, D. G., Cooper, K. H., & Gibbons, L. W. (1989). Physical fitness and all-cause mortality: A prospective study of healthy men and women. *Journal of the American Medical Association, 262,* 2395–2401.

Blake, J. S. (2011). *Nutrition and you.* Upper Saddle River, NJ: Pearson.

Blakemore, J. E. O., Berenbaum, S. A., & Liben, L. S. (2009). *Gender development.* Clifton, NJ: Psychology Press.

Blakemore, S. J., Burnett, S., & Dahl, R. E. (2010). The role of puberty in the developing adolescent brain. *Human Brain Mapping, 31,* 926–933.

Blakemore, S. J., Dahl, R. E., Frith, U., & Pine, D. S. (2011, in press). Developmental cognitive neuroscience. *Developmental Cognitive Neuroscience.*

Blanchard-Fields, F. (2007). Everyday problem solving and emotion. *Current Directions in Psychological Science, 16,* 26–31.

Blanco, M., & others. (2009). *Investigating critical incidents, driver restart period, sleep quantity, and crash countermeasures in commercial operations using naturalistic data collection: Final report* (Contract No. DTFH61-01-C-00049, Task Order # 23). Washington, DC: Federal Motor Carrier Safety Administration.

Blandthorn, J., Forster, D. A., & Love, V. (2011). Neonatal and maternal outcomes following maternal use of buprenorphine or methadone during pregnancy: Findings of a retrospective audit. *Women and Birth, 24,* 32–39.

Blass, E. (2008). Suckling. In M. M. Haith & J. B. Benson (Eds.), *Encyclopedia of infant and early childhood development.* Oxford, UK: Elsevier.

Blood-Siegfried, J., & Rende, E. K. (2010). The long-term effects of prenatal nicotine exposure on neurologic development. *Journal of Midwifery and Women's Health, 55,* 143–152.

Bloom, B. (1985). *Developing talent in young people.* New York: Ballantine.

Bloom, L. (1998). Language acquisition in its developmental context. In W. Damon (Ed.), *Handbook of child psychology* (5th ed., Vol. 2). New York: Wiley.

Bloom, L., Lifter, K., & Broughton, J. (1985). The convergence of early cognition and language in the second year of life: Problems in conceptualization and measurement. In M. Barrett (Ed.), *Single word speech.* London: Wiley.

Bloom, P., & German, T. P. (2000). Two reasons to abandon the false belief task as a test of theory of mind. *Cognition, 77,* B25–B31.

Bloomer, R. J., & others. (2011, in press). A 21-day Daniel Fast improves selected biomarkers of antioxidant status and oxidative stress in men and women. *Nutrition and Metabolism.*

Bloor, C., & White, F. (1983). Unpublished manuscript. University of California at San Diego, La Jolla, CA.

Boden, J. S., Fischer, J. L., & Niehuis, S. (2010). Predicting marital adjustment from young adults' initial levels of and changes in emotional intimacy over time: A 25-year longitudinal study. *Journal of Adult Development, 17,* 121–134.

Bodrova, E., & Leong, D. J. (2007). *Tools of the mind* (2nd ed.). Geneva, Switzerland: International Bureau of Education, UNESCO.

Boelen, P. A., & Prigerson, H. G. (2007). The influence of symptoms of prolonged grief disorder, depression, and anxiety on quality of life among bereaved adults: A prospective study. *European Archives of Psychiatry and Clinical Neuroscience, 259,* 442–452.

Boldo, E., & others. (2010). Health impact assessment of environmental tobacco smoke in European children: Sudden infant death syndrome and asthma episodes. *Public Health, 125*(3), 478–487.

Bonanno, G. A., Mancini, A. D., & Westphal, M. (2011). Resilience to extreme adversity. *Annual Review of Clinical Psychology* (Vol. 7). Palo Alto, CA: Annual Reviews.

Bonanno, G. A., Wortman, C. B., & Nesse, R. M. (2004). Prospective patterns of resilience and maladjustment during widowhood. *Psychology and Aging, 19,* 260–271.

Bond, M., Wyatt, K., Lloyd, J., & Taylor, R. (2010). Systematic review of the effectiveness of weight management schemes for the under fives. *Obesity Reviews, 13*(61), 1–75.

Bonda, D. J., & others. (2010). Oxidative stress in Alzheimer's disease: A possibility for prevention. *Neuropharmacology, 59*(4–5), 290–294.

Bonney, C., & Sternberg, R. J. (2011). Learning to think critically. In P. A. Alexander & R. E. Mayer (Eds.), *Handbook of research on learning and instruction.* New York: Routledge.

Bonvillian, J. (2005). Unpublished review of J. W. Santrock's *Topical life-span development,* 3rd ed. New York: McGraw-Hill.

Bookwala, J., & Jacobs, J. (2004). Age, marital processes, and depressed affect. *The Gerontologist, 44,* 328–338.

Borges, N. J., McNally, C. J., Maguire, C. P., Werth, J. L., & Britton, P. J. (2008). Work, health, diversity, and social justice: Expanding and extending the discussion. *The Counseling Psychologist, 36,* 127–131.

Borich, G. D. (2011). *Effective teaching methods* (7th ed.). Boston: Allyn & Bacon.

Borjas, G. J. (2011). Poverty and program participation by immigrant children. *Future of Children, 21,* 247–266.

Borjas, L., & others. (2010). Intragenic polymorphisms of factor VIII and IX genes and their utility in the indirect diagnosis of carriers of Haemophilias A and B. *Investigacion Clinica, 51,* 391–401.

Bornstein, M. H. (1975). Qualities of color vision in infancy. *Journal of Experimental Child Psychology, 19,* 401–409.

Bouman, W. P. (2008). Sexuality in later life. In R. Jacoby, C. Oppenheimer, T. Dening, & A. Thomas (Eds.), *Oxford textbook of old age psychiatry.* New York: Oxford University Press.

Boutot, E. A., & Myles, B. S. (2011). *Autism spectrum disorders.* Upper Saddle River, NJ: Merrill.

Bowen, C. E., Noack, M. G., & Staudinger, U. M. (2011). Aging in the work context. In K. W. Schaie & S. L. Willis (Eds.), *Handbook of the psychology of aging* (7th ed.). New York: Elsevier.

Bower, T. G. R. (1966). Slant perception and shape constancy in infants, *Science, 151,* 832–834.

Bowlby, J. (1969). *Attachment and loss* (Vol. 1). London: Hogarth Press.

Bowlby, J. (1980). *Attachment and loss, Vol. 3: Loss, sadness, and depression.* New York: Basic Books.

Bowlby, J. (1989). *Secure and insecure attachment.* New York: Basic Books.

Boyer, K., & Diamond, A. (1992). Development of memory for temporal order in infants and young children. In A. Diamond (Ed.), *Development and neural bases of higher cognitive function.* New York: New York Academy of Sciences.

Boyle, J., & Cropley, M. (2004). Children's sleep: Problems and solutions. *Journal of Family Health Care. 14*, 61–63.

Boyle, J. R., & Provost, M. C. (2012). *Strategies for teaching students with disabilities in inclusive classrooms: A case method approach.* Upper Saddle River, NJ: Pearson.

Brabek, M. M., & Brabek, K. M. (2006). Women and relationships. In J. Worell & C. D. Goodheart (Eds.), *Handbook of girls' and women's psychological health.* New York: Oxford University Press.

Brabyn, J. A., Schneck, M. E., Haegerstrom-Portnoy, G., & Lott, L. (2001). The Smith-Kettlewell Institute (SKI). Longitudinal study of vision function and its impact among the elderly: An overview. *Ophthalmology and Vision Science, 78*, 2464–2469.

Brainerd, C. J., & Reyna, V. F. (1993). Domains of fuzzy-trace theory. In M. L. Howe & R. Pasnak (Eds.), *Emerging themes in cognitive development.* New York: Springer.

Brainerd, C. J., & Reyna, V. F. (2004). Fuzzy-trace theory and memory development. *Developmental Review, 24*, 396–439.

Brand, M. (2011). Mitochondrial functioning and aging. In E. Masoro & S. Austad (Eds.), *Handbook of the biology of aging* (7th ed.). New York: Elsevier.

Brand, M., & Markowitsch, H. J. (2010). Aging and decision-making: A neurocognitive perspective. *Gerontology, 56*, 319–324.

Brandstädter, J. (1999). Sources of resilience in the aging self: Toward integrated perspectives. In T. M. Hess & F. Blanchard-Fields (Eds.), *Social cognition and aging.* San Diego: Academic Press.

Brandtstädter, J., & Renner, G. (1990). Tenacious goal pursuit and flexible goal adjustment: Explication and age-related analysis of assimilative and accommodative strategies of coping. *Psychology and Aging, 5*, 58–67.

Brannon, L. (2012). *Gender* (6th ed.). Upper Saddle River, NJ: Prentice Hall.

Bransford, J., & others. (2006). Learning theories in education. In P. A. Alexander & P. H. Winne (Eds.), *Handbook of educational psychology* (2nd ed.). Mahwah, NJ: Erlbaum.

Braun-Courville, D. K., & Roijas, M. (2009). Exposure to sexually explicit web sites and adolescent sexual attitudes and behavior. *Journal of Adolescent Health, 45*, 156–162.

Brechwald, W. A., & Prinstein, M. J. (2011). Beyond homophily: A decade of advances in understanding peer influence processes. *Journal of Research on Adolescence, 21*, 166–179.

Brecklin, L. R., & Ullman, S. E. (2010). The roles of victim and offender substance use in sexual assault outcomes. *Journal of Interpersonal Violence, 25*, 1503–1522.

Bredekamp, S. (2011). *Effective practices in early childhood education.* Upper Saddle River, NJ: Merrill.

Breheny, M., & Stephens, C. (2004). Barriers to effective contraception and strategies for overcoming them among adolescent mothers. *Public Health Nursing, 21*, 220–227.

Bremner, J. G., Slater, A. M., Johnson, S. P., Mason, U. C., Spring, J., & Bremner, M. E. (2010, in press). Two- to 8-month-old infants' cross-modal perception of dynamic auditory-visual spatial co-location. *Child Development.*

Brendgen, M., Lamarche, V., Wanner, B., & Vitaro, F. (2010). Links between friendship relations and early adolescents' trajectories of depressed mood. *Developmental Psychology, 46*, 491–501.

Brennan, M., Horowitz, A., & Su, Y. P. (2005). Dual sensory loss and its impact on everyday competence. *Gerontologist, 45*, 337–346.

Brennan, T., & others. (2010). Disease management to promote blood pressure control among African Americans. *Population Health Management, 13*, 65–72.

Brent, R. L. (2009). Saving lives and changing family histories: Appropriate counseling of pregnant women and men and women of reproductive age concerning the risk of diagnostic radiation exposure during and before pregnancy. *American Journal of Obstetrics and Gynecology, 200*, 4–24.

Brent, R. L. (2011, in press). The pulmonologist's role in caring for pregnant women with regard to reproductive risks of diagnostic radiological studies or radiation therapy. *Clinics in Chest Medicine.*

Brent, R. L., Christian, M. S., & Diener, R. M. (2011, in press). Evaluation of the reproductive and developmental risks of caffeine. *Birth Defects Research B: Developmental and Reproductive Toxicology.*

Breslau, J., & others. (2011, in press). A multinational study of mental disorders, marriage, and divorce. *Acta Psychiatrica Scandinavica.*

Brewer, M. B., & Campbell, D. T. (1976). *Ethnocentrism and intergroup attitudes.* New York: Wiley.

Bridgeland, J. M., Dilulio, J. J., & Wulsin, S. C. (2008). *Engaged for success.* Washington, DC: Civic Enterprises.

Bridgett, D. J., & others. (2009). Maternal and contextual influences and the effect of temperament development during infancy on parenting in toddlerhood. *Infant Behavior and Development, 32*, 103–116.

Brim, O. (1999). *The MacArthur Foundation study of midlife development.* Vero Beach, FL: MacArthur Foundation.

Brislin, R. (1993). *Understanding culture's influence on behavior.* Fort Worth, TX: Harcourt Brace.

Brodsky, J. L., Viner-Brown, S., & Handler, A. S. (2009). Change in maternal cigarette smoking among pregnant WIC participants in Rhode Island. *Maternal and Child Health Journal, 13*, 822–831.

Brody, L. R., & Hall, J. A. (2008). Gender, emotion, and expression. In M. Lewis & J. M. Haviland-Jones (Eds.), *Handbook of emotions* (2nd ed.). New York: Guilford.

Brody, N. (2000). Intelligence. In A. Kazdin (Ed.), *Encyclopedia of psychology.* New York: Oxford University Press.

Brody, N. (2007). Does education influence intelligence? In P. C. Kyllonen, R. D. Roberts, & L. Stankov (Eds.), *Extending intelligence.* Mahwah, NJ: Erlbaum.

Brody, S. (2010). The relative health benefits of different sexual activities. *Journal of Sexual Medicine, 7*, 1336–1361.

Brody, S., & Costa, R. M. (2009). Satisfaction (sexual, life, relationship, and mental health) is associated directly with penile-vaginal intercourse, but inversely related to other sexual behavior frequencies. *Journal of Sexual Medicine, 6*, 1947–1954.

Brodzinsky, D. M., & Pinderhughes, E. (2002). Parenting and child development in adoptive families. In M. H. Bornstein (Ed.), *Handbook of parenting* (Vol. 1). Mahwah, NJ: Erlbaum.

Broekhuizen, L. N., & others. (2011). Physical activity, metabolic syndrome, and coronary risk: The EPIC-Norfolk prospective population study. *European Journal of Cardiovascular Prevention and Rehabilitation, 18*, 209–217.

Bronfenbrenner, U. (1986). Ecology of the family as a context for human development: Research perspectives. *Developmental Psychology, 22*, 723–742.

Bronfenbrenner, U. (2004). *Making human beings human.* Thousand Oaks. CA: Sage.

Bronfenbrenner, U., & Morris, P. (1998). The ecology of developmental processes. In W. Damon (Ed.), *Handbook of child psychology* (5th ed., Vol. 1). New York: Wiley.

Bronfenbrenner, U., & Morris, P. A. (2006). The ecology of developmental processes. In W. Damon & R. Lerner (Eds.), *Handbook of child psychology* (6th ed.). New York: Wiley.

Bronstein, P. (2006). The family environment: Where gender role socialization begins. In J. Worell & C. D. Goodheart (Eds.), *Handbook of girls' and women's psychological health.* New York: Oxford University Press.

Brook, J. S., Brook, D. W., Gordon, A. S., Whiteman, M., & Cohen, P. (1990). The psychological etiology of adolescent drug use: A family interactional approach. *Genetic, Social, and General Psychology Monographs, 116*, 111–267.

Brooker, R. (2011). *Biology* (2nd ed.). New York: McGraw-Hill.

Brooks, J. G., & Brooks, M. G. (1993). *The case for constructivist classrooms.* Alexandria, VA: Association for Supervision and Curriculum.

Brooks, J. G., & Brooks, M. G. (2001). *The case for constructivist classrooms* (2nd ed.). Upper Saddle River, NJ: Erlbaum.

Brooks, R., & Meltzoff, A. N. (2005). The development of gaze in relation to language. *Developmental Science, 8*, 535–543.

Brooks-Gunn, J. (2003). Do you believe in magic?: What we can expect from early childhood programs. *Social Policy Report, Society for Research in Child Development, XVII* (1), 1–13.

Brooks-Gunn, J., Han, W-J., & Waldfogel, J. (2010). First-year maternal employment and child development in the first seven years. *Monographs of the Society for Research in Child Development, 75*(2), 1–147.

Brooks-Gunn, J., & Warren, M. F. (1989). The psychological significance of secondary sexual characteristics in 9- to 11-year-old girls. *Child Development, 59,* 161–169.

Broverman, I., Vogel, S., Broverman, D., Clarkson, F., & Rosenkranz, P. (1972). Sex-role stereotypes: A current appraisal. *Journal of Social Issues, 28,* 59–78.

Brown, B. B. (1999). Measuring the peer environment of American adolescents. In S. L. Friedman & T. D. Wachs (Eds.), *Measuring environment across the life span.* Washington, DC: American Psychological Association.

Brown, B. B., Bakken, J. P., Ameringer, S. W., & Mahon, S. D. (2008). A comprehensive conceptualization of the peer influence process in adolescence. In M. J. Prinstein & K. A. Dodge (Eds.), *Understanding peer influence in children and adolescents.* New York: Guilford.

Brown, B. B., & Dietz, E. L. (2009). Informal peer groups in middle childhood and adolescence. In K. H. Rubin, W. M. Bukowski, & B. Laursen (Eds.), *Handbook of peer interaction, relationships, and groups.* New York: Guilford.

Brown, B. B., & Larson, J. (2009). Peer relationships in adolescence. In R. M. Lerner & L. Steinberg (Eds.), *Handbook of adolescent psychology* (3rd ed.). New York: Wiley.

Brown, J. D., & Bobkowski, P. S. (2011). Older and newer media: Patterns of use and effects on adolescents' health and well-being. *Journal of Research on Adolescence, 21,* 95–113.

Brown, J. D., & Strasburger, V. C. (2007). From Calvin Klein to Paris Hilton and MySpace: Adolescents, sex, and the media. *Adolescent Medicine: State of the Art Reviews, 18,* 484–507.

Brown, L. S. (1989). New voices, new visions: Toward a lesbian/gay paradigm for psychology. *Psychology of Women Quarterly, 13,* 445–458.

Brown, R. (1968). *Words and things.* Glencoe, IL: Free Press.

Brown, R. (1973). *A first language: The early stages.* Cambridge, MA: Harvard University Press.

Brown, S. L., Brown, R. M., House, J. S., & Smith, D. M. (2008). Coping with spousal loss: Potential buffering effects of self-reported helping behavior. *Personality and Social Psychology Bulletin, 34,* 849–861.

Brown, S. L., Lee, G. R., & Bulanda, J. R. (2006). Cohabitation among older adults: A national portrait. *Journals of Gerontology B: Psychological Sciences and Social Sciences, 61,* S71–S79.

Brown, S. L., Nesse, R. M., House, J. S., & Utz, R. L. (2004). Religion and emotional compensation: Results from a prospective study of widowhood. *Personality and Social Psychology Bulletin, 30,* 1165–1174.

Brown, S. L., Nesse, R. M., Vinoker, A. D., & Smith, D. M. (2003). Providing social support

may be more beneficial than receiving it: Results from a prospective study of mortality. *Psychological Science, 14,* 320–327.

Brownell, C. (2009). *Brownell—Early social development lab.* Retrieved November 9, 2009, from www.pitt.edu/~toddlers/ESDL/brownell.html

Brownell, C. A., Nichols, S., Svetlova, M., Zerwas, S., & Ramani, G. (2009). The head bone's connected to the neck bone: When do toddlers represent their own body topography? *Child Development, 81*(3), 797–810.

Brownell, C. A., Ramani, G. B., & Zerwas, S. (2006). Becoming a social partner with peers: Cooperation and social understanding in one- and two-year-olds. *Child Development, 77,* 803–821.

Brownridge, D. A. (2008). The elevated risk for violence against cohabiting women: A comparison of three nationally representative surveys of Canada. *Violence Against Women, 14,* 809–832.

Bruce, A. (2007). Time(lessness): Buddhist perspectives and end-of-life. *Nursing Philosophy, 8,* 151–157.

Bruck, M., & Ceci, S. J. (1999). The suggestibility of children's memory. *Annual Review of Psychology, 50,* 419–439.

Bruck, M., Ceci, S. J., & Principe, G. F. (2006). The child and the law. In W. Damon & R. Lerner (Eds.), *Handbook of child psychology* (6th ed.). New York: Wiley.

Bruck, M., & Melnyk, L. (2004). Individual difference in children's suggestibility: A review and a synthesis. *Applied Cognitive Psychology, 18,* 947–996.

Bruera, E., & others. (2010). AAHPM position paper: Requirements for the successful development of academic palliative care programs. *Journal of Pain and Symptom Management, 39,* 743–745.

Brumariu, L. E., & Kerns, K. A. (2011). Parent-child attachment in early and middle childhood. In P. K. Smith & C. H. Hart (Eds.), *Wiley-Blackwell handbook of social development* (2nd ed.). New York: Wiley.

Brune, C. W., & Woodward, A. L. (2007). Social cognition and social responsiveness in 10-month-old infants. *Journal of Cognition and Development, 2,* 3–27.

Brunstein Klomek, A., Marrocco, F., Kleinman, M., Schofeld, I. S., & Gould, M. S. (2007). Bullying, depression, and suicidality in adolescents. *Journal of the American Academy of Child and Adolescent Psychiatry, 46,* 40–49.

Brunton, P. J., & Russell, J. A. (2011, in press). Neuroendocrine control of maternal stress responses and fetal programming by stress in pregnancy. *Progress in Neuro-Pharmacology and Biological Psychiatry.*

Bryant, J. B. (2009). Language in social contexts: Communication competence in the preschool years. In J. Berko Gleason & N. Ratner (Eds.), *The development of language* (7th ed.). Boston: Allyn & Bacon.

Buchman, A. S., & others. (2009). Association between late-life social activity and motor

decline in older adults. *Archives of Internal Medicine, 169,* 1139–1146.

Buckner, J. C., Mezzacappa, E., & Beardslee, W. R. (2009). Self-regulation and its relations to adaptive functioning in low-income youths. *American Journal of Orthopsychiatry, 79,* 19–30.

Bucur, B., & Madden, D. J. (2007). Information processing/cognition. In J. E. Birren (Ed.), *Encyclopedia of gerontology* (2nd ed.). San Diego: Academic Press.

Bucur, B., & Madden, D. J. (2010). Effects of adult age and blood pressure on executive function and speed of processing. *Experimental Aging Research, 36,* 153–168.

Budde, H., Voelcker-Rehage, C., Pietrabyk-Kendziorra, P., Ribeiro, P., & Tidow, G. (2008). Acute aerobic exercise improves attentional performance in adolescence. *Neuroscience Letters, 441,* 219–223.

Bueler, H. (2010). Mitochondrial dynamics, cell death, and the pathogenesis of Parkinson's disease. *Apoptosis, 15*(11), 1336–1353.

Buglass, E. (2010). Grief and bereavement theories. *Nursing Standard, 24,* 44–47.

Buhrmester, D. (1998). Need fulfillment, interpersonal competence, and the developmental contexts of early adolescent friendship. In W. M. Bukowski & A. F. Newcomb (Eds.), *The company they keep: Friendship in childhood and adolescence.* New York: Cambridge University Press.

Buhs, E. S., & Ladd, G. W. (2002). Peer rejection as antecedent of young children's school adjustment: An examination of mediating processes. *Developmental Psychology, 37,* 550–560.

Bukowski, R., & others. (2008, January). *Folic acid and preterm birth.* Paper presented at the meeting of the Society for Maternal-Fetal Medicine, Dallas.

Bukowski, W. M., Buhrmester, D., & Underwood, M. K. (2011). Peer relations as a developmental context. In M. K. Underwood & L. H. Rosen (Eds.), *Social development.* New York: Guilford.

Bukowski, W. M., Motzoi, C., & Meyer, F. (2009). Friendship as process, function, and outcome. In K. H. Rubin, W. M. Bukowski, & B. Laursen (Eds.), *Handbook of peer interactions, relationships, and groups.* New York: Guilford.

Bullock, M., & Lutkenhaus, P. (1990). Who am I? Self-understanding in toddlers. *Merrill-Palmer Quarterly, 36,* 217–238.

Bumpass, L., & Aquilino, W. (1994). *A social map of midlife: Family and work over the middle life course.* Center for Demography and Ecology, University of Wisconsin, Madison, WI.

Bumpus, M. F., Crouter, A. C., & McHale, S. M. (2001). Parental autonomy granting during adolescence: Exploring gender differences in context. *Developmental Psychology, 37,* 163–173.

Burchinal, M. R., Peisner-Feinberg, E., Pianta, R., & Howes, C. (2002). Development of academic skills from preschool through second grade: Family and classroom predictors of developmental trajectories. *Journal of School Psychology, 40*(5), 415–436.

Burgard, S. (2009). Job characteristics and job stress. In D. Carr (Ed.), *Encyclopedia of the life course and human development.* Boston: Gale Cengage.

Burger, J. M. (2011). *Personality* (8th ed.). Boston: Cengage.

Burke, D. M., & Shafto, M. A. (2004). Aging and language production. *Current Directions in Psychological Science, 13,* 21–24.

Burke, H. M., Zautra, A. J., Davis, M. C., Schultz, A. S., & Reich, J. W. (2003). Arthritis and musculoskeletal conditions. In I. B. Weiner (Ed.), *Handbook of psychology* (Vol. IX). New York: Wiley.

Burke-Adams, A. (2007). The benefits of equalizing standards and creativity: Discovering a balance in instruction. *Gifted Child Quarterly, 30,* 58–63.

Bursuck, W. D., & Damer, M. (2011). *Teaching reading to students who are at-risk or have disabilities* (2nd ed.). Upper Saddle River, NJ: Merrill.

Burt, S. A., McGue, M., & Iacono, W. G. (2010). Environmental contributions to the stability of antisocial behavior over time: Are they shared or non-shared? *Journal of Abnormal Child Psychology, 38,* 327–337.

Burton, R. V. (1984). A paradox in theories and research in moral development. In W. M. Kurtines & J. L. Gewirtz (Eds.), *Morality, moral behavior, and moral development.* New York: Wiley.

Bushnell, I. W. R. (2003). Newborn face recognition. In O. Pascalis & A. Slater (Eds.), *The development of face processing in infancy and early childhood.* New York: NOVA Science.

Buss, D. M. (2008). *Evolutionary psychology* (3rd ed.). Boston: Allyn & Bacon.

Buss, D. M. (2012). *Evolutionary psychology* (4th ed.). Boston: Allyn & Bacon.

Buss, D. M., & others. (1990). International preferences in selecting mates: A study of 37 cultures. *Journal of Cross-Cultural Psychology, 21,* 5–47.

Buss, K. A., & Goldsmith, H. H. (2007). Biobehavioral approaches to early socioemotional development. In C. A. Brownell & C. B. Kopp (Eds.), *Socioemotional development in the toddler years.* New York: Guilford.

Bussey, K., & Bandura, A. (1999). Social cognitive theory of gender development and differentiation. *Psychological Review, 106,* 676–713.

Butcher, K., Sallis, J. F., Mayer, J. A., & Woodruff, S. (2008). Correlates of physical activity guideline compliance for adolescents in 100 cities. *Journal of Adolescent Health, 42,* 360–368.

Butler, R. N., & Lewis, M. (2002). *The new love and sex after 60.* New York: Ballantine.

Butz, A. M., & others. (2010, in press). Household smoking behavior: Effects on indoor air quality and health of urban children with asthma. *Maternal and Child Health Journal.*

Buzwell, S., & Rosenthal, D. (1996). Constructing a sexual self: Adolescents' sexual self-perceptions and sexual risk-taking. *Journal of Research on Adolescence, 6,* 489–513.

Byrom, S., & Symon, A. (2011). Developing the midwife's role in public health. *Practicing Midwife, 14,* 16–17.

C

Cabeza, R. (2002). Hemispheric asymmetry reduction in older adults: The HAROLD model. *Psychology and Aging, 17,* 85–100.

Cabeza, R., Nyberg, L., & Park, D. (Eds.). (2009). *Cognitive neuroscience of aging.* New York: Oxford University Press.

Calkins, S. D., & Marcovitch, S. (2010). Emotion regulation and executive functioning in early development: Integrated mechanisms of control supporting adaptive functioning. In S. D. Calkins & M. A. Bell (Eds.), *Child development at the intersection of emotion and cognition.* Washington, DC: American Psychological Association.

Callahan, D. (2009). Death, mourning, and medical practice. *Perspectives in Biological Medicine, 52,* 103–115.

Cameron, J., & Pierce, D. (2008). Intrinsic versus extrinsic motivation. In N. J. Salkind (Ed.), *Encyclopedia of educational psychology.* Thousand Oaks, CA: Sage.

Cameron, J. M., Heidelberg, N., Simmons, L., Lyle, S. B., Kathakali, M-V., & Correia, C. (2010). Drinking game participation among undergraduate students attending National Alcohol Screening Day. *Journal of American College Health, 58,* 499–506.

Campbell, A. (2010). Oxytocin and human social behavior. *Personality and Social Psychology Review, 14*(3), 281–295.

Campbell, C. A. (2009). AIDS. In D. Carr (Ed.), *Encyclopedia of the life course and human development.* Boston: Gale Cengage.

Campbell, D. T., & LeVine, K. A. (1968). Ethnocentrism and intergroup relations. In R. Abelson & others (Eds.), *Theories and cognitive consistency: A sourcebook.* Chicago: Rand-McNally.

Campbell, F. A. (2007). The malleability of the cognitive development of children of low-income African-American families: Intellectual test performance over twenty-one years. In P. C. Kyllonen, R. D. Roberts, & L. Stankov (Eds.), *Extending intelligence.* Mahwah, NJ: Erlbaum.

Campbell, F. A., Pungello, E. P., Miller-Johnson, S., Burchinal, M., & Ramey, C. T. (2001). The development of cognitive and academic abilities: Growth curves from an early childhood educational experiment. *Developmental Psychology, 37,* 231–243.

Campbell, G. R., & Mahad, D. J. (2011, in press). Mitochondria as crucial players in demyelinated axons: Lessons from neuropathology and experimental demyelination. *Autoimmune Diseases.*

Campbell, L., Campbell, B., & Dickinson, D. (2004). *Teaching and learning through multiple intelligence* (3rd ed.). Boston: Allyn & Bacon.

Campos, J. J. (2005). Unpublished review of J. W. Santrock's *Life-span development,* 11th ed. (New York: McGraw-Hill).

Campos, J. J. (2009). Unpublished review of J. W. Santrock's *Life-span development,* 13th ed. (New York: McGraw-Hill).

Campos, J. J., Langer, A., & Krowiz, A. (1970). Cardiac responses on the visual cliff in prelocomotor human infants. *Science, 170,* 196–197.

Candore, G., Caruso, C., & Collona-Romano, G. (2010). Inflammation, genetic background, and longevity. *Biogerontology, 11*(5), 565–573.

Candow, D. G., & Chilibeck, P. D. (2005). Differences in size, strength, and power of upper and lower body muscle groups in young and older men. *Journals of Gerontology A: Biological Sciences and Medical Sciences, 60,* 148A–156A.

Cansino, S. (2009). Episodic memory decay along the adult lifespan: A review of behavioral and neurophysiological evidence. *International Journal of Psychophysiology, 71,* 64–69.

Capaldi, D. M., Stoolmiller, M., Clark, S., & Owen, L. D. (2002). Heterosexual risk behaviors in at-risk young men from early adolescence to young adulthood: Prevalence, prediction, and association with STD contraction. *Developmental Psychology, 38,* 394–406.

Caplan, D., DeDe, G., Waters, G., Michaud, J., & Tripodis, Y. (2011, in press). Effects of age, speed of processing, and working memory on comprehension of sentences with relative clauses. *Psychology and Aging.*

Cardelle-Elawar, M. (1992). Effects of teaching metacognitive skills to students with low mathematics ability. *Teaching and Teacher Education, 8*(2), 109–121.

Carey, D. P. (2007). Is bigger really better? The search for brain size and intelligence in the twenty-first century. In S. Della Sala (Ed.), *Tall tales about the mind and brain: Separating fact from fiction.* Oxford, UK: Oxford University Press.

Carlo, G., Knight, G. P., McGinley, M., Zamboanga, B. L., & Jarvis, L. H. (2010). The multidimensionality of prosocial behaviors and evidence of measurement equivalence in Mexican American and European American early adolescents. *Journal of Research on Adolescence, 20,* 334–358.

Carlson, M. J., Pilkauskas, N. V., McLanahan, S. S., & Brooks-Gunn, J. (2011). Couples as partners and parents over children's early years. *Journal of Marriage and the Family, 73,* 317–334.

Carlson, S. M. (2010). Development of conscious control and imagination. In R. F. Baumeister, R. Mele, & K. D. Vohs (Eds.), *Free will and consciousness: How might they work?* New York: Oxford.

Carlson, S. M., Davis, A. C., & Leach, J. G. (2005). Executive function and symbolic representation in preschool children. *Psychological Science, 16*, 609–616.

Carlson, S. M., & White, R. (2011). Unpublished research, Institute of Child Development, University of Minnesota, Minneapolis.

Carlson, S. M., & Zelazo, P. D. (2008). Symbolic thought. In M. M. Haith & J. B. Benson (Eds.), *Encyclopedia of infant and early childhood development.* Oxford, UK: Elsevier.

Carnagey, N. L., Anderson, C. A., & Bushman, B. J. (2007). The effect of video game violence on physiological desensitization to real-life violence. *Journal of Experimental Social Psychology, 43,* 489–496.

Carnegie Foundation. (1989). *Turning points: Preparing youth for the 21st century.* New York: Author.

Carpendale, J. I., & Chandler, M. J. (1996). On the distinction between false belief: Understanding and subscribing to an interpretive theory of mind. *Child Development, 67,* 1686–1706.

Carpendale, J. I. M., Muller, U., & Bibok, M. B. (2008). Piaget's theory of cognitive development. In N. J. Salkind (Ed.), *Encyclopedia of educational psychology.* Thousand Oaks, CA: Sage.

Carpendale, J. L. M., & Lewis, C. (2010). The development of social understanding: A relational perspective. In R. M. Lerner, W.F. Overton, A. M. Freund, & M. E. Lamb (Eds.), *Handbook of life-span development.* New York: Wiley.

Carpenter, M. (2011). Social cognition and social motivations in infancy. In U. Goswami (Ed.), *Wiley-Blackwell handbook of childhood cognitive development* (2nd ed.). New York: Wiley.

Carr, D. (2008). Character education as the cultivation of virtue. In L. Nucci & D. Narváez (Eds.), *Handbook of moral and character education.* Clifton, NJ: Psychology Press.

Carr, D. (2009). Death and dying. In D. Carr (Eds.), *Encyclopedia of the life course and human development.* Boston: Gale Cengage.

Carr, D., & Pudrovska, T. (2011, in press). Divorce and widowhood in later life. In R. Blieszner & V. H. Bedford (Eds.), *Handbook of aging and the family.* Santa Barbara, CA: Praeger.

Carrell, S. E., Malmstrom, F. V., & West, J. E. (2008). Peer effects in academic cheating. *Journal of Human Resources, 43,* 173–207.

Carriere, J. S., Cheyne, J. A., Solman, G. J., & Smilek, D. (2010). Age trends for failures in sustained attention. *Psychology and Aging, 25*(3), 569–574.

Carroll, J. L. (2010). *Sexuality now* (3rd ed.). Boston: Cengage.

Carskadon, M. A. (Ed.). (2002). *Adolescent sleep patterns.* New York: Cambridge University Press.

Carskadon, M. A. (2004). Sleep difficulties in young people. *Archives of Pediatric and Adolescent Health, 158,* 597–598.

Carskadon, M. A. (2005). Sleep and circadian rhythms in children and adolescents: Relevance for athletic performance of young people. *Clinical Sports Medicine, 24,* 319–328.

Carskadon, M. A. (2006, April). *Adolescent sleep: The perfect storm.* Paper presented at the meeting of the Society for Research on Adolescence, San Francisco.

Carstensen, L. L. (1991). Selectivity theory: Social activity in life-span context. *Annual Review of Gerontology and Geriatrics, 11,* 195–217.

Carstensen, L. L. (1998). A life-span approach to social motivation. In J. Heckhausen & C. Dweck (Eds.), *Motivation and self-regulation across the life span.* New York: Cambridge University Press.

Carstensen, L. L. (2006). The influence of a sense of time on human development. *Science, 312,* 1913–1915.

Carstensen, L. L. (2008, May). *Long life in the 21st century.* Paper presented at the meeting of the Association for Psychological Science, Chicago.

Carstensen, L. L. (2009). *A long bright future.* New York: Random House.

Carstensen, L. L., & Freund, A. M. (1994). Commentary: The resilience of the aging self. *Developmental Review, 14,* 81–92.

Carstensen, L. L., & others. (2011). Emotional experience improves with age: Evidence based on over 10 years of experience sampling. *Psychology & Aging, 26,* 21–33.

Carstensen, L. L., Mikels, J. A., & Mather, M. (2006). Aging and the intersection of cognition, motivation and emotion. In J. Birren & K. W. Schaie (Eds.), *Handbook of the psychology of aging* (6th ed.). San Diego: Academic Press.

Cartwright, K. B., Galupo, M. P., Tyree, S. D., & Jennings, J. G. (2009). Reliability and validity of the Complex Postformal Thought Questionnaire: Assessing adults' cognitive development. *Journal of Adult Development, 16,* 183–189.

Cartwright, R., Agargun, M. Y., Kirkby, J., & Friedman, J. K. (2006). Relation of dreams to waking concerns. *Psychiatry Research, 141,* 261–270.

Carver, K., Joyner, K., & Udry, J. R. (2003). National estimates of adolescent romantic relationships. In P. Florsheim (Eds.), *Adolescent romantic relationships and sexual behavior.* Mahwah, NJ: Erlbaum.

Casas, M. (2011). *Enhancing student learning in middle school.* New York: Routledge.

Case, R. (1987). Neo-Piagetian theory: Retrospect and prospect. *International Journal of Psychology, 22,* 773–791.

Case, R. (1999). Conceptual development in the child and the field: A personal view of the Piagetian legacy. In E. K. Skolnick, K. Nelson, S. A. Gelman, & P. H. Miller (Eds.), *Conceptual development.* Mahwah, NJ: Erlbaum.

Case, R., Kurland, D. M., & Goldberg, J. (1982). Operational efficiency and the growth of short-term memory span. *Journal of Experimental Child Psychology, 33,* 386–404.

Casey, B. J., & others. (2010). The storm and stress of adolescence: Insights from human imaging and mouse genetics. *Developmental Psychobiology, 52,* 225–235.

Casey, B. J., Duhoux, S., & Malter Cohen, M. (2010). Adolescence: What do transmission, transition, and translation have to do with it? *Neuron, 67,* 749–760.

Casey, J. R., & others. (2011, in press). A simple scoring system to improve clinical assessment of otitis media. *Clinical Pediatrics.*

Casey, P. H. (2008). Growth of low birth weight preterm children. *Seminars in Perinatology, 32,* 20–27.

Caspers, K. M., Paraiso, S., Yucuis, R., Troutman, B., Arndt, S., & Philibert, R. (2009). Association between the serotonin transporter polymorphism (5-HTTLPR) and adult unresolved attachment. *Developmental Psychology, 45,* 64–76.

Caspi, A., & others. (2003). Influence of life stress on depression: Moderation by a polymorphism in the 5-HTT gene. *Science, 301,* 386–389.

Caspi, A., Hariri, A. R., Holmes, A., Uher, R., & Moffitt, T. E. (2011). Genetic sensitivity to the environment: The case of the serotonin transporter gene and its implications for studying complex diseases and traits. In K. A. Dodge & M. Rutter (Eds.), *Gene-environment interaction and developmental psychopathology.* New York: Guilford.

Caspi, A., & Roberts, B. W. (2001). Personality development across the life course: The argument for change and continuity. *Psychological Inquiry, 12,* 49–66.

Cassell, E. J., & Rich, B. A. (2010). Intractable end-of-life suffering and the ethics of palliative sedation. *Pain Medicine, 11*(3), 440–441.

Cassidy, J. (2008). The nature of the child's ties. In J. Cassidy & P. R. Shaver (Eds.), *Handbook of attachment* (2nd ed.). New York: Guilford.

Castle, J., & others. (2010). Parents' evaluation of adoption success: A follow-up study of intercountry and domestic adoptions. *American Journal of Orthopsychiatry, 79,* 522–531.

Catalano, R. F., Gavin, L. E., & Markham, C. M. (2010). Future directions for positive youth development as a strategy to promote adolescent sexual and reproductive health. *Journal of Adolescent Health, 46*(Suppl. 1), S92–S96.

Catani, C., Gewirtz, A. H., Wieling, E., Schauer, E., Elbert, T., & Neuner, F. (2010). Tsunami, war, and cumulative risk in the lives of Sri Lankan school children. *Child Development, 81,* 1176–1191.

Caufman, E., & others. (2010). Age differences in affective decision making as indexed by performance on the Iowa Gambling Task. *Developmental Psychology, 46,* 193–207.

Caughey, A. B., Hopkins, L. M., & Norton, M. E. (2006). Chorionic villus sampling compared with amniocentesis and the difference in the rate of pregnancy loss. *Obstetrics and Gynecology, 108,* 612–616.

Cavanagh, S. E. (2009). Puberty. In D. Carr (Ed.), *Encyclopedia of the life course and human development.* Boston: Gale Cengage.

Cavazos-Rehg, P. A., & others. (2010a). Number of sexual partners and associations with initiation and intensity of substance abuse. *AIDS Behavior, 15*(4), 869–874.

Cavazos-Rehg, P. A., & others. (2010b). Understanding adolescent parenthood from a multisystematic perspective. *Journal of Adolescent Health, 46,* 525–531.

Cave, R. K. (2002, August). *Early adolescent language: A content analysis of child development and educational psychology textbooks.* Unpublished doctoral dissertation, University of Nevada, Reno.

Cease, A. T., King, W. D., & Monroe, K. W. (2011). Analysis of child passenger safety restraint use at a pediatric emergency department. *Pediatric Emergency Care, 27,* 102–105.

Ceci, S. J. (2000). Bronfenbrenner, Urie. In A. Kazdin (Ed.), *Encyclopedia of psychology.* Washington, DC, & New York: American Psychological Association and Oxford University Press.

Ceci, S. J., Fitneva, S., Aydin, C., & Chernyak, N. L. (2010). The legal context of memory development. In A. Slater and G. Bremner (Eds.), *An introduction to developmental psychology* (2nd ed.). London: Blackwell.

Ceci, S. J., & Gilstrap, L. L. (2000). Determinants of intelligence: Schooling and intelligence. In A. Kazdin (Ed.), *Encyclopedia of Psychology.* New York: Oxford University Press.

Ceci, S. J., Papierno, P. B., & Kulkofsky, S. (2007). Representational constraints on children's suggestibility. *Psychological Science, 18,* 503–509.

Center for Survey Research at the University of Connecticut. (2000). *Hours on the job.* Storrs: University of Connecticut, Center for Survey Research.

Centers for Disease Control and Prevention. (2008). *National Health Interview Study.* Atlanta: Author.

Centers for Disease Control and Prevention. (2008, June 5). *Teen sexual activity increases, condom use decreases.* Atlanta: Author.

Centers for Disease Control and Prevention. (2010a). *Aging.* Atlanta: Author.

Centers for Disease Control and Prevention. (2010b). *Autism spectrum disorders.* Atlanta: Author.

Centers for Disease Control and Prevention. (2011a). *Body mass index for children and teens.* Atlanta: Author.

Centers for Disease Control and Prevention. (2011b). *SIDS.* Retrieved January 10, 2011, from www.cdc.gov/SIDS/index.htm

Cerda, M., Sagdeo, A., Johnson, J., & Galea, S. (2010). Genetic and environmental influences on psychiatric comorbidity: A systematic review. *Journal of Affective Disorders, 126*(1–2): 14–38.

Chambers, B., Cheung, A. C. K., & Slavin, R. F. (2006). Effective preschool programs for children at risk of school failure: A best-evidence synthesis. In B. Spodek & O. N. Saracho (Eds.), *Handbook of research on the education of young children.* Mahwah, NJ: Erlbaum.

Chan, R., & Webster, J. (2010). End-of-life care pathways for improving outcomes in caring for the dying. *Cochrane Database of Systematic Reviews,* (1), CD008006.

Chang, M. Y., Chen, C. H., & Huang, K. F. (2006). A comparison of massage effects on labor pain using the McGill Pain Questionnaire. *Journal of Nursing Research, 14,* 190–197.

Chao, R., & Tseng, V. (2002). Parenting of Asians. In M. H. Bornstein (Ed.), *Handbook of parenting* (2nd ed., Vol. 4). Mahwah, NJ: Erlbaum.

Chao, R. K. (2005, April). *The importance of Guan in describing control of immigrant Chinese.* Paper presented at the meeting of the Society for Research in Child Development, Atlanta.

Chao, R. K. (2007, March). *Research with Asian Americans: Looking back and moving forward.* Paper presented at the meeting of the Society for Research in Child Development, Boston.

Chao, R. K., & Otsuki-Clutter, M. (2011). Racial and ethnic differences: Sociocultural and contextual explanations. *Journal of Research on Adolescence, 21,* 47–60.

Charles, S. T. (2011). Emotional experience and regulation in later life. In K. W. Schaie & S. L. Willis (Eds.), *Handbook of the psychology of aging* (7th ed.). New York: Elsevier.

Charles, S. T., & Carstensen, L. L. (2010). Social and emotional aging. In S. Fiske & S. Taylor (Eds). *Annual Review of Psychology* (Vol. 61). Palo Alto, CA: Annual Reviews.

Charles, S. T., Luong, G., Almeida, D. M., Ryff, C., Sturm, M., & Love, G. (2010). Fewer ups and downs: Daily stressors mediate age differences in negative affect. *Journals of Gerontology B: Psychological Sciences and Social Sciences, 65B,* 279–286.

Charles, S. T., & Piazza, J. R. (2007). Memories of social interactions: Age differences in emotional intensity. *Psychology and Aging, 22,* 300–309.

Charlton, R. A., Barrick, T. R., Lawes, N. C., Markus, H. S., & Morris, R. G. (2010). White matter pathways associated with working memory in normal aging. *Cortex, 46,* 474–489.

Charness, N., & Bosman, E. A. (1992). Human factors and aging. In F. I. M. Craik & T. A. Salthouse (Eds.), *The handbook of aging and cognition.* Hillsdale, NJ: Erlbaum.

Charness, N., Fox, M. C., & Mitchum, A. L. (2011). Life-span cognition and information technology. In K. L. Fingerman, C. A. Berg, J. Smith, & T. C. Antonucci (Eds.), *Handbook of life-span development.* New York: Springer.

Chassin, L., & others. (2008). Multiple trajectories of cigarette smoking and the intergenerational transmission of smoking: A multigenerational, longitudinal study of a midwestern community sample. *Health Psychology, 27,* 819–828.

Chaytor, N., & Schmitter-Edgecombe, M. (2004). Working memory and aging: A cross-sectional and longitudinal analysis using a self-ordered pointing task. *Journal of the International Neuropsychological Society, 10,* 489–503.

Cheah, C. S. L., & Yeung, C. (2011). The social development of immigrant children: A focus on Asian and Hispanic children in the U.S. In P. K. Smith & C. H. Hart (Eds.), *Wiley Blackwell handbook of social development* (2nd ed.). New York: Wiley.

Chemtob, C. M., Nomura, Y., Rajendran, K., Yehuda, R., Schwartz, D., & Abramovitz, R. (2010). Impact of maternal posttraumatic stress disorder and depression following exposure to the September 11 attacks on preschool children's behavior. *Child Development, 81,* 1129–1141.

Chen, C., & Stevenson, H. W. (1989). Homework: A cross-cultural examination. *Child Development, 60*(3), 551–561.

Chen, D., & Guarente, L. (2007). SIR2: A potential target for calorie restriction mimetics. *Trends in Molecular Medicine, 13,* 64–71.

Chen, G., & others. (2010). Role of osteopontin in synovial Th17 differentiation in rheumatoid arthritis. *Arthritis and Rheumatis, 62*(10), 2900–2908.

Chen, J. J., Howard, K. S., & Brooks-Gunn, J. (2011). How do neighborhoods matter across the life span? In K. L. Fingerman, C. A. Berg, J. Smith, & T. C. Antonucci (Eds.), *Handbook of life-span development.* New York: Springer.

Chen, X., Chung, J., Lechier-Kimel, R., & French, D. (2011) Culture and social development. In P. K. Smith & C. H. Hart (Eds.), *Wiley-Blackwell handbook of social development* (2nd ed.). New York: Wiley.

Chen, X., Hastings, P. D., Rubin, K. H., Chen, H., Cen, G., & Stewart, S. L. (1998). Childrearing attitudes and behavioral inhibition in Chinese and Canadian toddlers: A cross-cultural study. *Developmental Psychology, 34,* 677–686.

Chen, Z-Y. (2009a). Parenting style. In D. Carr (Ed.), *Encyclopedia of the life course and human development.* Boston: Gale Cengage.

Chen, Z-Y. (2009b). Parent-child relationships, childhood, and adolescence. In D. Carr (Ed.), *Encyclopedia of the life course and human development.* Boston: Gale Cengage.

Cheng, M. H., Lee, S. J., Wang, P. H., & Fuh, J. L. (2007). Does menopausal transition affect the quality of life? A longitudinal study of middle-aged women in Kinmen. *Menopause, 14,* 885–890.

Cheng, S., Maeda, T., Yoichi, S., Yamagata, Z., Tomiwa, K., & Japan Children's Study Group. (2010). Early television exposure and children's behavioral and social outcomes at age 30 months. *Journal of Epidemiology* (Suppl. 2), S482–S489.

Cheng, S. T., Lee, C. K., & Chow, P. K. (2010). Social support and psychological well-being of nursing home residents in Hong Kong. *International Geriatrics, 22*(7), 1185–1190.

Cherkas, L. F., & others. (2008). The association between physical activity in leisure time and leukocyte telomere length. *Archives of Internal Medicine, 168,* 154–158.

Cherlin, A. J. (2009). *The marriage-go-round.* New York: Random House.

Cherlin, A. J., & Furstenberg, F. F. (1994). Stepfamilies in the United States: A reconsideration. In J. Blake & J. Hagen (Eds.), *Annual Review of Sociology* (Vol. 20). Palo Alto, CA: Annual Reviews.

Chess, S., & Thomas, A. (1977). Temperamental individuality from childhood to adolescence. *Journal of Child Psychiatry, 16,* 218–226.

Chi, M. T. (1978). Knowledge structures and memory development. In R. S. Siegler (Ed.), *Children's thinking: What develops?* Hillsdale, NJ: Erlbaum.

Chia, P., Sellick, K., & Gan, S. (2006). The attitudes and practices of neonatal nurses in the use of kangaroo care. *Australian Journal of Advanced Nursing, 23,* 20–27.

Chiambretto, P., Moroni, L., Guarnerio, C., Bertolotti, G., & Prigerson, H. G. (2010). Prolonged grief and depression in caregivers of patients in vegetative state. *Brain Injury, 24,* 581–588.

Chiang, K. J., & others. (2010). The effects of reminiscence therapy on psychological well-being, depression, and loneliness among the institutionalized aged. *International Journal of Geriatric Psychiatry, 25,* 380–388.

Chiappe, D., & MacDonald, K. (2005). The evolution of domain-general mechanisms in intelligence and learning. *Journal of General Psychology, 132,* 5–40.

Child Trends. (2006). *Facts at a glance.* Washington, DC: Child Trends.

Child Trends. (2008). *Facts at a glance.* Washington, DC: Child Trends.

Childers, J. B., & Tomasello, M. (2002). Two-year-olds learn novel nouns, verbs, and conventional actions from massed or distributed exposures. *Developmental Psychology, 38,* 967–978.

Children's Defense Fund. (1992). *The state of America's children, 1992.* Washington, DC: Author.

Children's Defense Fund. (2011). *The state of America's children, 2011.* Washington, DC: Author.

Childstats.gov. (2010). *America's children in brief: Key national indicators of well-being 2010.* Retrieved October 21, 2010, from www.childstats.gov/americaschildren/eco.asp

Chlebowski, R. T., & others. (2010). Estrogen plus progestin and breast cancer in postmenopausal women.

Choi, H., & Marks, N. F. (2011). Socioeconomic status, marital status continuity and change, and mortality. *Journal of Aging and Health, 23,* 714–742.

Choi, S. & Gopnik, A. (1995). Early acquisition of verbs in Korean: A cross-linguistic study. *Journal of Child Language, 22,* 497–529.

Chomsky, N. (1957). *Syntactic structures.* The Hague: Mouton.

Choufani, S., Shuman, C., & Weksberg, R. (2011). Beckwith-Wiedemann syndrome.

American Journal of Medical Genetics: Part C, Seminars in Medical Genetics, 154C, 343–354.

Chouinard, R., Karsenti, T., & Roy, N. (2007). Relations among competence beliefs, utility value, achievement goals, and effort in mathematics. *British Journal of Educational Psychology, 77,* 501–517.

Christakis, D. A., & others. (2009). Audible television and decreased adult words, infant vocalizations, and conversational turns. *Archives of Pediatric & Adolescent Medicine, 163,* 554–558.

Christakis, D. A., Zimmerman, F. J., DiGiuseppe, D. L., & McCarty, C. A. (2004). Early television exposure and subsequent attentional problems in children. *Pediatrics, 113,* 708–713.

Christensen, L. B., Johnson, R. B., & Turner, L. A. (2011). *Research methods, design, & analysis* (11th ed.). Upper Saddle River, NJ: Pearson.

Christensen, M., Knopo, F. K., Vilsbell, T., & Hoist, J. J. (2010). Lixisenatide for type 2 diabetes mellitus. *Expert Opinion on Investigational Drugs, 20,* 549–557.

Christie, J., Enz, B. J., & Vukelich, C. (2011). *Teaching language and literacy* (4th ed.). Boston: Allyn & Bacon.

Chung, J. K., Park, S. H., Lee, W. J., & Lee, S. J. (2009). Bilateral cataract surgery: A controlled clinical trial. *Japan Journal of Ophthalmology, 53,* 107–113.

Cicchetti, D. (2010). Developmental psychopathology. In R. M. Lerner, W. F. Overton, A. M. Freund, & M. E. Lamb (Eds.), *Handbook of life-span development.* New York: Wiley.

Cicchetti, D. (2011). Pathways to resilient functioning in maltreated children: From single to multilevel investigations. In D. Cicchetti & G. I. Roisman (Eds.), *The origins and organization of adaptation and maladaptation: Minnesota Symposia on Child Psychology* (Vol. 36). New York: Wiley.

Cicchetti, D. (2012). Developmental psychopathology. In P. Zelazo (Ed.), *Oxford handbook of developmental psychology.* New York: Oxford University Press.

Cicchetti, D., & Toth, S. L. (2006). Developmental psychopathology and preventive intervention. In W. Damon & R. Lerner (Eds.), *Handbook of child psychology* (6th ed.). New York: Wiley.

Cicchetti, D., & Toth, S. L. (2011). Child maltreatment: The research imperative and the exploration of results to clinical contexts. In B. Lester & J. D. Sparrow (Eds.), *Nurturing children and families.* New York: Wiley.

Cicchetti, D., Toth, S. L., & Rogusch, F. A. (2005). *A prevention program for child maltreatment.* Unpublished manuscript, University of Rochester, Rochester, NY.

Cicirelli, V. G. (1994). Sibling relationships in cross-cultural perspective. *Journal of Marriage and Family, 56,* 7–20.

Cicirelli, V. G. (2009). Sibling relationships, later life. In D. Carr (Eds.), *Encyclopedia of the life course and human development.* Boston: Gale Cengage.

Cifani, C., Polidori, C., Melotto, S., Ciccocioppo, R., & Massi, M. (2009). A preclinical model of binge eating elicited by yo-yo dieting and stressful exposure to food: Effect of sibutramine, fluoxetine, topiramate, and midazolam. *Psychopharmacology, 204,* 113–125.

Cignini, P., & others. (2010). The role of ultrasonography in the diagnosis of fetal isolated complete agenesis of the corpus callosum: A long-term prospective study. *Journal of Maternal-Fetal and Neonatal Medicine, 23*(12), 1504–1509.

Cillessen, A. H. N., & Bellmore, A. D. (2011). Social skills and social competence in interactions with peers. In P. K. Smith & C. H. Hart (Eds.), *Wiley-Blackwell handbook of childhood social development* (2nd ed.). New York: Wiley.

Ciol, M. A., Shumway-Cook, A., Hoffman, J. M., Yorkston, K. M., Dudgeon, B. J., & Chan, L. (2008). Minority disparities in disability between Medicare beneficiaries. *Journal of the American Geriatrics Society, 56,* 444–453.

Citkovitz, C., Schnyer, R. N., & Hoskins, I. A. (2011). Acupuncture during labour: Data are more promising than a recent review suggests. *British Journal of Obstetrics and Gynecology, 118,* 101.

Civelek, E., & others. (2011). Risk factors for current wheezing and its phenotypes among elementary school children. *Pediatric Pulmonology, 46,* 166–174.

Claes, H. I. (2010). Understanding the effects of sildenafil treatment on erection maintenance and erection hardness. *Journal of Sexual Medicine, 7,* 2184–2191.

Clancy, S. M., & Hoyer, W. J. (1994). Age and skill in visual search. *Developmental Psychology, 30,* 545–552.

Clark, B. (2008). *Growing up gifted* (7th ed.). Upper Saddle River, NJ: Prentice Hall.

Clark, D. J., Patten, C., Reid, K. F., Carabello, R. J., Phillips, E. M., & Fielding, R. A. (2010). Impaired voluntary neuromuscular activation limits muscle power in mobility-limited older adults. *Journals of Gerontology A: Biological Sciences and Medical Sciences, 65A,* 495–502.

Clark, D. J., Patten, C., Reid, K. F., Carabello, R. J., Phillips, E. M., & Fielding, R. A. (2011). Muscle performance and physical function are associated with voluntary rate of neuromuscular activation in older adults. *Journals of Gerontology A: Biological Sciences and Medical Sciences, 66A,* 115–121.

Clark, E. (1993). *The lexicon in acquisition.* New York: Cambridge University Press.

Clark, E. V. (2009). What shapes children's language? Child-directed speech and the process of acquisition. In V. C. M. Gathercole (Ed.), *Routes to language: Essays in honor of Melissa Bowerman.* New York: Psychology Press.

Clark-Cotton, M. R., Williams, R. K., & Goral, M. (2007). Language and communication in aging. In J. E. Birren (Ed.), *Encyclopedia of gerontology* (2nd ed.). San Diego: Academic Press.

Clarke, A., & Thirlaway, K. (2011, in press). "Genomic counseling"? Genetic counseling in the genomic era. *Genome Medicine.*

Clarke-Stewart, A. K., & Miner, J. L. (2008). Child and day care, effects of. In M. M. Haith & J. B. Benson (Eds.), *Encyclopedia of infant and early childhood development.* Oxford, UK: Elsevier.

Class, Q. A., Lichtenstein, P., Langstrom, N., & D'Onofrio, B. M. (2011, in press). Timing of prenatal maternal exposure to severe life events and adverse pregnancy outcomes: A population study of 2.6 million pregnancies. *Psychosomatic Medicine.*

Clausen, J. A. (1993). *American lives.* New York Free Press.

Clay, O. J., & others. (2009). Visual function and cognitive speed of procession mediate age-related decline in memory span and fluid intelligence. *Journal of Aging and Health, 21,* 547–566.

Clearfield, M. W., Diedrich, F. J., Smith, L. B., & Thelen, E. (2006). Young infants reach correctly in A-not-B tasks: On the development of stability and perseveration. *Infant Behavior and Development, 29,* 435–444.

Clearfield, M. W., Dineva, E., Smith, L. B., Diedrich, F. J., & Thelen, E. (2009). Cue salience and infant preservative reaching: Tests of the dynamic field theory. *Developmental Science, 12,* 26–40.

Cliffordson, C., & Gustafsson, J-E. (2008). Effects of age and schooling on intellectual performance: Estimates obtained from analysis of continuous variation in age and length of schooling. *Intelligence, 36,* 143–152.

Clifton, R. K., Morrongiello, B. A., Kulig, J. W., & Dowd, J. M. (1981). Developmental changes in auditory localization in infancy. In R. N. Aslin, J. R. Alberts, & M. R. Petersen (Eds.), *Development of perception* (Vol. 1). Orlando, FL: Academic Press.

Clifton, R. K., Muir, D. W., Ashmead, D. H., & Clarkson, M. G. (1993). Is visually guided reaching in early infancy a myth? *Child Development, 64,* 1099–1110.

Cluett, E. R., & Burns, E. (2009). Immersion in water in labour and birth. *Cochrane Database of Systematic Reviews,* CD000111.

Cohen, D. (2009). *What every man should know about being a dad.* New York: Psychology Press.

Cohen, F., Kemeny, M. E., Zegans, L. S., Johnson, P., Kearney, K. A., & Stites, D. P. (2007). Immune function declines with unemployment and recovers after stressor termination. *Psychosomatic Medicine, 69,* 225–234.

Cohen, N. J., Lojkasek, M., Zadeh, Z. Y., Pugliese, M., & Kiefer, H. (2008). Children adopted in China: A prospective study of their growth and development. *Journal of Child Psychology and Psychiatry, 49*(4), 458–468

Coie, J. D. (2004). The impact of negative social experiences on the development of antisocial behavior. In J. B. Kupersmidt & K. A. Dodge (Eds.), *Children's peer relations: From development to intervention.* Washington, DC: American Psychological Association.

Coker, R. H., Williams, R. H., Kortebein, P. M., Sullivan, D. H., & Evans, W. J. (2009). Influence of exercise intensity on abdominal fat and adiponectin in elderly adults. *Metabolic Syndrome and Related Disorders, 7,* 363–368.

Colangelo, N. C., Assouline, S. G., & Gross, M. U. M. (2004). *A nation deceived: How schools hold back America's brightest students.* The Templeton National Report on Acceleration. Retrieved March 6, 2005, from http://nationdeceived.org/

Colapinto, J. (2000). *As nature made him.* New York: Simon & Schuster.

Colby, A., Kohlberg, L., Gibbs, J., & Lieberman, M. (1983). A longitudinal study of moral judgment. *Monographs of the Society for Research in Child Development, 48*(21, Serial No. 201).

Colcombe, S. J., & Kramer, A. F. (2003). Fitness effects on the cognitive function of older adults: A meta-analytic study. *Psychological Science, 14,* 125–130.

Colcombe, S. J., & others. (2006). Aerobic exercise training increases brain volume in aging humans. *Journals of Gerontology: Medical Sciences, 61A,* 1166–1170.

Cole, M., & Packer, M. (2011). Culture in development. In M. H. Bornstein & M. E. Lamb (Eds.), *Cognitive development.* New York: Psychology Press.

Cole, P. M., Dennis, T. A., Smith-Simon, K. E., & Cohen, L. H. (2009). Preschoolers' emotion regulation strategy understanding: Relations with emotion socialization and child self-regulation. *Social Development, 18*(2), 324–352.

Cole, P. M., & Tan, P. Z. (2007). Emotion socialization from a cultural perspective. In J. E. Grusec & P. D. Hastings (Eds.), *Handbook of socialization.* New York: Guilford.

Coleman, P. D. (1986, August). *Regulation of dendritic extent: Human aging brain and Alzheimer's disease.* Paper presented at the meeting of the American Psychological Association, Washington, DC.

Coleman-Phox, K., Odouli, R., & Li, D-K. (2008). Use of a fan during sleep and the risk of sudden infant death syndrome. *Archives of Pediatric and Adolescent Medicine, 162,* 963–968.

Collier, R. (2011). Prolonged grief proposed as a mental disorder. *CMAJ, 183,* E439–E440.

Collins, M. (1996, Winter). The job outlook for 96 grads. *Journal of Career Planning,* 51–54.

Collins, W. A., & Steinberg, L. (2006). Adolescent development in interpersonal context. In W. Damon & R. Lerner (Eds.), *Handbook of child psychology* (6th ed.). New York: Wiley.

Collins, W. A., & van Dulmen, M. (2006). The significance of middle childhood peer competence for work and relationships in early adulthood. In A. C. Huston & M. N. Ripke (Eds.), *Developmental contexts in middle childhood.* New York: Cambridge University Press.

Collins, W. A., Welsh, D. P., & Furman, W. (2009). Adolescent romantic relationships. *Annual Review of Clinical Psychology* (Vol. 5). Palo Alto, CA: Annual Reviews.

Colom, R., & others. (2009). Gray matter correlates of fluid, crystallized, and spatial intelligence. *Intelligence, 37,* 124–135.

Colom, R., Karama, S., Jung, R. E., & Haier, R. J. (2010). Human intelligence and brain networks. *Dialogues in Clinical Neuroscience, 12,* 489–501.

Columbo, J., Kapa, L., & Curtendale, L. (2011). Varieties of attention in infancy. In L. Oakes (Ed.), *Infant perception and cognition.* New York: Oxford University Press.

Comer, J. (2004). *Leave no child behind.* New Haven, CT: Yale University Press.

Comer, J. (2006). Child development: The under-weighted aspect of intelligence. In P. C. Kyllonen, R. D. Roberts, & L. Stankov (Eds.), *Extending intelligence.* Mahwah, NJ: Erlbaum.

Comer, J. (2010). Comer School Development Program. In J. Meece & J. Eccles (Eds.), *Handbook of research on schools, schooling, and human development.* New York: Routledge.

Comings, J. (2007). Persistence: Helping adult students reach their goals. In J. Comings, B. Garner, & C. Smith (Eds.), *Review of adult learning and literacy* (Vol. 7). Mahwah, NJ: Erlbaum.

Commoner, B. (2002). Unraveling the DNA myth: The spurious foundation of genetic engineering. *Harper's Magazine, 304,* 39–47.

Commons, M. L., & Richards, F. A. (2003). Four postformal stages. In J. Demick & C. Andreoletti (Eds.), *Handbook of adult development.* New York: Kluwer.

Commons, M. L., Sinnott, J. D., Richards, F. A., & Armon, C. (1989). *Adult development. Vol. 1: Comparisons and applications of developmental models.* New York: Praeger.

Comstock, G., & Scharrer, E. (2006). Media and popular culture. In W. Damon & R. Lerner (Eds.), *Handbook of child psychology* (6th ed.). New York: Wiley.

Conduct Problems Prevention Research Group. (2007). The Fast Track randomized controlled trial to prevent externalizing psychiatric disorders: Findings from grades 3 to 9. *Journal of the American Academy of Child and Adolescent Psychiatry, 46* 1250–1262.

Conduct Problems Prevention Research Group. (2010a). Fast Track intervention effects on youth arrests and delinquency. *Journal of Experimental Criminology, 6,* 131–157.

Conduct Problems Prevention Research Group. (2010b). The difficulty of maintaining positive intervention effects: A look at disruptive behavior, deviant peer relations, and social skills during the middle school years. *Journal of Early Adolescence, 30,* 593–624.

Conduct Problems Prevention Research Group. (2011, in press). The effects of the Fast

Track preventive intervention on the development of conduct disorder across childhood. *Child Development.*

Cong, X., Ludington-Hoe, S. M., & Walsh, S. (2011, in press). Randomized crossover trial of kangaroo care to reduce biobehavioral pain responses in preterm infants: A pilot study. *Biological Research for Nursing.*

Conger, R., & Conger, R. J. (2008). Understanding the processes through which economic hardship influences rural families and children. In D. R. Crane & T. B. Heaton (Eds.), *Handbook of families and poverty.* Thousand Oaks, CA: Sage.

Connell-Carrick, K. (2011). Child abuse and neglect. In G. Bremner & T. Wachs (Eds.), *Wiley-Blackwell handbook of infant development* (2nd ed.). New York: Wiley.

Connolly, J., Craig, W., Goldberg, A., & Pepler, D. (2004). Mixed-gender groups, dating, and romantic relationships in early adolescence. *Journal of Research on Adolescence, 14,* 185–207.

Connolly, J. A., & McIsaac, C. (2009). Romantic relationships in adolescence. In R. M. Lerner & L. Steinberg (Eds.), *Handbook of adolescence psychology* (3rd ed.). New York: Wiley.

Conradt, E., & Ablow, J. (2010). Infant physiological response to the still-face paradigm: Contributions of maternal sensitivity and infants' early regulatory behavior. *Infant Behavior and Development, 33,* 251–265.

Constant, C., & others. (2011). Environmental tobacco smoke (ETS) exposure and respiratory morbidity in school age children. *Portuguese Journal of Pulmonology,17,* 20–26.

Constantine, N. A. (2008). Editorial: Converging evidence leaves policy behind: Sex education in the United States. *Journal of Adolescent Health, 42,* 324–326.

Contestabile, A. (2009). Benefits of caloric restriction on brain aging and related pathological states: Understanding mechanisms to devise novel therapies. *Current Medicinal Chemistry, 16,* 350–361.

Cook, M., & Birch, R. (1984). Infant perception of the shapes of tilted plane forms. *Infant Behavior and Development, 7,* 389–402.

Cook, P. J., MacCoun, R., Muschkin, C., & Vigdor, J. (2008). The negative impacts of starting middle school in the sixth grade. *Journal of Policy Analysis and Management, 27,* 104–121.

Cook, T. D., Deng, Y., & Morgano, E. (2007). Friendship influences during early adolescence: The special role of friends' grade point average. *Journal of Research on Adolescence, 17,* 325–356.

Cooksey, E. C. (2009). Sexual activity, adolescent. In D. Carr (Ed.), *Encyclopedia of the life course and human development.* Boston: Gale Cengage.

Coontz, S. (2005). *Marriage: A history.* New York: Penguin.

Cooper, C. R. (2011). *Bridging multiple worlds.* New York: Oxford University Press.

Cooper, C. R., Behrens, R., & Trinh, N. (2009). Identity development. In R. A. Shweder,

T. R. Bidell, A. C. Daily, S. D. Dixon, P. J. Miller, & J. Model (Eds.), *The Chicago companion to the child.* Chicago: University of Chicago Press.

Cooper, C. R., & Grotevant, H. D. (1989, April). *Individuality and connectedness in the family and adolescent's self and relational competence.* Paper presented at the meeting of the Society for Research in Child Development, Kansas City.

Cooper, C. R., Grotevant, H. D., Moore, M. S., & Condon, S. M. (1982, August). *Family support and conflict: Both foster adolescent identity and role taking.* Paper presented at the meeting of the American Psychological Association, Washington, DC.

Cooper, M. L. (2002). Alcohol use and risky sexual behavior among college students and youth: Evaluating the evidence. *Journal of Studies on Alcohol, 14,* 101–107.

Copeland, W., Shanahan, L., Miller, S., Costello, E. J., Angold, A., & Maughan, B. (2010). Outcomes of early pubertal timing in young women: A prospective population-based study. *American Journal of Psychiatry, 167,* 1218–1225.

Corbetta, D., & Snapp-Childs, W. (2009). Seeing and touching: The role of sensory-motor experience on the development of reaching. *Infant Behavior and Development, 32,* 44–58.

Cordier, S. (2008). Evidence for a role of paternal exposure in developmental toxicity. *Basic and Clinical Pharmacology and Toxicology, 102,* 176–181.

Corna, D. R., Cukrowicz, K. C., Linton, K., & Prabhu, F. (2010). The mediating effect of perceived burdensomeness on the relation between depressive symptoms and suicide ideation in a community sample of older adults. *Aging and Mental Health, 50,* 785–797.

Cornelius, J. R., Clark, D. B., Reynolds, M., Kirisci, L., & Tarter, R. (2007). Early age of first sexual intercourse and affiliation with deviant peers predict development of SUD: A prospective longitudinal study. *Addictive Behavior, 32,* 850–854.

Cornish, K. M., Gray, K. M., & Rinehart, N. J. (2010). Fragile X syndrome and associated disorders. *Advances in Child Development and Behavior, 39,* 211–235.

Cornwell, B., Laumann, E. O., & Schumm, L. P. (2008). The social connectedness of older adults. *American Sociological Review, 73,* 185–203.

Cornwell, B., Schumm, L. P., & Laumann, E. O. (2008). The social connectedness of older adults. *American Sociological Review, 73,* 185–203.

Corso, J. F. (1977). Auditory perception and communication. In J. E. Birren & K. W. Schaie (Eds.), *Handbook of the psychology of aging* (2nd ed.). New York: Van Nostrand Reinhold.

Corso, P. S., & Fertig, A. R. (2010). The economic impact of child maltreatment in the United States: Are the estimates credible? *Child Abuse and Neglect, 34*(5), 296–304.

Cortes, E., Basra, R., & Kelleher, C. J. (2011). Waterbirth and pelvic floor injury: A retrospective study and postal survey using ICIQ modular long form questionnaires. *European*

Journal of Obstetrics, Gynecology, and Reproductive Biology, 155, 27–30.

Cosentino, S., Brickman, A. M., & Manley, J. L. (2011). Neuropsychological assessment of the dementias of late life. In K. W. Schaie & S. L. Willis (Eds.), *Handbook of the psychology of aging* (7th ed.). New York: Elsevier.

Cosmides, L. (2011). Evolutionary psychology. *Annual Review of Psychology* (Vol. 62). Palo Alto, CA: Annual Reviews.

Costa, P. T., & McCrae, R. R. (1995). Solid ground on the wetlands of personality: A reply to Black. *Psychological Bulletin, 117,* 216–220.

Costa, P. T., & McCrae, R. R. (1998). Personality assessment. In H. S. Friedman (Ed.), *Encyclopedia of mental health* (Vol. 3). San Diego: Academic Press.

Coté, J. E. (2009). Identity formation and self-development in adolescence. In R. M. Lerner & L. Steinberg (Eds.), *Handbook of adolescent psychology* (3rd ed.). New York: Wiley.

Cotton, S. R., McCullough, B. M., & Adams, R. G. (2011). Technological influences on social ties across the life span. In K. L. Fingerman, C. A. Berg, J. Smith, & T. C Antonucci (Eds.), *Handbook of life-span development.* New York: Springer.

Cotugno, G., & others. (2011, in press). Adherence to diet and quality of life in patients with phenylketonuria. *Acta Pediatrica.*

Couillard-Despres, S., Iglseder, B., & Aigner, L. (2011, in press). Neurogenesis, cellular plasticity, and cognition: The impact of stem cells in the adult and aging brain. *Gerontology.*

Council of Economic Advisors. (2000). *Teens and their parents in the 21st century: An examination of trends in teen behavior and the role of parent involvement.* Washington, DC: Author.

Courage, M. L., Edison, S. C., & Howe, M. L. (2004). Variability in the early development of visual self-recognition. *Infant Behavior and Development, 27,* 509–532.

Courage, M. L., & Richards, J. E. (2008). Attention. In M. M. Haith & J. B. Benson (Eds.), *Encyclopedia of infant and early childhood development.* Oxford, UK: Elsevier.

Cousineau, T. M., Goldstein, M., & Franco, D. L. (2005). A collaborative approach to nutrition education for college students. *Journal of American College Health, 53,* 79–84.

Cowan, P., & Cowan, C. (2000). *When partners become parents: The big life change for couples.* Mahwah, NJ: Erlbaum.

Cowan, P. A., & Cowan, C. P. (2009). How working with couples fosters children's development: From prevention science to public policy. In M. S. Schultz, M. K. Pruett, P. K. Kerig, & R. D. Parke (Eds.), *Feathering the nest: Couple relationships, couples interventions, and children's development.* Washington, DC: American Psychological Association.

Cox, K. S., Wilt, J., Olson, B., & McAdams, D. P. (2010). Generativity, the Big Five, and psychosocial adaptation in midlife adults. *Journal of Personality, 78,* 1185–1208.

Cox, M. J., Neilbron, N., Mills-Koonce, W. R., Pressel, A., Oppenheimer, C. W., & Szwedo, D. E. (2008). Marital relationship. In M. M. Haith & J. B. Benson (Eds.), *Encyclopedia of infant and early childhood development*. Oxford, UK: Elsevier.

Coyne, S. M., Nelson, D. A., & Underwood, M. (2011). Aggression in children. In P. K. Smith & C. H. Hart (Eds.), *Wiley-Blackwell handbook of childhood social development* (2nd ed.). New York: Wiley.

Cozzi, B., & others. (2010). Ontogenesis and migration of metallothionein I/II-containing glial cells in the human telencephalon during the second trimester. *Brain Research, 1327,* 16–23.

Crawford, D., & others. (2010). The longitudinal influence of home and neighborhood environments on children's body mass index and physical activity over 5 years: The CLAN study. *International Journal of Obesity, 34,* 1177–1187.

Crean, H. F. (2008). Conflict in the Latino parent-youth dyad: The role of emotional support from the opposite parent. *Journal of Family Psychology, 22,* 484–493.

Creed, M. C., & Milgram, N. W. (2010). Amyloid-modifying therapies for Alzheimer's disease: Therapeutic progress and its implications. *Age, 32*(3), 365–384.

Cremation Association of North America. (2011). *Statistics about cremation trends.* Retrieved January 22, 2011, from www.cremationassociation/org/Media/Cremation Statistics/tabid/95/Default.aspx

Cresci, M. K., Yarandi, H. N., & Morrell, R. W. (2010). The digital divide and urban older adults. *Computers, Informatics, Nursing, 28,* 88–94.

Crespo, C., Kielpikowski, M., Jose, P. E., & Pryor, J. (2010). Relationships between family connectedness and body satisfaction: A longitudinal study of adolescent girls and boys. *Journal of Youth and Adolescence, 39,* 1392–1401.

Crews, J. E., & Campbell, V. A. (2004). Vision impairment and hearing loss among community-dwelling older Americans: Implications for health and functioning. *American Journal of Public Health, 94,* 823–829.

Crick, N. R., Murray-Close, D., Marks, P. E. L., & Mohajeri-Nelson, N. (2009). Aggression and peer relationships in school-age children: Relational and physical aggression in group and dyadic contexts. In K. H. Rubin, W. M. Bukowski, & B. Laursen (Eds.), *Handbook of peer interactions, relationships, and groups.* New York: Guilford.

Crockett, L. J., Raffaelli, M., & Shen, Y-L. (2006). Linking self-regulation and risk proneness to risky sexual behavior: Pathways through peer pressure and early substance use. *Journal of Research on Adolescence, 16,* 503–525.

Crooks, R. L., & Baur, K. (2011). *Our sexuality* (11th ed.). Belmont, CA: Wadsworth.

Crosnoe, R., Riegle-Crumb, C., Field, S., Frank, K., & Muller, C. (2008). Peer group contexts of girls' and boys' academic experiences. *Child Development, 79,* 139–155.

Cross, S., & Markus, H. (1991). Possible selves across the lifespan. *Human Development, 34,* 230–255.

Croucher, E. (2010). Comments on shaken baby syndrome. *Nursing for Women's Health, 14,* 9–10.

Crouter, A. C. (2006). Mothers and fathers at work. In A. Clarke-Stewart & J. Dunn (Eds.), *Families count.* New York: Cambridge University Press.

Crouter, A. C., & McHale, S. (2005). The long arm of the job revisited: Parenting in dual-earner families. In T. Luster & L. Okagaki (Eds.), *Parenting.* Mahwah, NJ: Erlbaum.

Crowell, J. A., Treboux, D., & Brockmeyer, S. (2009). Parental divorce and adult children's attachment representations and marital status. *Attachment and Human Development, 11,* 87–101.

Crowley, K., Callahan, M. A., Tenenbaum, H. R., & Allen, E. (2001). Parents explain more to boys than to girls during shared scientific thinking. *Psychological Science, 12,* 258–261.

Cruikshank, D. R., Jenkins, D. B., & Metcalf, K. K. (2012). *The act of teaching* (6th ed.). New York: McGraw-Hill.

Csikszentmihalyi, M. (1996). *Creativity.* New York: HarperCollins.

Cubbin, C., Brindis, C. D., Jain, S., Snelli, J., & Braveman, P. (2010). Neighborhood poverty, aspirations and expectations, and initiation of sex. *Journal of Adolescent Health, 47,* 399–406.

Cuddy-Casey, M., & Orvaschel, H. (1997). Children's understanding of death in relation to child suicidality and homicidality. *Death Studies, 17,* 33–45.

Cui, X., & Vaillant, G. E. (1996). Antecedents and consequents of negative life events in adulthood: A longitudinal study. *American Journal of Psychiatry, 153,* 123–126.

Cumming, E., & Henry, W. (1961). *Growing old.* New York: Basic Books.

Cummings, D. M., Dubose, K. D., Imal, S., & Collier, D. N. (2010). Fitness versus fatness and insulin resistance in U.S. adolescents. *Journal of Obesity,* Article ID 195729, 7 pages.

Cummings, E. M., & Davies, P. T. (2010). *Marital conflict and children: An emotional security perspective.* New York: Guilford.

Cummings, E. M., & Kouros, C. D. (2008). Stress and coping. In M. M. Haith & J. B. Benson (Eds.), *Encyclopedia of infant and early childhood development* (Vol. 3, pp. 267–281). San Diego: Academic Press.

Cummings, E. M., & Merrilees, C. E. (2009). Identifying the dynamic processes underlying links between marital conflict and child adjustment. In M. S. Schulz, P. K. Kerig, M. K. Pruett, & R. D. Parke (Eds.), *Feathering the nest.* Washington, DC: American Psychological Association.

Cummings, E. M., El-Sheikh, M., & Kouros, C. D. (2009). Children and violence: The role of children's regulation in the marital aggression–child adjustment link. *Clinical Child and Family Psychology Review, 12*(1), 3–15.

Cunningham, M. (2004). Old is a three-letter word. *Geriatric Nursing, 25,* 277–280.

Cunningham, M. (2009). Housework. In D. Carr (Ed.), *Encyclopedia of the life course and human development.* Boston: Gale Cengage.

Cunningham, P. M., & Allington, R. L. (2011). *Classrooms that work: They can all read and write* (5th ed.). Boston: Allyn & Bacon.

Cunningham, W., & Hyson, D. (2006). The skinny on high-protein, low-carbohydrate diets. *Preventive Cardiology, 9,* 166–171.

Curran, K., DuCette, J., Eisenstein, J., & Hyman, I. A. (2001, August). *Statistical analysis of the cross-cultural data: The third year.* Paper presented at the meeting of the American Psychological Association, San Francisco.

Cutler, S. J. (2009). Media and technology use, later life. In D. Carr (Ed.), *Encyclopedia of the life course and human development.* Boston: Gale Cengage.

Czaja, S. J., & others. (2006). Factors predicting the use of technology: Findings from the Center for Research and Education on Aging and Technology (CREATE). *Psychology and Aging, 21,* 333–352.

D

da Fonseca, E. B., Bittar, R. E., Damiao, R., & Zugiab, M. (2009). Prematurity prevention: The role of progesterone. *Current Opinion in Obstetrics and Gynecology, 21,* 142–147.

da Rocha, A. F., Rocha, F. T., & Massad, E. (2011). The brain as a distributed intelligent processing system: An EEG study. *PLoS One, 6,* e17355.

Dahl, R. E. (2004). Adolescent brain development: A period of vulnerabilities and opportunities. *Annals of the New York Academy of Sciences, 1021,* 1–22.

Dahlen, H. G., Jackson, M., & Stevens, J. (2011). Homebirth, freebirth, and doulas: Casualty and consequences of a broken maternity system. *Women and Birth, 24,* 47–50.

Dalen, K., Bruaroy, S., Wentzel-Larsen, T., & Laegreid, L. M. (2009). Cognitive functioning in children prenatally exposed to alcohol and psychotropic drugs. *Neuropediatrics, 40,* 162–167.

Daley, A. J., MacArthur, C., & Winter, H. (2007). The role of exercise in treating postpartum depression: A review of the literature. *Journal of Midwifery & Women's Health, 52,* 56–62.

Dallongeville, J., & others. (2011, in press). Relation between body mass index, waist circumference, and cardiovascular outcomes in 19,579 diabetic patients with established vascular disease: The REACH registry. *European Journal of Cardiovascular Prevention and Rehabilitation.*

Damon, W. (1988). *The moral child.* New York: Free Press.

Damon, W. (2008). *The path to purpose.* New York: Free Press.

Daniels, H. (2011). Vygotsky and psychology. In U. Goswami (Ed.), *Wiley-Blackwell handbook of* *childhood cognitive development* (2nd ed.). New York: Wiley-Blackwell.

Danner, D., Snowdon, D., & Friesen, W. (2001). Positive emotions in early life and longevity: Findings from the Nun Study. *Journal of Personality and Social Psychology, 80*(5), 804–813.

Dare, J. S. (2011). Transitions in women's lives: Contemporary experiences. *Health Care for Women International, 32*, 111–133.

Darling-Hammond, N. (2011). Testing, No Child Left Behind, and educational equity. In L. M. Stulberg & S. L. Weinberg (Eds.), *Diversity in higher education.* New York: Routledge.

Darwin, C. (1859). *On the origin of species.* London: John Murray.

Das, A. (2009). Sexual harassment at work in the United States. *Archives of Sexual Behavior, 38,* 909–921.

Das, D. K., Mukherjee, S., & Ray, D. (2010). Resveratrol and red wine, healthy heart and longevity. *Heart Failure Reviews, 15*(5), 467–477.

Davanzo, R., & others. (2011). Antidepressant drugs and breastfeeding: A review of the literature. *Breastfeeding Medicine, 6,* 89–98.

Dave, D., & Rashad, I. (2009). Overweight status, self-perception, and suicide behaviors among adolescents. *Social Science & Medicine, 68,* 1685–1691.

Davey, A., Tucker, C. J., Fingerman, K. L., & Savia, J. (2009). Variability in representations of past relationships with parents. *Journals of Gerontology: Social Science, 64,* 125–136.

Davidson, D. (1996). The effects of decision characteristics on children's selective search of predecisional information. *Acta Psychologica, 92,* 263–281.

Davidson, J., & Davidson, B. (2004). *Genius denied: How to stop wasting our brightest young minds.* New York: Simon & Schuster.

Davidson, J., & Kemp, I. A. (2011). Contemporary models of intelligence. In R. J. Sternberg & S. B. Kaufman (Eds.), *Cambridge handbook of intelligence.* New York: Cambridge University Press.

Davidson, J. R. (2010). Major depressive disorder treatment guidelines in America and Europe. *Journal of Clinical Psychiatry, 71*(Suppl. E1), E04.

Davidson, M. R., & others. (2012). *Olds' maternal-newborn nursing and women's health across the lifespan: International edition* (9th ed.). Upper Saddle River, NJ: Pearson.

Davidson, M., Lickona, T., & Khmelkov, V. (2008). A new paradigm for high school character education. In L. Nucci & D. Narváez (Eds.), *Handbook of moral and character education.* Clifton, NJ: Psychology Press.

Davidson, W. S., Jimenez, T. R., Onifade, E., & Hankins, S. S. (2010). Student experiences of the adolescent diversion project: A community-based exemplar in the pedagogy of service-learning. *American Journal of Community Psychology, 46,* 442–458.

Davies, J., & Brember, I. (1999). Reading and mathematics attainments and self-esteem in

years 2 and 6: An eight-year cross-sectional study. *Educational Studies, 25,* 145–157.

Davioli, T., Denchi, E. L., & Lange, T. (2010). Persistent telomere damage induces bypass of mitosis and tetraploidy. *Cell, 141,* 81–93.

Davis, B. E., Moon, R. Y., Sachs, M. C., & Ottolini, M. C. (1998). Effects of sleep position on infant motor development: *Pediatrics, 102,* 1135–1140.

Davis, C. F., Lazariu, V., & Sekhobo, J. P. (2010). Smoking cessation in the WIC program. *Maternal and Child Health Journal, 14,* 474–477.

Davis, C. L., & others. (2007). Effects of aerobic exercise on overweight children's cognitive functioning: A randomized controlled trial. *Research Quarterly for Exercise and Sport, 78,* 510–519.

Davis, C. L., & others. (2011, in press). Exercise improves executive function and alters neural activation in overweight children. *Health Psychology.*

Davis, K., Christodoulou, J., Seider, S., & Gardner, H. (2011). The theory of multiple intelligences. In R. J. Sternberg & S. B. Kaufman (Eds.), *Cambridge handbook of intelligence.* New York: Cambridge University Press.

Davis, K. E., Norris, J., Hessler, D. M., Zawacki, T., Morrison, D. M., & George, W. H. (2010). College women's decision making: Cognitive mediation of alcohol expectancy effects. *Journal of American College Health, 58,* 481–488.

Davis, K. F., Parker, K. P., & Montgomery, G. L. (2004). Sleep in infants and young children: Part one: Normal sleep. *Journal of Pediatric Health Care, 18,* 65–71.

Davis, L., & Keyser, J. (1997). *Becoming the parent you want to be: A sourcebook of strategies for the first five years.* New York: Broadway Books.

Dawson, J. D., Uc, E. Y., Anderson, S. W., Johnson, A. M., & Rizzo, M. (2010). Neuropsychological predictors of driving errors in older adults. *Journal of the American Geriatric Society, 58*(6), 1090–1096.

Day, N. L., Goldschmidt, L., & Thomas, C. A. (2006). Prenatal marijuana exposure contributes to the prediction of marijuana use at age 14. *Addiction, 101,* 1313–1322.

Day, R. H., & McKenzie, B. E. (1973). Perceptual shape constancy in early infancy. *Perception, 2,* 315–320.

de Fine Olivarius, N., Siersma, V., Almind, G. J., & Nielson, N. V. (2011, in press). Prevalence and progression of visual impairment in patients newly diagnosed with clinical type 2 diabetes: A 6-year follow-up study. *BMC Public Health.*

de Haan, M., & Gunnar, M. R. (Eds.). (2009). *Handbook of developmental social neuroscience.* New York: Guilford.

de la Cuesta-Benjumea, C. (2011, in press). Strategies for the relief of burden in advanced dementia care-giving. *Journal of Advanced Nursing.*

de la Paz, S., & McCutchen, D. (2011). Learning to write. In P. A. Alexander & R. E. Mayer (Eds.), *Handbook of research on learning and instruction.* New York: Routledge.

De Leo, D. (2002). Struggling against suicide: The need for an integrative approach. *Crisis, 23,* 23–31.

De Meyer, G., & others. (2010). Diagnosis-independent Alzheimer disease biomarker signature in cognitively normal elderly people. *Archives of Neurology, 67,* 949–956.

de Wit, L., & others. (2010). Depression and obesity: A meta-analysis of community-based studies. *Psychiatry Research, 178,* 230–235.

Deary, I. (2012). Intelligence. *Annual Review of Psychology* (Vol. 63). Palo Alto, CA: Annual Reviews.

Deary, I. J., Johnson, W., & Starr, J. M. (2010). Are processing speed tasks biomarkers of aging? *Psychology and Aging, 25,* 219–228.

Deary, I. J., Penke, L., & Johnson, W. (2010). The neuroscience of human intelligence differences. *Nature Review: Neuroscience, 11,* 201–211.

Deary, I. J., Strand, S., Smith, P., & Fernandes, C. (2007). Intelligence and educational achievement. *Intelligence, 35,* 13–21.

Deater-Deckard, K., & Dodge, K. (1997). Externalizing behavior problems and discipline revisited: Non-linear effects and variation by culture, context and gender. *Psychological Inquiry, 8,* 161–175.

Debats, D. L. (1990). The Life Regard Index: Reliability and validity. *Psychological Reports, 67,* 27–34.

DeCasper, A. J., & Spence, M. J. (1986). Prenatal maternal speech influences newborn's perception of speech sounds. *Infant Behavior and Development, 9,* 133–150.

deCharms, R. (1984). Motivation enhancement in educational setting. In R. Arnes & C. Arnes (Eds.), *Research on motivation in education* (Vol. 1). Orlando, FL: Academic Press.

Deci, E. L., Koestner, R., & Ryan, R. M. (2001). Extrinsic rewards and intrinsic motivation in education: Reconsidered once again. *Review of Educational Research, 71,* 1–28.

DeJong, W., DeRicco, B., & Schneider, S. K. (2010). Pregaming: An exploratory study of strategic drinking by college students in Pennsylvania. *Journal of American College Health, 58,* 307–316.

Delaloye, C., & others. (2009). The contribution of aging to the understanding of the dimensionality of executive functions. *Archives of Gerontology and Geriatrics, 49,* e51–e59.

Delisle, T. T., Werch, C. E., Wong, A. H., Bian, H., & Weiler, R. (2010). Relationship between frequency and intensity of physical activity and health behaviors of adolescents. *Journal of School Health, 80,* 134–140.

Dell'osso, L., & others. (2011, in press). Complicated grief and suicidality: The impact of subthreshold mood symptoms. *CNS Spectrum.*

DeLoache, J. S. (2011). Early development of the understanding and use of symbolic artifacts. In U. Goswami (Ed.), *Wiley-Blackwell handbook of childhood cognitive development* (2nd ed.). New York: Wiley.

DeLoache, J. S., Simcock, G., & Macari, S. (2007). Planes, trains, automobiles—and tea-sets: Extremely intense interests in very young children. *Developmental Psychology, 43,* 1579–1586.

Demetriou, A., Mouyi, A., & Spanoudis, G. (2010). The development of mental processing In W. Overton & R. W. Lerner (Eds.), *Handbook of life-span development.* New York: Wiley.

Demiray, B., Gulgoz, S., & Bluck, S. (2009). Examining the life story account of the reminiscence bump: Why we remember more from early adulthood. *Memory, 17,* 708–723.

Demircin, S., Akkoyun, M., Yilmaz, R., & Gokdogan, M. R. (2011). Suicide of elderly persons: Towards a framework for prevention. *Geriatrics & Gerontology International, 11,* 107–113.

Dempster, F. N. (1981). Memory span: Sources of individual and developmental differences. *Psychological Bulletin, 80,* 63–100.

Dencker, M., Buge, A., Hermansen, B., Froberg, K., & Andersen, L. B. (2010). Aerobic fitness in pre-pubertal children according to level of body fat. *Acta Pediatrica, 99*(12), 1854–1860.

Denham, S. A., Bassett, H. H., & Wyatt, T. (2007). The socialization of emotional competence. In J. E. Grusec & P. D. Hastings (Eds.), *Handbook of socialization.* New York: Guilford.

Denham, S., & others. (2011). Emotions and social development in childhood. In P. K. Smith & C. H. Hart (Eds.), *Wiley-Blackwell handbook of childhood social development* (2nd ed.). New York: Wiley.

Denham, S., Warren, H., von Salisch, M., Benga, O., Chin, J-C., & Geangu, E. (2011). Social skills and social development in childhood. In P. K. Smith & C. H. Hart (Eds.), *Wiley-Blackwell handbook of childhood social development* (2nd ed.). New York: Wiley.

Denmark, F. L., Russo, N. F., Frieze, I. H., & Eschuzur, J. (1988). Guidelines for avoiding sexism in psychological research: A report of the ad hoc committee on nonsexist research. *American Psychologist, 43,* 582–585.

Denney, N. W. (1986, August). *Practical problem solving.* Paper presented at the meeting of the American Psychological Association, Washington, DC.

Denney, N. W. (1990). Adult age differences in traditional and practical problem solving. *Advances in Psychology, 72,* 329–349.

Dennis, N. A., & Cabeza, R. (2008). Neuroimaging of healthy cognitive aging. In F. I. M. Craik & T. A. Salthouse (Eds.), *Handbook of aging and cognition* (3rd ed.). Mahwah, NJ: Erlbaum.

DePaulo, B. (2006). *Singled out.* New York: St. Martin's Press.

DePaulo, B. (2011). Living single: Lightening up those dark, dopey myths. In W. R. Cupach & B. H. Spitzberg (Eds.), *The dark side of close relationships.* New York: Routledge.

Depp, C., & Jeste, D. V. (2010). Successful aging. *Annual Review of Clinical Psychology,* Vol. 6. Palo Alto, CA: Annual Reviews.

Der Ananian, C., & Prohaska, T. R. (2007). Exercise and physical activity. In J. E. Birren (Ed.), *Encyclopedia of gerontology* (2nd ed.). San Diego: Academic Press.

Deutsch, R., & Pruett, M. K. (2009). Child adjustment and high conflict divorce. In R. M. Galatzer-Levy, L. Kraus, & J. Galatzer-Levy (Eds.), *The scientific basis of custody decisions* (2nd ed.). New York: Wiley.

Devos, T. (2006). Implicit bicultural identity among Mexican American and Asian American college students. *Cultural Diversity and Ethnic Minority Psychology, 12,* 381–402.

Dew, J., & Wilcox, W. B. (2011). "If momma ain't happy": Explaining declines in marital satisfaction among new mothers. *Journal of Marriage and the Family, 73,* 1–12.

Dewey, J. (1933). *How we think.* Lexington, MA: D. C. Heath.

DeZolt, D. M., & Hull, S. H. (2001). Classroom and school climate. In J. Worell (Ed.), *Encyclopedia of women and gender.* San Diego: Academic Press.

Diamond, A. D. (1985). Development of the ability to use recall to guide action as indicated by infants' performance on A$\overline{\text{B}}$. *Child Development, 56,* 868–883.

Diamond, A. D. (2009). The interplay of biology and the environment broadly defined. *Developmental Psychology, 45,* 1–8.

Diamond, A. D., Casey, B. J., & Munakata, Y. (2011). *Developmental cognitive neuroscience.* New York: Oxford University Press.

Diamond, L. M., Fagundes, C. P., & Butterworth, M. R. (2010). Intimate relationships across the life span. In R. M. Lerner, A. Freund, & M. Lamb (Eds.), *Handbook of life-span development.* New York: Wiley.

Diamond, L. M., & Savin-Williams, R. C. (2011). Same-sex activity in adolescence: Multiple meanings and implications. In R. F. Fassinger & S. L. Morrow (Eds.), *Sex in the margins.* Washington, DC: American Psychological Association.

Diamond, M., & Sigmundson, H. K. (1997). Sex reassignment at birth: Long-term review and clinical implications. *Archives of Pediatric and Adolescent Medicine, 151,* 295–304.

Diaz, M. T., Barrett, K. T., & Hogstrom, L. J. (2011). The influence of sentence novelty and figurativeness on brain activity. *Neuropsychologia, 49,* 320–330.

Diaz-Rico, L. T. (2012). *Course for teaching English language learners* (2nd ed.). Boston: Allyn & Bacon.

Dickinson, W. J., & others. (2011, in press). Change in stress and social support as predictors of cognitive decline in older adults with and without depression. *International Journal of Geriatric Psychiatry.*

Diego, M. A., Field, T., & Hernandez-Reif, M. (2008). Temperature increases in preterm infants during massage therapy. *Infant Behavior and Development, 31,* 149–152.

Diekmann, A., & Schmidheiny, K. (2004). Do parents of girls have a higher risk of divorce? An eighteen-country study. *Journal of Marriage and the Family, 66,* 651–660.

Diener, E. (2011). *Subjective well-being.* Retrieved January 19, 2011, from http://internal.psychology.illinois.edu/~ediener/SWLS.html

Diener, E., Emmons, R. A., Larson, R. J., & Griffin, S. (1985). The Satisfaction with Life Scale. *Journal of Personality Assessment, 49,* 71–75.

Diener, E., & Seligman, M. E. P. (2002). Very happy people. *Psychological Science, 13,* 81–84.

Dietz, L. J., Jennings, K. D., Kelley, S. A., & Marshal, M. (2009). Maternal depression, paternal psychopathology, and toddlers' behavior problems. *Journal of Clinical Child and Adolescent Psychology, 38,* 48–61.

Dietz, P. M., & others. (2010). Infant morbidity and mortality attributable to prenatal smoking in the U.S. *American Journal of Preventive Medicine, 39,* 45–62.

Dillon, C. F., Gu, Q., Hoffman, H. J., & Ko, C. W. (2010). Vision, hearing, balance, and sensory impairment in Americans aged 70 years and over: United States, 1999–2006. *NCHS Data Brief, 31,* 1–8.

Dillon, J. (2003). Reincarnation: The technology of death. In C. D. Bryant (Ed.), *Handbook of death and dying.* Thousand Oaks, CA: Sage.

Dionyssiotis, Y., Paspati, I., Trovas, G., Galanos, A., & Lyritis, G. P. (2010, in press). Association of physical exercise and calcium intake bone mass measured by quantitative ultrasound. *BMC Women's Health.*

DiPietro, J. (2008). Unpublished review of J. W. Santrock's *Children,* 11th ed. (New York: McGraw-Hill).

Dishion, T. J., & Piehler, T. F. (2009). Deviant by design: Peer contagion in development, interventions, and schools. In K. H. Rubin, W. M. Bukowski, & B. Laursen (Eds.), *Handbook of peer interactions, relationships, and groups.* New York: Guilford.

Dishion, T. J., & Tipsord, J. M. (2011). Peer contagion in child and adolescent social and emotional development. *Annual Review of Psychology* (Vol. 62). Palo Alto, CA: Annual Reviews.

Dixon, L., Browne, K., & Hamilton-Giachritsis, C. (2005). Risk factors of parents abused as children: A mediational analysis of the intergenerational continuity of child maltreatment (Part I). *Journal of Child Psychology and Psychiatry and Allied Disciplines, 46,* 47–54.

Dixon, S. V., Graber, J. A., & Brooks-Gunn, J. (2008). The roles of respect for parental authority and parenting practices in parent-child conflict among African American, Latino, and European American families. *Journal of Family Psychology, 22,* 1–10.

Dodge, K. A. (1983). Behavioral antecedents of peer social status. *Child Development, 54,* 1386–1399.

Dodge, K. A., & McCourt, S. N. (2010). Translating models of antisocial behavioral development into efficacious intervention policy to prevent adolescent violence. *Developmental Psychobiology, 52*(3), 277–285.

Dodge, K. A., & Rutter, M. (Eds.). (2011). *Gene-environment interaction and developmental psychopathology.* New York: Guilford.

Doherty, M. (2008). *Theory of mind.* Philadelphia: Psychology Press.

Domsch, H., Lohaus, A., & Thomas, H. (2009). Influence of information processing and disengagement on infants' looking behavior. *Infant and Child Development, 19,* 161–174.

Donatelle, R. J. (2011). *Health* (9th ed.). Upper Saddle River, NJ: Pearson.

Dondi, M., Simion, F., & Caltran, G. (1999). Can newborns discriminate between their own cry and the cry of another newborn infant? *Developmental Psychology, 35*(2), 418–426.

Donegan, S., Maluccio, J. A., Myers, C. K., Menon, P., Ruel, M. T., & Habicht, J. P. (2010). Two food-assisted maternal and child health nutrition programs helped mitigate the impact of economic hardship on child stunting in Haiti. *Journal of Nutrition, 140,* 1139–1145.

Donnellan, M. B., & Lucas, R. E. (2008). Age differences in the big five across the life span: Evidence from two national samples. *Psychology and Aging, 23,* 558–566.

Donnellan, M. B., & Robins, R. W. (2009). The development of personality across the life span. In G. Matthews and P. Corr (Eds.), *Cambridge handbook of personality.* Cambridge, UK: Cambridge University Press.

Dontigny, L., & others. (2008). Rubella in pregnancy. *Journal of Obstetrics and Gynecology Canada, 30,* 152–168.

Doremus-Fitzwater, T. L., Varlinskaya, E. I., & Spear, L. P. (2010). Motivational systems in adolescence: Possible implications for age differences in substance abuse and other risk-taking behaviors. *Brain and Cognition, 72,* 114–123.

Dorrian, J., & others. (2008). Sleep and errors in a group of Australian hospital nurses at work and during the commute. *Applied Ergonomics, 39,* 605–613.

Doss, B. D., Rhoades, G. K., Stanley, S. M., Markman, H. J., & Johnson, C. A. (2009). Differential use of premarital education in first and second marriages. *Journal of Family Psychology, 23,* 268–273.

Doty, R. L., & Shah, M. (2008). Taste and smell. In M. M. Haith & J. B. Benson (Eds.), *Encyclopedia of infant and early childhood development.* Oxford, UK: Elsevier.

Dowda, M., & others. (2009). Policies and characteristics of the preschool environment and physical activity of young children. *Pediatrics, 123,* e261–e266.

Dozier, M., Stovall-McClough, K. C., & Albus, K. E. (2009). Attachment and psychopathology in adulthood. In J. Cassidy & P. R. Shaver (Eds.), *Handbook of attachment* (2nd ed.). New York: Guilford.

Draghi-Lorenz, R. (2007, July). *Self-conscious emotions in young infants and the direct perception of self and others in interaction.* Paper presented at the meeting of the International Society for Research on Emotions, Sunshine Coast, Australia.

Dregan, A., & Armstrong, D. (2010). Adolescence sleep disturbances as predictors of adulthood sleep disturbances—a cohort study. *Journal of Adolescent Health, 46*(5), 482–487.

Dryfoos, J. G., & Barkin, C. (2006). *Adolescence: Growing up in America today.* New York: Oxford University Press.

Du, Y., & others. (2011). Hypomethylated DSCR4 is a placenta-derived epigenetic marker for trisomy 21. *Prenatal Diagnostics, 31,* 207–214.

Duck, S. (2011). *Rethinking relationships.* Thousand Oaks, CA: Sage.

Dudley, R. L. (1999). Youth religious commitment over time: Longitudinal study of retention. *Review of Religious Research, 41,* 110–121.

Duggan, P. M., Lapsley, D. K., & Norman, K. (2000, April). *Adolescent invulnerability and personal uniqueness: Scale development and initial contact validation.* Paper presented at the biennial meeting of the Society for Research in Child Development, Chicago.

Duke, J., & others. (2011, in press). A study of burn hospitalizations for children younger than 5 years of age: 1983–2008. *Pediatrics.*

Duncan, A. F., & others. (2011, in press). Elevated systolic blood pressure in preterm very-low-birthweight infants at 3 years of life. *Pediatric Nephrology.*

Duncan, J. R., & others. (2010). Brainstem serotonergic deficiency in sudden infant death. *Journal of the American Medical Association, 303,* 430–437.

Dunkel Schetter, C. (2011). Psychological science in the study of pregnancy and birth. *Annual Review of Psychology* (Vol. 62). Palo Alto, CA: Annual Reviews.

Dunn, J. (1984). Sibling studies and the developmental impact of critical incidents. In P. B. Baltes & O. G. Brim (Eds.), *Life-span development and behavior* (Vol. 6). Orlando, FL: Academic Press.

Dunn, J. (2007). Siblings and socialization. In J. E. Grusec & P. D. Hastings (Eds.), *Handbook of socialization.* New York: Guilford.

Dunn, J., & Kendrick, C. (1982). *Siblings.* Cambridge, MA: Harvard University Press.

Dupre, M. E., & Meadows, S. O. (2007). Disaggregating the effects of marital trajectories on health. *Journal of Family Issue, 28,* 623–652.

Dupree, C. S. (2010). Primary prevention of failure: An update. *Current Opinion in Cardiology, 22,* 478–483.

Durbin, D. R., & others. (2011, in press). Technical report—child passenger safety. *Pediatrics.*

Durrant, J. E. (2008). Physical punishment, culture, and rights: Current issues for professionals. *Journal of Developmental and Behavioral Pediatrics, 29,* 55–66.

Durston, S. (2010). Imaging genetics in ADHD. *Neuroimage, 53*(3), 832–838.

Durston, S., & others. (2006). A shift from diffuse to focal cortical activity with development. *Developmental Science, 9,* 1–8.

Duschi, R., & Hamilton, R. (2011). Learning science. In P. A. Alexander & R. E. Mayer (Eds.), *Handbook of research on learning and instruction.* New York: Routledge.

Dweck, C. S. (2006). *Mindset.* New York: Random House.

Dweck, C. S. (2007). Boosting achievement with messages that motivate. *Education Canada, 47,* 6–10.

Dweck, C. S. (2009). Augmenting cognition: Psychological studies of children. *Frontiers of Neuroscience.*

Dweck, C. S. (2012). Social development. In P. Zelazo (Ed.), *Oxford handbook of developmental psychology.* New York: Oxford University Press.

Dweck, C. S., & Elliott, E. (1983). Achievement motivation. In P. Mussen (Ed.), *Handbook of child psychology* (4th ed., Vol. 4). New York: Wiley.

Dweck, C. S., Mangels, J. A., & Good, C. (2004). Motivational effects on attention, cognition, and performance. In D. Y. Dai & R. J. Sternberg (Eds.), *Motivation, emotion and cognition.* Mahwah, NJ: Erlbaum.

Dweck, C. S., & Master, A. (2009). Self-theories and motivation: Students' beliefs about intelligence. In K. R. Wentzel & A. Wigfield (Eds.), *Handbook of motivation at school.* New York: Routledge.

Dworkin, S. L., & Santelli, J. (2007). Do abstinence-plus interventions reduce sexual risk behavior among youth? *PLoS Medicine, 4,* 1437–1439.

Dworkis, D. A., & others. (2011). Severe sickle-cell anemia is associated with increased plasma levels of TNF-R1 and VCAM-1. *American Journal of Hematology, 86,* 220–223.

Dykas, M. J., & Cassidy, J. (2011). Attachment and the processing of information across the life span: Theory and evidence. *Psychological Bulletin, 137,* 19–46.

Dykes, F. (2011). Twenty-five years of breast-feeding research in midwifery. *Midwifery, 27,* 8–14.

E

Eagly, A. H. (2001). Social role theory of sex differences and similarities. In J. Worrell (Ed.), *Encyclopedia of women and gender.* San Diego: Academic Press.

Eagly, A. H. (2010). Gender roles. In J. Levine & M. Hogg (Eds.), *Encyclopedia of group process and intergroup relations.* Thousand Oaks, CA: Sage.

Eagly, A. H., & Crowley, M. (1986). Gender and helping behavior: A meta-analytic review of the social psychological literature. *Psychological Bulletin, 100,* 283–308.

Eagly, A. H., & Steffen, V. J. (1986). Gender and aggressive behavior: A meta-analytic review of the social psychological literature. *Psychological Bulletin, 100,* 309–330.

Eagly, A., & Wood, W. (2011). Gender roles in a biosocial world. In P. van Lange, A. Kruglanski, & E. T. Higgins (Eds.), *Handbook of theories in social psychology.* Thousand Oaks, CA: Sage.

East, P. (2009). Adolescent relationships with siblings. In R. M. Lerner & L. Steinberg (Eds.), *Handbook of adolescent psychology* (3rd ed.). New York: Wiley.

Eaton, D. K., & others. (2006). Youth risk behavior surveillance—United States, 2005. *MMWR Surveillance Summaries, 55,* 1–108.

Eaton, D. K., & others. (2008). Youth risk behavior surveillance—United States, 2007. *MMWR, 57,* 1–131.

Eaton, D. K., & others. (2010). Youth risk behavior surveillance—United States, 2009. *MMWR Surveillance Summary, 59*(5), 1–142.

Eaton, W. O. (2008). Milestones: Physical. In M. M. Haith & J. B. Benson (Eds.), *Encyclopedia of infant and early childhood development.* Oxford, UK: Elsevier.

Eby, J. W., Herrell, A. L., & Jordan, M. L. (2011). *Teaching in elementary school: A reflective approach* (6th ed.). Boston: Allyn & Bacon.

Eccles, J. (2003). Education: Junior and high school. In G. Adams & M. Berzonsky (Eds.), *Blackwell handbook of adolescence.* Malden, MA: Blackwell.

Eccles, J. S. (2004). Schools, academic motivation, and stage-environment fit. In R. Lerner & L. Steinberg (Eds.), *Handbook of adolescent psychology.* New York: Wiley.

Eccles, J. S. (2007). Families, schools, and developing achievement-related motivations and engagement. In J. E. Grusec & P. D. Hastings (Eds.), *Handbook of socialization.* New York: Guilford.

Eccles, J. S., & Roeser, R. W. (2010). Schools, academic motivation, and stage-environment fit. In J. Meece & J. Eccles (Eds.), *Handbook of research on schools, schooling, and human development.* New York: Routledge.

Eccles, J. S., & Roeser, R. W. (2011). Schools as developmental contexts during adolescence. *Journal of Research on Adolescence, 21,* 225–241.

Echevarria, J. L., & Vogt, M. J. (2011). *Response to intervention (RPI) and the English learners: Making it happen.* Boston: Allyn & Bacon.

Eckenrode, J., & others. (2010). Long-term effects of prenatal and infancy nurse home visitation on the life course of youths: 19-year follow-up of a randomized trial. *Archives of Pediatric and Adolescent Medicine, 164,* 9–15.

Ednick, M., & others. (2010). Sleep-related respiratory abnormalities and arousal pattern in achondroplasia during early infancy. *Journal of Pediatrics, 155,* 510–515.

Edwards, J. D., Bart, E., O'Connor, M. L., & Cissell, G. (2010). Ten years down the road: Predictors of driving cessation. *Gerontologist, 50,* 393–399.

Edwards, J. D., Delahunt, P. B., & Mahncke, H. W. (2009). Cognitive speed of processing training delays driving cessation. *Journal of Gerontology B: Psychological Sciences and Social Sciences, 64B,* 1262–1267.

Edwards, S., McCreanor, T., Ormsby, M., Tuwhangal, N., & Tipene-Leach, D. (2009). Maori men and the grief of SIDS. *Death Studies, 33,* 130–152.

Edwardson, C. L., & Gorely, T. (2010). Activity-related parenting practices and children's objectively measured physical activity. *Pediatric Exercise Science, 22,* 105–113.

Egan, S. K., & Perry, D. G. (2001). Gender identity: A multidimensional analysis with implications of psychological adjustment. *Developmental Psychology,* 451–463.

Ehrhardt, A. A., & Baker, S. W. (1974). Fetal androgens, human central nervous system differentiation, and behavior sex differences. In R. C. Friedman, R. M. Richart, & R. L. Vande Wiele (Eds.), *Sex differences in behavior.* New York: Wiley.

Eichorn, D. H., Clausen, J. A., Haan, N., Honzik, M. P., & Mussen, P. H. (Eds.). (1981). *Present and past in middle life.* New York: Academic Press.

Eidar-Avidan, D., Haj-Yahia, M. M., & Greenbaum, C. W. (2009). Divorce is part of my life . . . resilience, survival, and vulnerability: Young adults' perceptions of the implications of parental divorce. *Journal of Marital and Family Therapy, 35,* 30–46.

Einstein, G. O., & McDaniel, M. A. (2005). Prospective memory. *Current Directions in Psychological Science, 14,* 286–290.

Eisdorfer, C. (1996, December). Interview. *APA Monitor,* p. 35.

Eisenberg, M. E., Bernat, D. H., Bearinger, L. H., & Resnick, M. D. (2008). Support for comprehensive sexuality education: Perspectives from parents of school-aged youth. *Journal of Adolescent Research, 42,* 352–359.

Eisenberg, N. (2010). Emotion regulation in children. *Annual Review of Clinical Psychology* (Vol. 6). Palo Alto, CA: Annual Reviews.

Eisenberg, N., Fabes, R. A., Guthrie, I. K., & Reiser, M. (2002). The role of emotionality and regulation in children's social competence and adjustment. In L. Pulkkinen & A. Caspi (Eds.), *Paths to successful development.* New York: Cambridge University Press.

Eisenberg, N., & Morris, A. S. (2004). Moral cognitions and prosocial responding in adolescence. In R. Lerner & L. Steinberg (Eds.), *Handbook of adolescent psychology* (2nd ed.). New York: Wiley.

Eisenberg, N., Morris, A. S., McDaniel, B., & Spinrad, T. L. (2009). Moral cognitions and prosocial responding in adolescence. In R. M. Lerner & Steinberg (Eds.), *Handbook of adolescent psychology* (3rd ed.). New York: Wiley.

Eisenberg, N., Spinrad, T. R., & Eggum, N. D. (2010). Emotion-focused self-regulation and its relation to children's maladjustment. *Annual Review of Clinical Psychology* (Vol. 61). Palo Alto, CA: Annual Reviews.

Eisenberg, N., & Valiente, C. (2002). Parenting and children's prosocial and moral development. In M. H. Bornstein (Ed.), *Handbook of parenting* (2nd ed.). Mahwah, NJ: Erlbaum.

Elder, G. H. (1980). Adolescence in historical perspective. In J. Adelson (Ed.), *Handbook of adolescent psychology.* New York: Wiley.

Elder, G. H., & Shanahan, M. J. (2006). The life course and human development. In W. Damon & R. Lerner (Eds.), *Handbook of child psychology* (6th ed.). New York: Wiley.

El-Fishawy, P., & State, M. W. (2010). The genetics of autism: Key issues, recent findings, and clinical implications. *Psychiatric Clinics of North America, 33,* 83–105.

Elias, J. W., & Wagster, M. V. (2007). Developing context and background underlying cognitive intervention/training studies in older populations. *Journals of Gerontology B: Psychological Sciences and Social Sciences, 62,* 5–10.

Eliasieh, K., Liets, L. C., & Chalupa, L. M. (2007). Cellular reorganization in the human retina during normal aging. *Investigative Ophthalmology and Visual Science, 48,* 2824–2830.

Elkind, D. (1976). *Child development and education: A Piagetian perspective.* New York: Oxford University Press.

Elkind, D. (1978). Understanding the young adolescent. *Adolescence, 13,* 127–134.

Elks, C. E., & others. (2010). Thirty new loci for age of menarche identified by a meta-analysis of genome-wide association studies. *Nature Genetics, 42,* 1077–1085.

Ellenberg, D., & St. Louis-Deschenes, M. (2010). The effect of acute physical activity on cognitive function during development. *Psychology of Sport and Exercise, 11,* 122–126.

Elliott, A. F., Burgio, L. D., & Decoster, J. (2010). Enhancing caregiver health: Findings from the resources for enhancing Alzheimer's caregiver health II intervention. *Journal of the American Geriatrics Society, 58,* 30–37.

Ellis, L., & Ames, M. A. (1987). Neurohormonal functioning and sexual orientation. *Psychological Bulletin, 101,* 233–258.

Emery, R. E. (1999). *Renegotiating family relationships* (2nd ed.). New York: Guilford Press.

Emre, M., & others. (2010). Drug profile: Transdermal rivastigmine patch in the treatment of Alzheimer diseases. *CNS Neuroscience and Therapeutics, 16*(4), 246–253.

Enfield, A., & Collins, D. (2008). The relationships of service-learning, social justice, multicultural competence, and civic engagement. *Journal of College Student Development, 49,* 95–109.

Engler, C., & Marillonnet, S. (2011). Generation of families of construct variants using golden gate shuffling. *Methods in Molecular Biology, 729,* 167–181.

Englund, M. M., Egeland, B., & Collins, W. A. (2008). Exceptions to high school dropout predictions in a low-income sample: Do adults make a difference? *Journal of Social Issues, 64,* 77–93.

Englund, M. M., Luckner, A. E., Whaley, G. J. L., & Egeland, B. (2004). Children's achievement in early elementary school: Longitudinal effects of parental involvement, expectations, and quality of assistance. *Journal of educational Psychology, 96*, 723–730.

Engvig, A., & others. (2010). Effects of memory training on cortical thickness in the elderly. *Neuroimage, 52*, 1667–1676.

Ennett, S. T., Bauman, K. E., Hussong, A., Faris, R., Foshee, V. A., & Cai, L. (2006). The peer context of adolescent substance use: Findings from social network analysis. *Journal of Research on Adolescence, 16*, 159–166.

Enright, R. D., Santos, M. J., & Al-Mabuk, R. (1989). The adolescent as forgiver. *Journal of Adolescence, 12*, 95–110.

Ensembl Human. (2008). *Explore the Homo sapiens genome.* Retrieved April 14, 2008, from www.ensembl.org/Homo_sapiens/index.html

Ensor, R., Spencer, D., & Hughes, C. (2010). "You feel sad?" Emotion understanding mediates effects of verbal ability and mother-child mutuality on prosocial behaviors: Findings from 2 to 4 years. *Social Development, 20*(1), 93–110.

Entwisle, D., Alexander, K., & Olson, L. (2010). The long reach of socioeconomic status in education. In J. Meece & J. Eccles (Eds.), *Handbook of research on schools, schooling, and human development.* New York: Routledge.

Erath, S. E., Flanagan, K. S., & Bierman, K. B. (2010). Friendships moderate psychological maladjustment in socially anxious early adolescents. *Journal of Applied Developmental Psychology, 31*, 15–26.

Erickson, K. I., & Kramer, A. F. (2009). Aerobic exercise effects on cognitive and neural plasticity in older adults. *British Journal of Sports Medicine, 43*, 22–24.

Erickson, K. I., & others. (2009). Aerobic fitness is associated with hippocampal volume in elderly humans. *Hippocampus, 19*, 1030–1039.

Erickson, K. I., & others. (2011, in press). Physical activity predicts gray matter volume in late adulthood: The Cardiovascular Health Study. *Neurology.*

Ericsson, K. A., Krampe, R., & Tesch-Romer, C. (1993). The role of deliberate practice in the acquisition of expert performance. *Psychological Review, 100*, 363–406.

Erikson, E. H. (1950). *Childhood and society.* New York: W. W. Norton.

Erikson, E. H. (1962). *Young man Luther.* New York: W. W. Norton.

Erikson, E. H. (1968). *Identity: Youth and crisis.* New York: W. W. Norton.

Erikson, E. H. (1969). *Gandhi's truth.* New York: W. W. Norton.

Eriksson, U. J. (2009). Congenital malformations in diabetic pregnancy. *Seminar in Fetal and Neonatal Medicine, 14*, 85–93.

Erkal, S. (2010). Identification of the number of home accidents per year involving children in the 0–6 age group and the measures taken by mothers to prevent home accidents. *Turkish Journal of Pediatrics, 52*, 150–157.

Escobar-Chaves, S. L., & Anderson, C. A. (2008). Media and risky behavior. *The Future of Children, 18*(1), 147–180.

Eshkoli, T., Sheiner, E., Ben-Zvi, Z., & Holcberg, G. (2011, in press). Drug transport across the placenta. *Current Pharmaceutical Biotechnology.*

ESHRE Capri Workshop Group. (2011, in press). Perimenopausal risk factors and future health. *Human Reproduction Update.*

Eskildsen, M., & Price, T. (2009). Nursing home care in the USA. *Geriatrics and Gerontology International, 9*, 1–6.

Espelage, D., Holt, M., & Poteat, P. (2010). The school context of bullying and victimization. In J. Meece & J. Eccles (Eds.), *Handbook of research on schools, schooling, and human development.* New York: Routledge.

Etaugh, C., & Bridges, J. S. (2010). *Women's lives* (2nd ed.). Boston: Allyn & Bacon.

Evans, G. W. (2004). The environment of childhood poverty. *American Psychologist, 59*, 77–92.

Evans, G. W., & English, G. W. (2002). The environment of poverty. *Child Development, 73*, 1238–1248.

Evans, G. W., & Kim, P. (2007). Childhood poverty and health: Cumulative risk exposure and stress dysregulation. *Psychological Science, 18*, 953–957.

F

Fabiano, G. A., Pelham, W. W., Coles, E. K., Gnagy, E. M., Chronis-Tuscano, A., & O'Connor, B. C. (2009). A meta-analysis of behavioral treatments for attention deficit/hyperactivity disorder. *Clinical Psychology Review, 29*(2), 129–140.

Fabricius, W. V., Braver, S. L., Diaz, P., & Schenck, C. (2010). Custody and parenting time: Links to family relationships and well-being after divorce. In M. E. Lamb (Ed.), *The role of the father in child development* (5th ed.). New York: Wiley.

Facciorusso, A., Stanilslao, M., Fanelli, M., Valori, M., & Valle, G. (2011, in press). Ethical issues on defibrillator deactivation in end-of-life patients. *Journal of Cardiovascular Medicine.*

Fagan, J. F. (1992). Intelligence: A theoretical viewpoint. *Current Directions in Psychological Science, 1*, 82–86.

Fagan, J. F. (2011). Intelligence in infancy. In R. J. Sternberg & S. B. Kaufman (Eds.), *Cambridge handbook of intelligence.* New York: Cambridge University Press.

Fagan, J. F., Holland, C. R., & Wheeler, K. (2007). The prediction, from infancy, of adult IQ and achievement. *Intelligence, 35*, 225–231.

Fahey, T. D., Insel, P. M., & Roth, W. T. (2011). *Fit and well* (9th ed.). New York: McGraw-Hill.

Fairweather, A. K., Anstey, K. J., Rodgers, B., & Butterworth, P. (2006). Factors distinguishing suicide attempters from suicide ideators in a community sample: Social issues and physical health problems. *Psychological Medicine, 31*, 1–11.

Fairweather, E., & Cramond, B. (2011). Infusing creative and critical thinking into the classroom. In R. A. Beghetto & J. C. Kaufman (Eds.), *Nurturing creativity in the classroom.* New York: Cambridge University Press.

Faissner, A., & others. (2010). Contributions of astrocytes to synapse formation and maturation—Potential functions of the perisynaptic extracellular matrix. *Brain Research Reviews, 63*(1–2), 26–38.

Fakhoury, J., Nimmo, G. A., & Autexier, C. (2007). Harnessing telomerase in cancer therapeutics. *Anticancer Agents and Medicinal Chemistry, 7*, 475–484.

Falbo, T., & Poston, D. L. (1993). The academic personality and physical outcomes of only children in China. *Child Development, 64*, 18–35.

Fallu, J. S., & others. (2010). Preventing disruptive boys from becoming heavy substance users during adolescence: A longitudinal study of familial and peer-related protective factors. *Addictive Behaviors, 35*(12), 1074–1082.

Fanconi, M., & Lips, U. (2010). Shaken baby syndrome in Switzerland: Results of a prospective follow-up study, 2002–2007. *European Journal of Pediatrics, 169*(8), 1023–1028.

Fantasia, H. C. (2008). Concept analysis: Sexual decision-making in adolescence. *Nursing Forum, 43*, 80–90.

Fantz, R. L. (1963). Pattern vision in newborn infants. *Science, 140*, 286–297.

Farage, M. A., Miller, K. W., Berardesca, E., & Malbach, H. l. (2009). Clinical implications of aging skin: Cutaneous disorders in the elderly. *American Journal of Clinical Dermatology, 10*, 73–86.

Faraone, S. V., & Mick, E. (2010). Molecular genetics of attention deficit hyperactivity disorder. *Psychiatric Clinics of North America, 33*, 159–180.

Farooqui, T., & Farooqui, A. A. (2009). Aging: An important factor for the pathogenesis of neurogenerative diseases. *Mechanisms of Aging and Development, 130*, 203–215.

Farrell, M. P., & Rosenberg, S. D. (1981). *Men at mid-life.* Boston: Auburn House.

Farrell, S. W., Fitzgerald, S. J., McAuley, P., & Barlow, C. E. (2010). Cardiorespiratory fitness, adiposity, and all-cause mortality in women. *Medicine and Science in Sports Exercise, 42*(11), 2006–2012.

Farrington, D. (2004). Conduct disorder, aggression, and delinquency. In R. Lerner & L. Steinberg (Eds.), *Handbook of adolescent psychology.* New York: Wiley.

Farrington, D. P. (2009). Conduct disorder, aggression, and delinquency. In R. M. Lerner & L. Steinberg (Eds.), *Handbook of adolescent psychology* (3rd ed.). New York: Wiley.

Fasig, L. (2000). Toddlers' understanding of ownership: Implications for self-concept development. *Social Development, 9*, 370–382.

Fass, J., & Fass, A. (2011). Physician-assisted suicide: Ongoing challenges for pharmacists.

American Journal of Health-System Pharmacy, 68, 846–849.

Fatusi, A. O., & Hindin, M. J. (2010). Adolescents and youths in developing countries: Health and development issues in context. *Journal of Adolescence, 33,* 499–508.

Fearon, R. P., & others. (2010). The significance of insecure attachment and disorganization in the development of children's externalizing behavior: A meta-analytic study. *Child Development, 81,* 435–456.

Fechtner, R. D., & others. (2010). Prevalence of ocular surface complaints in patients with glaucoma using topical intraocular pressure-lowering medications. *Cornea, 29*(6), 618–621.

Federal Interagency Forum on Child and Family Statistics. (2010). *America's Children: Key indicators of well-being.* Washington, DC: U.S. Government Printing Office.

Feeney, B. C., & Monin, J. K. (2008). An attachment-theoretical perspective on divorce. In J. Cassidy & P. R. Shaver (Eds.), *Handbook of attachment* (2nd ed.). New York: Guilford.

Feeney, M. P., & Sanford, C. A. (2004). Age effects in the middle ear: Wideband acoustical measures. *Journal of the Acoustical Society of America, 116,* 3546–3558.

Feldhusen, J. (1999). Giftedness and creativity. In M. A. Runco & S. R. Pritzker (Eds.), *Encyclopedia of creativity.* San Diego: Academic Press.

Feldman, S. S., Turner, R., & Araujo, K. (1999). Interpersonal context as an influence on sexual timetables of youths: Gender and ethnic effects. *Journal of Research on Adolescence, 9,* 25–52.

Fenzel, L. M. (1994, February). *A prospective study of the effects of chronic strains on early adolescent self-worth and school adjustment.* Paper presented at the meeting of the Society for Research on Adolescence, San Diego.

Fergusson, D. M., Horwood, L. J., & Shannon, F. T. (1987). Breastfeeding and subsequent social adjustment in 6-to-8-year-old children. *Journal of Child Psychology and Psychiatry, 28,* 378–386.

Field, D. (1999). A cross-cultural perspective on continuity and change in social relations in old age: Introduction to a special issue. *International Journal of Aging and Human Development, 48,* 257–262.

Field, T., Diego, M., & Hernandez-Reif, M. (2008). Prematurity and potential predictors. *International Journal of Neuroscience, 118,* 277–289.

Field, T., Diego, M., & Hernandez-Reif, M. (2010). Preterm infant massage therapy research: A review. *Infant Behavior and Development, 33*(2), 115–124.

Field, T., Figueiredo, B., Hernandez-Reif, M., Diego, M., Deeds, O., & Ascencio, A. (2008). Massage therapy reduces pain in pregnant women, alleviates prenatal depression in both parents and improves their relationships. *Journal of Bodywork and Movement Therapies, 12,* 146–150.

Field, T., & others. (1986). Tactile/kinesthetic stimulation effects on preterm neonates. *Pediatrics, 77,* 654–658.

Field, T. M. (2001). Massage therapy facilitates weight gain in preterm infants. *Current Directions in Psychological Science, 10,* 51–55.

Field, T. M. (2007). *The amazing infant.* Malden, MA: Blackwell.

Field, T. M. (2010). Postpartum depression effects on early interactions, parenting, and safety practices: A review. *Infant Behavior and Development, 33,* 1–6.

Field, T. M. (2011). Prenatal depression effects on early development: A review. *Infant Behavior and Development, 34,* 1–14.

Finch, C. E. (2009). The neurobiology of middle-age has arrived. *Neurobiology of Aging, 30,* 515–520.

Finch, C. E. (2011). Inflammation and aging. In E. Masoro & S. Austad (Eds.), *Handbook of the biology of aging* (7th ed.). New York: Elsevier.

Finger, B., Hans, S. L., Bernstein, V. J., & Cox, S. M. (2009). Parent relationship quality and infant-mother attachment. *Attachment and Human Development, 11,* 285–306.

Fingerhut, A. W., & Peplau, L. A. (2012). Sexual orientation and romantic relationships. In C. J. Patterson & A. R. D'Augelli (Eds.), *Handbook of psychology and sexual orientation.* New York: Oxford University Press.

Fingerman, K. L., & Birditt, K. S. (2011a). Adult children and aging parents. In K. W. Schaie (Ed.), *Handbook of the psychology of aging* (7th ed.). New York: Elsevier.

Fingerman, K. L., & Birditt, K. S. (2011b). Intergenerational communication practices. In K. W. Schaie & S. L. Willis (Eds.), *Handbook of the psychology of aging* (7th ed.). New York: Elsevier.

Fingerman, K. L., Brown, B. G., & Blieszner, R. (2011). Informal ties across the lifespan: Peers, consequential strangers, and people we encounter in daily life. In K. L. Fingerman, C. A. Berg, J. Smith, & T. C. Antonucci (Eds.), *Handbook of life-span development.* New York: Springer.

Fingerman, K. L., Chan, W., Pitzer, L. M., Birditt, K. S., Franks, M. M., & Zarit, S. (2011). Who gets what and why: Help middle-aged adults provide to parents and grown children. *Journal of Gerontology B: Psychological Sciences and Social Sciences, 66,* 87–98.

Fingerman, K. L., Cheng, Y. P., Tighe, L., Birditt, K. S., & Zarit, S. (2011). Parent-child relationships in young adulthood. In A. Booth & others (Eds.), *Early adulthood in a family context.* New York: Springer.

Fingerman, K. L., Pitzer, L., Lefkowitz, E. S., Birditt, K. S., & Mroczek, D. (2008). Ambivalent relationship qualities between adults and their parents: Implications for both parties' well-being. *Journal of Gerontology B: Psychological Sciences and Social Sciences, 63,* 362–371.

Finkelstein, L. M., & Farrell, S. K. (2007). An expanded view of age bias in the workplace. In K. S. Shultz & G. A. Adams (Eds.), *Aging and work in the 21st century.* Mahwah, NJ: Erlbaum.

Fiori, K. L., Antonucci, T. C., & Cortina, K. S. (2006). Social network typologies and mental health among older adults. *Journal of Gerontology B: Psychological Sciences and Social Sciences, 61,* P25–P32.

Fiori, K. L., Smith, J., & Antonucci, T. C. (2007). Social network types among older adults: A multidimensional approach. *Journals of Gerontology B: Psychological Sciences and Social Sciences, 62,* P322–P330.

Fischhoff, B., Bruine de Bruin, W., Parker, A. M., Millstein, S. G., & Halpern-Felsher, B. L. (2010). Adolescents' perceived risk of dying. *Journal of Adolescent Health, 46,* 265–269.

Fisher, C. A., Hetrick, S. E., & Rushford, N. (2010, April 14). Family therapy for anorexia nervosa. *Cochrane Database of Systematic Reviews, 4,* CD004780.

Fisher, P. A. (2005, April). *Translational research on underlying mechanisms of risk among foster children: Implications for prevention science.* Paper presented at the meeting of the Society for Research in Child Development, Washington, DC.

Fiske, A., Wetherell, J. L., & Gatz, M. (2009). Depression in older adults. *Annual Review of Clinical Psychology* (Vol. 5). Palo Alto, CA: Annual Reviews.

Flavell, J. H. (2004). Theory-of-mind development. *Merrill-Palmer Quarterly, 50,* 274–290.

Flavell, J. H., Friedrichs, A., & Hoyt, J. (1970). Developmental changes in memorization processes. *Cognitive Psychology, 1,* 324–340.

Flavell, J. H., Green, F. L., & Flavell, E. R. (1993). Children's understanding of the stream of consciousness. *Child Development, 64,* 95–120.

Flavell, J. H., Green, F. L., & Flavell, E. R. (1995). The development of children's knowledge about intentional focus. *Developmental Psychology, 31,* 706–712.

Flavell, J. H., Green, F. L., & Flavell, E. R. (1998). The mind has a mind of its own: Developing knowledge about mental uncontrollability. *Cognitive Development, 13,* 127–138.

Flavell, J. H., Green, F. L., & Flavell, E. R. (2000). Development of children's awareness of their own thoughts. *Journal of Cognition and Development, 1,* 97–112.

Flavell, J. H., Miller, P. H., & Miller, S. (2002). *Cognitive development* (4th ed.). Upper Saddle River, NJ: Prentice Hall.

Flavell, J. H., Mumme, D., Green, F., and Flavell, E. (1992). Young children's understanding of different types of beliefs. *Child Development, 63,* 960–977.

Flegal, K. M., Carroll, M. D., Ogden, C. L., & Curtin, L. R. (2010). Prevalence and trends in obesity among U.S. adults, 1999–2008. *Journal of the American Medical Association, 303,* 235–241.

Flicker, L. (2010). Cardiovascular risk factors, cerebrovascular disease burden, and healthy brain aging. *Clinics in Geriatric Medicine, 26,* 17–27.

Flint, M. S., Baum, A., Chambers, W. H., & Jenkins, F. J. (2007). Induction of DNA damage, alteration of DNA repair, and transcriptional activation by stress hormones. *Psychoneuroendocrinology, 32,* 470–479.

Flom, R., & Pick, A. D. (2003). Verbal encouragement and joint attention in 18-month-old infants. *Infant Behavior and Development, 26,* 121–134.

Flores, I., & Blasco, M. A. (2010). The role of telomeres and telomerase in stem cell aging. *FEBS Letters, 584*(17), 3826–3830.

Florin, T., & Ludwig, S. (2011). *Netter's Pediatrics.* New York: Elsevier.

Florsheim, P., Moore, D., & Edgington, C. (2003). Romantic relationships among pregnant and parenting adolescents. In P. Florsheim (Ed.), *Adolescent romantic relations and sexual behavior.* Mahwah, NJ: Erlbaum.

Flynn, J. R. (1999). Searching for justice: The discovery of IQ gains over time. *American Psychologist, 54,* 5–20.

Flynn, J. R. (2007). The history of the American mind in the 20th century: A scenario to explain gains over time and a case for the irrelevance of *g.* In P. C. Kyllonen, R. D. Roberts, & L. Stankov (Eds.), *Extending intelligence.* Mahwah, NJ: Erlbaum.

Flynn, J. R. (2011). Secular changes in intelligence. In R. J. Sternberg & S. B. Kaufman (Eds.), *Cambridge handbook of intelligence.* New York: Cambridge University Press.

Follari, L. (2011). *Foundations and best practices in early childhood education* (2nd ed.). Upper Saddle River, NJ: Merrill.

Fontaine, R. G., Tanha, M., Yang, C., Dodge, K. A., Bates, J. E., & Pettit, G. S. (2010). Does response evaluation and decision (RED) mediate the relation between hostile attributional style and antisocial behavior in adolescence? *Journal of Abnormal Child Psychology, 38,* 615–626.

Fontenot, H. B. (2007). Transition and adaptation to adoptive motherhood. *Journal of Obstetric, Gynecologic, and Neonatal Nursing, 36,* 175–182.

Food & Nutrition Service. (2009). *The new look of the women, infants, and children (WIC) program.* Retrieved January 21, 2009, from www.health.state.ny.us/prevention/nutrition/wic/the_new_look_of_wic.htm

Forbes, E. E., & others. (2010). Healthy adolescents' neural response to reward: Associations with puberty, positive affect, and depressive symptoms. *Journal of the American Academy of Child and Adolescent Psychiatry, 49,* 162–172.

Ford, M. E., & Smith, P. E. (2007). Thriving with social purpose: An integrative approach to the development of optimal human functioning. *Educational Psychologist, 42,* 153–171.

Forgatch, M. S., Patterson, G. R., Degarmo, D. S., & Beldavs, Z. G. (2009). Testing the Oregon delinquency model with 9-year follow-up of the Oregon Divorce Study. *Development and Psychopathology, 21,* 637–660.

Forrester, M. B., & Merz, R. D. (2007). Risk of selected birth defects with prenatal illicit drug use, Hawaii, 1986–2002. *Journal of Toxicology and Environmental Health, 70,* 7–18.

Forsyth, A. L., Quon, D. V., & Konkle, B. A. (2011, in press). Role of exercise and physical activity on haemophilic arthropathy, fall prevention, and osteoporosis. *Haemophilia.*

Fosco, G. M., & Grych, J. H. (2010). Adolescent triangulation into parental conflicts: Longitudinal implications for appraisals and adolescent-parent relations. *Journal of Marriage and the Family, 72,* 254–266.

Foster, G. D., & others. (2010). Weight and metabolic outcomes after 2 years on a low-carbohydrate versus low-fat diet: A randomized trial. *Annals of Internal Medicine, 153,* 147–157.

Fowler, C. G., & Leigh-Paffenroth, E. D. (2007). Hearing. In J. E. Birren (Ed.), *Encyclopedia of gerontology* (2nd ed.). San Diego: Academic Press.

Fowler-Brown, A., & Kahwati, L. C. (2004). Prevention and treatment of overweight in children and adolescents. *American Family Physician, 69,* 2591–2598.

Fox, B. J. (2010). *Phonics and structural analysis for the teacher of reading* (10th ed.). Boston: Allyn & Bacon.

Fox, B. J. (2012). *Word identification strategies* (5th ed.). Boston: Allyn & Bacon.

Fox, E., & Alexander, P. A. (2011). Learning to read. In P. A. Alexander & R. E. Mayer (Eds.), *Handbook of research on learning and instruction.* New York: Routledge.

Fox, S. E., Levitt, P., & Nelson, C. A. (2010). How the timing and quality of early experiences influence the development of brain architecture. *Child Development, 81,* 28–40.

Fozard, J. L., & Gordon-Salant, S. (2001). Changes in vision and hearing with aging. In J. E. Birren & K. W. Schaie (Eds.), *Handbook of the psychology of aging* (5th ed.). San Diego: Academic Press.

Franchak, J. M., Kretch, K. S., Soska, K. C., Babcock, J. S., & Adolph, K. E. (2010). Head-mounted eye-tracking in infants' natural interactions: A new method. *Proceedings of the 2010 Symposium on Eye Tracking Research and Applications,* Austin, TX.

Francis, J., Fraser, G., & Marcia, J. E. (1989). *Cognitive and experimental factors in moratorium-achievement (MAMA) cycles.* Unpublished manuscript, Department of Psychology, Simon Fraser University, Burnaby, British Columbia.

Franco, P., Kato, I., Richardson, H. L., Yang, J. S., Montemitro, E., & Horne, R. S. (2010). Arousal from sleep mechanisms in infants. *Sleep Medicine, 11,* 603–614.

Frankl, V. (1984). *Man's search for meaning.* New York: Basic Books.

Franklin, A., Vevis, L., Ling, Y., & Hurlbert, A. (2010). Biological components of color preference in infancy. *Developmental Science, 13,* 346–354.

Fraser, J. (2011). *Teach.* New York: McGraw-Hill.

Fraser, S. (Ed.). (1995). *The bell curve wars: Race, intelligence, and the future of America.* New York: Basic Books.

Fraser-Abder, P. (2011). *Teaching budding scientists.* Boston: Allyn & Bacon.

Frazier, P. A., & Cook, S. W. (1993). Correlates of distress following heterosexual relationship dissolution. *Journal of Social and Personal Relationships, 10,* 55–67.

Frederikse, M., Lu, A., Aylward, E., Barta, P., Sharma, T., & Pearlson, G. (2000). Sex differences in inferior lobule volume in schizophrenia. *American Journal of Psychiatry, 157,* 422–427.

Freud, S. (1917). *A general introduction to psychoanalysis.* New York: Washington Square Press.

Freund, A. M., & Baltes, P. B. (2002). Life-management strategies of selection, optimization, and compensation: Measurement by self-report and construct validity. *Journal of Personality and Social Psychology, 82,* 642–662.

Frey, B. S. (2011). Happy people live longer. *Science, 331,* 542–543.

Frey, W. H. (2007). *Mapping the growth of older America: Seniors and boomers in the early 21st century.* Washington, DC: The Brookings Institution.

Fricker-Gates, R. A., & Gates, M. A. (2010). Stem cell–derived dopamine neurons for brain repair in Parkinson's disease. *Regenerative Medicine, 5,* 267–278.

Friederici, A. D., Mueller, J. L., & Oberecker, R. (2011). Precursors to natural grammar learning: Preliminary evidence from 4-month-olds. *PLoS One, 6,* e17920.

Friedman, S. L., Melhuish, E., & Hill, C. (2011). Childcare research at the dawn of a new millennium: Update. In J. G. Bremner & T. D. Wachs (Eds.), *Wiley-Blackwell handbook of infant development* (2nd ed.). New York: Wiley.

Friend, M. (2011). *Special education* (3rd ed.). Upper Saddle River, NJ: Merrill.

Friend, M., & Bursuck, W. D. (2012). *Including students with special needs* (6th ed.). Upper Saddle River, NJ: Pearson.

Frimer, J. A., Walker, L. J., Dunlop, W. L., Lee, B. H., & Riches, A. (2011, in press). The integration of agency and communion in moral personality: Evidence of enlightened self-interest. *Journal of Personality and Social Psychology.*

Frisen, A., & Holmqvist, K. (2010). What characterizes early adolescents with a positive body image? A qualitative investigation of Swedish boys and girls. *Body Image, 7,* 205–212.

Froh, J. J., Yurkewicz, C., & Kashdan, T. B. (2009). Gratitude and subjective well-being in early adolescence: Examining gender differences. *Journal of Adolescence, 32,* 633–650.

Frost, E. A., Gist, R. S., & Adriano, E. (2011). Drugs, alcohol, pregnancy, and fetal alcohol syndrome. *International Anesthesiology Clinics, 49,* 119–133.

Fry, P. S. (2001). The unique contribution of key existential factors to the prediction of psychological well-being of older adults following spousal loss. *The Gerontologist, 41,* 69–81.

Frydenberg, E. (2008). *Adolescent coping.* Clifton, NJ: Psychology Press.

Fujisawa, D., Miyashita, M., Nakajima, S., Ito, M., Kato, M., & Kim, Y. (2010). Prevalence and determinants of complicated grief in general population. *Journal of Affective Disorders, 127*(1–3), 352–358.

Fukunaga, A., Uematsu, H., & Sugimoto, K. (2005). Influences of age on taste perception and oral somatic sensation. *Journals of Gerontology A: Biological Sciences and Medical Sciences, 60,* 109A–113A.

Fulop, T., & others. (2010). Potential role of immunosenescence in cancer development. *Annals of the New York Academy of Sciences, 1197,* 158–165.

Fung, Y. L., & Chan, Z. C. (2011, in press). A systematic review of suicidal behavior in old age: A gender perspective. *Journal of Clinical Nursing.*

Furman, W., Low, S., & Ho, M. (2009). Romantic experience and psychosocial adjustment in middle adolescence. *Journal of Clinical Child and Adolescent Psychology, 38,* 1–16.

Furstenberg, F. F. (2006). Growing up healthy: Are adolescents the right target group? *Journal of Adolescent Health, 39,* 303–304.

Furth, H. G., & Wachs, H. (1975). *Thinking goes to school.* New York: Oxford University Press.

G

Gable, S., Chang, Y., & Krull, J. L. (2007). Television watching and frequency of family meals are predictive of overweight onset and persistence in a national sample of preschool children. *Journal of the American Dietetic Association, 107,* 53–61.

Gaesser, B., Sacchetti, D. C., Addis, D. R., & Schachter, D. L. (2011). Characterizing age-related changes in remembering the past and imagining the future. *Psychology and Aging, 26,* 80–84.

Gagliese, L. (2009). Pain and aging: The emergence of a new subfield of pain research. *Journal of Pain, 10,* 343–353.

Galambos, N. L. (2004). Gender and gender role development in adolescence. In R. Lerner & L. Steinberg (Eds.), *Handbook of adolescence.* New York: Wiley.

Galambos, N. L., Berenbaum, S. A., & McHale, S. M. (2009). Gender development in adolescence. In R. M. Lerner & L. Steinberg (Eds.), *Handbook of adolescent psychology.* New York: Wiley.

Galambos, N. L., Howard, A. L., & Maggs, J. L. (2011, in press). Rise and fall of sleep quality with student experiences across the first year of the university. *Journal of Research on Adolescence.*

Galimberti, D., & Scarpini, E. (2010). Treatment of Alzheimer's disease: Symptomatic and disease-modifying approaches. *Current Aging Science, 3,* 46–56.

Galinsky, E. (2010). *Mind in the making.* New York: HarperCollins.

Galinsky, E., & David, J. (1988). *The preschool years: Family strategies that work—from experts and parents.* New York: Times Books.

Gallo, W. T., & others. (2006). The persistence of depressive symptoms in older workers who experience involuntary job loss: Results from the health and retirement survey. *Journals of Gerontology B: Psychological Sciences and Social Sciences, 61,* S221–S228.

Galloway, J. C., & Thelen, E. (2004). Feet first: Object exploration in young infants. *Infant Behavior & Development, 27,* 107–112.

Gallup, G. W., & Bezilla, R. (1992). *The religious life of young Americans.* Princeton, NJ: Gallup Institute.

Galupo, M. P., Cartwright, K. B., & Savage, L. S. (2010). Cross-category friendships and postformal thought among college students. *Journal of Adult Development, 17,* 208–214.

Galvin, J. E. (2011, in press). Dementia screening, biomarkers, and protein misfolding: Implications for public health and diagnosis. *Prion.*

Gamble, W. C., & Modry-Mandell, K. (2008). Family relations and the adjustment of young children of Mexican descent: Do family cultural values moderate these associations? *Social Development, 17,* 358–379.

Ganong, L., Coleman, M., & Hans, J. (2006). Divorce as a prelude to stepfamily living and the consequences of re-divorce. In M. Fine & J.H. Harvey (Eds.), *Handbook of divorce and relationship dissolution.* Mahwah, NJ: Erlbaum.

Ganong, L., Coleman, M., & Jamison, T. (2011). Patterns of stepchild-stepparent relationship development. *Journal of Marriage and the Family, 73,* 396–413.

Gao, X., Yuan, S., Jayaraman, S., & Gursky, O. (2009). Differential stability of high-density lipoprotein subclasses: Effects of particle size and protein composition. *Journal of Molecular Biology, 387,* 628–638.

Garand, L., Mitchell, A. M., Dietrick, A., Hijjawi, S. P., & Pan, D. (2006). Suicide in older adults: Nursing assessment of suicide risk. *Issues in Mental Health Nursing, 27,* 355–370.

Garbarino, J. (1999). *Lost boys: Why our sons turn violent and how we can save them.* New York: Free Press.

Garbarino, J., & Asp, C. E. (1981). *Successful schools and competent students.* Lexington, MA: Lexington Books.

Garcia-Sierra, A., & others. (2011, in press). Socio-cultural environment and bilingual language learning: A longitudinal event-related potential study. *Journal of Phonetics.*

Gardner, H. (1983). *Frames of mind.* New York: Basic Books.

Gardner, H. (1993). *Multiple intelligences.* New York: Basic Books.

Gardner, H. (2002). The pursuit of excellence through education. In M. Ferrari (Ed.), *Learning from extraordinary minds.* Mahwah, NJ: Erlbaum.

Gardner, M., & Steinberg, L. (2005). Peer influence on risk taking, risk preference, and risky decision making in adolescence and adulthood. *Developmental Psychology, 41,* 625–635.

Garlow, S. J., Purselle, D., & Heninger, M. (2005). Ethnic differences in patterns of suicide across the life cycle. *American Journal of Psychiatry, 162,* 319–323.

Garofalo, R. (2010). Cytokines in human milk. *Journal of Pediatrics, 156*(Suppl. 2), S36–S40.

Garofalo, R., Wolf, R. C., Wissow, L. S., Woods, E. R., & Goodman, E. (1999). Sexual orientation and risk of suicide attempts among a representative sample of youth. *Archives of Pediatrics and Adolescent Medicine, 153,* 487–493.

Garshasbi, A., & Faghih Zadeh, S. (2005). The effect of exercise on the intensity of low back pain in pregnant women. *International Journal of Gynecology and Obstetrics, 88,* 271–275.

Gartner, J., Larson, D. B., & Allen, G. D. (1991). Religious commitment and mental health: A review of the empirical literature. *Journal of Psychology and Theology, 19,* 6–25.

Garvey, C. (2000). *Play* (enlarged ed.). Cambridge, MA: Harvard University Press.

Gasser, L., & Keller, M. (2009). Are the competent morally good? Perspective taking and moral motivation of children involved in bullying. *Social Development, 18*(4), 798–816.

Gates, W. (1998, July 20). Charity begins when I'm ready (interview). *Fortune Magazine.*

Gatz, M., & Karel, M. J. (1993). Individual change in perceived control over 20 years. Special issue: Planning and control processes across the life span. *International Journal of Behavioral Development, 16*(2), 305–322.

Gaudernack, L. C., Forbord, S., & Hole, E. (2006). Acupuncture administered after spontaneous rupture of membranes at term significantly reduces the length of birth and use of oxytocin. *Acta Obstetricia et Gynecologica Scandinavica, 85,* 1348–1353.

Gaudineau, A., Ehlinger, V., Vayssiere, C., Jouret, B., Arnaud, C., & Godeau, E. (2010). Factors associated with early menarche: Results from the French Health Behavior in School-Aged Children (HBSC) Study. *BMC Public Health, 10,* 175.

Gauthier, A. H., & Furstenberg, F. F. (2005). Historical trends in the patterns of time use among young adults in developed countries. In R. A. Setterson, F. F. Furstenberg, & R. G. Rumbaut (Eds.), *On the frontier of adulthood: Theories, research, and social policy.* Chicago: University of Chicago Press.

Gauvain, M. (2008). Vygotsky's sociocultural theory. In M. M. Haith & J. B. Benson (Eds.), *Encyclopedia of infant and early childhood development.* Oxford, UK: Elsevier.

Gauvain, M., & Parke, R. D. (2010). Socialization. In M. H. Bornstein (Ed.), *Handbook of cultural developmental science.* New York: Psychology Press.

Gavin, L. E., Catalano, R. F., David-Ferdon, C., Gloppen, K. M., & Markham, C. M. (2010). A review of positive youth development programs that promote adolescent sexual and reproductive health. *Journal of Adolescent Health, 46*(Suppl. 1), S75–S91.

Gaziano, J. M., & others. (2009). Vitamins E and C in prevention of prostate and total cancer in men: The Physicians Health Study II randomized controlled trial. *Journal of the American Medical Association, 301,* 52–62.

Geborek, A., & Hjelte, L. (2011, in press). Association between genotype and pulmonary phenotype in cystic fibrosis patients with severe mutations. *Journal of Cystic Fibrosis.*

Gee, C. L., & Heyman, G. D. (2007). Children's evaluations of other people's self-descriptions. *Social Development, 16,* 800–810.

Geldhof, G. J., Little, T. D., & Colombo, J. (2010). Self-regulation across the life span. In A. Freund, M. Lamb, & R. Lerner (Eds.), *Handbook of life-span development,* New York: Wiley.

Gelman, R. (1969). Conservation acquisition: A problem of learning to attend to relevant attributes. *Journal of Experimental Child Psychology, 7,* 67–87.

Gelman, R., & Williams, E. M. (1998). Enabling constraints for cognitive development and learning. In W. Damon (Ed.), *Handbook of child psychology* (5th ed., Vol. 4). New York: Wiley.

Gelman, S. A. (2009). Learning from others: Children's construction of concepts. *Annual Review of Psychology* (Vol. 60). Palo Alto, CA: Annual Reviews.

Gelman, S. A., & Kalish, C. W. (2006). Conceptual development. In W. Damon & R. Lerner (Eds.), *Handbook of child psychology* (6th ed.). New York: Wiley.

Gelman, S. A., & Opfer, J. E. (2004). Development of the animate-inanimate distinction. In U. Goswami (Ed.), *Blackwell handbook of childhood cognitive development.* Malden, MA: Blackwell.

Gelman, S. A., Taylor, M. G., & Nguyen, S. P. (2004). Mother-child conversations about gender. *Monographs of the Society for Research in Child Development, 69*(1, Serial No. 275).

Gennetian, L. A., & Miller, C. (2002). Children and welfare reform: A view from an experimental welfare reform program in Minnesota. *Child Development, 73,* 601–620.

Genovesi, S., & others. (2010). Hypertension, prehypertension, and transient elevated blood pressure in children: Association with weight excess and waist circumference. *American Journal of Hypertension, 23*(7), 756–761.

Gentile, D. A., Mathieson, L. C., & Crick, N. R. (2010). Media violence associations with the form and function of aggression among elementary school children. *Social Development, 20*(2), 213–232.

George, L. K. (2009). Religious and spirituality, later life. In D. Carr (Ed.), *Encyclopedia of the life course and human development.* Boston: Gale Cengage.

George, L. K. (2010). Still happy after all these years: Research frontiers on subjective well-being in later life. *Journals of Gerontology B: Psychological Sciences and Social Sciences, 65B,* 331–339.

Gershoff, E. T. (2002). Corporal punishment by parents and associated child behaviors and experiences: A meta-analysis and theoretical review. *Psychological Bulletin, 128,* 539–579.

Gershoff, E. T., & others. (2010). Parent discipline practices in an international sample: Associations with child behaviors and moderation by perceived normativeness. *Child Development, 81,* 487–502.

Gesell, A. (1934). *An atlas of infant behavior.* New Haven, CT: Yale University Press.

Gewirtz, J. (1977). Maternal responding and the conditioning of infant crying: Directions of influence within the attachment-acquisition process. In B. C. Etzel, J. M. LeBlanc, & D. M. Baer (Eds.), *New developments in behavioral research.* Hillsdale, NJ: Erlbaum.

Ghazarian, S. R., & Roche, K. M. (2010). Social support and low-income, urban mothers: Longitudinal associations with delinquency. *Journal of Youth and Adolescence, 39,* 1097–1108.

Ghetti, S., & Alexander, K. W. (2004). "If it happened, I would remember it": Strategic use of event memorability in the rejection of false autobiographical events. *Child Development, 75,* 542–561.

Ghosh, S., & others. (2010). Prospective randomized comparative study of macular thickness following phacoemulsification and manual small incision cataract surgery. *Acta Ophthalmologica, 88*(4), e102–e106.

Ghosh, S., Feingold, E., Chakaborty, S., & Dey, S. K. (2010). Telomere length is associated with types of chromosome 21 nondisjunction: A new insight into the maternal age effect on Down syndrome birth. *Human Genetics, 127*(4), 403–409.

Giarrusso, R., & Bengtson, V. L. (2007). Self-esteem. In J. E. Birren (Ed.), *Encyclopedia of gerontology* (2nd ed.). San Diego: Academic Press.

Gibbons, R. D., Hedeker, D., & DuToit, S. (2010). Advance in analysis of longitudinal data. *Annual Review of Clinical Psychology* (Vol. 6). Palo Alto, CA: Annual Reviews.

Gibbs, J. C. (2010). *Moral development and reality: Beyond the theories of Kohlberg and Hoffman* (2nd ed.). Boston: Allyn & Bacon.

Gibbs, J. C., Basinger, K. S., Grime, R. L., & Snarey, J. R. (2007). Moral judgment across cultures: Revisiting Kohlberg's universality claims. *Developmental Review, 27,* 443–500.

Gibbs, J. T., & Huang, L. N. (1989). A conceptual framework for assessing and treating minority youth. In J. T. Gibbs & L. N. Huang (Eds.), *Children of color.* San Francisco: Jossey-Bass.

Gibson, E. J. (1969). *Principles of perceptual learning and development.* New York: Appleton-Century-Crofts.

Gibson, E. J. (1989). Exploratory behavior in the development of perceiving, acting, and the acquiring of knowledge. *Annual Review of Psychology* (Vol. 39). Palo Alto, CA: Annual Reviews.

Gibson, E. J. (2001). *Perceiving the affordances.* Mahwah, NJ: Erlbaum.

Gibson, E. J., Riccio, G., Schmuckler, M. A. Stoffregen, T. A., Rosenberg, D., & Taormina, J. (1987). Detection of the traversability of surfaces by crawling and walking infants. *Journal of Experimental Psychology: Human Perception and Performance, 13,* 533–544.

Gibson, E. J., & Walk, R. D. (1960). The "visual cliff." *Scientific American, 202,* 64–71.

Gibson, J. J. (1966). *The senses considered as perceptual systems.* Boston: Houghton Mifflin.

Gibson, J. J. (1979). *The ecological approach to visual perception.* Boston: Houghton Mifflin.

Gibson, L. Y., Bryne, S. M., Blair, E., Davis, E. A., Jacoby, P., & Zubrick, S. R. (2008). Clustering of psychological symptoms in over-weight children. *Australian and New Zealand Journal of Psychiatry, 42,* 118–125.

Giedd, J. N. (2007, September 27). Commentary in S. Jayson, "Teens driven to distraction." *USA Today,* pp. D1–2.

Gielen, S., Sandri, M., Erbs, S., & Adams, V. (2011, in press). Exercise-induced modulation of endothelial nitric oxide production. *Current Pharmaceutical Biotechnology.*

Gilbert, G., & Graham, S. (2010). Teaching writing to students in grades 4–6: A national survey. *Elementary School Journal, 110,* 494–518.

Gillig, P. M., & Sanders, R. D. (2011). Higher cortical functions: Attention and vigilance. *Innovations in Clinical Neuroscience, 8,* 43–46.

Gilligan, C. (1982). *In a different voice.* Cambridge, MA: Harvard University Press.

Gilligan, C. (1992, May). *Joining the resistance: Girls' development in adolescence.* Paper presented at the symposium on development and vulnerability in close relationships, Montreal.

Gilligan, C. (1996). The centrality of relationships in psychological development: A puzzle, some evidence, and a theory. In G. G. Noam & K. W. Fischer (Eds.), *Development and vulnerability in close relationships.* Hillsdale, NJ: Erlbaum.

Gilligan, C., Spencer, R., Weinberg, M. K., & Bertsch, T. (2003). On the listening guide: A voice-centered relational model. In P. M. Carnic & J. E. Rhodes (Eds.), *Qualitative research in psychology.* Washington, DC: American Psychological Association.

Gillum, R. F., & Ingram, D. D. (2007). Frequency of attendance at religious services, hypertension, and blood pressure: The third National Health and Nutrition Examination Survey. *Psychosomatic Medicine, 68,* 382–385.

Gillum, R. F., King, D. E., Obisesan, T. O., & Koenig, H. G. (2008). Frequency of attendance at religious services and mortality in a U.S. national cohort. *Annals of Epidemiology, 18,* 124–129.

Girls, Inc. (1991). *Truth, trusting, and technology: New research on preventing adolescent pregnancy.* Indianapolis: Author.

Giunta, N. (2010). The national family caregiver support program: A multivariate examination of state-level implementation. *Journal of Aging and Social Policy, 22,* 249–266.

Givens, J. L., & Mitchell, J. L. (2009). Concerns about end-of-life care and support for euthanasia. *Journal of Pain and Symptom Management, 38,* 167–173.

Givens, J. L., Prigerson, H. G., Kiely, D. K., Shaffer, M. L., & Mitchell, S. L. (2011). Grief among family members of nursing home residents with advanced dementia. *American Journal of Geriatric Psychiatry, 19*, 543–550.

Glaser, R., & Kiecolt-Glaser, J. K. (2005). Stress-induced immune dysfunction: Implications for health. *Nature Review: Immunology, 5*, 243–251.

Glover, M. B., Mullineaux, P. Y., Deater-Deckard, K., & Petrill, S. A. (2010). Parents' feelings toward their adoptive and non-adoptive children. *Infant and Child Development, 19*(3), 238–251.

Gluck, M. E., Venti, C. A., Lindsay, R. S., Knowler, W. C., Salbe, A. D., & Krakoff, J. (2009). Maternal influence, not diabetic intrauterine environment, predicts children's energy intake. *Obesity, 17*, 772–777.

Goel, A., Sinha, R. J., Delela, D., Sankhwar, S., & Singh, V. (2009). Andropause in Indian men: A preliminary cross-sectional study. *Urology Journal, 6*, 40–46.

Gogtay, N., & Thompson, P. M. (2010). Mapping gray matter development: Implications for typical development and vulnerability to psychopathology. *Brain and Cognition, 72*, 6–15.

Goh, J. O. (2011). Functional dedifferentiation and altered connectivity in older adults: Neural accounts of cognitive aging. *Aging and Disease, 2*, 30–48.

Gold, D. (2011). Death and dying. In R. H. Binstock & L. K. George (Eds.), *Handbook of aging and the social sciences* (7th ed.). New York: Elsevier.

Gold, S. J., & Amthor, R. F. (2011). Life-span development and international migration. In K. L. Fingerman, C. A. Berg, J. Smith, & T. C. Antonucci (Eds.), *Handbook of life-span development.* New York: Springer.

Goldberg, W. A., & Lucas-Thompson, R. (2008). Effects if maternal and paternal employment. In M. M. Haith & J. B. Benson (Eds.), *Encyclopedia of infant and early childhood development.* Oxford, UK: Elsevier.

Goldenberg, R. L., & Culhane, J. F. (2007). Low birth weight in the United States. *American Journal of Clinical Nutrition, 85*(Suppl.), S584–S590.

Goldfield, B. A., & Snow, C. E. (2009). Individual differences: Implications for the study of language acquisition. In J. Berko Gleason & N. B. Ratner (Eds.), *The development of language.* Boston: Allyn & Bacon.

Goldin-Meadow, S., & Iverson, J. (2010). Gesturing across the lifespan. In R. M. Lerner (Ed.), *Handbook of life-span development.* New York: Wiley.

Goldman, N., Giel, D. A., Lin, Y. H., & Weinstein, M. (2010). The serotonin transporter polymorphism (5-HTTLPR): Allelic variation and its link with depressive symptoms. *Depression and Anxiety, 27*, 260–269.

Goldschmidt, L., Richardson, G. A., Willford, J., & Day, N. L. (2008). Prenatal marijuana exposure and intelligence test performance at age 6. *Journal of the American Academy of Child and Adolescent Psychiatry, 47*(3), 254–263.

Goldsmith, B., Borrison, R. S., Vanderwerker, L. C., & Prigerson, H. G. (2008). Elevated rates of prolonged grief disorder in African Americans. *Death Studies, 32*, 352–365.

Goldstein, M. H., King, A. P., & West, M. J. (2003). Social interaction shapes babbling: Testing parallels between birdsong and speech. *Proceedings of the National Academy of Sciences, 100*, 8030–8035.

Goldston, D. B., Molock, S. D., Whitebeck, L. B., Murakami, J. L., Zayas, L. H., & Hall, G. C. (2008). Cultural considerations in adolescent suicide prevention and psychosocial treatment. *American Psychologist, 63*, 14–31.

Goldwater, P. N. (2011, in press). A perspective on SIDS pathogenesis. The hypothesis: Plausibility and evidence.

Goleman, D. (1995). *Emotional intelligence.* New York: Basic Books.

Goleman, D., Kaufman, P., & Ray, M. (1993). *The creative spirit.* New York: Plume.

Golombok, S. (2011a). Why I study lesbian families. In S. Ellis, V. Clarke, E. Peel, & D. Riggs (Eds.), *LGBTQ psychologies.* New York: Cambridge University Press.

Golombok, S. (2011b). Children in new family forms. In R. Gross (Ed.), *Psychology* (6th ed.). London: Hodder.

Golombok, S., Rust, J., Zervoulis, K., Croudace, T., Golding, J., & Hines, M. (2008). Development trajectories of sex-typed behavior in boys and girls: A longitudinal general population study of children aged 2.5–8 years. *Child Development, 79*, 1583–1593.

Golombok, S., & Tasker, F. (2010). Gay fathers. In M. E. Lamb (Ed.), *The role of the father in child development* (5th ed.). New York: Wiley.

Gong, X., & others. (2009). An investigation of ribosomal protein L10 gene in autism spectrum disorders. *BMC Medical Genetics, 10*, 7.

Gonzalez, A., Atkinson, L., & Fleming, A. S. (2009). Attachment and the comparative psychobiology of mothering. In M. de Haan & M. R. Gunnar (Eds.), *Handbook of developmental social neuroscience.* New York: Guilford.

Good, M., & Willoughby, T. (2008). Adolescence as a sensitive period for spiritual development. *Child Development Perspectives, 2*, 32–37.

Good, M., & Willoughby, T. (2010). Evaluating the direction of effects in the relationship between religious versus non-religious activities, academic success, and substance use. *Journal of Youth and Adolescence, 40*(6), 680–693.

Goodenough, J., & McGuire, B. A. (2012). *Biology of humans* (4th ed.). Upper Saddle River, NJ: Pearson.

Goodie, J. A., & McGlory, G. (2010). Compassionate care: A focus on dying well. *Nursing, 40*, 12–14.

Goodman, G. S., Batterman-Faunce, J. M., & Kenney, R. (1992). Optimizing children's testimony: Research and social policy issues concerning allegations of child sexual abuse. In D. Cicchetti & S. Toth (Eds.), *Child abuse, child development and social policy.* Norwood, NJ: Ablex.

Goodman, W. B., & others. (2011). Parental work stress and latent profiles of father-infant parenting quality. *Journal of Marriage and the Family, 73*, 588–604.

Goodwin, P. V., Mosher, W. D., & Chandra, A. (2010). Marriage and cohabitation in the United States: A statistical portrait based on cycle 6 (2002) of the National Survey of Family Growth. *Vital Health Statistics, 23*, 1–45.

Gooren, L. (2006). The biology of human psychosexual differentiation. *Hormones and Behavior, 50*, 589–601.

Gopnik, A. (2010). Commentary in E. Galinsky (2010), *Mind in the making.* New York: Harper Collins.

Gorby, H. E., Brownell, A. M., & Falk, M. C. (2010). Do specific dietary constituents and supplements affect mental energy? Review of the evidence. *Nutrition Reviews, 68*, 697–718.

Gordon, S., & Gordon, J. (1989). *Raising a child conservatively in a sexually permissive world.* New York: Simon & Schuster.

Gordon-Salant, S., Veni-Komshian, G. H., Fitzgibbons, P. J., & Barrett, S. (2006). Age-related differences in identification of temporal cues in speech segments. *Journal of the Acoustical Society of America, 129*, 2455–2466.

Gorin, S. H. (2010). Health care reform and older adults. *Health and Social Work, 35*, 3–6.

Gosselin, J. (2010). Individual and family factors related to psychosocial adjustment in stepmother families with adolescents. *Journal of Divorce and Remarriage, 51*, 108–123.

Gottfried, A. E., Marcoulides, G. A., Gottfried, A. W., & Oliver, P. H. (2009). A latent curve model of motivational practices and developmental decline in math and science academic intrinsic motivation. *Journal of Educational Psychology, 101*, 729–739.

Gottlieb, G. (2007). Probabilistic epigenesis. *Developmental Science, 10*, 1–11.

Gottman, J. M. (1994). *Why marriages succeed or fail.* New York: Simon & Schuster.

Gottman, J. M. (2008). *Research on parenting.* Retrieved March 25, 2008, from www.gottman.com/parenting/research

Gottman, J. M. (2011). *Research on parenting.* Retrieved January 5, 2011, from www.gottman.com/parenting/research

Gottman, J. M., Coan, J., Carrere, S., & Swanson, C. (1998). Predicting marital happiness and stability from newlywed interactions. *Journal of Marriage and the Family, 60*, 5–22.

Gottman, J. M., & DeClaire, J. (1997). *The heart of parenting: Raising an emotionally intelligent child.* New York: Simon & Schuster.

Gottman, J. M., & Gottman, J. S. (2009). Gottman method of couple therapy. In A. S.

Gurman (Ed.), *Clinical handbook of couple therapy* (4th ed.). New York: Guilford.

Gottman, J. M., Gottman, J. S., & Shapiro, A. (2009). A new couples approach to interventions for the transition to parenthood. In M. S. Schultz, M. K. Pruett, P. K. Kerig, & R. D. Parke (Eds.), *Feathering the nest: Couple relationships, couples interventions, and children's development.* Washington, DC: American Psychological Association.

Gottman, J. M., & Parker, J. G. (Eds.). (1987). *Conversations of friends.* New York: Cambridge University Press.

Gottman, J. M., & Silver, N. (1999). *The seven principles for making marriages work.* New York: Crown.

Gouin, K., & others. (2011, in press). Effects of cocaine use during pregnancy on low birthweight and preterm birth: Systematic and metanalyses. *American Journal of Obstetrics and Gynecology.*

Gove, W. R., Style, C. B., & Hughes, M. (1990). The effect of marriage on the well-being of adults: A theoretical analysis. *Journal of Health and Social Behavior, 24,* 122–131.

Govia, I. O., Jackson, J. S., & Sellers, S. L. (2011). Social inequalities. In K. L. Fingerman, C. A. Berg, J. Smith, & T. C. Antonucci (Eds.), *Handbook of life-span development.* New York: Springer.

Gowan, D. E. (2003). Christian beliefs concerning death and life after death. In C. D. Bryant (Ed.), *Handbook of death and dying.* Thousand Oaks, CA: Sage.

Graber, J. A. (2008). Pubertal and neuroendocrine development and risk for depressive disorders. In N. B. Allen & L. Sheeber (Eds.), *Adolescent emotional development and the emergence of depressive disorders.* New York: Cambridge University Press.

Graber, J. A., Nichols, T. R., & Brooks-Gunn, J. (2010). Putting pubertal timing in developmental context: Implications for prevention. *Developmental Psychobiology, 52,* 254–262.

Grady, C. L. (2008). Cognitive neuroscience of aging. *Annals of the New York Academy of Sciences, 1124,* 127–144.

Grafenhain, M., Behne, T., Carpenter, M., & Tomasello, M. (2009). Young children's understanding of joint commitments. *Developmental Psychology, 45*(5), 1430–1443.

Graff-Radford, N. R. (2011, in press). Can aerobic exercise protect against dementia? *Alzheimer's Research and Therapy, 28.*

Graham, G. M., Holt/Hale, S. A., & Parker, M. A. (2010). *Children moving* (8th ed.). New York: McGraw-Hill.

Graham, J. E., Christian, L. M., & Kiecolt-Glaser, J. K. (2006). Stress, age, and immune function: Toward a lifespan approach. *Journal of Behavioral Medicine, 29,* 389–400.

Graham, J. H., & Beller, A. H. (2002). Non-resident fathers and their children: Child support and visitation from an economic perspective. In C. S. Tamis-LeMonda & N. Cabrera (Eds.), *The handbook of father involvement.* Mahwah, NJ: Erlbaum.

Graham, S. (1986, August). *Can attribution theory tell us something about motivation in Blacks?* Paper presented at the meeting of the American Psychological Association, Washington, DC.

Graham, S. (1990). Motivation in Afro-Americans. In G. L. Berry & J. K. Asamen (Eds.), *Black students: Psychosocial issues and academic achievement.* Newbury Park, CA: Sage.

Graham, S. (2005, February 16). Commentary in *USA Today,* p. 2D.

Graham, S. (Ed.). (2006). Our children too: A history of the first 25 years of the Society for Research in Child Development. *Monographs of the Society for Research in Child Development, 71*(1), 1–227.

Graham, S., & Perin, D. (2007). A meta-analysis of writing instruction for adolescent students. *Journal of Educational Psychology, 99,* 445–476.

Grammas, P. (2011, in press). Neurovascular dysfunction, inflammation, and endothelial activation: Implications for the pathogenesis of Alzheimer's disease. *Journal of Neuroinflammation.*

Granger, D. N., Rodrigues, S. F., Yildirim, A., & Senchenkova, E. Y. (2010). Microvascular responses to cardiovascular risk factors. *Microcirculation, 17,* 192–205.

Grant, A. M., & Gino, F. (2010). A little thanks goes a long way: Explaining why gratitude expressions motivate prosocial behavior. *Journal of Personality and Social Psychology, 98,* 946–955.

Grausland, J. (2011, in press). Eye complications and markers of morbidity and mortality in long-term type 1 diabetes. *Acta Ophthalmologica.*

Graven, S. (2006). Sleep and brain development. *Clinical Perinatology, 33,* 693–706.

Gravetter, R. J., & Forzano, L. B. (2012). *Research methods for the behavioral sciences* (4th ed.). Boston: Cengage.

Gray, J. (1992). *Men are from Mars, women are from Venus.* New York: HarperCollins.

Gredeback, G., Johnson, S., & von Hofsten, C. (2010). Eye tracking in infancy research. *Developmental Neuropsychology, 35,* 1–19.

Greder, K. A., & Allen, W. D. (2007). Parenting in color: Culturally diverse perspectives on parenting. In B. S. Trask & R. R. Hamon (Eds.), *Cultural diversity and families.* Thousand Oaks, CA: Sage.

Gredler, M. E. (2009). Hiding in plain sight: The stages of mastery/self-regulation in Vygotsky's cultural-history theory. *Educational Psychologist, 44,* 1–19.

Greenberger, E., & Steinberg, L. (1986). *When teenagers work: The psychological and social costs of adolescent employment.* New York: Basic Books.

Greenfield, L. A., & Marks, N. F. (2004). Formal volunteering as a protective factor for older adults' psychological well-being. *Journals of Gerontology B: Psychological Sciences and Social Sciences, 59,* S258–S264.

Greenfield, P. M. (2009). Linking social change and developmental change: Shifting pathways of human development. *Developmental Psychology, 43,* 401–418.

Greer, F. R., Sicherer, S. H., Burks, A. W., & the Committee on Nutrition and Section on Allergy and Immunology. (2008). Effect of early nutritional interventions on the development of atopic disease in infants and children: The role of maternal dietary restriction, breast feeding, timing of introduction of complementary foods, and hydrolyzed formulas. *Pediatrics, 121,* 183–191.

Gregory, A. M., Ball, H. A., & Button, T. M. M. (2011). Behavioral genetics. In P. K. Smith & C. H. Hart (Eds.), *Wiley-Blackwell handbook of childhood social development* (2nd ed.). New York: Wiley.

Gregory, P. C., & others. (2011, in press). Education predicts incidence of preclinical mobility disability in initially high-functioning older women. The Women's Health and Aging Study II. *Journals of Gerontology A: Biological Sciences and Medical Sciences, 66A.*

Gregory, R. J. (2011). *Psychological testing* (6th ed.). Upper Saddle River, NJ: Pearson.

Grello, C. M., Welsh, D. P., & Harper, M. S. (2006). No strings attached: The nature of casual sex in college students. *The Journal of Sex Research, 43,* 255–267.

Grevers, G. (2010). Challenges in reducing the burden of otitis media disease: An ENT perspective on improving management and prospects for prevention. *International Journal of Pediatric Otorhinolaryngology, 74,* 572–577.

Griffiths, R., Horsfall, J., Moore, M., Lane, D., Kroon, V., & Langdon, R. (2007). Assessment of health, well-being, and social connections: A survey of women living in western Sydney. *International Journal of Nursing Practice, 13,* 3–13.

Grigorenko, E. (2000). Heritability and intelligence. In R. J. Sternberg (Ed.), *Handbook of intelligence.* New York: Cambridge University Press.

Grigorenko, E. L., & Takanishi, R. (2010). *Immigration, diversity, and education.* New York: Routledge.

Gross, A., & Rebok, G. W. (2011, in press). Memory training and strategy use in older adults: Results from the ACTIVE Study. *Psychology and Aging.*

Gross, D., Garvey, C., Julion, W., Fogg, L., Tucker, S., & Mokros, H. (2009). Efficacy of the Chicago Parent Program with low-income African American and Latino parents of young children. *Prevention Science, 10,* 54–65.

Gross, J. J., Frederickson, B. L., & Levenson, R. W. (1994). The psychology of crying. *Psychophysiology, 31,* 460–468.

Grossmann, K., Grossmann, K. E., Spangler, G., Suess, G., & Unzner, L. (1985). Maternal sensitivity and newborns' orientation responses as related to quality of attachment in northern Germany. In I. Bretherton & E. Waters (Eds.), Growing points of attachment theory and research. *Monographs of the Society for Research in Child Development, 50* (1–2, Serial No. 209).

Grossmann, T., & Johnson, M. H. (2010). Selective prefrontal cortex responses to joint attention in early infancy. *Biological Letters, 6,* 540–543.

Grunwald, H. E., Lockwood, B., Harris, P. W., & Mennis, J. (2010). Influences of neighborhood context, individual history, and parenting behavior on recidivism among juvenile delinquents. *Journal of Youth and Adolescence, 39,* 1067–1079.

Grusec, J. (2006). Development of moral behavior and a conscience from a socialization perspective. In M. Killen & J. G. Smetana (Eds.), *Handbook of moral development.* Mahwah, NJ: Erlbaum.

Grusec, J. E. (2011). Socialization processes in the family: Social and emotional development. *Annual Review of Psychology* (Vol. 62). Palo Alto, CA: Annual Reviews.

Grusec, J. E., Hastings, P., & Almas, A. (2011). Prosocial behavior. In P. K. Smith & C. H. Hart (Eds.), *Wiley-Blackwell handbook of childhood social development* (2nd ed.). New York: Wiley.

Grusec, J. E., & Sherman, A. (2011). Prosocial behavior. In M. K. Underwood & L. Rosen (Eds.), *Social development.* New York: Guilford.

Grych, J. H. (2002). Marital relationships and parenting. In M. H. Bornstein (Ed.), *Handbook of parenting.* Mahwah, NJ: Erlbaum.

Grzywacz, J. G. (2009). Work-family conflict. In D. Carr (Ed.), *Encyclopedia of the life course and human development.* Boston: Gale Cengage.

Gu, M. L., & Zhao, J. (2011). Mapping and localization of susceptible genes in asthma. *China Medicine, 124,* 132–143.

Guerra, N. G., & Williams, K. R. (2010). Implementing bullying prevention in diverse settings: Geographic, economic, and cultural influences. In E. M. Vernberg & B. K. Biggs (Eds.), *Preventing and treating bullying and victimization.* New York: Oxford University Press.

Guilford, J. P. (1967). *The structure of intellect.* New York: McGraw-Hill.

Guillot, M. (2009). Life expectancy. In D. Carr (Ed.), *Encyclopedia of the life course and human development.* Boston: Gale Cengage.

Guldin, M. B., O'Connor, M., Sokolowski, I., Jensen, A. B., & Vedsted, P. (2011, in press). Identifying bereaved subjects at risk for complicated grief: Predictive value of questionnaire items in a cohort study. *BMC Palliative Care.*

Gumbo, F. Z., & others. (2010). Rising mother-to-child transmission in a resource-limited breastfeeding population. *Tropical Doctor, 40,* 70–73.

Gump, B., & Matthews, K. (2000, March). *Annual vacations, health, and death.* Paper presented at the meeting of the American Psychosomatic Society, Savannah, GA.

Gunnar, M., & Quevado, K. (2007). The neurobiology of stress and development. *Annual Review of Psychology* (Vol. 58). Palo Alto, CA: Annual Reviews.

Gunnar, M. R., & Fisher, P. A. (2006). Bringing basic research on early experience and stress neurobiology to bear on preventive interventions for neglected and maltreated children. *Development and Psychopathology, 18,* 651–677.

Gunnar, M. R., Malone, S., & Fisch, R. O. (1987). The psychobiology of stress and coping in the human neonate: Studies of the adrenocortical activity in response to stress in the first week of life. In T. Field, P. McCasbe, & N. Scheiderman (Eds.), *Stress and coping.* Hillsdale, NJ: Erlbaum.

Guo, G., & Tillman, K. H. (2009). Trajectories of depressive symptoms, dopamine D2 and D4 receptors, family socioeconomic status, and social support in adolescence and young adulthood. *Psychiatric Genetics, 19,* 14–26.

Guo, S. S., Wu, W., Chumlea, W. C., & Roche, A. F. (2002). Predicting overweight and obesity in adulthood from body mass index values in childhood and adolescence. *American Journal of Clinical Nutrition, 76,* 653–658.

Gur, R. C., & others. (1995). Sex differences in regional cerebral glucose metabolism during a resting state. *Science, 267,* 528–531.

Gurwitch, R. H., Silovksy, J. F., Schultz, S., Kees, M., & Burlingame, S. (2001). *Reactions and guidelines for children following trauma/disaster.* Norman, OK: Department of Pediatrics, University of Oklahoma Health Sciences Center.

Gutman, L. M., Eccles, J. S., Peck, S., & Malanchuk, O. (2011, in press). The influence of early family relations on trajectories of cigarette and alcohol use from early to late adolescence. *Journal of Adolescence.*

Gutmann, D. L. (1975). Parenthood: A key to the comparative study of the life cycle. In N. Datan & L. Ginsberg (Eds.), *Life-span developmental psychology: Normative life crises.* New York: Academic Press.

Guzzetta, A., & others. (2008). Language organization in left perinatal stroke. *Neuropediatrics, 39,* 157–163.

H

Ha, H. H., & Ingersoll-Dayton, B. (2011). Moderators in the relationship between social contact and psychological distress among widowed adults. *Aging and Mental Health, 15,* 354–363.

Hackney, M. E., & Earhart, G. M. (2010a). Effects of dance on balance and gait in severe Parkinson disease: A case study. *Disability and Rehabilitation, 32,* 679–684.

Hackney, M. E., & Earhart, G. M. (2010b). Effects of dance on gait and balance in Parkinson's disease: A comparison of partnered and nonpartnered dance movement. *Neurorehabilitation and Neural Repair, 24,* 384–392.

Hadley, W., & others. (2011). Monitoring challenges: A closer look at parental monitoring, maternal psychopathology, and adolescent sexual risk. *Journal of Family Psychology, 25,* 319–323.

Hagen, J. W., & Lamb-Parker, F. G. (2008). Head Start. In M. M. Haith & J. B. Benson (Eds.), *Encyclopedia of infant and early childhood development.* Oxford, UK: Elsevier.

Hagestad, G. O. (1985). Continuity and connectedness. In V. L. Bengtson (Ed.), *Grandparent-hood.* Beverly Hills, CA: Sage.

Hagestad, G. O., & Uhlenberg, P. (2007). The impact of demographic changes on relations between the age groups and generations: A comparative perspective. In K. W. Schaie & P. Uhlenberg (Eds.), *Demographic changes and the well-being of older persons.* New York: Springer.

Hahn, D. B., Payne, W. A., & Lucas, E. B. (2011). *Focus on health* (10th ed.). New York: McGraw-Hill.

Hahn, E. A., Cichy, K. E., Almeida, D. M., & Haley, W. E. (2011). Time use and well-being in older widows: Adaptation and resilience. *Journal of Women and Aging, 23,* 149–159.

Haier, R. J. (2011). Biological bases of intelligence. In R. J. Sternberg & S. B. Kaufman (Eds.), *Cambridge handbook of intelligence.* New York: Cambridge University Press.

Hakuta, K. (2001, April 5). *Key policy milestones and directions in the education of English language learners.* Paper prepared for the Rockefeller Foundation Symposium, Leveraging change: An emerging framework for educational equity. Washington, DC.

Hakuta, K. (2005, April). *Bilingualism at the intersection of research and public policy.* Paper presented at the meeting of the Society for Research in Child Development, Atlanta.

Hakuta, K., Butler, Y. G., & Witt, D. (2001). *How long does it take English learners to attain proficiency?* Berkeley, CA: The University of California Linguistic Minority Research Institute Policy Report 2000–1.

Hale, S. (1990). A global developmental trend in cognitive processing speed. *Child Development, 61,* 653–663.

Hales, D. (2011). *An invitation to health* (14th ed.). Boston: Cengage.

Haley, M. H. (2010). *Brain-compatible differentiated instruction for English Language Learners.* Boston: Allyn & Bacon.

Halford, G. S., & Andrews, G. (2011). Information-processing models of cognitive development. In U. Goswami (Ed.), *Wiley-Blackwell handbook of childhood cognitive development.* New York: Wiley.

Halford, W. K., Markman, H. J., & Stanley, S. (2008). Strengthening couples' relationships with education: Social policy and public health perspectives. *Journal of Family Psychology, 22,* 497–505.

Hall, C. B., & others. (2009). Cognitive activities delay onset of memory decline in persons who develop dementia. *Neurology, 73,* 356–361.

Hall, C. M., & others. (2004). Behavioral and physical masculinization are related to genotype in girls with congenital adrenal hyperplasia. *Journal of Clinical Endocrinology and Metabolism, 89,* 419–424.

Hall, G. S. (1904). *Adolescence* (Vols. 1 & 2). Englewood Cliffs, NJ: Prentice Hall.

Hall, L. (2009). *Autism spectrum disorders: From theory to practice.* Upper Saddle River, NJ: Prentice Hall.

Hall, W. J. (2008). Centenarians: Metaphor becomes reality. *Archives of Internal Medicine, 168,* 262–263.

Hallahan, D. P., Kauffman, J. M., & Pullen, P. C. (2012). *Exceptional learners* (12th ed.). Upper Saddle River, NJ: Prentice Hall.

Halmi, K. A. (2009). Anorexia nervosa: An increasing problem in children and adolescents. *Dialogues in Clinical Neuroscience, 11,* 100–103.

Halpern, D. F. (2006). Girls and academic success: Changing patterns of academic achievement. In J. Worell & C. D. Goodheart (Eds.), *Handbook of girls' and women's psychological health.* New York: Oxford University Press.

Halpern, D. F., Benhow, C. P., Geary, D. C., Gur, R. C., & Hyde, J. S. (2007). The science of sex differences in science and mathematics. *Psychological Science in the Public Interest, 8,* 1–51.

Halpin, K. S., Smith, K. Y., Widen, J. E., & Chertoff, M. E. (2010). Effects of universal newborn hearing screening on an early intervention program for children with hearing loss, birth to 3 yr of age. *Journal of the American Academy of Audiology, 21,* 169–175.

Hamilton, B. E., Martin, J. A., & Ventura, J. A. (2010, April). Births: Preliminary data for 2008. *National Vital Statistics Reports, 58*(16). Hyattsville, MD: National Center for Health Statistics.

Hamilton, B. E., Martin, J. A., & Ventura, S. J. (2009, March 18). Births: Preliminary data for 2007. *National Vital Statistics Reports, 57*(12), 1–23.

Hamilton, S. F., & Hamilton, M. A. (2006). School, work, and emerging adulthood. In J. J. Arnett & J. L. Tanner (Eds.), *Emerging adults in America.* Washington, DC: American Psychological Association.

Hamilton, S. F., & Hamilton, M. A. (2009). The transition to adulthood: Challenges of poverty and structural lag. In R. M. Lerner & L. Steinberg (Eds.), *Handbook of adolescent psychology* (3rd ed.). New York: Wiley.

Hammer, L. D., & others. (2010). Increasing immunization coverage. *Pediatrics, 125,* 1295–1304.

Han, W-J. (2009). Maternal employment. In D. Carr (Ed.), *Encyclopedia of the life course and human development.* Boston: Cengage.

Hanania, R., & Smith, L. B. (2010). Selective attention and attention switching: Towards a unified developmental approach. *Developmental Science, 13,* 622–635.

Hancox, R. J., Milne, B. J., & Poulton, R. (2004). Association between child and adolescent television viewing and adult health: A longitudinal birth cohort study. *Lancet, 364,* 257–262.

Hanish, L. D., & Guerra, N. G. (2004). Aggressive victims, passive victims, and bullies: Developmental continuity or developmental change? *Merrill-Palmer Quarterly, 50,* 17–38.

Hanna-Pladdy, B., & Heilman, K. M. (2010). Dopaminergic modulation of the planning phase of skill acquisition in Parkinson's disease. *Neurocase, 16,* 182–190.

Hanowski, R. J., Olson, R. L., Hickman, J. S., & Bocanegra, J. (2009, September). *Driver distraction in commercial vehicle operations.* Paper presented at the First International Conference on Driver Distraction and Inattention, Gothenburg, Sweden.

Hantera, M. M., Hamed, A. M., Fekry, Y., & Shoheib, E. A. (2010). Initial experience with an accommodating intraocular lens: Controlled perspective study. *Journal of Cataract and Refractive Surgery Journal, 36,* 1167–1172.

Hantman, S., & Cohen, O. (2010). Forgiveness in late life. *Journal of Gerontological Social Work, 53,* 613–630.

Harakeh, Z., Scholte, R. H. J., Vermulst, A. A., de Vries, H., & Engels, R. C. (2010). The relations between parents' smoking, general parenting, parental smoking communication, and adolescents' smoking. *Journal of Research on Adolescence, 20,* 140–165.

Hardy, M. (2006). Older workers. In R. H. Binstock & L. K. George (Eds.), *Handbook of aging and the social sciences* (6th ed.). San Diego: Academic Press.

Hardy, S. A., Bhattacharjee, A., Reed, A., & Aquino, K. (2010). Moral identity and psychological distance: The case of adolescent socialization. *Journal of Adolescence, 33,* 111–123.

Harkness, S., & Super, E. M. (1995). Culture and parenting. In M. M. Bornstein (Ed.), *Handbook of parenting* (Vol. 3). Hillsdale, NJ: Erlbaum.

Harlow, H. F. (1958). The nature of love. *American Psychologist, 13,* 673–685.

Harmon, O. R., Lambrinos, J., & Kennedy, P. Are online exams an invitation to cheat? *Journal of Economic Education, 39,* 116–125.

Harold, R. D., Colarossi, L. G., & Mercier, L. R. (2007). *Smooth sailing or stormy waters: Family transitions through adolescence and their implications for practice and policy.* Mahwah, NJ: Erlbaum.

Harper, M., O'Connor, R., Dickson, A., & O'Carroll, R. (2011). Mothers' continuing bonds and ambivalence to personal mortality after the death of their child—an interpretative phenomenological analysis. *Psychology, Health, and Medicine, 16,* 203–214.

Harris, G. (2002). *Grandparenting: How to meet its responsibilities.* Los Angeles: The Americas Group.

Harris, L. (1975). *The myth and reality of aging in America.* Washington, DC: National Council on Aging.

Harris, P. L. (2000). *The work of the imagination.* New York: Oxford University Press.

Harris, P. L. (2006). Social cognition. In W. Damon & R. Lerner (Eds.), *Handbook of child psychology* (6th ed.). New York: Wiley.

Harris, Y. R., & Graham, J. A. (2007). *The African American child.* New York: Springer.

Harrison-Hale, A. O., McLoyd, V. C., & Smedley, B. (2004). Racial and ethnic status: Risk and protective processes among African-American families. In K. L. Maton, C. J. Schellenbach, B. J. Leadbetter, & A. L. Solarz (Eds.), *Investing in children, families, and communities.* Washington, DC: American Psychological Association.

Harrist, A. W. (1993, March). *Family interaction styles as predictors of children's competence: The role of synchrony and nonsynchrony.* Paper presented at the biennial meeting of the Society for Research in Child Development, New Orleans.

Hart, B., & Risley, T. R. (1995). *Meaningful differences.* Baltimore. MD: Paul Brookes.

Hart, C. H., Yang, C., Charlesworth, R., & Burts, D. C. (2003, April). *Early childhood teachers' curriculum beliefs, classroom practices, and children's outcomes: What are the connections?* Paper presented at the biennial meeting of the Society for Research in Child Development, Tampa, FL.

Hart, C. L., Ksir, C. J., & Ray, O. S. (2011). *Drugs, society, and human behavior* (14th ed.). New York: McGraw-Hill.

Hart, D., Burock, D., London, B., & Atkins, R. (2003). Prosocial development, antisocial development, and moral development. In A. M. Slater & G. Bremner (Eds.), *An introduction to developmental psychology.* Malden, MA: Blackwell.

Hart, D., & Karmel, M. P. (1996). Self-awareness and self-knowledge in humans, great apes, and monkeys. In A. Russon, K. Bard, & S. Parker (Eds.), *Reaching into thought.* New York: Cambridge University Press.

Hart, D., Matsuba, M. K., & Atkins, R. (2008). The moral and civic effects of learning to serve. In L. Nucci & D. Narváez (Eds.), *Handbook of moral and character education.* Clifton, NJ: Psychology Press.

Hart, S., & Carrington, H. (2002). Jealousy in 6-month-old infants. *Infancy, 3,* 395–402.

Hart, S., Carrington, H., Tronick, E. Z., & Carroll, S. R. (2004). When infants lose exclusive maternal attention: Is it jealousy? *Infancy, 6,* 57–78.

Harter, S. (1981). A new self-report scale of intrinsic versus extrinsic orientation in the classroom: Motivational and informational components. *Development Psychology, 17,* 300–312.

Harter, S. (1986). Processes underlying the construction, maintenance, and enhancement of the self-concept of children. In J. Suls & A. Greenwald (Eds.), *Psychological perspectives on the self* (Vol. 3). Hillsdale, NJ: Erlbaum.

Harter, S. (1990). Processes underlying adolescent self-concept formation. In R. Montemayor, G. R. Adams, & T. P Gullotta (Eds.), *From childhood to adolescence: A transitional period?* Newbury Park, CA: Sage.

Harter, S. (1996). Teacher and classmate influences on scholastic motivation, self-esteem, and level of voice in adolescents. In J. Juvonen & K. R. Wentzel (Eds.), *Social motivation.* New York: Cambridge University Press.

Harter, S. (1998). The development of self-representations. In W. Damon (Ed.), *Handbook of child psychology* (5th ed., Vol. 3). New York: Wiley.

Harter, S. (1999). *The construction of the self.* New York: Guilford.

Harter, S. (2006). The self. In W. Damon & R. Lerner (Eds.), *Handbook of child psychology* (6th ed.). New York: Wiley.

Hartshorne, H., & May, M. S. (1928–1930). *Moral studies in the nature of character. Studies in deceit* (Vol. 1); *Studies in self-control* (Vol. 2); *Studies in the organization of character* (Vol. 3). New York: Macmillan.

Hartup, W. W. (1983). The peer system. In P. H. Mussen (Ed.), *Handbook of child psychology* (4th ed., Vol. 4). New York: Wiley.

Hartup, W. W. (2008). Peer interaction: What causes what? *Journal of Abnormal Child Psychology, 33,* 387–394.

Hartup, W. W. (2009). Critical issues and theoretical viewpoints. In K. H. Rubin, W. M. Bukowski, & B. Laursen (Eds.), *Handbook of peer interactions, relationships, and groups.* New York: Guilford.

Harwood, R., Leyendecker, B., Carlson, V., Asencio, M., & Miller, A. (2002). Parenting among Latino families in the U.S. In M. H. Bornstein (Ed.), *Handbook of parenting* (2nd ed.). Mahwah, NJ: Erlbaum.

Hasher, L. (2003, February 28). Commentary in "The wisdom of the wizened." *Science, 299,* 1300–1302.

Hasher, L., Chung, C., May, C. P., & Foong, N. (2001). Age, time of testing, and proactive interference. *Canadian Journal of Experimental Psychology, 56,* 200–207.

Hashimoto-Toril, Kawasawa, Y. I., Kuhn, A., & Rakic, P. (2011, in press). Combined transcriptome analysis of fetal human and mouse cerebral cortex exposed to alcohol. *Proceedings of the National Academy of Sciences U.S.A.*

Hattery, A. J., & Smith, E. (2007). *African American families.* Thousand Oaks, CA: Sage.

Hatton, H., Donnellan, M. B., Maysn, K., Feldman, B. J., Larsen-Riffe, D., & Conger, R. D. (2008). Family and individual difference predictors of trait aspects of negative interpersonal behavioral during emerging adulthood. *Journal of Family Psychology, 22,* 448–455.

Hauksdottir, A., Steineck, G., Furst, C. J., & Valdimarsdottir, U. (2010). Long-term harm of low preparedness for wife's death from cancer—a population-based study of widowers 4–5 years after the loss. *American Journal of Epidemiology, 172*(4), 389–396.

Hawkes, C. (2006). Olfaction in neurogenerative disorder. *Advances in Otorhinolaryngology, 63,* 133–151.

Hawkley, L. C., Thisted, R. A., Masi, C. M., & Cacioppo, J. T. (2010). Loneliness predicts increased blood pressure: 5-year cross-lagged analyses in middle-aged and older adults. *Psychology and Aging, 25,* 132–141.

Hayashino, D., & Chopra, S. B. (2009). Parenting and raising families. In N. Tewari & A. Alvarez (Eds.), *Asian American psychology.* Clifton, NJ: Psychology Press.

Haydon, A., & Halpern, G. T. (2010). Older romantic partners and depressive symptoms during adolescence. *Journal of Youth and Adolescence, 39,* 1240–1251.

Hayflick, L. (1977). The cellular basis for biological aging. In C. E. Finch & L. Hayflick (Eds.), *Handbook of the biology of aging.* New York: Van Nostrand.

Hayslip, B., & Hansson, R. (2003). Death awareness and adjustment across the life span. In C. D. Bryant (Ed.), *Handbook of death and dying.* Thousand Oaks, CA: Sage.

Hayslip, B., & Hansson, R. O. (2007). Hospice. In J. E. Birren (Eds.), *Encyclopedia of gerontology* (2nd ed.). San Diego: Academic Press.

Hazan, C., & Shaver, P. R. (1987). Romantic love conceptualized as an attachment process. *Journal of Personality and Social Psychology, 52,* 522–524.

He, C., & others. (2010). A large-scale candidate gene association study of age at menarche and age at natural menopause. *Human Genetics, 128,* 515–527.

Healey, M. K., Campbell, K. L., Hasher, L., & Ossher, L. (2010). Direct evidence for the role of inhibition in resolving interference. *Psychological Science, 21*(10), 1464–1470.

Healey, M. K., & Hasher, L. (2009). Limitations to the deficit attenuation hypothesis: Aging and decision making. *Journal of Consumer Psychology, 19,* 17–22.

Heard, E., & others. (2011). Mediating effects of social support on the relationship among perceived stress, depression, and hypertension in African Americans. *Journal of the National Medical Association, 103,* 116–122.

Hebebrand, J., & Bulik, C. M. (2011, in press). Critical appraisal of provisional DSM-criteria for anorexia nervosa and an alternative proposal. *International Journal of Eating Disorders.*

Hedden, T., & Gabrielli, J. D. E. (2004). Insights into the aging mind: A view from cognitive neuroscience. *Nature Reviews: Neuroscience, 5,* 87–97.

Hegaard, H. K., Hedegaard, M., Damm, P., Ottesen, B., Petersson, K., & Henriksen, T. B. (2008). Leisure time physical activity is associated with a reduced risk of preterm delivery. *American Journal of Obstetrics and Gynecology, 198,* e1–e5.

Heidelbaugh, J. J. (2010). Management of erectile dysfunction. *American Family Physician, 81,* 305–312.

Heiman, G. W. (2011). *Basic statistics for the behavioral sciences* (6th ed.). Boston: Cengage.

Heimann, M., Strid, K., Smith, L., Tjus, T., Ulvund, S. E., & Meltzoff, A. N. (2006). Exploring the relation between memory, gestural communication, and the emergence of language in infancy: A longitudinal study. *Infant and Child Development, 75,* 233–249.

Heisel, M. J. (2006). Suicide and its prevention in older adults. *Canadian Journal of Psychiatry, 51,* 143–154.

Heitzler, C. D., & others. (2010). Evaluating a model of youth physical activity. *American Journal of Health Behavior, 34,* 593–606.

Helman, C. (2008). Inside T. Boone Pickens' brain. *Forbes.* Retrieved June 15, 2008, from http://www.forbes.com/billionaires/forbes/2008/0630/076.html

Helman, R., VanDerhei. J., & Copeland, C. (2007). The retirement system in transition: The 2007 Retirement Confidence Survey. *Employment Benefit Research Institute Issue Brief, 304*(1), 4–24.

Helmuth, L. (2003). The wisdom of the wizened. *Science, 299,* 1300–1302.

Helson, R. (1997, August). *Personality change: When is it adult development?* Paper presented at the meeting of the American Psychological Association, Chicago.

Helson, R., & Wink, P. (1992). Personality change in women from the early 40s to early 50s. *Psychology and Aging, 7,* 46–55.

Helwig, C. C., & Turiel, E. (2011). Children's social and moral reasoning. In P. K. Smith & C. H. Hart (Eds.), *Wiley-Blackwell handbook of childhood social development* (2nd ed.). New York: Wiley.

Helzner, E. P., & others. (2009). Contribution of vascular risk factors to the progression of Alzheimer disease. *Archives of Neurology, 66,* 343–348.

Henderson, S., Gagnon, S., Belanger, A., Tabone, R., & Collin, C. (2010). Near peripheral motion detection threshold correlates with self-reported failures of attention in younger and older drivers. *Accident Analysis and Prevention, 42,* 1189–1194.

Henderson, V. W. (2011, in press). Gonadal hormones and cognitive aging: A midlife perspective. *Women's Health.*

Hendry, C. (2009). Incarceration and the tasks of grief: A narrative review. *Journal of Advanced Nursing, 65,* 270–278.

Hendry, J. (1999). *Social anthropology.* New York: Macmillan.

Hennessey, B. (2011). Intrinsic motivation and creativity: Have we come full circle? In R. A. Beghetto & J. C. Kaufman (Eds.), *Nurturing creativity in the classroom.* New York: Cambridge University Press.

Hennessey, B. A., & Amabile, T. M. (2010). Creativity. *Annual Review of Psychology* (Vol. 61). Palto Alto, CA: Annual Reviews.

Henninger, D. E., Madden, D. J., & Huettel, S. A. (2010). Processing speed and memory mediate age-related differences in decision making. *Psychology and Aging, 25,* 262–270.

Henretta, J. C. (2010). Lifetime marital history and mortality after age 50. *Journal of Aging and Health, 22*(8), 1198–1212.

Henriksen, T. B., & others. (2004). Alcohol consumption at the time of conception and spontaneous abortion. *American Journal of Epidemiology, 160,* 661–667.

Henrikson, C. A. (2010). Advance directives and surrogate decision making before death. *New England Journal of Medicine, 363,* 296.

Herd, P., Robert, S. A., & House, J. A. (2011). Health disparities among older adults: Life course influences and policy solutions. In R. H. Binstock & L. K. George (Eds.), *Handbook of aging and the social sciences* (7th ed.). New York: Elsevier.

Hernandez-Reif, M., Diego, M., & Field, T. (2007). Preterm infants show reduced stress behaviors and activity after 5 days of massage therapy. *Infant Behavior and Development, 30,* 557–561.

Herrera, S. G., & Murry, K. G. (2011). *Mastering ESL and bilingual methods* (2nd ed.). Boston: Allyn & Bacon.

Herrera, V. M., Koss, M. P., Bailey, J., Yuan, N. P., & Lichter, E. L. (2006). Survivors of male violence. In J. Worell & C. D. Goodheart (Eds.), *Handbook of girls' and women's psychological health.* New York: Oxford University Press.

Hertenstein, M. J., & Keltner, D. (2010). Gender and the communication of emotion via touch. *Sex Roles, 64,* 70–80.

Hertzog, C., & Dixon, R. A. (2005). Metacognition in midlife. In S. L. Willis & M. Martin (Eds.), *Middle adulthood: A lifespan perspective.* Thousand Oaks, CA: Sage.

Hertzog, C., Kramer, A. F., Wilson, R. S., & Lindenberger, U. (2009). Enrichment effects on adult cognitive development. *Psychological Science in the Public Interest, 9,* 1–65.

Hess, T. M., Auman, C., Colcombe, S. J., & Rahhal, T. A. (2003). The impact of stereotype threat on age differences in memory performance. *Journals of Gerontology: Psychological and Social Sciences, 58B,* P3–P11.

Hetherington, E. M. (1993). An overview of the Virginia Longitudinal Study of Divorce and Remarriage with a focus on early adolescence. *Journal of Family Psychology, 7,* 39–56.

Hetherington, E. M. (2006). The influence of conflict, marital problem solving, and parenting on children's adjustment in nondivorced, divorced, and remarried families. In A. Clarke-Stewart & J. Dunn (Eds.), *Families count.* New York: Cambridge University Press.

Hetherington, E. M., & Kelly, J. (2002). *For better or for worse: Divorce reconsidered.* New York: Norton.

Hetherington, E. M., & Stanley-Hagan, M. (2002). Parenting in divorced and remarried families. In M. Bornstein (Ed.), *Handbook of parenting* (2nd ed.). Mahwah, NJ: Erlbaum.

Heulens, I., & Kooy, F. (2011). Fragile X syndrome: From gene discovery to therapy. *Frontiers in Bioscience, 16,* 1211–1232.

Heuwinkel, M. K. (1996). New ways of learning: Five new ways of teaching. *Childhood Education, 72,* 27–31.

Hewlett, B. S. (1991). *Intimate fathers.* Ann Arbor, MI: University of Michigan Press.

Hewlett, B. S. (2000). Culture, history and sex: Anthropological perspectives on father involvement. *Marriage and Family Review, 29,* 324–340.

Hewlett, B. S., & MacFarlan, S. J. (2010). Fathers' roles in hunter-gatherer and other small-scale cultures. In M. E. Lamb (Ed.), *The role of the father in child development* (5th ed.). New York: Wiley.

Heyman, G. D., & Legare, C. H. (2005). Children's evaluation of sources of information about traits. *Developmental Psychology, 41,* 636–647.

Hibell, B., Andersson, B., Bjarnasson, T., & others. (2004). *The ESPAD report 2003: Alcohol and other drug use among students in 35 European countries.* The Swedish Council for Information on Alcohol and Other Drugs (CAN) and Council of Europe Pompidou Group.

Highfield, R. (2008, April 30). *Harvard's baby brain research lab.* Retrieved on January 24, 2009, from www.telegraph.co.uk/scienceandtechnology/science/sciencenews/3341166/Harvard

Hill, J. P., & Lynch, M. E. (1983). The intensification of gender-related role expectations during early adolescence. In J. Brooks-Gunn & A. C. Petersen (Eds.), *Girls at puberty: Biological and psychosocial perspectives.* New York: Plenum Press.

Hill, P. C., & Butter, E. M. (1995). The role of religion in promoting physical health. *Journal of Psychology and Christianity, 14,* 141–155.

Hill, T. D., Burdette, A. M., Angel, J. L., & Angel, R. J. (2006). Religious attendance and cognitive functioning among older Mexican Americans. *Journals of Gerontology B: Psychological Sciences and Social Sciences, 61,* P31–P39.

Hillman, C. H., Erickson, K. I., & Kramer, A. F. (2008). Be smart, exercise your heart: Exercise effects on the brain and cognition. *Nature Reviews: Neuroscience, 9,* 58–65.

Hillman, C. H., & others. (2009). The effect of acute treadmill walking on cognitive control and academic achievement in preadolescent children. *Neuroscience, 3,* 1044–1054.

Himes, C. L., Hogan, D. P., & Eggebeen, D. J. (1996). Living arrangements of minority elders. *Journal of Gerontology, 51A,* S42–S48.

Hindman, A. H., Skibbek, L. E., Miller, A., & Zimmerman, M. (2010). Ecological contexts and early learning: Contributions of child, family, and classroom factors during Head Start to literacy and mathematics growth through first grade. *Early Childhood Research Quarterly, 25,* 235–250.

Hinkle, J. S., Tuckman, B. W., & Sampson, J. P. (1993). The psychology, physiology, and the creativity of middle school aerobic exercisers. *Elementary School Guidance & Counseling, 28,* 133–145.

Hinrichsen, G. A. (2006). Why multicultural issues matter for practitioners working with older adults. *Psychology and Aging, 37,* 29–35.

Hipwell, A. E., Stepp, S. D., Keenan, K., Chung, T., & Loeber, R. (2011, in press). Brief report: Parsing the heterogeneity of adolescent girls' sexual behavior: Relationships to individual and interpersonal factors. *Journal of Adolescence.*

Hjelmeland, H. (2011). Cultural context is crucial in suicide research and prevention. *Crisis, 32,* 61–64.

Ho, A. J., & others. (2010). The effects of physical activity, education, and body mass index on the aging brain. *Human Brain Mapping.* http://onlinelibrary.wiley.com/doi/10.1002/hbm.21113/abstract

Hock, R. R. (2010). *Human sexuality* (2nd ed.). Upper Saddle River, NJ: Prentice Hall.

Hockenberry, M., & Wilson, D. (2011). *Wong's nursing care of infants and children* (9th ed.). New York: Elsevier.

Hodapp, R. M., Griffin, M. M., Burke, M., & Fisher, M. H. (2011). Intellectual disabilities. In R. J. Sternberg & S. B. Kaufman (Eds.), *Cambridge handbook of intelligence.* New York: Cambridge University Press.

Hodson, R. (2009). Employment. In D. Carr (Ed.), *Encyclopedia of the life course and human development.* Boston: Gale Cengage.

Hoeksema, E., & others. (2010). Enhanced neural activity in frontal and cerebellar circuits after cognitive training in children with attention deficit hyperactivity disorder. *Human Brain Mapping, 31*(12), 1942–1950.

Hoekstra, R. A., Happe, F., Baron-Cohen, S., & Ronald, A. (2010). Limited genetic covariance between autistic traits and intelligence: Findings from a longitudinal twin study. *American Journal of Medical Genetics, B. Neuropsychiatric Genetics, 153B*(5), 994–1007.

Hoelter, L. (2009). Divorce and separation. In D. Carr (Ed.), *Encyclopedia of the life course and human development.* Boston: Gale Cengage.

Hoff, E., Laursen, B., & Tardiff, T. (2002). Socioeconomic status and perverting. In M. H. Bornstein (Ed.), *Handbook of parenting* (2nd ed.). Mahwah, NJ: Erlbaum.

Hoffman, E., & Ewen, D. (2007). Supporting families, nurturing young children. *CLASP Policy Brief No. 9.* Retrieved May 22, 2011, from http://www.clasp.org/admin/site/publications/files/0386.pdf

Holden, G. W., Vittrup, B., & Rosen, L. H. (2011). Families, parenting, and discipline. In M. K. Underwood & L. H. Rosen (Eds.), *Social development.* New York: Guilford.

Holland, A. S., & Roisman, G. I. (2010). Adult attachment security and young adults' dating relationships over time: Self-reported, observational, and physiological evidence. *Developmental Psychology, 46,* 552–557.

Hollar, D., & others. (2010). Effect of a two-year obesity prevention intervention on percentile changes in body mass index and academic performance in low-income elementary school children. *American Journal of Public Health, 100,* 646–653.

Hollich, G. (2011). Early language development. In J. G. Bremner & T. D. Wachs (Eds.), *Wiley-Blackwell handbook of infant development* (2nd ed.). New York: Wiley.

Hollis, J. F., & others. (2008). Weight loss during the intensive intervention phase of the weight-loss maintenance trial. *American Journal of Preventive Medicine, 35,* 118–126.

Holloway, D. (2010). Clinical update on hormone replacement therapy. *British Journal of Nursing, 19,* 496, 498–504.

Holmes, R. M., Little, K. C., & Welsh, D. (2009). Dating and romantic relationships, adulthood. In D. Carr (Ed.), *Encyclopedia of the life course and human development.* Boston: Gale Cengage.

Holmes, T. H., & Rahe, R. H. (1967). The social readjustment rating scale. *Journal of Psychosomatic Research, 11,* 213–218.

Holtzman, D. M., Morris, J. C., & Goate, A. M. (2011, in press). Alzheimer's disease: The challenge of the second century. *Science Translational Medicine.*

Holzman, L. (2009). *Vygotsky at work and play.* Clifton, NJ: Psychology Press.

Honzik, M. P., MacFarlane, I. W., & Allen, L. (1948). The stability of mental test performance between two and eighteen years. *Journal of Experimental Education, 17,* 309–324.

Hood, B. M. (1995). Gravity rules for 2- to 4-year-olds? *Cognitive Development, 10,* 577–598.

Hooyman, N. R., & Kiyak, H. A. (2011). *Social gerontology* (9th ed.). Upper Saddle River, NJ: Pearson.

Hope, D. A. (2009). Contemporary perspectives on lesbian, gay, and bisexual identities: Introduction. *Nebraska Symposium on Motivation, 54,* 1–4.

Hopkins, B. (1991). Facilitating early motor development: An intercultural study of West Indian mothers and their infants living in Britain. In J. K. Nugent, B. M. Lester, & T. B. Brazelton (Eds.), *The cultural context of infancy, Vol. 2: Multicultural and interdisciplinary approaches to parent-infant relations.* New York: Ablex.

Hopkins, B., & Westra, T. (1990). Motor development, maternal expectations, and the role of handling. *Infant Behavior and Development, 13,* 117–122.

Hoppmann, C. A., Gerstorf, D., Smith, J., & Klumb, P. L. (2007). Linking possible selves and behavior: Do domain-specific hopes and fears translate into activities in very old age? *Journals of Gerontology B: Psychological Sciences and Social Sciences, 62,* P104–P111.

Hopwood, C. J., & others. (2011). Genetic and environmental influences on personality trait stability and growth during the transition to adulthood: A three-wave longitudinal study. *Journal of Personality and Social Psychology, 100,* 545–556.

Horn, J. (2007). Spearman, *g,* expertise, and the nature of human cognitive capacity. In P. C. Kyllonen, R. D. Robberts, & L. Stankov (Eds.), *Extending intelligence.* Mahwah, NJ: Erlbaum.

Horn, J. L., & Donaldson, G. (1980). Cognitive development II: Adulthood development of human abilities. In O. G. Brim & J. Kagan (Eds.), *Constancy and change in human development.* Cambridge, MA: Harvard University Press.

Horn, L., & Nevill, S. (2006). *Profile of undergraduates in U.S. postsecondary education institutions: 2003–2004, with a special analysis of community college students* (NCES 2006-184). Washington, DC: National Center for Education Statistics.

Horne, R. S., Franco, P., Adamson, T. M., Groswasser, J., & Kahn, A. (2002). Effects of body position on sleep and arousal characteristics in infants. *Early Human Development, 69,* 25–33.

Horowitz, F. D. (2009). Introduction: A developmental understanding of giftedness and talent. In F. D. Horowitz, R. F. Subotnik, & D. J. Matthews (Eds.), *The development of giftedness across the life span.* Washington, DC: American Psychological Association.

Hospital for Sick Children & others. (2010). *Infant sleep.* Toronto: Author.

Hotta, H., & Uchida, S. (2010). Aging of the autonomic nervous system and possible improvements in autonomic activity using somatic afferent stimulation. *Geriatrics & Gerontology International, 10*(Suppl. 1), S127–S136.

House, L. D., Mueller, T., Reininger, B., Brown, K., & Markham, C. M. (2010). Character as a predictor of reproductive health outcomes for youth: A systematic review. *Journal of Adolescent Health, 46*(Suppl. 1), S59–S74.

Howard, K., & others. (2011, in press). Biological and environmental factors as predictors of language skills in very preterm children at 5 years of age. *Journal of Developmental and Behavioral Pediatrics.*

Howe, M. J. A., Davidson, J. W., Moore, D. G., & Sloboda, J. A. (1995). Are there early childhood signs of musical ability? *Psychology of Music, 23,* 162–176.

Howe, N., Ross, H. S., & Recchia, H. (2011). Sibling relationships in early and middle childhood. In P. K. Smith & C. H. Hart (Eds.), *Wiley-Blackwell handbook of social development* New York: Wiley.

Howel, D. (2010). Trends in the prevalence of obesity and overweight in English adults by age and birth cohort, 1991–2006. *Public Health and Nutrition, 14*(1), 27–33.

Howell, A., & Evans, G. D. (2011). Hormone replacement therapy and cancer. *Recent Results in Cancer Research, 188,* 115–124.

Howes, C. (2009). Friendship in early childhood. In K. H. Rubin, W. M. Bukowski, & B. Laursen (Eds.), *Handbook of peer interactions, relationships, and groups.* New York: Guilford.

Howlin, P., Magiati, I., & Charman, T. (2009). Systematic review of early intensive behavioral interventions with autism. *American Journal on Intellectual and Developmental Disabilities, 114,* 23–41.

Hoyer, W. J., & Roodin, P. A. (2009). *Adult development and aging* (6th ed). New York: McGraw-Hill.

Hrabosky, J. I., Masheb, R. M., White, M. A., & Grilo, C. M. (2007). Overvaluation of shape and weight in binge eating disorder. *Journal of Consulting and Clinical Psychology, 75,* 175–180.

HSBC Insurance. (2007). *The future of retirement: The new age—global report.* London: HSBC.

Huang, J. H., DeJong, W., Towvim, L. G., & Schneider, S. K. (2009). Sociodemographic and psychobehavioral characteristics of U.S. college students who abstain from alcohol. *Journal of American College Health, 57,* 395–410.

Huang, Q., & Tang, J. (2010). Age-related hearing loss or presbycusis. *European European Archives of Oto-Rhino-Laryngology, 267,* 1179–1191.

Huber, K., & Superti-Furga, G. (2011, in press). After the grape rush: Sirtuins as epigenetic drug targets in neurodegenerative disorders. *Bioorganic & Medicinal Chemistry.*

Huda, S. S., Brodie, L. E., & Sattar, N. (2010). Obesity in pregnancy: Prevalence and metabolic consequences. *Seminars in pregnancy: Prevalence and metabolic consequences, 15,* 70–76.

Huerta, M., Cortina, L. M., Pang, J. S., Torges, C. M., & Magley, V. J. (2006). Sex and power in the academy: Modeling sexual harassment in the lives of college women. *Personality and Social Psychology Bulletin, 32,* 616–628.

Hughes, C., & Ensor, R. (2010). Do early social cognition and executive functions predict individual differences in preschoolers' prosocial and antisocial behavior? In B. Sokol, U. Muller, J. Carpendale, A. Young, & G. Iarocci (Eds.), *Self- and social cognition.* New York: Oxford University Press.

Hughes, J. P., McDowell, M. A., & Brody, D. J. (2008). Leisure-time physical activity among U.S. adults 60 or more years of age: Result from NHANES 1999–2004. *Journal of Physical Activity and Health, 5,* 347–358.

Hughes, M. E., Waite, L. J., LaPierre, T. A., & Luo, Y. (2007). All in the family: The impact of caring for grandchildren on grandparents' health. *Journal of Gerontology B: Psychological Sciences and Social Sciences, 62,* S108–S119.

Hughes, P. C. (1978). In J. L. Fozard & S. J. Popkin, Optimizing adult development. *American Psychologist, 33,* 975–989.

Hughes, T. F. (2010). Promotion of cognitive health through cognitive activity in the aging population. *Aging and Health, 6,* 111–121.

Hui, W. S., Liu, Z., & Ho, S. C. (2010). Metabolic syndrome and all-cause mortality: A meta-analysis of prospective cohort studies. *European Journal of Epidemiology, 25*(6), 375–384.

Hultsch, D. F., Hertzog, C., Small, B. J., & **Dixon, R. A.** (1999). Use it or lose it: Engaged lifestyle as a buffer of cognitive decline in aging? *Psychology and Aging, 14,* 245–263.

Hultsch, D. F., & Plemons, J. K. (1979). Life events and life-span development. In P. B. Baltes & O. G. Brim (Eds.), *Life-span development and behavior.* New York: Academic Press.

Hummert, M. L. (2011). Age stereotypes and aging. In K. W. Schaie & S. L. Willis (Eds.), *Handbook of the psychology of aging* (7th ed.). New York: Elsevier.

Hunes, K., & Davis, K. D. (2009). Gender in the workplace. In D. Carr (Ed.), *Encyclopedia of the life course and human development.* Boston: Gale Cengage.

Hunt, E. (1995). *Will we be smart enough? A cognitive analysis of the coming work force.* New York: Russell Sage.

Hunt, E. (2011). *Human intelligence.* New York: Cambridge University Press.

Hunter, K. I., & Linn, M. W. (1980). Psychosocial differences between elderly volunteers and non-volunteers. *International Journal of Aging and Human Development, 12,* 205–213.

Hurley, B. F., Hanson, E. D., & Sheaff, A. K. (2011, in press). Strength training as a countermeasure to aging muscle and chronic disease. *Sports Medicine.*

Hurt, H., Brodsky, N. L., Roth, H., Malmud, F., & Giannetta, J. M. (2005). School performance of children with gestational cocaine exposure. *Neurotoxicology and Teratology, 27,* 203–211.

Huston, A. C., & Bentley, A. C. (2010). Human development in societal context. *Annual Review of Psychology* (Vol. 61). Palo Alto, CA: Annual Reviews.

Huston, A. C., & others. (2006). Effects of a poverty intervention program last from middle childhood to adolescence. In A. C. Huston & M. N. Ripke (Eds.), *Developmental contexts of middle childhood: Bridge to adolescence and adulthood.* New York: Cambridge University Press.

Huston, A. C., & Ripke, M. N. (2006). Experiences in middle childhood and children's development: A summary and integration of research. In A. C. Huston & M. N. Ripke (Eds.), *Developmental contexts in middle childhood.* New York: Cambridge University Press.

Hutchinson, D. M., & Rapee, R. M. (2007). Do friends share similar body image and eating problems? The role of social networks and peer influences in early adolescence. *Behavior Research and Therapy, 45,* 1557–1577.

Huttenlocher, J., Haight, W., Bruk, A., Seltzer, M., & Lyons, T. (1991). Early vocabulary growth: Relation to language input and gender. *Developmental Psychology, 27,* 236–248.

Huttenlocher, P. R., & Dabholkar, A. S. (1997). Regional differences in synaptogenesis in human cerebral cortex. *Journal of Comparative Neurology, 37*(2), 167–178.

Huyck, M. H. (1995). Marriage and close relationships of the martial kind. In R. Blieszner

& V. H. Bedford (Eds.), *Handbook of aging and the family.* Westport, CT: Greenwood Press.

Hyde, D. C., & Spelke, E. S. (2011). Neural signatures of number processing in human infants: Evidence for two core systems underlying numerical cognition. *Developmental Science, 14,* 360–371.

Hyde, J. S. (2005). The gender similarities hypothesis. *American Psychologist, 60,* 581–592.

Hyde, J. S. (2007). *Half the human experience* (7th ed.). Boston: Houghton Mifflin.

Hyde, J. S., & DeLamater, J. D. (2011). *Understanding human sexuality* (11th ed.). New York: McGraw-Hill.

Hyde, J. S., Krajnik, M., & Skuldt-Niederberger, K. (1991). Androgyny across the life span: A replication and longitudinal follow-up. *Developmental Psychology, 27,* 516–519.

Hyde, J. S., Lindberg, S. M., Linn, M. C., Eillis, A. B., & Williams, C. C. (2008). Gender similarities characterize math performance. *Science, 321,* 494–495.

Hymel, S., Closson, L. M., Caravita, C. S., & Vaillancourt, T. (2011). Social status among peers: From sociometric attraction to peer acceptance to perceived popularity. In P. K. Smith & C. H. Hart (Eds.), *Wiley-Blackwell handbook of childhood social development* (2nd ed.). New York: Wiley.

Hyson, M. C., Copple, C., & Jones, J. (2006). Early childhood development and education. In W. Damon & R. Lerner (Eds.), *Handbook of child psychology* (6th ed.). New York: Wiley.

I

"I Have a Dream" Foundation. (2010). *About us.* Retrieved October 23, 2010, from http://www.ihad.org

Ickovics, J. R., & others. (2011). Effects of group prenatal care on psychosocial risk in pregnancy: Results from a randomized controlled trial. *Psychology and Health, 26,* 235–250.

Idler, E. (2006). Religion and aging. In R. H. Binstock & L. K. George (Eds.), *Handbook of aging and the social sciences* (6th ed.). San Diego: Academic Press.

Ige, F., & Shelton, D. (2004). Reducing the risk of sudden infant death syndrome (SIDS) in African-American communities. *Journal of Pediatric Nursing, 19,* 290–292.

Imdad, A., Sadig, K., & Bhutta, Z. A. (2011, in press). Evidence-based prevention of childhood malnutrition. *Current Opinion in Clinical Nutrition and Metabolic Care.*

Insel, P. N., & Roth, W. T. (2012). *Connect core concepts in health* (12th ed.). New York: McGraw-Hill.

International Montessori Council. (2006). Much of their success on prime-time television. Retrieved June 24, 2006, from www.Montessori.org/enews/Barbara_Walters.html

Ip, S., Chung, M., Raman, G., Trikaliinos, T. A., & Lau, J. (2009). A summary of the Agency for Healthcare Research and Quality's evidence

report on breastfeeding in developed countries. *Breastfeeding Medicine, 4*(Suppl. 1), S17–S30.

Ireland, J. (2010). Palliative care: A case study and reflections on some spiritual issues. *British Journal of Nursing, 19,* 237–240.

Irwin, C. E. (2010). Young adults are worse off than adolescents. *Journal of Adolescent Health, 46,* 405–406.

Isella, V., Mapelli, C., Morielli, N., Pelati, O., Franceschi, M., & Appollonio, I. M. (2008). Age-related quantitative and qualitative changes in decision-making ability. *Behavioral Neurology, 19,* 59–63.

Isingrini, M., Perrotin, A., & Souchay, C. (2008). Aging, metamemory regulation, and executive functioning. *Progress in Brain Research, 169,* 377–392.

Issel, L. M., & others. (2011, in press). A review of prenatal home-visiting effectiveness for improving birth outcomes. *Journal of Obstetric, Gynecologic, and Neonatal Nursing.*

Iwasaki, Y. (2008). Pathways to meaning-making through leisure-like pursuits in global contexts. *Journal of Leisure Research, 40,* 231–249.

J

Jackson, J. S. (2011). Race, ethnicity, and aging. In R. H. Binstock & L. K. George (Eds.), *Handbook of aging and the social sciences* (7th ed.). New York: Elsevier.

Jackson, J. S., Govia, I. O., & Sellers, S. L. (2011). Racial and ethnic influences over the life course. In R. H. Binstock & L. K. George (Eds.), *Handbook of aging and the social sciences* (7th ed.). New York: Elsevier.

Jackson, S. L. (2011). *Research methods* (2nd ed.). Boston: Cengage.

Jacobs, J. M., Hammerman-Rozenberg, R., Cohen, A., & Stressman, J. (2008). Reading daily predicts reduced mortality among men from a cohort of community-dwelling 70-year-olds. *Journals of Gerontology B: Psychological Sciences and Social Sciences, 63,* S73–S80.

Jacobs-Lawson, J. M., Hershey, D. A., & Neukam, K. A. (2005). Gender differences in factors that influence time spent planning for retirement. *Journal of Women and Aging, 16,* 55–69.

Jacques, S., & Marcovitch, S. (2010). Development of executive function across the life span. In W. F. Overton & R. H. Lerner (Eds.), *Handbook of life-span development.* New York: Wiley.

Jaeggi, S. M., Berman, M. G., & Jonides, J. (2009). Training attentional processes. *Trends in Cognitive Science, 37,* 644–654.

Jaffee, S., & Hyde, J. S. (2000). Gender differences in moral orientation: A meta-analysis. *Psychological Bulletin, 126,* 703–726.

Jago, R., Frobert, K., Cooper, A. R., Eiberg, S., & Anderson, L. B. (2010). Three-year changes in fitness and adiposity are independently associated with cardiovascular risk factors among young Danish children. *Journal of Physical Activity and Health, 7,* 37–44.

Jalongo, M. R. (2011). *Early childhood language arts* (5th ed.). Boston: Allyn & Bacon.

Jalongo, M. R., & Isenberg, J. (2012). *Exploring your role in early childhood education* (4th ed.). Upper Saddle River, NJ: Pearson.

James, A. H., Brancazio, L. R., & Price, T. (2008). Aspirin and reproductive outcomes. *Obstetrical and Gynecological Survey, 63*, 49–57.

James, B. D., & Bennett, D. A. (2011). Smoking in midlife and dementia in old age: Risk across the life course. *Archives of Neurology, 68*, 365–368.

James, B. D., Boyle, P. A., Buchman, A. S., & Bennett, D. A. (2011). Relation of late-life social activity with incident disability among community-dwelling older adults. *Journals of Gerontology A: Biological Sciences and Medical Sciences, 66*, 467–473.

James, D. C., & Dobson, B. (2005). Position of the American Dietetic Association: Promoting and supporting breastfeeding. *Journal of the American Dietetic Association, 105*, 810–818.

James, W. (1890/1950). *The principles of psychology.* New York: Dover.

Jan, J. E., & others. (2010). Long-term sleep disturbances in children: A cause of neuronal loss. *European Journal of Pediatric Neurology, 14*(5), 380–390.

Janssen, I., & others. (2005). Comparison of overweight and obesity prevalence in school-aged youth from 34 countries and their relationships with physical activity and dietary patterns. *Obesity Reviews, 6*, 123–132.

Jarrett, R. L. (1995). Growing up poor: The family experiences of socially mobile youth in low-income African-American neighborhoods. *Journal of Adolescent Research, 10*, 111–135.

Jayakody, A., & others. (2011, in press). Early sexual risk among black and minority ethnicity teenagers: A mixed methods study. *Journal of Adolescent Health.*

Jencks, C. (1979). *Who gets ahead? The determinants of economic success in America.* New York: Basic Books.

Jenik, A. G., & Vain, N. (2010). The pacifier debate. *Early Human Development, 85*(Suppl. 10), S89–S91.

Jenkins, J. M., & Astington, J. W. (1996). Cognitive factors and family structure associated with theory of mind development in young children. *Developmental Psychology, 32*, 70–78.

Jensen, A. R. (2008). Book review. *Intelligence, 36*, 96–97.

Jensen, G. L., & Hsiao, P. Y. (2010). Obesity in older adults: Relationship to functional limitation. *Current Opinion in Clinical Nutrition and Metabolic Care, 13*, 46–51.

Ji, B. T., & others. (1999). Parental cigarette smoking and the risk of childhood cancer among the offspring of nonsmoking mothers. *Journal of the National Cancer Institute, 89*, 238–244.

Jia, R., & Schoppe-Sullivan, S. J. (2011). Relations between coparenting and father involvement in families with preschool-age children. *Developmental Psychology, 47*, 106–118.

Jimerson, S. R. (2009). High school dropout. In D. Carr (Ed.), *Encyclopedia of the life course and human development.* Boston: Gale Cengage.

Joffe, H., & others. (2011, in press). Increased estradiol and improved sleep, but not hot flashes, predict enhanced mood during the menopausal transition. *Journal of Clinical Endocrinology and Metabolism.*

Johnson, G. B., & Losos, J. (2010). *The living world* (6th ed.). New York: McGraw-Hill.

Johnson, H. L., Erbelding, E. J., & Ghanem, K. G. (2007). Sexually transmitted infections during pregnancy. *Current Infectious Disease Reports, 9*, 125–133.

Johnson, J. G., Zhang, B., Greer, J. A., & Prigerson, H. G. (2007). Parental control, partner dependency, and complicated grief among widowed adults in the community. *Journal of Nervous and Mental Disease, 195*, 26–30.

Johnson, J. S., & Newport, E. L. (1991). Critical period effects on universal properties of language: The status of subjacency in the acquisition of a second language. *Cognition, 39*, 215–258.

Johnson, L., Giordano, P. C., Manning, W. D., & Longmore, M. A. (2011, in press). Parent-child relations and offending during young adulthood. *Journal of Youth and Adolescence.*

Johnson, M. (2008, April 30). Commentary in R. Highfield, *Harvard's baby brain research lab.* Retrieved January 24, 2008, from www.telegraph.co.uk/scienceandtechnology/science/sciencenews/3341166/Harvards-baby-brain-research-labl.html

Johnson, M. D. (2012). *Human biology* (6th ed.). Upper Saddle River, NJ: Pearson.

Johnson, M. H., & de Haan, M. (2010). *Developmental cognitive neuroscience* (3rd ed.). New York: Wiley-Blackwell.

Johnson, M. H., & de Haan, M. (2012). *Developmental cognitive neuroscience* (4th ed.). New York: Wiley-Blackwell.

Johnson, M. H., Grossmann, T., & Cohen-Kadosh, K. (2009). Mapping functional brain development: Building a social brain through interactive specialization. *Developmental Psychology, 45*, 151–159.

Johnson, S. P. (2010a). How infants learn about the visual world. *Cognitive Science, 34*(7), 1158–1184.

Johnson, S. P. (2010b). Perceptual completion in infancy. In S. P. Johnson (Ed.), *Neoconstructivism: The new science of cognitive development* (pp. 45–60). New York: Oxford University Press.

Johnson, S. P. (2011a). A constructivist view of object perception in infancy. In L. M. Oakes, C. H. Cashon, M. Casasola, & D. H. Rakison (Eds.), *Early perceptual and cognitive development.* New York: Oxford University Press.

Johnson, S. P. (2011b). Object perception. In P. D. Zelazo (Ed.), *Handbook of developmental psychology.* New York: Oxford University Press.

Johnson, W., te Nijenhuis, J., & Bouchard, T. J. (2008). Still just 1 *g*: Consistent results from five test batteries. *Intelligence, 36*, 81–95.

Johnston, C. C., & others. (2009). Enhanced kangaroo care for heel lance in preterm neonates: A crossover trial. *Journal of Perinatology, 29*, 51–56.

Johnston, L. D., O'Malley, P. M., Bachman, J. G., & Schulenberg, J. E. (2010a). *Monitoring the Future national survey results on drug use, 1975–2009. Volume II: College students and adults ages 19–50.* Bethesda, MD: National Institute on Drug Abuse.

Johnston, L. D., O'Malley, P. M., Bachman, J. G., & Schulenberg, J. E. (2010b). *Monitoring the Future national survey results on adolescent drug use: Overview of key findings, 2009.* Bethesda, MD: National Institute on Drug Abuse.

Johnston, L. D., O'Malley, P. M., Bachman, J. G., & Schulenberg, J. E. (2011). *Monitoring the Future national results on adolescent drug use: Overview of key findings.* Ann Arbor: Institute for Social Research, The University of Michigan.

Joint Economic Committee. (2007, February). *Investing in raising children.* Washington, DC: U.S. Senate.

Jolly, C. A. (2005). Diet manipulation and prevention of aging, cancer, and autoimmune disease. *Current Opinions in Clinical Nutrition and Metabolic Care, 8*, 382–387.

Jones, D., & others. (2010). The impact of the Fast Track prevention trial on health services utilization by youth at risk for conduct problems. *Pediatrics, 125*, 130–136.

Jones, M. C. (1965). Psychological correlates of somatic development. *Child Development, 36*, 899–911.

Jones, M. D., & Galliher, R. V. (2007). Navajo ethnic identity: Predictors of psychosocial outcomes in Navajo adolescents. *Journal of Research on Adolescence, 17*, 683–696.

Jordan, C. E., Campbell, R., & Follingstad, D. (2010). Violence and women's mental health: The impact of physical, sexual, and psychological aggression. *Annual Review of Clinical Psychology* (Vol. 6). Palo Alto, CA: Annual Reviews.

Jose, A., O'Leary, K. D., & Moyer, A. (2010). Does premarital cohabitation predict subsequent marital stability and marital quality? A meta-analysis. *Journal of Marriage and the Family, 72*, 105–116.

Josephson Institute of Ethics. (2006). *2006 Josephson Institute report card on the ethics of American youth. Part one—integrity.* Los Angeles: Josephson Institute.

Joyner, K. (2009). Transition to parenthood. In D. Carr (Ed.), *Encyclopedia of the life course and human development.* Boston: Gale Cengage.

Juang, L., & Syed, M. (2010). Family cultural socialization practices and ethnic identity in college-going emerging adults. *Journal of Adolescence, 33*(3), 347–354.

Judd, F. K., Hickey, M., & Bryant, C. (2011, in press). Depression and midlife: Are we overpathologising the menopause? *Journal of Affective Disorders.*

Juffer, F., & van IJzendoorn, M. H. (2005). Behavior problems and mental health referrals of international adoptees: A meta-analysis. *Journal of the American Medical Association, 293*, 2501–2513.

Juffer, F., & van IJzendoorn, M. H. (2007). Adoptees do not lack self-esteem: A meta-analysis of studies on self-esteem of transracial, international, and domestic adoptees. *Psychological Bulletin, 133,* 1067–1083.

Jylhava, J., & others. (2009). Genetics of C-reactive protein and complement factor H have an epistatic effect on carotid artery compliance: The Cardiovascular Risk in Young Finns Study. *Clinical and Experimental Immunology, 155,* 53–58.

K

Kaakinen, M., & others. (2010). Life-course analysis of a fat mass and obesity-associated (FTO) gene variant and body mass index in the Northern Finland birth cohort 1966 using structural equation modeling. *American Journal of Epidemiology, 172*(6), 653–665.

Kadenbach, B., Ramzan, R., & Vogt, S. (2009). Degenerative diseases, oxidative stress, and cytochrome c oxidase function. *Trends in Molecular Medicine, 15*(4), 139–147.

Kaeberlein, M. (2010). Resveratrol and rapamycin: Are they anti-aging drugs? *BioEssays, 32,* 96–99.

Kagan, J. (2000). Temperament. In A. Kazdin (Ed.), *Encyclopedia of psychology.* New York: Oxford University Press.

Kagan, J. (2002). Behavioral inhibition as a temperamental category. In R. J. Davidson, K. R. Scherer, & H. H. Goldsmith (Eds.), *Handbook of affective sciences.* New York: Oxford University Press.

Kagan, J. (2008). Fear and wariness. In M. M. Haith & J. B. Benson (Eds.), *Encyclopedia of infant and early childhood development.* Oxford, UK: Elsevier.

Kagan, J. (2010). Emotions and temperament. In M. H. Bornstein (Ed.), *Handbook of cultural developmental science.* New York: Psychology Press.

Kagan, J. J., Kearsley, R. B., & Zelazo, P. R. (1978). *Infancy: Its place in human development.* Cambridge, MA: Harvard University Press.

Kagan, S. H. (2008). Faculty profile, University of Pennsylvania School of Nursing. Retrieved April 25, 2008, from www.nursing.upenn.edu/faculty/profile.asp?pid=33

Kahana, E., Kahana, B., & Wykle, M. (2010). "Care-getting": A conceptual model of marshalling support near the end of life. *Current Aging Science, 3,* 71–78.

Kail, R. V. (2007). Longitudinal evidence that increases in processing speed and working memory enhance children's reasoning. *Psychological Science, 18,* 312–313.

Kalder, M., Knoblauch, K., Hrgovic, I., & Munstedt, K. (2011). Use of complementary and alternative medicine during pregnancy and delivery. *Archives of Gynecology and Obstetrics, 283*(3), 475–482.

Kalish, R. A. (1981). *Death, grief, and caring relationships.* Monterey, CA: Brooks/Cole.

Kalish, R. A. (1987). Death. In G. L. Maddox (Ed.), *Encyclopedia of aging.* New York: Springer.

Kalish, R. A., & Reynolds, D. K. (1976). *An overview of death and ethnicity.* Farmingdale, NY: Baywood.

Kamii, C. (1985). *Young children reinvent arithmetic: Implications of Piaget's theory.* New York: Teachers College Press.

Kamii, C. (1989). *Young children continue to reinvent arithmetic.* New York: Teachers College Press.

Kane, R. L. (2007). Health care and services. In J. E. Birren (Ed.), *Encyclopedia of gerontology* (2nd ed.). San Diego: Academic Press.

Kang, P. P., & Romo, L. F. (2010). The role of religious involvement on depression, risky behavior, and academic performance among Korean American adolescents. *Journal of Adolescence.*

Kanoy, K., Ulku-Steiner, B., Cox, M., & Burchinal, M. (2003). Marital relationship and individual psychological characteristics that predict physical punishment of children. *Journal of Family Psychology, 17,* 20–28.

Kaplan, H. B. (2009). Self-esteem. In D. Carr (Ed.), *Encyclopedia of the life course and human development.* Boston: Gale Cengage.

Kaplowitz, P. B. (2008). Link between body fat and timing of puberty. *Pediatrics, 121*(Suppl. 3), S208–S217.

Kapogiannis, D., & Mattson, M. P. (2011). Disrupted energy metabolism and neuronal circuit dysfunction in cognitive impairment and Alzheimer's disease. *Lancet Neurology, 10,* 187–198.

Karelitz, T. M., Jarvin, L., & Sternberg, R. J. (2010). The meaning of wisdom and its development throughout life. In R. M. Lerner & W. F. Overton (Eds.), *Handbook of life-span development* (Vol. 1). New York: Wiley.

Karlsson, M., Milberg, A., & Strang, P. (2011, in press). Dying cancer patients' own opinions on euthanasia: An expression of autonomy? A qualitative study. *Palliative Medicine.*

Karnes, F. A., & Stephens, K. R. (2008). *Achieving excellence: Educating the gifted and talented.* Upper Saddle River, NJ: Prentice Hall.

Karney, B. R., Garvin, C. W., & Thomas, M. S. (2003). *Family formation in Florida 2003 baseline survey of attitudes, beliefs, and demographics relating to marriage and family formation.* Gainesville, FL: The University of Florida. Retrieved from http://www.phhp.ufl.edu/~uspringe/FMP/Publications/REPORT.pdf

Karpov, Y. V. (2006). *The neo-Vygotskian approach to child development.* New York: Cambridge University Press.

Karreman, A., van Tuijl, C., van Aken, M. A. G., & Dekovic, M. (2008). Parenting, coparenting, and effortful control in preschoolers. *Journal of Family Psychology, 22,* 30–40.

Kasari, C., & Lawton, K. (2010). New directions in behavioral treatment of autism spectrum disorders. *Current Opinion in Neurology, 23,* 137–143.

Kastenbaum, R. J. (2004). *Death, society, and human experience* (8th ed.). Boston: Allyn & Bacon.

Kastenbaum, R. J. (2007). *Death, society, and human experience* (9th ed.). Boston: Allyn & Bacon.

Kastenbaum, R. J. (2009). *Death, society, and human experience* (10th ed.). Boston: Allyn & Bacon.

Kato, T. (2005). The relationship between coping with stress due to romantic break-ups and mental health. *Japanese Journal of Social Psychology, 20,* 171–180.

Katz, L. (1999). Curriculum disputes in early childhood education. *ERIC Clearinghouse on Elementary and Early Childhood Education,* Document EDO-PS-99-13.

Katz, P. R., Karuza, J., Intrator, O., & Mor, V. (2009). Nursing home physician specialists: A response to the workforce crisis in long-term care. *Annals of Internal Medicine, 150,* 411–413.

Kauffman, J. M., McGee, K., & Brigham, M. (2004). Enabling or disabling? Observations on changes in special education. *Phi Delta Kappan, 85,* 613–620.

Kaufman, J. C., & Sternberg, R. J. (2007). Resource review: Creativity. *Change, 39,* 55–58.

Kaufman, S. B., & Plucker, J. A. (2011). Intelligence and creativity. In R. J. Sternberg & S. B. Kaufman (Eds.), *Cambridge handbook of intelligence.* New York: Cambridge University Press.

Kavale, K. A., & Spaulding, L. S. (2011). Efficacy of special education. In M. A. Bray & T. J. Kehle (Eds.), *Oxford handbook of school psychology.* New York: Oxford University Press.

Kavsek, M. (2009). The perception of subjective contours and neon color spreading figures in young infants. *Attention, Perception, and Psychophysics, 71,* 412–420.

Kawai, M., & others. (2010). Developmental trends in mother-infant interaction from 4 months to 42 months: Using an observation technique. *Journal of Epidemiology, 20*(Suppl. 2), S427–S434.

Keating, D. P. (1990). Adolescent thinking. In S. S. Feldman & G. R. Elliott (Eds.), *At the threshold: The developing adolescent.* Cambridge, MA: Harvard University Press.

Keating, D. P. (2004). Cognitive and brain development. In R. Lerner & L. Steinberg (Eds.), *Handbook of adolescent psychology* (2nd ed.). New York: Wiley.

Keen, R. (2005). Unpublished review of J. W. Santrock, *A topical approach to life-span development,* 3rd ed. (New York: McGraw-Hill).

Keen, R. (2011). The development of problem solving in young children: A critical cognitive skill. *Annual Review of Psychology* (Vol. 63). Palo Alto, CA: Annual Reviews.

Keers, R., & others. (2011). Interaction between serotonin transporter gene variants and life events predicts response to antidepressants in the GENDEP project. *Pharmacogenetics, 11*(2), 138–145.

Keijer, J., & van Schothorst, E. M. (2008). Adipose tissue failure and mitochondria as a possible target for improvement by bioactive food components. *Current Opinion in Lipidology, 19*, 4–10.

Keijsers, L., & Laird, R. D. (2010). Introduction to special issue. Careful conversations: Adolescents managing their parents' access to information. *Journal of Adolescence, 33*, 255–259.

Keller, P., & El-Sheikh, M. (2010). Children's emotional security and sleep: Longitudinal relations and directions of effects. *Journal of Child Psychology and Psychiatry, 52*(1), 64–71.

Kellman, P. J., & Banks, M. S. (1998). Infant visual perception. In W. Damon (Ed.), *Handbook of child psychology* (5th ed., Vol. 2). New York: Wiley.

Kelly, D. J., & others. (2007). Cross-race preferences for same-race face extend beyond the African versus Caucasian contrast in 3-month-old infants. *Infancy, 11*, 87–95.

Kelly, D. J., & others. (2009). Development of the other-race effect in infancy: Evidence towards universality? *Journal of Experimental Child Psychology, 104*, 105–114.

Kelly, G. F. (2011). *Sexuality today* (10th ed.). New York: McGraw-Hill.

Kelly, J. P., Borchert, J., & Teller, D. Y. (1997). The development of chromatic and achromatic sensitivity in infancy as tested with the sweep VEP. *Vision Research, 37*, 2057–2072.

Kelly, J. R. (1996). Leisure. In J. E. Birren (Ed.), *Encyclopedia of gerontology* (Vol. 2). San Diego: Academic Press.

Kelmanson, I. A. (2010). Sleep disturbances in two-month-old infants sharing the bed with parent(s). *Minerva Pediatrica, 62*, 162–169.

Kelsey, S. G., Laditka, S. B., & Laditka, J. N. (2010). Caregiver perspectives on transitions in assisted living and memory care. *American Journal of Alzheimer's Disease and Other Dementias, 25*(3), 255–264

Kemnitz, J. W. (2011). Calorie restriction and aging in nonhuman primates. *ILAR Journal, 52*, 66–77.

Kennedy, M. A. (2009). Child abuse. In D. Carr (Ed.), *Encyclopedia of the life course and human development.* Boston: Gale Cengage.

Kennell, J. H. (2006). Randomized controlled trial of skin-to-skin contact from birth versus conventional incubator for physiological stabilization in 1200 g to 2199 g newborns. *Acta Paediatica (Sweden), 95*, 15–16.

Kennell, J. H., & McGrath, S. K. (1999). Commentary: Practical and humanistic lessons from the third world for perinatal caregivers everywhere. *Birth, 26*, 9–10.

Kensinger, E. A. (2009). *Emotional memory across the adult lifespan.* New York: Psychology Press.

Kersting, A., Brahler, E., Glaesmer, H., & Wagner, B. (2011). Prevalence of complicated grief in a representative population-based sample. *Journal of Affective Disorders, 131*, 339–343.

Ketcham, C. J., & Stelmack, G. E. (2001). Age-related declines in motor control. In J. E. Birren & K. W. Schaie (Eds.), *Handbook of the psychology of aging* (5th ed.). San Diego: Academic Press.

Keyes, C. L., & Ryff, C. D. (1998). Generativity in adult lives: Social structural contours and quality of life consequences. In D. P. McAdams & E. de St. Aubin (Eds.), *Generativity and adult development.* Washington, DC: American Psychological Association.

Keyes, K. M., Hatzenbuehler, M. L., & Hasin, D. S. (2011, in press). Stressful life experiences, alcohol consumption, and alcohol use disorders: The epidemiological evidence for four main types of stressors. *Psychopharmacology.*

Khabour, O. F., & Barnawi, J. M. (2010). Association of longevity with IL-10-1082 G/A and TNF-alpha-308 G/A polymorphisms. *International Journal of Immunogenetics, 37*(4), 293–298.

Khera, A. V., & Radar, D. J. (2010). Future therapeutic directions in reverse cholesterol transport. *Current Atherosclerosis Report, 12*, 73–81.

Kiang, L., & Fuligni, A. J. (2010). Meaning in life as a mediator of ethnic identity and adjustment among adolescents from Latin, Asian, and European American backgrounds. *Journal of Youth and Adolescence, 39*, 1253–1264.

Kiecolt-Glaser, J. K., Preacher, K. J., MacCallum, R. C., Atkinson, C., Malarkey, W. B., & Glaser, R. (2003). Chronic stress and age-related increases in the proinflammatory cytokine IL-6. *Proceedings of the National Academy of Science USA, 100*, 9090–9095.

Kim, G., Walden, T. A., & Knieps, L. J. (2010). Impact and characteristics of positive and fearful emotional messages during infant social referencing. *Infant Behavior and Development, 33*, 189–195.

Kim, H. J., & Pedersen, S. (2010). Young adolescents' metacognition and domain knowledge as predictors of hypothesis-development performance in a computer-supported context. *Educational Psychology, 30*, 565–582.

Kim, H. K., & others. (2011). Cardiovascular anomalies in Turner syndrome: Spectrum, prevalence, and cardiac MRI findings in a pediatric and young adult population. *AJR American Journal of Roentgenology, 196*, 454–460.

Kim, J., & Cicchetti, D. (2004). A longitudinal study of child maltreatment, mother-child relationship quality and maladjustment: The role of self-esteem and social competence. *Journal of Abnormal Child Psychology, 32*, 341–354.

Kim, J. A., Wei, Y., & Sowers, J. R. (2008). Role of mitochondrial dysfunction in insulin resistance. *Circulation Research, 102*, 401–414.

Kim, J. E., & Moen, P. (2002). Retirement transitions, gender, and psychological well-being: A life-course, ecological model. *Journals of Gerontology B: Psychological Sciences and Social Sciences, 57*, P212–P222.

Kim, J. H., Kwon, T. H., Koh, S. B., & Park, J. H. (2010). Parkinsonism-hyperpyrexia syndrome after deep brain stimulation surgery: Case report. *Neurosurgery, 66*, E1029.

Kim, K. H. (2010, July 10). Interview. *Newsweek*, 42–48.

Kim, S., & Hasher, L. (2005). The attraction effect in decision making: Superior performance by older adults. *Quarterly Journal of Experimental Psychology, 58A*, 120–133.

Kim, S. E., & others. (2010). Treadmill exercise prevents age-induced failure of memory through an increase in neurogenesis and suppression of apoptosis in rat hippocampus. *Experimental Gerontology, 45*, 357–365.

Kim, S. H. (2009). The influence of finding meaning and worldview of accepting death on anger among bereaved older spouses. *Aging and Mental Health, 13*, 38–45.

Kimble, M., Neacsiu, A. D., Flack, W. F., & Horner, J. (2008). Risk of unwanted sex for college women: Evidence for a red zone. *Journal of American College Health, 57*, 331–338.

King, L. A. (2011). *Psychology* (2nd ed.). New York: McGraw-Hill.

King, L. A., & Hicks, J. A. (2007). Whatever happened to "What might have been?" Regrets, happiness, and maturity. *American Psychologist, 62*, 625–636.

King, P. E., Carr, A., & Boiter, C. (2011). Spirituality, religiosity, and youth thriving. In R. M. Lerner, J. V. Lerner, & J. B. Benson (Eds.), *Advances in child development and behavior: Positive youth development.* New York: Elsevier.

King, P. E., & Roeser, R. W. (2009). Religion and spirituality in adolescent development. In R. M. Lerner & L. Steinberg (Eds.), *Handbook of adolescent psychology* (3rd ed.). New York: Wiley.

King, V., & Scott, M. E. (2005). A comparison of cohabiting relationships among older and younger adults. *Journal of Marriage and the Family, 67*, 271–285.

Kingston, E. R., & Bartholomew, J. (2009). Social Security. In D. Carr (Ed.), *Encyclopedia of the life course and human development.* Boston: Gale Cengage.

Kinney, J. (2012). *Loosening the grip: A handbook of alcohol information* (12th ed.). New York: McGraw-Hill.

Kinzler, K. D., Dupoux, E., & Spelke, E. S. (2011, in press). "Native" objects and collaborators: Infants' object choices and acts of giving reflect favor for native over foreign speakers. *Journal of Cognition and Development.*

Kirby, D. B., Laris, B. A., & Rolleri, L. A. (2007). Sex and HIV education programs: Their impact on sexual behavior of young people throughout the world. *Journal of Adolescent Health, 40*, 206–217.

Kirkorian, H. L., Wartella, E. A., & Anderson, D. A. (2008). Media and young children's learning. *Future of Children, 18*(1), 39–61.

Kisilevsky, B. S., & others. (2009). Fetal sensitivity to properties of maternal speech and language. *Infant Behavior and Development, 32,* 59–71.

Kistner, J., Counts-Allan, C., Dunkel, S., Drew, C. H., David-Ferton, C., & Lopez, C. (2010). Sex differences in relational and overt aggression in the late elementary school years. *Aggressive Behavior, 36,* 282–291.

Kitayama, S., & Uskul, A. K. (2011). Culture, mind, and the brain: Current evidence and future directions. *Annual Review of Psychology* (Vol. 62). Palo Alto, CA: Annual Reviews.

Kitsantas, P., & Gaffney, K. F. (2010). Racial/ethnic disparities in infant mortality. *Journal of Perinatal Medicine, 38,* 87–94.

Kittas, A. (2010). Evolution of the rate of biological aging using a phenotype based computational model. *Journal of Theoretical Biology, 266*(3), 401–407.

Kitzinger, S. (2011). Human rights and midwifery. *Birth, 38,* 86–87.

Kiuhara, S. A., Graham, S., & Hawken, L. S. (2009). Teaching writing to high school students: A national survey. *Journal of Educational Psychology, 101,* 136–160.

Klaczynski, P. (2001). The influence of analytic and heuristic processing on adolescent reasoning and decision making. *Child Development, 72,* 844–861.

Klatt, J., & Enright, R. (2009). Investigating the place of forgiveness within the positive youth development paradigm. *Journal of Moral Education, 38,* 35–52.

Klaus, M., & Kennell, H. H. (1976). *Maternal-infant bonding.* St. Louis: Mosby.

Klein, S. B. (2009). *Learning.* Thousand Oaks, CA: Sage.

Klepitskaya, O., Cole, W., Henderson, J., & Bronte-Stewart, H. (2011). Deep brain stimulation in "on"-state Parkinson hyperpyrexia. *Neurology, 15*(76)(Suppl. 2), S69–S71.

Klima, C., Norr, K., Conderheld, S., & Handler, A. (2009). Introduction of Centering Pregnancy in a public health clinic. *Journal of Midwifery and Women's Health, 54,* 27–34.

Klimstra, T. A., Hale, W. W., Raaijmakers, Q. A., Branje, S. J. T., & Meeus, W. H. (2010). Identity formation in adolescence: Change or stability? *Journal of Youth and Adolescence, 39,* 150–162.

Kling, K. C., Hyde, J. S., Showers, C. J., & Buswell, B. N. (1999). Gender differences in self-esteem: A meta-analysis. *Psychological Bulletin, 125,* 470–500.

Klingenberg, C. P., & others. (2010). Prenatal alcohol exposure alters the patterns of facial asymmetry. *Alcohol, 44*(7–8), 649–657.

Knoll, S., Bulik, C. M., & Hebebrand, J. (2011, in press). Do the currently proposed DSM-5 criteria for anorexia nervosa adequately consider developmental aspects of children and adolescents? *European Child and Adolescent Psychiatry.*

Knopik, V. S. (2009). Maternal smoking during pregnancy and child outcomes: Real or spurious effect? *Developmental Neuropsychology, 34,* 1–36.

Knox, M. (2010). On hitting children: A review of corporal punishment in the United States. *Journal of Pediatric Health Care, 24,* 103–107.

Knussmann, R., Christiansen, K., & Couwenbergs, C. (1986). Relations between sex hormone levels and sexual behavior in men. *Archives of Sexual Behavior, 15,* 429–445.

Koch, A., Homoe, P., Pipper, C., Hjuler, T., & Melbye, M. (2011). Chronic suppurative otitis media in a birth cohort of children in Greenland: Population-based study of incidence and risk factors. *Pediatric Infectious Disease Journal, 30,* 25–29.

Kochanska, G., & Aksan, N. (2007). Conscience in childhood: Past, present, and future. *Merrill-Palmer Quarterly, 50,* 299–310.

Kochanska, G., Aksan N., Prisco, T. R., & Adams, E. E. (2008). Mother-child and father-child mutually responsive orientation in the first two years and children's outcomes at preschool age: Mechanisms of influence. *Child Development, 79,* 30–44.

Kochanska, G., Barry, R. A., Stellern, S. A., & O'Bleness, J. J. (2010). Early attachment organization moderates the parent-child mutually coercive pathway to children's antisocial conduct. *Child Development, 80,* 1288–1300.

Kochanska, G., Forman, D. R., Aksan, N., & Dunbar, S. B. (2005). Pathways to conscience: Early mother-child mutually responsive orientation and children's moral emotion, conduct, and cognition. *Journal of Child Psychology and Psychiatry, 46,* 19–34.

Kochanska, G., Gross, J. N., Lin, M., & Nichols, K. E. (2002). Guilt in young children: Development, determinants, and relations with a broader set of standards. *Child Development, 73,* 461–482.

Kochanska, G., Koenig, J. L., Barry, R. A., Kim, S., & Yoon, J. E. (2010). Children's conscience during toddler and preschool years, moral self, and a competent, adaptive development trajectory. *Development Psychology, 46,* 1320–1332.

Kochanska, G., Woodard, J., Kim, S., Koenig, J. L., Yoon, J. E., & Barry, R. A. (2010). Positive socialization mechanisms in secure and insecure parent-child dyads: Two longitudinal studies. *Journal of Child Psychology and Psychiatry, 51,* 998–1009.

Koenig, H. G. (2004). Religion, spirituality, and medicine: Research findings and implications for clinical practice. *Southern Medical Journal, 97,* 1194–2000.

Koenig, H. G., & Larson, D. B. (1998). Religion and mental health. In H. S. Friedman (Ed.), *Encyclopedia of mental health* (Vol. 3). San Diego: Academic Press.

Koenig, L. B., McGue, M., & Iacono, W. G. (2008). Stability and change in religiousness during emerging adulthood. *Developmental Psychology, 44,* 523–543.

Kohen, D. E., Leventhal, T., Dahinten, V. S., & McIntosh, C. N. (2008). Neighborhood disadvantage: Pathways of effects for young children. *Child Development, 79,* 156–169.

Kohlberg, L. (1958). *The development of modes of moral thinking and choice in the years 10 to 16.* Unpublished doctoral dissertation, University of Chicago.

Kohlberg, L. (1969). Stage and sequence: The cognitive-developmental approach to socialization. In D. A. Goslin (Ed.), *Handbook of socialization theory and research.* Chicago: Rand McNally.

Kohlberg, L. (1986). A current statement on some theoretical issues. In S. Modgil & C. Modgil (Eds.), *Lawrence Kohlberg.* Philadelphia: Falmer.

Kohler, P. K., Manhart, L. E., & Lafferty, W. E. (2008). Abstinence-only and comprehensive sex education and the initiation of sexual activity and teen pregnancy. *Journal of Adolescent Health, 42,* 344–351.

Kohler, T. S., & others. (2008). Prevalence of androgen deficiency in men with erectile dysfunction. *Urology, 71,* 693–697.

Koolhof, R., Loeber, R., Wei, E. H., Pardini, D., & D'Escury, A. C. (2007). Inhibition deficits of serious delinquent boys of low intelligence. *Criminal Behavior and Mental Health, 17,* 274–292.

Kopp, C. B. (1982). The antecedents of self-regulation. *Developmental Psychology, 18,* 199–214.

Kopp, C. B. (1987). The growth of self-regulation: Caregivers and children. In N. Eisenberg (Ed.), *Contemporary topics in developmental psychology.* New York: Wiley.

Kopp, C. B. (2008). Self-regulatory processes. In M. M. Haith & J. B. Benson (Eds.), *Encyclopedia of infant and early childhood development.* Oxford, UK: Elsevier.

Kopp, C. B. (2011). Development in the early years: Socialization, motor development, and consciousness. *Annual Review of Psychology* (Vol. 62). Palo Alto, CA: Annual Reviews.

Kopp, F., & Lindenberger, U. (2011, in press). Effects of joint attention on long-term memory in 9-month-old infants: An event-related potentials study. *Developmental Science.*

Koppelman, K., & Goodhart, L. (2011). *Understanding human differences* (3rd ed.). Boston: Allyn & Bacon.

Kornblum, J. (2006, March 9). How to monitor the kids? *USA Today,* 1D, p.1.

Koropeckyj-Cox, T. (2009a). Loneliness, later life. In D. Carr (Ed.), *Encyclopedia of the life course and human development.* Boston: Gale Cengage.

Koropeckyj-Cox, T. (2009b). Singlehood. In D. Carr (Ed.), *Encyclopedia of the life course and human development.* Boston: Gale Cengage.

Kostelnik, M. J., Soderman, A. K., & Whiren, A. P. (2011). *Developmentally appropriate curricula* (5th ed.). Upper Saddle River, NJ: Merrill.

Kotovsky, L., & Baillargeon, R. (1994). Calibration-based reasoning about collision events in 11-month-old infants. *Cognition, 51,* 107–129.

Kotre, J. (1984). *Outliving the self: Generativity and the interpretation of lives.* Baltimore: Johns Hopkins University Press.

Kozol, J. (2005). *The shame of the nation.* New York: Crown.

Kramer, A. F., & Madden, D. J. (2008). Attention. In F. I. M. Craik & T. A. Salthouse (Eds.), *Handbook of aging and cognition* (3rd ed.). Mahwah, NJ: Erlbaum.

Kramer, A. F., & Morrow, D. (2009). Cognitive training and expertise. In D. Park & N. Schwartz (Eds.), *Cognitive aging: A primer.* New York: Psychology Press.

Kramer, L. (2006, July 10). Commentary in "How your siblings make you who you are" by J. Kluger. *Time,* 46–55.

Kramer, L., & Perozynski, L. (1999). Parental beliefs about managing sibling conflict. *Developmental Psychology, 35,* 489–499.

Kramer, L., & Radey, C. (1997). Improving sibling relationships among young children: A social skills training model. *Family Relations, 46,* 237–246.

Krause, N. (1995). Religiosity and self-esteem among older adults. *Journal of Gerontology B: Psychological Science, 50,* P236–P246.

Krause, N. (2003). Religious meaning and subjective well-being in late life. *Journal of Gerontology B: Psychological Science and Social Science, 58,* S160–S170.

Krause, N. (2008). The social foundations of religious meaning in life. *Research on Aging, 30*(4), 395–427.

Krause, N. (2009). Deriving a sense of meaning in late life. In V. L. Bengtson, D. Gans, N. M. Putney, & M. Silverstein (Eds.), *Handbook of theories of aging.* New York: Springer.

Kremen, W. S., & Lyons, M. J. (2011). Behavior genetics of aging. In K. W. Schaie & S. L. Willis (Eds.), *Handbook of the psychology of aging* (7th ed.). New York: Elsevier.

Kreutzer, M. A., Leonard, C., & Flavell, J. H. (1975). An interview study of children's knowledge about memory. *Monographs of the Society for Research in Child Development, 40*(1, Serial No. 159).

Kriemler, S., & others. (2010). Effect of school based physical activity programme (KISS) on fitness and adiposity in primary schoolchildren: Cluster randomised controlled trial. *British Medical Journal.*

Kring, A. M. (2000). Gender and anger. In A. H. Fischer (Ed.), *Gender and emotion.* New York: Cambridge University Press.

Kristjuhan, U., & Taidre, E. (2010). Postponed aging in university teachers. *Rejuvenation Research, 13*(2–3), 353–355.

Kroger, J. (2007). *Identity development: Adolescence through adulthood* (2nd ed.). Thousand Oaks, CA: Sage

Kroger, J., Martinussen, M., & Marcia, J. E. (2010). Identity change during adolescence and young adulthood: A meta-analysis. *Journal of Adolescence, 33,* 683–698.

Krueger, P. M., & Chang, V. W. (2008). Being poor and coping with stress: Health behaviors and the risk of death. *American Journal of Public Health, 98,* 889–896.

Kruger, J., Blanck, H. M., & Gillespie, C. (2006). Dietary and physical activity behaviors among adults successful at weight loss management. *International Journal of Behavioral Nutrition and Physical Activity, 3,* 17.

Ksir, C. J., Chart, C. L., & Ray, O. S. (2008), *Drugs, society, and human behavior* (12th ed.). New York: McGraw-Hill.

Kubicek, B., Korunka, C., Raymo, J. M., & Hoonakker, P. (2011). Psychological well-being in retirement: The effects of personal and gendered contextual resources. *Journal of Occupational Health Psychology, 16,* 230–246.

Kübler-Ross, E. (1969). *On death and dying.* New York: Macmillan.

Kuebli, J. (1994, March). Young children's understanding of everyday emotions. *Young Children,* pp. 36–48.

Kuehn, B. M. (2011). Scientists find promising therapies for fragile X and Down syndromes. *Journal of the American Medical Association, 305,* 344–346.

Kuhl, P. K. (1993). Infant speech perception: A window on psycholinguistic development. *International Journal of Psycholinguistics. 9,* 33–56.

Kuhl, P. K. (2000). A new view of language acquisition. *Proceedings of the National Academy of Science, 97*(22), 11850–11857.

Kuhl, P. K. (2007). Is speech learning "gated" by the social brain? *Developmental Science, 10,* 110–120.

Kuhl, P. K. (2009). Linking infant speech perception to language acquisition: Phonetic learning predicts language growth. In J. Colombo, P. McCardle, & L. Freund (Eds.), *Infant pathways to language.* New York: Psychology Press.

Kuhl, P. K. (2011). Social mechanisms in early language acquisition: Understanding integrated brain systems and supporting language. In J. Decety & J. Cacioppo (Eds.), *Handbook of social neuroscience.* New York: Oxford University Press.

Kuhl, P. K., & Damasio, A. (2011). Language. In E. R. Kandel & others (Eds.), *Principles of neural science* (5th ed.). New York: McGraw-Hill.

Kuhlmann, B. G., & Touron, D. R. (2011). Older adults' use of metacognitive knowledge in source monitoring: Spared monitoring but impaired control. *Psychology and Aging, 26,* 143–149.

Kuhn, D. (2008). Formal operations from a twenty-first-century perspective. *Human Development, 51,* 48–55.

Kuhn, C., & others. (2010). The emergence of gonadal hormone influences on dopaminergic function during puberty. *Hormones and Behavior, 58,* 122–137.

Kuhn, D. (1998). Afterword to Volume 2: Cognition, perception, and language. In W. Damon (Ed.), *Handbook of child psychology* (5th ed., Vol. 2). New York: Wiley.

Kuhn, D. (2008). Formal operations from a twenty-first-century perspective. *Human Development, 51,* 48–55.

Kuhn, D. (2009). Adolescent thinking. In R. M. Lerner & L. Steinberg (Eds.), *Handbook of adolescent psychology* (3rd ed.). New York: Wiley.

Kuhn, D. (2011). What is scientific thinking and how does it develop? In U. Goswami (Ed.), *Wiley-Blackwell handbook of childhood cognitive development* (2nd ed.). New York: Wiley-Blackwell.

Kuhn, D., Cheney, R., & Weinstock, M. (2000). The development of epistemological understanding. *Cognitive Development, 15,* 309–328.

Kuhn, D., & Franklin, S. (2006). The second decade: What develops (and how)? In W. Damon & R. Lerner (Eds.), *Handbook of child psychology* (6th ed.). New York: Wiley.

Kuhn, D., Schauble, L., & Garcia-Mila, M. (1992). Cross-domain development of scientific reasoning. *Cognition and Instruction, 9,* 285–327.

Kulik, L., & Heine-Cohen, E. (2011). Coping resources, perceived stress, and adjustment among Israeli women: Assessing effects. *Journal of Social Psychology, 151,* 5–30.

Kunz, J., & Kunz, J. (2011). *THINK marriages and families.* Upper Saddle River, NJ: Pearson.

Kurdek, L. A. (2008). Change in relationship quality for partners from lesbian, gay male, and heterosexual couples. *Journal of Family Psychology, 22,* 701–711.

L

La Vignera, S., Condorelli, R., Vicari, E., D'Agata, R., & Calogero, A. (2011, in press). Physical activity and erectile dysfunction in middle-aged men: A brief review. *Journal of Andrology.*

Labouvie-Vief, G. (1986, August). *Modes of knowing and life-span cognition.* Paper presented at the meeting of the American Psychological Association, Washington, DC.

Labouvie-Vief, G. (2009). Cognition and equilibrium regulation in development and aging. In V. Bengtson & others (Eds.), *Handbook of theories of aging.* New York: Springer.

Labouvie-Vief, G., Gruhn, D., & Studer, J. (2010). Dynamic integration of emotion and cognition: Equilibrium regulation in development and aging. In M. E. Lamb, A. Freund, & R. M. Lerner (Eds.), *Handbook of life-span development* (Vol. 2). New York: Wiley.

Lachman, M. E. (2004). Development in midlife. *Annual Review of Psychology* (Vol. 55). Palo Alto, CA: Annual Reviews.

Lachman, M. E., Agrigoroaei, S., Murphy, C., & Tun, P. A. (2010). Frequent cognitive activity compensates for education difference in episodic memory. *American Journal of Geriatric Psychiatry, 18,* 4–10.

Lachman, M., & Kranz, E. (2010). The midlife crisis. In I. Wiener & E. Craighead (Eds.), *The Corsini encyclopedia of psychology* (4th ed.). New York: Wiley.

Lachman, M., Neupert, S., & Agrigoroaei, S. (2011). The relevance of a sense of control for health and aging. In K. W. Schaie & S. L. Willis (Eds.), *Handbook of the psychology of aging* (7th ed.). New York: Elsevier.

Ladd, G., Buhs, E., & Troop, W. (2004). School adjustment and social skills training. In P. K. Smith & C. H. Hart (Eds.), *Wiley-Blackwell handbook of childhood social development*. Malden, MA: Blackwell.

Ladd, G. W., Kochenderfer-Ladd, B., & Rydell, A-M. (2011). Children's interpersonal skills and school-based relationships. In P. K. Smith & C. H. Hart (Eds.), *Wiley-Blackwell handbook of childhood social development* (2nd ed.). New York: Wiley.

LaFrance, M., Hecht, M. A., & Paluck, E. L. (2003). The contingent smile: A meta-analysis of sex differences in smiling. *Psychological Bulletin, 129,* 305–334.

Lafreniere, D., & Mann, N. (2009). Anosmia: Loss of smell in the elderly. *Otolaryngologic Clinics of North America, 42,* 123–131.

Lahey, B. B., Van Hulle, C. A., D'Onofrio, B. M., Roders, J. L., & Waldman, I. D. (2008). Is parental knowledge of their offspring's whereabouts and peer associations spuriously associated with offspring delinquency? *Journal of Abnormal Child Psychology, 36,* 807–823.

Laible, D., & Thompson, R. A. (2000). Mother-child discourse, attachment security, shared positive affect, and early conscience development. *Child Development, 71,* 1424–1440.

Laible, D., & Thompson, R. A. (2007). Early socialization: A relationship perspective. In J. E. Grusec & P. D. Hastings (Eds.), *Handbook of socialization.* New York: Guilford.

Laird, R. D., Criss, M. M., Pettit, G. S., Dodge, K. A., & Bates, J. E. (2008). Parents' monitoring knowledge attenuates the link between antisocial friends and adolescent delinquent behavior. *Journal of Abnormal Child Psychology, 36,* 299–310.

Laird, R. D., Marrero, M. D., & Sentse, M. (2010). Revisiting parental monitoring: Evidence that parental solicitation can be effective when needed most. *Journal of Youth and Adolescence, 39,* 1431–1441.

Lamb, M. E. (1994). Infant care practices and the application of knowledge. In C. B. Fisher & R. M. Lerner (Eds.), *Applied developmental psychology.* New York: McGraw-Hill.

Lamb, M. E. (2005). Attachments, social networks, and developmental contexts. *Human Development, 43,* 108–112.

Lamb, M. E. (2010). How do fathers influence children's development? In M. E. Lamb (Ed.), *The role of the father in child development* (5th ed.). New York: Wiley.

Lamb, M. E., Bornstein, M. H., & Teti, D. M. (2002). *Development in infancy* (4th ed.). Mahwah, NJ: Erlbaum.

Lamb, M. M., & others. (2010). Early-life predictors of higher body mass index in healthy children. *Annals of Nutrition & Metabolism, 56,* 16–22.

Landale, N. S., Thomas, K. J., & Van Hook, J. (2011). The living arrangements of children of immigrants. *Future of Children, 21,* 43–70.

Landgren, H., & Curtis, M. A. (2010). Locating and labeling neural stem cells in the brain. *Journal of Cellular Physiology, 226*(1), 1–7.

Landi, D., & Rossini, P. M. (2010). Cerebral restorative plasticity from normal aging to brain diseases: A "never ending story." *Restorative Neurology and Neuroscience, 28,* 349–366.

Landor, A., Simons, L. G., Simons, R. L., Brody, G. H., & Gibbons, F. X. (2011). The role of religiosity in the relationship between parents, peers, and adolescent risky sexual behavior. *Journal of Youth and Adolescence, 40,* 296–309.

Lane, H. (1976). *The wild boy of Aveyron.* Cambridge, MA: Harvard University Press.

Lang, F. R., & Carstensen, L. L. (1994). Close emotional relationship in late life: Further support for proactive aging in the social domain. *Psychology and Aging, 9,* 315–324.

Lange, B. S., & others. (2010). The potential of virtual reality and gaming to assist successful aging with disability. *Physical Medicine and Rehabilitation Clinics of North America, 21,* 339–356.

Langer, E. J. (2005). *On becoming an artist.* New York: Ballantine.

Langer, E. J. (2007, August). *Counterclockwise: Mindfulness and aging.* Paper presented at the meeting of the American Psychological Association, San Francisco.

Langston, W. (2011). *Research methods laboratory manual for psychology* (3rd ed.). Boston: Cengage.

Langstrom, N., Rahman, Q., Carlstrom, E., & Lichtenstein, P. (2010). Genetic and environmental effects on same-sex behavior: A population study of twins in Sweden. *Archives of Sexual Behavior, 39,* 75–80.

Lansford, J. E. (2009). Parental divorce and children's adjustment. *Perspectives on Psychological Science, 4,* 140–152.

Lansford, J. E., Malone, P. S., Dodge, K. A., Petti, G. S., & Bates, J. E. (2010). Developmental cascades of peer rejection, social information processing biases, and aggression during middle school. *Development and Psychopathology, 22,* 593–602.

Lansford, J. E., Yu, T., Erath, S., Pettit, G. S., Bates, J. E., & Dodge, K. A. (2010). Developmental precursors of number of sexual partners from age 16 to 22. *Journal of Research on Adolescence, 20,* 651–677.

Lapierre, S., & others. (2011). A systematic review of elderly suicide prevention programs. *Crisis, 32,* 88–98.

Lapsley, D. K., & Hill, P. L. (2010). Subjective invulnerability, optimism bias, and adjustment in emerging adulthood. *Journal of Youth and Adolescence, 39,* 847–857.

LaRocca, T. J., Seals, D. R., & Pierce, G. L. (2010). Leukocyte telomere length is preserved with aging in endurance exercise-trained adults and related to maximum aerobic capacity. *Mechanisms of Aging and Development, 131,* 165–167.

Larson, R. W. (2001). How U.S. children spend time: What it does (and doesn't) tell us about their development. *Current Directions in Psychological Science, 10,* 160–164.

Larson, R. W., Wilson, S., & Rickman, A. (2009). Globalization, societal change, and adolescence across the world. In R. M. Lerner & L. Steinberg (Eds.), *Handbook of adolescent psychology* (3rd ed.). New York: Wiley.

Larson, R., & Richards, M. H. (1994). *Divergent realities.* New York: Basic Books.

Larson, R., & Verma, S. (1999). How children and adolescents spent their time around the world: Work, play, and developmental opportunities. *Psychological Bulletin, 125,* 701–736.

Larzelere, R. E., & Kuhn, B. R. (2005). Comparing child outcomes of physical punishment and alternative disciplinary tactics: A meta-analysis. *Clinical Child and Family Psychology Review, 8,* 1–37.

Laumann, E. O., Glasser, D. B., Never, R. C., & Moreira, E. D. (2009). A population-based survey of sexual activity, sexual problems, and associated help-seeking behavior patterns in mature adults in the United States of America. *International Journal of Impotence Research, 21,* 171–178.

Laursen, B., & Collins, W. A. (2009). Parent-child relationships during adolescence. In R. M. Lerner & L. Steinberg (Eds.), *Handbook of adolescent psychology* (3rd ed.). New York: Wiley.

Lavalliere, M., & others. (2011). Changing lanes in a simulator: Effects of aging on the control of the vehicle and visual inspection of mirrors and the blind spot. *Traffic Injury Prevention, 12,* 191–200.

Lavie, C. J., & Milani, R. V. (2011). Depression, autonomic function, and cardiorespiratory fitness: Comment on Hughes et al. (2010). *Perceptual and Motor Skills, 112,* 319–321.

Lavik, E., Kuehn, M. H., & Kwon, Y. H. (2011, in press). Novel drug delivery systems for glaucoma. *Eye.*

Lavoie, B. A., Mehta, R., & Thornton, A. R. (2008). Linear and nonlinear changes in the auditory brainstem response of aging humans. *Clinical Neuropsychology, 119,* 772–785.

Lawyer, S., Resnick, H., Bakanic, V., Burkett, T., & Kilpatrick, D. (2010). Forcible, drug-facilitated, and incapacitated rape and sexual assault among undergraduate women. *Journal of American College Health, 58,* 453–460.

Le Couteur, D. G., & Simpson, S. J. (2011). Adaptive senectitude: The prolongevity effects on aging. *Journals of Gerontology A: Biological Sciences and Medical Sciences, 66A,* 179–182.

Leach, P. (1990). *Your baby and child: From birth to age five.* New York: Knopf.

Leadbeater, B. J., & Way, N. (2000). *Growing up fast.* Mahwah, NJ: Erlbaum.

Leaper, C., & Bigler, R. S. (2011). Gender. In M. K. Underwood & L. S. Rosen (Eds.), *Social development.* New York: Guilford.

Leaper, C., & Smith, T. E. (2004). A meta-analytic review of gender variations in children's language use: Talkativeness, affiliative speech, and assertive speech. *Development Psychology, 40,* 993–1027.

Leatherdale, S. T. (2010). Factors associated with communication-based sedentary behaviors among youth: Are talking on the phone, texting, and instant messaging new sedentary behaviors to be concerned about? *Journal of Adolescent Health, 47,* 315–318.

Lee, H. C., El-Sayed, Y. Y., & Gould, J. B. (2008). Population trends in cesarean delivery for breech presentation in the United States, 1997–2003. *American Journal of Obstetrics and Gynecology, 199,* e1–e8.

Lee, I. M., & Skerrett, P. J. (2001). Physical activity and all-cause mortality: What is the dose-response relation? *Medical Science and Sports Exercise, 33*(Suppl. 6), S459–S471.

Lee, K., Cameron, C. A., Doucette, J., & Talwar, V. (2002). Phantoms and fabrications: Young children's detection of implausible lies. *Child Development, 73,* 1688–1702.

Lee, K., Quinn, P. C., Pascalis, O., & Slater, A. (2011). Development of face processing ability in childhood. In P. D. Zelazo (Ed.), *Oxford handbook of developmental psychology.* Oxford, UK: Oxford University Press.

Lee, K. Y., & others. (2011). Effects of combined radiofrequency radiation exposure on the cell cycle and its regulatory proteins. *Bioelectromagnetics, 32,* 169–178.

Lefkowitz, E. S., Boone, T. L., & Shearer, T. L. (2004). Communication with best friends about sex-related topics during emerging adulthood. *Journal of Youth and Adolescence, 33,* 339–351.

Lefkowitz, E. S., & Gillen, M. M. (2006). "Sex is just a normal part of life": Sexuality in emerging adulthood. In J. J. Arnett & J. L. Tanner (Eds.), *Emerging adults in America.* Washington, DC: American Psychological Association.

Legerstee, M. (1997). Contingency effects of people and objects on subsequent cognitive functioning in 3-month-old infants. *Social Development, 6,* 307–321.

Lehman, H. C. (1960). The age decrement in outstanding scientific creativity. *American Psychologist, 15,* 128–134.

Lehrer, R., & Schauble, L. (2006). Scientific thinking and scientific literacy: In W. Damon & R. Lerner (Eds.), *Handbook of child psychology* (6th ed.). New York: Wiley.

Leifer, G. (2011). *Introduction to maternity and pediatric nursing* (6th ed.). New York: Elsevier.

Leifheit-Limson, E., & Levy, B. (2009). Ageism/age discrimination. In D. Carr (Ed.), *Encyclopedia of the life course and human development.* Boston: Gale Cengage.

Leming, M. R., & Dickinson, G. E. (2011). *Understanding death, dying, and bereavement* (7th ed.). Boston: Cengage.

Lempers, J. D., Flavell, E. R., & Flavell, J. H. (1977). The development in very young children of tacit knowledge concerning visual perception. *Genetic Psychology Monographs, 95,* 3–53.

Lenhart, A., Purcel, K., Smith, A., & Zickuhr, K. (2010). *Social media and mobile Internet use among teens and young adults.* Washington, DC: Pew Research Center.

Lennon, E. M., Gardner, J. M., Karmel, B. Z., & Flory, M. J. (2008). Bayley Scales of Infant Development. In M. M. Haith & J. B. Benson (Eds.), *Encyclopedia of infant and early childhood development.* Oxford, UK: Elsevier.

Lenoir, C. P., Mallet, E., & Calenda, E. (2000). Siblings of sudden infant death syndrome and near miss in about 30 families: Is there a genetic link? *Medical Hypotheses, 54,* 408–411.

Leonardi-Bee, J. A., Smyth, A. R., Britton, J., & Coleman, T. (2008). Environmental tobacco smoke and fetal health: Systematic review and analysis. *Archives of Disease in Childhood: Fetal and Neonatal Edition, 93*(5), F351–F361.

Leppanen, J. M., Moulson, M., Vogel-Farley, V. K., & Nelson, C. A. (2007). An ERP study of emotional face processing in the adult and infant brain. *Child Development, 78,* 232–245.

Lerch, C., Cordes, M., & Baumeister, J. (2011). Effectiveness of prevention programs in female youth soccer: A systematic review. *British Journal of Sports Medicine, 45,* 359.

Lerner, H. G. (1989). *The dance of intimacy.* New York: Harper & Row.

Lerner, R. M., & others. (2011). Positive youth development: Contemporary theoretical perspectives. In A. C. Fonseca (Ed.), *Criancas e adolescents.* Coimbra, Portugal: Nova Almedina.

Lerner, R. M., Boyd, M., & Du, D. (2008). Adolescent development. In I. B. Weiner & C. B. Craighead (Eds.), *Encyclopedia of psychology* (4th ed.). Hoboken, NJ: Wiley.

Lerner-Geva, L., Boyko, V., Blumstein, T., & Benyamini, Y. (2010). The impact of education, cultural background, and lifestyle on symptoms of the menopausal transition: The Women's Health at Midlife Study. *Journal of Women's Health, 19*(5), 975–985.

Lesaux, N. K., & Siegel, L. S. (2003). The development of reading in children who speak English as a second language. *Developmental Psychology, 39,* 1005–1019.

Leshikar, E. D., Gutchess, A. H., Hebrank, A. C., Sutton, B. P., & Park, D. C. (2010). The impact of increased relational encoding demands in frontal and hippocampal function in older adults. *Cortex, 46,* 507–521.

Lester, B. M., & others. (2002). The maternal lifestyle study: Effects of substance exposure during pregnancy on neurodevelopmental outcome in 1-month-old infants. *Pediatrics, 110,* 1182–1192.

Levant, R. F. (2001). Men and masculinity. In J. Worell (Ed.), *Encyclopedia of women and gender.* San Diego: Academic Press.

Levelt, W. J. M. (1989). *Speaking: From intention to articulation.* Cambridge, MA: MIT Press.

Levene, M. I., & Chervenak, F. A. (2009). *Fetal and neonatal neurology and neurosurgery* (4th Ed.). New York: Elsevier.

Lever-Duffy, J., & McDonald, J. B. (2011). *Teaching and learning with technology* (4th ed.). Boston: Allyn & Bacon.

Levin, J., & Fox, J. A. (2011). *Elementary statistics in social research* (3rd ed.). Upper Saddle River, NJ: Pearson.

Levine, T. P., & others. (2008). Effects of prenatal cocaine exposure on special education in school-aged children. *Pediatrics, 122,* e83–e91.

Levinson, D. J. (1978). *The seasons of a man's life.* New York: Knopf.

Levinson, D. J. (1987, August). *The seasons of a woman's life.* Paper presented at the meeting of the American Psychological Association, New York.

Levinson, D. J. (1996). *Seasons of a woman's life.* New York: Knopf.

Levitt, M. J., & Cici-Gokaltun, A. (2011). Close relationships across the life span. In K. L. Fingerman, C. A. Berg, J. Smith, & T. C. Antonucci (Eds.), *Handbook of life-span development.* New York: Springer.

Levy, B. R., Slade, M. D., & Gill, T. M. (2006). Hearing decline predicted by elders' stereotypes. *Journals of Gerontology B: Psychological Sciences and Social Sciences, 61B,* P82–P87.

Levy, G. D., Sadovsky, A. L., & Troseth, G. L. (2000). Aspects of young children's perceptions of gender-typed occupations. *Sex Roles, 42,* 993–1006.

Lewin-Bizan, S., Bowers, E., & Lerner, R. M. (2011, in press). One good thing leads to another: Cascades of positive youth development among American adolescents. *Development and Psychopathology.*

Lewis, A. C. (2007). Looking beyond NCLB. *Phi Delta Kappan, 88,* 483–484.

Lewis, C., & Carpendale, J. (2011). Social cognition. In P. K. Smith & C. H. Hart (Eds.), *Wiley-Blackwell handbook of childhood social development* (2nd ed.). New York: Wiley.

Lewis, M. (1997). *Altering fate: Why the past does not predict the future.* New York: Guilford.

Lewis, M. (2005). Selfhood. In B. Hopkins (Ed.), *The Cambridge encyclopedia of child development.* Cambridge, UK: Cambridge University Press.

Lewis, M. (2007). Early emotional development. In A. Slater & M. Lewis (Eds.), *Introduction to infant development.* Malden, MA: Blackwell.

Lewis, M. (2008). The emergence of human emotions. In M. Lewis, J. M. Haviland Jones, & L. Feldman Barrett (Eds.), *Handbook of emotions* (3rd ed.). New York: Guilford.

Lewis, M. (2010). The emergence of consciousness and its role in human development. In W. F. Overton & R. M. Lerner (Eds.), *Handbook of life-span development.* New York: Wiley.

Lewis, M., & Brooks-Gunn, J. (1979). *Social cognition and the acquisition of the self.* New York: Plenum.

Lewis, M., Feiring, C., & Rosenthal, S. (2000). Attachment over time. *Child Development, 71,* 707–720.

Lewis, R. (2010). *Human genetics* (8th ed.). New York: McGraw-Hill.

Li, C., Ford, E. S., McGuire, L. C., & Mokdad, A. H. (2007). Increasing trends in waist circumference and abdominal obesity among U.S. adults. *Obesity, 15,* 216–224.

Li, J., Olsen, J., Vestergaard, M., & Obel, C. (2011, in press). Low Apgar scores and risk of childhood attention deficit hyperactivity disorder. *Journal of Pediatrics.*

Li, M. D., Lou, X. Y., Chen, G., Ma, J. Z., & Elston, R. C. (2008). Gene-gene interactions among CHRNA4, CHRNB2, BDNF, and NTRK2 in nicotine dependence. *Biological Psychiatry, 64,* 951–957.

Li, Y. (2007). Recovering from spousal bereavement in later life: Does volunteer participation play a role? *Journals of Gerontology B: Psychological Sciences and Social Sciences, 62,* S257–S266.

Liao, W. C., & others. (2011). Healthy behaviors and onset of functional disability in older adults: Results of a national longitudinal study. *Journal of the American Geriatrics Society, 59,* 200–206.

Liben, L. S. (1995). Psychology meets geography: Exploring the gender gap on the national geography bee. *Psychological Science Agenda, 8,* 8–9.

Libertus, K., & Needham, A. (2010). Teach to reach: The effects of active vs. passive reaching experiences on action and perception. *Vision Research, 50,* 2750–2757.

Lidz, J. (2010). The abstract nature of syntactic representations: Consequences for a theory of learning. In E. Hoff & M. Shatz (Eds.), *Blackwell handbook of language development* (2nd ed.). Malden, MA: Blackwell.

Lie, E., & Newcombe, N. (1999). Elementary school children's explicit and implicit memory for faces of preschool classmates. *Developmental Psychology, 35,* 102–112.

Lieberman, E., Davidson, K., Lee-Parritz, A., & Shearer, E. (2005). Changes in fetal position during labor and their association with epidural analgesia. *Obstetrics and Gynecology, 105,* 974–982.

Liechty, J. M. (2010). Body image distortion and three types of weight loss behaviors among nonoverweight girls in the United States. *Journal of Adolescent Health, 47,* 176–182.

Lifton, R. J. (1977). The sense of immortality: On death and the continuity of life. In H. Feifel (Ed.), *New meanings of death.* New York: McGraw-Hill.

Lillard, A. (2006). Pretend play in toddlers. In C. A. Brownell & C. B. Kopp (Eds.), *Socioemotional development in the toddler years.* New York: Oxford University Press.

Lillard, A., Pinkham, A. M., & Smith, E. (2011). Pretend play and cognitive development. In U. Goswami (Ed.), *Wiley-Blackwell handbook of childhood cognitive development* (2nd ed.). New York: Wiley.

Lin, F. R., Thorpe, R., Gordon-Salant, S., & Ferrucci, L. (2011, in press). Hearing loss prevalence and risk factors among older adults in the United States. *Journals of Gerontology A: Biological Sciences and Medical Sciences.*

Lin, J. N., & others. (2010). Resveratrol modulates tumor cell proliferation and protein translation via SIRT1-dependent AMPK activation. *Journal of Agricultural and Food Chemistry, 58,* 1584–1592.

Lin, J., & others. (2009). Vitamins C and E and beta-carotene supplementation and cancer risk: A randomized controlled trial. *Journal of the National Cancer Institute, 101,* 14–23.

Lindau, S. T., & Gavrilova, N. (2010). Sex, health, and years of sexually active life gained due to good health: Evidence from two U.S. population based cross sectional surveys of aging. *British Medical Journal, 340,* c810.

Lindau, S. T., Schumm, L. P., Laumann, E. O., Levinson, W., O'Muircheartaigh, C. A., & Waite, L. J. (2007). A study of sexuality and health among older adults in the United States. *New England Journal of Medicine, 357,* 762–774.

Lindberg, S. M., Hyde, S. S., Petersen, J. L., & Lin, M. C. (2010). New trends in gender and mathematics performance: A meta-analysis. *Psychological Bulletin, 136,* 1123–1135.

Lindblad, F., & Hjern, A. (2010). ADHD after fetal exposure to maternal smoking. *Nicotine and Tobacco Research, 12,* 408–415.

Linn, S. (2008). *The case for make believe: Saving play in a commercialized world.* New York: The New Press.

Lippa, R. A., (2005). *Gender, nature, and nurture* (2nd ed.). Mahwah, NJ: Erlbaum.

Lippman, L. A., & Keith, J. D. (2006). The demographics of spirituality among youth: International perspectives. In E. Roehlkepartain, P. E. King, L. Wagener, & P. L. Benson (Eds.), *The handbook of spirituality in childhood and adolescence.* Thousand Oaks, CA: Sage.

Littleton, H. L. (2010). The impact of social support and negative self-disclosure reactions on sexual assault victims: A cross-sectional and longitudinal investigation. *Journal of Trauma and Dissociation, 11,* 210–227.

Liu, C. H., Murakami, J., Iap, S., Nagayama Hall, G. C. (2009). Who are Asian Americans? An overview of history, immigration, and communities. In N. Tewari & A. Alvarez (Eds.), *Asian American psychology.* Clifton, NJ: Psychology Press.

Liu, D., Wellman, H. M., Tardif, T., & Sabbagh, M. A. (2008). Theory of mind development in Chinese children: A meta-analysis of false-belief understanding across cultures and languages. *Developmental Psychology, 44,* 523–531.

Liu, S., Quinn, P. C., Wheeler, A., Xiao, N., Ge, L., & Lee, K. (2011, in press). Similarity and difference in the processing of same- and other-race faces as revealed by eye-tracking in 4- to 9-month-old infants. *Journal of Experimental Child Psychology.*

Liu, T., Shi, J., Zhang, Q., Zhao, D., & Yang, J. (2007). Neural mechanisms of auditory sensory processing in children with high intelligence. *Neuroreport, 18*(15), 1571–1575.

Liu, X., & Liu, L. (2005). Sleep habits and insomnia in a sample of elderly persons in China. *Sleep, 28,* 1579–1587.

Liu-Ambrose, T., & others. (2010). Resistance training and executive functions: A 12-month randomized controlled trial. *Archives of Internal Medicine, 170,* 170–178.

Locher, J. L., Ritchie, C. S., Roth, D. L., Baker, P. S., Bodner, E. V., & Allman, R. M. (2005). Social isolation, support, and capital and nutritional risk in an older sample: Ethnic and gender differences. *Social Science Medicine, 60,* 747–761.

Lock, A., & Zukow-Goldring, P. (2010). Preverbal communication. In J. G. Bremner & T. D. Wachs (Eds.), *Wiley-Blackwell handbook of infant development* (2nd ed.). New York: Wiley.

Lock, M. (1998). Menopause: Lessons from anthropology. *Psychosomatic Medicine, 60,* 410–419.

Lockey, K., Jennings, M. B., & Shaw, L. (2010). Exploring hearing aid use in older women through narratives. *International Journal of Audiology, 49*(8), 542–549.

Lockl, K., & Schneider, W. (2007). Knowledge about the mind: Links between theory of mind and later metamemory. *Child Development, 78,* 147–167.

Loeber, R., Burke, J., & Pardini, D. (2009). The etiology and development of antisocial and delinquent behavior. *Annual Review of Psychology* (Vol. 60). Palo Alto, CA: Annual Reviews.

Loeber, R., & Farrington, D. P. (Eds.). (2001). *Child delinquents: Development, intervention and service needs.* Thousand Oaks, CA: Sage.

Loehlin, J. C. (2010). Is there an active gene-environment correlation in adolescent drinking behavior? *Behavior Genetics, 40*(4), 447–451.

Loehlin, J. C., Horn, J. M., & Ernst, J. L. (2007). Genetic and environmental influences on adult life outcomes: Evidence from the Texas adoption project. *Behavior Genetics, 37,* 463–476.

Lomas, J., Stough, C., Hansen, K., & Downey, L. A. (2011, in press). Brief report: Emotional intelligence, victimization, and bullying in adolescents. *Journal of Adolescence.*

Longhese, M. P., Bonetti, D., Manfrini, N., & Clerici, M. (2010). Mechanisms and regulation of DNA and resection. *EMBO Journal, 29,* 2864–2874.

Lonner, W. J. (1988). *The introductory psychology text and cross-cultural psychology: A survey of cross-cultural psychologists.* Bellingham: Western Washington University, Center for Cross-Cultural Research.

Loprinzi, P. D., & Trost, S. G. (2010). Parental influences on physical activity behavior in preschool children. *Preventive Medicine, 50,* 129–133.

Lorenz, K. Z. (1965). *Evolution and the modification of behavior.* Chicago: University of Chicago Press.

Loukas, A., Suizzo, M.-A., & Prelow, H. M. (2007). Examining resource and protective factors in the adjustment of Latino youth in low-income families: What role does maternal acculturation play? *Journal of Youth and Adolescence, 36,* 489–501.

Lovden, M., Backman, L., Lindenberger,, U., Schaefer, S., & Schmiedek, F. (2010). A theoretical framework for the study of adult cognitive plasticity. *Psychological Bulletin, 136,* 659–676.

Lovden, M., & Lindenberger, U. (2007). Intelligence. In J. E. Birren (Ed.), *Encyclopedia of gerontology* (2nd ed.). San Diego: Academic Press.

Lovelady, C. (2011, in press). Balancing exercise and food intake with lactation to promote post-partum weight loss. *Proceedings of the Nutrition Society.*

Lowdermilk, D. L., Perry, S. E., & Cashion, M. C. (2011). *Maternity nursing* (8th ed.). New York: Elsevier.

Lu, M. C., & Lu, J. S. (2008). Prenatal care. In M. M. Haith & J. B. Benson (Eds.), *Encyclopedia of infant and early childhood development.* Oxford, UK: Elsevier.

Lu, T., Litovsky, R., & Zeng, F. G. (2010). Binaural masking level differences in actual and simulated bilateral cochlear implant listeners. *Journal of the Acoustical Society of America, 127,* 1479–1490.

Lubart, T. I. (2003). In search of creative intelligence. In R. J. Sternberg, J. Lautrey, & T. I. Lubart (Eds.), *Models of intelligence: International perspectives.* Washington, DC: American Psychological Association.

Lubinski, D. (2000). Measures of intelligence: Intelligence tests. In A. Kazdin (Ed.), *Encyclopedia of psychology.* New York: Oxford University Press.

Lucas, R. E., Clark, A. E., Yannis, G., & Diener, E. (2004). Unemployment alters the setpoint for life satisfaction. *Psychological Science, 15,* 8–13.

Luciana, M. (2010). Adolescent brain development: Current themes and future directions. *Brain and Cognition, 72,* 1–17.

Lucifero, D. (2010). Stem cells—Smi's second annual conference: Achieving success in science and commercialization. *IDrugs, 13,* 232–234.

Luders, E., & others. (2004). Gender difference in cortical complexity. *Nature Neuroscience, 7,* 799–800.

Luders, E., Narr, K. L., Thompson, P. M., & Toga, A. W. (2009). Neuroanatomical correlates of intelligence. *Intelligence, 37,* 156–163.

Lugert, S., & others. (2010). Quiescent and active hippocampal neural stem cells with distinct morphologies respond selectively to physiological and pathological stimuli and aging. *Cell Stem Cell, 6*(5), 445–456.

Lumpkin, A. (2011). *Introduction to physical education, exercise science, and sport studies.* New York: McGraw-Hill.

Luna, B., Padmanabhan, A., & O'Hearn, K. (2010). What has fMRI told us about the development of cognitive control in adolescence? *Brain and Cognition, 72,* 101–113.

Lund, D. A., Utz, R., Caserta, M. S., & De Vries, B. (2009). Humor, laughter, and happiness in the lives of recently bereaved spouses. *Omega, 58,* 87–105.

Lund, H. G., Reider, B. D., Whiting, A. B., & Prichard, J. R. (2010). Sleep patterns and predictors of disturbed sleep in a large population of college students. *Journal of Adolescent Health, 46,* 124–136.

Lunkenheimer, E. S., Shields, A. M., & Cortina, K. S. (2007). Parental emotion coaching and dismissing in family interaction. *Social Development, 16,* 232–248.

Luria, A., & Herzog, E. (1985, April). *Gender segregation across and within settings.* Paper presented at the biennial meeting of the Society for Research in Child Development, Toronto.

Luszcz, M. A. (2010). Editorial: 100 not out: Lifestyle and psychosocial factors associated with living a century or more. *Gerontology, 56,* 80–82.

Luthar, S. S. (2006). Resilience in development: A synthesis of research across five decades. In D. Cicchetti & D. J. Cohen (Eds.), *Developmental psychopathology: Vol. 3. Risk, disorder, and adaptation* (2nd ed.). Hoboken, NJ: Wiley.

Luthar, S. S., & Goldstein, A. S. (2008). Substance use and related behaviors among suburban late adolescents: The importance of perceived parent containment. *Development and Psychopathology, 20,* 591–614.

Lynch, S. M., & Brown, J. S. (2011). Stratification and inequality over the life course. In R. H. Binstock & L. K. George (Eds.), *Handbook of aging and the social sciences* (7th ed.). New York: Elsevier.

Lyndaker, C., & Hulton, L. (2004). The influence of age on symptoms of perimenopause. *Journal of Obstetric, Gynecological, and Neonatal Nursing, 33,* 340–347.

Lynn, R. (1996). Racial and ethnic differences in intelligence in the U.S. on the Differential Ability Scale. *Personality and Individual Differences, 26,* 271–273.

Lynn, R. (2009). What caused the Flynn effect? Secular increases in the development quotients of infants. *Intelligence, 37,* 16–24.

Lyon, T. D., & Flavell, J. H. (1993). Young children's understanding of forgetting over time. *Child Development, 64,* 789–800.

Lyons, D. M., & others. (2010). Stress coping stimulates hippocampal neurogenesis in adult monkeys. *Proceedings of the National Academy of Sciences U.S.A.*

M

Maccoby, E. E. (1998). *The two sexes: Growing up apart, coming together.* Cambridge, MA: Harvard University Press.

Maccoby, E. E. (2002). Gender and group process: A developmental perspective. *Current Directions in Psychological Science, 11,* 54–57.

Maccoby, E. E. (2007). Historical overview of socialization theory and research. In J. E. Grusec

& P. D. Hastings (Eds.), *Handbook of socialization.* New York: Guilford.

Maccoby, E. E., & Martin, J. A. (1983). Socialization in the context of the family: Parent-child interaction. In P. H. Mussen (Ed.), *Handbook of child psychology* (4th ed., Vol. 4). New York: Wiley.

MacFarlane, J. A. (1975). Olfaction in the development of social preferences in the human neonate. In *Parent–infant interaction.* Ciba Foundation Symposium No. 33. Amsterdam: Elsevier.

Maciejewski, P. K., Zhang, B., Block, S. D., & Prigerson, H. G. (2007). An empirical examination of the stage theory of grief. *Journal of the American Medical Association, 297,* 716–723.

Maciejewski, P. K., & others (2011, in press). Religious coping and behavioral disengagement: Opposing influences on advance care planning and receive of intensive care near death. *Psychooncology.*

Maciokas, J. B., & Crognale, M. A. (2003). Cognitive and attentional changes with age: Evidence from attentional blink deficits. *Experimental/Aging Research, 29,* 137–153.

MacWhinney, B. (2010). Language development. In W. F. Overton & R. M. Lerner (Eds.), *Handbook of life-span development.* New York: Wiley.

Madden, D. J. (2007). Aging and visual attention. *Current Directions in Psychological Science, 16,* 70–74.

Madden, D. J., & others. (1999). Aging and recognition memory: Changes in regional cerebral blood flow associated with components of reaction time distributions. *Journal of Cognitive Neuroscience, 11,* 511–520.

Mader, S. S. (2011). *Biology* (13th ed.). New York: McGraw-Hill.

Madkour, A. S., Farhat, T., Halpern, C. T., Godeu, E., & Gabhainn, S. N. (2010). Early adolescent sexual initiation as a problem behavior: A comparative study of five nations. *Journal of Adolescent Health, 47*(4), 389–398.

Madole, K. L., Oakes, L. M., & Rakison, D. H. (2011). Information processing approaches to infants' developing representation of dynamic features. In L. Oakes & others (Eds.), *Infant perception and cognition.* New York: Oxford University Press.

Madronal, N., & others. (2010). Effects of enriched physical and social environments on motor performance, associative learning, and hippocampal neurogenesis in mice. *PLoS One, 5,* e11130.

Maehr, M. L., & Zusho, A. (2009). Achievement goal theory: The past, present, and future. In K. R. Wentzel & A. Wigfield (Eds.), *Handbook of motivation in school.* New York: Taylor Francis.

Magno, C. (2010). The role of metacognitive skills in developing critical thinking. *Metacognition and Learning, 5,* 137–156.

Mahbub, S., Brubaker, A. L., & Kovacs, E. J. (2011). Aging of the innate immune system: An update. *Current Immunology Reviews, 7,* 104–115.

Mahoney, J. L., Larson, R. W., & Eccles, J. S. (Eds.). (2004). *Organized activities as contexts of development.* Mahwah, NJ: Erlbaum.

Mahoney, J., Parente, M. E., & Zigler, E. (2010). After-school program engagement and in-school competence: Program quality, content, and staffing. In J. Meece & J. Eccles (Eds.), *Handbook of research on schools, schooling, and human development.* Clifton, NJ: Psychology Press.

Mahoney, J. R., Verghese, J., Goldin, Y., Lipton, R., & Holtzer, R. (2010). Altering orienting, and executive attention in older adults. *Journal of the International Neuropsychological Society, 16*(5), 877–889.

Maimoun, L., & Sultan, C. (2010). Effects of physical activity on bone remodeling. *Metabolism, 60*(3), 373–388.

Malamitsi-Puchner, A., & Boutsikou, T. (2006). Adolescent pregnancy and perinatal outcome. *Pediatric Endocrinology Review, 3*(Suppl. 1), 170–171.

Malizia, B. A., Hacker, M. R., & Penzias, A. S. (2009). Cumulative live-birth rates after in vitro fertilization. *New England Journal of Medicine, 360,* 236–243.

Maloy, R. W., Verock-O'Loughlin, R-E., Edwards, S. A., & Woolf, B. P. (2011). *Transforming learning with new technologies.* Boston: Allyn & Bacon.

Malti, T., & Buchmann, M. (2010). Socialization and individual antecedents of adolescents' and young adults' moral motivation. *Journal of Youth and Adolescence, 39,* 138–149.

Malti, T., & Latzko, B. (2010). Children's moral emotions and moral cognition: Towards an integrative perspective. *New Directions for Child and Adolescent Development, 129,* 1–10.

Maltseva, D. V., & others. (2011). Killer cell immunoglobulin-like receptors and exercise. *Exercise Immunology Review, 17,* 150–163.

Mandal, B., Ayyagari, P., & Gallo, W. T. (2011). Job loss and depression: The role of subjective expectations. *Social Science & Medicine, 72,* 576–583.

Mandelman, S. D., & Grigorenko, E. L. (2011). Intelligence, genes, and their interactions. In R. J. Sternberg & S. B. Kaufman (Eds.), *Cambridge handbook of intelligence.* New York: Cambridge University Press.

Mandler, J. M. (2000). Unpublished review of J. W. Santrock's *Life-span development,* 8th ed. (New York: McGraw-Hill).

Mandler, J. M. (2004). *The functions of mind.* New York: Oxford University Press.

Mandler, J. M. (2006). Jean Mandler. Retrieved January 15, 2006, from http://cogsci.ucsd.edu/~jean/

Mandler, J. M., & McDonough, L. (1993). Concept formation in infancy. *Cognitive Development, 8,* 291–318.

Manenti, R., Cotelli, M., & Miniussi, C. (2010). Successful physiological aging and episodic memory: A brain stimulation study. *Behavioral Brain Research, 216*(1), 153–158.

Mangione, R., & others. (2011). Neurodevelopmental outcome following prenatal diagnosis of an isolated anomaly of the corpus callosum. *Ultrasound in Obstetrics and Gynecology, 37,* 290–295.

Mannell, R. C. (2000). Older adults, leisure, and wellness. *Journal of Leisurability, 26,* 3–10.

Manongdo, J. A., & Garcia, J. I. (2011). Maternal parenting and mental health of Mexican American youth: A bidirectional and prospective approach. *Developmental Psychology, 25,* 261–270.

Maraldi, C., & others. (2009). Moderate alcohol intake and risk of functional decline: The Health, Aging, and Body Composition study. *Journal of the American Geriatrics Society, 57,* 1767–1175.

Marcdante, K., Kliegman, R. M., & Behrman, R. E. (2011). *Nelson's essentials of pediatrics* (6th ed.). New York: Elsevier.

Marcia, J. E. (1980). Ego identity development. In J. Adelson (Ed.), *Handbook of adolescent psychology.* New York: Wiley.

Marcia, J. E. (1987). The identity status approach to the study of ego identity development. In T. Honess & K. Yardley (Eds.), *Self and identity: Perspectives across the lifespan.* London: Routledge & Kegan Paul.

Marcia, J. E. (1994). The empirical study of ego identity. In H. A. Bosma, T. L. G. Graafsma, H. D. Grotevant, & D. J. De Levita (Eds.), *Identity and development.* Newbury Park, CA: Sage.

Marcia, J. E. (1996). Unpublished review of J. W. Santrock's *Adolescence,* 7th ed. (Dubuque, IA: Brown & Benchmark).

Marcia, J. E. (2002). Identity and psychosocial development in adulthood. *Identity, 2,* 7–28.

Marcia, J. E., & Carpendale, J. (2004). Identity: Does thinking make it so? In C. Lightfoot, C. Lalonde, & M. Chandler (Eds.), *Changing conceptions of psychological life.* Mahwah, NJ: Erlbaum.

Marecek, J., Finn, S. E., & Cardell, M. (1988). Gender roles in the relationships of lesbians and gay men. In J. P. De Cecco (Ed.), *Gay relationships.* New York: Harrington Park Press.

Margran, T. H., & Boulton, M. (2005). Sensory impairment. In M. L. Johnson (Ed.), *The Cambridge handbook of age and aging.* New York: Cambridge University Press.

Margrett, J. A., & Deshpande-Kamat, N. (2009). Cognitive functioning and decline. In D. Carr (Ed.), *Encyclopedia of the life course and human development.* Boston: Gale Cengage.

Marion, M. C. (2010). *Introduction to early childhood education.* Upper Saddle River, NJ: Pearson.

Markey, C. N. (2010). Invited commentary: Why body image is important to adolescent development. *Journal of Youth and Adolescence, 39,* 1387–1391.

Markham, C. M., & others. (2010). Neighborhood poverty, aspirations and expectations, and initiation of sex. *Journal of Adolescent Health, 47,* 399–406.

Marko, M. G., Ahmed, T., Bunnell, S. C., Wu, D., Chung, H., Huber, B. T., & Meydani, S. N. (2007). Age-associated decline in effective immune synapse formation of CD4(+) T cells is reversed by vitamin E supplementation. *Journal of Immunology, 178,* 1443–1449.

Marks, B. L., Katz, L. M., & Smith, J. K. (2009). Exercise and the aging mind: Buffing the baby boomer's body and brain. *The Physician and Sports Medicine, 37,* 119–125.

Markus, H. R., & Kitayama, S. (2010). Cultures and selves: A cycle of multiple constitution. *Perspectives on Psychological Science, 5,* 420–430.

Markus, H. R., & Nurius, P. (1986). Possible selves. *American Psychologist, 41,* 954–969.

Marquez, F. Z., Markus, M. A., & Morris, B. J. (2010). The molecular basis of longevity, and clinical implications. *Maturitas, 65,* 87–91.

Marret, S., & others. (2010). Prenatal low-dose aspirin and neurobehavioral outcomes of children born very preterm. *Pediatrics, 125,* e29–e34.

Martin, C. L. (1990). Attitudes and expectations about children with nontraditional gender roles. *Sex Roles, 22,* 151–165.

Martin, C. L., & Fabes, R. A. (2001). The stability and consequences of young children's same-sex peer interactions. *Developmental Psychology, 37,* 431–446.

Martin, C. L., & Ruble, D. N. (2010). Patterns of gender development. *Annual Review of Psychology* (Vol. 61). Palo Alto, CA: Annual Reviews.

Martin, C. L., Ruble, D. N., & Szkrybalo, J. (2002). Cognitive theories of early gender development. *Psychological Bulletin, 128,* 903–933.

Martin, J. A., Hamilton, B. E., Sutton, P. D., Ventura, S. J., Menacker, F., & Munson, M. L. (2005, September). Births: Final data for 2003. *National Vital Statistics Reports, 54*(2), 1–116.

Martin, L. G. (2011). Demography and aging. In R. H. Binstock & L. K. George (Eds.), *Handbook of aging and the social sciences* (7th ed.). New York: Elsevier.

Martin, L. R., Friedman, H. S., & Schwartz, J. E. (2007). Personality and mortality risk across the lifespan: The importance of conscientiousness as a biopsychosocial attribute. *Health Psychology, 26,* 428–436.

Martinez, M. E. (2010). *Learning and cognition.* Upper Saddle River, NJ: Merrill.

Martini, T. S., & Busseri, M. A. (2010). Emotion regulation strategies and goals as predictors of older mothers' and daughters' helping-related subjective well-being. *Psychology and Aging, 25*(1), 48–59.

Mascolo, M. F., & Fischer, K. (2007). The co-development of self and socio-moral emotions during the toddler years. In C. A. Brownell & C. B. Kopp (Eds.), *Transitions in early development.* New York: Guilford.

Mascolo, M. F., & Fischer, K. W. (2010). The dynamic development of thinking, feeling, and acting over the life span. In W. F. Overton & R. M. Lerner (Eds.), *Handbook of life-span development* (Vol.1). New York: Wiley.

Mashburn, A. J., Justice, L. M., Downer, J. T., & Pianta, R. C. (2009). Peer effects on children's language achievement during pre-kindergarten. *Child Development, 80,* 686–702.

Masselli, G., & others. (2011, in press). MR imaging in the evaluation of placental abruption: Correlation with sonographic findings. *Radiology.*

Masten, A. S. (2005). Peer relationships and psychopathology in developmental perspective: Reflections on progress and promise. *Journal of Clinical Child and Adolescent Psychology, 34,* 87–92.

Masten, A. S. (2011). Risk and resilience in development. In P. D. Zelazo (Ed.), *Oxford handbook of developmental psychology.* New York: Oxford University Press.

Masten, A. S., & Osofsky, J. D. (2010). Disasters and their impact on child development: Introduction to the special section. *Child Development, 81,* 1029–1039.

Masters, C. (2008, January 17). We just clicked. *Time,* 84–89.

Mata, R., von Helversen, B., & Rieskamp, J. (2010). Learning to choose: Cognitive aging and strategy selection learning in decision making. *Psychology and Aging, 25,* 299–309.

Match.com. (2011). The Match.com Single in America Study. Retrieved February 7 from http://blog.match.com/singles-study

Mather, K. A., Jorm, A. F., Parslow, R. A., & Christensen, H. (2011). Is telomere length a biomarker of aging? A review. *Journals of Gerontology A: Biological Sciences and Medical Sciences, 66A,* 202–213.

Mathes, W. F., & others. (2010). Dopaminergic dysregulation in mice selectively bred for excessive exercise or obesity. *Behavioral Brain Research, 210,* 155–163.

Matlin, M. W. (2012). The *psychology of women* (7th ed.). Belmont, CA: Wadsworth.

Matsuba, M. K., & Walker, L. J. (2004). Extraordinary moral commitment: Young adults involved in social organizations. *Journal of Personality, 72,* 413–436.

Matthews, C. E., & others. (2007). Influence of exercise, walking, cycling, and overall nonexercise physical activity on mortality in Chinese women. *American Journal of Epidemiology, 165,* 1343–1350.

Matthews, G., Zeidner, M., & Roberts, R. D. (2006). Models of personality and affect for education: A review and synthesis. In P. A. Alexander & P. H. Wynne (Eds.), *Handbook of educational psychology* (2nd ed.). Mahwah, NJ: Erlbaum.

Mattson, S., & Smith, J. E. (2011). *Core curriculum for maternal-newborn nursing* (4th ed.). New York: Elsevier.

Mausbach, B. T., & others. (2007). Stress-related reduction in personal mastery is associated with reduced immune cell beta2-adrenergic receptor sensitivity. *International Psychogeriatrics, 4,* 1–13.

Maxwell, B., & DesRoches, S. (2010). Empathy and social-emotional learning: Pitfalls and touchstones for school-based programs. *New Directions for Child and Adolescent Development, 129,* 33–53.

Mayer, J. D., Salovey, P., Caruso, D., & Cherkasskly, L. (2011). Emotional intelligence. In R. J. Sternberg & S. B. Kaufman (Eds.), *Cambridge handbook of intelligence.* New York: Cambridge University Press.

Mayer, K. D., & Zhang, L. (2009). Short- and long-term effects of cocaine abuse during pregnancy on heart development. *Therapeutic Advances in Cardiovascular Disease, 3,* 7–16.

Mayer, R. E. (2008). *Curriculum and instruction* (2nd ed.). Upper Saddle River, NJ: Prentice Hall.

Mbugua Gitau, G., Liversedge, H., Goffey, D., Hawton, A., Liversedge, N., & Taylor, M. (2009). The influence of maternal age on the outcomes of pregnancy complicated by bleeding at less than 12 weeks. *Acta Obstetricia et Gynecologica Scandinavica, 88,* 116–118.

McAdams, D. P., & Cox, K. S. (2011). Self and identity across the life span. In A. Freund, M. Lamb, & R. Lerner (Eds.), *Handbook of life-span development* (Vol. 2). New York: Wiley.

McAdams, D. P., Josselson, R., & Lieblich, A. (Eds.). (2006). *Identity and story: Creating self in narrative.* Washington, DC: American Psychological Association Press.

McAdams, D. P., & Olson, B. D. (2010). Personality development: Continuity and change over the life course. *Annual Review of Psychology* (Vol. 61). Palo Alto, CA: Annual Reviews.

McAlister, A., & Peterson, C. (2007). A longitudinal study of child siblings and theory of mind development. *Cognitive Development, 22,* 258–270.

McBride-Chang, C. (2004). *Children's literacy development* (Texts in Developmental Psychology Series). London: Edward Arnold/Oxford Press.

McBride-Chang, C., & others. (2005). Changing models across cultures: Associations of phonological and morphological awareness to reading in Beijing, Hong Kong, Korea, and America. *Journal of Experimental Child Psychology, 92,* 140–160.

McBride-Chang, C., & others. (2008). Word recognition and cognitive profiles of Chinese preschool children at-risk for dyslexia through language delay or familial history of dyslexia. *Journal of Child Psychology and Psychiatry, 49,* 211–218.

McCall, R. B., Applebaum, M. I., & Hogarty, P. S. (1973). Developmental changes in mental performance. *Monographs of the Society for Research in Child Development, 38* (Serial No. 150).

McCartney, K. (2003, July 16). Interview with Kathleen McCartney in A. Bucuvalas, "Child care and behavior," *HGSE News,* 1–4. Cambridge, MA: Harvard Graduate School of Education.

McClain, C. S., Rosenfeld, B., & Breitbart, W. S. (2003). *The influence of spirituality on end-of-life despair in cancer patients close to death.* Paper presented at the meeting of the American Psychosomatic Society, Phoenix.

McCloskey, E. (2011). Preventing osteoporotic fractures in older people. *Practitioner, 255,* 19–22.

McClure, A. C., Tanski, S. E., Kingsbury, J., Gerrard, M., & Sargent, J. D. (2010).

Characteristics associated with low self-esteem among U.S. adolescents. *Academic Pediatrics, 10,* 238–244.

McCoy, M. K., & Cookson, M. R. (2011, in press). Dj-1 regulation of mitochondrial function and autophagy through oxidative press. *Autophagy.*

McCrae, R. R., & Costa, P. T. (1990). *Personality in adulthood.* New York: Guilford.

McCrae, R. R., & Costa, P. T. (2006). Cross-cultural perspectives on adult personality trait development. In D. K. Mroczek & T. D. Little (Eds.), *Handbook of personality development.* Mahwah, NJ: Erlbaum.

McCullough, M. E., & Willoughby, B. L. (2009). Religion, self-regulation, and self-control: Associations, explanations, and implications. *Psychological Bulletin, 135,* 69–93.

McDonald, J. A., Manlove, J., & Ikramullah, E. N. (2009). Immigration measures and reproductive health among Hispanic youth: Findings from the National Longitudinal Survey of Youth, 1997–2003. *Journal of Adolescent Health, 44,* 14–24.

McDowell, D. J., & Parke, R. D. (2009). Parental correlates of children's peer relations: An empirical test of a tripartite model. *Developmental Psychology, 45,* 224–235.

McElhaney, K. B., Allen, J. P., Stephenson, J. C., & Hare, A. L. (2009). Attachment and autonomy during adolescence. In R. M. Lerner & L. Steinberg (Eds.), *Handbook of adolescent psychology* (3rd ed.). New York: Wiley.

McEvoy, L. K., & others. (2011, in press). Mild cognitive impairment: Baseline and longitudinal structural MR imaging measures improve predictive diagnosis. *Radiology.*

McEwen, B. S. (1998). Protective and damaging effects of stress mediators. *New England Journal of Medicine, 338,* 171–180.

McGarry, J., Kim, H., Sheng, X., Egger, M., & Baksh, L. (2009). Postpartum depression and help-seeking behavior. *Journal of Midwifery and Women's Health, 54,* 50–56.

McGarvey, C., McDonnell, M., Hamilton, K., O'Regan, M., & Matthews, T. (2006). An eight-year study of risk factors for SIDS: Bed-sharing versus non-sharing. *Archives of Disease in Childhood, 91,* 318–323.

McGee, C. A., Caputi, P., & Iverson, D. C. (2010). Is sleep duration associated with obesity in older Australian adults? *Journal of Aging and Health, 22*(8), 1235–1255.

McGrath, A. P., Vohr, B., & O'Neil, C. A. (2010). Newborn hearing assessment in 2010. *Medical Health Rhode Island, 93,* 142–144.

McGregor, K. M., & others. (2011, in press). Physical activity and neural correlates of aging: A combined TMS/fMRI study. *Behavioral Brain Research.*

McGue, M., Hirsch, B., & Lykken, D. T. (1993). Age and the self-perception of ability: A twin analysis. *Psychology and Aging, 8,* 72–80.

McHale, S. M., Kim, J.-Y., Dotterer, A. M., Crouter, A. C., & Booth, A. (2009). The development of gendered interests and personality qualities from middle childhood through adolescence: A biosocial analysis. *Child Development, 80,* 482–495.

McHale, S. M., Kim, J. Y., Kan, M., & Updegraff, K. A. (2010, in press). Sleep in Mexican-American adolescents: Social ecological and well-being correlates. *Journal of Youth and Adolescence.*

McIntosh, C. G., Tonkin, S. L., & Gunn, A. J. (2010). What is the mechanism of sudden infant deaths associated with co-sleeping? *New Zealand Medical Journal, 122,* 69–75.

McIntosh, E., Gillanders, D., & Rodgers, S. (2010). Rumination, goal linking, daily hassles, and life events in major depression. *Clinical Psychology and Psychotherapy, 17,* 33–43.

McKain, W. C. (1972). A new look at older marriages. *The Family Coordinator, 21,* 61–69.

McLaughlin, K. (2003, December 30). Commentary in K. Painter, "Nurse dispenses dignity for dying." *USA Today,* pp. D1–D2.

McLean, I. A., Balding, V., & White, C. (2005). Further aspects of male-on-male rape and sexual assault in greater Manchester. *Medical Science and Law, 45,* 225–232.

McLean, K. C., & Breen, A. V. (2009). Processes and content of narrative identity development in adolescence: Gender and well-being. *Developmental Psychology, 45,* 702–710.

McLean, K. C., Breen, A. V., & Fournier, M. A. (2010). Constructing the self in early, middle, and late adolescent boys: Narrative identity, individuation, and well-being. *Journal of Research on Adolescence, 20,* 166–187.

McLean, K. C., & Pasupathi, M. (Eds.). (2010). *Narrative development in adolescence: Creating the storied self.* New York: Springer.

McLoyd, V. C. (1990). The impact of economic hardship on Black families and children: Psychological distress, parenting, and socio-emotional development. *Child Development, 61,* 311–346.

McLoyd, V. C. (1998). Children in poverty: Development, public policy, and practice. In W. Damon (Ed.), *Handbook of child psychology* (5th ed., Vol. 4). New York: Wiley.

McLoyd, V. C., Kaplan, R., Purtell, K. M., Bagley, E., Hardaway, C. R., & Smalls, C. (2009). Poverty and social disadvantage in adolescence. In R. M. Lerner & L. Steinberg (Eds.), *Handbook of adolescent psychology* (3rd ed.). New York: Wiley.

McLoyd, V. C., Kaplan, R., Purtell, K. M., & Huston, A. C. (2011). Assessing the effects of a work-based antipoverty program for parents on youth's future orientation and employment experiences. *Child Development, 82,* 113–132.

McMahon, M., & Stryjewski, G. (2011). *Pediatrics.* New York: Elsevier.

McMillan, J. H., & Schumacher, S. (2010). *Research in education: Evidence-based inquiry.* (7th ed.). Upper Saddle River, NJ: Merrill.

McNamara, F., & Sullivan, C. E. (2000). Obstructive sleep apnea in infants. *Journal of Pediatrics, 136,* 318–323.

McWilliams, L. A., & Bailey, S. J. (2010). Association between adult attachment rating and health conditions: Evidence from the National Comorbidity Survey replication. *Health Psychology, 29,* 446–453.

Mead, M. (1978, Dec. 30–Jan. 5). The American family: An endangered species. *TV Guide,* 21–24.

Meade, C. S., Kershaw, T. S., & Ickovics, J. R. (2008). The intergenerational cycle of teenage motherhood: An ecological approach. *Health Psychology, 27,* 419–429.

Mechakra-Tahiri, S. D., Zunzunegui, M. V., Preville, M., & Dube, M. (2010). Gender, social relationships and depressive disorders in adults aged 65 and over in Quebec. *Chronic Diseases in Canada, 30,* 56–65.

Meece, J., & Eccles, J. (Eds.). (2009). *Handbook of research on schools, schooling, and human development.* Clifton, NJ: Psychology Press.

Meerlo, P., Sgoifo, A., & Suchecki, D. (2008). Restricted and disrupted sleep: Effects on autonomic function, neuroendocrine stress systems, and stress responsivity. *Sleep Medicine Review, 12,* 197–210.

Meert, K. L., & others. (2011). Follow-up study of complicated grief among parents eighteen months after a child's death in the pediatric intensive care unit. *Journal of Palliative Medicine, 14,* 207–214.

Meeus, W., van de Schoot, R., Keijser, L., Branje, S., & Schwartz, S. J. (2010). On the progression and stability of adolescent identity formation: A five-wave longitudinal study in early-to-middle and middle-to-late adolescence. *Child Development, 81,* 1565–1581.

Mehta, C. M., & Strough, J. (2009) Sex segregation in friendships and normative contexts across the life span. *Development Review, 29,* 201–220.

Mehta, C. M., & Strough, J. (2010). Gender segregation and gender-typing in adolescence. *Sex Roles, 63,* 251–263.

Mellor, J. M., & Freeborn, B. A. (2010). Religious participation and risky health behaviors among adolescents. *Health Economics* (Wiley Online Library), DOI: 10. 1002/hec. 1666.

Meltzoff, A. N. (2011). Social cognition and the origins of imitation, empathy, and theory of mind. In U. Goswami (Ed.), *Wiley-Blackwell handbook of childhood cognitive development* (2nd ed.). New York: Wiley.

Meltzoff, A. N., & Brooks, R. (2009). Social cognition: The role of gaze following in early word learning In J. Colombo, P. McCardle, & L. Freund (Eds.), *Infant pathways in language.* Clifton, NJ: Psychology Press.

Melzi, G., & Ely, R. (2009). Language development in the school years. In J. B. Gleason & N. Ratner (Eds.), *The development of language* (7th ed.). Boston: Allyn & Bacon.

Melzi, G., Schick, A. R., & Kennedy, J. L. (2011, in press). Narrative elaboration and participation: Two dimensions of maternal elicitation style. *Child Development.*

Menec, V. H. (2003). The relation between everyday activities and successful aging: A 6-year longitudinal study. *Journal of Gerontology B: Psychological Sciences and Social Sciences, 58,* 574–582.

Menn, L., & Stoel-Gammon, C. (2009). Phonological development: Learning sounds and sound patterns. In J. Berko Gleason (Ed.), *The development of language* (7th ed.). Boston: Allyn & Bacon.

Mennella, J. A. (2009). Taste and smell. In R. A. Shweder & others (Eds.), *The child: An encyclopedic companion.* Chicago: University of Chicago Press.

Menon, R., & others. (2011, in press). Cigarette smoking induces oxidative stress and atopsis in normal fetal membranes. *Placenta.*

Mensah, G. A., & Brown, D. W. (2007). An overview of cardiovascular disease burden in the United States. *Health Affairs, 26,* 38–48.

Menshikova, E. V., Ritov, B. V., Fairfull, L., Ferrell, R. E., Kelley, D. E., & Goodpaster, B. H. (2006). Effects of exercise on mitochondrial content and function in aging human skeletal muscle. *Journals of Gerontology A: Biological Sciences and Medical Sciences, 61,* 534–540.

Menyuk, P., Liebergott, J., & Schultz, M. (1995). *Early language development in full-term and premature infants.* Hillsdale, NJ: Erlbaum.

Mercer, N. (2008). Talk and the development of reasoning and understanding. *Human Development, 51,* 90–100.

Meredith, N. V. (1978). Research between 1960 and 1970 on the standing height of young children in different parts of the world. In H. W. Reece & L. P. Lipsitt (Eds.), *Advances in child development and behavior* (Vol. 12). New York Academic Press.

Merrill, D. M. (2009). Parent-child relationships: Later-life. In D. Carr (Ed.), *Encyclopedia of the life course and human development.* Boston: Gale Cengage.

Meschia, G. (2011). Fetal oxygenation and maternal ventilation. *Clinics in Chest Medicine, 32,* 15–19.

Messiah, S. E., Miller, T. L., Lipshultz, S. E., & Bandstra, E. S. (2011). Potential latent effects of prenatal cocaine exposure on growth and the risk of cardiovascular and metabolic disease in childhood. *Progress in Pediatric Cardiology, 31,* 59–65.

Messinger, D. (2008). Smiling. In M. M. Haith & J. B. Benson (Eds.), *Encyclopedia of infant and early childhood development.* Oxford, UK: Elsevier.

Messinger, J. C. (1971). Sex and repression in an Irish folk community. In D. S. Marshall & R. C. Suggs (Eds.), *Human sexual behavior: Variations in the ethnic spectrum.* New York: Basic Books.

Metts, S., & Cupach, W. R. (2007). Responses to relational transgressions. In M. Tafoya & B. H. Spitzberg (Eds.), *The dark side of interpersonal communication.* Mahwah, NJ: Erlbaum.

Metz, E. C., & Youniss, J. (2005). Longitudinal gains in civic development through school-based required service. *Political Psychology, 26,* 413–437.

Meyer, M. D., & Parker, W. M. (2011). Gender, aging, and social policy. In R. H. Binstock & L. K. George (Eds.), *Handbook of aging and the social sciences* (7th ed.). New York: Elsevier.

Meyer, M. H. (2011). Gender, aging, and social policy. In R. H. Binstock & L. K. George (Eds.), *Handbook of aging and the social sciences* (7th ed.). New York: Elsevier.

Meyer, M. H., & Parker, W. M. (2011). Gender, aging, and social policy. In R. H. Binstock & L. K. George (Eds.), *Handbook of aging and the social sciences* (7th ed.). New York: Elsevier.

Meyer, S. L., Weible, C. M., & Woeber, K. (2010). Perceptions and practice of waterbirth: A survey of Georgia midwives. *Journal of Midwifery and Women's Health, 55,* 55–59.

Michael, R. T., Gagnon, J. H., Laumann, E. O., & Kolate, G. (1994). *Sex in America.* Boston: Little Brown.

Mikels, J. A., & others. (2010). Following your heart or your head: Focusing on emotions versus information differentially influences the decisions of younger and older adults. *Journal of Experimental Psychology: Applied, 17,* 87–95.

Mikulincer, M., & Shaver, P. R. (2008). Adult attachment and affect regulation. In J. Cassidy & P. R. Shaver (Eds.), *Handbook of attachment* (2nd ed.). New York: Guilford.

Mikulincer, M., Shaver, P. R., Bar-on, N., & ein-Dor, T. (2010). The pushes and pulls of close relationships: Attachment insecurities and relational ambivalence. *Journal of Personality and Social Psychology, 98,* 450–468.

Miller, B. C., Benson, B., & Galbraith, K. A. (2001). Family relationships and adolescent pregnancy risk: A research synthesis. *Developmental Review, 21,* 1–38.

Miller, B. C., Fan, X., Christensen, M., Grotevant, H. D., & von Dulmen, M. (2000). Comparisons of adopted and nonadopted adolescents in a large, nationally representative sample. *Child Development, 71,* 1458–1473.

Miller, C. F., Lurye, L. E., Zosuls, K. M., & Ruble, D. N. (2009). Accessibility of gender stereotype domains: Developmental and gender differences in children. *Sex Roles, 60,* 870–881.

Miller, D. I., Taler, V., Davidson, P. S., & Messier, C. (2011, in press). Measuring the impact of exercise on cognitive aging: Methodological issues. *Neurobiology of Aging.*

Miller, J. B. (1986). *Toward a new psychology of women* (2nd ed.). Boston: Beacon Press.

Miller, J. G. (2007). Insights into moral development from cultural psychology. In M. Killen & J. G. Smetana (Eds.), *Handbook of moral development.* Mahwah, NJ: Erlbaum.

Miller, L. J., & Larusso, E. M. (2011). Preventing postpartum depression. *Psychiatric Clinics of North America, 34,* 53–65.

Miller, M. A., & Cappuccio, F. P. (2007). Inflammation, sleep, obesity, and cardiovascular disease. *Current Vascular Pharmacology, 5,* 92–102.

Miller, P., & Plant, M. (2010). Parental guidance about drinking: Relationship with teenage psychoactive substance use. *Journal of Adolescence 33,* 55–68.

Miller, P. H. (2011). Piaget's theory: Past, present, and future. In U. Goswami (Ed.), *Wiley-Blackwell handbook of childhood cognitive development* (2nd ed.). New York: Wiley-Blackwell.

Miller, R. A. (2009). Cell stress and aging: New emphasis on multiplex resistance mechanisms. *Journals of Gerontology A: Biological Sciences and Medical Sciences, 64,* 179–182.

Miller, S., Malone, P., Dodge, K. A., & Conduct Problems Prevention Research Group. (2011, in press). Developmental trajectories of boys' and girls' delinquency: Sex differences and links to later adolescent outcomes. *Journal of Abnormal Child Psychology.*

Miller, W. D., Sadegh Nobari, T., & Lillie-Blanton, M. (2011). Healthy starts for all: Policy prescriptions. *American Journal of Preventive Medicine, 40*(Suppl. 1), S19–S37.

Mills, B., Reyna, V., & Estrada, S. (2008). Explaining contradictory relations between risk perception and risk taking. *Psychological Science, 19,* 429–433.

Mills, C. M., Elashi, F. B., & Archacki, M. A. (2011, March). *Evaluating sources of information and misinformation: Developmental and individual differences in the elementary school years.* Paper presented at the biennial meeting of the Society for Research in Child Development, Montreal.

Mills, D., & Mills, C. (2000). *Hungarian kindergarten curriculum translation.* London: Mills Production.

Milot, T., Ethier, L. S., St-Laurent, D., & Provost, M. A. (2010). The role of trauma symptoms in the development of behavioral problems in maltreated preschoolers. *Child Abuse and Neglect, 34*(4), 225–234.

Minde, K., & Zelkowitz, P. (2008). Premature babies. In M. M. Haith & J. B. Benson (Eds.), *Encyclopedia of infancy and early childhood.* Oxford, UK: Elsevier.

Minguez-Milio, J. A., & others. (2011, in press). Perinatal outcome and long-term follow-up of extremely low birth weight infants depending on the mode of delivery. *Journal of Maternal-Fetal and Neonatal Medicine.*

Minkler, M., & Fuller-Thompson, E. (2005). African American grandparents raising grandchildren: A national study using the Census 2000 American Community Survey. *Journal of Gerontology B: Psychological Sciences and Social Sciences, 60,* S82–S92.

Minnes, S., & others. (2010). The effects of prenatal cocaine exposure on problem behavior in children 4–10 years. *Neurotoxicology and Teratology, 32,* 443–451.

Minnesota Family Investment Program. (2009). *Longitudinal study of early MFIP recipients.* Retrieved on January 12, 2009, from www.dhs.state.mn.us/main/

Minuchin, P. O., & Shapiro, E. K. (1983). The school as a context for social development. In P. H. Mussen (Ed.), *Handbook of child psychology* (4th ed., Vol. 4). New York: Wiley.

Mischel, W. (1968). *Personality and assessment.* New York: Wiley.

Mischel, W. (1974). Process in delay of gratification. In L. Berkowitz (Ed.), *Advances in experimental social psychology* (Vol. 7). New York: Academic Press.

Mischel, W. (2004). Toward an integrative science of the person. *Annual Review of Psychology* (Vol. 55). Palo Alto, CA: Annual Reviews.

Mischel, W., & Mischel, H. (1975, April). *A cognitive social-learning analysis of moral development.* Paper presented at the meeting of the Society for Research in Child Development, Denver.

Mishra, G. D., Cooper, R., Tom, S. E., & Kuh, D. (2009). Early life circumstances and their impact on menarche and menopause. *Women's Health, 5,* 175–190.

Mistry, R. S., Vandewater, E. A., Huston, A. C., & McLoyd, V. C. (2002). Economic well-being and children's social adjustment: The role of family process in an ethnically diverse low-income sample. *Child Development, 3,* 935–951.

Mitchell, E. A. (2009). What is the mechanism of SIDS? Clues from epidemiology. *Developmental Psychobiology, 51,* 215–222.

Mitchell, E. A., Stewart, A. W., Crampton, P., & Salmond, C. (2000). Deprivation and sudden infant death syndrome. *Social Science and Medicine, 51,* 147–150.

Mitchell, M. L., & Jolley, J. M. (2010). *Research design explained* (7th ed.). Boston: Cengage.

Miyake, K., Chen, S., & Campos, J. (1985). Infants' temperament, mothers' mode of interaction and attachment in Japan: An interim report. In I. Bretherton & F. Waters (Eds.), Growing points of attachment theory and research, *Monographs of the Society for Research in Child Development, 50*(1–2, Serial No. 109), 276–297.

MMWR. (2010, June 4). Youth risk behavior surveillance—United States, 2009. *MMWR, 59*(SS-5), 9.

Moen, P. (1998). Recasting careers: Changing reference groups, risks and realities. *Generations, 22,* 40–45.

Moen, P. (2007). Unpublished review of J. W. Santrock's *Life-span development,* 12th ed. (New York: McGraw-Hill).

Moen, P. (2009a). Careers. In D. Carr (Ed.), *Encyclopedia of the life course and human development.* Boston: Gale Cengage.

Moen, P. (2009b). Dual-career couples. In D. Carr (Ed.), *Encyclopedia of the life course and human development.* Boston: Gale Cengage.

Moen, P., Kelly, E. L., & Magennis, R. (2008). Gender strategies: Social and institutional clocks, convoys, and cycles of control. In M. C. Smith and N. DeFrates-Densch (Eds.), *The handbook of research on adult development and learning.* New York: Routledge.

Moen, P., & Spencer, D. (2006). Converging divergences in age, gender, health, and well-being. In R. H. Binstock & L. K. George (Eds.), *Handbook of aging and the social sciences* (6th ed.). San Diego: Academic Press.

Moise, K. J. (2005). Fetal RhD typing with free DNA in maternal plasma. *American Journal of Obstetrics and Gynecology, 192,* 663–665.

Mollenkopf, H. (2007). Mobility and flexibility. In J. E. Birren (Ed.), *Encyclopedia of gerontology* (2nd ed.). San Diego: Academic Press.

Moller, J., Bjorkeenstam, E., Ljung, R., & Yngwe, M. A. (2011). Widowhood and the risk of psychiatric care, psychotropic medication, and all-cause mortality: A cohort of 658,022 elderly people in Sweden. *Aging and Mental Health, 15,* 259–266.

Momtaz, Y. A., Ibrahim, R., Hamid, T. A., & Yahaya, N. (2010). Mediating effects of social and personal religiosity on the psychological well-being of widowed elderly people. *Omega, 61,* 145–162.

Monahan, K. C., Lee, J. M., & Steinberg, L. (2011). Revisiting the impact of part-time work on adolescent adjustment: Distinguishing between selection and socialization using propensity score matching. *Child Development, 82,* 96–112.

Mond, J., & others. (2011). Obesity, body dissatisfaction, and emotional well-being in early and late adolescence: Findings from the Project EAT study. *Journal of Adolescent Health, 48,* 373–378.

Money, J. (1975). Ablatio penis: Normal male infant sex-reassigned as a girl. *Archives of Sexual Behavior, 4,* 65–71.

Monica, K. C., & du Plessis, R. A. (2011). Discussion of health benefits of breastfeeding within small groups. *Community Practice, 84,* 31–34.

Monserud, M. A. (2008). Intergenerational relationships and affectual solidarity between grandparents and young adults. *Journal of Marriage and the Family, 70,* 182–195.

Montagna, P., & Chokroverty, S. (2011). *Sleep disorders.* New York: Elsevier.

Montemayor, R. (1982). The relationship between parent-adolescent conflict and the amount of time adolescents spend with parents, peers, and alone. *Child Development, 53,* 1512–1519.

Montgomery-Downs, H. E., Insana, S. P., Clegg-Kraynok, M. M., & Mancini, L. M. (2010). Normative longitudinal maternal sleep: The first four postpartum months. *American Journal of Obstetrics and Gynecology, 203,* e1–e7.

Moore, B., & Stanley, T. (2010). *Critical thinking and formative assessments: Increasing the rigor in your classroom.* Larchmont, NY: Eye on Education.

Moore, D. (2001). *The dependent gene.* New York: W. H. Freeman.

Moos, B. (2007). Who'll care for aging boomers? *Dallas Morning News,* pp. A1–A2.

Morasch, K. C., & Bell, M. A. (2011). The role of inhibitory control in behavioral and physiological expressions of toddler executive function. *Journal of Experimental Psychology, 108,* 593–606.

Morley, J. E., & others. (2010). Nutritional recommendations for the management of sarcopenia. *Journal of the American Medical Directors Association, 11,* 391–396.

Morokuma, S., & others. (2008). Developmental change in fetal response to repeated low-intensity sound. *Developmental Science, 11,* 47–52.

Morra, S., Gobbo, C., Marini, Z., & Sheese, R. (2007). *Cognitive development: Neo-Piagetian perspectives.* Mahwah, NJ: Erlbaum.

Morrison, G. S. (2011). *Fundamentals of early childhood education* (6th ed.). Upper Saddle River, NJ: Merrill.

Morrison, G. S. (2012). *Early childhood education today* (12th ed.). Upper Saddle River, NJ: Merrill.

Morrissey, T. W. (2009). Multiple child-care arrangements and young children's behavioral outcomes. *Child Development, 80,* 59–76.

Morrow-Howell, N. (2010). Volunteering in later life: Research frontiers. *Journals of Gerontology B: Psychological Sciences and Social Sciences, 65,* 461–469.

Moshman, D. (2011). *Adolescent rationality and development: Cognition, morality, and identity* (3rd ed.). New York: Psychology Press.

Moulson, M. C., & Nelson, C. A. (2008). Neurological development. In M. M. Haith & J. B. Benson (Eds.), *Encyclopedia of infant and early childhood development.* Oxford, UK: Elsevier.

Mroczek, D. K., & Kolarz, C. M. (1998). The effect of age on positive and negative affect: A developmental perspective on happiness. *Journal of Personality and Social Psychology, 75,* 1333–1349.

Mroczek, D. K., & Spiro, A. (2007). Personality change influences mortality in older men. *Psychological Science, 18,* 371–376.

Mroczek, D. K., Spiro, A., & Griffin, P. W. (2006). Personality and aging. In J. E. Birren & K. W. Schaie (Eds.), *Handbook of the psychology of aging* (6th ed.). San Diego: Academic Press.

Mueller, A. S. (2009). Body image, childhood and adolescence. In D. Carr (Ed.), *Encyclopedia of the life course and human development.* Boston: Gale Cengage.

Murphy, M. C., & Dweck, C. S. (2011, in press). A culture of genius: How an organization's lay theories shape people's cognition, affect, and behavior. *Personality and Social Psychology Bulletin.*

Murray, J. P., & Murray, A. D. (2008). Television: Uses and effects. In M. M. Haith & J. B. Benson (Eds.), *Encyclopedia of infant and early childhood development.* Oxford, UK: Elsevier.

Murray, K. M., Byrne, D. C., & Rieger, E. (2010). Investigating adolescent stress and body image. *Journal of Adolescence, 34*(2), 269–278.

Murray, S. S., & McKinney, E. L. (2010). *Foundations of maternal-newborn and women's health* (5th ed.). New York: Elsevier.

Musch, D. C., & others. (2009). Visual field progression in the Collaborative Initial Glaucoma Treatment Study: The impact of treatment and other baseline factors. *Ophthalmology, 116*(2), 200–207.

Mussen, P. H., Honzik, M., & Eichorn, D. (1982). Early adult antecedents of life satisfaction at age 70. *Journal of Gerontology, 37,* 316–322.

Mwiru, R. S., & others. (2011, in press). Relationship of exclusive breast-feeding to infections and growth of Tanzanian children born to HIV-infected women. *Public Health Nutrition.*

Myer, G. D., & others. (2011). Integrative training for children and adolescents: Techniques and practices for reducing sports-related injuries and enhancing athletic performance. *The Physician and Sports Medicine, 39,* 74–84.

Myers, D. G. (2000). *The American paradox.* New Haven, CT: Yale University Press.

Myers, D. G. (2008, June 2). Commentary in S. Begley & Interlandi, The dumbest generation? Don't be dumb. Retrieved July 22, 2008, from www.newsweek.com/id/13856/

Myers, D. G. (2010). *Psychology* (9th ed.). New York: Worth.

Myers, D. L. (1999). *Excluding violent youths from juvenile court: The effectiveness of legislative waiver.* Doctoral dissertation, University of Maryland, College Park.

Myerson, J., Rank, M. R., Raines, F. Q., & Schnitzler, M. A. (1998). Race and general cognitive ability: The myth of diminishing returns in education. *Psychological Science, 9,* 139–142.

N

Nader, P. R., & others. (2006). Identifying risk for obesity in early childhood. *Pediatrics, 118,* e594–e601.

Nader, P. R., Bradley, R. H., Houts, R. M., McRitchie, S. L., & O'Brian, M. (2008). Moderate-to-vigorous physical activity from 9 to 15 years. *Journal of the American Medical Association, 300,* 295–305.

NAEYC (National Association for the Education of Young Children). (2009). *Developmentally appropriate practice in early childhood programs serving children from birth through age 8.* Washington, DC: Author.

Nagashima, J., & others. (2010). Three-month exercise and weight loss program improves heart rate recovery in obese persons along with cardiopulmonary function. *Journal of Cardiology, 56*(1), 79–84.

Nagy, M. (1948). The child's theories concerning death. *Journal of Genetic Psychology, 73,* 3–27.

Najman, J. M., Hayatbakhsh, M. R., Heron, M. A., Bor, W., O'Calaghan, M. J., & Williams, G. M. (2009). The impact of episodic and chronic poverty on child cognitive development. *Journal of Pediatrics, 154,* 284–289.

Najman, J. M., & others. (2010). Timing and chronicity of family poverty and development of unhealthy behaviors in children: A longitudinal study. *Journal of Adolescent Health, 46,* 538–544.

Nakamoto, J., & Schwartz, D. (2010). Is peer victimization associated with academic achievement? A meta-analytic review. *Social Development, 19,* 221–242.

Nansel, T. R., Overpeck, M., Pilla, R., Ruan, W., Simons-Morton, B., & Scheidt, P. (2001). Bullying behaviors among U.S. youth. *Journal of the American Medical Association, 285,* 2094–2100.

Narváez, D. (2006). Integrative moral education. In M. Killen & J. Smetana (ed.), *Handbook of moral development.* Mahwah, NJ: Erlbaum.

Narváez, D. (2008). Four Component Model. In F. C. Power, R. J. Nuzzi, D. Narváez, D. K. Lapsley, & T. C. Hunt (Eds.), *Moral education: A handbook.* Westport, CT: Greenwood Publishing.

Narváez, D. (2010a). Building a sustaining classroom climate for purposeful ethical citizenship. In T. Lovat, R. Toomey, & N. Clement (Eds.), *International research handbook of values education and student well-being.* New York: Springer.

Narváez, D. (2010b). The embodied dynamism of moral becoming. *Perspectives on Psychological Science, 5*(2), 185–186.

Narváez, D., Bock, T., Endicott, L., & Lies, J. (2004). Minnesota's Community Voices and Character Education Project. *Journal of Research in Character Education, 2,* 89–112.

Narváez, D., & Hill, P. L. (2010). The relation of multicultural experiences to moral judgment and mindsets. *Journal of Diversity in Higher Education, 3,* 43–55.

Narváez, D., & Lapsley, D. (2009). *Moral personality, identity, and character: An interdisciplinary future.* New York: Cambridge University Press.

Nash, J. M. (1997, February 3). Fertile minds. *Time,* 50–54.

Nash-Ditzel, S. (2010). Metacognitive reading strategies can improve comprehension. *Journal of College Reading and Learning, 40,* 45–63.

National Assessment of Educational Progress. (2005). *The nation's report card: 2005.* Washington, DC: U.S. Department of Education.

National Assessment of Educational Progress. (2007). *The nation's report card: 2007.* Washington, DC: U.S. Department of Education.

National Autism Association. (2010). *All about autism.* Retrieved January 5, 2010, from www.nationalautismassociation.org/definitions.php

National Center for Education Statistics. (2002). *Work during college.* Washington, DC: U.S. Office of Education.

National Center for Education Statistics. (2008). *The condition of education 2008. School dropout rates.* Washington, DC: U.S. Department of Education.

National Center for Education Statistics. (2010a). *The condition of education 2010.* Washington, DC: U.S. Department of Education.

National Center for Education Statistics. (2010b). *School dropouts.* Washington, DC: U.S. Department of Education.

National Center for Health Statistics. (2000). *Health United States, 1999.* Atlanta: Centers for Disease Control and Prevention.

National Center for Health Statistics. (2002). *Health United States, 2002.* Hyattsville, MD: Centers for Disease Control and Prevention.

National Center for Health Statistics. (2002). *Sexual behavior and selected health measures: Men and women 15–44 years of age, United States, 2002, PHS 2003–1250.* Atlanta: Centers for Disease Control and Prevention.

National Center for Health Statistics. (2008a). *Table 115: Deaths and death rates by leading causes of death and age: 2005.* Atlanta: Centers for Disease Control and Prevention.

National Center for Health Statistics. (2008b). *Table 117: Death rates from heart disease, by selected characteristics: 1980 to 2005.* Atlanta: Centers for Disease Control and Prevention.

National Center for Health Statistics. (2008c). *Table 119: Death rates from malignant neoplasms, by selected characteristics: 1990 to 2005.* Atlanta: Centers for Disease Control and Prevention.

National Center for Health Statistics. (2009, January 7). *Public Release Statement: Preterm births rise 36 percent since early 1980s.* Atlanta: Centers for Disease Control and Prevention.

National Center for Health Statistics. (2010). Deaths, percentage of total deaths, and death rates for 10 leading causes of death in selected age groups, by race and sex: United States, 2006. *National Vital Statistics Reports, 58*(14), 25.

National Center for Health Statistics. (2010a). *HIV/AIDS statistics and surveillance.* Atlanta: Centers for Disease Control and Prevention.

National Center for Health Statistics. (2010b). *Sexually transmitted diseases.* Atlanta: Centers for Disease Control and Prevention.

National Center for Vital Statistics. (2010). Births, marriages, divorces, deaths: Provisional data for November 2009. *National Vital Statistics Reports, 58*(23), 1–5.

National Center on Shaken Baby Syndrome. (2008). *Shaken baby syndrome.* Retrieved January 10, 2011, from www.dontshake.org/

National Clearinghouse on Child Abuse and Neglect. (2004). *What is child abuse and neglect?* Washington, DC: U.S. Department of Health and Human Services.

National Institute of Mental Health. (2008). *Autism spectrum disorders (pervasive developmental disorders).* Retrieved January 6, 2008, from http://www.nimh.nih.gov/publicat/autism.cfm

National Institute of Neurological Disorders and Stroke. (2011). *Understanding sleep.* Bethesda, MD: Author.

National Institutes of Health. (2004). *Women's Health Initiative Hormone Therapy Study.* Bethesda, MD: National Institutes of Health.

National Sleep Foundation. (2007). *Sleep in America poll 2007.* Washington, DC: Author.

National Sleep Foundation (2011). *Children and sleep.* Retrieved January 15, 2011, from www.sleepfoundation.org/site/c.hulXKjM0IxF/b.2418873/k.B9AD/Children_and_Sl . . .

Natsuaki, M. N., & others. (2010). Early pubertal maturation and internalizing problems in adolescence: Sex differences in the role of cortical reactivity to impersonal stress. *Journal of Clinical Child and Adolescent Psychology, 38,* 513–524.

Neal, A. R. (2009). Autism. In D. Carr (Ed.), *Encyclopedia of the life course and human development.* Boston: Gale Cengage.

Needham, A. (2009). Learning in infants' object perception, object-directed action, and tool use. In A. Needham & A. Woodward (Eds.), *Learning and the infant mind.* New York: Oxford University Press.

Needham, A., Barrett, T., & Peterman, K. (2002). A pick-me-up for infants' exploratory skills: Early simulated experiences reaching for object using "sticky mittens" enhances young infants' object exploration skills. *Infant Behavior and Development, 25,* 279–295.

Neer, R. M., & SWAN Investigators. (2010). Bone loss across menopausal transition. *Annals of the New York Academy of Sciences, 1192,* 66–71.

Neikrug, A. B., & Ancoli-Israel, S. (2010). Sleep disorders in the older adult: A mini-review. *Gerontology, 56,* 181–189.

Neisser, U. (2004). Memory development: New questions and old. *Developmental Review, 24,* 154–158.

Neisser, U., & others. (1996). Intelligence: Knowns and unknowns. *American Psychologist, 51,* 77–101.

Nelson, C. (2006). Unpublished review of J. W. Santrock's *Topical life-span development,* 4th ed. (New York: McGraw-Hill).

Nelson, C. A. (2003). Neural development and lifelong plasticity. In R. M. Lerner, R. Jacobs, & D. Wertlieb (Eds.), *Handbook of applied developmental science* (Vol. 1). Thousand Oaks, CA: Sage.

Nelson, C. A. (2007). A developmental cognitive neuroscience approach to the study of atypical development: A model system involving infants of diabetic mothers. In D. Coch, G. Dawson, & K. W. Fischer (Eds.), *Human behavior, learning, and the developing brain.* New York: Guilford.

Nelson, C. A. (2008). Unpublished review of J. W. Santrock's *Life-span development: A topical approach,* 5th ed. (New York: McGraw-Hill).

Nelson, C. A. (2011a). Brain development and behavior. In A. M. Rudolph, C. Rudolf, L. First,

G. Lister, & A. A. Gershon (Eds.), *Rudolph's pediatrics* (22nd ed.). New York: McGraw-Hill.

Nelson, C. A. (2011b). Neurobehavioral constructivism in the context of biocultural co-constructionism. In P. B. Baltes, P. A. Reuter-Lorenz, & F. Rosler (Eds.), *Lifespan development and the brain*. New York: Cambridge University Press.

Nelson, F. A., Yu, L. M., Williams, S., & International Child Care Practices Study Group Members. (2005). International Child Care Practices Study: Breastfeeding and pacifier use. *Journal of Human Lactation, 21,* 289–295.

Nelson, K. (1999). Levels and modes of representation: Issues for the theory of conceptual change and development. In E. K. Skolnick, K. Nelson, S. A. Gelman, & P. H. Miller (Eds.), *Conceptual development*. Mahwah, NJ: Erlbaum.

Nelson, L. J., Padilla-Walker, L. M., Christensen, K. J. Evans, C. A., & Carroll, J. S. (2010). Parenting in emerging adulthood: An examination of parenting clusters and correlates. *Journal of Youth and Adolescence, 40*(6), 730–743.

Nemec, S. F., & others. (2011, in press). Male sexual development in utero: Testicular descent on prenatal MRI. *Ultrasound in Obstetrics and Gynecology.*

Neugarten, B. L., Havighurst, R. J., & Tobin, S. S. (1968). Personality and patterns of aging. In B. L. Neugarten (Ed.), *Middle age and aging*. Chicago: University of Chicago Press.

Neugarten, B. L., & Weinstein, K. K. (1964). The changing American grandparent. *Journal of Marriage and the Family, 26,* 199–204.

Neukrug, E. S., & Fawcett, R. C. (2010). *Essentials of testing and assessment* (2nd ed.). Boston: Cengage.

Nevarez, M. D., & others. (2010). Associations of early life risk factors with infant sleep duration. *Academic Pediatrics, 10,* 187–193.

Neville, H. J. (2006). Different profiles of plasticity within human cognition. In Y. Munakata & M. H. Johnson (Eds.), *Attention and Performance XXI: Processes of change in brain and cognitive development*. Oxford, UK: Oxford University Press.

Nevsimalova, S. (2009). Narcolepsy in childhood. *Sleep Medicine Reviews, 13,* 169–180.

New, M. (2008, October). *Binge eating disorder.* Retrieved on February 27, 2011, from http://kidshealth.org/parent/emotions/behavior/binge_eating.html

Newcombe, N., & Fox, N. (1994). Infantile amnesia: Through a glass darkly. *Child Development, 65,* 31–40.

Newell, K., Scully, D. M., McDonald, P. V., & Baillargeon, R. (1989). Task constraints and infant grip configurations. *Developmental Psychobiology, 22,* 817–832.

Newman, A. B., & others. (2006). Association of long-distance corridor walk performance with mortality, cardiovascular disease, mobility limitation, and disability. *Journal of the American Medical Association, 295,* 2018–2026.

Newton, A. W., & Vandeven, A. M. (2010). Child abuse and neglect: A worldwide concern. *Current Opinion in Pediatrics, 22,* 226–233.

NICHD. (2011). *SIDS.* Retrieved January 14, 2011, from www.nichd.nih.gov/publications/pubs/safe_sleep_gen.cfm

NICHD Early Child Care Research Network. (2001). Nonmaternal care and family factors in early development: An overview of the NICHD study of Early Child Care. *Journal of Applied Development Psychology, 22,* 457–492.

NICHD Early Child Care Research Network. (2002). Structure → Process → Outcome: Direct and indirect effects and child care quality on young children's development. *Psychological Science, 13,* 199–206.

NICHD Early Child Care Research Network. (2003). Does amount of time spent in child care predict socioemotional adjustment during the transition to kindergarten? *Child Development, 74,* 976–1005.

NICHD Early Child Care Research Network. (2004). Type of child care and children's development at 54 months. *Early Childhood Research Quarterly, 19,* 203–230.

NICHD Early Child Care Research Network. (2005). *Child care and development.* New York: Guilford.

NICHD Early Child Care Research Network. (2005a). Duration and developmental timing of poverty and children's cognitive and social development from birth through third grade. *Child Development, 76,* 795–810.

NICHD Early Child Care Research Network. (2005b). Predicting individual differences in attention, memory, and planning in first graders from experiences at home, child care, and school. *Developmental Psychology, 41,* 99–114.

NICHD Early Child Care Research Network. (2006). Infant-mother attachment classification: Risk and protection in relation to changing maternal caregiving quality. *Developmental Psychology, 42,* 38–58.

Nieto, S., & Bode, P. (2012). *Affirming diversity* (6th ed.). Boston: Allyn & Bacon.

Nigro, G., & others. (2011, in press). Role of the infections in recurrent spontaneous abortion. *Journal of Maternal-Fetal and Neonatal Medicine.*

Nippold, M. A. (2009). School-age children talk about chess: Does knowledge drive syntactic complexity? *Journal of Speech, Language, and Hearing Research,* 856–871.

Nisbett, R. (2003). *The geography of thought.* New York: Free Press.

Nitko, A. J., & Brookhart, S. M. (2011). *Educational assessment of students* (6th ed.). Boston: Allyn & Bacon.

Noble, J. M., & others (2010). Association of C-reactive protein with cognitive impairment. *Archives of Neurology, 67,* 87–92.

Noddings, N. (2008). Caring and moral education. In L. Nucci & D. Narváez (Eds.), *Handbook of moral and character education*. Clifton, NJ: Psychology Press.

Noel-Miller, C. M. (2011). Partner caregiving in older cohabiting couples. *Journals of Gerontology B: Psychological Sciences and Social Sciences, 66,* 341–353.

Noftle, E. E., & Fleeson, W. (2010). Age differences in Big Five factor behavior averages and variabilities across the adult life span: Moving beyond retrospective, global summary accounts of personality. *Psychology and Aging, 25,* 95–107.

Noftle, E. E., & Robins, R. W. (2007). Personality predictors of academic outcomes: Big Five correlates of GPA and SAT scores. *Journal of Personality and Social Psychology, 93,* 116–130.

Nolen-Hoeksema, S. (2011). *Abnormal psychology* (5th ed.). New York: McGraw-Hill.

Nomoto, M., & others. (2009). Inter- and intra-individual variation in L-dopa pharmacokinetics in the treatment of Parkinson's disease. *Parkinsonism and Related Disorders, 15*(Suppl. 1), S21–S24.

Norman, J. E., & others. (2009). Progesterone for the prevention of preterm birth in twin pregnancy (STOPPIT): A randomized, double-blind, placebo-controlled study and meta-analysis. *Lancet, 373,* 2034–2040.

Norton, P. J., & Grellner, K. W. (2010, in press). A retrospective study on infant bed-sharing in a clinical population. *Maternal and Child Health Journal.*

Nottelmann, E. D., & others. (1987). Gonadal and adrenal hormone correlates of adjustment in early adolescence. In R. M. Leiner & T. T. Foch (Eds.), *Biological psychological interactions in early adolescence*. Hillsdale, NJ: Erlbaum.

Nrugham, L., Holen, A., & Sund, A. M. (2010). Associations between attempted suicide, life events, depressive symptoms, and resilience in adolescents and young adults. *Journal of Nervous and Mental Disease, 198,* 131–136.

Nucci, L. (2006). Education for moral development. In M. Killen & J. Smetana (Eds.), *Handbook of moral development*. Mahwah, NJ: Erlbaum.

Nultman-Shwartz, O., & Gadot, L. (2011, in press). Social factors and mental health symptoms among women who have experienced involuntary job loss. *Anxiety, Stress, and Coping.*

Nyakas, C., Granic, I., Halmy, L. G., Banerjee, P., & Luiten, P. G. (2010, in press). The basal forebrain cholinergic system in aging and dementia. *Behavioral Brain Research.*

Nyaronga, D., & Wickrama, K. A. S. (2009). Health behaviors, childhood and adolescence. In D. Carr (Ed.), *Encyclopedia of the life course and human development*. Boston: Gale Cengage.

Nyberg, L., & Backman, L. (2011a). Influences of biological and self-initiated factors on brain and cognition in adulthood and aging. In P. B. Baltes, P. A. Reuter-Lorenz, & F. Rosler (Eds.), *Lifespan development and the brain*. New York: Cambridge University Press.

Nyberg, L., & Backman, L. (2011b). Memory changes and the aging brain: A multimodal imaging approach. In K. W. Schaie & S. L. Willis (Eds.), *Handbook of the psychology of aging* (7th ed.). New York: Elsevier.

Nyqvist, K. H., & others. (2010). Towards universal kangaroo mother care: Recommendations and report from the First European conference and Seventh International Workshop on Kangaroo Mother Care. *Acta Pediatrica, 99*(6), 820–826.

O

O'Brien, J. M., & Lewis, D. F. (2009). Progestins for the prevention of spontaneous preterm birth: Review and implications of recent studies. *Journal of Reproductive Medicine, 54,* 73–87.

O'Brien, L., Albert, D., Cehin, J., & Steinberg, L. (2011, in press). Adolescents prefer more immediate rewards when in the presence of their peers. *Journal of Research on Adolescence.*

O'Brien, M., & Moss, P. (2010). Fathers, work, and family policies in Europe. In M. E. Lamb (Ed.), *The father's role in child development* (5th ed.). New York: Wiley.

O'Callaghan, F. V., & others. (2010). The link between sleep problems in infancy and early childhood and attention problems at 5 and 14 years: Evidence from a birth cohort study. *Early Human Development, 86,* 419–424.

O'Connor, D. B., Conner, M., Jones, F., McMillan, B., & Ferguson, E. (2009). Exploring the benefits of conscientiousness: An investigation of the role of daily stressors and health benefits. *Annals of Behavioral Medicine, 37,* 184–196.

O'Donnell, L., O'Donnell, C., Wardlaw, D. M., & Stueve, A. (2004). Risk and resiliency factors influencing suicidality among urban African-American and Latino youth. *American Journal of Community Psychology, 33,* 37–49.

O'Keefe, G. S., & others. (2011). The impact of social media on children, adolescents, and families. *Pediatrics, 127,* 800–804.

Oakes, L. M., Kannass, K. N., & Shaddy, D. J. (2002). Developmental changes in endogenous control of attention: The role of target familiarity on infants' distraction latency. *Child Development, 73,* 1644–1655.

Oates, J., & Abraham, S. (2010). *Llewellyn-Jones fundamentals of obstetrics and gynecology* (9th ed.). New York: Elsevier.

Oberg, M., & others. (2011). Worldwide burden of disease from exposure to second-hand smoke: A retrospective analysis of data from 192 countries. *Lancet, 377,* 139–146.

Oberlander, S. E., Black, M. M., & Starr, R. H. (2007). African American adolescent mothers and grandmothers: A multigenerational approach to parenting. *American Journal of Community Psychology, 39,* 37–46.

Obler, L. K. (2009). Developments in the adult years. In J. Berko Gleason & N. B. Ratner (Eds.), *The development of language* (7th ed.). Boston: Allyn & Bacon.

Obradovic, J., Shaffer, A., & Masten, A. S. (2011). Risk in developmental psychopathology: Progress and future directions. In L. C. Mayes & M. Lewis (Eds.), *The environment of human development: A handbook of theory and measurement.* New York: Cambridge University Press.

Obrenovich, M. E., & others. (2011). Antioxidants in health and disease. *CNS and Neurological Disorders Drug Targets, 10,* 192–207.

Occupational Outlook Handbook. (2010–2011). Washington, DC: U.S. Department of Labor, Bureau of Labor Statistics.

Odegard, T. N., & others. (2009). Children's eyewitness memory for multiple real-life events. *Child Development, 80,* 1877–1890.

OECD. (2010a). *Obesity and the economics of prevention—Fit or fat.* Paris: OECD.

OECD. (2010b). *Strong performers and successful reformers in education: Lessons from PISA for the United States.* Paris, France: OECD.

Offer, D., Ostrove, E., Howard, K. I., & Atkinson, R. (1988). *The teenage world: Adolescents' self-image in ten countries.* New York: Plenum Press.

Ogbu, J., & Stern, P. (2001). Caste status and intellectual development. In R. J. Sternberg & E. L. Grigorenko (Eds.), *Environmental effects on cognitive abilities.* Mahwah, NJ: Erlbaum.

Ogden, C. L., Carroll, M. D., & Flegal. K. M. (2008). High body mass index for age among U.S. children and adolescents, 2003–2006. *Journal of the American Medical Association, 299,* 2401–2405.

Ohta, Y., Tsuchihashi, T., Onaka, U., & Hasegawa, E. (2010). Clustering of cardiovascular risk factors and blood pressure control in hypertensive patients. *Internal Medicine, 49,* 1483–1487.

Okonkwo, O. C., & others. (2010). Longitudinal trajectories of cognitive decline in older adults with cardiovascular disease. *Cerebrovascular Diseases, 30,* 362–373.

Okun, E., Griffioen, K. J., & Mattson, M. P. (2011, in press). Toll-like receptor signaling in neural plasticity and disease. *Trends in Neuroscience.*

Okun, M. A., August, K. J., Rook, K. S., & Newsom, J. T. (2010). Does volunteering moderate the relation between functional limitations and mortality? *Social Science Medicine, 71,* 1662–1668.

Oldehinkel, A. J., Ormel, J., Veenstra, R., De Winter, A., & Verhulst F. C. (2008). Parental divorce and offspring depressive symptoms: Dutch developmental trends during early adolescence. *Journal of Marriage and the Family, 70,* 284–293.

Olds, D. L., & others. (2004). Effect of home visits by paraprofessionals and nurses: Age four follow-up of a randomized trial. *Pediatrics, 114,* 1560–1568.

Olds, D. L., & others. (2007). Effects of nurse home visiting on maternal and child functioning: Age-9 follow-up of a randomized trial. *Pediatrics, 120,* e832–e845.

Oliveira, B. F., Nogueira-Machado, J. A., & Chaves, M. M. (2010). The role of oxidative stress in the aging process. *Scientific World Journal, 10,* 1121–1128.

Oliver, S. R., & others. (2010). Increased oxidative stress and altered substrate metabolism in obese children. *International Journal of Pediatric Obesity, 5*(5), 436–444.

Oller, D. K., & Jarmulowicz, L. (2010). Language and literacy in bilingual children in the early school years. In E. Hoff & M. Shatz (Eds.), *Blackwell handbook of language development* (2nd ed.). Malden, MA: Blackwell.

Olson, B. H., Haider, S. J., Vangjel, L., Bolton, T. A., & Gold, J. G. (2010). A quasi-experimental evaluation of a breastfeeding support program for low income women in Michigan. *Maternal and Child Health Journal, 14,* 86–93.

Olson, M., & Hergenhahn, B. R. (2011). *Introduction to theories of personality* (8th ed.). Upper Saddle River, NJ: Pearson.

Olweus, D. (2003). Prevalence estimation of school bullying with the Olweus bully/victim questionnaire. *Aggressive Behavior, 29*(3), 239–269.

Oman, D., & Thoresen, C. E. (2006). Do religion and spirituality influence health? In R. F. Paloutzian & C. L. Park (Eds.), *Handbook of the psychology of religion and spirituality.* New York: Guilford.

Onwuteaka-Philipsen, B. D., Rurup, M. L., Pasman, H. R., & van der Heide, A. (2010). The last phase of life: Who requests and who receives euthanasia or physician-assisted suicide? *Medical Care, 48,* 596–603.

Opalach, K., Rangaraju, S., Madorsky, I., Leeuwenburgh, C., & Notterpek, L. (2010). Lifelong calorie restriction alleviates age-related oxidative damage on peripheral nerves. *Rejuvenation Research, 13,* 65–74.

Opfer, J. E., & Gelman, S. A. (2011). Development of the animate-inanimate distinction. In U. Goswami (Ed.), *Wiley-Blackwell handbook of childhood cognitive development* (2nd ed.). New York: Wiley.

Ophir, E., Nass, C., & Wagner, A. D. (2009). Cognitive control in media multitaskers. *Proceedings of the National Academy of Sciences USA, 106,* 15583–15587.

Ornstein, P. A., Coffman, J. L., & Grammer, J. K., (2007, April). *Teachers' memory-relevant conversations and children's memory performance.* Paper presented at the biennial meeting of the Society for Research in Child Development, Boston.

Ornstein, P. A., Coffman, J. L., Grammer, J. K., San Souci, P. P., & McCall, L. E. (2010). Linking the classroom context and the development of children's memory skills. In J. Meece & J. Eccles (Eds.), *The handbook of research on schools, schooling, and human development.* New York: Routledge.

Ornstein, P. A., Gordon, B. N., & Larus, D. (1992). Children's memory for a personally experienced event: Implications for testimony. *Applied Cognition and Psychology, 6,* 49–60.

Ornstein, P. A., Grammer, J., & Coffman, J. (2010). Teacher's "mnemonic style" and the development of skilled memory. In H. S. Waters & W. Schneider (Eds.), *Metacognition, strategy use, and instruction.* New York: Guilford.

Ornstein, P. A., Haden, C. A., & Coffman, J. L. (2010). Learning to remember: Mothers and teachers talking with children. In N. L. Stein & S. Raudenbush (Eds.), *Development science goes to school.* New York: Taylor & Francis.

Ornstein, P. A., & Light, L. L. (2010). Memory development across the life span. In W. F. Overton & R. H. Lerner (Eds.), *Handbook of life-span development.* New York: Wiley.

Ortigosa Gomez, S., & others. (2011, in press). Use of illicit drugs over gestation and their neonatal impact: Comparison between periods 1982–1988 and 2002–2008. *Medicina Clinica.*

Oswald, D. L., & Clark, E. M. (2003). Best friends forever? High school best friendships and the transition to college. *Personal Relationships, 10,* 187–196.

Otto, B. W. (2010). *Language development in early childhood* (3rd ed.). Upper Saddle River, NJ: Merrill.

Owen, J. J., Rhoades, G. K., Stanley, S. M., & Markman, H. J. (2011). The role of leaders' working alliance in premarital education. *Journal of Family Psychology, 25,* 49–57.

Owens, J. A., Belon, K., & Moss, P. (2010). Impact of delaying school start time on adolescent sleep, mood, and behavior. *Archives of Pediatric and Adolescent Medicine, 164,* 608–614.

Owens, J. A., Rosen, C. L., Mindell, J. A., & Kirchner, H. L. (2010). Use of pharmaco-therapy for insomnia in child psychiatry practice: A national survey. *Sleep Medicine, 11,* 692–700.

Oxford, M. L., Gilchrist, L. D., Gillmore, M. R., & Lohr, M. J. (2006). Predicting variation in the life course of adolescent mothers as they enter adulthood. *Journal of Adolescent Health, 39,* 20–36.

Ozer, E. M., & Irwin, C. (2009). Adolescent and youth adult health: From basic health status to clinical interventions. In R. M. Lerner & L. Steinberg (Eds.), *Handbook of adolescent psychology* (3rd ed.). New York: Wiley.

P

Padilla-Walker, L. M., & Coyne, S. M. (2011, in press). "Turn that thing off!" Parent and adolescent predictors of proactive media monitoring. *Journal of Youth and Adolescence.*

Padilla-Walker, L. M., Nelson, L. J., Carroll, J. S., & Jensen, A. C. (2010). More than just a game: Video game and Internet use during emerging adulthood. *Journal of Youth and Adolescence, 39,* 103–113.

Painter, K. (2008, June 16). Older, wiser, but less active. *USA Today,* p. 4D.

Palfrey, J., Sacco, D., Boyd, D., & Debones, L. (2009). *Enhancing child safety and online technologies.*

Cambridge, MA: Berman Center for Internet & Society.

Palmore, E. B. (2004). Research note: Ageism in Canada and the United States. *Journal of Cross Cultural Gerontology, 19,* 41–46.

Paloutzian, R. F. (2000). *Invitation to the psychology of religion* (3rd ed.). Needham Heights, MA: Allyn & Bacon.

Pan, B. A., Rowe, M. L., Singer, J. D., & Snow, C. E. (2005). Maternal correlates of growth in toddler vocabulary production in low-income families. *Child Development, 76,* 763–782.

Pan, B. A., & Uccelli, P. (2009). Semantic development. In J. Berko Gleason & N. B. Ratner (Eds.), *The development of language* (7th ed.). Boston: Allyn & Bacon.

Pandit, S. R., & others. (2011). Functional effects of adult human olfactory stem cells on early-onset sensorineural hearing loss. *Stem Cells, 29,* 670–677.

Pang, E. W., Wang, F., Malone, M., Kadis, D. S., & Donner, E. J. (2011). Localization of Broca's area using verb generation tasks in the MEG: Validation against fMRI. *Neuroscience Letters, 490,* 215–219.

Pann, K. M., & Crosbie-Burnett, M. (2005). Remarriage and re-coupling: A stress perspective. In P. C. Mckenry & S. J. Price (Eds.), *Families and change* (3rd ed.). Thousand Oaks, CA: Sage.

Paquette, J., & others. (2010). Risk of autoimmune diabetes in APECED: Association with short alleles of the 5'insulin VNTR. *Genes and Immunity, 11*(7), 590–597.

Parade, S. H., Leerkes, E. M., & Blankson, A. N. (2010). Attachment to parents, social anxiety, and close relationships of female students over the transition to college. *Journal of Youth and Adolescence, 39,* 127–137.

Parens, E., & Johnston, J. (2009). Facts, values, and attention-deficit hyperactivity disorder (ADHD): An update on the controversies. *Child and Adolescent Psychiatry and Mental Health, 3,* 1.

Park, C. L. (2005). Religion as a meaning-making system. *Psychology of Religion Newsletter, 30*(2), 1–9.

Park, C. L. (2007). Religiousness/spirituality and health: A meaning systems perspective. *Journal of Behavioral Medicine, 30,* 319–328.

Park, C. L. (2008). Estimated longevity and changes in spirituality in the context of advanced congestive heart failure. *Palliative and Supportive Care, 6,* 1–9.

Park, C. L. (2009). Meaning making in cancer survivorship. In P. T. P. Wong (Ed.), *The human quest for meaning* (2nd ed.). New York: Psychology Press.

Park, C. L. (2010). Making sense out of the meaning literature: An integrative review of meaning making and its effect on adjustment to stressful life events. *Psychological Bulletin, 136,* 257–301.

Park, C. L. (2011). Meaning making in cancer survivorship. In P. T. P. Wong (Ed.), *Handbook of meaning* (2nd ed.). Thousand Oaks, CA: Sage.

Park, C. L., Malone, M. R., Suresh, D. P., Bliss, D., & Rosen, R. I. (2008). Coping, meaning in life, and quality of life in congestive heart failure patients. *Quality of Life Research, 17,* 21–26.

Park, D. C., & Bischof, G. N. (2011). Neuroplasticity, aging, and cognitive function. In K. W. Schaie & S. L. Willis (Eds.), *Handbook of the psychology of aging* (7th ed.). New York: Elsevier.

Park, D. C., & Huang, C. M. (2010). Culture wires the brain: A cognitive neuroscience perspective. *Perspectives on Psychological Science, 5*(4), 391–400.

Park, D. C., & Reuter-Lorenz, P. (2009). The adaptive brain: Aging and neurocognitive scaffolding. *Annual Review of Psychology* (Vol. 60). Palo Alto, CA: Annual Reviews.

Park, M. J., Brindis, C. D., Chang, F., & Irwin, C. E. (2008). A midcourse review of the Healthy People 2010: 21 critical health objectives for adolescents and young adults. *Journal of Adolescent Health, 42,* 329–334.

Park, M. J., Fertig, A., & Allison, P. (2011, in press). Physical and mental health, cognitive development, and health care use by housing status of low-income young children in 20 American cities: A prospective cohort study. *American Journal of Public Health.*

Park, M. J., Mulye, T. P., Adams, S. H., Brindis, C. D., & Irwin, C. E. (2006). The health status of young adults in the United States. *Journal of Adolescent Health, 39,* 305–317.

Parke, R. D., & Buriel, R. (1998). Socialization in the family. In N. Eisenberg (Ed.), *Handbook of child psychology* (5th ed., Vol. 3). New York: Wiley.

Parke, R. D., & Buriel, R. (2006). Socialization in the family: Ethnic and ecological perspectives. In W. Damon & R. Lerner (Eds.), *Handbook of child psychology* (6th ed.). New York: Wiley.

Parke, R. D., & Clarke-Stewart, A. K. (2011). *Social development.* New York: Wiley.

Parke, R. D., Coltrane, S., & Schofield, T. (2011). The bicultural advantage. In J. Marsh, R. Menoza-Denton, & J. A. Smith (Eds.), *Are we born racist?* Boston: Beacon Press.

Parker, J. D., Keefer, K. V., & Wood, L. M. (2011, in press). Toward a brief multidimensional assessment of emotional intelligence: Psychometric properties of the Emotional Quotient Inventory-Short-form. *Psychological Assessment.*

Parker, M. A. (2011, in press). Biotechnology in the treatment of sensorineural hearing loss: Foundations and future of hair cell regeneration. *Journal of Speech, Language, and Hearing Research.*

Parsons, C. E., Young, K. S., Murray, L., Stein, A., & Kringelbach, M. L. (2010). The functional neuroanatomy of the evolving parent-infant relationship. *Progress in Neurobiology, 91*(3), 220–241.

Pasterski, V., Golombok, S., & Hines, M. (2011). Sex differences in social behavior. In P. K. Smith & C. H. Hart (Eds.), *Wiley-Blackwell handbook of childhood social development* (2nd ed.). New York: Wiley.

Patrick, M. E., Abar, C., & Maggs, J. L. (2009). Adolescent drinking. In D. Carr (Ed.). *Encyclopedia of the life course and human development*. Boston: Gale Cengage.

Patterson, C. J. (2004). What differences does a civil union make? Changing public policies and the experiences of same-sex couples: Comment on Solomon, Rothblum, and Balsam (2004). *Journal of Family Psychology, 18,* 287–289.

Patterson, C. J. (2009). Lesbian and gay parents and their children: A social sciences perspective. *Nebraska Symposium on Motivation, 54,* 142–182.

Patterson, C. J., & Wainright, J. L. (2010). Adolescents with same-sex parents: Findings from the National Longitudinal Study of Adolescent Health. In D. Brodzinsky, A. Pertman, & D. Kunz (Eds.), *Lesbian and gay adoption: A new American reality*. New York: Oxford University Press.

Patton, G. C., & others. (2011, in press). Overweight and obesity between adolescence and early adulthood: A 10-year prospective study. *Journal of Adolescent Health*.

Paul, E. L., McManus, B., & Hayes, A. (2000). "Hookups": Characteristics and correlates of college students' spontaneous and anonymous sexual experiences. *Journal of Sexual Research, 37,* 76–88.

Paulhus, D. L. (2008). Birth order. In M. M. Haith & J. B. Benson (Eds.), *Encyclopedia of infant and early childhood development*. Oxford, UK: Elsevier.

Paus, T. (2010). Growth of white matter in the adolescent brain: Myelin or axon? *Brain and Cognition, 72,* 26–35.

Paus, T., & others. (2008). Morphological properties of the action–observation cortical network in adolescents with low and high resistance to peer influence. *Social Neuroscience, 3,* 303–316,

Payer, L. (1991). The menopause in various cultures. In H. Burger & M. Boulet (Eds.), *A portrait of the menopause*. Park Ridge, NJ: Parthenon.

Pazainanas, M., Cooper, C., Ebetino, F. H., & Russell, R. G. (2010). Long-term treatment with bisphosphonates and their safety in postmenopausal osteoporosis. *Therapeutics, and Clinical Risk Management, 6,* 325–343.

Pederson, D. R., & Moran, G. (1996). Expressions of the attachment relationship outside of the Strange Situation. *Child Development, 67,* 915–927.

Pedroso, F. S. (2008). Reflexes. In M. M. Haith & J. B. Benson (Eds.), *Infant and early childhood development*. Oxford, UK: Elsevier.

Peek, L., & Stough, L. M. (2010). Children with disabilities in the context of disaster: A social vulnerability perspective. *Child Development, 81,* 1260–1270.

Peek, M. K. (2009). Marriage in later life. In D. Carr (Ed.), *Encyclopedia of the life course and human development*. Boston: Gale Cengage.

Peiffer, J. J., & others. (2010). Strength and functional characteristics of men and women 65 years and older. *Rejuvenation Research, 13,* 75–82.

Pelton, S. I., & Leibovitz, E. (2009). Recent advances in otitis media. *Pediatric and Infectious Disease Journal, 28*(Suppl. 10), S133–S137.

Pena, E., & Bedore, J. A. (2009). Bilingualism. In R. G. Schwartz (Ed.), *Handbook of childhood language disorders*. New York: Psychology Press.

Peng, X. D., Huang, C. Q., Chen, L. J., & Lu, Z. C. (2009). Cognitive behavioral therapy and reminiscence techniques for the treatment of depression in the elderly: A systematic review. *Journal of International Medical Research, 37,* 975–982.

Peplau, L. A., & Fingerhut, A. W. (2007). The close relationships of lesbians and gay men. *Annual Review of Psychology* (Vol. 58). Palo Alto, CA: Annual Reviews.

Perkins, D. (1994, September). Creativity by design. *Educational Leadership, 51,* 18–25.

Perls, T. T. (2007). Centenarians. In J. E. Birren (Ed.), *Encyclopedia of gerontology* (2nd ed.). San Diego: Academic Press.

Perry, D. G., & Pauletti, R. E. (2011). Gender and adolescent development. *Journal of Research in Adolescence, 21,* 61–74.

Perry, N. E., & Rahim, A. (2011). Supporting self-regulated learning in classrooms. In B. J. Zimmerman & D. H. Schunk (Eds.), *Handbook of self-regulation of learning and performance*. New York: Routledge.

Perry, W. G. (1970). *Forms of intellectual and ethical development in the college years*. New York: Holt, Rinehart & Winston.

Perry-Jenkins, M., & Claxton, A. (2011). The transition to parenthood and the reasons "Momma ain't happy." *Journal of Marriage and the Family, 73,* 23–28.

Persky, H. R., Dane, M. C., & Jin, Y. (2003). *The nation's report card: Writing 2002*. U.S. Department of Education.

Persson, K. E., Fridlund, B., Kvist, L. J., & Dykes, A. K. (2011). Mothers' sense of security in the first postnatal week: Interview study. *Journal of Advanced Nursing, 67,* 105–116.

Pesce, C., Crova, L., Cereatti, L., Casella, R., & Bellucci, M. (2009). Physical activity and mental performance in preadolescents: Effects of acute exercise on free-recall memory. *Mental Health and Physical Activity, 2,* 16–22.

Peskin, H. (1967). Pubertal onset ego functioning. *Journal of Abnormal Psychology, 72,* 1–15.

Peters, J. M., & Stout, D. L. (2011). *Science in elementary education* (11th ed.). Boston: Allyn & Bacon.

Peters, K. F., & Petrill, S. A. (2011, in press). Comparison of background, needs, and expectations for genetic counseling of adults with experience with Down syndrome, Marfan syndrome, and neurofibromatosis. *American Journal of Medical Genetics A*.

Peterson, C. C. (2005). Mind and body: Concepts of human cognition, physiology and false belief in children with autism or typical development. *Journal of Autism and Developmental Disorders, 35,* 487–497.

Peterson, J. L., & Hyde, J. S. (2010). A meta-analytic review of research on gender differences in sexuality, 1973–2007. *Psychological Bulletin, 136,* 21–38.

Peterson, M. D., & Gordon, P. M. (2011). Resistance exercise for the aging adult: Clinical implications and prescription guidelines. *American Journal of Medicine, 124,* 194–198.

Peterson, M. D., Rhea, M. R., Sen, A., & Gordon, P. M. (2010). Resistance exercise for muscular strength in older adults: A meta-analysis. *Aging Research Reviews, 9*(3), 226–237.

Pew Research Center. (2008). *Pew forum on religion and public life: U.S. Religious Landscape Survey*. Washington, DC: Author.

Pew Research Center. (2010a). *The decline of marriage and rise of new families*. Washington, DC: Author.

Pew Research Center. (2010b). *Millennials*. Washington, DC: Author.

Pfluger, M., Winkler, C., Hummel, S., & Ziegler, A. G. (2010). Early infant diet in children at risk for type 1 diabetes. *Hormone and Metabolic Research, 42,* 143–148.

Phan, M. L., & Vicario, D. S. (2010). Hemispheric differences in processing of vocalizations depend on early experience. *Proceedings of the National Academy of Sciences USA, 107,* 2301–2306.

Phelan, S., & others. (2011, in press). Randomized trial of a behavioral intervention to prevent excessive gestational weight gain: The Fit for Delivery Study. *American Journal of Clinical Nutrition*.

Phillips, D. A., & Lowenstein, A. E. (2011). Early care, education, and child development. *Annual Review of Psychology* (Vol. 62). Palo Alto, CA: Annual Reviews.

Phillips, L. H., & Andres, P. (2010). The cognitive neuroscience of aging: New findings on compensation and connectivity. *Cortex, 46,* 421–424.

Phinney, J. S. (1996). When we talk about American ethnic groups, what do we mean? *American Psychologist, 51,* 918–927.

Phinney, J. S. (2006, April). *Acculturation and adaptation of immigrant adolescents in thirteen countries*. Paper presented at the meeting of the Society for Research on Adolescence, San Francisco.

Phinney, J. S. (2008). Bridging identities and disciplines: Advances and challenges in understanding multiple identities. *New Directions for Child and Adolescent Development, 120,* 97–109.

Phinney, J. S., & Baldelomar, O. (2011). Identity development in multiple contexts. In L. Jensen (Ed.), *Bridging cultural and developmental approaches to psychology*. New York: Oxford University Press.

Piaget, J. (1932). *The moral judgment of the child*. New York: Harcourt Brace Jovanovich.

Piaget, J. (1954). *The construction of reality in the child*. New York: Basic Books.

Piaget, J. (1962). *Play, dreams, and imitation in childhood.* New York: W. W. Norton.

Piaget, J., & Inhelder, B. (1969). *The child's conception of space* (F. J. Langdon & J. L. Lunger, Trans.). New York: W. W. Norton.

Piazza, J. R., Almeida, D. M., Dmitrieva, N. O., & Klein, L. C. (2010). Frontiers in the use of biomarkers of health in research on stress and aging. *Journals of Gerontology B: Psychological Sciences and Social Sciences, 65B,* 513–525.

Pinette, M., Wax, J. & Wilson, E. (2004). The risks of underwater birth. *American Journal of Obstetrics & Gynecology, 190,* 1211–1215.

Ping, H., & Hagopian, W. (2006). Environmental factors in the development of type 1 diabetes. *Reviews in Endocrine and Metabolic Disorders, 7,* 149–162.

Pinker, S. (1994). *The language instinct.* New York: HarperCollins.

Pinto, J. G., Hornby, K. R., Jones, D. G., & Murphy, K. M. (2010). Developmental changes in GABAergic mechanisms in human visual cortex across the lifespan. *Frontiers in Cellular Neuroscience, 4,* 16.

Pipe, M-E., & Salmon, K. (2009). Memory development and the forensic context. In M. Courage & N. Cowan (Eds.), *The development of memory in infancy and childhood.* New York: Psychology Press.

Piper, B. J., & others. (2011, in press). Abnormalities in parentally rated executive function in methamphetamine/polysubstance exposed children. *Pharmacology, Biochemistry, and Behavior.*

Pitkanen, T., Lyyra, A. L., & Pulkkinen, L. (2005). Age of onset of drinking and the use of alcohol in adulthood: A follow-up study from age 8–42 for females and males. *Addiction, 100,* 652–661.

Pleck, J. H. (1995). The gender-role strain paradigm. In R. F. Levant & W. S. Pollack (Eds.), *A new psychology of men.* New York: Basic Books.

Plomin, R. (1999). Genetics and general cognitive ability. *Nature, 402*(Suppl.), C25–C29.

Plomin, R. (2004). Genetics and developmental psychology. *Merrill-Palmer Quarterly, 50,* 341–352.

Plucker, J. (2010, July 10). Interview. In P. Bronson & A. Merryman, The creativity crisis. *Newsweek,* 42–48.

Pluess, M., & Belsky, J. (2009). Differential susceptibility to rearing experience: The case of childcare. *Journal of Child Psychology and Psychiatry, 50,* 396–404.

Pollack, S., & others. (2010). Neurodevelopmental effects of early deprivation in postinstitutionalized children, *Child Development, 81,* 224–236.

Pollack, W. (1999). *Real boys.* New York: Owl Books.

Poole, D. A., & Lindsay, D. S. (1996). *Effects of parents' suggestions, interviewing techniques, and age on young children's event reports.* Presented at the NATO Advanced Study Institute, Port de Bourgenay, France.

Popenoe, D. (2008). *Cohabitation, marriage, and child wellbeing: A cross-national perspective.* Piscataway, NJ: The National Marriage Project, Rutgers University.

Popenoe, D. (2009). *The state of our unions 2008. Updates of social indicators: Tables and charts.* Piscataway, NJ: The National Marriage Project.

Popham, W. J. (2011). *Classroom assessment* (6th ed.). Boston: Allyn & Bacon.

Posada, G., & Kaloustian, G. (2011). Parent-infant interaction. In J. G. Bremner & T. D. Wachs (Eds.), *Wiley-Blackwell handbook of infant development* (2nd ed.). New York: Wiley.

Posada, G., & others. (2002). Maternal caregiving and infant security in two cultures. *Developmental Psychology, 38,* 67–78.

Posner, M. I., & Rothbart, M. K. (2007a). *Educating the human brain.* Washington, DC: American Psychological Association.

Posner, M. I., & Rothbart, M. K. (2007b). Research on attention networks as a model for the integration of psychological sciences. *Annual Review of Psychology, 58,* 1–23.

Poston, L., & others. (2011). Obesity in pregnancy: Implications for the mother and lifelong health of the child. A consensus statement. *Pediatric Research, 69,* 175–180.

Pot, A. M., & others. (2010). The impact of life review on depression in older adults: A randomized controlled trial. *International Psychogeriatrics, 22*(4), 572–581.

Potard, C., Courtois, R., & Rusch, E. (2008). The influence of peers on risky behavior during adolescence. *European Journal of Contraception and Reproductive Health Care, 13,* 264–270.

Poulin, F., & Pedersen, S. (2007). Developmental changes in gender composition of friendship networks in adolescent girls and boys. *Developmental Psychology, 43,* 1484–1496.

Powell, E. C., Malanchinski, J., & Sheehan, K. M. (2010). A randomized trial of a home safety education intervention using a safe home model. *Journal of Trauma, 69*(Suppl. 4), S233–S236.

Powell, J. L. (2009). Global aging. In D. Carr (Ed.), *Encyclopedia of the life course and human development.* Boston: Gale Cengage.

Powell, S. D. (2012). *Your introduction to education* (2nd ed.). Upper Saddle River, NJ: Pearson.

Power, F. C., & Higgins-D'Alessandro, A. (2008). The Just Community approach to moral education and moral atmosphere of the school. In L. Nucci & D. Narváez (Eds.), *Handbook of moral and character education.* Clifton, NJ: Psychology Press.

Power, S. (2011). Social play. In P. K. Smith & C. H. Hart (Eds.), *Wiley-Blackwell handbook of childhood social development* (2nd ed.). New York: Wiley.

Powers, S. K., Dodd, S. L., & Jackson, E. M. (2011). *Total fitness and wellness* (3rd ed.). Upper Saddle River, NJ: Prentice Hall.

Prabhakar, H. (2007). Hopkins Interactive Guest Blog: *The public health experience at Johns Hopkins.* Retrieved January 31, 2008, from http://hopkins.typepad.com/guest/2007/03/the_public_heal.html

Pratt, C., & Bryant, P. E. (1990). Young children understand that looking leads to knowing (so long as they are looking in a single barrel). *Child Development, 61,* 973–982.

Preiss, D. D., & Sternberg, R. J. (Eds.). (2010). *Innovations in educational psychology.* New York: Springer.

Preiss, H. A., & Lindberg, S. M. (2011, in press). Gender intensification. In R. J. R. Levesque (Ed.), *Encyclcopedia of adolescence.* New York: Springer.

Pressler, S. J., & others. (2010). Cognitive deficits in chronic heart failure. *Nursing Research, 59,* 127–139.

Pressley, M. (2003). Psychology of literacy and literacy instruction. In I. B. Weiner (Ed.), *Handbook of psychology* (Vol. 7). New York: Wiley.

Pressley, M. (2007a). Achieving best practices. In L. B. Bambrell, L. M. Morrow, & M. Pressley (Eds.), *Best practices in literacy instruction.* New York: Guilford.

Pressley, M. (2007b). An interview with Michael Pressley by Terri Flowerday and Michael Shaughnessy. *Educational Psychology Review, 19,* 1–12.

Pressley, M., Allington, R., Wharton-McDonald, R., Block, C. C., & Morrow, L. M. (2001). *Learning to read: Lessons from exemplary first grades.* New York: Guilford.

Pressley, M., Dolezal, S. E., Raphael, L. M., Welsh, L. M., Bogner, K., & Roehrig, A. D. (2003). *Motivating primary-grades teachers.* New York: Guilford.

Pressley, M., Raphael, L. Gallagher, D., & DiBella, J. (2004). Providence–St. Mel School: How a school that works for African-American students works. *Journal of Educational Psychology, 96,* 216–235.

Presson, J. C., & Jenner, J. C. (2008). *Biology.* New York: McGraw-Hill.

Preusse, F., & others. (2011, in press). Fluid intelligence allows flexible recruitment of the parieto-frontal network in analogical reasoning. *Frontiers in Human Neuroscience.*

Price, C. A., & Joo, E. (2005). Exploring the relationship between marital status and women's retirement satisfaction. *International Journal of Aging and Human Development, 61,* 37–55.

Priess, H. A., & Lindberg, S. M. (2011a). Gender roles. In B. B. Brown & M. Prinstein (Eds.), *Encyclopedia of adolescence.* San Diego: Academic Press.

Priess, H. A., & Lindberg, S. M. (2011b). Gender intensification. In B. B. Brown & M. Prinstein (Eds.), *Encyclopedia of adolescence.* San Diego: Academic Press.

Priess, H. A., Lindberg, S. M., & Hyde, J. S. (2009) Adolescent gender-role identity and mental health: Gender intensification revisited. *Child Development, 80,* 1531–1544.

Prinstein, M. J., Brechwald, W. A., & Cohen, G. L. (2011, in press). Susceptibility to peer influence: Using a performance-based measure to identify adolescent males at heightened risk for deviant peer socialization. *Developmental Psychology.*

Prinstein, M. J., & Dodge, K. A. (2010). Current issues in peer influence research. In M. J. Prinstein & K. A. Dodge (Eds.), *Understanding peer influence in children and adolescents.* New York: Guilford.

Prinstein, M. J., Rancourt, D., Guerry, J. D., & Browne, C. B. (2009). Peer reputations and psychological adjustment. In K. H. Rubin, W. M. Bukowksi, & B. Laursen (Eds.), *Handbook of peer interactions, relationships, and groups.* New York: Guilford.

Prinz, J. (2009). *The emotional construction of morals.* New York: Oxford University Press.

Prinz, R. J., Sanders, M. R., Shapiro, C. J., Witaker, D. J., & Lutzker, J. R. (2009). Population-based prevention of child maltreatment: The U.S. Triple P System Population Trial. *Prevention Science, 10,* 1–12.

Prior, J. C., & Hitchcock, C. L. (2011). The endocrinology of perimenopause: Need for a paradigm shift. *Frontiers in Bioscience, 3,* 474–486.

Provenzo, E. F. (2002). *Teaching, learning, and schooling in American culture: A critical perspective.* Boston: Allyn & Bacon.

Pryor, J. H., Hurtado, S., DeAngelo, L., Blake, L. P., & Tran, S. (2009). *The American college freshman 2009.* Los Angeles: Higher Education Research Institute, UCLA.

Pryor, J. H., Hurtado, S., DeAngelo, L., Blake, L. P., & Tran, S. (2010). *The American freshman: National norms for fall 2010.* Los Angeles: Higher Education Institute, UCLA.

Pudrovska, T. (2009). Midlife crises and transitions. In D. Carr (Ed.), *Encyclopedia of the life course and human development.* Boston: Gale Cengage.

Puma, M., & others. (2010). *Head Start impact study: Final report.* Washington, DC: Administration for Children and Families.

Pungello, E. P., & others. (2010). Early educational intervention, early cumulative risks, and the early home environment as predictors of young adult outcomes within a high-risk sample. *Child Development, 81,* 410–426.

Putallaz, M., Grimes, C. L., Foster, K. J., Kupersmidt, J. B., Clie, J. D., & Dearing, K. (2007). Overt and relational aggression and victimization: Multiple perspectives within the school setting. *Journal of School Psychology, 45,* 523–547.

Putnam Investments. (2006). *Survey of the working retired.* Franklin, MA: Author.

Q

Queen, B. L., & Tollefsbol, T. O. (2010). Polyphenols and aging. *Current Aging Science, 3,* 34–42.

Quinn, P. C. (2011). Born to categorize. In U. Goswami (Ed.), *Wiley-Blackwell handbook of childhood cognitive development* (2nd ed.). New York: Wiley-Blackwell.

R

Racine, E., Karczewska, M., Seidler, M., Amaram, R., & Illes, J. (2010). How the public responded to the Schiavo controversy: Evidence from letters to editors. *Journal of Medical Ethics, 36,* 571–573.

Raffaelli, M., & Ontai, L. (2001). "She's sixteen years old and there's boys calling over to the house": An exploratory study of sexual socialization in Latino families. *Culture, Health, and Sexuality, 3,* 295–310.

Raffaelli, M., & Ontai, L. L. (2004). Gender socialization in Latino/a families: Results from two retrospective studies. *Sex Roles, 50,* 287–299.

Rafii, M. S., & Aisen, P. S. (2009). Recent developments in Alzheimer's disease therapeutics. *BMC Medicine, 7,* 7.

Raghuveer, G. (2010). Lifetime cardiovascular risk of childhood obesity. *American Journal of Clinical Nutrition, 91*(5), 1514S–1519S.

Rahilly-Tierney, C. R., Spiro, A., Vokonas, P., & Gaziano, J. M. (2011). *American Journal of Cardiology, 107,* 1173–1177.

Raikes, H., & others. (2006). Mother-child bookreading in low-income families: Correlates and outcomes during the first three years of life. *Child Development, 77,* 924–953.

Raikes, H. A., & Thompson, R. A. (2009). Attachment security and parenting quality predict children's problem-solving, attributions, and loneliness with peers. *Attachment and Human Development, 10,* 319–344.

Ram, N., Gerstorf, D., Lindenberger, U., & Smith, J. (2011, in press). Developmental change and intraindividual variability: Relating cognitive aging to cognitive plasticity, cardiovascular lability, and emotional diversity. *Psychology and Aging.*

Ram, N., Morelli, S., Lindberg, C., & Carstensen, L. L. (2008). From static to dynamic: The ongoing dialectic about human development. In K. W. Schaie & R. P. Abeles (Eds.), *Social structures and aging individuals: Continuing challenges.* Mahwah, NJ: Erlbaum.

Ramey, C. T., & Campbell, F. A. (1984). Preventive education for high-risk children: Cognitive consequences of the Carolina Abecedarian Project. *American Journal of Mental Deficiency, 88,* 515–523.

Ramey, C. T., & Ramey, S. L. (1998). Early prevention and early experience. *American Psychologist, 53,* 109–120.

Ramey, C. T., Ramey, S. L., & Lanzi, R. G. (2001). Intelligence and experience. In R. J. Sternberg & E. L. Grigorenko (Eds.), *Environment effects on cognitive development.* Mahwah, NJ: Erlbaum.

Ramey, S. L. (2005). Human developmental science serving children and families: Contributions of the NICHD study of early child care. In NICHD Early Child Care Network (Eds.), *Child care and development.* New York: Guilford.

Ramsey-Rennels, J. L., & Langlois, J. H. (2007). How infants perceive and process faces. In A. Slater & M. Lewis (Eds.), *Introduction to infant development* (2nd ed.). Malden, MA: Blackwell.

Ranke, M. B., & Lindberg, A. (2011, in press). Observed and predicted total pubertal growth during treatment with growth hormone in adolescents with idiopathic growth hormone deficiency, Turner syndrome, short stature, born small for gestational age, and idiopathic short stature: KIGS analysis and review. *Hormone Research in Pediatrics.*

Rasmussen, M. M., & Clemmensen, D. (2010). Folic acid supplementation in pregnant women. *Danish Medical Bulletin, 57,* A4134.

Rasulo, D., Christensen, K., & Tomassini, C. (2005). The influence of social relations on mortality in later life: A study on elderly Danish twins. *The Gerontologist, 45,* 601–608.

Rathunde, K., & Csikszentmihalyi, M. (2006). The developing person: An experiential perspective. In W. Damon & R. Lerner (Eds.), *Handbook of child psychology* (6th ed.). New York: Wiley.

Raven, P. H. (2011). *Biology* (9th ed.). New York: McGraw-Hill.

Rawlins, W. K. (2009). *The compass of friendship.* Thousand Oaks, CA: Sage.

Raymo, J. M., & Sweeney, M. M. (2006). Work-family conflict and retirement preferences. *Journals of Gerontology B: Psychological Sciences and Social Sciences, 61,* S161–S169.

Read, J. P., Merrill, J. E., & Bytschkow, K. (2010). Before the party starts: Risk factors and reasons for "pregaming" in college students. *Journal of American College Health, 58,* 461–472.

Realini, J. P., Buzi, R. S., Smith, P. B., & Martinez, M. (2010). Evaluation of "big decisions": An abstinence-plus sexuality. *Journal of Sex and Marital Therapy, 36,* 313–326.

Ream, G. L., & Savin-Williams, R. (2003). Religious development in adolescence. In G. Adams & M. Berzonsky (Eds.), *Blackwell handbook of adolescence.* Malden, MA: Blackwell.

Reed, I. C. (2005). Creativity: Self-perceptions over time. *International Journal of Aging & Development, 60,* 1–18.

Reedy, M. N., Birren, J. E., & Schaie, K. W. (1981). Age and sex differences in satisfying relationships across the adult life span. *Human Development, 24,* 52–66.

Regalado, M., Sareen, H., Inkelas, M., Wissow, L. S., & Halfon, N. (2004). Parents' discipline of young children: Results from the National Survey of Early Childhood Health. *Pediatrics, 113,* 1952–1958.

Regenerus, M., & Uecker, J. (2011). *Premarital sex in America.* New York: Oxford University Press.

Regev, R. H., & others. (2003). Excess mortality and morbidity among small-for-gestational-age premature infants: A population based study. *Journal of Pediatrics, 143,* 186–191.

Reibis, R. K., Treszi, A., Wegscheider, K., Ehrlich, B., Dissmann, R., & Voller, H. (2010). Exercise capacity is the most powerful predictor of 2-year mortality in patients with left ventricular systolic dysfunction. *Herz, 35,* 104–110.

Reich, S. M., & Vandell, D. L. (2011). The interplay between parents and peers as socializing influences in children's development.

In P. K. Smith & C. H. Hart (Eds.), *Wiley-Blackwell handbook of childhood social development* (2nd ed.). New York: Wiley.

Reichstadt, J., Depp, C. A., Palinkas, L. A., Folsom, D. P., & Jeste, D. V. (2007). Building blocks of successful aging: A focus group study of older adults' perceived contributors to successful aging. *American Journal of Geriatric Psychiatry, 15,* 194–201.

Reid, P. T., & Zalk, S. R. (2001). Academic environments: Gender and ethnicity in U.S. higher education. In J. Worell (Ed.), *Encyclopedia of women and gender.* San Diego: Academic Press.

Reijmerink, N. E., & others. (2011, in press). Toll-like receptors and microbial exposure: Gene-gene and gene-environment interaction in the development of atopy. *European Respiratory Journal.*

Reiner, W. G., & Gearhart, J. P. (2004). Discordant sexual identity in some genetic males with cloacal exstrophy assigned to female sex at birth. *New England Journal of Medicine, 350,* 333–341.

Reis, O., & Youniss, J. (2004). Patterns of identity change and development in relationships with mothers and friends. *Journal of Adolescent Research, 19,* 31–44.

Reis, S. M., & Renzulli, J. S. (2011). Intellectual giftedness. In R. J. Sternberg & S. B. Kaufman (Eds.), *Cambridge handbook of intelligence.* New York: Cambridge University Press.

Reiss, J. (2012). *120 content strategies for teaching English language learners* (2nd ed.). Boston: Allyn & Bacon.

Rejeski, W. J., & others. (2011, in press). Translating weight loss and physical activity into the community to preserve mobility in older, obese adults in poor cardiovascular health. *Archives of Internal Medicine.*

Renju, J. R., & others. (2011). Scaling up adolescent sexual and reproductive health interventions through existing government systems? A detailed process evaluation of a school-based intervention in the Mwanza region in the northwest of Tanzania. *Journal of Adolescent Health, 48,* 79–86.

Reno, V. P., & Veghte, B. (2011). Economic status of the aged in the United States. In R. H. Binstock & L. K. George (Eds.), *Handbook of aging and the social sciences* (7th ed.). New York: Elsevier.

Repacholi, B. M., & Gopnik, A. (1997). Early reasoning about desires: Evidence from 14- and 18-month-olds. *Developmental Psychology, 33,* 12–21.

Rest, J. R. (1995). *Concerns for the social-psychological development of youth and educational strategies: Report for the Kaufmann Foundation.* Minneapolis: University of Minnesota, Department of Educational Psychology.

Reuter-Lorenz, P. A., & others. (2000). Age difference in the frontal lateralization of verbal and spatial working memory revealed by PET. *Journal of Cognitive Neuroscience, 12,* 174–187.

Reuter-Lorenz, P. A., & Mikels, J. A. (2011). The aging mind and brain: Implications of enduring plasticity for behavioral and cultural change. In P. B. Baltes, P. A. Reuter-Lorenz, & F. Rosler (Eds.), *Lifespan development and the brain.* New York: Cambridge University Press.

Reuter-Lorenz, P. A., & Park, D. C. (2010). Human neuroscience and the aging mind: A new look at old problems. *Journals of Gerontology B: Psychological Sciences and Social Sciences, 65B,* 405–415.

Reuter-Lorenz, P., & Park, D. C. (2011, in press). Human neuroscience and the aging mind: A new look at old problems. *Journals of Gerontology B: Psychological Sciences and Social Sciences.*

Reutzel, D. R., & Cooter, R. B. (2012). *Teaching children to read* (6th ed.). Boston: Allyn & Bacon.

Reyna, V. F., & Rivers, S. E. (2008). Current theories of risk and rational decision making. *Developmental Review, 28,* 1–11.

Reyna, V., & Farley, F. (2006). Risk and rationality in adolescent decision-making: Implications of theory, practice, and public policy. *Psychological Science in the Public Interest, 7,* 1–44.

Reynolds, F. (2010). The effects of maternal labour analgesia on the fetus. *Best Practices & Research. Clinical Obstetrics & Gynecology, 65*(4), 405–415.

Rhoades, G. K., Stanley, S. M., & Markman, H. J. (2009). The pre-engagement cohabitation effect: A replication and extension of previous findings. *Journal of Family Psychology, 23,* 107–111.

Rhodes, A. E., & Bethell, J. (2008). Suicide ideators without major depression—whom are we not reaching? *Canadian Journal of Psychiatry, 53,* 125–130.

Richard, M. B., Taylor, S. R., & Greer, C. A. (2010). Age-induced disruption of selective olfactory bulb synaptic circuits. *Proceedings of the National Academy of Sciences U.S.A., 107*(35): 15613–15618.

Richards, J. E. (2009). Attention to the brain in infancy. In S. Johnson (Ed.), *Neuroconstructivism: The new science of cognitive development.* New York: Oxford University Press.

Richards, J. E. (2010). Infant attention, arousal, and the brain. In L. M. Oaks, C. H. Cashon, M. Casaola, & D. H. Rakison (Eds.), *Infant perception and cognition.* New York: Oxford University Press.

Richards, J. E. (2011). Infant attention, arousal, and the brain. In L. Oakes & others (Eds.), *Infant perception and cognition.* New York: Oxford University Press.

Richards, J. E., Reynolds, G. D., & Courage, M. I. (2010). The neural bases of infant attention. *Current Directions in Psychological Science, 19,* 41–46.

Richardson, E. D., & Marottoli, R. A. (2003). Visual attention and driving behaviors among community-living older persons. *Journals of Gerontology A: Biological Sciences and Medical Sciences, 58,* M832–M836.

Richardson, G. A., Goldschmidt, L., Leech, S., & Williford, J. (2011). Prenatal cocaine exposure: Effects on mother- and teacher-rated behavior problems and growth in school-aged children. *Neurotoxicology and Teratology, 33,* 69–77.

Richardson, G. A., Goldschmidt, L., & Williford, J. (2008). The effects of prenatal cocaine use on infant development. *Neurotoxicology and Teratology, 30,* 96–106.

Richardson, T. M., & others. (2011, in press). Depression and its correlates among older adults accessing social services. *Journal of Nursing Care Quality.*

Richardson, V. E. (2007). A dual process model of grief counseling: Findings from the Changing Lives of Older Couples (CLOC) study. *Journal of Gerontological Social Work, 48,* 311–329.

Richmond, E. J., & Rogol, A. D. (2007). Male pubertal development and the role of androgen therapy. *Nature Clinical Practice: Endocrinology and Metabolism, 3,* 338–344.

Rideout, V. J., Foehr, U. G., & Roberts, D. F. (2010). *Generation M: Media in the lives of 8- to 18-year-olds.* Menlo Park, CA: Kaiser Family Foundation.

Rideout, V. J., Roberts, D. F., & Foehr, U. G. (2005). *Generation M.* Menlo Park, CA: Kaiser Family Foundation.

Rider, O. J., & others. (2010). The effect of obesity and weight loss on aortic pulse wave velocity as assessed by magnetic resonance imaging. *Obesity, 18*(12), 2311–2316.

Riesch, S. K., Gray, J., Hoefs, M., Keenan, T., Ertil, T., & Mathison, K. (2003). Conflict and conflict resolution: Parent and young teen perceptions. *Journal of Pediatric Health Care, 17,* 22–31.

Riley, K. P., Snowdon, D. A., Derosiers, M. F., & Markesbery, W. R. (2005). Early life linguistic ability, late life cognitive function, and neuropathology: Findings from the Nun Study. *Neurobiology of Aging, 26,* 341–347.

Rimmer, J. H., Rauworth, A. E., Wang, E. C., Nicola, T. L., & Hill, B. (2009). A preliminary study to examine the effects of aerobic and therapeutic (nonaerobic) exercise on cardiorespiratory fitness and coronary risk reduction in stroke survivors. *Archives of Physical Medicine and Rehabilitation, 90,* 407–412.

Risch, N., & others. (2009). Interaction between the serotonin transporter gene (5-HTTLPR), stressful life events, and risk of depression: A meta-analysis. *Journal of the American Medical Association, 302*(5), 492.

Ristow, M., & Zarse, K. (2010). How increased oxidative stress promotes longevity and metabolic health: The concept of mitochondrial hormesis (mitohormesis). *Experimental Gerontology, 45,* 410–416.

Ritchie, R. O. (2010). How does human bone resist fracture? *Annals of the New York Academy of Sciences, 1192,* 72–80.

Rivas-Drake, D. (2011, in press). Ethnic-racial socialization and adjustment among Latino college students: The mediating roles of ethnic centrality, public regards, and perceived barriers to opportunity. *Journal of Youth and Adolescence.*

Rix, S. (2011). Employment and aging. In R. H. Binstock & L. K. George (Eds.), *Handbook of aging and the social sciences* (7th ed.). New York: Elsevier.

Rizzo, M. S. (1999, May 8). Genetic counseling combines science with a human touch. *Kansas City Star*, p. 3.

Roberto, K. A., & Skoglund, R. R. (1996). Interactions with grandparents and great-grandparents: A comparison of activities, influences, and relationships. *International Journal of Aging and Human Development, 43,* 107–117.

Roberts, B. W., Helson, R., & Klohnen, E. C. (2002). Personality development and growth in women across 30 years: Three perspectives. *Journal of Personality, 70,* 79–102.

Roberts, B. W., & Mroczek, D. (2008). Personality trait change in adulthood. *Current Directions in Psychological Science, 17,* 31–35,

Roberts, B. W., Walton, K. E., & Bogg, T. (2005). Conscientiousness and health across the life course. *Review of General Psychology, 9,* 156–168.

Roberts, B. W., Walton, K. E., & Viechtbauer, W. (2006). Pattern of mean-level change in personality traits across the life course: A meta-analysis of longitudinal studies. *Psychological Bulletin, 132,* 1–25.

Roberts, B. W., & Wood, D. (2006). Personality development in the context of the Neo-Socioanalytic Model of personality. In D. Mroczek & T. Little (Eds.), *Handbook of personality development.* Mahwah, NJ: Erlbaum.

Roberts, B. W., Wood, D, & Caspi, A. (2009). Personality development. In O. P. John, R. W. Robins, & L. A. Pervin (Eds.), *Handbook of personality: Theory and research* (3rd ed.). New York: Guilford.

Roberts, D., Jacobson, L., & Taylor, R. D. (1996, March). *Neighborhood characteristics, stressful life events, and African-American adolescents' adjustment.* Paper presented at the meeting of the Society for Research on Adolescence, Boston.

Roberts, D. F., & Foehr, U. G. (2008). Trends in media use. *The Future of Children, 18,* 11–37.

Roberts, M. A. (2010). Toward a theory of culturally relevant critical teacher care: African American teachers' definitions and perceptions of care for African American students. *Journal of Moral Education, 39,* 449–467.

Roberts, S. B., & Rosenberg, I. (2006). Nutrition and aging: Changes in the regulation of energy metabolism with aging. *Physiology Review, 86,* 651–667.

Robins, R. W., Trzesniewski, K. H., Tracev, J. L., Potter, J., & Gosling, S. D. (2002). Age differences in self-esteem from age 9 to 90. *Psychology and Aging, 17,* 423–434.

Rochlen, A. B., McKelley, R. A., Suizzo, M-A., & Scaringi, V. (2008). Predictors of relationship satisfaction, psychological well-being, and life-satisfaction among stay-at-home fathers. *Psychology of Men and Masculinity, 9,* 17–28.

Rode, S. S., Chang, P., Fisch, R. O., & Sroufe, L. A. (1981). Attachment patterns of infants separated at birth. *Developmental Psychology, 17,* 188–191.

Rodin, J., & Langer, E. J. (1977). Long-term effects of a control-relevant intervention with the institutionalized aged. *Journal of Personality and Social Psychology, 35,* 397–402.

Rodriguez, E. T., & others. (2009). The formative role of home literacy experiences across the first three years of life in children from low-income families. *Journal of Applied Developmental Psychology, 30,* 677–694.

Roese, N. J., & Summerville, A. (2005). What we regret most … and why. *Personality and Social Psychology Bulletin, 31,* 1273–1285.

Rogers, W. A., & Fisk, A. D. (2001). Attention in cognitive aging research. In J. E. Birren & K. W. Schaie (Eds.), *Handbook of the psychology of aging* (5th ed.). San Diego: Academic Press.

Roisman, G. I., Aguillar, B., & Egelund, B. (2004). Antisocial behavior in the transition to adulthood: The independent and interactive roles of developmental history and emerging development tasks. *Development and Psychopathology, 16,* 857–872.

Rojas, A., & Storch, E. A. (2010). Psychological complications of obesity. *Pediatric Annals, 39,* 174–180.

Rokholm, B., Baker, J. L., & Sorensen, T. I. (2010). The leveling off of the obesity epidemic since the year 1999—a review of evidence and perspectives. *Obesity Reviews, 11,* 835–846.

Romans, S., Cohen, M., & Forte T. (2011). Rates of depression and anxiety in urban and rural Canada. *Social Psychiatry and Psychiatric Epidemiology, 46,* 567–575.

Rondou, P., Haegeman, G., & Van Craenenbroeck, K. (2010). The dopamine D4 receptor: Biochemical and signaling properties. *Cellular and Molecular Life Sciences, 67*(12), 1971–1986.

Rönnlund, M., Nyberg, L., Bäckman, L., & Nilsson, L.-G. (2005). Stability, growth, and decline in adult life span development of declarative memory: Cross-sectional and longitudinal data from a population-based study. *Psychology and Aging, 20,* 3–18.

Rook, K. S., Mavandadi, S., Sorkin, D. H., & Zettel, L. A. (2007). Optimizing social relationships as a source for the health and well-being in later life. In C. M. Aldwin, C. L. Park, & A. Spiro (Eds.), *Handbook of health psychology and aging.* New York: Guilford.

Rose, A. J., Carlson, W., & Waller, E. M. (2007). Prospective associations of co-rumination with friendship and emotional adjustment: Considering the socioemotional trade-offs of co-rumination. *Developmental Psychology, 43,* 1019–1031.

Rose, A. J., & Smith, R. J. (2009). Sex difference in peer relationships. In K. H. Rubin, W. M. Bukowski, & B. Laursen (Eds.), *Handbook of peer interactions, relationships, and groups.* New York: Guilford.

Rosen, L., Cheever, N., & Carrier, L. M. (2008). The association of parenting style and age with parental limit setting and adolescent MySpace behavior. *Journal of Applied Developmental Psychology, 29,* 459–471.

Rosenberg, M. S., Westling, D. L., & McLeskey, J. (2011). *Special education for today's teachers* (2nd ed.). Upper Saddle River, NJ: Merrill.

Rosenblith, J. F. (1992). *In the beginning* (2nd ed.). Newbury Park, CA: Sage.

Rosenblum, G. D., & Lewis, M. (2003). Emotional development in adolescence. In G. Adams & M. Berzonsky (Eds.), *Blackwell handbook of adolescence.* Malden, MA: Blackwell.

Rosenblum, S., Aloni, T., & Josman, N. (2010). Relationships between handwriting performance and organizational abilities among children with and without dysgraphia: A preliminary study. *Research in Developmental Disabilities, 31,* 502–509.

Rosenfeld, A., & Stark, E. (1987, May). The prime of our lives. *Psychology Today,* pp. 62–72.

Rosengard, C. (2009). Confronting the intendedness of adolescent rapid repeat pregnancy. *Journal of Adolescent Health, 44,* 5–6.

Rosenstein, D., & Oster, H. (1988). Differential facial responses to four basic tastes in newborns. *Child Development, 59,* 1555–1568.

Rosenthal, N. L., & Kobak, R. (2010). Assessing adolescents' attachment hierarchies: Differences across developmental periods and associations with individual adaptation. *Journal of Research on Adolescence, 20*(3), 678–706.

Rosnati, R., Montirosso, R., & Barni, D. (2008). Behavioral and emotional problems among Italian international adoptees and non-adopted children: Father's and mother's reports. *Journal of Family Psychology, 22,* 541–549.

Rosnow, R. L., & Rosenthal, R. (1996). *Beginning behavioral research* (2nd ed.). Upper Saddle River, NJ: Prentice Hall.

Ross, H., & Howe, N. (2009). Family influences on children's peer relationships. In K. H. Rubin, W. M. Bukowksi, & B. Laursen (Eds.), *Handbook of peer interactions, relationships, and groups.* New York: Guilford.

Ross, K., Handal, P. J., Clark, E. M., & Vander Wal, J. S. (2009). The relationship between religion and religious coping: Religious coping as a moderator between coping and adjustment. *Journal of Religion and Health, 48,* 454–467.

Rossi, A. S. (1989). A life-course approach to gender, aging, and intergenerational relations. In K. W. Schaie & C. Schooler (Eds.), *Social structure and aging.* Hillsdale, NJ: Erlbaum.

Rossi, S., Miniussi, C., Pasqualetti, P., Babiloni, C., Rossini, P. M., & Cappa, S. F. (2005). Age-related functional changes of prefrontal cortex in long-term memory: A repetitive transcranial magnetic stimulation study. *Journal of Neuroscience, 24,* 7939–7944.

Rostosky, S. S., Riggle, E. D., Horner, S. G., Denton, F. N., & Huellemeier, J. D. (2010). Lesbian, gay and bisexual individuals' psychological reactions to amendments denying access to civil marriage. *American Journal of Orthopsychiatry, 80,* 302–310.

Roth, J. L., Brooks-Gunn, J., Murray, L., & Foster, W. (1998). Promoting healthy adolescents: Synthesis of youth development program evaluations. *Journal of Research on Adolescence, 8,* 423–459.

Rothbart, M. K. (2004). Temperament and the pursuit of an integrated developmental psychology. *Merrill-Palmer Quarterly, 50,* 492–505.

Rothbart, M. K. (2007). Temperament, development, and personality. *Current Directions in Psychological Science, 16,* 207–212.

Rothbart, M. K. (2011). *Becoming who we are.* New York: Guilford.

Rothbart, M. K., & Bates, J. E. (2006). Temperament. In W. Damon & R. Lerner (Eds.), *Handbook of child psychology* (6th ed.). New York: Wiley.

Rothbart, M. K., & Gartstein, M. A. (2008). Temperament. In M. M. Haith & J. B. Benson (Eds.), *Encyclopedia of infant and early childhood development.* Oxford, UK: Elsevier.

Rothbaum, F., Poll, M., Azuma, H., Miyake, K., & Weisz, J. (2000). The development of close relationships in Japan and the United States: Paths of symbiotic harmony and generative tension. *Child Development, 71,* 1121–1142.

Rothbaum, F., & Trommsdorff, G. (2007). Do roots and wings complement or oppose one another? The socialization of relatedness and autonomy in cultural context. In J. E. Grusec & P. D. Hastings (Eds.), *Handbook of socialization.* New York: Guilford.

Rothbaum, F., Weisz, J., Pott, M., Miyake, K., & Morelli, G. (2000). Attachment and culture: Security in the United States and Japan. *American Psychologist, 55,* 1093–1104.

Roth-Hanania, R., Davidov, M., & Zahn-Waxler, C. (2011, in press). Empathy development from 8 to 16 months: Early signs of concern for others. *Infant Behavior and Development.*

Rousssotte, F. F. (2011). Abnormal brain activation during working memory in children with prenatal exposure to drugs of abuse: The effects of methamphetamine, alcohol, and polydrug exposure. *NeuroImage, 54,* 3067–3075.

Rovee-Collier, C. (1987). Learning and memory in children. In J. D. Osofsky (Ed.), *Handbook of infant development* (2nd ed.). New York: Wiley.

Rovee-Collier, C. (2004). Infant learning and memory. In U. Goswami (Ed.), *Blackwell handbook of childhood cognitive development.* Malden, MA: Blackwell.

Rovee-Collier, C. (2007). The development of infant memory. In N. Cowan & M. Courage (Eds.), *The development of memory in childhood.* Philadelphia: Psychology Press.

Rovee-Collier, C., & Barr, R. (2010). Infant learning and memory. In U. J. G. Bremner & T. D. Wachs (Ed.), *Wiley-Blackwell handbook of infant development* (2nd ed.). New York: Wiley.

Rowe, M. L., & Goldin-Meadow, S. (2009). Differences in early gesture explain SES disparities in child vocabulary size at school entry. *Science, 323,* 951–953.

Rowley, S. R., Kurtz-Costas, B., & Cooper, S. M. (2010). The role of schooling in ethnic minority achievement and attainment, In J. Meece & J. Eccles (Eds.), *Handbook of research on schools, schooling, and human development.* Clifton, NJ: Psychology Press.

Roza, S. J., & others. (2010). Maternal folic acid supplement use in early pregnancy and child behavioral problems: The Generation R Study. *British Journal of Nursing, 103,* 445–452.

Rozzini, R., Ranhoff, A., & Trabucchi, M. (2007). Alcoholic beverage and long-term mortality in elderly people living at home. *Journals of Gerontology A: Biological Sciences and Medical Science, 62A,* M1313–M1314.

Rubie-Davies, C. M. (2007). Classroom interactions: Exploring the practices of high- and low-expectation teachers. *British Journal of Educational Psychology, 77,* 289–306.

Rubie-Davies, C. M. (Ed.). (2011). *Educational psychology.* New York: Routledge.

Rubin, K. H., Bukowski, W., & Parker, J. (2006). Peer interactions, relationships, and groups. In W. Damon & R. Lerner (Eds.), *Handbook of child psychology* (6th ed.). New York: Wiley.

Rubin, K. H., Caplan, R. J., Bowker, J. C., & Menzer, M. (2011). Social withdrawal and shyness. In P. K. Smith & C. H. Hart (Eds.), *Wiley-Blackwell handbook of childhood social development* (2nd ed.). New York: Wiley.

Rudang, R., Mellstrom, D., Clark, E., Ohlsson, C., & Lorentzon, M. (2011, in press). Advancing maternal age is associated with lower bone mineral density in young adult male offspring. *Osteoporosis International.*

Rueda, M. R., Posner, M. I., & Rothbart, M. K. (2005). The development of executive attention: Contributions to the emergence of self-regulation. *Developmental Neuropsychology, 28,* 573–594.

Ruffman, T., Slade, L., & Crowe, B. (2002). The relation between children's and mothers' mental state language and theory-of-mind understanding. *Child Development, 73,* 734–751.

Rumberger, R. W. (1995). Dropping out of middle school: A multilevel analysis of students and schools. *American Education Research Journal, 3,* 583–625.

Runco, M. (Ed.). (2011). *Encyclopedia of creativity* (3rd ed.). New York: Elsevier.

Runco, M., & Pritzker, S. (Eds.). (2010). *Encyclopedia of creativity* (2nd ed.). New York: Elsevier.

Rupp, D. E., Vodanovich, S. J., & Crede, M. (2005). The multidimensional nature of ageism: Construct validity and group differences. *Journal of Social Psychology, 145,* 335–362.

Russ, S. A., Hanna, D., DesGeorges, J., & Forsman, I. (2010). Improving follow-up to newborn hearing screening: A learning-collaborative experience. *Pediatrics, 126*(Suppl. 1), S59–S69.

Russell, A. (2011). Parent-child relationships and influences. In P. K. Smith & C. H. Hart (Eds.), *Wiley-Blackwell handbook of social development.* New York: Wiley.

Russell, M., & Airasian, P. W. (2012). *Classroom assessment* (7th ed.). New York: McGraw-Hill.

Russell, S. T., Crockett, L. J., & Chao, R. K. (2010). *Asian American parenting and parent-adolescent relationships.* New York: Springer.

Rutter, M., & Dodge, K. A. (2011). Gene-environment interaction: State of the science. In K. A. Dodge & M. Rutter (Eds.), *Gene-environment interaction and developmental psychopathology.* New York: Guilford.

Ryan, A. S. (2010). Exercise in aging: Its important role in mortality, obesity, and insulin resistance. *Aging and Health, 6,* 551–556.

Ryan, R. M., & Deci, E. L. (2009). Promoting self-determined school engagement: Motivation, learning, and well-being. In K. Wentzel & A. Wigfield (Eds.), *Handbook of motivation at school.* New York: Routledge.

Ryff, C. D. (1984). Personality development from the inside: The subjective experience of change in adulthood and aging. In P. B. Baltes & O. G. Brim (Eds.), *Life-span development and behavior.* New York: Academic Press.

Rykhlevskaia, E., Uddin, L. Q., Kondos, L., & Menon, V. (2010). Neuroanatomical correlates of developmental dyscalculia: Combined evidence from morphometry and tractography. *Frontiers in Human Neuroscience, 3,* 51.

S

Saarni, C. (1999). *The development of emotional competence.* New York: Guilford.

Saarni, C., Campos, J., Camras, L. A., & Witherington, D. (2006). Emotional development. In W. Damon & R. Lerner (Eds.), *Handbook of child psychology* (6th ed.). New York: Wiley.

Sabbagh, K. (2009). *Remembering our childhood: How memory betrays us.* New York: Oxford University Press.

Sabbagh, M. A., Xu, F., Carlson, S. M., Moses, L. J., & Lee, K. (2006). The development of executive functioning and theory of mind: A comparison of Chinese and U.S. preschoolers. *Psychological Science, 17,* 74–81.

Sabini, J. (1995). *Social psychology* (2nd ed.). New York: Norton.

Sachs, J. (2009). Communication development in infancy. In J. Berko Gleason & N. B. Ratner (Eds.), *The development of language* (7th ed.). Boston: Allyn & Bacon.

Sadeh, A. (2008). Sleep. In M. M. Haith & J. B. Benson (Eds.), *Encyclopedia of infant and early childhood development.* Oxford, UK: Elsevier.

Saewyc, E. M. (2011). Research on adolescent sexual orientation: Development, health disparities, stigma, and resilience. *Journal of Research on Adolescence, 21,* 256–272.

Saffran, J. R., Werker, J. F., & Werner, L. A. (2006). The infant's auditory world: Hearing, speech, and the beginnings of language. In W. Damon & R. Lerner (Eds.), *Handbook of child psychology* (6th ed.). New York: Wiley.

Sahin, E., & Depinho, R. A. (2010). Linking functional decline of telomeres, mitochondria, and stem cells during aging. *Nature, 464,* 520–528.

Saint Onge, J. M. (2009). Mortality. In D. Carr (Ed.), *Encyclopedia of the life course and human development.* Boston: Gale Cengage.

Sakamoto, Y., & others. (2009). Effect of exercise, aging, and functional capacity on acute secretory immunoglobulin: A response in elderly people over 75 years of age. *Geriatrics and Gerontology International, 9,* 81–88.

Sakuma, K., & Yamaguchi, A. (2010). Molecular mechanisms in aging and current strategies to counteract sarcopenia. *Current Aging Science, 3*(2), 90–101.

Sala, S., Agosta, F., Pagani, E., Copetti, M., Comi, G., & Filippi, M. (2010, in press). Microstructural changes and atrophy in brain white matter tracts with aging. *Neurobiology of Aging.*

Salmivalli, C., & Peets, K. (2009). Bullies, victims, and bully-victim relationships in middle childhood and adolescence. In K. H. Rubin, W. M. Bukowski, & B. Laursen (Eds.), *Handbook of peer interactions, relationships, and groups.* New York: Guilford.

Salmivalli, C., Peets, K., & Hodges, E. V. E. (2011). Bullying. In P. K. Smith & C. H. Hart (Eds.), *Wiley-Blackwell handbook of childhood social development* (2nd ed.). New York: Wiley.

Salovey, P., & Mayer, J. D. (1990). Emotional intelligence. *Imagination, Cognition, and Personality, 9,* 185–211.

Salthouse, T. A. (1991). *Theoretical perspectives on cognitive aging.* Hillsdale, NJ: Erlbaum.

Salthouse, T. A. (1994). The nature of the influence of speed on adult age differences in cognition. *Developmental Psychology, 30,* 240–259.

Salthouse, T. A. (2007). Reaction time. In J. E. Birren (Ed.), *Encyclopedia of gerontology* (2nd ed.). San Diego: Academic Press.

Salthouse, T. A. (2009). When does age-related cognitive decline begin? *Neurobiology of Aging, 30,* 507–514.

Salthouse, T. A. (2010). The paradox of cognitive change. *Journal of Clinical and Experimental Neuropsychology, 32*(6), 622–629.

Salthouse, T. A. (2012). Consequences of age-related cognitive decline. *Annual Review of psychology* (Vol. 63). Palo Alto, CA: Annual Reviews.

Sameroff, A. J. (2009). The transactional model. In A. J. Sameroff (Ed.), *The transactional model of development: How children and contexts shape each other.* Washington, DC: American Psychological Association.

Sanchez-Johnsen, L. A., Fitzgibbon, M. L., Martinovich, Z., Stolley, M. R., Dyer, A. R., & Van Horn, L. (2004). Ethnic differences in correlates of obesity between Latin-American and black women. *Obesity Research, 12,* 652–660.

Sandler, I., Wolchik, S., & Schoenfelder, E. (2011). Evidence-based family-focused prevention programs for children. *Annual Review of Psychology* (Vol. 62). Palo Alto, CA: Annual Reviews.

Sanger, M. N. (2008). What we need to prepare teachers for the moral nature of their work. *Journal of Curriculum Studies, 40,* 169–185.

Sangree, W. H. (1989). Age and power: Life-course trajectories and age structuring of power relations in East and West Africa. In D. I. Kertzer & K. W. Schaie (Eds.), *Age structuring in comparative perspective.* Hillsdale, NJ: Erlbaum.

Sanson, A., & Rothbart, M. K. (1995). Child temperament and parenting. In M. H. Bornstein (Ed.), *Handbook of parenting* (Vol. 4). Hillsdale, NJ: Erlbaum.

Santelli, J. S., Abraido-Lanza, A. F., & Melnikas, A. J. (2009). Migration, acculturation, and sexual and reproductive health of Latino adolescents. *Journal of Adolescent Health, 44,* 3–4.

Santiago, C. D., Etter, E. M., Wadsworth, M. E., & Raviv, T. (2011, in press). Predictors of responses to stress among families coping with poverty-related stress. *Anxiety, Stress, and Coping.*

Santo, J. L., Portuguez, M. W., & Nunes, M. L. (2009). Cognitive and behavioral status of low birth weight preterm children raised in a developing country at preschool age. *Journal of Pediatrics, 85,* 35–41.

Santrock, J. W., & Halonen, J. A. (2009). *Your guide to college success* (6th ed.). Belmont, CA: Wadsworth.

Santrock, J. W., Sitterle, K. A., & Warshak, R. A. (1988). Parent-child relationship in stepfather families. In P. Bronstein & C. P. Cowan (Eds.), *Fatherhood today: Men's changing roles in the family.* New York: Wiley.

Sasaki, T., Unno, K., Tahara, S., & Kaneko, T. (2010). Age-related increase of reactive oxygen generation in the brains of mammals and birds: Is reactive oxygen a signaling molecule to determine the aging process and life span? *Geriatrics and Gerontology International, 10*(Suppl. I), S10–S24.

Savage, R. S., Abrami, P., Hipps, G., & Dealut, L. (2009). A randomized controlled trial study of the ABRACADABRA reading intervention program in grade 1. *Journal of Educational Psychology, 101,* 590–604.

Savin-Williams, R. C. (2006). *The new gay teenager.* Cambridge, MA: Harvard University Press.

Savin-Williams, R. C. (2011). Identity development in sexual minority youth. In S. Schwartz, K. Ulyckx, & V. Vignoles (Eds.), *Handbook of identity theory and research.* New York: Springer.

Sawyer, R. K., & DeZutter, S. (2007). Improvisation: A lens for play and literacy research. In K. A. Roskos & J. F. Christie (Eds.), *Play and literacy in early childhood.* Mahwah, NJ: Erlbaum.

Sayer, L. C. (2006). Economic aspects of divorce and relationship dissolution. In M. A. Fine & J. H. Harvey (Eds.), *Handbook of divorce and relationship dissolution.* Mahwah, NJ: Erlbaum.

Scalia, G. M., Khoo, S. K., & O'Neill, S. (2010, in press). Age-related changes in heart function by serial echocardiography in women aged 48–80 years. *Journal of Women's Health.*

Scarlett, W. G., & Warren, A. E. A. (2010). Religious and spiritual development across the life span: A behavioral and social science perspective. In M. E. Lamb, A. M. Freund, & R. M. Lerner (Eds.), *Handbook of life-span development.* New York: Wiley.

Scarr, S. (1993). Biological and cultural diversity: The legacy of Darwin for development. *Child Development, 64,* 1333–1353.

Scarr, S., & Weinberg, R. A. (1983). The Minnesota adoption studies: Genetic differences and malleability. *Child Development, 54,* 182–259.

Schachter, A. D., & Kohane, I. S. (2011). Drug target-gene signatures that predict teratogenicity are enrichers for developmentally related genes. *Reproductive Toxicology.*

Schaffer, H. R. (1996). *Social development.* Cambridge, MA: Blackwell.

Schaie, K. W. (1977). Toward a stage theory of adult cognitive development. *Aging and Human Development, 8,* 129–138.

Schaie, K. W. (1983). Consistency and changes in cognitive functioning of the young-old and old-old. In M. Bergner, U. Lehr, E. Lang, & R. Schmidt-Scherzer (Eds.), *Aging in the eighties and beyond.* New York: Springer.

Schaie, K. W. (1994). The life course of adult intellectual abilities. *American Psychologist, 49,* 304–313.

Schaie, K. W. (1996). *Intellectual development in adulthood: The Seattle Longitudinal Study.* New York: Cambridge University Press.

Schaie, K. W. (2000a). The impact of longitudinal studies on understanding development from young adulthood to old age. *International Journal of Behavioral Development, 24,* 257–266.

Schaie, K. W. (2000b). Unpublished review of J. W. Santrock's *Life-span development,* 8th ed. (New York: McGraw-Hill).

Schaie, K. W. (2005). *Developmental influences on adult intelligence: The Seattle Longitudinal Study.* New York: Oxford University Press.

Schaie, K. W. (2007). Generational differences: The age-period cohort. In J. E. Birren (Ed.), *Encyclopedia of gerontology* (2nd ed.). New York: Elsevier.

Schaie, K. W. (2010). Adult intellectual abilities. *Corsini encyclopedia of psychology.* New York: Wiley.

Schaie, K. W. (2011). *Developmental influences on adult intellectual development.* New York: Oxford University Press.

Schaie, K. W., & Willis, S. L. (2012). *Adult development and aging* (6th ed.). Upper Saddle River, NJ: Pearson.

Scheibe, S., & Carstensen, L. L. (2010). Emotional aging: Recent and future trends. *Journal of Gerontology B: Psychological Sciences, 65,* 135–144.

Scher, A., & Harel, J. (2008). Separation and stranger anxiety. In M. M. Haith & J. B. Benson (Eds.), *Encyclopedia of infant and early childhood development*. Oxford, UK: Elsevier.

Schermerhorn, A. C., Chow, S-M., & Cummings, E. M. (2010). Developmental family processes and interparental conflict: Patterns of micro-level influences. *Developmental Psychology, 46*, 869–885.

Schiff, W. J. (2011). *Nutrition for healthy living* (2nd ed.). New York: McGraw-Hill.

Schiffman, S. S. (2007). Smell and taste. In J. E. Birren (Ed.), *Encyclopedia of gerontology* (2nd ed.), San Diego: Academic Press.

Schilling, E. A., Aseltine, R. H., Glanovsky, J. L., James, A., & Jacobs, D. (2009). Adolescent alcohol use, suicidal ideation, and suicide attempts. *Journal of Adolescent Health, 44*, 335–341.

Schlegel, M. (2000). All work and play. *Monitor on Psychology, 31*(11), 50–51.

Schmader, K. E., & others. (2010). Treatment considerations for elderly and frail patients with neuropathic pain. *Mayo Clinic Proceedings, 85*(Suppl. 3), S26–S32.

Schmid, M., & others. (2011, in press). Maternal smoking and fetal lung volume—an in utero MRI investigation. *Prenatal Diagnosis.*

Schmidt, M. E., & Vandewater, E. A. (2008). Media and attention, cognition, and school achievement. *Future of Children, 18*(1), 64–85.

Schneider, B. H., & others. (2011). Cooperation and competition. In P. K. Smith & C. H. Hart (Eds.), *Wiley-Blackwell handbook of childhood social development* (2nd ed.). New York: Wiley.

Schneider, W. (2011). Memory development in childhood. In U. Goswami (Ed.), *Wiley-Blackwell handbook of childhood cognitive development*. New York: Wiley.

Schnittker, J. (2007). Look (closely) at all the lonely people: Age and social psychology of school support. *Journal of Aging and Health, 19*, 659–682.

Schnitzer, P. G., Covington, T. M., & Kruse, R. L. (2011). Assessment of caregiver responsibility in unintentional child injury deaths: Challenges for injury prevention. *Injury Prevention, 17*(Suppl. 1), S45–S54.

Schoffstall, C. L., & Cohen, R. (2011, in press). Cyber aggression: The relation between online offenders and offline social competence. *Social Development.*

Schofield, H. L., Bierman, K. L., Heinrichs, B., Nix, R. L., & the Conduct Problems Prevention Research Group. (2008). Predicting early sexual activity with behavior problems exhibited at school entry and in early adolescence. *Journal of Abnormal Child Psychology, 36*(8), 1175–1188.

Schooler, C. (2007). Use it—and keep it longer, probably: A reply to Salthouse (2006). *Perspectives on Psychological Science, 2*, 24–29.

Schooler, C., Mulatu, S., & Oates, G. (1999). The continuing effects of substantively complex work on the intellectual functioning of older workers. *Psychology and Aging, 14*, 483–506.

Schoon, I., Jones, E., Cheng, H., & Maughan, B. (2011, in press). Family hardship, family instability, and cognitive development. *Journal of Epidemiology and Community Health.*

Schreiber, L. R. (1990). *The parents' guide to kids' sports*. Boston: Little, Brown.

Schrijvers, D. L., Bollen, J., & Sabbe, B. G. (2011, in press). The gender paradox in suicidal behavior and its impact on the suicidal process. *Journal of Affective Disorders.*

Schulenberg, J. E., & Zarrett, N. R. (2006). Mental health during emerging adulthood: Continuities and discontinuities in course, content, and meaning. In J. J. Arnett & J. Tanner (Eds.), *Advances in emerging adulthood*. Washington, DC: American Psychological Association.

Schultz, T. R. (2011). Computational modeling of infant concept learning: The developmental shift from features to correlations. In L. Oakes & others (Eds.), *Infant perception and cognition*. New York: Oxford University Press.

Schulz, R., & Curnow, C. (1988). Peak performance and age among super athletes: Track and field, swimming, baseball, and golf. *Journal of Gerontology, 43*, P113–P120.

Schulz, R., Hebert, R., & Boerner, K. (2008). Bereavement after caregiving. *Geriatrics, 63*, 20–22.

Schumm, L. P., & others. (2009). Assessment of sensory function in the National Social Life, Health, and Aging Project. *Journals of Gerontology B: Psychological Sciences and Social Sciences, 64B* (Suppl. 1), S76–S85.

Schunk, D. H. (2012). *Learning theories: An educational perspective* (6th ed.). Upper Saddle River, NJ: Prentice Hall.

Schunk, D. H., Pintrich, P. R., & Meece, J. L. (2008). *Motivation in education: Theory, research, and applications* (3rd ed.). Upper Saddle River, NJ: Prentice Hall.

Schwartz, D., Kelly, B. M., Duong, M., & Badaly, D. (2010). Contextual perspective on intervention and prevention efforts for bully/ victim problems. In E. M. Vernberg & B. K. Biggs (Eds.), *Preventing and treating bullying and victimization*. New York: Oxford University Press.

Schwartz, T. T., Kim, M., Uno, M., Mortimer, J., & O'Brien, K. B. (2011). Safety nets and scaffolds: Parental support in the transition to adulthood. *Journal of Marriage and the Family, 73*, 414–429.

Schweinhart, L. J., Montie, J., Xiang, Z., Barnett, W. S., Belfield, C. R., & Nores, M. (2005). *Lifetime effects: The High/Scope Perry Preschool Study through age 40*. Ypsilanti, MI: High/ Scope Press.

Scialfa, C. T., & Kline, D. W. (2007). Vision. In J. E. Birren (Ed.), *Encyclopedia of gerontology* (2nd ed.). San Diego: Academic Press.

Scott, M. (2012). *THINK race and ethnicity*. Upper Saddle River, NJ: Pearson.

Scourfield, J., Van den Bree, M., Martin, N., & McGuffin, P. (2004). Conduct problems in children and adolescents: A twin study. *Archives of General Psychiatry, 61*, 489–496.

Scupin, R. (2012). *Race and ethnicity* (2nd ed.). Upper Saddle River, NJ: Pearson.

Seaton, E. K. (2010). The influence of cognitive development and perceived racial discrimination on the psychological well-being of African American youth. *Journal of Youth and Adolescence, 39*, 694–703.

Seay, G. (2011, in press). Euthanasia and common sense: A reply to Garcia. *Journal of Medical Philosophy.*

Sebastiani, P., & others. (2010, in press). Genetic signatures of exceptional longevity in humans. *Science.*

Segal, B. (2007). Addiction: General. In J. E. Birren (Ed.), *Encyclopedia of gerontology* (2nd ed.). San Diego: Academic Press.

Segal, M., & others. (2012). *All about child care and early education* (2nd ed.). Upper Saddle River, NJ: Pearson.

Sekhobo, J. P., Edmunds, L. S., Reynolds, D. K., Dalenius, K., & Sharma, A. (2010). Trends in the prevalence of obesity overweight among children enrolled in the New York State WIC program, 2002–2007. *Public Health Reports, 125*, 218–224.

Selman, R. L. (1980). *The growth of interpersonal understanding*. New York: Academic Press.

Sen, B. (2010). The relationship between frequency of family dinner and adolescent problem behaviors after adjusting for other characteristics. *Journal of Adolescence, 33*, 187–196.

Sener, A., Terzioglu, R. G., & Karabulut, E. (2007). Life satisfaction and leisure activities during men's retirement: A Turkish sample. *Aging and Mental Health, 11*, 30–36.

Senter, L., Sackoff, J., Landi, K., & Boyd, L. (2010). Studying sudden and unexpected deaths in a time of changing death certification and investigation practices: Evaluating sleep-related risk factors for infant death in New York City. *Maternal and Child Health, 15*(2), 242–248.

Serido, J. (2009). Life events. In D. Carr (Ed.), *Encyclopedia of the life course and human development*. Boston: Gale Cengage.

Sesso, H. D., & others. (2008). Vitamins E and C in the prevention of cardiovascular disease in men: The Physicians' Health Study II randomized controlled trial. *Journal of the American Psychological Association, 300*, 2095–2202.

Seto, C. K., Statuta, S. M., & Solari, I. L. (2010). Pediatric running injuries. *Clinics in Sports Medicine, 29*, 499–511.

Settersten, R. A., Furstenberg, F. F., & Rumbaut, R. G. (Eds.). (2005). *On the frontier of adulthood: Theory, research, and public policy*. Chicago: University of Chicago Press.

Shafer, V. L., & Garrido-Nag, K. (2010). The neurodevelopmental bases of language. In E. Hoff & M. Shatz (Eds.), *Blackwell handbook of language development* (2nd ed.). Malden, MA: Blackwell.

Shah, A. (2008). The relationship between elderly suicide rates and the human development index: A cross-national study of secondary data from the World Health Organization and the United Nations. *International Psychogeriatrics, 16,* 1–16.

Shah, A., & Bhandarkar, R. (2011). Does adversity early in life affect general population suicide rates? A cross-sectional study. *Journal of Injury and Violence Research, 3,* 25–27.

Shan, Z. Y., Liu, J. Z., Sahgal, V., Wang, B., & Yue, G. H. (2005). Selective atrophy of left hemisphere and frontal lobe of the brain in older men. *Journals of Gerontology A: Biological Sciences and Medical Sciences, 60,* A165–A174.

Shankaran, S., & others. (2010). Prenatal cocaine exposure and BMI and blood pressure at 9 years of age. *Journal of Hypertension, 28,* 1166–1175.

Shankaran, S., & others. (2011, in press). Risk for obesity in adolescence starts in childhood. *Journal of Perinatology.*

Shapiro, A. F., & Gottman, J. M. (2005). Effects on marriage of a psycho-education intervention with couples undergoing the transition to parenthood: Evaluation at 1-year post intervention. *Journal of Family Communication, 5,* 1–24.

Sharkey, W. (1993). Who embarrasses whom? Relational and sex differences in the use of intentional embarrassment. In P. J. Kalbfleisch (Ed.), *Interpersonal communication.* Mahwah, NJ: Erlbaum.

Sharma, A. R., McGue, M. K., & Benson, P. L. (1996). The emotional and behavioral adjustment of adopted adolescents: Part II: Age at adoption. *Children and Youth Services Review, 18,* 101–114.

Shatz, M., & Gelman, R. (1973). The development of communication skills: Modifications in the speech of young children as a function of the listener. *Monographs of the Society for Research in Child Development, 38* (Serial No. 152).

Shaver, P. R., & Mikulincer, M. (2012). Recent advances in the study of close relationships. *Annual Review of Psychology* (Vol. 63). Palo Alto, CA: Annual Reviews.

Shaw, A. C., Joshi, S., Greenwood, H., Panda, A., & Lord, J. M. (2010). Aging of the innate immune system. *Current Opinion in Immunology, 22*(4), 507–513.

Shaw, C. S., Clark, J., & Wagenmakers, A. J. (2010). The effects of exercise and nutrition on intramuscular fat metabolism and insulin sensitivity. *Annual Review of Nutrition* (Vol. 30). Palo Alto, CA: Annual Reviews.

Shaw, P., & others. (2007). Attention-deficit/hyperactivity disorder is characterized by a delay in cortical maturation. *Proceedings of the National Academy of Science, 104*(49), 19649–19654.

Shaywitz, B. A., Lyon, G. R., & Shaywitz, S. E. (2006). The role of functional magnetic resonance imaging in understanding reading and dyslexia. *Developmental Neuropsychology, 30,* 613–632.

Shaywitz, S. E., Gruen, J. R., & Shaywitz, B. A. (2007). Management of dyslexia, its rationale, and underlying neurobiology. *Pediatric Clinics of North America, 54,* 609–623.

Shebloski, B., Conger, K. J., & Widaman, K. F. (2005). Reciprocal links among differential parenting, perceived partiality, and self worth: A three-wave longitudinal study. *Journal of Family Psychology, 19,* 633–642.

Shen, Y., & others. (2010). Clinical genetic testing for patients with autism spectrum disorders. *Pediatrics, 125,* e727–e735.

Sher-Censor, E., Parke, R. D., & Coltrane, S. (2010). Parents' promotion of psychological autonomy, psychological control, and Mexican-American adolescents' adjustment. *Journal of Youth and Adolescence, 40*(5), 620–632.

Sheridan, M., & Nelson, C. A. (2008). Neurobiology of fetal and infant development: implications for mental health. In C. H. Zeanah (Ed.), *Handbook of infant mental health* (3rd ed.). New York: Guilford.

Shields, M. (2006). Overweight and obesity among children and youth. *Health Reports, 17,* 27–42.

Shields, S. A. (1998, August). *What Jerry Maguire can tell us about gender and emotion.* Paper presented at the meeting of the International Society for Research on Emotions, Würzburg, Germany.

Shin, D., Pregenzer, G., & Gardin, J. M. (2011). Erectile dysfunction: A disease marker for cardiovascular disease. *Cardiology Review, 19,* 5–11.

Shin, S. H., Hong, H. G., & Hazen, A. L. (2010). Childhood sexual abuse and adolescence substance use: A latent class analysis. *Drug and Alcohol Dependence, 109*(1–3), 226–235.

Shiraev, E. (2011). *A history of psychology: A global perspective.* Thousand Oaks, CA: Sage.

Shiraev, E., & Levy, D. A. (2010). *Cross-cultural psychology* (4th ed.). Boston: Allyn & Bacon.

Shirom, A., Toker, S., Alkaly, Y., Jacobson, O., & Balicer, R. (2011). Work-based predictors of mortality: A 20-year follow-up of healthy employees. *Health Psychology, 30,* 268–275.

Shomaker, L. B., & Furman, W. (2009). Parent-adolescent relationship qualities, internal working models, and styles as predictors of adolescents' observed interactions with friends. *Journal of Social and Personal Relationships, 26,* 579.

Shore, L. M., & Goldberg, C. B. (2005). Age discrimination in the workplace. In R. L. Dipobye & A. Colella (Eds.), *Discrimination at work.* Mahwah, NJ: Erlbaum.

Shors, T. J. (2009). Saving new brain cells. *Scientific American, 300,* 46–52.

Shultz, K. S., & Adams, G. A. (Eds.). (2007). *Aging and work in the 21st century.* Mahwah, NJ: Erlbaum.

Siegal, M., & Surian, L. (2010). Conversational understanding in young children. In E. Hoff & M. Shatz (Eds.), *Blackwell handbook of language development* (2nd ed.). Malden, MA: Blackwell.

Siegler, R. S. (2006). Microgenetic analysis of learning. In W. Damon & R. Lerner (Eds.), *Handbook of child psychology* (6th ed.). New York: Wiley.

Siegler, R. S. (2007). Cognitive variability. *Developmental Science, 10,* 104–109.

Siegler, R. S. (2009). Improving preschoolers' number sense using information processing theory. In O. A. Barbarin & K. Miller (Eds.), *Handbook of child development and early education.* New York: Guilford.

Sieving, R. E., & others. (2011, in press). A clinic-based youth development program to reduce sexual risk behaviors among adolescent girls: Prime Time Pilot Study. *Health Promotion Practice.*

Sigal, A., Sandler, I., Wolchik, S., & Braver, S. (2011). Do parent education programs promote healthy post-divorce parenting? Critical directions and distinctions and a review of the evidence. *Family Court Review, 49,* 120–129.

Silberg, J. L., Maes, H., & Eaves, L. J. (2010). Genetic and environmental influences on the transmission of parental depression to children's depression and conduct disturbance: An extended Children of Twins study. *Journal of Child Psychology and Psychiatry, 51*(6), 734–744.

Silfverdal, S. A. (2011). Important to overcome barriers in translating evidence-based breast-feeding information into practice. *Acta Pediatrica, 100,* 482–483.

Silva, C. (2005, October 31). When teen dynamo talks, city listens. *Boston Globe,* pp. 81–84.

Silver, E. J., & Bauman, L. J. (2006). The association of sexual experience with attitudes, beliefs, and risk behaviors of inner-city adolescents. *Journal of Research on Adolescence, 16,* 29–45.

Silverman, P. R., & Kelly, M. (2009). *A parent's guide to raising grieving children.* New York: Oxford University Press.

Silverstein, M. (2009). Caregiving. In D. Carr (Ed.), *Encyclopedia of the life course and human development.* Boston: Gale Cengage.

Silverstein, M., Conroy, S. J., Wang, H., Giarrusso, R., & Bengtson, V. L. (2002). Reciprocity in parent-child relations over the adult life course. *Journal of Gerontology B: Social Sciences, 57,* S3–S13.

Silverstein, N. M., Wong, C. M., & Brueck, K. E. (2010). Adult day health care for participants with Alzheimer's disease. *American Journal of Alzheimer's Disease and Other Dementias, 25*(3), 276–283.

Simkin, P., & Bolding, A. (2004). Update on nonpharmacological approaches to relieve labor pain and prevent suffering. *Journal of Midwifery and Women's Health, 49,* 489–504.

Simonetti, G. D., & others. (2011). Determinants of blood pressure in preschool children: The role of parental smoking. *Circulation, 123,* 292–298.

Simonton, D. K. (1996). Creativity. In J. E. Birren (Ed.), *Encyclopedia of aging.* San Diego: Academic Press.

Singh, A. A., Orpinas, P., & Horne, A. M. (2010). Empowering schools to prevent bullying: A holistic approach. In E. Vernberg & B. K. Biggs

(Eds.), *Preventing and treating bullying and victimization.* New York: Oxford University Press.

Singh, S., Wulf, D., Samara, R., & Cuca, Y. P. (2000). Gender differences in the timing of first intercourse: Data from 14 countries. *International Family Planning Perspectives, 26,* 21–28, 43.

Singleton, D., & Ryan, L. (2009). *Understanding child language acquisition.* New York: Oxford University Press.

Sinha, J. W., Cnaan, R. A., & Gelles, R. J. (2007). Adolescent risk behaviors and religion: Findings from a national study. *Journal of Adolescence, 30,* 231–249.

Sinnott, J. D. (2003). Postformal thought and adult development: Living in balance. In J. Demick & C. Andreolett (Eds.), *Handbook of adult development.* New York: Kluwer.

Sinnott, J. D., & Johnson, L. (1997). Brief report: Complex formal thought in skilled research administrators. *Journal of Adult Development, 4,* 45–53.

Sisson, S. B., Broyles, S. T., Baker, B. L., & Katzmarzyk, P. T. (2010). Screen time, physical activity, and overweight in U.S. youth: National Survey of Children's Health 2003. *Journal of Adolescent Health, 47,* 309–311.

Skinner, B. F. (1938). *The behavior of organisms: An experimental analysis.* New York: Appleton-Century-Crofts.

Skinner, B. F. (1957). *Verbal behavior.* New York: Appleton-Century-Crofts.

Slater, A. M., Bremner, J. G., Johnson, S. P., & Hayes, R. (2011). The role of perceptual processes in infant addition/subtraction events. In L. M. Oakes, C. H. Cashon, M. Casasola, & D. H Rakison (Eds.), *Early perceptual and cognitive development.* New York: Oxford University Press.

Slater, A., Morison, V., & Somers, M. (1988). Orientation discrimination and cortical function in the human newborn. *Perception, 17,* 597–602.

Slater, A., Riddell, P., Quinn, P. C., Pascalis, O., Lee, K., & Kelly, D. J. (2010). Visual perception. In J. G. Bremner & T. D. Wachs (Eds.), *Wiley-Blackwell handbook of infant development* (2nd ed.). New York: Wiley.

Slavin, R. E. (2011). Instruction based on cooperative learning. In P. A. Alexander & R. E. Mayer (Eds.), *Handbook of research on learning and instruction.* New York: Routledge.

Slobin, D. (1972, July). Children and language: They learn the same way around the world. *Psychology Today,* pp. 71–76.

Slomkowski, C., Rende, R., Conger, K. J., Simons, R. L., & Conger, R. D. (2001). Sisters, brothers, and delinquency: Social influence during early and middle adolescence. *Child Development, 72,* 271–283.

Smaldone, A., Honig, J. C., & Byrne, M. W. (2007). Sleepless in America: Inadequate sleep and relationships to health and well-being of our nation's children. *Pediatrics, 119*(Suppl. 1), S29–S37.

Small, S. A. (1990). *Preventive programs that support families with adolescents.* Washington, DC: Carnegie Council on Adolescent Development.

Smetana, J. G. (2008). "It's 10 o'clock: Do you know where your children are?" Recent advances in understanding parental monitoring and adolescents' information management. *Child Development Perspectives, 2,* 19–25.

Smetana, J. G. (2010). The role of trust in adolescent-parent relationships: To trust you is to tell you. In K. Rotenberg (Ed.), *Trust and trustworthiness during childhood and adolescence* (pp. 223–246). New York: Cambridge University Press.

Smetana, J. G. (2011a). *Adolescents, families, and social development.* New York: Wiley-Blackwell.

Smetana, J. G. (2011b). Adolescents' social reasoning and relationships with parents: Conflicts and coordinations within and across domains. In E. Amsel & J. Smetana (Eds.), *Adolescent vulnerabilities and opportunities: Constructivist and developmental perspectives.* New York: Cambridge University Press.

Smetana, J. G. (2011c). Parenting beliefs, parenting, and parent-adolescent communication in African American families. In N. E. Hill, T. Mann, & H. Fitzgerald (Eds.), *African American children's mental health.* New York: Praeger.

Smets, T., & others. (2010). Euthanasia in patients dying at home in Belgium: Interview study on adherence to legal standards. *British Journal of General Practice, 60,* e163–e170.

Smith, G. E., & others. (2009). A cognitive training program based on principles of brain plasticity: Results from the improvement in memory with plasticity-based adaptive cognitive training (IMPACT) study. *Journal of the American Geriatrics Society, 57,* 594–603.

Smith, J. (2009). Self. In D. Carr (Ed.), *Encyclopedia of the life course and human development.* Boston: Gale Cengage.

Smith, J. B. (2009). High school organization. In D. Carr (Ed.), *Encyclopedia of the life course and human development.* Boston: Gale Cengage.

Smith, L. E., & Howard, K. S. (2008). Continuity of paternal social support and depressive symptoms among new mothers. *Journal of Family Psychology, 22,* 763–773.

Smith, M. A., & Berger, J. B. (2010). Women's ways of drinking: College women, high-risk alcohol use, and negative consequences. *Journal of College Student Development, 51,* 35–49.

Smith, M. C., & Reio, T. G. (2007). *The handbook on adult development and learning.* Mahwah, NJ: Erlbaum.

Smith, N. G., Tarakeshwar, N., Hansen, N. B., Kochman, A., & Sikkema, K. J. (2009). Coping mediates outcome following a randomized group intervention for HIV-positive bereaved individuals. *Journal of Clinical Psychology, 65,* 319–325.

Smith, P. K. (2007). Pretend play and children's cognitive and literacy development: Sources of evidence and some lessons from the past. In

K. A. Roskos & J. F. Christie (Eds.), *Play and literacy in early childhood.* Mahwah, NJ: Erlbaum.

Smith, R. L., Rose, A. J., & Schwartz-Mette, R. A. (2010). Relational and overt aggression in childhood and adolescence: Clarifying mean-level gender differences and associations with peer acceptance. *Social Development, 19,* 243–269.

Smith, T. B., McCullough, M. E., & Poll, J. (2003). Religiousness and depression: Evidence for a main effect and the moderating influences of stressful life events. *Psychological Bulletin, 129,* 614–636.

Smith, T. E., Polloway, E. A., Patton, J. R., & Dowdy, C. A. (2012). *Teaching students with special needs in inclusive settings* (6th ed.). Upper Saddle River, NJ: Pearson.

Smoreda, Z., & Licoppe, C. (2000). Gender-specific use of the domestic telephone. *Social Psychology Quarterly, 63,* 238–252.

Snarey, J. (1987, June). A question of morality. *Psychology Today,* pp. 6–8.

Snow, C. E., Burns, M. S., & Griffin, P. (1998). *Preventing reading difficulties in young children.* Washington, DC: National Academies Press.

Snow, C. E., & Kang, J. Y. (2006). Becoming bilingual, biliterate, and bicultural. In W. Damon & R. Lerner (Eds.), *Handbook of child psychology* (6th ed.). New York: Wiley.

Snowdon, D. A. (1997). Aging and Alzheimer's disease: Lessons from the nun study. *Gerontologist, 37,* 150–156.

Snowdon, D. A. (2002). *Aging with grace: What the Nun Study teaches us about leading longer, healthier, and more meaningful lives.* New York: Bantam.

Snowdon, D. A. (2003). Healthy aging and dementia: Findings from the Nun Study. *Annals of Internal Medicine, 139,* 450–454.

Snowling, M. J., & Gobel, S. M. (2011). Reading development and dyslexia. In U. Goswami (Ed.), *Wiley-Blackwell handbook of childhood cognitive development.* New York: Wiley.

Snyder, H. N., & Sickmund, M. (1999, October). *Juvenile offenders and victims: 1999 national report.* Washington, DC: National Center for Juvenile Justice.

Snyder, K. A., & Torrence, C. M. (2008). Habituation and novelty. In M. M. Haith & J. B. Benson (Eds.), *Encyclopedia of infant and early childhood development.* Oxford, UK: Elsevier.

Sokol, B. W., Snjezana, H., & Muller, U. (2010). Social understanding and self-regulation: From perspective-taking to theory of mind. In B. Sokol, U. Muller, J. Carpendale, A. Young, & G. Iarocci (Eds.), *Self- and social cognition.* New York: Oxford University Press.

Solheim, K. N., & others. (2011, in press). The effect of cesarean delivery rates on the future incidence of placenta previa, placenta accrete, and maternal mortality. *Journal of Maternal-Fetal and Neonatal Medicine.*

Solmeyer, A. R., McHale, S. M., Killoren, S. E., & Updegraff, K. A. (2011). Coparenting around siblings' differential treatment in Mexican-origin families. *Developmental Psychology, 25,* 251–260.

Solomon, D., Watson, P., & Battistich, V. A. (2002). Teaching and school effects on moral/prosocial development. In V. Richardson (Ed.), *Handbook for research on teaching.* Washington, DC: American Educational Research Association.

Solomon, D., Watson, P., Schapes, E., Battistich, V., & Solomon, J. (1990). Cooperative learning as part of a comprehensive program designed to promote prosocial development. In S. Sharan (Ed.), *Cooperative learning.* New York: Praeger.

Song, A. V., & Halpern-Felsher, B. L. (2010). Predictive relationship between adolescent oral and vaginal sex: Results from a prospective, longitudinal study. *Archives of Pediatric and Adolescent Medicine, 165*(3), 243–249.

Song, L. J., & others. (2010). The differential effects of general mental ability and emotional intelligence on academic performance and social interactions. *Intelligence, 38,* 137–143.

Sontag, L. M., Clemans, K. H., Graber, J. A., & Lyndon, S. T. (2011). Traditional and cyber aggressors and victims: A comparison of social characteristics. *Journal of Youth and Adolescence, 40*(4), 392–404.

Sophian, C. (1985). Perseveration and infants' search: A comparison of two- and three-location tasks. *Developmental Psychology, 21,* 187–194.

Sorensen, T. L., & Kemp, H. (2010). Ranibizumab treatment in patients with neovascular age-related macular degeneration and very low vision. *Acta Ophthalmologica, 89*(1), e97.

Sorta-Bilajac, I., & others. (2011). How nurses and physicians face ethical dilemmas—the Croatian experience. *Nursing Ethics, 18,* 341–355.

Sorte, J., Daeschel, I., & Amador, C. (2011). *Nutrition, health, and wellness.* Upper Saddle River, NJ: Prentice Hall.

Spandel, V. (2009). *Creating young writers* (3rd ed.). Boston: Allyn & Bacon.

Spangler, G., Johann, M., Ronai, Z., & Zimmermann, P. (2009). Genetic and environmental influence on attachment disorganization. *Journal of Child Psychology and Psychiatry, 50,* 952–961.

Spelke, E. S. (1979). Perceiving bimodally specified events in infancy. *Developmental Psychology, 5,* 626–636.

Spelke, E. S. (1991). Physical knowledge in infancy. Reflections on Piaget's theory. In S. Carey & R. Gelman (Eds.), *The epigenesis of mind: Essays on biology and cognition.* Hillsdale, NJ: Erlbaum.

Spelke, E. S. (2000). Core knowledge. *American Psychologist, 55,* 1233–1243.

Spelke, E. S., & Hespos. S. J. (2001). Continuity, competence, and the object concept. In E. Dupoux (Ed.), *Language, brain, and behavior.* Cambridge, MA: Bradford/MIT Press.

Spelke, E. S., & Kinzler, K. D. (2007). Core knowledge. *Developmental Science, 10,* 89–96.

Spelke, E. S., & Kinzler, K. D. (2009). Innateness, learning and rationality. *Cognitive Development Perspectives, 3,* 96–98.

Spelke, E. S., & Owsley, C. J. (1979). Intermodal exploration and knowledge in infancy. *Infant Behavior and Development, 2,* 13–28.

Spelke, E. S., Breinlinger, K., Macomber, J., & Jacobson, K. (1992). Origins of knowledge. *Psychology Review, 99,* 605–632.

Spence, A. P. (1989). *Biology of human aging.* Englewood Cliffs, NJ: Prentice Hall.

Spencer, J. (2009). *Dynamic systems and connectionist approaches to development.* New York: Oxford University Press.

Speranza, M., & others. (2005). Depressive personality dimensions and alexithymia in eating disorders. *Psychiatry Research, 135,* 153–163.

Sperling, H., Debruyne, F., Boermans, A., Beneke, M., Ulbrich, E., & Ewald, S. (2010). The POTENT I randomized trial: Efficacy and safety of an orodispersible vardenafil formulation of the treatment of erectile dysfunction. *Journal of Sexual Medicine, 7,* 1497–1507.

Sprei, J. E., & Courtois, C. A. (1988). The treatment of women's sexual dysfunctions arising from sexual assault. In R. A. Brown & J. R. Fields (Eds.), *Treatment of sexual problems in individual and group therapy.* Great Neck, NY: PMA.

Spring, J. (2012). *American education* (15th ed.). New York: McGraw-Hill.

Srabstein, J. C., McCarter, R. J., Shao, C., & Huanz, Z. J. (2006). Morbidities associated with bullying behaviors in adolescents: School-based study of American adolescents. *International Journal of Adolescent Medicine and Health, 18,* 587–596.

Sroufe, L. A. (2000, Spring). The inside scoop on child development: Interview. *Cutting through the hype.* Minneapolis: College of Education and Human Development, University of Minnesota.

Sroufe, L. A., Coffino, B., & Carlson, E. A. (2010). Conceptualizing the role of early experience: Lessons from the Minnesota longitudinal study. *Developmental Review, 30,* 36–51.

Sroufe, L. A., Egeland, B., Carlson, E., & Collins, W. A. (2005). The place of early attachment in developmental context. In K. E. Grossman, K. Grossmann, & E. Waters (Eds.), *The power of longitudinal attachment research: From infancy and childhood to adulthood.* New York: Guilford.

Staff, J., Messersmith, E. E., & Schulenberg, J. E. (2009). Adolescents and the world of work. In R. M. Lerner & L. Steinberg (Eds.), *Handbook of adolescent psychology* (3rd ed.). New York: Wiley.

Stafford, A. C., Alswayan, M. S., & Tenni, P. C. (2010). Inappropriate prescribing in older residents of Australian care homes. *Journal of Clinical Pharmacy and Therapeutics, 36,* 33–44.

Stager, L. (2009–2010). Supporting women during labor and birth. *Midwifery Today with International Midwife, 23,* 12–15.

Stake, R. E. (2010). *Qualitative research.* New York: Guilford.

Stanford Center for Longevity. (2011). *Experts' consensus on brain health.* Retrieved April 30, 2011, from http://longevity.stanford.edu/mymind/cognitiveagingstatement

Stangor, C. (2011). *Research methods for the behavioral sciences* (4th ed.). Boston: Cengage.

Stanley, S. M., Amato, P. R., Johnson, C. A., & Markman, H. J. (2006). Premarital education, marital quality, and marital stability: Findings from a large, household survey. *Journal of Family Psychology, 20,* 117–126.

Stanley, S. M., Rhoades, G. K., Amato, P. R., Markman, H. J., & Johnson, C. A. (2010). The timing of cohabitation and engagement: Impact on first and second marriages. *Journal of Marriage and the Family, 72,* 906–918.

Staplin, L., Lococo, K., & Sim, J. (1993). *Traffic maneuver problems of older drivers.* Report No. FHWA-RD-92-092. McLean, VA: Federal Highway Administration.

Starr, C. (2011). *Biology* (8th ed.). Boston: Cengage.

Staudinger, U. M. (1996). Psychologische produktivitat and delbstenfaltung im alter. In M. M. Baltes & L. Montada (Eds.), *Produktives leben im alter.* Frankfurt: Campus.

Staudinger, U. M., & Gluck, J. (2011a). Intelligence and wisdom. In R. J. Sternberg & S. B. Kaufman (Eds.), *Cambridge handbook of intelligence.* New York: Cambridge University Press.

Staudinger, U. M., & Gluck, J. (2011b). Psychological wisdom research. *Annual Review of Psychology* (Vol. 62). Palo Alto, CA: Annual Reviews.

Staudinger, U. M., & Jacobs, C. B. (2010). Life-span perspectives on positive personality development in adulthood and old age. In R. M. Lerner, W. F. Overton, A. M. Freund, & M. E. Lamb (Eds.), *Handbook of life-span development.* New York: Wiley.

Steca, P., Bassi, M., Caprara, G. V., & Fave, A. D. (2011, in press). Parents' self-efficacy beliefs and their children's psychosocial adaptation during adolescence. *Journal of Youth and Adolescence.*

Steele, J., Waters, E., Crowell, J., & Treboux, D. (1998, June). *Self-report measures of attachment: Secure bonds to other attachment measures and attachment theory.* Paper presented at the meeting of the International Society for the Study of Personal Relationships, Saratoga Springs, NY.

Steinberg, L. (2008). A social neuroscience perspective on adolescent risk-taking *Developmental Review, 28,* 78–106.

Steinberg, L. (2009). Adolescent development and juvenile justice. *Annual Review of Clinical Psychology* (Vol. 5). Palo Alto, CA: Annual Reviews.

Steinberg, L. (2010). A behavioral scientist looks at the science of adolescent brain development. *Brain and Cognition, 72,* 160–164.

Steinberg, L., & others. (2008). Age differences in sensation-seeking and impulsivity as indexed by behavior and self-report: Evidence for a dual systems model. *Developmental Psychology, 44,* 1764–1778.

Steinberg, L., & others. (2009). Age differences in future discounting and delay discounting. *Child Development, 80,* 28–44.

Steinberg, L., Blatt-Eisengart, I., & Cauffman, E. (2006). Patterns of competence and adjustment among adolescents from authoritative, authoritarian, indulgent, and neglectful homes: A replication in a sample of serious juvenile offenders. *Journal of Research on Adolescence, 16,* 47–58.

Steinberg, L. D. (2011). Adolescent risk-taking: A social neuroscience perspective. In E. Amsel & J. Smetana (Eds.), *Adolescent vulnerabilities and opportunities: Constructivist developmental perspectives.* New York: Cambridge University Press.

Steiner, J. E. (1979). Human facial expression in response to taste and smell stimulation. In H. Reese & L. Lipsitt (Eds.), *Advances in child development and behavior* (Vol. 13). New York: Academic Press.

Steinhausen, H. C., Blattmann, B., & Pfund, F. (2007). Developmental outcome in children with intrauterine exposure to substances. *European Addiction Research, 13,* 94–100.

Steming, C. (2008). Centering Pregnancy: Group prenatal care. *Creative Nursing, 14,* 182–183.

Stephens, J. M. (2008). Cheating. In N. J. Salkind (Ed.), *Encyclopedia of educational psychology.* Thousand Oaks, CA: Sage.

Stern, D. N., Beebe, B., Jaffe, J., & Bennett, S. L. (1977). Infants' stimulus world during social interaction: A study of caregiver behaviors with particular reference to repetition and timing. In H. R. Schaffer (Ed.), *Studies in mother-infant interaction.* London: Academic Press.

Stern, W. (1912). The psychological methods of testing intelligence. *Educational Psychology Monographs* (No. 13).

Sternberg, K., & Sternberg, R. J. (2010). Love. In H. Pashler (Ed.), *Encyclopedia of the mind.* Thousand Oaks, CA: Sage.

Sternberg, R. J. (1986). *Intelligence applied.* San Diego: Harcourt Brace Jovanovich.

Sternberg, R. J. (1988). *The triangle of love.* New York: Basic Books.

Sternberg, R. J. (2003). Contemporary theories of intelligence. In I. B. Weiner (Ed.), *Handbook of psychology* (Vol. 7). New York: Wiley.

Sternberg, R. J. (2004). Individual differences in cognitive development. In U. Goswami (Ed.), *Blackwell handbook of childhood cognitive development.* Malden, MA: Blackwell.

Sternberg, R. J. (2010). The triarchic theory of successful intelligence. In B. Kerr (Ed.), *Encyclopedia of giftedness, creativity, and talent.* Thousand Oaks, CA: Sage.

Sternberg, R. J. (2011a, in press). Individual differences in cognitive development. In U. Goswami (Ed.), *Blackwell handbook of childhood cognitive development.* Malden, MA: Blackwell.

Sternberg, R. J. (2011b, in press). Intelligence. In B. McGaw, P. Peterson, & E. Baker (Eds.), *International encyclopedia of education* (3rd ed.). New York: Elsevier.

Sternberg, R. J. (2011c, in press). Intelligence in cultural context. In M. Gelfand, C-Y. Chiu, & Y-Y. Hong (Eds.), *Advances in cultures and psychology* (Vol. 2). New York: Oxford University Press.

Sternberg, R. J. (2011d). Componential models of creativity. In M. Runco & S. Pritzker (Eds.), *Encyclopedia of creativity* (2nd ed.). New York: Elsevier.

Sternberg, R. J., & Grigorenko, E. L. (2008). Ability testing across cultures. In L. A. Suzuki & J. G. Ponterotto (Eds.), *Handbook of multicultural assessment* (3rd ed.). San Francisco: Jossey-Bass.

Sternberg, R. J., Jarvin, L., & Grigorenko, E. L. (2011). *Explorations of the nature of giftedness.* New York: Cambridge University Press.

Sternberg, R. J., & Kaufman, J. C. (2010). Intelligence (as related to creativity). In M. Runco & S. Pritzker (Ed.), *Encyclopedia of creativity* (2nd ed.). New York: Elsevier.

Sternberg, R. J., Kaufman, J. C., & Grigorenko, E. L. (2008). *Applied intelligence.* New York: Cambridge University Press.

Sternberg, R. J., & Williams, W. M. (1996). *How to develop student creativity.* Alexandria, VA: ASCD.

Sternberg, R. J., & others. (2001). The relationship between academic and practical intelligence: A case study in Kenya. *Intelligence, 29,* 401–418.

Sterns, H. L., Barrett, G. V., & Alexander, R. A. (1985). Accidents and the aging individual. In J. E. Birren & K. W. Schaie (Eds.), *Handbook of the psychology of aging.* New York: Van Nostrand Reinhold.

Sterns, H. L., & Huyck, H. (2001). The role of work in midlife. In M. E. Lachman (Ed.), *Handbook of midlife development.* New York: John Wiley.

Stevenson, H. W. (1995). Mathematics achievement of American students: First in the word by the year 2000? In C. A. Nelson (Ed.), *Basic and applied perspectives on learning, cognition, and development.* Minneapolis: University of Minnesota Press.

Stevenson, H. W. (2000). Middle childhood: Education and schooling. In A. Kazdin (Ed.), *Encyclopedia of psychology.* Washington, DC, & New York: American Psychological Association and Oxford University Press.

Stevenson, H. W., & Zusho, A. (2002). Adolescence in China and Japan: Adapting to a changing environment. In B. B. Brown, R. W. Larson, & T. S. Saraswathi (Eds.), *The world's youth.* New York: Cambridge University Press.

Stevenson, H. W., Hofer, B. K., & Randel, B. (1999). *Middle childhood: Education and schooling.* Unpublished manuscript, Department of Psychology, University of Michigan, Ann Arbor.

Stevenson, H. W., Lee, S., Chen, C., Stigler, J. W., Hsu, C., & Kitamura, S. (1990). Contexts of achievement. *Monograph of the Society for Research in Child Development, 55* (Serial No. 221).

Stevenson, H. W., Lee, S., & Stigler, J. W. (1986). Mathematics achievement of Chinese, Japanese, and American children. *Science, 231,* 693–699.

Stewart, A. J., Ostrove, J. M., & Helson, R. (2001). Middle aging in women: Patterns of personality change from the 30s to the 50s. *Journal of Adult Development, 8,* 23–37.

Stice, F., Presnell, K., & Spangler, D. (2002). Risk factors for binge eating onset in adolescent girls: A 2-year prospective investigation. *Health Psychology, 21,* 131–138.

Stiggins, R. (2008). *Introduction to student-involved assessment for learning* (5th ed.). Upper Saddle River, NJ: Prentice Hall.

Stine-Morrow, E. A. L., & Basak, C. (2011). Cognitive interventions. In K. W. Schaie & S. L. Willis (Eds.), *Handbook of the psychology of aging* (7th ed.). New York: Elsevier.

Stine-Morrow, E. A. L., Miller, L. M., & Hertzog, C. (2006). Aging and self-regulated language processing. *Psychological Bulletin, 132,* 582–606.

Stine-Morrow, E. A. L., Parisi, J. M., Morrow, D. G., Greene, J., & Park, D. C. (2007). An engagement model of cognitive optimization through adulthood. *Journals of Gerontology B: Psychological Sciences and Social Science, 62,* P62–P69.

Stipek, D. J. (2002). *Motivation to learn* (4th ed.). Boston: Allyn & Bacon.

Stipek, D. J. (2005, February 16). Commentary in *USA Today,* p. ID.

Stirling, E. (2011). *Valuing older people.* New York: Wiley.

Stocker, C., & Dunn, J. (1990). Sibling relationships in childhood: Links with friendships and peer relationships. *British Journal of Developmental Psychology, 8,* 227–244.

Stoel-Gammon, C., & Sosa, A. V. (2010). Phonological development. In E. Hoff & M. Shatz (Eds.), *Blackwell handbook of language development* (2nd ed.). New York: Wiley.

Stokes, C. E., & Raley, R. K. (2009). Cohabitation. In D. Carr (Ed.), *Encyclopedia of the life course and human development.* Boston: Gale Cengage.

Stoll, C., Dott, B., Alembik, Y., & Roth, M. P. (2011, in press). Associated malformations among infants with neural tube defects. *American Journal of Medical Genetics A.*

Stolzer, J. M. (2009). Attention deficit/hyperactivity disorder. In D. Carr (Ed.), *Encyclopedia of the life course and human development.* Boston: Gale Cengage.

Stonach, E. P., & others. (2011, in press). Child maltreatment, attachment security, and internal representations of mother and mother-child relationships. *Child Maltreatment.*

Stone, A. A., Schwartz, J. E., Broderick, J. E., & Deaton, A. (2010). A snapshot of the age distribution of psychological well-being in the United States. *Proceedings of the National Academy of Sciences U.S.A., 107,* 9985–9990.

Stoppa, T. M., & Lefkowitz, E. S. (2010). Longitudinal changes in religiosity among emerging adult college students. *Journal of Research on Adolescence, 20,* 23–38.

Stouthamer-Loeber, M., Loeber, R., Wei, E., Farrington, D. P., & Wikstrom, P. H. (2002). Risk and promotive effects in the explanation of persistent serious delinquency in boys. *Journal of Consulting and Clinical Psychology, 70,* 111–123.

Stouthamer-Loeber, M., Wei, E., Loeber, R., & Masten, A. (2004). Desistance from serious delinquency in the transition to adulthood. *Development and Psychopathology, 16,* 897–918.

Strasburger, V. (2010). Children, adolescents, and the media: Seven key issues. *Pediatric Annals, 39,* 556–564.

Strathearn, L. (2007). Exploring the neurobiology of attachment. In L. C. Mayes, P. Fonagy, & M. Target (Eds.), *Developmental science and psychoanalysis.* London: Karnac Press.

Stray, L. L., Ellertsen, B., & Stray, T. (2010). Motor function and methylphenidate effect in children with attention deficit hyperactivity disorder. *Acta Pediatrica, 99*(8), 1199–1204.

Streib, H. (1999). Off-road religion? A narrative approach to fundamentalist and occult orientations of adolescents. *Journal of Adolescence, 22,* 255–267.

Stright, A. D., Herr, M. Y., & Neitzel, C. (2009). Maternal scaffolding of children's problem solving and children's adjustment in kindergarten: Hmong families in the United States. *Journal of Educational Psychology, 101,* 207–218.

Stroebe, M., Schut, H., & Boerner, K. (2010). Continuing bonds in adaptation to bereavement: Toward theoretical integration. *Clinical Psychology Review, 30,* 259–268.

Stroebe, M., Schut, H., & Stroebe, W. (2005). Attachment in coping with bereavement: A theoretical integration. *Review of General Psychology, 9,* 48–66.

Stroobant, N., Buijs, D., & Vingerhoets, G. (2009). Variation in brain lateralization during various language tasks: A functional transcranial Doppler study. *Behavioral Brain Research, 199,* 190–196.

Strough, J., Leszczynski, J. P., Neely, T. L., Flinn, J. A., & Margrett, J. (2007). From adolescence to later adulthood: Femininity, masculinity and androgyny in six age groups. *Sex Roles, 57,* 385–396.

Studd, J. (2010). Ten reasons to be happy about hormone replacement therapy: A guide for patients. *Menopause, 16,* 44–46.

Studenski, S., Carlson, M. C., Fillet, H., Greenough, W. T., Kramer, A. F., & Rebok, G. W. (2006). From bedside to bench: Does mental and physical activity promote cognitive vitality in late life? *Science of Aging, Knowledge, and Environment, 10,* e21.

Stuebe, A. (2009). The risk of not breastfeeding for mothers and infant. *Reviews in Obstetrics and Gynecology, 2,* 222–231.

Stuebe, A. M., & Schwarz, E. G. (2010). The risks and benefits of infant feeding practices for women and their children. *Journal of Perinatology, 30,* 155–162.

Stukenborg, J. B., Colon, E., & Soder, O. (2010). Ontogenesis of testis development and function in humans. *Sexual Development, 4,* 199–212.

Sturm, R. (2005). Childhood obesity—what we can learn from existing data and social trends. *Prevention of Chronic Diseases, 2,* A12.

Substance Abuse and Mental Health Services Administration. (2005). Substance use tables [online database]. Retrieved November 15, 2005, from http://www.icpsr.umich.edu/

Sugimoto, M., Kuze, M., & Uji, Y. (2008). Ultrasound biomicroscopy for membranous congenital cataract. *Canadian Journal of Ophthalmology, 43,* 7–8.

Sugita, Y. (2004). Experience in early infancy is indispensable for color perception. *Current Biology, 14,* 1267–1271.

Sullivan, C. J., Childs, K. K., & O'Connell, D. (2010). Adolescent risk behavior subgroups: An empirical assessment. *Journal of Youth and Adolescence, 39,* 541–562.

Sullivan, H. S. (1953). *The interpersonal theory of psychiatry.* New York: W. W. Norton.

Sullivan, K., & Sullivan, A. (1980). Adolescent-parent separation. *Developmental Psychology, 16,* 93–99.

Sumaroka, M., & Bornstein, M. H. (2008). Play. In M. M. Haith & J. B. Benson (Eds.), *Encyclopedia of infant and early childhood development.* Oxford, UK: Elsevier.

Sund, A. M., Larsson, B., & Wichstrom, L. (2010, in press). Role of physical and sedentary activities in the development of depressive symptoms in early adolescence. *Social Psychiatry and Psychiatric Epidemiology.*

Sung, S. C., & others. (2011, in press). Complicated grief among individuals with major depression: Prevalence, comorbidity, and associated features. *Journal of Affective Disorders.*

Super, C. M., & Harkness, S. (2011). Culture and infancy. In J. G. Bremner & T. D. Wachs (Eds.), *Wiley-Blackwell handbook of infant development* (2nd ed.). New York: Wiley.

Susman, E. J., & Dorn, L. D. (2009). Puberty: Its role in development. In R. M. Lerner & L. Steinberg (Eds.), *Handbook of adolescent psychology* (3rd ed.). New York: Wiley.

Susman, E. J., & others. (2010). Longitudinal development of secondary sexual characteristics in girls and boys between 9½ and 15½ years. *Archives of Pediatric and Adolescent Medicine, 164,* 166–173.

Sveistrup, H., Schneiberg, S., McKinley, P. A., McGadyen, B. J., & Levin, M. F. (2008). Head, arm and trunk coordination during reaching in children. *Experimental Brain Research, 188,* 237–247.

Sviri, S., & others. (2009). Contraindications in end-of-life decisions for self and others, expressed by relatives of chronically ventilated persons. *Journal of Critical Care, 24,* 293–301.

Swaab, D. F., Chung, W. C., Kruijver, F. P., Hofman, M. A., & Ishunina, T. A. (2001). Structural and functional sex differences in the human hypothalamus. *Hormones and Behavior, 40,* 93–98.

Swahn, M. H., & others. (2011, in press). Early substance use initiation and suicide ideation and attempts among students in France and the United States. *International Journal of Public Health.*

Swain, S. O. (1992). Men's friendships with women. In P. M. Nardi (Ed.), *Gender in intimate relationships.* Belmont, CA: Wadsworth.

Swamy, G. K., Ostbye, T., & Skjaerven, R. (2008). Association of preterm birth with long-term survival, reproduction, and next generation preterm birth. *Journal of the American Medical Association, 299,* 1429–1436.

Swanson, D. P. (2010). Adolescent psychosocial processes: Identity, stress, and competence. In D. P. Swanson, M. C. Edwards, & M. B. Spencer (Eds.), *Adolescence: Development in a global era.* San Diego: Academic Press.

Swartz, T. T., Kim, M., Uno, M. Mortimer, J., & O'Brien, K. B. (2011). Safety nets and scaffolds: Parental support in the transition to adulthood. *Journal of Marriage and the Family, 73,* 414–429.

Sweeney, M. M. (2009). Remarriage. In D. Carr (Ed.), *Encyclopedia of the life course and human development.* Boston: Gale Cengage.

Sweeney, M. M. (2010). Remarriage and stepfamilies: Strategic sites for family scholarship in the 21st century. *Journal of Marriage and the Family, 72*(3), 667–684.

Swing, E. L., Gentile, D. A., Anderson, C. A., & Walsh, D. A. (2010). Television and video game exposure and the development of attention problems. *Pediatrics, 126,* 214–221.

Syed, M. (2010). Memorable everyday events in college: Narratives of the intersection of college and academia. *Journal of Diversity in Higher Education, 3,* 56–59.

Syed, M. (2011, in press). Developing an integrated self: Academic and ethnic identities among ethnically-diverse college students. *Developmental Psychology.*

Syed, M., & Azmitia, M. (2010). Narrative and ethnic identity exploration: A longitudinal account of emerging adults' ethnicity-related experiences. *Developmental Psychology, 46,* 208–219.

Sykes, C. J. (1995). *Dumbing down our kids: Why America's children feel good about themselves but can't read, write, or add.* New York: St. Martin's Press.

Szinovacz, M. E. (2009). Grandparenthood. In D. Carr (Ed.), *Encyclopedia of the life course and human development.* Boston: Gale Cengage.

Szwedo, D. E., Mikami, A. Y., & Allen, J. P. (2011, in press). Qualities of peer relations on social networking websites: Predictions from negative mother-teen interactions. *Journal of Research on Adolescence.*

T

Taddio, A. (2008). Circumcision. In M. M. Haith & J. B. Benson (Eds.), *Encyclopedia of infant and early childhood development.* Oxford, UK: Elsevier.

Tager-Flusberg, H., & Zukowski, A. (2009). Putting words together: Morphology and syntax in the preschool years. In J. Berko Gleason & N. Ratner (Eds.), *The development of language* (7th ed.). Boston: Allyn & Bacon.

Tahir, L., & Gruber, H. E. (2003). Developmental trajectories and creative work in late life. In. J. Demick & C. Andreoletti (Eds.), *Handbook of adult development*. New York: Kluwer.

Taige, N. M., & others. (2007). Antenatal maternal stress and long-term effects on child neurodevelopment: How and why? *Journal of Child Psychology and Psychiatry, 48,* 245–261.

Takeuchi, H., & others. (2011, in press). Regional gray matter density associated with emotional intelligence: Evidence from voxel-based morphometry. *Human Brain Mapping.*

Talbot, J., Baker, J. K., & McHale, J. P. (2009). Sharing the love: Prebirth adult attachment status and coparenting adjustment during infancy. The transition to parenthood. *Parenting: Science & Practice, 9,* 56–77.

Taler, S. J. (2009). Hypertensions in women. *Current Hypertensions Reports, 11,* 23–28.

Tamis-LeMonda, C. S., & McFadden, K. E. (2010). The United States of America. In M. H. Bornstein (Ed.), *Handbook of cultural developmental science*. New York: Psychology Press.

Tamis-LeMonda, C. S., Way, N., Hughes, D., Yoshikawa, H., Kallman, R. K., & Niwa, E. Y. (2008). Parents' goals for children: The dynamic coexistence of individualism and collectivism in cultures and individuals. *Social Development, 17,* 183–209.

Tang, F., Choi, E., & Morrow-Howell, N. (2010). Organizational support and volunteering benefits older adults. *Gerontologist, 50,* 603–612.

Tang, Y., & Posner, M. I. (2009). Attention training and attention state training. *Trends in Cognitive Science, 13,* 222–227.

Tannen, D. (1990). *You just don't understand: Women and men in conversation.* New York: Ballantine.

Tashiro, T., & Frazier, P. (2003). "I'll never be in a relationship like that again": Personal growth following romantic relationship breakups. *Personal Relationships, 10,* 113–128.

Tashiro, T., Frazier, P., & Berman, M. (2006). Stress-related growth following divorce and relationship dissolution. In M. A. Fine & J. H. Harvey (Eds.), *Handbook of divorce and relationship dissolution*. Mahwah, NJ: Erlbaum.

Tauman, R., & Gozal, D. (2006). Obesity and obstructive sleep apnea in children. *Pediatric Respiratory Reviews, 7,* 247–259.

Taupin, P. (2011). Neurogenic drugs and compounds. *Recent Patents on CNS Drug Discovery, 11*(1), 35–37.

Tavris, C., & Wade, C. (1984). *The longest war: Sex differences in perspective* (2nd ed.). San Diego: Harcourt Brace Jovanovich.

Taylor, R. J., Chatters, L. M., & Jackson, J. S. (2007). Religious and spiritual involvement among older African Americans, Caribbean Blacks, and non-Hispanic Whites: Findings from the National Survey of American life. *Journals of Gerontology B: Psychological Sciences and Social Sciences, 62,* S238–S250.

Teichert, M., & others. (2010). Isotretinoin and compliance with the Dutch pregnancy prevention program: A retrospective cohort study in females of reproductive age using pharmacy dispensing data. *Drug Safety, 33,* 315–326.

Temple, C., Nathan, R., Temple, F., & Burris, N. A. (1993). *The beginnings of writing* (3rd ed.). Boston: Allyn & Bacon.

Templeton, J. L., & Eccles, J. S. (2006). The relation between spiritual development and identity processes. In E. Roehlkepartain, P. E. King, L. Wagener, & P. L. Benson (Eds.), *The handbook of spirituality in childhood and adolescence*. Thousand Oaks, CA: Sage.

Terman, L. (1925). *Genetic studies of genius. Vol. 1: Mental and physical traits of a thousand gifted children.* Stanford, CA: Stanford University Press.

Terry, D. F., Nolan, V. G., Andersen, S. L., Perls, T. T., & Cawthon, R. (2008). Association of longer telomeres with better health in centenarians. *Journals of Gerontology A: Biological Sciences and Medical Sciences, 63,* 809–812.

Terry, D. F., Sebastian, P., Andersen, P. S., & Perls, T. T. (2008). Disentangling the roles of disability and morbidity in survival to exceptional old age. *Archives of Internal Medicine, 168,* 277–283.

Teti, D. (2001). Retrospect and prospect in the psychological study of sibling relationships. In J. P. McHale & W. S. Grolnick (Eds.), *Retrospect and prospect in the psychological study of families.* Mahwah, NJ: Erlbaum.

Teti, D. M., Kim, B. R., Mayer G., & Countermine, M. (2010). Maternal emotional availability at bedtime predicts infant sleep quality. *Journal of Family Psychology, 24,* 307–315.

Thabet, A. A., Ibraheem, A. N., Shivram, R., Winter, E. A., & Vostanis, P. (2009). Parenting support and PTSD in children of a war zone. *International Journal of Social Psychiatry, 55,* 225–227.

Tharp, R. G. (1994). Intergroup differences among Native Americans in socialization and child cognition: An erythrogenetic analysis. In P. M. Greenfield & R. Cocking (Eds.), *Cross-cultural roots of minority child development*. Mahwah, NJ: Erlbaum.

The, N. S., & others. (2010). Association of adolescent obesity with risk of severe obesity in adulthood. *Journal of the American Psychological Association, 304,* 2042–2047.

Thelen, E. (2000). Perception and motor development. In A. Kazdin (Ed.), *Encyclopedia of psychology*. Washington, DC, & New York: American Psychological Association and Oxford University Press.

Thelen, E., Corbetta, D., Kamm, K., Spencer, J. P., Schneider, K., & Zernicke, R. F. (1993). The transition to reaching: Mapping intention and intrinsic dynamics. *Child Development, 64,* 1058–1098.

Thelen, E., & Smith, L. B. (1998). Dynamic systems theory. In W. Damon (Ed.), *Handbook of child psychology* (5th ed., Vol. 1). New York: Wiley.

Thelen, E., & Smith, L. B. (2006). Dynamic development of action and thought. In W. Damon & R. Lerner (Eds.), *Handbook of child psychology* (6th ed.). New York: Wiley.

Theokas, C. (2009). Youth sports participation—A view of the issues: Introduction to the special section. *Developmental Psychology, 45,* 303–306.

Therrell, B. L., & others. (2010). Newborn Screening System Performance Evaluation Assessment (PEAS). *Seminars in Perinatology, 34,* 105–120.

Thio, A. (2010). *Deviant behavior* (10th ed.). Boston: Allyn & Bacon.

Thomas, A., & Chess, S. (1991). Temperament in adolescence and its functional significance. In R. M. Lerner, A. C. Petersen, & J. Brooks-Gunn (Eds.), *Encyclopedia of adolescence* (Vol. 2). New York: Garland.

Thomas, M. S. C., & Johnson, M. H. (2008). New advances in understanding sensitive periods in brain development. *Current Directions in Psychological Science, 17,* 1–5.

Thompson, D. R., & others. (2007). Childhood overweight and cardiovascular disease risk factors: The National Health, Lung, and Blood Institute Growth and Health Study. *Journal of Pediatrics, 150,* 18–25.

Thompson, J., Monroe, M., & Vaughn, L. (2011). *Science of nutrition* (2nd ed.). Upper Saddle River, NJ: Pearson.

Thompson, M., Kuruwita, C., & Foster, E. M. (2009). Transitions in suicide risk in a nationally representative sample of adolescents. *Journal of Adolescent Health, 44,* 458–463.

Thompson, M. P., & Light, L. S. (2011, in press). Examining gender differences in risk factors in suicide attempts made 1 and 7 years later in a nationally representative sample. *Journal of Adolescent Health.*

Thompson, R., & Murachver, T. (2001). Predicting gender from electronic discourse. *British Journal of Social Psychology, 40,* 193–201.

Thompson, R. A. (2006). The development of the person. In W. Damon & R. Lerner (Eds.), *Handbook of child psychology* (6th ed.). New York: Wiley.

Thompson, R. A. (2008). Unpublished review of J. W. Santrock's *Life-span development,* 12th ed. (New York: McGraw-Hill).

Thompson, R. A. (2009a). Early foundations: Conscience and the development of moral character. In D. Narváez & D. Lapsley (Eds.), *Moral self, identity and character: Prospects for a new field of study.* New York: Cambridge University Press.

Thompson, R. A. (2009b). Emotional development. In R. A. Schweder (Ed.), *The Chicago companion to the child.* Chicago: University of Chicago Press.

Thompson, R. A. (2009c). Unpublished review of J. W. Santrock's *Life-span development,* 13th ed. (New York: McGraw-Hill).

Thompson, R. A. (2010). Feeling and understanding through the prism of relationships. In S. D. Calkins & M. A. Bell (Eds.), *Child development at the intersection of emotion and cognition.* Washington, DC: American Psychological Association.

Thompson, R. A. (2011a). Attachment and development: Precis and prospect. In P. Zelazo (Ed.), *Oxford handbook of developmental psychology*. New York: Oxford University Press.

Thompson, R. A. (2011b). The emotionate child. In D. Cicchetti & G. I. Roissman (Eds.), *The origins and organization of adaptation and maladaptation*. *Minnesota Symposium on Child Psychology* (Vol. 36). New York: Wiley.

Thompson, R. A. (2011c). Emotion and emotion regulation: Two sides of the developing coin. *Emotion Review, 3*, 53–61.

Thompson, R. A., & Goodman, M. (2010). Development of emotion regulation: More than meets the eye. In A. Kring & D. Sloan (Eds.), *Emotion regulation and psychopathology* (pp. 38–58). New York: Guilford.

Thompson, R. A., & Goodman, M. (2011). The architecture of social developmental science: Theoretical and historical perspectives. In M. K. Underwood & L. H. Rosen (Eds.), *Social development*. New York: Guilford.

Thompson, R. A., & Goodvin, R. (2007). Taming the tempest in the teapot: Emotion regulation in toddlers. In C. A. Brownell & C. B. Kopp (Eds.), *Socioemotional development in toddlers*. New York: Guilford.

Thompson, R. A., McGinley, M., & Meyer, S. (2006). Understanding values in relationships. In M. Killen & J. G. Smetana (Eds.), *Handbook of moral development*. Mahwah, NJ: Erlbaum.

Thompson, R. A., Meyer, S., Virmani, E., Waters, S., Raikes, H. A., & Jochem, R. (2009, April). *Parent-child relationships, conversation, and developing emotion regulation*. Paper presented at the meeting of the Society for Research in Child Development, Denver.

Thompson, R. A., & Nelson, C. A. (2001). Developmental science and the media: *American Psychologist, 56*, 5–15.

Thompson, R. A., & Newton, E. K. (2011). Emotion in early conscience. In W. Arsenio & E. Lemerise (Eds.), *Emotions, aggression, and morality: Bridging development and psychopathology*. Washington, DC: American Psychological Association.

Thompson, R. A., & Waters, S. F. (2011). The development of emotion regulation: Parent and peer influences. In R. Sanchez-Aragon (Ed.), *Emotion regulation*. Mexico: Miguel Angel Porrua.

Thompson, R. A., Winer, A. C., & Goodvin, R. (2011). The individual child: Temperament, emotion, self, and personality. In M. Bornstein & M. E. Lamb (Eds.), *Developmental science: An advanced textbook* (6th ed.). New York: Psychology Press / Taylor & Francis.

Thornton, R., & Light, L. L. (2006). Language comprehension and production in normal aging. In J. E. Birren & K. W. Schaie (Eds.), *Handbook of the psychology of aging* (6th ed.). San Diego: Academic Press.

Thornton, W. J. L., & Dumke, H. A. (2005). Age differences in everyday problem-solving and decision-making effectiveness: A meta-analytic review. *Psychology and Aging, 20*, 85–99.

Thorton, A., & Camburn, D. (1989). Religious participation and sexual behavior and attitudes. *Journal of Marriage and the Family, 49*, 117–128.

Tikotzky, L., Sadeh, A., & Glickman-Gavrieli, T. (2010). Infant sleep and paternal involvement in infant caregiving during the first 6 months of life. *Journal of Pediatric Psychology, 36*(1), 36–46.

TIMMS. (2008). *Trends in international mathematics and science study, 2007*. Washington, DC: National Center for Education Statistics.

Tobler, A. L., & Komro, K. A. (2010). Trajectories of parental monitoring and communication and effects on drug use among urban young adolescents. *Journal of Adolescent Health, 6*(5), 560–568.

Toh, S., Hernandez-Diaz, S., Logan, R., Rossuw, J. E., & Hernan, M. A. (2010). Coronary heart disease in postmenopausal recipients of estrogen plus progestin therapy: Does the increased risk ever disappear? A randomized trial. *Annals of Internal Medicine, 152*, 211–217.

Tolani, N., & Brooks-Gunn, J. (2008). Family support, international trends. In M. M. Haith & J. B. Benson (Eds.), *Encyclopedia of infant and early childhood development*. Oxford, UK: Elsevier.

Toledo-Pereyra, L. H. (2010). Good life good death according to Christian Barnard. *Journal of Investigative Surgery, 23*, 125–128.

Tolman, D. L., & McClelland, S. I. (2011). Normative sexuality development in adolescence: A decade in review, 2000–2009. *Journal of Research on Adolescence, 21*, 242–255.

Tomasello, M. (2011a). *Human culture in evolutionary perspective*. New York: Oxford University Press.

Tomasello, M. (2011b). Language development. In U. Goswami (Ed.), *Wiley-Blackwell handbook of childhood cognitive development* (2nd ed.). New York: Wiley.

Tomiyama, H., & others. (2010). Continuous smoking and progression of arterial stiffening: A prospective study. *Journal of the American College of Cardiology, 55*, 1979–1987.

Tompkins, G. E. (2011). *Literacy in the early grades* (3rd ed.). Boston: Allyn & Bacon.

Tompkins, S. A., & Bell, P. A. (2009). Examination of a psychoeducational intervention and a respite grant in relieving psychosocial stressors associated with being an Alzheimer's caregiver. *Journal of Gerontological Social Work, 52*, 89–104.

Tonnesen, J., & others. (2011). Functional integration of grafted neural stem cell–derived dopaminergic neurons monitored by optogenetics in an in vitro Parkinson model. *PLoS One, 6*, e17560.

Torbic, H. (2011). Children and grief: But what about the children?: A guide for home care and hospice clinicians. *Home Healthcare Nurse, 29*, 67–77.

Touati, S., & others. (2010). Exercise reverses metabolic syndrome in high fat diet–induced obese rats. *Medicine and Science in Sports and Exercise, 43*(3), 398–407.

Townsend-Roccichelli, J., Sanford, J. T., & VandeWaa, E. (2010). Managing sleep disorders in the elderly. *Nurse Practitioner, 35*, 30–37.

Towse, J. N., Hitch, G. J., Horton, N., & Harvey, K. (2010). Synergies between processing and memory in children's reading span. *Developmental Science, 13*, 779–789.

Trafimow, D., Triandis, H. C., & Goto, S. G. (1991). Some tests of the distinction between the prime and collective self. *Journal of Personality and Social Psychology, 60*, 649–655.

Trehub, S. E., Schneider, B. A., Thorpe, L. A., & Judge, P. (1991). Observational measure of auditory sensitivity in early infancy. *Developmental Psychology, 27*, 40–49.

Triandis, H. C. (1994). *Culture and social behavior*. New York: McGraw-Hill.

Triandis, H. C. (2001). Individualism and collectivism. In D. Matsumoto (Eds.), *The handbook of culture and psychology*. New York: Oxford University Press.

Triandis, H. C. (2007). Culture and psychology: A history of their relationship. In S. Kitayama & D. Cohen (Eds.), *Handbook of cultural psychology*. New York: Guilford.

Trickett, P. K., & Negriff, S. (2011). Child maltreatment and social relationships. In M. H. Underwood & L. H. Rosen (Eds.), *Social development*. New York: Guilford.

Trimble, J. E. (1988, August). *The enculturation of contemporary psychology*. Paper presented at the meeting of the American Psychological Association, New Orleans.

Triulzi, F., Manganaro, L., & Volpe, P. (2011, in press). Fetal magnetic resonance imaging: Indications, study protocols, and safety. *La Radiologia Medica*.

Troiano, A. R., & others. (2010). Dopamine transporter PET in normal aging: Dopamine transporter decline and its possible role in preservation of motor function. *Synapse, 64*, 146–151.

Truog, R. D. (2008). End-of-life decision-making in the United States. *European Journal of Anesthesiology, 42*(Suppl. 1), S43–S50.

Trzesniewski, K. H., Donnellan, M. B., Moffitt, T. E., Robins, R. W., Poulton, R., & Caspi, A. (2006). Low self-esteem during adolescence predicts poor health, criminal behavior, and limited economic prospects during adulthood. *Developmental Psychology, 42*, 381–390.

Tschann, J. M., Flores, E., de Groat, C. L., Deardorff, J., & Wibbelsman, C. J. (2010). Condom negotiation strategies and actual condom use among Latino youth. *Journal of Adolescent Health, 47*, 254–262.

Tucker, C. J., McHale, S. M., & Crouter, A. C. (2003). Conflict resolution: Links with adolescents' family relationships and individual well-being. *Journal of Family Issues, 24*, 715–726.

Tucker, J. S., Ellickson, P. L., & Klein, M. S. (2003). Predictors of the transition to regular smoking during adolescence and young adulthood. *Journal of Adolescent Health, 32,* 314–324.

Tun, P. A., & Lachman, M. E. (2010). The association between computer use and cognition across adulthood: Use it so you won't lose it? *Psychology and Aging, 25*(3), 560–568.

Turner, B. F. (1982). Sex-related differences in aging. In B. B. Wolman (Ed.), *Handbook of developmental psychology*. Englewood Cliffs, NJ: Prentice Hall.

Turrigiano, G. (2010). Synaptic homeostasis. *Annual Review of Neuroscience* (Vol. 33). Palo Alto, CA: Annual Reviews.

Tyas, S. L., & others. (2007). Transitions to mild cognitive impairments, dementia, and death: Findings from the Nun Study. *American Journal of Epidemiology, 165,* 1231–1238.

U

Udry, J. R., & others. (1985), Serum androgenic hormones motivate sexual behavior in adolescent boys. *Fertility and Sterility, 43,* 90–94.

Ueno, K., & McWilliams, S. (2010). Gender-typed behaviors and school adjustment. *Sex Roles, 63,* 580–591.

Umana-Taylor, A. J. (2009). Research with Latino early adolescents. *Journal of Early Adolescence, 29,* 5–15.

Umana-Taylor, A. J., Updegraff, K. A., & Gonzales-Bracken, M. A. (2010). Mexican-origin adolescent mothers' stressors and psychological functioning: Examining ethnic identity affirmation and families as moderators. *Journal of Youth and Adolescence, 40*(2), 140–157.

UNAIDS. (2009). *What countries need: Investments needed for 2010 targets.* New York: United Nations.

Underhill, K., Montgomery, P., & Operario, D. (2007). Sexual abstinence programs to prevent HIV infection in high-income countries. *British Medical Journal, 335,* 248.

Underwood, M. K. (2011). Aggression. In M. K. Underwood and L. H. Rosen (Eds.), *Social development*. New York: Guilford.

UNICEF. (2006). *The state of the world's children 2006*. Geneva, Switzerland: Author.

UNICEF. (2007). *The state of the world's children 2007*. Geneva, Switzerland: Author.

UNICEF. (2010). *The state of the world's children 2010*. Geneva, Switzerland: Author.

UNICEF. (2011). *The state of the world's children 2011*. Geneva, Switzerland: Author.

Urbina, S. (2011). Tests of intelligence. In R. J. Sternberg & S. B. Kaufman (Eds.), *Cambridge handbook of intelligence*. New York: Cambridge University Press.

U.S. Bureau of Labor Statistics. (2008). *Employment of older workers*. Washington, DC: U.S. Department of Labor.

U.S. Census Bureau. (2006). *Statistical abstracts of the United States*. Washington, DC: U.S. Government Printing Office.

U.S. Census Bureau. (2008a). *Death statistics*. Washington, DC: U.S. Census Bureau.

U.S. Census Bureau. (2008b). *Population statistics*. Washington, DC: U.S. Department of Labor.

U.S. Census Bureau. (2010a). *Deaths*. Washington, DC: U.S. Department of Labor.

U.S. Census Bureau. (2010b). *Facts for features: Older Americans month: May 2010*. Washington, DC: U.S. Census Bureau.

U.S. Census Bureau. (2010c). *Marriage*. Washington, DC: U.S. Department of Labor.

U.S. Census Bureau. (2011). *Death statistics*. Washington, DC: Author.

U.S. Census Bureau. (2011). *The 2011 statistical abstract*. Washington, DC: U.S. Department of Labor.

U.S. Department of Energy. (2001). *The human genome project*. Washington, DC: U.S. Department of Energy.

U.S. Department of Health and Human Services. (2009a). *Child maltreatment 2007*. Washington, DC: Government Printing Office.

U.S. Department of Health and Human Services. (2009b). *CDC folic acid homepage*. Retrieved January 19, 2009, from http://www.cdc.gov/ncbddd/folicacid/

Uusitupa, M., Tuomilehto, J., & Puska, P. (2011, in press). Are we really active in the prevention of obesity and type 2 diabetes at the community level? *Nutrition, Metabolism, and Cardiovascular Disease*.

V

Vahia, I. V., & others. (2011a). Correlates of spirituality in older women. *Aging and Mental Health, 15*(1), 97–102.

Vahia, I. V., & others. (2011b). Psychological protective factors across the lifespan: Implications for psychiatry. *Psychiatric Clinics of North America, 34,* 231–248.

Vaillant, G. E. (1977). *Adaptation to life*. Boston: Little Brown.

Vaillant, G. E. (2002). *Aging well*. Boston: Little Brown.

Valkenburg, P. M., & Peter, J. (2011). Online communication among adolescents: An integrated model of its attraction, opportunities, and risks. *Journal of Adolescent Health, 48,* 121–127.

Van Beveren, T. T. (2011, March). *Personal conversation*. Richardson, TX: Department of Psychology, University of Texas at Dallas.

van den Boom, D. C. (1989). Neonatal irritability and the development of attachment. In G. A. Kohnstamm, J. E. Bates, & M. K. Rothbart (Eds.), *Temperament in childhood*. New York: Wiley.

van den Dries, L., Juffer, F., van IJzendoorn, M. H., & Bakersman-Kranenburg, M. J. (2010). Infants' physical and cognitive development after international adoption from foster care or institutions in China. *Journal of Developmental and Behavioral Pediatrics, 31,* 144–150.

van der Heijden, G. J., & others. (2010). Strength exercise improves muscle mass and hepatic insulin sensitivity in obese youth. *Medicine and Science in Sports and Exercise, 42*(11), 1973–1980.

van der Stel, M., & Veenman, M. V. J. (2010). Development of metacognitive skillfulness: A longitudinal study. *Learning and Individual Differences, 20,* 220–224.

van Ettinger-Veenstra, H. M., & others. (2010). Right-hemispheric brain activation correlates to language performance. *NeuroImage, 49,* 3481–3488.

van Harmelen, A. L., de Jong, P. J., Glashouwer, K. A., Spinhoven, P., Penninx, B. W., & Elzinga, B. M. (2010). Child abuse and negative explicit and automatic self-associations: The cognitive scars of emotional maltreatment. *Behavior Research and Therapy, 48*(6), 486–494.

van Hof, P., van der Kamp, J., & Savelsbergh, G. J. (2008). The relation between infants' perception of catchableness and the control of catching. *Developmental Psychology, 44,* 182–194.

van IJzendoorn, M. H., Kranenburg, M. J., Pannebakker, F., & Out, D. (2010). In defense of situational morality: Genetic, dispositional, and situational determinants of children's donating to charity. *Journal of Moral Education, 39,* 1–20.

van IJzendoorn, M. H., & Kroonenberg, P. M. (1988). Cross-cultural patterns of attachment: A meta-analysis of the Strange Situation. *Child Development, 59,* 147–156.

van IJzendoorn, M. H., & Sagi-Schwartz, A. (2008). Cross-cultural patterns of attachment: Universal and contextual dimensions. In J. Cassidy & P. R. Shaver (Eds.), *Handbook of attachment* (2nd ed.). New York: Guilford.

Van Leijenhorst, L., & others. (2010). Adolescent risky decision-making: Neurocognitive development of reward and control regions. *NeuroImage, 51,* 345–355.

Van Praag, H. (2009). Exercise and the brain: Something to chew on. *Trends in Neuroscience, 32,* 283–290.

Van Ryzin, M. J., Johnson, A. B., Leve, L. D., & Kim, H. K. (2011, in press). The number of sexual partners and health-risking sexual behavior: Prediction from high school entry to high school exit. *Archives of Sexual Behavior*.

Van Solinge, H., & Henkens, K. (2005). Couples' adjustment to retirement: A multi-actor panel study. *Journals of Gerontology B: Psychological Sciences and Social Sciences, 60,* S11–S20.

van Spronsen, F. J., & Enns, G. M. (2010). Future treatment strategies in phenylketonuria. *Molecular Genetics and Metabolism, 99*(Suppl. 1), S90–S95.

Van Voorhees, B. W., & others. (2008). Protective and vulnerability factors predicting new-onset depressive episode in a representative of U.S. adolescents. *Journal of Adolescent Health, 42,* 605–616.

Vandehey, M., Diekhoff, G., & LaBeff, E. (2007). College cheating: A 20-year follow-up and the addition of an honor code. *Journal of College Development, 48,* 468–480.

Vandell, D. L., & others. (2010). Do effects of early childcare extend to age 15 years? From the NICHD Study of Early Child Care and Young Development. *Child Development, 81,* 737–756.

VanRemmen, H. (2011). The oxidative stress theory of aging: Where do we stand? In E. Masoro & S. Austad (Eds.), *Handbook of the biology of aging* (7th ed.). New York: Elsevier.

Vasan, N. (2002). Commentary in "18-year-old inductees." Retrieved April 4, 2009, from http://thekidshalloffame.com/CustomPage19.html

Vasdev, G. (2008). *Obstetric anesthesia.* Oxford, UK: Elsevier.

Vatner, D. (2011). Aging alterations in cardiovascular function. In E. Masoro & S. Austad (Eds.), *Handbook of the biology of aging* (7th ed.). New York: Elsevier.

Vazsonyi, A. T., & Huang, L. (2010). Where self-control comes from: On the development of self-control and its relationship to deviance over time. *Developmental Psychology, 46,* 245–257.

Veenman, M. V. J. (2011). Learning to self-monitor and self-regulate. In P. A. Alexander & R. E. Mayer (Eds.), *Handbook of research on learning and instruction.* New York: Routledge.

Veenstra, A., Lindenberg, S., Munniksma, A., & Dijkstra, J. K. (2010). The complex relationship between bullying, victimization, acceptance, and rejection: Giving special attention to status, affection, and sex differences. *Social Development, 19,* 480–486.

Velez, C. E., Wolchik, S. A., Tein, J. Y., & Sandler, I. (2011). Protecting children from the consequences of divorce: A longitudinal study of the effects of parenting on children's coping responses. *Child Development, 82,* 244–257.

Vellas, B., & Aisen, P. S. (2010). Editorial: Early Alzheimer's trials: New developments. *Journal of Nutrition, Health, and Aging, 14,* 293.

Vemuri, P., & others (2010). Effects of apolipoprotein E on biomarkers of amyloid and neuronal pathology in Alzheimer disease. *Annals of Neurology* (Vol. 67). Palo Alto, CA: Annual Reviews.

Vendelbo, M. H., & Nair, K. S. (2011). Mitochondrial longevity pathways. *Biochemica et Biophysica Acta, 1813,* 634–644.

Venners, S. A., & others. (2004). Paternal smoking and pregnancy loss: A prospective study using a biomarker of pregnancy. *American Journal of Epidemiology, 159,* 993–1001.

Ventura, S. J., Abma, C., Mosher, W. D., & Henshaw, S. K. (2008). Estimated pregnancy rates by outcome for the United States, 1990–2004. *National Vital Statistics Reports, 56,* 1–25, 28.

Vernberg, E. M., & Biggs, B. K. (2010). Empowering schools to prevent bullying: A holistic approach. In E. Vernberg & B. K. Biggs (Eds.), *Preventing and treating bullying and victimization.* New York: Oxford University Press.

Villanueva, C. M., & Buriel, R. (2010). Speaking on behalf of others: A qualitative study of the perceptions and feelings of adolescent Latina language brokers. *Journal of Social Issues, 66,* 197–210.

Villegas, R., & others. (2008). Duration of breast-feeding and the incidence of type 2 diabetes mellitus in the Shanghai Women's Health Study. *Diabetologia, 51,* 258–266.

Vina, J., Borras, C., Garnbini, J., Sastre, J., & Pallardo, F. V. (2005). Why females live longer than males: Control of longevity by hormones. *Science of Aging Knowledge Environment, 23,* e17.

Vincent, H. K., Vincent, K. R., & Lamb, K. M. (2010). Obesity and mobility disability in the older adult. *Obesity Reviews, 11,* 568–579.

Visher, E., & Visher, J. (1989). Parenting coalitions after remarriage: Dynamics and therapeutic guidelines. *Family Relations, 38,* 65–70.

Vitaro, F., Pedersen, S., & Brendgen, M. (2007). Children's disruptiveness, peer rejection, friends' deviancy, and delinquent behaviors: A process-oriented approach. *Development and Psychopathology, 19,* 433–453.

Volbrecht, M. M., & Goldsmith, H. H. (2010). Early temperamental and family predictors of shyness and anxiety. *Developmental Psychology, 46,* 1192–1205.

Von Hofsten, C. (2008). Motor and physical development manual. In M. M. Haith & J. B. Benson (Eds.), *Encyclopedia of infant and early childhood development.* Oxford, UK: Elsevier.

Vondracek, S. F. (2010). Managing osteoporosis in postmenopausal women. *American Journal of Health-System Pharmacy, 67*(7) (Suppl. 3), S9–S19.

Voorpostel, M., & Blieszner, R. (2008). Intergenerational solidarity and support between adult siblings. *Journal of Marriage and the Family, 70,* 157–167.

Vos, J., & others. (2011, in press). Family communication matters: The impact of telling relatives about unclassified variants and uninformative DNA-test results. *Genetics in Medicine.*

Vreeman, R. C., & Carroll, A. E. (2007). A systematic review of school-based interventions to prevent bullying. *Archives of Pediatric and Adolescent Medicine, 161,* 78–88.

Vrklijan, B. H., & others. (2010). Supporting safe driving with arthritis: Developing a driving toolkit for clinical practice and consumer use. *American Journal of Occupational Therapy, 64,* 259–267.

Vurpillot, E. (1968). The development of scanning strategies and their relation to visual differentiation. *Journal of Experimental Child Psychology, 6,* 632–650.

Vygotsky, L. S. (1962). *Thought and language.* Cambridge, MA: MIT Press.

W

Waber, D. P. (2010). *Rethinking learning disabilities.* New York: Guilford.

Wachs, T. D. (2000). *Necessary but not sufficient.* Washington, DC: American Psychological Association.

Wachs, T. D., & Bates, J. E. (2011). Temperament. In J. G. Bremner & T. D. Wachs (Eds.), *Wiley-Blackwell handbook of infant development* (2nd ed.). New York: Wiley.

Wagner, D. A. (2010). Literacy. In M. H. Bornstein (Ed.), *Handbook of cultural developmental science.* New York: Psychology Press.

Wagner, R. K., & Sternberg, R. J. (1986). Tacit knowledge and intelligent functioning in the everyday world. In R. J. Sternberg & R. K. Wagner (Eds.), *Practical intelligence.* New York: Cambridge University Press.

Wahlstrom, K. (2010). School start time and sleepy teens. *Archives of Pediatric and Adolescent Medicine, 164,* 676–677.

Waite, L. (2005, June). *The case for marriage.* Paper presented at the 9th annual Smart Marriages conference, Dallas.

Waite, L. J. (2009). Marriage. In D. Carr (Ed.), *Encyclopedia of the life course and human development.* Boston: Gale Cengage.

Waiter, G. D., & others. (2009). Exploring possible neural mechanisms of intelligence differences using processing speed and working memory tasks. *Intelligence, 37,* 199–206.

Wakeling, E. L. (2011, in press). Silver-Russell syndrome. *Archives of Disease in Childhood.*

Wald, E. R. (2011). Acute otitis media and acute bacterial sinusitis. *Clinical Infectious Diseases, 52*(Suppl. 4), S277–S283.

Waldinger, R. J., & Schulz, M. C. (2010). What's love got to do with it? Social functioning, perceived health, and daily happiness in married octogenarians. *Psychology and Aging, 25,* 422–431.

Walker, K. Z., O'Dea, K., Gomez, M., Girgis, S., & Colagiuri, R. (2010). Diet and exercise in the prevention of diabetes. *Journal of Human Nutrition and Diet, 23*(4), 344–352.

Walker, L. J. (1982). The sequentiality of Kohlberg's stages of moral development. *Child Development, 53,* 1130–1136.

Walker, L. J. (2002). Moral exemplarity. In W. Damon (Ed.), *Bringing in a new era of character education.* Stanford, CA: Hoover Press.

Walker, L. J. (2004). Progress and prospects in the psychology of moral development. *Merrill-Palmer Quarterly, 50,* 546–557.

Walker, L. J. (2006). Gender and morality. In M. Killen & J. G. Smetana (Eds.), *Handbook of moral development.* Mahwah, NJ: Erlbaum.

Walker, L. J., & Frimer, J. A. (2009). Moral personality exemplified. In D. Narváez & D. K. Lapsley (Eds.), *Personality, identity and character. Explorations in moral psychology* (pp. 232–255). New York: Cambridge University Press.

Walker, L. J., & Frimer, J. A. (2011). The science of moral development. In M. K. Underwood & L. Rosen (Eds.), *Social development.* New York: Guilford.

Walker, L. J., Frimer, J. A., & Dunlop, W. L. (2011, in press). Varieties of moral personality: Beyond the banality of heroism. *Journal of Personality.*

Walker, L. J., Hennig, K. H., & Krettenauer, T. (2000). Parent and peer contexts for children's moral reasoning development. *Child Development, 71*, 1033–1048.

Wallenborg, K., & others. (2009). Red wine triggers cell death and thiroredoxin reductase inhibition: Effects beyond resveratrol and SIRT 1. *Experimental Cell Research, 315*(8), 1360–1371.

Wallerstein, J. S. (2008). Divorce. In M. M. Haith & J. B. Benson (Eds.), *Encyclopedia of infant and early childhood development.* Oxford, UK: Elsevier.

Walsh, L. A. (2000, Spring). The inside scoop on child development: Interview. *Cutting through the hype.* Minneapolis: College of Education and Human Development, University of Minnesota.

Walsh, N. P., & others. (2011). Position statement. Part one: Immune function and exercise. *Exercise Immunology Review, 17*, 6–63.

Walsh, R. (2011, in press). Lifestyle and mental health. *American Psychologist.*

Walter, K. H., Horsey, K. J., Palmieri, P. A., & Hobfoll, S. E. (2010). The role of protective self-cognitions in the relationship between childhood trauma and later loss. *Journal of Trauma and Stress, 23*, 264–273.

Walters, E., & Kendler, K. S. (1994). Anorexia nervosa and anorexia-like symptoms in a population-based twin sample. *American Journal of Psychiatry, 152*, 62–71.

Wandell, P. E., Carlsson, A. C., & Theobald, H. (2009). The association between BMI value and long-term mortality. *International Journal of Obesity, 33*, 577–582.

Wang, Q., & Pomerantz, E. M. (2009). The motivational landscape of early adolescence in the United States and China: A longitudinal study. *Child Development, 80*, 1272–1287.

Wang, W., & others. (2010). Neural interface technology for rehabilitation: Exploiting and promoting neural plasticity. *Physical Medicine and Rehabilitation Clinics of North America, 21*, 157–178.

Wang, W., Dew, I. T. Z, & Giovanello, K. S. (2010). Effects of aging and prospective memory on recognition of item and associative information. *Psychology and Aging, 25*, 486–491.

Wankowska, M., & Polkowska, J. (2010). The pituitary endocrine mechanisms involved in mammalian maturation: Maternal and photoperiodic influences. *Reproductive Biology, 10*, 3–18.

Ward, W. F., Qi, W., Van Remmen, H., Zackert, W. E., Roberts, L. J., & Richardson, A. (2005). Effects of age and caloric restriction on lipid peroxidation: Measurement of oxidative stress by F2-isoprostane levels. *Journals of Gerontology A: Biological Sciences and Medical Sciences, 60*, 847–851.

Wardlaw, G. M., & Smith, A. M. (2011). *Contemporary nutrition* (8th ed.). New York: McGraw-Hill.

Ware, J. E., Kosinski, M., & Dewey, J. E. (2000). *How to score Version 2 of the SF-36 Health Survey.* Boston: Quality Metric.

Warr, P. (1994). Age and employment. In M. Dunnette, L. Hough, & H. Triandis (Eds.), *Handbook of industrial and organizational psychology* (Vol. 4). Palo Alto, CA: Consulting Psychologists Press.

Warren, M. P. (2007). Historical perspectives on postmenopausal hormone therapy: Defining the right dose and duration. *Mayo Clinic Proceedings, 82*, 219–226.

Warshak, R. A. (2008, January). Personal communication. Department of Psychology, University of Texas at Dallas, Richardson.

Watamura, S. E., Phillips, D. A., Morrissey, D. A., McCartney, T. W., & Bub, K. (2011). Double jeopardy: Poorer social-emotional outcomes for children in the NICHD SECCYD who experience home and child-care environments that convey risk. *Child Development, 82*, 48–65.

Waterman, A. S. (1985). Identity in the context of adolescent psychology. In A. S. Waterman (Ed.), *Identity in adolescence: Processes and contents.* San Francisco: Jossey-Bass.

Waterman, A. S. (1992). Identity as an aspect of optimal psychological functioning. In G. R. Adams, T. P. Gulotta, & R. Montemayor (Eds.), *Adolescent identity formation.* Newbury Park, CA: Sage.

Watson, J. A., Randolph, S. M., & Lyons, J. L. (2005). African-American grandmothers as health educators in the family. *International Journal of Aging and Human Development, 60*, 343–356.

Watson, J. B. (1928). *Psychological care of infant and child.* New York: W. W. Norton.

Watson, R. (2009). Luxembourg is to allow euthanasia from 1 April. *British Medical Journal, 338*, 1248.

Watts, C., & Zimmerman, C. (2002). Violence against women: Global scope and magnitude. *Lancet, 359*, 1232–1237.

Watts, C. E. & Caldwell, L. L. (2011, in press). The influence of parenting practices, adolescent self-determination and adolescent initiative on structured and unstructured activity involvement of adolescents. *Journal of Leisure Research.*

Waxman, S. (2009). How infants discover distinct word types and map them to distinctive meanings. In J. Colombo, P. McCardle, & L. Freund (Eds.), *Infant pathways to language.* Clifton, NJ: Psychology Press.

Webb, J. T., Gore, J. L., Mend, E. R., & DeVries, A. R. (2007). *A parent's guide to gifted children.* Scottsdale, AZ: Great Potential Press.

Webber, S. C., Porter, M. M., & Menec, V. H. (2010). Mobility in older adults: A comprehensive framework. *Gerontologist, 50*(4), 443–450.

Webster, N. S., & Worrell, F. C. (2008). Academically-talented adolescents' attitudes toward service in the community. *Gifted Child Quarterly, 52*, 170–179.

Wechsler, D. (1939). *The measurement of adult intelligence.* Baltimore: Williams & Wilkins.

Wechsler, H., Davenport, A., Sowdall, G., Moetykens, B., & Castillo, S. (1994). Health and behavioral consequences of binge drinking in college. *Journal of the American Medical Association, 272*, 1672–1677.

Weikert, D. P. (1993). *Long-term positive effects in the Perry Preschool Head Start Program.* Unpublished data. High/Scope Foundation, Ypsilanti, MI.

Weiner, C. P., & Buhimschi, C. (2009). *Drugs for pregnant and lactating women* (2nd ed.). London: Elsevier.

Weinstein, R. S. (2004). *Reaching higher: The power of expectations in schooling.* Cambridge, MA: Harvard University Press.

Weismiller, D. G. (2009). Menopause. *Primary Care, 36*, 199–226.

Weisner, T. S. (2011). Culture. In M. K. Underwood & L. H. Rosen (Eds.), *Social development.* New York: Guilford.

Weiss, L. A., & others. (2008). Association between microdeletion and microduplication at 16p 11.2 and autism. *New England Journal of Medicine, 358*, 667–675.

Weissglas-Volkov, D., & Pajukanta, P. (2010). Genetic causes of high and low serum HDL-cholesterol. *Journal of Lipid Research, 51*(8), 2032–2057.

Wekerle, C., & others. (2009). The contribution of childhood emotional abuse to teen dating violence among child protective services–involved youth. *Child Abuse and Neglect, 33*(1), 45–58.

Welch, K. J. (2011). *THINK human sexuality.* Upper Saddle River, NJ: Pearson.

Wellman, H. M. (2011). Developing a theory of mind. In U. Goswami (Ed.), *The Blackwell handbook of childhood cognitive development* (2nd ed.). New York: Wiley.

Wellman, H. M., Cross, D., & Watson, J. (2001). Meta-analysis of theory-of-mind development: The truth about false belief. *Child Development, 72*, 655–684.

Wellman, H. M., & Woolley, J. D. (1990). From simple desires to ordinary beliefs: The early development of everyday psychology. *Cognition, 35*, 245–275.

Welsh, J. A., Nix, R. L., Blair, C., Bierman, K. L., & Nelson, K. E. (2010). The development of cognitive skills and gains in academic school readiness for children from low-income families. *Journal of Educational Psychology, 102*, 43–53.

Wenestam, C. G., & Wass, H. (1987). Swedish and U.S. children's thinking about death: A qualitative study and cross-cultural comparison. *Death Studies, 11*, 99–121.

Weng, X., Odouli, R., & Li, D. K. (2008). Maternal caffeine consumption during pregnancy and the risk of miscarriage: A prospective cohort study. *American Journal of Obstetrics and Gynecology, 198*, e1–e8.

Wenger, N. S., & others. (2003). The quality of medical care provided to vulnerable community-dwelling older patients. *Annals of Internal Medicine, 139*, 740–747.

Wentzel, K. (1997). Student motivation in middle school: The role of perceived pedagogical caring. *Journal of Educational Psychology, 89,* 411–419.

Wentzel, K. R., & Asher, S. R. (1995). The academic lives of neglected, rejected, popular, and controversial children. *Child Development, 66,* 754–763.

Wertsch, J. (2008). From social interaction to higher psychological processes. *Human Development, 51,* 66–79.

Westerlund, M., & Lagerberg, D. (2008). Expressive vocabulary in 18-month-old children in relation to demographic factors, mother and child characteristics, communication style, and shared reading. *Child: Care, Health, and Development, 34,* 257–266.

Westlake, C., Evangelista, L. S., Stromberg, A., Ter-Galstanyan, A., Vazirani, S., & Dracup, K. (2007). Evaluation of a web-based education and counseling pilot for older heart failure patients. *Progress in Cardiovascular Nursing, 22,* 20–26.

Westling, E., Andrews, J. A., Hampson, S. E., & Peterson, M. (2008). Pubertal timing and substance use: The effects of gender, parental monitoring, and deviant peers. *Journal of Adolescent Health, 42*(6), 555–563.

Weston, M. J. (2010). Magnetic resonance imaging in fetal medicine: A pictorial review of current and developing indications. *Postgraduate Medicine Journal, 86,* 42–51.

Westphal, D. M., & McKee, S. A. (2009). End-of-life decision making in the intensive care unit: Physician and nurse perspective. *American Journal of Medical Quality, 24,* 222–228.

Wethington, E., Kessler, R., & Pixley, J. (2004). Turning points in adulthood. In G. Brim, C. D. Ryff, & R. Kessler (Eds.), *How healthy we are: A national study of well-being in midlife.* Chicago: University of Chicago Press.

Whitbourne, S. K., & Meeks, S. (2011). Psychopathology, bereavement, and aging. In K. W. Schaie & S. L. Willis (Eds.), *Handbook of the psychology of aging* (7th ed.). New York: Elsevier.

White, H. R., Fleming, C. B., Catalano, R. F., & Bailey, J. A (2009). Prospective association among alcohol use–related sexual enhancement expectancies, sex after alcohol use, and casual sex. *Psychology of Addictive Behaviors, 23,* 702–707.

White, L. (1994). Stepfamilies over the life course: Social support. In A. Booth and J. Dunne (Eds.), *Stepfamilies: Who benefits and who does not.* Hillsdale, NJ: Lawrence Erlbaum.

White, M. A., & Grillo, C. M. (2011). Diagnostic efficiency of DSM-IV indicators for binge eating episodes. *Journal of Consulting and Clinical Psychology, 79,* 75–83.

Whitehead, B. D., & Popenoe, D. (2003). *The state of our unions.* Piscataway, NJ: The National Marriage Project, Rutgers University.

Whitehead, K. A., Ainsworth, A. T., Wittig, M. A., & Gadino, B. (2009). Implications of ethnic identity exploration and ethnic identity affirmation and belonging for intergroup attitudes among adolescents. *Journal of Research on Adolescence, 19,* 123–135.

Whitfield, K. E., Thorpe, R., & Szanton, S. (2011). Health disparities, social class, and aging. In K. W. Schaie & S. L. Willis (Eds.), *Handbook of the psychology of aging* (7th ed.). New York: Elsevier.

Whittle, S., & others. (2008). Prefrontal and amygdala volumes are related to adolescents' affective behaviors during parent-adolescent interactions. *Proceedings of the National Academy of Sciences USA, 105,* 3652–3657.

WIC New York. (2010). *WIC program: Women, infants, and children.* Retrieved August 12, 2010, from www.health.state.ny.us/prevention/nutrition/wic/

Wickelgren, I. (1999). Nurture helps to mold able minds. *Science, 283,* 1832–1834.

Wickrama, K. A. S., Bryant, C. M., Conger, R. D., & Meehan, J. M. (2004). Change and continuity in marital relationships during the middle years. In R. D. Conger, F. O. Lorenz, & K. A. S. Wickrama (Eds.), *Continuity and change in family relations.* Mahwah, NJ: Erlbaum.

Wiesel, A., & others. (2011, in press). Maternal occupation exposure to ionizing radiation and birth defects. *Radiation and Environmental Biophysics.*

Wiesner, M., & Ittel, A. (2002). Relations of pubertal timing and depressing symptoms to substance use in early adolescence. *Journal of Early Adolescence, 22,* 5–23.

Wigfield, A., Byrnes, J. P., & Eccles, J. S. (2006). Development during early and middle adolescence. In P. A. Alexander & P. H. Winne (Eds.), *Handbook of educational psychology* (2nd ed.). Mahwah, NJ: Erlbaum.

Wigfield, A., & Cambria, J. (2010). Students' achievement values, goal orientations, and interest: Definitions, development, and relations to achievement outcomes. *Developmental Review, 30,* 1–35.

Wigfield, A., Eccles, J. S., Schiefele, U., Roeser, R., & Davis-Kean, P. (2006). Development of achievement motivation. In W. Damon & R. Lerner (Eds.), *Handbook of child psychology* (6th ed.). New York: Wiley.

Wigfield, A., Klauda, S. L., & Cambria, J. (2011). Motivational sources and outcomes of self-regulated learning and performance. In B. J. Zimmerman & D. H. Schunk (Eds.), *Handbook of self-regulation of learning and performance.* New York: Routledge.

Wilcox, S., Evenson, K. R., Aragaki, A., Wassertheil-Smoller, S., Mouton, C. P., & Loevinger, B. L. (2003). The effects of widowhood on physical and mental health, health behaviors, and health outcomes: The women's health initiative. *Health Psychology, 22,* 513–522.

Wildman, L., & McNulty, J. K. (2010). Sexual narcissism and the perpetration of sexual aggression. *Archives of Sexual Behavior, 39,* 926–939.

Williams, D. D., Yancher, S. C., Jensen, L. C., & Lewis, C. (2003). Character education in a public high school: A multi-year inquiry into unified studies. *Journal of Moral Education, 32,* 3–33.

Williams, D. R., & Sternthal, M. J. (2007). Spirituality, religion, and health: Evidence and research directions. *Medical Journal of Australia, 186*(Suppl.), S47–S50.

Williams, G. L., Keigher, S., & Williams, A. V. (2011, in press). Spiritual well-being among older African Americans in a midwestern city. *Journal of Religion and Health.*

Williams, K. M., Nathanson, C., & Paulhus, D. L. (2010). Identifying and profiling academic cheaters: Their personality, cognitive ability, and motivation. *Journal of Experimental Psychology: Applied, 16,* 293–307.

Williams, K. N., & Kemper, S. (2010). Interventions to reduce cognitive decline in aging. *Journal of Psychosocial Nursing and Mental Health Services, 48,* 42–51.

Williams, M. E. (1995). *The American Geriatric Society's complete guide to aging and health.* New York: Harmony Books.

Williams, R., & Hazell, P. (2011). Austerity, poverty, resilience, and the future of mental health services for children and adolescents. *Current Opinion in Psychiatry, 24,* 263–266.

Williamson, D. L., Raue, U., Slivka, D. R., & Trappe, S. (2010). Resistance exercise, skeletal muscle FOXO3A, and 85-year-old women. *Journals of Gerontology A: Biological Sciences and Medical Sciences, 65A,* 335–343.

Williamson, J. (2011). The future of retirement security. In R. H. Binstock & L. K. George (Eds.), *Handbook of aging and the social sciences* (7th ed.). New York: Elsevier.

Williamson, J. D., & others. (2009). Changes in cognitive function in a randomized trial of physical activity: Results of the Lifestyle interventions and independence for Elders Pilot Study. *Journals of Gerontology A: Biological Sciences and Medical Sciences, 64*(6), 688–694.

Willis, S. L., & Nesselroade, C. S. (1990). Long-term effects of fluid ability training in old age. *Developmental Psychology, 26,* 905–910.

Wilson, A. C., Dugger, B. N., Dickson, D. W., & Wang, D. S. (2011). TDP-43 in aging and Alzheimer's disease—a review. *International Journal of Clinical and Experimental Pathology, 4,* 147–155.

Wilson, B. J. (2008). Media and children's aggression, fear, and altruism. *Future of Children, 18*(1), 87–118.

Wilson, R. S., Mendes de Leon, C. F., Barnes, L. L., Schneider, J. A., Evans, D. A., & Bennett, D. A. (2002). Participation in cognitively stimulating activities and risk of incident Alzheimer disease. *Journal of the American Medical Association, 287,* 742–748.

Wilson, R. S., Mendes de Leon, C. F., Bienas, J. L., Evans, D. A., & Bennett, D. A. (2004). Personality and mortality in old age. *Journals of Gerontology B: Psychological Sciences and Social Sciences, 59,* 110B–116B.

Winerman, L. (2005, January). Leading the way. *Monitor on Psychology, 36*(1), 64–67.

Wink, P., & Dillon, M. (2002). Spiritual development across the adult life course:

Findings from a longitudinal study. *Journal of Adult Development, 9,* 79–94.

Winne, P. H., & Nesbit, J. C. (2010). The psychology of academic achievement. *Annual Review of Psychology* (Vol. 61). Palo Alto, CA: Annual Reviews.

Winner, E. (1986, August). Where pelicans kiss seals. *Psychology Today,* pp. 24–35.

Winner, E. (1996). *Gifted children: Myths and realities.* New York: Basic Books.

Winner, E. (2000). The origins and ends of giftedness. *American Psychologist, 55,* 159–169.

Winner, E. (2006). Development in the arts: Drawing and music. In W. Damon & R. Lerner (Eds.), *Handbook of child psychology* (6th ed.). New York: Wiley.

Winner, E. (2009). Toward broadening our understanding of giftedness: The spatial domain. In F. D. Horowitz, R. F. Subotnik, & D. J. Matthews (Eds.), *The development of giftedness and talent across the life span.* Washington, DC: American Psychological Association.

Wintre, M. G., & Vallance, D. D. (1994). A developmental sequence in the comprehension of emotions: Intensity, multiple emotions, and valence. *Developmental Psychology, 30,* 509–514.

Wise, P. M. (2006). Aging of the female reproductive system. In E. J. Masor & S. N. Austad (Eds.), *Handbook of the biology of aging* (6th ed.). New York: Elsevier.

Wit, J. M., Kiess, W., & Mullis, P. (2011). Genetic evaluation of short stature. *Best Practices & Research: Clinical Endocrinology and Metabolism, 25,* 1–17.

Witelson, S. F., Kigar, D. L., & Harvey, T. (1999). The exceptional brain of Albert Einstein. *The Lancet, 353,* 2149–2153.

Witherington, D. C., Campos, J. J., Harriger, J. A., Bryan, C., & Margett, T. E. (2011). Emotion and its development in infancy. In J. G. Bremner & T. D. Wachs (Eds.), *Wiley-Blackwell handbook of infant development* (2nd ed.). New York: Wiley.

Witkin, H. A., & others. (1976). Criminality in XYY and XXY men. *Science, 193,* 547–555.

Witte, A. V., & others. (2009). Caloric restriction improves memory in elderly humans. *Proceedings of the National Academy of Sciences, U.S.A., 106,* 1255–1260.

Witte, R. (2012). *Classroom assessment for teachers.* New York: McGraw-Hill.

Witvliet, M., & others. (2010). Peer group affiliation in children: The role of perceived popularity, likeability, and behavioral similarity in bullying. *Social Development, 19,* 285–303.

Woelders, L. C. S., Larsen, J. K., Scholte, R., Cillessen, T., & Engles, R. C. M. E. (2010). Friendship group influences on body dissatisfaction and dieting among adolescent girls: A prospective study. *Journal of Adolescent Health, 47*(5), 456–462.

Wolff, J. M., & Crockett, L. J. (2011, in press). The role of deliberative decision making, parenting, and friends in adolescent risk behaviors. *Journal of Youth and Adolescence.*

Wolfgram, S. M. (2008). Openness in adoption: What we know so far—a critical review of the literature. *Social Work, 53,* 133–142.

Wolfinger, N. H. (2011). More evidence for trends in the intergenerational transmission of divorce: A completed cohort approach using data from the General Social Survey. *Demography, 48,* 581–592.

Wolkowitz, O. M., Epel, E. S., Reus, V. I., & Mellon, S. H. (2010). Depression gets old fast: Do stress and depression accelerate cell aging? *Depression and Anxiety, 27,* 327–338.

Women's Sports Foundation. (2001). *The 10 commandments for parents and coaches in youth sports.* Eisenhower Park, NY: Author.

Wong Briggs, T. (2004, October 14). *USA Today's* 2004 all-USA teacher team. *USA Today,* p. 6D.

Wong Briggs, T. (2007, October 18). An early start for learning. *USA Today,* p. 6D.

Wong, M. M., Brower, K. J., Nigg, J. T., & Zucker, R. A. (2010). Childhood sleep problems, response inhibition, and alcohol and drug outcomes in adolescence and young adulthood. *Alcoholism, Clinical and Experimental Research, 34,* 10033–10044.

Wong, P. T. P., & Watt, L. M. (1991). What types of reminiscence are associated with successful aging? *Psychology and Aging, 6,* 272–279.

Wood, J. T. (2011). *Communication mosaics* (6th ed.). Boston: Cengage.

Wood, J. T. (2012). *Communication in our lives* (6th ed.). Boston: Cengage.

Wood, J., Chaparrow, A., Carberry, T., & Chu, B. S. (2010). Effect of simulated visual impairment on nighttime driving performance. *Optometry and Vision Science, 87*(6), 379–386.

Wood, J., Lacherez, P., Black, A., Cole, M., Boon, M., & Kerr, G. (2011, in press). Risk of falls, injurious falls, and other injuries resulting from visual impairment among older adults with age-related macular degeneration. *Investigative Ophthalmology & Visual Science.*

Wood, L. D. (2010). Clinical review and treatment of select adverse effect of dopamine receptor agonists in Parkinson's disease. *Drugs and Aging, 27,* 295–310.

Woodward, A., Markman, E., & Fitzsimmons, C. (1994). Rapid word learning in 13- and 18-month-olds. *Developmental Psychology, 30,* 553–556.

Woodward, A. L., & Markman, E. M. (1998). Early word learning. In D. Kuhn & R. S. Siegler (Eds.), *Handbook of child psychology* (5th ed., Vol. 2). New York: Wiley

Woolett, L. A. (2011). Review: Transport of maternal cholesterol to the fetal circulation. *Placenta, 3*(Suppl. 2), S18–S21.

World Health Organization. (2000, February 2). *Adolescent health behavior in 28 countries.* Geneva, Switzerland: World Health Organization.

World Health Organization. (2009). *Suicide rates.* Geneva, Switzerland: Author.

Worthington, E. L. (1989). Religious faith across the life span: Implications for counseling and research. *Counseling Psychologist, 17,* 555–612.

Wortmann, J. H., & Park, C. L. (2008). Religion and spirituality in adjustment following bereavement: An integrative review. *Death Studies, 32,* 703–736.

Wouters, H., & others. (2011, in press). Does adaptive cognitive testing combine efficiency with precision? *Journal of Alzheimer's Disease.*

Wright, R. H., Mindel, C. H., Tran, T. V., & Habenstein, R. W. (2012). *Ethnic families in America* (5th ed.). Upper Saddle River, NJ: Pearson.

Wright, R. O., & Christiani, D. (2010). Gene-environment interaction and children's health and development. *Current Opinion in Pediatrics, 22*(2), 197–201.

Wu, J. M., & Hsieh, T. C. (2011). Resveratol: A cardioprotective substance. *Annals of the New York Academy of Sciences, 1215,* 16–21.

Wu, T., Gao, X., Chen, M., & van Dam, R. M. (2009). Long-term effectiveness of diet-plus-exercise interventions vs. diet-only interventions for weight loss: A meta-analysis. *Obesity Reviews, 10,* 313–323.

Wu, W. T. (2010). Botox facial slimming/facial sculpting: The role of botulinum toxin-A in the treatment of hypertrophic masseteric muscle and parotid enlargement to narrow the lower facial width. *Facial Plastic Surgery Units of North America, 18,* 133–140.

X

Xia, N. (2010). *Family factors and student outcomes.* Unpublished doctoral dissertation, RAND Corporation, Pardee RAND Graduate School, Pittsburgh.

Xie, Q., & Young, M. E. (1999). Integrated child development in rural China. *Education: The World Bank.* Washington, DC: The World Bank.

Xu, J., Kochanek, K. D., Murphy, S. L., & Tejada-Vera, B. (2010, May). Deaths: Final data for 2007. *National Vital Statistics Reports, 58*(19), 1–72.

Xu, Q., Parks, C. G., Derro, L. A., Cawthon, R. M., Sandler, D. P., & Chen, H. (2009). Multivitamin use and telomere length in women. *American Journal of Clinical Nutrition, 89,* 1857–1863.

Y

Yang, X. P., & Reckelhoff, J. F. (2011). Estrogen, hormonal replacement therapy, and cardiovascular disease. *Current Opinion in Nephrology and Hypertension, 20,* 133–138.

Yang, Y. (2008). Social inequalities in happiness in the United States, 1972–2004: An age-period-cohort analysis. *American Sociological Review, 73,* 204–226.

Yang, Y. (2011). Aging, cohorts, and methods. In R. H. Binstock & L. K. George (Eds.),

Handbook of aging and the social sciences (7th ed.). New York: Elsevier.

Yarber, W., Sayad, B., & Strong, B. (2010). *Human sexuality* (7th ed.). New York: McGraw-Hill.

Yassin, A. A., Akhras, F., El-Sakka, A. I., & Saad, F. (2011, in press). Cardiovascular diseases and erectile dysfunction: The two faces of the coin on androgen deficiency. *Andrologia*.

Yates, L. B., Djuousse, L., Kurth, T., Buring, J. E., & Gaziano, J. M. (2008). Exceptional longevity in men: Modifiable factors associated with survival and function to age 90 years. *Archives of Internal Medicine, 168,* 284–290.

Yazdy, M. M., Liu, S., Mitchell, A. A., & Werler, N. M. (2010). Maternal dietary glycemic intake and the risk of neural tube defects. *American Journal of Epidemiology, 171,* 407–414.

Yell, M. L., & Drasgow, E. (2009). *What every teacher should know about No Child Left Behind* (2nd ed.). Upper Saddle River, NJ: Prentice Hall.

Yen, S. C. (2008). Short-term memory. In N. J. Salkind (Ed.), *Encyclopedia of educational psychology*. Thousand Oaks CA: Sage.

Yi, S., & others. (2010). Role of risk and protective factors in risky sexual behavior among high school students in Cambodia. *BMC Public Health, 12*(10), 477.

Yokoya, T., Demura, S., & Sato, S. (2009). Three-year follow-up of the fall risk and physical function characteristics of the elderly participating in a community exercise class. *Journal of Physiological Anthropology, 28,* 55–62.

Yoon, C., Cole, C. A., & Lee, M. P. (2009). Consumer decision making and aging: Current knowledge and future directions. *Journal of Consumer Psychology, 19,* 2–16.

Yoshida, S., Kozu, T., Gotoda, T., & Saito, D. (2006). Detection and treatment of early cancer in high-risk populations. *Best Practice and Research: Clinical Gastroenterology, 20,* 745–765.

Young, K. T. (1990). American conceptions of infant development from 1955 to 1984: What the experts are telling parents. *Child Development, 61,* 17–28.

Youniss, J., McLellan, J. A., & Yates, M. (1999). Religion, community service, and identity in American youth. *Journal of Adolescence, 22,* 243–253.

Ystad, M., Eichele, T., Lundervold, A. J., & Lundervold, A. (2010). Subcortical functional connectivity and verbal episodic memory in healthy elderly—A resting state fMRI study. *NeuroImage, 52*(1), 379–388.

Yuan, A. S. V. (2010). Body perceptions, weight control behavior, and changes in adolescents' psychological well-being over time: A longitudinal examination of gender. *Journal of Youth and Adolescence, 39,* 927–939.

Yun, Y. H., & others. (2011, in press). Attitudes of cancer patients, family caregivers, oncologists, and members of the general public toward critical interventions at the end of life of terminally ill patients. *CMAJ*.

Z

Zaff, J. F., Hart, D., Flanagan, C., Youniss, J., & Levine, P. (2010). Developing civic engagement within a civic context. In M. E. Lamb, A. M. Freund, & R. M. Lerner (Eds.), *Handbook of life-span development* (Vol. 2). New York: Wiley.

Zagorsky, J. L. (2007). Do you have to be smart to be rich? The impact of IQ on wealth, income, and financial distress. *Intelligence, 35,* 489–501.

Zamperetti, N., & Bellomo, R. (2009). Total brain failure: A new contribution by the President's Council of Bioethics to the definition of death according to the neurological standard. *Intensive Care Medicine, 35,* 1305–1307.

Zarit, S. H., & Knight, B. G. (Eds.). (1996). *A guide to psychotherapy and aging.* Washington, DC: American Psychological Association.

Zayas, L., Gulbas, L. E., Fedoravivicus, N., & Cabassa, L. J. (2010). Patterns of distress, precipitating events, and reflections on suicide attempts by young Latinas. *Social Science & Medicine, 70*(11), 1773–1779.

Zeeck, A., Stelzer, N., Linster, H. W., Joos, A., & Hartmann, A. (2011, in press). Emotion and eating in binge eating disorder and obesity. *European Eating Disorders Review*.

Zeifman, D., & Hazan, C. (2008). Pair bonds as attachments: Reevaluating the evidence. In J. Cassidy & P. R. Shaver (Eds.), *Handbook of attachment* (2nd ed.). New York: Guilford.

Zelazo, P. D., & Lee, W. S. C. (2010). Brain development: An overview. In W. F. Overton (Ed.), *Handbook of life-span development* (Vol. 1). New York: Wiley.

Zelazo, P. D., & Muller, U. (2011). Executive function in typical and atypical development. In U. Goswami (Ed.), *Wiley-Blackwell handbook of childhood cognitive development*. New York: Wiley.

Zelazo, P. D., Qu, L., & Kesek, A. C. (2010). Hot executive function: Emotion and the development of cognitive control. In S. D. Calkins & M. A. Bell (Eds.), *Child development at the intersection of emotion and cognition*. Washington, DC: American Psychological Association.

Zelinski, E. M., & Kennison, R. F. (2007). Not your parents' test scores: Cohort reduces psychometric aging effects. *Psychology and Aging, 22,* 546–557.

Zeskind, P. S. (2007). Impact of the cry of the infant at risk on psychosocial development. In R. E. Tremblay, R. de V. Peters, M. Boivin, & R. G. Barr (Eds.), *Encyclopedia of early childhood development*. Montreal: Centre of Excellence for Early Childhood Development. Retrieved November 24, 2008, from www.child-encyclopedia.com/en-ca/list-of-topics.html

Zettel-Watson, L., & Rook, K. S. (2009). Friendship, later life. In D. Carr (Ed.), *Encyclopedia of the life course and human development*. Boston: Gale Cengage.

Zhang, L-F., & Sternberg, R. J. (2011). Learning in cross-cultural perspective. In T. Husen & T. N. Postlethwaite (Eds.), *International encyclopedia of education* (3rd ed.). New York: Elsevier.

Zhao, X., & others. (2010). Telomerase-immortalized human mammary stem/progenitor cells with ability to self-renew and differentiate. *Proceedings of the National Academy of Sciences U.S.A., 107*(32), 14146–14151.

Zhao, Y., Shay, J. W., & Wright, W. E. (2011). Telomere terminal G/C strand synthesis: Measuring telomerase action and C-rich fill-in. *Methods in Molecular Biology, 735,* 63–75.

Zhou, M., & others. (2010). Forebrain overexpression of CK1delta leads to down-regulation of dopamine receptors and altered locomotor activity reminiscent of ADHD. *Proceedings of the National Academy of Sciences, 107,* 4401–4406.

Zielinski, D. S. (2009). Child maltreatment and adult socioeconomic well-being. *Child Abuse and Neglect, 33,* 666–678.

Zigler, E. F., & Styfco, S. J. (1994). Head Start: Criticisms in a constructive context. *American Psychologist, 49,* 127–132.

Zigler, E. F., & Styfco, S. J. (2010). *The hidden history of Head Start*. New York: Oxford University Press.

Zimmerman, F. J., Christakis, D. A., & Meltzoff, A. N. (2007). Association between media viewing and language development in children under age 2 years. *Journal of Pediatrics, 151,* 364–368.

Zinn, M. B., & Wells, B. (2000). Diversity within Latino families: New lessons for family social science. In D. M. Demo, K. R. Allen, & M. A. Fine (Eds.), *Handbook of family diversity*. New York: Oxford University Press.

Ziol-Guest, K. M. (2009). Child custody and support. In D. Carr (Ed.), *Encyclopedia of the life course and human development*. Boston: Cengage.

Zisook, S., & others. (2010). Bereavement, complicated grief, and DSM, part 1: Depression. *Journal of Clinical Psychiatry, 71,* 955–956.

Zosuls, K. M., Ruble, D. N., Tamis-LeMonda, C. S., Shrout, P. E., Bornstein, M. H., & Greulich, F. K. (2009). The acquisition of gender labels in infancy: Implications for gender-typed play. *Developmental Psychology, 45,* 688–701.

Zuckoff, A., Shear, K., Frank, E., Daley, D. C., Seligman, K., & Silowash, R. (2006). Treating complicated grief and substance use disorders: A pilot study. *Journal of Substance Abuse and Treatment, 30,* 205–211.

credits

Corbis; p. 394: © Marilyn Humphries/The Image Works; p. 396: © Michael Ray; p. 398: Courtesy of Lynn Blankenship; p. 399: © Frank Fournier; p. 400: © Ocean/Corbis; p. 401: © McGraw-Hill Companies, Inc./Suzie Ross, Photographer; p. 402: © Rhoda Sidney/PhotoEdit; p. 403: © Emma Rian/zefa/Corbis

Chapter 13

p. 407: © Simon Jarratt/Corbis; p. 408: © Yves De Braine/Black Star/Stock Photos; p. 409 (top): © Tom Grill/Corbis; p. 412 (top): © Arthur Tilley/Taxi/Getty Images; p. 412 (bottom): Photo by Joyce Ravid and Courtesy of Dr. Carol Gilligan; p. 413: © Jim Craigmyle/Corbis; p. 415: © Martin Harvey/Corbis; p. 418 (left): © Bettmann/Corbis; p. 418 (right): © Alain Nogues/Corbis Sygma; p. 419: © Corbis RF; p. 421: © Copyright 2005, Globe Newspaper Company, Matthew J. Lee photographer/Landov Images; p. 422: Eric Audras/PhotoAlto Agency RF Collections/Getty Images; p. 424: © Norbert Schaefer/Corbis; p. 425: © Dallas Morning News, photographer Jim Mahoney; p. 426: © Stockdisc/PunchStock; p. 427: Comstock Images/Alamy; p. 428 (top): Courtesy of Rodney Hammond; p. 428 (bottom): © David Young-Wolff/Getty Images; p. 431: Courtesy of Nina Vasan/© Newscom; p. 432: © BigStock Photo; p. 433: © Stone/Getty Images; p. 434 (top): © Erik S. Lesser/epa/Corbis; p. 434 (bottom): © Hill Street Studios/age Fotostock; p. 436: PunchStock RF; p. 437: © Michael Prince/Corbis

Chapter 14

p. 444: Blend Images/Jasper Cole/Getty Images; p. 445: © Floresco Productions/Corbis; p. 446: Jamie Grill/Getty Images; p. 447 (left): © Tom & Dee Ann McCarthy/Corbis; p. 447 (right): © Franco Vogt/Corbis; p. 450 (top): © Corbis RF; p. 450 (bottom): © Steve Cole/Getty RF; p. 452 (left to right): © Johner Images/Getty Images; © ShutterStock; BLOOMimage/Getty Images; p. 453: © Courtesy Dr. John Gottman, The Gottman Institute; p. 454 (top): Image Source Pink/Alamy; p. 454 (bottom): © Ronnie Kaufman/Corbis; p. 455: Image Source/Getty Images; p. 456: © Denkou Images/Alamy; p. 457 (left): © 2009 Jupiterimages RF; p. 457 (right): © Jack Star/PhotoLink/Getty RF; p. 459: © Corbis RF; p. 460: Courtesy of Janis Keyser; p. 462: © Ariel Skelley/Corbis; p. 463: © Jose Luis Pelaez, Inc./Corbis; p. 464: © Corbis RF; p. 465 (top): Courtesy of Darla Botkin; p. 465 (bottom): © Jim Craigmyle/Corbis; p. 466: © Prevent Child Abuse America. Also reprinted by permission of Grant and Tamia Hill; p. 468 (top): © Myrleen Ferguson Cate/PhotoEdit; p. 468 (bottom): © BananaStock/PunchStock; p. 469 (top): © BananaStock/PunchStock; p. 469 (bottom): © Pat Vasquez-Cunningham 1999, USA Today; p. 470: © David Young-Wolff/PhotoEdit; p. 471: Photodisc Collection/Getty Images; p. 472: © PunchStock RF; p. 474: Todd Wright/Blend Images/Getty Images; p. 475: © Newscom; p. 476: Photodisc/Getty Images; p. 477 (all): Rubberball Productions/Getty Images; p. 478: Image Source/Getty Images; p. 479: © Jose Luis Pelaez, Inc./

Corbis; p. 480 (top): John Santrock; p. 480 (bottom): © Reza/National Geographic/Getty; p. 481: © Steve Casimiro/The Image Bank/Getty Images

Chapter 15

p. 486: © Rolf Bruderer/Corbis; p. 487: © Ariel Skelley/Corbis; p. 488: © MM Productions/Corbis RF; p. 489: © Rachel Epstein/PhotoEdit; p. 490: © Blend Images/age Fotostock; p. 491: © BananaStock/PunchStock; p. 492: Design Pics Inc./Alamy; p. 494: Jose Luis Pelaez Inc./Blend Images/Getty Images; p. 496: © Rolf Bruderer/Corbis; p. 498 (left to right): © Stockbyte/PunchStock; © BananaStock Ltd.; © Ingram Publishing/age Fotostock; p. 499: © George Shelley/Corbis; p. 500: © istockphoto.com; p. 501: © LWA-Dann Tardif/Corbis; p. 502: Laurence Mouton/Photoalto/PictureQuest; p. 503 (top): Allan Shoemake/Getty Images; p. 503 (bottom): © Mark Romanelli/Getty Images; p. 505 (top): © Claro Cortes IV/Reuters/Corbis; p. 505 (bottom): © Frank Conaway/Index Stock/Photolibrary; p. 506 (top): © Digital Vision/Getty RF; p. 506 (bottom): © NASA/Liaison Agency/Getty Images News Service; p. 507 (top): Cartesia/Getty Images; p. 507 (bottom): Annabelle Breakey/The Image Bank/Getty Images; p. 509: © iStockphoto.com/Dan Wilton; p. 510: imagebroker.net/PhotoLibrary; p. 511: © Davo Blair/Alamy; p. 512 (top): Digital Vision/Alamy; p. 512 (bottom): Sami Sarkis/Getty Images; p. 513 (top): © Suzi-Moore-McGregor/Woodfin Camp & Associates; p. 513 (bottom): BananaStock/PunchStock RF; p. 515 (top left): © Janet Jarman/Corbis; p. 515 (top right): © Joseph Sohm/Corbis; p. 515 (bottom): Courtesy of Vonnie McLoyd; p. 516: © Syracuse Newspapers/S. Cannerelli/The Image Works; p. 517: © Alison Wright/Corbis; p. 518: © Spencer Grant/PhotoEdit; p. 519: Courtesy of Norma Thomas

Chapter 16

p. 524: © Superstock/PhotoLibrary; p. 525: © Michael Newman/PhotoEdit; p. 526 (top): Tony Cordoza/Alamy; p. 526 (bottom): Image Source/Alamy; p. 527 (top): © image100/Corbis RF; p. 527 (bottom): Michael Grecco/Hulton Archive/Getty Images; p. 529 (top): Courtesy of Yolanda Garcia; p. 529 (bottom): © Newscom; p. 530 (top): Blend Images/Getty Images; p. 530 (bottom): © Creatas/PunchStock; p. 531: © Ed Kashi/Corbis; p. 532 (top): © Ray A. Llanos; p. 532 (bottom): © Stockbyte/PunchStock; p. 533: © ZUMA Press/Newscom; p. 534: © AP Wide World Photos; p. 535: © David Young-Wolff/PhotoEdit; p. 536 (top): © Pixland/PunchStock; p. 536 (bottom): Crown copyright MMVI, www.thetransporters.com, Courtesy Changing Media Development; p. 537: © Creatas/PunchStock; p. 538 (top): © 2004, USA Today. Reprinted with permission; p. 538 (bottom): © AP Wide World Photos; p. 539 (top): © Chris Volpe Photography; p. 539 (bottom): McGraw-Hill Companies Inc./Ken Karp, photographer; p. 544: © Ralf-Finn Hestoft/Corbis; p. 545: Courtesy of Sandra Graham; p. 546: © Eiji Miyazawa/Stock Photo; p. 548: Courtesy of Grace Leaf; p. 549:

Corey Lowenstein/MCT/Landov; p. 550: © Jose Luis Perez/Corbis; p. 551 (top): © LWA-Dann Tardif/Corbis; p. 551 (bottom): Photo by Scott Olson/Getty Images; p. 552: Image Source/Getty Images; p. 553: © Greg Sailor; p. 555 (top): © Ronnie Kaufman/Blend Images LLC; p. 555 (bottom): © Bronwyn Kidd/Getty RF

Chapter 17

p. 562: © Fuse/Getty Images; p. 563: © Lynsey Addario; p. 564: © Robert Galbrait/Reuters/Corbis; p. 565: © Patrick Ward/Stock Boston; p. 567 (top to bottom): © Handout Courtesy of the Schiavo Family/Corbis; © The Detroit News; Comstock Images/PictureQuest; p. 568: © 2003 USA Today, photographer Tim Dillon; p. 570 (top): Per-Anders Pettersson/Getty Images; p. 570 (bottom): Photo by Molly Hayden, U.S. Army Garrison-Hawaii Public Affairs; p. 571: © Corbis; p. 574: © Corbis; p. 577: Stockbroker/PhotoLibrary; p. 578: © Digital Vision; p. 579: © Jennifer S. Altman; p. 581 (top): Matt Moyer/Getty Images; p. 581 (bottom left): © Mike Kemp/Rubberball/Corbis; p. 581 (bottom right): © Hermine Dreyfuss; p. 582 (top): Courtesy of The Baltimore Sun Company, Inc. All Rights Reserved; p. 582 (bottom): © Gil Cohen Magen/Reuters

TEXT AND LINE ART CREDITS

Front Matter pp. xxii–xxv

Copyright © 2007 by the American Psychological Association. Reproduced with permission. American Psychological Association (2007). *APA guidelines for the undergraduate psychology major*. Washington, DC: Author. Retrieved from http://www.apa.org/ed/precollege/about/psymajor-guidelines.pdf. No further reproduction or distribution is permitted without written permission from the American Psychological Association.

Chapter 1

Figure 1.1: From Santrock, *Life-Span Development,* 10e. Copyright © 2006 The McGraw-Hill Companies. Reproduced with permission of The McGraw-Hill Companies, Inc. **Figure 1.3:** From Santrock, *Life-Span Development,* 13e. Copyright © 2011 The McGraw-Hill Companies. Reproduced with permission of The McGraw-Hill Companies, Inc. **Figure 1.4:** From Santrock, *Life-Span Development,* 13e. Copyright © 2011 The McGraw-Hill Companies. Reproduced with permission of The McGraw-Hill Companies, Inc. **Figure 1.5:** From Santrock, *Life-Span Development,* 13e. Copyright © 2011 The McGraw-Hill Companies. Reproduced with permission of The McGraw-Hill Companies, Inc. **Figure 1.7:** From Santrock, *Life-Span Development,* 12e. Copyright © 2009 The McGraw-Hill Companies. Reproduced with permission of The McGraw-Hill Companies, Inc. **Figure 1.8:** From E. Diener, R.A. Emmons, R. J. Larsen and S. Griffin. 1985. The Satisfaction with Life Scale. The scale is in the public domain provided credit is given to the authors of the scale: Ed Diener, Robert A. Emmons, Randy J. Larsen and Sharon Griffin as noted in the 1985 article in the *Journal of Personality Assessment, 49,* 71–75. **Figure 1.9:** From Santrock, *Life-Span Development,* 13e. Copyright © 2011 The McGraw-Hill Companies. Reproduced with permission of The McGraw-Hill Companies, Inc. **Figure 1.10:** From Santrock, *Life-Span Development,* 8e. Copyright © 2002 The McGraw-Hill Companies. Reproduced with permission of The McGraw-Hill Companies, Inc. **Figure 1.11:** From Santrock, *Child Development,* 9e. Copyright © 2001 The McGraw-Hill Companies. Reproduced with permission of The McGraw-Hill Companies, Inc. **Figure 1.12 (text):** From Santrock, *Life-Span Development,* 13e. Copyright © 2011 The McGraw-Hill Companies. Reproduced with permission of The McGraw-Hill Companies, Inc. **Figure 1.13:** From Santrock, *Children,* 5e. Copyright © 1997 The McGraw-Hill Companies. Reproduced with permission of The McGraw-Hill Companies, Inc. **Figure 1.14:** Adapted from Claire B. Kopp & Joanne B. Krakow, *The Child: Development in Social Context.* Copyright © 1982, p. 648. Prentice-Hall Publishing/Pearson Education. **Figure 1.15:** From Santrock, *Life-Span Development,* 12e. Copyright © 2009 The McGraw-Hill Companies. Reproduced with permission of The McGraw-Hill Companies, Inc. **Figure 1.16:** From K. Crowley, et al., 2001, "Parents Explain More Often to Boys Than to Girls During Shared Scientific Thinking," *Psychological Science,* 12(3), pp. 258–261. Copyright © Association for Psychological Science. Reprinted by permission of SAGE Publications. **Figure 1.17:** From Santrock, *Children,* 5e. Copyright © 1997 The McGraw-Hill Companies. Reproduced with permission of The McGraw-Hill Companies, Inc. **Figure 1.18:** From Santrock, *Child Development,* 9e. Copyright © 2001 The McGraw-Hill Companies. Reproduced with permission of The McGraw-Hill Companies, Inc.

Chapter 2

Figure 2.2: From P.B. Baltes, U.M. Staudinger & U. Lindenberger, 1999, "Lifespan Psychology," *Annual Review of Psychology,* 50, p. 474, Figure 1. Reprinted with permission from the *Annual Review of Psychology,* Volume 50. Copyright © 1999 by Annual Reviews, www.annualreviews.org. Used by permission of Annual Reviews via Copyright Clearance Center, Inc. **Figure 2.3:** From Santrock, *Child Development,* 9e. Copyright © 2001 The McGraw-Hill Companies. Reproduced with permission of The McGraw-Hill Companies, Inc. **Figure 2.6:** From Santrock, *Life-Span Development,* 8e. Copyright © 2002 The McGraw-Hill Companies. Reproduced with permission of The McGraw-Hill Companies, Inc. **Figure 2.7:** From Santrock, *Life-Span Development,* 8e. Copyright © 2002 The McGraw-Hill Companies. Reproduced with permission of The McGraw-Hill Companies, Inc. **Figure 2.8:** From Santrock, *Children,* 7e. Copyright © 2003 The McGraw-Hill Companies. Reproduced with permission of The McGraw-Hill Companies, Inc. **Figure 2.10 (text):** From Santrock, *Children,* 5e. Copyright © 1997 The McGraw-Hill Companies. Reproduced with permission of The McGraw-Hill Companies, Inc. **Figure 2.13:** Adapted from K.L. Moore and

T.V.N. Persaud from *Before We Are Born,* p. 130. Copyright 1993 by the W.B. Saunders Company. Used with permission from Elsevier. **Figure 2.14 (text):** Figure based on The Apgar Scale, from Virginia A. Apgar, 1953, "A Proposal for a New Method of Evaluation of a Newborn Infant," in *Anesthesia and Analgesia,* Vol. 32, p. 261. **Figure 2.16:** From Santrock, *Life-Span Development,* 13e. Copyright © The McGraw-Hill Companies. Reproduced with permission of The McGraw-Hill Companies, Inc. **Figure 2.17:** From Santrock, *Life-Span Development,* 13e. Copyright © 2011 The McGraw-Hill Companies. Reproduced with permission of The McGraw-Hill Companies, Inc. **Figure 2.18:** From Santrock, *Life-Span Development,* 13e. Copyright © 2011 The McGraw-Hill Companies. Reproduced with permission of The McGraw-Hill Companies, Inc.

Chapter 3

Figure 3.3: From Santrock, *Children,* 10e. Copyright © 2008 The McGraw-Hill Companies. Reproduced with permission of The McGraw-Hill Companies, Inc. **Figure 3.6:** From Santrock, *Life-Span Development,* 13e. Copyright © 2011 The McGraw-Hill Companies. Reproduced with permission of The McGraw-Hill Companies, Inc. **Figure 3.7:** From Santrock, *Child Development,* 9e. Copyright © 2001 The McGraw-Hill Companies. Reproduced with permission of The McGraw-Hill Companies, Inc. **Figure 3.12:** From Santrock, *Psychology,* 7e. Copyright © 2003 The McGraw-Hill Companies. Reproduced with permission of The McGraw-Hill Companies, Inc. **Figure 3.13:** From *Human Biology and Ecology,* Second Edition, by Albert Damon. W.W. Norton & Company, Inc., 1977. **Figure 3.14:** From Santrock, *Essentials of Life-Span Development,* 1e. Copyright © 2008 The McGraw-Hill Companies. Reproduced with permission of The McGraw-Hill Companies, Inc. **Figure 3.19:** From data in D.J. Eaton, et al., 2008. *Youth Risk Behavior Surveillance—United States, MMWR,* Vol. 57, 131, after data from Table 95. Atlanta: Centers for Disease Control & Prevention. **Figure 3.20:** From *The Psychology of Death, Dying and Bereavement,* by Richard Schulz. Copyright © 1978 The McGraw-Hill Companies. Reproduced with permission of The McGraw-Hill Companies, Inc.

Chapter 4

Figure 4.2: From M.J. Park, et al., 2006, "The Health Status of Young Adults in the U.S.," *Journal of Adolescent Health,* 39(3), Figure. 1, p. 310. Reprinted with permission from Elsevier via RightsLink. http://www.elsevier.com. **Figure 4.4:** Reprinted from *Alzheimer's & Dementia,* Vol. 6(2), 2010, 158–194. Alzheimer's Association. Copyright © 2010 with permission from Elsevier. http://www.elsevier.com. **Figure 4.6:** Adapted from Janice K. Kiecolt-Glaser, et al., 2003, "Chronic Stress and Age-Related Increases in the Proinflammatory Cytokine IL-6," *Proceedings of the National Academy of Science USA,* 100(15), after Figure 1. Copyright © 2003 National Academy of Sciences, U.S.A. Used with permission. **Figure 4.7:** From "Nursing home

use by the "Oldest Old" sharply declines," by Lisa Alecxih, The Lewin Group, November 21, 2006, Reprinted with permission.

Chapter 5

Figure 5.3 (graph): Reprinted from *Journal of Pediatrics,* Vol. 71(2), W.K. Frankenburg and J.B. Dobbs, "The Denver Development Screening Test" pp. 181–191. Copyright Journal of Pediatrics 1967. Used with permission from Elsevier. **p. 159 text:** From *Parents' Guide to Girls' Sports.* Reprinted by permission of the Women's Sports Foundation. **Figure 5.6a:** Adapted from Alexander Semenoick, in R.L. Franz, "The Origin of Form Perception," *Scientific American,* 1961. **Figure 5.7:** From A. Slater, V. Morison, & M. Somers, 1988, "Orientation Discrimination and Cortical Functions in the Human Newborn," *Perception,* Vol. 17, pp. 597–602, Figure 1 and Table 1. Reprinted by permission. **Figure 5.10:** From B.I. Bertenthal, M.R. Longo, and S. Kenny, "Phenomenal Permanence and the Development of Predictive Tracking in Infancy," 2007. *Child Development,* 78, p. 354. Reprinted by permission of John Wiley and Sons, Inc. **Figure 5.13:** Adapted from J.A. Brabyn, et al., "The Smith-Kettlewell Institute (SKI) Longitudinal Study of Vision Function and Its Impact on the Elderly: An Overview," *Optometry and Vision Science,* 78(5): 264–269, May 2001. Used with permission by Dr. John Brabyn. **Figure 5.16:** From Santrock, *Life-Span Development,* 8e. Copyright © 2002 The McGraw-Hill Companies. Reproduced with permission of The McGraw-Hill Companies, Inc.

Chapter 6

Figure 6.4: From R. Baillargeon & J. DeVos, 1991, "Object Permanence in Young Infants: Further Evidence," *Child Development,* 62(6), pp. 1227–1246. Reprinted by permission from John Wiley and Sons, Inc. **Figure 6.5:** From Santrock, *Psychology,* 7e. Copyright © 2003 The McGraw-Hill Companies. Reproduced with permission of The McGraw-Hill Companies, Inc. **Figure 6.6:** From *The Symbolic Drawings of Young Children,* by Dennie Palmer Wolf, Annenberg Institute, Brown University. Reprinted by permission. **Figure 6.7 (line art):** From Santrock, *Life-Span Development,* 8e. Copyright © 2002 The McGraw-Hill Companies. Reproduced with permission of The McGraw-Hill Companies, Inc. **Figure 6.8:** From Santrock, *Life-Span Development,* 8e. Copyright © 2002 The McGraw-Hill Companies. Reproduced with permission of The McGraw-Hill Companies, Inc. **Figure 6.9:** From Santrock, *Life-Span Development,* 8e. Copyright © 2002 The McGraw-Hill Companies. Reproduced with permission of The McGraw-Hill Companies, Inc. **Figure 6.11:** Figures from Writing Progress, drawings from Aaron's journal from E. Bodrova & D. Leong, 2001, *Tools of the Mind: A Case Study of Implementing the Vygotskian Approach in American Early Childhood and Primary Classrooms,* pp. 36, 38. Copyright © UNESCO: IBE 2001. **Figure 6.13:** Figure after J.D. Sinnott & L. Johnson, 1997, "Brief report: Complex postformal thought in skilled research administrators," *Journal of Adult*

Development, 4(1), 45–53. Reprinted with kind permission from Springer Science + Business Media.

Chapter 7

Figure 7.2: From S.C. Li et al., 2004, *Psychological Science,* 15(3), p. 158. Copyright © Association for Psychological Science. Reprinted by permission of Sage Publications. **Figure 7.4:** From E. Vurpillot, 1968, "The Development of Scanning Strategies," *Journal of Experimental Child Psychology,* 6(4), 632–650, Figure 1. Reprinted with permission from Elsevier, via RightsLink. http://www.elsevier.com. **Figure 7.7:** From P.J. Bauer, *Learning and the Infant Mind,* A. Woodward & A. Needham (eds.), Table 1, p. 12. © 2009 by Amanda Woodward and Amy Needham. Used by permission of Oxford University Press, Inc. **Figure 7.8:** From F. Dempster, 1981, "Memory Span," *Psychological Bulletin,* Vol. 89(1), pp. 63–100. Copyright © 1981 American Psychological Association. Adapted with permission. **Figure 7.10:** From Santrock, *Life-Span Development* 13e. Copyright © 2011 The McGraw-Hill Companies. Reproduced with permission of The McGraw-Hill Companies, Inc. **Figure 7.11:** From M. Rönnlund, et al., 2005, "Stability, Growth, and Decline in Adult Life Span Development of Declarative Memory," *Psychology and Aging,* 20, p. 11, Figure 2. Copyright © 2005 American Psychological Association. Reprinted with permission. **Figure 7.14:** From "Planes, Trains, Automobiles—and Tea Sets: Extremely Intense Interests in Very Young Children," 2007, DeLoache, Judy S.; Simcock, Gabrielle; Macari, Suzanne. *Developmental Psychology,* 2007(Nov), Vol. 43(6), 1579–1586. Copyright © 2007 American Psychological Association. Reprinted with permission. **Figure 7.16:** After Wellman, Cross & Watson, 2001, "Meta-Analysis of Theory-of-Mind Development: The Truth About False Belief," *Child Development,* 72(3), pp. 655–684. Reprinted by permission of John Wiley and Sons, Inc. **Figure 7.17:** From Uta Frith, *Autism: Explaining the Enigma,* p. 83. Blackwell Publishing, 1989. Reprinted by permission of Blackwell Publishing Ltd.

Chapter 8

Figure 8.1: From Santrock, *Children,* 5e. Copyright © 1997 The McGraw-Hill Companies. Reproduced with permission of The McGraw-Hill Companies, Inc. **Figure 8.5:** From Robert Sternberg (ed.), 2000, *Handbook of Intelligence.* New York: Cambridge University Press. **Figure 8.6:** From "The Increase in IQ Scores from 1932 to 1997," by Dr. Ulric Neisser. Reprinted by permission. **Figure 8.7:** From Santrock, *Life-Span Development,* 8e. Copyright © 2002 The McGraw-Hill Companies. Reproduced with permission of The McGraw-Hill Companies, Inc. **Figure 8.8:** From K.W. Schaie, *Developmental Influences on Adult Intelligence: The Seattle Longitudinal Study,* 2005, p. 127, Figure 5.7a. © 2005 by Oxford University Press. Used by permission of Oxford University Press, Inc. **Figure 8.9:** From Santrock, *Life-Span Development,* 8e. Copyright © 2002 The McGraw-

Hill Companies. Reproduced with permission of The McGraw-Hill Companies, Inc. **Figure 8.10:** From Santrock, *Life-Span Development,* 10e. Copyright © 2006 The McGraw-Hill Companies. Reproduced with permission of The McGraw-Hill Companies, Inc. **Figure 8.11:** From Santrock, *Educational Psychology,* 1e. Copyright © 2001 The McGraw-Hill Companies. Reproduced with permission of The McGraw-Hill Companies, Inc. **Figure 8.12:** Classification of Mental Retardation Based on Levels of Support Needed, Based on Morton Hunt, *The Universe Within: A New Science Explores the Human Mind,* 1982.

Chapter 9

Figure 9.1: Reprinted by permission of Sherrel Haight, Ph.D. **Figure 9.3:** From Santrock, *Children,* 7e. Copyright © 2003 The McGraw-Hill Companies. Reproduced with permission of The McGraw-Hill Companies, Inc. **Figure 9.4:** From Santrock, *Children,* 7e. Copyright © 2003 The McGraw-Hill Companies. Reproduced with permission of The McGraw-Hill Companies, Inc. **Figure 9.5:** From Jean Berko, 1958, "The Child's Learning of English Morphology," in *Word,* Vol. 14, p. 154. Reprinted by permission of Jean Berko Gleason. **Figure 9.7:** From Santrock, *Child Development,* 10e. Copyright © 2005 The McGraw-Hill Companies. Reproduced with permission of The McGraw-Hill Companies, Inc.

Chapter 10

Figure 10.6: From D. Mroczek and C.M. Kolarz, 1998, "The Effect of Age in Positive and Negative Affect," in *Journal of Personality and Social Psychology,* Vol. 75(5), pp. 1333–1349. Copyright © 1998 by the American Psychological Association. Reproduced with permission. **Figure 10.7:** From L. Carstensen, et al., "The Social Context of Emotional Experience," *Annual Review of Gerontology and Geriatrics,* Schaie/Lawton, eds., Vol. 17, p. 331, Figure 12.2. Copyright 1997. Reproduced with the permission of Springer Publishing Company, LLC. **Figure 10.9 (graph):** From Santrock, *Life-Span Development,* 11e. Copyright © 2008 The McGraw-Hill Companies. Reproduced with permission of The McGraw-Hill Companies, Inc. **Figure 10.10:** From M.H. van IJzendoorn & P.M. Kroonenberg, 1988, "Cross-Cultural Patterns of Attachment: A Meta-Analysis of the Strange Situation," *Child Development,* 59(1), pp. 147–156. © 1988. Reprinted by permission of Blackwell Publishing Ltd. **Figure 10.11:** From Santrock, *Child Development: An Introduction,* 13e, p. 313. Copyright © 2011 The McGraw-Hill Companies. Used by permission of The McGraw-Hill Companies, Inc. **Figure 10.13:** From A.K. Clarke-Stewart and J.L. Miner, "Child and day care, effects of," from M.M. Haith and J.B. Benson (Eds.), *Encyclopedia of Infant and Early Childhood Development,* Vol. 1, Figure 2, p. 269. Copyright © 2008 with permission from Elsevier. http://www.elsevier.com. **Figure 10.14:** From M.N. Reedy, J.E. Birren & K.W. Schaie, 1981, "Age and Sex Differences in Satisfying Relationships Across the Adult Life Span," *Human Development,* 24, pp. 52–66. Reprinted

with permission, S. Karger AG, Basel, Switzerland. **Figure 10.15:** From Robert J. Sternberg, 1988, *The Triangle of Love,* New York: Basic Books. **Figure 10.16:** From T. Tashiro & P. Frazier, 2003, "I'll Never Be in a Relationship Like That Again: Personal Growth Following Romantic Relationship Breakups," *Personal Relationships,* 10(1), pp. 113–128, after Table 1, p. 120. Reprinted by permission of John Wiley and Sons, Inc.

Chapter 11

Figure 11.1 (graph): From M. Lewis & J. Brooks-Gunn, "The Development of Self-Recognition in Infancy," *Social Cognition and the Acquisition of the Self,* 1979, p. 64. Reprinted with kind permission from Springer Science + Business Media. **Figure 11.2:** From S. Harter, 1999, *The Construction of the Self,* Table 6.1. New York: Guilford Press. Reprinted by permission of Guilford Press. **Figure 11.3:** From R.W. Robins, et al., 2002, "Global Self-Esteem Across the Life-Span," in *Psychology and Aging,* Vol. 17(3), pp. 423–434. Copyright © 2002 by the American Psychological Association. Reproduced with permission. **Figure 11.5:** From Santrock, *Life-Span Development,* 8e. Copyright © 2002 The McGraw-Hill Companies. Reproduced with permission of The McGraw-Hill Companies, Inc. **Figure 11.6:** From Santrock, *Psychology,* 6e. Copyright © 2000 The McGraw-Hill Companies. Reproduced with permission of The McGraw-Hill Companies, Inc. **Figure 11.8:** From Nansel et al., 2001. "Bullying Behaviors Among U.S. Youth," *Journal of the American Medical Association,* Vol. 285, pp. 2094–2100. **Figure 11.10:** From "Items Used to Assess Generativity and Identity Certainty," from A.J. Stewart, J.M. Ostrove & R. Helson, 2001, "Middle Aging in Women: Patterns of Personality Change from the 30s to the 50s, "Table II, *Journal of Adult Development,* Vol. 8(1), pp. 23–37, with kind permission of Springer Science + Business Media. **Figure 11.11:** From D.K. Mroczek and A. Spiro, 2007, "Personality Change Influences Mortality in Older Men," *Psychological Science,* 18(5), Figure 1, p. 375. Copyright © Association for Psychological Science. Reprinted by permission of Sage Publications.

Chapter 12

Figure 12.2: From G. Levy, A. Sadovsky & G. Troseth, 2000, "Aspects of Young Children's Perceptions of Gender-Typed Occupations," *Sex Roles,* 42(11/12), Table 1. p. 1000. Reprinted with kind permission from Springer Science + Business Media. **Figure 12.4:** From *Sex in America,* by Robert Michael et al. Copyright © 1994 CSG Enterprises, Inc., Edward O. Laumann, Robert T. Michael, and Gina Kolata. By permission of Hachette Book Group, on behalf of Edward O. Laumann. **Figure 12.5:** From Santrock, *Children,* 9e. Copyright © 2007 The McGraw-Hill Companies. Reproduced with permission of The McGraw-Hill Companies, Inc. **Figure 12.8:** From Santrock, *Life-Span Development,* 12e. Copyright © 2009 The McGraw-Hill Companies. Reproduced with permission of The McGraw-Hill Companies, Inc.

Chapter 13

Figure 13.3: From Santrock, *Adolescence*, 8e. Copyright © 2001 The McGraw-Hill Companies. Reproduced with permission of The McGraw-Hill Companies, Inc. **Figure 13.5:** From P. Wink & M. Dillon, 2002, "Spiritual Development Across the Adult Life Course: Findings From a Longitudinal Study," *Journal of Adult Development*, 9(1), pp. 79–84. With kind permission of Springer Science + Business Media.

Chapter 14

Figure 14.1: From Jay Belsky, "Early Human Experiences: A Family Perspective," in *Developmental Psychology*, Vol. 17(1), pp. 3–23. Copyright © 1981 by the American Psychological Association. **Figure 14.2:** "The Increase in Cohabitation in the United States," from U.S. Bureau of the Census, 2000. **Figure 14.3:** The National Marriage Project, Figure 4, Copyright © 2008 by The National Marriage Project at the University of Virginia. Reprinted by permission of the National Marriage Project. **Figure 14.4:** From Karney, B.R. & Bradbury, T.N., 2005, "Contextual Influences on Marriage: Implications for Policy and Intervention," *Current Directions in Psychological Science*, (14)4, pp. 171–174, Figure 2. Copyright © Association for Psychological Science. Reprinted by permission of SAGE Publications. **Figure 14.5:** "The Divorce Rate in Relation to Number of Years Married," from U.S. Bureau of the Census, 2000. **p. 455 Coping with Divorce:** From *For Better or Worse: Divorce Reconsidered*, by E. Mavis Hetherington and John Kelly. Copyright © 2002 by E. Mavis Hetherington and John Kelly. Used by permission of W.W. Norton & Company, Inc. **Figure 14.7:** From "Corporal Punishment in Different Countries," K. Curran, J. DuCette, J. Eisenstein, I. Hyman, August 2001, "Statistical Analysis of the Cross-Cultural Data: The Third Year." Paper presented at APA meeting, San Francisco, CA. Reprinted with permission. **Figure 14.8:** From M.R. Gunnar, P.A. Fisher, 2006, "The Early Experience Stress and Prevention Network: Bringing Basic Research on Early Experience and Stress Neurobiology to Bear on Preventative Interventions for Neglected and Maltreated Children," *Development and Psychopathology*, 18(3), 651–677. Figure 4 on p. 666. Cambridge Journals. © 2006 Cambridge University Press. Used with permission of Cambridge University Press via Copyright Clearance Center. **Figure 14.10:** From Santrock, *Child Development*, 13e. Copyright © 2011 The McGraw-Hill Companies. Used by permission of The McGraw-Hill Companies, Inc. **Figure 14.11:** From Santrock, *Life-Span Development*, 11e. Copyright © 2008 The McGraw-Hill Companies. Reproduced with permission of The McGraw-Hill Companies, Inc.

Chapter 15

Figure 15.1: From T. Nansel, et al., 2001, "Bullying Behaviors Among U.S. Youth," *Journal of the American Medical Association*, Vol. 285, pp. 2094–2100. **Figure 15.2:** From E.E. Maccoby & C.N. Jacklin, 1987, "Gender Segregation in Childhood," in H.W. Reese (ed.), *Advances in Child Development and Behavior*, Vol. 20, pp. 239–287, San Diego: Academic Press. Copyright 1987 with permission from Elsevier. http://www .elsevier.com. **Figure 15.3:** From Santrock, *Child Development*, 11e. Copyright © 2007 The McGraw-Hill Companies. Reproduced with permission of The McGraw-Hill Companies, Inc. **Figure 15.5:** From R.W. Larson, 2001, "How U.S. Children and Adolescents Spend Time: What it Does (and Doesn't) Tell Us About Their Development," *Current Directions in Psychological Science*, 10(5), pp. 160–164, Table 1. Copyright © Association for Psychological Science. Reprinted by permission of SAGE Publications. **Figure 15.6:** From H.C. Triandis, 1995, *Individualism & Collectivism*. Boulder, CO: Westview Press. Copyright © 1995 Harry C. Triandis. Reprinted by permission of Westview Press, a member of the Perseus Books Group. **Figure 15.7:** From D. Trafimow, et al., 1997, "The Effects of Language and Priming on the Relative Accessibility of the Private Self and the Collective Self," *Journal of Cross-Cultural Psychology*, 28(1), pp. 107–123. Reprinted by permission via RightsLink. **Figure 15.9:** From Santrock, *Adolescence*, 8e.

Copyright © 2001 The McGraw-Hill Companies. Reproduced with permission of The McGraw-Hill Companies, Inc. **Figure 15.10:** "Actual and Projected Number of U.S. Adolescents Aged 10 to 19, 2000–2100," from U.S. Bureau of the Census, 2002, *National Population Projects, Summary Files*.

Chapter 16

Figure 16.2: From E. Diener & M.E. Seligman, 2002, "Very Happy People," *Psychological Science*, 13(1), pp. 81–84. Copyright © Association for Psychological Science. Reprinted by permission of SAGE Publications. **Figure 16.3:** Figure from the National Center for Education Statistics, 2003. **Figure 16.5:** From P. Shaw et al., 2007, "Attention Deficit/Hyperactivity Disorder is Characterized by a Delay in Cortical Maturation," *Proceedings of the National Academy of Sciences*, Vol. 104(49), p. 19650, Figure. 2. Copyright © 2007 National Academy of Sciences, USA. Used with permission. **Figure 16.7:** From D. Stipek, *Motivation to Learn*, 4e, Table 5.3. Boston: Allyn & Bacon. Copyright © 2002. Reproduced with permission of Pearson Education, Inc. **Figure 16.9:** From Stevenson, Lee & Stigler, 1986, "Mathematics Achievement of Chinese, Japanese and American Children" *Science*, Vol. 231(4739), pp. 693–699, Figure 6. Reprinted with permission from AAAS via RightsLink. http://www .sciencemag.org/content/231/4739/693.abstract. **Figure 16.10:** From Santrock, *Adolescence*, 11e. Copyright © 2007 The McGraw-Hill Companies. Reproduced with permission of The McGraw-Hill Companies, Inc. **Figure 16.11:** U.S. Bureau of Labor Statistics. **Figure 16.12:** U.S. Bureau of Labor Statistics. **Figure 16.14:** From HSBC 2007 report *The Future of Retirement: The new old age*. Reprinted by permission.

Chapter 17

Figure 17.3 From D.B. Goldston, et al., 2008, "Cultural Consideration in Adolescent Suicide Prevention and Psychosocial Treatment," *American Psychologist*, 63(1), 14–31, Figure 2, p. 15. Copyright © 2008 by the American Psychological Association. Reproduced with permission.

name index

Bukowski, W. M., 490, 493, 496, 497
Bulanda, J. R., 450
Bulik, C. M., 13, 136
Bullock, M., 340
Bumpass, L., 481
Bumpus, M. F., 468
Burchinal, M. R, 544
Burgard, S., 551
Burgio, L. D., 128
Buriel, R., 36, 448, 459, 462, 518
Burke, D. M., 289
Burke, H. M., 96
Burke, J., 427
Burke-Adams, A., 268
Burns, F., 79
Burns, M. S., 283
Burraston, B., 429
Bursuck, W. D., 534, 537
Burt, S. A., 61
Burton, R. V., 414
Bushman, B. J., 510
Bushnell, E. W., 175
Buss, D. M., 18, 19, 49, 373, 380, 452
Buss, K. A., 314
Busseri, M. A., 480
Bussey, K., 373
Butcher, K., 141
Butler, R. N., 402
Butler, Y. G., 288
Butter, E. M., 434
Butterworth, M. R., 389, 458
Butz, A. M., 124
Buzwell, S., 394
Byrne, D. C., 94
Byrne, M. W., 112
Byrnes, J. P., 198
Byrom, S., 77
Bytschkow, K., 147

C

Cabeza, R., 107, 235
Caldwell, E. L., 503
Calenda, E., 111
Calkins, S. D., 302, 306
Callahan, D., 582
Caltran, G., 305
Cambria, J., 544
Camburn, D., 394
Cameron, J. M., 147
Campbell, A., 324
Campbell, B., 251
Campbell, C. A., 390
Campbell, D. T., 507
Campbell, G. R., 100
Campbell, L., 251
Campbell, R., 391
Campbell, R. A., 256
Campbell, V. A., 172
Campos, J., 322
Campos, J. J., 168, 304, 305, 306, 312, 323
Candore, G., 116
Candow, D. G., 96
Cansino, S., 224
Capaldi, D. M., 400
Caplan, D., 223

Cappuccio, F. P., 113
Caputi, P., 113
Cardell, M., 457
Cardelle-Elawar, M., 238
Carey, D. P., 252
Carlo, G., 424, 425
Carlow, J. J., 572
Carlson, E. A., 7, 19, 322, 323, 330
Carlson, M. J., 446
Carlson, S. M., 191, 218, 228
Carlson, W., 497
Carlsson, A. C., 139
Carnagy, N. L., 510
Carnegie Foundation, 530
Carpendale, J., 341, 342, 490
Carpendale, J. I., 240, 340
Carpendale, J. I. M., 198, 340
Carpenter, M., 215, 319
Carr, D., 420, 456, 565, 567, 575, 579
Carrell, S. E., 422
Carrier, L. M., 512
Carriere, J. S., 217
Carrington, H., 304
Carroll, A. E., 493
Carroll, J. L., 391, 392
Carroll, M. D., 134, 135, 387
Carskadon, M. A., 112, 113
Carstensen, L. L., 17, 310, 311, 347, 351, 499, 504, 506
Carter, C. S., 324
Cartwright, K. B., 206, 207
Cartwright, R., 110
Caruso, C., 116
Carver, K., 330
Casas, M., 530
Case, R., 199, 220
Casey, B. J., 13, 102, 103, 104, 105, 187, 190, 220, 227, 228, 235, 317, 349
Casey, P. H., 82
Cashion, M. C., 8, 78, 82
Caspers, K. M., 62
Caspi, A., 62, 366
Cassell, E. J., 567
Cassey, J. R., 171
Cassidy, J., 320, 330
Catalano, R. F., 396
Catani, C., 309
Cauffman, E., 104, 462
Caughey, A. B., 68
Cavanagh, S. E., 95
Cavazos-Rehg, P. A., 398
Cave, R. K., 289
Cease, A. T., 123
Ceci, S. J., 27, 221, 222, 254
Center for Survey Research at the University of Connecticut, 551
Centers for Disease Control and Prevention, 111, 134, 144, 397, 536
Cerda, M., 61
Chalupa, L. M., 107
Chambers, B., 528
Chan, R., 567
Chan, W., 481
Chan, Z. C., 572
Chandler, M. J., 240

Chandra, A., 449
Chang, M. Y., 79
Chang, V. W., 516
Chang, Y., 141
Chao, R., 462
Chao, R. K., 462
Charles, S. T., 310, 311, 351, 362, 499, 504, 506
Charlton, R. A., 235
Charman, T., 536
Charness, N., 172, 447, 512
Chassin, L., 481
Chatters, L. M., 435
Chaytor, N., 223
Cheah, C. S., 518
Cheah, C. W., 517
Cheah, S. L., 447
Cheever, N., 512
Chemtob, C. M., 309
Chen, C., 546
Chen, C. H., 79
Chen, D., 139
Chen, G., 56
Chen, J. J., 513, 537
Chen, S., 322
Chen, X., 315, 447, 508
Chen, Z-Y., 461
Cheney, R., 240
Cheng, M. H., 97
Cheng, S., 510
Cheng, S. T., 505
Cheng, Y. P., 470
Cherkas, L. F., 144
Cherlin, A. J., 448, 450, 473
Chervenak, F. A., 73
Chess, S., 312, 314
Cheung, A. C. K., 528
Chevreul, H., 270
Chi, M. T., 223
Chia, P., 82
Chiambretto, P., 577
Chiang, K. J., 345
Chiappe, D., 252
Childers, J. B., 282
Children's Defense Fund, 514
Childs, K. L., 105
Childstats.gov, 10, 514
Chilibeck, P. D., 96
Chlebowski, R. T., 401
Choi, H., 454
Choi, S., 279
Chokroverty, S., 111
Chomsky, N., 291–292
Chopra, S. B., 518
Choufani, S., 56
Chouinard, R., 542
Chow, P. K., 505
Chow, S-M., 471
Christakis, D. A., 510
Christensen, K., 454, 499
Christensen, L. B., 32
Christensen, M., 94
Christian, L. M., 129
Christian, M. S., 70
Christiani, D., 62
Christiansen, K., 386
Christie, J., 285, 286
Chung, J. K., 170

Cicchetti, D., 464, 465, 466, 467
Cici-Gokaltun, T. C., 505
Cicirelli, V. G., 478, 479
Cifani, C., 139
Cignini, P., 67
Cillessen, A. H. N., 490
Ciol, M. A., 519
Citkovitz, C., 79
Civelek, E., 70
Claes, H. I., 402
Clancy, S. M., 233
Clark, B., 266
Clark, D. J., 160
Clark, E., 282
Clark, E. V., 292
Clark, J., 142
Clark-Cotton, M. R., 289, 290
Clarke, A., 58
Clarke-Stewart, A. K., 3, 8, 27, 63, 323, 324, 325, 326, 445, 471, 472
Class, Q. A., 73
Clausen, J. A., 365, 434
Claxton, A., 459
Clay, O. J., 169
Clearfield, M. W., 189
Clemmensen, D., 67, 73
Cliffordson, C., 254
Clifton, R. K., 160, 174
Cluett, E. R., 79
Cnaan, R. A., 433
Coangelo, N. C., 266
Coffino, B., 7, 19, 322, 323, 330
Coffman, J. L., 223
Cohen, D., 324
Cohen, F., 551
Cohen, M., 551
Cohen, N. J., 475
Cohen, O., 425
Cohen, R., 511
Coie, J. D., 491
Coker, R. H., 144
Colapinto, J., 372
Colarossi, L. G., 468
Colby, A., 411
Colcombe, S. J., 236, 237
Cole, C., 224
Cole, C. A., 234
Cole, M., 199
Cole, P. M., 302, 307, 315
Coleman, M., 456, 473
Coleman, P. D., 107
Coleman-Phox, K., 111
Collier, R., 578
Collins, D., 422
Collins, M., 550
Collins, W. A., 329, 467, 468, 469, 498, 532
Colom, R., 252
Colombo, J., 349
Colon, E., 94
Colonna-Romano, G., 116
Coltrane, S., 468
Columbo, J., 214
Comer, J., 539
Comings, J., 533
Commoner, B., 53
Commons, M. L., 207

Durbin, D. R., 123
Durrant, J. E., 464, 466
Durston, S., 103, 535
Duschi, R., 230
DuToit, S., 33
Dweck, C. S., 542, 543
Dworkin, S. L., 395
Dworkis, D. A., 58
Dwyer, D. S., 124
Dykas, M. J., 320
Dykes, F., 131
Dy-Liacco, G., 435

E

Eagly, A., 9, 35, 373, 379, 380
Eagly, A. H., 379
Earhart, G. M., 129
East, P., 477
Eaton, D. K., 112, 135, 142, 156, 391, 395, 396
Eaves, L. J., 60
Eby, J. W., 525
Eccles, J., 530, 531, 542
Eccles, J. S., 198, 433, 503, 531, 538, 541, 544
Echevarria, J. K. L., 288
Eckenrode, J., 76
Edelman, M. W., 10
Edgington, C., 329
Edison, S. C., 340
Ednick, M., 111
Edwards, J. D., 213, 237
Edwardson, C. L., 141
Egan, S. K., 371
Egeland, B., 427, 532
Eggebeen, D. J., 519
Eggum, N. D., 349, 380
Ehrhardt, A. A., 372
Eidar-Avidan, D., 455
Einstein, A., 252–253
Einstein, G. O., 225
Eisdoerfer, C., 556
Eisenberg, N., 302, 349, 380, 415, 419, 421, 423, 425
Elashi, F. B., 341
Elder, G. H., 446, 447
El-Fishawy, P., 536
Elias, J. W., 234
Eliasieh, K., 107
Elkind, D., 192, 195, 197
Elks, C. E., 94
Ellenberg, D., 141
Ellertson, B., 535
Ellickson, P. L., 147
Elliott, A. F., 128
Elliott, E., 542
Ellis, L., 388
El-Sayed, Y. Y., 79
El-Sheikh, M., 112, 471
Ely, P., 285
Emery, R. E., 472
Emre, M., 128
Enfield, A., 422
English, G. W., 10, 515
Englund, M. M., 532
Engvig, A., 237
Ennett, S. T., 147
Enns, G. M., 58

Enright, R., 425
Ensembl Human, 53
Ensor, R., 307, 340
Entwisle, D., 513, 538
Enz, B. J., 285, 286
Erath, S. E., 496
Erbelding, E. J., 72
Erickson, K. I., 73, 106, 213, 235, 236, 237, 506
Ericsson, K. A., 265
Erikson, E., 21–22, 320, 353, 357, 363, 427
Erikson, E. H., 432
Erikson, J., 22
Erkal, S., 123
Ernst, J. L., 60
Eshkoll, T., 65
ESHRE Capri Workshop Group, 400
Eskildsen, M., 130
Eskilsson, G., 171
Espelage, D., 492
Estrada, S., 232
Etaugh, C., 480, 482
Evans, G. D., 401
Evans, G. W., 10, 515
Ewen, D., 528
Eysenck, M., 219

F

Fabiano, G. A., 535
Fabricius, W. V., 472
Facciorusso, A., 566
Fagan, J. F., 259
Faghih Zadeh, S., 75
Fagundes, C. P., 389, 458
Fahey, T. D., 138, 141
Fairweather, A. K., 573
Fairweather, E., 228, 268
Faissner, A., 102
Fakhoury, J., 117
Falbo, T., 478
Falk, M. C., 237
Fallu, J. S., 105
Fanconi, M., 100
Fantasia, H. C., 396
Fantz, R. L., 164, 166
Farage, M. A., 96
Faraone, S. V., 534
Farley, F., 232
Farooq, A., 127
Farooqui, A., 118
Farooqui, T., 118
Farrell, M. P., 361
Farrell, S. K., 553
Farrell, S. W., 143
Farrington, D. P., 427
Fass, A., 566
Fass, J., 566
Fatusi, A. O., 124
Fawcett, R. C., 247, 249
Fearon, R. P., 322
Fechtner, R. D., 170
Federal Interagency Forum on Child and Family Statistics, 515
Feeney, M. P., 171
Feeny, B. C., 331, 332

Feiring, C., 330
Feldhusen, J., 264
Feldman, S. S., 394, 395
Fenzel, L. M., 346
Fergusson, D. M., 132
Fertig, A., 514, 515
Fertig, A. R., 467
Field, D., 481
Field, T., 79
Field, T. M., 71, 73, 83, 85
Finch, C. E., 212
Finch, E., 118
Finger, B., 323
Fingerhut, A. W., 388, 389
Fingerman, K. L., 19, 470, 480, 481, 505
Fingerman, L., 481
Finkelstein, L. M., 553
Finlayson, M., 434
Finn, S. E., 457
Fischer, J. L., 454
Fischer, K., 339
Fischer, K. W., 206
Fischoff, B., 196, 570
Fisher, C. A., 136
Fisher, D., 391
Fisher, P. A., 467
Fisk, A. D., 217
Fiske, A., 345
Fitzsimmons, C., 282
Flannery, D., 196
Flavell, E. R., 239
Flavell, J. H., 212, 222, 238, 239, 240, 241
Fleeson, W., 364
Flegal, K. M., 135, 138
Flegal, R. M., 134
Fleming, A. S., 324
Flicker, L., 235
Flint, M. S., 53
Flom, R., 215
Flores, I., 117
Flori, K. L., 499
Florin, T., 92
Florsheim, P., 329
Flynn, J. R., 254
Foehr, U. G., 216, 509
Follingstad, D., 391
Fontaine, R. G., 490
Fontenot, H. B., 476
Food & Nutrition Service, 133
Forbes, E. E., 103
Ford, M. E., 544
Forgatch, M. S., 428
Forrester, M. B., 7
Forster, D. A., 72
Forsyth, A. L., 126
Forte, T., 551
Forzano, L. B., 29
Fosco, G. M., 446
Foster, E. M., 572
Foster, G. D., 139
Fournier, M. A., 355
Fowler-Brown, A., 136
Fox, E., 285
Fox, J. A., 31
Fox, M. C., 447, 512
Fox, N., 220

Fox, N. A., 102
Fox, S. E., 100
Fox, S. P., 100
Fozard, J. L., 169
Franchak, J. M., 165
Francis, J., 356
Franco, D. L., 125
Franco, P., 111
Frankl, V., 436
Franklin, A., 167
Franklin, B., 269–270
Franklin, S., 231, 242
Fraser, G., 356
Fraser, J., 525
Fraser, S., 253
Frazier, P., 334, 455
Frederickson, B. L., 379
Frederikse, M., 378
Freeborn, B. A., 433
Freud, S., 20–21
Freund, A. M., 347, 351
Frey, B. S., 310
Frey, W. H., 554
Frick, J., 318
Fricker-Gates, R. A., 129
Friedman, H. S., 17, 364
Friedman, S. L., 325, 327
Friedrichs, A., 241
Friedrici, A. D., 291
Friend, M., 536, 537
Friesen, W., 108
Frimer, J. A., 417
Frisen, A., 95
Froh, J. J., 425
Frost, E. A., 70
Fruen, J. R., 534
Fry, P. S., 580
Frydenberg, E., 348
Fujisawa, D., 578
Fuligni, A. J., 357
Fuller-Thompson, E., 480
Fulop, T., 118
Fung, Y. L., 572
Furman, W., 328, 329
Furstenberg, F. F., 124, 473, 549, 550
Furth, H. G., 194

G

Gable, S., 141
Gabrielli, J. D. E., 235
Gackney, M. E., 129
Gadot, L., 551
Gaesser, B., 218, 224
Gaffney, K. F., 111
Gagliese, L., 173
Galambos, N. L., 113, 374, 378, 380, 382
Galimberti, D., 126
Galinsky, E., 284, 294, 343, 473
Galliher, R. V., 357
Galloway, J. C., 90
Gallup, G. W., 435
Galupo, M. P., 207
Galvin, J. E., 126
Gamble, W. C., 518
Gan, S., 82
Ganong, L., 456, 473

Ladd, G. W., 488, 491
LaFrance, M., 379
Lafreniere, D., 173
Lagerberg, D., 293
Lahey, B. B., 8
Laible, D., 318, 419, 420
Laible, L. D., 340
Laird, R. D., 428
Lamaze, F., 78
Lamb, K. M., 160
Lamb, M. E., 84, 183, 323, 324, 325
Lamb, M. M., 132
Lamb-Parker, F. G., 528
Lambrinos, J., 422
Landale, N. S., 517
Landgren, H., 106
Landi, D., 108
Landor, A., 433
Lane, H., 275
Lang, F. R., 311
Lange, B. S., 237
Lange, T., 117
Langer, A., 168
Langer, E. J., 130, 228, 237, 575
Langlois, J. H., 317
Langston, W., 29
Langstrom, N., 388
Lansdorp, P. M., 117
Lansford, J. E., 396, 471, 472, 490, 513, 519
Lanzi, R. G., 256
Lapierre, S., 571
Lapp, S. I., 285, 292
Lapsley, D., 417, 420
Lapsley, D. K., 104, 196
Laris, B. A., 399
Larkina, M., 190, 198, 219, 220, 227
La Rocca, T. J., 144
Larson, D. B., 434, 436
Larson, J., 488, 494
Larson, R., 310, 502, 503
Larson, R. W., 503, 549
Larsson, B., 142
Larus, D., 221
Larusso, E. M., 85
Larzelere, R. E., 464
Lathrop, A. L., 166
Latzko, B., 416
Laumann, E. O., 15, 402, 425
Laursen, B., 467, 468, 469, 514
Lavalliere, M., 177
Laven, M., 417
Lavie, C. J., 144
La Vignera, S., 402
Lavik, E., 170
Lavoie, B. A., 172
Lawton, K., 536
Lawyer, S., 148
Lazariu, V., 133
Leadbeater, B. J., 398
Leaf, G., 548
Leaper, C., 374, 377
Leatherdale, S. T., 142
Le Couteur, D. G., 117
Lee, C., 546

Lee, C. K., 505
Lee, G. R., 450
Lee, H. C., 79
Lee, I. M., 144
Lee, K., 168, 341
Lee, M. P., 224, 234
Lee, W. S. C., 100
Leerkes, E. M., 331
Lefkowitz, E. S., 399, 400, 432
Legare, C. H., 343
Legerstee, M., 318
Lehman, H. C., 269
Lehrer, R., 230
Leibovitz, E., 132
Leifer, G., 91
Leifheit-Limson, E., 385, 505
Leigh-Paffenroth, E. D., 172
Leming, M. R., 569
Lempers, J. D., 239
Lenhart, A., 511
Lennon, E. M., 258
Lenoir, C. P., 111
Leonard, C., 241
Leonardi-Bee, J. A., 71
Leong, D. J., 202
Leppanen, J. M., 318
Lerch, C., 159
Lerner, H. G., 383
Lerner, R. M., 104, 396
Lerner-Geva, L., 97, 401
Lesaux, N. K., 288
Leshikar, E. D., 235
Lester, B. M., 71
Levant, R. F., 385
Levelt, W. J. M., 6
Levene, M. I., 73
Levenson, R. W., 379
Lever-Duffy, J., 509, 511
Levin, J., 31
LeVine, K. A., 507
Levine, T. P., 71
Levinson, D. J., 360
Levitt, M. J., 505
Levitt, P., 100
Levy, B., 385, 505
Levy, D. A., 257, 507
Levy, G. D., 376
Lewin-Bizan, S., 396
Lewis, C., 340, 341, 342, 490
Lewis, D. F., 81
Lewis, M., 54, 304, 307, 309, 310, 322, 330, 340, 402, 526
Li, C., 138
Li, D. K., 70, 111
Li, J., 80
Li, Y., 581
Liao, W. C., 144
Liben, L. S., 373, 375, 377, 378, 379, 380, 413, 493, 497
Libertus, K., 161
Lickona, T., 420
Licoppe, C., 383
Lidz, J., 284
Lie, N., 220
Liebergott, J., 279
Lieberman, E., 78
Lieblich, A., 355
Liechty, J. M., 136

Liets, L. C., 107
Lieven, E. V. M., 293
Lifter, K., 279
Lifton, A. J., 575
Light, L. L., 236, 238, 289, 290
Light, L. S., 572
Lillard, A., 500, 501
Lin, F. R., 172
Lin, J. N., 149
Lindau, S. T., 144, 402
Lindberg, A., 57, 379, 380
Lindberg, S. M., 380, 382
Lindblad, F., 535
Lindenberger, U., 215, 261, 262, 350, 351
Lindenberger, V., 6, 107
Lindsay, D. S., 221
Linn, M. W., 426
Linn, S., 500
Lippman, L. A., 432
Lips, U., 100
Litovsky, R., 172
Little, K. C., 332
Little, T. D., 349
Littleton, H. L., 391
Liu, D., 239
Liu, L., 113
Liu, S., 166
Liu, T., 253
Liu, X., 113
Liu-Ambrose, T., 235
Lock, A., 277
Lock, M., 98
Lockey, K., 172
Lockl, K., 239
Lococo, K., 169
Loeber, R., 427
Loehlin, J. C., 60
Lohaus, A., 259
Lomas, J., 251
Longhese, M. P., 117
Longo, M. R., 167
Lonner, W. J., 508
Lorenz, K. Z., 25–26
Losos, J., 49
Loukas, A., 428
Lovden, M., 236
Love, V., 72
Lovelady, C., 75
Low, S., 329
Lowdermilk, D. L., 75, 78, 82
Lowenstein, A. E., 10, 255, 325, 516, 528
Lu, J. S., 69
Lu, M. C., 69
Lu, T., 172
Lubart, T. I., 267
Lucas, E. B., 8
Lucas, R. E., 363, 551
Lucas-Thompson, R., 471
Luciana, M., 104
Lucifero, D., 170
Luden, E., 378
Luders, E., 252, 253
Ludington-Hoe, S. M., 82
Ludwig, S., 92
Lugert, S., 107
Lumpkin, A., 141

Lund, D. A., 577
Lund, H. G., 113
Lundgren, I., 78
Lunkenheimer, E. S., 302
Luria, A., 375
Luszcz, M. A., 117
Luthar, S. S., 514
Lutkenhaus, P., 340
Lykken, D. T., 347
Lynch, M. E., 382
Lynch, S. M., 512, 517, 518
Lyndaker, C., 400
Lynn, R., 255, 257
Lyon, G. R., 534
Lyon, T. D., 241
Lyons, D. M., 106
Lyons, M. J., 18
Lyrra, A. L., 147

M

Ma, Yo-Yo, 266
Macari, S., 227
MacArthur, C., 85
Maccoby, E. E., 462, 463, 497
MacDonald, K., 252
MacFarlane, I. W., 259
MacFarlane, J. A., 173
Maciejewski, P. K., 578
Maciokas, J. B., 217
MacWhinney, B., 276, 293
Madden, D. J., 107, 217, 224, 234, 235
Mader, S. S., 49
Madkour, A. S., 395
Madole, K. L., 227
Madronal, N., 106
Maehr, M. L., 544
Maes, H., 60
Magennis, R., 544
Maggs, J. L., 113, 147
Magiati, I., 536
Magno, C., 238, 242
Mahad, D. J., 100
Mahbub, A. L., 118
Mahncke, H. W., 213
Mahoney, J., 217, 531
Mahoney, J. L., 503
Maimoun, L., 144
Malamitsi-Puchner, A., 398
Maliza, B. A., 73
Mallet, E., 111
Malmstrom, F. V., 422
Maloy, R. W., 509, 511
Malter Cohen, M., 104, 105
Malti, T., 416
Maltseva, D. V., 144
Mancini, A. D., 308
Mandelman, S. D., 255
Mandler, J., 219
Mandler, J. M., 226, 227
Manenti, R., 107
Manganaro, L., 68
Mangels, J. A., 542
Mangione, R., 67
Manhart, L. E., 399
Manley, J. L., 126
Manlove, J., 394
Mann, N., 173

subject index

Education for All Handicapped Children Act (Public Law 94–142), 536
efficacy, need for sense of, 437
effortful control (self-regulation), 314
egocentrism, 191
egocentrism concept, 341
ego ideal, 415
elaboration, 222
electronic media, 510–511
elementary school, 530
embryonic period, 64–65
emerging adults. *See also* adulthood; adults; middle adulthood
  drug use among, 147–148
  friendships, 498
  health of, 124–125
  relationships with parents, 469–470
  sexuality among, 399–400
  substance use by, 145–148
  work and, 549–550
emotional abuse, 466
emotional competence, 303
emotional intelligence, 251
emotional states and stress, effect of, on prenatal development, 73
emotions, 239, 301
  in adolescence, 309–310
  cognition and, 205, 206
  defined, 301–302
  developmental changes in, 308
  in early childhood, 307
  expression of and social relationships, 305–306
  gender differences in, 379–380
  in infancy, 304–307
  positive, longevity and, 108
  primary, 304, 305
  regulating, 302, 306–307, 490
  role of in moral development, 416
  self-conscious, 304, 305
emotion security theory, 471–472
empathy, 415–416
empiricists, 175
encoding, 212
endoderm, 64
engagement model of cognitive optimization, 236
environmental hazards, effect of, on prenatal development, 74
epidural block, 78
epigenetic view and gene × environment (G × E) interaction, 62
episodic memory, 224
equality, 424
equilibration, 184
erectile dysfunction (ED), 402
Erikson's theory, 20, 21–22
estradiol, 93–94
estrogens, 371, 386, 400–401
ethics, in research, 34–35
ethnic bias, 35

ethnic gloss, 35
ethnic identity, 357
ethnicity, 9, 517
  aging and, 519
  families and, 517–519
  immigration and, 517
  in schools, 538–540, 545
ethnocentrism, 508
ethology, 25–26
euthanasia, 566
evocative genotype-environment correlations, 60, 61
evolution
  language development and, 291
  life-span development and, 50–51
evolutionary developmental psychology, 50–51
evolutionary psychology, 49–51
  gender in, 372–373
evolutionary theory of aging, 117
evolutionary perspective, 49
evolutionary psychology, 49–51
  natural selection and adaptive behavior, 49
executive attention, 214
executive functioning, 227–228
exercise, 140
  in adulthood, 138–139, 142–143
  aerobic, 142–143
  in childhood and adolescence, 141–142
  effect of, on aging and longevity, 143–145
existentialist intelligence, 251
exosystem, 27, 445
expanding, of language, 293
experiment, 31
experimental research, 31
expertise, 233
explicit memory, 219, 224
expressive traits, 377
extraversion, 359, 364
extraversion/surgency, 313
extreme binge drinking, 147
extremely preterm infants, 82
extrinsic motivation, 540–541
eye, diseases of, 170
eye-tracking equipment, 165

F

Facebook, 511
face-to-face play, 318
Fagan Test of Infant Intelligence, 259
fairness, concept of, 424
falls, as cause of injury and death among adults, 160
false beliefs, 239
families, 445. *See also* parenting
  adoption in, 45–76
  birth order in, 478–479
  ethnicity and, 517–519
  intergenerational relationships in, 480–482
  moral development within, 412
  multiple developmental trajectories in, 448

poverty and, 516
  reciprocal socialization in, 445–446
  sibling relationships, 477–478, 479
  sociocultural and historical influences on, 446–448
  stepfamilies, 473–474
  as systems, 446
families and relationships, careers in, 45
family and consumer science education, as career, 42
family policy, 11
fast mapping, 282
Fast Track, 429
fathers. *See also* parenting; parents
  as caregivers, 324–325
  socialization strategies of, 374
fear, in infancy, 306
females
  anorexia nervosa in, 136–137
  bereavement among, 580
  binge eating disorder in, 137
  body image during puberty, 95
  bulimia nervosa in, 137
  communication traits of, 383–384
  feminization of poverty, 515–516
  gender development in, 383–384
  life expectancy for, 115
  puberty in, 92–95
  reasons for divorce, 456
feminization of poverty, 515–516
fertilization, 53
fetal alcohol spectrum disorders (FASD), 70
fetal MRI, 67–68
fetal period, 65
  transition to newborn, 79–80
fetus, hearing in, 170
fine motor skills, 160
  adult development and, 162
  in childhood and adolescence, 161–162
  in infancy, 160–161
first habits, 185
5-HTTLPR gene, 62, 323
fixed mindset, 542
fluid intelligence, 260
fluid mechanics, 261
Flynn effect, 254
folic acid, 67
forgiveness, 425
formal operational stage, 23, 194
  abstract, idealistic, and logical thinking, 194–195
fragile X syndrome, 57, 264
free-radical theory of aging, 117–118, 127
friendship
  in adolescence, 496–498
  in adulthood, 498–499
  in childhood, 496
  in emerging adulthood, 498
  in late adulthood, 499
  strategies for making friends, 496

frontal lobe, 99, 100, 102
functional magnetic resonance imaging (fMRI), 30
fuzzy trace theory, 222

G

games, 502
gamma-aminobutyric acid (GABA), 106
Gandhi's Truth (Erikson), 353
gaze following, 215
gender, 9, 371. *See also* sexuality
  autonomy and, 467–468
  biological influences on, 371–373
  care perspective and, 412–413
  cognitive influences on, 375
  cognitive similarities and differences, 378–379
  communication and, 383
  in context, 380–381
  controversy over, 380
  dropout rates and, 531–532
  evolutionary psychology view of, 372–373
  friendship and, 498–499
  intergenerational relationships and, 482
  learning disabilities and, 536
  peer relations and, 493–494
  physical similarities and differences, 378
  prosocial behavior and, 425
  social influences on, 373–375
  socioemotional similarities and differences, 379–380
  suicide and, 571–572
gender bias, 35
gender development, 381
  in adolescence, 382–383
  in childhood, 381–382
gender identity, 371
gender-intensification hypothesis, 382–383
gender schemas, 375, 376
gender schema theory, 375
gender stereotypes, 377
gender-typing, 371
gene-gene interaction, 56
gene-linked abnormalities, 57–58
generativity, versus stagnation, 22, 362–363
genes, 52–53
  Alzheimer disease and, 127
  dominant and recessive, 55
  5-HTTLPR gene, 62
  longevity, 55
  mutated, 54
  sex-linked, 55–56
  susceptibility, 54–55, 116
genetic counseling, as career, 45
genetic expression, 53
genetic imprinting, 56
genetic loading, 63
genetics
  chromosomal and gene-linked abnormalities, 56–58
  collaborative gene, 52–53

differences between males and females, 54
as foundation of development, 52
genes and chromosomes, 53–55
principles of, 55–56
genetic susceptibility to teratogens, 69
gene × environment (G × E) interaction, 62
Genie, 275, 293
genital herpes, 389
genital stage, 21
genital warts, 389
Genius Denied: How to Stop Wasting Our Brightest Young Minds (Davidson & Davidson), 266
genotype, 54
geriatric nursing, as career, 44–45
geriatrics, as career, 44
germinal period, 64
gerontology, as career, 42–43
gestational diabetes, 73
gestures, as language, 278
giftedness, 264–266
gingko biloba, 237
gist, 222
glaucoma, 170
global empathy, 416
goal-directed behavior, 318–319
goal-setting, 543–555
gonadotropins, 93
gonads, 93
gonorrhea, 389
goodness of fit, 315–316
Google, 511
grammar, development of, 284
grandparenting and great-grandparenting, 479–480
Grant Study, 361, 365
grasping reflex, 155
gratitude, 425
Great Depression, 446–447
grief, 576–577
coping and type of death, 579
dimensions of, 577–578
disenfranchised, 578
dual-process model of, 578–579
forms of mourning, 581–583
losing a life partner, 579–581
making sense of the world, 579
prolonged, 578
gross motor skills, 155
in adolescence and adulthood, 159–160
in childhood, 158–159
cultural variations in guiding development, 157–158
first-year development, 156
milestones in, 157
posture development, 155
second-year development, 156–157
walking, 155–156

growth mindset, 542
gynecology, as career, 43–44

H

habituation, 164, 214–215, 259
HDL cholesterol, 96–97
Head Start, 528–529
health, 123
in adolescents, 124
aging and, 125–130
in children, 123–124
cognitive functioning and, 235
in emerging and young adults, 124–125
in life-span perspective, 8
poverty and, 124
religion and, 434–445
health-care system, 11
hearing aids, 172
helpless orientation, 542
hemophilia, 58
heredity-environment correlations, 60–61, 253–255
heritability, 54
heroin, prenatal exposure to, 71–72
heteronomous morality, 408, 410
heterosexual attitudes and behavior, 387–388
hidden curriculum, 420
high-amplitude sucking, 164
hippocampus, 100, 107
home health aide, career as, 45
hormonal stress theory of aging, 118
hormone replacement therapy (HRT), 401
hormones
during puberty, 93–94
effect of, on gender, 371–372
hospice, 567
hostility, punishment of children and, 464
Human Genome Project, 53
human immunodeficiency virus (HIV), 390–391
Huntington's disease, 58
hypertension, 125
hypothalamus, 93
hypothesis, 20
hypothetical-deductive reasoning, 195

I

idea density, 108
idealism, 204
idealistic thinking, 194–195, 343
Identity: Youth and Crisis (Erikson), 353
identity, 339, 352–353
contemporary thoughts on, 353–354
developmental changes in, 354–356
Erikson's view, 353
ethnic, 357
family influences on, 356–357
identity achievement, 355

identity consolidation, 356
identity development, religion and, 432–433
identity diffusion, 354, 355
identity foreclosure, 354, 355
identity moratorium, 355
identity versus identity confusion, 353
"I Have a Dream" (IHAD) program, 532
imagery, 222
imaginary audience, 195
imitation, 25
immanent justice, 409
immigration, changes in families and, 447
immunization schedule, 123
implantation, 64
implicit memory, 219, 224–225
imprinting, 25, 26
inclusion, 537
incompatible blood types, prenatal effects of, 72
incremental theory, 543
independent variable, 32
individualism, 508–509
individualism, instrumental purpose, and exchange in Kohlberg's theory, 410
individuality, 356
individualized education plan (IEP), 537
Individuals with Disabilities Education Act (IDEA), 536–537
inductive reasoning, 260
indulgent parenting, 462
industry versus inferiority, 21
infancy, 14
attachment in, 317–328
attention in, 214–215
brain development in, 100–102
breast versus bottle feeding, 131–133
concept formation and categorization in, 226–227
crying in, 305
emotions in, 304–307
fear in, 306
fine motor skills in, 160–161
grasping skills in, 160–161
height and weight in, 91
intelligence in, 258–259
language development in, 278–280, 294
locomotion during, 318
low birth weight and preterm infants, 80–81
memory in, 219–220
nutrition during, 131–133
orienting response in, 165
reflexes in, 154–155
self-understanding in, 339–340
sensorimotor stage in, 184–190
separation protest in, 306, 307
shared sleeping during, 110–111
SIDS in, 111
sleep patterns in, 109–110

smiling in, 305
social sophistication and insight during, 319
stranger anxiety in, 306, 307
studying perception in, 164–165
touch and pain senses in, 173
visual perception in, 166–168
infantile amnesia, 220
infinite generativity, 275
information
speed of processing, 212–213
strategies for processing, 222
information-processing approach, 211–213
information-processing theory, 24
inhibition to the unfamiliar, 313
initiative versus guilt, 21
insecure avoidant babies, 320, 321
insecure disorganized babies, 320, 321
insecure resistant babies, 320, 321
instrumental traits, 377
integrative approach to moral education, 422–423
integrative ethical education, 423
integrity versus despair, 22
intelligence, 247
in adulthood, 260–263
analytical, 250
bodily-kinesthetic, 251
creative, 250
cross-cultural comparisons, 256
crystallized, 260
cultural bias in testing, 256–257
defined, 247
emotional, 251
ethnic comparisons, 257–258
existentialist, 251
fluid, 260
in infants, 258–259
influence of heredity and environment, 253–255
interpersonal, 251
intrapersonal, 251
mathematical, 251
multiple, theories of, 250
musical, 251
naturalist, 251
neuroscience of, 252–253
practical, 250
spatial, 251
stability and change through adolescence, 29
tests of, 247–250
verbal, 251
intelligence quotient (IQ), 248
intention, 318–319
interactionist view of language, 293–295
interleukin-6, 129
intermodal perception, 174–175
Internet, the, 511–512
interpersonal intelligence, 251
interviews, 29–30
intimacy, 333
in friendships, 495
versus isolation, 21–22
intrapersonal intelligence, 251

mild cognitive impairment (MCI), 127
Mills College studies, 365
mind, theory of, 239–241
mindfulness, 228–229
mindset, 542–543
Minnesota Family Investment Program (MFIP), 11, 516
mitochondrial theory of aging, 118
mitosis, 53–54
mobile media, 509
modeling, 25
Montessori approach to education, 527
moral behavior, 413–414
moral character, 417
moral development
    antisocial behavior and, 426–430
    defined, 408
    emotion and, 416
    moral thought, 408–413
    parenting and, 418–420
    prosocial behavior, 423–426
moral exemplars, 417–418
moral feeling, 414–415
    emotion and, 416
    empathy and, 415–416
    psychoanalytic theory of, 415
moral identity, 417
moral motivation, 493
moral personality, 417
moral thought
    Kohlberg's theory of, 409–413
    Piaget's theory of, 408–409
Moro reflex, 154
morphology, 276, 277, 280–281
mothers. See also parenting; parents
    as caregivers, 324–325
    socialization strategies of, 374
motor development, 153
    dynamic systems view, 153–154
    fine motor skills, 160–162
    gross motor skills, 155–160
    perceptual-motor coupling, 176–177
    reflexes, 154–155
mourning, forms of, 581–583
multiple developmental trajectories, 448
multiple intelligences, theory of, 250–251
multitasking, 217
musical intelligence, 251
mutated genes, 54
mutual interpersonal expectations, relationships, and interpersonal conformity, in Kohlberg's theory, 41
myelination, 99, 100, 101, 102, 103, 161

N

National Association for the Education of Young Children (NAEYC), 529
National Longitudinal Survey of Youth, 397–398

Nation Deceived, A: How Schools Hold Back America's Brightest Students (Colangelo, Assouline, & Cross), 266
nativists, 175
natural childbirth, 78
natural death, 566
naturalistic observation, 29
naturalist intelligence, 251
natural selection, 49
nature-nurture debate, 18, 59
    behavior genetics, 60
    conclusions about, 62–63
    epigenetic view and gene × environment (G × E) interaction, 62
    heredity-environment correlations, 60–61
    in infant development, 189–190
    intelligence, 253–255
    perceptual development and, 175
    shared and nonshared environmental influences, 61–62
negative affectivity, 313
neglected children, 491
neglectful parenting, 462
neonatal intensive care unit (NICU), 73, 82
neonatal nursing, as career, 44
neo-Piagetians, 199
neural tube, 66–67
neurofibrillary tangles, 126
neurogenesis, 67, 106–107
neuronal migration, 67
neurons, 66, 100, 101–102, 128
neuroticism, 359, 364
neurotransmitters, 100, 106
newborn
    hearing in, 170–171
    perception in, 164
    reflexes in, 154–155
    smell sense in, 173
    transition from fetus, 79–80
New Hope program, 516
niche-picking, 61
nicotine, prenatal exposure to, 70–71
No Child Left Behind (NCLB), 266, 268, 526, 542
nonnormative life events, 8
nonprescription drugs, prenatal exposure to, 70
nonshared environmental experiences, 61–62
normal distribution, 248
normative age-graded influences, 7
normative history-graded influences, 7
novelty, 186
Nurse Family Partnership, 76
nurse-midwifery, as career, 44
nursing homes, 130
nutrition, 131
    in adolescence, 135–137
    in childhood, 133–135

during adult development and aging, 137–140
    in infancy, 131–133

O

obesity
    in adolescence, 135–136
    in adulthood, 138
    breast feeding and, 132
    in childhood, 134–135
    mobility limitation and, 160
object permanence, 187, 188
observation, 29
observational learning, 25
obstetrics, as career, 43–44
occipital lobe, 99, 100, 253
occluded objects, perception of, 167–168
Occupational Outlook Handbook, 548
occupational therapy, as career, 45
occupations, gender schema about, 376
Odyssey of the Mind, 237
olfactory bulb, 107
openness, 359
operant conditioning, 24
operations, 190–191
oppositional defiant disorder, 429
optic nerve, 163
oral stage, 21
organic retardation, 264
organization, 184
organogenesis, 64, 70
orienting/investigative process, 214
orienting response, 165
osteoporosis, 126
otitis media, 171
    breast feeding and, 132
overextension, of words, 280
oxidative stress, 127
oxytocin, 78, 324

P

pain, sense of, 173
pain cry, 305
palliative care, 567
palmer grasp, 160
parental leave, 325
parenting. See also families
    adopted children, 476
    child maltreatment and, 465–467
    coparenting, 465
    discipline and, 463–464
    effective monitoring, 460
    juvenile delinquency and, 428–429
    in life-span perspective, 8
    moral development and, 418–420
    parent-adolescent and parent-emerging adult relationships, 467–470
    parental roles, 458–460
    peer relations and, 488
    styles of, 460–463
    temperament and, 315–316

parents
    adoptive, 475–476
    attachment to, 328
    development of child's identity and, 356–357
    drug use and, 147
    facilitation of language development by, 294
    gay and lesbian, 474
    working parents, 470–471
parietal lobe, 99, 100, 252–253
Parkinson disease, 128–129
passion, 333
passive euthanasia, 566
passive genotype-environment correlations, 60, 61
paternal factors, effect of on prenatal development, 73–74
Path to Purpose, The: Helping Children Find Their Calling in Life (Damon), 431
pediatric nursing, as career, 44
pediatrics, as career, 44
peer pressure, 494
    drug use and, 147
peer relations, 487–490
    in adolescence, 494–495
    bullying, 492–493
    friendship, 495–498
    gender and, 493–494
    peer statuses, 490–492
peers, 487
pelvic field defect, 372
perception, 163
perceptual categorization, 226–227
perceptual constancy, in infants, 167
perceptual development, 189
perceptual-motor coupling, 176–177
perceptual speed, 260
performance orientation, 542
perimenopause, 400
Perry Preschool program, 529
personal fable, 195–196
personality, 339, 358–359
    adult personality development, 360–362
    Big Five factors of, 359–360
    generativity and, 362–363
    stability and change in, 363–366
    trait theories of, 359–360
perspective taking, 342, 493, 539
phallic stage, 21
phenotype, 55
phenylketonuria (PKU), 57–58
phoneme, 276
phonics, 285
phonology, 275–276, 277, 280–281
physical abuse, 466
physical appearance, in middle adulthood, 96
physical descriptions, 340–341
physical development, 90. See also brain
    during puberty, 92–95
    in early adulthood, 95–96
    growth patterns, 90

self-understanding, 339
  in adolescence, 343–344
  in adulthood, 344–345
  in early childhood, 340–342
  in infancy, 339–340
  in middle and late childhood, 342–343
self-worth, need for, 437
semantic memory, 224
semantics, 276–277, 281–282
Senior Odyssey, 217
sensation, 163
sensitive period, 26
sensorimotor play, 501
sensorimotor stage of cognitive development, 22, 23, 184
  A-not-B error, 187, 189
  evaluation of, 187
  object permanence, 187
  substages, 184–186
sensory and perceptual development, 162–163
  ecological view of, 163–165
  hearing, 170–173
  intermodal perception, 174–175
  nature/nurture and, 175
  perceptual-motor coupling, 176–177
  smell, 173–174
  taste, 174
  touch and pain, 173
  visual perception, 166–170
sensory receptors, 163
service learning, 421–422
Sex in America survey, 387–388, 402
sex-linked chromosomal abnormalities, 56–57
sex-linked genes, 55–56
sexual abuse, 466
sexual harassment, 392
sexual identity, 393–394
sexuality, 386. See also gender
  in adolescence, 393–400
  biological factors, 386
  in childhood, 393
  cultural factors, 386–387
  forcible sexual behavior, 391–392
  in middle adulthood, 97
  sexual orientation, 387–389
sexually transmitted infections (STIs), 389–391, 396–397
sexual reassignment, 372
sexual scripts, 387
shaken baby syndrome, 100
shape constancy, 167
shared environmental experiences, 61–62
shared sleeping, 110–111
sharing, concept of, 424
short-term memory, 220
sibling relationships, 477–478, 479
sickle-cell anemia, 58
SIDS (sudden infant death syndrome), 111, 569

simple reflexes, 185
sinus problems, 125
SIRTL, 149
size constancy, 167
sleep, 109
  in adolescence and emerging adulthood, 112–113
  in adulthood and aging, 113–114
  in childhood, 112
  in infancy, 109–110
sleep deprivation, in pregnant and postpartum women, 84
sleep/wake cycle, 109–110
slow-to-warm child, 312–313
small for date infants, 80–81
smell, sense of, 173
smiling, in infancy, 305
smoking. See cigarettes
social age, 17
social cognition, 48–90
social cognitive theory
  of development, 24–25
  of gender, 373–375
  of morality, 414
social comparison, 341
social constructivist approach, 203
social contract or utility and individual rights, in Kohlberg's theory, 411
social conventional reasoning, 413
social media, 511
social orientation, in infancy, 317–318
social play, 501
social policy, 9–12
social referencing, 319
social relationships, emotional expression and, 305–306
social role theory of gender, 373
social smile, 305
social system morality, in Kohlberg's theory, 411
social work, as career, 43
sociocultural cognitive theory, 23–24
sociocultural influences, 507
  culture, 507–513
  ethnicity, 517–519
  socioeconomic status and poverty, 513–517
socioeconomic status (SES), 9
  aging and, 516–517
  defined, 513
  education and, 537–538
  language and literacy development and, 283
  poverty and, 514–517
  variations in neighborhoods and families, 513–514
socioemotional processes, in development, 13
socioemotional selectivity theory, 310–311, 504
source memory, 225
spatial intelligence, 251, 260
special education, as career, 41–42

speech therapy, as career, 45
spina bifida, 58
spirituality. See religion and spirituality
sports, motor skills development and, 158–159
stability-change issue, 18–19
stage-crisis view of personality, 360–361
standardized test, 30
Stanford-Binet 5, 248, 254
still-face paradigm, 318
stranger anxiety, 306, 307
Strange Situation, 320, 321–322
strategies, for information processing, 222
strategy construction, 212
strength, in middle adulthood, 96
strength training, 143
stress
  coping with, 308–309
  effect of, on prenatal development, 73
  home care of Alzheimer patients and, 129
  oxidative, 127
substance use, 145
  in adolescence and emerging adulthood, 145–148
subtractive bilingualism, 287
sucking reflex, 154
suicide, 571–573
superego, 415
surveys, 29–30
susceptibility genes, 54–55
sustained attention, 214
symbolic function substage, 191
synapses, 100
syntax, 276, 277, 281–282
syphilis, 389
  effect of, on prenatal development, 72

T

taste, sense of, 174
Tay-Sachs disease, 58
teaching, as career, 41
technology, effect of, on families, 447
Teen Outreach Program (TOP), 399
telegraphic speech, 280
television, 509–510
telomerase, 117
telomeres, 117
temperament, 312
  biological influences on, 314
  describing and classifying, 312–314
  developmental connections, 314–315
  goodness of fit and, 315–316
  parenting and, 315–316
temporal lobe, 100, 253
teratogen, 68–70
tertiary circular reactions, 186
testosterone, 93, 97, 372, 401–402

theory, 20
theory of mind, 239–241
therapeutic/recreational therapy, as career, 45
thinking, 226
  abstract, 194–195
  in adulthood, 233–235
  in childhood, 226–231
  contextual, 205–206
  critical, 228–229, 233
  idealistic, 194–195
  logical, 194–195
  pragmatic, 204–205
  provisional, 206
  realistic, 204–205, 206
  reflective, 205–206
  relativistic, 205–206
  scientific, 229–230
  in Vygotsky's theory, 200–201
thyroid gland, 93
time of exposure, to teratogens, 69
time out, 464
tip-of-the-tongue phenomenon, 224, 289–290
Tools of the Mind, 202
top-dog phenomenon, 530
touch, sense of, 173
traditional religious script, 387
trait-situation interaction, 359–360
trait theories of personality, 359–360
tranquilizers, abuse of, 146
transactional interchanges, 445
traumatic events, emotional development and, 308–309
triangular theory of love, 333
triarchic theory of intelligence, 250
trimesters, 65, 66
trust versus mistrust, 21
Turner syndrome, 57
twin study, 60

U

ultrasound sonography, 67
umbilical cord, 64, 65, 79
underextension, of words, 280
unemployment, 551–552
universal ethical principles, in Kohlberg's theory, 411
unrealistic positive overestimation, 341

V

Vaillant's studies, 365
values, 430–431
  need for, 437
values clarification, 421
variables, 32
vasopressin, 323
verbal aggression, 379
verbal intelligence, 251, 260
verbal memory, 260
verbatim memory trace, 222
very preterm infants, 82
viability, 65
vigilance, 217

visual acuity
  in adults, 169
  in infants, 166
visual perception, 166
  in infancy, 166–168
visual preference method, 164
vitamins, aging and, 140
vocabulary. *See also* language;
    literacy
  first words, 279–280
  growth of, 279–280
  in middle and late childhood,
    284–285
  receptive, 279
  socioeconomic status and
    development of, 283
  spoken, 279

volunteerism, 425–426
Vygotsky's theory of cognitive
    development, 23–24,
    199–200
  in education, 201
  evaluation of, 203–204
  language and thought, 200–201
  scaffolding, 200
  zone of proximal development
    (ZPD), 200

W

walking, as gross motor skill,
    155–156
waterbirth, 79
Wechsler Scales, 248–249
Wernicke's area, 291

whole-language approach to
    reading, 285
WIC (Women, Infants, and
    Children) program,
    133–134
Widowed Person's Service, 581
widowhood, 580
Wild Boy of Aveyron, 275,
    292, 293
wisdom, 261–263
work, 548
  in adolescence, 548–549
  cognitive functioning and,
    234–235
working memory, 221, 223
writing, in middle and late
    childhood, 286

X

X chromosomes, 54
X-linked inheritance, 55–56
XYY syndrome, 57

Y

Y chromosomes, 54
You Just Don't Understand
    (Tannen), 380
Young Man Luther (Erikson), 353

Z

zone of proximal development
    (ZPD), 200, 201
zygote, 53, 64